P9-CAY-360

For the professor

- **Teaching Resources** provide material contributed by professors throughout the world—including teaching tips, techniques, academic papers, and sample syllabi—and **Talk to the Team**, a moderated faculty chat room.
- **Online Faculty Support** includes downloadable supplements, additional cases, articles, links, and suggested answers to Current Events Activities.
- **What's New** gives you one-click access to all newly posted PHLIP resources.

For the student

- **Talk to the Tutor** schedules virtual office hours that allow students to post questions from any supported discipline and receive responses from the dedicated PHLIP/CW faculty team.
- **Writing Resource Center** provides an online writing center that supplies links to online directories, thesauruses, writing tutors, style and grammar guides, and additional tools.
- **Career Center** helps students access career information, view sample résumés, even apply for jobs online.
- **Study Tips** provides an area where students can learn to develop better study skills.

ONLINE LEARNING SOLUTIONS
IN BLACKBOARD, WEBCT, AND PEARSON COURSECOMPASS

STANDARD COURSES

(Free with New Text Purchase) Standard courses include traditional online course features:

- Online Testing
- Course Management and Page Tracking
- Gradebook
- Course Information

- Multiple-Section Chat Rooms
- Bulletin Board Conferencing
- Syllabus and Calendar Functions
- E-mail Capability

WWW.PRENHALL.COM/HORNGREN

Introduction to Financial Accounting

Charles T. Horngren Series in Accounting
Charles T. Horngren, Consulting Editor

Auditing: An Integrated Approach, 8/E
Arens/Loebbecke

Financial Statement Analysis, 2/E
Foster

Governmental and Nonprofit Accounting: Theory & Practice, 6/E
Freeman/Shoulders

Financial Accounting, 4/E
Harrison/Horngren

Cases in Financial Reporting, 3/E
Hirst/McAnally

Cost Accounting: A Managerial Emphasis, 10/E
Horngren/Foster/Datar

Accounting, 5/E
Horngren/Harrison/Bamber

Introduction to Financial Accounting, 8/E
Horngren/Sundem/Elliott

Introduction to Management Accounting, 12/E
Horngren/Sundem/Stratton

INTRODUCTION TO FINANCIAL ACCOUNTING

Eighth Edition

CHARLES T. HORNGREN
Stanford University

GARY L. SUNDEM
University of Washington—Seattle

JOHN A. ELLIOTT
Cornell University

PRENTICE HALL, *Upper Saddle River, NJ 07458*

Library of Congress Cataloging-in-Publication Data

Horngren, Charles T., 1926-
    Introduction to financial accounting / Charlaes T. Horngren, Gary L. Sundem,
John A. Elliot.—8th ed.
        p. cm.
    Includes bibliographical references and index.
    ISBN 0-13-03237-3
    1. Accounting.   I. Sundem, Gary L.   II. Elliott, John A.

HF5635 .H813 2001
657—dc21   2001033948

Executive Editor: Deborah Hoffman
Editor-in-Chief: P. J. Boardman
Senior Editorial Assistant: Jane Avery
Associate Editor: Kathryn Sheehan
Media Project Manager: Nancy Welcher
Executive Marketing Manager: Beth Toland
Marketing Assistant: Brian Rappelfeld
Managing Editor (Production):   Cynthia Regan
Production Editor: Michael Reynolds
Production Assistant: Dianne Falcone
Permissions Supervisor: Suzanne Grappi
Associate Director, Manufacturing: Vincent Scelta
Production Manager: Arnold Vila
Accounting Hotline Customer Service Representative: Walter Mendez
Design Manager: Patricia Smythe
Interior Design/Cover Design/Photo Montage: Michael J. Fruhbeis
Photo Credits: David R. Frazier/*Photo Researchers Inc.;* Randy Wells/*Stone;*
Siegfried Layda/*Stone;* Brad Rickerby/*Stone;* Jeremy Woodhouse/*Photodisc;* Mark
Segal/*Stone; Corbis Digital Stock*
Associate Director, Multimedia Production: Karen Goldsmith
Manager, Multimedia Production: Christy Mahon
Print Production Liaison: Ashley Scattergood
Composition: Progressive Information Technologies
Full-Service Project Management: Progressive Publishing Alternatives
Printer/Binder: R. R. Donnelley, Willard
Cover Printer: Phoenix Color

Credits and acknowledgments borrowed from other sources and reproduced, with
permission, in this textbook appear on page P1.

Copyright © 2002 by Pearson Education, Inc., Upper Saddle River, New Jersey, 07458.
All rights reserved. Printed in the United States of America. This publication is
protected by Copyright and permission should be obtained from the publisher prior to
any prohibited reproduction, storage in a retrieval system, or transmission in any form
or by any means, electronic, mechanical, photocopying, recording, or likewise. For
information regarding permission(s), write to: Rights and Permissions Department.

10 9 8 7 6 5 4 3 2 1
ISBN 0-13-032371-3

To Joan, Scott, Mary, Susie,

Cathy, Liz, Garth, Jens,

Laura, Dawn, and Jesse

Charles T. Horngren   is the Edmund W. Littlefield Professor of Accounting, Emeritus, at Stanford University. A graduate of Marquette University, he received his MBA from Harvard University and his Ph.D. from the University of Chicago. He is also the recipient of honorary doctorates from Marquette University and DePaul University.

A Certified Public Accountant, Horngren served on the Accounting Principles Board for six years, the Financial Accounting Standards Board Advisory Council for five years, and the Council of the American Institute of Certified Public Accountants for three years. For six years, he served as a trustee of the Financial Accounting Foundation, which oversees the Financial Accounting Standards Board and the Government Accounting Standards Board.

Horngren is a member of the Accounting Hall of Fame.

A member of the American Accounting Association, Horngren has been its President and its Director of Research. He received its first annual Outstanding Accounting Educator Award.

The California Certified Public Accountants Foundation gave Horngren its Faculty Excellence Award and its Distinguished Professor Award. He is the first person to have received both awards.

The American Institute of Certified Public Accountants presented its first Outstanding Educator Award to Horngren.

Horngren was named Accountant of the Year, Education, by the national professional accounting fraternity, Beta Alpha Psi.

Professor Horngren is also a member of the Institute of Management Accountants, where he received its Distinguished Service Award. He was a member of the Institute's Board of Regents, which administers the Certified Management Accountant examinations.

Horngren is the author of these books published by Prentice-Hall: *Cost Accounting: A Managerial Emphasis,* Tenth Edition, 2000 (with George Foster and Srikant Datar); *Introduction to Management Accounting,* Twelfth Edition, 2002 (with Gary L. Sundem and William O. Stratton); *Introduction to Financial Accounting,* Eighth Edition, 2002 (with Gary L. Sundem and John A. Elliott; *Accounting,* Fifth Edition, 2002 (with Walter T. Harrison, Jr. and Linda Bamber); and *Financial Accounting,* Fourth Edition, 2001 (with Walter J. Harrison, Jr.).

Horngren is the Consulting Editor for the Charles T. Horngren Series in Accounting.

Gary L. Sundem   is the Julius A. Roller Professor of Accounting and Co-Chair of the Department of Accounting at the University of Washington, Seattle. He received his B.A. degree from Carleton College and his MBA and Ph.D. degrees from Stanford University.

Professor Sundem was the 1992–93 President of the American Accounting Association. He was Executive Director of the Accounting Education Change Commission, 1989–91, and served as Editor of *The Accounting Review,* 1982–86.

A member of the National Association of Accountants, Sundem is past president of the Seattle chapter. He has served on NAA's national Board of Directors, the Committee on Academic Relations, and the Research Committee.

Professor Sundem has numerous publications in accounting and finance journals including *Issues in Accounting Education, The Accounting Review, Journal of Accounting Research,* and *The Journal of Finance.* He was selected as the Outstanding Accounting Educator by the American Accounting Association in 1998 and by the Washington Soci-

ety of CPAs in 1987. He has made more than 150 presentations at universities in the United States and abroad.

John A. Elliott is Associate Dean and Professor of Accounting at the Johnson Graduate School of Management at Cornell University. He received his B.S. and MBA degrees from the University of Maryland and his Ph.D. degree from Cornell University.

A certified public accountant, Elliott worked for Arthur Andersen & Co. and for Westinghouse before returning for his advanced degrees. He currently teaches financial accounting and international accounting at the Johnson School. Prior teaching experience has included auditing and taxation as well as intermediate accounting and financial statement analysis. With over 25 years as an educator, Professor Elliott has taught at the University of Maryland, St. Lawrence University, Central Washington State College, and the University of Chicago. In addition to executive teaching for Cornell, he has conducted various corporate training programs in the United States and internationally.

As a member of the American Accounting Association, he was the founding president of the Financial Accounting and Reporting Section. As a member of the Financial Accounting Standards Committee he frequently responded to FASB exposure drafts and worked to integrate academic study with practice. His research has been published in accounting and economics journals and deals primarily with the use of accounting information to assess the financial condition of an enterprise.

Professor Elliott served on the Hangar Theatre Board of Trustees for nine years, and was president for four of those years. He also served on the Board of the Cayuga Medical Center at Ithaca for nine years and was president for the final three years.

BRIEF CONTENTS

CONTENTS

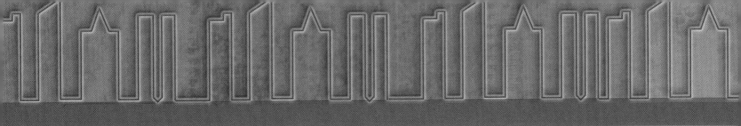

PREFACE

"You have to know what something is before you know how to use it."

Introduction to Financial Accounting, 8/E, describes the most widely used accounting theory and practice with an emphasis on what accounting is rather than on what it should be.

IFA, 8/E, takes the view that business is an exciting process and that accounting is the perfect window through which to see how economic events affect businesses. Because we believe that accounting aids the understanding of economic events and that accounting builds on simple principles, this book introduces a number of concepts earlier than other textbooks. These early introductions are at the simplest level and are illustrated with carefully chosen examples from real companies.

OUR PHILOSOPHY

Introduce the simple concepts early, revisit concepts at more complex levels as students gain understanding, and provide appropriate real-company examples at every stage—that's our philosophy.

We want students to view accounting as a tool that enhances their understanding of economic events. Students should be asking, "After this transaction, are we better or worse off?"

One of our colleagues, Hal Bierman, often focuses on an economic event by asking, "Are you happy or are you sad?" We believe that accounting provides a way to understand what is happening and to answer that question. You might think of the basic financial statements as scorecards in the most fundamental economic contests. Each year the financial statements help you answer the most important questions: Are you happy or sad? Did you make or lose money? Are you prospering or just surviving? Will you have the cash you need for the next big step?

WHO SHOULD USE THIS BOOK?

IFA, 8/E, presupposes no prior knowledge of accounting and is suitable for any undergraduate or MBA student enrolled in a financial accounting course. It deals with important topics that all business students should study. Our goals have been to choose relevant subject matter, and to present it clearly and accessibly.

This text is oriented to the user of financial statements but gives ample attention to the needs of potential accounting practitioners. *IFA,* 8/E, stresses underlying concepts yet makes them concrete with numerous illustrations, many taken from recent corporate annual reports. Moreover, accounting procedures such as transaction analysis, journalizing, and posting are given due consideration where appropriate.

NEW AND RETAINED FEATURES

- NEW and revised Chapter Opening vignettes, many with corresponding "On Location!" videos

    Chapter openers help students understand accounting's role in current business practice. "On Location!" video segments, specially produced for this text, reinforce and expand upon chapter openers. New segments include Three Dog Bakery, Nantucket Nectars, Oracle, and Teva Sandals.

- NEW Cisco Annual Report

    Based on reviewer feedback, the annual report from a leading technology company is packaged with all new text copies. Cases at the end of each chapter help students analyze Cisco's financial position.

- NEW "Take 5's"

    Study Breaks appear throughout each chapter and encourage students to stop and think about material just read. Answers immediately follow.

- NEW Cognitive Exercises

    Based on focus group feedback, short cognitive exercises serve as critical-thinking "warm-ups" to more complex case material.

- NEW Business First Boxes

    Provide insights into operations at well-known domestic and international companies, including technology and E-Commerce companies.

- Updated material includes simple, straightforward presentation of the Statement of Cash Flows in Chapter 1 and new material on EVA and MVA added to Chapter 13.

- *Introduction to Financial Accounting,* 8/E, and its companion text, *Introduction to Management Accounting,* 12/E, provide a seamless presentation for any first year accounting course. Please ask your Prentice Hall representative about cost-saving discounts when you adopt and package both books together.

ONLINE AND TECHNOLOGY SOLUTIONS

- myPHLIP offers FREE one-click, personalized access to free Web resources for faculty and students. Resources include chapter-by-chapter current events, Internet resources and hotlinks, online study guide, online tutor, and much more! Go to www.prenhall.com/myphlip and register today.

- NEW Online courses available in WebCT, Blackboard and Pearson Course Compass, Prentice Hall's nationally hosted distance learning solution.

- NEW Student CD-ROM contains PH Re-Enforcer tutorial software, PHAS General Ledger software, Spreadsheet Templates, and Powerpoints.

- NEW Instructor Resource CD-ROM contains all print and technology supplements so that instructors can provide seamless classroom presentations.

- NEW Getting Started Series provides fundamental instruction on how to use Peachtree, Quickbooks, or Simply Accounting.

- NEW Mastering Accounting CD-ROM
Students watch professionally written, acted, and filmed videos about a fictional Internet start-up company to see how accounting concepts are related to workplace events and challenges.
- Accounting Made Easy CD-ROM

SUPPLEMENTS FOR INSTRUCTORS

NEW INSTRUCTOR'S RESOURCE CD-ROM (see description under "Online and Technology Solutions")

INSTRUCTOR'S RESOURCE MANUAL BY SCOTT YETMAR (DRAKE UNIVERSITY) Contains the following elements for each chapter of the text: chapter overviews, chapter outlines organized by objectives, teaching tips, chapter quiz, transparency masters derived from textbook exhibits, and suggested readings.

SOLUTIONS MANUAL AND SOLUTIONS TRANSPARENCIES BY TEXT AUTHORS Special thanks to Thomas Hoar, Houston Community College, and Jerry D. Siebel, University of South Florida, for their technical reviews.

TEST ITEM FILE BY ALICE B. SINEATH (FORSYTH TECHNICAL COMMUNITY COLLEGE) The Test Item File includes multiple choice, true/false, exercises, comprehensive problems, short answer problems, critical thinking essay questions, etc. Each test item is tied to the corresponding learning objective, has an assigned difficulty level, and provides a page reference. Special thanks to Beth Woods for her reviewing, which contributed to the accuracy of the tests.

PRENTICE HALL WINDOWS CUSTOM TEST MANAGER, BY ENGINEERING SOFTWARE ASSOCIATES (ESA), INC. This easy-to-use computerized testing program can create exams, evaluate, and track student results. The PH Test Manager also provides on-line testing capabilities. You may ***call 1-800-550-1701, our Test Paper Preparation Center,*** to have a hardcopy of your custom test created to suit your classroom needs.

ON LOCATION! A CUSTOM VIDEO LIBRARY BY BEVERLY AMER (NORTHERN ARIZONA UNIVERSITY) Highlighted companies include Three Dog Bakery, Oracle, Teva Sport Sandals, and Nantucket Nectars. A Video Guide in the Instructor's Resource Manual helps integrate the videos into your classroom lectures.

SUPPLEMENTS FOR STUDENTS

WORKING PAPERS BY LYNN MAZZOLA (NASSAU COMMUNITY COLLEGE) This supplement includes tear-out forms to solve all the end-of-chapter assignments in the text. Forms are numbered and arranged in the same order as the textbook.

STUDY GUIDE BY LYNN MAZZOLA (NASSAU COMMUNITY COLLEGE) For each chapter of the text, the study guide contains a pretest, a chapter overview, a detailed chapter review including study tips, practice test questions and demonstration problems with worked-out solutions.

NEW STUDENT RESOURCE CD-ROM (see description under "Online and Technology Solutions")

ADDITIONAL RESOURCES

NEW "GETTING STARTED" SERIES OF MANUALS ON PEACHTREE COMPLETE 8.0, QUICKBOOKS PRO 2001, AND SIMPLY ACCOUNTING 8.0   Package your choice of one of these brief manuals free with new copies of the student text. In addition, you can package your choice of the full software for Peachtree Complete Release 8.0 (a $200.00 value) or Simply Accounting 8.0 (a $150.00 value) for only $10.00 net with new copies of the student text.

INTERPRETING AND ANALYZING FINANCIAL STATEMENTS, SECOND EDITION BY KAREN P. SCHOENEBECK

New WALL STREET JOURNAL Offer: 10 weeks for $10.00 net with new student texts.

ACTIVITIES IN FINANCIAL ACCOUNTING BY MARTHA DORAN (SAN DIEGO STATE UNIVERSITY)   This workbook contains interactive learning assignments designed to help students see beyond the technical aspects of accounting through active learning. In addition, these group activities fulfill the AECC recommendations by providing students with the chance to practice and improve their writing, speaking, and reasoning skills. An Instructor's Guide provides an overview of each activity, highlights important content and process objectives, and provides step-by-step instructions for running each activity.

MoviesDoortoDoor.com BY MARK S. BEASLEY AND FRANK A. BUCKLESS (NORTH CAROLINA STATE UNIVERSITY)

Free eBiz FOR ACCOUNTING Booklet may be packaged with new student texts.

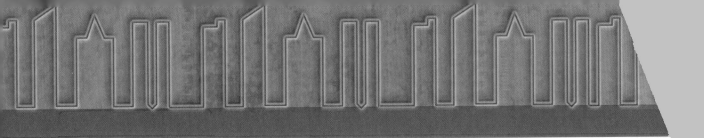

ACKNOWLEDGMENTS

Our appreciation extends to our present and former mentors, colleagues, and students. This book and our enthusiasm for accounting grew out of their collective contributions to our knowledge and experience. We particularly appreciate the following individuals who supplied helpful comments and reviews of drafts of this edition: Frances Ayers, University of Oklahoma; Roderick S. Barclay, University of Texas at Dallas; Ronald S. Barden, Georgia State University; LuAnn Bean, Pittsburg State University; Michele J. Daley, Rice University; Patricia A. Doherty, Boston University; Philip D. Drake, Thunderbird, The American Graduate School of International Management; Allan R. Drebin, Northwestern University; D. Jacque Grinnell, University of Vermont; M. Zafar Iqbal, California Polytechnic State University-San Luis Obispo; John L. Norman Jr., Keller Graduate School of Management; Renee A. Price, University of Nebraska; and James A. Schweikart, Rhode Island College. We would also like to thank those who gave valuable feedback on previous editions: Roderick S. Barclay, University of Texas at Dallas; Mary Barth, Stanford University; Marianne Bradford, The University of Tennessee; David T. Collins, Bellarmine College; Ray D. Dillon, Georgia State University; Patricia A. Doherty, Boston University; Alan H. Falcon, Loyola Marymount University; Anita Feller, University of Illinois; Richard Frankel, University of Michigan; John D. Gould, Western Carolina University; Leon J. Hanouille, Syracuse University; Al Hartgraves, Emory University; Suzanne Hartley, Franklin University; Peter Huey, Collin County Community College; Yuji Ijiri, Carnegie Mellon University; Joan Luft, Michigan State University; Maureen McNichols, Stanford University; Mohamed Onsi, Syracuse University; Patrick M. Premo, St. Bonaventure University; Leo A. Ruggle, Mankato State University; James A. Schweikart, University of Richmond; Robert Swieringa, Cornell University; Katherene P. Terrell, University of Central Oklahoma; Michael G. Vasilou, DeVry Institute of Technology, Chicago; Deborah Welch, Tyler Junior College; Christine Wiedman, College of William and Mary; and Peter D. Woodlock, Youngstown State University.

Finally, our thanks to the following people at Prentice Hall: Deborah Hoffman, PJ Boardman, Jane Avery, Beth Toland, Vincent Scelta, Richard Bretan, Pat Smythe, Kathlyn Sheehan, Brian Rappelfeld, Arnold Vila, Michael Reynolds, Michael Fruhbeis, Christy Mahon, Nancy Welcher, and Walter Mendez.

The solutions manual was skillfully produced by Donna Phoenix. Proofing help was provided by Eugene A. Imhoff, University of Michigan; Barbara Longee, University of California, Irvine; and Robin Tarpley, George Washington University.

Comments from users are welcome.

Charles T. Horngren
Gary L. Sundem
John A. Elliott

1

ACCOUNTING: THE LANGUAGE OF BUSINESS

Cisco Systems helps customers discover and deliver all that is possible on the Internet.

www.prenhall.com/horngren

Learning Objectives

After studying this chapter, you should be able to

1. Explain how accounting information assists in making decisions.

2. Describe the components of the balance sheet.

3. Analyze business transactions and relate them to changes in the balance sheet.

4. Classify operating, investing, and financing activities in a cash flow statement.

5. Compare the features of proprietorships, partnerships, and corporations.

6. Describe auditing and how it enhances the value of financial information.

7. Distinguish between public and private accounting.

8. Evaluate the role of ethics in the accounting process.

The Internet or World Wide Web is booming, providing electronic connections among individuals, companies, organizations, and governments. One study revealed that the Internet economy grew to $523.9 billion in 1999, and now directly supports 2.5 million workers. So many activities have moved to the Internet that it is the centerpiece of what is called the "new economy." In this new economy there are newly created companies that have emerged to meet new business needs and to meet old business needs in new ways. Amazon.com is an example of the latter, a Web-based company that began selling books exclusively via electronic contact with customers and delivered books directly and quickly. Cisco Systems is an example of the former. Cisco is a company that emerged to make the Internet possible and has grown as the size and scope of the Internet has grown.

Cisco is the worldwide leader in networking for the Internet. The Internet is simply the sum of all the computers that comprise it, connected together in a manner that allows efficient communication. That is where Cisco comes in, efficient connections and communication. The company's router products connect computers and computer networks around the globe and help form the backbone infrastructure for the Internet. Cisco shipped its first products in 1986 and has seen its annual revenues explode to almost $19 billion in 2000. Revenues in 2000 were up 50% from the prior year and there is no sign of slowing growth. The company constantly acquires smaller firms to fuel its growth. How to keep track of it all? Accounting systems crunch all the transaction details. Analysts, accountants, and staff must design, develop, and operate these systems. Because Cisco is a publicly held company with stockholders, the accounting systems and people must be prepared to generate financial reports quickly and accurately for use by decision makers around the globe.

Cisco does not just build hardware to carry and direct electronic signals. It builds complete integrated systems to support companies in their quest for inexpensive reliable

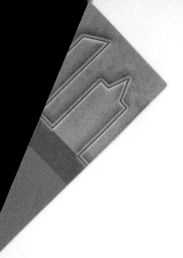

systems. Charles Schwab, the innovator in low-cost security transactions, has 1.9 million brokerage accounts on line and is adding thousands each day. Half of its trades now occur on the Web. Cisco partnered with Schwab to develop this capability. Cisco has an Alliance with IBM to develop and implement networking applications for all manner of clients. Because IBM and Cisco are separate companies, they need a good accounting system to figure how they are doing in their alliance and to figure out how to split their profits.

As we embark on your journey into the world of financial accounting, we explore what it takes for a company such as Cisco to manage its financial activities with ease and how investors use this accounting information to better understand Cisco. Keep this in mind: The same basic accounting needs and procedures that support the new economy support businesses big and small, old and new, worldwide.

BUSINESS FIRST

Did you ever wonder how McDonald's, which started as a small Pasadena, California, hamburger stand, became a 27,000-location restaurant chain with stores in 119 countries? The first McDonald's employed three carhops to serve hot dogs and shakes to drive-in customers in Pasadena in 1937. In 1940, the two McDonald brothers, Dick and Mac, added a larger drive-in in San Bernardino where 20 carhops served a 25-item menu of sandwiches and ribs. Business was good, and the brothers shared $50,000 per year in profits (and in 1940 $50,000 would buy as much as $550,000 today).

How did accounting affect these entrepreneurs? When they analyzed their sales and costs, they found that 80% of their business came from hamburgers. Other sandwiches and ribs might taste good, but they generated little business. So the McDonald brothers streamlined their product line and focused on low prices, high volume, and a small standardized menu. They cut 25 items to 9, and slashed the price of a burger from $.30 to $.15. Sales and profits soared. This simple menu and value pricing served McDonald's well for years.

A few people noticed this money machine besides the nightly customers. Carnation Corporation noticed it was selling the McDonald brothers frozen milk shake

mix in enormous quantities. The company figured that anyone selling that many shakes was on to something, so Carnation tried to buy the right to open additional McDonald's stores. Dick and Mac declined. Then, in 1954, Ray Kroc entered the picture.

Ray Kroc sold five-spindle "multi-mixers," machines that made five milk shakes simultaneously. You guessed it: He sold so many of these machines to the McDonald brothers that he eventually decided to visit the burger stand that made so many shakes. Kroc spent a day watching the McDonald's operation. He saw an opportunity to sell more shake machines as the company opened more stores, but within days he decided the real golden opportunity was in selling the McDonald's formula to entrepreneurs who wanted to open similar burger stands around the country. A persistent man, Kroc convinced the McDonald brothers to allow him to sell franchises. Kroc's golden opportunity became the golden arches, and a small California burger stand became one of the world's strongest marketing engines. Today McDonald's has become one of the most recognized brand names in the world, mostly by sticking to the strategy worked out years ago using accounting information.

---

accounting The process of identifying, recording, summarizing, and reporting economic information to decision makers.

This book is an introduction to financial accounting. **Accounting** is a process of identifying, recording, summarizing, and reporting economic information to decision makers. **Financial accounting** focuses on the specific needs of decision makers external to the organization such as stockholders, suppliers, banks, and government agencies. You probably expect to see a bunch of rules and procedures about how to record and report financial information. Well, you are correct. You will see all those. However, our philosophy about financial accounting goes beyond rules and procedures. To use your financial accounting training effectively you must also understand the underlying business transactions that give rise to the economic information and why the information is helpful in making the financial decisions.

We hope that you want to know how businesses work. When you understand that McDonald's sales information by product helped its management make decisions about what products to sell, you will see why we track sales and profitability by product line. Both outside investors and internal managers need this information.

Our goal is to help you understand business transactions—to know how they create accounting information and how decision makers both inside the company (managers) and outside the company (investors) use this information in deciding how, when, and what to buy or sell. In the process you get to know some of the world's premier companies. You may wonder about what it costs to develop a theme park such as Disney World. Are these parks worth that kind of huge investment? How many people visit these Disney destinations each year? Can Disney keep track of them all, and are there enough visitors to make the parks profitable? If investors consider purchasing Disney stock, what do they need to know to decide that the current price is a good one? We cannot answer every such question you might ask, but we explore some exciting aspects of business and use business examples to illustrate the uses of accounting information.

financial accounting The field of accounting that serves external decision makers, such as stockholders, suppliers, banks, and government agencies.

Objective 1
Explain how accounting information assists in making decisions.

Exhibit 1-1

Dow Industrials

Assets and Owners' Equity as of Spring 2000 ($ in billions)

Symbol	Company	Total Assets	Total Owners' Equity
AA	Aluminum Company of America	$ 30.8	$ 11.0
AXP	American Express	148.5	10.5
T	AT&T	243.5	110.1
BA	Boeing	37.5	12.0
CAT	Caterpillar	27.9	5.5
C	Citigroup	716.9	49.7
KO	Coca-Cola	23.3	9.2
DIS	Disney	44.7	23.8
DD	DuPont	40.2	13.0
EK	Eastman Kodak	14.4	3.9
XOM	ExxonMobil	146.6	66.9
GE	General Electric	424.0	45.9
GM	General Motors	291.3	29.0
HWP	Hewlett-Packard	1.2	1.0
HD	Home Depot	20.2	13.9
HON	Honeywell	24.9	9.5
INTC	Intel	48.5	36.6
IBM	International Business Machines	82.9	18.9
IP	International Paper	30.3	10.3
JNJ	Johnson & Johnson	29.2	16.2
JPM	JP Morgan	266.3	11.1
MCD	McDonald's	21.2	9.0
MRK	Merck	37.4	12.7
MSFT	Microsoft	50.4	40.7
MMM	Minnesota Mining & Manufacturing	14.9	6.4
MO	Philip Morris	59.8	15.1
PG	Procter & Gamble	35.2	10.6
SBC	SBC Communications	91.2	28.4
UTX	United Technologies	24.3	6.8
WMT	Wal-Mart	73.4	28.1

In pursuing actual business examples, we consider details about many of the 30 companies in the Dow Jones Industrial Average (the Dow), the most commonly reported stock market index in the world. Both Disney and McDonald's are among these 30 companies along with many other large, familiar companies listed in Exhibit 1-1. We also consider some younger and faster growing companies such as Cisco, Apple, Timberland, and Gap Inc. For now, we start with the basics.

THE NATURE OF ACCOUNTING

Accounting organizes and summarizes economic information so that decision makers can use it. The information is presented in reports called financial statements. To prepare these statements, accountants analyze, record, quantify, accumulate, summarize, classify, report, and interpret economic events and their financial effects on the organization.

The series of steps involved in initially recording information and converting it into financial statements is called the accounting system. Accountants analyze the information needed by managers and other decision makers and create the accounting system that best meets those needs. Bookkeepers and computers then perform the routine tasks of collecting and compiling economic information. The real value of any accounting system lies in the information it provides.

Consider the accounting system at your school. It collects information about tuition charges and payments and tracks the status of each student. Your school must be able to bill individuals whose balances are unpaid. It must be able to schedule courses and hire faculty to meet the course demands of students. It must ensure that tuition and other cash inflows are sufficient to pay the faculty and keep the buildings warm (or cool) and well lit. If your experience is like that of most students, you can find some flaws with your school's accounting system. Perhaps there are too many waiting lines at registration or too many complicated procedures in filing for financial aid. If you are lucky, you have experienced electronic registration for courses and made all your tuition payments in response to bills received in the mail. The right information system can streamline your life.

Every business maintains an accounting system, from the store where you bought this book to the company that issued the credit card you used. Mastercard and Visa maintain very fast, very complicated accounting systems. At any moment, thousands of credit card transactions are occurring around the globe, and accounting systems are keeping track of them all. When you use your charge card, it is read electronically and linked to the cash register, which transmits the transaction amount over phone lines to the card company's central computer. The computer verifies that your charges are within acceptable limits and approves or denies the transaction. At the same time the computer also conducts some fairly careful security checks. For example, if your credit card were being used simultaneously to buy groceries in Ithaca and to make long distance phone calls in Korea, the credit card computer might sense that something is wrong and require you to call a customer service representative before the charges could be approved. Without reliable accounting systems, credit cards simply could not exist.

ACCOUNTING AS AN AID TO DECISION MAKING

Accounting information is useful to anyone who must make decisions that have economic consequences. Such decision makers include managers, owners, investors, and politicians. For example,

- When the engineering department of Apple Computer developed the iMac, an accountant developed a report on the potential profitability of the product, including estimated sales and estimated production and selling costs. Managers used the report to help decide whether to produce and market the product.

- Jill runs a small consulting firm and has five employees who service clients. In deciding who to promote (and who to fire), Jill produces reports each month of the productivity of each employee and compares productivity to the salary and other costs associated with the employees' work for the month.
- An investor considering buying stock in either General Motors or Volvo would consult published accounting reports to compare the most recent financial results of the companies. The information in the reports helps the buyer decide which company would be the better investment choice.
- A senator debating a new low-income housing plan needs to know how the proposed plan will affect the country's budget. Accounting information shows how much the plan will cost and where the money will come from.
- A lender considering a loan to a company that wants to expand would examine the historical performance of the company and projections the company provided about how the borrowed funds are to be used to produce new business.

Accounting helps decision making by showing where and when money has been spent and commitments have been made, by evaluating performance, and by indicating the financial implications of choosing one plan instead of another. Accounting also helps predict the future effects of decisions, and it helps direct attention to current problems, imperfections, and inefficiencies, as well as opportunities.

Consider some basic relationships in the decision-making process:

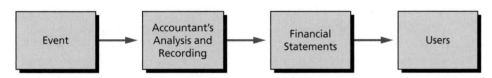

Our focus includes all four boxes. All financial accounting courses cover analysis and recording and preparing financial statements. We pay more attention to the underlying business process and to the way in which the financial reports help decision makers to take action.

FINANCIAL AND MANAGEMENT ACCOUNTING

The financial statements discussed in this book are common to all areas of accounting. "Financial accounting" is often distinguished from "management accounting." The major distinction between them is their use by two different classes of decision makers. The field of financial accounting serves external decision makers, such as stockholders, suppliers, banks, and government agencies. **Management accounting** serves internal decision makers, such as top executives, department heads, college deans, hospital administrators, and people at other management levels within an organization.[1] The two fields of accounting share many of the same procedures for analyzing and recording the effect of individual transactions.

The primary questions concerning a firm's financial success that decision makers want answered are:

What is the financial picture of the organization on a given day?

How well did it do during a given period?

The accountant answers these questions with three major financial statements: balance sheet, income statement, and statement of cash flows. The balance sheet focuses on the financial picture as of a given day. The other financial statements focus on the performance over time.

management accounting
The field of accounting that serves internal decision makers, such as top executives, department heads, college deans, hospital administrators, and people at other management levels within an organization.

---

[1] *For a book-length presentation of the field, see Charles T. Horngren, Gary L. Sundem, and William O. Stratton, Introduction to Management Accounting, 12th ed. (Upper Saddle River, NJ: Prentice Hall, 2002), the companion volume to this textbook.*

The annual report is the traditional, primary communication to shareholders. It includes financial statements and other information. The *New York Times* assessed and graded one component of such reports, the "letters to shareholders" in which the company's chief executive officer (CEO) discusses the year's results. They gave First Chicago, a major bank, a D for the following explanation of a 14% decline in performance: ". . . trading results were significantly lower, due largely to very difficult market conditions." In other words, times were hard because times were hard.

In contrast, Intel suffered a $475 million loss because of a problem with one of their Pentium computer chips that made an infrequent, but predictable, mistake in certain calculations. Chairman Gordon Moore reported that "1994 was the best of times—and the worst of times. We received a crash course in consumer relations." This forthright discussion of the problem and management's actions earned Intel an A from the *New York Times*.

The annual report is also a marketing piece, with colorful pictures and often a striking cover. The 1999 annual report covers for IBM and Coca Cola are interesting examples of powerful images that need no words. The company name is not on either cover. For example, IBM's cover is simply ".com" to emphasize IBM's critical role in the Internet.

The annual report is being transformed in today's economy. While the information contained inside is important, the printed copy takes a long time to produce and is not always widely available. The Web has helped to solve that. Today, most companies have a Web site where they provide direct access to the annual report as a downloadable file. They typically produce various abbreviated financial summaries. The Securities Exchange Commission (SEC) has its own Web site where investors can electronically access all documents filed with the SEC.

Sources: Patrice Samuels, Annual Reports: Upfront and Unstarched, *New York Times*, April 9, 1995, p. f5; Coca Cola and IBM 1999 annual reports.

---

annual report A combination of financial statements, management discussion and analysis, and graphs and charts that is provided annually to investors.

The most common source of financial information used by investors and managers is the annual report. The **annual report** is a document prepared by management and distributed to current and potential investors to inform them about the company's past performance and future prospects. Firms distribute their annual report to stockholders automatically. Interested investors may request the report by calling the investor relations department of the company or visiting its Web site.

You may want to skim over Cisco System's annual report in appendix A to see how firms use photographs extensively to communicate their message. Also, in addition to the financial statements, annual reports include:

1. A letter from corporate management
2. A discussion and analysis by management of recent economic events
3. Footnotes that explain many elements of the financial statements in more detail
4. The report of the independent auditors
5. A statement of management's responsibility for preparation of the financial statements
6. Other corporate information

Although all of the annual report is important, we concentrate on the principal financial statements and how accountants collect and report this information.

THE BALANCE SHEET

One of the major financial statements prepared by the accounting system is the **balance sheet,** which shows the financial status of a company at a particular instant in time. The balance sheet has two counterbalancing sections. The left side lists assets, which represent the resources of the firm (everything the firm owns and controls—from cash to buildings, etc.). The right side lists liabilities and owners' equity, which represent the sources of resources used to acquire the assets. Liabilities and owners' equity might be thought of as claims against the resources.

Although balance sheet is a widely used term, it is not as descriptive as its newer substitute terms: **statement of financial position** or **statement of financial condition.** Nevertheless, old terms die hard, so balance sheet is used in this book.

To illustrate the balance sheet, suppose George Smith, a salaried employee of a local bicycle company, quits his job and opens his own bicycle shop. Smith has heard about the troubles of new businesses that lack money, so he invests plenty: $400,000. Then Smith, acting for the business (which he names Biwheels Company), borrows $100,000 from a local bank for business purposes. That gives Biwheels $500,000 in assets, all currently in the form of cash. The opening balance sheet of this new business enterprise follows:

Biwheels Company
Balance Sheet December 31, 20X1

Assets		Liabilities and Owners' Equity	
Cash	$500,000	Liabilities (note payable)	$100,000
	....	Smith, capital	400,000
Total assets	$500,000	Total liabilities and owners' equity	$500,000

The elements in this balance sheet show the financial status of the Biwheels Company as of December 31, 20X1. The company's assets at this point in time ($500,000) are listed on the left. They are balanced on the right by an equal amount of liability and owners' equity ($100,000 liability owed to the bank plus $400,000 paid in by Smith). The double underscores (double ruling) under the column totals are used to denote final numbers.

Because the balance sheet shows the financial status at a particular point in time, it is always dated. Also, the left and right sides are always kept in balance (thus the name balance sheet). The elements in the balance sheet form the **balance sheet equation:**

$$\text{Assets} = \text{Liabilities} + \text{Owners' equity}$$

The terms in this equation are specifically defined as follows:

Assets are economic resources that are expected to help generate future cash inflows or reduce or prevent future cash outflows. Examples are cash, inventories, and equipment.

Liabilities are economic obligations of the organization to outsiders, or claims against its assets by outsiders. An example is a debt to a bank. When a company takes out a loan or other type of liability, a promissory note that states the terms of repayment is usually exchanged. Accountants use the term **notes payable** to describe the existence of promissory notes.

Owners' equity is the residual interest in, or remaining claims against, the organization's assets after deducting liabilities. When the business is first started, the owners' equity is measured by the total amount invested by the owners. As illustrated by "Smith, capital" in the Biwheels Company example, the accountant often uses the term capital instead of owners' equity to designate an owner's investment in the business. The residual, or "leftover," nature of owners' equity is often emphasized by reexpressing the balance sheet equation as follows:

$$\text{Owners' equity} = \text{Assets} - \text{Liabilities}$$

balance sheet (statement of financial position, statement of financial condition) A financial statement that shows the financial status of a business entity at a particular instant in time.

Objective 2
Describe the components of the balance sheet.

balance sheet equation Assets = Liabilities + Owners' equity

assets Economic resources that are expected to help generate future cash inflows or help reduce future cash outflows.

liabilities Economic obligations of the organization to outsiders, or claims against its assets by outsiders.

notes payable Promissory notes that are evidence of a debt and state the terms of payment.

owners' equity The residual interest in the organization's assets after deducting liabilities.

BALANCE SHEET TRANSACTIONS

entity An organization or a section of an organization that stands apart from other organizations and individuals as a separate economic unit.

transaction Any event that both affects the financial position of an entity and can be reliably recorded in money terms.

Objective 3
Analyze business transactions and relate them to changes in the balance sheet.

Balance sheets are affected by every transaction that a company, or an entity, has. An **entity** is an organization or a section of an organization that stands apart from other organizations and individuals as a separate economic unit. A **transaction** is any event that both affects the financial position of an entity and can be reliably recorded in money terms. Each transaction has counterbalancing entries on the balance sheet so that the total assets always equal the total liabilities and owners' equity. That is, the equality of the balance sheet equation is maintained for every transaction. An accountant who prepares a balance sheet that does not balance has made a mistake somewhere because the balance sheet must balance.

Let us take a look at some transactions of Biwheels Company to see how typical transactions affect the balance sheet.

Transaction 1, Initial Investment. The first Biwheels transaction was the investment by the owner on December 31, 20X1. Smith deposited $400,000 in a business bank account entitled Biwheels Company. The accounting equation is affected as follows:

	Assets	=	Liabilities	+	Owners' Equity
	Cash				Smith, Capital
(1)	+$400,000	=			+$400,000 (Owner investment)

This transaction increases both the assets, specifically Cash, and the owners' equity of the business, specifically Smith, Capital. Liabilities are unaffected. Why? Because Smith's business has no obligation to an outside party because of this transaction. A parenthetical note, "Owner investment," is used to identify the reason for the transaction's effect on owners' equity. The total amounts on the left side of the equation are equal to the total amounts on the right side, as they should be.

Transaction 2, Loan from Bank. On January 2, 20X2, Biwheels Company borrows from a bank, signing a promissory note for $100,000. The $100,000 is added to the business's cash. The effect of this loan transaction on the accounting equation is:

	Assets	=	Liabilities	+ Owners' Equity
			Note	
	Cash		Payable	Smith, Capital
(1)	+$400,000	=		+$400,000
(2)	+ 100,000	=	+$100,000	
Bal.	500,000	=	100,000	400,000
	$500,000			$500,000

The loan increases the asset, Cash, and increases the liability, Note Payable, by the same amount, $100,000. After the transaction is completed, Biwheels has assets of $500,000, liabilities of $100,000, and owners' equity of $400,000. As always, the sums of the individual account balances (abbreviated Bal.) on each side of the equation are equal.

Transaction 3, Acquire Inventory for Cash. On January 2, 20X2, Biwheels acquires bicycles from a manufacturer for $150,000 cash.

	Assets		=	Liabilities	+	Owners' Equity
	Cash	Merchandise Inventory	=	Note Payable		Smith, Capital
Bal.	$500,000		=	$100,000		$400,000
(3)	−150,000	+150,000	=			
Bal.	350,000	150,000	=	100,000		400,000
	$500,000				$500,000	

This transaction, the cash purchase of inventory, increases one asset, Merchandise Inventory, and decreases another asset, Cash, by the same amount. **Inventory** refers to goods held by the company for the purpose of sale to customers. The form of the assets changed, but the total amount of assets is unchanged. Moreover, the right-side items are completely unchanged.

inventory Goods held by a company for the purpose of sale to customers.

Biwheels can prepare a balance sheet at any point in time, even after every transaction. The balance sheet for January 2, after the first three transactions, would look like this:

Biwheels Company
Balance Sheet January 2, 20X2

Assets		Liabilities and Owners' Equity	
Cash	$350,000	Liabilities (note payable)	$100,000
Merchandise inventory	150,000	Smith, capital	400,000
Total assets	$500,000	Total liabilities and owners' equity	$500,000

TRANSACTION ANALYSIS

Accountants record transactions in an organization's accounts. An **account** is a summary record of the changes in a particular asset, liability, or owners' equity, and the account balance is the total of all entries to the account to date. The analysis of transactions is the heart of accounting. For each transaction, the accountant determines (1) which specific accounts are affected, (2) whether the account balances are increased or decreased, and (3) the amount of the change in each account balance.

account A summary record of the changes in a particular asset, liability, or owners' equity.

Exhibit 1-2 shows how a series of transactions may be analyzed using the balance sheet equation. The transactions are numbered for easy reference. Please examine how the first three transactions that were discussed earlier are analyzed in Exhibit 1-2.

Consider how each of the following additional transactions is analyzed:

4. January 3. Biwheels buys bicycles for $10,000 from a manufacturer. The manufacturer requires $4,000 by January 10 and the balance in 30 days.

5. January 4. Biwheels acquires assorted store equipment for a total of $15,000. A cash down payment of $4,000 is made. The remaining balance must be paid in 60 days.

6. January 5. Biwheels sells a store showcase to a business neighbor after Smith decides he dislikes it. Its selling price, $1,000, happens to be exactly equal to its cost. The neighbor agrees to pay within 30 days.

7. January 6. Biwheels returns some inventory (which had been acquired on January 3 for $800) to the manufacturer for full credit (an $800 reduction of the amount that Biwheels owes the manufacturer).

8. January 10. Biwheels pays $4,000 to the manufacturer described in transaction 4.

Exhibit 1-2

Biwheels Company

Analysis of Transactions for December 31, 20X1 – January 12, 20X2

Description of Transactions	Assets				=	Liabilities + Owners' Equity		
	Cash	+ Accounts Receivable +	Merchandise Inventory +	Store Equipment =		Note Payable +	Accounts Payable +	Smith, Capital
(1) Initial investment	+$400,000				=			+ $400,000
(2) Loan from bank	+ 100,000				=	+100,000		
(3) Acquire inventory for cash	− 150,000		+150,000		=			
(4) Acquire inventory on credit			+ 10,000		=		+10,000	
(5) Acquire store equipment for cash plus credit	− 4,000			+15,000 =			+11,000	
(6) Sale of equipment		+1,000		− 1,000 =				
(7) Return of inventory acquired on January 3			− 800		=		− 800	
(8) Payments to creditors	− 4,000				=		− 4,000	
(9) Collections from debtors	+ 700	− 700						
Balance, January 12, 20X2	342,700	+ 300 +	159,200 +	14,000 =		100,000 +	16,200 +	400,000
		$516,200					$516,200	

9. January 12. Biwheels collects $700 of the $1,000 owed by the business neighbor for transaction 6.

10. January 12. Smith remodels his home for $35,000, paying by check from his personal bank account.

Use the format in Exhibit 1-2 to analyze each transaction. Try to do your own analysis of each transaction before looking at the entries shown for it in the exhibit. For example, you could cover the numerical entries with a sheet of paper or a ruler and then proceed through each transaction, one by one.

Transaction 10 does not appear in Exhibit 1-2. Why not?

ANSWER

Transaction 10 is a personal transaction by Smith and does not involve Biwheels as a business.

open account Buying or selling on credit, usually by just an "authorized signature" of the buyer.

account payable A liability that results from a purchase of goods or services on open account.

Transaction 4, Purchase on Credit. Most purchases by various types of companies throughout the world are made on a credit basis instead of a cash basis. An authorized signature of the buyer is usually good enough to assure payment. No formal promissory note is necessary. This practice is known as buying on **open account.** The money owed is shown on the buyer's balance sheet as an account payable. Thus an **account payable** is a liability that results from a purchase of goods or services on open account. As Exhibit 1-2 shows for this merchandise purchase on account, the merchandise inventory (an asset account) of Biwheels is increased and an account payable (a liability account) is also increased in the amount of $10,000 to keep the equation in balance.

		Assets	=	Liabilities		+	Owner's Equity
	Cash	Merchandise Inventory		Note Payable	Accounts Payable		Smith, Capital
Bal.	$350,000	$150,000	=	$100,000			$400,000
(4)		+10,000	=		+10,000		
Bal.	350,000	160,000	=	100,000	10,000		400,000
		$510,000			$510,000		

Transaction 5, Purchase for Cash Plus Credit. This transaction illustrates a **compound entry** because it affects more than two balance sheet accounts (two asset accounts and one liability account in this case). Store equipment is increased by the full amount of its cost regardless of whether payment is made in full now, in full later, or partially now and partially later. Therefore Biwheels' Store Equipment (an asset account) is increased by $15,000, Cash (an asset account) is decreased by $4,000, and Accounts Payable (a liability account) is increased by the difference, $11,000.

compound entry A transaction that affects more than two accounts.

		Assets		=	Liabilities		+	Owners' Equity
	Cash	Merchandise Inventory	Store Equipment		Note Payable	Accounts Payable		Smith, Capital
Bal.	$350,000	$160,000		=	$100,000	$10,000		$400,000
(5)	−4,000		+15,000	=		+11,000		
Bal.	346,000	160,000	15,000	=	100,000	21,000		400,000
		$521,000				$521,000		

Transaction 6, Sale on Credit. This transaction is similar to a purchase on credit except that Biwheels is now the seller. Thus, Biwheels is owed money. The cash payment that has been promised counts as an asset. Accounts Receivable (an asset account) of $1,000 is thus created, and Store Equipment (an asset account) is decreased by $1,000. In this case, the transaction affects asset accounts only. One increases and one decreases with no change in total assets. Liabilities and owners' equity are unchanged.

			Assets			=	Liabilities		+	Owners' Equity
	Cash	Accounts Receivable	Merchandise Inventory	Store Equipment			Note Payable	Accounts Payable		Smith, Capital
Bal.	$346,000		$160,000	$15,000		=	$100,000	$21,000		$400,000
(6)		+1,000		−1,000		=				
Bal.	346,000	1,000	160,000	14,000		=	100,000	21,000		400,000
			$521,000					$521,000		

Transaction 7, Return of Inventory to Supplier. When a company returns merchandise to its suppliers for credit, its merchandise inventory account is reduced and its liabilities are reduced. In this instance, the amount of the decrease on each side of the equation is $800.

	Assets				=	Liabilities		+	Owners' Equity
	Cash	Accounts Receivable	Merchandise Inventory	Store Equipment		Note Payable	Accounts Payable		Smith, Capital
Bal.	$346,000	$1,000	$160,000	$14,000	=	$100,000	$21,000		$400,000
			−800		=		−800		
Bal.	346,000	1,000	159,200	14,000	=	100,000	20,200		400,000
		$520,200					$520,200		

creditor A person or entity to whom money is owed.

Transaction 8, Payments to Creditors. A **creditor** is one to whom money is owed. For Biwheels, the manufacturer who supplied the bikes on credit is an example of a creditor. Payments to the manufacturer decrease both assets (Cash) and liabilities (Accounts Payable) by $4,000.

	Assets				=	Liabilities		+	Owners' Equity
	Cash	Accounts Receivable	Merchandise Inventory	Store Equipment		Note Payable	Accounts Payable		Smith, Capital
Bal.	$346,000	$1,000	$159,200	$14,000	=	$100,000	$20,200		$400,000
(8)	−4,000				=		−4,000		
Bal.	342,000	1,000	159,200	14,000	=	100,000	16,200		400,000
		$516,200					$516,200		

debtor A person or entity that owes money to another.

Transaction 9, Collections from Debtors. A **debtor** is one who owes money. Biwheels' business neighbor is a debtor, and Biwheels is the creditor. Collections from the neighbor increase one of Biwheels' assets (Cash) and decrease another asset (Accounts Receivable) by $700.

	Assets				=	Liabilities		+	Owners' Equity
	Cash	Accounts Receivable	Merchandise Inventory	Store Equipment		Note Payable	Accounts Payable		Smith, Capital
Bal.	$342,000	$1,000	$159,200	$14,000	=	$100,000	$16,200		$400,000
(9)	+700	−700			=				
Bal.	342,700	300	159,200	14,000	=	100,000	16,200		400,000
		$516,200					$516,200		

PREPARING THE BALANCE SHEET

A cumulative total may be drawn at any date for each account in Exhibit 1-2. The following balance sheet uses the totals at the bottom of Exhibit 1-2. Observe once again that a balance sheet represents the financial impact of all transactions up to a specific point in time, here January 12, 20X2.

Biwheels Company
Balance Sheet January 12, 20X2

Assets		Liabilities and Owner's Equity	
Cash	$342,700	Note payable	$100,000
Accounts receivable	300	Accounts payable	16,200
Merchandise		Total liabilities	$116,200
inventory	159,200		
Store equipment	14,000	Smith, capital	400,000
Total	$516,200	Total	$516,200

As noted earlier, Biwheels could prepare a new balance sheet after each transaction. Obviously, such a practice would be awkward and unnecessary. Therefore balance sheets are usually produced once a month.

EXAMPLES OF ACTUAL CORPORATE BALANCE SHEETS

To become more familiar with the balance sheet and its equation, consider the condensed balance sheet information for Cisco Systems and for DuPont shown in Exhibit 1-3. The

Exhibit 1-3

Comparative Consolidated Condensed Balance Sheets
(Dollars in millions, except per share)

	DuPont December 31, 1999	Cisco July 29, 2000
Assets		
Current Assets		
Cash and cash equivalents	$ 1,466	$ 4,234
Marketable securities	116	1,291
Accounts and notes receivable	5,318	2,299
Inventories	5,057	1,232
Other	696	2,054
Total current assets	12,653	11,110
Net property, plant and equipment	14,871	1,426
Investment	1,459	13,688
Other assets	11,794	6,646
Total	$40,777	$32,870
Liabilities and Stockholders' Equity		
Current Liabilities		
Accounts payable	$ 2,780	$ 739
Short-term borrowings and capital lease obligations	4,941	—
Income taxes	359	233
Other accrued liabilities	3,148	4,224
Total current liabilities	11,228	5,196
Long-Term Borrowings and Capital Lease Obligations	6,625	—
Other Liabilities	7,872	—
Deferred Income Taxes	1,660	1,132
Total liabilities	27,385	6,328
Minority Interests	517	45
Total Stockholders' Equity	12,875	26,497
Total	$40,777	$32,870

DuPont 1999 balance sheet shows that property, plant, and equipment comprise the major assets for this chemical company, accounting for more than one-third of total assets. In contrast, on its balance sheet for 2000, Cisco has only $801 million of similar assets, which is less than 10% of its total assets. The two companies also differ in the financing of their activities. DuPont relies on debt for about two-thirds of its total financing while Cisco has only 21% debt.

Appendix A at the end of this book contains a complete set of the actual 2000 financial statements of Cisco. As you proceed from chapter to chapter, you should examine the pertinent parts of these financial statements. In this way, you will become increasingly comfortable with actual financial reports. For example, the general format and some major items in Cisco's balance sheet (appendix A) should be familiar by now. Details will gradually become more understandable as each chapter explains the nature of the various major financial statements and examines their components.

INTRODUCTION TO STATEMENT OF CASH FLOWS

Objective 4
Classify operating, investing, and financing activities in a cash flow statement.

While the balance sheet provides very important information about the company's status at a point in time, it is also important to know what happens over time. One way to do this is to trace the flow of cash during the period. Companies do three basic things; they invest in assets to conduct business, they raise money to finance these assets, and they use the assets and the money they raise to operate their business. These activities lead naturally to a system for classifying each cash flow as an operating, investing, or financing activity. Companies then prepare a cash flow statement to report this information.

The creation of the statement of cash flows is simple. First, list the activities that increased cash (i.e., cash inflows) and those that decreased cash (i.e., cash outflows). Second, place each cash inflow and outflow into one of the three categories according to the type of activity that caused it: operating activities, investing activities, or financing activities.

Operating activities include the sale and the purchase or production of goods and services, including collecting payments from customers, paying suppliers or employees, and paying for items such as rent, taxes, and interest. Investing activities include acquiring and selling assets and securities held for long-term investment purposes. Financing activities include obtaining resources from owners and creditors and repaying amounts borrowed. When The Gap sells you clothing, it is an operating cash flow. When The Gap buys a new storefront in New York City to open a new store, it is an investing activity. When The Gap issues additional common stock to investors to raise money to finance growth and the new store, it is a financing activity.

Consider our Biwheels example from its inception in December 20X1 through the end of January 12, 20X2. Part I of Exhibit 1-4 lists the transactions that affect cash, and part II shows the statement of cash flows. Notice that at the bottom of the statement the change in cash during this period is added to the beginning balance to give the January 12, 20X2 balance in the cash account of $342,700.

The statement of cash flows gives a direct picture of where cash came from and where it went. The dominant reason that Biwheels' cash increased by $342,700 is that the company obtained $500,000 of new financing. No cash came in from operating activities. In fact, a total of $154,000 was paid to support operating activities. It is not unusual to have large cash outflows for operating activities in the early periods of a company's life or when an entity is growing quickly. Cash payments for inventories and prepayments for operating expenses often exceed receipts. In the Biwheels example, no sales have yet occurred, so all operating cash flows were outflows.

Exhibit 1-4

Biwheels Company

Statement of Cash Flows for the Period Ended January 12, 20X2

PART I: TRANSACTIONS AFFECTING CASH

Transaction	Amount	Type of Activity
(1) Initial investment	$ 400,000	Financing
(2) Loan from bank	100,000	Financing
(3) Acquire inventory for cash	(150,000)	Operating
(5) Acquire store equipment for cash	(4,000)	Investing
(8) Payments to trade creditors	(4,000)	Operating
(9) Sale of store equipment	700	Investing

PART II: STATEMENT OF CASH FLOWS

Cash Flows from Operating Activities	
Cash payments to suppliers	$(154,000)
Net cash used for operating activities	$(154,000)
Cash Flows from Investing Activities	
Cash payments for purchases of equipment	$ (4,000)
Cash receipts from sales of equipment	700
Net cash used for investing activities	$ (3,300)
Cash Flows from Financing Activities	
Proceeds from initial investment	$ 400,000
Proceeds from bank loan	100,000
Net cash provided by financing activities	$ 500,000
Net increase in cash	$ 342,700
Cash balance, December 31, 20X1	0
Cash balance, January 12, 20X2	$ 342,700

TYPES OF OWNERSHIP

Although there are countless different types of companies, there are only three basic forms of ownership structures for business entities: sole proprietorships, partnerships, and corporations.

> **Objective 5**
> Compare the features of proprietorships, partnerships, and corporations.

SOLE PROPRIETORSHIPS

A **sole proprietorship** is a separate organization with a single owner. Most often the owner is also the manager. Therefore, sole proprietorships tend to be small retail establishments and individual professional businesses such as those of dentists, physicians, and attorneys. From an accounting viewpoint, each sole proprietorship is a separate entity that is distinct from the proprietor. Thus, the cash in the dentist's business account is an asset of the dental practice, whereas the cash in the dentist's personal account is not.

> **sole proprietorship** A separate organization with a single owner.

PARTNERSHIPS

A **partnership** is an organization that joins two or more individuals who act as co-owners. Many retail establishments are partnerships, and dentists, physicians, attorneys, and accountants often conduct their activities as partnerships. Partnerships can be gigantic. The largest international accounting firms have thousands of partners. Again, from an accounting viewpoint, each partnership is an individual entity that is separate from the personal activities of each partner.

> **partnership** A form of organization that joins two or more individuals together as co-owners.

CORPORATIONS

corporation A business organization that is created by individual state laws.

Corporations are business organizations created under state law in the United States. The most notable characteristic of a corporation is **limited liability** of the owners, which means that corporate creditors (such as banks or suppliers) ordinarily have claims against the corporate assets only. Individuals form a corporation by applying to the state for approval of the company's articles of incorporation, which include information on shares of ownership. Most large corporations are **publicly owned** in that shares in the ownership are sold to the public. The owners of the corporation are then identified as shareholders (or stockholders). Large publicly owned corporations often have thousands of shareholders. Some corporations are **privately owned** by families, small groups of shareholders, or a single individual, with shares of ownership not publicly sold.

limited liability A feature of the corporate form of organization whereby corporate creditors ordinarily have claims against the corporate assets only. The owners' personal assets are not subject to the creditors' grasp.

In the United States, the laws governing the creation of a corporation vary from state to state. In spite of its small size, Delaware is the state in which many corporations are legally created because its rules are less restrictive than are those of most other states. In addition, its legal and incorporating fees are low, and its legal system and the judges who hear business cases are experienced and efficient at resolving disputes and lawsuits. The exact rights and privileges of a corporation vary from state to state and from country to country.

publicly owned A corporation in which shares in the ownership are sold to the public.

Internationally, organizational forms similar to corporations are common. In the United Kingdom they are frequently indicated by the word "limited" (Ltd.) in the name. In many countries whose laws trace back to Spain, the initials S.A. refer to a "society anonymous" meaning that multiple unidentified owners stand behind the company. Not surprisingly, countries in the former Soviet Union are formulating legal systems that permit corporate-style companies. They are also creating markets where the owners of these companies can buy and sell their ownership interests.

privately owned A corporation owned by a family, a small group of shareholders, or a single individual, in which shares of ownership are not publicly sold.

Whereas the owners of proprietorships and partnerships are typically active managers of the business as well, corporate managers often own only a small part of the public corporation. Because the corporate form is the form in which the majority of U.S. business is conducted, we use corporate accounting practice almost exclusively.

A NOTE ON NONPROFIT ORGANIZATIONS

The major focus of this book is on profit-seeking organizations, such as business firms. However, the fundamental accounting principles also apply to nonprofit, that is, not-for-profit, organizations. Managers and accountants in hospitals, universities, government agencies, and other nonprofit organizations use financial statements. Money must be raised and spent, budgets must be prepared, and financial performance must be judged.

ADVANTAGES AND DISADVANTAGES OF THE CORPORATE FORM

The corporate form of organization has many advantages. Limited liability is foremost. If a corporation drifts into financial trouble, its creditors cannot look for repayment beyond the corporation itself. In other words, the owners' personal assets are not subject to the creditors' grasp. In contrast, the owners of proprietorships and partnerships typically have unlimited liability, which means that business creditors can look to the owners' personal assets for repayment. For example, if Biwheels were a partnership, each partner would bear a personal liability for full payment of the $100,000 bank loan.

capital stock certificate (stock certificate) Formal evidence of ownership shares in a corporation.

Another advantage of the corporation is easy transfer of ownership. In selling shares in its ownership, the corporation usually issues **capital stock certificates** (often called simply **stock certificates**) as formal evidence of ownership. These shares may be sold and resold among present and potential owners. Numerous stock exchanges exist in the United States and worldwide where long established rules for trading facilitate daily buying and selling of shares. About 1 billion shares are bought and sold on an average day on the New York Stock Exchange (NYSE) alone. Further, trading is not limited to U.S. markets. Shares of many large U.S. firms are also traded on international exchanges such as those in Tokyo and London. Many Japanese and British firms have shares traded on the NYSE. Examples include Nissan, Toyota, and Honda from Japan, BPAmoco, and Glaxo Wellcome from the United Kingdom.

Biwheels is organized as a sole proprietorship. What would be the biggest advantage for Mr. Smith in converting it to a corporation?

ANSWER

As a sole proprietorship Mr. Smith is personally liable for all of the liabilities of Biwheels. If it were a corporation, his liability would be limited to his investment.

In contrast to proprietorships and partnerships, corporations have the advantage of ease in raising ownership capital from hundreds or thousands of potential stockholders. AT&T has over 4.2 million stockholders, owning a total of more than 3 billion shares of stock. More than 11 million shares trade hands daily as investors buy and sell this popular stock.

The corporation also has the advantage of continuity of existence. The life of a corporation is indefinite in the sense that it continues even if its ownership changes. In contrast, proprietorships and partnerships officially terminate on the death or complete withdrawal of an owner.

The effects of the form of ownership on income taxes may vary significantly. For example, a corporation is taxed as a separate entity (as a corporation). However, no income taxes are levied on a proprietorship (as a proprietorship) or on a partnership (as a partnership). Instead the income earned by proprietorships and partnerships is attributed to the owners as personal taxpayers. In short, the income tax laws regard corporations as taxable entities, but proprietorships or partnerships as not taxable entities. Whether the corporate form provides tax advantages or disadvantages depends heavily on the personal tax situations of the owners.

Regardless of the economic and legal advantages or disadvantages of each type of organization, some small-business owners incorporate simply for prestige. That is, they feel more important if they can refer to "my corporation" and if they can refer to themselves as "chairman of the board" or "president" instead of "business owner" or "partner."

Although there are fewer corporations in the United States than there are proprietorships or partnerships, the corporation has far more economic significance. Therefore, this book emphasizes the corporate form of ownership.

ACCOUNTING FOR OWNERS' EQUITY

The basic accounting concepts that underlie the owners' equity section of the balance sheet are the same for all three forms of ownership. However, owners' equities for proprietorships and partnerships are often identified by the word capital. In contrast, owners' equity for a corporation is usually called **stockholders' equity** or **shareholders' equity.** Examine the possibilities for the Biwheels Company that are shown in Exhibit 1-5.

The accounts for the proprietorship and the partnership show owners' equity as straightforward records of the capital invested by the owners. For a corporation, though, the total capital investment by its owners, both at the start of the company and thereafter, is called **paid-in capital.** It is recorded in two parts: capital stock at par value and paid-in capital in excess of par value.

stockholders' equity (shareholders' equity) Owners' equity of a corporation. The excess of assets over liabilities of a corporation.

paid-in capital The total capital investment in a corporation by its owners both at and subsequent to the inception of business.

Newscasters often report on the performance of the stock market by saying, "Today the Dow gained 100 points" or "The Dow closed at 11,000." The Dow Jones Industrial Average is one of many indices used to describe performance of stock markets around the world. All indices are designed to provide a picture of what is happening on average to the value of securities owned by investors. Although the details vary a bit from one to another, most indices calculate the ongoing value of an assumed investment. For example, the Dow began as the average value of an investment in one share of each of 12 stocks and was first published in 1896 by Charles Dow. To calculate it you simply added the prices of the 12 stocks and divided by 12. It began at 40.94 but fell to an all-time low of 28.48 in August of that year. The calculation today is more complex due to several factors that you will better understand at the end of this course than today.

Since 1928, the number of stocks in the Dow has been constant at 30, but there have been 38 changes in the composition of the Dow. These changes reflect the dynamic nature of American industry. The original Dow had several auto and petroleum companies to capture the massive importance of these industries. Today only ExxonMobil and General Motors remain. McDonald's replaced American Tobacco in 1985, Wal-Mart replaced Woolworth in 1997, and Home Depot replaced Sears in 1999. Technology companies have only appeared in the Dow in significant numbers recently with Hewlett-Packard, Microsoft, and Intel all added since 1997.

Dow's goal was to create an average of a small number of companies that gave a good indication about how all investments were doing. At the time, calculations were difficult and having just 30 stocks eased calculation and permitted timely reporting. Today, indices commonly have hundreds or thousands of companies included and the index values are recalculated instantly throughout the day and reported electronically to brokerage houses and individual computers around the world. Today you can find many indices reported including the Standard and Poor's Five Hundred, the Nasdaq, and so forth. Each is intended to give a quick picture of the average result for investors in a particular group of companies.

Exhibit 1-5

Owners' Equity for Different Organizations

OWNERS' EQUITY FOR A PROPRIETORSHIP (ASSUME GEORGE SMITH IS THE SOLE OWNER)	
George Smith, capital	$400,000

OWNERS' EQUITY FOR A PARTNERSHIP (ASSUME SMITH HAS TWO PARTNERS)	
George Smith, capital	$320,000
Alex Handl, capital	40,000
Susan Eastman, capital	40,000
Total partners' capital	$400,000

OWNERS' EQUITY FOR A CORPORATION	
Stockholders' equity:	
Paid-in capital:	
Capital stock, 10,000 shares issued at par value of $10 per share	$100,000
Paid-in capital in excess of par value of capital stock	300,000
Total paid-in capital	$400,000

THE MEANING OF PAR VALUE

Most states require stock certificates to have some dollar amount printed on them. This amount is determined by the board of directors and is usually called **par value** or **stated value.** Typically, the stock is sold at a price that is higher than its par value. The difference between the total amount received for the stock and the par value is called **paid-in capital in excess of par value.** This distinction is of little economic importance and we introduce it here only because you will frequently encounter it in actual financial statements.

par value (stated value) The nominal dollar amount printed on stock certificates.

paid-in capital in excess of par value When issuing stock, the difference between the total amount received and the par value.

Let us take a closer look at par value by altering our Biwheels example. We now assume that Biwheels is a corporation and that 10,000 shares of its stock have been sold for $40 per share. The par value is $10 per share, and therefore the paid-in capital in excess of par value is $30 per share. Thus, the total ownership claim of $400,000 arising from the investment is split between two equity claims, one for $100,000 capital stock, at par and one for $300,000 paid-in capital in excess of par or additional paid-in capital.

The following formulas show these components of the total paid-in capital account:

$$\text{Total paid-in capital} = \text{Capital stock at par} + \text{Paid-in capital in excess of par}$$

$$\$400,000 = \$100,000 + \$300,000$$

$$\text{Capital stock at par} = \text{Number of shares issued} \times \text{Par value per share}$$

$$\$100,000 = 10,000 \times \$10$$

$$\text{Paid-in capital in excess of par} = \text{Total paid-in capital} - \text{Capital stock at par}$$

$$\$300,000 = \$400,000 - \$100,000$$

$$\text{Total paid-in capital} = \text{Number of shares issued} \times \text{Average issue price per share}$$

$$\$400,000 = 10,000 \times \$40$$

Exhibit 1-6 shows par value and paid-in capital for McDonald's and Gap Inc. in panel A. Panel B shows the relationship between par value and market value of common stock, including AT&T. As you see, there is no relationship.

Shares of AT&T have a par value of $1, while those of Gap have a par value of $.05, and those of McDonald's have a $.01 par value. AT&T refers to its shares as common shares while Gap and McDonald's use the phrase common stock. Whether called common shares or **common stock,** the word represents the class of owners having a "residual" ownership of the corporation. Although it would be nice to stick to one phrase at every point in this textbook, the reality is that the world is full of different words for some accounting items. One of our goals is to help you to prepare yourself for reading and understanding actual financial statements and reports. Therefore, we use many of the various synonyms you are likely to come across when reading financial statements. Another of our goals is to identify distinctions that are important and those that are not. For example, there are different par values for these companies, but these values bear no relation to the companies' market prices, as illustrated in panel B of Exhibit 1-6.

common stock (capital stock) Stock representing the class of owners having a "residual" ownership of a corporation.

The extremely small amount of par value as compared with the additional paid-in capital is common in practice and illustrates the insignificance of par value in today's business world. McDonald's uses the frequently encountered term, "additional paid-in capital," as a short synonym for "paid-in capital in excess of par value of common stock." Finally, note that the number of "shares authorized" is the maximum number of shares that the company can issue as designated by the company's articles of incorporation.

Exhibit 1-6

Owners' Equity: McDonald's and Gap

PANEL A: COMPARATIVE BALANCE SHEET AND DATA

Gap Inc. ($000 Except par value)	January 29, 2000	January 30, 1999
Shareholders' Equity		
Common stock $.05 par value	$ 50,386	$ 49,875
Additional paid-in-capital	669,490	349,037
Retained earnings	4,172,796	3,121,360
Other comprehensive income (loss)	(6,759)	(12,518)
Other	(2,652,850)	(1,934,075)
Total Shareholders' Equity	$ 2,233,063	$1,573,679

McDonald's (in millions, except per share data)	December 31, 1999	1998
Shareholders' Equity		
Common Stock $.01 par value	$ 16.6	$ 16.6
Additional Paid-in Capital	1,288.3	989.2
Retained Earnings	15,562.8	13,879.6
Accumulated Other Comprehensive Income	(886.8)	(522.5)
Other	(6,341.8)	(4,898.2)
Total Shareholders' Equity	$ 9,639.1	$ 9,464.7

PANEL B: COMPARATIVE PAR AND MARKET VALUES

	AT&T	Gap	McDonald's
Par value	$ 1.00	$ .05	$ .01
Market (7/2000)	$33.00	$38.00	$31.00

McDonald's shows "retained earnings" and "other" as part of owners' equity. These values arise from various sources with the passage of time. Our current focus is on the first two lines—common stock and additional paid-in capital. These amounts can be described accurately with a simple term, total paid-in capital. An important point about paid-in capital is that it shows amounts that owners actively contributed to the firm.

Individuals buy shares of stock as investments. Sometimes they purchase the stock from the company, and the previous discussion describes what happens. The company records cash received and records the par value of shares issued with the excess shown as an increase in paid-in capital. However, the majority of stock transactions involving purchase and sale of stock occur between individuals. When Mary sells 100 shares of DuPont to Carlos, the transaction has no effect on DuPont. Mary may have a gain if the shares are sold for more than she paid for them. She will have a loss on the sale otherwise, but this affects DuPont only in terms of keeping track of its owners. When the shares change hands, Mary will be replaced by Carlos on the corporate records as an owner, and Carlos will begin to receive the dividends on the shares and will be allowed to vote on corporate issues.

STOCKHOLDERS AND THE BOARD OF DIRECTORS

In partnerships, the managerial tasks may be shared by the owners. In corporations, the ultimate responsibility for management is delegated by the stockholders to the board of directors, as indicated in the following diagram:

An advantage of the corporate form of organization is that it separates ownership and management. Stockholders invest resources but do not need to devote time to managing, and managers can be selected for their managerial skills, not their ability to invest large sums in the firm. The board of directors is the link between stockholders and the actual managers. The board's duty is to ensure that managers act in the interests of shareholders.

The board of directors is elected by the shareholders, but the slate of candidates is often selected by management. Sometimes, the chairman of the board is also the top manager and the major shareholder. For example, for over 30 years Henry Ford II was the major stockholder, the chairman of the board, and the CEO of the Ford Motor Company. Other top company managers, such as the president, financial vice president, and marketing vice president, are routinely elected to the board of directors of the company they manage. Therefore, the interests of both stockholders and managers are usually represented on the board of directors.

Membership on a board of directors is often extended to CEOs and presidents of other corporations, to university presidents and professors, and to attorneys. For example, the 9-member board of Oracle in 2000 included three members of Oracle management, a professor, former senator and presidential aspirant Jack Kemp, the chairman of Lucent Technologies, a venture capitalist, and two other CEOs. Although boards once had 15 to 20 members, many companies are moving toward having smaller boards of directors that include fewer members of the company's management team.

CREDIBILITY AND THE ROLE OF AUDITING

If someone told you that smoking cigarettes was not related to the risk of lung cancer, your reaction would be based on when the conversation occurred, on who the speaker was, and on your own knowledge at the time. For instance, when Europeans arrived in North America and first witnessed the act of smoking tobacco, no one knew what lung cancer was, and no one linked disease to behavior. By the middle of the twentieth century, people understood that what you did to your body could easily make you sick, but there was not enough evidence about the health risks of smoking. Were people who smoked more likely to have lung cancer? By the mid-1990s, evidence showed that the answer to this question was most certainly yes, although it was not until 1997 that executives of tobacco companies acknowledged a link. Some people continue to consider the additional risk of cancer small and continue to smoke.

Objective 6
Describe auditing and how it enhances the value of financial information.

This little history lesson emphasizes that peoples' statements are often affected by the position of the speaker. Many tobacco executives refuse to say that tobacco causes cancer for to do so would acknowledge prior lies and invite lawsuits. Some smokers cannot say that tobacco is really dangerous because to do so would call into question their own behavior. As listeners we discount certain claims because we know the motives of the person or organization making the claim.

Corporate managers provide financial statements to both internal and external decision makers. They may have incentives to make the company's performance look better than it really is. Perhaps doing so will make it easier to raise money to open new stores, or perhaps it would lead to increases in managers' compensation. Managers often believe that company conditions are better than they really are because managers are optimistic about the good decisions they have made and the plans they are implementing. The problem we face as investors is that we must rely on managers to tell the truth, because we cannot see personally what is going on in the firm.

One way to solve this credibility problem is to introduce an honorable, expert third party. In the area of financial statements this third party is called the auditor. The **auditor** examines the information that managers use to prepare the financial statements and provides assurances about the credibility of those statements. On seeing the auditor's assurance that the financial statements provide a fair and accurate picture of a company's economic circumstances, investors can feel more comfortable about using the information to guide their investing activity. Another way to ensure truthful reporting by managers is by handing out stiff legal penalties for lying. A manager who knowingly misstates performance is subject to both fines and jail sentences under U.S. law.

auditor A person who examines the information used by managers to prepare the financial statements and attests to the credibility of those statements.

THE CERTIFIED PUBLIC ACCOUNTANT

The desire for third-party assurance about the credibility of financial statements gave rise naturally to a profession dedicated to that purpose. Providing credibility requires individuals who have both the technical knowledge to assess financial statements and the reputation for integrity and independence that assures they will honestly tell investors and other interested parties if management has not produced fair financial statements. Enter the certified public accountant (CPA).

certified public accountant (CPA) In the United States, a person earns this designation by a combination of education, qualifying experience, and the passing of a 2-day written national examination.

Certified public accountants in the United States earn their certification by a combination of education, qualifying experience, and passing a 2-day written national examination. The examination is administered and graded by a national organization, the American Institute of Certified Public Accountants (AICPA). The institute is the principal professional association in the private sector that regulates the quality of the public accounting profession. Other English-speaking nations have similar arrangements but use the term *chartered accountant* (*CA*) instead of CPA.

The CPA examination covers four major topic areas: auditing, accounting theory, business law, and accounting practice. The last is a series of accounting problems covering a wide variety of topics, including income taxes, cost accounting, and accounting for non-profit institutions.

Although the AICPA prepares and grades the CPA examination on a national basis, the individual states have their own regulations concerning the qualifications for taking and passing the examination and for earning the right to practice as a CPA. These regulations are determined and enforced by state boards of accountancy.

THE AUDITOR'S OPINION

audit An examination of transactions and financial statements made in accordance with generally accepted auditing standards.

To assess management's financial disclosure, public accountants conduct an **audit,** which is an examination of transactions and financial statements made in accordance with generally accepted auditing standards developed primarily by the AICPA. This audit includes miscellaneous tests of the accounting records, internal control systems, and other auditing

Exhibit 1-7
Report of Independent Auditors

The Board of Directors and Shareholders
McDonald's Corporation

We have audited the accompanying consolidated balance sheets of McDonald's Corporation as of December 31, 1999 and 1998, and the related consolidated statements of income, shareholders' equity and cash flows for each of the three years in the period ended December 31, 1999. These financial statements are the responsibility of McDonald's Corporation management. Our responsibility is to express an opinion on these financial statements based on our audits.

We conducted our audits in accordance with auditing standards generally accepted in the United States. Those standards require that we plan and perform the audit to obtain reasonable assurance about whether the financial statements are free of material misstatement. An audit includes examining, on a test basis, evidence supporting the amounts and disclosures in the financial statements. An audit also includes assessing the accounting principles used and significant estimates made by management, as well as evaluating the overall financial statement presentation. We believe that our audits provide a reasonable basis for our opinion.

In our opinion, the financial statements referred to above present fairly, in all material respects, the consolidated financial position of McDonald's Corporation at December 31, 1999 and 1998, and the consolidated results of its operations and its cash flows for each of the three years in the period ended December 31, 1999, in conformity with accounting principles generally accepted in the United States.

Ernst & Young LLP
Chicago, Illinois
January 26, 2000

---

procedures as deemed necessary. The examination is described in the **auditor's opinion** (also called an **independent opinion**) that is included with the financial statements in a corporation's annual report. Standard phrasing is used for auditors' opinions, as illustrated by the January 26, 2000 opinion rendered by a large CPA firm, Ernst & Young, for McDonald's Corporation which appears in Exhibit 1-7.

This book explores the meaning of such phrases as "present fairly" and "generally accepted accounting principles." For now, reflect on the fact that auditors do not prepare a company's financial statements. Instead, the auditor's opinion is the public accountant's stamp of approval on financial statements prepared by management.

auditor's opinion (independent opinion) A report describing the auditor's examination of transactions and financial statements. It is included with the financial statements in an annual report issued by the corporation.

THE ACCOUNTING PROFESSION

There are many ways to classify accountants, but the easiest and most common way is to divide them into public and private accountants. **Public accountants** are those whose services are offered to the general public on a fee basis. Such services include auditing, preparing income taxes, and management consulting. All other accountants would be **private accountants.** This category consists not only of those individuals who work for businesses but also of those who work for government agencies, including the Internal Revenue Service (IRS), and other nonprofit organizations.

Objective 7
Distinguish between public and private accounting

public accountants Accountants who offer services to the general public on a fee basis including auditing, tax work, and management consulting.

PUBLIC ACCOUNTING FIRMS

Public accounting firms vary in their size and in the type of accounting services they perform. There are small proprietorships, where auditing may represent as little as 10% or

private accountants
Accountants who work for businesses, as well as government agencies, and other nonprofit organizations.

less of annual billings. Billings are the total amounts charged to clients for services rendered to them. The bulk of the work of these small proprietorships is usually income taxes and "write-up" work (the actual bookkeeping services for clients who are not equipped to do their own accounting).

There are also a handful of gigantic firms that have more than 2,000 partners with offices located throughout the world. Such enormous firms are necessary because their clients also tend to be enormous. For instance, one large CPA firm reported that its annual audit of one client takes the equivalent of 72 accountants working a full year. Another client has 300 separate corporate entities in 40 countries that must ultimately be consolidated into one set of overall financial statements.

The five largest public international accounting firms are known collectively as the "Big-Five":

- Andersen
- Deloitte & Touche
- Ernst & Young
- KPMG Peat Marwick
- PricewaterhouseCoopers

Many of these firms trace their origins to England and Scotland during the colonial period when audit firms came to the United States to oversee investments in the colonies. Of the companies listed on the NYSE, 97% are clients of the Big-Five. These accounting firms have annual billings in excess of a billion dollars each. A large part of the billings is attributable to auditing services. The top partners in big accounting firms are compensated on about the same scale as their corporate counterparts. Huge accounting firms tend to receive more publicity than other firms. However, please remember that there are thousands of other able accounting firms, varying in size from sole practitioners to giant international partnerships.

PROFESSIONAL ETHICS

Objective 8
Evaluate the role of ethics in the accounting process.

Members of the AICPA must abide by a code of professional conduct. Surveys of public attitudes toward CPAs have consistently ranked the accounting profession as having high ethical standards. The code of professional conduct is especially concerned with integrity and independence.

Many public accounting firms have practices that involve providing audit services but also providing tax and consulting services to clients. People have worried for many years about how auditors can remain independent if they or their partners stand to reap substantial fees from the continuing relationship or from investing in stock in their clients. One rule to minimize this risk prohibits professional staff and partners from investing in the shares of client firms. In a recent SEC investigation, one of the Big Five was found to have many partners who were violating this rule. The firm has been forced to resign from several audits and has suffered significant embarrassment and loss of public confidence.

The emphasis on ethics extends beyond public accounting. For example, members of the Institute of Management Accountants are expected to abide by that organization's code of ethics for management accountants. Auditors and management accountants have professional responsibilities concerning competence, confidentiality, integrity, and objectivity. Professional accounting organizations and state regulatory bodies have procedures for reviewing behavior alleged to violate codes of professional conduct.

OTHER OPPORTUNITIES FOR ACCOUNTANTS

In the accompanying diagram, the long arrows indicate how accountants often move from public accounting firms to positions in business or government. Obviously, these movements can occur at any level or in any direction.

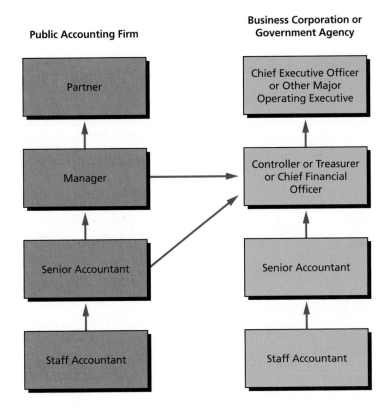

Public Accounting Firm

- Partner
- Manager
- Senior Accountant
- Staff Accountant

Business Corporation or Government Agency

- Chief Executive Officer or Other Major Operating Executive
- Controller or Treasurer or Chief Financial Officer
- Senior Accountant
- Staff Accountant

Accounting cuts across all management functions, including purchasing, manufacturing, wholesaling, retailing, and a variety of marketing and transportation activities. It provides an excellent opportunity for gaining broad knowledge. The people responsible for collecting and interpreting financial information about the company develop detailed knowledge about what is occurring and close relationships with key decision makers. Senior accountants or controllers in a corporation are often picked as production or marketing executives. Why? Because they may have impressed other executives as having acquired general management skills.

Accounting is ranked as the most important business school course for future managers. *Business Week* recently reported that "more CEOs [chief executive officers] started out in finance or accounting than in any other area." It is easy to see why accounting is called the language of business.

SUMMARY PROBLEMS FOR YOUR REVIEW

PROBLEM ONE

Analyze the following additional transactions of Biwheels Company. Begin with the balances shown for January 12, 20X2, in Exhibit 1-2 on p. 12. Prepare an ending balance sheet for Biwheels Company (e.g., on January 16 after these additional transactions).

  i.   Biwheels pays $10,000 on the bank loan (ignore interest).

 ii.   Smith buys furniture for his home for $5,000, using his family charge account at Macy's.

iii.   Biwheels buys merchandise inventory for $50,000. Half the amount is paid in cash, and half is owed on open account.

 iv.   Biwheels collects $200 more from its business debtor.

Exhibit 1-8

Biwheels Company

Analysis of Additional January Transactions

Description of Transaction	Assets							=	Liabilities + Owners' Equity				
	Cash	+	Accounts Receivable	+	Merchandise Inventory	+	Store Equipment	=	Note Payable	+	Accounts Payable	+	Smith, Capital
Balance, January 12, 20X2	$342,700	+	$ 300	+	$159,200	+	$14,000	=	$100,000	+	$ 16,200	+	$400,000
(i) Payment on bank loan	−10,000							=	−10,000				
(ii) Personal; no effect													
(iii) Acquire inventory, half for cash	−25,000				+	50,000			=		+	25,000	
(iv) Collection of receivable	+ 200		−200										
Balance, January 16	$307,900	+	$ 100	+	$209,200	+	$14,000	=	$ 90,000	+	$ 41,200	+	$400,000
			$531,200					=			$531,200		

SOLUTION TO PROBLEM ONE

See Exhibits 1-8 and 1-9. Note that transaction ii is ignored because it is wholly personal. However, visualize how Smith's personal balance sheet would be affected. His assets, Home Furniture, would rise by $5,000 and his liabilities, Accounts Payable, would also rise by $5,000.

PROBLEM TWO

"If I purchase 100 shares of the outstanding stock of General Motors Corporation (or Biwheels Company), I invest my money directly in that corporation. General Motors must record that event." Do you agree? Explain.

SOLUTION TO PROBLEM TWO

Money is invested directly in a corporation when the corporation originally issues the stock. For example, 100,000 shares of stock may be issued at $80 per share, bringing in $8 million to the corporation. This is a transaction between the corporation and the stockholders. It affects the corporate financial position:

Cash $8,000,000   Stockholders' equity $8,000,000

Subsequently, 100 shares of that stock may be sold by an original stockholder (Michael Jordan) to another individual (Meg Ryan) for $130 per share. This is a private transaction; no cash is received by the corporation. Of course, the corporation records the

Exhibit 1-9

Biwheels Company

Balance Sheet January 16, 20X2

Assets		Liabilities and Owner's Equity	
		Liabilities:	
Cash	$307,900	Note payable	$ 90,000
Accounts receivable	100	Accounts payable	41,200
Merchandise inventory	209,200	Total liabilities	$131,200
Store equipment	14,000	Smith, capital	400,000
Total	$531,200	Total	$531,200

fact that 100 shares originally owned by Jordan are now owned by Ryan, but the corporate financial position is unchanged. Accounting focuses on the business entity; subsequently, private dealings of the owners have no effect on the financial position of the entity, although the corporation records the owners' identities.

PROBLEM THREE

"One individual can be an owner, an employee, and a creditor of a corporation." Do you agree? Explain.

SOLUTION TO PROBLEM THREE

The corporation enters contracts, hires employees, buys buildings, and conducts other business. The chairman of the board, the president, the other officers, and all the workers are employees of the corporation. Thus Katharine Graham could own some of the capital stock of the *Washington Post* and also be an employee (CEO). Because money owed to employees for salaries is a liability, she could be an owner, an employee, and a creditor. Similarly, an employee of a telephone company who is a stockholder of the company could also be receiving telephone services from the same company. She is an owner, employee, customer, creditor, and debtor of the company.

PROBLEM FOUR

Refer to the Cisco financial statements reproduced in appendix A to respond to the following questions.

1. As of what date is the consolidated balance sheet prepared?
2. What are total assets for the 2 years shown in the consolidated balance sheets? What elements explain the difference in the asset levels for the 2 years?
3. What is the par value of the common stock?
4. How many share of common stock are authorized and how many shares are outstanding at the latest year-end?

SOLUTION TO PROBLEM FOUR

1. Two balance sheets are presented. One is dated as of July 29, 2000 and the other is dated as of July 31, 1999. The more recent one is in the left column. The first sentence in note 2, "Summary of Significant Accounting Policies," explains that the company uses a fiscal year for either 52 or 53 weeks that end on the last Saturday in July. Thus fiscal 2000 refers to the year ending July 29, 2000.
2. Total assets more than doubled from $14,893,000,000 in 1999 to $32,870,000,000 in 2000. Note that the numbers in the annual report are expressed "in millions" as indicated in the parenthetical note under the words "Consolidated Balance Sheets" at the top of the page. All asset accounts increased from 1999 to 2000, but the biggest percentage gains were in Cash and cash equivalents (up from $913 million to $4,234 million or 464%) and in Goodwill and purchased intangible assets (up from $460 million to $4,087 million or 888%). The percentage increases are calculated as the final value divided by the beginning value times 100. Thus, $4,234 \div $913 \times 100 = 464\%$. The largest absolute increase was in Investments, which grew by $6,656 million.
3. The par value is $0.001 per share as indicated in the Shareholders' equity section of the balance sheet.
4. Cisco has authorized 20,000,000,000 shares. At the end of fiscal 2000, 7,138,000,000 shares are issued and outstanding. Note that the reference to numbers "in millions" included numbers of shares. Only the par value is not expressed in millions.

Highlights to Remember

1. **Explain how accounting information assists in making decisions.** Financial statements provide information for decision making to managers, creditors, and owners of all types of organizations. The balance sheet (or statement of financial position) provides a "snapshot" of the financial position of an organization at any instant. That is, it answers the basic question, Where are we?

2. **Describe the components of the balance sheet.** The balance sheet equation is Assets = Liabilities + Owners' Equity. This equation must always be in balance. The balance sheet presents the balances of the components of Assets, Liabilities, and Owners' Equity at a specific point in time.

3. **Analyze business transactions and relate them to changes in the balance sheet.** Transaction analysis is the heart of accounting. A transaction is any event that both affects the financial position of an entity and can be reliably recorded in money terms. For each transaction, an accountant must determine what accounts are affected and the amount involved.

4. **Classify operating, investing, and financing activities in a cash flow statement.** The cash flow statement summarizes the changes during a period in the cash balance for the firm. The changes are classified as to whether they relate to an operating activity, financing activity, or investing activity. Operating activities relate to the purchase, production and sale of goods, and services on an ongoing basis. Financing activities relate to raising capital via issuance of capital stock or borrowing. Investing is the use of capital to acquire assets such as buildings and equipment.

5. **Compare the features of proprietorships, partnerships, and corporations.** Corporations are the most important form of business ownership because so much business is conducted by corporations. The ownership equity of a corporation is usually called stockholders' equity. It initially takes the form of common stock at par, or stated, value plus additional paid-in capital.

6. **Describe auditing and how it enhances the value of financial information.** Separation of ownership from management in corporations creates a demand for auditing, a third-party examination of financial statements. Auditors evaluate the record-keeping system of the firm and test specific transactions and account balances to assure that the balances fairly reflect the financial position of the company.

7. **Distinguish between public and private accounting.** Public accounting involves providing services, especially audit services, to client companies. The public accounting profession gives credibility to audits by specifying qualifications for certified public accountants, including ethical standards, and by developing generally accepted auditing standards to ensure thoroughness of audits. Private accounting refers to performing accounting functions as an employee of a firm. The treasurer of Cisco and a cost analyst at Boeing are both engaged in private accounting. Because accountants work with managers in all management functions, accounting positions are fertile training grounds for future top managers.

8. **Evaluate the role of ethics in the accounting process.** Ethical behavior is critically important in professional activities such as accounting. In public accounting, the value of an audit is directly linked to the credibility of the auditor as an ethical, independent professional who is qualified to evaluate the financial statements of the firm and is also reliably committed to disclosing problems or concerns uncovered in the evaluation.

Accounting Vocabulary

account, p. 11
accounting, p. 4
account payable, p. 12

annual report, p. 8
assets, p. 9
audit, p. 24

auditor, p. 24
auditor's opinion, p. 25
balance sheet, p. 8

Assignment Material

The assignment material for each chapter is divided into Questions, Cognitive Exercises, and Problems. The assignment material contains problems based on fictitious companies and problems based on real-life situations. We hope our use of actual companies and news events enhances your interest in accounting.

We identify problems based on real companies by highlighting the name in blue. These problems underscore a major objective of this book: to increase your ability to read, understand, and use published financial reports and news articles. In later chapters, these problems provide the principal means of reviewing not only the immediate chapter but also the previous chapters. Note that the last four problems in each chapter are (1) a problem based on Cisco Systems, whose financial statements are in appendix A, (2) a financial statement research problem, (3) a Collaborative Learning Exercise, and (4) an Internet-based problem.

QUESTIONS

1-1 Describe *accounting.*

1-2 "It's easier to learn accounting if you avoid real-world examples." Do you agree? Explain.

1-3 Give three examples of decisions that are likely to be influenced by financial statements.

1-4 Give three examples of users of financial statements.

1-5 Briefly distinguish between *financial accounting* and *management accounting.*

1-6 Give two synonyms for *balance sheet.*

1-7 "The balance sheet may be out of balance after some transactions, but it is never out of balance at the end of an accounting period." Do you agree? Explain.

1-8 "When a company buys inventory for cash, total assets do not change. However, when it buys inventory on open account, total assets increase." Explain.

1-9 Explain the difference between a *note payable* and an *account payable.*

1-10 Give two synonyms for *owners' equity.*

1-11 Explain the meaning of *limited liability.*

1-12 Why does this book emphasize the corporation instead of the proprietorship or the partnership?

1-13 "International companies with Ltd. or S.A. after their name are essentially the same in organizational form as U.S. companies with Corp. after their name." Do you agree? Explain.

1-14 "The accounting systems described in this book apply to corporations and are not appropriate for nonprofit organizations." Do you agree? Explain.

1-15 "The idea of par value is insignificant." Explain.

1-16 Explain the relationship between the board of directors and top management of a company.

1-17 What is a CPA and how does someone become one?

COGNITIVE EXERCISES

1-18 The Auditor's Opinion

In reviewing the annual report of a company that you might invest in, you noted that you did not recognize the name of the audit firm that signed the audit opinion. What questions would this raise in your mind and how might you resolve them?

1-19 The Corporation

Some historians were arguing over the most important innovation in the history of business. Most thought of things and processes such as the railroad, the automobile, the printing press, the telephone, television, or more recently, the computer chip, fiberoptic cable, or even the Internet. One person argued that the really important innovation was the corporation and business law. How would this person argue for this idea?

1-20 Double-Entry Accounting
The accounting process in use today is typically called "double-entry" bookkeeping. Discuss the meaning and possible importance of this name.

1-21 Accountants as Historians
Critics sometimes refer to accountants as historians and do not mean it kindly. In what sense are accountants historians, and do you believe this is a compliment or a criticism?

EXERCISES

1-22 Describing Underlying Transactions
LaTech Company, which was recently formed, is engaging in some preliminary transactions before beginning full-scale operations for retailing laptop computers. The balances of each item in the company's accounting equation are given next for May 10 and for each of the next nine business days.

	Cash	Accounts Receivable	Computer Inventory	Store Fixtures	Accounts Payable	Owners' Equity
May 10	$ 6,000	$ 4,000	$18,000	$ 3,000	$ 4,000	$27,000
11	12,000	4,000	18,000	3,000	4,000	33,000
12	12,000	4,000	18,000	7,000	4,000	37,000
15	9,000	4,000	21,000	7,000	4,000	37,000
16	9,000	4,000	26,000	7,000	9,000	37,000
17	12,000	1,000	26,000	7,000	9,000	37,000
18	7,000	1,000	26,000	13,000	10,000	37,000
19	5,000	1,000	26,000	13,000	8,000	37,000
22	5,000	1,000	25,600	13,000	7,600	37,000
23	2,000	1,000	25,600	13,000	7,600	34,000

Required State briefly what you think took place on each of these nine days, assuming that only one transaction occurred each day.

1-23 Describing Underlying Transactions
The balances of each item in Monterrey Company's accounting equation are given next for August 31 and for each of the next nine business days.

Required State briefly what you think took place on each of these nine days, assuming that only one transaction occurred each day.

	Cash	Accounts Receivable	Computer Inventory	Store Fixtures	Accounts Payable	Owners' Equity
Aug. 31	$2,000	$ 8,000	$ 9,000	$ 7,500	$ 5,500	$21,000
Sept. 1	4,000	6,000	9,000	7,500	5,500	21,000
2	4,000	6,000	9,000	10,000	8,000	21,000
3	1,000	6,000	9,000	10,000	8,000	18,000
4	2,000	10,000	4,000	10,000	8,000	18,000
5	2,000	10,000	11,000	10,000	8,000	25,000
8	1,500	10,000	11,000	10,000	7,500	25,000
9	1,000	10,000	11,000	13,000	10,000	25,000
10	1,000	10,000	11,000	12,700	9,700	25,000
11	4,000	7,000	11,000	12,700	9,700	25,000

1-24 Prepare Balance Sheet

Albany Corporation's balance sheet at March 30, 20X1, contained only the following items (arranged here in random order):

Cash	$10,000	Accounts payable	$ 8,000
Notes payable	10,000	Furniture and fixtures	3,000
Merchandise inventory	40,000	Long-term debt payable	12,000
Paid-in capital	80,000	Building	20,000
Land	6,000	Notes receivable	2,000
Accounts receivable	14,000	Machinery and equipment	15,000

On March 31, 20X1, these transactions and events took place:

1. Purchased merchandise on account, $3,000.
2. Sold at cost for $1,000 cash some furniture that was not needed.
3. Issued additional capital stock for machinery and equipment valued at $12,000.
4. Purchased land for $25,000, of which $5,000 was paid in cash, the remaining being represented by a 5-year note (long-term debt).
5. The building was valued by professional appraisers at $45,000.

Required

Prepare in good form a balance sheet for March 31, 20X1, showing supporting computations for all new amounts.

1-25 Prepare Balance Sheet

Broadway Corporation's balance sheet at November 29, 20X1 contained only the following items (arranged here in random order):

Paid-in capital	$19,000	Machinery and equipment	$ 20,000
Notes payable	20,000	Furniture and fixtures	8,000
Cash	22,000	Notes receivable	8,000
Accounts receivable	10,000	Accounts payable	16,000
Merchandise inventory	29,000	Building	230,000
Land	41,000	Long-term debt payable	142,000

On the following day, November 30, these transactions and events occurred:

1. Purchased machinery and equipment for $14,000, paying $3,000 in cash and signing a 90-day note for the balance.
2. Paid $6,000 on accounts payable.
3. Sold on account some land that was not needed for $6,000, which was the Broadway Corporation's acquisition cost of the land.
4. The remaining land was valued at $240,000 by professional appraisers.
5. Issued capital stock as payment for $23,000 of the long-term debt, that is, debt due beyond 1 year.

Required

Prepare in good form a balance sheet for November 30, 20X1, showing supporting computations for all new amounts.

1-26 Balance Sheet

General Electric (GE) is one of the largest companies in the world with sales of nearly $61 billion. The company's balance sheet on January 1, 2000, had total assets of $405 billion and stockholders' equity (called shareowners' equity by GE) of $43 billion.

Required

1. Compute GE's total liabilities on January 1, 2000.
2. As of January 1, 2000, GE had issued 3,715,018,000 shares of common stock. The par value was $.16 per share. Compute the balance in the account, "Common stock, par value" on GE's balance sheet.

1-27 Prepare Balance Sheet

Sophia Brentano is a realtor. She buys and sells properties on her own account, and she also earns commissions as a real estate agent for buyers and sellers. Her business was organized on November 24, 20X1, as a sole proprietorship. Brentano also owns her own personal residence. Consider the following on November 30, 20X1:

1. Brentano owes $95,000 on a mortgage on some undeveloped land, which was acquired by her business for a total price of $180,000.
2. Brentano had spent $15,000 cash for a Century 21 real estate franchise. Century 21 is a national affiliation of independent real estate brokers. This franchise is an asset.
3. Brentano owes $100,000 on a personal mortgage on her residence, which was acquired on November 20, 20X1, for a total price of $180,000.
4. Brentano owes $3,800 on a personal charge account with Nordstrom's Department Store.
5. On November 28, Brentano hired Benjamin Goldstein as her first employee. He was to begin work on December 1. Brentano was pleased because Goldstein was one of the best real estate salesmen in the area. On November 29, Goldstein was killed in an automobile accident.
6. Business furniture was acquired for $17,000 on November 25, for $6,000 on open account plus $11,000 of business cash. On November 26, Brentano sold a $1,000 business chair for $1,000 to her next-door business neighbor on open account.
7. Brentano's balance at November 30 in her business checking account after all transactions was $9,000.

Required   Prepare a balance sheet as of November 30, 20X1, for Sophia Brentano, realtor.

1-28 Analysis of Transactions

Use the format of Exhibit 1-2 to analyze the following transactions for April of Crystal Cleaners. Then prepare a balance sheet as of April 30, 20X1. Crystal was founded on April 1.

1. Issued 1,000 shares of $1 par common stock for cash, $40,000.
2. Issued 500 shares of $1 par common stock for equipment, $20,000.
3. Borrowed cash, signing a note payable for $35,000.
4. Purchased equipment for cash, $30,000.
5. Purchased office furniture on account, $10,000.
6. Disbursed cash on account (to reduce the account payable), $4,000.
7. Sold equipment on account at cost, $8,000.
8. Discovered that the most prominent competitor in the area was bankrupt and was closing its doors on April 30.
9. Collected cash on account, $3,000. See transaction 7.

1-29 Analysis of Transactions

Walgreen Company is a well-known drugstore chain. A condensed balance sheet for August 31, 2000 follows ($ in millions):

Assets		Liabilities and Stockholders' Equity	
Cash	$ 13		
Accounts receivable	614	Accounts payable	$1,364
Inventories	2,831	Other liabilities	1,506
Property and other assets	3,646	Stockholders' equity	4,234
Total	$7,104	Total	$7,104

 Required   Use a format similar to Exhibit 1-2 to analyze the following transactions for the first 2 days of September ($ amounts are in millions). Then prepare a balance sheet as of September 2.

1. Issued 1,000,000 shares of common stock to employees for cash, $30.
2. Issued 1,500,000 shares of common stock for the acquisition of special equipment from a supplier, $45.
3. Borrowed cash, signing a note payable for $12.
4. Purchased equipment for cash, $13.
5. Purchased inventories on account, $90.
6. Disbursed cash on account (to reduce the accounts payable), $35.
7. Sold display equipment to retailer on account at cost, $1.
8. Collected cash on account, $8.

1-30   Analysis of Transactions

Nike, Inc. had the following condensed balance sheet on May 31, 2000 ($ in millions):

Assets		Liabilities and Owners' Equity	
Cash	$ 254		
Accounts receivable	1,567		
Inventories	1,446		
Equipment and		Total liabilities	$2,721
other assets	2,590	Owners' equity	3,136
		Total liabilities and	
Total assets	$5,857	owners' equity	$5,857

Consider the following transactions that occurred during the first 3 days of June ($ in thousands):

1. Inventories were acquired for cash, $16.
2. Inventories were acquired on open account, $19.
3. Unsatisfactory shoes acquired on open account in March were returned for full credit, $4.
4. Equipment of $12 was acquired for a cash down payment of $3 plus a 2-year promissory note of $9.
5. To encourage wider displays, special store equipment was sold on account to New York area stores for $40. The equipment had cost $40 in the preceding month.
6. Jodie Foster produced, directed, and starred in a movie. As a favor to a Nike executive, she agreed to display Nike shoes in a basketball scene. No fee was paid by Nike.
7. Cash was disbursed on account (to reduce accounts payable), $17.
8. Collected cash on account, $18.
9. Borrowed cash from a bank, $50.
10. Sold additional common stock for cash to new investors, $90.
11. The president of the company sold 5,000 shares of his personal holdings of Nike stock through his stockbroker.

Required

1. By using a format similar to Exhibit 1-2 (p. 12), prepare an analysis showing the effects of the June transactions on the financial position of Nike.
2. Prepare a balance sheet as of June 3.

1-31   Analysis of Transactions

Consider the following January transactions:

1. XYZ Corporation is formed on January 1, 20X1, by three persons, Xiao, Yergen, and Zimbel. XYZ will be a wholesale distributor of PC software. Each of the three investors is issued 10,000 shares of common stock ($1 par value) for $10 cash per share. Use two stockholders' equity accounts: Capital Stock (at par) and Additional Paid-in Capital.
2. Merchandise inventory of $80,000 is acquired for cash.
3. Merchandise inventory of $85,000 is acquired on open account.
4. Unsatisfactory merchandise that cost $11,000 in transaction 3 is returned for full credit.

5. Equipment of $40,000 is acquired for a cash down payment of $10,000 plus a 3-month promissory note of $30,000.

6. As a favor, XYZ sells equipment of $4,000 to a business neighbor on open account. The equipment had cost $4,000.

7. XYZ pays $20,000 on the account described in transaction 3.

8. XYZ collects $2,000 from the business neighbor. See transaction 6.

9. XYZ buys merchandise inventory of $100,000. One-half of the amount is paid in cash, and one-half is owed on open account.

10. Zimbel sells half of his common stock to Quigley for $12 per share.

Required

1. By using a format similar to Exhibit 1-2, prepare an analysis showing the effects of January transactions on the financial position of XYZ Corporation.

2. Prepare a balance sheet as of January 31, 20X1.

1-32 Analysis of Transactions

You began a business as a wholesaler of woolen goods. The following events have occurred:

1. On March 1, 20X1, you invested $60,000 cash in your new sole proprietorship, which you call Yukon Products.

2. Acquired $10,000 inventory for cash.

3. Acquired $8,000 inventory on open account.

4. Acquired equipment for $15,000 in exchange for a $5,000 cash down payment and a $10,000 promissory note.

5. A large retail store, which you had hoped would be a big customer, discontinued operations.

6. You take gloves home for your family. The gloves were carried in Yukon's inventory at $600. (Regard this as a borrowing by you from Yukon Products.)

7. Gloves that cost $300 in transaction 2 were of the wrong style. You returned them and obtained a full cash refund.

8. Gloves that cost $800 in transaction 3 were of the wrong color. You returned them and obtained gloves of the correct color in exchange.

9. Caps that cost $500 in transaction 3 had an unacceptable quality. You returned them and obtained full credit on your account.

10. Paid $1,000 on promissory note.

11. You use your personal cash savings of $5,000 to acquire some equipment for Yukon. You consider this as an additional investment in your business.

12. Paid $3,000 on open account.

13. Two scarf manufacturers who are suppliers for Yukon announced a 7% rise in prices, effective in 60 days.

14. You use your personal cash savings of $1,000 to acquire a new TV set for your family.

15. You exchange equipment that cost $4,000 in transaction 4 with another wholesaler. However, the equipment received, which is almost new, is smaller and is worth only $1,500. Therefore, the other wholesaler also agrees to pay you $500 in cash now and an additional $2,000 in cash in 60 days. (No gain or loss is recognized on this transaction.)

Required

1. By using Exhibit 1-2 (p. 12) as a guide, prepare an analysis of Yukon's transactions for March. Confine your analysis to the effects on the financial position of Yukon Products.

2. Prepare a balance sheet for Yukon Products as of March 31, 20X1.

1-33 Personal and Professional Entities

Jose Gomez, a recent graduate of a law school, was penniless on December 25, 20X1.

1. On December 26, Gomez inherited an enormous sum of money.

2. On December 27, he placed $40,000 in a business checking account for his unincorporated law practice.

3. On December 28, he purchased a home for a down payment of $100,000 plus a home mortgage payable of $250,000.

4. On December 28, Gomez agreed to rent a law office. He provided a $1,000 cash damage deposit (from his business cash), which will be fully refundable when he vacates the premises. This deposit is a business asset. Rental payments are to be made in advance on the first business day of each month. (The first payment of $700 is not to be made until January 2, 20X2.)

5. On December 28, Gomez purchased a computer for his law practice for $2,000 cash plus a $2,000 promissory note due in 90 days.

6. On December 28, he also purchased legal supplies for $1,000 on open account.

7. On December 28, Gomez purchased office furniture for his practice for $4,000 cash.

8. On December 29, Gomez hired a legal assistant receptionist for $380 per week. She was to report to work on January 2.

9. On December 30, Gomez's law practice lent $2,000 of cash in return for a 1-year note from Genie Kulp, a local candy store owner. Kulp had indicated that she would spread the news about the new lawyer.

Required

1. Use the format demonstrated in Exhibit 1-2 (p. 12) to analyze the transactions of Jose Gomez, lawyer. To avoid crowding, put your numbers in thousands of dollars. Do not restrict yourself to the account titles in Exhibit 1-2.

2. Prepare a balance sheet as of December 31, 20X1.

1-34   Bank Balance Sheet

Consider the following balance sheet accounts of Citigroup Inc. (in millions of $):

Assets		Liabilities and Stockholders' Equity	
Cash	$ 14,158	Deposits	$261,091
Investment securities	371,338	Other liabilities	406,160
Loans receivable	237,527	Total liabilities	667,251
Other assets	93,914	Stockholders' equity	49,686
Total assets	$716,937	Total liabilities and	
		stockholders' equity	$716,937

This balance sheet illustrates how it gathers and uses money. More than 80% of the total assets are in the form of investments and loans, and more than 35% of the total liabilities and stockholders' equity are in the form of deposits, a major liability. That is, these financial institutions are in the business of raising funds from depositors and, in turn, lending those funds to businesses, homeowners, and others. The stockholders' equity is usually tiny in comparison with the deposits (only about 7% in this case).

Required

1. What Citigroup accounts would be affected if you deposited $1,000?
2. Why are deposits listed as liabilities?
3. What accounts would be affected if the bank loaned John Solvang $50,000 for home renovations?
4. What accounts would be affected if Isabel Ramos withdrew $4,000 from her savings account?

1-35   Balance Sheet

KLM Royal Dutch Airlines is an international airline with a home base at Schiphol Airport in Amsterdam. It is the world's first scheduled airline still operating under its original name. It has more than 26,000 employees, 80% of them located in the Netherlands. On March 31, 2000, KLM's noncash assets were $9,046 million. Total assets were $10,549 million, and total liabilities were $8,105 million. Dollar amounts are translated from the Netherlands' monetary unit, the guilder.

1. Compute the following:
   a. KLM's cash on March 31, 2000.
   b. KLM's stockholders' equity on March 31, 2000.
2. Explain the easiest way to determine KLM's total liabilities and stockholders' equity from the information given in this problem.

1-36 Presenting Paid-In Capital

Consider excerpts from two balance sheets (amounts in millions):

CITIGROUP

Common stock ($.01 par value; authorized shares: 6.0 billion), issued shares 3,612,385,458	$ 36
Additional paid-in capital	10,036

IBM

Common stock, par value $.20 per share—shares authorized: 4,687,500,000; shares issued: 1,876,665,245 shares (includes capital in excess of par value)	$7,752,000

1. How would the presentation of Citigroup stockholders' equity accounts be affected if 1 billion more shares were issued for $70 cash per share?
2. How would the presentation of IBM's stockholders' equity accounts be affected if 1 million more shares were issued for $100 cash per share? Be specific.

1-37 Presenting Paid-In Capital

Honeywell, Inc., maker of thermostats and a variety of complex control systems, presented the following in its balance sheet shortly before it was purchased by GE in 2000.

Common stock—$1.00 par value, 957,599,006 shares issued	?
Additional paid-in capital	$2,318,000,000

What amount should be shown on the common stock line? What was the average price per share paid by the original investors for the Honeywell common stock? How do your answers compare with the $50 market price of the stock? Comment briefly.

1-38 Presenting Paid-In Capital

Honda Motor Company is the largest producer of motorcycles in the world, as well as a major auto manufacturer. The following items were presented in a recent balance sheet:

Common stock—¥50 par value, 974 million shares issued and outstanding	?
Additional paid-in capital (in millions of yen)	¥171,910

Note: ¥ is the symbol for Japanese yen.

1. What amount should be shown on the common stock line?
2. What was the average price per share paid by the original investors for the Honda common stock?
3. How do your answers compare with the ¥580 market price of the stock? Comment briefly.

1-39 Prepare Balance Sheet

Amazon is the world's leading e-retailer. Amazon's December 31, 1999 balance sheet included the following items ($ in millions):

Property, plant, and equipment	$ 317
Accounts payable	463
Capital stock	3
Cash	?
Total stockholders' equity	?
Long-term debt	1,466
Total assets	2,471
Other assets	1,564
Other stockholders' equity	?
Other liabilities	$ 276

Required

Prepare a condensed balance sheet, including amounts for

1. Cash.
2. Additional and total stockholders' equity.
3. Total liabilities.

1-40 Prepare Balance Sheet

May Department Stores, headquartered in St. Louis, operates Lord & Taylor, Filene's, and six other department store chains. Its balance sheet of January 29, 2000 contained the following items ($ in millions):

Long-term debt payable	$ 3,560
Cash	(1)
Total shareholders' equity	(2)
Total liabilities	(3)
Accounts receivable	2,173
Common stock	163
Inventories	2,817
Accounts payable	1,030
Property, plant, and equipment	4,769
Additional shareholders' equity	3,914
Other assets	1,160
Other liabilities	2,268
Total assets	10,935

Required

Prepare a condensed balance sheet, including amounts for

1. Cash. What do you think of its relative size?
2. Total shareholders' equity.
3. Total liabilities.

1-41 Accounting and Ethics

Required

A survey of high school seniors and college freshmen by the AICPA showed that accountants are given high marks for their ethics. Professional associations for both internal accountants and external auditors place much emphasis on their standards of ethical conduct. Discuss why maintaining a reputation for ethical conduct is important for (1) accountants within an organization, and (2) external auditors. What can accountants do to foster a reputation for high ethical standards and conduct?

ANNUAL REPORT CASE

1-42   The Cisco Annual Report

This and similar problems in succeeding chapters focus on the financial statements of an actual company. Cisco is the worldwide leader in networking for the Internet. As each of these homework problems is solved, readers gradually strengthen their understanding of actual financial statements in their entirety.

Required

Refer to Cisco's balance sheet in appendix A at the end of the book and answer the following questions:

1. How much cash did Cisco have on July 29, 2000? (Include cash equivalent as part of cash.)
2. What were the total assets on July 29, 2000 and on July 31, 1999?
3. Write the company's accounting equation as of July 29, 2000, by filling in the dollar amounts: Assets = Liabilities + Stockholders' equity.

Consider minority interests and deferred income taxes to be liabilities.

1-43   Financial Statement Research

Select the financial statements of any company, and focus on the balance sheet.

Required

1. Identify the amount of cash (including cash equivalents, if any) shown on the most recent balance sheet.
2. What were the total assets shown on the most recent balance sheet, and the total liabilities plus stockholders' equity? How do these two amounts compare?
3. Compute total liabilities and total stockholders' equity. (Assume that all items on the right side of the balance sheet that are not explicitly listed as stockholders' equity are liabilities.) Compare the size of the liabilities to stockholders' equity, and comment on the comparison. Write the company's accounting equation as of the most recent balance sheet date, by filling in the dollar amounts.

COLLABORATIVE LEARNING EXERCISE

1-44   Understanding Transactions

Form groups of three to five students each. Each group should choose one of the companies included in the Dow Jones Industrial Average (see Exhibit 1-1), and find its most recent balance sheet. (You might try the company's home page on the Internet; the majority of Dow companies include their financial statements on their Web site.) Ignore much of the detail on the balance sheet, focusing on the following accounts: cash, inventory, notes payable, accounts payable, and total stockholders' equity.

Divide the following six assumed transactions among the members of the group:

1. Sold 1 million shares of common stock for a total of $10 million (ignore par value).
2. Bought inventory for cash of $3 million.
3. Borrowed $5 million from the bank, receiving the $5 million in cash.
4. Bought inventory for $6 on open account.
5. Paid $4 million to suppliers for inventory bought on open account.
6. Bought equipment for $8 million cash.

Required

1. The student responsible for each transaction should explain to the group how the transaction would affect the company's balance sheet, using the accounts listed earlier.
2. By using the most recent published balance sheet as a starting point, prepare a balance sheet for the company assuming that the preceding six transactions are the only transactions since the date of the latest balance sheet.

INTERNET EXERCISE

1-45   Internet Case

Go to www.cisco.com to locate the Cisco annual report. Click on *Investor Relations*. Then, locate the *View Annual Report* button, and select it to view the latest annual report.

Answer the following questions concerning Cisco:

Required

1. Select *Letter to Shareholders* from the menu. Does Cisco intend to grow during the coming year? What is fueling Cisco's growth?

2. Select *Corporate Profile* from the menu. In how many countries does Cisco operate? How many employees work at Cisco?

3. Move on to *Management's Discussion and Analysis*. What has been the trend for net sales? Net income? What does management have to say about the trends? Which region of the world contributed the most to sales?

4. What does management say about its accounts receivable and inventories assets? Are the trends favorable?

5. What "risk factors" does Cisco face? How might these factors affect future business?

6. Select the *Report of Independent Accountants*. Who is responsible for the preparation, integrity, and fair presentation of Cisco's financial statements? What is the auditor's responsibility?

chapter 2

MEASURING INCOME TO ASSESS PERFORMANCE

IT'S just LUNCH!, a young, fast-growing company, helped these two professionals meet for lunch.

www.prenhall.com/horngren

Learning Objectives

After studying this chapter, you should be able to

1. Explain how accountants measure income.

2. Use the concepts of recognition, matching, and cost recovery to record revenues and expenses.

3. Prepare an income statement and show how it is related to a balance sheet.

4. Calculate operating cash flows and show how cash flow differs from income.

5. Account for cash dividends and prepare a statement of retained income.

6. Compute and explain earnings per share, price–earnings ratio, dividend–yield ratio, and dividend–payout ratio.

When Andrea McGinty's fiancé walked out on her just weeks before their wedding, the 29-year-old jewelry marketing representative was faced with the prospect of reentering the dating scene. She did not like what she found: singles bars, video dating services, and personal ads. None of the available choices appealed to her instincts as a sophisticated, professional person, and none of them really fit into her lifestyle. Then she hit on an idea. What if there were a service that fit the lifestyle of today's busy professionals, one that let people date over the lunch hour instead of during an entire evening? Ready to take on the challenge, McGinty formed It's Just Lunch! in downtown Chicago.

By using her accounting education as a foundation, McGinty knew that she would need some capital to start the business and generate income. So she used $6,000 from her personal savings to print flyers and lease office space. She also knew that the sales revenue she hoped to generate would be reduced by the expenses of running the business, so she priced her services to be sure she made an acceptable return on her investment. She charged $400 for arranging six dates.

What started as a simple idea for helping single professionals find matches has grown into a multimillion-dollar-a-year business. Sales recently exceeded $2.1 million, and net income totaled $400,000. McGinty relies on her accrual-based income statement and balance sheet reports each month to assess how well the company is doing. Because It's Just Lunch! now has many locations across the country, she gets reports for each location. These reports allow her to quickly identify a location that is not performing up to expectations and focus her energy on correcting any problems.

What about McGinty's own dating life? A Chicago lawyer came in for help and decided he wanted to date the owner. After thinking about it, McGinty refunded his fees and accepted the date. They are now married.

The measurement of income is one of the most important and controversial topics in accounting. Income is calculated as the difference between revenue and expense. The resulting income number is a measure of accomplishment—a means of evaluating an organization's performance over a period of time.

Investors eagerly await reports about a company's annual income. Stock prices generally reflect investors' expectations about income. However, actual reported income often differs from what was expected, which tends to result in large swings in stock prices. For example, in the week ending July 14 of 2000, Yahoo stock traded as low as $100 per share before rising to $128 at week's end. What happened? Yahoo announced earnings for the quarter of 12 cents per share which was 2 cents higher than expected. Yahoo is variously described as an online community, a portal or "the only place anyone has to go to get connected to anything or anybody." Yahoo is one of several market leaders whose earnings results and stock performance are believed to signal results for other companies as well. Andrew Bary summed up the week in *Barron's* magazine and indicated that Yahoo's spectacular rise " . . . helped ignite other depressed Internet stocks, including America Online, Amazon.com, and eBay which scored big gains in Friday's session—up $7\frac{3}{4}$ Friday to $61\frac{3}{16}$; Amazon added $7\frac{5}{8}$ to $42\frac{5}{8}$ and AOL rose $3\frac{3}{4}$ to 62."

The Yahoo example was the reaction to an actual announcement, but even rumors can have a major effect on stock prices. The September 10, 1997 *Wall Street Journal* attributed the previous day's 2.8% decline in IBM to "rumors about profit problems at IBM, stemming from adverse markets in Southeast Asia." Consider investors in IBM stock during recent years. They saw profits fall from $5.8 billion in 1988 to a loss of $2.8 billion in 1991 before reaching profits of $3.0 billion in 1994, $5.4 billion in 1996, and $8.1 billion in 2000. Share prices followed profits. One IBM share was $60 in 1988, fell to about $22 during 1993 before recovering to $83 at the end of 1996. In July of 2000, IBM traded at $115. Meanwhile, investors in McDonald's Corporation saw a steady increase in profits from $0.6 billion in 1988 to $0.9 billion in 1991, $1.2 billion in 1994, $1.6 billion in 1996, and $2.0 billion in 2000. These investors experienced a fairly steady increase in share values as well. One McDonald's share sold for $6 in 1988 and $8 in 1991, reaching $24 by the end of 1996, and $33 in late 2000. For comparison sake, $100 invested in a bank account in 1988 would be worth about $179 in 2000. In IBM, a $100 investment would have grown to only $192. However, $100 investment in McDonald's in 1988 would be worth $550 by 2000. Of course, the secret for IBM investors was to buy in 1993, not 1988. These profitability numbers and various other pieces of information in financial statements allow investors to make intelligent decisions about whether to invest more or less in a particular firm.

So profits are a key measure of performance and value. This chapter presents the basics of measuring income, with a special focus on revenues and expenses. It also defines three basic financial statements prepared by accountants: the income statement, statement of cash flows, and statement of retained income.

INTRODUCTION TO INCOME MEASUREMENT

Objective 1
Explain how accountants measure income.

Measuring income is important to everyone, from individuals to businesses, because we all need to know how well we are doing economically. Income is a tool for keeping score. Nevertheless, measuring income is not straightforward. Income is generally regarded as a measure of the increase in the "wealth" of an entity over a period of time. What is wealth and how do you measure it over a period of time? Accountants have agreed on a common

Earnings are a critical measure of company performance, and investors watch earnings carefully. *Barron's* is a financial weekly published by Dow Jones with a Web site at **www.barrons.com**. The banner heading on the July 17, 2000 issue said "Strong Earnings Boost NASDAQ 5.5%." What does this mean? First, we need to understand the language. The NASDAQ is a national securities market where particular firms have their shares traded, including well-known companies such as Microsoft. The reference to strong earnings meant that a number of high-technology stocks such as Yahoo, Juniper Networks, and Cisco Systems reported earnings during the week that were significantly higher than analysts and investors expected them to be. Cisco, for example, had sales that were six times higher than the year before and generated high profits of 8 cents per share. Its stock rose by $27.50 per share, or 19%. The story was repeated for company after company to give the overall result for the NASDAQ.

So earnings are very important. Note that it is not only the specific companies that announce earnings that experience a growth in share price. Although announcements by Yahoo, Juniper Networks, and Cisco led to huge increases in their share prices, these announcements also affected other companies in this industry. If these companies were doing well, the logic went, so were others who did the same types of business, so these other shares should also be more valuable. Thus, a few announcements led to changes in share values for many companies.

Another indicator of the importance of earnings is *Barron's* weekly listing of companies who are expected to announce earnings in the coming week. On page 13 of the July 17, 2000 issue, *Barron's* summarizes the companies who are expected to announce earnings during the next week and reports the expected day of announcement, the earnings level reported in the prior year, and the consensus expectation of analysts for what earnings should be this year. People anticipate these announcements and revise their beliefs about the company when the results become known. So how do investors know when companies report what *Barron's* would call "strong earnings?" These are the companies whose actual reported earnings exceed the expectation that *Barron's* reported the week before as the agreed on average number that analysts thought the company would report. For example, IBM had earnings of $.91 in the second quarter of 1999. *Barron's* reported that analysts expected second quarter earnings of $1.00 per share to be reported Wednesday, July 19, 2000. Actual reported earnings on Wednesday were $1.06 per share. The stock price rose about 10% in response to these results because they substantially exceeded the forecasts.

Source: *Barron's*, July 17, 2000; IBM Web site.

---

set of rules for measuring income that should be applied by all companies. Decision makers such as investors can more easily compare the performance of one company with that of another when the "measuring stick," net income, is fairly standard. Let us now take a look at the foundations of these rules.

OPERATING CYCLE

Most companies follow a similar operating cycle (also called a cash cycle or earnings cycle). During the **operating cycle,** the company uses cash to acquire goods and services, which in turn are sold to customers. The customers in turn pay for their purchases with cash, which brings us back to the beginning of the cycle. Consider the following example:

operating cycle The time span during which cash is used to acquire goods and services, which in turn are sold to customers, who in turn pay for their purchases with cash.

Cash $100,000 — Buy → Merchandise Inventory $100,000 — Sell → Accounts Receivable $160,000 — Collect →

The box for Accounts Receivable (amounts owed to the entity by customers) is larger than the other two boxes because the company's objective is to sell its goods at a price higher than it paid for them. The amount that the selling price rises over costs/expenses is, of course, known as profit. The total amount of profit earned during a particular period depends on the difference between selling price and costs and on the speed of the operating cycle.

The operating cycle is simplified in the preceding example. It suggests that the company would have $160,000 in cash after collecting the accounts receivable. What is missing?

ANSWER

Rarely can we buy something and sell it without incurring any other expenses. Perhaps we paid a sales person to make the sale. Perhaps we paid a delivery service to deliver the goods to the customer. The point is that some part of the $60,000 excess of the $160,000 sales price over the $100,000 cost to buy the merchandise will be used up in completing the sale.

THE ACCOUNTING TIME PERIOD

Because it is hard to measure accurately the success of an ongoing operation, the only way to be certain of how successfully a business has performed is to close its doors, sell all its assets, pay all liabilities, and return any leftover cash to the owner. Actually, in the 1400s, Venetian merchant traders did exactly that for each and every voyage. Successful investors might combine their cash to initiate another voyage while investors in failed voyages might have to sell other assets to cover unpaid liabilities. Of course, that system would not be feasible for companies today (imagine a company that needed to close down and restart after every business deal!). Instead, companies need to be able to measure their performances over discrete time periods.

fiscal year The year established for accounting purposes.

The calendar year is the most popular time period for measuring income or profits. However, about 40% of large companies use a **fiscal year.** Established purely for accounting purposes, the fiscal year does not end on December 31. Instead, the fiscal year-end date is often the low point in annual business activity. For example, Kmart and JCPenney use a fiscal year ending on January 31. Why? Christmas sales and post-Christmas sales are over, and inventories, which are at their lowest point of the year, can be counted more easily and valued with greater accuracy.

interim periods The time spans established for accounting purposes that are less than a year.

Of course, users of financial statements cannot wait an entire year for financial information. They want to know how well the business is doing each month, each quarter, and each half year. Therefore, companies prepare financial statements for these **interim periods.**

revenues (sales) Increases in owners' equity arising from increases in assets received in exchange for the delivery of goods or services to customers.

REVENUES AND EXPENSES

Now that we know the "when" and "why" of measuring income, we need to examine the "how." Revenues and expenses are the key components in measuring income. These terms apply to the inflows and outflows of assets that occur during a business's operating cycle. The **revenues** (inflows), also called **sales,** increase the owner's interest (equity) in the business while **expenses** (outflows) decrease the owner's interest. Together these items define the fundamental meaning of **income** (or **profit** or **earnings**), which can be

expenses Decreases in owners' equity that arise because goods or services are delivered to customers.

income (profit, earnings) The excess of revenues over expenses.

Exhibit 2-1

Biwheels Company

Analysis of Transactions for December 31, 20X1 to January 12, 20X2 (in $)

Description of Transactions	Cash	+ Accounts Receivable +	Merchandise Inventory +	Store Equipment =	Note Payable +	Accounts Payable +	Stockholders' Equity
			Assets		**=**	**Liabilities**	**+ Stockholders' Equity**
(1) Initial investment	+400,000			=			+400,000
(2) Loan from bank	+100,000			=	+100,000		
(3) Acquire inventory for cash	−150,000		+150,000	=			
(4) Acquire inventory on credit			+ 10,000	=		+10,000	
(5) Acquire store equipment for cash plus credit	− 4,000			+15,000 =		+11,000	
(6) Sales of equipment		+1,000		− 1,000 =			
(7) Return of inventory acquired on January 3			− 800	=		− 800	
(8) Payments to creditors	− 4,000			=		− 4,000	
(9) Collections from debtors	+ 700	− 700					
Balance January 12, 20X2	+342,700 +	300 +	159,200 +	14,000 =	100,000 +	16,200 +	400,000
			516,200			516,200	

defined simply as the excess of revenues over expenses. Revenues arise when McDonald's collects cash in exchange for a "happy meal." Expenses arise when McDonald's uses hamburger, buns, and other materials and pays the workers to deliver a completed meal to the customers. The McDonald's store owner is happy when the cash received exceeds the cost to produce and deliver the meal. The additional owners' equity generated by income or profits is called **retained income** (or **retained earnings** or **reinvested earnings**).

Consider again the Biwheels Company we examined in chapter 1. Exhibit 2-1 is almost a direct reproduction of Exhibit 1-2, which summarized the nine transactions of George Smith's business. However, the company has now been incorporated, and the owners' equity account is no longer George Smith, Capital. In Exhibit 2-1, it is stockholders' equity.

Now consider some additional transactions. Suppose Biwheels' sales for the entire month of January amount to $160,000 on open account. The cost to Biwheels of the inventory sold is $100,000. Note that the January sales and other transactions illustrated here are recorded as summarized transactions. The company's sales, purchases of inventory, collections from customers, or disbursements to suppliers do not all take place at once. Actual accounting systems would record every sale, on a cash register, for example, and would then record summary data daily.

The accounting for the summarized sales transaction has two phases, a revenue phase (10a) and an expense phase (10b):

retained income (retained earnings, reinvested earnings) Additional owners' equity generated by income or profits.

	Assets		=	Liabilities	+	Stockholders' Equity
	Accounts Receivable	*Merchandise Inventory*				*Retained Income*
(10a) Sales on open account	+160,000		=			+160,000 (sales revenues)
(10b) Cost of merchandise inventory sold		−100,000	=			−100,000 (cost of goods sold expenses)

This transaction is somewhat complex and can be best understood as two steps happening simultaneously in the balance sheet equation: an inflow of assets in the form of accounts receivable (10a) in exchange for an outflow of assets in the form of merchandise inventory (10b). This exchange of assets does not affect liabilities, so to keep the equation equal, stockholders' equity must rise by $60,000 [$160,000 (sales revenues) − $100,000 (cost of goods sold expense)].

As entries 10a and 10b show, revenue from sales is recorded as an increase in the asset Accounts Receivable and an increase in Retained Income. In contrast, the expense of the goods sold is recorded as a decrease in the asset Merchandise Inventory and a decrease in Retained Income. You can thus see that revenues are positive entries to stockholder's equity accounts, and expenses are negative entries to stockholders' equity accounts. These relationships can be illustrated as follows:

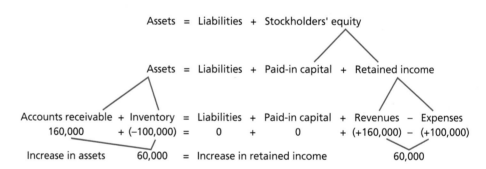

MEASURING INCOME

ACCRUAL BASIS AND CASH BASIS

accrual basis Accounting method that recognizes the impact of transactions on the financial statements in the time periods when revenues and expenses occur.

cash basis Accounting method that recognizes the impact of transactions on the financial statements only when cash is received or disbursed.

There are multiple ways to measure income, the most compelling of which are the cash basis and the accrual basis. The **accrual basis** recognizes the impact of transactions in the financial statements for the time periods when revenues and expenses occur. That is, revenue is recorded as it is earned, and expenses are recorded as they are incurred—not necessarily when cash changes hands. In contrast, the **cash basis** recognizes the impact of transactions in the financial statements only when cash is received or disbursed.

For many years accountants debated the merits of accrual-basis versus cash-basis accounting. Supporters of the accrual basis maintained that the cash basis ignores activities that increase or decrease assets other than cash. Supporters of the cash basis pointed out that a company, no matter how well it seems to be doing, can go bankrupt if it does not manage its cash properly. In the end, the debate has been declared a draw. Companies include both an accrual-basis income statement and a cash-basis statement of cash flows in their annual reports. Although companies must prepare cash flow statements, the results are not labeled "income". For the calculation of income over a period of time, the accrual basis won out. It is the current standard for income measurement. Although both bases have their merits, the accrual basis has the advantage of presenting a more complete summary of the entity's value-producing activities. The accrual basis recognizes revenues as they are earned and matches costs to revenues. This accrual process was illustrated in our analysis of the sale on open account in transaction 10. Revenue was recognized although no cash was received and an expense was recorded although no cash was paid. Let us now take a look at some of the specifics of the accrual basis.

RECOGNITION OF REVENUES

A major convention accountants use to measure income on an accrual basis is **recognition** of revenues, which is a test for determining whether revenues should be recorded in the financial statements of a given period. To be recognized, revenues must ordinarily meet two criteria:

recognition A test for determining whether revenues should be recorded in the financial statements of a given period. To be recognized, revenues must be earned and realized.

1. They must be earned. Revenues are considered earned when a company delivers goods or services to a customer.
2. They must be realized. Revenues are realized when cash or claims to cash are received in exchange for goods or services. "Claims to cash" usually mean credit or some other promise to pay. For a promise to pay to justify revenue recognition, the company must be relatively certain that it will receive the cash it has been promised.

Revenue recognition for most retail companies, such as Wal-Mart, Safeway, and McDonald's, is straightforward. Revenue is both earned and realized at the point of sale—when a customer makes payment and takes possession of the goods. For other companies, revenue may be earned and realized at different times. When revenues are earned and realized at different times, the revenue is not recognized until the second event. Consider the following examples:

Objective 2
Use the concepts of recognition, matching, and cost recovery to record revenues and expenses.

- *Newsweek* receives prepaid subscriptions. The revenue is realized when the subscription is received, but it is not earned until delivery of each issue.
- A dealer in oriental rugs lets a potential customer take a rug home on a trial basis. The customer has possession of the goods, but no revenue is recorded until the customer formally promises to accept the rug and pay for it.

A new theater company sells a subscription series that allows patrons to attend all nine of its productions that occur monthly from September through May. During August and September, the company sells 1,000 subscriptions for the 2001–2002 season at $180 each and collects the cash. How much revenue would the theater recognize in its income statement for the year ended December 31, 2001 from these subscriptions?

ANSWER

Total collections are $180,000 and this amount is realized in cash. However, at December 31, 2001, only four out of nine productions have been provided to the customers so the company has only earned 4/9 of the total or $80,000.

MATCHING AND COST RECOVERY

Now that we have seen how revenues are recognized, we should turn our attention to expenses. There are two types of expenses in every accounting period: (1) those linked with the revenues earned that period, and (2) those linked with the time period itself.

product costs Costs that are linked with revenues and are charged as expenses when the related revenue is recognized.

cost of goods sold (cost of sales) The original acquisition cost of the inventory that was sold to customers during the reporting period.

matching The recording of expenses in the same time period as the related revenues are recognized.

period costs Items identified directly as expenses of the time period in which they are incurred.

cost recovery The concept by which some purchases of goods or services are recorded as assets because their costs are expected to be recovered in the form of cash inflows (or reduced cash outflows) in future periods.

Some expenses, called **product costs,** are naturally linked with revenues. **Cost of goods sold,** that is, the acquisition cost of the inventory that was sold (also called **cost of sales**), and sales commissions are good examples. If there are no revenues, there is no cost of goods sold or sales commissions. When are product costs recognized? Accountants match such expenses to the revenues they help produce. Expenses are best recognized and recorded in the same period as their related revenues are recognized. This process is known as **matching.**

Other expenses, such as rent and many administrative expenses, cannot be linked directly to specific revenues. These expenses go toward supporting a company's operations for a given period and are thus called **period costs.** Period costs are recognized as expense in the period in which they are incurred. Rent expense arises because of the passage of time regardless of the sales level, and therefore rent is a good example of a period cost. Consider a McDonald's store. The rent expense for May gives the store operator the right to do business for the month and is best matched to May sales, regardless of whether the sales are high or low.

Some expenses can be tricky in that a transaction occurs well before the revenues or benefits they ultimately help produce. To record the expense in the proper period accountants use the **cost recovery** concept. Under cost recovery, some purchases of goods or services are recorded as assets because the costs are expected to be recovered in the form of cash inflows (or reduced cash outflows) in future periods. For example, the purchase price of goods or services that are acquired in the current period but will be sold or used in a future period should be initially recorded as an asset. When the good or service is sold or used, the accountant reduces the asset account and records an expense.

Rent paid in advance is such an asset. Suppose a firm pays an annual rental of $12,000 on January 1. An asset account, prepaid rent, is increased by $12,000 because the rental services have not yet been used. Each month the prepaid rent account is reduced by $1,000, and rent expense is increased by $1,000, recognizing the using up of the prepaid rent asset.

APPLYING MATCHING AND COST RECOVERY

To focus on the matching and cost recovery concepts, assume that the Biwheels Company has only two expenses other than the cost of goods sold: rent expense and depreciation expense. Rent is $2,000 per month, payable quarterly in advance. Transaction 11 (see Exhibit 2-2, which merely continues Exhibit 2-1) is the payment of $6,000 worth of store rent, covering January, February, and March of 20X2. (Assume that this initial payment was made on January 16, although rent is commonly paid at the start of the rental period.)

The rent payment gives the company the right to use store facilities for the next 3 months. The use of the facilities constitutes a future benefit, so the $6,000 is recorded in an asset account, Prepaid Rent.

Transaction 11, the rent payment, shows no effect on stockholders' equity in the balance sheet equation. One asset, cash, is simply exchanged for another, prepaid rent.

Transaction 12 is recorded at the end of January. It recognizes that 1 month (one-third of the total) of the rental services has been used up, so that asset is reduced, and stockholders' equity is also reduced by $2,000 as rent expense for January. This recognition of rent expense means that $2,000 of the asset, Prepaid Rent, has been "used up" in the conduct of operations during January. That $2,000 worth of rent was a period cost for January and is recognized at the end of that period.

Prepaid rent of $4,000 remains an asset as of January 31. Why? Because without the prepayment, Biwheels would have to pay $2,000 in both February and March for rent. So the cost of the prepayment will be recovered in the sense that future cash outflows will be reduced by $4,000.

Exhibit 2-2

Biwheels Company

Analysis of Transactions for January 20X2 (in $)

Description of Transactions	Cash	+	Accounts Receivable	+	Merchandise Inventory	+	Prepaid Rent	+	Store Equipment	=	Note Payable	+	Accounts Payable	+	Paid-in Capital	+	Retained Income
					Assets					=			**Liabilities**		+		**Stockholders' Equity**
(1)–(9) See Exhibit 2-1 Balance, January 12, 20X2	342,700	+	300	+	159,200	+		+	14,000	=	100,000	+	16,200	+	400,000	+	
(10a) Sales on open account (inflow of assets)			+160,000							=						+	160,000 (Sales revenue)
(10b) Cost of merchandise inventory sold (outflow of assets)					−100,000					=						−	100,000 (Increase cost of goods sold expense)
(11) Pay rent in advance	−6,000						+6,000			=							
(12) Recognize expiration of rental services							−2,000			=						−	2,000 (Increase rent expense)
(13) Recognized expiration of equipment services (depreciation)									−100	=						−	100 (Increase depreciation expense)
Balance January 31, 20X2	336,700	+	160,300	+	59,200	+	4,000	+	13,900	=	100,000	+	16,200	+	400,000	+	57,900
					574,100												574,100

depreciation The systematic allocation of the acquisition cost of long-lived or fixed assets to the expense accounts of particular periods that benefit from the use of the assets.

The same matching and cost recovery concepts that underlie the accounting for prepaid rent apply to **depreciation,** which is the systematic allocation of the acquisition cost of long-lived or fixed assets to the expense accounts of particular periods that benefit from the use of the assets. These assets are tangible physical assets such as buildings, equipment, furniture, and fixtures owned by the entity. Land is not subject to depreciation because it does not deteriorate over time.

In both prepaid rent and depreciation, the business purchases an asset that gradually wears out or is used up. As the asset is being used, more and more of its original cost is transferred from an asset account to an expense account. The sole difference between depreciation and prepaid rent is the length of time taken before the asset loses its usefulness. Buildings, equipment, and furniture remain useful for many years; prepaid rent and other prepaid expenses usually expire within a year.

Transaction 13 in Exhibit 2-2 records the depreciation expense for the Biwheels equipment. A portion of the original cost of $14,000 becomes depreciation expense in each month of the equipment's useful life, say, 140 months. Under the matching concept, the depreciation expense for January is $14,000/140 months, or $100 per month:

	Assets	=	Liabilities	+	Stockholders' Equity
	Store Equipment				*Retained Income*
(13) Recognize depreciation expense	-100	=			-100 (Increase depreciation expense)

In this transaction, the asset account, Store Equipment, is decreased as is the stockholders' equity account, Retained Income. The general concept of expense under the accrual basis should be clear by now. The purchases and uses of goods and services, for example, inventories, rent, and equipment, ordinarily consist of two basic steps: (1) the acquisition of the assets (transactions 3, 4, and 5 in Exhibit 2-1 and transaction 11 in Exhibit 2-2), and (2) the expiration of the assets as expenses (transactions 10b, 12, and 13 in Exhibit 2-2). As these examples show, when prepaid expenses and fixed assets are used up, the total assets and owners' equity are decreased. Expense accounts are basically deductions from stockholders' equity.

RECOGNITION OF EXPIRED ASSETS

Assets such as inventory, prepaid rent, and equipment may be thought of as costs that are stored to be carried forward to future periods and recorded as expenses in the future. For inventory, the future period of expense recognition is identified by the sale of the item and the recognition of revenue at the time of sale. For rent, the future period of recognition is the period to which the rent applies. For equipment, the total cost of the long-lived asset is split up into smaller pieces and a part of that total cost is recognized in each of the periods that benefits from the use of the asset. You might say that inventory costs are product costs that are matched to the revenue they produce. Rent is a period cost that is matched to the period it benefits. Equipment benefits many periods, and its cost is spread over those periods as depreciation expense:

The analysis of the inventory, rent, and depreciation transactions in Exhibit 2-2 distinguishes between acquisition and expiration. Inventory, rent, and equipment are all recorded as assets when they are acquired. The unexpired costs of inventory, prepaid rent, and equipment then remain assets until they are used up and become expenses. What happens if acquired assets expire, or are used, almost immediately? For example, services such as advertising are often used almost as soon as they are acquired. Conceptually, these costs should, at least momentarily, be viewed as assets on acquisition before being written off as expenses. For example, suppose a company purchased newspaper advertising for $1,000 cash. To abide by the acquisition–expiration sequence, the transaction could be analyzed in two phases (see alternative 1 that follows).

		Assets		=	Liabilities	+	Stockholders' Equity	
Transaction	*Cash*	+ *Other Assets*	+ *Prepaid Advertising* =				*Paid-in Capital* +	*Retained Income*
Alternative 1: Two Phases								
Phase (a) Prepay for advertising	−1,000		+1,000 =					
Phase (b) Use up advertising			−1,000 =					−1,000 (Advertising expense)
Alternative 2: One Phase								
Phases (a) and (b) together	−1,000			=				−1,000 (Advertising expense)

In practice, however, prepaid advertising and many other services are acquired and used up so quickly that accountants do not bother recording them as assets. Instead accountants use the recording shortcut shown in alternative 2. When financial statements are prepared, this alternative presents the correct result, although the two-step alternative 1 more accurately portrays the events.

Although this chapter focuses on the income statement, it is important to realize that the income statement is really just a way of explaining changes between one balance sheet and another. The balance sheet equation shows revenue and expense items as subparts of owners' equity. The income statement just collects all these changes in owners' equity for the accounting period and combines them in one place.

(1) Assets (A) = Liabilities (L) + Stockholders' equity (SE)

(2) Assets   = Liabilities   + Paid-in capital + Retained income

(3) Assets   = Liabilities   + Paid-in capital + Revenues − Expenses

Revenue and expense accounts are nothing more than subdivisions of stockholders' equity—temporary stockholders' equity accounts, as it were. Their purpose is to summarize the volume of sales and the various expenses so that income can be measured.

The analysis of each transaction in Exhibits 2-1 and 2-2 illustrates the dual nature of the balance sheet equation, which is always kept in balance. If the items affected are confined to one side of the equation, the total amount added is equal to the total amount subtracted on that side. If the items affected are on both sides, then equal amounts are simultaneously added or simultaneously subtracted on each side.

The striking feature of the balance sheet equation is its universal applicability. No transaction has ever been conceived, no matter how simple or complex, that cannot be analyzed via the equation. Business leaders and accountants employ the balance sheet equation constantly to be sure they understand the effects of business transactions they are planning.

 A company starts its business on January 1, 2001 and rents an office for $4,000 per month and pays 4 months of rent in advance. During January, no revenue is earned. How much rent expense should the company report on its income statement for January?

ANSWER

Rent expense is $4,000 for January and this expense should appear on the income statement. Some expenses are matched with revenue, but rent is a period expense that is incurred because the space was used.

THE INCOME STATEMENT

Objective 3
Prepare an income statement and show how it is related to a balance sheet.

income statement (statement of earnings, operating statement) A report of all revenues and expenses pertaining to a specific time period.

net income The remainder after all expenses have been deducted from revenues.

By now you should understand when revenues and expenses are recorded and how they can be used to measure income. How are they recorded in the financial statements? Chapter 1 introduced the balance sheet as a snapshot-in-time summary of a company's financial status and the statement of cash flow as a summary of cash flow during the period for operating, investing, and financing purposes. To report overall economic activity from operations during the period, we need another basic financial statement, the income statement. An **income statement** (also called **statement of earnings** or **operating statement**) is a report of all revenues and expenses pertaining to a specific time period. **Net income** is the famous "bottom line" on an income statement—the remainder after all expenses have been deducted from revenues.

Look back at Exhibit 2-2 and notice that four of the accounting events affect the Biwheels Company's retained income account: sales revenue, cost of goods sold expense, rent expense, and depreciation expense. Exhibit 2-3 shows how an income statement arranges these transactions to arrive at a net income of $57,900.

Because the income statement measures performance, in terms of revenues and expenses, over a period of time, whether it be a month, a quarter, or longer, it must always indicate the exact period covered. In Exhibit 2-3, the Biwheels income statement clearly shows it covers the month ended January 31, 20X2.

Public companies in the United States generally publish income statements quarterly. In some other countries, companies publish only semiannual or annual statements. Worldwide, most companies prepare such statements monthly or weekly for internal management purposes.

Exhibit 2-3

Biwheels Company

Income Statement for the Month Ended January 31, 20X2

Sales (revenues)		$160,000
Deduct expenses		
Cost of goods sold	$100,000	
Rent	2,000	
Depreciation	100	
Total expenses		102,100
Net income		$ 57,900

Dollar signs are customarily used at the beginning of each column of dollar amounts and for totals such as net income, as shown in Exhibit 2-3. Double underscores (double rulings) are typically used to denote final numbers.

Decision makers both inside and outside the company use the income statement to assess the company's performance over a span of time. The income statement shows how the entity's operations for the period have increased net assets through revenues and decreased net assets through expenses. Net income measures the amount by which the increase in newly acquired assets (revenues) exceeds the expiration of other assets (expenses). (A net loss means that expenses exceeded revenues.) In essence, net income is one measure of the wealth created by an entity during the accounting period. By tracking net income from period to period and examining changes in the components of net income, investors and other decision makers can evaluate the success of the period's operations.

For example, the management of Lucent Technologies explained its 46% increase in net income in 1999 by discussing revenue growth of different business units. Revenues rose by 20% overall, but different parts of the business grew at different rates. Sales of network systems grew 24%, while sales of business communication systems grew by 5% and microelectronics grew by 18%. Lucent also emphasized the strength of its business internationally, by reporting growth of 47%. Because revenue is growing more rapidly internationally, the international business is becoming more important to Lucent. In 1999, it represented 32% of total revenue, up from 23% when Lucent was separated from AT&T in 1996. Note that net income increased more than did revenue. Why? Because Lucent was able to produce the 20% higher revenue while controlling expenses carefully so that expenses increased by only 18%.

RELATIONSHIP BETWEEN INCOME STATEMENT AND BALANCE SHEET

The income statement is the major link between two balance sheets:

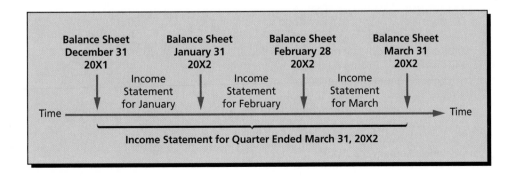

You can think of income statements as filling in the gaps between balance sheets. The balance sheets show the financial position of the company at discrete points in time, and the income statements explain the changes that have taken place between those points.

For example, the balance sheet for Biwheels Company on December 31, 20X1 showed assets of $500,000 and, to balance the equation, liabilities of $100,000 plus stockholders' equity of $400,000. There was no retained income. The January transactions analyzed in Exhibit 2-2 showed revenues of $160,000 and expenses of $102,100 recorded in the retained income account. The income statement in Exhibit 2-3 displays these revenues and expenses for the time span, the month of January, and shows the resulting net income of $57,900. On the balance sheet on January 31, 20X2, the stockholders' equity account, Retained Income, will be $57,900 greater than it was on December 31, 20X1.

STATEMENT OF CASH FLOWS

INCOME VERSUS CASH FLOWS

Objective 4
Calculate operating cash flows and show how cash flow differs from income.

You can think of income as a measure of the entity's performance in generating net assets, that is, assets less liabilities. Increases in retained income are accompanied by increases in assets or decreases in liabilities. However, income, especially when using accrual-basis accounting, does not measure the entity's performance in generating cash. Because a business enterprise is usually formed to return cash to the owners, and because creditors

Exhibit 2-4

Biwheels Company
Statement of Cash Flows for the Two Months Ended January 31, 20X2

PART I: TRANSACTIONS AFFECTING CASH

Transaction	Amount	Type of Activity
(1) Initial investment	$400,000	Financing
(2) Loan from bank	100,000	Financing
(3) Acquire inventory for cash	(150,000)	Operating
(5) Acquire store equipment for cash	(4,000)	Investing
(8) Payments to trade creditors	(4,000)	Operating
(9) Sale of store equipment	700	Investing
(11) Pay rent in cash	(6,000)	Operating

PART II: STATEMENT OF CASH FLOWS

Cash Flows from Operating Activities	
Cash payments to suppliers	$(154,000)
Cash payments for rent	(6,000)
Net cash used for operating activities	$(160,000)
Cash Flows from Investing Activities	
Cash payments for purchases of equipment	$ (4,000)
Cash receipts from sales of equipment	700
Net cash used for investing activities	$ (3,300)
Cash Flows from Financing Activities	
Proceeds from initial investment	$ 400,000
Proceeds from bank loan	100,000
Net cash provided by financing activities	$ 500,000
Net increase in cash	$ 336,700
Cash balance, December 1, 20X1	0
Cash balance, January 31, 20X2	$ 336,700

must be paid in cash, many decision makers want a financial statement focused on cash in addition to the income statement that focuses on changes in net assets. The statement of cash flows is prepared to fill this need. Since the 1970s, companies have been required to provide this statement in addition to the income statement. This is why we said earlier that the debate over whether to use cash or accrual accounting was really a draw. Accountants do both.

The **statement of cash flows** (or **cash flow statement**) reports the cash receipts and cash payments of an entity during a particular period. Like the income statement, it summarizes activities over a span of time, so it must be labeled with the exact period covered. Furthermore, like the income statement, which shows details about how operating activities produce changes in retained income, the statement of cash flows details the changes in one balance sheet account, the cash account. Exhibit 2-4 updates the Biwheels Company statement of cash flows through the end of January. Notice that from a cash flow standpoint only one of the new transactions shown is relevant, the $6,000 payment for rent. Thus, the only difference between this cash flow statement and the statement on January 12 shown in chapter 1 (Exhibit 1-4) is a $6,000 increase in net cash used in operating activities and a $6,000 decrease in the cash balance. Despite having income of $57,900 on the income statement, Biwheels has not yet begun to generate any cash from operations.

statement of cash flows (cash flow statement) A required statement that reports the cash receipts and cash payments of an entity during a particular period.

SUMMARY PROBLEM FOR YOUR REVIEW

PROBLEM ONE

Biwheels' transactions for January were analyzed in Exhibits 2-1 and 2-2. The balance sheet, January 31, 20X2, follows.

Biwheels Company
Balance Sheet January 31, 20X2

Assets		Liabilities and Stockholders' Equity		
Cash	$336,700	Liabilities:		
Accounts receivable	160,300	Note payable		$100,000
Merchandise		Accounts payable		16,200
inventory	59,200	Total liabilities		$116,200
Prepaid rent	4,000	Stockholders' equity:		
Store equipment	13,900	Paid-in capital	$400,000	
		Retained income	57,900	
		Total stockholders' equity		457,900
		Total liabilities and		
Total assets	$574,100	stockholders' equity		$574,100

The following series of transactions occurred during February:

(14) Collection of accounts receivable, $130,000.

(15) Payments of accounts payable, $15,000.

(16) Acquisitions of inventory on open account, $80,000, and for cash, $10,000.

(17) Merchandise carried in inventory at a cost of $110,000 was sold for $176,000, of which $125,000 was on open account and $51,000 was for cash.

(18) Recognition of rent expense for February.

(19) Recognition of depreciation expense for February.

(20) Borrowing of $10,000 from the bank was used to buy $10,000 of store equipment on February 28.

1. Prepare an analysis of transactions, employing the equation approach demonstrated in Exhibit 2-2.

2. Prepare a balance sheet as of February 28, 20X2, and an income statement and statement of cash flows for the month of February.

SOLUTION TO PROBLEM ONE

1. Analysis of transactions. The answer is in Exhibit 2-5. All transactions are straightforward extensions or repetitions of the January transactions.

2. Preparation of financial statements. Exhibit 2-6 contains the balance sheet, income statement, and statement of cash flows, which have been described earlier. Notice that the balance sheet lists the ending balances in all the accounts in Exhibit 2-5. The income statement summarizes the revenue and expense entries in retained income, and the statement of cash flows summarizes the entries to the cash account.

ACCOUNTING FOR DIVIDENDS AND RETAINED INCOME

Objective 5
Account for cash dividends and prepare a statement of retained income.

net loss The difference between revenues and expenses when expenses exceed revenues.

cash dividends
Distributions of cash to stockholders that reduce retained income.

A corporation's revenues and expenses for a particular time period are recorded in the stockholders' equity account, Retained Income. Because net income is the excess of revenues over expenses, retained income increases by the amount of net income reported during the period. If expenses exceed revenues, retained income decreases by the amount of the period's **net loss.**

CASH DIVIDENDS

In addition to revenues and expenses, **cash dividends,** distributions of cash to stockholders, are recorded in the Retained Income account. These distributions reduce retained income. Corporations pay out cash dividends to stockholders to provide a return on the stockholders' investment in the corporation. The ability to pay dividends is fundamentally a result of profitable operations. Retained income increases as profits accumulate, and it decreases as dividends are paid out. Although cash dividends decrease retained income, they are not expenses like rent and depreciation. They should not be deducted from revenues because dividends are not directly linked to the generation of revenue or the costs of operating activities. They are transactions with shareholders. For example, assume that on February 28, cash dividends of $50,000 are disbursed to stockholders. This transaction (21) is analyzed as follows:

	Assets	=	Liabilities	+	Stockholders' Equity
	Cash				*Retained Income*
(21) Declaration and payment of cash dividends	−$50,000	=			−$50,000 (Dividends)

Exhibit 2-5

Biwheels Company

Analysis of Transactions for February 20X2 (in $)

Description of Transactions	Assets					=	Liabilities		+	Stockholders' Equity	
	Cash +	Accounts Receivable +	Merchandise Inventory +	Prepaid Rent +	Store Equipment	=	Notes Payable +	Accounts Payable	+	Paid-in Capital +	Retained Income
Balance, January 31, 20X2	336,700 +	160,300 +	59,200 +	4,000 +	13,900	=	100,000 +	16,200	+	400,000 +	57,900
(14) Collection of accounts receivable	+130,000	−130,000									
(15) Payments of accounts payable	− 15,000					=		−15,000			
(16) Acquisitions of inventory on open account and for cash	− 10,000		+ 90,000			=		+80,000			
(17a) Sales on open account and for cash	+ 51,000	+125,000				=				+	176,000 (Increase sales revenue)
(17b) Cost of inventory sold			−110,000			=				−	110,000 (Increase cost of goods sold expense)
(18) Recognize expiration of rental services				−2,000		=				−	2,000 (Increase rent expense)
(19) Recognize expiration of equipment services (depreciation)					− 100	=				−	100 (Increase depreciation expense)
(20a) Borrow from bank	+ 10,000					=	+10,000				
(20b) Purchase store equipment	− 10,000				+10,000	=					
Balance February 28, 20X2	492,700 +	155,300 +	39,200 +	2,000 +	23,800	=	110,00 +	81,200	+	400,000 +	121,800
	713,000										
							713,000				
										713,000	

59

Exhibit 2-6

Biwheels Company

Balance Sheet February 28, 20X2

Assets		Liabilities and Stockholders' Equity		
Cash	$492,700	Liabilities		
Accounts receivable	155,300	Notes payable	$110,000	
Merchandise		Accounts payable	81,200	$191,200
inventory	39,200			
Prepaid rent	2,000	Stockholders' equity		
Store equipment	23,800	Paid-in capital	$400,000	
		Retained income	121,800	521,800
Total	$713,000	Total		$713,000

Biwheels Company

Income Statement for the Month Ended February 28, 20X2

Sales		$176,000
Deduct expenses		
Cost of goods sold	$110,000	
Rent	2,000	
Depreciation	100	112,100
Net income		$ 63,900

Biwheels Company

Statement of Cash Flows for the Month Ended February 28, 20X2

Cash Flows from Operating Activities	
Cash collections from customers	$181,000
Cash payments to suppliers	(25,000)
Net cash provided by operating activities	$156,000
Cash Flows from Investing Activities	
Purchase of store equipment	$(10,000)
Net cash used for investing activities	$(10,000)
Cash Flows from Financing Activities	
Loan from bank	$ 10,000
Net cash provided by financing activities	$ 10,000
Net increase in cash	$156,000
Cash balance, February 1, 20X2	336,700
Cash balance, February 28, 20X2	$492,700

Transaction 21 presented the payment of a dividend as a single transaction. However, corporations usually approach dividend matters in steps. The board of directors declares—announces its intention to pay—a dividend on one date (declaration date), payable to those stockholders on record as owning the stock on a second date (record date), and actually pays the dividend on a third date (payment date).

Cash dividends distribute some of the company's assets (cash) to shareholders, thus reducing the economic value of their remaining interest in Biwheels. Of course, companies must have sufficient cash on hand to pay cash dividends. Because dividends require so much cash, many companies try to avoid paying dividends that exceed the amount of cash provided by operating activities.

Not all companies pay dividends. Microsoft retains all its income to finance future growth. McDonald's also paid no dividends during its early, highest growth years. However, as a successful company grows, the Retained Income account can soar enormously if dividends are not paid. It can easily be the largest stockholders' equity account. Its balance is the cumulative, lifetime earnings of the company less its cumulative, lifetime losses and dividends. For example, on January 1, 2000, Eli Lilly, the pharmaceutical company, had retained earnings of $4,986 million while total stockholders' equity was only $5,013 million.

RETAINED INCOME AND CASH

The existence of retained income and cash enable a board of directors to declare a dividend. However, Cash and Retained Income are two entirely separate accounts, sharing no necessary relationship. Consider the following illustration:

Step 1. Assume an opening balance sheet of:

Cash	$100	Paid-in capital	$100

Step 2. Purchase inventory for $50 cash. The balance sheet now reads:

Cash	$ 50	Paid-in capital	$100
Inventory	50		
Total assets	$100		

Step 3. Now sell the inventory for $80 cash, which produces a retained income of $80 − $50 = $30:

Cash	$130	Paid-in capital	$100
		Retained income	30
		Total owners' equity	$130

At this stage, the retained income seems to be directly linked to the cash increase of $30. It is, but do not think that retained income is a claim against the cash specifically. Remember, it is a claim against total assets. This relationship can be clarified by the transaction that follows.

Step 4. Purchase inventory and equipment, in the amounts of $60 and $50, respectively. Now,

Cash	$ 20	Paid-in capital	$100
Inventory	60	Retained income	30
Equipment	50		
Total assets	$130	Total owners' equity	$130

Where is the $30 in retained income reflected? Is it reflected in Cash? It cannot be, because there is only $20 in Cash, and Retained Income is $30. Part of the cash from profitable sales has been reinvested in inventory and equipment. This example helps to explain the nature of the Retained Income account. It is a residual claim, not a pot of gold. A residual claim means that if the company went out of business, and all its assets were sold and converted to cash, the owners would receive the amount left over after all the liabilities were paid.

Exhibit 2-7

Biwheels Company

Statement of Retained Income for the Month Ended
February 28, 20X2

Retained income, January 31, 20X2	$ 57,900
Net income for February	63,900
Total	$121,800
Dividends declared	50,000
Retained income, February 28, 20X2	$ 71,800

STATEMENT OF RETAINED INCOME

statement of retained income A statement that lists the beginning balance in retained income, followed by a description of any changes that occurred during the period, and the ending balance.

statement of income and retained income A statement that includes a statement of retained income at the bottom of an income statement.

Because owners are interested in tracing the amount of retained income in a company, accountants have created a financial statement to do just that. Exhibit 2-7 shows the **statement of retained income,** which lists the beginning balance (in this case, January 31) in Retained Income, followed by a description of any major changes (in this case, net income and dividends) that occurred during the period, and the ending balance (February 28) for the Biwheels Company.

Frequently, the statement of retained income is added to the bottom of the income statement. In such cases, the combined statements are called a **statement of income and retained income.** For example, the income statement in Exhibit 2-6 combined with the statement of retained income in Exhibit 2-7 appear reformatted, and retitled, in Exhibit 2-8 as a statement of income and retained income.

Note how Exhibit 2-8 is anchored to the balance sheet equation:

Asset	=	Liabilities	+	Paid-in capital	+	Retained income

Ending Retained Income balance	=	[Beginning balance	+	Revenues	−	Expenses	−	Dividends]		
Bal. Feb 28 after dividends	=	[57,900	+	176,000	−	112,100	−	$50,000]	=	71,800

Exhibit 2-8

Biwheels Company

Statement of Income and Retained Income for the Month
Ended February 28, 20X2

Sales		$176,000
Deduct expenses		
Cost of goods sold	$110,000	
Rent	2,000	
Depreciation	100	112,100
Net income		$ 63,900*
Retained income, January 31, 20X2		57,900
Total		$121,800
Dividends declared		50,000
Retained income, February 28, 20X2		$ 71,800

* Note how the income statement ends here. The $63,900 simultaneously becomes the initial item on the statement of retained income portion of this combined statement.

If we observe a company with revenues of $50,000 and expenses of $40,000 whose retained earnings grows from $15,000 at the beginning of the year to $17,000 at the end of the year, what can we conclude about dividends paid?

ANSWER

We know that net income = revenue − expenses, so net income is $10,000 = $50,000 − $40,000. Further, ending retained income = beginning retained income + net income − dividends. This means that $17,000 = $15,000 + $10,000 − dividends. Retained income would have been $15,000 + $10,000 = $25,000 if no dividends were paid, but it was only $17,000. Therefore, $8,000 must have been paid as dividends.

SUMMARY PROBLEM FOR YOUR REVIEW

PROBLEM TWO

The following interpretations and remarks are frequently encountered with regard to financial statements. Do you agree or disagree? Explain fully.

1. "Sales show the cash coming in from customers, and the various expenses show the cash going out for goods and services. The difference is net income."

2. Consider the following December 31, 1999 accounts of Motorola, Inc., a U.S. company that is a leading worldwide provider of wireless communications, semiconductors, and advanced electronic systems, and components and services. You may have used one of their cell phones:

Motorola, Inc
Consolidated Balance Sheets
(In millions, except per share amounts)

January 1	**2000**	**1999**
Stockholders' equity		
Preferred stock, $100 par value issuable in series		
Authorized shares: 0.5 (none issued)	—	—
Common stock, $3 par value		
Authorized shares: 2000 and 1999, 1,400		
Issued and outstanding shares: 2000, 612.8; 1999, 601.1	1,838	1,804
Additional paid-in capital	2,572	1,894
Retained earnings	8,780	8,254
Non-owner changes to equity	3,154	270
Total stockholders' equity	$16,344	$12,222

A Motorola employee commented, "Why can't that big company pay higher wages and dividends too? It can use its hundreds of millions of dollars of retained earnings to do so."

3. "The total Motorola stockholders' equity measures the amount that the shareholders would get today if the corporation were liquidated."

SOLUTION TO PROBLEM TWO

1. Cash receipts and disbursements are not the basis for the accrual accounting recognition of revenues and expenses. Sales could easily be credit sales for which no cash has yet been received, and expenses could be those that have been incurred but not yet paid out. Depreciation is another example where the expense recognition does

not coincide with the payment of cash. Depreciation recorded in today's income statement may result from the use of equipment that was acquired for cash years ago. Therefore, under accrual accounting sales and expenses are not equivalent to cash inflows and outflows. To determine net income under accrual accounting, expenses are subtracted from revenues (expenses are linked to revenues via matching). Cash flow from operations can be larger or smaller than net income.

2. As the chapter indicated, retained earnings is not cash. It is a stockholders' equity account that represents the accumulated increase in ownership claims due to profitable operations. This claim may be lowered by the payment of cash dividends, but a growing company will reinvest cash in receivables, inventories, plant, equipment, and other assets so necessary for expansion. Paying higher wages may make it impossible to compete effectively and stay in business. Paying higher dividends may make it impossible to grow. The level of retained earnings does not lead to a specific wage or dividend policy for the firm.

3. Stockholders' equity is the excess of assets over liabilities. If the assets were carried in the accounting records at their liquidating value today and the liabilities were represented exactly at their market values, the remark would be true. However, the numbers on the balance sheet are historical numbers, not current numbers. Intervening changes in markets and general price levels in inflationary times may mean that the assets are woefully understated. Investors make a critical error if they think that balance sheets indicate current values.

FOUR POPULAR FINANCIAL RATIOS

Objective 6
Compute and explain earnings per share, price–earnings ratio, dividend–yield ratio, and dividend–payout ratio.

earnings per share (EPS)
Net income divided by average number of common shares outstanding.

Now that you know quite a bit about financial statements, you are ready to learn how the information in these statements is used. Numbers are hard to understand out of context. Is $10 a lot to pay for a share of stock? Is $1 a good dividend? To show you how investors think about such questions, we gradually introduce you to various financial ratios.

A financial ratio is computed by dividing one number by another. For a set of complex financial statements, literally hundreds of ratios can be computed if desired. Every analyst has a set of favorite ratios, but one is so popular that it dwarfs all others: **earnings per share of common stock (EPS).** In fact, EPS data must appear on the face of the income statement of publicly held corporations. This is the only instance in which a financial ratio is required as a part of the body of financial statements. Let us now examine some popular ratios based on financial statement information.

EARNINGS PER SHARE (EPS)

When the owners' equity is relatively simple, the computation of EPS is straightforward. For example, consider McDonald's. It reported EPS of $.55, $.73, $1.11, and $1.44 in 1990, 1993, 1996, and 1999, respectively. The 1999 EPS is calculated by dividing 1999 income of $1,946 million by average shares outstanding of 1,351,389,000 during the year.

$$EPS = \frac{Net\ income}{Average\ number\ of\ shares\ outstanding}$$

$$1999\ EPS = \frac{\$1,946,000,000}{1,351,389,000} = \$1.44$$

The McDonald's computation is relatively simple because the company has only one type of capital stock, little fluctuation of shares outstanding throughout the year, and no unusual items affecting the computation of net income. EPS calculations can become more difficult when such complications arise. Investors interested in McDonald's might ask whether EPS was growing over time and would calculate about an 11% per year growth in EPS from 1990 through 1999.

PRICE–EARNINGS (P-E) RATIO

Another popular ratio is the **price–earnings (P-E) ratio:**

price-earnings ratio (P-E)
Market price per share of common stock divided by earnings per share of common stock.

$$\text{P-E ratio} = \frac{\text{Market price per share of common stock}}{\text{Earnings per share of common stock}}$$

The numerator is typically today's market price for a share of the company's stock. The denominator is the EPS for the most recent 12 months. Thus, the P-E ratio varies throughout a given year, depending on the fluctuations in the company's stock price. For example, McDonald's P-E ratio would be:

McDonald's

	Using Market Price at Year-End
1999 P-E	$\dfrac{\$40.31}{\$1.44} = 28.0$
1996 P-E	$\dfrac{\$22.69}{\$1.11} = 20.44$
1993 P-E	$\dfrac{\$14.25}{\$.73} = 19.52$
1990 P-E	$\dfrac{\$7.25}{\$.55} = 13.18$

The P-E ratio is sometimes called the earnings multiple. It measures how much the investing public is willing to pay for a chance to share the company's potential earnings. Note especially that the P-E ratio is determined by the marketplace. This earnings multiplier may differ considerably for two companies within the same industry. It may also change for the same company through the years. McDonald's P-E increases in each of the 4 years we calculated. This is partly due specifically to McDonald's performance and partly reflects the overall positive performance in the financial markets during the 1990s as we entered an era of peace and prosperity characterized by low interest rates and substantial growth.

In general, a high P-E ratio indicates that investors predict the company's net income will grow rapidly. Consider Cisco's 2000 ratio of 173 compared with the P-E ratio of 7 for General Motors (GM). These ratios tell us that Cisco's earnings are expected to grow much more rapidly than GM's. History certainly suggests this is likely. Cisco's earnings per share have grown almost 45% each year during the last decade while GM's EPS growth during the period cannot be calculated because it had losses in 1990. Since 1994, GM's EPS have grown about 3.5% per year. The *Wall Street Journal* publishes P-E ratios daily on its stock pages.

From 1995 to 2000, Microsoft's stock price rose from about $10 per share to about $100 per share. Give two explanations for this 10-fold increase in value.

ANSWER

One possibility is that the P-E ratio rose by a factor of 10. Another possibility is that earnings grew by a factor of 10. In fact, the explanation is a mixture of the two. Earnings grew from about $.28 to $1.70 over the 5-year period, by a factor of 6. Thus, part of the explanation was earnings growth, but there was also an increase in the P-E ratio. In early 2000, the ratio was about 60 whereas 5 years earlier it was about 36.

Dividend–Yield Ratio

dividend–yield ratio
Common dividends per share divided by market price per share.

Individual investors are usually interested in the profitability of their personal investments in common stock. That profitability takes two forms: cash dividends and market-price appreciation of the stock. The **dividend–yield ratio** (the current dividend per share divided by the current market price of the stock), also simply called dividend yield, gauges dividend payouts. It is computed as follows for McDonald's:

McDonald's

	Using Market Price at Year-End
1999 Dividend yield =	$\dfrac{\$.20}{\$40.31} = .5\%$
1996 Dividend yield =	$\dfrac{\$.15}{\$22.69} = .7\%$
1993 Dividend yield =	$\dfrac{\$.11}{\$14.25} = .8\%$
1990 Dividend yield =	$\dfrac{\$.09}{\$7.25} = 1.2\%$

Dividend ratios may be of particular importance to those investors in common stock who seek regular cash returns on their investments. For example, an investor who favored high current returns would not buy stock in growth companies. Growth companies have conservative dividend policies because they are using most of their profit-generated resources to help finance expansion of their operations.

Market prices at which stocks are traded in organized marketplaces, such as the New York Stock Exchange (NYSE), are quoted in the daily newspapers. The dividend yields are also published, as measured by annual disbursements based on the last quarterly dividends.

Consider the following stock quotations for McDonald's concerning trading for the week ended July 15, 2000 as published in *Barron's:*

52 Weeks									
High	**Low**	**Stock**	**Sales 100s**	**Ticker Symbol**	**Yield %**	**P-E Ratio**	**High**	**Low**	**Close**	**Net Change**
49.56	29.81	McDonald's	188,770	MCD	.6	22	33.44	31.00	31.38	−1.69

Reading from left to right, the highest price at which McDonald's common stock was traded in the preceding 52 weeks was $49.56 per share; the lowest price, $29.81. During the day over 18 million shares were traded. MCD is the ticker symbol for McDonald's. All listed stocks have short ticker symbols that identify them. These symbols were created years ago to facilitate communication via ticker tape, but they remain effective for computer communication today. The current dividend yield is .6% based on the day's closing price of the stock. The P-E ratio is 22, also based on the closing price. The highest price at which the stock was traded was $33.44 per share; the lowest $31.00. The closing price was that of the last trade for the day, $31.38, which was $1.69 lower than the preceding week's last trade.

Keep in mind that transactions in publicly traded shares are between individual investors in the stock, not between the corporation and the individuals. Thus, a "typical trade" results in the selling of, for example, 100 shares of McDonald's stock held by Ms.

Johnson in Minneapolis to Ms. Davis in Atlanta for $3,138 in cash. These parties would ordinarily transact the trade through their respective stockbrokers. McDonald's would not be directly affected by the trade except that its records of shareholders would be changed to show that 100 shares were now held by Davis, not Johnson.

DIVIDEND – PAYOUT RATIO

Although not routinely published, the **dividend–payout ratio** also receives much attention from analysts. The formula for computing the dividend–payout ratio is given below, followed by McDonald's ratio, using figures from its 1999 annual report:

dividend–payout ratio Common dividends per share divided by earnings per share.

$$\text{Dividend–payout ratio} = \frac{\text{Common dividends per share}}{\text{Earnings per share}}$$

$$\text{1999 Dividend–payout ratio} = \frac{\$.20}{\$1.44} = 14\%$$

$$\text{1996 Dividend–payout ratio} = \frac{\$.15}{\$1.11} = 14\%$$

$$\text{1993 Dividend–payout ratio} = \frac{\$.11}{\$.73} = 15\%$$

$$\text{1990 Dividend–payout ratio} = \frac{\$.09}{\$.55} = 16\%$$

McDonald's fits into the category of a low-payout company. As long as McDonald's continues its worldwide expansion, a minimal payout can be anticipated. Some fast-growing companies such as Microsoft pay no dividends. In contrast, companies without

BUSINESS FIRST
From GM to Cisco in Just Four Decades

The title for this box is the title for a February 7, 2000 *Business Week* article that illustrated the incredible changes in the sizes of firms and the industry from which the largest came during the 30 years from 1969 to 1999. Their table is reproduced on page 68. The market value of a firm is determined by multiplying the number of shares outstanding at year-end by price per share. Note that IBM was the largest company in both 1969 and 1979 although it lost some $4 billion dollars in value over the decade. More telling is the shift in dominant industries over time. In 1969 and 1979, the natural resources companies dominated, with 13 of the top 25 in 1979. By 1999, only Exxon Mobil remained in the top 25 and a merger of Exxon and Mobil was required for it to attain the number 5 position. The dominant industry in 1999 again had 13 companies representing it, but in this case it was high-tech/telcom. Moreover, 10 of the members had not been on the list in 1989. (If you are auditing the count, you should know that we are counting both Lucent and AT&T as if they were on the list in 1989 since Lucent was formerly part of AT&T).

The article is especially appropriate since Cisco is the company we chose to feature in this book. Although it was not the most valuable company at the end of 1999, it grew to that status in 2000, while Microsoft suffered a drop in share price due partly to antitrust action by the U.S. government. Please do not feel too sorry for Bill Gates, the CEO of Microsoft and a major shareholder. We recently saw the following question: If Bill Gates had to spend the same proportion of his wealth to take his spouse to the movies as the average couple spends for this entertainment, what would the evening cost? The answer is $17 million.

Source: *Business Week*, February 7, 2000.

THE TOP 25 U.S. COMPANIES BY MARKET VALUE

1969			1979			1989			1999		
RANK	COMPANY	MARKET VALUE BILLIONS	RANK	COMPANY	MARKET VALUE BILLIONS	RANK	COMPANY	MARKET VALUE BILLIONS	RANK	COMPANY	MARKET VALUE BILLIONS
1	IBM	$41.5	1	IBM	$37.6	1	EXXON	$62.5	1	MICROSOFT	$601.0
2	AT&T	26.7	2	AT&T	36.6	2	GE	58.4	2	GE	507.2
3	GENERAL MOTORS	19.8	3	EXXON	24.2	3	IBM	54.1	3	CISCO	355.1
4	EASTMAN KODAK	13.3	4	GENERAL MOTORS	14.5	4	AT&T	48.9	4	WAL-MART	307.9
5	EXXON	13.3	5	SCHLUMBERGER	11.9	5	PHILIP MORRIS	38.7	5	EXXON MOBIL	278.7
6	SEARS, ROEBUCK	10.5	6	AMOCO	11.8	6	MERCK	30.6	6	INTEL	275.0
7	TEXACO	8.3	7	MOBIL	11.7	7	BRISTOL-MEYERS SQUIBB	29.4	7	LUCENT	228.7
8	XEROX	8.2	8	GE	11.5	8	DUPONT	28.1	8	AT&T	226.7
9	GE	7.0	9	SOHIO	10.8	9	AMOCO	27.9	9	IBM	196.6
10	GULF OIL	6.4	10	CHEVRON	9.6	10	BELLSOUTH	27.9	10	CITIGROUP	187.5
11	3M	6.0	11	ATLANTIC RICHFIELD	9.3	11	COCA-COLA	26.0	11	AMERICA ONLINE	169.5
12	DUPONT	4.9	12	TEXACO	7.8	12	GENERAL MOTORS	25.6	12	AIG	167.4
13	AVON PRODUCTS	4.9	13	EASTMAN KODAK	7.8	13	MOBIL	25.6	13	ORACLE	159.5
14	COCA-COLA	4.7	14	PHILLIPS PETROLEUM	7.4	14	WAL-MART	25.4	14	HOME DEPOT	158.2
15	MOBIL OIL	4.7	15	GULF OIL	6.8	15	PROCTER & GAMBLE	24.3	15	MERCK	157.1
16	PROCTER & GAMBLE	4.5	16	PROCTER & GAMBLE	6.1	16	CHEVRON	24.1	16	MCI WORLDCOM	149.3
17	CHEVRON	4.3	17	GETTY OIL	6.1	17	GTE	23.1	17	PROCTER & GAMBLE	144.2
18	POLAROID	4.1	18	3M	5.9	18	BELL ATLANTIC	21.9	18	COCA-COLA	143.9
19	MERCK	4.1	19	DUPONT	5.8	19	PACIFIC TELESIS	21.0	19	DELL COMPUTER	130.1
20	ATLANTIC RICHFIELD	3.8	20	DOW CHEMICAL	5.8	20	FORD MOTOR	20.6	20	BRISTOL-MEYERS SQUIBB	127.3
21	AMERICAN HOME PROD.	3.6	21	SEARS, ROEBUCK	5.7	21	JOHNSON & JOHNSON	19.8	21	PFIZER	125.6
22	ITT	3.5	22	MERCK	5.4	22	DOW CHEMICAL	19.2	22	JOHNSON & JOHNSON	125.3
23	AMOCO	3.4	23	XEROX	5.2	23	SBC COMMUNICATIONS	19.2	23	SUN MICROSYSTEMS	121.0
24	JOHNSON & JOHNSON	3.3	24	CONOCO	5.1	24	ELI LILLY	19.1	24	HEWLETT-PACKARD	115.9
25	GTE	3.2	25	HALLIBURTON	5.0	25	AMERITECH	18.4	25	YAHOO!	113.9

Note: Market Value is equal to yearend share price multiplied by shares outstanding.
DATA: FOR 1969. CRSP, CENTER FOR RESEARCH IN SECURITY PRICES. THE UNIVERSITY OF CHICAGO, GRADUATE SCHOOL OF BUSINESS. USED WITH PERMISSION. ALL RIGHTS RESERVED.
FOR 1979, 1989 AND 1999, COMPUSTAT PROVIDED BY STANDARD & POOR'S INSTITUTIONAL MARKET SERVICES.

exceptional growth tend to pay a higher percentage of their earnings as dividends. Public utilities ordinarily have high payout ratios. For instance, recently FPL, a Florida based company paid dividends amounting to 53% of its earnings. GM falls between the extremes, with a 1999 payout ratio of 26%.

THE LANGUAGE OF ACCOUNTING IN THE REAL WORLD

At this point you have learned a great number of accounting terms. Unfortunately, organizations use different terms to describe the same concept or account. As a result, the terms you see in real financial statements might not correspond exactly with the ones you just learned. To ease your potential terminology worries, a number of synonyms are presented in Exhibit 2-9. These terms are not introduced here to confuse you. Our objective is to acquaint you with the real world of accounting vocabulary so that you are not surprised when a company's financial statement uses different terms than you learned initially.

Exhibit 2-9

Some Synonyms in Accounting

Term Initially Used in This Book	Examples of Synonyms	Example of Companies
1. Net income		Anheuser-Busch, H. J. Heinz, Colgate-Palmolive
	Net earnings	General Mills, Chrysler, Johnson & Johnson
	Profit	Caterpillar
2. Retained income		General Motors
	Retained earnings	Anheuser-Busch, H. J. Heinz, Colgate-Palmolive
	Reinvested earnings	Coca-Cola
	Earnings retained for use in the business	Ford Motor
	Profit employed in the business	Caterpillar

SUMMARY PROBLEM FOR YOUR REVIEW

PROBLEM THREE

During 1999, Liz Claiborne stock sold for about $40 per share. The company had net income of $192 million, had an average of 61.5 million shares outstanding during the year, and paid dividends of $.45 per share. Calculate the following:

Earnings per share   Dividend–yield ratio
Price–earnings ratio   Dividend–payout ratio

SOLUTION TO PROBLEM THREE

$$\text{Earnings per share} = \frac{\$192}{\$61.5} = \$3.12$$

$$\text{Price–earnings ratio} = \frac{\$40}{\$3.12} = 12.82$$

$$\text{Dividend–yield ratio} = \frac{\$.45}{\$40} = 1.1\%$$

$$\text{Dividend–payout ratio} = \frac{\$.45}{\$3.12} = 14.4\%$$

Highlights to Remember

1. **Explain how accountants measure income.** Accountants can measure income, the excess of revenues over expenses for a particular time period, on an accrual or cash basis. In accrual accounting, revenue is recorded when it is earned, and expenses are recorded when they are incurred. In cash accounting, revenues and expenses are recorded only when cash changes hands. Accrual accounting is the standard basis for accounting today.

2. **Use the concepts of recognition, matching, and cost recovery to record revenues and expenses.** The concept of revenue recognition means that revenues are assigned to the period in which they are earned and realized. Under the concepts of matching and cost recovery, expenses are assigned to a period in which the pertinent goods and services either are used or apparently have no future benefit. Revenues and expenses are components of stockholders' equity. Revenues increase stockholders' equity, and expenses decrease stockholders' equity.

3. **Prepare an income statement and show how it is related to a balance sheet.** An income statement shows an entity's revenues and expenses for a particular span of time. The net income (loss) during the period increases (decreases) the amount of retained income on the balance sheet.

4. **Calculate operating cash flows and show how cash flow differs from income.** Accrual accounting is an excellent way to follow a company's use of its overall assets, but it does not trace cash flows. To satisfy decision makers' need to follow a company's use of cash, accountants use a statement of cash flows. On the statement of cash flows, cash provided by operating activities is reported as the difference between cash provided by customers and cash used to service those customers. Cash provided by customers differs from revenue because some sales are on account and are not received in the same period the sale is made. Similarly, some expenses are incurred and recognized for purposes of determining net income before or after the actual cash is paid out. For example, inventory may be acquired and paid for in the period before it is sold.

5. **Account for cash dividends and prepare a statement of retained income.** Cash dividends are not expenses. They are distributions of cash to stockholders that reduce retained income. Corporations are not obligated to pay dividends, but once dividends are declared by the board of directors they become a legal liability until paid in cash. A statement of retained income shows how net income increases the beginning balance in retained earnings and dividends decrease it to calculate the ending balance.

6. **Compute and explain earnings per share, price–earnings ratio, dividend–yield ratio, and dividend–payout ratio.** Ratios relate one element of a company's economic activity to another. EPS expresses overall earnings on a scale that individual investors can link to their own ownership level. The P-E ratio relates accounting earnings to market prices. The dividend–yield ratio relates dividends paid per share to market prices and the dividend–payout ratio relates those same dividends to the earnings during the period.

Accounting Vocabulary

Assignment Material

QUESTIONS

2-1 How long is a company's operating cycle?

2-2 "Expenses are negative stockholders' equity accounts." Explain.

2-3 What is the major defect of the cash basis of accounting?

2-4 What are the two tests of recognition of revenue?

2-5 Give two examples where revenue is not recognized at the point of sale, one where recognition is delayed because the revenue is not yet earned, and one because it is not yet realized.

2-6 "Expenses are assets that have been used up." Explain.

2-7 "The manager acquires goods and services, not expenses per se." Explain.

2-8 "The income statement is like a moving picture; in contrast, a balance sheet is like a snapshot." Explain.

2-9 "Cash dividends are not expenses." Explain.

2-10 Identify the three categories of cash flows found on the statement of cash flows and list two activities that might appear in each of the categories.

2-11 "Retained income is not a pot of gold." Explain.

2-12 "Financial ratios are important tools for analyzing financial statements, but no ratios are shown on the statements." Do you agree? Explain.

2-13 "Fast growing companies have high P-E ratios." Explain.

2-14 Give two ratios that give information about a company's dividends, and explain what each means.

2-15 "Companies with a high dividend–payout ratio are good investments because stockholders get more of their share of earnings in cash." Do you agree? Explain.

2-16 Give two synonyms for *income statement*.

2-17 Give two synonyms for *income* and for *retained income*.

2-18 Why is it important to learn synonyms that are used for various accounting terms?

COGNITIVE EXERCISES

2-19 Quarterly versus Annual Financial Statements
In the United States it is common to provide abbreviated financial data quarterly with full financial statements provided annually. In some countries only annual data are provided. Discuss the tradeoffs.

2-20 Statement of Cash Flows versus Income Statement
Which would you rather have, a statement of cash flows or an income statement? Why?

2-21 Dividends and Stock Prices
Suppose a company was going to pay out half of its total assets in a cash dividend. What would you expect to happen to the value of the company's stock as a result of the dividend?

2-22 Interpretation of the Price–Earnings Ratio
Would you rather own a company with a high price–earnings ratio or a low price–earnings ratio? Why?

EXERCISES

2-23 Synonyms and Antonyms
Consider the following terms: (1) expenses, (2) unexpired costs, (3) reinvested earnings, (4) net earnings, (5) prepaid expenses, (6) undistributed earnings, (7) statement of earnings, (8) used-up costs, (9) net profits, (10) net income, (11) revenues, (12) retained income, (13) sales, (14) statement of financial condition, (15) statement of income, (16) statement of financial position, (17) retained earnings, (18) operating statement, and (19) cost of goods sold.

Required

Group the items into two major categories, the income statement and the balance sheet. Answer by indicating the numbered items that belong in each group. Specify items that are assets and items that are expenses.

2-24 Special Meanings of Terms
A news story described the disappointing sales of a new model car, the Nova. An auto dealer said: "Even if the Nova is a little slow to move out of dealerships, it is more of a plus than a minus. . . . We're now selling 14 more cars per month than before. That's revenue. That's the bottom line."

Required

Is the dealer confused about accounting terms? Explain.

2-25 Nature of Retained Income

This is an exercise on the relationships between assets, liabilities, and ownership equities. The numbers are small, but the underlying concepts are large.

1. Assume an opening balance sheet of:

Cash	$1,500	Paid-in capital	$1,500

2. Purchase inventory for $800 cash. Prepare a balance sheet. A heading is unnecessary in this and subsequent requirements.
3. Sell the entire inventory for $950 cash. Prepare a balance sheet. Where is the retained income in terms of relationships within the balance sheet? That is, what is the meaning of the retained income? Explain in your own words.
4. Buy inventory for $300 cash and equipment for $800 cash. Prepare a balance sheet. Where is the retained income in terms of relationships within the balance sheet? That is, what is the meaning of the retained income? Explain in your own words.
5. Buy inventory for $500 on open account. Prepare a balance sheet. Where is the retained income and account payable in terms of the relationships within the balance sheet? That is, what is the meaning of the account payable and the retained income? Explain in your own words.

2-26 Asset Acquisition and Expiration

The Lougee Company had the following transactions:

a. Paid $2,000 for stationery and wrapping supplies.
b. Paid $18,000 cash for rent for the next 6 months.
c. Paid $4,000 cash for an advertisement in the *New York Times*.
d. Paid $9,000 cash for a training program for employees.

Required

Show the effects on the balance sheet equation in two phases: at acquisition and on expiration at the end of the month of acquisition. Show all amounts in thousands.

2-27 Find Unknowns

The following data pertain to the Cruz Corporation. Total assets at January 1, 20X1 were $100,000; at December 31, 20X1, $124,000. During 20X1, sales were $354,000, cash dividends were $5,000, and operating expenses (exclusive of cost of goods sold) were $200,000. Total liabilities at December 31, 20X1 were $55,000; at January 1, 20X1, $40,000. There was no additional capital paid in during 20X1. Compute the following:

1. Stockholders' equity, January 1, 20X1 and December 31, 20X1.
2. Net income for 20X1.
3. Cost of goods sold for 20X1.

2-28 Income Statement

A statement of an automobile dealer follows:

Warner Toyota, Inc.
Statement of Profit and Loss
December 31, 20X3

Revenues		
Sales	$1,000,000	
Increase in market value of land and building	200,000	$1,200,000
Deduct expenses		
Advertising	$ 100,000	
Sales commissions	50,000	
Utilities	20,000	
Wages	160,000	
Dividends	100,000	
Cost of cars purchased	700,000	1,130,000
Net profit		$ 70,000

Required

List and describe any shortcomings of this statement.

2-29 Income Statement and Cash Flow Statement

KLM Royal Dutch Airlines flies to more than 350 cities in 80 countries. In the year ended March 31, 2000, KLM had revenues of NLG 13,666 million (where NLG is Netherlands guilders). Total expenses were NLG 12,923 million. Cash flows from operating activities were NLG 616 million, cash flows from investing were NLG (197), and cash flows from financing activities were NLG (892) million.

1. Compute KLM's net income for the year ended March 31, 2000.
2. Compute the increase (decrease) in cash for KLM for the year ended March 31, 2000.

2-30 Balance Sheet Equation

(Alternates are 2-31 and 2-46.) For each of the independent cases columns 1, 2, and 3, compute the amounts ($ in thousands) for the items indicated by letters, and show your supporting computations:

	Case		
	1	2	3
Revenues	$140	$K	$280
Expenses	120	200	240
Dividends declared	—	5	Q
Additional investment by stockholders	—	40	35
Net income	E	20	P
Retained income			
Beginning of year	30	60	100
End of year	D	J	110
Paid-in capital			
Beginning of year	15	10	N
End of year	C	H	85
Total assets			
Beginning of year	80	F	L
End of year	95	280	M
Total liabilities			
Beginning of year	A	90	105
End of year	B	G	95

2-31 Balance Sheet Equation

(Alternates are 2-30 and 2-46.) Intuit, producer of Quicken and TurboTax software, has the following actual data ($ in thousands) for the year 2000:

Total costs	$ B
Net earnings	305,661
Dividends	162
Assets, beginning of period	2,447,460
Assets, end of period	D
Liabilities, beginning of period	A
Liabilities, end of period	807,613
Shareholders' equity, beginning of period	1,561,388
Shareholders' equity, end of period	2,071,289
Retained earnings, beginning of period	215,167
Retained earnings, end of period	C
Total revenues	1,093,825

Find the unknowns ($ in millions), showing computations to support your answers.

Required

2-32 Nonprofit Operating Statement

Examine the accompanying statement of the Edinburgh University Faculty Club. Identify the Edinburgh classifications and terms that would not be used by a profit-seeking hotel and restaurant. Suggest terms that the profit-seeking entity would use instead (£ is the British pound).

Edinburgh Faculty Club
Statement of Income and Expenses for Fiscal Year

Food Service

Sales		£545,130
Expenses		
Food	£287,088	
Labor	272,849	
Operating costs	30,537	590,474
Deficit		£(45,344)

Bar

Sales		£90,549
Expenses		
Cost of liquor	£29,302	
Labor	5,591	
Operating costs	6,125	41,018
Surplus		49,531

Hotel

Sales		£33,771
Expenses		23,803
Surplus		9,968
Total Surplus from operations		£ 14,155
General income (members' dues, room fees, etc.)		95,546
General administration and operating expenses		(134,347)
Deficit before university subsidy		£ (24,646)
University subsidy		31,000
Net surplus after university subsidy		£ 6,354

2-33 Earnings and Dividend Ratios

Cadbury Schweppes, the British candy and beverage company, had 1999 earnings of £642 million. Cash dividends were £202. The company had an average of 2,026 million common shares outstanding. No other type of stock was outstanding. The market price of the stock at the end of the year was £3.75 per share.

Required

Compute (1) earnings per share, (2) price–earnings ratio, (3) dividend yield, and (4) dividend–payout ratio.

2-34 Earnings and Dividend Ratios

Chevron Corporation is one of the largest oil companies in the world. The company's revenue in 1999 was $31.5 billion. Net income was $2.07 billion. EPS was $3.14. The company's common stock is the only type of shares outstanding.

Required

1. Compute the average number of common shares outstanding during the year.
2. The dividend–payout ratio was 83%. What was the amount of dividends per share?
3. The average market price of the stock for the year was $83 per share. Compute (a) dividend yield and (b) price–earnings ratio.

PROBLEMS

2-35 Fundamental Revenue and Expense

Bowen Corporation was formed on June 1, 20X2, when some stockholders invested $100,000 in cash in the company. During the first week of June, $80,000 cash was spent for merchandise inventory (sportswear). During the remainder of the month, total sales reached $110,000, of which $70,000 was on open account. The cost of the inventory sold was $60,000. For simplicity, assume that no other transactions occurred except that on June 28, Bowen Corporation acquired $26,000 additional inventory on open account.

Required

1. By using the balance sheet equation approach demonstrated in Exhibit 2-2 (p. 51), analyze all transactions for June. Show all amounts in thousands.
2. Prepare a balance sheet, June 30, 20X2.
3. Prepare two statements for June, side by side. The first should use the accrual basis of accounting to compute net income, and the second, the cash basis to compute net cash provided by (or used by) operating activities. Which basis provides a more informative measure of economic performance? Why?

2-36 Accounting for Prepayments

(Alternates are 2-38, 2-40, 2-42, and 2-45). The Ordonez Company, a wholesale distributor of home appliances, began business on July 1, 20X2. The following summarized transactions occurred during July.

1. Ordonez's stockholders contributed $240,000 in cash in exchange for their common stock.
2. On July 1, Ordonez signed a 1-year lease on a warehouse, paying $60,000 cash in advance for occupancy of 12 months.
3. On July 1, Ordonez acquired warehouse equipment for $100,000. A cash down payment of $40,000 was made and a note payable was signed for the balance.
4. On July 1, Ordonez paid $24,000 cash for a 2-year insurance policy covering fire, casualty, and related risks.
5. Ordonez acquired assorted merchandise for $35,000 cash.
6. Ordonez acquired assorted merchandise for $190,000 on open account.
7. Total sales were $200,000, of which $30,000 were for cash.
8. Cost of inventory sold was $160,000.
9. Rent expense was recognized for the month of July.
10. Depreciation expense of $2,000 was recognized for the month.
11. Insurance expense was recognized for the month.
12. Collected $35,000 from credit customers.
13. Disbursed $80,000 to trade creditors.

For simplicity, ignore all other possible expenses.

Required

1. By using the balance sheet equation format demonstrated in Exhibit 2-2 (p. 51), prepare an analysis of each transaction. Show all amounts in thousands. What do transactions 8 to 11 illustrate about the theory of assets and expenses? (Use a Prepaid Insurance account, which is not illustrated in Exhibit 2-2.)
2. Prepare an income statement for July on the accrual basis.
3. Prepare a balance sheet, July 31, 20X2.

2-37 Net Income and Cash Flows from Operating Activities

(Alternates are 2-39, 2-41, and 2-43.) Refer to the preceding problem. Suppose Ordonez measured performance on the cash basis instead of the accrual basis. Compute the net cash provided by (or used for) operating activities. Which measure, net income or net cash provided by (or used for) operating activities, provides a better measure of overall performance? Why?

2-38 Analysis of Transactions, Preparation of Statements

(Alternates are 2-36, 2-40, 2-42, and 2-45.) The Guenther Company was incorporated on April 1, 20X2. Guenther had 10 holders of common stock. Rita Guenther, who was the president and chief executive officer, held 51% of the shares. The company rented space in chain discount stores and specialized in selling ladies' shoes. Guenther's first location was in a store that was part of The Old Market in Omaha.

The following events occurred during April:

1. The company was incorporated. Common stockholders invested $150,000 cash.
2. Purchased merchandise inventory for cash, $45,000.
3. Purchased merchandise inventory on open account, $35,000.

4. Merchandise carried in inventory at a cost of $37,000 was sold for cash for $25,000 and on open account for $65,000, a grand total of $90,000. Guenther (not The Old Market) carries and collects these accounts receivable.

5. Collection of the preceding accounts receivable, $15,000.

6. Payments of accounts payable $30,000. See transaction 3.

7. Special display equipment and fixtures were acquired on April 1 for $36,000. Their expected useful life was 36 months. This equipment was removable. Guenther paid $12,000 as a down payment and signed a promissory note for $24,000. Also see transaction 11.

8. On April 1, Guenther signed a rental agreement with The Old Market. The agreement called for a flat $2,000 per month, payable quarterly in advance. Therefore, Guenther paid $6,000 cash on April 1.

9. The rental agreement also called for a payment of 10% of all sales. This payment was in addition to the flat $2,000 per month. In this way, The Old Market would share in any success of the venture and be compensated for general services such as cleaning and utilities. This payment was to be made in cash on the last day of each month as soon as the sales for the month had been tabulated. Therefore, Guenther made the payment on April 30.

10. Employee wages and sales commissions were all paid for in cash. The amount was $34,000.

11. Depreciation expense of $1,000 was recognized ($36,000/36 months). See transaction 7.

12. The expiration of an appropriate amount of prepaid rental services was recognized. See transaction 8.

Required

1. Prepare an analysis of Guenther Company's transactions, employing the equation approach demonstrated in Exhibit 2-2 (p. 51). Show all amounts in thousands.

2. Prepare a balance sheet as of April 30, 20X2, and an income statement for the month of April. Ignore income taxes.

3. Given these sparse facts, analyze Guenther's performance for April and its financial position as of April 30, 20X2.

2-39 Net Income and Cash Flows from Operating Activities
(Alternates are 2-37, 2-41, and 2-43.) Refer to the preceding problem. Suppose Guenther measured performance on the cash basis instead of the accrual basis. Compute the net cash provided by (or used for) operating activities. Which measure, net income or net cash provided by (or used for) operating activities, provides a better measure of overall performance? Why?

2-40 Analysis of Transactions, Preparation of Statements
(Alternates are 2-36, 2-38, 2-42, and 2-45.) H. J. Heinz Company's actual condensed balance sheet data for May 1, 2000 follows ($ in millions):

Cash	$ 138	Accounts payable	$1,027
Accounts receivable	1,237	Other liabilities	6,227
Inventories	1,600		
Other assets	3,517	Owner's equity	1,596
Property, plant, and equipment	2,358		
Total	$8,850	Total	$8,850

The following summarizes some transactions during May ($ in millions):

1. Ketchup carried in inventory at a cost of $3 was sold for cash of $3 and on open account of $8, a grand total of $11.

2. Acquired inventory on account, $6.

3. Collected receivables, $4.

4. On May 2, used $12 cash to prepay some rent and insurance for 12 months.
5. Payments on accounts payable (for inventories), $2.
6. Paid selling and administrative expenses in cash, $1.
7. Prepaid expenses of $1 for rent and insurance expired in May.
8. Depreciation expense of $1 was recognized for May.

Required

1. Prepare an analysis of Heinz's transactions, employing the equation approach demonstrated in Exhibit 2-2 (p. 51). Show all amounts in millions. (For simplicity, only a few transactions are illustrated here.)
2. Prepare a statement of earnings for the month ended May 31 and a balance sheet, May 31. Ignore income taxes.

2-41 Net Income and Cash Flows from Operating Activities
(Alternates are 2-37, 2-39, and 2-43.) Refer to the preceding problem. Suppose Heinz measured performance on the cash basis instead of the accrual basis. Compute the net cash provided by (or used for) operating activities. Which measure, net income or net cash provided by (or used for) operating activities, provides a better measure of overall performance? Why?

2-42 Analysis of Transactions, Preparation of Statements
(Alternates are 2-36, 2-38, 2-40, and 2-45.) Wm. Wrigley Jr. Company manufactures and sells chewing gum. The company's actual condensed balance sheet data for January 1, 2000 follows ($ in millions):

Cash	$ 288	Accounts payable	$ 87
Receivables	182	Dividends payable	40
Inventories	258	Other liabilities	282
Other current assets	76	Owner's equity	1,139
Property, plant, and equipment	559		
Other assets	185		
Total	$1,548	Total	$1,548

The following summarizes some major transactions during January ($ in millions):

1. Gum carried in inventory at a cost of $40 was sold for cash of $30 and on open account of $40, a grand total of $70.
2. Collection of receivables, $45.
3. Depreciation expense of $3 was recognized.
4. Selling and administrative expenses of $24 were paid in cash.
5. Prepaid expenses of $5 expired in January. These included fire insurance premiums paid in the previous year that applied to future months. The expiration increases selling and administrative expense and reduces other current assets.
6. The January 1 liability for dividends was paid in cash on January 25.

Required

1. Prepare an analysis of Wrigley's transactions, employing the equation approach demonstrated in Exhibit 2-2 (p. 51). Show all amounts in millions. (For simplicity, only a few major transactions are illustrated here.)
2. Prepare a statement of earnings. Also prepare a balance sheet, January 31. Ignore income taxes.

2-43 Net Income and Cash Flows from Operating Activities
(Alternates are 2-37, 2-39, and 2-41.) Refer to the preceding problem. Suppose Wrigley measured performance on the cash basis instead of the accrual basis. Compute the net cash provided by (or used for) operating activities. Which measure, net income or net cash provided by (or used for) operating activities, provides a better measure of overall performance? Why?

2-44 Prepare Financial Statements

The Loretti Corporation does not use the services of a professional accountant. At the end of its second year of operations, 20X2, the company's financial statements were prepared by its office manager. Listed next in random order are the items appearing in these statements:

Accounts receivable	$ 27,800	Office supplies inventory	$ 2,000
Paid-in capital	100,000	Notes payable	7,000
Trucks	33,700	Merchandise inventory	61,000
Cost of goods sold	156,000	Accounts payable	14,000
Salary expense	86,000	Notes receivable	2,500
Unexpired insurance	1,800	Utilities expenses	5,000
Rent expense	19,500	Net income	4,200
Sales	280,000	Retained income	
Advertising expense	9,300	January 1, 20X2	18,000
Cash	14,400	December 31, 20X2	22,200

You are satisfied that the statements in which these items appear are correct except for several matters that the office manager overlooked. The following information should have been entered on the books and reflected in the financial statements:

a. The amount shown for rent expense includes $1,500 that is actually prepaid for the first month in 20X3.

b. Of the amount shown for unexpired insurance, only $800 is prepaid for periods after 20X2.

c. Depreciation of trucks for 20X2 is $5,000.

d. About $1,200 of the office supplies in the inventory shown earlier was actually issued and used during 20X2 operations.

e. Cash dividends of $4,000 were declared in December 20X2 by the board of directors. These dividends are to be distributed in February 20X3.

Required

Prepare in good form the following corrected financial statements, ignoring income taxes:

1. Income statement for 20X2.

2. Statement of retained income for 20X2.

3. Balance sheet at December 31, 20X2.

It is not necessary to prepare a columnar analysis to show the transaction effects on each of the elements of the accounting equation.

2-45 Transaction Analysis and Financial Statements, Including Dividends

(Alternates are 2-36, 2-38, 2-40, and 2-42.) Consider the following balance sheet of a wholesaler of party supplies:

Partco Supplies Company
Balance Sheet December 31, 20X7

Assets		Liabilities and Stockholders' Equity		
		Liabilities		
Cash	$ 300,000	Accounts payable		$ 800,000
Accounts receivable	400,000	Stockholders' equity		
Merchandise inventory	860,000	Paid-in capital	$300,000	
Prepaid rent	40,000	Retained income	600,000	
Equipment	100,000	Total stockholders'		
		equity		900,000
Total	$1,700,000	Total		$1,700,000

The following is a summary of transactions that occurred during 20X8:

a. Acquisitions of inventory on open account, $1 million.

b. Sales on open account, $1.5 million; and for cash, $200,000. Therefore, total sales were $1.7 million.

c. Merchandise carried in inventory at a cost of $1.2 million was sold as described in b.

d. The warehouse 12-month lease expired on September 1, 20X8. However, the lease was immediately renewed at a rate of $84,000 for the next 12-month period. The entire rent was paid in cash in advance.

e. Depreciation expense for 20X8 for the warehouse equipment was $20,000.

f. Collections on accounts receivable, $1.25 million.

g. Wages for 20X8 were paid in full in cash, $200,000.

h. Miscellaneous expenses for 20X8 were paid in full in cash, $70,000.

i. Payments on accounts payable, $900,000.

j. Cash dividends for 20X8 were paid in full in December, $100,000.

Required

1. Prepare an analysis of transactions, employing the equation approach demonstrated in Exhibit 2-2 (p. 51). Show the amounts in thousands of dollars.
2. Prepare a balance sheet, statement of income, and statement of retained income. Also prepare a combined statement of income and retained income.
3. Reconsider transaction j. Suppose the dividends were declared on December 15, payable on January 31, 20X9, to shareholders of record on January 20. Indicate which accounts and financial statements in requirement 2 would be changed and by how much. Be complete and specific.

2-46 Balance Sheet Equation

(Alternates are 2-30 and 2-31.) Nordstrom, Inc., the fashion retailer, had the following actual data for fiscal year ended January 31, 2000 ($ in millions):

Assets, beginning of period	$ 3,088
Assets, end of period	3,062
Liabilities, beginning of period	A
Liabilities, end of period	D
Other shareholders' equity, beginning of period	227
Other shareholders' equity, end of period	47
Retained earnings, beginning of period	1,074
Retained earnings, end of period	C
Sales and other revenues	5,124
Cost of sales and all other expenses	4,921
Net earnings	B
Dividends	44

Find the unknowns ($ in millions), showing computations to support your answers.

Required

2-47 Statement of Cash Flows

D. Ng Company imports Asian goods and sells them in eight import stores on the East Coast. On August 1, 20X4, Ng's cash balance was $156,000. Summarized transactions during August were:

1. Sales on open account, $580,000.
2. Collections of accounts receivable, $460,000.
3. Purchases of inventory on open account, $305,000.

4. Payment of accounts payable, $280,000.
5. Cost of goods sold, $325,000.
6. Salaries and wages expense, $100,000, of which $90,000 was paid in cash and $10,000 remained payable on August 31.
7. Rent expense for August, $35,000, paid in advance in July.
8. Depreciation expense, $46,000.
9. Other operating expenses, $70,000, all paid in cash.
10. Borrowed from bank on August 31, $50,000, with repayment (including interest) due on December 31.
11. Purchased fixtures and equipment for the Baltimore store on August 31, $120,000; half paid in cash and half due in October.

Required

1. Prepare a statement of cash flows, including the cash balance on August 31.
2. Prepare an income statement.
3. Explain why net income differs from net cash provided by (or used for) operating activities.

2-48 Two Sides of a Transaction

For each of the following transactions, show the effects on the entities involved. As was illustrated in the chapter, use the A = L + OE equation to demonstrate the effects. Also name each amount affected, show the dollar amount, and indicate whether the effects are increases or decreases. The following transaction is completed as an illustration.

ILLUSTRATION

The Seattle General Hospital collects $1,000 from the Blue Cross Health Care Plan.

		A		=	L + OE
Entity	*Cash*	*Receivables*	*Trucks*		*Payables*
Hospital	+1,000	−1,000		=	
Blue Cross	−1,000			=	−1,000

1. Borrowing of $100,000 on a home mortgage from Fidelity Savings by Kenneth Berg.
2. Payment of $10,000 principal on the preceding mortgage. Ignore interest.
3. Purchase of a 2-year subscription to *Time* magazine for $90 cash by Carla Paperman.
4. Purchase of trucks by the U.S. Postal Service for $10 million cash from the U.S. General Services Administration. The trucks were carried in the accounts at $10 million by the General Services Administration.
5. Purchase of U.S. government bonds for $100,000 cash by Lockheed Corporation.
6. Cash deposits of $11 on the returnable bottles sold by Safeway Stores to a retail customer, Philomena Simon.
7. Collections on open account of $100 by Sears store from a retail customer, Kenneth Debreu.
8. Purchase of traveler's checks of $1,000 from American Express Company by Michael Sharpe.
9. Cash deposit of $600 in a checking account in Bank of America by David Kennedy.
10. Purchase of a United Airlines "supersaver" airline ticket for $400 cash by Robert Peecher on June 15. The trip will be taken on September 10.

2-49 Net Income and Retained Income

McDonald's Corporation is a well-known fast-food restaurant company. The following data are from the 1999 annual report ($ in millions):

McDonald's Corporation

Retained earnings,		Dividends paid	$ 264.7
beginning of year	$13,879.6	General, administrative,	
Revenues	13,259.3	and selling expenses	1,372.4
Interest and other		Franchise expenses	737.7
nonoperating expenses	435.5	Retained earnings,	
Provisions for income taxes	936.2	end of year	15,562.8
Food and packaging expense	3,204.6	Occupancy and other	
Payroll and employee benefit	2,418.3	operating expenses	2,206.7

Required

1. Prepare the following for the year:
    a. Income statement. The final three lines of the income statement were labeled as income before provision for income taxes, provisions for income taxes, and net income.
    b. Statement of retained earnings.
2. Comment briefly on the relative size of the cash dividend.

2-50 Earnings Statement, Retained Earnings

Compaq is a computer company. The following amounts were in the financial statements contained in its 1999 annual report ($ in millions):

Total revenues	$38,525	Retained earnings at	
Cash	2,666	beginning of year	$ 4,501
Provision for income taxes	365	Cost of goods sold	29,798
Accounts payable	4,380	Dividends declared	122
Cash provided by operations	1,161	Other expenses	7,793

Required

Choose the relevant data and prepare (1) the income statement for the year and (2) the statement of retained income for the year. The final three lines of the income statement were labeled as earnings before income taxes, provision for income taxes, and net earnings.

2-51 Financial Ratios

Following is a list of several well-known companies and selected financial data of the sort typically included in letters sent by stock brokerage firms to clients:

	Per-Share Data				Ratios and Percentages	
Company	Price	Earnings	Dividends	P-E	Dividend Yield	Dividend Payout
Airborne	$15.13	$1.85	$—	—	—	9%
Federal Express	—	2.32	—	17	—	0%
UPS	55.75	—	—	27	1.2%	—

The missing figures for this schedule can be computed from the data given.

1. Compute the missing figures and identify the company with:
    a. The highest dividend yield.
    b. The highest dividend–payout percentage.
    c. The lowest market price relative to earnings.
2. Assume that you know nothing about any of these companies other than the data given and the computations you have made from the data. Which company would you choose as:
    a. The most attractive investment? Why?
    b. The least attractive investment? Why?

2-52 Financial Ratios

Following is a list of several well-known companies and selected financial data of the sort typically included in letters sent by stock brokerage firms to clients:

	Per-Share Data			Ratios and Percentages		
Company	Price	Earnings	Dividends	P-E	Dividend Yield	Dividend Payout
BP	53.13	1.54	1.33	—	—	—
Exxon Mobil	81.13	—	—	22.6	2.2%	—
Texaco	—	2.14	—	23.3	—	84%

The missing figures for this schedule can be computed from the data given.

1. Compute the missing figures and identify the company with:
   a. The highest dividend yield.
   b. The highest dividend-payout percentage.
   c. The lowest market price relative to earnings.
2. Assume that you know nothing about any of these companies other than the data given and the computations you have made from the data. Which company would you choose as:
   a. The most attractive investment? Why?
   b. The least attractive investment? Why?

2-53 Revenue Recognition and Ethics

Kendall Square Research Corporation (KSR), located in Waltham, Massachusetts, produced high-speed computers and competed against companies such as Cray Research and Sun Microsystems.

In August 1993, the common stock of KSR reached an all-time high of $25.75 a share; by mid-December it had plummeted to $5.25. Its financial policies were called into question in an article in *Financial Shenanigan Busters,* Winter 1994, p. 3. The main charge was that the company was recording revenues before it was appropriate.

KSR sold expensive computers to universities and other research institutions. Often the customers took delivery before they knew how they might pay for the computers. Sometimes they anticipated receiving grants that would pay for the computers, but other times they had no prospective funding. KSR also recorded revenue when computers were shipped to distributors who did not yet have customers to buy them and when computers were sold contingent on future upgrades.

Required Comment on the ethical implications of KSR's revenue recognition practices.

ANNUAL REPORT CASE

2-54 Cisco Annual Report

Refer to the financial statements of the actual company, Cisco, in appendix A at the end of the text and answer the following questions:

Required
1. What was the amount of net sales (total revenues), and the net earnings for the year ended July 29, 2000?
2. What was the total amount of cash provided by financing activities for the year ended July 29, 2000?
3. Compute the increase in retained earnings for the year ended July 29, 2000.

2-55 Financial Statement Research

Select the financial statements of any company.

1. What was the amount of sales or total revenues, and the net income for the most recent year?
2. What was the total amount of cash dividends for the most recent year?

3. What was the amount of cash provided by (or used for) operating activities in the most recent year? Compare the amount to the net income.

4. What was the ending balance in retained income in the most recent year? What were the two most significant items during the year that affected the retained income balance?

COLLABORATIVE LEARNING EXERCISE

2-56 Financial Ratios

Form groups of four to six persons each. Each member of the group should pick a different company and find the most recent annual report for that company. (If you do not have printed annual reports, try searching the Internet for one.)

1. Members should compute the following ratios for their company:
   a. Earnings per share
   b. P-E ratio
   c. Dividend–yield ratio
   d. Dividend–payout ratio

Required

2. As a group, list two possible reasons that each ratio differs across the selected companies. Focus on comparing the companies with the highest and lowest values for each ratio, and explain how the nature of the company might be the reason for the differences in ratios.

INTERNET EXERCISE

2-57 Internet Case

It's Just Lunch does not have a Web site, but because many of its clients' dates take place in restaurants, we examine the financial statements of a popular steakhouse. Go to www.outback.com, the home page for Outback Steakhouse. Locate *Company & Jobs,* then *Investor Relations.* Find *Financial Reports* and click on the most recent annual report.
Answer the following questions:

www.prenhall.com/horngren

Required

1. Locate Outback's revenue recognition policy in the *Notes to Consolidated Financial Statements.* When does Outback recognize revenue? Does it differ for franchise sales (i.e., the sale of a franchise to an investor)? How?

2. Why does Outback have "unearned revenue"? Where is it found in the financial statements?

3. Refer to Outback's *Results of Operations.* What are the restaurant brands that contribute to system-wide sales? Why does it make sense to track them separately?

4. What specific items comprise *Cost of Sales?* Is labor considered part of this line item?

5. Is Outback's income statement prepared using the cash or accrual basis? What items on the balance sheet are clues to answering this question?

6. Do you think Outback Steakhouse is a profit-seeking organization? What clues on the financial statements help you answer this?

3

RECORDING TRANSACTIONS

One Gap storefront from a firm with over 3,000 casual apparel specialty stores, including Bannana Republic and Old Navy locations.

www.prenhall.com/horngren

Learning Objectives

After studying this chapter, you should be able to

1. Use double-entry accounting.

2. Analyze and journalize transactions.

3. Post journal entries to the ledgers.

4. Prepare and use a trial balance.

5. Close revenue and expense accounts and update retained income.

6. Correct erroneous journal entries and describe how errors affect accounts.

7. Use T-accounts to analyze accounting relationships.

8. Explain how computers have transformed processing of accounting data.

Have you ever bought a shirt, a pair of jeans, or anything else from a Gap store? If so, your purchase was just one of hundreds of thousands of transactions that Gap Inc. had to record that day. With so many transactions happening, you might think that yours would get lost in the shuffle. Yet you can read a report on your transaction combined with millions of others in any major newspaper in news articles built on press releases such as this one from *Business Wire* dated August 10, 2000 and time-stamped 7:02 AM:

> *Gap Inc. (NYSE:GPS) today announced sales and earnings for the second quarter which ended July 29, 2000. Earnings per share during the quarter decreased 5 percent to $.21 versus $.22 the prior year. Second quarter net sales rose 20 percent to $2.95 billion, compared with $2.45 billion in 1999. Comparable store sales decreased 2 percent versus an 8 percent increase last year. . . . Net earnings decreased 6 percent in the second quarter to $184 million compared with $196 million last year.*

Are you not seeing that shirt you bought? The information contained in this news article comes directly from Gap's corporate headquarters and is designed to inform investors, stockholders, and other interested parties about the financial performance of the organization. Gap's corporate headquarters gets this information directly from the company's accounting records. Of course, these records contain every single Gap transaction—including your shirt purchase.

Gap Inc.'s transactions can take many forms—for example, merchandise sales for cash or credit or purchases of inventory for its stores. When summarized at the end of the month, quarter, or year, the totals for each account are used to prepare the financial reports that tell the financial story for that period. As you can see from Gap, Inc.'s press release, their net sales totaled $2.95 billion for the quarter. After deducting expenses and other items, net earnings came to $184 million, or 6.2% of net sales ($184/$2,950). Now you know that only 6.2% of what you paid for your shirt was actually net earnings for Gap.

The information in this press release led to major price changes for Gap stock. Shares fell some 14% to close at $27 at the end of August 10, 2000. The earnings release and the results for the quarter were significant information and caused investors to change their valuation of shares of Gap. There had been earlier hints of trouble for Gap, whose stock had peaked at more than $50 per share in early 2000. Retailers such as Gap provide information every month on sales levels. May sales were up 19% from the year earlier level, which looks like good news at first glance. It turns out that Gap was opening new stores at a furious pace, and the store count was up 23% during the same period. When only stores open for both years were considered, sales declined by 2%. Such "same store" sales were down 2% again in June and down 1% in July. Thus, the August press release confirmed developing concerns and clarified how sales patterns would translate into earnings. The news was not good. By the night of August 10, Gap was down about 50% from its high, and news about sales and profit levels was a primary driving force in helping investors decide on an appropriate value for Gap.

Methods of processing accounting data have changed dramatically in the last decade or two, as computerized systems have replaced manual ones. However, the steps in recording, storing, and processing accounting data have not changed. Switching from pencil-and-paper accounting records to computerized ones is a little like switching from a car with a stick shift to one with an automatic transmission. You spend less time worrying about routine tasks, but you still need to understand the way the basic system works. Whether the data are entered into the system by pencil, keyboard, or optical scanner, the same basic data must be input, summarized, and reported.

To use intelligently the financial statements we learned about in the last two chapters, decision makers must understand the methods used to record and analyze the data in those reports. This chapter focuses on those methods. In particular, this chapter explains the double-entry accounting system that is universally used to record and process information about a company's transactions. As you will find, a working knowledge of this system is essential for anyone engaged in business. Ultimately, the accounting practices comprise language that managers in all organizations use to understand the economic progress of their organization.

THE DOUBLE-ENTRY ACCOUNTING SYSTEM

Objective 1
Use double-entry accounting.

double-entry system
The method usually followed for recording transactions, whereby at least two accounts are always affected by each transaction.

In large businesses such as McDonald's and AT&T, hundreds or thousands of transactions occur hourly. With so much activity, it is easy to lose track of one or two transactions. However, even one lost transaction could wreak havoc on a company's accounting (just think of what happens when you miss one transaction in your checking account record) and lead to some very serious consequences. As a result, accountants must record these transactions in a systematic manner. Worldwide, the dominant recording process is a **double-entry system,** in which at least two accounts are always affected by each transaction. Each transaction must be analyzed to determine which accounts are involved, whether the accounts are increased or decreased, and how much each account balance will change.

BUSINESS FIRST

Meeting a Web User's Needs

Increasingly, investors are going to the Web to get financial information, and companies are tailoring their Web sites to respond to this demand. *CFO* magazine performed a study of the contents and performance of 50 randomly selected Web sites. Two stood out: Dayton Hudson Corporation (**www.dhc.com**) and Motorola (**www.motorola.com**). CCBN, a provider of investor relations Web site management, reports that over 80% of visitors to investor relations pages of corporate Web sites are seeking stock quotes, financial releases, Securities Exchange Commission (SEC) filings, and a stock price chart. The best Web sites provide these items and more. Moreover, the best companies assure that investors can find this information with a minimum number of clicks of the mouse.

CFO's critical factors for an excellent investor Web site include the following:

1. Easy access to key data: Most sites route the visitor to the well-labeled investor relations pages immediately and to the latest earnings release in three clicks or less. The worst sites do not even use this common label or make it very hard to find.

2. A clear and unique message: CFO liked Dayton Hudson's clear direct presentation of the "value proposition" for buying the shares. "We remain confident that Dayton Hudson can continue to deliver 15% annual earnings per share growth over time."

3. Multimedia disclosures: Studies indicate 13% of companies are now Web-casting their quarterly conferences to release earnings results. Many are providing archived audiotapes of recent talks and access to the power-point slides that were used.

4. "Push" technology: The best sites give visitors the chance to leave their e-mail address and begin to receive data such as press releases or announcements of speeches or conferences.

5. Standard investor data: The best sites provided answers to a list of frequently asked questions, links to other Web sites, compilation of general investor information, and even analysts' forecasts and recommendations.

Source: CFO Magazine, February 2000.

Recall the first three transactions of the Biwheels Company introduced in chapter 1:

	Cash	Merchandise Inventory	=	Note Payable	Paid-in Capital
	A		**=**	**L** +	**SE**
(1) Initial investment by owner	+400,000		=		+400,000
(2) Loan from bank	+100,000		=	+100,000	
(3) Acquire inventory for cash	−150,000	+150,000	=		

This balance sheet equation format illustrates the basic concepts of the double-entry system by showing two entries for each transaction. It also emphasizes that the equation Assets = Liabilities + Stockholders' Equity must always remain in balance. Unfortunately, this format is too unwieldy for recording each and every transaction that occurs. In practice, accountants record the individual transactions as they occur and then organize the elements of the transaction into accounts that group similar items together. For example, the elements that affect cash are collected in the cash column.

LEDGER ACCOUNTS

A **ledger** contains the records for a group of related accounts. The ledger may be in the form of a bound record book, a loose-leaf set of pages, or some kind of electronic storage

ledger The records for a group of related accounts kept current in a systematic manner.

element such as magnetic tape or disk, but it is always kept current in a systematic manner. For simplicity's sake, you can think of a ledger as a book with one page for each account. When you hear about "keeping the books" or "auditing the books," the word *books* refers to the ledger. A firm's **general ledger** is the collection of accounts that accumulate the amounts reported in the firm's major financial statements.

general ledger The collection of accounts that accumulates the amounts reported in the major financial statements.

The ledger accounts used here are simplified versions of those used in practice. They are called **T-accounts** because they take the form of the capital letter T. They capture the essence of the accounting process we need to understand as accountants and managers without burdening us with too many details that bookkeepers use. The vertical line in the T divides the account into left and right sides for recording increases and decreases in the account. The account title is on the horizontal line. For example, consider the format of the Cash account:

T-account Simplified version of ledger accounts that takes the form of the capital letter T.

Cash	
Left side	Right side
Increases in cash	Decreases in cash

The T-accounts for the first three Biwheels Company transactions are as follows:

Assets		=	Liabilities + Stockholders' Equity	

Cash			Note Payable	
Increases	Decreases		Decreases	Increases
(1) 400,000	(3) 150,000			(2) 100,000
(2) 100,000				

Merchandise Inventory			Paid-in Capital	
Increases	Decreases		Decreases	Increases
(3) 150,000				(1) 400,000

Note that two accounts are affected by each numbered transaction, as is the rule under the double-entry system. In practice, accounts are created as needed. The process of creating a new T-account in preparation for recording a transaction is called opening the account. For transaction 1, we opened Cash and Paid-in Capital. For transaction 2, we opened Note Payable, and for transaction 3, we opened Merchandise Inventory.

Each T-account summarizes the changes in a particular asset, liability, or owners' equity. Because T-accounts show only amounts and not transaction descriptions, each transaction is keyed in some way, such as by the numbering used in this illustration, by the date, or by both. This keying helps the rechecking (auditing) process by aiding the tracing of entries in the ledger account to the original transactions, which are written down in chronological order as they occur.

balance The difference between the total left-side and right-side amounts in an account at any particular time.

A **balance** is the difference between the total left-side and right-side amounts in an account at any particular time. Asset accounts have left-side balances. They are increased by entries on the left side and decreased by entries on the right side. This process is exactly reversed for liabilities and owners' equity accounts that have right-side balances. They are increased by entries on the right side and decreased by entries on the left side.

Take a look at the analysis of the entries for each Biwheels transaction. Notice that each transaction generates a left-side entry in one T-account and a right-side entry of the same amount in another T-account. *Helpful hint:* When analyzing a transaction, initially pinpoint the effects (if any) on cash. Did cash increase or decrease? Then think of the effects on other accounts. Usually, it is much easier to identify the effects of a transaction on cash than it is to identify the effects on other accounts.

1. Transaction: Initial Investment by owners, $400,000 cash.
     Analysis: The asset **Cash** is increased.
                 The stockholders' equity **Paid-in-Capital** is increased.

Cash		Paid-in Capital	
(1) (400,000)			(1) (400,000)

2. Transaction: Loan from bank, $100,000.
     Analysis: The asset **Cash** is increased.
                 The liability **Note Payable** is increased.

Cash		Note Payable	
(1) 400,000			(2) (100,000)
(2) (100,000)			

3. Transaction: Acquired inventory for cash, $150,000.
     Analysis: The asset **Cash** is decreased.
                 The asset **Merchandise Inventory** is increased.

Cash			
(1) 400,000	(3) (150,000)
(2) 100,000	

Merchandise Inventory	
(3) (150,000)	

Accounts keep a record of the changes in specific assets and equities. Financial statements can be prepared at any instant if the account balances are up to date. The information accumulated in the accounts provides the necessary summary balances for the financial statements. For example, Biwheels' balance sheet after its first three transactions would contain the following account balances:

Assets		Liabilities + Owners' Equity	
Cash	$350,000	Liabilities	
Merchandise		Note payable	$100,000
inventory	150,000	Stockholders' equity	
		Paid-in capital	400,000
Total	$500,000	Total	$500,000

Most of the accounts have only one transaction and are easily summed. For cash, the balance of $350,000 is the difference between the total increases on the left side of $500,000 (400,000 + 100,000) and the total decreases of $150,000 on the right side.

DEBITS AND CREDITS

You have just seen that the double-entry system features entries on left sides and right sides of various accounts. Accountants use the term **debit** (abbreviated dr.) to denote an entry on the left side of any account and the term **credit** (abbreviated cr.) to denote an entry on the right side of any account. Many people make the mistake of thinking that credit means increase and debit means decrease. Trust us—when used in accounting, they do not. Left and right would be much easier and more descriptive to use, but debit and credit are the standard terms for the double-entry system. The word **charge** is often used instead of debit, but no single word is used as a synonym for credit. Just remember that debit means left and credit means right, and you will be fine.

debit An entry or balance on the left side of an account.

credit An entry or balance on the right side of an account.

charge A word often used instead of debit.

Debit and credit are used as verbs, adjectives, and nouns. "Debit $1,000 to cash," and "credit $1,000 to accounts receivable" are examples of uses as verbs, meaning that $1,000 should be placed on the left side of the Cash account and on the right side of the Accounts Receivable account. Similarly, in phrases such as "a debit is made to cash" or "cash has a debit balance of $12,000," the word debit is a noun or an adjective that describes the status of a particular account. From this point on you will be seeing an awful lot of debit and credit. Be sure you understand their uses completely before moving on.

THE RECORDING PROCESS

In the preceding section we entered Biwheels' transactions 1, 2, and 3 directly in the ledger. In actual practice the recording process does not start with the ledger. The sequence of steps in recording transactions is as follows:

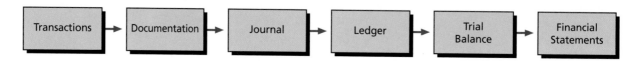

Transactions → Documentation → Journal → Ledger → Trial Balance → Financial Statements

source documents The supporting original records of any transaction.

The recording process begins with **source documents.** These are the original records of any transaction. Examples of source documents include sales slips or invoices, check stubs, purchase orders, receiving reports, cash receipt slips, and minutes of the board of directors. As soon as a transaction occurs, it generates a source document. For example, when a company sells a product to a customer, a receipt is made for the sale. Source documents are kept on file so they can be used to verify the details of a transaction and the accuracy of subsequent records if necessary.

book of original entry A formal chronological record of how the entity's transactions affect the balances in pertinent accounts.

In the second step of the recording process, an analysis of the transaction, based on the source documents, is placed in a **book of original entry,** which is a formal chronological listing of each transaction and how it affects the balances in particular accounts. The most common example of a book of original entry is the general journal. The **general journal** is basically a diary of all the events (transactions) in an entity's life. Each transaction is listed in its entirety in one place in the journal.

general journal The most common example of a book of original entry; a complete chronological record of transactions.

When transactions are entered into the ledger, which is the third step of the recording process, they are not entered in a single place. Instead, as we have seen, each component is entered into the left side or the right side of the appropriate accounts. The timing of the steps differ. Transactions occur constantly and source documents are prepared continuously. Depending on the size and nature of the organization, transaction analysis may occur continuously, weekly, or monthly. Basically, the timing of the steps in the recording process must conform to the needs of the users of the data.

trial balance A list of all accounts in the general ledger with their balances.

The fourth step of the recording process is the preparation of the **trial balance,** which is a simple listing of the accounts in the general ledger together with their balances. This listing aids in verifying clerical accuracy and in preparing financial statements. Thus, it occurs as needed, perhaps each month or each quarter as the firm prepares its financial statements. The final step, the preparation of financial statements, occurs at least once a quarter, every 3 months, for publicly traded companies in the United States. Although they are required to produce financial statements only once a quarter for external reporting, some companies prepare financial statements more frequently for management's benefit. For example, Springfield ReManufacturing Corporation in the Ozark Mountains of southern Missouri prepares monthly financial statements. Springfield is a leader in "open-book management," which refers to the open availability of the company's accounting results. Management and all employees meet monthly to examine the results in detail. Extensive training is provided to employees on how the accounting process works and what the numbers mean. This new management process focused the attention of every employee and increased efficiency and profitability at Springfield.

JOURNALIZING TRANSACTIONS

The process of entering transactions into the journal is called **journalizing.** A **journal entry** is an analysis of all the effects of a single transaction on the various accounts, usually accompanied by an explanation. For each transaction, this analysis identifies the accounts to be debited and credited. The top of Exhibit 3-1 shows how the opening three transactions for Biwheels are journalized.

The conventional form for recording in the general journal includes the following:

1. The date and identification number of the entry make up the first two columns.

2. The accounts affected are shown in the next column, Accounts and Explanation. The title of the account or accounts to be debited is placed flush left. The title of the account or accounts to be credited is indented in a consistent way. The journal entry is followed by the narrative explanation of the transaction, which can be brief or extensive. The length of the explanation depends on the complexity of the transaction and whether management wants the journal itself to contain all relevant information. Most often, explanations are brief because details are available in the file of supporting documents.

3. The Post Ref. (posting reference) column contains the number that is assigned to each account and is used for cross-referencing to the ledger accounts.

4. The debit and credit columns are for recording the amounts that are to be debited (left) or credited (right) for each account. No dollar signs are used.

CHART OF ACCOUNTS

To assure consistent record keeping, organizations specify a **chart of accounts,** which is normally a numbered or coded list of all account titles. This list specifies the accounts (or categories) that the organization uses in recording its activities. These account numbers are used as references in the Post Ref. column of the journal, as Exhibit 3-1 demonstrates. The following is the chart of accounts for Biwheels:

Account Number	Account Title	Account Number	Account Title
100	Cash	202	Note payable
120	Accounts receivable	203	Accounts payable
		300	Paid-in capital
130	Merchandise inventory	400	Retained income
		500	Sales revenues
140	Prepaid rent	600	Cost of goods sold
170	Store equipment	601	Rent expense
170A	Accumulated depreciation, store equipment (explained later)	602	Depreciation expense

Outsiders and new employees would refer to the chart of accounts to learn the accounts being used and their numbers, but the longer term accounting employees become so familiar with the various codes that they think, talk, and write in terms of account numbers instead of account names. Thus, an outside auditor may find Biwheels'

journalizing The process of entering transactions into the journal.

journal entry An analysis of the effects of a transaction on the accounts, usually accompanied by an explanation.

Objective 2
Analyze and journalize transactions.

chart of accounts A numbered or coded list of all account titles.

Exhibit 3-1

Journal Entries—Recorded in General Journal and Posted to General Ledger Accounts

General Journal

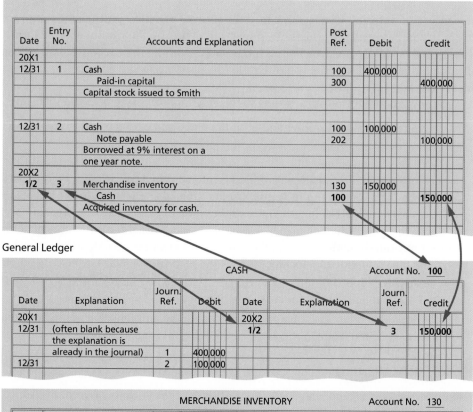

Date	Entry No.	Accounts and Explanation	Post Ref.	Debit	Credit
20X1					
12/31	1	Cash	100	400,000	
		Paid-in capital	300		400,000
		Capital stock issued to Smith			
12/31	2	Cash	100	100,000	
		Note payable	202		100,000
		Borrowed at 9% interest on a			
		one year note.			
20X2					
1/2	3	Merchandise inventory	130	150,000	
		Cash	100		150,000
		Acquired inventory for cash.			

General Ledger

CASH   Account No. **100**

Date	Explanation	Journ. Ref.	Debit	Date	Explanation	Journ. Ref.	Credit
20X1				20X2			
12/31	(often blank because the explanation is already in the journal)	1	400,000	1/2		3	150,000
12/31		2	100,000				

MERCHANDISE INVENTORY   Account No. 130

Date	Explanation	Journ. Ref.	Debit	Date	Explanation	Journ. Ref.	Credit
20X2							
1/2		3	150,000				

NOTE PAYABLE   Account No. 202

Date	Explanation	Journ. Ref.	Debit	Date	Explanation	Journ. Ref.	Credit
				20X1			
				12/31		2	100,000

PAID-IN CAPITAL   Account No. 300

Date	Explanation	Journ. Ref.	Debit	Date	Explanation	Journ. Ref.	Credit
				20X1			
				12/31		1	400,000

entry 3, the acquisition of Merchandise Inventory (Account 130) for Cash (Account 100), journalized as follows:

20X2			dr.	cr.
Jan. 2	130	....	150,000	
	100	....		150,000

This journal entry was made using the employee's shorthand, which uses codes and does not bother with account names. Its brevity and lack of explanation would hamper any outsider's understanding of the transaction, but the entry's meaning would be clear to anyone within the organization.

POSTING TRANSACTIONS TO THE LEDGER

Posting is the transferring of amounts from the journal to the appropriate accounts in the ledger. To demonstrate, consider transaction 3 for Biwheels. Exhibit 3-1 shows with bold arrows how the credit to cash is posted using the information and values from the journal entry. Note that the sample of the general ledger in Exhibit 3-1 uses fairly complete structures for the account instead of the simplified T-accounts format. Dates, explanations, and journal references are provided in detail on paper formatted with special columns. The structure is repeated for debits on the left side of the page and for credits on the right side.

Because posting is strictly a mechanical process of moving numbers from the journal to the ledger, many accountants feel it is most efficiently done by a computer. In such cases, the accountant would journalize a transaction in an electronic general journal, and the computer would automatically transfer the information to an electronic version of the ledger. Note how cross-referencing occurs between the journal and the ledger. The date is recorded in the journal and the ledger, and the journal entry number for each transaction is placed in the reference column of the ledger. The process of using numbering, dating, and/or some other form of identification to relate each posting to the appropriate journal entry is known as **cross-referencing.** Transactions from the journal are often posted to several different accounts, but cross-referencing allows users to find all the components of the transactions in the ledger no matter where they start. It also helps auditors to find and correct errors and reduces the frequency of initial errors.

posting The transferring of amounts from the journal to the appropriate accounts in the ledger.

Objective 3
Post journal entries to the ledgers.

cross-referencing The process of numbering or otherwise specifically identifying each journal entry and each posting.

RUNNING BALANCE COLUMN

Ledger entries do not always take the form of a T-account. Exhibit 3-2 shows another popular ledger account format, one that adds an additional column to the presentation to provide a running balance of the account holdings. This format should look familiar to you because it is very similar to the format found in a checkbook. The running

Exhibit 3-2
Ledger Account with Running Balance Column

	Cash				Account No. 100	
Date	Explanation	Journ. Ref.	Debit	Credit	Balance	
20X1						
12/31	(often blank because the explanation is already	1	400,000		400,000	
12/31	in the journal)	2	100,000		500,000	
20X2						
1/2		3		150,000	350,000	

balance feature is a nice addition because it provides a status report for an account at a glance. Although many accounting systems are now fully computerized, the reports generated by computers often look much like the paper-based ledgers and journals described previously. Over hundreds of years these formats have become traditional and familiar.

ANALYZING, JOURNALIZING, AND POSTING THE BIWHEELS TRANSACTIONS

We have seen that the accountant reviews source documents about a transaction, mentally analyzes the transaction, records that analysis in a journal entry, and then posts the result to the general ledger where all transactions affecting an account are grouped together. We can now apply this process to additional transactions from the Biwheels company. We will systematically omit explanations for the journal entry because they are already presented in the statement of the transaction. The posting of the elements of the transaction to the T-accounts are indicated by encircling the new number.

4. Transaction: Acquired inventory on credit, $10,000.
    Analysis: The asset **Merchandise Inventory** is increased.
                The liability **Accounts Payable** is increased.
Journal Entry: Merchandise inventory 10,000
                Accounts payable   10,000
     Posting:

	Merchandise Inventory*			Accounts Payable	
(3)	150,000			(4)	(10,000)
(4)	(10,000)				

*If it is the only type of inventory account, it is often simply called Inventory.

simple entry An entry for a transaction that affects only two accounts.

Transaction 4, like transactions 1, 2, and 3, is a **simple entry** in that only the two accounts shown are affected by the transaction. Note that the balance sheet equation always remains in balance.

5. Transaction: Acquired store equipment for $4,000 cash plus $11,000 trade credit.
    Analysis: The asset **Cash** is decreased.
                The asset **Store Equipment** is increased.
                The liability **Accounts Payable** is increased.
Journal Entry: Store equipment 15,000
                Cash   4,000
                Accounts payable   11,000
     Posting:

	Cash					Accounts Payable	
(1)	400,000	(3)		150,000		(4)	10,000
(2)	100,000	(5)		(4,000)		(5)	(11,000)

	Store Equipment	
(5)	(15,000)	

compound entry An entry for a transaction that affects more than two accounts.

Transaction 5 is a **compound entry,** which means that more than two accounts are affected by a single transaction. Whether transactions are simple (like transactions 1 through 4) or compound, the total of all left-side entries always equals the total of all right-side entries. The net effect is always to keep the accounting equation in balance:

$$\text{Assets} = \text{Liabilities} + \text{Stockholders' equity}$$
$$15,000 - 4,000 = +11,000$$

6. Transaction: Sold unneeded showcase to neighbor for $1,000 on open account.
    Analysis: The asset **Accounts Receivable** is increased.
           The asset **Store Equipment** is decreased.
Journal Entry: Accounts receivable   1,000
                Store equipment   1,000
    Posting:

Accounts Receivable			Store Equipment		
(6)	(1,000)		(5)	15,000	(6)	(1,000)

In transaction 6, one asset goes up, and another asset goes down. Only one side of the accounting equation is involved because no liability or owners' equity account is affected.

7. Transaction: Returned inventory to supplier for full credit, $800.
    Analysis: The asset **Merchandise Inventory** is decreased.
           The liability **Accounts Payable** is decreased.
Journal Entry: Accounts payable   800
                Merchandise inventory   800
    Posting:

Merchandise Inventory				Accounts Payable			
(3)	150,000	(7)	(800)	(7)	(800)	(4)	10,000
(4)	10,000					(5)	11,000

8. Transaction: Paid cash to creditors, $4,000.
    Analysis: The asset **Cash** is decreased.
           The liability **Accounts Payable** is decreased.
Journal Entry: Accounts payable   4,000
                Cash   4,000
    Posting:

Cash				Accounts Payable			
(1)	400,000	(3)	150,000	(7)	800	(4)	10,000
(2)	100,000	(5)	4,000	(8)	(4,000)	(5)	11,000
		(8)	(4,000)				

9. Transaction: Collected cash from debtors, $700.
    Analysis: The asset **Cash** is increased.
           The asset **Accounts Receivable** is decreased.
Journal Entry: Cash   700
                Accounts receivable   700
    Posting:

Cash				Accounts Receivable			
(1)	400,000	(3)	150,000	(6)	1,000	(9)	(700)
(2)	100,000	(5)	4,000				
(9)	(700)	(8)	4,000				

Transactions 7, 8, and 9 are all simple entries. In transactions 7 and 8, an asset and a liability both go down. In transaction 9, one asset goes up while another asset goes down.

Do you agree with the following statements? Explain.
    1. To charge an account means to credit it.
    2. One person's debit is another person's credit.

ANSWER

Remember that in accounting, debit means left side and credit means right side.
    1. No. Charge and debit and left side are synonyms.
    2. Yes, in certain situations. The clearest example is probably the sale of merchandise on open account. The buyer's account payable would have a credit (right) balance, and the seller's account receivable would have a debit (left) balance.

REVENUE AND EXPENSE TRANSACTIONS

Revenue and expense transactions deserve special attention because their relation to the balance sheet equation is less obvious. To help focus on this relationship, you should review how the owners' equity section of the balance sheet equation can be broken down as follows:

$$\text{Assets} = \text{Liabilities} + \text{Stockholders' equity} \tag{1}$$
$$\text{Assets} = \text{Liabilities} + (\text{Paid-in capital} + \text{Retained income}) \tag{2}$$

Recall from chapter 2 that if we ignore dividends, retained income is merely accumulated revenue less expenses. Therefore the T-accounts can be grouped as follows:

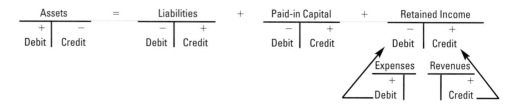

You may wonder why we do not simply increase the Retained Income account directly. To do so would make it harder to prepare an income statement because revenue and expense items would be mixed together in the Retained Income account. By accumulating information separately for categories of revenue and expense, a more meaningful income statement can be easily prepared.

Expense and Revenue accounts are part of Retained Income. You can think of them as separate compartments within the larger Retained Income account. Expense and Revenue accounts are types of accounts, just as an asset account is a type. Cash is a specific asset account and we discuss a variety of specific revenue and expense accounts. A Revenue account collects items that increase retained income. Thus, any credit to Revenue is essentially a credit to Retained Income (both revenue and retained income are increased by such a credit entry). Sales revenue is an example of a revenue account. The Expense account collects items that decrease retained income. Thus, a debit to Expense is essentially a debit to Retained Income. Although a debit entry increases expenses, it results in a decrease in retained income. Wage expense is an example of an expense account. Revenue and expense accounts are really "little" stockholders' equity accounts. That is, they are fundamentally a part of stockholders' equity.

We can now examine a few transactions involving revenues and expenses. Consider Biwheels' transactions 10a and 10b in detail:

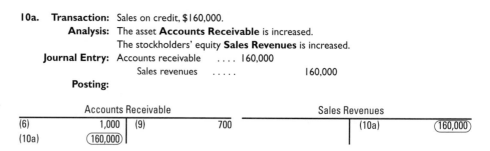

The Sales Revenues account is increased by a credit, or right-side, entry in this transaction, essentially increasing the stockholders' equity account, Retained Income. In this transaction, the expense account, Cost of Goods Sold, is increased by a debit, or left-side, entry. The effect is to decrease the stockholders' equity account, Retained Income.

10b. Transaction: Cost of merchandise inventory sold, $100,000.

Analysis: The asset **Merchandise Inventory** is decreased.

The stockholders' equity is decreased by creating an expense account, **Cost of Goods Sold,** which is essentially a negative stockholders' equity account.

Journal Entry: Cost of goods sold 100,000

Merchandise inventory   100,000

Posting:

Merchandise Inventory					Cost of Goods Sold	
(3)	150,000	(7)	800	(10b)	(100,000)	
(4)	10,000	(10b)	(100,000)			

Before proceeding, reflect on the logic illustrated by transactions 10a and 10b. These transactions illustrate the general relationship of revenue and expense to retained income using actual journal entries and showing the effects on the ledger accounts. Revenues increase stockholders' equity because the revenue accounts and the stockholders' equity accounts are right-side balance accounts. Expenses decrease stockholders' equity because expenses are left-side balance accounts. They are offsets to the normal right-side balances of stockholders' equity. Therefore, increases in expenses are decreases in stockholders' equity. The following analysis shows that the $100,000 Cost of Goods Sold expense could be recorded directly in the Stockholders' Equity account, in the Retained Income account, or in an expense account. This third alternative captures the most information.

If only a lone stockholder's equity account is used:			Stockholders' Equity			
			Decreases	Increases		
			(100,000)			
If two stockholders' equity accounts are used without a revenue or expense account:	Paid-in Capital		Retained Income			
	Decreases	Increases	Decreases	Increases		
			(100,000)			
If revenue and expense accounts are created that will eventually be summarized into a single net effect on retained income:	Expenses			Revenues		
	Increases				Increases	
	(100,000)					

Exhibit 3-3 presents the rules of debit and credit and the normal balances of the accounts discussed in this section. It demonstrates the basic principles of the balance sheet equation and the double-entry accounting system:

$$\text{Left side} = \text{Right side}$$
$$\text{Debit} = \text{Credit}$$

The exhibit also emphasizes that revenues increase stockholders' equity; hence, they are recorded as credits whereas expenses decrease stockholders' equity and are recorded as debits. Keeping revenues and expenses, which are changes in retained income resulting from operations, in separate accounts makes it easier to prepare an income statement. Revenues and expenses are summarized and used to calculate net income (or net loss) on the income statement providing a detailed explanation of how operations caused the retained income shown on the balance sheet to change during the period.

PREPAID EXPENSES AND DEPRECIATION TRANSACTIONS

Recall from chapter 2 that prepaid expenses, such as prepaid rent and depreciation expenses, relate to assets having a useful life that will expire some time in the future.

Exhibit 3-3

Rules of Debit and Credit and Normal Balances of Accounts

RULES OF DEBIT AND CREDIT

Assets	=	Liabilities	+	Owners' Equity

Assets		=	Liabilities		+	Paid-in Capital		+	Retained Income	
+	−		−	+		−	+		−	+
Increase	Decrease		Decrease	Increase		Decrease	Increase		Decrease	Increase
Debit	Credit		Debit	Credit		Debit	Credit		Debit	Credit
Left	Right		Left	Right		Left	Right		Left	Right
Normal Bal.				Normal Bal.			Normal Bal.			Normal Bal.

Normal Balances

			Expenses		Revenues	
Assets	Debit		+*	−	−	+
Liabilities		Credit	Increase	Decrease	Decrease	Increase
Owners' Equity (overall)		Credit	Debit	Credit	Debit	Credit
Paid-in Capital		Credit	Left	Right	Left	Right
Revenues		Credit	Normal Bal.			Normal Bal.
Expenses	Debit					

*Remember that *increases* in expenses *decrease* retained income.

Biwheels' transactions 11, 12, and 13 demonstrate the analysis for journalizing and posting of prepaid rent expenses and depreciation of store equipment.

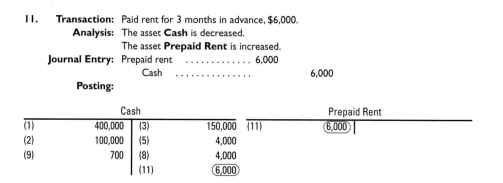

11.   Transaction: Paid rent for 3 months in advance, $6,000.
   Analysis: The asset **Cash** is decreased.
   The asset **Prepaid Rent** is increased.
   Journal Entry: Prepaid rent 6,000
   Cash 6,000
   Posting:

Cash				Prepaid Rent	
(1)	400,000	(3)	150,000	(11)	(6,000)
(2)	100,000	(5)	4,000		
(9)	700	(8)	4,000		
		(11)	(6,000)		

Transaction 11 represents the prepayment of rent as the acquisition of an asset. It affects only asset accounts—Cash is decreased (credited) and Prepaid Rent is increased (debited). Transaction 12 represents the subsequent expiration of one-third of the asset as an expense.

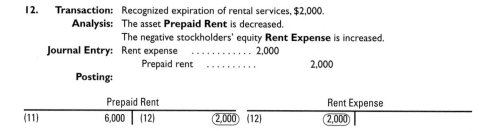

12.   Transaction: Recognized expiration of rental services, $2,000.
   Analysis: The asset **Prepaid Rent** is decreased.
   The negative stockholders' equity **Rent Expense** is increased.
   Journal Entry: Rent expense 2,000
   Prepaid rent 2,000
   Posting:

Prepaid Rent				Rent Expense	
(11)	6,000	(12)	(2,000)	(12)	(2,000)

Remember that in this transaction, the effect of the $2,000 increase in Rent Expense is a decrease in stockholders' equity on the balance sheet.

13. Transaction: Recognized depreciation, $100.

  Analysis: The asset-reduction account **Accumulated Depreciation, Store Equipment** is increased.

  The negative stockholders' equity **Depreciation Expense** is increased.

Journal Entry: Depreciation expense 100

  Accumulated depreciation, store equipment ... 100

Posting:

Accumulated Depreciation, Store Equipment		Depreciation Expense	
(13)	(100)	(13) (100)	

In transaction 13, a new account, Accumulated Depreciation, is opened. Although it is described as an asset-reduction account in our analysis and corresponding journal entry, a more popular term is contra account. A **contra account** is a separate but related account that offsets or is a deduction from a companion account. A contra account has two distinguishing features: (1) it always has a companion account, and (2) it has a balance on the opposite side from the companion account. In our illustration, accumulated depreciation is a **contra asset** account because it is a contra account offsetting an asset. Although the normal balance of the asset account is a debit, the normal balance of accumulated depreciation is a credit. The asset and contra asset accounts on January 31, 20X2, are:

contra account A separate but related account that offsets or is a deduction from a companion account. An example is accumulated depreciation.

contra asset A contra account that offsets an asset.

Asset:	Store equipment	$14,000
Contra asset:	Accumulated depreciation, equipment	100
Net asset:	Book value	$13,900

The **book value,** also called **net book value, carrying amount,** or **carrying value,** is defined as the balance of an account shown on the books, net of any contra accounts. In our example, the book value of Store Equipment is $13,900, the original acquisition cost less the contra account for accumulated depreciation.

book value (net book value, carrying amount, carrying value) The balance of an account shown on the books, net of any contra accounts. For example, the book value of equipment is its acquisition cost minus accumulated depreciation.

A NOTE ON ACCUMULATED DEPRECIATION

The balance sheet distinguishes between the store equipment's original cost and its accumulated depreciation. As the name implies, **accumulated depreciation** (sometimes called **allowance for depreciation**) is the cumulative sum of all depreciation recognized since the date of acquisition of the particular assets described. Published balance sheets routinely report both the original cost and accumulated depreciation.

Why is there an Accumulated Depreciation account? Why do we not reduce Store Equipment directly by $100? Conceptually, a direct reduction is indeed justified. However, accountants have traditionally preserved the original cost in the original asset account throughout the asset's useful life. Accountants can then readily refer to that account to learn the asset's initial cost. Such information may be sought for reports to management, government regulators, and tax authorities. Moreover, the original $14,000 cost is the height of accuracy—it is a reliable, objective number. In contrast, the Accumulated Depreciation is an estimate, the result of a calculation whose accuracy depends heavily on the accountant's less reliable prediction of an asset's useful life. Recall that the $100 of depreciation was calculated by dividing the $14,000 cost by an assumed useful life of 140 months. We have no assurance concerning how long an asset will be useful. Some cars run for several hundred thousand miles over 20 years, while others become impossible to keep running after 10 years of use. In calculating depreciation, we must

accumulated depreciation (allowance for depreciation) The cumulative sum of all depreciation recognized since the date of acquisition of the particular assets described.

make estimates that are imperfect, but there is no other way to allocate the cost of the equipment over the periods that it benefits.

In practice, investors can estimate the average age of the assets by computing the percentage of the original cost that has been depreciated. For example, recently Microsoft had accumulated depreciation of $314 million on an original cost of plant and equipment of $1,037 million, making it 30% depreciated. Most of Microsoft's assets must be quite young, which is what would be expected for a fast-growing company. In contrast, the German diversified industrial company VIAG Aktiengesellschaft has accumulated depreciation of DM 17.1 billion on an original cost of DM 24.5 billion (DM stands for deutsche marks, the German currency). Therefore, its assets are 17.1/24.5 = 70% depreciated.

BIWHEELS' TRANSACTIONS IN THE JOURNAL AND LEDGER

Exhibit 3-4 shows the formal journal entries for Biwheels' transactions 4 through 13 as analyzed in the previous section. The posting reference (Post Ref.) column uses the account numbers from the Biwheels chart of accounts on page 91. These account numbers also appear on each account in the Biwheels general ledger. Exhibit 3-5 shows the Biwheels general ledger in T-account form.

Pause and trace each of the following journal entries to its posting in the ledger in Exhibit 3-5. Recall that the first three journal entries were summarized in Exhibit 3-1, the remainder appear in Exhibit 3-4.

1. Initial investment
2. Loan from bank
3. Acquire merchandise inventory for cash
4. Acquire merchandise inventory for credit
5. Acquire store equipment for cash plus credit
6. Sale of equipment on credit
7. Return of merchandise inventory for credit
8. Payments to creditors
9. Collections from debtors
10a. Sales on credit
10b. Cost of merchandise inventory sold
11. Pay rent in advance
12. Recognize expiration of rental services
13. Recognize depreciation

ANSWER

As you trace these items you should understand why they appear on the left or right side of each account. You might find it useful to say the relationships explicitly as follows. The initial investment was a debit to Cash and a credit to Paid-in-Capital. The posting shows an entry on the left-hand side of the Cash account, which increases the balance in this asset account, and a right-hand side entry to the Paid-in-Capital account, which increases the balance in this owners' equity account.

It is customary not to use dollar signs in either the journal or the ledger. You should also note that negative numbers are never used in the journal or the ledger to show the effect of a given transaction on an account. Instead the effect on the account is conveyed

Exhibit 3-4

General Journal of Biwheels Company

Date	Entry No.	Accounts and Explanation	Post Ref.	Debit	Credit
20X2	4	Merchandise inventory	130	10,000	
		Accounts payable	203		10,000
		Acquired inventory on credit			
	5	Store Equipment	170	15,000	
		Cash	100		4,000
		Accounts payable	203		11,000
		Acquired store equipment for cash plus credit			
		(This is an example of a *compound journal entry*			
		whereby more than two accounts are affected by			
		the same transaction)			
	6	Accounts receivable	120	1,000	
		Store equipment	170		1,000
		Sold store equipment to business neighbor			
	7	Accounts payable	203	800	
		Merchandise inventory	130		800
		Returned some inventory to supplier			
	8	Accounts payable	203	4,000	
		Cash	100		4,000
		Payments to creditors			
	9	Cash	100	700	
		Accounts receivable	120		700
		Collections from debtors			
	10a	Accounts receivable	120	160,000	
		Sales	500		160,000
		Sales to customers on credit			
	10b	Cost of goods sold	600	100,000	
		Merchandise inventory	130		100,000
		To record the cost of inventory sold			
	11	Prepaid rent	140	6,000	
		Cash	100		6,000
		Payment of rent in advance			
	12	Rent expense	601	2,000	
		Prepaid rent	140		2,000
		Recognize expiration of rental service			
	13	Depreciation expense	602	100	
		Accumulated depreciation, store equipment	170A		100
		Recognize depreciation for January			

by the side on which the number appears. Debits and credits tell the whole story in the recording process, so be sure you understand them fully.

In the ledgers that do not keep a running balance column, the account balance may be updated from time to time as desired. There are many acceptable techniques for updating, and accountants' preferences vary. The double horizontal lines in Exhibit 3-5 signify that these accounts have been updated. (Many accountants prefer to use single horizontal lines instead of the double lines used in this book.) All postings above the double lines are summarized as a single balance immediately below the double lines. Accountants would use this single balance as a starting point for computing the next updated balance.

Exhibit 3-5

General Ledger of Biwheels Company

Assets	=	Liabilities and Stockholders' Equity
(Increases on left, decreases on right)		*(Decreases on left, increases on right)*

	Cash	Account No. 100			Note Payable	202			Paid-in Capital	300
(1)	400,000	(3) 150,000				(2) 100,000				(1) 400,000
(2)	100,000	(5) 4,000								
(9)	700	(8) 4,000								
		(11) 6,000								
1/31 Bal.	336,700									

	Accounts Receivable	120			Accounts Payable	203			Retained Income	400
(6)	1,000	(9) 700		(7)	800	(4) 10,000				1/31 Bal. 57,900*
(10a)	160,000			(8)	4,000	(5) 11,000				
1/31 Bal.	160,300					1/31 Bal. 16,200				

Expense and Revenue Accounts

	Merchandise Inventory	130			Cost of Goods Sold	600			Sales Revenues	500
(3)	150,000	(7) 800		(10b)	100,000					(10a) 160,000
(4)	10,000	(10b) 100,000								
1/31 Bal.	59,200									

*The details of the revenue and expense accounts appear in the income statement. Their net effect is then transferred to a single account, Retained Income, in the balance sheet. In this case, $160,000 − $100,000 − $2,000 − $100 = $57,900.

	Prepaid Rent	140			Rent Expense	601
(11)	6,000	(12) 2,000		(12)	2,000	
1/31 Bal.	4,000					

	Store Equipment	170			Depreciation Expense	602
(5)	15,000	(6) 1,000		(13)	100	
1/31 Bal.	14,000					

	Accumulated Depreciation, Store Equipment	170A
		(13) 100

Note: An ending balance is shown on the side of the account with the larger total.

The accounts in Exhibit 3-5 that contain only one lone number do not have a double line. Why? If there is only one number in a given account, this number automatically serves also as the ending balance. For example, the Note Payable entry of $100,000 also serves as the ending balance for the account.

PREPARING THE TRIAL BALANCE

Objective 4
Prepare and use a trial balance.

Once journal entries have been posted to the ledger, the next step in the process of recording transactions is the preparation of a trial balance. A trial balance is a list of all the accounts with their balances. It is prepared as a test or check — a trial as the name says — before proceeding further. Thus, the purpose of the trial balance is twofold: (1) to help check on accuracy of posting by proving whether the total debits equal the total credits, and (2) to establish a convenient summary of balances in all accounts for the preparation of formal financial statements. A trial balance may be taken at any time the accounts are up to date. For example, we might take a trial balance for Biwheels on January 2, 20X2, after the company's first three transactions:

Biwheels Company
Trial Balance January 2, 20X2

Account Number	Account Title	Balance Debit	Balance Credit
100	Cash	$350,000	
130	Merchandise inventory	150,000	
202	Note payable		$100,000
300	Paid-in capital		400,000
	Total	$500,000	$500,000

Obviously, the more accounts there are, the more detailed (and the more essential for checking multiple figures) the trial balance becomes.

Exhibit 3-6 shows the trial balance of the general ledger in Exhibit 3-5. As shown, the trial balance is normally prepared with the balance sheet accounts listed first, in the order of assets, liabilities, and stockholders' equity. These are followed by the income statement accounts, Revenues and Expenses. Note that the last stockholders' equity account listed, Retained Income, has no balance here because it was zero at the start of the period in our example. The revenues and expenses for the current period that are on the list constitute the change in retained income for the current period. When the accountant prepares a formal balance sheet, the revenue and expense accounts are deleted and their net effect is added to the Retained Income account.

Exhibit 3-6

Biwheels Company
Trial Balance January 31, 20X2

	Debits	Credits
Cash	336,700	
Accounts receivable	160,300	
Merchandise inventory	59,200	
Prepaid rent	4,000	
Store equipment	14,000	
Accumulated depreciation, store equipment		$ 100
Note payable		100,000
Accounts payable		16,200
Paid-in capital		400,000
Retained income		0*
Sales revenues		160,000
Cost of goods sold	100,000	
Rent expense	2,000	
Depreciation expense	100	
Total	$676,300	$676,300

*If a Retained Income balance existed at the start of the accounting period, it would appear here. However, in our example, Retained Income was zero at the start of the period.

Exhibit 3-7

Trial Balance, Balance Sheet, and Income Statement

Biwheels Company
Trial Balance
January 31, 20X2

	Debits	Credits
Cash	336,700	
Accounts receivable	160,300	
Merchandise inventory	59,200	
Prepaid rent	4,000	
Store equipment	14,000	
Accumulated depreciation, store equipment		$ 100
Note payable		100,000
Accounts payable		16,200
Paid-in capital		400,000
Retained income		0
Sales revenue		160,000
Cost of goods sold	100,000	
Rent expense	2,000	
Depreciation expense	100	
Total	$676,300	$676,300

Biwheels Company
Balance Sheet January 31, 20X2

Assets			Liabilities and Stockholders' Equity		
			Liabilities		
Cash		$336,700	Note payable		$100,000
Accounts receivable		160,300	Accounts payable		16,200
Merchandise inventory		59,200	Total liabilities		$116,200
Prepaid rent		4,000	**Stockholders' equity**		
Store equipment	14,000		Paid-in capital	$400,000	
Less: accumulated depreciation	100	13,900	Retained income	57,900	
			Total stockholders' equity		457,900
Total assets		$574,100	Total liabilities and stockholders' equity		$574,100

Biwheels Company
Income Statement
For the Month Ended January 31, 20X2

Sales revenues		$160,000
Deduct expenses		
Cost of goods sold	$100,000	
Rent	2,000	
Depreciation	100	
Total expenses		102,100
Net income		$ 57,900

DERIVING FINANCIAL STATEMENTS FROM THE TRIAL BALANCE

As you can see, the trial balance assures the accountant that the debits and credits are equal. It is also the springboard for the preparation of the balance sheet and the income statement, as shown in Exhibit 3-7. The income statement accounts are summarized later as a single number, net income, which then becomes part of Retained Income in the formal balance sheet. Note that the retained income in the balance sheet in Exhibit 3-7 is $57,900 although the retained income in the trial balance is $0. This is because the balance sheet shows the ending balance in retained income, the beginning balance of zero plus net income during the period. In future periods when the trial balance is prepared, the beginning balance will be the ending balance of the previous period. The beginning balance for February will be $57,900.

Although the trial balance helps alert the accountant to possible errors, a trial balance may balance even when there are recording errors. For example, an accountant may misread a $10,000 cash receipt on account as a $1,000 receipt and record the erroneous amount in both the Cash and Accounts Receivable accounts. Then both Cash and Accounts Receivable would be in error by offsetting amounts of $9,000. Another example would be the recording of a $10,000 cash receipt on account as a credit to Sales Revenues instead of a credit reducing Accounts Receivable. Sales Revenues and Accounts Receivable would both be overstated by $10,000. Nevertheless, the trial balance would still show total debits equal to total credits.

CLOSING THE ACCOUNTS

After preparing financial statements, accountants must prepare the ledger accounts to record the next period's transactions. This process is called closing the books, although transferring, summarizing, or clearing might be better labels. All balances in the "temporary" stockholders' equity accounts (revenue and expense accounts) are summarized and transferred to a "permanent" stockholders' equity account, Retained Income. Closing entries perform this transfer.

Objective 5
Close revenue and expense accounts and update retained income.

For Biwheels the closing process is illustrated in Exhibit 3-8. The process closes the revenue accounts in one entry, the expense accounts in another entry and transfers the total net income for the period into retained income in the final step. A new account called the income summary account is used, but it is only used for this instant and merely keeps track of the process. Slight variations on this process occur in different

Exhibit 3-8

Closing the Accounts
Data are from Exhibit 3-7

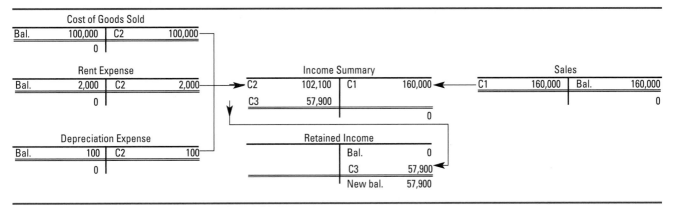

Note: Balances are as shown in Trial Balance in Exhibit 3-7.

companies, but the end result is always the same, revenue and expense account balances are "reset" to zero and the net income generated during the period increases retained income.

DETAILED ANALYSIS OF CLOSING TRANSACTIONS

Exhibit 3-8 shows the posting but does not show formal journal entries recorded in the general journal. The following analysis gives the journal entries for the closing transactions:

C1. Transaction: Clerical procedure of transferring the ending balances of revenue accounts to the Income Summary account.

Analysis: The stockholders' equity account **Sales** is decreased.
The stockholders' equity account **Income Summary** is increased.

Journal Entry: Sales 160,000
Income summary 160,000

C2. Transaction: Clerical procedure of transferring the ending balances of expense accounts to the Income Summary account.

Analysis: The negative stockholders' equity accounts **Cost of Goods Sold, Rent Expense,** etc., are decreased.
The stockholders equity account **Income Summary** is decreased.

Journal Entry: Income summary 102,100
Cost of goods sold 100,000
Rent expense 2,000
Depreciation expense 100

C3. Transaction: Clerical procedure of transferring the ending balance of Income Summary account to the Retained Income account.

Analysis: The stockholders' equity account **Income Summary** is decreased.
The stockholders' equity account **Retained Income** is increased.

Journal Entry: Income summary 57,900
Retained income 57,900

EFFECTS OF ERRORS

Objective 6
Correct erroneous journal entries and describe how errors affect accounts.

When a journal entry contains an error, the entry can be erased or crossed out and corrected—if the error is discovered immediately. However, if the error is detected after posting to ledger accounts, the accountant makes a correcting entry (as distinguished from a correct entry). Basically, the idea behind correcting entries is to counteract the erroneous entries into the incorrect accounts and to assure the correct accounts are credited or debited. The correcting entry is recorded in the general journal and posted to the general ledger exactly as regular entries are. However, the end result is that the balances in the accounts are corrected to what they should have been originally. The focus is on the final balances, not on the flow of entries through the accounts. The balances are used in preparing the financial statements and therefore the balances must be correct.

Consider the following examples:

1. A repair expense was erroneously debited to Equipment on December 27. The error is discovered on December 31:

CORRECT ENTRY	12/27 Repair Expense 500	
	Cash	500
ERRONEOUS ENTRY	12/27 Equipment 500	
	Cash	500
CORRECTING ENTRY	12/31 Repair Expense 500	
	Equipment	500

The correcting entry shows a credit to Equipment to cancel or offset the erroneous debit to Equipment. Moreover, the correcting entry debits Repair Expense as it should have been on 12/27. Notice that the credit to Cash was correct and therefore was not changed.

2. A collection on account was erroneously credited to Sales on November 2. The error is discovered on November 28:

CORRECT ENTRY	11/2	Cash	3,000	
		Accounts Receivable ..		3,000
ERRONEOUS ENTRY	11/2	Cash	3,000	
		Sales		3,000
CORRECTING ENTRY	11/28	Sales	3,000	
		Accounts Receivable ..		3,000

The debit to Sales in the correcting entry offsets the incorrect credit to Sales in the erroneous entry. The credit to Accounts Receivable in the correcting entry places the collected amount where it belongs. The correcting entry moves the 3,000 from the Sales account to the Accounts Receivable account where it belongs. The correct debit to Cash in the erroneous entry is unaffected by the correcting entry.

SOME ERRORS ARE COUNTERBALANCED

Accountants' errors that are undetected can affect a variety of items, including revenues and expenses for a given period. Some errors are counterbalanced by offsetting errors in the ordinary bookkeeping process in the next period. Such errors misstate net income in both periods, but by the end of the second period the errors counterbalance or cancel each other out, and they affect the balance sheet of only the first period, not the second.

Consider a payment of $1,000 in December 20X1 for rent. Suppose this was for January 20X2's rent. Instead of recording it as prepaid rent, the payment was listed as Rent Expense:

INCORRECT ENTRY	12/X1	Rent expense	1,000	
		Cash		1,000
		One month's rent.		
CORRECT ENTRY	12/X1	Prepaid rent	1,000	
		Cash		1,000
		Payment for January's 20X2's rent.		
	1/X2	Rent Expense	1,000	
		Prepaid rent		1,000
		Expiration of January's rent.		

The effects of this recording error would be to (1) overstate rent expense (which understates pretax income) and understate year-end assets by $1,000 (because the prepayment would not be listed as an asset waiting to be expired) for the first year and (2) understate rent expense (which overstates income by $1,000) for the second year. These errors have no effect on the second year's ending assets because the same total assets exist whether the rent is recorded as used in January of that year or recorded as used in full the previous year. The total of the incorrect pretax incomes for the 2 years would be identical with the total of the correct pretax incomes for the 2 years because the first year's understatement of pretax income by $1,000 would counterbalance the second year's overstatement of $1,000. The retained income balance at the end of the second year would thus be correct on a pretax basis.

SOME ERRORS ARE NOT COUNTERBALANCED

Errors that are not counterbalanced in the ordinary bookkeeping process will keep subsequent balance sheets in error until specific correcting entries are made. For example, overlooking a depreciation expense of $2,000 in only 1 year would (1) overstate pretax income, assets, and retained income by $2,000 in that year, and (2) continue to overstate assets and retained income on successive balance sheets for the life of the fixed asset. However, observe that pretax income for each subsequent year would not be affected unless the same error is committed again.

INCOMPLETE RECORDS

Objective 7
Use T-accounts to analyze accounting relationships.

A company's accounting records are not always perfect. Records may be stolen, destroyed, or lost, and accountants are left to make journal and ledger entries and create financial statements with incomplete records. Luckily, T-accounts can help accountants to discover unknown amounts. For example, suppose the proprietor of a local sports shop asks you for help in calculating her sales for 20X5. She provides the following accurate but incomplete information:

List of customers who owe money	
December 31, 20X4	$ 4,000
December 31, 20X5	6,000
Cash receipts from customers during 20X5	
appropriately credited to customer's accounts	280,000

She further tells you that all sales were on credit, not cash. How can you use T-accounts to solve for the missing credit sales figure? There are two basic steps to follow:

Step 1: Enter all known items into the key T-account. Of course, you need to understand this account and all its components to properly work the problem. In this case, we are looking for credit sales, which are debited to Accounts Receivable. By substituting S for the unknown credit sales, we get the following T-account values:

Accounts Receivable			
Bal. 12/31/X4	4,000	Collections	280,000
Sales	S		
Total debits	(4,000+S)	Total credits	280,000
Bal. 12/31/X5	6,000		

Step 2: Solve for the unknown. Finding this solution is usually just a simple arithmetic exercise. However, we can also use the debit and credit relationships we have just learned to solve our problem:

$$\text{Total debits} - \text{Total credits} = \text{Balance}$$
$$(4,000 + S) - 280,000 = 6,000$$
$$S = 6,000 + 280,000 - 4,000$$
$$S = 282,000$$

Obviously, the analyses of missing data become more complicated if there are more entries in a particular account and if there is more than one unknown value. Nevertheless, the key idea is to fill in the account with all known debits, credits, and balances, and then solve for the unknown.

DATA PROCESSING AND COMPUTERS

Data processing is a general term referring to the procedures used to record, analyze, store, and report on chosen activities. An accounting system is a data-processing system. Computers have been refining data-processing systems for the last decade, and the accounting system is no exception (although for simplicity's sake, we focus on manual methods for record keeping). Today almost all organizations use advanced technology, ranging from a simple cash register to bar-code scanners at grocery store checkouts to massive computer systems that automatically record and bill billions of telephone transactions per month.

Today journals and ledgers are more likely to be computerized than they are to be in the traditional paper book format. Regardless of their format, journals and ledgers still maintain the same form and still require the same inputs. So, whether you enter them into a book or into a computer, the transaction data in ledgers and journals remain the same. Of course, if you enter journal amounts into a computerized accounting program, the computer can automatically generate the subsequent ledger postings.

data processing The totality of the procedures used to record, analyze store, and report on chosen activities.

Objective 8
Explain how computers have transformed processing of accounting data.

BUSINESS FIRST
Cisco Insights

Cisco is not only a key supporter of Web users, but also a committed user of the latest technology internally. Chief financial officer (CFO) Larry Carter made a commitment to providing Web-based services and cutting the time to deliver services to employees and customers. Within the company, the basics were implemented quickly. Travel expenses, purchasing, employee benefit information, and an electronic employee directory were "low-hanging fruit" important to the employees, but fairly easy to do. All this is now done online, reducing the handling of paper and the introduction of errors by multiple people inputting information into different systems. More important to the business were initiation of ordering status information, revenue tracking, operating expense tracking, and systems for managing hiring activities. In a nutshell, if the customer needs to know it, Cisco people can provide the information. Equally important, if Cisco managers need to manage it, the data are there to help them.

The bigger task was to fully integrate the accounting system so that everything worked together. The idea was to be sure that information was maintained current at all times and that the system could be "closed" to produce financial statements and important management data whenever required. The system now permits the production of financial statements in 1 day. Not long ago it took 14 days. By redesigning the system and pushing for integration, the time to close has been cut, and so has the cost, by 50%. However, these are not even the biggest advantages. The new system permits managers to constantly view up-to-date data for tracking and decision-making purposes. Orders can be tracked by business unit, by country, or by product line. Carter calls the outcome of this system "ubiquitous" connectivity, essentially worldwide access to timely information for anyone who needs it. He credits the system with helping Cisco deliver strong but steady earnings performance to Wall Street. In this case it is 40 consecutive quarters of increasing revenue and earnings.

Source: *CFO Magazine*, February 2000.

The personal computer has enabled small organizations to process data more efficiently than ever. In fact, managers can get computers to produce daily financial statements. However, the benefits of computers affect not only the outputs of a recording system, but the inputs as well. When you check out at a CVS drugstore or The Limited clothing store, the cash register often does more than just record a sale. It may be linked to a computer that also records a decrease in inventory. It may activate an order to a supplier if the inventory level is low. If a sale is on credit, the computer may check a customer's credit limit, update the accounts receivable, and eventually prepare monthly statements for mailing to the customer. Most importantly, the computer can automatically enter each and every transaction into the journal as each transaction occurs, thereby reducing the amount of source document paperwork and moving from step 2 of the recording process to step 3 in the blink of an eye.

Because computers reduce the need for paperwork and for accountants to analyze every transaction, data processing costs have plummeted recently. Consider the oil companies. ExxonMobil would receive more than 1 million separate sales slips daily if its system were manual. However, today most credit sales are recorded by computers reading the magnetic strips on credit cards. Many gas stations have the card-reading equipment built into the gasoline pumps, eliminating the need for sales clerks. Information about each credit sale is electronically submitted to a central computer, which prepares all billing documents and financial statements. Millions of transactions are recorded automatically into the general journal without any paperwork or keyboard entry, producing huge savings in time and money while increasing accuracy.

Computers have speeded the process of closing the books and preparing financial statements as well. IBM's 1999 annual report contains an audit opinion dated January 19, 2000. IBM announced its results for 2000 in a webcast at 4:30 PM ET on Wednesday, January 17, 2001. It takes less than three weeks for a company with some $25 billion in sales to finalize its results.

SUMMARY PROBLEMS FOR YOUR REVIEW

PROBLEM ONE

Do you agree with the following statements? Explain.

1. My credit is my most valuable asset.
2. When I give credit, I debit my customer's account.

SOLUTION TO PROBLEM ONE

Remember that in accounting, debit means left side and credit means right side.

1. As used in this statement, "my credit" refers to "my ability to borrow," not which side of a balance sheet is affected. "My ability to borrow" may indeed be a valuable right, but the accountant does not recognize that ability (as such) as an asset to be measured and reported in the balance sheet. When borrowing occurs, the borrower's assets are increased (debited, increased on the left side) and the liabilities are increased (credited, increased on the right side).
2. Yes. Accounts Receivable is debited (left). "Give credit" in this context means that the seller is allowing the customer to defer payment. The corresponding account payable on the customer's accounting records will be increased (credited, right).

PROBLEM TWO

The trial balance of Hassan Used Auto Company, on March 31, 20X1, follows:

| | Balance | |
Account Title	*Debit*	*Credit*
Cash	$ 10,000	
Accounts receivable	20,000	
Automobile inventory	100,000	
Accounts payable		$ 3,000
Notes payable		70,000
Hassan, owner's equity		57,000
Total	$130,000	$130,000

The Hassan business is a proprietorship, thus the equity account used here is Hassan, Owner's Equity. In practice, it is often called Hassan, Capital.

Hassan rented operating space and equipment on a month-to-month basis. During April, the business had the following summarized transactions:

a. Invested an additional $20,000 cash in the business.

b. Collected $10,000 on accounts receivable.

c. Paid $2,000 on accounts payable.

d. Sold autos for $120,000 cash.

e. Cost of autos sold was $70,000.

f. Replenished inventory for $60,000 cash.

g. Paid rent expense in cash, $14,000.

h. Paid utilities in cash, $1,000.

i. Paid selling expense in cash, $30,000.

j. Paid interest expense in cash, $1,000.

1. Journalize transactions a to j and post the entries to the ledger. Key entries by **Required** transaction letter.

2. Open the following T-accounts in the general ledger: cash; accounts receivable; automobile inventory; accounts payable; notes payable; Hassan, owners' equity; sales; cost of goods sold; rent expense; utilities expense; selling expense; and interest expense. Enter the March 31 balances in the appropriate accounts.

3. Prepare the trial balance at April 30, 20X1.

4. Prepare an income statement for April. Ignore income taxes.

5. Give the closing entries.

SOLUTION TO PROBLEM TWO

The solutions to requirements 1 through 5 are in Exhibits 3-9 through 3-12. The journal entries are prepared in Exhibit 3-9 and posted to the ledger in Exhibit 3-10. Opening balances are placed in the appropriate accounts in Exhibit 3-10. A trial balance is prepared in Exhibit 3-11 with the income statement. The closing entries appear in Exhibit 3-12.

Exhibit 3-9

Hassan Used Auto Company
General Journal

ENTRY	ACCOUNTS AND EXPLANATION	POST REF.*	DEBIT	CREDIT
a.	Cash	✓	20,000	
	Hassan, owners' equity	✓		20,000
	Investment in business by Hassan			
b.	Cash	✓	10,000	
	Accounts receivable	✓		10,000
	Collected cash on accounts			
c.	Accounts payable	✓	2,000	
	Cash	✓		2,000
	Disbursed cash on accounts owed to others			
d.	Cash	✓	120,000	
	Sales (or Sales Revenue)	✓		120,000
	Sales for cash			
e.	Cost of goods sold	✓	70,000	
	Automobile inventory	✓		70,000
	Cost of inventory that was sold to customers			
f.	Automobile inventory	✓	60,000	
	Cash	✓		60,000
	Replenished inventory			
g.	Rent expense	✓	14,000	
	Cash	✓		14,000
	Paid April rent			
h.	Utilities expense	✓	1,000	
	Cash	✓		1,000
	Paid April utilities			
i.	Selling expense	✓	30,000	
	Cash	✓		30,000
	Paid April selling expenses			
j.	Interest expense	✓	1,000	
	Cash	✓		1,000
	Paid April interest expense			

* Ordinarily, account numbers are used to denote specific posting references. Otherwise check marks are used to indicate that the entry has been posted to the general ledger.

PROBLEM THREE

An annual report of Kobe Steel, Ltd., one of the world's largest producers of iron and steel, showed (Japanese yen in billions):

Property, plant, and equipment, at cost	¥2,062	
Accumulated depreciation	1,051	¥1,011

1. Open T-accounts for (a) Property, Plant, and Equipment, (b) Accumulated Depreciation, and (c) Depreciation Expense. Enter these amounts therein.

2. Assume that during the ensuing year no additional property, plant, and equipment were acquired, but depreciation expense of ¥80 billion was incurred. Prepare the journal entry, and post to the T-accounts.

3. Show how Kobe Steel would present its property, plant, and equipment accounts in its balance sheet after the journal entry in requirement 2.

Exhibit 3-10

Hassan Used Auto Company
General Ledger

Cash

Bal.*	10,000	(c)	2,000
(a)	20,000	(f)	60,000
(b)	10,000	(g)	14,000
(d)	120,000	(h)	1,000
	160,000	(i)	30,000
		(j)	1,000
			108,000†
Bal.	52,000		

Accounts Receivable

Bal.*	20,000	(b)	10,000
Bal.	10,000		

Automobile Inventory

Bal.*	100,000	(e)	70,000
(f)	60,000		
Bal.	90,000		

Accounts Payable

(c)	2,000	Bal.*	3,000
		Bal.	1,000

Notes Payable

	Bal.*	70,000

Cost of Goods Sold

(e)	70,000

Selling Expense

(i)	30,000

Utilities Expense

(h)	1,000

Hassan, Owners' Equity

	Bal.*	57,000
	(a)	20,000
	Bal.	77,000

Sales

	(d)	120,000

Rent Expense

(g)	14,000

Interest Expense

(j)	1,000

*Balances denoted with an asterisk are as of March 31; balances without asterisks are as of April 30. A lone number in any account also serves as an ending balance.

† Subtotals are included in the Cash account. They are not an essential part of T-accounts. However, when an account contains many postings, subtotals ease the checking of arithmetic.

SOLUTION TO PROBLEM THREE

1. Amounts are in billions of Japanese yen.

Property, Plant, and Equipment

2,062	

Accumulated Depreciation, Property Plant, and Equipment

		1,051
	(2)	80
	Bal.	1,131

Depreciation Expense

(2)	80

Exhibit 3-11

Hassan Used Auto Company
Trial Balance April 30, 20X1

	Balance	
Account Title	*Debit*	*Credit*
Cash	$52,000	
Accounts receivable	10,000	
Automobile inventory	90,000	
Accounts payable		$1,000
Notes payable		70,000
Hassan, owners' equity		77,000
Sales		120,000
Cost of goods sold	70,000	
Rent expense	14,000	
Utilities expense	1,000	
Selling expense	30,000	
Interest expense	1,000	
Total	$268,000	$268,000

Hassan Used Auto Company
Income Statement For the Month Ended April 30, 20X1

Sales		$120,000
Deduct expenses		
Cost of goods sold	$70,000	
Rent expense	14,000	
Utilities expense	1,000	
Selling expense	30,000	
Interest expense	1,000	116,000
Net income		$ 4,000

Exhibit 3-12

Hassan Used Auto Company

Closing Entries

C1.	Sales	....	120,000	
	Income summary	....		120,000
C2.	Income summary	....	116,000	
	Cost of goods sold	.....		70,000
	Selling expense	....		30,000
	Utilities expense	....		1,000
	Rent expense	....		14,000
	Interest expense	....		1,000
C3.	Income summary	....	4,000	
	Retained income	....		4,000

2. Depreciation expense   80

     Accumulated depreciation, property, plant, and equipment   80

3. The plant and equipment section would appear as follows:

Property, plant, and equipment, at cost   ¥2,062

Accumulated depreciation   <u>1,131</u>   <u>¥931</u>

Highlights to Remember

1. **Use double-entry accounting.** Double-entry accounting refers to the fact that every transaction can be thought of as affecting two elements in the fundamental accounting equation. We not only keep track of an increase in cash but also keep track of whether that increase arose from making a sale or borrowing money.

2. **Analyze and journalize transactions.** Two very important steps in the accountant's recording process involve the journal and the general ledger. The journal provides a chronological record of transactions, whereas the general ledger provides a dated summary of the effects of the transactions on each account, account by account.

3. **Post journal entries to the ledgers.** Transactions are recorded as journal entries in the general journal and the elements of each transaction are then posted to the proper accounts in the general ledger. The general ledger accounts accumulate all the transactions affecting the account over time, and the balance in a specific general ledger account can be found by adding all the debits and all the credits and subtracting the totals. This textbook uses a simplified version of general ledger accounts called T-accounts. Accountants at all levels use T-accounts to help think through complex transactions. Accountants use the terms debit and credit repeatedly. Remember that debit simply means "left side" and credit means "right side."

4. **Prepare and use a trial balance.** Trial balances are internal reports that list each account in the general ledger together with the balance in that account as of the trial balance date. They are used for detecting errors in the accounts and in preparing financial statements. Trial balances that fail to balance are inevitably the result of careless or rushed journalizing or posting. The good news is that the out-of-balance condition lets you know that an error has been made.

5. **Close revenue and expense accounts and update retained income.** At the end of each accounting period, the temporary revenue and expense accounts are "closed," which involves resetting them to zero by transferring their balances for the period into the Retained Income account.

6. **Correct erroneous journal entries and describe how errors affect accounts.** Despite precautions, errors sometimes occur in accounting entries. Such errors are corrected when discovered by making a correcting entry that reverses the error and adjusts

account balances so that they equal the amounts that would have existed if the correct entry had been made.

7. **Use T-accounts to analyze accounting relationships.** T-accounts help organize thinking and provide a natural structure for discovering unknown amounts. The key idea is to fill in the related accounts with all known debits, credits, and balances, and then solve for the unknown amounts.

8. **Explain how computers have transformed processing of accounting data.** Computers are fast and efficient and enable the performance of repetitive tasks with complete accuracy. In many accounting processes human effort and error creation have been eliminated. Computers perform tasks from initial recording of a sale, to journalizing and posting, to creation of trial balances and financial statements, and finally to sending financial information to interested parties over the Web.

Accounting Vocabulary

accumulated depreciation, p. 99

allowance for depreciation, p. 99

balance, p. 88

book of original entry, p. 90

book value, p. 99

carrying amount, p. 99

carrying value, p. 99

charge, p. 89

chart of accounts, p. 91

compound entry, p. 94

contra account, p. 99

contra asset, p. 99

credit, p. 89

cross-referencing, p. 93

data processing, p. 109

debit, p. 89

double-entry system, p. 86

general journal, p. 90

general ledger, p. 88

journal entry, p. 91

journalizing, p. 91

ledger, p. 87

net book value, p. 99

posting, p. 93

simple entry, p. 94

source documents, p. 90

T-account, p. 88

trial balance, p. 90

Assignment Material

QUESTIONS

3-1 "Double entry means that amounts are shown in the journal and ledger." Do you agree? Explain.

3-2 "Increases in cash and stockholders' equity are shown on the right side of their respective accounts." Do you agree? Explain.

3-3 "Debit and credit are used as verbs, adjectives, or nouns." Give examples of how debit may be used in these three meanings.

3-4 Name three source documents for transactions.

3-5 "The ledger is the major book of original entry because it is more essential than the journal." Do you agree? Explain.

3-6 "Revenue and expense accounts are really little stockholders' equity accounts." Explain.

3-7 "Accumulated depreciation is the total depreciation expense for the year." Do you agree? Explain.

3-8 Give two synonyms for book value.

3-9 "A trial balance assumes that the amounts in the financial statements are correct." Do you agree? Explain.

3-10 "If debits equal credits in a trial balance, you can be assured that no errors were made." Do you agree? Explain.

3-11 "In double-entry accounting, errors are not a problem because they are self-correcting." Do you agree? Explain.

3-12 Are all data processing systems computerized? Explain.

COGNITIVE EXERCISES

3-13 The Chart of Accounts

As a new auditor you are beginning your second audit of a fast-food company. You are surprised that this client has a chart of accounts with twice as many accounts as the first company that you worked on even though the current client's sales are half as large. You are tempted to write a very critical memo to your senior about this issue. You have asked a more experienced friend for advice. What might this friend ask you about these clients?

3-14 Manual versus Computerized Accounting Systems

As a new auditor you have just been assigned to an audit of a highly computerized accounting system. How would you expect an audit of such a system to differ from the audit of a small company whose records were maintained manually?

3-15 Reconstructing Transactions

As a new auditor you have been asked to trace transactions from the general journal to the general ledger. You are part way into the task when you find at the top of one page in the general journal that part of a transaction has been obliterated by a coffee spill. You can see that the debit portion of the transaction was for $1,000 to rent expense, but the credit portion is illegible. How might you go about recreating what happened?

3-16 The Importance of Accounting for Cash

Why is a whole financial statement devoted to explaining what happened to cash during the period?

EXERCISES

3-17 Debits and Credits

For each of the following accounts, indicate whether it normally possesses a debit or a credit balance. Use dr. or cr.:

1. Sales
2. Accounts payable
3. Accounts receivable
4. Supplies expense
5. Supplies inventory
6. Retained income
7. Depreciation expense
8. Dividends payable
9. Paid-in capital
10. Subscription revenue

3-18 Debits and Credits

Indicate for each of the following transactions whether the account named in parentheses is to be debited or credited:

1. Bought merchandise on account (Merchandise Inventory), $4,000.
2. Paid Napoli Associates $3,000 owed them (Accounts Payable).
3. Received cash from customers on accounts due (Accounts Receivable), $2,000.
4. Bought merchandise on open account (Accounts Payable), $5,000.
5. Sold merchandise (Merchandise Inventory), $1,500.
6. Borrowed money from a bank (Notes Payable), $10,000.

3-19 Debits and Credits

For the following transactions, indicate whether the accounts in parentheses are to be debited or credited. Use dr. or cr.:

1. Merchandise was sold on credit (Accounts Receivable).
2. Dividends were declared and paid in cash (Retained Income).
3. A county government received property taxes (Tax Revenue).
4. Wages were paid to employees (Wages Expense).
5. A newsstand sold magazines (Sales Revenue).
6. A 3-year fire insurance policy was acquired (Prepaid Expenses).

3-20 True or False

Use T or F to indicate whether each of the following statements is true or false:

1. Repayments of bank loans should be charged to Notes Payable and credited to Cash.
2. Asset debits should be on the right and liability debits should be on the left.
3. Inventory purchases on account should be credited to Accounts Payable and debited to an expense account.
4. In general, all debit entries are recorded on the left side of accounts and represent decreases in the account balances.
5. Cash collections of accounts receivable should be recorded as debits to Cash and credits to Accounts Receivable.
6. Credit purchases of equipment should be debited to Equipment and charged to Accounts Payable.
7. In general, entries on the right side of asset accounts represent decreases in the account balances.

8. Increases in liability and revenue accounts should be recorded on the left side of the accounts.
9. Decreases in retained income are recorded as debits.
10. Both increases in assets and decreases in liabilities are recorded on the debit sides of accounts.
11. In some cases, increases in account balances are recorded on the right sides of accounts.
12. Cash payments of accounts payable should be recorded by a debit to Cash and a credit to Accounts Payable.

3-21 Matching Transaction Accounts

Listed here are a series of accounts that are numbered for identification. Accompanying this problem are columns in which you are to write the identification numbers of the accounts affected by the transactions described. The same account may be used in several answers. For each transaction, indicate which account or accounts are to be debited and which are to be credited.

1. Cash
2. Accounts receivable
3. Inventory
4. Equipment
5. Accumulated depreciation, equipment
6. Prepaid insurance
7. Accounts payable

8. Notes payable
9. Paid-in capital
10. Retained earnings
11. Sales revenues
12. Costs of goods sold
13. Operating expense

	Debit	Credit
(a) Purchased new equipment for cash plus a short-term note	4	1,8
(b) Bought regular merchandise on credit		
(c) Made sales on credit. Inventory is accounted for as each sale is made		
(d) Paid cash for salaries and wages for work done during the current fiscal period		
(e) Collected cash from customers on account		
(f) Paid some old trade bills with cash		
(g) Purchased 3-year insurance policy on credit		
(h) Sold for cash some old equipment at cost		
(i) Paid off note owed to bank		
(j) Paid cash for inventory that arrived today		
(k) To secure additional funds, 400 new shares of common stock were sold for cash		
(l) Recorded the entry for depreciation on equipment for the current fiscal period		
(m) Paid cash for ad in today's *Chicago Tribune*		
(n) Some insurance premiums have expired		

3-22 Prepaid Expenses

Continental Aktiengesellschaft is a large German supplier of auto parts. Continental has DM35.6 million of prepaid expenses on a recent balance sheet as of January 1. (DM stands for German deutsch marks.) A footnote to the company's financial statements indicates that this is "primarily rental, leasing, and interest prepayments." Assume that all these prepayments were for services that were used during the year. In addition, DM150 million was spent in cash during the year for rent, leasing, and interest, of which DM38 million was a prepayment of expenses for the subsequent year.

Required

1. Prepare a journal entry recognizing the use of the DM35.6 million of prepaid assets during the year.
2. Prepare a compound journal entry for the cash payment of DM150 million for rent, leasing, and interest during the year, with the proper amounts going to expense and prepaid expenses.

3-23 Journalizing and Posting

(Alternate is 3-24.) Prepare journal entries and post to T-accounts the following transactions of Eduardo's Catering Company:

a. Cash sales, $10,000.
b. Collections on accounts, $6,000.
c. Paid cash for wages, $3,000.

d. Acquired inventory on open account, $5,000.

e. Paid cash for janitorial services, $600.

3-24 Journalizing and Posting

(Alternate is 3-23.) Prepare journal entries and post to T-accounts the following transactions of Joie Leonhardt, realtor.

a. Acquired office supplies of $700 on open account. Use a Supplies Inventory account.

b. Sold a house and collected a $9,000 commission on the sale. Use a Commissions Revenue account.

c. Paid cash of $700 to a local newspaper for current advertisements.

d. Paid $600 for a previous credit purchase of office supplies.

e. Recorded office supplies used of $300.

3-25 Reconstruct Journal Entries

(Alternate is 3-26.) Reconstruct the journal entries (omit explanations) that resulted in the postings to the following T-accounts of a consulting firm:

Cash					Equipment		Revenue from Fees		
(a)	60,000	(b)	1,000	(c)	15,000			(d)	80,000
		(c)	5,000						

Accounts Receivable		Note Payable		
(d)	80,000		(c)	10,000

Supplies Inventory			Paid-in Capital		Supplies Expense	
(b)	1,000	(e) 300		(a) 60,000	(e)	300

3-26 Reconstruct Journal Entries

(Alternate is 3-25.) Reconstruct the journal entries (omit explanations) that resulted in the postings to the following T-accounts of a small computer retailer:

Cash				Accounts Payable			Paid-in Capital		
(a)	40,000	(e)	25,000	(e) 25,000	(b)	90,000		(a)	40,000

Accounts Receivable	
(c)	100,000

Inventory				Cost of Goods Sold		Sales		
(b)	90,000	(d)	57,000	(d) 57,000			(c)	100,000

3-27 Effects of Errors

The bookkeeper of Beenair Dunnit Legal Services included the cost of a new computer, purchased on December 30 for $9,000 and to be paid in January, as an operating expense instead of an addition to the proper asset account. What was the effect of this error ("no effect," "overstated," or "understated"? — use symbols n, o, or u, respectively) on:

---

1. Operating expenses for the year ended December 31 . . . . _____

2. Profit from operations for the year . . . . _____

3. Retained earnings as of December 31 after the books are closed . . . . _____

4. Total assets as of December 31 . . . . _____

5. Total liabilities as of December 31 . . . . _____

3-28 Effects of Errors

Analyze the effect of the following errors on the net profit figures of EuroPac Trading Company for 20X7 and 20X8. Choose one of three answers: understated (u), overstated (o), or no effect (n). Problem a has been answered as an illustration.

a. Example: Failure to adjust at end of 20X7 for prepaid rent that had expired during December 20X7. The remaining prepaid rent was charged in 20X8. 20X7: o; 20X8: u. (Explanation: In 20X7, expenses would be understated and profits overstated. This error would carry forward so that expenses in 20X8 would be overstated and profits understated.)

b. Omission of Depreciation on Office Machines in 20X7 only. Correct depreciation was taken in 20X8.

c. During 20X8, $300 of office supplies were purchased and debited to Office Supplies, an asset account. At the end of 20X8, only $100 worth of office supplies were left. No entry had recognized the use of $200 of office supplies during 20X8.

d. Machinery, cost price $500, bought in 20X7, was not entered in the books until paid for in 20X8. Ignore depreciation; answer in terms of the specific error described.

e. Three months' rent, paid in advance in December 20X7, for the first quarter of 20X8 was debited directly to Rent Expense in 20X7. No prepaid rent was on the books at the end of 20X7.

PROBLEMS

3-29 Account Numbers, Journal, Ledger, Trial Balance

Journalize and post the entries required by the following transactions for Lombardi Construction Company. Prepare a trial balance, April 30, 20X6. Ignore interest. Use dates, posting references, and the following account numbers:

Cash	100	Note payable	130
Accounts receivable	101	Paid-in capital	140
Equipment	111	Retained income	150
Accumulated depreciation,		Revenues	200
equipment	111A	Expenses	300, 301, etc.
Accounts payable	120		

- April 1, 20X6. The Lombardi Construction Company was formed with $90,000 cash on the issuance of common stock.
- April 2. Equipment was acquired for $75,000. A cash down payment of $25,000 was made. In addition, a note for $50,000 was signed.
- April 3. Sales on credit to a local hotel, $2,200.
- April 3. Supplies acquired (and used) on open account, $200.
- April 3. Wages paid in cash, $700.
- April 30. Depreciation expense for April, $2,000.

3-30 Account Numbers, T-Accounts, and Transaction Analysis

Consider the following ($ in thousands):

Ontario Computing
Trial Balance December 31, 20X7

Account Number	Account Titles	Balance Debit	Balance Credit
10	Cash	$ 50	
20	Accounts receivable	115	
21	Note receivable	100	
30	Inventory	130	
40	Prepaid insurance	12	
70	Equipment	120	
70A	Accumulated depreciation, equipment		$ 30
80	Accounts payable		135
100	Paid-in capital		60
110	Retained income		182
130	Sales		950
150	Cost of goods sold	550	
160	Wages expense	200	
170	Miscellaneous expense	80	
		$1,357	$1,357

The following information had not been considered before preparing the trial balance:

a. The note receivable was signed by a major customer. It is a 3-month note dated November 1, 20X7. Interest earned during November and December was collected at 4 P.M. on December 31. The interest rate is 12% per year.

b. The Prepaid Insurance account reflects a 1-year fire insurance policy acquired for cash on August 1, 20X7.

c. Depreciation for 20X7 was $16,000.

d. Wages of $12,000 were paid in cash at 5 P.M. on December 31.

Required

1. Enter the December 31 balances in a general ledger. Number the accounts. Allow room for additional T-accounts.

2. Prepare the journal entries prompted by the additional information. Show amounts in thousands.

3. Post the journal entries to the ledger. Key your postings. Create logical new account numbers as necessary.

4. Prepare a new trial balance, December 31, 20X7.

3-31 Trial Balance Errors

Consider the following trial balance ($ in thousands)

Winslow Auto Parts Store
Trial Balance for the Year Ended December 31, 20X7

Cash	$ 16	
Equipment	33	
Accumulated depreciation, equipment	15	
Accounts payable	42	
Accounts receivable	14	
Prepaid insurance	1	
Prepaid rent		$ 4
Inventory	129	
Paid-in capital		12
Retained income		10
Cost of goods sold	500	
Wages expense	100	
Miscellaneous expenses	80	
Advertising expense		30
Sales		788
Note payable	40	
	$970	$844

Required

List and describe all the errors in the preceding trial balance. Be specific. On the basis of the available data, prepare a corrected trial balance.

3-32 Journal, Ledger, and Trial Balance

(Alternates are 3-34 through 3-39.) The Clothes Hanger is a retailer. The entity's balance sheet accounts had the following balances on October 31, 20X5:

Cash	$ 39,000	
Accounts receivable	90,000	
Inventory	70,000	
Prepaid rent	2,000	
Accounts payable		$ 25,000
Paid-in capital		160,000
Retained income		16,000
	$201,000	$201,000

Following is a summary of the transactions that occurred during November:

a. Collections of accounts receivable, $85,000.
b. Payments of accounts payable, $19,000.
c. Acquisitions of inventory on open account, $80,000.
d. Merchandise carried in inventory at a cost of $70,000 was sold on open account for $86,000.
e. Recognition of rent expense for November, $1,000.
f. Wages paid in cash for November, $8,000.
g. Cash dividends declared and disbursed to stockholders on November 29, $10,000.

Required

1. Prepare journal entries ($ in thousands).
2. Enter beginning balances in T-accounts. Post the journal entries to T-accounts. Use the transaction letters to key your postings.
3. Prepare a trial balance, November 30, 20X5.
4. Explain why accounts payable increased by so much during November.

3-33 Financial Statements

Refer to problem 3-32. Prepare a balance sheet as of November 30, 20X5, and an income statement for the month of November. Prepare a statement of retained income. Prepare the income statement first.

3-34 Journal, Ledger, and Trial Balance

(Alternates are 3-32, and 3-35 through 3-39.) The final trial balance of Solvang Appliance Company on December 31, 20X8, follows:

| | Balance | |
Account Title	Debit	Credit
Cash	$ 35,000	
Accounts receivable	30,000	
Merchandise inventory	120,000	
Accounts payable		$ 35,000
Notes payable		80,000
Paid-in capital		39,000
Retained income		31,000
Total	$185,000	$185,000

Operating space and equipment are rented on a month-to-month basis. A summary of January transactions follows:

a. Collected $26,000 on accounts receivable.
b. Sold appliances for $60,000 cash and $50,000 on open account.
c. Cost of appliances sold was $50,000.
d. Paid $19,000 on accounts payable.
e. Replenished inventory for $64,000 on open account.
f. Paid selling expense in cash, $33,000.
g. Paid rent expense in cash, $7,000.
h. Paid interest expense in cash, $1,000.

Required

1. Open the appropriate T-accounts in the general ledger. In addition to the seven accounts listed in the trial balance of December 31, open accounts for Sales, Cost of Goods Sold, Selling Expense, Rent Expense, and Interest Expense. Enter the December 31 balances in the accounts.
2. Journalize transactions a to h. Post the entries to the ledger, keying by transaction letter.
3. Prepare a trial balance, January 31, 20X9.

3-35 Journal, Ledger, and Trial Balance

(Alternates are 3-32, 3-34, 3-36, 3-37, 3-38, and 3-39.) Norma Nielsen owned and managed a franchise of Seattle Expresso, Incorporated. The accompanying trial balance existed on September 1, 20X8, the beginning of a fiscal year.

Norma's Seattle Expresso
Trial Balance September 1, 20X8

Cash	$ 2,600	
Accounts receivable	25,200	
Merchandise inventory	77,800	
Prepaid rent	4,000	
Store equipment	21,000	
Accumulated depreciation, store equipment		$ 5,750
Accounts payable		45,000
Paid-in capital		30,000
Retained income		49,850
	$130,600	$130,600

Summarized transactions for September were:

1. Acquisitions of merchandise inventory on account, $52,000.
2. Sales for cash, $39,250.
3. Payments to creditors, $29,000.
4. Sales on account, $38,000.
5. Advertising in newspapers, paid in cash, $3,000.
6. Cost of goods sold, $40,000.
7. Collections on account, $33,150.
8. Miscellaneous expenses paid in cash, $8,000.
9. Wages paid in cash, $9,000.
10. Entry for rent expense. (Rent was paid quarterly in advance, $6,000 per quarter. Payments were due on February 1, May 1, August 1, and November 1.)
11. Depreciation of store equipment, $250.

Required

1. Enter the September 1 balances in a general ledger.
2. Prepare journal entries for each transaction.
3. Post the journal entries to the ledger. Key your postings.
4. Prepare an income statement for September and a balance sheet as of September 30, 20X8.

3-36 Journalizing, Posting, Trial Balance

(Alternates are 3-32, 3-34, 3-35, 3-37, 3-38, and 3-39.) Canseco Gardens, a retailer of garden supplies and equipment, had the accompanying balance sheet accounts, December 31, 20X7:

Assets			Liabilities and Stockholders' Equity	
Cash		$22,000	Accounts payable*	$111,000
Accounts receivable		37,000	Paid-in capital	40,000
Inventory		131,000	Retained income	79,000
Prepaid rent		4,000		
Store equipment	$60,000			
Less: Accumulated depreciation	24,000	36,000		
Total		$230,000	Total	$230,000

*For merchandise only.

Following is a summary of transactions that occurred during 20X8:

a. Purchases of merchandise inventory on open account, $550,000.

b. Sales, all on credit, $800,000.

c. Cost of merchandise sold to customers, $440,000.

d. On June 1, 20X4, borrowed $80,000 from a supplier. The note is payable at the end of 20X8. Interest is payable yearly on December 31 at a rate of 15% per annum.

e. Disbursed $25,000 for the rent of the store. Add to Prepaid Rent.

f. Disbursed $165,000 for wages through November.

g. Disbursed $76,000 for miscellaneous expenses such as utilities, advertising, and legal help. (Combined here to save space. Debit Miscellaneous expenses.)

h. On July 1, 20X8, lent $20,000 to the office manager. He signed a note that will mature on July 1, 20X9, together with interest at 10% per annum. Interest for 20X8 is due on December 31, 20X8.

i. Collections on accounts receivable, $691,000.

j. Payments on accounts payable $471,000.

The following entries were made on December 31, 20X8:

k. Previous rent payments applicable to 20X9 amounted to $3,000.

l. Depreciation for 20X8 was $6,000.

m. Wages earned by employees during December were paid on December 31, $6,000.

n. Interest on the loan from the supplier was disbursed.

o. Interest on the loan made to the office manager was received.

Required

1. Prepare journal entries in thousands of dollars.

2. Post the entries to the ledger, keying your postings by transaction letter.

3. Prepare a trial balance, December 31, 20X8.

3-37 Transaction Analysis, Trial Balance and Closing entries

(Alternates are 3-32, 3-34, 3-35, 3-36, 3-38, and 3-39.) Hawkeye Appliance Repair Service, Incorporated, had the accompanying trial balance on January 1, 20X8

Hawkeye Appliance Repair Service, Inc.
Trial Balance January 1, 19X8

Cash	$ 5,000	
Accounts receivable	4,000	
Parts inventory	2,000	
Prepaid rent	2,000	
Trucks	36,000	
Equipment	8,000	
Accumulated depreciation, trucks		$15,000
Accumulated depreciation, equipment		5,000
Accounts payable		2,900
Paid-in capital		17,000
Retained income		17,100
Total	$57,000	$57,000

During January, the following summarized transactions occurred:

January 2 Collected accounts receivable, $3,000.

3 Rendered services to customers for cash, $4,200 ($700 collected for parts, $3,500 for labor). Use two accounts, Parts Revenue and Labor Revenue.

3 Cost of parts used for services rendered, $300.

7 Paid legal expenses, $500 cash.

9 Acquired parts on open account, $900.

11 Paid cash for wages, $1,000.

13 Paid cash for truck repairs, $500.
19 Billed customer for services, $3,600 ($800 for parts and $2,800 for labor).
19 Cost of parts used for services rendered, $500.
24 Paid cash for wages, $1,300.
27 Paid cash on accounts payable, $1,500.
31 Rent expense for January, $1,000 (reduce Prepaid Rent).
31 Depreciation for January: trucks, $600; equipment, $200.
31 Paid cash to local gas station for gasoline for trucks for January, $300.
31 Paid cash for wages, $900.

Required

1. Enter the January 1 balances in T-accounts. Leave room for additional accounts.

2. Record the transactions in the journal.

3. Post the journal entries to the T-accounts. Key your entries by date. (Note how keying by date is not as precise as by transaction number or letter. Why? There is usually more than one transaction on any given date.)

4. Prepare a trial balance, January 31, 20X8.

5. Prepare closing entries

3-38 Transaction Analysis, Trial Balance

(Alternates are 3-32, 3-34 through 3-37, and 3-39.) McDonald's Corporation is a well-known fast-foods restaurant company. Examine the accompanying condensed trial balance, which is based on McDonald's annual report and actual terminology.

Consider the following assumed partial summary of transactions for 2000 ($ in millions):

McDonald's Corporation
Trial Balance January 1, 2000 ($ in millions)

Cash	$ 420	
Accounts and notes receivable	708	
Inventories	83	
Prepaid expenses	362	
Property and equipment, at cost	22,451	
Other assets	3,085	
Accumulated depreciation		$ 6,126
Notes and accounts payable		1,659
Other liabilities		9,685
Paid-in capital		1,305
Retained earnings		8,334
Total	$27,109	$27,109

a. Revenues in cash, company-owned restaurants, $2,100.

b. Revenues, on open account from franchised restaurants, $500. Set up a separate revenue account for these sales.

c. Inventories acquired on open account, $827.

d. Cost of the inventories sold, $820.

e. Depreciation, $226 (Debit Depreciation Expenses).

f. Paid rents and insurance premiums in cash in advance, $42 (Debit Prepaid Expenses).

g. Prepaid expenses expired, $37 (Debit Operating Expenses).

h. Paid other liabilities, $148.

i. Cash collections on receivables, $590.

j. Cash disbursements on notes and accounts payable, $747.

k. Paid interest expense in cash, $100.

l. Paid other expenses in cash, mostly payroll and advertising, $1,510 (Debit Operating Expenses).

1. Record the transactions in the journal.
2. Enter beginning balances in T-accounts. Post the journal entries to the T-accounts. Key your entries with the transaction letters used here.
3. Prepare a trial balance, December 31, 2000.

Required

3-39 Transaction Analysis, Trial Balance
(Alternates are 3-32, and 3-34 through 3-38.) Kellogg Company's major product line is ready-to-eat breakfast cereals. Examine the following condensed trial balance, which is based on Kellogg's annual report.

Kellogg Company Trial Balance
January 1, 2000 ($ in millions)

Cash	$ 151	
Accounts receivable	679	
Inventories	504	
Property and equipment, net	2,641	
Other assets	834	
Accounts payable		$ 305
Other liabilities		3,691
Paid-in capital		208
Retained earnings		605
Total	$4,809	$4,809

Consider the following assumed partial summary of transactions for 2000 ($ in millions):

a. Acquired inventories for $1,750 on open account.
b. Sold inventories that cost $1,600 for $2,500 on open account.
c. Collected $2,550 on open account.
d. Disbursed $1,650 on open accounts payable.
e. Paid cash of $300 for advertising expenses (use an Operating Expenses account).
f. Paid rent and insurance premiums in cash in advance, $20 (use a Prepaid Expenses account).
g. Prepaid expenses expired, $18 (use an Operating Expenses account).
h. Other liabilities paid in cash, $110.
i. Interest expense of $13 was paid in cash (use an Interest Expense account).
j. Depreciation of $50 was recognized (use an Operating Expenses account; instead of creating an accumulated depreciation account, reduce the Property and Equipment (net) account directly).
k. Additional shares were sold for $10 in cash (record as increase to paid-in-capital).

Required

1. Record the transactions in the journal.
2. Enter beginning balances in T-accounts. Post the journal entries to the T-accounts. Key your entries with the transaction letters used here.
3. Prepare a trial balance, December 31, 2000.
4. Explain why cash increased more than fourfold during 2000.

3-40 Preparation of Financial Statements from Trial Balance
Pepsico produces snack foods such as Fritos and Lay's potato chips as well as beverages such as Pepsi and Mug Root Beer. The company had the following trial balance for the year ended December 28, 1999 ($ in millions):

Pepsico Trial Balance

	Debits	Credits
Current assets	$ 4,173	
Property and equipment, net	5,266	
Intangible assets, net	4,735	
Other assets	3,377	
Current liabilities		$ 3,788
Long-term debt and other liabilities		6,882
Stockholders' equity*		5,609
Net sales		20,367
Cost of sales	8,198	
Selling, general, and administrative expenses	9,103	
Other expenses	2,217	
Other income		1,201
Cash dividends	778	
Total	$37,847	$37,847

*Includes *beginning* retained earnings.

Required

1. Prepare Pepsico's income statement for the year ended December 28, 1999.
2. Prepare Pepsico's balance sheet as of December 28, 1999.

3-41 Accumulated Depreciation

Michelin, the French tire company, had the following balances on a recent January 1 balance sheet [FF (French franc) in thousands]:

Tangible fixed assets, at cost	FF20,121
Accumulated depreciation	15,812
Net tangible fixed assets	FF4,309

Michelin depreciates most of its tangible fixed assets over 10 years.

Required

1. What is the approximate average age of Michelin's tangible fixed assets?
2. Michelin invested FF620,000 in tangible fixed assets during the prior year. Is this surprising, given your answer in requirement 1? Explain.

3-42 Reconstructing Journal Entries, Posting

Sony Corporation is a leading international supplier of audio and video equipment. The Sony annual report at the end of a recent fiscal year included the following balance sheet items (Japanese yen in millions):

Cash	¥ 428,518
Receivables	1,066,314
Prepaid expenses	240,195
Land	179,011
Accounts payable, trade	653,826

Consider the following assumed transactions that occurred immediately subsequent to the balance sheet date (Japanese yen in millions):

a. Collections from customers	¥820,000
b. Purchase of land for cash	20,000
c. Purchase of insurance policies on account	12,000
d. Disbursements to trade creditors	590,000

1. Enter the five account balances in T-accounts.
2. Journalize each transaction.
3. Post the journal entries to T-accounts. Key each posting by transaction letter.

3-43 Reconstructing Journal Entries, Posting

(Alternate is 3-44.) Gap owns department stores including Old Navy stores. A partial income statement from its annual report for the fiscal year ending in January 2000 showed the following actual numbers, nomenclature, and format ($ in millions):

Net sales	$11,635
Costs and expenses	
Cost of retail sales and occupancy	6,775
Operating	3,043
Interest expense, net	32
Income taxes	658
	10,508
Net earnings	$ 1,127

1. Prepare five summary journal entries for the given data. Label your entries a through e. Omit explanations. For simplicity, assume that all transactions (except for cost of products sold) were for cash. One-fourth of the cost of retail sales and occupancy was paid in cash. The other three-fourths represented a decrease in inventories.
2. Post to a ledger for all affected accounts. Key your postings by transaction letter.

3-44 Reconstructing Journal Entries, Posting

(Alternate is 3-43.) Linens 'n Things is a specialty retailer with more than 170 stores throughout the United States. A partial income statement from its annual report for the fiscal year ending in January 2000 showed the following actual numbers and nomenclature ($ in millions):

Net sales		$1,301
Cost and expenses		
Cost of sales	$772	
Selling, general, and administrative expenses	444	
Total costs and expenses		1,216
Earnings before income taxes		$ 85

1. Prepare three summary journal entries for the given data. Label your entries a through c. Omit explanations. For simplicity, assume that all transactions except for cost of sales were for cash.
2. Post to a ledger for all affected accounts. Key your postings by transaction letter.

3-45 Plant Assets and Accumulated Depreciation

Georgia-Pacific, the pulp, paper, and building products company, had the following in its balance sheet dated January 1, 2000 ($ in millions):

Total property, plant, and equipment, at cost	$15,816
Accumulated depreciation	8,756
Property, plant, and equipment, net	$ 7,060

1. Open T-accounts for (a) Property, Plant, and Equipment; (b) Accumulated Depreciation, Property, Plant, and Equipment; and (c) Depreciation Expense. Enter these amounts into the T-accounts.

2. Assume that in 2000 no assets were purchased or sold. Depreciation expense for 2000 was $750 million. Prepare the journal entry, and post to the T-accounts.

3. Prepare the property, plant, and equipment section of Georgia-Pacific's balance sheet at the end of 2000.

4. Land comprises $476 million of Georgia-Pacific's property, plant, and equipment, and land is not depreciated. Comment on the age of the company's depreciable assets—that is, all property, plant, and equipment except land—at the January 1, 2000 balance sheet date.

3-46 Management Incentives, Financial Statements, and Ethics

Juanita Reynolds was controller of the San Leandro Electronic Components (SLEC) division of a major medical instruments company. On December 30, 2000, Reynolds prepared a preliminary income statement and compared it with the 2000 budget:

San Leandro Electronic Components Division
Income Statement for the Year Ended December 31, 2000 ($ in thousands)

	Budget	Preliminary Actual
Sales revenues	$1,200	$1,600
Cost of goods sold	600	800
Gross margin	600	800
Other operating expenses	450	500
Operating income	$ 150	$ 300

The top managers of each division had a bonus plan that paid each a 10% bonus if operating income exceeded budgeted income by more than 20%. It was obvious to Reynolds that the SLEC division had easily exceeded the $180,000 of operating income needed for a bonus. In fact, she wondered if it would not be desirable to reduce operating income this year—after all, the higher the income this year, the higher top management is likely to set the budget next year. Besides, if some of December's sales could just be held back and recorded in January, the division would have a running start on next year.

Reynolds had always been a team player, and she saw holding back sales as the best strategy for her team of managers. Therefore, she recorded only $1,500,000 of sales in 2000—the other $100,000 was recorded as January 2001 sales. Operating income for 2000 then became $250,000 and there was a head start of $50,000 on 2001's operating income.

Comment on the ethical implications of Reynold's decision.

ANNUAL REPORT CASE

3-47 Cisco Annual Report

Refer to the financial statements of Cisco in appendix A at the end of the book. Note the following summarized items from the income statement for the year ended July 29, 2000 ($ in millions):

Net sales		$18,928
Cost of sales	$6,746	
Operating expenses	8,947	
Net gains realized on minority investments	(531)	
Interest and other income (net)	(577)	14,585
		$ 4,343

1. Prepare four summary journal entries for the given data. Use Cisco's account titles and label your entries a through d. Omit explanations. For simplicity, assume that all transactions (except for cost of sales) were for cash.

2. Why are there brackets on the Net gains and Interest and other income numbers?

3-48 Financial Statement Research
Select the financial statements of any company.

1. Prepare an income statement in the following format:

   Total sales (or revenues)
   Cost of goods sold
   Gross margin
   Other expenses
   Income before income taxes

   Be sure that all revenues are included in the first line and that all expenses (except income taxes) are included in either Cost of goods sold or Other expenses.

2. Prepare three summary journal entries for the income statement data you prepared. Use the given account titles and label your entries a, b, and c. Omit explanations. For simplicity, assume that all "Other expenses" were paid in cash.

3. Post to a ledger for all affected accounts. Key your postings by transaction letter.

COLLABORATIVE LEARNING EXERCISE

3-49 Income Statement and Balance Sheet Accounts
Form teams of two persons each. Each person should make a list of 10 account names, with approximately half being income statement accounts and half being balance sheet accounts. Give the list to the other member of the team, who is to write beside each account name the financial statement (I for income statement or B for balance sheet) on which it belongs. If there are errors or disagreements in classification, discuss the account and come to an agreement about which financial statement it belongs to.

INTERNET EXERCISE

3-50 Internet Case
Go to www.gap.com. Locate Gap Inc. and click on *Company Info*. Enter the site and click on *Performance* and *Annual Reports*. Select the most recent annual report.
   Answer the following questions about Gap, Inc.:

www.prenhall.com/horngren

1. Locate Gap's entry for accumulated depreciation and amortization. Does this represent an expense for Gap? Why does Gap keep track of accumulated depreciation?

2. The amounts reported on the financial statements are interrelated. In addition to the *Consolidated Statement of Earnings,* which other statements contain *Net Earnings?*

3. Locate *Cash and Equivalents at End of Year* on the Consolidated Statements of Cash Flows. Which other statement contains this amount? Do the numbers match?

4. Locate *Shareholders' Equity* on the Consolidated Balance Sheets. There are two amounts: Common Stock at par value and Additional Paid-in Capital. Which other statement contains these two amounts? Do the amounts for the current year-end match?

5. Suppose Gap overstated its merchandise inventory amount this year. What is the effect on cost of goods sold, on net earnings, and on ending shareholders' equity? If no other errors are made, what will be the effect on these reported amounts next year?

Go to the "Deferrals (Unearned Revenues and Prepaid Expenses)" episode on the *Mastering Accounting* CD-ROM for an interactive, video-enhanced exercise explaining the principles of income statements and the timing of recorded transactions to CanGo managers to help them interpret financial reports.

USING FINANCIAL STATEMENTS

Lands' End rugby shirts symbolize comfortable fashion and fit, by mail order, at a profit.

www.prenhall.com/horngren

Learning Objectives

After studying this chapter, you should be able to

1. Make adjustments for the expiration or consumption of assets.

2. Make adjustments for the earning of unearned revenues.

3. Make adjustments for the accrual of unrecorded expenses.

4. Make adjustments for the accrual of unrecorded revenues.

5. Describe the sequence of the final steps in the recording process and relate cash flows to adjusting entries.

6. Prepare a classified balance sheet and use it to assess solvency.

7. Prepare single- and multiple-step income statements and use ratios to assess profitability.

8. Relate generally accepted accounting principles (GAAP) to the accounting practices we have learned.

Chances are you or someone you know is one of the 8 million customers who has purchased something from Lands' End, the Wisconsin-based mail-order company. Selling clothes from socks to winter coats, from business suits and dresses to rain boots, Lands' End has built a great reputation based on quality, affordable prices, and excellent customer service—factors that concern, and have won over, discerning shoppers. Lands' End managers are also concerned about these factors, and they take pride in their high ratings for customer satisfaction. However, customer satisfaction alone does not pay their salaries, so managers also want to know whether the company is making a profit. Do managers have to turn to complicated equations and formulas to figure out the company's profit? No, they can turn to Lands' End's financial statements—just as we can.

Information in Lands' End's financial statements comes straight from the company's financial accounting system. The system provides information about the company's financial success. Most important to managers, it also provides detailed information about the financial results of each product. As Don Hughes, Lands' End Vice President of Finance, says, "We record all the activities [of Lands' End] in the financial statements. We make decisions primarily from the financial information about individual products."

Suppose you want to buy Lands' End stock instead of their clothes. Then you, too, would be interested in the company's financial statements. You would want to know the company's financial position and prospects to judge whether it is wise to invest in Lands' End stock. You need to understand the fundamentals of financial accounting if you want to read and understand Lands' End financial statements and compare them to the statements of other companies.

Entities as large as IBM and as small as Rosa Mexicana use accrual accounting and must make adjusting entries before preparing financial statements. Financial managers in nonprofit as well as for-profit organizations, whether located in France, China, the United States, or elsewhere in the world, must understand the consequences of these adjustments when interpreting financial statements.

ADJUSTMENTS TO THE ACCOUNTS

We have already seen how accountants record the majority of a company's transactions in journals and ledgers when they occur. However, transactions such as depreciation and expiration of prepaid rent are a little trickier to handle. In fact, they might not even seem like transactions at all and are recognized only at the end of an accounting period. The difference between these transactions and normal transactions stems from how obvious or explicit they are.

explicit transactions
Events such as cash receipts and disbursements, credit purchases, and credit sales that trigger nearly all day-to-day routine entries.

Explicit transactions are obvious events, such as cash receipts and disbursements, credit purchases, and credit sales. For every explicit transaction, you can easily show that something has happened and must be recorded in a routine day-to-day entry. Recording explicit transactions is straightforward. Entries for these transactions are supported by source documents, for example, sales slips, purchase invoices, and employee payroll checks, or other tangible evidence. Note that some explicit transactions do not involve actual exchanges of goods and services between the entity and another party. For instance, the losses of assets from fire or theft are also explicit transactions even though no market exchange occurs. In all cases, though, explicit transactions involve events that you know have happened.

implicit transactions
Events (such as the passage of time) that do not generate source documents or visible evidence of the event and are not recognized in the accounting records until the end of an accounting period.

Conversely, the events that trigger implicit transactions are not as obvious. **Implicit transactions** are events (such as the passage of time) that do not generate source documents or any visible evidence that the event actually happened. Because bookkeepers do not receive specific notification to record such events, they are not formally recognized in the accounting records until the end of an accounting period. For example, accountants prepare entries for depreciation expense and expiration of prepaid rent at the end of an accounting period from special schedules or memorandums, not because an explicit event occurred. You cannot point to an actual event that used up part of the rent asset, yet at the end of the month you must make an entry showing the expiration of a month's worth of rent.

adjustments (adjusting entries) End-of-period entries that assign the financial effects of implicit transactions to the appropriate time periods.

The end-of-period entries used to acknowledge these implicit events are known as adjustments. These **adjustments** (also called **adjusting entries**) help assign the financial effects of implicit transactions to the appropriate time periods. Thus, adjustments occur at periodic intervals, usually when the financial statements are about to be prepared. The adjustments consist of journal entries that are recorded in the general journal and then posted to the general ledger. After we recognize these adjustments for implicit transactions, we update the balances in the general ledger accounts through the end of the period and use these balances for preparing financial statements.

accrue To accumulate a receivable or payable during a given period even though no explicit transaction occurs.

Adjusting entries are at the heart of accrual accounting. **Accrue** means to accumulate a receivable (asset) or payable (liability) during a given period even though no explicit transaction occurs. The receivables or payables grow as the clock ticks, but no physical assets change hands. Examples of accruals are the wages earned by employees for partial payroll periods and the interest earned on borrowed money before the interest payment date. Usually we recognize wage expense when wages are paid. However, if wages are paid every Friday and the accounting period ends on Wednesday, a problem arises. Three days of wages have been earned but not recorded. The accrual adjusting entry for wages payable corrects this. Because accruals are not based on explicit transactions, we do not record them on a day-to-day basis. Thus, we need to make adjusting entries at the end of each period to recognize unrecorded but relevant accruals.

You will note that our ensuing discussions involve both the income statement and the balance sheet. Our goal is to assure that all the assets, liabilities, and owners' equity of the company are properly stated. In the process we consider whether the passage of time or other events have lead to the creation of assets, the using up of assets, or the creation or discharge of liabilities.

Adjustments are essential for understanding the logic behind accounts because they help in the matching of revenues and expenses to a particular period in addition to assuring that assets and liabilities are correctly stated. For example, consider an $8 million annual contract for a baseball star, such as Ken Griffey, Jr., Mark Maguire, or Barry Bonds, for the 2002 season. If the player receives all $8 million in cash in 2002, it is an obvious explicit transaction. In contrast, suppose he receives only $3 million in cash and defers $5 million until 2003 or later. The $3 million cash payment is an explicit transaction that is recorded as an expense when the payment is made. Because no explicit transaction for the additional $5 million occurs during the period, it is not routinely entered into the accounting record. However, the player has earned the full $8 million as a result of playing the whole season and the employer has the obligation, so a liability exists. Moreover, the entire $8 million contract was incurred for the benefit of the 2002 season, so the $5 million deferred payment is an expense for 2002 that arises because of an implicit transaction for the period. Thus, at the end of the period, when preparing the 2002 financial statements, an adjustment is necessary to record the deferred $5 million payment as an expense and to record a $5 million liability for its payment.

The principal adjustments arise from four basic types of implicit transactions:

   I. Expiration of unexpired costs

  II. Earning of revenues received in advance

 III. Accrual of unrecorded expenses

 IV. Accrual of unrecorded revenues

Let us now examine each of these categories in detail.

I. EXPIRATION OF UNEXPIRED COSTS

Objective 1
Make adjustments for the expiration or consumption of assets.

As you should recall from previous chapters, some costs expire because of the passage of time. For example, prepaid rent is used up in increments at the end of every month, until it is completely used (expires). As we have already seen, we make adjustments at the end of each month to mark the gradual expiration of these costs. Other examples of adjusting for asset expirations include the write-offs to expense of such assets as Office Supplies Inventory, Prepaid Fire Insurance, and even Depreciation Expense. Originally the company pays cash and creates an asset. The adjustment recognizes an expense (debits an expense account) and reduces the corresponding asset (credits the asset account). The key characteristic of unexpired items is that an explicit transaction in the past has created an asset, and a subsequent implicit transaction serves to adjust the value of this asset.

II. EARNING OF REVENUES RECEIVED IN ADVANCE

Objective 2
Make adjustments for the earning of unearned revenues.

unearned revenue (revenue received in advance, deferred revenue, deferred credit) Revenue received and recorded before it is earned.

Just as some assets are acquired and then expire over time, some revenue is received and then earned over time. **Unearned revenue** (also called **revenue received in advance, deferred revenue,** or **deferred credit**) is revenue that is received and recorded before it is earned. That is, a company may receive payment in exchange for a commitment to provide services (or goods) at a later date. This commitment is a liability and must be recorded when received. At that moment a liability to perform offsets the asset received. Over time, as the obligation is discharged the liability must be reduced accordingly.

The analysis of adjusting entries for unearned revenue is easier to understand if we visualize the financial positions of both parties to a contract. For example, recall the Biwheels Company's January advance payment of $6,000 for 3 months of rent. Compare the financial impact on Biwheels Company with the impact on the owner of the property, who received the rental payment:

	Owner of Property (Landlord, Lessor)				Biwheels Company (Tenant, Lessee)			
	A	=	L	+	SE	A		= L + SE
	Cash		Unearned Rent Revenue		Rent Revenue	Cash	Prepaid Rent	Rent Expense
(a) Explicit transaction (advance payment of 3 months of rent)	+6,000	=	+6,000			−6,000	+6,000	=
(b) January adjustment (for 1 month of rent)		=	−2,000		+2,000		−2,000	= −2,000
(c) February adjustment (for 1 month of rent)		=	−2,000		+2,000		−2,000	= −2,000
(d) March adjustment (for 1 month of rent)		=	−2,000		+2,000		−2,000	= −2,000

The journal entries for (a) and (b) follow:

OWNER (LANDLORD)

(a) Cash	6,000	
Unearned rent revenue		6,000
(b) Unearned rent revenue	2,000	
Rent revenue		2,000

BIWHEELS COMPANY (TENANT)

(a) Prepaid rent	6,000	
Cash		6,000
(b) Rent expense	2,000	
Prepaid rent		2,000

[Entries for (c) and (d) are the same as for (b).]

We are already familiar with the analysis from Biwheels' point of view. The $2,000 monthly entries for Biwheels are examples of the first type of adjustments, the expiration of a prepaid asset. From the viewpoint of the owner of the rental property, though, transaction (a) is an explicit transaction that recognizes the receipt of unearned revenue. The balancing amount for the increase in cash is recorded in a liability account because the lessor is now obligated to deliver the rental services (or to refund the money if the services are not delivered). Sometimes this account is called Rent Collected in Advance instead of Unearned Rent Revenue, as in our example. Regardless of its title, it is an

In a franchise arrangement, a central organization, such as McDonald's or the National Basketball Association, sells the right to use the company name and company products to a franchisee. The franchisee also receives the benefit of advertising through the larger company, along with management assistance and product development. There are more than 500,000 franchise outlets of various types in the United States, with sales totaling more than $1 trillion. This is about half of all retail sales. It is hard to know exactly how many franchises are out there, but in fast food alone, the largest category, there are well over 200 franchised names.

Franchising raises an interesting accounting problem. How does the central organization account for the franchise fees? At first glance, it might seem clear that companies should record such fees as revenue. However, under accrual accounting, companies should record revenue only after two conditions have been satisfied: (1) The company has completed the "work," that is, the revenue has been earned, and (2) there is reasonable assurance the fee can be collected (it is realized in cash or will be collectible).

Jiffy Lube, a subsidiary of Pennzoil–Quaker State Company, is a franchisor of fast oil-change centers with more than 1,600 locations. It provides an example of receipt of franchise fees before the related work is performed. Jiffy Lube sells its franchisees area development rights, which grant the franchisee the exclusive right to develop Jiffy Lube outlets in a certain area. In return for these rights, Jiffy Lube receives an upfront fee. Should Jiffy Lube record the fee as revenue? It should not because Jiffy Lube's work is not done until the franchisee actually opens the outlets. In the interim, Jiffy Lube must report the fees as unearned revenue.

McDonald's was named *Entrepreneur Magazine's* number one franchising organization. McDonald's just opened its 25,000th location with franchisee Ilene Porter, a former school teacher. Ilene joins 5,000 other owner operators. In 1999, McDonald's had $39 billion in system-wide sales of which franchisees and affiliates generated $29.5 billion. However, when we look at the income statement, we only see total revenue of $13.3 billion: $9.5 billion from company-owned restaurants and $3.8 billion from franchisees and affiliates. Why? McDonald's only recognizes as revenues the franchise fees, not the total sales of its franchisees.

unearned revenue type of liability account. That is, it is revenue collected in advance that has not been earned, and it obligates the landlord to provide services in the future.

Notice that transaction (a) does not affect stockholders' equity because it does not recognize any revenue. The revenue is recognized (earned) only when the adjusting entries are made in transactions (b), (c), and (d). That is, as the liability Unearned Rent Revenue is decreased (debited), the stockholders' equity account Rent Revenue is increased (credited). The net effect is an increase in stockholders' equity at the time the revenue is recognized.

By looking at both sides of the Biwheels rent contract, you should see that adjustment categories I and II are really mirror images of each other. If a contract causes one party to have a prepaid expense, it must cause the other party to have an unearned revenue. This basic relationship holds for any prepayment situation, from a 3-year fire insurance policy to a 3-year magazine subscription. The buyer—we use the magazine buyer here—recognizes a prepaid expense (asset) and uses adjustments to spread the initial cost to an expense account over the useful life of the subscription. In turn, the seller, the magazine publisher, must initially record its liability, Unearned Subscription Revenue, on receipt of payment for the 3-year subscription. For example, Time Warner, the publisher of *Time* magazine showed a liability of $762 million as of January 1, 2000, calling it Unearned Portion of Paid Subscriptions. The unearned revenue of this liability is then systematically recognized as earned revenue when magazines are delivered throughout the life of the subscription. The following diagrams show that the initial explicit cash transactions in such situations are recorded as balance sheet items but, thanks to periodic adjustments for the implicit transactions, are later transformed into income statement items:

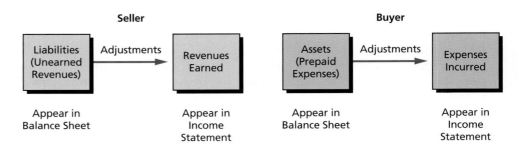

Unearned revenues are essentially advances from customers who have paid for goods or services to be delivered at a future date. For instance, airlines often require advance payments for special-fare tickets. American Airlines showed a recent balance of more than $2.2 billion in an unearned revenue account labeled Air Traffic Liability.

III. ACCRUAL OF UNRECORDED EXPENSES

Objective 3
Make adjustments for the accrual of unrecorded expenses.

Wages are an example of a liability that grows moment to moment as employees perform their duties. The services the employees provide are expenses. It is awkward and unnecessary to make hourly, daily, or even weekly formal recordings in the accounts for many accrued expenses. Remember, these liabilities and related expenses continually grow over the length of a given period, so the cost of such frequent recording would certainly exceed the benefits. This is true, even though computers can perform these tasks somewhat effortlessly. The costs of computing may be small, but the benefits are even smaller. These balances are only important when we prepare financial statements and this rarely needs to be done hourly or daily. Consequently, adjustments are made to bring each accrued expense (and corresponding liability) account up to date at the end of the period, just before the formal financial statements are prepared to match the expense to the period.

ACCOUNTING FOR PAYMENT OF WAGES

Consider wages. Most companies pay their employees at predetermined times. A sample calendar for January follows:

January						
S	M	T	W	T	F	S
	1	2	3	4	5	6
7	8	9	10	11	12	13
14	15	16	17	18	19	20
21	22	23	24	25	26	27
28	29	30	31			

The Calvin Corporation, for example, pays its employees each Friday for services rendered during that week. Thus, wages paid on January 26 are compensation for the week ended January 26 and wage expense accrues for an entire week before it is finally paid. The cumulative total wages paid on the four Fridays during January amount to $20,000, $5,000 per 5-day workweek, or $1,000 per day. Calvin Corporation would make routine entries for wage payments at the end of each week in January. As wages were paid, wage expense would be recorded while cash was decreased. During the January shown in the preceding calendar, wages would be paid on the 5th, 12th, 19th, and 26th. These events were explicit transactions, driven by writing a payroll check. At the end of January, the balance sheet shows the summarized amounts and their effect on the accounting equation:

	Assets		Liabilities		Stockholders' Equity
	A	=	L	+	SE
	Cash				Wages Expense
(a) Routine entries for explicit transactions	−20,000	=			−20,000

ACCOUNTING FOR ACCRUAL OF WAGES

Suppose that Calvin's accountant wishes to prepare financial statements at the end of January. In addition to the $20,000 actually paid to employees during the month, Calvin owes $3,000 for employee services rendered during the last 3 days of the month. The employees will not be paid for these services until Friday, February 2. To ensure an accurate accounting of wage expenses for the month of January an adjustment must be made. Transaction (a) shows the total of the routine entries in the journal for the explicit wage payments made to employees, and transaction (b) shows the entries for the accrued wages to recognize both the expense and the liability.

(a) Wages expense	20,000	
Cash		20,000
(b) Wages expense	3,000	
Accrued wages payable		3,000

The total effect of wages on the balance sheet equation for the month of January, including transactions (a) and (b), are as follows:

	A	=	L	+	SE
			Accrued Wages		Wages
	Cash		Payable		Expense
(a) Routine entries for explicit transactions	−20,000	=			−20,000
(b) Adjustment for implicit transaction, the accrual of unrecorded wages		=	+3,000		− 3,000
Total effects	−20,000	=	+3,000		−23,000

The adjustment in entry (b) is the first adjusting entry we have examined that shows an expense that is offset by an increase in a liability instead of a decrease in an asset. You can see that the accountant's problem is different for this type of accrual than it was for prepaid rent. With prepaid rent, there is a record in the accounts of an asset and the accountant might recognize the necessity for an adjustment by asking, is the balance shown on the books correct or is an adjustment required to reduce it? With accrued wages, the accountant's question is a little harder. Is there something that does not appear in the records at all that should appear there? Of course, most adjustments at the end of the period are routine. We know to check for used up rent and for accrued wages because we experience these items every period.

On February 2, the liability will be paid off, together with the wages expense for February 1 and 2:

```
Wages expense (February 1 and 2)      ...............  2,000
Accrued wages payable       .........................  3,000
    Cash    ....................................            5,000
(To record wages expense for February 1 and 2
and to pay wages for the week ended February 2)
```

These entries clearly demonstrate the matching principle. The routine entries and the adjusting entries match the wage expenses to the periods in which they help generate revenues.

ACCRUAL OF INTEREST

Other examples of accrued expenses include sales commissions, property taxes, income taxes, and interest paid on borrowed money. You can think of interest as "rent" paid for the use of money, just as rent is paid for the use of buildings. The interest accumulates (accrues) as time unfolds, regardless of when the actual cash for interest is paid.

Suppose Calvin Corporation borrowed $100,000 on December 31, 20X1. The loan is for 1 year with interest at 9%. This means that on December 31, 20X2, Calvin must repay the lender the $100,000 that was borrowed plus interest. Interest for 1 year is calculated as follows:

$$\text{Principal} \times \text{Interest rate} \times \text{Fraction of a year} = \text{Interest}$$
$$\$100,000 \times \quad .09 \quad \times \quad 1 \quad = \$9,000$$

Principal is the amount borrowed ($100,000). The interest rate is expressed as an annual percentage (.09). The time is recorded as the fraction of a year (1 for a full year).

As of January 31, Calvin has had the benefit of a $100,000 bank loan for 1 month. Calvin owes the bank for the use of this money, and the amount owed has been accruing for the entire month of January. The amount owed is $1/12 \times .09 \times \$100,000 = \$750$. (*Note:* We multiply the interest rate and the principal by 1/12 because the interest rate is for an entire year, and here we are calculating the interest paid for 1 month, or 1/12 of a year.) The monthly benefit from the loan is $750. Because it has already been acquired and used up for January, an adjusting entry is required for the month of January. The interest is not actually due to be paid until December 31, 20X2, but at the end of January, there is a liability for 1 month of accrued interest payable. The adjustment is analyzed and recorded in a fashion similar to the adjustment for accrued wages:

	A	**=**	**L**	**+**	**SE**
			Accrued Interest Payable		*Interest Expense*
Adjustment to accrue January interest not yet recorded		=	+750		−750

The adjusting journal entry is:

```
Interest expense    .............................  750
    Accrued interest payable    ....................        750
```

At the end of January, Calvin Corporation owes the bank $100,750, not $100,000. The adjusting entry matches the $750 interest expense with the period in which it occurred. If the adjusting entry is omitted, liabilities will be understated at the end of January.

ACCRUAL OF INCOME TAXES

As a company generates income, it accrues income tax expense. Income taxes exist worldwide, although rates and details differ from country to country and from state to state. Corporations in the United States are subject to federal and state corporate income taxes. For many corporations, the federal-plus-state income tax rates hover around 40%. Thus, for every dollar of income a company makes, it accrues 40 cents worth of income tax expense. Of course, this 40 cents is not paid out as each dollar comes in. Instead, it accrues over the period, and an adjustment is made at the end of the period when the financial statements are prepared.

Companies use various labels to denote income taxes on their income statements: income tax expense, provision for income taxes, and just plain income taxes are found most frequently. For multinational firms, income tax expense may include tax obligations in every country in which they operate. In preparing their income statements, about 85% of publicly held U.S. companies calculate a subtotal called income before taxes and then show income taxes as a separate income statement item just before net income. This arrangement is logical because income tax expense is based on income before taxes. **Pretax income** is a synonym for income before taxes. In contrast, the other 15% list income taxes along with other operating expenses such as wages. The 2000 Qualcomm annual report contains the format adopted by the vast majority of companies:

pretax income Income before income taxes.

Income before income taxes	$1,196,805,000
Income tax expense	526,594,000
Net income	$ 670,211,000

IV. ACCRUAL OF UNRECORDED REVENUES

Just as the realization of unearned revenues was the mirror image of the expiration of unexpired costs, the accrual of unrecorded revenues is the mirror image of the accrual of unrecorded expenses. The adjusting entries show the recognition of revenues that have been earned but not yet received. Because no payment has occurred, nothing has been entered in the accounts. According to the revenue recognition principle, revenues affect stockholders' equity in the period they are earned, not the period in which cash is received. Thus, an adjustment is required.

Objective 4
Make adjustments for the accrual of unrecorded revenues.

Suppose First National Bank had loaned the $100,000 to Calvin. As of January 31, First National Bank has earned $750 on the loan. The following tabulation shows the mirror-image effect:

	First National Bank, as a Lender				Calvin, as a Borrower			
	A	= L +	SE		A =	L	+	SE
	Accrued Interest Receivable		*Interest Revenue*			*Accrued Interest Payable*		*Interest Expense*
January interest	+750	=	+750		=	+750		−750

An example of accrued revenues and receivables is "unbilled" fees. For example, attorneys, public accountants, physicians, and advertising agencies may earn hourly fees during a particular month but not send out bills to their clients until the completion of an entire contract or engagement. Under the accrual basis of accounting, such revenues should be recorded in the month in which they were earned, not at a later time. Suppose an attorney renders $10,000 of services during January, but will not bill for these services until March 31. Before the attorney's financial statements can be prepared for January, an adjustment for unrecorded revenue for the month must be made:

	A	=	L	+	SE
	Accrued (Unbilled) Fees Receivable				Fee Revenue
Adjustment for fees earned	+10,000	=			+10,000

Utility companies often recognize unbilled revenues for services provided but not yet billed. In fact, American Water Works Company, a utility that provides water supply services to more than 10 million customers in 23 states, includes nearly as many unbilled revenues as accounts receivable among its current assets:

Customer accounts receivable	$103,975,000
Unbilled revenues	83,878,000

THE ADJUSTING PROCESS IN PERSPECTIVE

Chapter 3 presented the various steps in the recording process as follows:

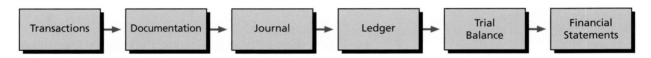

This process has a final aim: the preparation of accurate financial statements prepared on the accrual basis. To accomplish this goal, the process must include adjusting entries to record implicit transactions. When we consider the adjustments, the final steps in the recording process can be divided further as follows:

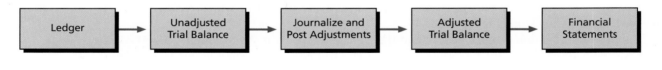

Objective 5
Describe the sequence of the final steps in the recording process and relate cash flows to adjusting entries.

Each adjusting entry affects at least one income statement account—a revenue or an expense—and one balance sheet account—an asset or a liability. No adjusting entry debits or credits cash. Why?

ANSWER

If transactions affect cash, they are explicit transactions that are routinely recorded as they happen. The end-of-period adjustment process is reserved for the implicit transactions that must be recognized by the accrual basis of accounting.

Cash flows—that is, explicit transactions of cash receipts or disbursements—may precede or follow the adjusting entry that recognizes the related revenue or expense. The diagrams on page 141 underscore the basic differences between the cash flows and the accrual accounting entries.

Entries for adjustments I and II, expiration of unexpired costs and realization of unearned revenues, are usually made subsequent to the cash flows. For example, the cash received or disbursed for rent had an initial impact on the balance sheet. The adjustment process was used to show the later impact on the income statement.

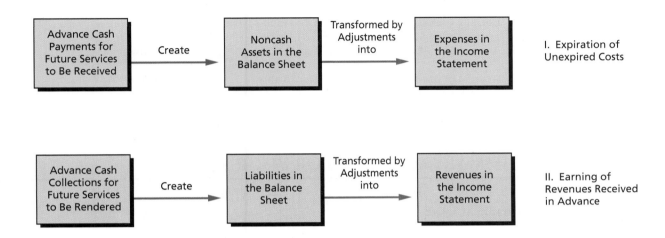

Entries for adjustments III and IV, accrual of unrecorded expenses and accrual of unrecorded revenues, are made before the related cash flows. The income statement is affected before the cash receipts and disbursements occur. The accounting entity must compute the amount of goods or services provided or received prior to any cash receipt or payment. Exhibit 4-1 summarizes the major adjusting entries.

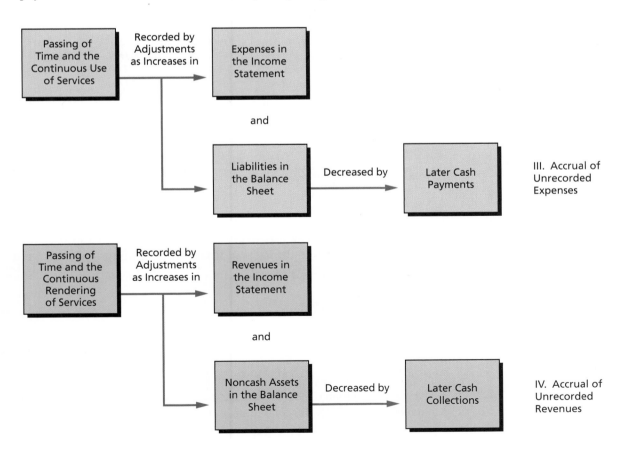

Exhibit 4-1

Summary of Adjusting Entries

Adjusting Entry	Type of Account Debited	Type of Account Credited
I. Expiration of unexpired costs	Expense	Prepaid expense, accumulated depreciation
II. Earning of revenues received in advance	Unearned revenue	Revenue
III. Accrual of unrecorded expenses	Expense	Payable
IV. Accrual of unrecorded revenues	Receivable	Revenue

SUMMARY PROBLEM FOR YOUR REVIEW

PROBLEM ONE

Chan Audio Company is a retailer of stereo equipment. Chan Audio has been in business 1 month. The company's unadjusted trial balance, January 31, 20X2, has the following accounts:

Cash	$ 71,700	
Accounts receivable	160,300	
Note receivable	40,000	
Merchandise inventory	250,200	
Prepaid rent	15,000	
Store equipment	114,900	
Note payable		$100,000
Accounts payable		117,100
Unearned rent revenue		3,000
Paid-in capital		400,000
Sales		160,000
Cost of goods sold	100,000	
Wages expense	28,000	
Total	$780,100	$780,100

Consider the following adjustments on January 31:

a. January depreciation, $1,000.

b. On January 2, rent of $15,000 was paid in advance for the first quarter of 20X2, as shown by the debit balance in the Prepaid Rent account. Adjust for January rent.

c. Wages earned by employees during January but not paid as of January 31 were $3,750.

d. Chan borrowed $100,000 from the bank on January 1. This explicit transaction was recorded when the business began, as shown by the credit balance in the Note Payable account. The principal and 9% interest are to be paid 1 year later (January 1, 20X3). However, an adjustment is necessary now for the interest expense of $1/12 \times .09 \times \$100,000 = \$750$ for January.

e. On January 1, a cash loan of $40,000 was made to a local supplier, as shown by the debit balance in the Note Receivable account. The promissory note stated that the loan is to be repaid 1 year later (January 1, 20X3), together with interest at

12% per annum. On January 31, an adjustment is needed to recognize the interest earned on the note receivable.

f. On January 15, a nearby corporation paid $3,000 cash to Chan Audio Company as an advance rental for Chan's storage space and equipment to be used temporarily from January 15 to April 15 (3 months). This $3,000 is the credit balance in the Unearned Revenue account. On January 31, an adjustment is needed to recognize the rent revenue earned for half a month.

g. Income tax expense must be accrued on January income at a rate of 50% of income before taxes.

1. Enter the trial-balance amounts in the general ledger. Set up the new asset account, Accrued Interest Receivable, and the new asset-reduction account, the contra account, Accumulated Depreciation, Store Equipment. Set up the following new liability accounts: Accrued Wages Payable, Accrued Interest Payable, and Accrued Income Taxes Payable. Set up the following new expense and revenue accounts: Depreciation Expense, Rent Expense, Interest Expense, Interest Revenue, Rent Revenue, and Income Tax Expense. **Required**

2. Journalize adjustments a to g and post the entries to the ledger. Key entries by transaction letter.

3. Prepare an adjusted trial balance as of January 31, 20X2.

SOLUTION TO PROBLEM ONE

The solutions to requirements 1 through 3 are in Exhibits 4-2, 4-3, and 4-4. Accountants often refer to the final trial balance, Exhibit 4-4, as the adjusted trial balance. Why? All the necessary adjustments have been made; thus, the trial balance provides the data necessary for creating the formal financial statements.

Exhibit 4-2

Chan Audio Company
Journal Entries

(a)	Depreciation expense	1,000	
	Accumulated depreciation, store equipment		1,000
	Depreciation for January		
(b)	Rent expense	5,000	
	Prepaid rent		5,000
	Rent expense for January		
(c)	Wages expense	3,750	
	Accrued wages payable		3,750
	Wages earned but not paid		
(d)	Interest expense	750	
	Accrued interest payable		750
	Interest for January		
(e)	Accrued interest receivable	400	
	Interest revenue		400
	Interest earned for January:		
	$\frac{1}{12} \times \$40,000 \times .12 = \$400$		
(f)	Unearned rent revenue	500	
	Rent revenue		500
	Rent earned for January, rent per month,		
	$\$3,000 \div 3 = \$1,000$; for half a month, $500		
(g)	Income tax expense	11,200	
	Accrued income taxes payable		11,200
	Income tax on January income:		
	$.50 \times [160,000 + 400 + 500 - 100,000 - 31,750 - 1,000 - 5,000 - 750]$		

Exhibit 4-3

Chan Audio Company
General Ledger

Assets	=	Liabilities + Stockholders' Equity		
(Increases Left, Decreases Right)		(Decreases Left, Increases Right)		

Cash

Bal.	71,700	

Note Payable

		Bal.	100,000

Paid-in Capital

		Bal.	400,000

Accounts Receivable

Bal.	160,300	

Accounts Payable

		Bal.	117,100

Sales

		Bal.	160,000

Note Receivable

Bal.	40,000	

Unearned Rent Revenue

(f)	500	Bal.	3,000
		Bal.	2,500

Cost of Goods Sold

Bal.	100,000	

Merchandise Inventory

Bal.	250,200	

Accrued Wages Payable

		(c)	3,750

Wages Expense

Bal.	28,000	
(c)	3,750	
Bal.	31,750	

Prepaid Rent

Bal.	15,000	(b)	5,000
Bal.	10,000		

Accrued Interest Payable

		(d)	750

Depreciation Expense

(a)	1,000	

Store Equipment

Bal.	114,900	

Accrued Income Tax Payable

		(g)	11,200

Rent Expense

(b)	5,000	

Accumulated Depreciation, Store Equipment

		(a)	1,000

Interest Expense

(d)	750	

Accrued Interest Receivable

(e)	400	

Interest Revenue

		(e)	400

Rent Revenue

		(f)	500

Income Tax Expense

(g)	11,200	

CLASSIFIED BALANCE SHEET

Objective 6
Prepare a classified balance sheet and use it to assess solvency.

classified balance sheet A balance sheet that groups the accounts into subcategories to help readers quickly gain a perspective on the company's financial position.

As we have seen throughout this book thus far, accounts are listed on the balance sheet according to the major categories of assets, liabilities, and owners' equity. A **classified balance sheet** further groups the accounts into subcategories to help readers quickly gain a perspective on the company's financial position. The classifications help to draw attention to certain amounts or groups of accounts. Assets are frequently classified into two groupings: current assets and long-term assets. Liabilities are similarly classified into current liabilities and long-term liabilities. This distinction is useful in assessing the company's ability to meet obligations as they fall due. For the most part, current assets give rise to the cash needed to pay current liabilities, so the relationship between these categories is important. In this section we concentrate on these current elements and on a ratio that is useful in analyzing them.

CURRENT ASSETS AND LIABILITIES

Current assets are cash and those other assets that are expected to be converted to cash, sold, or consumed during the next 12 months (or within the normal operating cycle if

Exhibit 4-4

Chan Audio Company

Adjusted Trial Balance January 31, 20X2

Account Title	Balance		
	Debit	*Credit*	
Cash	$ 71,700		
Accounts receivable	160,300		
Note receivable	40,000		
Merchandise inventory	250,200		
Prepaid rent	10,000		
Store equipment	114,900		
Accumulated depreciation, store equipment		$ 1,000	Balance
Accrued interest receivable	400		Sheet
Note payable		100,000	Exhibit 4-5
Accounts payable		117,100	
Unearned rent revenue		2,500	
Acrued waves payable		3,750	
Accrued interest payable		750	
Accrued income taxes payable		11,200	
Paid-in capital		400,000	
Sales		160,000	
Cost of goods sold	100,000		
Wages expense	31,750		
Depreciation expense	1,000		
Rent expense	5,000		Income
Interest expense	750		Statement,
Interest revenue		400	Exhibit 4-8
Rent revenue		500	
Income tax expense	11,200		
Total	$797,200	$797,200	

longer than a year). Similarly, **current liabilities** are those liabilities that fall due within the coming year (or within the normal operating cycle if longer than a year).

Exhibit 4-5 shows the classified balance sheet for Chan Audio Company, which is prepared from the adjusted trial balance for the company (shown in Exhibit 4-4). On the classified balance sheet, the current asset accounts are generally listed in the order in which they will be converted to cash during the coming year. Cash is thus listed first because it is, obviously, already in the form of cash. Accounts Receivable are listed next because cash payments for these accounts should be received within weeks or months. Note Receivable and Accrued Interest Receivable, which are listed as the third and fourth accounts, will be converted to cash by the end of the year. Nonmonetary assets, such as inventories and prepaid expenses (in this case, Merchandise Inventory and Prepaid Rent) are usually listed last in the current assets section of the balance sheet. Prepaid Rent will not be converted to cash, but it is a current asset in the sense that it is consumed and its existence reduces the obligation to pay cash within the next year.

As shown in Exhibit 4-5, current liability accounts are also listed in the approximate order in which they will draw on, or decrease, cash during the coming year. Wages tend to be paid weekly or monthly, while interest tend to be paid monthly, quarterly, or annually and taxes are also paid monthly, quarterly, or annually.

The excess of current assets over current liabilities is known as **working capital.** In the case of the Chan Audio Company, the working capital on January 31, 20X2, is $297,300 ($532,600 − $235,300). The name conveys the idea that this mix of current assets and

current assets Cash plus assets that are expected to be converted to cash or sold or consumed during the next 12 months or within the normal operating cycle if longer than a year.

current liabilities Liabilities that fall due within the coming year or within the normal operating cycle if longer than a year.

working capital The excess of current assets over current liabilities.

Exhibit 4-5

Chan Audio Company

Balance Sheet, January 31, 20X2

Assets			Liabilities and Owners' Equity		
Current assets			Current liabilities		
Cash		$ 71,700	Note payable		$100,000
Accounts receivable		160,300	Accounts payable		117,100
Note receivable		40,000	Unearned rent revenue		2,500
Accrued interest receivable		400	Accrued wages payable		3,750
Merchandise inventory		250,200	Accrued interest payable		750
Prepaid rent		10,000	Accrued inome taxes payable		11,200
Total current assets		$532,600	Total current liabilities		$235,300
Long-term asset			Stockholders' equity		
Store equipment	$114,900		Paid-in capital	$400,000	
Accumulated			Retained income	11,200	411,200
depreciation	1,000	113,900			
Total		$646,500	Total		$646,500

liabilities is working hard for the company and its components are constantly changing. The number is important because it connects assets and liabilities. Working capital normally grows larger as the company grows, so it is proportional to the size of the firm and is normally evaluated with the current ratio.

CURRENT RATIO

Current assets tell you how much cash a company will have on hand in the near future; current liabilities tell you how much debt the company will have to pay off with that cash in the near future. Comparing the two amounts can help readers of financial statements assess a business entity's **solvency,** which is its ability to meet its immediate financial obligations with cash and near-cash assets as those obligations become due. The **current ratio** (also called the **working capital ratio**), which is calculated by dividing current assets by current liabilities, is widely used to evaluate solvency. Chan Audio's current ratio, for example, is:

solvency An entity's ability to meet its immediate financial obligations as they become due.

current ratio (working capital ratio) Current assets divided by current liabilities.

$$\text{Current ratio} = \frac{\text{Current assets}}{\text{Current liabilities}} = \frac{\$532,600}{\$235,300} = 2.3$$

Other things being equal, the higher the current ratio, the more assurance creditors have about being paid in full and on time. Conversely, from a manager's perspective, a current ratio that is too high may indicate excessive holdings of cash, accounts receivable, or inventories. Excessive holdings of this nature are bad for a company because it ties up money that could be more effectively used elsewhere. Analysts will compare a company's current ratio with those of past years and with those of similar companies to make judgments about the company's solvency.

An old rule of thumb was that the current ratio should be greater than 2.0. However, today current ratios are more commonly close to one. One useful assessment can be made by comparing a company's current ratio with the average in its industry. For example, recently IBM's ratio was 1.1, compared with an industry average of 1.7. Although below the average, IBM's ratio is certainly not a cause for concern. Microsoft's current ratio of 2.3 was more than twice as large as IBM's. Microsoft is a rapidly growing firm that maintains very large cash balances, $21 billion as of March 2000. Microsoft tends to use this cash to grow the business by investing in new technology and buying other companies, but the balance keeps growing. Utilities often have low current ratios because of low inventories and stable cash flows. For example,

Verizon, the company formed by the recent merger of Bell Atlantic with GTE, has a current ratio of only .7.

Although the current ratio is widely used as a measure of short-term debt-paying ability, a budget (prediction) of cash receipts and disbursements is more useful. Whether a company's level of cash is too low or too high really depends on the predictions of operating requirements over the coming months. For example, a company such as a small comic book and baseball card retailer might need very little cash on hand because upcoming debts and operating needs will be small in the next few months. Conversely, Marvel Comics, the corporation that produces the comic books sold by the small retailer, might need hundreds of thousands of dollars worth of cash to meet upcoming debt and short-term operating needs. As a rule, companies should try to keep as little cash as possible on hand because intelligent management calls for trying to invest any temporary excess cash to generate additional income.

BUSINESS FIRST
Managing Working Capital

The traditional view is that large amounts of working capital and high current ratios are good—they show that a company is likely to remain solvent. However, maintaining solvency is not as big a problem for most companies as is generating profits. Large amounts of working capital may needlessly tie up funds that could profitably be used elsewhere in the company.

The main components of working capital for the typical company are accounts receivable plus inventories less accounts payable. In the 1990s, holding large amounts of inventories and accounts receivable fell out of fashion. Each dollar not invested in working capital is a dollar of free cash available for investing in value-adding activities—activities that actually create and deliver products or services to customers. In addition, there is another downside to large accounts receivable or inventories. Receivables may grow because of increasing sales, but they can also zoom upward when collection of receivables slows down. Soaring inventories may mean increased ability to deliver orders on time. They may also mean that sales are not keeping up with production or that the company is incurring excessive storage and handling costs for inventory. Companies with large inventories may also lack the ability to adapt products quickly to customers' wishes.

You can see that there are mixed signals in measures such as working capital and current ratio. In the 1990s, many companies have made a concerted effort to reduce working capital and hence lower their current ratios. For example, between January 1998 and January 2000, Gap Inc. reduced its working capital by $394 million. This meant that Gap had an extra $394 million to invest in new products, corporate acquisitions, or whatever other opportunity presented itself. A food company, Quaker Oats, reduced its working capital by $200 million, primarily by smoothing out its production runs. Instead of building inventories and then offering huge discounts to entice customers to take delivery, Quaker now produces its cereals and other products just in time to ship them. Each product is produced once a week instead of once every 6 weeks or so. Of course, this requires more time resetting machines to produce a different product. By streamlining its procedures, one Quaker Oats factory spent only $20,000 a year on the extra machine setups compared with the annual savings of $500,000 from lowering inventories.

A measure of working capital that is increasingly popular is working capital per dollar of sales. The Fortune 500 firms have an average ratio of $.20 for every dollar of sales. Gap was at $.04 in January 2000.

Reduction of working capital is not just a U.S. phenomenon. Consider Wabco UK, the British auto products manufacturer. In the 1990s, its working capital went from $13 million to a negative $154,000. Currently, payables exceed receivables by $2.35 million and inventories are only $2.2 million. How did it accomplish this? Partly by cutting cycle time—the time from receipt of an order to delivery of the product. For example, a vacuum pump that formerly took 3 weeks to build can now be built in 6 minutes. Wabco is also collecting receivables more quickly—42 days compared with 54 days 5 years earlier.

Many companies have set a target of zero working capital and therefore a current ratio of 1.0. As these efforts prove to be successful, the rule of thumb of a desirable current ratio of 2.0 is being revised. Companies with twice as many current assets as current liabilities may be solvent but may lose out in the long run. Why? They may not be using their capital as profitably as possible.

FORMATS OF BALANCE SHEETS

The particular details and formats of balance sheets and other financial statements vary among companies. Yet, all balance sheets contain the same basic information, regardless of format. For example, consider the reproduction of the balance sheet of Walgreen Company, the drugstore chain, as shown in Exhibit 4-6. The format and classifications are those actually used by Walgreen. Note the "noncurrent" terminology used to denote long-term items. Headings such as long-term assets and long-term liabilities might be used instead of noncurrent assets and noncurrent liabilities, respectively. Some accountants prefer to omit a general heading for noncurrent items when there are only one or two items within a specific class.

report format A classified balance sheet with the assets at the top.

account format A classified balance sheet with the assets at the left.

Exhibit 4-6 presents a classified balance sheet in the **report format** (assets at top) in contrast to the **account format** (assets at left) that has previously been illustrated (Exhibit 4-5). Either format is acceptable. A recent survey of 600 U.S. companies indicated that 70% use the report format and 30% use the account format.

Exhibit 4-6
Walgreen Company
At August 31, 1999 and 1998 ($ in Millions)

Assets	1999	1998
Current assets		
Cash and cash equivalents	$ 142	$ 144
Accounts receivable	487	373
Inventories	2,463	2,027
Other current assets	130	79
Total current assets	3,222	2,623
Noncurrent assets		
Property and equipment, at cost, less accumulated depreciation and amortization	2,594	2,144
Other noncurrent assets	91	135
Total assets	$5,907	$4,902

Liabilities and Shareholders' Equity		
Current liabilities		
Trade accounts payable	$1,130	$ 907
Accrued expenses and other liabilities	730	618
Income taxes	63	55
Total current liabilities	1,923	1,580
Noncurrent liabilities		
Deferred income taxes	75	89
Other noncurrent liabilities	424	384
Total noncurrent liabilities	499	473
Shareholders' equity		
Preferred stock, $.0625 par value; authorized 32 million shares; none issued		
Common stock, $.078125 par value; authorized 3.2 billion shares; issued and outstanding 1,004,022,258 in 1999 and 996,487,044 in 1998	78	78
Paid-in capital	259	118
Retained earnings	3,148	2,653
Total shareholders' equity	3,485	2,849
Total liabilities and shareholders' equity	$5,907	$4,902

Exhibit 4-7

BP Amoco Balance Sheet
December 31, 2000 (£ millions)

Fixed assets		£103,819
Current assets	£40,119	
Current liabilities	37,147	
Net current assets		2,972
Total assets less current liabilities		£106,791
Long-term liabilities		33,375
Shareholders' interests		£ 73,416

Non-U.S. companies may use formats other than those presented in Exhibits 4-5 and 4-6. Exhibit 4-7 shows a condensed balance sheet for BP Amoco. Notice that fixed assets, that is, long-term assets, are listed before current assets. Current liabilities are deducted from current assets to give a direct measure of working capital (called net current assets by BP Amoco). Again, regardless of the format, balance sheets always contain the same basic information. Note that BP Amoco has working capital of £2,972 million. Current assets and current liabilities are close to equal. As suggested in the preceding Business First example, "Managing Working Capital," zero or negative working capital is becoming more common as companies reduce their inventories and accounts receivable.

INCOME STATEMENT

As we have just seen, balance sheets can provide decision makers with information about a company's ability to meet its short-term operating and debt needs. However, most investors are much more concerned about a company's ability to produce long-run earnings and dividends—information that can be gleaned from the income statement. In this regard, income statements are often considered to be more important than are balance sheets. To be most informative, income statements, like balance sheets, may be prepared with subcategories that help focus attention on certain accounts or groups of accounts.

SINGLE- AND MULTIPLE-STEP INCOME STATEMENTS

The adjusted trial balance for Chan Audio Company (Exhibit 4-4) provides the data for the two formats of income statements shown in Exhibit 4-8. The statement in Part A of the exhibit is called a **single-step income statement** because it groups all revenues together (sales plus interest and rent revenues) and then lists and deducts all expenses together without drawing any intermediate subtotals.

Another major form of income statement is the **multiple-step income statement.** It contains one or more subtotals that highlight significant relationships. For example, Exhibit 4-8, Part B, shows a gross profit figure. **Gross profit** (also called **gross margin**) is the excess of sales revenue over the cost of the inventory that was sold. Most multiple-step income statements start with this section.

The next section of a multiple-step income statement usually contains the operating expenses, which is a group of recurring expenses that pertain to the firm's routine, ongoing operations. Examples of such expenses are wages, rent, depreciation, and various other operation-oriented expenses, such as telephone, heat, and advertising. These

Objective 7
Prepare single- and multiple-step income statements and use ratios to assess profitability.

single-step income statement An income statement that groups all revenues together and then lists and deducts all expenses together without drawing any intermediate subtotals.

multiple-step income statement An income statement that contains one or more subtotals that highlight significant relationships.

gross profit (gross margin) The excess of sales revenue over the cost of the inventory that was sold.

Exhibit 4-8, Part A

Chan Audio Company

Single-Step Income Statement
Income Statement for the Month Ended January 31, 20X2

Sales		$160,000
Rent revenue		500
Interest revenue		400
Total sales and other revenues		$160,900
Expenses		
Cost of goods sold	$100,000	
Wages	31,750	
Depreciation	1,000	
Rent	5,000	
Interest	750	
Income taxes	11,200	
Total expenses		149,700
Net income		$ 11,200

Exhibit 4-8, Part B

Chan Audio Company

Multiple-Step Income Statement
Income Statement for the Month Ended January 31, 20X2

Sales			$160,000
Cost of goods sold			100,000
Gross profit			$ 60,000
Operating expenses			
Wages	$31,750		
Depreciation	1,000		
Rent	5,000		37,750
Operating income			$ 22,250
Other revenues and expenses			
Rent revenue	$ 500		
Interest revenue	400		
Total other revenue	$ 900		
Deduct: interest expense	750		150
Income before income taxes			$ 22,400
Income taxes (at 50%)			11,200
Net income			$ 11,200

operating income (operating profit) Gross profit less all operating expenses.

operating expenses are deducted from the gross profit to obtain **operating income,** which is also called **operating profit.**

The next grouping in the multiple-step income statement is usually called other revenue and expense (or other income or other expense, or nonoperating items, or some similar catchall title). These categories are not directly related to the mainstream of a firm's operations. The revenues are usually minor in relation to the revenues shown at the top of the income statement. The expenses are also minor, with one likely exception—interest expense. There is no theoretical or practical reason to prefer one of these formats over another. Experienced readers of financial statements can easily adjust from one to another. For the newcomer to accounting it can seem confusing. As you begin to read and evaluate actual statements, do not let the superficial differences between one structure and the other confuse you.

Accountants have usually regarded interest revenue and interest expense as "other" items because they arise from lending and borrowing money—activities that are distinct from most companies' ordinary operations of selling of goods or services. Of course, the exceptions are companies in the business of lending and borrowing money: banks, credit unions, insurance companies, and other financial intermediaries. Some operating companies make heavy use of debt, which causes high interest expenses, whereas other companies incur little debt and have low interest expenses. Because interest revenue and expense appear in a separate category, comparisons of operating income between years and between companies can be made easily. Comparisons of operating income focus attention on selling the product and controlling the costs of doing so. Success in this arena is the ultimate test of a company. Recently, many analysts have noted that corporate earnings are significantly improving. However, these analysts make a major distinction between those whose earnings are growing because interest cost is falling or because production costs are being aggressively reduced and those whose earnings are growing because sales are soaring. The first two sources of earnings growth depend on outside forces or one-time changes, but when more and more people want to buy your product, the long-term potential for growth is better.

EXAMPLES OF ACTUAL INCOME STATEMENTS

Exhibits 4-9 and 4-10 demonstrate how two different companies use assorted terminology and formats for their individual income statements. Note that extremely condensed income statement information is provided in both of these published reports. This level of detail is appropriate for external analysts and investors. In contrast, firms also prepare income statements to be used by managers inside the firm. Suppose you were the person responsible for managing inventory at a Gap store. You would want a very detailed financial statement for your store. You would want to know what the inventory was for spring merchandise and for summer merchandise, for men's wear and ladies' wear, and for clothing and accessories. You would need detail about the balance sheet. The same is true for the income statement. You would want sales and cost information for all those categories. You need this detail to manage your operation and to evaluate your performance against that of other Gap stores. Outside investors are more concerned with the overall performance of Gap as a whole relative to competing retailers, so summarized company-wide information is sufficient.

Exhibit 4-9

H. J. Heinz Company
Statement of Income ($ in Millions) for the Year Ended
April 28, 1999

Sales	$9,300
Cost of products sold	5,945
Gross profit	3,355
Selling, general and administrative expenses	2,245
Operating income	1,110
Interest income	25
Interest expense	259
Other expenses, net	41
Income before income taxes	835
Provision for income taxes	361
Net income	$ 474

Exhibit 4-10

Wm. Wrigley Jr. Company

Consolidated Statement of Earnings for the Year Ended
December 31, 2000

	($ in Millions)
Revenues	
Net sales	$2,146
Investment income	19
Total revenues	$2,165
Costs and expenses	
Cost of sales	904
Selling and general administrative	778
Other expense	4
Total costs and expenses	$1,686
Earnings before income taxes	479
Income taxes	150
Net earnings	$ 329

The H. J. Heinz income statement in Exhibit 4-9 uses a multiple-step format, as do 65% of all corporate external reports in the United States. The multiple-step format highlights significant relationships, especially two key measures of performance, gross profit and operating income. In all financial statements, accountants use the label net to denote that some amounts have been deducted in computing the final result. Thus, Other Expenses, Net in the Heinz statement means that some revenue items and some expense items have been combined into one number. Wm. Wrigley Jr. Company, maker of chewing gum, uses a single-step format for its income statement in Exhibit 4-10, as do 35% of corporate external reports in the United States. Wrigley follows the single-step model and

BUSINESS FIRST
Accounting for Hospitals

Some hospitals are for-profit corporations and some are not-for-profit community-based institutions. Historically, the two types of hospitals often used different accounting practices, but in recent years their accounting practices have converged. However, differences frequently remain in their internal cultures and the importance they place on the results of the accounting numbers.

The boards of directors and managers of for-profit hospitals are accountable for delivering profits. Their salaries may be linked to profits. Their stock price certainly is. They watch financial outcomes carefully and try to control salaries, minimize staffing, and buy new technology only when it can pay for itself from fees that are generated. In contrast, the boards of directors and managers of not-for-profit hospitals are accountable to their community for delivering good medical outcomes. There

is no stock price to watch that rises and falls with profits. When doctors or patients want new services, the question may be "Can we afford it?" instead of "Will it be profitable?"

What perspective is best? This is a hard question to answer. Both can be taken to an extreme. The for-profit hospital may fail to provide needed services, turn away patients on financial grounds, and otherwise fall short of fully serving the community. The not-for-profit hospital may become lazy. By not working to create efficient business systems and by not managing carefully, it can wind up less healthy financially than it should be. When the hospital lacks the resources to buy new equipment or to renovate the facility as needed, it ends up providing less service to the community than it should have been able to provide.

groups all revenues together and all expenses together without drawing subtotals within revenue and expense categories.

Note where income taxes appear in both of these income statements. Most companies follow this practice of showing income taxes as a separate item immediately above net income regardless of the grouping of other items on the income statement.

As the Wrigley income statement shows, the term costs and expenses is sometimes used in statements instead of just the phrase expenses. Of course, expenses would be an adequate description here. Why? The "costs" listed on the income statement are expired costs, such as cost of sales, and thus are really expenses of the current period.

PROFITABILITY EVALUATION RATIOS

We have learned to construct an income statement and a balance sheet, but they may seem a bit like tables of numbers without much meaning. In fact, for managers who work with them all the time these statements are the "language of business." These managers know what last month and last year looked like; they know their competitors' financial statements inside and out, and they know that high earnings (say $2 million) will cause them to earn a big bonus. How can we create meaning in these financial statements for individuals who do not have this deep company and industry knowledge? How can we use the data in these statements to enhance our understanding of these companies? What creates a context for interpreting them?

Earlier in this chapter, we saw that ratios such as the current ratio can help give meaning to the numbers in the balance sheet. The same is true for the income statement. Income statements are most useful in evaluating a company's profitability. In its ultimate sense, **profitability** is the ability of a company to provide its investors with a particular rate of return on their investment. Return on investment refers to the amount of money an investor receives because of a prior investment. If Mary invests $100 in Calvin Corporation and receives $10 every year as a result, $10 is her return on investment. However, absolute amounts are hard to evaluate. Had Mary given Calvin Corporation $200, a return of $10 would not be nearly as attractive. Thus, it is common to express the return as a rate of return, a return per dollar invested. In this case for a $100 investment, a $10 return is a 10% rate of return ($10/$100). For a $200 investment, a $10 return is a 5% rate of return ($10/$200).

> **profitability** The ability of a company to provide investors with a particular rate of return on their investment.

Profitability measures are useful decision-making tools for company managers. Investors use profitability measures to distinguish between different investment opportunities they are considering. Managers know that the profitability measures on their company will affect investors and that good profitability makes it easier to raise capital by selling stock or issuing debt securities. Managers are also often faced with a decision to buy another company, a division of a company, or a machine that makes a new product. In every such case, the manager will evaluate the profitability of the project as part of making the decision.

Profitability comparisons through time and within and among industries are used as a basis for predictions and decisions. By far, the easiest way to analyze a company's profitability is through three popular ratios:

1. A ratio based on gross profit (sales revenues minus cost of goods sold) is particularly useful to a retailer or manufacturer in choosing a pricing strategy and in judging its results. This measure, the **gross profit percentage,** or **gross margin percentage,** is defined as gross profit divided by sales. The Chan Audio gross profit percentage for January was (numbers from p. 150):

> **gross profit percentage (gross margin percentage)** Gross profit divided by sales.

$$\text{Gross profit percentage} = \text{Gross profit} \div \text{Sales}$$
$$= \$60,000 \div \$160,000$$
$$= 37.5\%$$

These relationships can also be presented as follows:

	Amount	Percentage
Sales	$160,000	100.0%
Cost of goods sold	100,000	62.5
Gross profit	$ 60,000	37.5%

Gross profit percentages vary greatly by industry. Software companies have high gross profit percentages (Microsoft's is 90%). Why? Because most costs in that industry are in research and development and sales and marketing, not in cost of goods sold. In contrast, retail companies have lower gross margin percentages because product costs are their main expense. For example, in 2000, the gross profit percentage for Safeway was 30%. Other gross margin percentages fall between the extremes, such as General Mills at 59% and Nike at 37%.

return on sales ratio Net income divided by sales.

2. A ratio based on a comparison of expenses and sales will be carefully followed by managers from month to month. The **return on sales ratio** shows the relationship of net income to sales revenue. Chan Audio's return on sales ratio is computed as follows:

$$\text{Return on sales} = \text{Net income} \div \text{sales}$$
$$= \$11,200 \div \$160,000$$
$$= 7\%$$

return on stockholders' equity ratio Net income divided by invested capital (measured by average stockholder's equity).

3. The **return on stockholders' equity ratio** also uses net income but compares it with invested capital (as measured by average stockholders' equity) instead of sales. This ratio is widely regarded as the ultimate measure of overall accomplishment. The return on stockholders' equity calculation for Chan Audio is:

$$\text{Return on stockholders' equity} = \text{Net income} \div \text{Average stockholders' equity}$$
$$= \$11,200 \div 1/2 \text{ (January 1 balance,}$$
$$\$400,000 + \text{January 31 balance, } \$411,200)$$
$$= \$11,200 \div \$405,600$$
$$= 2.8\% \text{ (for 1 month)}$$

Some recent examples of actual annual return on sales and return on stockholders' equity ratios are:

	Return on Sales (%)	Return on Stockholders' Equity (%)
Microsoft	41	28
Nike	6	14
McDonald's	15	20
Verizon	13	27
Walgreens	3	18
BP Amoco (United Kingdom)	6	12
Nordstrom	4	17
Kobe Steel (Japan)	1	1

Chan Audio's 37.5% gross profit is relatively low compared with the usual 40% to 45% for the retail stereo industry. However, Chan Audio has maintained excellent expense control because its 7% return on sales and its 33.6% return on stockholders' equity (a monthly rate of 2.8% $\times$ 12 = 33.6% as an annual rate) are higher than the 6% and 18% annual returns usually earned by the industry.

Which industry would you expect to have a higher gross margin percentage, the grocery industry or the pharmaceutical industry? Why?

ANSWER

There are many "right ways" to think about this issue. An example of a gross margin percentage for a grocery store is given in the text. The grocery industry is a retail activity where stores buy and resell items very quickly. As a result they can accept fairly low margins because they will hold the inventory briefly and face little risk of failure. In contrast, the pharmaceutical industry has to develop drugs, seek government approval to market them, and then aggressively sell them. Thus, the pharmaceutical industry has very high gross margin percentages. *Eli Lilly* has almost an 80% gross margin percentage. Two issues are important to realize. Cost of goods sold does not include very important selling, general, and administrative costs, which are larger in the pharmaceutical industry than in the grocery industry. More important, the pharmaceutical industry faces huge research and development costs (R&D), which GAAP treats as a period cost instead of a product cost. So R&D, which may be 15% or more of sales in the pharmaceutical industry, is not part of cost of goods sold and does not affect the gross margin percentage.

GENERALLY ACCEPTED ACCOUNTING PRINCIPLES AND BASIC CONCEPTS

Financial statements are the result of a measurement process that rests on a set of principles. If every accountant used a different set of measurement rules, decision makers would find it difficult to use and compare financial statements. For example, consider the recording of an asset such as a machine on the balance sheet. If one accountant listed the purchase cost, another the amount for which the used machine could be sold, and others listed various other amounts, the readers of financial statements would be confused. It would be as if each accountant were speaking a different language. Therefore, accountants have agreed to apply a common set of measurement principles—that is, a common language—to record information on financial statements.

> **Objective 8**
> Relate generally accepted accounting principles (GAAP) to the accounting practices we have learned.

Generally accepted accounting principles (GAAP) is the term that applies to all the broad concepts and detailed practices in accounting. It includes all the conventions, rules, and procedures that together make up accepted accounting practice. We concentrate on the GAAP that exists today in the United States. However, we frequently use practices from other countries and financial reports for non-U.S. firms to illustrate the extent of global diversity in practice. Although there is no single, perfect method for measuring an organization's performance, each country has found it useful to narrow the range of practices to a few acceptable ones. The general trend is to reduce international diversity and governments and accounting groups worldwide are cooperating in this effort.

> **generally accepted accounting principles (GAAP)** A term that applies to the broad concepts or guidelines and detailed practices in accounting, including all the conventions, rules, and procedures that make up accepted accounting practice at a given time.

Accounting principles become "generally accepted" by agreement. Such agreement is not influenced only by formal logical analysis. Experience, custom, usage, and practical necessity contribute to a set of principles. Therefore, it might be better to call them conventions. Why? Because "principles" erroneously connotes that GAAP is the product of airtight logic. Nevertheless, accountants use the term principles instead of conventions to describe the entire framework that guides their work.

STANDARD SETTING BODIES

The existence of GAAP implies that someone must decide which principles are generally accepted and which are not. This decision is made by regulatory agencies or professional associations. In the United States, GAAP is set primarily in the private sector (with government oversight), but in many countries, such as France, the government sets the standards directly.

Financial Accounting Standards Board (FASB) A private-sector body that determines generally accepted accounting standards in the United States.

AICPA American Institute of Certified Public Accountants, the leading organization of the auditors of corporate financial reports.

FASB Statements The FASB's rulings on generally accepted accounting principles (GAAP).

Accounting Principles Board (APB) The predecessor to the Financial Accounting Standards Board.

APB Opinions A series of 31 opinions of the Accounting Principles Board, many of which are still the "accounting law of the land."

Securities and Exchange Commission (SEC) The agency designated by the U.S. Congress to hold the ultimate responsibility for authorizing the generally accepted accounting principles for companies whose stock is held by the general investing public.

International Accounting Standards Board (IASB) An organization charged with responsibility for developing a common set of accounting standards to be used throughout the world.

The **Financial Accounting Standards Board (FASB)** is responsible for establishing GAAP in the United States. The FASB is an independent creature of the private sector consisting of seven qualified individuals who work full-time. The board is supported by a large staff and an annual $20 million budget provided by various professional accounting associations such as the leading organization of auditors, the American Institute of Certified Public Accountants (**AICPA**). The FASB's rulings on GAAP are called **FASB Statements.**

The FASB, established in 1973, replaced the **Accounting Principles Board (APB),** a group of 18 accountants (mostly partners in large accounting firms) who worked part-time. The APB issued a series of 31 **APB Opinions** during 1962 to 1973, many of which are still the "accounting law of the land."

The U.S. Congress has charged the **Securities and Exchange Commission (SEC)** with the ultimate responsibility for authorizing the GAAP for companies whose stock is held by the general investing public. However, the SEC has informally delegated much rule-making power to the FASB. This public sector/private sector authority relationship can be sketched as follows:

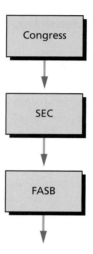

Issues pronouncements on various accounting issues. These pronouncements govern the preparation of typical financial statements.

Take a careful look at the preceding three-tiered structure. Note that Congress can overrule both the SEC and the FASB, and the SEC can overrule the FASB. Such undermining of the FASB occurs rarely, but pressure is exerted on all three tiers by corporations if they think an impending pronouncement is "wrong." Thus, the setting of accounting principles is a complex process involving heavy interactions among the affected parties: public regulators (Congress and the SEC), private regulators (FASB), companies, those in the public accounting profession, representatives of investors, and other interested groups.

International Accounting Standards. Recent years have seen a growing interest in developing a common set of accounting principles throughout the world. Often called harmonization of accounting standards, the movement seeks to eliminate differences in accounting principles that are not caused by cultural or environmental differences between countries. Leading the way is the **International Accounting Standards Board (IASB),** which was established "to develop, in the public interest, a single set of high quality, understandable and enforceable global accounting standards." On April 1, 2001, the IASB succeeded the International Accounting Standards Committee, formed in 1973, as the international accounting standard setter. It has 12 full-time and 2 part-time members, including one academic, Mary Barth of Stanford University. Sir David Tweedie of the

United Kingdom chairs the Board and is its CEO. The Board is appointed by and reports to the IASC Foundation Trustees, whose 19 members represent a diversity of geographic and professional backgrounds. Although compliance with IASB standards is voluntary, a growing number of countries and multinational companies are adopting the methods advocated by the IASB.

The motivation for this conformity movement lies in the explosive growth of international commerce. Increasingly, investors commit their money worldwide as individuals or through retirement accounts or mutual funds. Companies rely on international capital to finance their growth. In January of 2000, shares of more than 400 non-U.S. companies from more than 50 countries were listed on the New York Stock Exchange (NYSE). This phenomenon is even more pronounced in London where approximately two-thirds of the market value of traded firms on the London Stock Exchange are non-U.K. firms. Examples of major multinational firms that now publish their financial statements in conformity with IASC standards are Allianz (Germany), Nestlé (Switzerland), Nokia (Finland), Shanghai Petrochemical (China), and Microsoft (United States).

Also affecting international accounting standards is the European Union (EU). Via a series of directives, which have the force of law, the EU is reducing the variations in financial statements of companies in its member nations.

CONCEPTS AND CONVENTIONS OF GAAP

In the United States, the FASB sets many detailed rules that are part of GAAP. Some of the most difficult issues in accounting center on when an unexpired cost expires and becomes an expense. For example, some accountants believe that research and development costs should be accounted for as unexpired costs, shown on balance sheets among the assets, and written off to expense in some systematic manner over a period of years. After all, companies engage in research and product development activities because they expect them to create future benefits. However, the FASB in the United States and regulators in many other countries have ruled that such costs have vague future benefits that are difficult to measure reliably. Therefore, research and development costs are treated as expenses when incurred and do not appear on the balance sheet as assets. In contrast, Italy and Spain allow R&D costs to be recognized initially as an asset and to be shown on the balance sheet.

In addition to specific pronouncement by regulators such as the IASC and the FASB, there are a number of concepts and conventions that guide our accounting process.

The Entity Concept.   The first basic concept or principle in accounting is the entity concept. An accounting entity is an organization or a section of an organization that stands apart from other organizations and individuals as a separate economic unit. Accounting draws sharp boundaries around each entity to avoid confusing its affairs with those of other entities.

An example of an entity is General Motors Corporation, an enormous entity that encompasses many smaller entities such as the Chevrolet Division and the Buick Division. In turn, Chevrolet encompasses many smaller entities such as a Michigan assembly plant and an Ohio assembly plant. Managers want accounting reports that are confined to their particular entities.

The key point here is that the entity concept helps the accountant relate events to a clearly defined area of accountability. For example, business entities should not be confused with personal entities. A purchase of groceries for merchandise inventory is an accounting transaction of a grocery store (the business entity), but the store owner's purchase of a stereo set with a personal check is a transaction of the owner (the personal entity).

The Reliability Concept.   Users of financial statements want assurance that the numbers are not fabricated by management. Consequently, accountants regard reliability as an essential characteristic of measurement. **Reliability** is a quality of information that

reliability The quality of information that assures decision makers that the information captures the conditions or events it purports to represent.

assures decision makers that the information captures the conditions or events it purports to represent. Reliable data are supported by convincing evidence that can be verified by independent accountants.

The accounting process focuses on reliable recording of events that affect an organization. Although many events may affect a company—including wars, elections, and general economic booms or depressions—the accountant recognizes only specified types of events as being reliably recorded as accounting transactions.

Suppose the president of ExxonMobil is killed in an airplane crash, and the company carries no life insurance for its executive officer. The accountant would not record this event. Suppose further that Exxon discovers that an employee has embezzled $1,000 in cash, and the company carries no employee theft insurance. The accountant would record this event. The death of the president may have considerably more economic or financial significance for Exxon than does the embezzlement, but the monetary effect is hard to measure in any objective way. Accountants measure the impact of events in a systematic, reliable manner.

going concern convention (continuity convention)
The assumption that in all ordinary situations an entity persists indefinitely.

Going Concern Convention. The **going concern convention (continuity convention)** is the assumption that ordinarily an entity persists indefinitely. This notion implies that a company's existing resources, such as plant assets, will be used to fulfill the general business needs of the company rather than be sold in tomorrow's real estate or equipment markets. For a going concern it is reasonable to use historical cost to record long-lived assets. Also, for a going concern it is reasonable to report liabilities at the amount to be paid at maturity.

The opposite view of this going concern convention is an immediate liquidation assumption whereby all items on a balance sheet are valued at the amounts appropriate if the entity were to be liquidated in piecemeal fashion within a few days or months. This liquidation approach to valuation is usually used only when the probability is high that the company will be liquidated.

Materiality Convention. How does an accountant know what to include on financial statements? There are a lot of rules and regulations about what must appear in those statements, but what about items that are not covered by the rules? The **materiality convention** asserts that an item should be included in a financial statement if its omission or misstatement would tend to mislead the reader of the financial statements under consideration.

materiality convention
The concept that an item should be included in a financial statement if its omission or misstatement would tend to mislead the reader of the financial statements under consideration.

Most large items, such as cars and machinery, are clearly material. Smaller items, though, may not be so clear-cut. Many acquisitions that should theoretically be recorded as assets are immediately written off as expenses because of their insignificance. For example, coat hangers may last indefinitely but never appear in the balance sheet as assets. Many corporations require the immediate write-off to expense of all outlays under a specified minimum, such as $1,000, regardless of the useful life of the asset acquired. The resulting $1,000 understatement of assets and stockholders' equity is considered too trivial to worry about. In general, GAAP does not need to be applied to immaterial items. The FASB regularly includes the following statement in its standards: "The provisions of this statement need not be applied to immaterial items."

When is an item material? There will probably never be a universal, clear-cut answer. What is trivial to General Motors may be material to Evelyn's Boutique. A working rule is that an item is material if its proper accounting would probably affect the decision of a knowledgeable party. In sum, materiality is an important convention, but it is difficult to use anything other than prudent judgment to tell whether an item is material.

Cost-Benefit Criterion. Accounting systems vary in complexity—from the minimum crude records kept by a small business to satisfy government authorities, to the sophisticated budgeting and feedback schemes that are required to manage a huge,

BUSINESS FIRST
Accounting for Nonprofit Organizations and Governmental Entities

Most examples thus far have focused on profit-seeking organizations, but balance sheets and income statements are also used by nonprofit organizations. For example, hospitals and universities have income statements, although they are called statements of revenue and expense. The "bottom line" is frequently called "excess of revenue over expense" or "net financial result" rather than "net income." Part of the notion is that there are no shareholders to be the residual claimants. Non-Profits are run for the good of the community. But for an organization to be healthy and able to grow, invest and change, it must generate revenues in excess of its costs.

In response to abuses over the years regulators are bringing greater discipline to reporting by not-for-profit entities and governmental entities. The FASB now requires that financial statements for large not-for-profit firms include essentially equivalent financial statements to those required for businesses. A parallel organization that regulates governmental reporting is considering a requirement that governmental units such as cities and states use accrual-based accounting and the basic financial statements that businesses use.

Unfortunately, the federal government in the United States currently reports its financial results and does its planning on a cash basis. Worse yet, it does not produce

a balance sheet. Thus, when the citizens and their elected representatives try to make intelligent decisions, they lack good information for evaluating alternatives or even for carrying on an intelligent debate.

When Vice President Gore and Governor Bush were locked in a battle for the presidency, issues such as defense spending, Medicare, education, and tax cuts were very much in the news. To focus the debate, people should realize that defense spending has two components, current operating activity and investing in the future. Thus, budget authorization for more spending might refer to building new ships or planes that are long-lived assets or it might refer to amounts to be spent on payment to our armed forces. The two have very different consequences but are rarely separated in the debate. The same is true of education: Spending on teacher salaries and on school buildings are different. If the federal government produced a balance sheet that showed federal buildings as assets, national parks as assets, the national highway system as assets, etc., it might be the case that we would find, as a nation, that the country has "equity" in its assets. That is, imagine that the depreciated cost of all the assets of the country exceeded the often discussed national debt. Instead of thinking about each citizen's share of the national debt, we might find that the right way to think is about each citizen's share of the national assets.

multinational corporation. Of course, a system can start out small and get much bigger as is necessary. However, when are changes to an accounting system necessary? The **cost-benefit criterion** states that a system should be changed when the expected additional benefits of the change exceed its expected additional costs. Often the benefits are difficult to measure, but this criterion should always underlie the decisions about the design and change of accounting systems. In fact, the FASB uses a cost-benefit criterion in judging new standards. It safeguards the cost-effectiveness of its standards by (1) assuring that a standard does not "impose costs on the many for the benefit of a few," and (2) seeking alternative ways of handling an issue that are "less costly and only slightly less efficient."

cost-benefit criterion As a system is changed, its expected additional benefits should exceed its expected additional costs.

Stable Monetary Unit. The monetary unit (called the dollar in the United States, Canada, Australia, New Zealand, and elsewhere) is the principal means for measuring assets and equities. It is the common denominator for quantifying the effects of a wide variety of transactions. Accountants record, classify, summarize, and report in terms of the monetary unit. The ability to use historical cost accounting depends on a stable monetary unit. A stable monetary unit is simply one that is not expected to change in value significantly over time.

SUMMARY PROBLEM FOR YOUR REVIEW

PROBLEM TWO

Johnson & Johnson (maker of Tylenol, Band-Aids, and other health care and personal use products) uses a statement of earnings and retained earnings, as follows:

Johnson & Johnson
Statement of Earnings for the year ended December 31, 1999
($ in millions except per share figures)

Sales to customers	$27,471
Cost of products sold	8,442
Gross Profit	19,029
Selling, marketing, and administrative expenses	10,503
Research expense	2,600
Interest income	(246)
Interest expense	197
Other expense, net	222
	13,276
Earnings before provision for taxes on income	5,753
Provision for taxes on income	1,585
Net earnings	$ 4,168
Net earnings per share	$ 3.00

1. Is this a single-step or a multiple-step income statement? Explain your answer.

2. What term would H. J. Heinz use as a label for the line in Johnson and Johnson's statements having the $5,753 figure? (Refer to the Heinz income statement in Exhibit 4-9.)

3. Suggest an alternative term for interest income.

4. What is the amount of the famous "bottom line" that is so often referred to by managers?

5. Net earnings per share is defined as net earnings divided by the average number of common shares outstanding. Compute the average number of common shares outstanding during the year.

SOLUTION TO PROBLEM TWO

1. As is often the case, Johnson & Johnson uses a hybrid of single-step and multiple-step income statements. However, it is closer to a multiple-step statement. A purebred single-step statement would place interest income with sales to obtain total revenues and would not calculate a gross profit subtotal.

2. Heinz would use "income before income taxes" to describe the $5,753 figure.

3. Interest revenue is preferable to interest income.

4. The bottom line in total is net earnings of $4,167 million. The bottom line per average common share outstanding is $3.00.

5. As chapter 2 explains, net earnings per share is required to be shown on the face of the income statement.

$$\text{Earnings per share (EPS)} = \frac{\text{Net earnings}}{\text{Average number of common shares outstanding}}$$

$$\$3.00 = \frac{\$4,167,000,000}{\text{Average shares}}$$

Average shares = $\$4,167,000,000 \div 3.00$

Average shares = $1,389,000,000$

Highlights to Remember

1. **Make adjustments for the expiration or consumption of assets.**

2. **Make adjustments for the earning of unearned revenues.**

3. **Make adjustments for the accrual of unrecorded expenses.**

4. **Make adjustments for the accrual of unrecorded revenues.** At the end of each accounting period, adjustments must be made so that financial statements can be presented on a full-fledged accrual basis. The major adjustments are for (1) the expiration of unexpired costs, (2) the earning of unearned revenues, (3) the accrual of unrecorded expenses, and (4) the accrual of unrecorded revenues. Frequently, accounting adjustments are clarified when they are seen as mirror images by looking at both sides of the adjustment simultaneously. For example, (a) the expiration of unexpired costs (the tenant's rent expense) is accompanied by (b) the earning of unearned revenues (the landlord's rent revenue). Similarly, (a) the accrual of unrecorded expenses (a borrower's interest expense) is accompanied by (b) the accrual of unrecorded revenues (a lender's interest revenue).

5. **Describe the sequence of the final steps in the recording process and relate cash flows to adjusting entries.** The adjusting entries capture expense and revenue elements that either precede or follow the related cash flows. Entries for the expiration of unexpired costs and the recognition (earning) of unearned revenues follow the cash flows, while entries for the accrual of unrecorded expenses and the accrual of unrecorded revenues precede the cash flows. The adjusting entries provide a mechanism for capturing implicit transactions that do not necessarily generate documents that lead to them being recorded.

6. **Prepare a classified balance sheet and use it to assess solvency.** Classified balance sheets divide various items into subcategories. For example, assets and liabilities are separated into current and long term. These subcategories are used in analysis. For example, current assets minus current liabilities is called working capital. The current ratio, defined as current assets divided by current liabilities, is used to help assess solvency.

7. **Prepare single- and multiple-step income statements and use ratios to assess profitability.** Income statements may appear in single-step or multiple-step form. Single-step statements group all revenue items together and all expense items together, while the multiple-step forms calculate various subtotals such as gross profit and operating income. Regardless of the format, published income statements are highly condensed and summarized compared with reports used within an organization. Income statement ratios are used to assess profitability. Among the most useful are gross margin (or gross profit), return on sales, and return on stockholders' equity.

8. **Relate generally accepted accounting principles (GAAP) to the accounting practices we have learned.** Generally accepted accounting principles (GAAP) are

based on many concepts including the entity concept, the going concern assumption, materiality, and a stable monetary unit. GAAP in the United States is generally determined by the Financial Accounting Standards Board (FASB), with oversight by the Securities and Exchange Commission (SEC). Growing interest in a common international GAAP has moved the International Accounting Standards Board (IASB) into the forefront of standard setting.

Accounting Vocabulary

account format, p. 148
Accounting Principles Board (APB), p. 156
accrue, p. 132
adjusting entries, p. 132
adjustments, p. 132
AICPA, p. 156
APB Opinions, p. 156
classified balance sheet, p. 144
continuity convention, p. 156
cost-benefit criterion, p. 159
current assets, p. 145
current liabilities, p. 145
current ratio, p. 146
deferred credit, p. 134
deferred revenue, p. 134
explicit transactions, p. 132
FASB Statements, p. 156

Financial Accounting Standards Board (FASB), p. 156
generally accepted accounting principles (GAAP), p. 155
going concern convention, p. 158
gross margin, p. 149
gross margin percentage, p. 153
gross profit, p. 149
gross profit percentage, p. 153
implicit transactions, p. 132
International Accounting Standards Board (IASB), p. 156
materiality convention, p. 158
multiple-step income statement, p. 149
operating income, p. 150

operating profit, p. 150
pretax income, p. 139
profitability, p. 153
reliability, p. 157
report format, p. 148
return on sales ratio, p. 154
return on stockholders' equity ratio, p. 154
revenue received in advance, p. 134
Securities and Exchange Commission (SEC), p. 156
single-step income statement, p. 149
solvency, p. 146
unearned revenue, p. 134
working capital, p. 145
working capital ratio, p. 146

Assignment Material

QUESTIONS

4-1 Give two examples of explicit transactions.

4-2 Give two examples of implicit transactions.

4-3 Give two synonyms for *unearned revenue*.

4-4 Distinguish between the accrual of wages and the payment of wages.

4-5 Give a synonym for *income tax expense*.

4-6 Explain why income tax expense is usually the final deduction on both single-step and multiple-step income statements.

4-7 "The accrual of previously unrecorded revenues is the mirror image of the accrual of previously unrecorded expenses." Explain, by using an illustration.

4-8 What types of adjusting entries are made before the related cash flows? After the related cash flows?

4-9 Why are current assets and current liabilities grouped separately from long-term assets and long-term liabilities?

4-10 "Microsoft is much more profitable than IBM because its current ratio is more than four times larger than IBM's." Do you agree? Explain.

4-11 "Companies should always strive to avoid negative working capital." Do you agree? Explain.

4-12 Explain the difference between a *single-step* and a *multiple-step* income statement.

4-13 Why does interest expense appear below operating income on a multiple-step income statement?

4-14 The term *costs and expenses* is sometimes found instead of just *expenses* on the income statement. Would expenses be an adequate description? Why?

4-15 Name three popular ratios for measuring profitability, and indicate how to compute each of the three.

4-16 "Computer software companies are generally more profitable than grocery stores because their gross profit percentages are usually at least twice as large." Do you agree? Explain.

4-17 Distinguish between GAAP, FASB, SEC, and APB.

4-18 What functions does the International Accounting Standards Board (IASB) have in setting GAAP?

4-19 "This idea implies that existing equipment will be used instead of sold in tomorrow's equipment markets." What is the name of this idea?

4-20 "What is trivial to General Electric may be significant to Don's Hobby Shop." What idea is being described?

COGNITIVE EXERCISES

4-21 Accounting Errors
You have discovered an error in which a $2,000 payment on December 1 for rent for December and January was "incorrectly" recorded by the tenant as rent expense. As a young auditor you are not sure whether this must be corrected. You think it is a self-correcting error. What are the issues you should consider?

4-22 What Constitutes Revenue?
You have just started a program of selling gift certificates at your store. In the first month you sold $1,000 worth and customers redeemed $100 of these certificates for merchandise. Your average gross profit margin is 50%. What should you report as gift certificate revenue and how much gross margin will appear in the income statement?

4-23 GAAP and Cost-Benefit
How would you relate the term cost-benefit criterion to the concept of generally accepted accounting principles?

4-24 Accounting for Supplies
A company began business on July 1 and purchased $1,000 in supplies including paper, pens, paper clips, and so on. On December 31, as they prepared their financial statements, the accounting clerk asked how to treat the $1,000 that appeared in the supplies inventory account. What should this clerk do?

EXERCISES

4-25 True or False
Use T or F to indicate whether each of the following statements is true or false:

1. Retained earnings should be accounted for as a current asset item.
2. Cash should be classified as a stockholders' equity item.
3. Machinery used in the business should be recorded as a noncurrent asset item.
4. The cash balance is the best evidence of stockholders' equity.
5. From a single balance sheet you can find stockholders' equity for a period of time but not for a specific day.
6. It is not possible to determine changes in the condition of a business from a single balance sheet.

4-26 Tenant and Landlord
The Trucano Company, a retail hardware store, pays quarterly rent on its store at the beginning of each quarter. The rent per quarter is $15,000. The owner of the building in which the store is located is the Resing Corporation.

By using the balance sheet equation format, analyze the effects of the following on the tenant's and the landlord's financial position: **Required**

1. Trucano pays $15,000 rent on July 1.
2. Adjustment for July.
3. Adjustment for August.
4. Adjustment for September. Also prepare the journal entries for Trucano and Resing for September.

4-27 Customer and Airline
Kimberly Clark (KC), maker of Scott paper products decided to hold a managers' meeting in Hawaii in February. To take advantage of special fares, KC purchased airline tickets in advance from United Airlines at a total cost of $80,000. These were acquired on December 1 for cash.

By using the balance sheet equation format, analyze the impact of the December payment and the February travel on the financial position of both KC and United. Also prepare journal entries for February. **Required**

4-28 Accruals of Wages

Consider the following calendar:

		September				
S	M	T	W	T	F	S
		1	2	3	4	5
6	7	8	9	10	11	12
13	14	15	16	17	18	19
20	21	22	23	24	25	26
27	28	29	30			

The Montlake Department Store commenced business on September 1. It is open every day except Sunday. Its total payroll for all employees is $6,000 per day. Payments are made each Tuesday for the preceding week's work through Saturday.

Required

By using the balance sheet equation format, analyze the financial impact on Montlake of the following:

1. Disbursements for wages on September 8, 15, 22, and 29.
2. Adjustments for wages on September 30. Also prepare the journal entry.

4-29 Accrued Vacation Pay

Delta Airlines had the following as a current liability on its balance sheet, December 31, 2000:

Accrued salaries and vacation pay	$1,170,000,000

Under the accrual basis of accounting, vacation pay is ordinarily accrued throughout the year as workers are regularly paid. For example, suppose a Delta baggage handler earns $800 per week for 50 weeks and also gets paid $1,600 for 2 weeks' vacation. Accrual accounting requires that the obligation for the $1,600 be recognized as it is earned instead of when the payment is disbursed. Thus, in each of the 50 weeks Delta would recognize a wage expense (or vacation pay expense) of $1,600/50 = $32.

Required

1. Prepare the weekly Delta adjusting journal entry called for by the $32 example.
2. Prepare the entry for the $1,600 payment of vacation pay.

4-30 Placement of Interest in Income Statement

Two companies have the following balance sheets as of December 31, 20X8:

Jupiter Company

Cash	$ 50,000	Note payable*	$100,000
Other assets	150,000	Stockholders' equity	100,000
Total	$200,000	Total	$200,000

*12% interest.

Saturn Company

Cash	$ 50,000	Stockholders' equity	$200,000
Other assets	150,000		
Total	$200,000		

In 20X9, each company had sales of $550,000 and expenses (excluding interest) of $500,000. Ignore income taxes.

Required

Did the two companies earn the same net income and the same operating income? Explain, showing computations of operating income and net income.

4-31 Effects of Interest on Lenders and Borrowers

Prudential lent Dayglo Paint Company $1,000,000 on April 1, 20X1. The loan plus interest of 12% is payable on April 1, 20X2.

Required

1. By using the balance sheet equation format, prepare an analysis of the impact of the transaction on both Prudential's and Dayglo's financial position on April 1, 20X1. Show the summary adjustments on December 31, 20X1, for the period April 1 to December 31.
2. Prepare adjusting journal entries for Prudential and Dayglo on December 31, 20X1.

4-32 Identification of Transactions

Valenzuela Corporation's financial position is represented by the nine balances shown on the first line of the following schedule ($ in thousands). Assume that a single transaction took place for each of the following lines, and describe what you think happened, using one short sentence for each line.

	Cash	Accounts Receivable	Inven-tory	Equip-ment	Accounts Payable	Accrued Wages Payable	Unearned Rent Revenue	Paid-in Capital	Retained Income
Bal.	19	32	54	0	29	0	0	55	21
(1)	29	32	54	0	29	0	0	65	21
(2)	29	32	54	20	29	0	0	85	21
(3)	29	32	66	20	41	0	0	85	21
(4a)	29	47	66	20	41	0	0	85	36
(4b)	29	47	58	20	41	0	0	85	28
(5)	34	42	58	20	41	0	0	85	28
(6)	14	42	58	20	21	0	0	85	28
(7)	19	42	58	20	21	0	5	85	28
(8)	19	42	58	20	21	2	5	85	26
(9)	19	42	58	19	21	2	5	85	25
(10)	19	42	58	19	21	2	3	85	27

4-33 Effects on Balance Sheet Equation

Following is a list of effects of accounting transactions on the basic accounting equation: Assets = Liabilities + Stockholders' equity.

a. Increase in assets, increase in liabilities.
b. Increase in assets, decrease in liabilities.
c. Increase in assets, increase in stockholders' equity.
d. Increase in assets, decrease in assets.
e. Decrease in assets, decrease in liabilities.
f. Increase in liabilities, decrease in stockholders' equity.
g. Decrease in assets, increase in liabilities.
h. Decrease in liabilities, increase in stockholders' equity.
i. Decrease in assets, decrease in stockholders' equity.
j. None of these.

Required

Which of the relationships identified by letter above defines the accounting effect of each of the following transactions?

1. The adjusting entry to recognize periodic depreciation.
2. The adjusting entry to record accrued salaries.
3. The adjusting entry to record accrued interest receivable.
4. The collection of interest previously accrued.
5. The settlement of an account payable by the issuance of a note payable.
6. The recognition of an expense that had been paid for previously. A "prepaid" account was increased on payment.
7. The earning of revenue previously collected. Unearned revenue was increased when collection was made in advance.

4-34 Effects of Errors in Adjustments

What will be the effect—understated (u), overstated (o), or no effect (n)—on the income of the present and future periods if the following errors were made. In all cases assume that amounts carried over into 20X7 would affect 20X7 operations via the routine accounting entries of 20X7.

	Period	
	20X6	*20X7*
1. Revenue has been collected in advance, but earned amounts have not been recognized at the end of 20X6. Instead, all revenue was recognized as earned in 20X7.	_____	_____
2. Revenue for services rendered has been earned, but the unbilled amounts have not been recognized at the end of 20X6.	_____	_____
3. Accrued wages payable have not been recognized at the end of 20X6.	_____	_____
4. Prepaid items like rent have been paid (in late 20X6), but not adjusted at the end of 20X6. The payments have been debited to prepaid rent. They were transferred to expense in mid-20X7.	_____	_____

4-35 Effects of Adjustments and Corrections

Listed next are a series of accounts that are numbered for identification. All accounts needed to answer the parts of this question are included. Prepare an answer sheet with columns in which you are to write the identification numbers of the accounts affected by your answers. The same account may be used in several answers.

1. Cash
2. Accounts receivable
3. Notes receivable
4. Inventory
5. Accrued interest receivable
6. Accrued rent receivable
7. Fuel on hand
8. Unexpired rent
9. Unexpired insurance
10. Unexpired repairs and maintenance
11. Land
12. Buildings
13. Machinery and equipment
14. Accounts payable

15. Notes payable
16. Accrued wages and salaries payable
17. Accrued interest payable
18. Unearned subscription revenue
19. Capital stock
20. Sales
21. Fuel expense
22. Sales and wages
23. Insurance expense
24. Repairs and maintenance expense
25. Rent expense
26. Rent revenue
27. Subscription revenue
28. Interest revenue
29. Interest expense

Required

Prepare any necessary adjusting or correcting entries called for by the following situations, which were discovered at the end of the calendar year. With respect to each situation, assume that no entries have been made concerning the situation other than those specifically described (i.e., no monthly adjustments have been made during the year). Consider each situation separately. These transactions were not necessarily conducted by one business firm. Amounts are in thousands of dollars. An illustration follows: purchased new equipment for $100 cash, plus a $300 short-term note. The bookkeeper failed to record the transaction. The answer would appear as follows:

	Account		Amount (in $)	
	Debit	*Credit*	*Debit*	*Credit*
Illustration	13	1 & 15	400	100 & 300
a.	___	_____	___	_____
b.	___	_____	___	_____
c.	___	_____	___	_____
etc.	___	_____	___	_____

a. A $500 purchase of equipment on December 5 was erroneously debited to Accounts Payable. The credit was correctly made to Cash.

b. A business made several purchases of fuel oil. Some purchases ($800) were debited to Fuel Expense, while others ($1,100) were charged to an asset account. An oil gauge revealed $400 of fuel on hand at the end of the year. There was no fuel on hand at the beginning of the year.

c. On April 1, a business took out a fire insurance policy. The policy was for 2 years, and the premium paid was $800. It was debited to Insurance Expense on April 1.

d. On December 1, $400 was paid in advance to the landlord for 4 months of rent. The tenant debited Unexpired Rent for $400 on December 1. What adjustment is necessary on December 31 on the tenant's books?

e. Machinery is repaired and maintained by an outside maintenance company on an annual fee basis, payable in advance. The $240 fee was paid in advance on September 1 and charged to Repairs and Maintenance Expense. What adjustment is necessary on December 31?

f. On November 16, $800 of machinery was purchased, $200 cash was paid down, and a 90-day, 5% note payable was signed for the balance. The November 16 transaction was properly recorded. Prepare the adjustment for the interest.

g. A publisher sells subscriptions to magazines. Customers pay in advance. Receipts are originally credited to Unearned Subscription Revenue. On August 1, many 1-year subscriptions were collected and recorded, amounting to $12,000.

h. On December 30, certain merchandise was purchased for $1,000 on open account. The bookkeeper debited Machinery and Equipment and credited Accounts Payable for $1,000. Prepare a correcting entry.

i. A 120-day, 9%, $15,000 cash loan was made to a customer on November 1. The November 1 transaction was recorded correctly.

4-36 Working Capital and Current Ratio
The Royal Dutch/Shell Group of Companies operates the Shell Oil Company. Headquartered in both The Netherlands and the United Kingdom, the company's financial statements are in British pounds (£). In the late 1990s, Royal Dutch/Shell had current assets of £25,452 million and current liabilities of £19,525 million.

Compute Royal Dutch/Shell's working capital and current ratio.

Required

4-37 Profitability Ratios
Nestlé S.A., the Swiss chocolate company, sells many other food items in addition to various types of chocolates. Sales in 1999 were SF74,660 million (where SF means Swiss francs), cost of goods sold was SF36,241 million, net income was SF4,724 million, and average stockholders' equity was SF23,634 million.

Compute Nestlé's gross profit percentage, return on sales, and return on stockholders' equity.

Required

PROBLEMS

4-38 Adjusting Entries
(Alternates are 4-40, 4-41, and 4-42.) Christy Blair, certified public accountant, had the following transactions (among others) during 20X8:

a. For accurate measurement of performance and position, Blair uses the accrual basis of accounting. On August 1, she acquired office supplies for $2,000. Office Supplies Inventory was increased, and Cash was decreased by $2,000 on Blair's books. On December 31, her inventory of office supplies was $900.

b. On September 1, a client gave Blair a retainer fee of $36,000 cash for monthly services to be rendered over the following 12 months. Blair increased Cash and Unearned Fee Revenue.

c. Blair accepted an $8,000 note receivable from a client on October 1 for tax services. The note plus interest of 12% per year were due in 6 months. Blair increased Note Receivable and Fee Revenue by $8,000.

d. As of December 31, Blair had not recorded $600 of unpaid wages earned by her secretary during late December.

For the year ended December 31, 20X8, prepare all adjustments called for by the preceding transactions. Assume that appropriate entries were routinely made for the explicit transactions described earlier. However, no adjustments have been made before December 31. For each adjustment, prepare an analysis in the same format used when the adjustment process was explained in the chapter (i.e., the balance sheet equation format). Also prepare the adjusting journal entry.

4-39 Multiple-Step Income Statement

(Alternate is 4-43.) From the following data, prepare a multiple-step income statement for the Ortonville Company for the fiscal year ended May 31, 20X6 ($ in thousands except for percentage).

Sales	$900	Cost of goods sold	$500
Interest expense	68	Depreciation	30
Rent expense	55	Rent revenue	10
Interest revenue	14	Wages	200
Income tax rate	40%		

4-40 Four Major Adjustments

(Alternates are 4-38, 4-41, and 4-42) Jocelyn Noller, an attorney, had the following transactions (among others) during 20X8, her initial year in practicing law:

a. On August 1, Noller leased office space for 1 year. The landlord (lessor) insisted on full payment in advance. Prepaid Rent was increased and Cash was decreased by $24,000 on Noller's books. Similarly, the landlord increased Cash and increased Unearned Rent Revenue.

b. On October 1, Noller received a retainer fee of $12,000 cash for services to be rendered to her client, a local trucking company, over the succeeding 12 months. Noller increased Cash and Unearned Fee Revenue. The trucking company increased Prepaid Expenses and decreased Cash.

c. As of December 31, Noller had not recorded $500 of unpaid wages earned by her secretary during late December.

d. During November and December, Noller rendered services to another client, a utility company. She had intended to bill the company for $5,400 services through December 31, but she decided to delay formal billing until late January when the case would probably be settled.

1. For the year ended December 31, 20X8, prepare all adjustments called for by the preceding transactions. Assume that appropriate entries were routinely made for the explicit transactions described earlier. However, no adjustments have been made before December 31. For each adjustment, prepare an analysis in the same format used when the adjustment process was explained in the chapter (i.e., the balance sheet equation format). Prepare two adjustments for each transaction, one for Noller and one for the other party to the transaction. In part c, assume that the secretary uses the accrual basis for her entity.

2. For each transaction, prepare the journal entries for Jocelyn Noller and the other entities involved.

4-41 Four Major Adjustments

(Alternates are 4-38, 4-40, and 4-42). The Goodyear Tire & Rubber Company included the following items in its December 31, 2000 balance sheet ($ sheet in millions):

Prepaid expenses (a current asset)	$259.9
United States and foreign taxes (a current liability)	208.4

1. Analyze the impact of the following transactions on the financial position of Goodyear as of January 31, 2001. Prepare your analysis in the same format used when the adjustment process was explained in the chapter. Also show adjusting journal entries.

a. On January 31, an adjustment of $3 million was made for the rentals of various retail outlets that had originally increased Prepaid Expenses but had expired.

b. During December 2000, Goodyear sold tires for $2 million cash to U-Haul, but delivery was not made until January 28, 2001. Unearned Revenue had been increased in December. No other adjustments had been made since then. Prepare the adjustment on January 31.

c. Goodyear had loaned cash to several of its independent retail dealers. As of January 31, the dealers owed $5 million of interest that had been unrecorded.

d. On January 31, Goodyear increased its accrual of federal income taxes by $41 million.

2. Compute the ending balances on January 31, 2001 in prepaid expenses and in U.S. and foreign taxes.

4-42   Four Major Adjustments

(Alternates are 4-38, 4-40, and 4-41.) Alaska Airlines had the following items in its balance sheet, December 31, 1999, the end of the fiscal year ($ in millions):

Inventories and supplies	$ 44.1
Prepaid expenses and other current assets	107.5
Air traffic liability	178.6
Accrued wages, vacation, and payroll taxes	79.4

A footnote stated: "Passenger revenues are considered earned at the time service is provided. Tickets sold but not yet used are reported as Air Traffic Liability."

The 1999 income statement included ($ in millions):

Passenger revenues	$1,574.5
Wages and benefits expense	531.7

1. Analyze the impact of the following assumed 2000 transactions on the financial position of Alaska. Prepare your analysis in the same format used when the adjustment process was explained in the chapter. Also show adjusting journal entries.

   a. Rented sales offices for 1 year, beginning July 1, 2000, for $6 million cash.

   b. On December 31, 2000, an adjustment was made for the rent in requirement 1.

   c. Sold 20 charter flights to Apple Computer for $100,000 each. Cash of $2 million was received in advance on November 20, 2000. The flights were for transporting marketing personnel to business conventions.

   d. As the financial statements were being prepared on December 31, 2000, accountants for both Alaska and Apple Computer independently noted that the first 10 charter flights had occurred in December. The rest would occur in early 2001. An adjustment was made on December 31.

   e. Alaska had lent $30 million to Boeing. Interest of $1.6 was accrued on December 31.

   f. Additional wages of $30 million were accrued on December 31.

2. At year-end, in addition to liabilities for future charter flights from the preceding 1.b and 1.c, the company had $190 million of collections in advance for flights scheduled in 2001. Compute the proper year-end balance in the Air Traffic Liability account as of December 31, 2000.

4-43   Budweiser Financial Statements

(Alternate is 4-39.) Anheuser-Busch (maker of Budweiser beer) is the largest beer producer in the United States. Some actual financial data and nomenclature from its 1999 annual report were ($ in millions):

Anheuser-Busch, Incorporated

Interest expense	$ 307.8	Cash dividends declared	$ 541.7
Net sales	11,703.7	Other income	170.6
Gross profit	4,449.3	Retained earnings	
Operating income	2,302.3	Beginning of year	8,320.7
Marketing, distribution, and		End of year	9,181.2
administrative expenses	?	Provision for income taxes	
Cost of products sold	?	(income tax expense)	762.9

Required

1. Prepare a combined multiple-step statement of income and retained earnings for the year ended December 31, 1999.

2. Compute the percentage of gross profit on sales and the percentage of net income on sales.

3. The average stockholders' equity for the year was $4,069 million. What was the percentage of net income on average stockholders' equity?

4-44   Accounting for Dues

(Alternate is 4-45.) The Stone Beach Golf Club provided the following data from its comparative balance sheets:

	December 31	
	20X8	*20X7*
Dues receivable	$90,000	$75,000
Unearned dues revenue	—	$30,000

The income statement for 20X8, which was prepared on the accrual basis, showed dues revenue earned of $720,000. No dues were collected in advance during 20X8.
Prepare journal entries and post to T-accounts for the following:

1. Earning of dues collected in advance.

2. Billing of dues revenue during 20X8.

3. Collection of dues receivable in 20X8.

4-45   Accounting for Subscriptions

(Alternate is 4-44.) A French magazine company collects subscriptions in advance of delivery of its magazines. However, many magazines are delivered to magazine distributors (for newsstand sales), and these distributors are billed and pay later. The subscription revenue earned for the month of March on the accrual basis was FF200,000 (FF refers to the French franc). Other pertinent data were:

	March	
	31	*1*
Unearned subscription revenue	FF190,000	FF140,000
Accounts receivable	7,000	9,000

Required

Reconstruct the entries for March. Prepare journal entries and post to T-accounts for the following:

1. Collections of unearned subscription revenue of FF140,000 prior to March 1.

2. Billing of accounts receivable (a) of FF9,000 prior to March 1, and (b) of FF80,000 during March (Credit Revenue Earned).

3. Collections of cash during March and any other entries that are indicated by the given data.

4-46 Financial Statements and Adjustments

Marcella Wholesalers, Inc., has just completed its fourth year of business, 20X3. A set of financial statements was prepared by the principal stockholder's eldest child, a college student who is beginning the third week of an accounting course. Following is a list (in no systematic order) of the items appearing in the student's balance sheet, income statement, and statement of retained income:

Accounts receivable	$183,100	Advertising expense	$98,300
Note receivable	36,000	Cost of goods sold	590,000
Merchandise inventory	201,900	Unearned rent revenue	4,800
Cash	99,300	Insurance expense	2,500
Paid-in capital	620,000	Unexpired insurance	2,300
Building	300,000	Accounts payable	52,500
Accumulated depreciation,		Interest expense	600
building	20,000	Telephone expense	2,900
Land	169,200	Notes payable	20,000
Sales	936,800	Net income	110,500
Salary expense	124,300	Miscellaneous expense	3,400
Retained income		Maintenance expense	4,300
December 31, 20X2	164,000		
December 31, 20X3	274,500		

Assume that the statements in which these items appear are current and complete except for the following matters not taken into consideration by the student:

a. Salaries of $5,200 have been earned by employees for the last half of December 20X3. Payment by the company will be made on the next payday, January 2, 20X4.

b. Interest at 10% per annum on the note receivable has accrued for 2 months and is expected to be collected by the company when the note is due on January 31, 20X4.

c. Part of the building owned by the company was rented to a tenant on November 1, 20X3, for 6 months, payable in advance. This rent was collected in cash and is represented by the item labeled Unearned Rent Revenue.

d. Depreciation on the building for 20X3 is $6,100.

e. Cash dividends of $60,000 were declared in December 20X3, payable in January 20X4.

f. Income tax at 40% applies to 20X3, all of which is to be paid in the early part of 20X4.

Prepare the following corrected financial statements:

Required

1. Multiple-step income statement for 20X3.

2. Statement of retained income for 20X3.

3. Classified balance sheet at December 31, 20X3. (Show appropriate support for the dollar amounts you compute.)

4-47 Mirror Side of Adjustments

Problem 4-38 described some Blair adjustments. Repeat the requirement for each adjustment in transaction a as it would be made by the client in transactions b and c and by the secretary in transaction d. For our purposes here, assume that the secretary keeps personal books on the accrual basis.

4-48 Mirror Side of Adjustments

Problem 4-41 described some Goodyear adjustments. Repeat the requirements for each adjustment as it would be made by (a) landlords, (b) U-Haul, (c) retail dealers, and (d) U.S. and foreign governments. Assume that all use accrual accounting.

4-49 Mirror Side of Adjustments

Problem 4-42 described some Alaska Airlines adjustments lettered a through f. Repeat the requirements for each adjustment as it would be made by the other party in the transaction. Specifically, (a) and (b) landlord, (c) and (d) Apple Computer, (e) Boeing, and (f) employees. Assume that all use accrual accounting.

4-50 Journal Entries and Posting

Nike, Inc., has many well-known products, including footwear. The company's balance sheet included ($ in millions):

	May 31	
	1999	*1998*
Prepaid expenses	190.9	196.2
Income taxes payable	—	28.9

Suppose that during the fiscal year ended May 31, 1999, $210,000,000 cash was disbursed and charged to Prepaid Expenses. Similarly, $325,000,000 was disbursed for income taxes and charged to Income Taxes Payable.

Required

1. Assume that the Prepaid Expenses account relates to outlays for miscellaneous operating expenses, for example, supplies, insurance, and short-term rentals. Prepare summary journal entries for (a) the disbursements and (b) the expenses for fiscal 1999.
2. Assume that there were no other accounts related to income taxes. Prepare summary journal entries for (a) the disbursements and (b) the expenses for fiscal 1999.

4-51 Advance Service Contracts

Diebold, Incorporated, a manufacturer of automated teller machines (ATMs), showed the following balance sheet accounts on December 31, 2000 ($ amounts in thousands):

	December 31	
	2000	*1999*
Deferred income	$59,242	$88,319

Required

A footnote to the financial statements stated: "Deferred income is recognized for customer service billings in advance of the period in which the service will be performed and is recognized in income on a straight-line basis over the contract period."

1. Prepare summary journal entries for the creation in 1999 and subsequent earning in 2000 of the deferred income of $88,319,000. Use the following accounts: Accounts Receivable, Deferred Income, and Income from Advance Billings.
2. A 1-year job contract was billed to Keystone Bank on January 1, 2000, for $36,000. Work began on January 2. The full amount was collected on February 15. Prepare all pertinent journal entries through February 28, 2000. ("Straight-line" means an equal amount per month.)

4-52 Journal Entries and Adjustments

Xcel Energy, Inc. is a public utility in Minnesota. An annual report included the following footnote:
Revenues—We estimate and record unbilled revenues from the monthly meter-reading dates to month's end.

The income statements showed ($ in thousands):

	2000	**1999**
Operating revenues	$11,591,796	$7,895,543
Operating income	1,571,140	1,201,896

The balance sheet showed as part of current assets ($ in thousands):

	December 31	
	2000	*1999*
Accounts receivable	$1,289,724	$800,066
Accrued unbilled revenues	683,266	410,798

Prepare the adjusting journal entry for (a) the unbilled revenues at the end of 2000 and (b) the eventual billing and collection of the unbilled revenues. Ignore income taxes.

Required

4-53 Classified Balance Sheet and Current Ratio

Intel is the world's leading producer of microprocessors. The company's balance sheet for December 25, 1999 contained the following items ($ in millions):

Property and equipment, net	$11,715
Accrued compensation and benefits	1,454
Cash	3,695
Other assets	14,315
Other noncurrent liabilities	3,260
Short-term debt	230
Inventories	1,478
Other current liabilities	2,350
Income taxes payable	1,695
Other current assets	1,241
Accounts payable	1,370
Short-term investments	7,705
Accounts receivable	3,700
Long-term debt	?
Stockholders' equity	32,535

Required

1. Prepare a December 25, 1999 classified balance sheet for Intel. Include the correct amount for long-term debt.

2. Compute the company's working capital and current ratio.

3. Comment on the company's current ratio. In 1995, the ratio was 2.2.

4. During 1999, Intel increased its short-term investments by $2,433,000. Suppose the company had not increased its short-term investments but had instead increased its long-term investments by $2,433,000. How would this have affected Intel's current ratio? How would it have affected the company's solvency?

4-54 Multiple-Step Income Statement

Kimberly-Clark Corporation has many well-known products, including Kleenex and Huggies. Its 2000 annual report contained the following data and actual terms ($ in millions):

Cost of products sold	$8,228	Advertising, promotion,	
Research expense	277	and selling expense	$2,123
Interest expense	222	Provision for income taxes	
Interest and other income	24	(income tax expense)	758
Gross profit	5,753	General and other expense	720

Prepare a multiple-step statement of income.

Required

4-55 Single-Step Income Statement

A. T. Cross Company's best-known products are writing instruments such as ballpoint pens. A recent Cross annual report contained the following items ($ in thousands) for the year ending December 31:

Interest and other income	$ 2,091	Selling, general, and	
Cost of goods sold	94,093	administrative expenses	$ 70,627
		Other expenses	7,196
Provision for income taxes		Retained earnings at end	
(income tax expense)	2,772	of year	106,781
Sales	179,203	Cash dividends	10,568

1. Prepare a combined single-step statement of income and retained earnings for the year.
2. Compute the percentage of gross profit on sales and the percentage of net income on sales.
3. The average stockholders' equity for the year was about $129 million. What was the percentage of net income on average stockholders' equity?
4. Four years earlier the gross profit percentage was 47.0%, the percentage of net income to sales was 5.8%, and the return on average stockholders' equity was 6.9%. Comment on the changes over the 4 years.

4-56 Retail Company Financial Statements

Kmart Corporation is one of the world's largest retailers. The annual report for the year ended January 26, 2000 included the data shown below ($ in millions). Unless otherwise specified, the balance sheet amounts are the balances as of January 26, 2000.

Sales	$35,925	Interest expense	$ 280
Cash dividends	0	Long-term debt	1,759
Merchandise inventories	7,101	Cash	344
Cost of sales, buying,		Selling, general, and administrative	
and occupancy	28,102	expenses	6,523
Paid-in capital	2,036	Accrued payroll and other current	
Other expenses	280	liabilities	1,574
Retained earnings		Other current assets	715
Beginning of year	3,878	Provision for income taxes	337
End of year	4,281	Property and equipment, net	6,410
Accounts payable	2,204	Other noncurrent assets	534
		Other noncurrent liabilities	2,952
		Accrued taxes payable	298

1. Prepare a combined multiple-step statement of income and retained earnings.
2. Prepare a classified balance sheet.
3. The average stockholders' equity for the year was about $6,148 million. What was the percentage of net income (loss) on average stockholders' equity?
4. Compute (a) gross profit percentage and (b) percentage of net income to sales.

4-57 Preparation of Financial Statements from Trial Balance

ConAgra, the Omaha company that produces consumer foods such as Armour and Swift meats, Banquet and Morton frozen foods, and Healthy Choice brands, prepared the following (slightly modified) trial balance as of May 30, 1999, the end of the company's fiscal year:

ConAgra, Inc.
Trial Balance May 30, 1999 ($ in millions)

	Debits	Credits
Cash and cash equivalents	$ 62.8	
Receivables	1,637.5	
Inventories	3,639.9	
Prepaid expenses	315.9	
Property, plant, and equipment, at cost	6,213.8	
Accumulated depreciation, property, plant, and equipment		$2,599.6
Brands, trademarks, and goodwill, net	$2,408.7	
Other assets	467.1	
Notes payable		837.9
Accounts payable		2,036.5
Accrued payroll		269.4
Advances on sales (deferred revenues)		1,191.7

(continued)

Other current liabilities		1,050.9
Long-term debt		2,543.1
Other noncurrent liabilities		782.8
Preferred stock		525.0
Common stock, $5 par value		2,598.2
Retained earnings (May 30, 1998)		1,337.5
Additional paid-in capital		219.4
Treasury stock*	1,278.6	
Net sales		24,594.3
Cost of goods sold	20,556.2	
Selling, administrative, and general expenses	2,598.4	
Interest expense	316.6	
Nonrecurring charges	440.8	
Income taxes	323.9	
Cash dividends	326.1	
Total	$40,586.3	$40,586.3

*Part of stockholders' equity.

Required

1. Prepare ConAgra's income statement for the year ended May 30, 1999, using a multiple-step format.
2. Prepare ConAgra's income statement for the year ended May 30, 1999, using a single-step format. Which format for the income statement is more informative? Why?
3. Prepare ConAgra's classified balance sheet as of May 30, 1999.

4-58 Professional Football Income

Examine the accompanying condensed income statement of the Green Bay Packers, Inc.

Income		
Regular season		
Net receipts from home games	$ 3,223,803	
Out-of-town games	2,288,967	
Television and radio programs	14,322,244	$19,835,014
Preseason		
Net receipts from preseason games	1,356,751	
Television and radio programs	355,032	1,711,783
Miscellaneous		
Club allocation of league receipts	784,988	
Other income	511,516	1,296,504
Total income		22,843,301
Expenses		
Salaries and other season expenses	16,243,729	
Training expense	725,079	
Overhead expense	4,744,336	
Severance pay	656,250	22,369,394
Income from operations		473,907
Interest income		1,203,281
Income before taxes		1,677,188
Provision for income taxes		167,000
Net income		$ 1,510,188

Required

1. Do you agree with the choice of terms in this statement? If not, suggest where a preferable label should be used.
2. Is this a single-step income statement? If not, which items would you shift to prepare a single-step statement?
3. Identify the major factors that affect the Packers' net income.

4-59　Adjusting Entries and Ethics

By definition, adjusting entries are not triggered by an explicit event. Therefore, accountants must initiate adjusting entries. For each of the following adjusting entries, discuss a potential unethical behavior that an accountant or manager might undertake:

    a.　Recognition of expenses from the prepaid supplies account.

    b.　Recognition of revenue from the unearned revenue account.

    c.　Accrual of interest payable.

    d.　Accrual of fees receivable.

ANNUAL REPORT CASE

4-60　Cisco Annual Report

This problem uses an actual company's accounts to develop skill in preparing adjusting journal entries. Refer to the financial statements of Cisco (appendix A at the end of the book). Note the following balance sheet items ($ in millions):

	July 29, 2000	July 31, 1999
Prepaid expenses and other current assets	$ 963	$ 171
Other accrued liabilities	1,521	631

Suppose that during the year ended July 29, 2000, $1,200,000,000 cash was disbursed and charged to Prepaid Expenses and $1,600,000,000 of accrued liabilities were paid.

    1.　Assume that the Prepaid Expenses account relates to outlays for miscellaneous Operating Expenses, for example, supplies, insurance, and short-term rentals. Prepare summary journal entries for (a) the disbursements and (b) the expenses (for our purposes, debit Operating Expenses) for the year ended July 29, 2000. Post the entries to the T-accounts.

    2.　Prepare summary journal entries for (a) the disbursements and (b) the expenses related to the accrued liabilities for the year ended July 29, 2000. (For our purposes, debit Operating Expenses.) Post the entries to the T-accounts.

4-61　Financial Statement Research

Select any two companies.

    1.　For each company, determine the amount of working capital and the current ratio.

    2.　Compare the current ratios. Which company has the larger ratio, and what do the ratios tell you about the solvency of the companies?

    3.　Compute the gross margin percentage, the return on sales, and the return on stockholders' equity.

    4.　Compare the profitability of the two companies.

COLLABORATIVE LEARNING EXERCISE

4-62　Implicit Transactions

Form groups of from three to six "players." Each group should have a die and a paper (or board) with four columns labeled:

    1.　Expiration of unexpired costs.

    2.　Realization of unearned revenues.

    3.　Accrual of unrecorded expenses.

    4.　Accrual of unrecorded revenues.

The players should select an order in which they wish to play. Then, the first player rolls the die. If this player rolls a 5 or 6, the die passes to the next player. If the second player rolls a 1, 2, 3, or 4, this person must, within 20 seconds, name an example of a transaction that fits in the corresponding category; for example, if a 2 is rolled, the player must give an example of realization of unearned revenues. Each time a correct example is given, the player receives one point. If someone doubts the correctness of a given example, the player can challenge it. If the remaining players unanimously agree that the example is incorrect, the challenger gets a point and the player giving the example does not get a point for a correct example and is out of the game. If the remaining players do not unanimously agree that the answer is incorrect, the challenger loses a point and the player giving the example gets a point for a correct example. If a player fails to give an example within the time limit or gives an incorrect example, this person is out of the game (except for voting when an example is challenged), and the remaining players continue until everyone has failed to give a correct example within the time limit. Each correct answer should be listed under the appropriate column. The player with the most points is the group winner.

When all groups have finished a round of play, a second level of play can begin. All the groups can get together and list all the examples for each of the four categories by group. Discussion can establish the correctness of each entry; the faculty member or an appointed discussion leader will be the final arbitrator of the correctness of each entry. Each group gets one point for each correct example and loses one point for each incorrect entry. The group with the most points is the overall winner.

Internet Exercise

4-63   Internet Case
Go to http://www.landsend.com/cd/frontdoor/ to find Lands' End's home page. Select *Investor's corner* then *Annual reports* from the menus, and click on the most recent annual report.

www.prenhall.com/horngren

Answer the following questions:

1. Name two items on Lands' End's balance sheet that most likely represent unexpired (prepaid) costs. Name two items that most likely represent accruals of unrecorded expenses.

2. Does Lands' End prepare a single- or multi-step income statement? How can you tell?

3. Determine Lands' End's gross profit percentage for the past 2 years. Is the change favorable or not? What does Lands' End management have to say about the change? (*Hint:* Look in *Management's Discussion and Analysis.*) If nothing was said, why do you think management chose not to comment? How do you think management determines the reason that gross profit changed, given the condensed nature of the income statement?

4. Calculate Lands' End's current ratio for the past 2 years. Did this ratio improve or decline? Does management offer any comment about any particular problems that could have affected this ratio? (*Hint:* Look in the *Shareholders' Letter.*) Should management be concerned about changes in the current ratio?

5. Where can you find evidence in Lands' End's annual report that the financial statements were prepared using GAAP?

6. Explain how Lands' End's financial statements illustrate one of the basic concepts or principles found in this chapter of the text.

Go to the "Alternate Income Statement Formats and Extraordinary Items" and "Generally Accepted Accounting Principles and Audited Financial Statements" episodes on the *Mastering Accounting* CD-ROM for interactive, video-enhanced exercises that focus on CanGo's need to consider the different income statement formats and their effect on investors and CanGo's need for standardized accounting reports to prepare for an IPO and attract investors to fund new business projects.

5

ACCOUNTING FOR SALES

Oracle supplies the software that powers the Internet. All ten of the world's largest Web sites including Amazon and Yahoo and 98% of the Fortune 100 use Oracle.

www.prenhall.com/horngren

Learning Objectives

After studying this chapter, you should be able to

1. Recognize revenue items at the proper time on the income statement.

2. Account for cash and credit sales.

3. Record sales returns and allowances, sales discounts, and bank credit card sales.

4. Manage cash and explain its importance to the company.

5. Estimate and interpret uncollectible accounts receivable balances.

6. Assess the level of accounts receivable.

7. Develop and explain internal control procedures.

Not many companies seek the permission of the CIA when naming products. Yet that is precisely what System Development Laboratories did in 1977 when it created a new type of database. Called the "Oracle," this new relational database structure proved to be the world's most popular form, and for the company, now called Oracle Corporation, it was an explosive sales success story. Revenues for its most recent fiscal year-end topped $10 billion dollars for software sales worldwide.

Recording and managing this sales revenue is important to Oracle's success. For every sale generated, the company must either collect cash or record an accounts receivable from the customer. The accounts receivable must then be collected so that the company has adequate cash to continue its operations. On average it took Oracle 77 days to convert customer accounts to cash. This places Oracle below the average for its industry, 50 days, and the average for the Standard & Poors (S&P) 500 companies of 41 days.

Managing accounts receivable and collecting cash is a key activity for Oracle. The faster the company collects the cash, the more use of it the firm will have and the less it will need to borrow (and the less interest it will pay). Good accounts receivable management also plays other vital roles for the company. For example, at quarter-end and year-end, Oracle must report its financial results to the investment community. Recording sales revenue in the right time period is essential if Oracle is to follow the matching principle for sales and expenses on the income statement. There is a balance sheet effect too. The cash and receivables associated with sales revenue show up as current assets, and if not properly recorded, they will distort Oracle's financial position. Investors use this information to make stock purchase decisions, and what Oracle reports affects the price of its stock. For Oracle, whose very company name means "source of wisdom," efficient and accurate accounts receivable activity is smart business.

Would you like to invest in a stock whose price increases 54-fold in just 10 years? Anyone who bought Intel's stock in 1990 already has. Intel stock purchased for $100 in March of 1990 sold for about $5,400 in March of 2000.

If you had been able to read and understand Intel's financial statements in 1990, could you have predicted this large increase in stock price? Unfortunately, you probably could not. You also could not have predicted in March of 2000 that by January of 2001 your $5,400 investment would have collapsed to $2,300. If understanding financial statements were sufficient for making good investment decisions, there would be a lot of rich accountants in this world. However, looking at Intel's financial statement from 1990 through 2000 helps explain why the company did so well over that period. Understanding what made Intel successful helps you predict whether that success will continue.

Intel's revenues increased from $3.9 billion in 1990 to $33.7 billion in 2000, a rate of growth of more than 21% per year. Meanwhile, earnings per share grew from $.10 to $1.51. This growth in earnings per share is even more rapid than the revenue growth, nearly 28% per year. To support this growth in sales and earnings, Intel continued to invest heavily, spending over $3.9 billion in 2000 on research and development (R&D) in addition to another $2.4 billion on plant, property, and equipment.

Will Intel continue to be this successful? No one knows for sure, but there are some clues in the company's 2000 balance sheet. One clue is that Intel has nearly $14 billion in cash. That much cash can help Intel fund its expansion plans, or it can provide a shot in the arm in case sales drop. The microprocessor industry is cyclical, which means that sales throughout the industry rise and fall. Sales, of course, are the driving force behind any company's success. If Intel's sales remain strong, the company will continue to be successful. Even if the industry stumbles and Intel's sales fall, $14 billion makes a nice cushion.

RECOGNITION OF SALES REVENUE

Objective 1
Recognize revenue items at the proper time on the income statement.

Why is the timing of revenue recognition so important? It is critical to the measurement of net income. Revenue recognition affects net income in two ways. First, it directly affects net income because it is one element of the calculation net income = revenue − expense. Second, it indirectly affects net income because it determines when a company recognizes certain expenses. Under the matching principle, a company reports the cost of the items sold in the same period in which it recognizes the related revenue.

The timing of changes in sales and net income might not seem so important until you realize that these changes affect stock prices. Moreover, managers often receive higher salaries or greater bonuses for increasing sales and net income. Therefore, they prefer to recognize sales revenue as soon as possible. Owners and potential investors, however, want to be sure the economic benefits of the sale are guaranteed before recognizing revenue. In other words, financial statement users want to be sure that the company actually will receive payment before they recognize the accounting effects of a completed sale. Because of these different perspectives, accountants must carefully assess when revenue should be recognized.

A key feature of accrual-basis accounting is that recognition of revenue requires a two-pronged test: (1) goods or services must be delivered to the customers, that is, the revenue is earned; and (2) cash or an asset virtually assured of being converted into cash must be received, that is, the revenue is realized. Most revenue is recognized at the point of sale. Suppose you buy a compact disc at a local music store. Both revenue recognition tests are generally met at the time of purchase. You receive the merchandise, and the store receives cash, a check, or a credit card slip. Because both checks and credit card slips are readily converted to cash, the store can recognize revenue at the point of sale regardless of which of these three methods of payment you use.

Of course, the two revenue recognition tests are not always met at the same time. In such cases, revenue is generally recognized only when both tests are met. Consider magazine subscriptions. The realization test is met when the publisher receives cash. However, revenues are not earned until magazines are delivered. Therefore, revenue recognition is delayed until the time of delivery.

Sometimes accountants must make a judgment call on when the recognition criteria are met. A classic example is accounting for long-term contracts. Suppose Lockheed Martin Corporation signs a $40 million contract with the U.S. government to produce a part for the space shuttle. The contract is signed, and work begins on January 2, 20X1. The completion date is December 31, 20X4. Payment is to be made on delivery of the part. Lockheed Martin expects to complete one-fourth of the project each year. When should the $40 million of revenue be recorded on the company's income statement?

The most common answer is that one-fourth of the revenue is earned each year, so $10 million of the revenue should be recognized annually. Generally, the government and major corporations can be counted on to make payments on their contracts. Therefore, revenues on such contracts are recognized as the work is performed. Because payment is virtually certain, revenues can be realized as they are gradually earned. This is called the **percentage-of-completion method** for recognizing revenue on long-term contracts. Once the decision is made to recognize the revenue as production occurs, the matching principle requires that corresponding recognition be given to the associated expenses. When one-quarter of the revenue is recognized, one-quarter of the expected expenses are recorded as well.

percentage-of-completion method Method of recognizing revenue on long-term contracts as production occurs.

MEASUREMENT OF SALES REVENUE

After deciding when revenue is to be recognized, the accountant must determine how much revenue to record. In other words, how should accountants measure revenue?

A cash sale increases Sales Revenue, an income statement account, and increases Cash, a balance sheet account. A credit sale on open account is recorded much like a cash sale except that the balance sheet account Accounts Receivable is increased instead of Cash. To measure revenue, accountants approximate the net realizable value of the asset inflow from the customer. That is, the revenue is measured in terms of the cash equivalent value of the asset (either cash or accounts receivable) received.

Objective 2
Account for cash and credit sales.

Revenue is recorded equal to the asset received:

Cash	XXX	
Sales revenue		XXX
OR		
Accounts receivable	XXX	
Sales revenue		XXX

In fact, there are many ways in which prices are not what they appear to be and ultimately the revenue earned may not be equal to the original sales price. Merchants give discounts for prompt payment, or discounts for high-volume purchases. Sometimes, the customer is unable or unwilling to pay the full amount owed. The accounting system must deal with all these issues, and the manager must have information to determine how company policy is affecting its relationship with the customer.

MERCHANDISE RETURNS AND ALLOWANCES

Objective 3
Record sales returns and allowances, sales discounts, and bank credit card sales.

sales returns (purchase returns) Products returned by the customer.

sales allowance (purchase allowance) Reduction of the original selling price.

gross sales Total sales revenue before deducting sales returns and allowances.

net sales Total sales revenue reduced by sales returns and allowances.

Suppose revenue for a given sale is recognized at the point of that sale, but later the customer decides to return the merchandise. The purchaser may be unhappy with the product's color, size, style, or quality, or simply may have a change of heart. The supplier (vendor) calls these **sales returns;** the customer calls them **purchase returns.** Such merchandise returns are minor for manufacturers and wholesalers but are major for retail department stores. For instance, returns of 12% of gross sales are not abnormal for stores such as Marshall Field's or Macy's.

Sometimes, instead of returning merchandise, the customer demands a reduction of the selling price (the original price previously agreed to). For example, a customer may complain about finding scratches on a household appliance or about buying a cordless phone for $40 on Wednesday and seeing the same item for sale in the same store or elsewhere for $35 on Thursday. Such complaints are often settled by the seller's granting a **sales allowance** (the purchaser calls this a **purchase allowance**), which is essentially a reduction of the original selling price.

Naturally, sales allowances and returns are going to have an effect on net sales, but not on gross sales. **Gross sales** are equal to the initial revenues or asset inflows based on the sales price, and they must be decreased by the amount of the returns and allowances to give the **net sales.** Instead of directly reducing the revenue (or sales) account, managers of retail stores typically use a contra account, Sales Returns and Allowances, which combines both returns and allowances in a single account. Managers use a contra account so they can watch changes in the level of returns and allowances. For instance, a change in the percentage of returns in fashion merchandise may give early signals about changes in customer tastes. Similarly, a seller of fashion or fad merchandise may want to keep track of sales returns to help assess the quality of products and services of various suppliers. Also, it is useful to track sales and returns separately so that sales figures for commissions or bonuses are properly interpreted. Another reason managers use separate accounts for sales and returns is that the returns happen after the sales, and separate tracking avoids going back and changing the original entries for the sale, a messy and unreliable process. Let us take a look at how a retailer might adjust gross sales by accounting for sales returns and allowances. Suppose your local outlet of The Disney Store has $900,000 gross sales on credit and $80,000 sales returns and allowances. The analysis of transactions would show:

	A	=	L +	SE
Credit sales on open account	+900,000 Increase Accounts Receivable	=		+900,000 Increase Sales
Returns and allowances	−80,000 Decrease Accounts Receivable	=		−80,000 Increase Sales Returns and Allowances

The journal entries (without explanations) are:

Accounts receivable	900,000	
Sales		900,000
Sales returns and allowances	80,000	
Accounts receivable		80,000

The income statement would begin:

Gross sales	$900,000
Deduct: Sales returns and allowances	80,000
Net sales	$820,000
or	
Sales, net of $80,000 returns and allowances	$820,000

Returns and allowances are not the only factors that affect gross and net sales figures. Discounts also affect the reported sales. There are two major types of sales discounts: trade and cash. **Trade discounts** offer one or more reductions to the gross selling price for a particular class of customers. These discounts are generally price concessions or purchase incentives. An example is a discount for large-volume purchases. The seller might offer no discount on the first $10,000 of merchandise purchased per year but a 2% discount on the next $10,000 worth of purchases and a discount of 3% to a customer on all sales in excess of $20,000. The gross sales revenue recognized from a trade discount sale is the price received after deducting the discount.

trade discounts
Reductions to the gross selling price for a particular class of customers.

Companies set trade discount terms for various reasons. If such discounts are offered by competing firms, the seller may offer trade discounts to be competitive. Discounts may also be used to encourage certain customer behavior. For example, manufacturers with seasonal products (gardening supplies, snow shovels, fans, Christmas gifts, and so on) might offer price discounts on early orders and deliveries to smooth out production throughout the year and minimize the manufacturer's cost of storing the inventory. In deciding to accept early delivery, the buyer must weigh the storage costs it will incur against the reduced price the discount provides.

In contrast to trade discounts, **cash discounts** are rewards for prompt payment. The terms of the discount may be quoted in various ways on the invoice:

cash discounts
Reductions of invoice prices awarded for prompt payment.

Credit Terms	Meaning
n/30	The full billed price (net price) is due on the thirtieth day after the invoice date
1/5, n/30	A 1% discount can be taken for payment within 5 days of the invoice date; otherwise the full billed price is due in 30 days
15 E.O.M.	The full price is due within 15 days after the end-of-the-month of sale; an invoice dated December 20 is due January 15

For example, a manufacturer sells $30,000 of computer games to Toys "Я" Us, a retailer, on terms 2/10, n/60. Therefore, Toys "Я" Us may remit $30,000 less a cash discount of 0.02 × $30,000, or $30,000 − $600 = $29,400, if payment is made within 10 days after the invoice date. Otherwise the full $30,000 is due in 60 days.

Cash discounts entice prompt payment and reduce the manufacturer's need for cash. Early collection also reduces the risk of bad debts. Favorable credit terms with attractive cash discounts are also a way to compete with other sellers. Of course, once one seller grants such terms, competitors tend to do likewise.

Should purchasers take cash discounts? The answer is usually yes, but the decision depends on the relative costs of interest. Suppose Toys "Я" Us decides not to pay the $30,000 invoice for 60 days. It has the use of $29,400 for an extra 50 days (60 − 10) for an "interest" payment of $600. Think of this as if Toys "Я" Us had two choices. They could borrow the money from the bank and pay 10% interest per year. Interest for 50 days on $29,400 would be $403 ($29,400 × 10% × 50 ÷ 365). Alternatively, they could delay payment for 50 days and pay the higher invoice price. Notice that it is much cheaper to borrow the money, and that is what most companies should do. The total invoice is $600 higher than the discount price and the interest is only $403.

You could also calculate the annual interest rate equivalent of the discount using the following logic. If you pay $600 to use the money for 50 days, you are paying 2.04% for the 50 days ($600 ÷ $29,400). During a year there are 7.3 periods of 50 days (365 ÷ 50 days). If the interest rate is 2.04% for 50 days, it will be 14.9% for the year (2.04% per period × 7.3 periods per year). Most well-managed companies, such as Toys "Я" Us, can obtain funds for less than 14.9% interest per year, so their accounting systems are designed to take advantage of all cash discounts automatically. However, some retailers pass up the discounts. Why? Because they have trouble getting loans or other financing at interest rates lower than the annual rates implied by the cash discount terms offered by their suppliers. Usage of cash discounts varies through time and from one industry to another. You may be familiar with some gas stations that offer a lower price for cash payment, while other stations do not.

RECORDING CHARGE CARD TRANSACTIONS

Cash discounts also occur when retailers accept charge cards such as VISA, MasterCard, American Express, Carte Blanche, or Diner's Club. Retailers accept these cards for three major reasons: (1) to attract credit customers who would otherwise shop elsewhere, (2) to get cash immediately instead of waiting for customers to pay in due course, and (3) to avoid the cost of keeping track of many customers' accounts.

Retailers can deposit VISA slips in their bank accounts daily (just like cash). However, this service costs money (in the form of service charges on every credit sale), and this cost must be included in the calculations to determine net sales revenue. Card companies impose a service charge for card sales of anywhere from 1% to 3% of gross sales, although large-volume retailers bear less cost as a percentage of sales. For example, JCPenney had an arrangement where it accepted charge cards other than its own branded card. It paid 4.3 cents per transaction plus only 1.08% of the gross sales using charge cards.

With the 3% rate, credit sales of $10,000 will result in cash of only $10,000 − (0.03 × $10,000), or $10,000 − $300, or $9,700. The $300 amount may be separately tabulated for management control purposes:

	A	=	L	+	SE
Sales using VISA $\begin{bmatrix}\text{Increase}\\\text{Cash}\end{bmatrix}$	+9,700	=			+10,000 $\begin{bmatrix}\text{Increase}\\\text{Sales}\end{bmatrix}$ −300 $\begin{bmatrix}\text{Increase}\\\text{Cash Discounts}\\\text{for Bank Cards}\end{bmatrix}$

Cash	9,700	
Cash discounts for bank cards	300	
Sales		10,000

ACCOUNTING FOR NET SALES REVENUE

Cash discounts and sales returns and allowances are recorded as deductions from Gross Sales. Consequently, a detailed income statement often contains:

Gross sales		xxx
Deduct		
Sales returns and allowances	x	
Cash discounts on sales	<u>x</u>	<u>xx</u>
Net sales		<u><u>xxx</u></u>

Reports to shareholders often omit details and show only net revenues. For example, when Nike shows "Revenues . . . $8,777 million" on its income statement, the number refers to its net revenues. Note also that in many countries outside the United States, the word **turnover** is used as a synonym for sales or revenues. Thus, BP Amoco began its income statement with "Group Turnover . . . £148,062 million."

turnover A synonym for sales or revenues in many countries outside the United States.

An important feature of the income statement is the fact that returns, allowances, and most discounts are offsets to gross sales. Management may design an accounting system to use one account, Sales, or several accounts, as shown in the preceding sample income statement. If only one account is used, all returns, allowances, and cash discounts are direct decreases to the sales account. If a separate account is used for cash discounts on sales, the following analysis would be made for our Toys "Я" Us example:

	A	= L +	SE
1. Sell at terms of 2/10, n/60	+30,000 [Increase Accounts Receivable]	=	+30,000 [Increase Sales]
Followed by either 2 or 3			
2. Either collect $29,400 ($30,000 less 2%)	+29,400 [Increase Cash]	=	−600 [Increase Cash Discounts on Sales]
	−30,000 [Decrease Accounts Receivable]		
or			
3. Collect $30,000	+30,000 [Increase Cash]	=	(No effect)
	−30,000 [Decrease Accounts Receivable]		

The journal entries follow:

1.	Accounts receivable	30,000	
	Sales		30,000
2.	Cash...	29,400	
	Cash discounts on sales	600	
	Accounts receivable		30,000
	OR		
3.	Cash	30,000	
	Accounts receivable		30,000

CASH

Objective 4
Manage cash and explain its importance to the company.

cash equivalents Highly liquid short-term investments that can easily be converted into cash.

Many companies combine cash and cash equivalents on their balance sheets. **Cash equivalents** are highly liquid short-term investments that can easily and quickly be converted into cash. For example, the 2000 balance sheet of AOL Time Warner begins with "Cash and cash equivalents . . . $2,610 million." AOL describes its cash equivalents as ". . . highly liquid investments with a maturity of 3 months or less."

Cash has essentially the same meaning to organizations that it does to individuals. It is not just paper money and coins, though. Instead, cash encompasses all the items that are accepted for deposit by a bank, notably paper money and coins, money orders, and checks. Banks do not accept postage stamps, IOUs, or postdated checks as cash. Of course, not all the items a bank does accept for deposit are treated the same. For example, although all deposits may be credited to the accounts of bank customers on the date received, the bank may not provide the depositor with access to the funds from a deposited check until the check "clears" through the banking system (until payment is actually made from the check writer's account). If the check fails to clear because its writer has insufficient funds, its amount is deducted from the depositor's account.

COMPENSATING BALANCES

compensating balances Required minimum cash balances on deposit when money is borrowed from banks.

There are other reasons that the entire cash balance in a bank account may not be available for unrestricted use. Banks frequently require companies to maintain **compensating balances,** which are required minimum balances on deposit to compensate the bank for providing loans. The size of the minimum balance may depend on the amount borrowed, the amount of credit available, or both.

Compensating balances increase the effective interest rate paid by the borrower. When borrowing $100,000 at 10% per year, annual interest will be $10,000. With a 10% compensating balance, the borrower can use only $90,000 of the loan, raising the effective interest rate on the usable funds to 11.1% ($10,000 ÷ $90,000).

To prevent any misleading information concerning cash, annual reports must disclose the state of any significant compensating balances. For example, a footnote in the annual report of North Carolina Natural Gas Corporation disclosed a requirement for keeping a compensating balance "of 10% of the annual average loan outstanding" in its bank account. Without such a disclosure, financial statement readers might think that a company has more cash available than it really does.

MANAGEMENT OF CASH

reconcile a bank statement To verify that the bank balance for cash is consistent with the accounting records.

Cash is usually a small portion of the total assets of a company. Yet, managers spend much time managing cash. Why? For many reasons. First, although the cash balance may be small at any one time, the flow of cash can be enormous. Weekly receipts and disbursements of cash may be many times as large as the cash balance. Second, because cash is the most liquid asset, it is enticing to thieves and embezzlers. If companies do not watch their cash, someone might walk off with it. Third, adequate cash is essential to the smooth functioning of operations. Companies need it for everything from routine purchases to major investments, from purchasing lunch for a visiting business partner to purchasing another company. Finally, because cash itself does not earn income, it is important not to hold excess cash. The treasury department is responsible for managing the levels of cash efficiently and for assuring that unneeded cash is deposited in income generating accounts.

Most organizations have detailed, well-specified procedures for receiving, recording, and disbursing cash. It is usually placed in a bank account, and the company's books are periodically reconciled with the bank's records. To **reconcile a bank statement** means to verify that the bank balance and the accounting records are consistent. The two balances are rarely identical. A company accountant records a deposit when made and a payment when the check is written. The bank, however, may receive or record the deposit several days after the accountant recorded it because of postal delay, deposit on a bank holiday or weekend, and so on. The bank typically receives and processes a check days, weeks, or even months after it was issued.

The major internal control procedures set up to safeguard cash include the following:

1. The individuals who receive cash do not also disburse cash.
2. The individuals who handle cash cannot access accounting records.
3. Cash receipts are immediately recorded and deposited and are not used directly to make payments.
4. Disbursements are made by serially numbered checks, only with proper authorization by someone other than the person writing the check.
5. Bank accounts are reconciled monthly.

Why are such internal controls necessary? Consider a person who handles cash and makes entries into the accounting records. That person could take cash and cover it up by making the following entry in the books:

Operating expenses	xxx	
Cash		xxx

Besides guarding against dishonest actions, the listed procedures help ensure accurate accounting records. For example, suppose a check is written but not recorded in the books. Without serially numbered checks, there would be no way of discovering the error before receiving a bank statement showing that the check was paid. However, if checks are numbered, an unrecorded check can be identified, and such errors can be discovered early.

CREDIT SALES AND ACCOUNTS RECEIVABLE

Credit sales on open account increase **accounts receivable,** which are amounts owed to the company by its customers as a result of delivering goods or services. Accounts receivable, sometimes called **trade receivables** or simply **receivables,** arise when the company grants credit to its customer on an ongoing basis. This means the company agrees to accept payment in the future for goods or services delivered today.

accounts receivable (trade receivables, receivables) Amounts owed to a company by customers as a result of delivering goods or services and extending credit in the ordinary course of business.

UNCOLLECTIBLE ACCOUNTS

Granting credit entails costs and benefits. The main benefit is the boost in sales and profit that would otherwise be lost if credit were not extended. Many potential customers would not buy if credit were unavailable or they would buy from a competitor that offered credit. One cost is administration and collection of the credit amount. Another cost is the delay in receiving payment. The seller must finance its activities in other ways while awaiting payment. Perhaps the most significant cost is **uncollectible accounts** or **bad debts**—receivables that some credit customers are either unable or unwilling to pay. Accountants often label this major cost of granting credit that arises from uncollectible accounts as **bad debts expense.**

uncollectible accounts (bad debts) Receivables determined to be uncollectible because debtors are unable or unwilling to pay their debts.

The extent of nonpayment of debts varies. It often depends on the credit risks that managers are willing to accept. For instance, many smaller, local establishments, will accept a higher level of risk than will larger, national stores, such as Sears. The small stores know their customers personally. The extent of a nonpayment can also depend on the industry. For example, the problem of uncollectible accounts is especially difficult in the health-care field. The Bayfront Medical Center of St. Petersburg, Florida, suffered bad debts equal to 21% of gross revenue.

bad debts expense The cost of granting credit that arises from uncollectible accounts.

DECIDING WHEN AND HOW TO GRANT CREDIT

Competition and industry practice affect whether and how companies offer credit, and the final decision is based on cost-benefit trade-offs. In other words, companies offer credit only when the additional earnings on credit sales exceed the costs of offering credit. Suppose 5% of credit sales are bad debts, administrative costs of a credit department are $5,000 per year, and $20,000 of credit sales (with earnings of $8,000 before credit costs) are achieved. Assume that none of the credit sales would have been made without granting credit. Offering credit is worthwhile because the earnings of $8,000 exceeds the credit costs of $6,000 [(5% × $20,000) + $5,000].

MEASUREMENT OF UNCOLLECTIBLE ACCOUNTS

Objective 5
Estimate and interpret uncollectible accounts receivable balances.

Uncollectible accounts require special accounting procedures and thus deserve special attention here. Consider an example. Suppose Compuport has credit sales of $100,000 (200 customers averaging $500 each) during 20X1. Collections during 20X1 were $60,000. The December 31, 20X1, accounts receivable of $40,000 includes the accounts of 80 different customers who have not yet paid for their 20X1 purchases. During 20X1, there were no bad debts, but it turns out that 40% of the year's sales are still unpaid at year-end and some may never be paid. The outstanding balances are:

Customer	Amount Owed
1. Jones	$ 1,400
2. Slade	125
42. Monterro	600
79. Weinberg	700
80. Porras	11
Total receivables	$40,000

How should Compuport account for these receivables? Should we assume they will all be collected? Should we assume some will not be? If the latter, how do we decide which are collectible and which are not? Of course, we would never have initially made a credit sale to someone we really believed would not pay us.

There are two basic ways to record uncollectibles: by waiting to see which ones are unpaid or by making estimates today of the portion that will not be collected. The methods are called the specific write-off method and the allowance method.

SPECIFIC WRITE-OFF METHOD

specific write-off method
This method of accounting for bad debt losses assumes all sales are fully collectible until proved otherwise.

A company that rarely experiences a bad debt might use the **specific write-off method,** which assumes that all sales are fully collectible until proved otherwise. If uncollectibles are small and very infrequent, this practice will not misstate the economic situation in a material way. When a specific customer account is later identified as uncollectible, the Account Receivable is reduced. Because no specific customer's account is deemed to be uncollectible at the end of 20X1, the December 31, 20X1, Compuport balance sheet would simply show an Account Receivable of $40,000.

Now assume that during the next year, 20X2, the retailer identifies Jones and Monterro as customers who are not expected to pay. When the chances of collection from specific customers become dim, the amounts in the particular accounts are recognized as bad debts expense:

Specific Write-Off Method	A	= L +	SE
20X1 Sales	+100,000 [Increase Accounts Receivable]	=	+100,000 [Increase Sales]
20X2 Write-off	−2,000 [Decrease Accounts Receivable]	=	−2,000 [Increase Bad Debts Expense]

Unfortunately, the specific write-off method has been criticized justifiably because it fails to apply the matching principle of accrual accounting. The $2,000 bad debts expense in 20X2 is related to (or caused by) the $100,000 of 20X1 sales. Matching requires recognition of the bad debts expense at the same time as the related revenue, that is, in 20X1, not 20X2. As a result of not matching expenses to revenues, the specific write-off method produces two errors. First, 20X1 income is overstated by $2,000 because no bad debts expense is charged to that year. Second, 20X2 income is understated by $2,000. Why? Because 20X1's bad debts expense of $2,000 is charged in 20X2. Compare the specific write-off method with a correct matching of revenue and expense:

	Specific Write-off Method: Matching Violated		Matching Applied Correctly	
	20X1	*20X2*	*20X1*	*20X2*
Sales revenue	100,000	0	100,000	0
Bad debts expense	0	2,000	2,000	0

The principal arguments in favor of the specific write-off method are based on cost-benefit concerns and materiality. Basically, the method is simple and extremely inexpensive to use. Moreover, no great error in measurement of income occurs if amounts of bad debts are small and similar from one year to the next.

ALLOWANCE METHOD

Most accountants do not use the specific write-off method because it violates the matching principle. Instead, they use an alternate method that estimates the amount of uncollectible accounts to be matched to the related revenue. This method, known as the **allowance method**, has two basic elements: (1) an estimate of the amounts that will ultimately be uncollectible and (2) a contra account, which contains the estimate and is deducted from the accounts receivable. The contra account is usually called **allowance for uncollectible accounts** (or **allowance for doubtful accounts, allowance for bad debts,** or **reserve for doubtful accounts**). It contains the amount of receivables estimated to be uncollectible from as yet unidentified customers. In other words, using this contra account allows accountants to recognize bad debts in general during the proper period, before specific uncollectible accounts are identified in the following period.

Returning to our example, suppose that Compuport knows from experience that 2% of sales is never collected. Therefore, 2% × $100,000 = $2,000 of the 20X1 sales can be estimated to be uncollectible. However, the exact customer accounts that will not be

allowance method
Method of accounting for bad debt losses using estimates of the amount of sales that will ultimately be uncollectible and a contra asset account, allowance for doubtful accounts.

allowance for uncollectible accounts (allowance for doubtful accounts, allowance for bad debts, reserve for doubtful accounts) A contra asset account that measures the amount of receivables estimated to be uncollectible.

collected are unknown on December 31, 20X1. (Of course, all $2,000 must be among the $40,000 of accounts receivable at year-end because the other $60,000 has already been collected.) Compuport can still acknowledge the $2,000 worth of bad debt in 20X1, before the specific accounts of Jones and Monterro are identified in 20X2. The effects of the allowance method on the balance sheet equation in the Compuport example follow:

	A	= L +	SE
Allowance method			
20X1 Sales	+100,000 [Increase Accounts Receivable]	=	+100,000 [Increase Sales]
20X1 Allowance	−2,000 [Increase Allowance for Uncollectible Accounts]	=	−2,000 [Increase Bad Debts Expense]
20X2 Write-off	+2,000 [Decrease Allowance for Uncollectible Accounts] −2,000 [Decrease Accounts Receivable]	=	(No effect)

The associated journal entries are:

20X1 Sales	Accounts receivable	100,000	
	Sales		100,000
20X1 Allowances	Bad debts expense	2,000	
	Allowance for uncollectible accounts		2,000
20X2 Write-offs	Allowance for uncollectible accounts	2,000	
	Accounts receivable, Jones		1,400
	Accounts receivable, Monterro		600

Note in the 20X2 journal entry that two credit entries are made, one for $1,400 due to Jones and one for $600 due to Monterro. This is to emphasize that, for accounts receivable, records must be maintained for each individual customer. In a similar manner, the 20X1 increase of $100,000 to accounts receivable would actually be recorded as many (200 in this example) individual sales to specific customers.

The principal argument in favor of the allowance method is its superiority in measuring accrual accounting income in any given year. That is, under this method the $2,000 of 20X1 sales that is estimated never to be collected is recorded in 20X1, the period in which the $100,000 sales revenue is recognized.

The allowance method results in the following presentation in the Compuport balance sheet, December 31, 20X1:

Accounts receivable	$40,000
Less: Allowance for uncollectible accounts	2,000
Net accounts receivable	$38,000

Other formats for presenting the allowance method on recent balance sheets of actual companies include:

($ in millions)	2000	1999
IBM		
Notes and accounts receivable, trade, net of allowances	$10,447	$9,103
AOL Time Warner		
Trade accounts receivable, less allowances of $97 and $58	$ 464	$ 385

The various approaches to the allowance method are based on historical experience and assume the current year is similar to prior years in terms of economic circumstances (growth versus recession, interest rate levels, and so on) and in terms of customer composition. Of course, estimates are revised when conditions change. For example, if a local employer closed or drastically reduced employment and many local customers were thus suddenly unemployed, Compuport might increase expected bad debts.

APPLYING THE ALLOWANCE METHOD USING A PERCENTAGE OF SALES

How do managers and accountants estimate the percentage of bad debts in the allowance method? In our example, Compuport managers determined a 2% rate of bad debts, for a total of $2,000 (2% × $100,000), based on experience. Expressing the amount of bad debts as a percentage of total sales is known as the **percentage of sales method,** which relies on historical relationships between credit sales and uncollectible debts.

percentage of sales method
An approach to estimating bad debts expense and uncollectible accounts based on the historical relations between credit sales and uncollectibles.

The percentage of sales method is easier to understand if we look at the relationship between the general ledger item Accounts Receivable and its supporting detail. Each time a sale is made on account we record the amount in the general ledger but we also record it in a separate, supporting ledger called a subsidiary ledger. In the subsidiary ledger a separate page is maintained for each customer, recording both sales and payments. On December 31, 20X1, the sum of the balances of all the customer accounts in the subsidiary ledger must equal the accounts receivable balance in the general ledger. The schematic in Exhibit 5-1, panel A, illustrates this.

Note that the use of the allowance account enables us to record bad debt expense without identifying specific accounts that will be uncollectible. In 20X2, after exhausting all practical means of collection, the retailer decides the Jones and Monterro accounts are uncollectible. Recording the $2,000 write-off for Jones and Monterro in 20X2 reduces their individual subsidiary accounts, reduces the general ledger Accounts Receivable account, and eliminates the Allowance for Uncollectible accounts as shown in Panel B of Exhibit 5-1.

How does the ultimate write-off of the Monterro and Jones accounts affect total assets?

ANSWER

Convince yourself that the ultimate write-off has no effect on total assets:

	Before Write-off	After Write-off
Accounts receivable	$40,000	$38,000
Allowance for uncollectible accounts	2,000	—
Book value (net realized value)	$38,000	$38,000

Exhibit 5-1

Compuport General Ledger, December 31, 20X1

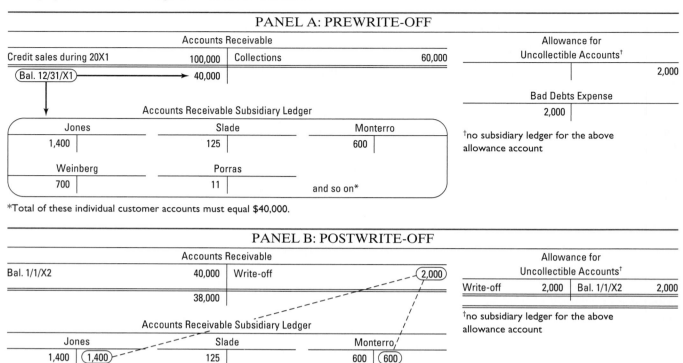

PANEL A: PREWRITE-OFF

Accounts Receivable

Credit sales during 20X1	100,000	Collections	60,000
Bal. 12/31/X1	40,000		

Accounts Receivable Subsidiary Ledger

Jones	Slade	Monterro
1,400	125	600

Weinberg	Porras	
700	11	and so on*

Allowance for
Uncollectible Accounts†

	2,000

Bad Debts Expense

2,000	

†no subsidiary ledger for the above allowance account

*Total of these individual customer accounts must equal $40,000.

PANEL B: POSTWRITE-OFF

Accounts Receivable

Bal. 1/1/X2	40,000	Write-off	2,000
	38,000		

Accounts Receivable Subsidiary Ledger

Jones	Slade	Monterro
1,400 1,400	125	600 600

Weinberg	Porras	
700	11	and so on*

Allowance for
Uncollectible Accounts†

Write-off	2,000	Bal. 1/1/X2	2,000

†no subsidiary ledger for the above allowance account

*Total of these individual customer accounts must equal $38,000.

APPLYING THE ALLOWANCE METHOD USING A PERCENTAGE OF ACCOUNTS RECEIVABLE

percentage of accounts receivable method An approach to estimating bad debts expense and uncollectible accounts at year-end using the historical relations of uncollectibles to accounts receivable.

Like the percentage of sales method, the **percentage of accounts receivable method** uses historical experience, but the estimate of uncollectible accounts is based on the historical relations of uncollectibles to year-end gross accounts receivable, not to total sales made during the year.

The Allowance for Bad Debts contra account is used to show the approximate amount of bad debts contained in the end-of-period accounts receivable. Under the percentage of accounts receivable method, additions to the Allowance for Bad Debts are calculated to achieve a desired ending balance in the Allowance account. Consider the historical experience in the table at the top of the next page.

At the end of 20X7, assume the accounts receivable balance is $115,000. The 20X7 addition to the Allowance for Bad Debts is computed as follows:

1. Divide average bad debt losses of $3,400 by average ending accounts receivable of $102,000 to calculate the historical average uncollectible percentage of 3.33.

2. Apply the percentage from step 1 to the ending Accounts Receivable balance for 20X7 to determine the ending balance that should be in the Allowance account at the end of the year: 3.33% × $115,000 receivables at the end of 20X7 is $3,830.

3. Prepare an adjusting entry to bring the Allowance to the appropriate amount determined in step 2. Suppose the books show a $700 credit balance in the Allowance

	Accounts Receivable at End of Year	Bad Debts Deemed Uncollectible and Written Off
20X1	$100,000	$ 3,500
20X2	80,000	2,450
20X3	90,000	2,550
20X4	110,000	4,100
20X5	120,000	5,600
20X6	112,000	2,200
Six-year total	$612,000	$ 20,400
Average (divide by 6)	$102,000	$ 3,400
Average percentage not collected = 3,400 ÷ 102,000 = 3.33%		

account at the end of 20X7. Then the adjusting entry for 20X7 is $3,830 − $700, or $3,130 to record the Bad Debts expense. The journal entry is:

```
Bad debts expense  ..............................    3,130
     Allowance for bad debts .......................              3,130
     To bring the Allowance to the level
     justified by bad debt experience during
     the past 6 years
```

The percentage of accounts receivable method differs from the percentage of sales method in two ways: (1) the percentage is based on the ending accounts receivable balance instead of sales, and (2) the dollar amount calculated using the percentage is the appropriate ending balance in the allowance account, not the amount added to the account for the year.

APPLYING THE ALLOWANCE METHOD USING THE AGING OF ACCOUNTS RECEIVABLE

A refinement on the percentage of accounts receivable approach is the **aging of accounts receivable method,** which considers the composition of the end-of-year accounts receivable based on the age of the debt. This method directly incorporates the customers' payment histories. The more time that elapses after the sale, the less likely collection becomes. The seller may send the buyer a late notice 30 days after the sale and a second reminder after 60 days, make a phone call after 90 days, and place the account with a collection agency after 120 days. Companies that analyze the age of their accounts receivable for credit management purposes naturally incorporate this information into estimates of the allowance for uncollectibles. For example, the $115,000 balance in Accounts Receivable on December 31, 20X7, for Compuport might be aged as shown in Exhibit 5-2.

This aging schedule in Exhibit 5-2 produces a different target balance for the Allowance account than the percentage of accounts receivable method did: $3,772 versus $3,830. Similarly, the journal entry is slightly different. Given the same $700 credit balance in the Allowance account, the journal entry to record the Bad Debts Expense is $3,772 − $700, or $3,072:

```
Bad debts expense  ....................................    $3,072
     Allowance for uncollectible accounts  .................              $3,072
     To bring the Allowance to the level justified by
        prior experience using the aging method.
```

Whether the percentage of sales, percentage of accounts receivable, or aging method is used to estimate bad debts expense and the Allowance for Uncollectible Accounts, the subsequent accounting for write-offs is the same—a decrease in Accounts Receivable and a decrease in the Allowance for Uncollectible Accounts.

aging of accounts receivable An analysis that considers the composition of year-end accounts receivable based on the age of the debt.

Exhibit 5-2

Aging of Accounts Receivable—Compuport—20X7

Name	Total	1–30 Days	31–60 Days	61–90 Days	Over 90 Days
Oxwall Tools	$ 20,000	$20,000			
Chicago Castings	10,000	10,000			
Estee	20,000	15,000	$ 5,000		
Sarasota Pipe	22,000		12,000	$10,000	
Ceilcote	4,000			3,000	$1,000
Other accounts (each detailed)	39,000	27,000	8,000	2,000	2,000
Total	$115,000	$72,000	$25,000	$15,000	$3,000
Historical bad debt percentages		0.1%	1%	5%	90%
Bad debt allowance to be provided	$ 3,772 =	$ 72 +	$ 250 +	$ 750 +	$2,700

BAD DEBT RECOVERIES

bad debt recoveries
Accounts receivable that
were written off as
uncollectible but then
collected at a later date.

Infrequently, accounts are written off as uncollectible, but then collection occurs at a later date. When such **bad debt recoveries** occur, the write-off should be reversed, and the collection handled as a normal receipt on account. In this way, a company will be better able to keep track of the customer's true payment history. Return to the earlier Compuport example and assume that Monterro's account for $600 is written off in February 20X2 and collected in October 20X2. The following journal entries produce a complete record of the transactions in Monterro's individual accounts receivable account.

20X1	Accounts receivable	600	
	Sales		600
	To record sales of $600 to Monterro, a specific customer		
Feb. 20X2	Allowance for uncollectible accounts	600	
	Accounts receivable		600
	To write off uncollectible account of Monterro		
Oct. 20X2	Accounts receivable	600	
	Allowance for uncollectible accounts		600
	To reverse February 20X2 write-off of account of Monterro		
	Cash	600	
	Accounts receivable		600
	To record the collection on account		

Note that these 20X2 entries have no effect on the level of bad debt expense estimated for 20X1. At the end of 20X1, using one of the three estimation methods we just examined, Compuport estimated bad debt expense based on the expected level of uncollectibles. These estimates are not changed whether future uncollectibles are greater or less than expected. The errors in estimate affect future periods but do not produce adjustments of prior periods. Briefly, in 20X2 Compuport thought that Monterro would be a nonpaying customer. This was not ultimately the case, and the records now reflect Monterro's payment, and the fact that it was delayed.

ASSESSING THE LEVEL OF ACCOUNTS RECEIVABLE

Objective 6
Assess the level of
accounts receivable.

You now know how to account for bad debts, but you should realize that the management issue is how to control bad debts at the proper level. The more credit a company provides, the greater the chances of bad debts occurring. Management and financial analysts like to monitor the firm's ability to control accounts receivable. Can the firm generate increasing sales without excessive growth in receivables? Do bad debt expenses rise sharply when sales grow, indicating a reduction in the credit quality of the store's customers? One measure of the ability to control receivables is the **accounts receivable turnover,** which is calculated by dividing the credit sales by the average accounts receivable for the period during which the sales were made:

$$\text{Accounts receivable turnover} = \frac{\text{Credit Sales}}{\text{Average accounts receivable}}$$

accounts receivable turnover Credit sales divided by average accounts receivable.

This ratio indicates how rapidly collections occur. If the turnover were 12, it would indicate that receivables are collected after 1 month on average. Higher turnovers indicate that receivables are collected quickly—lower turnovers indicate slower collection cycles. The level of the ratio is often driven by competitive conditions in the industry. Changes in the ratio provide important guidance concerning changes in the company's policies, changes in the industry, or changes in the general economic environment. For example, a decline in the general level of economic activity will slow collections across the board and this turnover measure will tend to rise for all firms.

Suppose credit sales (or sales on account) for Compuport in 20X8 were $1 million, and beginning and ending accounts receivable were $115,000 and $112,000, respectively.

$$\text{Accounts receivable turnover} = \frac{\$1,000,0000}{0.5\ (\$115,000 + \$112,000)} = 8.81$$

Receivables levels are also assessed in terms of how long it takes to collect them. This alternative to the turnover ratio has an appealing direct interpretation. How long does it take to get my money after I make a sale? The **days to collect accounts receivable,** or **average collection period,** is calculated by dividing 365 by the accounts receivable turnover. For our example:

days to collect accounts receivable (average collection period) 365 divided by accounts receivable turnover.

$$\begin{aligned}
\frac{\text{Days to collect}}{\text{accounts receivable}} &= \frac{365\ \text{days}}{\text{Accounts receivable turnover}} \\
&= \frac{365\ \text{days}}{8.81} \\
&= 41.4\ \text{days}
\end{aligned}$$

There is significant variability in accounts receivable turnover levels among industries, as shown in Exhibit 5-3. The high accounts receivable turnovers for automobile retailers and department stores are a result of the way customers finance their purchases. For automobiles, customers generally finance through banks or through the credit arms of the automobile manufacturer. For department stores, credit is often provided by national

Exhibit 5-3

Accounts Receivable Ratios

	Median Levels	
Industry	Accounts Receivable Turnover	Days to Collect Accounts Receivable
Automobile retailer	74.7	4.9
Department stores	26.0	14.0
Furniture retailer	63.0	5.8
Jewelry retailer	23.7	15.4
Book stores	57.1	6.4

Source: RMA, *Annual Statement Studies for 1999.*

BUSINESS FIRST
Managing Accounts Receivable

Years ago, a current ratio of 2 to 1 was normal, but increasingly aggressive companies have driven the working capital ratio below one. This is not accidental. It happens because these companies view money trapped in working capital as money that is not available to help grow the company, profitability. To improve the current ratio, companies are concentrating on reducing current assets, including control of accounts receivable. Reductions in accounts receivable must not damage the company's ability to profitably serve its customers.

Cash management involves careful planning of receipts and disbursements. When you know future cash flows, you avoid the need to keep idle cash "just in case." Many companies find their major collection problem is disputes over amounts billed. If disputes are discovered when a bill is overdue and more time is lost in solving the problem, significant payment delays result. One solution is to provide records on a web site so that customers can see exactly what the selling company has recorded. Early contact between the seller's accounts receivable staff and the buyer's accounts payable staff promptly resolve disputes.

Burlington Northern Santa Fe railroad speeded collection by breaking its receivable management into two steps. What they call "days-to-bill" measures the time between providing service and billing the customer, while "days-to-pay" measures the time between billing and collection. To reduce days-to-bill they executed technology initiatives to eliminate errors and get the billing process out of human hands. Today they have only 15,000 bills in process on any given day, down from about 50,000 in early 1998. By working closely with customers to resolve disputes, they have also cut their collection period almost in half.

Source: Cash Crop, *CFO Magazine*, August 2000.

credit cards, such as VISA and MasterCard. In both industries the seller receives cash quickly. The other three industries more frequently involve direct granting of credit by the selling firm. In other words, outside credit providers tend to pay off the sellers quickly, but when the sellers themselves provide the credit, payments come in much more slowly. In fact, if department stores provided their own credit to customers, as used to be the case, their accounts receivable turnover would drop sharply.

OVERVIEW OF INTERNAL CONTROL

Objective 7
Develop and explain internal control procedures.

internal control System of checks and balances that assures all actions occurring within the company are in accordance with organizational objectives.

Bank reconciliations and cash controls were discussed earlier, but internal control is broader than a focus on cash. The essence of **internal control** is the creation of a system of checks and balances that assures that all actions occurring within the company are in accord with organizational objectives and have the general approval of top management. At one level, this means that a highly placed manager should not expose the company to unauthorized, speculative losses from, for example, trading exotic derivatives securities. Here internal control seeks to tie daily decisions to corporate strategy. At another level, it means that a salesperson at the clothing-store giant, Gap, should not be able to walk out of the store with holiday gifts for the family without paying for them. Here internal control refers to the protection of firm assets from theft and loss. Therefore, an electronic tag on a leather coat is an internal control device and so is the requirement that checks over $2,000 have the approval of two people.

In its broadest sense, internal control refers to both administrative control and accounting control:

1. **Administrative controls** include the plan of organization, for example, the formal organizational chart concerning who reports to whom, and all methods and procedures that facilitate management planning and control of operations. Examples are departmental budgeting procedures, reports on performance, and procedures for granting credit to customers.

2. **Accounting controls** include the methods and procedures for authorizing transactions, safeguarding assets, and ensuring the accuracy of the financial records. Good accounting controls help maximize efficiency, and they help minimize waste, unintentional errors, and fraud.

administrative controls All methods and procedures that facilitate management planning and control of operations.

accounting controls The methods and procedures for authorizing transactions, safeguarding assets, and ensuring the accuracy of the financial records.

Our focus is on internal accounting controls, which should provide reasonable assurance concerning:

1. Authorization. Transactions are executed in accordance with management's general or specific intentions.

2. Recording. All authorized transactions are recorded in the correct amounts, periods, and accounts. No fictitious transactions are recorded.

3. Safeguarding. Precautions and procedures appropriately restrict access to assets.

4. Reconciliation. Records are compared with other independently kept records and physical counts. Such comparisons help ensure that other control objectives are attained.

5. Valuation. Recorded amounts are periodically reviewed for impairment of values and necessary write-downs.

The first three general objectives—authorization, recording, and safeguarding—relate to establishing the system of accountability and are aimed at the prevention of errors and irregularities. The final two objectives—reconciliation and valuation—are aimed at detecting errors and irregularities. A sixth objective of an internal control system should be added—promoting operating efficiency. Management should recognize that an internal control system's purpose is as much a positive one (promoting efficiency) as a negative one (preventing errors and fraud).

THE ACCOUNTING SYSTEM

An entity's **accounting system** is a set of records, procedures, and equipment that routinely deals with the events affecting the entity's financial performance and position. The system maintains accountability for the firm's assets and liabilities.

accounting system A set of records, procedures, and equipment that routinely deals with the events affecting the financial performance and position of the entity.

Chapters 3 and 4 provided an overview of the heart of the accounting system—source documents, journal entries, postings to ledgers, trial balances, adjustments, and financial reports. The focus of the system is on repetitive, voluminous transactions, which almost always fall into four categories:

1. Cash disbursements
2. Cash receipts
3. Purchase of goods and services, including employee payroll
4. Sales or other rendering of goods and services

The magnitude of the physical handling of records is often staggering. For example, telephone companies and credit card companies process millions of transactions daily. Without computers and data-processing systems, most modern organizations would be forced to halt operations.

Well-designed and well-run accounting systems are positive contributions to organizations and the economy. Credit card companies use sophisticated systems to evaluate transactions on your credit card and may refuse credit transactions that seem likely to be fraudulent use of your card by an unauthorized party. While such refusals sometimes inconvenience a legitimate card holder, they more frequently foil criminal use. Federal

Express Corporation created a dominant position in the overnight delivery market by developing an efficient system for continuous tracking of an item from pickup to delivery. Wal-Mart's extraordinary success as a low-price retailer is partly due to its development of an integrated inventory control and ordering system that allows its computer to interact automatically with suppliers such as Procter & Gamble to generate orders and reduce delivery times.

MANAGEMENT'S RESPONSIBILITY

management reports
Explicit statements in annual reports of publicly held companies that management is responsible for all audited and unaudited information in the annual report.

audit committee A committee of the board of directors that oversees the internal accounting controls, financial statements, and financial affairs of the corporation.

Although outside auditors attest to the financial reports of an entity, management bears the primary responsibility for a company's financial statements. Most annual reports of publicly held companies in the United States contain an explicit statement of management responsibility for its financial statements. These **management reports** state that management is responsible for all audited and unaudited information in the annual report, and they include a statement on the adequacy of internal control. They also include a description of the composition and duties of the audit committee as well as the duties of the independent auditor. You can review an example for Cisco in the appendix to the text.

The Audit Committee. Management's primary responsibility for the entity's financial statements extends upward to the board of directors. Most boards have an **audit committee,** which oversees the internal accounting controls, financial statements, and financial affairs of the corporation.

Audit committees typically have many "outside" board members who are not managers of the company. They are considered to be more independent than the "inside" directors—employees who serve as part of the corporation's management. Cisco has a typical board composition. Of 12 directors in 2000, 3 are also members of management and 9 are "outside" directors. Four of the outside directors form the audit committee. The committee provides contact and communication among the board, the external auditors, the internal auditors, the financial executives, and the operating executives.

CHECKLIST OF INTERNAL CONTROL

All good systems of internal control have certain features in common. These features can be summarized in a checklist of internal control, which may be used to appraise any specific procedures for cash, purchases, sales, payroll, and the like. The following checklist summarizes the guidance that is found in much of the systems and auditing literature.

1. Reliable Personnel with Clear Responsibilities

    The most important element of successful control is personnel. Incompetent or dishonest individuals can undermine a system, no matter how well it meets the other items on the checklist. Procedures to hire, train, motivate, and supervise employees are essential. Individuals must be given authority, responsibility, and duties commensurate with their abilities, interests, experience, and reliability. Yet, many employers use low-cost talent that may prove exceedingly expensive in the long run, not only because of fraud but also because of poor productivity.

    Assessing responsibility means tracking actions as far down in the organization as is feasible, so that results can be related to individuals. It means having salesclerks sign sales slips, inspectors initial packing slips, and workers sign time cards and requisitions. Grocery stores often assign each cashier a separate money tray; therefore, shortages can easily be traced to the person responsible. The psychological impact of fixing responsibility tends to promote care and efficiency.

    The National Mass Retailing Institute estimates that retailers lose about 2% of sales to theft and mistakes. Shoplifting accounts for part of this, but employee theft causes much larger losses than shoplifting. The institute estimates than an average retail store loses $10 per shift per clerk.

2. Separation of Duties

The separation of duties not only helps ensure accurate compilation of data but also limits the chances for fraud. Separation of duties makes it hard for one person, acting alone, to defraud the company. It is difficult, although not impossible, for two or more employees to collude in a fraud. This is why movie theaters have a cashier selling tickets and an usher taking them. The cashier takes in cash, the usher keeps the ticket stubs, and in an audit step performed by a third person, the cash is compared with the number of stubs. However, suppose they do collude. The ticket seller pockets the cash and issues a fake ticket. The usher accepts the fake ticket and allows entry. Separation of duties alone does not prevent collusive theft. Consider three additional examples where failure to separate duties allows easy theft.

In a computer system, a person with custody of assets should not have access to programming or any input of records. In a classic example, a programmer in a bank rounded transactions to the next lower cent instead of the nearest cent and had the computer put the fraction of a cent into his account. For example, a customer amount of $10.057 became $10.05, and the programmer's account received $.007. With millions of transactions, the programmers' account became very large.

The same individual should not authorize the payment of a supplier's invoice and also sign the check in payment of the bill. Also, an individual who handles cash receipts should not have the authority to indicate which accounts receivable should be written off as uncollectible.

The latter separation of powers prevents such embezzlement as the following: A bookkeeper opens the mail, removes a $1,000 check from a customer, and somehow cashes it. To hide the theft, the bookkeeper prepares the following journal entry to write off an amount owed by a customer:

Allowance for bad debts	1,000	
Accounts receivable		1,000

An accounts payable clerk at a pharmaceuticals company embezzled $25,000 by writing checks to companies that he created. Following a standard practice, his employer had an executive authorize payments by initialing invoices. The resulting checks, for small amounts, were created by the clerk, mechanically signed, and mailed. The extra payments to the clerk's companies were detected one day when the clerk called in sick and his co-worker noted checks written to an unfamiliar vendor. In another case, a bookkeeper wrote fraudulent paychecks to seasonal employees and cashed them himself. The theft was revealed when a seasonal employee objected that the W-2 form, sent to the government at year end to report his annual earnings for income tax purposes, reported too much income. Good systems of internal control would reduce such losses.

3. Proper Authorization

Authorization can be either general or specific. General authorization is usually found in writing. It often sets definite limits on what price to pay (whether to fly economy or first class), on what price to receive (whether to offer a sales discount), on what credit limits to grant to customers, and so forth. There may also be complete prohibitions (against paying extra fees or bribes or overtime premiums). Specific authorization usually means that a superior manager must permit (typically in writing) any particular deviations from the limits set by general authorization. For example, a manager may have to approve any overtime. The board of directors may have to approve expenditures for capital assets in excess of a specific limit.

4. Adequate Documents

Documents and records vary considerably, from source documents such as sales invoices and purchase orders to journals and ledgers. Immediate, complete, and tamper-proof recording is the aim. It is encouraged by optical scanning of bar-coded data, by having all source documents prenumbered and accounted for, by using devices such as cash registers, and by designing forms for ease of recording. Immediate recording is especially important for handling cash sales. Devices used to ensure immediate recording include "rewards" to customers if they are not offered a receipt at the time of sale and forcing clerks to make change by pricing items at $1.99, $2.99, and $3.99 instead of $2, $3, and $4. (Historically, such pricing was originally adopted to force clerks to make change as well as for its psychological impact on potential customers.) The need to access the change drawer forces the clerk to ring up the sale so the drawer will open.

5. Proper Procedures

Most organizations use procedures manuals to specify the flow of documents and provide information and instructions to facilitate adequate record keeping. Routine and automatic checks are major ways of attaining proper procedures. In a phrase, this means doing things "by the numbers." The use of general routines permits specialization of effort, division of duties, and automatic checks on previous steps in the routine.

6. Physical Safeguards

Obviously, losses of cash, inventories, and records are minimized by safes, locks, guards, guard dogs, special lighting, and limited access. For example, many companies (such as Boeing and Hewlett-Packard) require all visitors to sign a register and wear a name tag. Often, employees also wear name tags that are coded to show the facilities to which they have access. Doors to research areas or computer rooms often may be opened only with special keys or by use of a specific code.

7. Bonding, Vacations, and Rotation of Duties

Key people may be subject to excessive temptation. Thus, top executives, branch managers, and individuals who handle cash or inventories should have understudies, be required to take vacations, and be bonded.

Rotating employees and requiring them to take vacations ensures that at least two employees know how to do each job so that an absence due to illness or a sudden resignation does not create major problems. Further, the practice of having another employee periodically perform their duties discourages employees from engaging in fraudulent activities that might be discovered when someone else has access to their records.

Rotation of duties is illustrated by the common practice of having employees such as receivables and payables clerks periodically exchange duties. A receivables clerk may handle accounts from A to C for 3 months, and then be rotated to accounts M to P for 3 months, and so forth.

Bonding or buying insurance against embezzlement is not a substitute for vacations, rotation of duties, and similar precautions. Insurance companies pay only when a loss is proved; establishing proof is often difficult and costly in itself. Prevention of the loss is far better.

8. Independent Check

All phases of the system should be subjected to periodic review by outsiders, for example, by independent public accountants, and by internal auditors. Auditors have independence and a degree of objectivity that allows them to spot weaknesses overlooked by managers immersed in day-to-day operations. It is too costly for external auditors to examine all transactions, so they inspect a sample of the transactions. By first evaluating the system of internal control and testing the extent to which it is being followed, the auditor decides on the likelihood of undetected errors. If internal controls are weak, there is a greater probability of significant errors in the accounting records. Then the auditor must examine many transactions to provide reasonable assurance that existing errors are found. If internal controls are strong, the auditor can use a smaller sample to develop confidence in the accuracy of the accounting records.

Internal auditors are company employees who help design control systems and assess the degree of compliance with the existing systems. Their main goal is to enhance efficiency of operations by promoting adherence to both administrative and accounting controls and to continuously improve the system.

9. Cost-Benefit Analysis

Highly complex systems tend to strangle people in red tape, impeding instead of promoting efficiency. Investments in more costly systems must be compared with the expected benefits. Unfortunately, it is easier to relate new lathes or production methods to cost savings in manufacturing than to link a new computer to cost savings in inventory control. However, cost savings from improved information systems can be huge. The accounting firm of KPMG Peat Marwick completed a study of office automation for a client. After examining the jobs of 2,600 white-collar workers, KPMG Peat Marwick quantified a cost-benefit relationship: "A single investment of $10 million would result in a productivity savings equal to $8.4 million every year."

BUSINESS FIRST

The $346,770 Overdraft

Karen Smith was amazed when her credit union notified her that her account was overdrawn by $346,770. How could that kind of money turn up missing? Did she mistakenly add three extra zeros to a check? No, she left her bank card in her wallet, locked inside her van during a high school football game on a Friday night. Two thieves broke into the van, stole the bank card, and visited local cash machines.

Think about how bank internal control procedures should stop thieves. Automated teller machines (ATMs) require the use of a customer's specific personal identification number (the "pin" number). As a secondary precaution, ATM machines normally restrict withdrawals to a maximum amount, perhaps $200 per day, per account. Thieves cannot randomly guess pin numbers. The computer tracks "unauthorized" accesses. After several incorrect pin numbers the ATM keeps the card and notifies the user to reclaim it at the bank.

Nonetheless, these thieves hit the jackpot. Karen stored her pin number on her social security card, in the stolen wallet. Luckier yet, the Oregon TelCo Credit Union was updating some computer programs and their $200 limit per account per day was inoperative. To access all the funds in Karen's account, the thieves put the card in and withdrew $200, time after time. Eventually, the ATM ran out of bills, but the thieves visited many more on a circuitous, five-county, 500-mile route.

A third internal control should have limited the thieves to the balance in Karen's account. Something else went wrong. Most financial institutions permit immediate withdrawal of only certified checks or checks drawn on accounts at the institution. Deposits may be unavailable for days while the institution verifies that the check is written on a good bank against a bonafide account with sufficient funds. Checks on in-state institutions may take 2 days to "clear" while out-of-state checks take 3 or 4 days. Deposits into an ATM machine are generally unavailable until the next banking day so the bank can verify the deposit, subject to the rules just described.

Unfortunately, the TelCo system was giving immediate credit for deposits made into automated tellers. The thieves "deposited" $820,500 by inserting empty deposit envelopes and recording large deposits on the ATM keypad. They exhausted the cash in the ATM machines in their five-county area by 2:30 A.M. on Monday and headed to Reno to buy a new truck and enjoy their wealth.

One piece of TelCo's internal control worked. Hidden cameras photographed the thieves. The perpetrators, David Gallagher and his wife Terry, were easily identified. David has been in prison five times and has 21 felony convictions. Federal sentencing guidelines could bring up to 63 years in prison.

Source: *New York Times,* (February 12, 1995) p. 36.

Although many companies implement more complex procedures to improve internal control, a few have taken a reverse course. They have decided that the increased costs of additional scrutiny are not worth the expected savings from catching mistakes or crooks. For example, an aerospace manufacturer routinely pays the invoice amounts without checking supporting documentation except on a random-sampling basis. An aluminum company sends out a blank check with its purchase orders, and then the supplier fills out the check and deposits it.

No framework for internal control is perfect in the sense that it can prevent some shrewd individual from "beating the system" either by outright embezzlement or by producing inaccurate records. The goal is not total prevention of fraud, or implementation of operating perfection; instead, the goal is the design of a cost-effective tool that helps achieve efficient operations and reduce temptation.

SUMMARY PROBLEMS FOR YOUR REVIEW

PROBLEM ONE

Hector Lopez, marketing manager for Fireplace Distributors, sold 12 wood stoves to Woodside Condominiums, Inc. The sales contract was signed on April 27, 20X1. The list price of each wood stove was $1,200, but a 5% quantity discount was allowed. The wood stoves were to be delivered on May 10, and a cash discount of 2% of the amount owed was offered if payment was made by June 10. Fireplace Distributors delivered the wood stoves as promised and received the proper payment on June 9.

1. How much revenue should be recognized in April, in May, and in June? Explain.
2. Suppose Fireplace Distributors has a separate account titled "Cash Discounts on Sales." What journal entries would be made on June 9 when the cash payment is received?
3. Suppose Fireplace Distributors has another account titled "Sales Returns and Allowances." Suppose further that one of the wood stoves had a scratch, and Fireplace Distributors allowed Woodside to deduct $100 from the total amount due. What journal entries would be made on June 9 when the cash payment is received?

SOLUTION TO PROBLEM ONE

1. Revenue of $13,680 (12 × $1,200 less a 5% quantity discount of $720) would be recognized in May and none in April or June. The key to recognizing revenue is whether the revenue is earned and the asset received from the buyer is realized. The revenue is not earned until the merchandise is delivered. Therefore, revenue cannot be recognized in April because nothing was delivered then. Provided that Woodside Condominiums has a good credit rating, the receipt of cash is reasonably ensured before the cash is actually received. Therefore, recognition of revenue need not be delayed until June. On May 10, both revenue recognition tests were met, and the revenue would be recorded on May's income statement. However, if Woodside had a poor credit rating, the revenue would not be recognized and recorded until it was received in June.

2. The original revenue recorded was $13,680. The 2% cash discount is 2% × $13,680 = $273.60. Therefore, the cash payment is $13,680 − $273.60 = $13,406.40:

```
Cash ............................................  13,406.40
Cash discounts on sales  ..........................  273.60
     Accounts receivable  ..........................              13,680.00
```

3. The only difference from requirement 2 is a $100 smaller cash payment and a $100 debit to sales returns and allowances:

```
Cash ............................................  13,306.40
Cash discounts on sales  ..........................  273.60
Sales returns and allowances ......................  100.00
     Accounts receivable  ..........................              13,680.00
```

PROBLEM TWO

The balance sheet of Nautica, the sportswear company with annual sales of more than $600 million, showed accounts receivable at March 4, 2000 of $107,609,000, net of allowances of $9,046,000. Suppose a large discount chain that owed Nautica $2 million announced bankruptcy on March 5, 2000. Nautica decided that chances for collection were virtually zero and immediately wrote off the account. Show the accounts receivable and allowance account balances after the write-off, and explain the effect of the write-off on income for the year beginning March 5, 2000.

SOLUTION TO PROBLEM TWO

The write-off does not affect the net accounts receivable. Nevertheless, both gross accounts receivable and the allowance balance change. Gross accounts receivable were $116,655,000 at March 4 and the allowance was $9,046,000, giving a net accounts receivable of $107,609,000. When Nautica takes the write-off, gross accounts receivable go down by $2 million, but the allowance does also, with the following result:

Gross receivables ($116,655,000 − $2,000,000)	$114,655,000
Less allowance for doubtful accounts ($9,046,000 − $2,000,000)	7,046,000
Net receivables	$107,609,000

Highlights to Remember

1. **Recognize revenue items at the proper time on the income statement.** Revenue is generally recognized when two tests are met: (1) the revenue is earned, and (2) the asset received in return is realized. Most often, revenue is recognized at the point of sale, when the product is delivered to the customer. In offering products for sale, many special practices produce differences between the price at which a product is offered and the final price that a customer is charged. The term net sales represents the final proceeds to the seller—gross sales less offsetting amounts for returns, allowances, and cash discounts.

2. **Account for cash and credit sales.** At the moment a sale occurs we record the full amount of the sale so that sales revenue for the year show our full level of economic activity, regardless of whether the sale is on account or for cash, so long as the revenue recognition criteria are met. To do so we increase an asset account and increase the sales revenue account. For credit sales we also need to maintain detailed records about the individual customers in a subsidiary account.

3. **Record sales returns and allowances, sales discounts, and bank credit card sales.** We may not ultimately collect the total we initially record. Various discounts or allowances may be recorded and shown as reductions of gross sales to arrive at net sales on the income statement. Sales returns and allowances arise when merchandise is returned or discounts are given due to damaged goods or errors in filling the order.

Customers sometimes receive a cash discount as a result of prompt payment. Similarly bank cards create a known discount to compensate the bank for its collection services.

4. **Manage cash and explain its importance to the company.**   Cash is the fuel that runs a company and must be available to meet obligations as they come due. Cash creates a number of procedural problems for the firm. Protecting cash from theft or loss, adequately planning for the availability of cash as needed, and reconciling the firm's accounting records with the bank's records are just some of these problems.

5. **Estimate and interpret uncollectible accounts receivable balances.**   Potential uncollectible accounts reduce the amount of accounts receivable reported on the balance sheet. Reporting the uncollectible portion of credit sales requires estimates that may be based on a percentage of sales, a percentage of accounts receivable, or an aging of accounts receivable. These estimates permit the financial statements to (1) properly reflect asset levels on the balance sheet, and (2) properly match bad debts expense with revenue on the income statement.

6. **Assess the level of accounts receivable.**   Companies and analysts use ratios to assess the level of accounts receivable. The accounts receivable turnover ratio and the days to collect accounts receivable ratio both relate the average dollar value of accounts receivable to the level of credit sales during the year. Comparisons with other companies in the same industry or examination of a particular company over time draw attention to unusual circumstances and possible problems.

7. **Develop and explain internal control procedures.**   It is tempting to delegate internal control decisions to accountants. However, managers at all levels have a major responsibility for the success of internal controls. To help monitor internal control, boards of directors appoint audit committees, which oversee accounting controls, the financial statements, and general financial affairs of the company. Managers and accountants should recognize that the role of an internal control system is as much a positive one (enhancing efficiency) as a negative one (reducing errors and fraud). The following general characteristics form a checklist that serves as a starting point for judging the effectiveness of internal control:
   a. Reliable personnel with clear responsibilities
   b. Separation of duties
   c. Proper authorization
   d. Adequate documents
   e. Proper procedures
   f. Physical safeguards
   g. Bonding, vacations, and rotation of duties
   h. Independent check
   i. Cost-benefit analysis

Appendix 5A: Bank Reconciliations

Exhibit 5-4 displays a bank statement for account number 96848602, one of thousands of the bank's deposits. Together, these accounts form the subsidiary ledger that supports the bank's general ledger account Deposits, a liability.

The supporting documents for the detailed checks on the statement are canceled checks; for additional deposits, deposit slips. Notice that the minimum balance, $233.39, is negative. This indicates an overdraft, which is a negative account balance arising from the bank's paying a check even though the depositor had insufficient funds available at the instant the check was presented. Overdrafts are permitted as an occasional courtesy by the bank, although the bank may levy a fee (e.g., $10 or $30) for each overdraft.

Exhibit 5-5 shows selected records for another depositor in another bank. The bank balance on December 31 is an asset (Cash) on the depositor's books and a liability

Exhibit 5-4

An Actual Bank Statement

SEAFIRST BANK
University Branch
4701 University Way NE
Seattle WA 98145

		Account Number
Richard B. Sandstrom	777	96848602
2420 Highline Rd.		Statement Period
Redmond WA 98110		11-21-00 to 12-20-00

SUMMARY OF YOUR ACCOUNTS

CHECKING

First choice Minimum Balance	96848602
Beginning Balance	368.56
Deposits	5,074.00
Withdrawals	3,232.92
Service Charges/Fees	16.00
Ending Balance	2,193.64
Minimum Balance on 12-9-00	**−33.39**

CHECKING ACTIVITY

Deposits

Posted	Amount	Description
11-21	700.00	Deposit
11-25	1,810.00	Payroll Deposit
12-10	1,810.00	Payroll Deposit
12-16	754.00	Deposit

Withdrawals

Ck No.	Paid	Amount
1606	**12-02**	**1134.00**
1607	**11-28**	**561.00**
1609*	**12-09**	**12.00**
1617*	**12-05**	**7.00**
1629*	**11-26**	**10.00**
1630	**11-25**	**16.95**
1639*	**12-02**	**96.00**
1641*	**12-09**	**1025.00**
1642	**12-05**	**50.00**
1643	**12-15**	**236.25**
1644	**12-17**	**84.72**

* = Gap in check sequence.
Total number of checks = 11.

(Deposits) on the bank's books. The terms debit and credit as used by banks may seem strange. Banks credit the depositor's account for additional deposits because the bank has a liability to the depositor. Banks debit the account for checks written by the depositor and paid by the bank. When the $2,000 check drawn by the depositor on January 5 is paid by the bank on January 8, the bank's journal entry would be:

Exhibit 5-5

Comparative Cash Balances, January 31, 20X2

Depositor's Records			
Cash in Bank			
(receivable from bank)			
1/1/X2 Bal.	11,000	1/5	2,000
1/10	4,000	1/15	3,000
1/24	6,000	1/19	5,000
1/31	7,000	1/29	10,000
	28,000		20,000
1/31/X2 Bal.	8,000		

Bank's Records			
Deposits			
(payable to depositor)			
1/8	2,000	1/1/X2 Bal.	11,000
1/20	3,000	1/11	4,000
1/28	5,000	1/26	6,000
1/31	20 *		
	10,020		21,000
		1/31/X2 Bal.	10,980

*Service charge for printing checks.

Date	Depositor's General Journal	Debit	Credit
1/5	Accounts payable	2,000	
	Cash		2,000
	Check No. 1.		
1/10	Cash	4,000	
	Accounts receivable		4,000
	Deposit slip No. 1.		
1/15	Income taxes payable	3,000	
	Cash		3,000
	Check No. 2.		
1/19	Accounts payable	5,000	
	Cash		5,000
	Check No. 3.		
1/24	Cash	6,000	
	Accounts receivable		6,000
	Deposit No. 2.		
1/29	Accounts payable	10,000	
	Cash		10,000
	Check No. 4.		
1/31	Cash	7,000	
	Accounts receivable		7,000
	Deposit No. 3.		

Jan. 8 Deposits	$2,000	
Cash		$2,000
To decrease the depositor's account		

    A monthly bank reconciliation is conducted by the depositor to make sure that all cash receipts and disbursements are accounted for. Bank reconciliations take many forms, but the objective is to explain all differences in the cash balances shown on the bank statement and in the depositor's general ledger at a given date. By using the data in Exhibit 5-5:

Bank Reconciliation, January 31, 20X2

Balance per books (also called *balance per check register, register balance*)	$ 8,000
Deduct: Bank service charges for January not recorded on the books (also include any other charges by the bank not yet deducted)*	20
Adjusted (corrected) balance per books	$ 7,980
Balance per bank (also called *bank statement balance, statement balance*)	$10,980
Add: Deposits not recorded by bank (also called *unrecorded deposits, deposits in transit*), deposit of 1/31	7,000
Total	$17,980
Deduct: Outstanding checks, check of 1/29	10,000
Adjusted (corrected) balance per bank	$ 7,980

*Note that new entries on the depositor's books are required for all previously unrecorded additions and deductions made to achieve the adjusted balance per books.

The bank reconciliation indicates that an adjustment is necessary on the books of the depositor:

Jan. 31 Bank service charge expense	20	
Cash		20
To record bank charges for printing checks.		

The popular reconciliation format has two major sections. The first section begins with the balance per books, that is, the balance in the Cash T-account. Adjustments are made for items not entered on the books but already entered by the bank, such as deduction of the $20 service charge. These adjustments are then recorded in the records of the company. No additions are shown in the illustrated section, but an illustrative addition would be the bank's collection of a customer receivable on behalf of the company. The second section begins with the balance per bank. Adjustments are made for items not entered by the bank but already entered in the company's books. These items normally adjust automatically as deposits and checks reach the bank for processing. After adjustments, each section should end with identical adjusted cash balances. This is the amount that should appear as Cash in Bank on the depositor's balance sheet.

Accounting Vocabulary

accounting controls, p. 197

accounting system, p. 197

accounts receivable, p. 187

accounts receivable turnover, p. 195

administrative controls, p. 197

aging of accounts receivable, p. 193

allowance for bad debts, p. 189

allowance for doubtful accounts, p. 189

allowance for uncollectible accounts, p. 189

allowance method, p. 189

audit committee, p. 198

average collection period, p. 195

bad debt recoveries, p. 194

bad debts, p. 187

bad debts expense, p. 187

cash discounts, p. 183

cash equivalents, p. 186

compensating balances, p. 186

days to collect accounts receivable, p. 195

gross sales, p. 182

internal control, p. 196

management reports, p. 198

net sales, p. 182

percentage of accounts receivable method, p. 192

percentage of completion method, p. 181

percentage of sales method, p. 191

purchase allowance, p. 182

purchase returns, p. 182

receivables, p. 187

reconcile a bank statement, p. 186

reserve for doubtful accounts, p. 189

sales allowance, p. 182

sales returns, p. 182

specific write-off method, p. 188

trade discounts, p. 183

trade receivables, p. 187

turnover, p. 185

uncollectible accounts, p. 187

Assignment Material

QUESTIONS

5-1 Describe the timing of revenue recognition for a defense contractor on a $50 million long-term government contract with work spread evenly over 5 years.

5-2 Why is the realizable value of a credit sale often less than that of a cash sale?

5-3 Distinguish between a *sales* and a *purchase return*.

5-4 Distinguish between a *cash discount* and a *trade discount*.

5-5 "Trade discounts should not be recorded by the accountant." Do you agree? Explain.

5-6 "Retailers who accept VISA or MasterCard are foolish because they do not receive the full price for merchandise they sell." Comment.

5-7 Describe and give two examples of *cash equivalents*.

5-8 "A compensating balance essentially increases the interest rate on money borrowed." Explain.

5-9 "Cash is only 3% of our total assets. Therefore, we should not waste time designing systems to manage cash. We should use our time on matters that have a better chance of affecting our profits." Do you agree? Explain.

5-10 It is common in sub shops and pizza parlors around the Cornell University campus to find signs that say "Your purchase is free if the clerk does not give you a receipt" or "Two free lunches if your receipt has a red star." What is management trying to accomplish with these free offers?

5-11 "The cash balance on a company's books should always equal the cash balance shown by its bank." Do you agree? Explain.

5-12 List five internal control procedures used to safeguard cash.

5-13 "If everyone were honest, there would be no need for internal controls to safeguard cash." Do you agree? Explain.

5-14 What is the cost-benefit relationship in deciding whether to offer credit to customers, and whether to accept bank credit cards?

5-15 If a company accepts bank credit cards, why might it accept specific cards instead of all of them? For example, some retailers accept VISA and MasterCard, but not American Express or Diner's Club, while the exact opposite is true for some restaurants.

5-16 Distinguish between the allowance method and the specific write-off method for bad debts.

5-17 The El Camino Hospital uses the allowance method in accounting for bad debts. A journal entry was made for writing off the accounts of Jane Jensen, Eunice Belmont, and Samuel Maze: Do you agree with this entry? If not, show the correct entry and the correcting entry.

Bad debts expense	14,321	
Accounts receivable.		14,321

5-18 "The Allowance for Uncollectible Accounts account has no subsidiary ledger, but the Accounts Receivable account does." Explain.

5-19 "Under the allowance method, there are three popular ways to estimate the bad debts expense for a particular year." Name the three.

5-20 What is meant by "aging of accounts"?

5-21 Describe why a write-off of a bad debt should be reversed if collection occurs at a later date.

5-22 What is the relationship between the average collection period and the accounts receivable turnover?

5-23 Distinguish between the percentage of sales approach to applying the allowance method and the aging of accounts receivable approach.

5-24 Distinguish between *internal accounting control* and *internal administrative control*.

5-25 "The primary responsibility for internal controls rests with the outside auditors." Do you agree? Explain.

5-26 What is the primary responsibility of the audit committee?

5-27 Prepare a checklist of important factors to consider in judging an internal control system.

5-28 "The most important element of successful control is personnel." Explain.

5-29 What is the essential idea of separation of duties?

COGNITIVE EXERCISES

5-30 Revenue Recognition

A newly created weekly free newspaper has approached your bank seeking a loan. While the newspaper is free, it gets significant revenue from advertising. In the first 2 months of operations it reported profits of $10,000. It has receivables of $70,000 on $200,000 of advertising revenue. Some of the revenue reported for these 2 months included special promotional pricing that gave advertisers 4 months of ads for the price of 2. All this promotional revenue was included in the income statement for 2 months. Comment on the reported profit.

5-31 Using the Income Statement to Evaluate Sales Success

The net income of a company is the result of many factors. Sometimes managers want to measure the performance of one part of the organization separate from the effects of other parts. How might a company evaluate the success of its sales efforts using a classified income statement? Assume that the sales department is responsible for pricing and thus influences both the total amount sold and the margin on the items sold.

5-32 Criteria for Revenue Recognition

We generally treat revenue as earned when the company delivers merchandise to the customer. At that moment, what additional uncertainty remains about the proper amount of revenue that will ultimately be realized?

5-33 Revenue Recognition and Evaluation of Sales Staff

Revenue on an accrual-accounting basis must be both earned and realized before it is recognized in the income statement. Revenue in cash-basis accounting must be received in cash. Is accrual-basis or cash-basis recognition of revenue more relevant for evaluating the performance of a sales staff? Why?

EXERCISES

5-34 Revenue Recognition, Cash Discounts, and Returns

University Bookstore ordered 500 copies of an introductory economics textbook from Prentice Hall on July 17, 20X0. The books were delivered on August 12, at which time a bill was sent requesting payment of $40 per book. However, a 2% discount was allowed if Prentice Hall received payment by September 12. University Bookstore sent the proper payment, which was received by Prentice Hall on September 10. On December 18, University Bookstore returned 60 books to Prentice-Hall for a full cash refund.

Required

1. Prepare the journal entries (if any) for Prentice Hall on (a) July 17, (b) August 12, (c) September 10, and (d) December 18. Include appropriate explanations.
2. Suppose this was the only sales transaction in 20X0. Prepare the revenue section of Prentice-Hall's income statement.

5-35 Revenue Recognition

Cascade Logging Company hired Dmitri Construction Company to build a new bridge across the Logan River. The bridge would extend a logging road into a new stand of timber. The contract called for a payment of $10 million on completion of the bridge. Work was begun in 20X0 and completed in 20X2. Total costs were:

20X0	$2 million
20X1	3 million
20X2	4 million
Total	$9 million

Required

1. Suppose the accountant for Dmitri Construction Company judged that Cascade Logging might not be able to pay the $10 million. How much revenue would you recognize each year?
2. Suppose Cascade Logging is a subsidiary of a major wood products company. Therefore, receipt of payment on the contract is reasonably certain. How much revenue would you recognize each year?

5-36 Sales in Britain

The first line of the income statement of Cadbury Schweppes, the British candy and beverage company, showed:

Turnover	£5,115,000,000

The current assets on the company's balance sheet were shown as follows:

Current Assets

Stocks [inventories]		£ 436,000,000
Debtors		
Trade debtors	£643,000,000	
Other debtors	248,000,000	
Total		891,000,000
Investments		75,000,000
Cash at bank and in hand		91,000,000
Total current assets		£1,493,000,000

1. What term is used in the United States for the item called "trade debtors" on the Cadbury Schweppes balance sheet?

2. By using the account titles given in this exercise, make a journal entry for the sale of £150,000 of chocolates to Harrod's Department Store.

5-37 Compensating Balances

Gemini Company borrowed $100,000 from First Bank at 8% interest. The loan agreement stated that a compensating balance of $10,000 must be kept in the Gemini checking account at First Bank. The total Gemini cash balance at the end of the year was $45,000.

1. How much usable cash did Gemini Company receive for its $100,000 loan?
2. What was the real interest rate paid by Gemini?
3. Prepare a footnote for the annual report of Gemini Company explaining the compensating balance.

5-38 Sales Returns and Discounts

San Jose Electronics Wholesalers had gross sales of $800,000 during the month of March. Sales returns and allowances were $40,000. Cash discounts granted were $20,000.

Prepare an analysis of the impact of these transactions on the balance sheet equation. Also show the journal entries. Prepare a detailed presentation of the revenue section of the income statement.

5-39 Gross and Net Sales

Midwest Metal Products, Incorporated reported the following in 20X8 ($ in thousands):

Net sales	$600
Cash discounts on sales	20
Sales returns and allowances	30

1. Prepare the revenue section of the 20X8 income statement.
2. Prepare journal entries for (a) initial revenue recognition for 20X8 sales, (b) sales returns and allowances, and (c) collection of accounts receivable. Assume that all sales were on credit and all accounts receivable for 20X8 sales were collected in 20X8. Omit explanations.

5-40 Cash Discounts Transactions

Video Specialties is a wholesaler that sells on terms of 2/10, n/30. It sold video equipment to Video City for $200,000 on open account on January 10. Payment (net of cash discount) was received on January 19. By using the equation framework, analyze the two transactions for Video Specialties. Also prepare journal entries.

5-41 Entries for Cash Discounts and Returns on Sales

The Sonoma Wine Company is a wholesaler of California wine that sells on credit terms of 2/10, n/30. Consider the following transactions:

June 9	Sales on credit to Sierra Wines, $20,000
June 11	Sales on credit to Marty's Liquors, $10,000
June 18	Collected from Sierra Wines
June 26	Accepted the return of six cases from Marty's, $1,000
July 10	Collected from Marty's
July 12	Sierra returned some defective wine that it had acquired on June 9 for $100. Sonoma issued a cash refund immediately

Prepare journal entries for these transactions. Omit explanations. Assume that the full appropriate amounts were exchanged.

5-42 Credit Terms, Discounts, and Annual Interest Rates

As the struggling owner of a new Korean restaurant, you suffer from a habitual shortage of cash. Yesterday the following invoices arrived:

Vender	Face Amount	Terms
Cornation Produce	$ 600	n/30
Rose Exterminators	90	EOM
Nebraska Meat Supply	900	15, EOM
John's Fisheries	1,000	1/10, n/30
Garcia Equipment	2,000	2/10, n/30

Required

1. Write out the exact meaning of each of the terms.
2. You can borrow cash from the local bank on a 10-, 20-, or 30-day note bearing an annual interest rate of 16%. Should you borrow to take advantage of the cash discounts offered by the last two vendors? Why? Show computations. For interest rate computations, assume a 360-day year.

5-43 Accounting for Credit Cards

La Roux Designer Clothing Store has extended credit to customers on open account. Its average experience for each of the past 3 years has been:

	Cash	Credit	Total
Sales	$500,000	$300,000	$800,000
Bad debts expense	—	6,000	6,000
Administrative expense	—	10,000	10,000

Edith La Roux is considering whether to accept bank cards (e.g., VISA, MasterCard). She has resisted because she does not want to bear the cost of the service, which would be 5% of gross sales.

The representative of VISA claims that the availability of bank cards would have increased overall sales by at least 10%. However, regardless of the level of sales, the new mix of the sales would be 50% bank card and 50% cash.

Required

1. How would a bank card sale of $200 affect the accounting equation? Where would the discount appear on the income statement?
2. Should La Roux adopt the bank card if sales do not increase? Base your answer solely on the sparse facts given here.
3. Repeat requirement 2, but assume that total sales would increase 10%.

5-44 Trade-Ins versus Discounts

Many states base their sales tax on gross sales less any discount. Trade-in allowances are not discounts, so they are not deducted from the sales price for sales tax purposes. Suppose Michio Nagata had decided to trade in his old car for a new one with a list price of $20,000. He will pay cash of $13,000 plus sales tax. If he had not traded in a car, the dealer would have offered a discount of 15% of the list price. The sales tax is 8%.

Required

How much of the $8,000 price reduction should be called a discount? How much a trade-in? Mr. Nagata wants to pay as little sales tax as legally possible.

5-45 Uncollectible Accounts

During 20X8, the Rainbow Paint Store had credit sales of $700,000. The store manager expects that 2% of the credit sales will never be collected, although no accounts are written off until 10 assorted steps have been taken to attain collection. The 10 steps require a minimum of 14 months.

Assume that during 20X9, specific customers are identified who are never expected to pay $10,000 that they owe from the sales of 20X8. All 10 collection steps have been completed.

Required

1. Show the impact on the balance sheet equation of the preceding transactions in 20X8 and 20X9 under (a) the specific write-off method and (b) the allowance method. Which method do you prefer? Why?
2. Prepare journal entries for both methods. Omit explanations.

5-46 Specific Write-Off versus Allowance Methods

The Empire District Electric Company serves customers in the region where the states of Kansas, Missouri, Arkansas, and Oklahoma come together. Empire District uses the allowance method for recognizing uncollectible accounts. The company's January 1, 2000 balance sheet showed accounts receivable of $17,377,963. The footnotes revealed that this was net of uncollectible accounts of $372,000.

Required

1. Suppose Empire District wrote off a specific uncollectible account for $10,000 on January 2, 2000. Assume that this was the only transaction affecting the accounts receivable or allowance accounts on that day. Give the journal entry to record this write-off. What would the balance sheet show for accounts receivable at the end of the day on January 2.

2. Suppose Empire District used the specific write-off method instead of the allowance method for recognizing uncollectible accounts. Compute the accounts receivable balance that would be shown on the January 1, 2000, balance sheet.

5-47 Bad Debts

Prepare all journal entries concerning the following data for a medical clinic that performs elective laser surgery that corrects vision. Such procedures are not covered by third-party payers such as Blue Cross or Medicare. Consider the following balances of a medical clinic on December 31, 20X1: Receivables from individual patients, $200,000; and Allowance for Doubtful Receivables, $50,000. During 20X2, total billings to individual patients were $2.5 million. Past experience indicated that 10% of such individual billings would ultimately be uncollectible. Write-offs of receivables during 20X2 were $260,000.

5-48 Bad Debt Allowance

Myrick Appliance had sales of $1,000,000 during 20X8, including $600,000 of sales on credit. Balances on December 31, 20X7, were Accounts Receivable, $95,000; and Allowance for Bad Debts, $9,000. Data for 20X8: Collections on accounts receivable were $560,000. Bad debts expense was estimated at 2% of credit sales, as in previous years. Write-offs of bad debts during 20X8 were $11,000.

Required

1. Prepare journal entries concerning the preceding information for 20X8.
2. Show the ending balances of the balance sheet accounts, December 31, 20X8.
3. Based on the given data would you advise Alice Myrick, the president of the store, that the 2% estimated bad debt rate appears adequate?

5-49 Bad Debt Recoveries

Seneca Department Store has many accounts receivable. The Seneca balance sheet, December 31, 20X1, showed Accounts Receivable, $950,000 and Allowance for Uncollectible Accounts, $40,000. In early 20X2, write-offs of customer accounts of $30,000 were made. In late 20X2, a customer, whose $5,000 debt had been written off earlier, won a $1 million sweepstakes cash prize. The buyer immediately remitted $5,000 to Seneca. The store welcomed the purchaser's money and return to high credit standing.

Required

Prepare the journal entries for the $30,000 write-off in early 20X2 and the $5,000 receipt in late 20X2.

5-50 Subsidiary Ledger

An appliance store made credit sales of $800,000 in 20X4 to a thousand customers: Schumacher, $4,000; Cerruti, $7,000; others, $789,000. Total collections during 20X4 were $700,000 including $5,000 from Cerruti, but nothing was collected from Schumacher. At the end of 20X4, an allowance for uncollectible accounts was provided of 3% of credit sales.

Required

1. Set up appropriate general ledger accounts plus a subsidiary ledger for Accounts Receivable. The subsidiary ledger should consist of two individual accounts plus a third account called Others. Post the entries for 20X4. Prepare a statement of the ending balances of the individual accounts receivable to show that they reconcile with the general ledger account.

2. On March 24, 20X5, the Schumacher account was written off. Give the journal entry.

5-51 Accounts Receivable Turnover and Average Collection Period

Honda Motor Company had recent sales of ¥5,293,302 million. Beginning and ending accounts receivable for the fiscal year were ¥337,848 and ¥381,774, respectively.

Compute Honda's accounts receivable turnover and average collection period for the fiscal year. **Required** Assume that all sales are on open account.

5-52 Internal Control Weaknesses

Identify the internal control weaknesses in each of the following situations and indicate what change or changes you would recommend to eliminate the weaknesses.

a. The internal audit staff of MacDougall Aerospace, Inc., reports to the controller. However, internal audits are undertaken only when a department manager requests one, and audit reports are confidential documents prepared exclusively for the manager. Internal auditors are not allowed to talk to the external auditors.

b. Alice Walker, president of Northwestern State Bank, a small-town midwestern bank, wants to expand the size of her bank. She hired Fred Howell to begin a foreign-loan department. Howell had previously worked in the international department of a London bank. The president told him to consult with her on any large loans, but she never specified exactly what was meant by "large." At the end of Howell's first year, the president was surprised and pleased by his results. Although he had made several loans larger than any made by other sections of the bank and had not consulted with her on any of them, the president hesitated to say anything because the financial results were so good. Walker certainly did not want to upset the person most responsible for the bank's excellent growth in earnings.

c. Michael Grant is in charge of purchasing and receiving watches for Blumberg, Inc., a chain of jewelry stores. Grant places orders, fills out receiving documents when the watches are delivered, and authorizes payment to suppliers. According to Blumberg's procedures manual, Grant's activities should be reviewed by a purchasing supervisor. However, to save money, the supervisor was not replaced when she resigned 3 years ago. No one seems to miss the supervisor.

5-53 Assignment of Duties

Music Supplies, Inc., is a distributor of several popular lines of musical instruments and supplies. It purchases merchandise from several suppliers and sells to hundreds of retail stores. Here is a partial list of the company's necessary office routines:

1. Verifying and comparing related purchase documents: purchase orders, purchase invoices, receiving reports, etc.

2. Preparing vouchers for cash disbursements and attaching supporting purchase documents.

3. Signing vouchers to authorize payment (after examining vouchers with attached documents).

4. Preparing checks for 1 to 3.

5. Signing checks (after examining voucher authorization and supporting documents).

6. Mailing checks.

7. Daily sorting of incoming mail into items that contain money and items that do not.

8. Distributing the mail: money to cashier, reports of money received to accounting department, and remainder to various appropriate offices.

9. Making daily bank deposits.

10. Reconciling monthly bank statements.

The company's chief financial officer has decided that no more than five people will handle all these routines, including himself as necessary.

Required

Prepare a chart to show how these operations should be assigned to the five employees, including the chief financial officer. Use a row for each of the numbered routines and a column for each employee: Financial Officer, A, B, C, D. Place a check mark for each row in one or more of the columns. Observe the rules of the textbook checklist for internal control, especially separation of duties.

5-54 Simple Bank Reconciliation

Study appendix 5A. St. Luke's Hospital has a bank account. Consider the following information:

a. Balances as of July 31: per books, $48,000; per bank statement, $32,880.

b. Cash receipts of July 31 amounting to $10,000 were recorded and then deposited in the bank's night depository. The bank did not include this deposit on its July statement.

c. The bank statement included service charges of $120.

d. Patients had given the hospital some bad checks amounting to $11,000. The bank marked them NSF and returned them with the bank statement after charging the hospital for the $11,000. The hospital had made no entry for the return of these checks.

e. The hospital's outstanding checks amounted to $6,000.

Required

1. Prepare a bank reconciliation as of July 31.

2. Prepare the hospital journal entries required by the given information.

5-55 Allowance for Credit Losses

Thompkins Trustco Inc., a multibank holding company headquartered in Ithaca, New York, included the following in the footnotes to its 1999 annual report:

The following is a summary of changes in the reserve for loan/lease losses ($ in thousands):

	1999
Reserve at beginning of year	$7,405
Loans/leases charged off	(1,108)
Recoveries	476
Provision charged to operations	944
Other additions (deductions)	1,511
Reserve at end of year	$9,228

Required

1. Terminology in bank financial statements sometimes differs slightly from that in statements of industrial companies. Explain what is meant by "reserve for loan/lease losses," "provision charged to operations," and "loans/leases charged off" in the footnote.

2. Prepare the 1999 journal entries to record the writing off of specific credit losses, the recovery of previously written off credit losses, and the charge for credit losses against 1999 income. Omit explanations.

3. Suppose the bank analyzed its loans at the end of 1999 and decided that a reserve for losses equal to $10 million was required. Compute the provision that would be charged in 1999.

4. The bank had income before income taxes of $23,607 thousand in 1999. Compute the income before income taxes if the reserve for losses at the end of 1999 had been $10 million?

5-56 Aging of Accounts

Consider the following analysis of Accounts Receivable, February 28, 20X9:

Name of Customer	Total	Remarks
Ng Nurseries	$ 20,000	50% over 90 days, 50% 61–90 days
Michael's Landscaping	8,000	75% 31–60 days, 25% under 30 days
Shoven Garden Supply	12,000	60% 61–90 days, 40% 31–60 days
Bonner Perennial Farm	20,000	All under 30 days
Hjortshoj Florists	4,000	25% 61–90 days, 75% 1–30 days
Other accounts (each detailed)	80,000	50% 1–30 days, 30% 31–60 days, 15% 61–90 days, 5% over 90 days
Total	$144,000	

Prepare an aging schedule, classifying ages into four categories: 1 to 30 days, 31 to 60 days, 61 to 90 days, and over 90 days. Assume that the prospective bad debt percentages for each category are 0.2%, 0.8%, 10%, and 80%, respectively. What is the ending balance in the Allowance for Uncollectible Accounts?

Required

5-57 Percentage of Ending Accounts Receivable
Consider the following data:

	Accounts Receivable at End of Year	Accounts Receivable Deemed Uncollectible and Written off during Subsequent Years
20X1	$210,000	$ 8,000
20X2	170,000	6,000
20X3	195,000	7,000
20X4	230,000	9,000
20X5	250,000	12,000
20X6	220,000	9,000

Required

The unadjusted credit balance in Allowance for Uncollectible Accounts at December 31, 20X7, is $600. By using the percentage of ending accounts receivable method, prepare an adjusting entry to bring the Allowance to the appropriate amount at December 31, 20X7 when the Accounts Receivable balance is $240,000. Base your estimate of the percentage on the actual loss experience in the prior 6 years.

5-58 Estimates of Uncollectible Accounts
Rashid Company has made an analysis of its sales and accounts receivable for the past 5 years. Assume that all accounts written off in a year related to sales of the preceding year and were part of the accounts receivable at the end of that year. That is, no account is written off before the end of the year of the sale, and all accounts remaining unpaid are written off before the end of the year following the sale. The analysis showed:

	Sales	Ending Accounts Receivable	Bad Debts Written Off During the Year
20X1	$680,000	$ 90,000	$12,000
20X2	750,000	97,000	12,500
20X3	750,000	103,000	14,000
20X4	850,000	114,000	16,500
20X5	850,000	112,000	17,600

The balance in Allowance for Uncollectible Accounts on December 31, 20X4, was $16,000.

Required

1. Determine the bad debts expense for 20X5 and the balance of the Allowance for Uncollectible Accounts for December 31, 20X5, using the percentage of sales method.
2. Repeat requirement 1 using the percentage of ending accounts receivable method.

5-59 Percentage of Sales and Percentage of Ending Accounts Receivable
Teton Equipment Company had credit sales of $6 million during 20X7. Most customers paid promptly (within 30 days), but a few took longer; an average of 1.4% of credit sales were never paid. On December 31, 20X7, accounts receivable were $450,000. The Allowance for Bad Debts account, before any recognition of 20X7 bad debts, had a $1,200 debit balance.

Teton produces and sells mountaineering equipment and other outdoor gear. Most of the sales (about 80%) come in the period of March through August; the other 20% is spread almost evenly over the other 6 months. Over the last 6 years, an average of 18% of the December 31 accounts receivable has not been collected.

1. Suppose Teton Equipment uses the percentage of sales method to calculate an allowance for bad debts. Present the accounts receivable and allowance accounts as they should appear on the December 31, 20X7, balance sheet. Give the journal entry required to recognize the bad debts expense for 20X7.

2. Repeat requirement 1 except assume that Teton Equipment uses the percentage of ending accounts receivable method.

3. Which method do you prefer? Why?

5-60 Average Collection Period

Consider the following:

	20X8	20X7	20X6
Sales	$2,000,000	$2,500,000	$2,400,000

	December 31		
	20X8	*20X7*	*20X6*
Accounts receivable	$ 195,000	$ 190,000	$ 185,000

Of the total sales, 80% are on account.

Compute the days to collect accounts receivable for the years 20X7 and 20X8. Comment on the results.

5-61 Bank Cards

VISA and MasterCard are used to pay for a large percentage of retail purchases. The financial arrangements are similar for both bank cards. A news story said:

> *If a cardholder charges a $600 briefcase, for instance, the merchant deposits the sales draft with his bank, which immediately credits $600 less a small transaction fee (usually 2% of the sale) to the merchant's account. The bank that issued the customer his card then pays the merchant's bank $600 less a 1.5% transaction fee, allowing the merchant's bank a 0.5% profit on the transaction.*

1. Prepare the journal entry for the sale by the merchant.

2. Prepare the journal entries for the merchant's bank concerning (a) the merchant's deposit and (b) the collection from the customer's bank that issued the card.

3. Prepare the journal entry for the customer's bank that issued the card.

4. The national losses from bad debts for bank cards are about 1.8% of the total billings to cardholders. If so, how can the banks justify providing this service if their revenue from processing is typically 1.5% to 2.0%?

5-62 Student Loans

An annual report of the University of Washington includes information about its receivables from student loans in a footnote to the financial statements ($ in thousands):

	Year 1		Year 2	
Student loans				
Federal programs	$30,905		$33,109	
Less—allowances	2,793	$28,112	2,378	$30,731
University funds	$ 4,748		$ 4,999	
Less—allowances	337	4,411	271	4,728
Total, net		$32,523		$35,459

1. Compare the quality of the loans under federal programs with the quality of those using university funds. Compare the quality of the loans outstanding at the end of year 2 with the quality of those outstanding at the end of year 1.
2. By using the allowance method, which accounts would be affected by an allowance for bad debts of an appropriate percentage of $200,000 of new loans in year 2 from university funds? Choose a percentage.

5-63 Hospital Bad Debts

EquiMed, Inc., a medical management company based in State College, Pennsylvania, owned, operated, and managed 35 radiation oncology centers. Notes to a recent earnings statement reported the following about net revenue ($ in thousands):

Gross revenues	$159,944
Less provision for contractual adjustments	60,829
Net revenues	$ 99,115

1. Prepare a reasonable footnote to accompany the preceding presentation. What do you think is the purpose of contractual adjustments?
2. Prepare the summary journal entries for the $159,944 and the $60,829.

5-64 Discounts and Doubtful Items

Eli Lilly, a major pharmaceutical company, includes the following in its 1999 balance sheet ($ amounts in millions): Accounts receivable (net of allowances of $79.9): $1,443.2.

1. Compute the ratio of the allowance for discounts and doubtful items to gross accounts receivable for December 31, 1999. In 1995, this ratio was 4.1%. What are some possible reasons for the change in this ratio?
2. Independent of the actual balances, prepare a journal entry to write off an uncollectible account of $100,000 on January 2, 2000.

5-65 Uncollectible Accounts

Nike, Inc., is a worldwide supplier of athletic products. Its balance sheet on May 31, 2000, included the following data ($ in millions):

Accounts receivable, less allowance for doubtful accounts of $65.4	$1,567.2

1. The company uses the allowance method for accounting for bad debts. Suppose the company added $20 million to the allowance during the year ending May 31, 2000. Write-offs of uncollectible accounts were $19 million. Show (a) the impact on the balance sheet equation of these transactions and (b) the journal entries.
2. Suppose Nike had used the specific write-off method for accounting for bad debts. By using the same information as in requirement 1, show (a) the impact on the balance sheet equation and (b) the journal entry.
3. How would these Nike balance sheet amounts have been affected if the specific write-off method had been used up to that date? Be specific.

5-66 Uncollectible Accounts

Oracle is the world's largest supplier of database software. Its balance sheet included the following presentation:

	May 31	
	1999	1998
	($ in thousands)	
Trade receivables, net of allowance for doubtful accounts of $217,096 in 1999 and $195,609 in 1998	$2,238,204	$1,857,480

Required

1. Suppose that during 1999 Oracle had added $200 million to its allowance for estimated doubtful accounts. (a) Calculate the write-offs of uncollectible accounts and show (b) the impact on the balance sheet equation of these transactions and (c) the journal entries.
2. Assume that Oracle had used the specific write-off method for accounting for bad debts. By using the same information as in requirement 1, show (a) the impact on the balance sheet equation and (b) the journal entry.
3. How would the Oracle balance sheet amounts have been affected if the specific write-off method had been used? Be specific.

5-67 Allowance for Doubtful Accounts and 10-K Disclosures

The following is schedule II, taken from the 10-K filing of Nike, Inc. for the year ending May 31, 1999. The 10-K is a required filing that companies must make with the Securities and Exchange Commission (SEC) each year for their common stock to be traded publicly in the United States. It includes more detail than is often found in the annual report that is sent to all shareholders. This schedule describes exactly what occurred in the allowance for doubtful accounts. Use the information in schedule II to reproduce the journal entries affecting the allowance for doubtful accounts during the year ending May 31, 1999.

Required

Nike Corporation

Schedule II—Valuation and Qualifying Accounts ($ in millions)

Column A	Column B	Column C	Column D	Column E	Column F
Descriptions	Balance at Beginning of Period	Additions Charged to Cost and Expenses	Additions Charged to Other Accounts	Write-offs Net of Recoveries	Balance at End of Period
Allowance for doubtful accounts					
1998	$57.2	$39.8	$(7.0)	$(18.6)	$71.4
1999	$71.4	$ 7.8	$ 1.8	$ (7.8)	$73.2

5-68 Sales, Accounts Receivable, and Ethics

Writing in Corporate Cashflow, Howard Schillit described how the market value of Comptronix fell from $238 million to $67 million in a few hours when it was revealed that management had "cooked the books." Comptronix provided contract manufacturing services to makers of electronic equipment. Its 1991 financial results looked strong.

	1991	1990	Change
Sales	$102.0 million	$70.2 million	+45%
Accounts receivable	12.6 million	12.0 million	+5%
Accounts receivable turnover	8.1	5.9	

However, the relationship between sales and accounts receivable sent signals to knowledgeable analysts.

Required

1. Discuss the relationship that you would expect between sales and accounts receivable in a normal situation.

2. What unethical actions might cause sales to grow so much faster than accounts receivable? What unethical actions might cause the opposite, that is, for accounts receivable to grow faster than sales?

3. What is the most likely type of "cooking the books" that occurred at Comptronix?

5-69   Audit Committee Role

In a recent court decision, a U.S. corporation was required to delegate certain responsibilities to its audit committee. Management was required to:

1. Consult with its independent auditors before deciding any significant or material accounting question or policy.

2. Retain independent auditors to perform quarterly reviews of all financial statements prior to public issuance.

3. Conduct internal audits, with personnel reporting directly to the audit committee (internal auditors must report quarterly to the audit committee).

4. Retain or dismiss independent and internal auditors.

5. Consult with the independent auditors on their quarterly reviews of financial statements.

6. Review all monthly corporate and division financial statements and the auditor's management letter.

7. Receive quarterly reports from independent auditors on internal control deficiencies.

8. Review and approve all reports to shareholders and the SEC before dissemination.

The court also ruled that the audit committee must be composed of at least three outside directors who have no business dealing with the firm other than directors' fees and expense reimbursements.

Required

a. Prepare a partial corporation organization chart to depict these requirements. Use boxes only for Audit Committee, Independent Auditors, Internal Auditing, Finance Vice-President, and Board of Directors. Connect the appropriate boxes with lines: solid lines for direct responsibility, and dashed lines for information and communications. Place numbers on these lines to correspond to the eight items specified by the court decision.

b. Identify the main elements of the chapter checklist of internal control that seem most relevant to this system design.

5-70   Embezzlement of Cash Receipts

Braxton Company is a small wholesaler of pet supplies. It has only a few employees.

The owner of Braxton Company, who is also its president and general manager, makes daily deposits of customers' checks in the company bank account and writes all checks issued by the company. The president also reconciles the monthly bank statement with the books when the bank statement is received in the mail.

The assistant to Braxton Company's president renders secretarial services, which include taking dictation, typing letters, and processing all mail, both incoming and outgoing. Each day the assistant opens the incoming mail and gives the president the checks received from customers. The vouchers attached to the checks are separated by the assistant and sent to the bookkeeper, along with any other remittance advices that have been enclosed with the checks.

The bookkeeper makes prompt entries to credit customers' accounts for their remittances. From these accounts, the bookkeeper prepares monthly statements for mailing to customers.

Other employees include marketing and warehouse personnel.

Required

For the thefts described next, explain briefly how each could have been concealed and what precautions you would recommend for forestalling the theft and its concealment:

1. The president's assistant takes some customers' checks, forges the company's endorsements, deposits the checks in a personal bank account, and destroys the check vouchers and any other remittance advices that have accompanied these checks.

2. The same action is taken in 1, except that the vouchers and other remittance advices are sent intact to the bookkeeper.

5-71   Film Processing

Write not more than one page about the possible areas where internal controls should be instituted in the following business described briefly. Keep in mind the size of the business, and do not suggest controls of a type impossible to set up in a firm of this sort. Make any reasonable assumptions about management duties and policies not expressly described.

You have a film-developing service on Long Island, with 10 employees driving their own cars 6 days a week to contact about 40 places each, where film is left to be picked up and developed. Drivers bring film in 1 day and return the processed film the second or third day later. Stores pay the driver for his charges made on film picked up at their store, less a percentage for their work as an agency. The driver then turns this cash in to the Long Island office, where all film is developed and books are kept. From 6 to 10 employees work at the office in Long Island, depending on the volume of work. You run the office and have one full-time accounting–clerical employee. Route drivers are paid monthly by miles of route covered.

5-72 Appraisal of Internal Control System

From the *San Francisco Chronicle:*

> *The flap over missing ferry fares was peacefully—and openly—resolved at a meeting of the Golden Gate Bridge District finance committee yesterday.*
>
> *Only a week ago, the subject was a matter of furious dispute in which bridge manager Dale W. Luehring was twice called a liar and there were prospects of a closed meeting on personnel matters.*
>
> *But yesterday, after a week of investigation, the meeting turned out to be public after all, and attorney Thomas M. Jenkins revealed the full total of stolen ferry tickets equaled $26.20.*
>
> *The controversy began when auditor Gordon Dahlgren complained that there was an auditing "problem" and that he had not been informed when four children swiped $13.75 worth of tickets February 28. Committee chairman Ben K. Lerer, of San Francisco, ordered a full investigation.*
>
> *Jenkins said the situation was complicated because children under 5 have been allowed to ride the ferry without a ticket, but after May 1 everyone will have to have a ticket, allowing for a closer audit.*
>
> *Secondly, Jenkins explained, the "vault" in which tickets are deposited was proved insecure (resulting in two thefts totaling $26.20 worth of tickets) but has been replaced.*
>
> *In the future, it was decided, all thefts of cash or tickets must be reported immediately to the California Highway Patrol or the local police, the bridge lieutenant on duty, the general manager, the security officer, the auditor-controller, and the transit manager.*
>
> *In addition, employees must make a full written report within 24 hours to the president of the district board, the chairman of the finance-auditing committee, the auditor–controller, the attorney, the bus transit manager, the water transit manager, the toll captain, and the chief of administration and security.*

Required What is your reaction to the new system? Explain, giving particular attention to applicable criteria for appraising an internal control system.

5-73 Casino Skimming

An article in the *Wall Street Journal* reported that about $7 million in quarters disappeared from the slot machines of four casinos of Argent Corporation in an 18-month period. The coins weighed nearly 150 tons, and the odds against such a payout to players of the slot machines is one in 3,875,000,000,000,000,000,000,000,000,000,000,000,000,000,000,000—an extremely unlikely event, to say the least. The disappearance was part of the biggest known skim operation ever. Skimming is taking a portion of gambling revenues before they can be counted for tax purposes.

Internal control is especially important in casinos. Meters in the slot machines record the winnings paid to customers. Coins are taken immediately to the slot counting room when machines are emptied. In the counting rooms, coins are weighed, and a portion is returned to the change booths.

Required What items in the chapter checklist of internal control seem especially important concerning slot machine operations? How could the money from slot machine operations have been stolen in such large amounts?

5-74 Employee Dishonesty

Consider the following true newspaper reports of dishonesty:

a. At a small manufacturer, supervisors had access to time cards and gave out W-2 forms each year. The supervisors pocketed $80,000 a year in the paychecks for phantom workers.

b. A male manager at a busy branch office of a copying service had a receipt book of his own. Jobs of $200 and $300 were common. The manager stole cash by simply giving customers a receipt from his book instead of one of the company's numbered forms.

c. A purchasing agent received tiny kickbacks on buttons, zippers, and other trims used at a successful dress company. The agent got rich, and the company was overcharged $10 million.

Required

Specify what control or controls would have helped avoid each of the listed situations.

5-75 Internal Control Weaknesses

Identify the internal control weaknesses in each of the following situations.

a. Rodney Williams, a football star at the local university, was hired by D. A. Mount to work in the accounting department of Mount Electronics during summer vacation. Providing summer jobs is one way Mount supports the team. After a week of training, Williams opened the mail containing checks from customers, recorded the payment in the books, and prepared the bank deposit slip.

b. Jim Sanchez manages a local franchise of a major 24-hour convenience store. Sanchez brags that he keeps labor costs well below the average for such stores by operating with only one clerk. He has not granted a pay increase in 4 years. He loses a lot of clerks, but he can find replacements.

c. Martha McGuire operates an Exxon service station. Because it takes much extra time for attendants to walk from the gas pumps to the inside cash register, McGuire placed a locked cash box next to the pumps and gave each attendant a key. Cash and credit card slips are placed in the cash box. Each day the amounts are counted and entered in total into the cash register.

d. Lazlo Perconte trusts his employees. The former manager purchased fidelity bonds on employees who handle cash. Perconte decided that such bonds showed a lack of trust, so he ceased purchasing them. Besides, the money saved helped Perconte meet his budget for the year.

5-76 Cooking the Books

In *The Accounting Wars,* author Mark Stevens presents a chapter on "Book Cooking, Number Juggling, and Other Tricks of the Trade." He quotes Glen Perry, a former chief accountant of the SEC's Enforcement Division: "Companies play games with their financial reports for any number of reasons, the most common being the intense pressure on corporate management to produce an unbroken stream of increasing earnings reports." Stevens then lists Perry's "terrible 10 of accounting frauds—ploys used to misrepresent corporate financial statements":

1. Recognition of revenues before they are realized.
2. Recognition of rentals to customers as sales.
3. Inclusion of fictitious amounts in inventories.
4. Improper cutoffs at year-end.
5. Improper application of LIFO.
6. Creation of fraudulent year-end transactions to boost earnings.
7. Failure to recognize losses through write-offs and allowances.
8. Inconsistent accounting practices without disclosures.
9. Capitalization or improper deferral of expenses.
10. Inclusion of unusual gains in operating income.

Required

Suppose you were a division manager in a major corporation. Give a brief specific example of each of the 10 methods.

5-77 Straightforward Bank Reconciliation

Study appendix 5A. The City of Royalton has a checking account with First National Bank. The city's cash balance on February 28, 20X1, was $30,000. The deposit balance on the bank's books on February 28, 20X1, was also $30,000. The following transactions occurred during March.

Date	Check Number	Amount	Explanation
3/1	261	$11,000	Payment of previously billed consulting fee
3/6	262	9,000	Payment of accounts payable
3/10		12,000	Collection of taxes receivable
3/14	263	14,000	Acquisition of equipment for cash
3/17		16,000	Collection of license fees receivable
3/28	264	8,000	Payment of accounts payable
3/30	265	21,000	Payment of interest on municipal bonds
3/31		25,000	Collection of taxes receivable

All cash receipts are deposited via a night depository system after the close of the municipal business day. Therefore, the receipts are not recorded by the bank until the succeeding day.

On March 31, the bank charged the City of Royalton $95 for miscellaneous bank services.

Required

1. Prepare the journal entries on the bank's books for check 262 and the deposit of March 10.
2. Prepare the journal entries for all March transactions on the books of the City of Royalton.
3. Post all transactions for March to T-accounts for the City's Cash in Bank account and the bank's Deposit account. Assume that only checks 261 to 263 have been presented to the bank in March, each taking 4 days to clear the bank's records.
4. Prepare a bank reconciliation for the City of Royalton, March 31, 20X1. The final three City of Royalton transactions of March had not affected the bank's records as of March 31. What adjusting entry in the books of the City of Royalton is required on March 31?
5. What would be the cash balance shown on the balance sheet of the City of Royalton on March 31, 20X1?

5-78 Semicomplex Bank Reconciliation

Study appendix 5A. An employee, Sylvia Nelson, has a personal bank account. Her employer deposits her weekly paycheck automatically each Friday. The employee's check register (checkbook) for October is summarized as follows:

	October		
Reconciled cash balance, September 30, 20X1			$ 100
Additions			
Weekly payroll deposits			
	3		800
	10		800
	17		800
	24		800
Deposit of check received for gambling debt	25		500
Deposit of check received as winner of cereal contest	31		400
Subtotal			$4,200
Deductions			
Checks written No. 325–339	1–23	$3,300	
Check No. 340	26	70	
Check No. 341	30	90	
Check No. 342	31	340	3,800
Cash in bank, October 31, 20X1			$ 400

The bank statement is summarized in Exhibit 5-6. Note that NSF means "not sufficient funds." The check deposited on October 25 bounced; by prearrangement with Nelson, the bank automatically lends sufficient amounts (in multiples of $100) to ensure that her balance is never negative.

Required

1. Prepare Nelson's bank reconciliation, October 31, 20X1.
2. Assume that Nelson keeps a personal set of books on the accrual basis. Prepare the compound journal entry called for by the bank reconciliation.

Exhibit 5-6
Bank Statement of Sylvia Nelson

SUMMARY OF YOUR CHECKING ACCOUNTS	
Beginning balance	$ 100.00
Deposits	4,600.00
Withdrawals	3,870.00
Service charges/fees	25.00*
Ending balance	805.00
Minimum balance on 10-28	**−80.00**

*$10.00 for returned check;
  $15.00 monthly service charge.

CHECKING ACTIVITY		

Deposits

Posted	**Amount**	**Description**
10-03	800.00	Payroll deposit
10-10	800.00	Payroll deposit
10-17	800.00	Payroll deposit
10-24	800.00	Payroll deposit
10-25	500.00	Deposit
10-28	100.00	Automatic loan
10-31	800.00	Payroll deposit

Withdrawals

Ck. No.	**Paid**	**Amount**
325–339 Various dates in October. These would be shown by specific amounts, but are shown here as a total.		$3,300.00
340	10–27	70.00
NSF	10–28	500.00

Total number of checks = 16

5-79   Bank versus Book Records

Study appendix 5A. The Mead Corporation, primarily a forest products company, lists the following among its current assets and current liabilities ($ in millions):

	December 31,	
	1999	*1998*
As part of current assets		
Cash and cash equivalents	$ 56.4	$102.2
As part of current liabilities		
Accounts payable:		
Trade	209.1	199.2
Affiliated companies	11.1	32.5
Outstanding checks	45.9	44.2

It is unusual to find a liability account labeled "Outstanding Checks."

1. Most companies have checks outstanding at any balance sheet date. Why is it unusual to have a liability for outstanding checks?
2. Suppose you examined the "Cash and Cash Equivalents" account in Mead's general ledger. What balance would you find for December 31, 1999? for December 31, 1998?
3. Why do you suppose Mead reported outstanding checks as a liability?

5-80   Ethics and Bank Reconciliations

The Springfield Chamber of Commerce recently hired you as an accounting assistant. On assuming your position on September 15, one of your first tasks was to reconcile the August bank statement. Your immediate supervisor, Ms. Ratelli, had been in charge of nearly all accounting tasks, including paying bills, preparing the payroll, and recording all transactions in the books. She has been very helpful to you, providing assistance on all the tasks she has asked you to do. The reconciliation was no different. Without assistance, you were able to locate the following information from the bank statement and the Chamber's books:

Balance per books	$16,710
Balance per bank statement	16,500
Bank service charges	30
NSF check returned	3,000
Deposit in transit	4,600
Outstanding checks	9,750

You also found a deposit on the bank statement of $3,300 that was incorrectly recorded as $3,030 on the Chamber's books.

When you could not reconcile the book and bank balances, you asked Ms. Ratelli for help. She responded that an additional $2,600 deposit was in transit.

1. Assume that all the information that you obtained without Ms. Ratelli's help is accurate and complete. Prepare the August bank reconciliation with the original information, showing that the book and the bank balances do not reconcile.
2. Prepare a reconciliation using the new number, $7,200, for deposits in transit.
3. Why might Ms. Ratelli have instructed you to add $2,600 to the deposits in transit? What might she be trying to hide? If there were deceit, when might it be discovered?
4. What actions would you take if you were the accounting assistant?
5. By coincidence, you noticed a $2,600 cancelled check, signed by Ms. Ratelli, to an individual whose name you did not recognize. How would this change your answer to number 4?

ANNUAL REPORT CASE

5-81   Cisco Annual Report

Refer to Cisco's financial statements (appendix A).

1. Cisco combines cash and cash equivalents on the balance sheet. Define cash equivalents and give an example.
2. Calculate the average collection period for the year ended July 29, 2000, assuming all sales were on account.

5-82   Financial Statement Research

Select an industry and choose two companies within that industry.

Calculate the accounts receivable turnover and days to collect accounts receivable for the two companies for 2 years and comment on the results.

COLLABORATIVE LEARNING EXERCISE

5-83   Revenue Recognition

Form groups of three to six students. Each student should pick one of the six industries listed as follows. The Standard Industrial Classification (SIC) number is provided for each industry. This number may be helpful in locating companies in that industry, especially if using search routines in electronic media.

Members of each group should learn as much as possible about the revenue recognition issues in their industry. Select at least two companies in the industry, and examine the description of each company's revenue recognition policies in the footnotes (usually in footnote 1 or 2) to the financial statements. Two possible companies are listed for each industry, but do not feel restricted to using the companies listed.

After the individual research on a particular industry, get together as a team and report on what each member has learned. Compare and contrast the issues relating to when revenue is earned and realized in each industry. Discuss why issues that are important in one industry are unimportant in another.

- 2721—Periodicals Publishing and Printing
    Marvel Entertainment Group
    Readers Digest Association
- 4512—Air Transportation, Scheduled
    Alaska Air Group
    Southwest Airlines Company
- 4911—Electric Services
    Duke Power
    Puget Sound Energy
- 6311—Life Insurance
    Allstate Corporation
    USLIFE, Incorporated
- 7811—Motion Picture, Video Tape Production
    Dick Clark Productions
    Walt Disney Company
- 8062—General Medical and Surgical Hospitals
    Columbia/HCA Healthcare
    Regency Health Services

INTERNET EXERCISE

5-84   Oracle

Go to http://www.sec.gov/ to search for Oracle in the EDGAR database and find Oracle Corporation's latest 10K filing (annual report).

Answer the following questions about the company:

1. Under Part I *General,* how does Oracle categorize its software products? What do the categories contain?
2. Under *Research and Development,* is Oracle allowed to fully expense its software research and product development costs? What guidelines are followed in this area? What financial statement accounts reflect adherence to these guidelines?
3. Turn to the *Notes to Consolidated Financial Statements.* What is Oracle's revenue recognition policy?
4. Examine Oracle's balance sheet. Which method of accounting for uncollectible accounts does the company use? How can you tell? Which accounting principle does this method support?

www.prenhall.com/horngren

6

INVENTORIES AND COST OF GOODS SOLD

Bernie Marcus and Arthur Blank founded Home Depot in 1978 and drove its success by managing its inventory to assure customers would find what they wanted. They expect to have 1,900 stores such as this one by 2003.

www.prenhall.com/horngren

Learning Objectives

After studying this chapter, you should be able to

1. Link inventory valuation to gross profit.

2. Use both perpetual and periodic inventory systems.

3. Calculate the cost of merchandise acquired.

4. Choose one of the four principal inventory valuation methods.

5. Calculate the impact on net income of LIFO liquidations.

6. Use the lower-of-cost-or-market method to value inventories.

7. Show the effects of inventory errors on financial statements.

8. Evaluate the gross profit percentage and inventory turnover.

Have you ever gone to your local hardware store and been frustrated because they did not have what you wanted? A goal of Home Depot is to help you avoid this frustration. They do it by keeping a large inventory—40,000 to 50,000 different items, more than three times the number at a typical hardware store. As chief executive officer (CEO) and Chairman Bernie Marcus says, one of the three main values at Home Depot is assortment—"everything a do-it-yourselfer needs to complete a project."

Inventory requires a large investment by retail companies—$5.5 billion at Home Depot, about 32% of the company's total assets—and accounting for this inventory is important. By carefully monitoring inventory levels, Home Depot makes sure it does not lose sales by having too little inventory and does not lose money by investing in too much inventory.

In Chapter 5, we learned how to account for sales revenues. Of course, when a company sells a product, it also incurs costs. For example, Home Depot must buy the tools it sells. Similarly, a Toyota dealership has to pay for every car it sells. The cost of tools or Toyotas sold must be recognized along with the related revenues.

Determining the cost of the Toyota sold is easy enough—you look up the cost on the invoice for the specific car you sold. Unfortunately, the calculations are not always that simple. Because products such as tools sold by Home Depot are often purchased in quantity and held in inventory, tracing the precise cost of a single product can be difficult. As a result, companies must develop procedures to determine the value of their inventories and the cost of goods sold. Home Depot had sales of $45.7 billion in the year ended in January 2001 with costs of goods sold of $32.0 billion. This provides a gross margin of $13.7 billion or 30% of sales.

This chapter examines various methods for valuing and accounting for inventories that companies such as Toyota or Home Depot use to calculate cost of sales, inventory, and gross margin measures. Different inventory accounting practices are found around the globe, and multiple methods exist even in the same country or in the same industry. These differences make it hard to compare one firm to another. By understanding these differences, you are better able to evaluate the profitability of different companies. You are able to distinguish between apparent differences that arise solely from different accounting practices and real economic differences that distinguish two firms based on their profitability.

GROSS PROFIT AND COST OF GOODS SOLD

Objective 1
Link inventory valuation to gross profit.

For merchandising firms, an initial step in assessing profitability is gross profit (also called profit margin or gross margin), which is the difference between sales revenues and costs of the goods sold. Sales revenues must cover the cost of goods sold and provide a gross profit sufficient to cover all other costs, including research and development (R&D), selling and marketing, administration, and so on. As illustrated in Exhibit 6-1, products being held prior to sale are reported as inventory, a current asset in the balance sheet. When the goods are sold, the costs of the inventory become an expense, Cost of Goods Sold, in the income statement. This expense is deducted from Net Sales to determine Gross Profit, and additional expenses are deducted from Gross Profit to determine Net Income.

Exhibit 6-1
Merchandising Company (Retailer or Wholesaler)

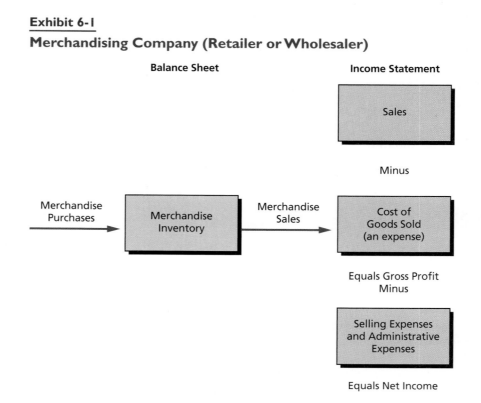

THE BASIC CONCEPT OF INVENTORY ACCOUNTING

In theory, the accounting for inventory and cost of goods sold is very simple. Suppose Christina sells T-shirts. Periodically, she orders many shirts of various sizes and colors. They sell, she orders more, and her business operating cycle continues on in this way. After a year, to evaluate her success, Christina prepares financial statements. To calculate the value of inventory on hand, she counts all the inventory items remaining at year-end (known as a physical count). She then develops a **cost valuation** by assigning a specific value from the historical cost records to each item in ending inventory. If the shirts cost $5.00 each and there are 100 shirts remaining in inventory, Christina's total ending inventory is $500. Suppose she had no shirts at the beginning of the year, and total purchases for the year were $26,000. Her cost of goods sold would thus be $25,500 ($26,000 of available shirts minus $500 of unsold shirts). Notice that the key to calculating the cost of goods sold is accounting for the remaining inventory.

> **cost valuation** Process of assigning specific historical costs to items counted in the physical inventory.

Unfortunately, determining the cost of goods sold and accounting for inventory are not this simple in practice. In the following sections, we show you some of the problems that can arise as well as how to deal with these problems. We also show you the major techniques for measuring inventories that various companies use. As a manager or investor, you want to know how inventory accounting can affect reported earnings. Especially important is how economic events, such as inflation, or management decisions, such as increasing or decreasing inventory levels, affect inventory values and thereby affect earnings.

PERPETUAL AND PERIODIC INVENTORY SYSTEMS

There are two main systems for keeping merchandise inventory records: perpetual and periodic. The **perpetual inventory system** has been used in prior examples in this text. It keeps a continuous record that tracks inventories and the cost of goods sold on a day-to-day basis. Such a record helps managers control inventory levels and prepare interim financial statements. The perpetual system does not eliminate the need for a physical count and valuation of the inventory. A **physical count** is the process of counting all of the items in inventory. It should be conducted at least once a year to check on the accuracy of the continuous records. The perpetual system was developed to provide managers with information to aid in pricing or ordering. At first it was extremely cumbersome and expensive to maintain constant records, but computerized inventory systems and optical scanning equipment at checkout counters have made implementation of perpetual inventory systems much less costly in many industries.

> **Objective 2**
> Use both perpetual and periodic inventory systems.

> **perpetual inventory system** A system that keeps a running, continuous record that tracks inventories and the cost of goods sold on a day-to-day basis.

> **physical count** The process of counting all the items in inventory at a moment in time.

Previous chapters have used the perpetual system to record inventory transactions without referring to it by name. It can be illustrated as follows:

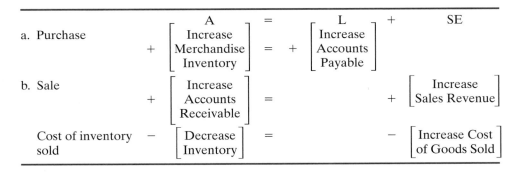

In the perpetual inventory system, the journal entries are:

```
a.  When inventory is purchased:
        Merchandise inventory ........................  xxx
            Accounts payable .........................           xxx
```

b. When inventory is sold:

Accounts receivable (or cash) xxx

    Sales revenue xxx

Cost of goods sold xxx

    Inventory xxx

Thus, in the perpetual inventory system, the sale of an item and the accompanying inventory reduction are recorded simultaneously.

    In contrast, the **periodic inventory system** does not involve a day-to-day record of inventories or of the cost of goods sold. Instead the cost of goods sold and an updated inventory balance are computed only at the end of an accounting period, when a physical count of inventory is taken. The physical count allows management to delete from inventory goods that are damaged or obsolete and thus helps reveal **inventory shrinkage,** which refers to losses from theft, breakage, and loss. Inventory shrinkage can be quite large in some businesses. This periodic inventory system was illustrated in the example of Christina's T-shirt business.

    Under the periodic system, calculations for the cost of goods sold start with the **cost of the goods available for sale.** This is the sum of the opening inventory for the period plus purchases during the period. The accountant computes the cost of goods sold by subtracting the ending inventory from this sum. Thus, the periodic system computes cost of goods sold as a residual amount.

    Although the cost of goods sold under the perpetual system is computed instantaneously as goods are sold, under the periodic system, the computation is delayed until a physical count is made:

$$\underbrace{\text{Beginning inventory} + \text{Purchases}}_{\text{Goods available for sale}} - \underbrace{\text{Ending inventory}}_{\text{Inventory left over}} = \underbrace{\text{Cost of goods sold}}_{\text{Cost of goods sold}}$$

    Exhibit 6-2 compares the perpetual and periodic inventory systems. Note that for annual financial statements, the two methods produce the same cost of goods sold figure. The perpetual system is more timely but it is also more costly to administer. Although the periodic system is less costly because there is no day-to-day processing concerning cost of goods sold, it is not always the best system. The perpetual system often provides managers with better assessments of levels of inventory and helps them order more appropriately to restock the shelves with the right merchandise.

Exhibit 6-2

Inventory Systems

Periodic System		Perpetual System
Beginning inventories		Cost of goods sold (kept on a
(by physical count)	xxx	day-to-day basis instead of
Add: Purchases	xxx	determined periodically)*
Cost of goods available for sale	xxx	
Less: Ending inventories		
(by physical count)	xxx	
Cost of goods sold	xxx	

*Such a condensed figure does not preclude the presentation of a supplementary schedule similar to that on the left.

---

periodic inventory system The system in which the cost of goods sold is computed periodically by relying solely on physical counts without keeping day-to-day records of units sold or on hand.

inventory shrinkage Inventory reductions from theft, breakage, or losses of inventory.

cost of goods available for sale Sum of beginning inventory plus current year purchases.

Home Depot is on a roll. Forbes predicts it will eclipse Sears Roebuck as the nation's second-largest retailer in 2000 (behind Wal-Mart). It has already replaced Sears on the Dow Jones Industrial Average. The company has generated revenue growth of 28% per year for the last 10 years and earnings per share growth of 27%. This is impressive as seen in the following data:

10-Year Average Growth Rates		
	Revenue	*EPS*
Home Depot	28%	27%
Wal-Mart	18	16
JCPenney	8	(14)
Kmart	.3	N/C
Sears	(4)	N/C

N/C = not calculable due to negative earnings.

Home Depot attends to details. Of its 50,000 items including precut venetian blinds, tool rentals, Christmas trees, and pretzels, 70% are responses to customer suggestions. Concluding a 2-year test, washers, dryers, and refrigerators will be added to the line by 2001. However, they will be sold Home Depot's way. A PC-based catalog will support salaried salesclerks. Some models will be stocked, but others will be direct shipped from the manufacturer.

Part of the success comes from aggressive negotiation with suppliers. Home Depot's top suppliers claim they can count on their fingers how often they have been granted a price increase in the past 3 years. When General Electric (GE) experienced shortages in lightbulb inventories, Marcus, the Home Depot founder and CEO immediately cut a deal with Phillips, the Dutch electronics company, to replace GE as lightbulb supplier. Experts believe a large part of the 1.75 percentage point improvement in Home Depot's gross margin over the last 5 years came at the expense of suppliers. Of course, Home Depot's suppliers push their own suppliers, and everyone wants to remain part of this important distribution network. Home Depot sells in huge volumes, and its suppliers prosper accordingly.

Home Depot also seeks new opportunities. In surveys of customers they found GE was named the third best brand for water heaters despite the fact that GE does not make water heaters. Solution: pay GE a royalty for use of the name, pay Rheem to manufacture water heaters with the GE name, and become the exclusive distributor for a great product. They played a similar game with riding lawn mowers, contracting with Deere to manufacture a mower with the Scott brand. They get quality, Scott gets a royalty, and their mower sells for under $4,000 versus the Deere-branded $4,250 at lawn and garden shops.

Home Depot uses technology. Inventory tracking and order placement occurs through wireless-pen-based PCs that staff wheel up and down aisles to transmit current inventory counts and to execute orders based on a database of sales history and forecasts. By the end of 2000, every store had information feeds enabling cashiers to fix jammed register tapes by watching a 20-second training film at their register. Today Home Depot's credit approvals take less than a second, an industry standard.

Home Depot's Web strategy is under construction, but current competition on the Web in its markets is not a big threat. Industry Web sales of about $100 million are in sharp contrast with the Home Depot annual revenue of $38 billion. When the company launches its Web site, the strategy is to provide service based on zip code. Customers will receive inventory and pricing consistent with their closest store and can either pick up or request delivery. This is not a one-price-fits-all strategy and Home Depot does not like Web-based competition. When Black & Decker and Whirlpool began to offer products directly to customers over the Web, Home Depot warned that it would be "hesitant" to retain suppliers who competed directly in the retail market.

Of course, today no one is safe from competition. Lowe's is running hard as second player in this market. Although it is only half the size of Home Depot, its own 10-year growth rates are impressive. Revenue growth was 21% and earnings per share (EPS) growth was 31%. Stay tuned.

Source: Profit in a Big Orange, *Forbes*, January 24, 2000; Financial analysis Web sites via the Excite browser.

PHYSICAL INVENTORY

Good inventory control procedures require a physical count of each item being held in inventory at least annually in both periodic and perpetual inventory systems. The physical count is an imposing, time-consuming, and expensive process. You may have seen "closed for inventory" signs. To simplify counting and valuation, firms often choose fiscal accounting periods so that the year ends when inventories are low. For example, as with Home Depot, Kmart and JCPenney have late January year-ends, which follow the holiday season.

The physical inventory is so important to income determination that external auditors usually observe the client's physical count and confirm the accuracy of the subsequent valuation. Some audit firms hire outside experts to assist them. For example, assessing a jeweler's inventory might require an expert to test the color, size, clarity, and imperfections in the diamonds on hand. Similarly, the client and auditor might rely on an engineer to measure the physical dimensions of an electric utility's coal pile so the volume and weight could be estimated without actually weighing the coal itself.

Inventory fraud is well illustrated by the Classic Salad Oil Swindle. On Thursday, November 21, 1963, reports linked the suspension of two Wall Street brokerage firms to uncollectible loans made to an obscure company named Allied Crude Vegetable Oil and Refining. Collateral for the loans had been $175 million worth of vegetable oil supposedly stored in 40 converted gasoline storage tanks in Bayonne, New Jersey. Investigation revealed that, instead of being filled with vegetable oil, the tanks contained seawater, soap stock, and "sludge."

Allied used some ingenious techniques to hide their shortfall from the watchful auditors. Because the 40 storage tanks were connected by pipes, a small quantity of vegetable oil was pumped from tank to tank during the week required to complete the inventory count. The same vegetable oil was counted over and over. Moreover, no one tank was ever completely filled with the oil. Allied welded shut all but one opening to the tank. Beneath this working opening the company then welded a pipe, which was filled with a few hundred pounds of real oil. When the auditors took samples, they were actually testing what was in this pipe, not what was in the tank. The tank itself was filled with seawater. After the fraud was uncovered, a faucet on one tank was opened, and water poured out for 12 days.

COST OF MERCHANDISE ACQUIRED

Objective 3
Calculate the cost of merchandise acquired.

Regardless of whether you use the periodic or perpetual system, the basis of inventory accounting is the cost of the merchandise a company purchases to then sell. What makes up that cost? To be more specific, does that cost include all or part of the following: invoice price, transportation charges, trade and cash discounts, cost of handling and placing in stock, storage, purchasing department, receiving department, and other indirect charges? In practice, accountants usually consider the cost of merchandise to include only the invoice price plus the directly identifiable inbound transportation charges less any offsetting discounts. The costs of the purchasing and receiving departments are treated as period costs and appear on the income statement as they are incurred.

TRANSPORTATION CHARGES

F.O.B. destination Seller pays freight costs from the shipping point of the seller to the receiving point of the buyer.

F.O.B. shipping point Buyer pays freight costs from the shipping point of the seller to the receiving point of the buyer.

The major cost of transporting merchandise is typically the freight charges from the shipping point of the seller to the receiving point of the buyer. When the seller bears this cost, the terms are stated on the sales invoice as free onboard **(F.O.B.) destination**. When the buyer bears this cost, the terms are stated as **F.O.B. shipping point.**

In theory, any transportation costs borne by the buyer should be added to the cost of the inventory acquired. In practice, though, transportation costs are not always easy to trace to specific inventory items. Companies tend to order several different items and have them shipped at the same time.

By not allocating freight costs, management can more easily manage these costs. For example, management may want to compile freight costs separately to see how they change over time and to compare costs using rail service to costs using trucks. Consequently, accountants frequently use a separate transportation cost account, labeled as Freight In, Transportation In, Inbound Transportation, or Inward Transportation.

Freight in (or **inward transportation**) appears in the purchases section of an income statement as an additional cost of the goods acquired during the period. **Freight Out** represents the costs borne by the seller and is shown as a "shipping expense," which is a form of selling expense. Thus, Freight In affects the gross profit section of an income statement for the buyer, and Freight Out appears below the gross profit line on the seller's income statement.

freight in (inward transportation) An additional cost of the goods acquired during the period, which is often shown in the purchases section of an income statement.

freight out The transportation costs borne by the seller of merchandise and often shown as a "shipping expense."

Suppose that Huang Company bought several items of inventory that were shipped in a single load. Should total freight costs be assigned to each of the components of the shipment based on weight, value, number of items, volume of the item, or some other process?

ANSWER

Each of these bases of assignment might be correct in certain cases. For example, if you thought of coal as the product, weight would be a very good basis for assigning delivery costs. If you thought of jewelry, you might have thought of assigning based on the number of items and their value, because outbound transportation costs would depend on packing and handling of the item and insurance for its value in case it were lost or damaged. Thus, assigning inbound transportation costs would require a lot of analysis to pick the best approach, followed by a lot of clerical work to apply the technique. Because of these difficulties and the modest benefit to the company from all this work, most companies do not assign freight costs to inventories. Instead, they charge them to expense when incurred.

RETURNS, ALLOWANCES, AND DISCOUNTS

The accounting for purchase returns, purchase allowances, and cash discounts on purchases is just the opposite of their sales counterparts. Using the periodic inventory system, suppose gross purchases are $960,000 and purchase returns and allowances are $75,000. The summary journal entries are:

Purchases	960,000	
Accounts payable		960,000
Accounts payable	75,000	
Purchase returns and allowances		75,000

Suppose also that cash discounts of $5,000 are taken on payment of the remaining $960,000 − $75,000 = $885,000 of payables. The summary journal entry is:

Accounts payable	885,000	
Cash discounts on purchases		5,000
Cash		880,000

The accounts Cash Discounts on Purchases and Purchase Returns and Allowances are deducted from Purchases in calculating cost of goods sold.

Exhibit 6-3

Detailed Gross Profit Calculation

($ in thousands)

Gross sales			$1,740
Deduct: Sales returns and allowances		$ 70	
Cash discounts on sales		100	170
Net sales			$1,570
Deduct: Cost of goods sold			
Merchandise inventory, December 31, 20X1		$ 100	
Purchases (gross)	$960		
Deduct: Purchase returns and allowances	$75		
Cash discounts on purchases	5	80	
Net purchases		$880	
Add: Freight in		30	
Total cost of merchandise acquired		910	
Cost of goods available for sale		$1,010	
Deduct: Merchandise inventory, December 31, 20X2		140	
Cost of goods sold			870
Gross profit			$ 700

Car dealers sometimes sell cars "below cost" or "$100 below invoice." Do dealers lose money on such sales? Probably they do not, because gross invoice cost to the dealer and final cost of goods sold may differ. Dealers receive incentives from the manufacturers such as volume discounts or special discounts to push particular models. The dealer's invoice shows the list price before discounts and allowances, not the final net dealer cost.

A detailed gross profit section in the income statement is often arranged as in Exhibit 6-3. Although management may find such detail valuable, summary information is much more common in the annual report to shareholders:

Net sales	$1,570
Cost of goods sold	870
Gross profit	$ 700

COMPARING ACCOUNTING PROCEDURES FOR PERIODIC AND PERPETUAL INVENTORY SYSTEMS

GoodEarth Products, Incorporated, has a balance of $100,000 in merchandise inventory at the beginning of 20X2 (December 31, 20X1). A summary of transactions for 20X2 follows:

a. Purchases	$990,000
b. Purchase returns and allowances	80,000

Net purchases were therefore $990,000 less $80,000, or $910,000. The physical count of the ending inventory for 20X2 led to a cost valuation of $140,000. Note how these figures can be used to compute the $870,000 cost of goods sold:

$$\underset{\text{inventory}}{\text{Beginning}} + \text{Net purchases} - \underset{\text{inventory}}{\text{Ending}} = \underset{\text{goods sold}}{\text{Cost of}}$$

$$\underbrace{\$100{,}000 + \$910{,}000}_{\substack{\text{Cost of goods} \\ \text{available for sale}}} - \underset{\substack{\text{Cost of goods} \\ \text{left over}}}{\$140{,}000} = \underset{\substack{\text{Cost of} \\ \text{goods sold}}}{\$870{,}000}$$

$$\$1{,}010{,}000 - \$140{,}000 = \$870{,}000$$

The periodic and perpetual procedures would record these transactions differently. As Exhibit 6-4 shows in the left side of panel A, the perpetual system entails directly increasing the Inventory account by the $990,000 purchases (entry a) and decreasing it by the $80,000 in returns and allowances (entry b) and the $870,000 cost of goods sold (entry c). The Cost of Goods Sold account would be increased daily as sales are made. The T-accounts reflect how these items would appear in the general ledger.

These summary amounts of $990,000 in purchases and $80,000 in returns and allowances represent many smaller transactions. GoodEarth Products would record each transaction as it occurs. Similarly, GoodEarth would make smaller daily entries as each sale occurs. While the method seems to create the correct $140 final inventory balance, recall that the company will also conduct a physical count to verify the number. Often there are minor differences between the valuation determined by the physical count and the value shown in the perpetual record. Such differences, often due to clerical error or

Exhibit 6-4

GoodEarth Products, Incorporated

Comparison of Perpetual and Periodic Inventory Procedures ($ Amounts in Thousands)

	Perpetual Records			**Periodic Records**		
			PANEL A: JOURNAL ENTRIES			
a. Gross purchases:	Inventory	990		Purchases	990	
	Accounts payable . .		990	Accounts payable		990
b. Returns and allowances:	Accounts payable	80		Accounts payable	80	
	Inventory		80	Purchase returns and allowances		80
c. As goods are sold:	Cost of goods sold	870		No entry		
	Inventory		870			
d. At the end of the accounting period:	d1. } No entry d2. }			d1. Cost of goods sold	1,010	
				Purchase returns and allowances	80	
				Purchases		990
				Inventory		100
				d2. Inventory	140	
				Cost of goods sold . . .		140

	PANEL B: GENERAL LEDGER EFFECTS	

Inventory (Perpetual)

Balance 12/31/X1	100	(b)	80
(a)	990	(c)	870
Balance 12/31/X2	140		

Cost of Goods Sold (Perpetual)

(c)	870		
Balance 12/31/X2	870		

Inventory (Periodic)

Balance 12/31/X1	100	(d1)	100
(d2)	140		
Balance 12/31/X2	140		

Cost of Goods Sold (Periodic)

(d1)	1,010	(d2)	140
Balance 12/31/X2	870		

shrinkage, result in appropriate adjustments to increase or decrease inventory and cost of sales.

Under the periodic system in the right side of panel A of Exhibit 6-4, Purchases and Purchase Returns and Allowances are each accounted for in a separate account, as entries a and b indicate. The periodic system is called *periodic* because neither the Cost of Goods Sold account nor the Inventory account is computed on a daily basis. Entries d1 and d2 at the bottom of Exhibit 6-4 show how these accounts are updated during the eventual periodic calculation of cost of goods sold.

Entry d1 transfers the beginning inventory balance, purchases, and purchase returns and allowances, totaling $1,010,000, to cost of goods sold, which provides the cost of goods available for sale. Next, the ending inventory is physically counted, and its cost is computed. Entry d2 recognizes the $140,000 ending inventory and reduces the $1,010,000 cost of goods available for sale by $140,000 to obtain a final cost of goods sold of $870,000.

Panel B of Exhibit 6-4 shows how these journal entries affect the general ledger accounts. Both sequences reach the same result, inventory of $140 and Cost of Goods Sold of $870.

PRINCIPAL INVENTORY VALUATION METHODS

Objective 4
Choose one of the four principal inventory valuation methods.

Each period, accountants must divide the cost of beginning inventory and merchandise acquired between cost of goods sold and cost of items remaining in ending inventory. Under a perpetual system, we must determine a cost for each item sold. Under a periodic system, we instead must determine the costs of the items remaining in ending inventory. In both systems, costs of individual items must be determined by some inventory valuation method. Four principal inventory valuation methods have been generally accepted in the United States: specific identification; first-in first-out (FIFO); last-in, first-out (LIFO); and weighted-average. Each is explained and compared in this section.

If unit prices and costs did not fluctuate, all four inventory methods would show identical results. However, prices change, and these changes raise central issues concerning cost of goods sold (income measurement) and inventories (asset measurement). As a simple example of the valuation method choices facing management, consider Emilio, a new vendor of a cola drink at the fairgrounds, who begins the week with no inventory. He buys one can on Monday for 30 cents, a second can on Tuesday for 40 cents, and a third can on Wednesday for 56 cents. He then sells one can on Thursday for 90 cents.

As panel I of Exhibit 6-5 shows, Emilio's choice of an inventory method can significantly affect the amount reported as cost of goods sold (and hence gross profit and net income) and ending inventory. The gross profit for Monday through Thursday ranges from 34 cents to 60 cents, depending on the method chosen. By using Exhibit 6-5 as a guide, let us now examine each of the four methods in detail.

SPECIFIC IDENTIFICATION

specific identification method This inventory method concentrates on the physical linking of the particular items sold.

The **specific identification method** concentrates on physically linking the particular items sold. Emilio could mark each can with its cost and record that cost as cost of goods sold when he hands the can to a customer. If he reached for the Monday can instead of the Wednesday can, the specific identification method would show different results. Thus, Panel I of Exhibit 6-5 indicates that gross profit for operations of Monday through Thursday could be 60 cents, 50 cents, or 34 cents, depending on the particular can handed to the customer. Emilio could choose which can to sell and affect reported results by doing so.

Exhibit 6-5

Emilio's Cola Sales
Comparison of Inventory Methods (All Monetary Amounts Are in Cents)

	(1) Specific Identification			(2) FIFO	(3) LIFO	(4) Weighted Average
	(1A)	(1B)	(1C)			
PANEL I						
Income Statement for the Period Monday through Thursday						
Sales	90	90	90	90	90	90
Deduct cost of goods sold						
1 30¢ (Monday) unit	30			30		
1 40¢ (Tuesday) unit		40				
1 56¢ (Wednesday) unit			56		56	
1 weighted-average unit [(30 + 40 + 56) ÷ 3 = 42]						42
Gross profit for Monday through Thursday	60	50	34	60	34	48
Thursday's ending inventory, 2 units						
Monday unit @ 30¢		30	30		30	
Tuesday unit @ 40¢	40		40	40	40	
Wednesday unit @ 56¢	56	56		56		
Weighted-average units @ 42¢						84
Total ending inventory on Thursday	96	86	70	96	70	84
PANEL II						
Income Statement for Friday						
Sales, 2 units @ 90¢	180	180	180	180	180	180
Cost of goods sold (Thursday ending inventory from Panel I)	96	86	70	96	70	84
Gross profit, Friday only	84	94	110	84	110	96
PANEL III						
Gross profit for full week						
Monday through Thursday (Panel I)	60	50	34	60	34	48
Friday (Panel II)	84	94	110	84	110	96
Total gross profit	144	144	144	144	144	144

Because the cost of goods sold is determined by the specific item handed to the customer, the specific identification method permits managers to manipulate income and inventory values by filling a sales order from a number of physically equivalent items with different historical costs. This method is relatively easy to use for relatively expensive low-volume merchandise, such as custom artwork, diamond jewelry, and automobiles. However, most organizations have vast segments of inventories that have too many items insufficiently valuable per unit to warrant such individualized attention.

FIFO

FIFO refers to **first-in, first-out.** The method is a cost assignment method and does not track the actual physical flow of individual items except by coincidence. For identical units, it assigns the cost of the earliest acquired units to cost of goods sold. Picture Emilio putting each new can of cola at the back of the cooler to chill and the oldest, coldest can being sold first. Thus, under FIFO, Emilio's Monday can of cola is deemed to have been sold—regardless of the actual can delivered. The costs of the newer stock are assigned to the units in ending inventory. This fact leads some to label this method last-in, still-here (LISH).

By using the more recent costs to measure the ending inventory, FIFO tends to provide inventory valuations that closely approximate the actual market value of the inventory at

first-in, first-out (FIFO)
This method of accounting for inventory assigns the cost of the earliest acquired units to cost of goods sold.

the balance sheet date. In addition, in periods of rising prices, FIFO leads to higher net income. Note that gross profit is 60 cents in Panel I of Exhibit 6-5 under FIFO because the oldest, cheapest unit is used in the calculation of cost of goods sold. Higher reported incomes may favorably affect investor attitudes toward the company. Similarly, higher reported incomes may lead to higher salaries, higher bonuses, or higher status for the management of the company. Unlike specific identification, FIFO specifies the order in which acquisition costs become cost of goods sold, so management cannot affect income by choosing to sell one identical item instead of another.

LIFO

last-in, first-out (LIFO)
This inventory method assigns the most recent costs to cost of goods sold.

LIFO refers to **last-in, first-out.** Whereas FIFO associates the most recent costs with ending inventories, LIFO assigns the most recent costs to costs of goods sold. The LIFO method assumes that the stock acquired most recently is sold first. Picture Emilio putting each new can, as it is acquired, into the top of a cooler. At each customer purchase, the top can is the one sold. This is the physical flow that corresponds to the LIFO cost system. Thus, under LIFO, Emilio's Wednesday can of cola is deemed to have been sold—regardless of the actual can delivered from the cooler.

LIFO provides an income statement perspective in the sense that net income measured using LIFO combines current sales prices and current acquisition costs. In a period of rising prices and constant or growing inventories, LIFO yields lower net income as shown by the 34 cents of gross margin in Panel I of Exhibit 6-5. Why is lower net income such an important feature of LIFO? In the United States, LIFO is an acceptable inventory accounting method for income tax purposes. When lower income is reported to the tax authorities, lower taxes are paid, so it is not surprising that almost two-thirds of U.S. corporations use LIFO for at least some of their inventories. However, the Internal Revenue Code requires that if LIFO is used for tax purposes, it must also be used for financial reporting purposes.

You might think of LIFO as the good news/bad news method. Lower income taxes provide the good news but the accompanying bad news is lower reported profits. During a period of higher inflation some years ago, the *Wall Street Journal* reported that many small firms changed from FIFO to LIFO. As an example, Chicago Heights Steel Company "boosted cash by 5% to 10% by lowering income taxes when it switched to LIFO." When Becton, Dickinson and Company changed to LIFO, its annual report stated that its "change to the LIFO method . . . for both financial reporting and income tax purposes resulted in improved cash flow due to lower income taxes paid." Indeed, some observers maintain that executives are guilty of serious mismanagement by not adopting LIFO when FIFO produces significantly higher taxable income.

The whole issue with respect to LIFO is driven by inflation. When inflation is low, as it has been for nearly a decade, the tax and income differences are small as well. The inventory method chosen matters little. Low inflation has been the norm in the United States during most of the last hundred years, but in 1974, the inflation rate in the United States reached double digits for the first time. In response, more than 40 U.S. corporations switched from FIFO to LIFO, apparently deciding the benefit of lower income taxes exceeded the cost of reporting lower profits. These tax savings were not trivial. For example, by switching from FIFO to LIFO, DuPont saved more than $200 million in taxes in 1974, and could anticipate greater savings in the future.

Why did some firms remain on FIFO? Some firms should choose FIFO because for them it lowers taxes. Even when prices were rising in general, some industries, such as computers, faced declining costs and prices, so FIFO minimized reported income and taxes. For those who could have lowered taxes by using LIFO, possible reasons to remain on LIFO include the high bookkeeping costs of implementing the switch, reluctance by management to make an accounting switch reducing reported income and possibly reducing management bonuses, fear that banks would view the reduction in income unfavorably in loan negotiations, and belief that lower reported income would result in a lower stock price.

LIFO permits management to influence reported income by the timing of purchases of inventory items. Consider Emilio's case. Suppose that acquisition prices increase from 56 cents on Wednesday to 68 cents on Thursday, the day of the sale of the one unit. How is net income affected if one more unit is acquired on Thursday? Under LIFO, cost of goods sold would change to 68 cents, and profit would fall by 12 cents. In contrast, under FIFO, cost of goods sold and gross profit would be unchanged.

	LIFO		FIFO	
	As in Exhibit 6-5	*If One More Unit Acquired*	*As in Exhibit 6-5*	*If One More Unit Acquired*
Sales	90¢	90¢	90¢	90¢
Cost of goods sold	56¢	68¢	30¢	30¢
Gross profit	34¢	22¢	60¢	60¢
Ending inventory				
First purchase, Monday	30¢	30¢		
Second purchase, Tuesday	40¢	40¢	40¢	40¢
Third purchase, Wednesday		56¢	56¢	56¢
Fourth purchase, Thursday				68¢
	70¢	126¢	96¢	164¢

WEIGHTED AVERAGE

The **weighted-average method** computes a unit cost by dividing the total acquisition cost of all items available for sale by the number of units available for sale. Picture Emilio dropping his cooler and not knowing which can was on top. Exhibit 6-5 shows the calculations Emilio would make to average the costs of these units. The average cost is 42 cents [(30 + 40 + 56) ÷ 3].

The averaging in the weighted-average method can be better understood by assuming Emilio bought two cans instead of one on Monday at 30 cents each. To get the weighted average, we must consider not only the price paid, but also the number of units purchased as follows:

Weighted average = Cost of goods available for sale ÷ Units available for sale
Weighted average = [(2 × 30¢) + (1 × 40¢) + (1 × 56¢)] ÷ 4
= 156¢ ÷ 4
= 39¢

The weighted-average method produces a gross profit somewhere between that obtained under FIFO and that under LIFO (48 cents as compared with 60 cents and 34 cents in panel I of Exhibit 6-5).

weighted-average method
This inventory method computes a unit cost by dividing the total acquisition cost of all items available for sale by the number of units available for sale.

COST FLOW ASSUMPTIONS

Because the actual physical flow of identical products is less important to the financial success of most businesses than is the flow of the units' costs, the accounting profession has concluded that companies may choose any of the four methods to record cost of goods sold. Basically, the units are all the same, but their costs differ, so tracing the flow or assignment of those costs is more important than is tracing where each specific unit goes. Because three out of the four methods are not linked to the physical flow of merchandise, inventory methods are often referred to as cost flow assumptions. For example, when we decide that the cost of the first inventory item purchased will be matched with the sales revenue from the first item sold to calculate the gross profit from the sale, we are adopting the FIFO cost flow assumption.

It is interesting to note that no matter what cost flow assumptions we use, the cumulative gross profit over the life of a company remains the same. Suppose Emilio sells his remaining inventory for 90¢ per can on Friday and enters a more attractive business. Panel II of Exhibit 6-5 shows Friday's gross profit. As you can see, the gross profit for this one period, Friday, varies with the cost flow assumption used. However, Panel III of Exhibit 6-5 shows that the cumulative gross profit over the life of Emilio's business would be the same $1.44 under any of the inventory methods. What makes the choice of method important is the need to match particular costs to particular periods during the life of the business in order to prepare periodic financial statements and evaluate performance.

INVENTORY COST RELATIONSHIPS

Note that all four methods work with the same basic numbers. Nothing in our choice of methods affects accounts payable. We record inventory purchases at cost and recognize a liability in the same way under all these methods. All that changes is how we allocate those costs between inventory and cost of sales.

Recall that during a period of rising prices, FIFO yields higher inventory and higher gross profit than does LIFO. This result is consistent with the accounting equation that requires that A = L + OE. If inventory is higher under FIFO (higher assets) and the equation is to balance, either liabilities or owners' equity must also be higher. Higher gross profit under FIFO implies higher net income and higher owners' equity (OE in the equation).

There are, of course, relationships other than those of the accounting equation that come into play in the various inventory methods. Consider also the link between cost of goods sold and the valuation of ending inventory. Emilio's three cola cans had a total cost of goods available for sale of $1.26. At the end of the period, this $1.26 must be allocated either to cans sold or to cans in ending inventory. The higher the cost of goods sold, the lower the ending inventory. Exhibit 6-6 illustrates that interdependence. At one extreme, FIFO treats the 30 cent cost of the first can acquired as cost of goods sold and 96 cents as ending inventory. At the other extreme, LIFO treats the 56 cent cost of the last can acquired as cost of goods sold and 70 cents as ending inventory.

Exhibit 6-6

Emilio's Cola Sales

Diagram of Inventory Methods (Data are from Panel I, Exhibit 6-5; Monetary Amounts Are in Cents)

Beginning inventory	+	Merchandise purchases	=	Cost of goods available for sale
0	+	126	=	126
Cost of goods available for sale	−	Cost of goods sold	=	Ending inventory

1 @ 30 1 @ 40 1 @ 56	126	−	30 or 40 or 56	=	96 or 86 or 70	Specific identification
	126	−	30	=	96	FIFO
	126	−	56	=	70	LIFO
	126	−	42	=	84	Weighted average

THE CONSISTENCY CONVENTION

Although companies can choose just about any inventory cost flow assumption they want, they have to be consistent over time and stick with whatever they choose. The Financial Accounting Standards Board (FASB) has referred to **consistency** as "conformity from period to period with unchanging policies and procedures." Interpreting financial performance over time involves comparing the results of different periods. If accounting methods for inventory were changed often, meaningful comparisons over time would be impossible.

consistency Conformity from period to period with unchanging policies and procedures.

Occasionally a change in market conditions or other circumstances may justify a change in inventory method. With its auditor's approval, a firm may change method. However, the firm is required to note the change in its financial statements, and the auditor also refers to the change in the audit opinion. Therefore, financial statement readers are alerted to the possible effects of the change on their analysis.

CHARACTERISTICS AND CONSEQUENCES OF LIFO

LIFO is just another method, but it is very widely used in the United States, has strong tax benefits for certain companies, and has some unusual features in application. Because of its dominant role in inventory accounting in the United States, LIFO gets a little extra attention from us in this section. Actually, LIFO is a fairly uncommon method in most countries. For example, in Brazil and Australia it is not permitted at all, and in Canada it is disallowed for tax purposes. The most popular method worldwide is the average cost method, and the next most common choice is FIFO.

HOLDING GAINS AND INVENTORY PROFITS

LIFO's income statement orientation provides a particular economic interpretation of operating performance in inflationary periods, based on replacement of inventory. A merchant such as Emilio is in the business of buying and selling on a daily basis. To continue in business, he must be able to maintain his stock of cola and must make sufficient profit on each transaction to make it worth his while to run his soda stand. So, before he can feel he has really made a profit, he will need to restock his inventory and be ready for the next day. If he must spend 56 cents to replace the can that was sold, we might call 56 cents the **replacement cost** of the inventory. Under LIFO we calculate his profit to be 34 cents, because we use that recent inventory acquisition cost of 56 cents to measure cost of goods sold. So LIFO approximates a replacement cost view of the transaction.

replacement cost The cost at which an inventory item could be acquired today.

In contrast, FIFO measures profit relative to the 30-cent can acquired on Monday and reports a profit of 60 cents. The difference between the 60 cents FIFO profit and the 34 cents LIFO profit is 26 cents, which is also the difference between the historical cost of 30 cents under FIFO and 56 cents under LIFO. This 26 cents difference that occurs because prices are rising is called a **holding gain** or an **inventory profit.** The idea is that between Monday and Thursday, Emilio's first can of cola acquired for 30 cents became more valuable as prices rose, and because he held it during those days he experienced a 26 cents gain.

holding gain (inventory profit) Increase in the replacement cost or other measure of current value of the inventory held during the current period.

Because LIFO matches the most recent acquisition costs with sales revenue, LIFO cost of goods sold typically offers a close approximation to replacement cost, and reported net income rarely contains significant holding gains. In contrast, FIFO reports a profit of 60 cents including the economic profit of 34 cents calculated as sales price less replacement costs, plus the inventory profit or holding gain of 26 cents that arose because the value of the inventory item rose with the passage of time.

This issue is more than an accounting complexity of academic interest. Whenever government begins to reconsider the tax law, this issue takes center stage. For example, a recent reduction in U.S. capital gains taxes relies on the notion that holding gains are economically different from true economic profit and should be taxed less.

LIFO LAYERS

LIFO layer (LIFO increment) A separately identifiable additional segment of LIFO inventory.

The ending inventory under LIFO will have one total value, but it may contain prices from many different periods. For example, Emilio's ending inventory contained two cans, one acquired on Monday at 30 cents and one acquired on Tuesday at 40 cents. Each distinct cost element of inventory might be called a **LIFO layer** (also called **LIFO increment**)—an addition to inventory at an identifiable cost level. As a company grows, the LIFO layers tend to pile on top of one another over the years. Suppose Emilio's business grew for years, ending each year with two more cans in inventory than were there the year before. Each year would have an identifiable LIFO layer, much like the annual rings on a tree. After 5 years of inventory growth and rising prices, his ending inventory might be structured as follows:

Year 1	Layer 1—1 can @.30	
	Layer 2—1 can @.40	.70
Year 2	Layer 3—2 cans @.45	.90
Year 3	Layer 4—2 cans @.50	1.00
Year 4	Layer 5—2 cans @.55	1.10
Total inventory—8 cans		$3.70

Many LIFO companies show inventories that have ancient layers going back as far as 1940, when LIFO was first used. Reported LIFO inventory values may therefore be far below what the true market value or current replacement value of the inventory might be. From a balance sheet perspective, this means that the book values being reported will have little relevance to investors interested in assessing the assets of the company. While LIFO presents the economic reality on the income statement well, FIFO provides more up to date valuations on the balance sheet.

LIFO INVENTORY LIQUIDATIONS

Objective 5
Calculate the impact on net income of LIFO liquidations.

The existence of old LIFO layers can cause problems in income measurement when inventory decreases after a period of rising prices. Examine Exhibit 6-7. Suppose Harbor Electronics bought 100 units of inventory at $10 per unit on December 31, 20X0 to begin its business operations. The company bought and sold 100 units each year, 20X1 through 20X4, at the purchase and selling prices shown. The example assumes replacement costs and sales prices rise by the same amount, with a difference between the two of $3 per unit. In 20X5, 100 units were sold but none were purchased.

Compare the gross profit each year under LIFO with that under FIFO in Exhibit 6-7. LIFO gross profit was generally less than FIFO gross profit because prices were rising, and the LIFO cost of goods sold reflected the latest prices, while the FIFO did not. What happened in 20X5? The old 20X0 inventory became the cost of goods sold under LIFO because inventory was depleted. As a result, gross profit under LIFO soared to $1,300, well above the FIFO gross profit, which was stable at $500. In general, when the physical amount of inventory decreases, under LIFO old, low inventory acquisition costs associated with old LIFO layers are used to calculate cost of goods sold. This is called a LIFO liquidation. This treatment can create a very low cost of goods sold and high gross profit. For example, LIFO inventory liquidations by Alcoa increased its 1999 net income by $31 million, about 3% of its $1,054 million net income. In a sense, a LIFO liquidation means that the cumulative inventory profit from years of increasing prices is reflected in the income statement in one year. An analyst tracking Alcoa's profitability would want to know that its profit increase that year was not due solely to opening new stations and selling more gasoline. It was partly due to the company's inventory accounting process.

The effect of LIFO liquidations is potentially large and security analysts like to remain aware of the effect of the choice between LIFO and FIFO on net income. The

Exhibit 6-7

Harbor Electronics

Effect of Inventory Liquidations under LIFO (Purchases and sales of 100 Units 20X1 through 20X4, Purchases but No Sales in 20X0; Sales but No Purchases in 20X5)

Year	Purchase Price Per Unit	Selling Price Per Unit	Revenue	FIFO Cost of Goods Sold	FIFO Gross Profit	FIFO Ending Inventory	LIFO Cost of Goods Sold	LIFO Gross Profit	LIFO Ending Inventory
20X0	$10	—	—	—	—	$1,000	—	—	$1,000
20X1	12	$15	$1,500	$1,000	$ 500	1,200	$1,200	$ 300	1,000
20X2	14	17	1,700	1,200	500	1,400	1,400	300	1,000
20X3	16	19	1,900	1,400	500	1,600	1,600	300	1,000
20X4	18	21	2,100	1,600	500	1,800	1,800	300	1,000
20X5		23	2,300	1,800	500	0	1,000	1,300	0
Total			$9,500	$7,000	$2,500		$7,000	$2,500	

difference between a company's LIFO inventory level and what it would be under FIFO is helpful in tracking these relations. This difference is called the **LIFO reserve.** Most companies that use LIFO explicitly measure and report this LIFO reserve on the front of the balance sheet or in the footnotes.

LIFO reserve The difference between a company's inventory valued at LIFO and what it would be under FIFO.

Refer to Exhibit 6-7. What is the Harbor Electronics LIFO reserve at the end of 20X1? It is $1,200 − $1,000 = $200, the difference in the LIFO and FIFO ending inventories. Note that it is the same as the difference in gross profit of $200 in the first year of the example. What about year 20X2? The LIFO reserve is $400 (FIFO ending inventory of $1,400 less LIFO ending inventory of $1,000). This difference represents the cumulative effect on earnings (or gross profit) over the first 2 years the company was in business. The specific effect on earnings during 20X2 is the change in the LIFO reserve, or $200. Exhibit 6-8 summarizes these effects.

From Exhibit 6-8 note that the annual difference between gross profit using FIFO and that using LIFO is the yearly change in the LIFO reserve. Finally, when all the inventory is sold in 20X5, the liquidation of the LIFO inventory leads to recognition of higher earnings than under FIFO by the amount of the LIFO reserve. LIFO recognizes inventory profits when inventory levels are reduced. The balance of the LIFO reserve at any point in time indicates the cumulative effect on gross profit over all prior years due to LIFO.

How significant are the effects of LIFO? Ford Motor Company reported 2000 inventory of $7.5 billion. LIFO was used for the U.S. inventories. If FIFO had been used for all inventories, the total inventory would have been $1.1 billion higher (more than a

Exhibit 6-8

Harbor Electronics

Annual and Cumulative Effects of LIFO Reserve

Year	Ending Inventory FIFO	Ending Inventory LIFO	LIFO Reserve	Change in Reserve	Gross Profit Effect Current	Gross Profit Effect Cumulative
X0	$1,000	$1,000	$ 0	$ 0	$ 0	$ 0
X1	1,200	1,000	200	200	200	200
X2	1,400	1,000	400	200	200	400
X3	1,600	1,000	600	200	200	600
X4	1,800	1,000	800	200	200	800
X5	0	0	0	(800)	(800)	0

15% difference). This means that over time, Ford has reported lower income on its tax returns by $1.1 billion and paid lower taxes of approximately $440 million ($1.1 billion times the approximate tax rate of 40%) as a result of its decision to use LIFO instead of FIFO.

This savings amounts to an interest-free loan from the government. If Ford ever goes out of business, the sale of old inventory items will create a large LIFO liquidation and all these delayed taxes will become due. In the meantime, Ford has the use of some $440 million it has not yet had to pay in taxes.

ADJUSTING FROM LIFO TO FIFO

As mentioned earlier, Ford Motor Company uses LIFO and therefore reports different cost of goods sold and inventory levels than it would if FIFO were used. Ford reported the following in 2000:

Ford Motor Company ($ in Millions)

	2000 Inventory		Cost of
	Beginning	*Ending*	**Goods Sold**
LIFO	5,684	7,514	126,120
LIFO reserve	1,000	1,100	
FIFO	6,684	8,614	126,020

*Change in LIFO reserve is ⟨$100⟩ ($1,000 − $1,100).

Note that Ford's LIFO reserve increased from $1.0 billion to $1.1 billion during the year. This increase of $100 million in the LIFO reserve is exactly the amount by which the cost of goods sold for the year under LIFO is more than the cost of goods sold under FIFO.

Why is the LIFO cost of goods sold higher? Because costs are rising and under LIFO the new higher costs flow directly to the cost of goods sold reported in the earnings statement. In contrast, under FIFO the new higher costs flow into ending inventory, while older lower costs are used to calculate cost of goods sold. Cumulatively, this process has happened year after year for Ford. The *change* in the LIFO reserve from one year to the next answers the question "How much did this year's LIFO cost of good sold differ from what the cost of goods sold would have been if FIFO were used?"

In contrast to this effect on costs of goods sold in a specific year, we can examine the cumulative effect of the inventory accounting choice over time. The end of year level of the LIFO reserve allows us to answer the question "During the years that Ford has used LIFO, what has the total, cumulative effect been on cost of goods sold over all those years?" To see this, do the mental experiment of having Ford sell all of its 2000 year-end inventory for $9,000 million. How would profit from this liquidation differ between LIFO and FIFO given inventory levels that would exist at year end 2000 under each method?

ANSWER

This complete liquidation would produce higher profits under LIFO. These higher profits in the final liquidation year are equal to the cumulative amount by which gross profits were lower under LIFO in past years. The hypothetical liquidation of Ford inventories would show:

	LIFO	FIFO	Difference
Sales	$9,000	$9,000	—
Cost of goods sold	7,514	8,614	1,100
Gross profit	$1,486	$ 386	($1,100)

LOWER-OF-COST-OR-MARKET METHOD

Objective 6
Use the lower-of-cost-or-market method to value inventories.

Sometimes obsolete or damaged inventory items cannot be easily sold at amounts equal to their historical cost. Investors want to know if the inventory can be sold to at least recover its cost. Under the **lower-of-cost-or-market method (LCM),** a market-price test is run on an inventory costing method. The current market price is compared with historical cost derived under one of the four primary methods: specific identification, FIFO, LIFO, or weighted average. The lower of the two—current market value or historical cost—is conservatively selected as the basis for the valuation of goods at a specific inventory date. When market value is lower and is used for valuing the ending inventory, the effect is to increase the amount reported as cost of goods sold.

lower-of-cost-or-market method (LCM) The superimposition of a market-price test on an inventory cost method.

LCM is an example of conservatism. **Conservatism** means selecting methods of measurement that yield lower net income, lower assets, and lower stockholders' equity. Conservatism was illustrated in accounts receivable with the use of an allowance for bad debts. We estimated and recorded losses on uncollectible accounts before they were certain. With inventories, conservatism dictates the use of the LCM method.

conservatism Selecting the methods of measurement that yield lower net income, lower assets, and lower stockholders' equity.

Accountants feel that erring in the direction of conservatism is better than erring in the direction of overstating assets and net income. The accountant's conservatism balances management's optimism. Management prepares the financial statements, but the conservatism principle moderates management's human tendency to hope for, and expect, the best.

ROLE OF REPLACEMENT COST

Under generally accepted accounting principles (GAAP), the definition of market price is complex. For our purposes we think of it as the replacement cost of the inventory item, that is, what it would cost to buy the inventory item today. Keep in mind, though, that this method assumes that when replacement costs decline in the wholesale market, so do the retail selling prices. Consider the following example. The Ripley Company has 100 units in its ending FIFO inventory on December 31, 20X1. Its gross profit of $990 for 20X1 has been tentatively computed as follows:

Sales		$2,180
Cost of goods available for sale	$1,980	
Ending inventory of 100 units, at cost	790	
Cost of goods sold		1,190
Gross profit		$ 990

Assume a sudden decline in market prices during the final week of December from $7.90 per unit to $4 per unit. If we assume that the sales price will drop along with the market price, an inventory write-down of ($7.90 − $4.00) × 100 units, or $390, is in order. A **write-down** reduces the recorded historical cost of an item in response to a decline in value. When a write-down occurs, the new $4 per unit replacement cost becomes, for accounting purposes, the unexpired cost of the inventory. Thus, if replacement prices subsequently rise to $8 per unit in January 20X2, the assigned cost of each

write-down A reduction in the assumed cost of an item in response to a decline in value.

unit will remain $4. In short, the lower-of-cost-or-market method would regard the $4 cost of December 31 as the "new historical cost" of the inventory. The required journal entry is:

Loss on write-down of inventory (or cost of goods
  sold)   390
    Inventory   390
To write down inventory from $790 cost to
$400 market value

The write-down of inventories increases cost of goods sold by $390. Therefore, reported income for 20X1 would be lowered by $390:

	Before $390 Write-Down	After $390 Write-Down	Difference
Sales	$2,180	$2,180	
Cost of goods available	$1,980	$1,980	
Ending inventory	790	400	−$390
Cost of goods sold	$1,190	$1,580	+$390
Gross profit	$ 990	$ 600	−$390

Why is $390 written down? LCM holds that of the $790 historical cost, $390 is considered to have expired during 20X1 because that cost cannot be justifiably carried forward to the future as an asset. However, if the market replacement cost falls but selling prices remain the same, items still have their original earnings power. No loss has occurred and no reduction in the book value of the inventory is necessary.

CONSERVATISM IN ACTION

Compared with a pure cost method, the lower-of-cost-or-market method reports less net income in the period of decline in the market value of the inventory and more net income in the period of sale. The lower-of-cost-or-market method affects how much income is reported in each year but not the total income over the company's life. Exhibit 6-9

Exhibit 6-9

The Ripley Company
Effects of Lower-of-Cost-or-Market

	Cost Method		Lower-of-Cost-or-Market Method	
	20X1	*20X2*	*20X1*	*20X2*
Sales	$2,180	$800	$2,180	$800
Cost of goods available	$1,980	$790	$1,980	$400
Ending inventory	790	—	400*	—
Cost of goods sold	$1,190	$790	$1,580	$400
Gross profit	$ 990	$ 10	$ 600	$400

Combined gross profit for 2 years
   Cost method: $990 + $10 = $1,000
   Lower-of-cost-or-market method: $600 + $400 = $1,000

*The inventory is shown here after being written down by $390, from $790 to $400. For internal purposes, many accountants prefer to show the write-down separately, presenting a gross profit before write-down of inventory, the write-down, and a gross profit after write-down.

underscores this point. Suppose the Ripley Company goes out of business in early 20X2. That is, it acquires no more units. There are no sales in 20X2 except for the disposal of the inventory at $8 per unit (100 × $8 = $800). The LCM method will affect neither combined gross profit nor combined net income for the two periods, as the bottom of Exhibit 6-9 reveals.

A full-blown lower-of-cost-or-market method is rarely encountered in practice. Why? Because it is expensive to get the correct replacement costs of hundreds or thousands of different products in inventory. Further, the benefit from doing so does not justify the cost. Auditors do watch for price trends in the industry that might indicate a serious concern. In particular, they watch for subclasses of inventory that are obsolete, shopworn, or otherwise of only nominal value and apply LCM to such inventory.

EFFECTS OF INVENTORY ERRORS

Inventory errors can arise from many sources. For example, incorrect physical counts might be taken because goods that were in receiving or shipping areas instead of in the inventory stockroom were not counted. A clerk might hit a 5 on the keyboard instead of a 6.

Objective 7
Show the effects of inventory errors on financial statements.

An undiscovered inventory error usually affects two reporting periods. Amounts will be misstated in the period in which the error occurred, but the effects will then be counterbalanced by identical offsetting amounts in the following period. Consider the income statements in Exhibit 6-10 (all numbers are in thousands), which assume ending 20X7 inventory shown in panel A is reported to be $10,000 too low.

Think about the effects of the uncorrected error on the following year, 20X8, shown in Panel B. The beginning inventory will be $60,000 instead of the correct $70,000. Therefore, all the errors in 20X7 will be offset by counterbalancing errors in 20X8. Thus, the retained income at the end of 20X8 would show a cumulative effect of zero. Why? Because the net income in 20X7 would be understated by $6,000, but the net income in 20X8 would be overstated by $6,000.

The point here is that the ending inventory of one period is also the beginning inventory of the succeeding period. The example assumes that the operations during 20X8 are a duplication of those of 20X7 except that the ending inventory is correctly counted as $40,000.

The complete analyses for 20X7 and 20X8 show the full detail of the inventory error, and they provide us with a handy rule of thumb. If ending inventory is understated, retained income is understated. If ending inventory is overstated, retained income is overstated. These relations are clear from the accounting equation. Including taxes in this rule of thumb is really just adding another piece of the accounting equation. Why? Understated inventory implies overstated cost of goods sold and therefore lower current-year income and lower tax liability. The shortcut analysis including taxes follows, assuming a 40% tax rate:

	A	**=**	**L**	**+**	**SE**
	Inventory		*Income Tax Liability*		*Retained Income*
Effects of error	$10,000 understated	=	$4,000 understated	+	$6,000 understated*

*Cost of goods overstated	$10,000
Pretax income understated	$10,000
Income taxes understated	4,000
Net income, which is included in ending retained income, understated	$ 6,000

In the second year, the income and taxes will be affected in the opposite direction and the total taxes over both years will be correct.

Exhibit 6-10

Effects of Inventory Errors

	PANEL A		
20X7	**Correct Reporting**	**Incorrect Reporting***	**Effects of Errors**
Sales	$980	$980	
Deduct: Cost of goods sold			
Beginning inventory	$100	$100	
Purchases	500	500	
Cost of goods available for sale	$600	$600	
Deduct: Ending inventory	70	60	Understated by $10
Cost of goods sold	530	540	Overstated by $10
Gross profit	$450	$440	Understated by $10
Other expenses	250	250	
Income before income taxes	$200	$190	Understated by $10
Income tax expense at 40%	80	76	Understated by $4
Net income	$120	$114	**Understated by $6**
Ending balance sheet items			
Inventory	$ 70	$ 60	Understated by $10
Retained income includes			Understated by $6
current net income of	120	114	
Income tax liability[†]	80	76	Understated by $4

*Because of error in ending inventory.

[†]For simplicity, assume that the entire income tax expense for the year will not be paid until the succeeding year. Therefore, the ending liability will equal the income tax expense.

	PANEL B		
20X8	**Correct Reporting**	**Incorrect Reporting***	**Effects of Errors**
Sales	$980	$980	
Deduct: Cost of goods sold			
Beginning inventory	$ 70	$ 60	Understated by $10
Purchases	500	500	
Cost of goods available for sale	$570	$560	Understated by $10
Deduct: Ending inventory	40	40	
Cost of goods sold	530	520	Understated by $10
Gross profit	$450	$460	Overstated by $10
Other expenses	250	250	
Income before income taxes	$200	$210	Overstated by $10
Income tax expense at 40%	80	84	Overstated by $4
Net income	$120	$126	**Overstated by $6**
Ending balance sheet items			
Inventory	$ 40	$ 40	**Correct**
Retained income includes			
Net income of previous year	120	114	Counterbalanced and
Net income of current year	120	126	thus now correct in total
Two-year total	240	240	
Income tax liability			
End of previous year	80	76	Counterbalanced and
End of current year	80	84	thus now correct in total[†]
Two-year total	160	160	

*Because of error in beginning inventory.

[†]The $84 really consists of the $4 that pertains to income of the previous year plus $80 that pertains to income of the current year.

The accrual basis of accounting should include the physical counting and careful valuation of inventory at least once yearly. Auditors routinely search for **cutoff errors,** which are failures to record transactions in the correct time period. For example, assume a periodic inventory system. Suppose a physical inventory is conducted on December 31. Inventory purchases of $100,000 arrive in the receiving room during the afternoon of December 31. The acquisition is included in Purchases and Accounts Payable but excluded from the ending inventory valuation. Such an error would understate ending inventory, thereby overstating cost of goods sold and understating gross profit. On the other hand, if the acquisition were not recorded until January 2, the error would understate both the ending inventory and Accounts Payable as of December 31. However, cost of goods sold and gross profit would be correct because Purchases and the ending inventory would be understated by the same amount.

cutoff error Failure to record transactions in the correct time period.

The general approach to recording purchases and sales is keyed to the legal transfer of ownership. Auditors are especially careful about cutoff tests because the pressure for profits sometimes causes managers to postpone the recording of bona fide purchases of goods and services. Similarly, the same managers may deliberately include sales orders near year-end (instead of bona fide completed sales) in revenues. For example, consider the case of Datapoint, a maker of small computers and telecommunications equipment. A news story reported: "Datapoint's hard-pressed sales force was still logging orders that might not hold up after shipment." In the wake of an accounting scandal, Datapoint's president declared a 3-week "amnesty period" during which scheduled shipments could be removed from the sales account, no questions asked.

A similar news story referred to difficulties at McCormick & Company, a firm known for its spices: "The investigation also found that improprieties included the company's accounting for sales. In a longstanding practice, the company recorded as sales, goods that had been selected and prepared for shipment rather than waiting until after they had been shipped as is the customary accounting practice."

THE IMPORTANCE OF GROSS PROFITS

We began this chapter by discussing gross profits, which are the result of sales revenue less the cost of goods sold. Management and investors are intensely interested in gross profit and how it changes over time. In comparing the gross profits of two firms, it is sometimes important to examine which inventory method they have used to calculate their gross profit.

Objective 8
Evaluate the gross profit percentage and inventory turnover.

GROSS PROFIT PERCENTAGE

Gross profit is often expressed as a percentage of sales. Consider the following information on a past year for a typical Safeway grocery store:

	Amount	Percentage
Sales	$10,000,000	100%
Net cost of goods sold	7,500,000	75%
Gross profit	$ 2,500,000	25%

The **gross profit percentage**—gross profit divided by sales—here is 25%. It is worth noting that financial analysts define the gross profit percentage this way, as a percent of sales. In marketing the profit percentage is sometimes expressed as a markup on cost. In this example, the markup on cost is $2,500,000 ÷ $7,500,000 = 33%.

gross profit percentage Gross profit as a percentage of sales.

The following table illustrates the extent to which gross profit percentages vary among industries.

Industry	Gross Profit (%)
Auto retailers	12.0
Auto manufacturers	18.1
Jewelry retailers	45.4
Grocery retailers	23.2
Grocery wholesalers	14.5
Drug manufacturers	41.1

Source: RMA, *Annual Statement Studies for 1999*.

wholesaler An intermediary that sells inventory items to retailers.

retailer A company that sells items directly to the final users, individuals.

What accounts for this wide variation in gross profit percentage? The nature of the business has a lot to do with it. **Wholesalers** sell in larger quantity and incur fewer selling costs because they sell to other companies instead of individuals. As a result of competition and high volumes, they have smaller gross profit percentages than do retailers. **Retailers** sell directly to the public—to individual buyers. Among retailers, jewelers have twice the gross profits of grocers because of extensive personal selling. Drug manufacturers earn high gross profits because of high drug prices, caused by the need for substantial research and development (R&D) outlays (up to 15% of sales) and allowed by patent protection on specific drugs. In contrast, auto manufacturers face more direct competition and earn lower gross profit percentages.

It is also important to note that R&D is a cost of developing a drug and therefore must be incurred to generate any sales from a drug. However, accounting practice treats the R&D costs as a period cost when incurred instead of a product cost to be matched to future sales of the drug. We do this because it is impossible to know as R&D costs are incurred, whether they will ultimately produce a viable drug whose therapeutic value will allow recovery of the costs of developing it.

ESTIMATING INTRAPERIOD GROSS PROFIT AND INVENTORY

The gross profit percentage can be extremely useful, especially when related information is unavailable. For example, exact ending inventory balances are not usually available for monthly or quarterly reports. To avoid costly physical counts, interim reports often rely on estimates derived from percentage or ratio methods. For example, assume that past sales of Tip Top Variety Store have usually resulted in a gross profit percentage of 25%. The accountant would estimate gross profit to be 25% of sales. If the monthly sales are $800,000, the cost of goods sold can be estimated as follows:

$$\text{Sales} - \text{Cost of goods sold} = \text{Gross profit}$$
$$\text{S} - \text{CGS} = \text{GP}$$
$$\$800,000 - \text{CGS} = .25 \times \$800,000 = \$200,000$$
$$\text{CGS} = \$600,000$$

If we know Tip Top's beginning inventory is $30,000 and purchases are $605,000, we can then estimate ending inventory to be $35,000 as follows:

$$\text{Beginning inventory} + \text{Purchases} - \text{Ending inventory} = \text{CGS}$$
$$\text{BI} + \text{P} - \text{EI} = \text{CGS}$$
$$\$30,000 + \$605,000 - \text{EI} = \$600,000$$
$$\text{EI} = \$35,000$$

GROSS PROFIT PERCENTAGE AND TURNOVER

Retailers often attempt to increase total profits by increasing sales levels. They may lower prices and hope to increase their total gross profits by selling their inventories more

A Pharmaceutical Firm's Answer to the Question: Are Drug Prices Fair?

Eli Lilly is a major pharmaceutical company whose major drugs include: Prozac, a leading antidepressant; Evista, a major drug for prevention and treatment of osteoporosis; and Takeda and Humalog, two of a series of Lilly drugs used in the battle against diabetes. In its 1999 annual report, Lilly addresses the question, Are Drug Prices Fair? Although you may or may not agree with them that the answer is yes, their coverage helps frame the debate. They restate the question as two questions: Can patients afford needed prescription drugs? And can pharmaceutical companies afford to conduct the research necessary to find new, effective drugs? Their answer can be summarized in the following.

Today's medicines are more expensive than in the past but they do more than ever before. Modern medicines are more cost effective than other treatments. For example, they point out that a year's treatment with new antipsychotic drugs costs about the same as 1 week of hospitalization for a patient with schizophrenia and improves the patient's quality of life.

Lilly points out that much of the public outcry over pharmaceutical cost is not about the specific costs of a specific drug but about the total cost of all drugs. According to Lilly, the price of existing drugs has been rising modestly, 3.2% in 1998 for example, while the total spending on drugs in 1998 rose by 12.5%. The 12.5% figure is what fuels public outrage, but underlying that figure is the sum of higher unit costs on existing drugs, plus

greater utilization of those drugs. More patients are being helped. The effect of new drugs being introduced is to improve our ability to manage disease or to attack previously untreatable medical conditions.

Finally, they cite the high cost of developing new treatments. Over the past 3 years they spent 18% of sales on R&D. In the process they would typically develop three new drugs that reached the marketplace and helped patients for every 15,000 compounds that they tested. A new drug that reaches the market typically costs $500 million to develop. Some barely recover that investment over their lifetimes, while others generate sales of more than a $1 billion per year.

Lilly's answer to the debate is that pharmaceuticals are a good value in the fight against disease and preserving the quality of life. Our society should try to help people afford such drugs, including better prescription benefits in insurance coverage. Doing so would raise the cost of health benefits for corporate employers and also for Medicare and other government sponsored insurance programs. Such costs are ultimately paid for by each citizen, either through the costs of products purchased from companies or taxes paid to the government. Insurance plans spread those costs over everyone in society instead of letting them fall heavily on those suffering from debilitating disease.

Source: 1999 Lilly annual report, p. 13.

---

quickly, replenishing, selling again, and so forth. In essence they are accepting a lower gross profit per unit but expecting to increase total sales more than enough to compensate. A high volume of sales activity allows a smaller gross margin per unit sold while providing high total profits. This is one of the reasons that stores such as Wal-Mart and Home Depot do well.

A way to measure sales levels is in terms of **inventory turnover,** which is defined as cost of goods sold divided by the average inventory held during a given period. Average inventory is usually the sum of beginning inventory and ending inventory divided by 2. For the Tip Top Variety Store, the average inventory is ($30,000 + $35,000)/2 = $32,500. The inventory turnover is computed as follows:

$$\text{Turnover} = \text{Cost of goods sold} \div \text{Average inventory}$$
$$= \$600,000 \div \$32,500 = 18.5$$

Suppose the inventory sells twice as quickly if prices are lowered. With a 5% reduction in sales price, sales revenue on the current level of business drops from $800,000 to (0.95 × $800,000), or $760,000. But twice as many units are sold, so total revenue becomes 2 × $760,000, or $1,520,000. How profitable is Tip Top? Cost of goods sold doubles from

inventory turnover The cost of goods sold divided by the average inventory held during the period.

$600,000 to $1,200,000. Total gross profit is $320,000. So gross profit during the month is $120,000 higher as a result of the lower price. The inventory turnover doubles: $1,200,000 divided by $32,500 (the unchanged average inventory) is 36.9. However, the gross profit percentage falls from 25% to 21% ($320,000 divided by $1,520,000).

Is the company better off? Maybe. Certainly, in the current month gross profit has risen. Long-term strategic concerns, though, raise the question: Is this new sales level maintainable? For some products, when prices fall, consumers sharply increase purchases and stockpile the extras for later consumption. There is little increase in underlying demand, just a shift of future purchases to the present. Therefore, the current good sales could result in terrible future sales.

Another strategic question is: What will the competition do? If Tip Top's increased sales came at a competitor's expense, the competitor's response may be a similar decrease in prices. The competition might recover most of its old customers, with each buying a little more at the new price than they did at the old. Assuming all competitors decrease prices similarly, the whole market would see, not a doubling of sales, but perhaps a 20% sales growth. In that case, Tip Top would be worse off overall because the 20% growth would not cover the 5% price reduction.

Exhibit 6-11 illustrates two principles. Panel A shows that if a firm can increase inventory turnover while maintaining a constant gross profit percentage, it should do so. However, as shown in Panel B, if the increased inventory turnover results from a decrease in sales price, the gross margin percentage may fall. The desirability of the change depends on whether the sales gain could offset the decreased margin. In the Tip Top Variety Store example, when a 5% price reduction produces only a 20% increase in units sold, the new gross margin of $192,000 is less than the initial margin of $200,000. Dropping the price is not justified even though the inventory turnover rises to 22.2 from 18.5. However, at a 50% increase in sales volume, the new gross margin of $240,000 would exceed the original $200,000. Basically, the lesson of Exhibit 6-11 is that you cannot focus on only one number or measure of company performance. Paying too much attention to one measure could cause you to miss the fact that another was falling fast.

Exhibit 6-11

Tip Top Variety Store
Effects of Increased Inventory Turnover ($ in Thousands)

	Unit Sales Increase			
	Original	*20%*	*50%*	*100%*
	PANEL A			
No change in sales price				
Sales	$800	$960	$1,200	$1,600
Cost of goods sold (75%)	600	720	900	1,200
Gross margin (25%)	$200	$240	$ 300	$ 400
Inventory turnover	18.5	22.2	27.7	36.9
	PANEL B			
5% reduction in sales price				
Sales (95% of above)	$760	$912	$1,140	$1,520
Cost of goods sold (as above)	600	720	900	1,200
Gross margin (21% of sales)	$160	$192	$ 240	$ 320
Inventory turnover (as above)	18.5	22.2	27.7	36.9

The industry variability in gross margin percentages referred to earlier is also reflected in inventory turnover percentages.

Industry	Gross Profit	Inventory Turnover
Auto retailers	12.0	7.0
Auto manufacturers	18.1	10.5
Jewelry retailers	45.4	1.5
Jewelry manufacturers	31.2	3.0
Grocery retailers	23.2	19.1
Grocery wholesalers	14.5	15.2
Drug manufacturers	41.1	3.2
Drugstores	24.0	5.9
Drug wholesalers	20.2	8.4
Computer and software retail	26.5	20.5
Semiconductor manufacturers	30.9	5.7
Computer manufacturers	31.5	7.8

Source: RMA Annual Statement Studies, 1999.

As you can see, the industries with the highest gross profit percentages tend to have the lowest inventory turnover. This reflects the observation earlier that firms must have gross margins high enough to cover other selling and administrative costs. The lower turnover for jewelers and pharmaceuticals relates to high costs of selling or research that must be covered by high margins.

Thus, the inventory turnover measure is especially effective for assessing companies in the same industry. If one industry member has a higher turnover than another, it is probably more efficient. That is, the higher turnover indicates an ability to use smaller inventory levels to attain a high sales level. This is good, because it reduces the investment in inventory. Fewer products are sitting on display shelves or in warehouses and less capital is tied up in maintaining, moving, and displaying inventory items.

When ratios are being calculated, it is important to keep the accounting methods in mind. Consider the data for Ford Motor Company given earlier on page 244. By using LIFO and FIFO results for Ford Motor Company, we can calculate the inventory turnover and gross profit percentages (sales of $136,973 million) to be:

LIFO
Gross profit percentage: ($141,230 − 126,120) ÷ $141,230 = 10.7%
Inventory turnover: $126,120 ÷ (($5,681 + $7,514) ÷ 2) = 19.11

FIFO
Gross profit percentage: ($141,230 − $126,120) ÷ $141,230 = 10.8%
Inventory turnover: $126,020 ÷ (($6,684 + $8,614) ÷ 2) = 16.48

In Ford's case LIFO decreased the gross profit percentage in the current year slightly and increased the inventory turnover significantly relative to FIFO. The modest change in the gross profit percentage is because the 2000 change in the LIFO reserve was small relative to the large size of cost of sales. In contrast, the significant change in inventory turnover is due to the total LIFO reserve being large relative to the size of the inventory level. Notice that the FIFO ending inventory balance is 15% larger than the LIFO inventory balance.

GROSS PROFIT PERCENTAGES AND ACCURACY OF RECORDS

Auditors, including those from the Internal Revenue Service (IRS), use the gross profit percentage to help satisfy themselves about the accuracy of records. For example, the IRS compiles gross profit percentages by types of retail establishment. If a company shows an unusually low percentage compared with similar companies, IRS auditors may suspect that the company has failed to record all cash sales to avoid taxes. Similarly, managers watch changes in gross profit percentages to judge operating profitability and to monitor how well employee theft and shoplifting are being controlled.

Suppose an internal revenue agent, a manager, or an outside auditor had gathered the following data for a particular jewelry company for the past 3 years ($ in millions):

	20X3	20X2	20X1
Net sales	$350	$325	$300
Cost of goods sold	210	165	150
Gross profit	$140	$160	$150
Gross profit percentage	40%	49%	50%

Comparing these data is a good acid test to see if there are any changes worth investigating. As you can see, the percentage for the jewelry company has been fairly steady, for 2 years. However, the decline in the percentage in year three could be a sign of trouble. Obviously, a decline in the percentage might be attributable to many factors, and not all of them are cause for concern. Possible explanations include the following:

1. Competition has intensified, resulting in intensive price wars that reduced selling prices.
2. The mix of goods sold has shifted so that, for instance, the $350 million of sales in 20X3 is composed of relatively more products bearing lower gross margins, for example, more costume jewelry bearing low margins and less diamond jewelry bearing high margins.
3. Shoplifting or embezzling has soared out of control. For example, a manager may be pocketing and not recording cash sales of $70 million. After all, given costs of sales of $210 million, sales in 20X3 would have been $210 × 2 = $420 million if the past 50% margin had been maintained. Similarly, given sales of $350 million we would have expected costs to be only $175 million, not $210 million.

REPORTS TO SHAREHOLDERS

The importance of gross profits to investors is demonstrated in the following example based on a quarterly report to shareholders of Superscope, Incorporated, a manufacturer and distributor of stereophonic equipment that encountered rocky times. The following condensed income statement was presented for a 3-month period ($ in thousands):

	Current Year	Previous Year
Net sales	$40,000	$40,200
Cost and expenses		
Cost of sales	33,100	28,200
Selling, general, and administrative	11,200	9,900
Interest	2,000	1,200
Total costs and expenses	46,300	39,300
Income (loss) before income tax		
provision (benefit)	(6,300)	900
Income tax provision (benefit)	(3,000)	200
Net income (loss)	$(3,300)	$ 700

Although the statement does not show the amount of gross profit, the gross profit percentages can readily be computed as ($40,000 − $33,100) ÷ $40,000 = 17% and

($40,200 − $28,200) ÷ $40,200 = 30%. To show how seriously these percentages are considered, the chairman's letter to shareholders began as follows:

> *I shall attempt herein to provide you with a candid analysis of the Company's present condition, the steps we have instituted to overcome current adversities, and the potential which we believe can, in due course, be realized by the Company's realistic positive determination to regain profitability.*
>
> *In the second quarter the Company's gross profit margins decreased to 17% compared to 30% in the corresponding quarter of a year ago. For the first six months gross profit margins were 22%, down from 31% for the corresponding period of a year ago.*
>
> *Essentially, the gross profits and consequential operating losses in the second quarter, as reflected in the condensed financial statements appearing in this report, resulted from lower than anticipated sales volume and from the following second quarter factors: liquidation of our entire citizens band inventory; increases in dealer cash discounts and sales incentive expenses; gross margin reductions resulting from sales of slow moving models at less than normal prices; and markdown of slow moving inventory on hand to a realistic net realizable market value.*

INTERNAL CONTROL OF INVENTORIES

In many organizations, inventories are more easily accessible than cash. Therefore, they can become a favorite target for thieves.

Retail merchants must contend with inventory shrinkage, a polite term for shoplifting by customers and embezzling by employees. Consider the following footnote from a recent annual report of Associated Dry Goods, one of the largest operators of department and discount stores in the country: "Physical inventories are taken twice each year. Department store inventory shrinkage at retail, as a percent of retail sales, was 2.4% this year compared with 2.1% last year. Discount store inventory shrinkage as a percent of retail sales was 0.4% and 0.3%, respectively." Some department stores have suffered shrinkage losses of 4% to 5% of their sales volume. Compare this with the typical net profit margin of 5% to 6%.

A management consulting firm has demonstrated how widespread shoplifting has become. The firm concentrated on a midtown New York City department store. Picked at random, 500 shoppers were followed from the moment they entered the store to the time they departed. Forty-two shoppers, or 1 out of every 12 took something. They stole $300 worth of merchandise, an average of $7.15 each. Similar experiments were conducted in Boston (1 of 20 shoplifted), in Philadelphia (1 of 10), and again in New York (1 of 12).

Experts on controlling inventory shrinkage generally agree that the best deterrent is an alert employee at the point of sale. Retail stores use sensitized tags on merchandise; if not detached or neutralized by a salesclerk, these miniature transmitters trip an alarm as the culprit begins to leave the store. Many libraries use a similar system to safeguard their books. Macy's in New York has continuous surveillance with over 50 television cameras.

Retailers must also scrutinize their own personnel, because they account for at least 30% to 40% of inventory shortages. Some stores have actors pose as shoplifters, who are then subjected to fake arrests. If potential thieves see the arrests, they may be deterred. Such ploys have helped reduce thefts by employees at major retail chains.

The imposing magnitude of retail inventory shrinkage demonstrates how management objectives may differ among industries. For example, consider the grocery business, where net income is about 1% of sales. You can readily see why a prime responsibility of the store manager is to control inventory shrinkage instead of boost gross sales volume.

The trade-off is clear: If the operating profit is 2% of sales, to offset a $1,000 increase in shrinkage requires a $50,000 boost in gross sales.

SHRINKAGE IN PERPETUAL AND PERIODIC INVENTORY SYSTEMS

Measuring inventory shrinkage is straightforward for companies that use a perpetual inventory system. Shrinkage is simply the difference between the cost of inventory identified by a physical count and the clerical inventory balance. Consider the following example:

Sales	$100,000
Cost of goods sold (perpetual inventory system)	80,000
Beginning inventory	15,000
Purchases	85,000
Ending inventory, per clerical records	20,000
Ending inventory, per physical count	18,000

Shrinkage is $20,000 − $18,000 = $2,000. The total cost of goods sold would be $80,000 + $2,000 = $82,000. The journal entries under a perpetual inventory system would be:

Inventory shrinkage	2,000	
Inventory		2,000
To adjust ending inventory to its balance per physical count		

Cost of goods sold	2,000	
Inventory shrinkage		2,000
The transfer inventory shrinkage to cost of goods sold		

By definition, a periodic inventory system has no continuing balance of the inventory account. Inventory shrinkage is automatically included in cost of goods sold. Why? Beginning inventory plus purchases less ending inventory measures all inventory that has flowed out, whether it went to customers, shoplifters, or embezzlers, or was simply lost or broken. Our example would show:

Beginning inventory	$ 15,000
Plus: Purchases	85,000
Goods available for sale	$100,000
Less: Ending inventory, per physical count	18,000
Cost of goods sold	$ 82,000

SUMMARY PROBLEMS FOR YOUR REVIEW

PROBLEM ONE

Examine Exhibit 6-12. The company uses the periodic inventory system. By using these facts, prepare a columnar comparison of income statements for the year ended December 31, 20X2. Compare the FIFO, LIFO, and weighted-average inventory methods. Assume that other expenses are $1,000. The income tax rate is 40%.

SOLUTION TO PROBLEM ONE

See Exhibit 6-13.

PROBLEM TWO

"When prices are rising, FIFO produces profits that confuse economic profit and holding profits because more resources are needed to maintain operations than previously." Do you agree? Explain.

Exhibit 6-12

Facts for Summary Problem One

	Purchases	Sales	Inventory
December 31, 20X1			200 @ $5 = $1,000
January 25	170 @ $6 = $1,020		
January 29		150*	
May 28	190 @ $7 = $1,330		
June 7		230*	
November 20	150 @ $8 = $1,200		
December 15		100*	
Total	510	$3,550	480*
December 31, 20X2			230 @ ?

*Selling prices were $9, $11, and $13, respectively, providing total sales of:

	150 @ $ 9 = $1,350	
	230 @ $11 = $2,530	
	100 @ $13 = $1,300	
Total sales	480	$5,180

Summary of costs:

Beginning inventory	$1,000
Purchases	$3,550
Cost of goods available for sale	$4,550

Exhibit 6-13

Comparison of Inventory Methods for the Year Ended December 31, 20X2

	FIFO		LIFO		Weighted Average
Sales, 480 units		$5,180		$5,180	$5,180
Deduct cost of goods sold					
Beginning inventory, 200 @ $5		$1,000		$1,000	$1,000
Purchases, 510 units (from Exhibit 6-12)*		3,550		3,550	3,550
Available for sale, 710 units†		$4,550		$4,550	$4,550
Ending inventory, 230 units‡					
150 @ $8	$1,200				
80 @ $7	560	1,760			
or					
200 @ $5			$1,000		
30 @ $6			180	1,180	
or					
230 @ $6.408					1,474
Cost of goods sold, 480 units		2,790		3,370	3,076
Gross profit		$2,390		$1,810	$2,104
Other expenses		1,000		1,000	1,000
Income before income taxes		$1,390		$ 810	$1,104
Income taxes at 40%		556		324	442
Net income		$ 834		$ 486	$ 662

*Always equal across all three methods.

†These amounts will not be equal in general across the three methods because beginning inventories will generally be different. They are equal here only because beginning inventories were assumed to be equal.

‡Under FIFO, the ending inventory is composed of the last purchases plus the second-last purchases, and so forth, until the costs of 230 units are compiled. Under LIFO, the ending inventory is composed of the beginning inventory plus the earliest purchases of the current years until the costs of 230 units are compiled. Under weighted average, the ending inventory and cost of goods sold are accumulations based on an average unit cost. The latter is the cost of goods available for sale divided by the number of units available for sale: $4,550 ÷ 710 = $6.408.

Solution to Problem Two

Whether FIFO profits confuse economic profit and holding profit depends on the concept of income favored. LIFO gives a better measure of "distributable" income than FIFO. Recall Emilio's Cola Sales example in Exhibit 6-5. The gross profit under FIFO was 60 cents, and under LIFO it was 34 cents. The 60 cents − 34¢ = 26 cents difference is a fool's profit because it must be reinvested to maintain the same inventory level as previously. It arises from a profit on holding inventory as prices change instead of buying at wholesale and selling at retail. Therefore, the 26 cents cannot be distributed as a cash dividend without reducing the current level of operations.

Problem Three

Hewlett-Packard (HP) designs, manufactures, and services a broad array of products including perhaps your calculator or printer. Some results for the year ended October 31, 1999 were ($ in millions):

Sales of products	$42,370
Cost of merchandise sold	29,720
Net earnings	3,491
Beginning merchandise inventory	6,184
Ending merchandise inventory	4,863

1. Calculate the 1999 gross profit and gross profit percentage for Hewlett-Packard.
2. Calculate the inventory turnover ratio.
3. What gross profit would have been reported if inventory turnover in 1999 had been 6, the gross profit percentage remained the same as that calculated in requirement 1, and the level of inventory was unchanged?

Solution to Problem Three

1. Gross profit = Sales − Cost of merchandise sold
   = $42,370 − 29,720
   = $12,650

   Gross profit percentage = Gross profit ÷ Sales
   = $12,650 ÷ $42,370
   = 30%

2. Inventory turnover = Cost of merchandise sold ÷ Average merchandise inventory
   = $29,720 ÷ [($6,184 + $4,863) × 2]
   = $29,720 ÷ $5,523
   = 5.4

3. To respond to this question you must first see that a higher inventory turnover given a constant average inventory implies an increase in sales. Increased sales with a constant gross profit percentage implies increased total gross profit. With these relationships in mind, answering the question is a process of working backward based on the ratios and relationships.

   Cost of merchandise sold = Inventory turnover × Average merchandise inventory
   = 6 × $5,523
   = $33,138

   Gross profit percentage = (Sales − Cost of merchandise sold) ÷ Sales
   30% = (S − $33,138) ÷ S

$$.30 \times S = S - \$33{,}138$$
$$S - (.30 \times S) = \$33{,}138$$
$$S \times (1 - 30) = \$33{,}138$$
$$S = \$33{,}138 \div (1 - .30)$$
$$S = \$47{,}340$$

$$\text{Gross profit} = \text{Sales} - \text{Cost of merchandise sold}$$
$$= \$47{,}340 - \$33{,}138$$
$$= \$14{,}202$$

The increase in inventory turnover from 5.4 to 6.0 would raise gross profit from \$12,650 to \$14,202.

PROBLEM FOUR

At the end of 20X1, a \$1,000 error was made in the physical inventory so the ending inventory value was understated. The error went undetected. The subsequent inventory at the end of 20X2 was done correctly. Assess the effect of this error on income before tax, taxes, net income, and retained earnings for 20X1 and 20X2, assuming a 40% tax rate.

SOLUTION TO PROBLEM FOUR

	20X1	20X2
Beginning inventory	OK	Too low
Purchases	OK	OK
Goods available for sale	OK	Too low
Ending inventory	Too low	OK
Cost of goods sold	Too high	Too low

Note that 20X1 Ending inventory becomes 20X2 Beginning inventory, reversing the effects on Cost of goods sold. The 20X1 Cost of goods sold being too high causes 20X1 income before tax to be too low by \$1,000. Therefore, taxes will be too low by .40 × \$1,000 = \$400 and net income will be too low by \$600, causing retained income to be too low by \$600 also. In 20X2, the effects reverse and by year-end retained income is correctly stated.

Highlights to Remember

1. **Link inventory valuation to gross profit.** Gross profit is the difference between sales and cost of goods sold. Inventory valuation is linked to gross profit because the inventory valuation involves allocating the cost of goods available for sale between cost of goods sold and ending inventory as of the balance sheet date. Under the perpetual inventory system, this allocation occurs continually, and cost of goods sold is recorded for each sale. Under the periodic inventory system, the allocation occurs via an adjusting entry at year-end. A physical inventory is conducted at the end of each period under either system. The goods on hand are counted, and a cost is calculated for each item from purchase records. The cost of an item of inventory includes not only purchase price but also inward transportation costs.

2. **Use both perpetual and periodic inventory systems.** Under the periodic system, the physical inventory is the basis for the year-end adjusting entry to recognize cost of goods sold. Under the perpetual system, the physical inventory is used to confirm the accounting records. Differences, if any, lead to adjustments to cost of goods sold and ending inventory.

3. **Calculate the cost of merchandise acquired.** The cost of merchandise acquired is the invoice price of the goods plus directly identifiable inbound transportation costs less any cash or quantity discounts and less any returns or allowances.

4. **Choose one of the four principal inventory valuation methods.** Valuation of inventories involves the assignment of specific historical costs of acquisition either to units sold or to units remaining in ending inventory. Four major inventory valuation methods are in use in the United States: specific identification, weighted average, FIFO, and LIFO. Specific identification is most common for low-volume, high-value products such as automobiles, boats, or jewelry. FIFO attributes the most recent, current prices to inventory items. LIFO attributes the most recent, current prices to cost of sales. When prices are rising and inventories are constant or growing, less income is shown by LIFO than by FIFO. LIFO is popular in the United States among companies who face rising prices, for whom lower profits under LIFO mean lower taxes. The U.S. tax law contains a conformity requirement that allows companies to use LIFO for tax purposes only if they use it also for financial reporting purposes. Weighted average provides results between LIFO and FIFO for both the income statement cost of sales and the balance sheet inventory number.

5. **Calculate the impact on net income of LIFO liquidations.** LIFO liquidation refers to the relatively higher profits generated under LIFO when reductions in inventory levels cause older, lower inventory costs to be used in calculating cost of goods sold. Notice that, even with declining inventories, with rising costs the cumulative taxable income is always less under LIFO than it is under FIFO because the inventory valuation is less and the cumulative cost of goods sold is higher.

6. **Use the lower-of-cost-or-market method to value inventories.** Conservatism leads to the lower-of-cost-or-market method, which treats cost as the maximum value of inventory. Inventory is reduced to replacement cost (with a corresponding increase in cost of goods sold) when acquisition prices fall below historical cost levels.

7. **Show the effects of inventory errors on financial statements.** The nature of accrual accounting for inventories creates a self-correcting quality about errors in counting or valuing the ending inventory. This occurs because the ending inventory in one period becomes the beginning inventory of the subsequent period.

8. **Evaluate the gross profit percentage and inventory turnover.** Financial analysts and managers use gross profit percentages as a measure of profitability and inventory turnover as a measure of efficient asset use. These measures are compared with prior levels to examine trends and with current levels of other industry members to assess relative performance.

Appendix 6: Inventory in a Manufacturing Environment

In this chapter, inventory accounting is covered from the viewpoint of a merchandiser. When a company manufactures products, the cost of inventory is a combination of the acquisition cost of raw material, the wages paid to workers who combine the raw materials into finished products, and an allocation of the costs of space, energy, and equipment used by the workers as they transform the various elements into a finished product.

Consider how costs are accumulated in a manufacturing environment for Packit, a company that makes backpacks. The raw materials are heavy fabric, glue, and thread. The transformation occurs when workers use cutters to make the panels that other workers sew and glue together. The costs of manufacture include depreciation on the manufacturing building, depreciation on the sewing machines and cutters, and utilities to support the effort in the form of heat, power, and light. The finished goods are backpacks.

The accounting process is easiest to understand when calculating the cost of a complete year of production. In the following example, 10,000 backpacks are produced during Packit's first year at a total cost of $800,000, providing a cost per backpack of $80.00 each ($800,000/10,000 units). At year-end, if all have been sold, the financial statements would include $800,000 in cost of goods sold.

Packit Company—Year 1

Beginning inventory	—
Fabric purchased and used	$200,000
Wages paid to workers	300,000
Thread and glue used	50,000
Depreciation on building and equipment	220,000
Utilities	30,000
Total costs to manufacture	$800,000
Cost per backpack ($800,000 ÷ 10,000)	$ 80.00

In the preceding example, all the materials acquired during the year are transformed into finished products before year-end and sold. In reality, if we take a snapshot of the typical backpack manufacturer at year-end, we would observe bolts of fabric, spools of thread,

Exhibit 6-14
Packit Company Accounting for Manufacturing Costs—Year 2

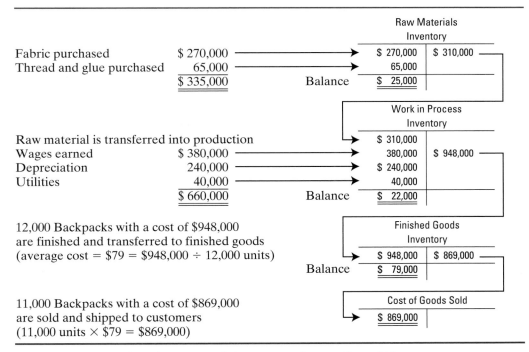

The summary journal entries to record these events for year 2 would be:

PURCHASE OF RAW MATERIAL:

Raw material inventory	335,000	
Accounts payable		335,000

PRODUCTION ACTIVITY:

Work in process inventory	310,000	
Raw materials inventory		310,000
Work in process inventory	660,000	
Wages payable		380,000
Accumulated depreciation		240,000
Utilities payable		40,000

COMPLETION OF PRODUCTION:

Finished goods inventory	948,000	
Work in process inventory		948,000

raw material inventory Includes the cost of materials held for use in the manufacturing of a product.

work in process inventory Includes the cost incurred for partially completed items, including raw materials, labor, and other costs.

finished goods inventory The accumulated costs of manufacture for goods that are complete and ready for sale.

and gallons of glue waiting to be put into production. We call these items held for use in the manufacturing of a product **raw material inventory.** In addition, we would also observe fabric already cut but not assembled and some partially completed backpacks. We refer to the material, labor, and other costs accumulated for partially completed items as **work in process inventory.** When manufacture is complete and the goods are ready to deliver to customers, the inventory is called **finished goods inventory.** The accounting system for managing these costs for the second year of production of our backpack manufacturer is illustrated in Exhibit 6-14. During this second year, 12,000 backpacks are completed and 11,000 are sold. Some remain in the assembly process at year-end, and unused fabric, thread, and glue are held in preparation for future production.

The schematic in Exhibit 6-14 captures the production process. You might think of each of the accounts as corresponding to a physical reality. The raw material is stored in a locked room, ready for use. The work-in-process is located in the production room and as it is finished it is physically transferred to a storage site. When goods are sold, they are removed from that storage site and are given to the customer in exchange for cash or an account receivable. Raw materials, work-in-process, and finished goods are all forms of inventory and appear on the balance sheet as current assets. They are simply in different stages of completion. The act of sale converts the asset into an expense to be reported on the income statement. At the end of year 2, Packit will show total inventory on its balance sheet of $126,000, as follows:

Raw materials inventory	$ 25,000
Work in process inventory	22,000
Finished goods inventory	79,000
Total inventory	$126,000

Accounting Vocabulary

conservatism, p. 245
consistency, p. 241
cost of goods available for sale, p. 230
cost valuation, p. 229
cutoff error, p. 249
finished goods inventory, p. 261
first-in, first-out (FIFO), p. 237
F.O.B. destination, p. 232
F.O.B. shipping point, p. 232
freight in, p. 233
freight out, p. 233
gross profit percentage, p. 249

holding gain, p. 241
inventory profit, p. 241
inventory shrinkage, p. 230
inventory turnover, p. 251
inward transportation, p. 233
last-in, first-out (LIFO), p.238
LIFO increment, p. 242
LIFO layer, p. 242
LIFO reserve, p. 243
lower-of-cost-or-market method (LCM), p. 245
periodic inventory system, p. 230

perpetual inventory system, p. 229
physical count, p. 229
raw material inventory, p. 261
replacement cost, p. 241
retailer, p. 250
specific identification method, p. 236
weighted-average method, p. 239
wholesaler, p. 250
work in process inventory, p.261
write-down, p. 245

Assignment Material

QUESTIONS

6-1 When a company records a sales transaction, it also records another related transaction. Explain the related transaction.

6-2 "There are two steps in the periodic system of accounting for inventories." What are they?

6-3 Distinguish between the *perpetual* and *periodic* inventory systems.

6-4 "An advantage of the perpetual inventory system is that a physical count of inventory is unnecessary. The peri-

odic method requires a physical count to compute cost of goods sold." Do you agree? Explain.

6-5 Distinguish between *F.O.B. destination* and *F.O.B. shipping point.*

6-6 "Freight out should be classified as a direct offset to sales, not as an expense." Do you agree? Explain.

6-7 Name the four inventory cost flow assumptions or valuation methods that are generally accepted in the United States. Give a brief phrase describing each.

6-8 Which of the following items would a company be likely to account for using the the specific identification inventory method?
  a. Corporate jet aircraft
  b. Large sailboats
  c. Pencils
  d. Diamond rings
  e. Timex watches
  f. Automobiles
  g. Books
  h. Compact discs

6-9 If a company uses a FIFO cost flow assumption, will it report the same cost of goods sold using the periodic inventory method that it reports using the perpetual method? Why or why not?

6-10 Why is LIFO a good news/bad news inventory method?

6-11 "Purchases of inventory at the end of a fiscal period can have a direct effect on income under LIFO." Do you agree? Explain.

6-12 "Gamma Company has five units of inventory, two purchased for $4 each and three purchased for $5 each. Thus, the weighted-average cost of the inventory is ($4 + $5) ÷ 2 = $4.50 per unit." Do you agree? Explain.

6-13 Assume that the physical level of inventory is constant at the beginning and end of year and that the cost of inventory items is rising. Which will produce a higher ending inventory value, LIFO or FIFO?

6-14 Will LIFO or FIFO produce higher cost of goods sold during a period of *falling* prices? Explain.

6-15 What is *consistency,* and why is it an important accounting principle?

6-16 "There is a single dominant reason why more and more U.S. companies have adopted LIFO." What is the reason?

6-17 "An inventory profit is a fictitious profit." Do you agree? Explain.

6-18 LIFO produces absurd inventory valuations. Why?

6-19 "Conservatism always results in lower reported profits." Do you agree? Explain.

6-20 "Accountants have traditionally favored taking some losses but no gains before an asset is exchanged." What is this tradition or convention called?

6-21 What does *market* mean in inventory accounting?

6-22 "The lower-of-cost-or-market method is inherently inconsistent." Do you agree? Explain.

6-23 "Inventory errors are counterbalancing." Explain.

6-24 Express the cost of goods sold section of the income statement as an equation.

6-25 "Gross profit percentages help in the preparation of interim financial statements." Explain.

6-26 The branch manager of a national retail grocery chain has stated: "My managers are judged more heavily on the basis of their merchandise-shrinkage control than on their overall sales volume." Why? Explain.

COGNITIVE EXERCISES

6-27 Deciding on a Discount Policy
You are debating with your boss whether or not to initiate a 2% discount for quantity purchases. You favor the idea, but your boss says, "Why give money away? If the customer buys more, we are out 2%." How do you reply?

6-28 Effect of Overstating Inventories
Phar Mor was a large, rapidly growing pharmacy chain that proved to have overstated assets by more than $400 million. The overstatement occurred by top executives inflating the company's inventories at numerous store locations. How would this affect the earnings statements of Phar Mor?

6-29 Purchasing Operations and LIFO versus FIFO
Suppose that the evaluation of the purchasing officer for a refinery is based on the gross margin on the oil products produced and sold during the year. During the year, the price of a barrel of oil has increased from $20 to $30. All the inventory of oil at the beginning of the year is valued at $20 or less. On the last day of the year, the purchasing agent is contemplating the purchase of additional oil at $30 per barrel. Is the agent more likely to purchase additional oil if the company uses the FIFO or LIFO method for its inventories? Explain.

6-30 Periodic versus Perpetual Inventory Systems
The Zen Bootist manufactures sheepskin slippers, mittens, gloves, jackets, and leather sandals to sell at craft fairs and similar events. The majority of the company's transactions occur over the winter gift-giving season. As the business has grown, the owner has become concerned about how to account for certain items and has asked your advice about whether to use the periodic or perpetual inventory system. What do you say?

EXERCISES

6-31 Gross Profit Section
Given the following, prepare a detailed gross profit section for Prag's Jewelry Wholesalers for the year ended December 31, 20X8 ($ in thousands):

Cash discounts on purchases	$	6	Cash discounts on sales	$	5
Sales returns and allowances		40	Purchase returns and allowances		27
Gross purchases		650			
Merchandise inventory, December 31, 20X7		103	Merchandise inventory, December 31, 20X8		170
Gross profit		355	Freight in		50

6-32 Gross Margin Computations and Inventory Costs

On January 15, 20X4, Malia Mayes valued her inventory at cost, $40,000. Her statements are based on the calendar year, so you find it necessary to establish an inventory figure as of January 1, 20X4. You find that from January 2 to January 15, sales were $71,200; sales returns, $2,300; goods purchased and placed in stock, $54,000; goods removed from stock and returned to suppliers, $2,000; freight in, $500. Calculate the inventory cost as of January 1, assuming that goods are priced to provide a 23% gross profit.

6-33 Journal Entries

Vadim Company had sales of $20 million during the year. The goods cost Vadim $15 million. Give the journal entry or entries at the time of sale under the perpetual and the periodic inventory systems.

6-34 Valuing Inventory and Cost of Goods Sold

Glasgow Metals Ltd. had the following inventory transactions during the month of January:

1/1 beginning inventory	4,000 units @ £2.00	£8,000
Week 1, purchases	2,000 units @ £2.10	4,200
Week 2, purchases	2,000 units @ £2.20	4,400
Week 3, purchases	1,000 units @ £2.30	2,300
Week 4, purchases	1,000 units @ £2.40	2,400

On January 31, a count of the ending inventory was completed, and 5,500 units were on hand. By using the periodic inventory system, calculate the cost of goods sold and ending inventory using LIFO, FIFO, and weighted-average inventory methods.

6-35 Entries for Purchase Transactions

The Volkert Company is a Swiss wholesaler of office supplies. Its unit of currency is the Swiss franc (CHF). Volkert uses a periodic inventory system. Prepare journal entries for the following summarized transactions (omit explanations):

Aug. 2	Purchased merchandise, CHF 300,000, terms 2/10, n/45.
Aug. 3	Paid cash for freight in, CHF 10,000.
Aug. 7	Volkert complained about some defects in the merchandise acquired on August 2. The supplier hand-delivered a credit memo granting an allowance of CHF 30,000.
Aug. 11	Cash disbursement to settle purchase of August 2.

6-36 Cost of Inventory Acquired

On July 5, Solanski Company purchased on account a shipment of sheet steel from Northwest Steel Co. The invoice price was $160,000, F.O.B. shipping point. Shipping cost from the steel mill to Solanski's plant was $10,000. When inspecting the shipment, the Solanski receiving clerk found several flaws in the steel. The clerk informed Northwest's sales representative of the flaws, and after some negotiation, Northwest granted an allowance of $15,000.

To encourage prompt payment, Northwest grants a 2% cash discount to customers who pay their accounts within 30 days of billing. Solanski paid the proper amount on August 1.

1. Compute the total cost of the sheet steel acquired.
2. Prepare the journal entries for the transaction. Omit explanations.

6-37 Entries for Periodic and Perpetual Systems

Gulick Co. had an inventory of $210,000, December 31, 20X7. Data for 20X8 follow:

Gross purchases	$960,000
Cost of goods sold	890,000
Inventory, December 31, 20X8	200,000
Purchase returns and allowances	80,000

Required

By using the data, prepare comparative journal entries, including closing entries, for a perpetual and a periodic inventory system.

6-38 Entries for Purchase Transactions

Pier Four Imports uses a periodic inventory system. Prepare journal entries for the following summarized transactions for 20X8 (omit explanations). For simplicity, assume that the beginning and ending balances in accounts payable were zero.

1. Purchases (all using trade credit), $900,000.
2. Purchase returns and allowances, $50,000.
3. Freight in, $72,000 paid in cash.
4. Payment for all credit purchases, less returns and allowances and cash discounts on purchases of $18,000.

6-39 Journal Entries, Periodic Inventory System

Refer to the data in the preceding problem. Inventories were December 31, 20X7, $81,000 and December 31, 20X8, $130,000. Sales were $1,250,000. Prepare summary journal entries for 20X8 for sales and cost of goods sold. Omit explanations.

6-40 Journal Entries, Periodic Inventory System

Consider the following data taken from the adjusted trial balance of the Emerald Bay Boat Company, December 31, 20X3 ($ in millions):

Purchases	$125	Sales	239
Sales returns and allowances	5	Purchase returns and	
Freight in	14	allowances	6
Cash discounts on purchases	1	Cash discounts on sales	8
Inventory (beginning of year)	25	Other expenses	80

Prepare summary journal entries. The ending inventory was $40 million.

Required

6-41 Reconstruction of Transaction

Apple Computer, Inc. produces the well-known Macintosh computer. Consider the following account balances ($ in millions):

	July 1, 2000	September 25, 1999
Inventories	$5	$20

The purchases of inventories during the 9 months between September 25, 1999 and July 1, 2000 were $1,282,000,000. The income statement for that 9-month period had an item "cost of sales." Compute its amount.

Required

6-42 Reconstruction of Records

An earthquake caused heavy damage to the Modern Jazz Record Store on May 3, 20X8. All the merchandise was destroyed. Some accounting data are missing. In conjunction with an insurance investigation, you have been asked to estimate the cost of the inventory destroyed. The following data for 20X8 are available:

Cash discounts on purchases	$ 1,000	Inventory, December 31, 20X7	$ 19,000
Gross sales	140,000	Purchase returns and allowances	4,000
Sales returns and allowances	12,000	Inward transportation	2,000
Gross purchases	80,000	Gross profit percentage on net sales	45%

6-43 Cost of Inventory Destroyed by Fire

Liao Company's insurance agent requires an estimate of the cost of merchandise lost by fire on March 9. Merchandise inventory on January 1 was $65,000. Purchases since January 1 were $195,000; freight in, $20,000; purchase returns and allowances, $10,000. Sales are made at a gross margin of 20% of sales and totaled $200,000 up to March 9. What was the cost of the merchandise destroyed?

6-44 Inventory Shortage

An accounting clerk of the Ayers Company absconded with cash and a truck full of the entire electronic merchandise on May 14, 20X8. The following data have been compiled:

Beginning inventory, January 1	$ 60,000
Sales to May 14, 20X8	280,000
Average gross profit rate	25%
Purchases to May 14, 20X8	200,000

Required Compute the estimated cost of the missing merchandise.

6-45 Inventory Errors

At the end of his first business year, Cal Stokes counted and priced the inventory. A few very high-value items were hidden in a dark corner of the storage shelves and Cal understated his 20X8 inventory by $10,000. His business financial statements and his tax return were affected. Assume a 40% tax rate.

Required
1. Calculate the effect on taxable income, taxes, net income, and retained earnings for 20X8.
2. Repeat requirement 1 for 20X9, assuming the 20X9 ending inventory is correctly calculated.

6-46 Decision about Pricing

Genuine Gems, Inc., a retail jewelry store, had gross profits of $880,000 on sales of $1,600,000 in 20X3. Average inventory was $720,000.

Required
1. Compute inventory turnover.
2. Aaron Siegl, owner of Genuine Gems, is considering whether to become a "discount" jeweler. For example, Aaron believes that a cut of 20% in average selling prices would have increased turnover to 1.5 times per year. Beginning and ending inventory would be unchanged. Suppose Aaron's beliefs are valid. What would his new gross profit percentage be? Would the total gross profit in 20X3 have improved? Show computations.

6-47 LIFO and FIFO

The inventory of the Alcon Gravel Company on June 30 shows 1,000 tons at $9 per ton. A physical inventory on July 31 shows a total of 1,100 tons on hand. Revenue from sales of gravel for July totals $98,000. The following purchases were made during July:

July 8	5,000 tons @ $10 per ton
July 13	1,000 tons @ $11 per ton
July 22	900 tons @ $12 per ton

Required
1. Compute the inventory cost as of July 31 using (a) LIFO and (b) FIFO.
2. Compute the gross profit using each method.

6-48 Lower-of-Cost-or-Market

(Alternate is 6-74.) Matsushita Company uses the inventory method "cost or market, whichever is lower." There were no sales or purchases during the periods indicated, although selling prices generally fluctuated in the same directions as replacement costs. At what amount would you value merchandise on the dates that follow?

	Invoice Cost	Replacement Cost
December 31, 20X1	$200,000	$180,000
April 30, 20X2	200,000	190,000
August 31, 20X2	200,000	220,000
December 31, 20X2	200,000	175,000

6-49 Reconstruction of Transactions

Consider the following account balances of Converse, Inc., maker of athletic shoes ($ in thousands):

	January 1	
	2000	1999
Inventories	$76,414	$71,292

The income statement for the fiscal year included the item "cost of sales" of $293,948. Compute the net cost of the acquisition of inventory for the fiscal year ending January 1, 2000.

Required

6-50 Gross Profit Percentage

Toys "Я" Us operates over 1,500 stores in the United States and abroad. Like most retailers, the managers of Toys "Я" Us monitor the company's gross margin percentage. The following information is from the company's income statement:

	For the Year Ended		
	January 29, 2000	*January 30, 1999*	*January 31, 1998*
Sales	$11,862	$11,170	$11,038
Cost of sales	8,321	8,191	7,710

Compute the gross profit percentage for each of the 3 years. Comment on the changes in gross profit percentage.

Required

6-51 Profitability and Turnover

Zeke's Building Supply began 20X1 with inventory of $160,000. Zeke's 20X1 sales were $800,000, purchases of inventory totaled $690,000, and ending inventory was $220,000.

1. Prepare a statement of gross profit for 20X1.
2. What was Zeke's inventory turnover?

Required

PROBLEMS

6-52 Detailed Income Statement

(Alternate is 6-55.) Following are accounts taken from the adjusted trial balance of the Marchesi Kitchen Supply Company, December 31, 20X5. The company uses the periodic inventory system.

Prepare a detailed income statement for 20X5. All amounts are in thousands:

Required

Sales salaries and commissions	$160	Freight in	$ 50
Inventory, December 31, 20X4	200	Miscellaneous expenses	13
Allowance for bad debts	14	Sales	1,085
Rent expense, office space	10	Bad debts expense	8
Gross purchases	600	Cash discounts on purchases	15
Depreciation expense, office equipment	3	Inventory, December 31, 20X5	300
Cash discounts on sales	10	Office salaries	46
Advertising expense	45	Rent expense, selling space	90
Purchase returns and allowances	40	Income tax expense	40
Delivery expense	20	Sales returns and allowances	50
		Office supplies used	6
		Depreciation expenses, trucks and store fixtures	29

6-53 Perpetual Inventory Calculations

Lincoln Electric is a wholesaler for commercial builders. The company uses a perpetual inventory system and a FIFO cost-flow assumption. The data concerning Lincoln Electric for the year 20X8 follows:

	Purchased		Sold	Balance
December 31, 20X7				110 @ $5 = $550
February 10, 20X8	80 @ $6 =	$480		
April 14			60	
May 9	110 @ $7 =	$770		
July 14			120	
October 21	100 @ $8 =	$800		
November 12			75	
Total	290	$2,050	255	

Required

Calculate the ending inventory balance in units and dollars.

6-54 Gross Profit and Turnover

Retailers closely watch a number of financial ratios, including the gross profit (gross margin) percentage and inventory turnover. Suppose the results for the furniture department in a large store in a given year were:

Sales	$3,000,000
Cost of goods sold	1,800,000
Gross profit	$1,200,000
Beginning inventory	$ 650,000
Ending inventory	550,000

Required

1. Compute the gross profit percentage and the inventory turnover.
2. Suppose the retailer is able to maintain a reduced inventory of $450,000 throughout the succeeding year. What inventory turnover would have to be obtained to achieve the same $1,200,000 gross profit? Assume that the gross profit percentage is unchanged.
3. Suppose the retailer maintains inventory at the $450,000 level throughout the succeeding year but cannot increase the inventory turnover from the level in requirement 1. What gross profit percentage would have to be obtained to achieve the same total gross profit?
4. Suppose the average inventory of $600,000 is maintained. Compute the total gross profit in the succeeding year if there is:
   a. A 10% increase of the gross profit percentage, that is, 10% of the percentage, not an additional 10 percentage points, and a 10% decrease of the inventory turnover.
   b. A 10% decrease of the gross profit percentage and a 10% increase of the inventory turnover.
5. Why do retailers find the preceding types of ratios helpful?

6-55 Detailed Income Statement

(Alternate is 6-52.) Hartmarx Corporation is a clothing company with many retail outlets, including Country Miss and Kuppenheimer. The company's annual report contained the following actual data for the year ended November 30, 1999 ($ in thousands):

Net sales	$729,699
Cost of goods sold	541,730
Selling, general, and administrative expenses	156,560
Other expenses (net)	11,195
Profit before tax	$ 20,214

The balance sheets included the following actual data ($ in thousands of dollars):

	November 30	
	1999	*1998*
Allowance for doubtful accounts	$ 8,639	$ 8,210
Inventories	176,214	207,679

Consider the following additional assumed data ($ in thousands of dollars):

Bad debts expense	$ 5,000	Freight in	$14,000
Gross purchases	509,265	Advertising expense	20,000
Cash discounts on sales	10,000	Sales returns and allowances	35,000
Sales salaries and compensation	64,560	Depreciation expense	15,000
Purchase returns and		Cash discounts on purchases	2,000
allowances	11,000	Rent expense	40,000
Freight out	12,000		

Required

Prepare a detailed multistep income statement that ends with profit (or loss) before tax. You need not subclassify the selling, general, and administrative expenses into three separate categories.

6-56 Comparison of Inventory Methods

(Alternates are 6-67 and 6-69.) The Hauck Company is a wholesaler for commercial builders. The company uses a periodic inventory system. The data concerning Zelton cooktops for the year 20X8 follow:

	Purchases	Sold	Balance
December 31, 20X7			110 @ $50 = $5,500
February 10, 20X8	80 @ $60 = $ 4,800		
April 14		60	
May 9	120 @ $70 = $ 8,400		
July 14		120	
October 21	100 @ $80 = $ 8,000		
November 12		80	
Total	300 $21,200	260	
December 31, 20X8			150 @ ?

The sales during 20X8 were made at the following selling prices:

60 @ $ 80 =	$ 4,800
120 @ 100 =	12,000
80 @ 110 =	8,800
260	$25,600

1. Prepare a comparative statement of gross profit for the year ended December 31, 20X8, using FIFO, LIFO, and weighted-average inventory methods.

2. By how much would income taxes differ if Hauck used LIFO instead of FIFO for Zelton cooktops? Assume a 40% income tax rate.

6-57 Effects of Late Purchases

(Alternates are 6-68 and 6-70.) Refer to the preceding problem. Suppose 100 extra units had been acquired on December 30 for $80 each, a total of $8,000. How would net income and income taxes have been affected under FIFO, and under LIFO? Show a tabulated comparison.

6-58 LIFO, FIFO, and Lower-of-Cost-or-Market

ASR Company began business on March 15, 20X0. The following are ASR's purchases of inventory.

March 17	100 units @ $10	$1,000
April 19	50 units @ $12	600
May 14	100 units @ $13	1,300
Total		$2,900

On May 25, 140 units were sold, leaving inventory of 110 units. ASR Company's accountant was preparing a balance sheet for June 1, at which time the replacement cost of the inventory was $12 per unit.

1. Suppose ASR Company uses LIFO, without applying lower-of-cost-or-market. Compute the June 1 inventory amount.

2. Suppose ASR Company uses lower-of-LIFO-cost-or-market. Compute the June 1 inventory amount.

3. Suppose ASR Company uses FIFO, without applying lower-of-cost-or-market. Compute the June 1 inventory amount.

4. Suppose ASR Company uses lower-of-FIFO-cost-or-market. Compute the June 1 inventory amount.

6-59 Inventory Errors

(Alternate is 6-66.) The following data are from the 20X1 income statement of the Oriental Rug Emporium ($ in thousands):

Sales		$1,700
Deduct cost of goods sold		
Beginning inventory	$ 390	
Purchases	820	
Cost of goods available for sale	$1,210	
Deduct: Ending inventory	370	
Cost of goods sold		840
Gross profit		$ 860
Other expenses		610
Income before income taxes		$ 250
Income tax expense at 40%		100
Net income		$ 150

The ending inventory was overstated by $20,000 because of errors in the physical count. The income tax rate was 40% in 20X1 and 20X2.

1. Which items in the income statement are incorrect and by how much? Use O for overstated, U for understated, and N for not affected. Complete the following tabulation:

	20X1	20X2
Beginning inventory	N	0 $30
Ending inventory	?	?
Cost of goods sold	?	?
Gross margin	?	?
Income before income taxes	?	?
Income tax expense	?	?
Net income	?	?

2. What is the dollar effect of the inventory error on retained income at the end of 20X1 and at the end of 20X2?

6-60 LIFO, FIFO, Prices Rising and Falling
The Fasano Company has a periodic inventory system. Inventory on December 31, 20X1, consisted of 10,000 units @ $10 = $100,000. Purchases during 20X2 were 13,000 units. Sales were 12,000 units for sales revenue of $21 per unit.

Prepare a four-column comparative statement of gross margin for 20X2:

Required

1. Assume purchases were at $12 per unit. Assume FIFO and then LIFO.
2. Assume purchases were at $8 per unit. Assume FIFO and then LIFO.
3. Assume an income tax rate of 40%. Suppose all transactions were for cash. Which inventory method in requirement 1 would result in more cash for Fasano Company and by how much?
4. Repeat requirement 3. Which inventory method in requirement 2 would result in more cash for Fasano Company and by how much?

6-61 LIFO, FIFO, Cash Effects
In 20X8, MacGregor Company had sales revenue of £360,000 for a line of woolen scarves. The company uses a periodic inventory system. Pertinent data for 20X8 included:

Inventory, December 31, 20X7	14,000 units @ £6	£ 84,000
January purchases	22,000 units @ £7	154,000
July purchases	30,000 units @ £8	240,000
Sales for the year	30,000 units	

Required

1. Prepare a statement of gross margin for 20X8. Use two columns, one assuming LIFO and one assuming FIFO.
2. Assume a 40% income tax rate. Suppose all transactions were for cash. Which inventory method would result in more cash for MacGregor Company, and by how much?

6-62 FIFO and LIFO
Two companies, the LIFO Company and the FIFO Company, are in the scrap metal warehousing business as arch competitors. They are about the same size and in 20X1 coincidentally encountered seemingly identical operating situations. Only their inventory accounting systems differed.

Their beginning inventory was 10,000 tons; it cost $50 per ton. During the year, each company purchased 50,000 tons at the following prices:

- 30,000 @ $60 on March 17
- 20,000 @ $70 on October 5

Each company sold 45,000 tons at average prices of $100 per ton. Other expenses in addition to cost of goods sold but excluding income taxes were $650,000. The income tax rate is 40%.

Required

1. Compute net income for the year for both companies. Show your calculations.
2. As a manager, which method would you prefer? Why? Explain fully. Include your estimate of the overall effect of these events on the cash balances of each company, assuming that all transactions during 20X1 were direct receipts or disbursements of cash.

6-63 Effects of LIFO and FIFO

The Karas Company is starting in business on December 31, 20X0. In each half year, from 20X1 through 20X4, it expects to purchase 1,000 units and sell 50 units for the amounts listed next. In 20X5, it expects to purchase no units and sell 4,000 units for the amount indicated in the following table:

	20X1	20X2	20X3	20X4	20X5
Purchases					
First 6 months	$ 2,000	$ 4,000	$ 6,000	$ 6,000	0
Second 6 months	4,000	5,000	6,000	8,000	0
Total	$ 6,000	$ 9,000	$12,000	$14,000	0
Sales (at selling price)	$10,000	$10,000	$10,000	$10,000	$40,000

Assume that there are no costs or expenses other than those shown earlier. The tax rate is 40%, and taxes for each year are payable on December 31 of each year. Karas Company is trying to decide whether to use periodic FIFO or LIFO throughout the 5-year period.

Required

1. What was net income under FIFO for each of the 5 years? under LIFO? Show calculations.
2. Explain briefly which method, LIFO or FIFO, seems more advantageous, and why.

6-64 Effects of LIFO on Purchase Decisions

The Ramayya Corporation is nearing the end of its first year in business. The following purchases of its single product have been made:

	Units	Unit Price	Total Cost
January	1,000	$10	$ 10,000
March	1,000	10	10,000
May	1,000	11	11,000
July	1,000	13	13,000
September	1,000	14	14,000
December	4,000	15	60,000
	9,000		$118,000

Sales for the year will be 5,000 units for $120,000. Expenses other than cost of goods sold will be $20,000.

The president is undecided about whether to adopt FIFO or LIFO for income tax purposes. The company has ample storage space for up to 7,000 units of inventory. Inventory prices are expected to stay at $15 per unit for the next few months.

Required

1. What would be the net income before taxes, the income taxes, and the net income after taxes for the year under (a) FIFO or (b) LIFO? Income tax rates are 40%.
2. If the company sells its year-end inventory in year two @ $24 per unit and goes out of business, what would be the net income before taxes, the income taxes, and the net income after taxes under (a) FIFO and (b) LIFO? Assume that other expenses in year two are $20,000.
3. Repeat requirements 1 and 2, assuming that the 4,000 units @ $15 purchased in December were not purchased until January of the second year. Generalize on the effect on net income of the timing of purchases under FIFO and LIFO.

6-65 Changing Quantities and LIFO Reserve

Consider the following data for the year 20X8:

	Units	Unit Cost
Beginning inventory	4	*
Purchases	6	24
	6	28
Ending inventory	4	†

*FIFO, $20; LIFO, $16.
†To be computed.

1. Prepare a comparative table computing the cost of goods sold, using columns for FIFO and LIFO. In a final column, show (a) the difference between FIFO and LIFO inventories (the LIFO reserve) at the beginning of the year and at the end of the year, and (b) how the change in this amount explains the difference in cost of goods sold.

2. Repeat requirement 1, except assume that the ending inventory consisted of (a) eight units, (b) zero units.

3. In your own words, explain why, for a given year, the increase in the LIFO reserve measures the amount by which cost of goods sold is higher under LIFO than FIFO.

6-66 Inventory Errors, 3 Years

(Alternate is 6-59.) The Janoski Company had the accompanying data for three successive years ($ in millions):

	20X3	20X2	20X1
Sales	$200	$160	$170
Deduct: Cost of goods sold			
Beginning inventory	15	25	40
Purchases	135	100	90
Cost of goods available for sale	150	125	130
Ending inventory	30	15	25
Cost of goods sold	120	110	105
Gross profit	80	50	65
Other expenses	70	30	30
Income before income taxes	10	20	35
Income tax expense at 40%	4	8	14
Net income	$ 6	$ 12	$ 21

In early 20X4, a team of internal auditors discovered that the ending inventory for 20X1 had been overstated by $15 million. Furthermore, the ending inventory for 20X3 had been understated by $5 million. The ending inventory for December 31, 20X2, was correct.

1. Which items in the income statement are incorrect and by how much? Prepare a tabulation covering each of the 3 years.

2. Is the amount of retained income correct at the end of 20X1, 20X2, and 20X3? If it is erroneous, indicate the amount and whether it is overstated (O) or understated (U).

6-67 Comparison of Inventory Methods

(Alternates are 6-56 and 6-69.) Tarpley Company produces computers. The following data and descriptions are from the company's fiscal 2001 annual report ($ in millions):

	December 31	
	2001	*2000*
Inventories	$177,359	$207,496

A footnote states: "Inventories are stated at the lower of cost (determined principally on the first-in, first-out method) or market."

Assume that Tarpley used the periodic inventory system. Suppose a division of Tarpley had the accompanying data concerning the use of its computer parts that it acquires and resells to customers for maintaining equipment ($ are not in millions):

	Units	Total
Inventory (December 31, 2001)	100	$ 400
Purchase (February 20, 2002)	200	1,000
Sales, March 17, 1996 (at $9 per unit)	150	
Purchase (June 25, 2002)	160	960
Sales, November 7, 2002 (at $10 per unit)	160	

1. For these computer parts only, prepare a tabulation of the cost of goods sold section of the income statement for the year ended December 31, 2002. Support your computations. Round totals to the nearest dollar. Show your tabulation for four different inventory methods: (a) FIFO, (b) LIFO, (c) weighted-average, and (d) specific identification. For requirement d, assume that the purchase of February 20 was identified with the sale of March 17. Also assume that the purchase of June 25 was identified with the sale of November 7.

2. By how much would income taxes differ if Tarpley used (a) LIFO instead of FIFO for this inventory item and (b) LIFO instead of weighted-average? Assume a 40% tax rate.

6-68 Effects of Late Purchases

(Alternates are 6-57 and 6-70.) Refer to the preceding problem. Suppose Tarpley acquired 60 extra units @ $7 each on December 29, 2002, a total of $420. How would gross profit and income taxes be affected under FIFO, that is, compare FIFO results before and after the purchase of 60 extra units; and under LIFO, that is, compare LIFO results before and after the purchase of 60 extra units. Show computations and explain.

6-69 Comparison of Inventory Methods

(Alternates are 6-56 and 6-67.) Texas Instruments is a major producer of semiconductors and other electrical and electronic products. Semiconductors are especially vulnerable to price fluctuations. The following are from the company's annual report ($ in millions):

	December 31	
	1999	*1998*
Inventories	$845	$596

Texas Instruments uses a variety of inventory methods, but for this problem assume that only FIFO is used.

Net revenues for the fiscal year ended December 31, 1999, were $9,468 million. Cost of revenues was $4,931 million.

Assume that Texas Instruments had the accompanying data concerning one of its semiconductors. Assume a periodic inventory system.

	In		Out	'Balance
December 31, 1998				80 @ $5 = 400
February 25, 1999	50 @ $6 = $	300		
March 29			60* @ ?	
May 28	80 @ $7 = $	560		
June 7			90* @ ?	
November 20	90 @ $8 = $	720		
December 15			50* @ ?	
Total	220	$1,580	200	
December 31, 1999				100 @ ?

*Selling prices were $9, $11, and $13, respectively:

	60 @ $9 = $ 540
	90 @ 11 = 990
	50 @ 13 = 650
Total sales	200 $2,180

Summary of costs to account for:

Beginning inventory	$ 400
Purchases	1,580
Cost of goods available for sale	$1,980
Other expenses for this product	$ 500
Income tax rate, 40%	

Required

1. Prepare a comparative income statement for the 1999 fiscal year for the product in question. Use the FIFO, LIFO, and weighted-average inventory methods.
2. By how much would income taxes have differed if Texas Instruments had used LIFO instead of FIFO for this product?
3. Suppose Texas Instruments had used the specific identification method. Compute the gross margin (or gross profit) if the ending inventory had consisted of (a) 90 units @ $8, and 10 units @ $7; and (b) 60 units @ $5, and 40 units @ $8.

6-70 Effects of Late Purchases
(Alternates are 6-57 and 6-68.) Refer to the preceding problem. Suppose Texas Instruments had acquired 50 extra units @ $8 each on December 30, 1999, a total of $400. How would income before income taxes have been affected under FIFO? That is, compare FIFO results before and after the purchase of 50 extra units. Under LIFO? That is, compare LIFO results before and after the purchase of 50 extra units. Show computations and explain.

6-71 Classic Switch from LIFO to FIFO
Effective January 1, 1970, Chrysler Corporation adopted the FIFO method for inventories previously valued by the LIFO method. The 1970 annual report stated: "This . . . makes the financial statements with respect to inventory valuation comparable with those of the other United States automobile manufacturers."

The *Wall Street Journal* reported:

> *The change improved Chrysler's 1970 financial results several ways. Besides narrowing the 1970 loss by $20 million it improved Chrysler's working capital. The change also made the comparison with 1969 earnings look somewhat more favorable because, upon restatement, Chrysler's 1969 profit was raised by only $10.2 million from the original figures.*
>
> *Finally, the change helped Chrysler's balance sheet by boosting inventories, and thus current assets, by $150 million at the end of 1970 over what they would have been under LIFO. As Chrysler's profit has collapsed over the last two years and its financial position tightened, auto analysts have eyed warily Chrysler's shrinking ratio of current assets to current liabilities.*
>
> *To get the improvements in its balance sheet and results, however, Chrysler paid a price. Roger Helder, vice president and comptroller, said Chrysler owed the government $53 million in tax savings it accumulated by using the LIFO method since it switched from FIFO in 1957. The major advantage of LIFO is that it holds down profit and thus tax liabilities. The other three major auto makers stayed on the FIFO method. Mr. Helder said Chrysler now has to pay back that $53 million to the government over 20 years, which will boost Chrysler's tax bills about $3 million a year.*

Required

Given the content of this text chapter, do you think the Chrysler decision to switch from LIFO to FIFO was beneficial to its stockholders? Explain, being as specific as you can.

6-72 LIFO, FIFO, Purchase Decisions, and Earnings Per Share
Hollywood Pet Supplies, a company with 1 million shares of common stock outstanding, had the following transactions during 20X1, its first year in business:

Sales	1,100,000 units @ $5
Purchases	900,000 units @ $2
	300,000 units @ $3

The current income tax rate is a flat 50%; the rate next year is expected to be 40%.

It is December 20 and Lane Braxton, the president, is trying to decide whether to buy the 400,000 units he needs for inventory now or early next year. The current price is $4 per unit. Prices on inventory are expected to remain stable; in any event, no decline in prices is anticipated.

Braxton has not chosen an inventory method as yet, but will pick either LIFO or FIFO. Other expenses for the year will be $1.4 million.

Required

1. By using LIFO, prepare a comparative income statement assuming the 400,000 units (a) are not purchased and (b) are purchased. The statement should end with reported earnings per share.

2. Repeat requirement 1, using FIFO.

3. Comment on the preceding results. Which method should Braxton choose? Why? Be specific.

4. Suppose that in year two the tax rate drops to 40%, prices remain stable, 1.1 million units are sold @ $5, enough units are purchased at $4 so that the ending inventory will be 700,000 units, and other expenses are reduced to $800,000.

   a. Prepare a comparative income statement for the second year showing the impact of each of the four alternatives on net income and earnings per share for the second year.

   b. Explain any differences in net income that you encounter among the four alternatives.

   c. Why is there a difference in ending inventory values under LIFO even though the same amount of physical inventory is in stock?

   d. What is the total cash outflow for income taxes for the 2 years together under the four alternatives?

   e. Would you change your answer in requirement 3 now that you have completed requirement 4? Why?

6-73 Eroding the LIFO Base

Many companies on LIFO are occasionally faced with strikes or material shortages that necessitate a reduction in their normal inventory levels to satisfy current sales demands. A few years ago several large steel companies requested special legislative relief from the additional taxes that ensued from such events.

A news story stated:

> As steelworkers slowly streamed back to the mills this week, most steel companies began adding up the tremendous losses imposed by the longest strike in history. At a significant number of plants across the country, however, the worry wasn't losses but profits—"windfall" bookkeeping profits that for some companies may mean painful increases in corporate income taxes.
>
> These outfits have been caught in the backfire of a special mechanism for figuring up inventory costs on tax returns. It's known to accountants as LIFO, or last in, first out. Ironically, it's designed to slice the corporate tax bill in a time of rising prices.
>
> Biggest Bite—Most of the big steel companies—16 out of the top 20—as well as 40 percent of all steel warehousers, use LIFO accounting in figuring their taxes. But the tax squeeze from paper LIFO profits won't affect them all equally. It will put the biggest bite on warehousers that kept going during the strike—and as a result, the American Steel Warehouse Assn. may ask Congress for a special tax exemption on these paper profits. . . .
>
> Companies such as Ryerson and Castle have been caught because they have had to strip their shelves bare in order to satisfy customer demands during the strike. And they probably won't be able to rebuild their stocks by the time they close their books for tax purposes.

To see how this situation can happen, consider the following example. Suppose a company adopted LIFO in 1976. At December 31, 1999, its LIFO inventory consisted of three "layers":

From 1976	100,000 units @ $1.00	$100,000
From 1977	50,000 units @ 1.10	55,000
From 1978	30,000 units @ 1.20	36,000
		$191,000

In 2000, prices rose enormously. Data follow:

Sales	500,000 units @ $3.00 = $1,500,000
Purchases	340,000 units @ $2.00 = $ 680,000
Operating expenses	500,000

A prolonged strike near the end of the year resulted in a severe depletion of the normal inventory stock of 180,000 units. The strike was settled on December 28, 2000. The company intended to replenish the inventory as soon as possible. The applicable income tax rate is 60%.

Required

1. Compute the income taxes for 2000.
2. Suppose the company had been able to meet the 500,000-unit demand out of current purchases. Compute the income taxes for 2000 under those circumstances.

6-74 Lower-of-Cost-or-Market

(Alternate is 6-48.) Polaroid Corporation's annual report stated: "Inventories are valued on a first-in, first-out basis at the lower of cost or market value." Assume that severe price competition in 2001 necessitated a write-down on December 31 for a class of camera inventories with a cost of $13 million. The appropriate valuation at market was deemed to be $8 million.

Suppose the product line was terminated in early 2002 and the remaining inventory was sold for $8 million.

Required

1. Assume that sales of this line of camera for 2001 were $20 million and cost of goods sold was $14 million. Prepare a statement of gross margin for 2001 and 2002. Show the results under a strict FIFO cost method in the first two columns and under a lower-of-FIFO-cost-or-market method in the next two columns.
2. Assume that Polaroid did not discontinue the product line. Instead a new marketing campaign spurred market demand. Replacement cost of the cameras in the December 31 inventory was $9 million on January 31, 2002. What inventory valuation would be appropriate if the inventory of December 31, 2001 was still held on January 31, 2002?

6-75 LIFO Liquidation

Maytag Corporation reported 1999 pretax operating income of $530,851,000. Footnotes to Maytag's financial statements read: "Inventories are stated at the lower of cost or market. Inventory costs are determined by the last-in, first-out (LIFO) method for approximately 77% of the company's inventory. . . . The footnote showed that if the FIFO method of inventory accounting, which approximates current cost, had been used for all inventories, they would have been $80.3 million and $79.0 million higher than reported at December 31, 1999 and 1998, respectively."

Required

1. Calculate the pretax income that Maytag would have reported if the FIFO inventory method had been used.
2. Suppose Maytag's income tax rate is 34%. What were Maytag's income taxes using LIFO? What would they have been if Maytag had used FIFO?
3. Was Maytag's use of LIFO a good choice from a tax perspective? What is the cumulative financial effect of the choice?

6-76 LIFO Reserve

Brunswick Corporation reported LIFO inventories of $444.9 million on a recent balance sheet. A footnote to the financial statements indicated that the "LIFO cost was $83.6 million lower than the FIFO cost of inventories."

1. Has the cost of Brunswick's inventory generally been increasing or decreasing? Explain.
2. Suppose Brunswick sold its entire inventory for $600 million the subsequent year and did not replace it. Compute the gross profit from the sale of this inventory (a) as Brunswick would report it using LIFO and (b) as it would have been reported if Brunswick had always used FIFO instead of LIFO. Which inventory method creates higher gross profit? Explain.

6-77 Inventory Errors

IBM had inventories of $4.8 billion at December 31, 1999, and $5.2 billion 1 year earlier.

Required

1. Suppose the beginning inventory for fiscal 1999 had been overstated by $30 million because of errors in physical counts. Which items in the financial statements would be incorrect and by how much? Use *O* for overstated, *U* for understated, and *N* for not affected. Assume a 40% tax rate.

	Effect on Fiscal Year	
	1999	*1998*
Beginning inventory	O by $30	N
Ending inventory	?	?
Cost of sales	?	?
Gross profit	?	?
Income before taxes on income	?	?
Taxes on income	?	?
Net income	?	?

2. What is the dollar effect of the inventory error on retained earnings at the end of fiscal 1998, and 1999?

6-78 LIFO Liquidation

The inventory footnote taken from the 1996 annual report of Monsanto is printed as follows. Monsanto reported Income before income taxes of $33 million in 1996.

	Inventories	
(in millions)	*1996*	*1995*
Inventories at FIFO cost		
Finished goods	$258	$266
Goods in process	47	53
Raw materials and supplies	126	145
Inventories, at FIFO cost	431	464
Excess of FIFO over LIFO cost	(140)	(153)
Total	$291	$311

In 1996 and 1995, inventory quantities were reduced, resulting in liquidations of LIFO inventory quantities carried at the lower costs prevailing in prior years. The effects of these liquidations increased pretax income by $5 million in 1996 and were immaterial in 1995.

Required

1. What would Monsanto have reported as Income before income taxes for 1996 had they used FIFO to account for all their inventories?
2. How does the change in the LIFO reserve relate to the effect of the LIFO liquidation?

6-79 Year-End Purchases and LIFO

A company engaged in the manufacture and sale of dental supplies maintained an inventory of gold for use in its business. The company used LIFO for the gold content of its products.

On the final day of its fiscal year, the company bought 10,000 ounces of gold at $380 per ounce. Had the purchase not been made, the company would have penetrated its LIFO layers for 8,000 ounces of gold acquired at $260 per ounce.

The applicable income tax rate is 40%.

Required

1. Compute the effect of the year-end purchase on the income taxes of the fiscal year.

2. On the second day of the next fiscal year, the company resold the 10,000 ounces of gold to its suppliers. What do you think the Internal Revenue Service should do if it discovers this resale? Explain.

6-80 Comparison of Gross Profit Percentages and Inventory Turnover

JCPenney and Kmart are competitors in the retail business, although they target slightly different markets. The gross margin for each company and average inventory follow for the indicated years (both have January year-ends; 2000 refers to the year ending in January of 2000).

JCPenney

	2000	1995
	(Millions)	
Retail sales	$32,510	$20,380
Cost of goods sold*	23,374	13,970
Gross profit	9,136	6,410
Average inventory	6,004	3,711

Kmart

	2000	1995
	(Millions)	
Retail sales	$35,925	$34,025
Cost of goods sold*	28,102	25,992
Gross profit	7,823	8,033
Average inventory	6,819	7,317

*Both companies classify costs of occupancy, buying, and warehousing with cost of goods sold.

Required

Calculate gross profit percentages and inventory turnovers for 1995 and 2000 for each company and compare them. What trends do you observe? Which company appears to perform better? To what extent do their different performances seem to relate to their relative positions in the retail market?

6-81 Gross Profit on German Income Statement

Most German companies use an income statement format called a "type-of-cost" format. Consider a slightly simplified version of the 1996 and 1995 income statements of Mannesman AG, the large engineering and manufacturing firm (German marks in millions):

	1996	1995
Net sales	DM34,683	DM32,094
Increase in inventories	746	830
Total operating output	35,429	32,924
Cost of goods manufactured	31,204	29,351
Other operating expenses (net)	3,215	2,662
Operating income	DM 1,010	DM 911

Note that the cost of goods manufactured includes the cost of the additional units produced to increase the inventories.

Compute the gross profit and gross profit percentage for Mannesman in 1995 and 1996. Comment on the change in gross profit percentage between 1995 and 1996.

6-82 LIFO and Ethical Issues

Yamaha Instrument Distributors is a wholesaler of electronic instruments. Yamaha has used the LIFO inventory method since 1971. Near the end of 2001, the company's inventory of a particular instrument listed three LIFO layers, two of which were from earlier years and one from 2001 purchases:

	No. of Units	Unit Cost
Layer one	4,000	$40
Layer two	2,500	50
2001 Purchases	30,000	60
Total available	36,500	

In 2001, Yamaha sold 32,500 units, leaving 4,000 units in inventory.

On December 27, 2001, Yamaha had a chance to buy a minimum of 15,000 units of the instrument at a unit cost of $70. The offer was good for 10 days, and delivery would be immediate on placing the order.

Suki Yamaguchi, chief purchasing manager of Yamaha, was trying to decide whether to make the purchase, and, if it is made, whether to make it in 2001 or 2002. The controller had told her that she should buy immediately, because the company would save $70,000 in taxes. The tax rate is 40%.

1. Explain why $70,000 of taxes would be saved.
2. Are there any ethical considerations that would influence this decision? Explain.

6-83 Inventory Shrinkage

Jim Rivera, owner of Village Hardware Company, was concerned about his control of inventory. In December 20X7, he installed a computerized perpetual inventory system. In April, his accountant brought him the following information for the first 3 months of 20X8:

Sales	$700,000
Cost of goods sold	590,000
Beginning inventory (per physical count)	130,000
Merchandise purchases	630,000

Rivera had asked his public accounting firm to conduct a physical count of inventory on April 1. The CPAs reported inventory of $140,000.

1. Compute the ending inventory shown in the books by the new perpetual inventory system.
2. Provide the journal entry to reconcile the book inventory with the physical count. What is the corrected cost of goods sold for the first 3 months of 20X8?
3. Do your calculations point out areas about which Rivera should be concerned? Why?

6-84 Cheating on Inventories

The *Wall Street Journal* reported: "Cheating on inventories is a common way for small businesses to chisel on their income taxes. . . . A New York garment maker, for example, evades a sizable amount of income tax by undervaluing his firm's inventory by 20% on his tax return. He hides about $500,000 out of a $2.5 million inventory."

The news story concluded: "When it's time to borrow, business owners generally want profits and assets to look fat." The garment maker uses a different fiscal period for financial statements to his bank. "After writing down the inventory as of Dec. 31, he writes it up six months later when the fiscal year ends. In this way, he underpays the IRS and impresses his banker. Some describe that kind of inventory accounting as WIFL—Whatever I Feel Like."

1. At a 40% income tax rate, what amount of federal income taxes would the owner evade according to the news story?
2. Consider the next year. By how much would the ending inventory have to be understated to evade the same amount of income taxes?

Use the following table and fill in the blanks:

	(in dollars)			
	Honest Reporting		**Dishonest Reporting**	
	First Year	*Second Year*	*First Year*	*Second Year*
Beginning inventory	$ 3,000,000	$?	$ 3,000,000	$?
Purchases	10,000,000	$ 10,000,000	10,000,000	10,000,000
Available for sale	13,000,000	?	13,000,000	?
Ending inventory	2,500,000	2,500,000	2,000,000	?
Cost of goods sold	$10,500,000	$?	$11,000,000	$?
Income tax savings @ 40%*	$ 4,200,000	$?	$?	$?
Income tax savings for 2 years together	$?		$?	

*This is the income tax effect of only the cost of goods sold. To shorten and simplify the analysis, sales, and operating expenses are assumed to be the same each year.

6-85   Manufacturing Costs
Study appendix 6. Sean O'Neal made custom T-shirts for himself and his friends for years before trying to treat it seriously as a business. January 1, 20X1, he decided to become more serious. He bought some screening equipment for $4,000 that he figured was good for 8,000 screenings. He decided to use units of production depreciation. He acquired 2,000 shirts for $4,000 and rented a studio for $500 per month. During the month, he paid an assistant $1,600 and together they created three designs, screened 1,500 shirts, and sold 1,200 at $8 each. At month-end, there were 500 shirts unused, 300 finished shirts ready for sale, and Sean was trying to figure out how he was doing.

1. Calculate the cost of goods sold and the value of ending inventory (including raw material and finished goods).
2. Prepare an income statement for Sean's first month of operations. Assume a 30% tax rate.

ANNUAL REPORT CASE

6-86   Cisco Annual Report
Refer to the financial statements for Cisco in appendix A. Assume that Cisco uses the periodic inventory procedure.

1. Compute the amount of merchandise inventory purchased during the year ended July 29, 2000. (*Hint:* Use the inventory T-account.)
2. Compute the inventory turnover for Cisco for the year ended July 29, 2000.
3. Calculate the gross margin percentage for each of the last 3 years. Comment on any changes.

6-87   Financial Reporting Research
Select an industry and identify two firms within that industry.

1. Identify the inventory accounting method used by each.
2. Calculate gross profit percentages and inventory turnovers for 2 years for each firm. Comment on the comparison and any trends.

COLLABORATIVE LEARNING EXERCISE

6-88   Understanding Inventory Methods

Form groups of three students each. (If there are more than three students in a group, extras can be paired up.) Each student should select or be assigned one of these three inventory methods:

1. Specific identification
2. FIFO
3. LIFO

Consider the following information from the annual report of Levitz Corporation, one of the largest specialty retailers of furniture in the United States which filed for bankruptcy in 1997. Hence no updated financial results are available, although the company continues to do business. Levitz uses the LIFO method to account for its inventories ($ amounts are in thousands).

For the year ended March 31, 1997	
Sales	$966,855
Cost of goods sold (using LIFO)	533,555
Other operating expenses	417,283
Operating income	$ 16,017
Purchases of inventory	$562,125
At March 31, 1997	
Inventories @ LIFO	$169,488
Inventories @ FIFO	180,688
At March 31, 1996	
Inventories @ LIFO	$140,918
Inventories @ FIFO	151,918

Assume that in the next fiscal year, Levitz had exactly the same physical sales as in the year reported, but prices were 5% higher. Thus, next year's sales were $1.05 \times \$966,855 = \$1,015,198$. Assume that other operating expenses were exactly the same as in the current year. Further assume that the physical level of inventories at the end of the next fiscal year were unchanged, but because of a 5% price increase on April 1, purchases of inventories in the next fiscal year were $560,233. (Note that if there had been no price increase, the purchases of inventories would have been $533,555.)

Required

1. Compute operating income for Levitz for the current year and next year using the inventory method to which you were assigned. Those using the LIFO and FIFO methods have all the information needed for the calculations. Those using specific identification must make some assumptions, and their operating income numbers will depend on the assumptions made.

2. Explain to the other members of the group how you computed the operating income, including an explanation of how you chose the assumptions you made.

INTERNET EXERCISE

6-89   Deckers Outdoor Corporation

Go to http://www.sec.gov/ to locate Deckers Outdoor Corporation's latest annual report information in the EDGAR database. Deckers Outdoor Corporation is the exclusive licensee for the manufacture of Teva footwear. Click on the latest 10K filing to find financial report data.

Answer the following questions about Deckers:

1. Under Part 1, *General,* what percentage of revenues does Teva represent? Have revenues related to Teva products increased or decreased over the past few years?

2. Scroll through several pages to locate *Inventory Risk*. What does Deckers say about its inventory policy?

3. Read the *Summary of Significant Accounting Policies* section of the *Notes to Consolidated Financial Statements.* How are inventories valued and accounted for? Why do you think the company uses this particular costing method?

4. Locate the *Selected Financial Data.* How much gross profit is reported for the most recent year? Has this amount increased or decreased compared with the previous year? What explanation does management give for the changes? (*Hint:* Look in the *Management's Discussion and Analysis* section.)

Go to the "Depreciation Methods and Inventory Cost Flow Assumptions" episode on the *Mastering Accounting* CD-ROM for an interactive, video-enhanced exercise focused on the different methods for depreciation and inventory. CanGo staff must prepare reports that present potential investors with the best possible financial outlook for the company.

7

LONG-LIVED ASSETS AND DEPRECIATION

More than 3,000 Gap stores, and every one has tables, shelves, doors, and walls: expensive assets to support the sales effort.

www.prenhall.com/horngren

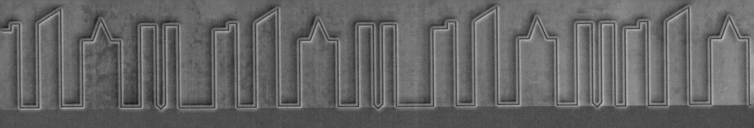

Learning Objectives

After studying this chapter, you should be able to

1. Measure the acquisition cost of tangible assets such as land, buildings, and equipment.

2. Compute depreciation for buildings and equipment using various depreciation methods.

3. Differentiate financial statement depreciation from income tax depreciation.

4. Explain depreciation's effects on cash flow.

5. Distinguish expenses from expenditures that should be capitalized.

6. Compute gains and losses on disposal of fixed assets.

7. Interpret depletion of natural resources.

8. Account for various intangible assets.

It was the late 1960s, and Don Fisher, like most people of his generation, liked blue jeans and music. Also like many of his peers, he was annoyed that existing clothing stores had disorganized and poorly stocked jeans departments, so he decided to do something about it. He opened a store that sold only blue jeans and music, and called it "Gap" in reference to the generation gap that was the buzz of the times.

That was 1969. As of February 3, 2001, Gap Inc. operated 3,676 stores including Gap, Banana Republic, and Old Navy locations. New stores are opening at a rapid rate with 731 in the most recent year and about 500 per year in the prior 2 years. Gap leases most of these stores, but it still must make a tremendous investment in long-lived assets such as fixtures to operate each location. For example, under the balance sheet asset category for Property and Equipment, leasehold improvements and furniture and equipment are listed at $1.9 billion and $2.8 billion, respectively. In the most recent year, Gap spent $1.8 billion in cash to purchase property and equipment and acquire lease rights. These assets have useful lives that vary, but they all last longer than the average pair of blue jeans.

By now you should understand how to account for short-lived assets, such as those in inventory. Their costs are easily matched to the single periods in which the associated revenues are recognized. What about assets that are not used up quickly? Many long-lived assets, such as buildings and heavy machinery, produce revenues in numerous periods and their costs must be spread across all those periods.

How important are long-lived assets? Depending on the industry, they can be the most important assets a company owns. For example, consider the plant and equipment accounts (the main long-lived asset accounts) in the balance sheets of the following companies ($ in millions):

| Company | Total Assets | Plant and Equipment | |
		Total	Percentage
Decker's	$ 73	$ 2	3
AOL Time Warner	5,348	657	12
Hewlett-Packard	35,297	4,333	12
Gap Inc.	5,189	2,715	52
ExxonMobil	144,521	94,043	65
Empire District	731	616	84

Why do these numbers vary so greatly? Because different types of businesses require different types of assets. Decker's "designs, manufactures, and markets innovative function-oriented footwear and apparel" under such brand names as Teva, Simple, Ugg, and Picante. The company outsources most of the manufacturing to Asian and Costa Rican subcontractors. It has little need for fixed assets. AOL Time Warner and Hewlett-Packard are high-tech companies that rely significantly on intellectual property. Their balance sheets show significant current investments and also longer term investments, but little plant, property, and equipment. Gap may lease its stores, but, as noted in the introduction, the "leasehold" improvements to the stores and the fixtures and equipment to outfit them are quite expensive. ExxonMobil has extensive plant, property, and equipment, including everything from oil wells, to drilling rigs, to buildings, to gas pumps. Empire District is a utility company, with most of its assets in the form of electric generation plant and equipment.

As you can imagine, accounting for long-lived assets presents some interesting and unique concerns. The main issue is when to charge the cost of a long-lived asset as an expense on the income statement. For example, if an asset lasts 10 years, how much of its cost should be assigned to each of the 10 years it is used? The answer to this question relies on the method chosen for recording depreciation.

This chapter shows how to account for long-lived assets. Most of this chapter focuses on depreciation—both understanding the nature of depreciation and learning about the various depreciation methods. We start off, though, with a look at long-lived assets in general.

OVERVIEW OF LONG-LIVED ASSETS

long-lived assets
Resources that are held for an extended time, such as land, buildings, equipment, natural resources, and patents.

Most business entities hold such major assets as land, buildings, equipment, natural resources, and patents. These **long-lived assets** help produce revenues over many periods by facilitating the production and sale of goods or services to customers. Because these assets are necessary in a company's day-to-day operations, companies do not sell them in the ordinary course of business. Keep in mind, though, that one company's long-lived asset might be another company's short-lived asset. For example, a delivery truck is a

It is important to know the strengths and weaknesses of the historical accounting model. Accounting for fixed assets has both. Assets are fairly valued at cost because cost can usually be observed. The cost is verifiable and reliable. Depreciation is calculated in one of many ways to allocate the acquisition cost over the useful life of the asset. From the moment of acquisition throughout the life of the assets, the book value may be out of touch with market values, and the depreciation may be unrelated to the change in market value for the period. These characteristics of the historical accounting model are very serviceable as long as we remember the strengths and weaknesses of the model.

The bigger problem is that the accounting model does not treat certain things as assets, even though they provide undeniable future benefits to the company. Key examples are human capital, advertising, and research and development (R&D). Ed Michaels of McKinsey & Company says, "The half-life of technology is growing shorter all the time. For many companies today, talented people are the prime source of competitive advantage." Investors and analysts realize this, and the extraordinary stock prices once attached to Cisco, Microsoft, Intel, and the like are in part a recognition of what the very able employees of those firms can do. However, the financial statements do not (and cannot independently and reliably) report a value for these assets. A key reason is that the firm does not own these talented employees, it only "rents" them. Talent is always susceptible to being lured away.

John T. Chambers, CEO of Cisco puts it this way:

The New Economy is heavy on intellectual capital. The sharing of knowledge is what really makes it go. In the New Economy, you expect lifelong learning, not necessarily lifelong employment. People used to work for wages. In the New Economy, they work for ownership. Security comes from the stock. Labor often fought management in the Old Economy. Today, teamwork and empowerment are crucial to success.

How do the financial statements help us to assess these elements? The companies with great human capital grow faster and earn more than the others. We can measure their growth and earnings and compare them using financial accounting outcomes.

Coca-Cola sells for more per ounce than does RC Cola or Branson Cola or a number of other very tasty competitors. Part of the reason is the century of advertising and impression making that is Coke's history. The brand name is an asset, and yet the financial statements do not reflect it. In the United States, we expense advertising costs as incurred and do not reflect the internal generation of an asset. Note that this is not as true elsewhere. Companies in the United Kingdom often report an asset on their balance sheet representing the value of the "brand." Again, the accounting process assures that we see how much is currently being expended on these efforts, and we can assess its effectiveness by looking at the outcomes. When Coke grows rapidly and earns high profits, we can see the evidence of a devoted workforce and a great brand.

Source: *Business Week*, October 4, 1999.

long-lived asset for most companies, but a truck dealer would regard a delivery truck as short-lived merchandise inventory.

Long-lived assets are divided into tangible and intangible categories. **Tangible assets** (also called **fixed assets** or **plant assets**) are physical items that can be seen and touched. Examples are land, natural resources, buildings, and equipment. In contrast, **intangible assets** are not physical in nature. They generally consist of rights or economic benefits, such as patents, trademarks, and copyrights.

As you might guess, we account for these different types of long-lived assets quite differently. Land is unique in that it does not wear out or become obsolete. Therefore, it is reported in the financial records at its historical cost. It is not depreciated. Other long-lived assets are used up or worn out, or become obsolete. As these assets expire over time, accountants convert their historical cost to expense.

tangible assets (fixed assets, plant assets) Physical items that can be seen and touched, such as land, natural resources, buildings, and equipment.

intangible assets Rights or economic benefits, such as franchises, patents, trademarks, copyrights, and goodwill, that are not physical in nature.

Exhibit 7-1

Summary of Accounting for Long-Lived Assets

Balance Sheet	Income Statement
Land ⟶	—
Buildings and equipment ⟶	Depreciation
Natural resources ⟶	Depletion
Intangible assets, for example, franchises or patents ⟶	Amortization

depletion The process of allocating the cost of natural resources to the periods in which the resources are used.

amortization When referring to long-lived assets, it usually means the allocation of the costs of intangible assets to the periods that benefit from these assets.

In practice, different words are used to describe the allocation of costs over time, as summarized in Exhibit 7-1. For tangible assets such as buildings, machinery, and equipment, the allocation is called depreciation. For natural resources the allocation is called **depletion.** Although it has a broader meaning, **amortization** is typically used specifically to refer to the allocation of the costs of intangible assets to the periods that benefit from these assets.

ACQUISITION COST OF TANGIBLE ASSETS

The acquisition cost of long-lived assets is the cash-equivalent purchase price, including incidental costs required to complete the purchase, to transport the asset, and to prepare it for use.

LAND

The acquisition cost of land includes charges to the purchaser for the cost of land surveys, legal fees, title fees, realtors' commissions, transfer taxes, and even the demolition costs of old structures that might be torn down to get the land ready for its intended use. Under historical-cost accounting, land is reported in the balance sheet at its original cost.

Objective 1
Measure the acquisition cost of tangible assets such as land, buildings, and equipment.

Of course, after years of rising real estate values and inflation, the carrying amount of land is likely to be far below its current market value. Should land acquired and held since 1940 still appear at its 1940 cost on balance sheets prepared 60 years later? Accountants do exactly that. For example, Weyerhaeuser listed on its balance sheet 5.9 million acres of land at $125 million (only $21 per acre). The current value of the land was in the billions of dollars. In some countries, periodic revaluation of assets is permitted, but in the United States the conservative bias using historical costs is firmly rooted in accounting for land and other long-lived assets.

BUILDINGS AND EQUIPMENT

The cost of buildings, plant, and equipment should include all costs of acquisition and preparation for use. Consider the following example for some used packaging equipment:

Invoice price, gross	$100,000
Deduct 2% cash discount for payment within 30 days	2,000
Invoice price, net	$ 98,000
State sales tax at 8% of $98,000	7,840
Transportation costs	3,000
Installation costs	8,000
Repair costs prior to use	7,000
Total acquisition cost	$123,840

288   CHAPTER 7   LONG-LIVED ASSETS AND DEPRECIATION

As you can see, several individual costs make up total acquisition cost. The total of $123,840 would be capitalized and added to the Equipment account. We describe a cost as being **capitalized** when we add it to an asset account, as distinguished from expensing it immediately. In the preceding example, we include repair costs in the amount that we capitalize as the cost of the asset. Normally we would expense repair costs in the income statement as incurred. The difference here is that repair costs prior to first use are part of getting the asset ready to produce and, therefore, they belong in acquisition cost on the balance sheet. Repair costs to maintain the productive ability of the machine should be charged as expenses in the income statement.

capitalized A cost that is added to an asset account, as distinguished from being expensed immediately.

DEPRECIATION OF BUILDINGS AND EQUIPMENT

Depreciation is frequently misunderstood. It is not a process of valuation. In everyday use, we might say that an auto depreciates in value, meaning that its current market value declines. But to an accountant, depreciation is not a technique for approximating current values such as replacement costs or resale values. It is simply a system for cost allocation. Companies in the United States freely select the depreciation method they believe best portrays their economic circumstance. Thus, we discuss several alternatives. In contrast, in countries such as Japan, Germany, and France, depreciation methods are specified by government (often tax) authorities.

Objective 2
Compute depreciation for buildings and equipment using various depreciation methods.

Depreciation is one of the key factors distinguishing accrual accounting from cash-basis accounting. If a company purchases a long-lived asset for cash, strict cash-basis accounting would treat the entire cost of the asset as an expense immediately. In contrast, accrual accounting initially capitalizes the cost and then allocates it in the form of depreciation over the periods the asset is used. This matches expenses with the revenues produced.

The amount of the acquisition cost to be depreciated or allocated over the total useful life of the asset is the **depreciable value.** It is the difference between the total acquisition cost and the predicted residual value. The **residual value,** also known as **terminal value, disposal value, salvage value,** and **scrap value,** is the amount predicted to be received from sale or disposal of a long-lived asset at the end of its useful life. The **useful (or economic) life** of an asset is determined as the shorter of the physical life of the asset before it wears out or the economic life of the asset before it is obsolete.

depreciable value The amount of the acquisition cost to be allocated as depreciation over the total useful life of an asset. It is the difference between the total acquisition cost and the predicted residual value.

Given the rapidly increasing speed and decreasing cost of computers in recent times, most companies replace them long before they wear out. That is, their economic life is shorter than their physical life. Sometimes an asset's life is measured directly in terms of the benefit it provides instead of the time period over which it is used. For example, the useful life of a truck might be measured as the total miles to be driven, perhaps 100,000, 200,000, or even 400,000 miles. If a truck were purchased for $50,000, the depreciation would be $.50 per mile if the truck were expected to last 100,000 miles with no salvage value.

residual value (terminal value, disposal value, salvage value, scrap value) The amount received from disposal of a long-lived asset at the end of its useful life.

Depreciation methods differ primarily in the amount of cost allocated to each period. A list of depreciation amounts for each year of an asset's useful life is called a **depreciation schedule.** We use the following symbols and amounts to compare the various depreciation schedules for a hypothetical $41,000 company truck:

useful life (economic life) The number of years before an asset wears out or becomes obsolete, whichever comes first.

Symbols	Amounts for Illustration
Let	
C = total acquisition cost on December 31, 20X2	$41,000
R = residual value	$ 1,000
n = useful life (in years or miles)	4 years;
	200,000 miles
D = amount of depreciation	Various

depreciation schedule The listing of depreciation amounts for each year of an asset's useful life.

Exhibit 7-2
Straight-Line Depreciation Schedule

	Balances at End of Year			
	1	*2*	*3*	*4*
Plant and equipment (at original acquisition cost)	$41,000	$41,000	$41,000	$41,000
Less: Accumulated depreciation (the portion of original cost that has already been charged to operations as expense)	10,000	20,000	30,000	40,000
Net book value (the portion of original cost that will be charged to future operations as expense)	$31,000	$21,000	$11,000	$ 1,000

STRAIGHT-LINE DEPRECIATION

straight-line depreciation
A method that spreads the depreciable value evenly over the useful life of an asset.

Straight-line depreciation spreads the depreciable value evenly over the useful life of an asset. It is by far the most popular method for corporate reporting to shareholders. In fact, it is used by almost 95% of major companies for at least part of their fixed assets, and 70% use it exclusively.

Exhibit 7-2 shows how our company truck would be displayed in the balance sheet if a straight-line method of depreciation were used. The annual depreciation expense that would appear on the income statement is:

$$\text{Depreciation expense} = \frac{\text{Acquisition cost} - \text{Residual value}}{\text{Years of useful life}}$$

$$= \frac{C - R}{n}$$

$$= \frac{\$41,000 - \$1,000}{4} = \$10,000 \text{ per year}$$

DEPRECIATION BASED ON UNITS

In some cases, time is not the limiting factor on the useful life of an asset. When physical wear and tear determines the useful life of the asset, accountants often base depreciation on units of service or units of production instead of the units of time (years) so commonly used. Depreciation based on units of service is called **unit depreciation.** Note that the shipping truck in our example has a useful life of 200,000 miles. Depreciation computed on a mileage basis is:

unit depreciation A depreciation method based on units of service when physical wear and tear is the dominating influence on the useful life of the asset.

$$D = \frac{C - R}{n}$$

$$= \frac{\$41,000 - \$1,000}{200,000 \text{ miles}}$$

$$= \$.20 \text{ per mile}$$

For some assets, such as transportation equipment, this depreciation pattern may have more logical appeal than the straight-line method. However, the unit depreciation method is not widely used, probably for two major reasons:

1. Unit-based depreciation frequently produces approximately the same yearly depreciation amounts as does straight-line depreciation.

2. Straight-line depreciation is easier. Under straight-line, the entire depreciation schedule can be set at the time of acquisition, but under unit depreciation, detailed records of units of service must be kept to determine the amount depreciated each year.

DECLINING-BALANCE DEPRECIATION

Any pattern of depreciation that writes off depreciable costs more quickly than does the ordinary straight-line method based on expected useful life is called accelerated depreciation. Although an infinite number of **accelerated depreciation** methods are possible, the most popular form of accelerated depreciation is the **double-declining-balance (DDB)** method. DDB is computed as follows:

1. Compute a rate by dividing 100% by the years of useful life. This result is the straight-line rate. You then double the rate. In our example, the straight-line rate is 100% ÷ 4 years = 25%. The DDB rate would be 2 × 25%, or 50%.

2. To compute the depreciation on an asset for any year, ignore the residual value and multiply the asset's book value at the beginning of the year by the DDB rate. Cease depreciation when the book value reaches the residual value.

The DDB method can be illustrated as follows:

$$\text{DDB rate} = 2 \times (100\% \div n)$$
$$\text{DDB rate, 4-year life} = 2 \times (100\% \div 4) = 50\%$$
$$\text{DDB depreciation} = \text{DDB rate} \times \text{Beginning book value}$$

For year 1: $D = .50\ (\$41,000)$
$\qquad = \$20,500$
For year 2: $D = .50\ (\$41,000 - \$20,500)$
$\qquad = \$10,250$
For year 3: $D = .50\ [\$41,000 - (\$20,500 + \$10,250)]$
$\qquad = \$5,125$
For year 4: $D = .50\ [\$41,000 - (\$35,875)]$
$\qquad = \$2,563$

Cumulative 3-year total = $35,875

In this example, by coincidence, the depreciation amount for each year happens to be half the preceding year's depreciation. However, this halving is a special case that happens only with a 4-year life. Remember, the basic approach of DDB is to apply the depreciation rate to the beginning book value. About 20% of U.S. companies use accelerated depreciation for part of their long-lived assets. While we have illustrated the declining balance method with DDB, other versions use different multiples. For example, the 150% declining balance method simply multiplies the straight-line rate by 1.5 instead of doubling it.

COMPARING AND CHOOSING DEPRECIATION METHODS

Exhibit 7-3 compares the results of straight-line and DDB depreciation for our shipping truck example. Note that the DDB method provides $38,438 of total depreciation and does not allocate the full $40,000 cost to expense. To compensate for this fact, some companies that use DDB change to the straight-line method part way through the asset's depreciable life. This is illustrated in the right-most columns of Exhibit 7-3.

To decide when to change, calculate the straight-line depreciation over the remaining life of the asset given the undepreciated cost. Change methods when the next year's

accelerated depreciation Any depreciation method that writes off depreciable costs more quickly than the ordinary straight-line method based on expected useful life.

double-declining-balance depreciation (DDB) The most popular form of accelerated depreciation. It is computed by doubling the straight-line rate and multiplying the resulting DDB rate by the beginning book value.

Exhibit 7-3

Depreciation: Two Popular Methods

(Assume Equipment Costs $41,000, 4-Year Life, Predicted Residual Value of $1,000)

	Straight-Line*		Declining Balance at Twice the Straight-Line Rate (DDB)†		Modified DDB–Switch to Straight-Line in Year 4‡	
	Annual Depreciation	*Book Value*	*Annual Depreciation*	*Book Value*	*Annual Depreciation*	*Book Value*
At acquisition		$41,000		$41,000		$41,000
Year 1	$10,000	31,000	$20,500	20,500	$20,500	20,500
Year 2	10,000	21,000	10,250	10,250	10,250	10,250
Year 3	10,000	11,000	5,125	5,125	5,125	5,125
Year 4	10,000	1,000	2,563	2,562	4,125	1,000
Total	$40,000		$38,438		$40,000	

* Depreciation is the same each year, 25% of ($41,000 − $1,000).

† 100%/4 = 25%. The double rate is 50%. Then 50% of $41,000; 50% of ($41,000 − $20,500); 50% of [$41,000 − ($20,500 + $10,250)]; etc. Unmodified, this method will never fully depreciate the existing book value.

‡ The switch to straight-line occurs in year four and the depreciation amount is the amount required to reduce the book value to the final salvage value.

straight-line depreciation first equals or exceeds the amount in the original DDB schedule. During year three, DDB gives depreciation of $5,125. Switching to straight-line would give depreciation of $4,625 for the remaining 2 years. [($10,250 − $1,000) ÷ 2]. DDB is used because it gives a higher depreciation amount. After year three, the undepreciated book value is $5,125. With 1 year remaining and a $1,000 salvage, this gives $4,125 to be recorded as straight-line depreciation for year four [($5,125 − $1,000) ÷ 1 year] as shown in the far right-hand column of Exhibit 7-3. Because $4,125 exceeds 2,563, the switch occurs for year four.

Companies do not necessarily use the same depreciation methods for all types of depreciable assets. For example, consider the annual report of Kobe Steel, Ltd., a major Japanese company: "Buildings and structures in all locations and machinery and equipment located in the Kakogawa Works, the Kobe Works, the Takasago Works, the Mooka Plant, and the Chofu Plant are depreciated using the straight-line method, and all other machinery and equipment are depreciated using the declining balance method over estimated useful lives."

How does a company choose among the alternatives? In some cases tradition leads one company to select the method used by other companies in its industry to enhance comparability. Sometimes one method provides far superior matching of expense and revenue as units of production would for certain types of equipment and manufacturing processes. Sometimes the method is chosen to present the life-cycle cost of the asset. Suppose a type of equipment requires little maintenance in the first years of its life but increasing maintenance later. Accelerated depreciation with decreasing depreciation charges each year, plus rising maintenance costs each year would provide a somewhat constant cost per year of use and production. Thus, the choice depends on the nature of the industry and the equipment and the goals of management.

CONTRASTING INCOME TAX AND SHAREHOLDER REPORTING

In accounting for long-lived assets, reporting to stockholders and reporting to the income tax authorities often differ. Reports to stockholders must abide by generally accepted accounting principles (GAAP). In contrast, reports to income tax authorities must abide by the income tax rules and regulations. These rules are often consistent with GAAP, but the two sometimes vary. Therefore, keeping two sets of records is neither immoral nor unethical; it is necessary.

Objective 3
Differentiate financial statement depreciation from income tax depreciation.

DEPRECIATION ON TAX REPORTS

Congress changes the U.S. tax rules in some way almost every year. However, since 1986 the tax authorities have required the use of the Modified Accelerated Cost Recovery System (MACRS) for computing accelerated depreciation. MACRS approximates declining-balance depreciation over very short lives. MACRS often provides lives for tax purposes much shorter than the real economic life of the depreciable asset.

The short useful lives are a key factor in MACRS. Why? Because the shorter the life, the earlier depreciation expense is realized. The earlier the depreciation expense is recognized, the earlier the company gets a reduction in income taxes (remember that higher expenses mean lower net income, which means lower income taxes). MACRS allows for higher depreciation in the early years of an asset's service life than does the straight-line method. When implementing MACRS, Congress purposely included accelerated depreciation with short lives as a means of lowering taxes to encourage companies to invest in long-lived assets.

If tax authorities allow a company to choose to depreciate an asset for tax purposes over a 5-year life using DDB or over a 7-year life using straight line, which should it choose?

ANSWER

The company should choose the 5-year option using DDB. Both the *shorter life* and the *accelerated DDB method* allow the company to depreciate the asset more quickly, which reduces current taxes and delays payments to the government.

SHAREHOLDER REPORTING

Although they use MACRS for tax purposes, most companies use straight-line depreciation for shareholder reporting. Tax authorities may use special rates, very short lives, or immediate write-off to increase the tax benefits of investing in long-lived assets, but shareholder reporting is driven by efforts to use depreciation to match the costs of an asset to all the periods in which that asset generates revenues.

There are several practical reasons for adopting straight-line depreciation, namely, simplicity, convenience, and reporting of higher earnings in early years than would be reported under accelerated depreciation. Managers tend not to choose accounting methods that hurt reported earnings in the early years of long-lived assets. Previously we noted that many firms choose LIFO, which reduces earnings in a period of rising prices. But they did so because they were required to use LIFO for financial reporting to do so on the tax return. That conformity feature does not exist for depreciation, so firms normally use straight-line for financial reporting and MACRS for tax reporting.

DEPRECIATION AND CASH FLOW

Too often, the relationships between depreciation expense, income tax expense, cash, and accumulated depreciation are confused. For example, the business press frequently

Objective 4
Explain depreciation's effects on cash flow.

contains misleading quotations such as " . . . we're looking for financing $3.75 billion. Of that, about 60% will be recovered in depreciation and amortization." As another example, consider a *Business Week* news report concerning an airline company: "And with a hefty boost from depreciation and the sale of $6 million worth of property, its cash balance rose by $10 million in the year's first quarter."

These statements imply that depreciation somehow generates cash. It does not. Depreciation simply allocates the original cost of an asset to the periods in which the asset is used—nothing more and nothing less. Furthermore, accumulated depreciation is merely the portion of an asset's original cost that has already been written off to expense in prior periods—not a pile of cash waiting to be used.

EFFECTS OF DEPRECIATION ON CASH

To illustrate depreciation's relationship to cash, consider Acme Service Company, which began business with cash and common stock equity of $100,000. On the same day, Acme acquired equipment for $40,000 cash. The equipment had an expected 4-year life and a predicted residual value of zero. The first year's operations generated cash sales of $103,000 and cash operating expenses of $53,000. The schematic in panel A of Exhibit 7-4 depicts these facts. Notice that the increase in cash is $50,000 for both straight-line and accelerated depreciation, although the two depreciation methods lead to different amounts of pretax income.

Assume straight-line depreciation of $10,000 and accelerated depreciation of $20,000. Note that the reported before-tax income in panel B of Exhibit 7-4 differs as a result of the depreciation method chosen, but cash flow from operations is the same, as shown in panel C of the exhibit. Comparing the before-tax amounts stresses the role of depreciation expense most vividly. Why? Because before taxes, changes in the depreciation method affect only the accumulated depreciation and retained earnings accounts. The before-tax ending cash balances are completely unaffected.

One final set of calculations should finish proving that the level of depreciation does not generate cash. Assume depreciation at Acme to now be $40,000, and compute the pretax income and increase in cash.

ANSWER

You should have obtained pretax income of only $10,000. However, the increase in cash remains at $50,000. Why? Because cash received from sales is $103,000, and cash expenses are $53,000, leaving $50,000 cash provided by operations regardless of how much depreciation exists, so long as we ignore taxes.

EFFECTS OF DEPRECIATION ON INCOME TAXES

Now consider the after-tax portions of panels B and C of Exhibit 7-4 in the two rightmost columns. Depreciation is a deductible noncash expense for income tax purposes. Thus, the higher the depreciation allowed to be deducted in any given year, the lower the taxable income, and therefore the lower the cash paid for income taxes. In short, if depreciation expense is higher, taxes are lower and more cash is conserved and kept for use in the business.

To emphasize the relationship between depreciation and cash and to simplify the comparison, we assume the depreciation method used for financial reporting is the same

Exhibit 7-4

Acme Service Company

Straight-Line and Accelerated Depreciation ($ in Thousands)

PANEL A: PRETAX COMPARISON—NO CASH DIFFERENCES

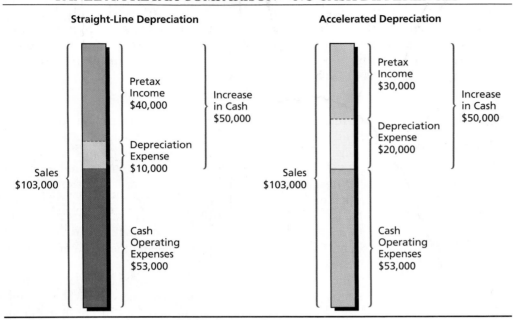

PANELS B & C: TAX EFFECTS

	Before Taxes		After Taxes	
	Straight-Line Depreciation	*Accelerated Depreciation*	*Straight-Line Depreciation*	*Accelerated Depreciation*
Panel B. Income Statement				
Sales	$103	$103	$103	$103
Operating expenses	53	53	53	53
Depreciation expense	10	20	10	20
Pretax income	40	30	40	30
Income tax expense (40%)	—	—	16	12
Net income	$ 40	$ 30	$ 24	$ 18
Panel C. Statement of Cash Flows				
Cash collections	$103	$103	$103	$103
Cash operating expenses	53	53	53	53
Cash tax payments	—	—	16	12
Cash provided by operations*	$ 50	$ 50	$ 34	$ 38

* Sometimes called cash flow from operations or just cash flow. But it is usually simply called cash provided by operations, which is basically defined as cash collected on sales (a) less all operating expenses requiring cash and (b) less cash paid for income taxes.

as for tax purposes. From the last two columns of Exhibit 7-4, you can see that Acme would pay $16,000 of income taxes using straight-line depreciation but only $12,000 using accelerated depreciation. Therefore, compared with the straight-line depreciation method, the accelerated method conserves $4,000 in cash. Depreciation does not generate cash, but it does have a cash benefit if it results in lower taxes.

CONTRASTING LONG-LIVED ASSET EXPENDITURES WITH EXPENSES

Objective 5
Distinguish expenses from expenditures that should be capitalized.

expenditures The purchases of goods or services, whether for cash or on credit.

Expenditures are purchases of goods or services, whether for cash or on credit. Asset-related expenditures that benefit more than the current accounting year are capitalized, that is, added to an asset account. Such capital expenditures add new fixed assets or increase the capacity, efficiency, or useful life of an existing fixed asset. In contrast, expenditures that provide a benefit lasting 1 year or less are charged as expenses in the current year.

THE DECISION TO CAPITALIZE

There are no hard and fast rules about which expenditures can be capitalized, but the topic gets the attention of both the public accounting firms and the income tax authorities. Consider whether an engine repair is properly classified as an asset or an expense. The public accountant might want to call it an expense, while an income tax auditor might want to call it an asset. Why? Because public accountants watch for tendencies to understate current expenses through the unjustified charging of a repair to an asset account. Public accountants know that investors can be misled by earnings patterns that are unusually high and increasing. In contrast, the income tax auditor is looking for unjustified charges to an expense account. This reduces reported income and therefore provides an immediate income tax deduction.

Wherever doubt exists, there is a tendency in practice to charge an expense instead of an asset account for repairs, parts, and similar items. First, many of these expenditures are minor, so the cost-benefit test of record keeping and the concept of materiality justifies this choice. For instance, many companies have a policy of charging to expense all expenditures that are less than a specified minimum such as $100, $1,000, or $5,000.

REPAIRS AND MAINTENANCE VERSUS CAPITAL IMPROVEMENTS

Repairs and maintenance costs are necessary to maintain a fixed asset in operating condition. The costs of repairs and maintenance are usually compiled in a single account and are regarded as expenses of the current period. Repairs are sometimes distinguished from maintenance as follows. Repairs include the occasional costs of restoring a fixed asset to its ordinary operating condition after breakdowns, accidents, or damage. Maintenance includes the routine recurring costs of oiling, polishing, painting, and adjusting. However, accountants spend little effort distinguishing between repairs and maintenance expenditures because both are period costs.

improvement (betterment, capital improvement) An expenditure that is intended to add to the future benefits from an existing fixed asset.

However, an **improvement** (sometimes called a **betterment** or a **capital improvement**) is an expenditure that is intended to add to the future benefits from an existing fixed asset by decreasing its operating cost, increasing its rate of output, or prolonging its useful life. Repairs and maintenance maintain the level of an asset's future benefits, while improvements increase those benefits. Improvements are generally capitalized. Examples of capital improvements or betterments include the rehabilitation of an apartment house that will allow increased rents and the rebuilding of a packaging machine that increases its speed or extends its useful life.

Suppose the $40,000 truck with a 4-year life and $1,000 salvage value presented earlier in the chapter experiences a major overhaul costing $7,000 at the start of year three. If this overhaul extends the useful life of our shipping truck from 4 to 5 years, the required accounting would be:

1. Increase the book value of the asset (now $41,000 − $20,000 = $21,000) by $7,000. This increase is usually done by adding the $7,000 to Equipment.

2. Revise the depreciation schedule so that the new unexpired cost is spread over the remaining 3 years, as follows (assume straight-line depreciation):

	Original Depreciation Schedule		Revised Depreciation Schedule	
	Year	Amount	Year	Amount
	1	$10,000	1	$10,000
	2	10,000	2	10,000
	3	10,000	3	9,000*
	4	10,000	4	9,000
			5	9,000
Accumulated depreciation		$40,000		$47,000†

*New depreciable amount is [($41,000 − $20,000 + $7,000) − $1,000 residual value] = $27,000. New depreciation expense is $27,000 divided by remaining useful life of 3 years, or $9,000 per year.

†Recapitulation:
Original cost	$41,000
Major overhaul	7,000
	48,000
Less residual	1,000
Depreciable cost	$47,000

GAINS AND LOSSES ON SALES OF TANGIBLE ASSETS

Objective 6
Compute gains and losses on disposal of fixed assets.

So far we have seen how to account for property, plant, and equipment assets, from calculating acquisitions cost to depreciating this cost up to the end of the asset's useful life. However, companies sometimes sell an asset before the end of its useful life. When they sell assets, gains or losses are inevitable. These gains or losses are usually measured in a cash sale by the difference between the cash received and the net book value (net carrying amount) of the asset given up. One could argue that these "gains and losses" are as much due to incorrect original estimates of life or salvage value as they are to real changes in the economic value of the assets.

RECORDING GAINS AND LOSSES

Suppose we sell the shipping truck in our earlier example at the end of year two for $21,000 when its book value was $21,000. There would be no gain or loss on the transaction. We would simply eliminate the asset and the accumulated depreciation from the records and record the cash received. The sale would have the following effects:

A					=	L + SE
+$21,000	−	$41,000	+	$20,000	=	$0
[Increase Cash]		[Decrease Equipment]		[Decrease Accumulated Depreciation]		

Note that the disposal of the equipment requires the removal of its carrying amount or book value, which appears in two accounts, not one. Therefore, dispositions affect both the Accumulated Depreciation account and the Equipment account.

If the selling price were $27,000 instead of $21,000, the sale would produce a gain of $6,000. The gain is the difference between the sales proceeds and the book value of the asset being sold:

Sales proceeds		$27,000
Less book value		
Cost	$41,000	
Accumulated depreciation	20,000	21,000
Gain		$ 6,000

This sale would have the following effects on the accounting equation:

A				=	L + SE
+$27,000	−	$41,000	+ $20,000	=	+$6,000
[Increase Cash]		[Decrease Equipment]	[Decrease Accumulated Depreciation]		[Increase Gain on Sale of Equipment]

If the selling price were $17,000 instead of $21,000, the sale would produce a $4,000 loss with the following effects:

				=	
+$17,000	−	$41,000	+ $20,000	=	−$4,000
[Increase Cash]		[Decrease Equipment]	[Decrease Accumulated Depreciation]		[Decrease Loss on Sale of Equipment]

The T-account presentations and journal entries for these transactions are shown in Exhibit 7-5. Note again that both the original cost of the equipment and the accompanying

Exhibit 7-5

Journal and Ledger Entries

Gain or Loss on Sale of Equipment ($ in Thousands)

Sale at $27,000:

			Cash	Equipment	Gain on Sale of Equipment
			27 |	* 41 | 41	| 6
Cash	27				
Accumulated depreciation	20			Accumulated	
Equipment		41		Depreciation,	
Gain on sale of equipment		6		Equipment	
				20 | * 20	

Sale at $17,000:

			Cash	Equipment	Loss on Sale of Equipment
			17 |	* 41 | 41	4 |
Cash	17			Accumulated	
Accumulated depreciation	20			Depreciation,	
Loss on sale of equipment	4			Equipment	
Equipment		41		20 | * 20	

*Beginning balance.

accumulated depreciation must be eliminated when the asset is sold. Of course, the net effect is to eliminate the $21,000 carrying amount of the equipment (cost of $41,000 less accumulated depreciation of $20,000).

INCOME STATEMENT PRESENTATION

In most instances, gains or losses on disposition of plant assets are not significant, so they are buried as a part of "other income" on the income statement and are not separately identified as shown in the following three lines from a recent DuPont statement ($ amounts in millions):

Sales	$26,918
Other income	974
Total	$27,892

Footnote 2 revealed that other income includes a loss of $30 million arising from the sales of assets. The $30 million is "not significant" in the sense that it is not a material thing for analysts to understand in evaluating the company. The focus is on ongoing selling activity of chemicals and other products produced to be sold. Occasionally, even large sales of plant, property, and equipment may be immaterial to understanding the company. To put things in perspective, remember that DuPont had nearly $41 billion in assets on January 1, 2000.

Other income, including gains from sales of assets, may be included with sales at the very top of the income statement, which is the choice DuPont made. Alternatively, the gain (or loss) may be excluded from the computation of major profit categories such as gross profit or operating profit. NW Natural, a natural gas local distribution company headquartered in Portland, Oregon, did this in its 1999 income statement. The company subtracted other income of $4.8 million after calculating gross profit and operating income. Footnotes reveal that this other income includes: "interest income; gain on sale of assets. . . ."

DEPLETION OF NATURAL RESOURCES

Objective 7
Interpret depletion of natural resources

We now turn our attention to another group of long-lived assets—natural resources, such as minerals, oil, and timber (sometimes called wasting assets). Depletion is the accounting measure used to allocate the acquisition cost of natural resources. Depletion differs from depreciation because depletion focuses specifically on the physical use and exhaustion of the natural resources, while depreciation focuses more broadly on any reduction of the economic value of a fixed asset, including physical deterioration and obsolescence.

The costs of natural resources are usually classified as fixed assets. However, buying natural resources is actually like buying massive quantities of inventories under the ground (iron ore) or above the ground (timber). Depletion expense is the measure of that portion of this "long-term inventory" that is used up in a particular period. For example, a coal mine may cost $20 million and originally contain an estimated 1 million tons of usable coal. The depletion rate would be $20 million ÷ 1 million tons = $20 per ton. If 100,000 tons were mined during the first year, the depletion would be 100,000 × $20, or $2 million for that year. Each year the amount of coal extracted would be measured, and the amount of depletion recorded would be based on that usage.

As our coal mine example shows, depletion is measured on a units-of-production basis. The annual depletion may be accounted for as a direct reduction of the mining asset, or it may be accumulated in a separate contra account similar to accumulated depreciation. Environmental laws and ethical responsibility often lead a firm to expend substantial amounts to return the site to a safe and attractive condition after exhausting the natural resources. When calculating the depletion per unit, companies should include these expected future costs in the total costs subject to depletion. Therefore, the depletion per unit would include not only the original cost of the resources but also future restoration costs. The portion of depletion that represents future costs for site restoration can be added to a Liability for Restoration account that grows as extraction continues.

AMORTIZATION OF INTANGIBLE ASSETS

Objective 8
Account for various intangible assets.

Our final category of long-lived assets is intangibles. These assets are not physical in nature. Instead they are rights or claims to expected benefits that tend to be contractual in nature. Examples of intangible assets are patents, copyrights, and franchises.

Intangible assets are accounted for in the same manner as plant and equipment. That is, their acquisition costs are capitalized as assets and are then gradually expensed [amortized] over the estimated useful lives of the assets. Because of obsolescence, the useful lives of intangible assets tend to be shorter than their legal lives.

An intangible asset is shown on a company's balance sheet only if the rights to some benefit are purchased. Equally valuable assets may be created by internal expenditures, but they are not recognized as assets in the accounting records. For example, suppose Pfizer paid $5 million to another company for that company's patent on a drug. Pfizer would record the $5 million as an intangible asset and amortize the cost over the useful life of the patent. In contrast, suppose Pfizer spent $5 million to internally develop and patent a new drug. Pfizer would charge the $5 million for this R&D to expense, and the patent would not be recognized as an asset.

Why does this discrepancy exist between external and internal items? The difference arises because it is difficult for management to value the results of its internal research and development efforts honestly and objectively. However, when another company purchases the results of those efforts, the purchase price that is negotiated more realistically measures the value. As a result, GAAP requires that the costs of internal research, advertising, and employee training be immediately expensed, although they surely have expected future benefits.

To gain a better understanding of exactly what constitutes an intangible asset, we will now examine some of those assets in detail.

EXAMPLES OF INTANGIBLE ASSETS

patents Grants by the federal government to an inventor, bestowing (in the United States) the exclusive right for 17 years to produce and sell the invention.

copyrights Exclusive rights to reproduce and sell a book, musical composition, film, and similar items.

Patents are grants by the federal government to an inventor, bestowing (in the United States) the exclusive right to produce and sell a given invention for 17 years. After that, others can produce and sell the invention themselves. Suppose a company acquires such a patent from the inventor for $170,000. Suppose further that because of fast-changing technology, the economic life of the patent is only 5 years. The amortization would be over the shorter of the economic or legal life—$170,000 ÷ 5 = $34,000 per year, instead of $170,000 ÷ 17 = $10,000 per year.

Copyrights are exclusive rights to reproduce and sell a book, musical composition, film, or similar creative items. These rights are issued (in the United States) by the federal government and provide protection to a company or individual for 75 years. The original costs of obtaining copyrights from the government are nominal, but a company may pay a large sum to purchase an existing asset from the owner. For example, a publisher of paperback books will pay the author of a popular novel in excess of a million dollars for the writer's copyright. Although copyrights last for 75 years, their economic lives may be no longer than 2 or 3 years, so amortization occurs accordingly.

Under GAAP, companies must immediately expense R&D expenditures. Why? The FASB decided that it is hard to determine whether R&D will be valuable, and, if it is valuable, it is hard to estimate over what period of time a company will realize its value. Some analysts believe it is important to treat R&D as an asset to fully understand the total commitment of resources a company has made. They somewhat arbitrarily choose to assume a life and develop a hypothetical value for R&D.

To illustrate, consider the following data for Eli Lilly. R&D spending in the 5-year period 1995 to 1999 rose each year from $1.0 billion in 1995 to $1.8 billion in 1999 and totaled $7.1 billion. Suppose these amounts were capitalized each year as incurred and then expensed over the subsequent 4 years on a straight-line basis (25% per year). Under this procedure the $1.0 billion spent in 1995 would appear as an asset of $1 billion at year-end and would give rise to amortization of $250 million in each of the next 4 years. By the end of 1999, it would be fully amortized and would not appear as an asset.

Consider Lilly's financial statements for 1999 ($ amounts are in millions). We can calculate the 1999 R&D expense of $1,324.75 and R&D asset of $3,201.25 as shown below.

Under this treatment, how would the financial statements differ from what Eli Lilly reported under GAAP?

Net earnings would be higher because expense on the income statement would be $1,324.75 million instead of the amount of the spending in 1999 of $1,784. This lowers expense by about $459.25 million. On the balance sheet, assets would be higher by $3.2 billion or about 25% greater than the actual reported assets of $12.9 billion. Of course, if assets are higher, there needs to be an offsetting effect on the other side of the accounting equation, and retained earnings and some liabilities for taxes would also be higher.

Lilly and other pharmaceutical companies are extreme cases since R&D typically represents more than 15% of sales (about 18% for Lilly in 1999). Some young, high-tech start-ups have even more substantial R&D spending on a proportional basis. Indeed, some of these start-ups have no sales, and if R&D is expensed immediately for accounting purposes, they sometimes have essentially no assets. Yet they may have very high market values because the ideas they have generated have great potential. Research-intensive firms and young start-up firms are two examples of cases where adjustments to the data from the historical cost-accounting model are often useful for analyzing the firm. The 4-year amortization period in this example is arbitrary and was chosen in part to simplify the example. In various industries different assumptions might be appropriate depending on how quickly technology is changing.

Year of R&D Expenditure	R&D Expenditure	1999 Income Statement Expense	% of Spending Unamortized at End of 1999	Balance Sheet Asset–12/31/99
1995	$1,000	$ 250.00	0	0
1996	1,190	297.50	25	297.50
1997	1,370	342.50	50	685.00
1998	1,739	434.75	75	434.75
1999	1,784	0	100	1,784.00
Total 1999 Value		$1,324.75		3,201.25

Trademarks are distinctive identifications of a manufactured product or of a service, taking the form of a name, a sign, a slogan, a logo, or an emblem. An example is an emblem for Coca-Cola or the Prentice Hall logo on the spine of this book. Trademarks, trade names, trade brands, secret formulas, and similar items are property rights with economic lives depending on their length of use. Of course, if you look on Coca-Cola's balance sheet you see no accounting recognition of its secret formula. It is internally developed, not purchased, so it is not recorded. In fact, the story is that they chose to keep it a secret instead of patenting it because they did not want patent protection to expire and leave others free to produce their product. Similarly, the Coca-Cola balance sheet does not report an intangible asset for its trademark, although Coke has spent millions of advertising dollars creating public awareness of the brand.

trademarks Distinctive identifications of a manufactured product or of a service taking the form of a name, a sign, a slogan, a logo, or an emblem.

If a company has trademarks or other intangible assets that cease to have value, they should be immediately written off as an expense. For example, Brown-Forman Corporation had $60 million of intangible assets associated with the brand California Cooler when it decided the assets no longer provided future benefits. The $60 million expense reduced the company's income before taxes from $218 million to $158 million.

Franchises and **licenses** are legal contracts that grant the buyer the right to sell a product or service. An example is a local McDonald's franchise. The buyer obtains the right to use the McDonald's name, to acquire branded products such as cups and bags, and to share in advertising and special promotions. In exchange, the franchisee promises to follow McDonald's procedures and maintain standards of quality, cleanliness, and pricing. The lengths of the franchises vary from 1 year to perpetuity. Again, the acquisition costs of franchises and licenses are amortized over their economic lives instead of their legal lives.

franchises (licenses)
Privileges granted by a government, manufacturer, or distributor to sell a product or service in accordance with specified conditions.

AMORTIZATION OF LEASEHOLDS AND LEASEHOLD IMPROVEMENTS

A **leasehold** is the right to use a fixed asset (such as a building or some portion thereof) for a specified period of time beyond 1 year. Leaseholds are frequently classified with plant assets although they are technically intangible assets. A company that owns its own plant clearly counts that plant as a tangible asset. However, if a company has a leasehold or leases its plant, then that company owns only the right to use the leased plant, not the plant itself. Because the leasehold allows for the recognition of future benefits (in this case, the use of the plant) but does not provide for the ownership of a tangible asset, it is an intangible asset.

Related to a leasehold is a **leasehold improvement**, which occurs when a lessee (tenant) spends money to add new materials to a leased property. These new materials then become part of the leased property and are no longer owned by the lessee. A leasehold improvement can take various forms. Examples are the installation of new fixtures, panels, walls, and air-conditioning equipment that are not permitted to be removed from the premises when a lease expires.

The costs of leases and leasehold improvements are amortized over the life of the lease, even if the physical life of the leasehold improvement is longer. The straight-line method is used almost exclusively, probably because accelerated methods have not been permitted for income tax purposes.

leasehold The right to use a fixed asset for a specified period of time, typically beyond 1 year.

leasehold improvement
Investments by a lessee in items that are not permitted to be removed from the premises when a lease expires, such as installation of new fixtures, panels, walls, and air-conditioning equipment.

AMORTIZATION OF DEFERRED CHARGES

Deferred charges are like prepaid expenses—in fact, the two often appear lumped together on a single line of the balance sheet—but deferred charges have longer term benefits. For example, the costs of relocating a mass of employees to a different geographic area, or the costs of rearranging an assembly line or developing new markets, must be paid before any benefit from these actions is realized. Of course, relocating and developing new markets are not done unless they will provide years worth of benefits. As a result, their costs may be carried forward as deferred charges and written off as expense over a 3- to 5-year period. This procedure is often described as the amortization of deferred charges.

deferred charges Similar to prepaid expenses, but they have longer term benefits.

BASKET PURCHASES

Frequently, companies acquire more than one type of long-lived asset for a single overall purchase price. The acquisition of two or more types of assets for a lump-sum cost is sometimes called a basket purchase. The acquisitions cost of a **basket purchase** is always split among assets according to some estimate of relative sales value for the assets. For instance, suppose a company acquires land and a building for $1 million. How much of the $1 million should the company allocate to land and how much to the building? If an

basket purchase The acquisition of two or more types of assets for a lump-sum cost.

appraiser indicates that the market values of the land and the building are $480,000 and $720,000, respectively, the cost would be allocated as follows:

	(1)	**(2)**	**(3)**	**(2) × (3)**
	Appraised Value	*Weighting*	*Total Cost to Allocate*	*Allocated Costs*
Land	$ 480,000	480/1,200 (or 40%)	$1,000,000	$ 400,000
Building	720,000	720/1,200 (or 60%)	1,000,000	600,000
Total	$1,200,000			$1,000,000

Allocating a basket purchase cost to the individual assets can significantly affect future reported income if the useful lives of various assets differ. In our example, if less cost is allocated to the land, more cost is allocated to the building, which is depreciable. In turn, depreciation expenses are higher, operating income is lower, and fewer income taxes are paid. Within the bounds of the law, tax-conscious managers load as much cost as possible on depreciable assets instead of land.

SUMMARY PROBLEMS FOR YOUR REVIEW

PROBLEM ONE

"The net book value of plant assets that appears on the balance sheet is the amount that would be spent today for their replacement." Do you agree? Explain.

SOLUTION TO PROBLEM ONE

Net book value of the plant assets on the balance sheet is the result of deducting accumulated depreciation from original cost. It is a result of cost allocation, not valuation. This process does not attempt to reflect all the technological and economic events that may affect replacement value. Consequently, there is little assurance that net book value will approximate replacement cost.

PROBLEM TWO

"Accumulated depreciation provides cash for the replacement of fixed assets." Do you agree with this quotation from a business magazine? Explain.

SOLUTION TO PROBLEM TWO

Accumulated depreciation does not generate cash. It is the amount of the asset already used up and in no way represents a direct stockpile of cash for replacement.

PROBLEM THREE

Refer to Exhibit 7-3, page 292. Suppose the predicted residual value had been $5,000 instead of $1,000.

Required

1. Compute depreciation for each of the first 2 years using straight-line and double-declining-balance methods.
2. Assume that DDB depreciation is used and that the equipment is sold for $20,000 cash at the end of the second year. Compute the gain or loss on the sale.

Show the effects of the sale in T-accounts for the equipment and accumulated depreciation. Where and how would the sale appear in the income statement?

3. Assume that straight-line depreciation is used and that the equipment is sold for $20,000 cash at the end of the second year. Compute the gain or loss on the sale. Compare this amount to the gain or loss computed in the previous question.

SOLUTION TO PROBLEM THREE

1.

	Straight-Line Depreciation $= \dfrac{C - R}{n}$	DDB Depreciation = Rate* × (Beginning Book Value)
Year 1	$36,000/4 = $9,000	.50 ($41,000) = $20,500
Year 2	$36,000/4 = $9,000	.50 ($41,000 − $20,500) = $10,250

*Rate = 2(100% ÷ n) = 2(100% ÷ 4) = 50%.

2.

Revenue	$20,000
Expense: Net book value of equipment sold is $41,000 − ($20,500 + $10,250), or $41,000 − $30,750 =	10,250
Gain on sale of equipment	$ 9,750

The effect of removing the book value is a $10,250 decrease in assets. Note that the effect of a decrease in Accumulated Depreciation (by itself) is an increase in assets:

Equipment			
Acquisition cost	41,000	Cost of equipment sold	41,000

Accumulated Depreciation, Equipment			
Accumulated depreciation on equipment sold	30,750	Depreciation for	
		Year 1	20,500
		Year 2	10,250
			30,750

The $9,750 gain is usually shown as a separate item on the income statement as Gain on Sale of Equipment or Gain on Disposal of Equipment or combined with similar transactions as Other Gains and Losses.

3.

Revenue	$20,000
Expense: $41,000 − ($9,000 + $9,000)	23,000
Loss on sale of equipment	$ 3,000

Even though the sales price is the same as in number 2, there is a loss of $3,000 instead of a gain of $9,750 because the book value is $12,750 higher. The amount of gains or losses on disposed-of equipment depends on the depreciation method used.

PROBLEM FOUR

Review the important chapter illustration in the section "Depreciation and Cash Flow" on page 293–295. Suppose the Acme Service equipment had been acquired for $80,000 instead of $40,000. The predicted residual value remains zero and the useful life remains 4 years.

1. Prepare a revised Exhibit 7-4, panels B and C. Assume an income tax rate of 40%; round all income tax computations to the nearest thousand.
2. Indicate all items affected by these changes. Also tabulate all differences between the final two columns in your revised exhibit as compared with Exhibit 7-4.

SOLUTION TO PROBLEM FOUR

1. The revised income statements are in Exhibit 7-6.
2. The following comparisons of Exhibits 7-6 and 7-4 are noteworthy. Sales, operating expenses, and cash provided by operations before income taxes are unaffected by the change in depreciation. Because of higher depreciation, net income would be lower in all four columns of Exhibit 7-6 than it was in Exhibit 7-4. Comparison of the final two columns of the exhibits follows:

	As Shown in		
	Exhibit 7-6	Exhibit 7-4	Difference
Straight-line depreciation	20	10	10 Higher
Accelerated depreciation	40	20	20 Higher
Income tax expense based on			
Straight-line depreciation	12	16	4 Lower
Accelerated depreciation	4	12	8 Lower
Net income based on			
Straight-line depreciation	18	24	6 Lower
Accelerated depreciation	6	18	12 Lower
Cash provided by operations based on			
Straight-line depreciation	38	34	4 Higher
Accelerated depreciation	46	38	8 Higher

Exhibit 7-6

Acme Service Company
Income Statement and Statement of Cash Flows ($ in Thousands)

	Before Taxes		After Taxes	
	Straight-Line Depreciation	Accelerated Depreciation	Straight-Line Depreciation	Accelerated Depreciation
PANEL 1. Income Statement				
Sales	$103	$103	$103	$103
Operating expenses	53	53	53	53
Depreciation expense	20	40	20	40
Pretax income	30	10	30	10
Income tax expense (40%)	—	—	12	4
Net income	$ 30	$ 10	$ 18	$ 6
PANEL 2. Statement of Cash Flows				
Cash collections	$103	$103	$103	$103
Cash operating expenses	53	53	53	53
Cash tax payments	—	—	12	4
Cash from operations	$ 50	$ 50	$ 38	$ 46

Especially noteworthy is the phenomenon that higher depreciation decreases net income but also decreases cash outflows for income taxes. As a result, cash provided by operations increases.

Highlights to Remember

1. **Measure the acquisition cost of tangible assets such as land, buildings, and equipment.** The acquisition cost includes both the purchase price and all incidental costs necessary to get the asset ready for use.

2. **Compute depreciation for buildings and equipment using various depreciation methods.** Depreciation is a systematic allocation of historical costs over the useful life of the asset. Three common depreciation methods discussed in the text are straight line, double-declining balance (DDB), and units of production. Straight line is a constant amount per year of use. It is calculated by dividing depreciable cost (cost less salvage value) by the shorter of physical or economically useful life. DDB is a declining balance method that records the largest annual amount in the first full year of use and declining amounts thereafter. The annual depreciation charge is a percentage of the then undepreciated book value. For DDB the percentage is twice the percentage used for straight line, that is, $2 \times (100\% \div \text{years of life})$. Units-of-production depreciation is based on the physical use of the asset, for example, miles for a vehicle or tons of production for iron ore. The cost per unit is the depreciable costs divided by the estimated units of use from the asset. This is multiplied by the actual units of use to determine the annual depreciation.

3. **Differentiate financial statement depreciation from income tax depreciation.** Financial reports to shareholders often differ from the reports to tax authorities. Financial rules governing financial statement presentation produce informative financial information for investors and managers. Tax rules governing determination of tax obligations achieve political and economic goals and give taxpayers the right to make certain choices with an eye to maximizing expenses and therefore minimizing the tax obligation. Keeping two sets of records to satisfy these two purposes is necessary, not illegal or immoral.

4. **Explain depreciation's effects on cash flow.** By itself, depreciation does not provide cash. Customers provide cash. However, depreciation is deductible for income tax purposes. Therefore, the larger the depreciation reported on the tax return in any given year, the lower the annual pretax income and subsequent income taxes, and the greater the amount of cash from customers that may be kept by the business instead of being disbursed to the income tax authorities.

5. **Distinguish expenses from expenditures that should be capitalized.** Expenditures can be capitalized or expensed. Expenditures with benefits extending beyond the current year should be capitalized—other expenditures should be expensed.

6. **Compute gains and losses on disposal of fixed assets.** Gains and losses on disposal of fixed assets arise because the proceeds of the sale are not identical to the book value of the asset sold (historical cost less accumulated depreciation). If the proceeds exceed the book value, a gain is realized. If proceeds are less, a loss is realized. Sometimes gains or losses occur because there was a significant change in the economic value of the item being sold. Often gains or losses are merely a result of imprecise depreciation because either the asset's life or its salvage value was misestimated.

7. **Interpret depletion of natural resources.** Depletion refers to the accounting process for allocating the cost of the natural resources over the period of extraction. Companies typically use the units-of-production method to allocate the cost of acquiring natural resources. In some cases, there are future costs to be incurred to minimize the environmental damage by returning the site to acceptable condition. Accountants estimate those future costs and include them in the annual depletion charges so as to appropriately match the full cost to the revenues generated over time.

8. **Account for various intangible assets.** Intangible assets are not physical in nature, instead they are legal or economic rights that have limited lives. Examples include, patents, trademarks, and copyrights. Companies capitalize such assets when purchased and then amortize them on a straight-line basis over their useful life. The unamortized book value appears on the balance sheet as an asset. Companies do not capitalize internally created intangible assets. Instead, they expense such outlays as incurred.

Accounting Vocabulary

accelerated depreciation, p. 291	double-declining-balance depreciation (DDB), p. 291	patents, p. 300
amortization, p. 288		plant assets, p. 287
basket purchase, p. 303	economic life, p. 289	residual value, p. 289
betterment, p. 296	expenditures, p. 296	salvage value, p. 289
capital improvement, p. 296	fixed assets, p. 287	scrap value, p. 289
capitalized, p. 289	franchises, p. 302	straight-line depreciation, p. 290
copyrights, p. 300	improvement, p. 296	
deferred charges, p. 302	intangible assets, p. 287	tangible assets, p. 287
depletion, p. 288	leasehold, p. 302	terminal value, p. 289
depreciable value, p. 289	leasehold improvement, p. 302	trademarks, p. 301
depreciation schedule, p. 289	licenses, p. 302	unit depreciation, p. 290
disposal value, p. 289	long-lived assets, p. 286	useful life, p. 289

Assignment Material

QUESTIONS

7-1 Distinguish between *tangible* and *intangible* assets.

7-2 Distinguish between *amortization, depreciation,* and *depletion.*

7-3 "The cash discount on the purchase of equipment is income to the buyer during the year of acquisition." Do you agree? Explain.

7-4 "When an expenditure is capitalized, stockholders' equity is credited." Do you agree? Explain.

7-5 "Accumulated depreciation is a sum of cash being accumulated for the replacement of fixed assets." Do you agree? Explain.

7-6 "The accounting process of depreciation is allocation, not valuation." Explain.

7-7 Criticize: "Depreciation is the loss in value of a fixed asset over a given span of time."

7-8 "Keeping two sets of books is immoral." Do you agree? Explain.

7-9 Compare the choice between straight-line and accelerated depreciation with the choice between FIFO and LIFO. Give at least one similarity and one difference.

7-10 "Most of the money we'll spend this year for replacing our equipment will be generated by depreciation." Do you agree? Explain.

7-11 "Accelerated depreciation saves cash but shows lower net income." Explain.

7-12 Contrast repairs and maintenance expenditures with expenditures for capital improvements or betterments.

7-13 The manager of a division reported to the president of the company: "Now that our major capital improvements are finished, the division's expenses will be much lower." Is this really what this manager means to say? Explain.

7-14 "The gain on sale of equipment should be reported fully on the income statement." Explain what the complete reporting would include.

7-15 Name and describe four kinds of intangible assets.

7-16 "Internally acquired patents are accounted for differently than externally acquired patents." Explain the difference.

7-17 "Accountants sometimes are too concerned with physical objects." Explain.

7-18 "Improvements by a tenant to leased property cannot be capitalized because they become part of the leased property and therefore belong to the lessor." Do you agree? Explain.

7-19 Individuals make deposits into their bank accounts and make security deposits on apartments they rent. Are these deposits assets for the individual? The bank? The landlord?

7-20 "In a basket purchase, all assets that are part of the purchase must be depreciated over the same useful lives." Do you agree? Explain.

COGNITIVE EXERCISES

7-21 Production Facilities and Depreciation

A manager complained about the amount of depreciation charged on the plant for which she was responsible: "The market value of my plant just continues to increase, yet I am hit with large depreciation charges on my income statement and the value of my plant and equipment on the balance sheet goes down each year. This doesn't seem fair." Comment on this statement, focusing on the relation of asset values on the balance sheet to market values of the assets.

7-22 Research and Development and the Recognition of Intangible Assets

In the United States, expenditures for research and development (R&D) are charged directly to expense. In some other countries such costs can be recognized as assets. Suppose you were a manager of an R&D department. Which method of accounting for R&D would be most consistent with the information you use for decision making? Explain.

7-23 Capital Investment and the Statement of Cash Flows

Growing companies often need capital to purchase or build additional facilities. There are many potential sources of such capital. Describe how an investor might use the statement of cash flows to learn how a company financed its capital expansion.

7-24 Accounting Valuation of Fixed Assets

Consider two types of assets held by Weyerhaeuser Company: timber-growing land purchased in 1910 when the company was known as Weyerhaeuser Timber Company and machinery purchased and installed at its paper processing plant in Saskatchewan, Canada, in 1998. How close do you suppose the December 31, 2001 balance sheet value of each asset is to the market value of the asset at that date?

EXERCISES

7-25 Computing Acquisition Costs

From the following data, calculate the cost to be added to the Land account and the Building account of Edmonton University.

On January 1, 20X2, the university acquired a 20-acre parcel of land immediately adjacent to its existing facilities. The land included a warehouse, parking lots, and driveways. The university paid $600,000 cash and also gave a note for $3 million, payable at $300,000 per year plus interest of 10% on the outstanding balance.

The warehouse was demolished at a cash cost of $150,000 so that it could be replaced by a new classroom building. The construction of the building required a cash down payment of $3 million plus a mortgage note of $7 million. The mortgage was payable at $250,000 per year plus interest of 10% on the outstanding balance.

Required Prepare journal entries (without explanations) to record the preceding transactions.

7-26 Government Equipment

An office of the Internal Revenue Service acquired some used computer equipment. Installation costs were $8,000. Repair costs prior to use were $9,000. The purchasing manager, with a salary of $54,000 per annum, spent 1 month evaluating equipment and completing the transaction. The invoice price was $400,000. The seller paid its salesman a commission of 4% and offered the buyer a cash discount of 2% if the invoice was paid within 60 days. Freight costs were $4,400, paid by the agency. Repairs during the first year of use were $10,000.

Required

Compute the total capitalized cost to be added to the Equipment account. The seller was paid within 60 days.

7-27 Journal Entries for Depreciation

(Alternates are 7-28 and 7-29.) On January 1, 20X1, the Dayton Auto Parts Company acquired nine assembly robots for a total of $594,000 cash. The robots had an expected useful life of 10 years and an expected terminal scrap value of $54,000 in total. Dayton uses straight-line depreciation.

Required

1. Set up T-accounts and prepare the journal entries for the acquisition and for the first annual depreciation charge. Post to T-accounts.
2. One of the robots with an original cost of $66,000 on January 1, 20X1, and an expected terminal scrap value of $6,000 was sold for $42,000 cash on December 31, 20X3. Prepare the journal entry for the sale.
3. Refer to requirement 2. Suppose the robot had been sold for $52,000 cash instead of $42,000. Prepare the journal entry for the sale.

7-28 Journal Entries for Depreciation

(Alternates are 7-27 and 7-29.) The USAirways quarterly balance sheet of June 30, 2000 included the following ($ in millions):

Property and equipment	
Flight equipment	$6,511
Ground property and equipment	1,083
Less accumulated depreciation	(3,051)
and amortization	$4,543

Assume that on July 1, 2000, some new maintenance equipment was acquired for $880,000 cash. The equipment had an expected useful life of 5 years and an expected terminal scrap value of $80,000. Straight-line depreciation was used.

Required

1. Prepare the journal entry that would be made annually for depreciation on the new equipment.
2. Suppose some of the equipment with an original cost of $220,000 on July 1, 2000, and an expected terminal scrap value of $20,000 was sold for $160,000 cash 2 years later. Prepare the journal entry for the sale.
3. Refer to requirement 2. Suppose the equipment had been sold for $110,000 cash instead of $150,000. Prepare the journal entry for the sale.

7-29 Journal Entries for Depreciation

(Alternates are 7-27 and 7-28.) The Coca-Cola Company balance sheet of December 31, 1999 included the following ($ in millions):

Property, plant, and equipment	$6,471
Less allowances for depreciation	2,204
	$4,267

Note that the company uses "allowances for" instead of "accumulated" depreciation. Assume that on January 1, 2000 some new bottling equipment was acquired for $2.4 million cash. The equipment had an expected useful life of 5 years and an expected terminal scrap value of $200,000. Straight-line depreciation was used.

1. Prepare the journal entry that would be made annually for depreciation.
2. Suppose some of the equipment with an original cost of $55,000 on January 1, 2000, and an expected terminal scrap value of $5,000 was sold for $32,000 cash 2 years later. Prepare the journal entry for the sale.
3. Refer to requirement 2. Suppose the equipment had been sold for $40,000 cash instead of $32,000. Prepare the journal entry for the sale.

7-30 Simple Depreciation Computations

A company acquired the following assets:

a. Conveyor, 5-year useful life, $38,000 cost, straight-line method, $5,000 residual value.
b. Truck, 3-year useful life, $18,000 cost, DDB method, $1,500 residual value.

Compute the first 3 years of depreciation.

7-31 Units-of-Production Method

The Rockland Transport Company has many trucks that are kept for a useful life of 300,000 miles. Depreciation is computed on a mileage basis. Suppose a new truck is purchased for $68,000 cash. Its expected residual value is $5,000. Its mileage during year 1 is 60,000 and during year 2 is 90,000.

1. What is the depreciation expense for each of the 2 years?
2. Compute the gain or loss if the truck is sold for $40,000 at the end of year two.

7-32 Fundamental Depreciation Approaches

(Alternates are 7-34 and 7-35.) U-Haul acquired some new trucks for $1 million. Their predicted useful life is 4 years, and predicted residual value is $200,000.

Prepare a depreciation schedule similar to Exhibit 7-3, p. 292, comparing straight-line and double-declining-balance.

7-33 Units-of-Production, Straight-Line, and DDB

Yukon Mining Company buys special drills for $440,000 each. Each drill can extract about 200,000 tons of ore, after which it has a $40,000 residual value. One such drill was bought in early January 20X1. Projected tonnage figures for the drill are 60,000 tons in 20X1, 45,000 tons in 20X2, and 45,000 tons in 20X3. The drill is scheduled for sale at the end of the third year at the $40,000 residual value. Yukon is considering units-of-production, straight-line, or double-declining-balance depreciation for the drill.

Compute depreciation for each year under each of the three methods.

7-34 Comparison of Popular Depreciation Methods

(Alternates are 7-32 and 7-35.) Port Angeles Cedar Company acquired a saw for $32,000 with an expected useful life of 5 years and a $2,000 expected residual value. Prepare a tabular comparison (similar to Exhibit 7-3, p. 292) of the annual depreciation and book value for each year under straight-line and double-declining-balance depreciation. If these two methods were available for tax reporting purposes, which would a company prefer to use?

7-35 Fundamental Depreciation Policies

(Alternates are 7-32 and 7-34.) Suppose the Printing department of Safeco Insurance acquired a new press for $200,000. The equipment's predicted useful life is 8 years and predicted residual value is $20,000.

Prepare a depreciation schedule similar to Exhibit 7-3 (p. 292), comparing straight-line and double-declining-balance. Show all amounts in thousands of dollars (rounded to the nearest tenth). Limit the schedule to each of the first 3 years of useful life. Show the depreciation for each year and the book value at the end of each year. (Note that this is a comparison of methods used for reporting to shareholders. Such methods may differ from those used for reporting to the income tax authorities.)

7-36 Balance Sheet Presentation of PPE

Boeing, the world's largest maker of commercial airplanes, had the following items under property, plant, and equipment on its 1999 balance sheet ($ in millions):

Construction in progress	$ 1,130
Land	430
Net property, plant, and equipment	8,245
Machines and equipment	10,411
Buildings	8,148
Accumulated depreciation	?

Required

Prepare the property, plant, and equipment section of Boeing's balance sheet in proper form. Include the appropriate amount for accumulated depreciation.

7-37 Accumulated Depreciation

Bethlehem Steel Company reported the following items on its January 1, 2000 balance sheet ($ in millions):

Property, plant, and equipment, net	$2,899.7
Accumulated depreciation	$4,263.6

Required

1. Compute Bethlehem Steel's historical cost of property, plant, and equipment on January 1, 2000.
2. Bethlehem Steel uses an 18-year economic life for computing straight-line depreciation on most of its assets. Are most of their assets more than or less than 9 years old? Explain how you can determine this.

7-38 Depreciation, Income Taxes, and Cash Flow

Fleck Company began business with cash and common stock equity of $150,000. The same day, December 31, 20X1, the company acquired equipment for $50,000 cash. The equipment had an expected useful life of 5 years and a predicted residual value of $5,000. The first year's operations generated cash sales of $180,000 and cash operating expenses of $100,000.

Required

1. Prepare an analysis of income and cash flow for the year 20X2, using the format illustrated in Exhibit 7-4 panels B and C. (p. 295). Assume (a) straight-line depreciation and (b) DDB depreciation. Assume an income tax rate of 40%. Income taxes are paid in cash. The company uses the same depreciation method for reporting to shareholders and to income tax authorities.
2. Examine your answer to requirement 1. Does depreciation provide cash? Explain as precisely as possible.
3. Suppose depreciation were tripled under straight-line and DDB methods. How would before-tax cash flow be affected? Be specific.

7-39 MACRS Versus Straight-Line Depreciation

Chicago Machinery bought special tooling equipment for $1.8 million. The useful life is 5 years, with no residual value. For tax purposes, assume MACRS specifies a 3-year, DDB depreciation schedule. Chicago Machinery uses the straight-line depreciation method for reporting to shareholders.

Required

1. Explain the two factors that account for acceleration of depreciation for tax purposes.
2. Compute the first year's depreciation (a) for shareholder reporting and (b) for tax purposes. (Ignore complications in the tax law that are not introduced in this chapter.)

7-40 Leasehold Improvements

Pizza Hut has a 10-year lease on space in a suburban shopping center. Near the end of the sixth year of the lease, Pizza Hut exercised its rights under the lease, removing walls and replacing floor coverings and lighting fixtures. These improvements would not be removable at the end of the lease term. The cost was $120,000. The useful life of the redesigned facilities was predicted to be 12 years.

What accounts would be affected by the $120,000 expenditure? What would be the annual amortization?

7-41 Classic Case from the Business Press

A news story concerning Chrysler Corporation stated:

> Yet the $7.5 billion that John J. Riccardo, its money man, estimates the company will need to finance a recovery over the next five years is huge by any standard. But, says Riccardo, "half is charged to the P&L [profit and loss] as incurred, so we're looking for $3.75 billion. Of that, about 60% will be recovered in depreciation and amortization. That leaves a balance of $1.5 billion over the five years, to be financed through earnings, borrowings, and divestitures. Over the period, that overall number is manageable."

Explain or comment on the following:

1. "Half is charged to the P&L as incurred, so we're looking for $3.75 billion."
2. "Of that, about 60% will be recovered in depreciation and amortization."

7-42 Capital Expenditures

Consider the following transactions:

a. Acquired building for a down payment plus a mortgage payable.
b. Paid plumbers for repair of leaky faucets.
c. Acquired new air-conditioning system for the building.
d. Paid interest on building mortgage.
e. Paid principal on building mortgage.
f. Paid cash dividends.
g. Replaced smashed front door (not covered by insurance).
h. Paid travel expenses of sales personnel.
i. Paid janitorial wages.
j. Paid security guard wages.

Answer by letter:

1. Indicate which transactions are capital expenditures.
2. Indicate which transactions are expenses in the current year.

7-43 Capital Expenditures

Consider each of the following transactions. For each one, indicate whether it is a capital expenditure (C) or an expense in the current year (E).

a. Paid organization costs to incorporate a new company.
b. Paid a consultant to advise on marketing strategy.
c. Installed new lighting fixtures in a leased building.
d. Paid for routine maintenance on equipment.
e. Developed a patent for a process that cost $50,000 in R&D.
f. Paid for overhaul of machinery that extends its useful life.
g. Acquired a patent from General Electric for $40,000.
h. Paid for a tune-up on one of the autos in the company's fleet.

7-44 Repairs and Improvements

Yakima Wheat Company acquired harvesting equipment for $90,000 with an expected useful life of 5 years and a $10,000 expected residual value. Straight-line depreciation was used. During its fourth year of service, expenditures related to the equipment were as follows:

1. Oiling and greasing, $200.
2. Replacing belts and hoses, $450.
3. Major overhaul during the final week of the year, including the replacement of an engine. The useful life of the equipment was extended from 5 to 7 years. The cost was $21,000. The residual value is now expected to be $11,000 instead of $10,000.

Indicate in words how each of the three items would affect the income statement and the balance sheet. Prepare a tabulation that compares the original depreciation schedule with the revised depreciation schedule.

Required

7-45 Disposal of Equipment

The Outpatient Clinic of Eastside Hospital acquired X-ray equipment for $29,000 with an expected useful life of 5 years and a $4,000 expected residual value. Straight-line depreciation was used. The equipment was sold at the end of the fourth year for $12,000 cash.

Required

1. Compute the gain or loss on the sale. Show the effects of the sale on the balance sheet equation, identifying all specific accounts by name. Where and how would the sale appear on the income statement?

2. (a) Show the journal entries for the transaction in requirement 1. (b) Repeat 2a, assuming that the cash sales price was $7,000 instead of $12,000.

7-46 Gain or Loss on Sales of Fixed Assets

Luigi's Pizza Company purchased a delivery van in early 20X1 for $30,000. It was being depreciated on a straight-line basis over its useful life of 5 years. Estimated residual value was $5,000. The van was sold in early 20X3 after 2 years of depreciation had been recognized.

Required

1. Suppose Luigi's Pizza received $21,000 for the van. Compute the gain or loss on the sale. Prepare the journal entries for the sale of the van.

2. Suppose Luigi's Pizza received $17,000 for the van. Compute the gain or loss on the sale. Prepare the journal entries for the sale of the van.

7-47 Depletion

A zinc mine contains an estimated 900,000 tons of zinc ore. The mine cost $14.4 million. The tonnage mined during 20X4, the first year of operations, was 120,000 tons.

Required

1. What was the depletion for 20X4?

2. Suppose that in 20X5 a total of 100,000 tons were mined. What depletion expense would be charged for 20X5?

7-48 Various Intangible Assets

Consider the following:

1. On December 29, 20X1, a publisher acquires the paperback copyright for a book by Steven King for $3 million. Most sales of this book are expected to take place uniformly during 20X2 and 20X3. What will be the amortization for 20X2?

2. In 20X1, company C spent $6 million in its research department, which resulted in new valuable patents. In December 20X1, company D paid $6 million to an outside inventor for some valuable new patents. How would the income statements of 20X1 for each company be affected? How would the balance sheets as of December 31, 20X1 be affected?

3. On December 28, 20X8, Black Electronics Company purchased a patent for a calculator for $420,000. The patent has 10 years of its legal life remaining. Technology changes fast, so Black Electronics expects the patent to be worthless in 4 years. What will be the amortization for 20X9?

7-49 Various Intangible Assets

1. On December 29, 2000, Sony Corporation purchased a patent on some broadcasting equipment for $800,000. The patent has 16 years of its legal life remaining. Because technology moves rapidly, Sony expects the patent to be worthless at the end of 5 years. What is the amortization for 2001?

2. (a) Amgen, a biotech firm with more than $3 billion in revenues, spent more than $800 million in its research departments in 1999, and this resulted in valuable new patents. (b) Suppose that in December 1999, Amgen had paid $800 million to various outside companies for the same new patents. How would the income statement for 1999 have been affected under a and b? How would the balance sheet on December 31, 1999 be affected?

7-50 Various Intangible Assets

1. (a) Dow Chemical Company's annual report indicated that R&D expenditures for the year were $761 million. How did this amount affect operating income, which was $3,087 million? (b) Suppose the entire $761 million arose from outlays for patents acquired from various outside parties on December 30. What would be the operating income for the year? (c) How would Dow's December 31 balance sheet be affected by b?

2. On January 1, American Telephone and Telegraph Company (AT&T) acquired new patents on some communications equipment for $5 million. Technology changes quickly. The equipment's useful life is expected to be 5 years instead of the 17-year life of the patent. What will be the amortization for the first year?

3. IBM reported $663 million of software as an asset on its 1999 balance sheet. The notes indicated that "Costs related to the conceptual formulation and design of licensed programs are expensed as research and development. . . . the company capitalizes costs to produce the finished product that are incurred after technological feasibility is established. The annual amortization is the greater of the amount computed based on the estimated revenue distribution over the products' revenue-producing lives, or the straight-line method, and is applied over periods ranging up to three years." Suppose that IBM spends the same amount on this activity every year and that all such software is amortized over 3 years on a straight-line basis. How would the income statement and balance sheet change if the minimum term were changed to 4 years and every dollar of capitalized software was amortized over 4 years?

7-51 Basket Purchase

On February 21, 20X2, Speed-Tune, an auto service chain, acquired an existing building and land for $720,000 from a local gas station that had failed. The tax assessor had placed an assessed valuation of $200,000 on the land and $400,000 on the building as of January 1, 20X2.

Land	$200,000
Building	400,000
Total	$600,000

Required How much of the $720,000 purchase price should be attributed to the building? Why?

7-52 Basket Purchase of Sports Franchise

Paul Allen, co-founder of Microsoft, purchased the Seattle Seahawks, an NFL football team. Assume a total purchase price of $300 million. The largest assets are the franchise and the contracts. Assume that for reporting to the IRS, the franchise has an indefinite useful life while the contracts have a 5-year useful life. Other assets are relatively minor. Suppose the seller shows the following book values of the assets ($ in millions):

Player contracts	$30
Franchise	50
Total book value	$80

Required As Allen, if you have complete discretion for tax purposes, how much of the $300 million price would you allocate to the contracts? Explain.

PROBLEMS

7-53 Popular Depreciation Methods

(Problem 7-67 is an extension of this problem.) The annual report of Alaska Airlines contained the following footnote:

PROPERTY, EQUIPMENT, AND DEPRECIATION—Property and equipment are recorded at cost and depreciated using the straight-line method over the estimated useful lives, which are as follows:

Aircraft and other flight equipment	14–20 years
Buildings	10–30 years
Capitalized leases and leasehold improvements	Term of lease
Other equipment	3–15 years

Required

Consider a Boeing 727-100 airplane, which was acquired for $30 million. Its useful life is 20 years, and its expected residual value is $6 million. Prepare a tabular comparison of the annual depreciation and book value for each of the first 3 years of service life under straight-line and double-declining-balance depreciation. Show all amounts in thousands of dollars (rounded to the nearest thousand). (Note that this is a comparison of methods used for reporting to shareholders. Such methods may differ from those used for reporting to the income tax authorities.) *Hint:* See Exhibit 7-3, p. 292.

7-54 Depreciation Practices

The 2000 annual report of General Mills, maker of *Wheaties, Cheerios,* and *Betty Crocker* baking products, contained the following ($ in millions):

	2000	1999
Total land, buildings, and equipment	$2,949.2	$2,718.9
Less accumulated depreciation	1,544.3	1,424.2
Net land, buildings, and equipment	$1,404.9	$1,294.7

During 2000, depreciation expense was $208.8 million, and General Mills acquired land, buildings, and equipment worth $368 million. Assume that no gain or loss arose from the disposition of land, buildings, and equipment and that cash of $49.0 million was received from such disposals.

Required

Compute (1) the gross amount of assets written off (sold or retired), (2) the amount of accumulated depreciation written off, and (3) the book value of the assets written off. *Hint:* The use of T-accounts may help your analysis.

7-55 Depreciation

Asahi Chemical Industry Co. Ltd., has sales greater than the equivalent of $11 billion U.S. dollars. The company included the following in its balance sheet (yen in millions):

Property, plant and equipment, net of accumulated depreciation (Note 7)	
Buildings	¥135,337
Machinery and equipment	188,428
Land	64,817
Construction in progress	20,929
Other	17,233
Total property, plant and equipment	¥426,744

Footnote 7 contains the following:

Accumulated depreciation comprises the following (yen in millions):	
Buildings	¥ 182,957
Machinery and equipment	745,911
Other	72,498
Total accumulated depreciation	¥1,001,366

Footnote 2 says: "Depreciation is provided under a declining-balance method at rates based on estimated useful lives of the assets."

Required

1. Compute the original acquisition cost of each of the five assets listed under property, plant, and equipment.
2. Explain why no accumulated depreciation is shown for land or construction in progress.
3. Suppose Asahi had used straight-line instead of declining-balance depreciation. How do you suppose this would affect the the preceding values shown for property, plant, and equipment? How would this influence your estimate of the average age of Asahi's assets?

7-56 Reconstruction of Plant Asset Transactions

The Ford Motor Company's footnotes included ($ in millions):

Ford Motor Company

	December 31	
	1999	*1998*
Property		
Land, plant, and equipment	$60,748	$56,043
Less accumulated depreciation	(27,832)	(26,840)
Net land, plant, and equipment	32,916	29,203
Special tools, net	9,401	8,117
Net property	$42,317	$37,320

The notes to the income statement for 1999 revealed depreciation and amortization of $5,895 million. The account Special Tools, net is increased by new investments in tools, dies, jigs, and fixtures necessary for new models and production processes. These investments are then amortized over various periods and the account is reduced directly.

Hint: Analyze with the help of T-accounts.

Required

1. Assume $4,000 million was spent on special tools in 1999. There were no disposals of special tools. How much amortization was recorded on special tools?
2. Given your answer to requirement 1, estimate the cost of the new acquisitions of land, plant, and equipment. Assume all disposals of plant, property, and equipment involved fully depreciated assets with zero book value.

7-57 Average Age of Assets

Southwestern Bell Telephone Company provides phone services in Texas and surrounding states. The company had the following on its January 1, 2000 balance sheet ($ in millions):

Total property, plant, and equipment	$116,332
Less: Accumulated depreciation	69,761
	$ 46,571

A footnote states that "property, plant, and equipment is depreciated using the straight-line method." Annual depreciation expense is approximately $8,500 million.

Required

1. Estimate the average useful life of Southwestern Bell's depreciable assets.
2. Estimate the average age of Southwestern Bell's depreciable assets on January 1, 2000.

7-58 Depreciation, Income Tax, and Cash Flow

(Alternates are 7-59 and 7-60.) Sanchez Metal Products Company had the following balances, among others, at the end of December 20X1: Cash, $300,000; Equipment, $400,000; Accumulated Depreciation, $100,000. Total revenues (all in cash) were $900,000. Cash operating expenses were $600,000. Straight-line depreciation expense was $50,000. If accelerated depreciation had been used, depreciation expense would have been $100,000.

Table for Problem 7-58
($ Amounts in Thousands)

	1. Zero Income Taxes		2. 40% Income Taxes	
	Straight-Line Depreciation	*Accelerated Depreciation*	*Straight-Line Depreciation*	*Accelerated Depreciation*
Revenues	$	$	$	$
Cash operating expenses				
Cash provided by operations before income taxes				
Depreciation expense				
Operating income				
Income tax expense				
Net income	$	$	$	$
Supplementary analysis				
Cash provided by operations before income taxes	$	$	$	$
Income tax payments				
Net cash provided by operations	$	$	$	$

Required

1. Assume zero income taxes. Fill in the blanks in the accompanying table. Show the amounts in thousands.

2. Repeat requirement 1, but assume an income tax rate of 40%. Assume also that Sanchez uses the same depreciation method for reporting to shareholders and to income tax authorities.

3. Compare your answers to requirements 1 and 2. Does depreciation provide cash? Explain as precisely as possible.

4. Assume that Sanchez had used straight-line depreciation for reporting to shareholders and to income tax authorities. Indicate the change (increase or decrease and amount) in the following balances if Sanchez had used accelerated depreciation instead of straight-line: Cash, Accumulated Depreciation, Operating Income, Income Tax Expense, and Retained Income.

5. Refer to requirement 1. Suppose depreciation were doubled under both straight-line and accelerated methods. How would cash be affected? Be specific.

7-59 Depreciation, Income Taxes, and Cash Flow

(Alternates are 7-58 and 7-60.) A recent annual report of Kmart, a major retailing company, listed the following property and equipment ($ in millions):

Property and equipment, at cost	$10,768
Less: Accumulated depreciation	5,028
Property and equipment, net	$ 5,740

The cash balance was $406,000,000.

Depreciation expense during the year was $654,000,000. The condensed income statement follows ($ in millions):

Revenues	$31,437
Expenses	30,654
Operating income	$ 783

For purposes of this problem, assume that all revenues and expenses, excluding depreciation, are for cash. Thus, cash operating expenses were $30,654,000,000 − $654,000,000 = $30,000,000,000.

Required

1. Kmart uses straight-line depreciation. Suppose accelerated depreciation had been $754,000,000 instead of $654,000,000. Assume zero income taxes. Fill in the blanks in the accompanying table ($ in millions).

Table for Problem 7-59
($ Amounts in Millions)

	1. Zero Income Taxes		2. 40% Income Taxes	
	Straight-Line Depreciation	*Accelerated Depreciation*	*Straight-Line Depreciation*	*Accelerated Depreciation*
Revenues	$	$	$	$
Cash operating expenses				
Cash provided by operations before income taxes				
Depreciation expense				
Operating income				
Income tax expense				
Net income	$	$	$	$
Supplementary analysis				
Cash provided by operations before income taxes	$	$	$	$
Income tax payments				
Net cash provided by operations	$	$	$	$

2. Repeat requirement 1, but assume an income tax rate of 40%. Assume also that Kmart uses the same depreciation method for reporting to shareholders and to income tax authorities.

3. Compare your answers to requirements 1 and 2. Does depreciation provide cash? Explain as precisely as possible.

4. Assume that Kmart had used straight-line depreciation for reporting to shareholders and to income tax authorities. Indicate the change (increase or decrease and amount) in the following balances if Kmart had used accelerated depreciation instead of straight-line during that year: Cash, Accumulated Depreciation, Operating Income, Income Tax Expense, and Retained Income. What would be the new balances in Cash and Accumulated Depreciation?

5. Refer to requirement 1. Suppose depreciation were increased by an extra $300,000,000 under both straight-line and accelerated methods. How would cash be affected? Be specific.

7-60 Depreciation, Income Taxes, and Cash Flow
(Alternates are 7-58 and 7-59.) The French auto company, PSA Peugeot Citroen, sells the majority of its cars outside France. The company's annual report showed the following balances (French francs in millions):

Revenues	FF 173,516
Operating expenses	171,841
Operating income	FF 1,675

PSA Peugeot Citroen had depreciation expense of FF7,089,000,000 (included in operating expenses). The company's ending cash balance was FF2,886,000,000.

PSA Peugeot Citroen reported its property and equipment in the following way (FF in millions):

Property, plant, and equipment, at cost	FF 107,044
Less: Accumulated depreciation	56,835
Net property and equipment	FF 50,209

For purposes of this problem, assume that all revenues and expenses, excluding depreciation, are for cash.

Required

1. PSA Peugeot Citroen used straight-line depreciation. Suppose accelerated depreciation had been FF7,589 million instead of FF 7,089 million. Assume zero income taxes. Fill in the blanks in the accompanying table (in thousands of French francs).

Table for Problem 7-60
(Amounts in Thousands of French francs)

	1. Zero Income Taxes		2. 60% Income Taxes	
	Straight-Line Depreciation	*Accelerated Depreciation*	*Straight-Line Depreciation*	*Accelerated Depreciation*
Revenues	FF	FF	FF	FF
Cash operating expenses	_____	_____	_____	_____
Cash provided by operations before income taxes				
Depreciation expense	_____	_____	_____	_____
Operating income				
Income tax expense	_____	_____	_____	_____
Net income	FF	FF	FF	FF
Supplementary analysis				
Cash provided by operations before income taxes	FF	FF	FF	FF
Income tax payments	_____	_____	_____	_____
Net cash provided by operations	FF	FF	FF	FF

2. Repeat requirement 1, but assume an income tax rate of 60%. Assume also that PSA Peugeot Citroen uses the same depreciation method for reporting to shareholders and to income tax authorities.

3. Compare your answers to requirements 1 and 2. Does depreciation provide cash? Explain as precisely as possible.

4. PSA Peugeot Citroen used straight-line depreciation for reporting to shareholders and to income tax authorities. Indicate the change (increase or decrease and amount) in the following balances if PSA Peugeot Citroen had used accelerated depreciation instead of straight-line: Cash, Accumulated Depreciation, Operating Income, Income Tax Expense, and Retained Income. What would be the new balances in Cash and Accumulated Depreciation?

5. Refer to requirement 1. Suppose depreciation were doubled under both straight-line and accelerated methods. How would cash be affected? Be specific.

7-61 Depreciation, Income Taxes, and Cash Flow

Mr. Brandt, president of the Bremen Shipping Company, had read a newspaper story that stated: "The Frankfurt Steel Company had a cash flow last year of 1,500,000 DM, consisting of 1,000,000 DM of net income plus 500,000 DM of depreciation. New plant facilities helped the cash flow, because depreciation was 25% higher than in the preceding year." "Cash flow" is frequently used as a synonym for "cash provided by operations," which, in turn, is cash revenue less cash operating expenses and income taxes. (DM stands for deutsch mark, the German unit of currency.)

Brandt was encouraged by the quotation because Bremen Shipping Company had just acquired a vast amount of new transportation equipment. These acquisitions had placed a severe financial strain on the company. Brandt was heartened because he thought that the added cash flow from the depreciation of the new equipment should ease the financial pressures on the company.

The income before income taxes of the Bremen Shipping Company last year (20X8) was 200,000 DM. Depreciation was 200,000 DM; it will also be 200,000 DM on the old equipment in 20X9.

Revenue in 20X8 was 2.1 million DM (all in cash), and operating expenses other than depreciation were 1.7 million DM (all in cash).

In 20X9, the new equipment is expected to help increase revenue by 1 million DM. Operating expenses other than depreciation will increase by 800,000 DM.

Required

1. Suppose depreciation on the new equipment for financial reporting purposes is 100,000 DM. What would be the cash flow from operations (cash provided by operations) for 20X9? Show computations. Ignore income taxes.

2. Repeat requirement 1, assuming that the depreciation on the new equipment is 50,000 DM. Ignore income taxes.

3. Assume an income tax rate of 30%. (a) Repeat requirement 1; (b) repeat requirement 2. Assume that the same amount of depreciation is shown for tax purposes and for financial reporting purposes.

4. In your own words, state as accurately as possible the effects of depreciation on cash flow. Comment on preceding requirements 1, 2, and 3 to bring out your points. This is a more important requirement than requirements 1, 2, and 3.

7-62 Rental Cars

Hertz was acquired by Ford Motor Company and is now a Ford subsidiary. Before the acquisition, an annual report of the Hertz rental car company contained the following footnote:

> *Depreciable assets—the provisions for depreciation and amortization are computed on a straight-line basis over the estimated useful lives of the respective assets. . . . Hertz follows the practice of charging maintenance and repairs, including the costs of minor replacements, to maintenance expense accounts. Costs of major replacement of units of property are charged to property and equipment accounts and depreciated. . . . Upon disposal of revenue earning equipment, depreciation expense is adjusted for the difference between the net proceeds from sale and the remaining book value.*

Required

1. Assume that some new cars are acquired on October 1, 2000, for $60 million. The useful life is 1 year. Expected residual values are $42 million. Prepare a summary journal entry for depreciation for 2000. The fiscal year ends on December 31.

2. Prepare a summary journal entry for depreciation for the first 9 months of 2001.

3. Assume that the automobiles are sold for $48 million cash on September 30, 2001. Prepare the journal entry for the sale. Automobiles are considered "revenue earning equipment."

4. What is the total depreciation expense on these automobiles for 2001? If the $48 million proceeds could have been predicted exactly when the cars were originally acquired, what would depreciation expense have been in 2000? In 2001? Explain.

7-63 Nature of Research Costs

Katherine Mori, a distinguished scientist of international repute, had developed many successful drugs for a well-established pharmaceutical company. Having an entrepreneurial spirit, she persuaded the board of directors that she should resign her position as vice-president of research and launch a subsidiary company to produce and market some powerful new drugs for treating arthritis. However, she did not predict overnight success. Instead, she expected to gather a first-rate research team that might take 3 to 5 years to generate any marketable products. Furthermore, she admitted that the risks were so high that conceivably no commercial success might result. Nevertheless, she had little trouble obtaining an initial investment of $5 million. The Mori Pharmaceuticals Company was 80% owned by the parent and 20% by Katherine.

Katherine acquired a team of researchers and began operations. By the end of the first year of the life of the new subsidiary, $2 million had been expended on research activities, mostly for researchers' salaries, but also for related research costs.

No marketable products had been developed, but Katherine and other top executives were extremely pleased about overall progress and were very optimistic about getting such products within the next 3 or 4 years.

Required

How would you account for the $2 million? Would you write it off as an expense in year one? Could it be capitalized as an intangible asset? If so, would you carry it indefinitely? Or would you write it off systematically over 3 years or some longer span? Why? Explain, giving particular attention to the idea of an asset as an unexpired cost.

7-64 Meaning of Book Value

Chavez Company purchased an office building 20 years ago for $1.3 million, $500,000 of which was attributable to land. The mortgage has been fully paid. The current balance sheet follows:

Cash		$300,000	Stockholders'
Land		500,000	equity	$1,000,000
Building at cost	$800,000		
Accumulated depreciation	600,000		
Net book value		200,000	
Total assets		$1,000,000	

The company is about to borrow $1.8 million on a first mortgage to modernize and expand the building. This amounts to 60% of the combined appraised value of the land and building before the modernization and expansion.

Required

Prepare a balance sheet after the loan is made and the building is expanded and modernized. Comment on its significance.

7-65 Capital Expenditures

Disputes sometimes arise between the taxpayer and the Internal Revenue Service concerning whether legal costs should be deductible as expenses in the year incurred or be considered as capital expenditures because they relate to defining or perfecting title to business property.

Consider three examples from court cases:

Example 1
Several years after Rock set up his stone-quarrying business, Smalltown passed an ordinance banning it. Rock spent $1,000 to invalidate the ordinance.

Example 2
Now suppose Rock decided to expand his business. He applied to Smalltown for a permit to build an additional crusher. It was denied because an ordinance prohibited the expansion of nonconforming uses, including quarrying. Rock sued to invalidate the ordinance and won after spending $2,000. He then built the crusher.

Example 3
Smalltown's zoning board established a restrictive building (setback) line across Rock's business property. The line lowered the property's value. Rock spent $3,000 trying unsuccessfully to challenge it.

Required

Indicate whether each example should be deemed (a) an expense or (b) a capital expenditure. Briefly explain your answer.

7-66 Change in Service Life

An annual report of TWA contained the following footnote:

> *Note 2, Change in accounting estimate. TWA extended the estimated useful lives of Boeing 727-100 aircraft from principally sixteen years to principally twenty years. As a result, depreciation and amortization expense was decreased by $9,000,000.*

The TWA annual report also contained the following data: depreciation, $235,518,000; net income, $42,233,000.

The cost of the 727-100 aircraft subject to depreciation was $800 million. Residual values were predicted to be 10% of acquisition cost.

Required

Assume a combined federal and state income tax rate of 46% throughout all parts of these requirements.

1. Was the effect of the change in estimated useful life a material difference? Explain, including computations.

2. The same year's annual report of Delta Air Lines contained the following footnote:

   > *Depreciation—Substantially all of the flight equipment is being depreciated on a straight-line basis to residual values (10% of cost) over a 10-year period from dates placed in service.*

   The Delta annual report also contained the following data: depreciation, $220,979,000; net income, $146,474,000. Suppose Delta had used a 20-year life instead of a 10-year life. Assume a 46% applicable income tax rate. Compute the new depreciation and net income.

3. Suppose TWA had used a 10-year life instead of a 20-year life on its 727-100 equipment. Compute the new depreciation and net income. For purposes of this requirement, assume that the equipment cost $800 million and has been in service 1 year and that reported net income based on a 20-year life was $42,233,000.

7-67 Disposal of Equipment

(Alternate is 7-68.) Alaska Airlines acquired a new Boeing 727-100 airplane for $26 million. Its expected residual value was $6 million. The company's annual report indicated that straight-line depreciation was used based on an estimated service life of 20 years. In addition, the company stated: "The cost and related accumulated depreciation of assets sold or retired are removed from the appropriate accounts, and gain or loss, if any, is recognized in Other Income (Expense)."

Show all amounts in millions of dollars.

1. Assume that the equipment is sold at the end of the sixth year for $22 million cash. Compute the gain or loss on the sale. Show the effects of the sale on the balance sheet equation, identifying all specific accounts by name. Where and how would the sale appear on the income statement?

2. (a) Show the journal entries for the transaction in requirement 1. (b) Repeat 2a, assuming that the cash sales price was $19 million instead of $22 million.

7-68 Disposal of Property and Equipment

(Alternate is 7-67.) Rockwell International is an advanced technology company operating primarily in aerospace and electronics. The company's annual report indicated that both accelerated and straight-line depreciation were used for its property and equipment. In addition, the annual report said: "Gains or losses on property transactions are recorded in income in the period of sale or retirement."

Rockwell received $27.9 million for property that it sold.

1. Assume that the total property in question was originally acquired for $150 million and the $27.9 million was received in cash. There was a gain of $8.5 million on the sale. Compute the accumulated depreciation on the property and equipment sold. Show the effects of the sale on the balance sheet equation, identifying all specific accounts by name.

2. (a) Show the journal entries and postings to T-accounts for the transaction in requirement 1. (b) Repeat 2a, assuming that the cash sales price was $17.9 million cash instead of $27.9 million.

7-69 Gain on Airplane Crash

A few years ago, a Delta Air Lines 727 crashed in Dallas. The crash resulted in a gain of $.11 per share for Delta. How could this happen? Consider the accounting for airplanes. Airlines insure their craft at market value, $6.5 million for Delta's 727. However, the planes' book values are often much less because of large accumulated depreciation amounts. The book value of Delta's 727 was only $962,000.

1. Suppose Delta received the insurance payment and immediately purchased another 727 for $6.5 million. Compute the effect of the crash on pretax income. Also compute the effect on Delta's total assets.

2. Do you think a casualty should generate a reported gain? Why?

7-70 Disposal of Equipment

Airline Executive reported on an airline as follows:

> Lufthansa's *highly successful policy of rolling over entire fleets in roughly ten years—before the aircrafts have outlived their usefulness—got started in a "spectacular" way when seven first-generation 747s were sold.*
> *The 747s were bought six to nine years earlier for $22–28 million each and sold for about the same price.*

1. Assume an average original cost of $25 million each, an average original expected useful life of 10 years, a $2.5 million expected residual value, and an average actual life of 8 years before disposal. Use straight-line depreciation. Compute the total gain or loss on the sale of the seven planes.

2. Prepare a summary journal entry for the sale.

7-71 Depreciation of Professional Sports Contracts

"Accounting Professor Says the Owners Lost $27 Million" read the headline. Major league baseball players and owners were engaged in contract negotiations. The owners claimed to have lost $43 million in the last year, and the Players Association maintained that the owners had made a profit of as much as $10 million. George Sorter, Professor of Accounting at New York University, fixed the loss at $27 million, primarily because he added back "initial roster depreciation" to adjust the owners' figure. "That depreciation, an amount that arises when a team is purchased and a portion of the purchase price that makes up player contracts is paid off [amortized] over several years, should not be

322   CHAPTER 7   LONG-LIVED ASSETS AND DEPRECIATION

treated as an operating expense," Sorter said. When a team is sold, an amount representing the value of current player contracts is put into an intangible asset account and amortized (or depreciated) over several years.

Required

Explain why such an intangible asset account is created. Should this asset be amortized (or depreciated), thereby reducing income? Why would Professor Sorter eliminate this expense when assessing the financial operating performance of the major league teams?

7-72 Valuation of Intangible Assets of Basketball Team

Suppose that new owners acquired a National Basketball Association team for $72 million. They valued the contracts of their 15 players at a total of $35 million, the franchise at $36 million, and other assets at $1 million. For income tax purposes, the team amortized the $35 million over 5 years; therefore, they took a tax deduction of $7 million annually.

The Internal Revenue Service (IRS) challenged the deductions. It maintained that only $3 million of the $72 million purchase price was attributable to the player contracts, and that $32 million of the $35 million in dispute should be attributed to the league franchise rights. Such franchise rights are regarded by the IRS as a valuable asset with an indefinite future life; therefore, no amortization is permitted for tax-reporting purposes.

Suppose the operating income for each of the 5 years (before any amortization) was $10 million.

Required

1. Consider the reporting to the IRS. Tabulate a comparison of annual operating income (after amortization) according to two approaches, (a) that of the NBA team and (b) that of the IRS. What is the difference in annual operating income?

2. Consider the reporting to shareholders. Reports to shareholders by American companies amortize franchise fees. The NBA team had been using a 5-year life for player contracts and a 40-year life for the league franchise rights. Tabulate a comparison of operating income (after amortization) using (a) this initial approach and (b) the approach whereby only $3 million would have been attributed to player contracts. What is the difference in annual operating income?

3. Comment on the results in requirements 1 and 2. Which alternative do you think provides the more informative report of operating results? Why?

7-73 Deferred Charges

Four Seasons Hotels, Inc., the Ontario-based operator of luxury hotels and resorts throughout the world, had the following items under assets in its 1999 balance sheet ($ in millions):

	1999	1998
Deferred development costs	$ 7	$ 6
Investment in management contracts	186	132

A footnote to the financial statements stated:

> The corporation defers legal, consulting, travel, and other costs directly relating to the negotiation, structuring, and execution of new contracts. . . . When the property is opened, these deferred charges are reclassified to "Investment in management contracts." The deferred charges associated with new management contracts developed by the corporation are amortized on a straight-line basis over a 10-year period commencing when the hotel is opened.

Required

1. In 1999, Four Seasons amortized $6 million of investment in management contracts. Compute the amount transferred from deferred charges to investment in management contracts during 1999.

2. Compute the amount of deferred development cost capitalized during 1999.

3. Prepare journal entries for amortization of investment in management contracts, for the recognition of deferred charges (assume the expenditures are paid in cash), and for the transfer from deferred charges to investment in management contracts.

4. Explain why investment in management contracts is a legitimate asset to be included on the balance sheet. Also explain why some accountants would not consider it an asset.

7-74 Software Development Costs

Microsoft, Incorporated, is one of the largest producers of software for personal computers. Special rules apply to accounting for the costs of developing software for sale or lease. Such costs are expensed until the technological feasibility of the product is established. Thereafter, they should be capitalized and amortized over the life of the product.

One of Microsoft's divisions began working on some special business applications software. Suppose $800,000 had been spent on the project by the end of 20X1, but it was not yet clear whether the software was technologically feasible.

On about July 1, 20X2, after spending another $400,000, management decided that the software was technologically feasible. During the second half of 20X2, the division spent another $1 million on this project. In December 20X2, the product was announced, with deliveries to begin in March 20X3. No R&D costs for the software were incurred after December 20X2. Projected sales were: 20X3, $800,000; 20X4, $1.4 million; 20X5, $1.2 million; 20X6, $400,000; and 20X7, $200,000.

Required

1. Prepare journal entries to account for the R&D expenses for the software for 20X1 and 20X2. Assume that all expenditures were paid in cash.
2. Would any R&D expenses affect income in 20X3? If so, prepare the appropriate journal entry. Actual 20X3 sales were $800,000.

7-75 Basket Purchase and Intangibles

A tax newsletter stated: "When a business is sold, part of the sales price may be allocated to tangible assets and part to a 'covenant not to compete.' How this allocation is made can have important tax consequences to both the buyer and seller."

A large law firm, organized as a professional services corporation, purchased a successful local firm for $100,000. The purchase included both tangible assets, which have an average remaining useful life of 10 years, and a 3-year covenant not to compete. Suppose the buyer has legally supportable latitude concerning how to allocate this amount, as follows:

	Allocation One	Allocation Two
Covenant	$ 72,000	$ 48,000
Tangible assets	28,000	52,000
Total for two assets	$100,000	$100,000

Required

1. For income tax purposes, which allocation would the buyer favor? Why?
2. For shareholder reporting purposes, which allocation would the buyer favor? Why?

7-76 Depreciation Policies and Ethics

Some companies have depreciation policies that differ substantially from the norm of their industry. For example, Cineplex Odeon depreciated its theater seats, carpets, and related equipment over 27 years, much longer than most of its competitors. Another example is Blockbuster Entertainment, which depreciated the videotapes it rents over 36 months. Others depreciate them over a period as short as 9 months.

Growing companies can increase their current income by depreciating fixed assets over a longer period of time. Sometimes companies lengthen the depreciable lives of their fixed assets when a boost in income is desired. Comment on the ethical implications of choosing an economic life for depreciation purposes, with special reference to the policies of Cineplex Odeon and Blockbuster.

ANNUAL REPORT CASE

7-77 Cisco Annual Report

Refer to the financial statements of Cisco in appendix A. Cisco uses straight-line depreciation for all assets, as explained in note 2. Depreciation and amortization expense was $863 million for the year ended July 29, 2000, according to the Consolidated Statement of Cash Flows.

Required

1. What lives does Cisco use for depreciating and amortizing its assets?
2. Suppose Cisco extended the lives of all its depreciable assets by 50%, so that depreciation was smaller each year. Estimate the effect of this on net earnings reported in the year 2000. Assume that the average tax rate in the current income statement applied to this

change in depreciation and that depreciation for financial reporting purposes and tax purposes were the same.

3. What would be the effect of the change described in number 2 on cash provided by operating activities?

7-78 Financial Statement Research
Select two distinct industries and identify two companies in each industry.

1. Identify the depreciation methods used by each company.

2. Calculate gross and net plant, property, and equipment as a percentage of total assets for each company. What differences do you observe between industries? Within industries?

3. Do the notes disclose any unusual practices with regard to long-lived assets?

COLLABORATIVE LEARNING EXERCISE

7-79 Accumulated Depreciation
Form groups of at least four students (this exercise can be done as an entire class, if desired). Individual students, on their own, should select a company and find the fixed asset section of its most recent balance sheet. From the balance sheet (and possibly the footnotes) find the original acquisition cost of property, plant, and equipment (the account title varies slightly by company) and the accumulated depreciation on property, plant, and equipment. Compute the ratio of accumulated depreciation to original acquisition cost. Also note the depreciation method used and the average economic life of the assets, if given. (For an extra bonus, find a company that uses accelerated depreciation for reporting to shareholders; such companies are harder to find.)

When everyone gets together, make four columns on the board or on a piece of paper. Find the 25% of the companies with the highest ratios and list them in the first column. Then list the 25% with the next highest ratios in the second column, and so on. As a group, make a list of explanations for the rankings of the companies. What characteristics of the company, its industry, or its depreciation methods distinguish the companies with high ratios from those with low ratios?

INTERNET EXERCISE

7-80 Gap, Inc.
Go to www.gapinc.com to find Gap Inc.'s home page. Select *financial and media* and enter the site. Then, select *Annual Reports,* and click on the most recent annual report.
Answer the following questions about Gap:

www.prenhall.com/horngren

1. Read the *Notes to Consolidated Financial Statements.* What is the nature of Gap's operations? What type of property and equipment would you expect would be included in Gap's property and equipment section of the balance sheet?

2. In which section of its financial statements does Gap provide information on the method of depreciation and amortization used? What other disclosures concerning depreciable assets are available in this same location?

3. Does Gap have any intangible assets? What type are they? What time period is used for cost allocation?

4. What does the amount listed on the balance sheet for property and equipment represent — cost, market, or some other amount? If no additional property and equipment assets are purchased, what will happen to the net book value over time?

5. How much depreciation and amortization expense did Gap report, as shown on its most recent annual report? Why is this amount not obvious from looking at the income statement? Which financial statement provides the depreciation and amortization amount?

Go to the "Depreciation Methods and Inventory Cost Flow Assumptions" episode on the *Mastering Accounting* CD-ROM for an interactive, video-enhanced exercise focused on the different methods for depreciation and inventory. CanGo staff must prepare reports that present potential investors with the best possible financial outlook for the company.

LIABILITIES AND INTEREST

America West Airlines is smaller than some of its competitors but nonetheless has major liabilities for airplanes and frequent flyer miles.

www.prenhall.com/horngren

Learning Objectives

After studying this chapter, you should be able to

1. Account for current liabilities.

2. Design an internal control system for cash disbursements.

3. Explain simple long-term liabilities.

4. Relate bond covenants to the riskiness of a bond.

5. Interpret deferred tax liabilities.

6. Locate and understand the contingent liabilities information in a company's financial statements.

7. Use ratio analysis to assess a company's debt levels.

From a marketing perspective, the idea is a simple one. On most of today's major air carriers, you can earn one mile of free travel credit for every paid mile you fly. Earn enough miles and you can travel to any number of dream destinations. What better way to reward loyal air travelers than with free tickets in the future? Yet the accounting behind the scenes for all this activity is quite a complex matter.

America West Airlines, based in Phoenix, Arizona, began offering its frequent flyer miles in 1987. Its program is called "Flight Fund" and has over 1 million active members. The miles accrued by members are a liability to the airline because they represent an obligation to provide air travel at some point in the future. This obligation is called "Air traffic liability" and appears as a current liability on America West's balance sheet. In fact, the program is now the company's single largest current liability.

The financial impact of this liability is estimated by considering how many people are eligible for free travel, how many will redeem mileage during the current period, and their possible destinations. Historical redemption patterns are factored into the estimation. Once the probable "free" travel is estimated as to the number of people and routes traveled, this free travel must be expressed in financial terms. The valuation technique is referred to as the "incremental cost method" and requires a charge to operations for the accumulated miles. Under this valuation method, the incremental costs reflect the additional gas and other cash costs incurred to serve additional passengers on existing flights. At the end of 2000, America West's air traffic liability amounted to $209 million, or 34% of current liabilities.

When individuals seek to buy a car or a house, lenders assess the buyer's financial position carefully and pay special attention to the size of the down payment the buyer will make. The larger the down payment, the more "equity" the borrower has in the purchase, and the more comfortable the lender is in making the loan. Similarly, potential investors in the common stock or bonds of a company carefully evaluate the amount of debt the company has relative to the amount of stockholders' equity to assess the potential risk of their investment. Thus, a major element of generally accepted accounting principles in the United States is the careful definition of what constitutes a liability and how best to disclose the liability to readers of financial statements.

LIABILITIES IN PERSPECTIVE

As stated in previous chapters, liabilities are one company's obligations to pay cash or to provide goods and services to other companies or individuals. Liabilities include wages due to employees, payables to suppliers, taxes owed the government, interest and principal due to lenders, obligations from losing a lawsuit, and so on. Such obligations usually stem from a transaction with an outside party such as a supplier, a lending institution, or an employee. Accrual accounting recognizes expenses as they occur, not necessarily when they are paid in cash. Whenever an obligation is recognized before it is paid, a liability is created.

Investors, financial analysts, management, and creditors consider existing liabilities of the firm when valuing the firm's common stock, when evaluating a new loan to the company, and when making many other decisions. Problems arise when companies appear to have excessive debt or seem to be unable to meet existing obligations. For example, suppliers who normally sell on credit may evaluate a customer's debt level; after concluding that it is excessive, they would refuse to ship new items or may ship only collect on delivery (C.O.D.). Also, lenders may refuse to provide new loans, and customers, worried that the company will not be around long enough to honor warranties, may prefer to buy elsewhere. Of course, once creditors and customers go, a company is not long for this world. Debt problems can snowball quickly.

Once a debt problem gets so bad that the company cannot pay, the creditors can take legal action to collect the debt. Depending on the type of obligation, creditors may be able to force the sale of specific assets, take over the board of directors, or force the company out of business. Because poorly managed debt can cause such problems, financial statements users tend to be very concerned about debt levels. Accountants preparing financial statements are thus careful to disclose fully the company's liabilities.

To get a better understanding of the reporting of liabilities, consider a real example. Exhibit 8-1 shows the balance sheet presentation of liabilities from the annual report of Deckers Outdoor Corporation, a footwear and apparel company known mainly for its Teva sandals.

As is common practice, Deckers classifies its liabilities as either current or long-term, which helps financial statement readers interpret the immediacy of the company's obligations. **Long-term liabilities** are those that fall due more than 1 year beyond the balance sheet date. Conversely, current liabilities fall due within the coming year or within the company's normal operating cycle (if that cycle is longer than a year). Companies pay some long-term obligations gradually, in yearly or monthly installments. You can see from Exhibit 8-1 that Deckers includes the current portion of these long-term obligations ($125,000 in 1999) as a part of the company's current liabilities.

In the general ledger, separate accounts are kept for different liabilities, such as wages, salaries, commissions, interest, and similar items. In the annual report, though, these liabilities may be combined and shown as a single current liability labeled accrued

long-term liabilities
Obligations that fall due beyond 1 year from the balance sheet date.

Exhibit 8-1

Deckers Outdoor Corporation

Consolidated Balance Sheets as of December 31, 1999 and 1998
($ in Thousands, Except per Share Data)

	1999	1998
Current liabilities		
Current installments of long-term debt	$ 125	$ 6,236
Trade accounts payable	7,261	7,947
Accrued expenses	3,000	2,991
Total current liabilities	10,386	17,174
Long-term debt	6,276	15,199
Total debt	$17,662	$32,373

liabilities or accrued expenses payable. Sometimes the adjective accrued is deleted so that these liabilities are labeled simply taxes payable, wages payable, and so on. Similarly, the term accrued may be used, and payable may be deleted.

Liabilities can be measured in different ways. Basically, though, they are best measured in terms of the amount of cash needed to meet or pay off an obligation. For current liabilities, measurement is relatively easy, and the accounting process is straightforward.

ACCOUNTING FOR CURRENT LIABILITIES

Not all current liabilities are recorded the same way. Some are recorded as a result of a transaction with an outside entity, such as a lender or supplier. Other liabilities are recorded with an adjusting journal entry to acknowledge an obligation arising over time, such as interest or wages. Let's take a look at the accounting procedures for different types of current liabilities.

Objective 1
Account for current liabilities.

ACCOUNTS PAYABLE

Accounts payable (or trade accounts payable) are amounts owed to suppliers. Over 90% of major U.S. companies show accounts payable as a separate line under current liabilities on their balance sheet. However, a few combine accounts payable with accrued liabilities. Payments on these amounts tend to be made frequently to the same suppliers. Large sums of money flow through these accounts payable systems. Therefore, data-processing and internal control systems are carefully designed for these transactions. The key is to assure that checks are only written for legitimate obligations of the company. The internal control system includes checks and balances to assure that products have been ordered, have been received in good condition, and are billed at agreed upon prices.

NOTES PAYABLE

When companies take out loans, they must sign promissory notes. A **promissory note** is a written promise to repay the loan principal plus interest at specific future dates. Most promissory notes are payable to banks and are called notes payable.

Balance sheet presentation of notes payable varies. Notes that are payable within 1 year are shown as current liabilities; others are long-term liabilities. Chevron reports the current portion of long-term debt with notes payable with the descriptive caption, "short-term debt." Merck, a pharmaceutical company included in the Dow, calls a similar account "loans payable and current portion of long-term debt."

promissory note A written promise to repay principal plus interest at specific future dates.

line of credit An
agreement with a bank to
provide automatically
short-term loans up to
some preestablished
maximum.

Instead of having to apply for small loans one at a time, many companies create lines of credit with a bank or other lender. A **line of credit** sets up a predetermined maximum amount that a company can borrow from a given lender without significant additional credit checking or other time-consuming procedures. Lines of credit benefit lenders and borrowers. The lender gets the advantage of not having to run credit checks and extensive paperwork every time the borrower wants a loan. The borrower gets the advantage of having a preset amount of borrowing available.

Companies do not always take out loans from banks to meet short-term needs for credit. **Commercial paper** is a debt contract issued by prominent companies that borrow directly from investors. They may work with financial intermediaries or dealers who match borrowers and lenders. The liability created by commercial paper always falls due in 9 months or less, usually in 60 days after issuance.

commercial paper A
short-term debt contract
issued by prominent
companies that borrow
directly from investors.

Coca-Cola showed $4.8 billion of loans and notes payable on its 2000 balance sheet, and the accompanying footnotes explained this amount as follows:

> *Loans and notes payable consist primarily of commercial paper
> issued in the United States. On December 31, 2000, we had $4.5 bil-
> lion outstanding in commercial paper borrowings. In addition, we
> had $3.0 billion in lines of credit . . . available, of which $246 mil-
> lion was outstanding. Our . . . interest rates for commercial paper
> were approximately 6.7 and 6.0 percent at December 31, 2000 and
> 1999, respectively.*

Coca-Cola borrows more in the commercial paper market than it does from banks because the interest rates are lower in the commercial paper market. However, only companies with the sort of visibility and creditworthiness of Coca-Cola can issue commercial paper.

ACCRUED EMPLOYEE COMPENSATION

Expenses that have been incurred and recognized on the income statement but not yet paid are accrued liabilities. Some accrued liabilities are obligations to employees for payment of wages. In fact, most companies have a separate current liability account for such items, with a label such as salaries, wages, and commissions payable.

In earlier chapters, we assumed that an employee earned, for example, $100 per week and, in turn, received $100 in cash on payday. In reality, however, payroll accounting is never that easy. For example, employers must withhold some employee earnings and pay them instead to the government, insurance companies, labor unions, charitable organizations, and so forth.

For example, consider the withholding of income taxes and Social Security taxes [also called Federal Insurance Contributions Act (FICA) taxes]. Assume a company has a $100,000 monthly payroll and, for simplicity, assume that the only amounts withheld are $15,000 for income taxes and $7,000 for Social Security taxes. The withholdings are not additional employer costs. They are simply part of the employee wages and salaries that are paid instead to third parties. The journal entry for this $100,000 payroll is:

Compensation expense...................	100,000	
Salaries and wages payable.............		78,000
Income tax withholding payable		15,000
Social Security withholding payable......		7,000

A second complication companies must deal with is payroll taxes and fringe benefits. These are employee-related costs in addition to salaries and wages. Payroll taxes are amounts paid to the government for items such as the employer's portion of Social Security, federal and state unemployment taxes, and workers' compensation taxes. Fringe benefits include employee pensions, life and health insurance, and vacation pay. At many organizations the fringe benefits exceed 30% of salary. Thus, a person who earns $30,000 per year in salary, effectively costs the company $39,000 ($30,000 + 30% of $30,000). Liabilities are accrued for each of these costs. If they have not yet been paid at the balance sheet date, they are included among the current liabilities.

Note that the Social Security taxes are paid in two parts. About half is withheld directly from the employee and a similar amount represents an additional amount paid by the employer. If employers pay an additional FICA tax equal to the $7,000 withheld from the employee and also pay 10% of gross wages into a retirement account, the following journal entry should be made:

Employee benefit expense...............	17,000	
Employer Social Security payable		7,000
Pension liability payable		10,000

INCOME TAXES PAYABLE

A corporation must pay income taxes as a percentage of its earnings. Instead of paying one lump sum at tax time, corporations make periodic installment payments based on their estimated tax for the year. Therefore, the accrued liability for income taxes at year-end is generally much smaller than the annual income tax expense.

To illustrate, suppose a corporation has an estimated taxable income of $100 million for the calendar year 20X0. At a 40% tax rate, the company's estimated taxes for the year are $40 million. Payments must be made as follows:

	April 15	June 15	September 15	December 15
Estimated taxes (in millions)	$10	$10	$10	$10

The final income tax return must be filed, and payment must be made by March 15, 20X1. Suppose the actual taxable income for the year turned out to be $110 million instead of the estimated $100 million. Total tax would then be calculated as $44 million. On March 15, the corporation must pay the $4 million additional tax on the additional $10 million of taxable income. The accrued liability on December 31, 20X0, would appear in the current liability section of the balance sheet as:

Income taxes payable	$4,000,000

For simplicity, the illustration assumed equal quarterly payments. However, the estimated taxable income for a calendar year may change as the year unfolds. The corporation must change its quarterly payments accordingly. Regardless of how a company changes its estimates, there will nearly always be a tax payment or refund due on March 15, and there will be an accrual adjustment at year-end.

CURRENT PORTION OF LONG-TERM DEBT

A company's long-term debt often includes some payments due within a year that should be reclassified as current liabilities. The journal entry for recognizing the current portion of long-term debt reclassifies a noncurrent liability as a current liability. By using the Deckers illustration in Exhibit 8-1, the reclassification journal entry for 1999 would be:

Long-term obligations.......................	125,000	
Current portion of long-term obligations		125,000

SALES TAX

When retailers collect sales taxes, they are collecting on behalf of the state or local government. For example, suppose a 7% sales tax is levied on sales of $10,000. The total collected from the customer must be $10,000 + $700, or $10,700. The transaction would affect the balance sheet as follows:

A	=	L	+	SE
+ 10,700	=	+ 700		+ 10,000
Increase Cash or Accounts Receivable		Increase Sales Tax Payable		Increase Sales

The sales shown on the income statement would be $10,000, not $10,700. The sales tax never affects the income statement. The $700 received for taxes affects the current liability account Sales Tax Payable and is shown on the balance sheet until it is paid to the government. The journal entries (without explanations) are:

Cash or accounts receivable	10,700	
Sales		10,000
Sales tax payable		700
Sales tax payable	700	
Cash		700

PRODUCT WARRANTIES

Not all current liabilities can be measured exactly. For example, a sales warranty creates a liability, but warranty claims will arise in the future and cannot be estimated precisely. If warranty obligations are material, they must be accrued when products are sold because the obligation arises then, not when the actual repair services are performed. Ford describes its warranty accounting as follows: "Estimated costs related to product warranty are accrued at the time of sale."

The estimated warranty expenses are typically based on past experience for replacing or remedying defective products. Although estimates should be close, they are rarely precisely correct. Differences between the estimated and actual results are usually added to or subtracted from the current warranty expense account as additional information unfolds. The accounting entry at the time of sale is:

Warranty expense	600,000	
Liability for warranties (or some similar title)		600,000
To record the estimated liability for warranties		
arising from current sales; the provision is 3%		
of current sales of $20 million, or $600,000		

When a warranty claim arises, an entry such as the following is made:

Liability for warranties	1,000	
Cash, accounts payable, accrued wages payable,		
and similar accounts		1,000
To record the acquisition of supplies,		
outside services, and employee services to		
satisfy claims for repairs		

If the estimate for warranty expense is accurate, the entries for all claims will total about $600,000.

RETURNABLE DEPOSITS

Customers occasionally must make money deposits that are to be returned in full, sometimes with interest and sometimes not. Well-known examples of returnable deposits are those for returnable containers such as soft drink bottles, oil drums, or beer kegs. Also, many landlords require security deposits that are to be returned in full at the end of a lease, as long as the tenants do not cause any damage to the property. These examples are actual exchanges of cash between the user and the seller. The credit card imprint that your local Blockbuster video store takes serves the same purpose; it assures that videos will be returned. However, because cash changes hands only if Blockbuster charges the credit card because the video is not returned, the act of taking the imprint does not lead to the recording of an item on Blockbuster's financial statements.

Companies that receive deposits record them as a form of payable, although the word payable may not be a part of their specific labeling. The accounting entries by the recipients of deposits have the following basic pattern (numbers assumed in thousands of dollars):

	Interest-Bearing			**Non-Interest-Bearing**		
1. Deposit	Cash	100		Cash	100	
	Deposits (payable)		100	Deposits (payable)		100
2. Interest	Interest expense	9		No entry		
recognized	Deposits		9			
3. Deposit	Deposits	109		Deposits	100	
returned	Cash		109	Cash		100

The account Deposits is a current liability of the company receiving the deposit. Ordinarily the recipient of the cash deposit may use the cash for investment purposes from the date of deposit to the date of its return to the depositor. For example, landlords may deposit security deposits in interest-bearing accounts. In some states the interest earned is kept by the landlord, in others the interest must be paid to the tenant.

UNEARNED REVENUE

Under accrual accounting, revenues that a company collects before it delivers services or goods are called unearned revenue. These unearned revenues are current liabilities because they require a company either to deliver the product or service or to make a full refund. Examples include lease rentals, magazine subscriptions, insurance premiums, advance airline or theater ticket sales, and advance repair service contracts. The journal entries to record $100,000 of prepayments for services and the subsequent performance of those services and appropriate revenue recognition would be as follows:

```
Cash .............................................  100,000
    Unearned sales revenues  ........................          100,000
To record advance collections from customers
Unearned sales revenues  ...........................  100,000
    Sales  ........................................          100,000
To record sales revenues when products are
delivered to customers who paid in advance
```

Companies use a variety of labels for unearned revenues or revenues collected in advance of their being earned. For example, Dow Jones & Company lists "Unexpired subscriptions," and Wang Laboratories shows "Unearned service revenue." Some people also refer to these advance collections as deferred credits. Why? Because as the second entry shows, the ultimate accounting entry is a "credit" to revenue, but such an entry has been deferred to a later accounting period.

Consider a basketball team that sells season tickets for $100 each, collected at the beginning of the season. The accounting period is a calendar year, but typically 40% of the games occur in November and December whereas the other 60% occur in January and February. The team sells all of its 15,000 seats to season ticket holders for the 2001 to 2002 season. Indicate how these facts would affect the income statement and the balance sheet for 2001 and the income statement for 2002.

ANSWER

In 2001, the team would collect $100 × 15,000 = $1,500,000. However, it would earn only 40% of it ($600,000) in 2001, so the 2001 income statement would show only $600,000 of revenue. The 2001 balance sheet would show a current liability of 60% × $1,500,000 = $900,000, labeled Revenue received in advance or unearned service revenue. This $900,000 is deferred and will be recognized as income on the 2001 income statement when it is earned by the playing of the remaining games.

INTERNAL CONTROL OVER PAYABLES

Objective 2
Design an internal control system for cash disbursements.

purchase order A document that specifies the items ordered and the price to be paid by the ordering company.

receiving report A document that specifies the items received by the company and the condition of the items.

invoice A bill from the seller to a buyer indicating the number of items shipped, their price, and any additional costs (such as shipping) along with payment terms, if any.

Huge sums flow through corporate bank accounts as sales are collected and payments for goods and services are made. It is important to create internal controls over cash disbursements to assure that all payments involve properly approved and valid obligations of the company. Thus, most disbursement systems require that all payments are made by check. Why? Prenumbered checks make record keeping easy, and companies can thus trace exactly how much of their money is going where.

Most payables systems require that all checks issued must be supported by source documents. This means that before a check is written a series of steps are completed to document the obligation. One document is the **purchase order,** which specifies that the items were ordered by the company at specific prices. A second document is the **receiving report,** which indicates that the shipment was received and verifies the number of items and their condition on receipt. The company does not want to pay for unordered merchandise or merchandise received in damaged condition. Once the purchase order, receiving report, and the invoice from the seller are matched and found to be in agreement, the check can be issued. The **invoice** is a bill from the seller specifying number of units and price per unit along with freight charges the buyer is responsible to pay, plus any payment terms such as cash discounts for prompt payment or quantity discounts.

Checks in excess of a specified amount typically require additional authorization and must be signed by two people (usually by a supervisor, manager, or accountant). This process leaves a paper trail that is easy to follow in case anything should go wrong. It permits periodic, systematic reviews to assure that nothing does go wrong. Because multiple people are involved, errors should be avoided or detected early before their consequences are large.

What can go wrong? An employee could create a bank account for a fictitious company (Fred's Fraud Inc.) and write checks to it. By requiring different employees to create the source documents, keep purchase records, and issue the checks, companies make it harder to succeed with such frauds. More people see the transactions and begin to wonder exactly what sort of business the company does with Fred's Fraud Inc.

With computer automation, a file of approved vendors can be maintained. Checks can be written only to approved vendors, and a high-level employee must approve all additions to the vendor list. Some corporations have created computer networks with their suppliers that generate automatic payments when the proper source information is provided electronically by the supplier.

Even with the best control system, mistakes can and do occur. The most common mistake is overpayment, which is usually caused by multiple billings. For various reasons, such as late payment, suppliers will sometimes send out two or more bills for the same goods. Companies can then mistakenly overpay by paying both bills instead of just one. Fortunately, most companies strive to provide honest and efficient service to both their customers and suppliers. Generally, the overpayment is detected by the supplier's internal control system over cash receipts and receivables. The supplier then either refunds the money or provides a credit on the payer's account with the supplier.

LONG-TERM LIABILITIES

Some long-term liabilities are similar to short-term liabilities except for the time frame. For example, long-term loans such as car loans or home mortgage loans are similar to notes payable. In these circumstances, money is borrowed and a contract is signed that defines the terms under which the borrower will repay the lender. The accounting for these contracts involves reporting the liability on the balance sheet and recording interest expense in the income statement. As time passes, interest and principal payments eliminate the loan obligation.

Objective 3
Explain simple long-term liabilities.

Consider Michelle Young's loan to purchase a $14,000 car on January 1, 20X0. She has only $4,000 cash, so she borrows $10,000 at 10% interest, agreeing to pay $3,154.71 each December 31 from 20X0 through 20X3. (Normally she would make payments monthly, but for simplicity we assume annual payments.) Exhibit 8-2 illustrates the loan amortization schedule. This schedule shows the amounts of interest accrued, cash paid, and remaining balance for each year over the life of the loan.

Michelle's total payments are $12,618.83, which consists of interest of $2,618.83 and her repayment of the $10,000 principal. These amounts are the totals of columns 2, 3, and 4, respectively, in Exhibit 8-2. Notice that her payments are $3,154.71 for 3 years and one cent less in the final year. In the first year the payment includes $1,000 in interest (10% × $10,000 of principal). The remainder of the payment, $2,154.71, is applied to reduce the principal amount to $7,845.29 as shown in column 5. That new balance then becomes the basis for interest calculation in year two. The journal entry to record the first year payment would be:

Interest expense	1,000.00	
Liability	2,154.71	
Cash		3,154.71

BONDS AND NOTES

Notes and bonds are common financial contracts that businesses use to raise money. Both are legal contracts that specify how much is to be borrowed as well as the dates and

Exhibit 8-2

Analysis of Car Loan

Year	(1) Beginning Liability	(2) End-of-Year Cash Payment	(3) Interest @ 10% (1) × 0.10	(4) Reduction of Principal (2) − (3)	(5) Ending Liability (1) − (4)
20X0	$10,000.00	$ 3,154.71	$1,000.00	$ 2,154.71	$7,845.29
20X1	7,845.29	3,154.71	784.53	2,370.18	5,475.11
20X2	5,475.11	3,154.71	547.51	2,607.20	2,867.91
20X3	2,867.91	3,154.70	286.79	2,867.91	0.00
		$12,618.83	$2,618.83	$10,000.00	

negotiable Legal financial contracts that can be transferred from one lender to another.

private placement A process whereby notes are issued by corporations when money is borrowed from a few sources, not from the general public.

bonds Formal certificates of debt that include (1) a promise to pay interest in cash at a specified annual rate plus (2) a promise to pay the principal at a specific maturity date.

nominal interest rate (contractual rate, coupon rate, stated rate) A contractual rate of interest paid on bonds.

principal (face amount) The loan amount that a borrower promises to repay at a specific maturity date.

interest rate The percentage applied to a principal amount to calculate the interest charged.

amounts for repayment by the borrower. Notes and bonds are often called **negotiable** financial instruments or securities because they can be transferred from one lender to another (thus the term negotiable). Sometimes these securities are created to borrow directly from a financial institution such as a pension plan or insurance company. Notes and bonds issued for these purposes are known as **private placements** because they are not held or traded among the general public. Private placements provide over half the capital borrowed by corporations in the United States. They are popular because they are generally easy to arrange and because they allow the lender to evaluate the creditworthiness of the borrower very carefully and directly. Specific features of the loan agreement can be tailored to the lender and borrower.

Corporations have heavy demands for borrowed capital, so they often borrow from the general public by issuing bonds in the financial markets. **Bonds** are formal certificates of debt that include (1) a promise to pay interest in cash at a specified annual rate (often called the **nominal interest rate, contractual rate, coupon rate,** or **stated rate**) plus (2) a promise to pay the **principal** (often called the **face amount**) of the loan amount at a specific maturity date. The interest is usually paid every 6 months. Fundamentally, bonds are individual promissory notes issued to many lenders.

The **interest rate** on the bond represents the return the lender earns for loaning the money. A basic principle about interest is that lenders charge higher interest rates for riskier loans. Compare a $1,000 bond issued by the U.S. government and a $1,000 bond issued by DaimlerChrysler. In 2000, the U.S. government bond might pay interest of 6% per year. On June 1, 2000, DaimlerChrysler issued $2 billion in "global E-bonds." One billion dollars of the issue had a 5-year maturity and paid just under 8% and the other $1 billion had a 10-year maturity and paid just over 8%. DaimlerChrysler bonds carry a slightly higher interest rate because they are riskier than the debt of the U.S. government. The global E-bonds are traded over Goldman Sachs' proprietary trading system called Web.ET. On this Web-based information system both buyers and sellers can have access to live market quotes for these bonds. This ability to obtain information and trade corporate securities electronically is another example of the broad effects that electronic innovations are having on all types of businesses.

BOND ACCOUNTING

Suppose that on December 31, 2000, a company issued 10,000 2-year, 10% debentures, at par. Par means that the company received exactly the amount of the bond principal. Bonds typically have a principal or face value of $1,000 each. Thus, in this case the total issue is for $10 million (10,000 × $1,000). Panel A of Exhibit 8-3 shows how the issuer would account for the bonds throughout their life, assuming that they are held to maturity. The interest expense equals the amount of the interest payments, 5% × $10 million = $500,000 each 6 months. The interest expense (and the cash payments for interest) totals $2,000,000 over the four semiannual periods. The journal entries for the issue appear in panel B of Exhibit 8-3.

The issuer's balance sheet at December 31, 2001 (at the end of the first year, after paying semiannual interest) shows:

Bonds payable, 10% due December 31, 2002	$10,000,000

We cover bond accounting in more detail in Chapter 9.

MORTGAGE BONDS AND DEBENTURES

mortgage bond A form of long-term debt that is secured by the pledge of specific property.

Different lenders have different priority claims in collecting their money. For example, **mortgage bonds** are a form of long-term debt that is secured by the pledge of specific property. In case of default, these bondholders can sell the pledged property to satisfy their

Exhibit 8-3

Bond Transactions: Issued at Par

($ in Thousands)

PANEL A: ANALYSIS					
	A	=	L	+	SE
	Cash		Bonds Payable		Retained Income
Issuer's records					
1. Issuance	+10,000	=	+10,000		
2. Semiannual interest (repeated twice a year for 2 years)	−500	=			−500 ⌈Increase⌉ Interest ⌊Expense⌋
3. Maturity value (final payment)	−10,000	=	−10,000		

PANEL B: JOURNAL ENTRIES		
1. Cash	10,000,000	
Bonds payable		10,000,000
To record proceeds upon issuance of 10% bonds maturing on December 31, 2002.		
2. Interest expense	500,000	
Cash		500,000
To record payment of interest each six-month period.		
3. Bonds payable	10,000,000	
Cash		10,000,000
To record payment of maturity value of bonds and their retirement.		

claims. Moreover, the holders of mortgage bonds have a further unsecured claim on the corporation if the proceeds from the pledged property are not enough to cover the debt.

In contrast, debenture holders have a lower priority claim to recover their loan amount. A **debenture** is a debt security with a general claim against the company's total assets, instead of a particular asset. To see how a debenture bond's claim works, suppose a company defaults and is liquidated to repay the creditors. An example of a default would be when a borrower does not make an interest or principal payment at the required time. **Liquidation** means converting assets to cash and paying off outside claims. The act of default often gives bondholder's the right to require liquidation. After liquidation, a debenture bondholder shares the available assets with other general creditors, such as trade creditors who seek to recover their accounts payable claims.

If all claims were of equal priority, individual claimants would receive a share in the liquidated assets proportional to their percentage of the total claim. However, as we have just seen, not all claims are equal. Mortgage bonds take priority over debenture bonds because they set aside certain assets for the claimants. Interestingly enough, not all general claims are equal. Some debenture bonds are **subordinated,** which means that their holders have claims against only the assets that remain after satisfying the claims of other general creditors.

To clarify these ideas, suppose a liquidated company had a single asset, a building, that was sold for $110,000 cash. The liabilities total $160,000 as follows:

debenture A debt security with a general claim against all assets instead of a specific claim against particular assets.

liquidation Converting assets to cash and paying off outside claims.

subordinated debentures Debt securities whose holders have claims against only the assets that remain after the claims of general creditors are satisfied.

Liabilities	
Accounts payable	$ 50,000
First-mortgage bonds	80,000
Subordinated bonds	30,000
Total liabilities	$160,000

The mortgage bondholders, having a direct claim on the building, will be paid in full ($80,000). The trade creditors (the company's suppliers, to whom the company owes money) will be paid the remaining $30,000 for their $50,000 claim ($0.60 on the dollar). The subordinated debenture claimants will get what is left over—nothing. Suppose their $30,000 of bonds were not subordinated. The bondholders would have a general claim on assets equivalent to that of the company suppliers. The $30,000 of cash remaining after paying $80,000 to the mortgage holders would then be used to settle the remaining $80,000 claims of the suppliers and bondholders proportionally as follows:

Liabilities		Payments	
Accounts payable	$ 50,000	5/8 × 30,000 =	18,750
First-mortgage bonds	80,000		80,000
Unsubordinated bonds	30,000	3/8 × 30,000 =	11,250
	$160,000		$110,000

In order of priority, we have the mortgage bond, then the debenture and accounts payable, and finally the subordinated debenture. Because interest rates are higher for riskier bonds, you can see that mortgage bonds would have the lowest interest rate and debentures would have the next lowest. Subordinated debentures would carry the highest interest rate.

BOND PROVISIONS

Objective 4
Relate bond covenants to the riskiness of a bond.

trust indenture A contract whereby the issuing corporation of a bond promises a trustee that it will abide by stated provisions.

protective covenant (covenant) A provision stated in a bond, usually to protect the bondholders' interests.

An issue of bonds is usually accompanied by a **trust indenture,** in which the issuing corporation promises a trustee (someone who will look after the interests of the lenders—usually a bank or trust company) that it will abide by stated provisions, often called **protective covenants** or simply **covenants.** The covenant provisions pertain to payments of principal and interest, sales of pledged property, restrictions on dividends, and like matters. In general, the indenture's purpose is to protect the bondholders' interests. Based on the concept of less risky bonds paying lower interest, you can see that these covenants have the ability to make the bond safer and to lower the interest rate.

Suppose you were thinking of investing in bonds but were worried that the company already had significant debt. You feared that after the company raised the current planned $1 million by issuing bonds, it would proceed to borrow more through various vehicles and eventually be unable to meet interest payments and repay principle. If the company would include a covenant in the bond indenture that promised "your" bond would be immediately repaid if other new debt were issued, your comfort level would increase significantly, and you might even be willing to lend the money at a lower interest rate than you were previously contemplating.

For example, Gap Inc. indicated "Borrowings under the Company's loan and credit agreements are subject to the Company maintaining certain levels of tangible net worth and financial ratios." If Gap failed to do so, the principal amount of the loans would become due immediately. Dockers' 1999 annual report discloses a revolving credit agreement. The agreement allows Dockers to borrow up to $50 million as needed at an agreed-upon interest rate. The borrowable amount is linked to the amount of accounts receivable and inventory that Dockers has. There is also a tangible net worth covenant that further restricts the loan size based on the company's financial condition. The Gap and Dockers examples illustrate the ways in which lending arrangements are easily tailored to specific borrowers and situations. In general, the more covenants there are, the more restricted the borrower is, and the more attractive the arrangement is to the lender.

BUSINESS FIRST
Bond Covenants

A simple bond is a promise to pay interest and to repay principle at specific times. However, investors have learned that to control the risk that a borrower cannot pay, it is useful to limit the borrower's freedom in a number of ways by writing restrictions into the bond contract. These covenants take many forms and may limit the ability to pay dividends, the ability to borrow additional amounts, and/or specify maintenance of certain ratios such as debt/equity, current ratio, etc.

For such covenants to be powerful, they typically require the borrower to provide the lender with audited financial statements every quarter and require the auditor to assure that no violations of the covenants have occurred. If the covenants are violated, the debt typically comes due immediately. Although the lender may not require repayment in full when this happens, the default provides the opportunity for the lender to renegotiate the terms of the loan. That may involve earlier repayment, a higher interest rate, issuance of common stock, or some other remedy.

Covenants tend to evolve in response to observed risks. It is currently common for bonds to have a "change of control" feature, which means that when the ownership of the equity (common stock) of a company changes hands, the bonds become immediately due and payable. This feature might be called the RJR provision because it became common after R.J. Reynolds Tobacco Company (RJR) was acquired. This major tobacco company had various bonds outstanding when it was acquired by Kohlberg, Kravis, Roberts & Co. (KKR), a leveraged buyout firm. In the transaction the buyer, KKR, issued many additional bonds that were equal to RJR's existing bonds in seniority. In the process the new company became very debt-heavy, and investors worried that the existing bonds would never be repaid. Existing bonds fell some 14% in value on the day the takeover was announced. Thereafter, many lenders inserted a change-of-control feature into their bonds to assure they had the right to get their full maturity value back whenever a takeover occurred.

CALLABLE, SINKING FUND, AND CONVERTIBLE BONDS

Most companies have an assortment of long-term debt, including a variety of bonds payable. There are too many types of bonds to discuss them all here. However, we can focus on some of the more important and popular types.

Some bonds are **callable**, which means that they are subject to redemption before maturity at the option of the issuer. Typically the call is at a redemption price in excess of par. The excess over par is referred to as a **call premium.** To illustrate, consider a bond issued in 2000 with a 2020 maturity date, which might be callable any time after 2015. Then it may be subject to call for an initial price in 2015 of 105 (105% of par), in 2016 of 104, in 2017 of 103, and so on. The call premium declines from $50 per $1,000 bond to $40 in 2016 and so on. This call feature is good for the borrower because the borrower has a choice to redeem the bond early or wait to maturity. The feature creates uncertainty for the lender, who might therefore require a slightly higher interest rate on callable bonds. The call premium compensates the lender for the risk of unexpected early redemption.

Sinking fund bonds require the issuer to make annual payments into a sinking fund. A **sinking fund** is a pool of cash or securities set aside solely for meeting certain obligations. It is an asset that is usually classified as part of a balance sheet category called "investments" or "other assets." The sinking fund helps assure the bondholders that enough cash will be on hand to repay the bond's principal at maturity. These provisions increase the attractiveness of the bond to lenders and lower the interest rate.

Convertible bonds are those bonds that may, at the lenders' option, be exchanged for other securities. The conversion is usually for a preset number of shares of the issuing company's common stock. Because of the conversion feature, convertible bondholders are willing to accept a lower interest rate than on a similar bond without the conversion privilege.

callable bonds Bonds subject to redemption before maturity at the option of the issuer.

call premium The amount by which the redemption price of a callable bond exceeds par.

sinking fund bonds Bonds with indentures that require the issuer to make annual payments to a sinking fund.

sinking fund A pool of cash or securities set aside for meeting certain obligations.

convertible bonds Bonds that may, at the holder's option, be exchanged for other securities.

The body of the balance sheet usually summarizes the various types of bonds and other long-term debt on one line with details in the footnotes. Coca-Cola recently listed five specific bonds and notes totaling $856 million. Coca-Cola only discloses U.S. dollar-based debt in 2000 although in 1996 one of the company's bond series was payable in yen and another in German marks. Many international companies borrow around the world. In 2000, for example, ExxonMobil had $331 million of Swiss franc obligations and an additional $598 million of assorted "foreign currency obligations."

RESTRUCTURING

restructuring   A significant makeover of part of the company typically involving the closing of plants, firing of employees, and relocation of activities.

During the 1990s many companies recorded restructuring charges, and some recognized significant liabilities for future costs. A **restructuring** is a significant makeover of part of the company. It typically involves the closing of one or more plants, firing of a significant number of employees, and termination or relocation of various activities. For example, Compaq recorded $868 million in restructuring and related charges in 1999, following recognition of $393 million of such costs in the prior year. By year-end 1999, Compaq had already paid $709 million of the $1,261 million total. It reported a liability for the remaining $552 million to be paid in future years. Note that the charge against the income statement is in anticipation of costs to be incurred as the company executes the plan. The liability at year-end is for the remaining unexecuted costs. It may be classified as current or long-term depending upon when the costs will actually be incurred.

DEFERRED TAXES

Objective 5
Interpret deferred tax liabilities.

We have previously seen that delays in payment of taxes between the time that income is earned and taxes are due leads to short-term taxes payable. There is another source of difference between when income is recognized in the financial statements and when it is reported to the tax authorities that arises because of differences between U.S. income tax rules and the GAAP requirements for financial reporting. Sometimes the difference between GAAP reporting and tax laws forces some income tax expense to be recorded long before it is paid and thus creates a deferred income tax liability. For example, General Electric (GE) reported income tax expense of $5.7 billion in its 2000 financial statements. However, GE paid only $4.6 billion in income taxes and deferred the remainder to future years.

The differences arise because GAAP is designed to provide useful information to investors, while the tax code is written to generate revenue for the government. Revenue recognition and expense recognition rules for tax purposes can differ from GAAP rules on two dimensions: (1) whether an item is recognized (permanent differences) and (2) when it is recognized (temporary differences).

To save their companies money, good managers struggle to pay the least amount of income tax at the latest possible moment permitted within the law. As a result, they delay the reporting of taxable revenue as long as possible, while deducting tax-deductible expense items as quickly as possible. This leads the tax return to report the smallest taxable income consistent with the law and the firm's financial results. Taxes paid to the government are calculated as a percentage of the taxable income that results from subtracting tax deductible expenses from taxable revenue. The percentage is called the **tax rate.** U.S. corporations face graduated tax rates ranging from 15% on incomes under $50,000 to 35% on incomes over $335,000. Many states also levy an income tax, with tax rates varying from state to state. To simplify our illustrations, we generally assume a flat tax rate of 40%. This is a reasonable approximation of the combination of the federal 35% statutory (legally set) rate plus a state tax rate.

Net income before taxes for financial reporting may differ from taxable income because differences in rules create the difference or because managers make different

tax rate   The percentage of taxable income paid to the government.

choices of accounting treatment for financial reporting than for tax. Although the company tries to minimize taxable income to minimize taxes, it does not have the same incentive for financial reporting purposes. Reporting higher net income may often be desirable for financial reporting purposes, to increase bonuses or to make the company appear more profitable. For simplicity, we illustrate these issues with one permanent difference, municipal bond interest, and two timing differences, depreciation and warranty expense.

PERMANENT DIFFERENCES

Permanent differences involve either revenue or expense items that a company recognizes for tax purposes but does not recognize under GAAP, or items that it does not recognize for tax purposes but recognizes under GAAP. For example, suppose a company owns a bond issued by the city of Seattle and periodically receives interest income on it. Under GAAP, this interest income is reported on the income statement. Under federal law, interest on municipal bonds issued by cities, states, and towns is not taxed. Dealing with this permanent difference is straightforward. It is included as income for financial reporting but no income tax expense is recognized because no income tax will ever be paid. Thus, permanent differences do not have a tax effect.

permanent differences
Revenue or expense items that are recognized for tax purposes but not recognized under GAAP, or vice versa.

TEMPORARY DIFFERENCES

Temporary or **timing differences** arise because some revenue and expense items are recognized at different times for tax purposes than for financial reporting purposes. A common temporary difference arises when firms use a special accelerated depreciation [Modified Accelerated Cost Recovery (MACRS)] for tax purposes, while using straight-line depreciation for financial reporting. Suppose a small company earns $40,000 per year before deducting depreciation and taxes and pays taxes at a rate of 40% of taxable income. The company acquires a $10,000 asset with a 2-year useful life. It can deduct the $10,000 immediately for tax purposes and will depreciate it at $5,000 per year for book purposes.

timing differences (temporary differences)
Differences between net income and taxable income that arise because some revenue and expense items are recognized at different times for tax purposes than for reporting purposes.

Examine panel A of Exhibit 8-4. The total tax paid to the government over the 2 years will be $12,000 + $16,000 = $28,000, which is 40% of the 2 years of combined taxable income $30,000 + $40,000 = $70,000. How should this fact be shown for financial reporting purposes? One approach is to report the amount actually paid to the government each year, but the Financial Accounting Standards Board (FASB) does not permit this alternative. When timing differences arise, GAAP requires a hypothetical tax expense number. It is the tax that would have been paid if the pretax income used for shareholder reporting had also been reported to the tax authorities. Panel B of Exhibit 8-4 illustrates both approaches.

In our example, the company has a stable economic earnings pattern. When the tax expense is based on the financial reporting numbers, that stable pattern is evident in a constant $21,000 net income over the 2 years. However, if the actual tax paid is used to measure tax expense, the apparent pattern of net income is a declining one, from $23,000 to $19,000. Because the use of the actual tax amount paid to the government tends to distort the pattern of reported earnings, the FASB requires companies to calculate tax expense based on the accounting methods used for financial reporting purposes. This requirement correctly matches the income tax expense with the income to which it relates.

How is this hypothetical income tax expense number to be recorded? The payable to the government in year one is $12,000, but tax expense of $14,000 is being recorded. Think of it as a current payable for the $12,000 currently owed to the government and a $2,000

Exhibit 8-4

The Logic of Financial Reporting of Tax Expense

	PANEL A: FINANCIAL REPORTING DIFFERS FROM TAX RETURN			
	Financial Reporting		**Income Tax Return**	
	Year 1	*Year 2*	*Year 1*	*Year 2*
Income before depreciation and taxes	$40,000	$40,000	$40,000	$40,000
Depreciation	5,000	5,000	10,000	0
Pretax income	$35,000	$35,000	$30,000	$40,000
Taxes payable at 40%			$12,000	$16,000

	PANEL B: CALCULATING NET INCOME			
	Tax Expense Based on Financial Reporting (Required)		**Tax Expense Based on Tax Paid (Not Allowed)**	
	Year 1	*Year 2*	*Year 1*	*Year 2*
Pretax income	$35,000	$35,000	$35,000	$35,000
Tax expense	14,000*	14,000*	12,000[†]	16,000[†]
Net income	$21,000	$21,000	$23,000	$19,000

* $14,000 is 40% of $35,000.

[†] From the tax return columns in panel A 40% $\times$ $30,000 = $12,000; 40% $\times$ $40,000 = $16,000.

deferred tax liability An obligation arising because of predictable future taxes, to be paid when a future tax return is filed.

liability that arises because of predictable future taxes. This $2,000 liability is called a **deferred tax liability,** because it will be paid only when a future tax return is filed. The journal entry would be:

```
Income tax expense  . . . . . . . . . . . . . . . . .   14,000
      Deferred tax liability  . . . . . . . . . . . . .           2,000
      Cash (or taxes payable)  . . . . . . . . . . .          12,000
```

Note that the deferred tax liability of $2,000 is shown on the balance sheet. It is equal to the tax rate of 40% times the $5,000 timing difference in depreciation expense ($5,000 on the books versus $10,000 on the tax return). This can be seen not only as a difference in depreciation but also as a difference in the book values of the assets. The undepreciated cost for financial reporting at the end of year one is $5,000 (cost of $10,000 less depreciation of $5,000). The undepreciated cost for tax purposes at the end of year one is $0 (cost of $10,000 less immediate deduction of $10,000). The deferred tax liability is the tax rate times the difference in undepreciated cost [40% of ($5,000 less $0)]. In this example we are assuming that tax rates are always constant at 40%. Details about how to treat changing tax rates are deferred to future courses.

Remember that differences between reported income and taxable income result in deferral of taxes, not cancellation of taxes. For almost a decade, General Dynamics Corporation, a large defense contractor took advantage of tax deferral. From 1973 through 1984, General Dynamics reported total pretax income of $2.7 billion and total federal income tax expense of $1 billion for financial reporting purposes. How much income tax did General Dynamics pay during this period? Zero! Thanks to a quirk in the tax law concerning revenue recognition on very long-term government contracts (that has since been changed), the company managed to defer income taxes completely. Eventually, in the years 1987 through 1992, the company paid income taxes totaling $1.6

billion. This amount exceeded income tax expense during these periods as the timing differences between tax and financial reporting reversed. General Dynamics' shareholders were happy though. The decade of delayed taxes was equivalent to an interest-free loan from the government.

Not all temporary differences result in early deduction for tax purposes and later deduction for financial reporting. Unlike depreciation expenses, expenses for warranty costs are typically deducted earlier for financial reporting purposes than they are for tax purposes. In such cases, a deferred tax asset is recorded to acknowledge that the taxes being paid now are higher than the tax expense provided, based on pretax income reported for financial purposes.

The balance sheet of nearly every company contains deferred tax liabilities. The following schedule illustrates the magnitude of the deferred tax liability as reported by various companies in 1999. We show the deferred tax liability along with the total stockholders' equity and total assets to provide perspective ($ in millions):

Company	Deferred Tax	Stockholders' Equity	Total Assets
ExxonMobil	$16,251	$63,466	$144,521
IBM	1,354	20,511	87,495
McDonald's	1,174	9,639	20,983
Merck	3,365	13,242	35,635

The deferred tax liability, expressed as a percentage of total assets, varies for these firms from 11% for ExxonMobil to 2% for IBM. For most companies the primary source of deferred taxes is timing differences related to depreciation. In a recent survey of international practice, 60% of the countries surveyed required the use of deferred taxes when financial reporting of expenses differed from the timing of reporting of corresponding tax deductions.

CONTINGENT LIABILITIES

A **contingent liability** is a potential (possible) liability that depends on a future event arising out of a past transaction. Sometimes it has a definite amount. For instance, company X may guarantee the payment on a related company Y's note payable. In other words, company X will pay if, and only if, company Y fails to pay. Such a note payable is the liability (either current or long-term) of the primary borrower (company Y) and the contingent liability of the guarantor (company X). More often, a contingent liability has an indefinite amount. A common example is a lawsuit. Many companies have lawsuits pending against them. These are possible obligations of indefinite amounts. Why? Because if a judge rules against the company, it will be obligated to pay an amount that is currently unknown. However, the judge may rule in the company's favor, in which case there is no obligation and may even be a receivable because the company has made counterclaims.

Some companies show contingent liabilities on the balance sheet. Most often they are listed after long-term liabilities but before stockholders' equity. United Technologies has sales of more than $26.6 billion in providing "high-technology products to customers in the aerospace, building systems, and automotive industries throughout the world." The 2000 balance sheet has a line labeled "Commitments and contingent liabilities (notes 4 and 14)" at the end of the liabilities. As is usually the case, no amount is shown in the body of the balance sheet. The item is listed solely to direct readers to the details in the footnotes. The United Technologies footnotes are lengthy. Note 4 describes the commitments that the company often makes to customers to provide relatively long-term financing for

contingent liability A potential liability that depends on a future event arising out of a past transaction.

Objective 6
Locate and understand the contingent liabilities information in a company's financial statements.

future purchases. Note 14 describes potential and actual liability for environmental contamination at various waste disposal sites (and other risks). It reveals that some amounts have already been accrued for some sites where responsibility has been established or clean-up is underway. These would be included in expenses when accrued and carried as part of "other liabilities" until paid.

Footnote disclosure of lawsuits is very common. Most companies have some lawsuits pending concerning the environment, product liability, or employment issues. The result of such litigation is extremely hard to estimate. Some years ago IBM lost a multimillion-dollar lawsuit for patent violation. On appeal, the verdict was reversed, and IBM ended up collecting damages from the plaintiff. The uncertainty involved in lawsuits does not always center on whether the verdict will be overturned. Sometimes the uncertainty concerns just how big the settlement will be. For example, Eagle Picher is a company that most recently makes auto parts but years ago did contracts for the federal government that required the use of asbestos for insulation. When the company became subject to extensive product liability claims over asbestos, it had trouble estimating the ultimate costs. The company initially estimated its costs to settle existing and future claims at $270

BUSINESS FIRST
Dow Corning, Inc.

A well-known product liability issue involved Dow Corning, Inc. In the 1980s, the company began facing many accusations from patients who were unhappy with silicone breast implants made by the company and surgically installed for reconstructive or cosmetic purposes. The accusations became lawsuits over time, and the company was confronted with a major product liability. Throughout the 1980s, Dow Corning regularly reported on its ongoing litigation. However, the lawsuits being heard in court were still fairly few, and no one knew how they might be resolved. So for several years the financial statements disclosed the litigation in some detail, but the balance sheet and income statement did not show specific numbers.

In 1991, the company recorded $25 million of pretax costs; in 1992, it recorded another $69 million. Remember that each of these amounts was intended to be a best estimate of future costs to be incurred. The product from which the claims stemmed had been produced and delivered years before. In fact, production of all silicone implants ceased in 1992. However, the liability estimates provided through 1992 were woefully inadequate. In 1993, Dow Corning recorded another pretax charge of $640 million. Combined with expected insurance coverage exceeding $600 million, the expected total cost of litigation exceeded $1.2 billion. Dow Corning and other manufacturers joined together to structure a settlement that would properly compensate plaintiffs, minimize legal costs, and allow the companies

to survive. The deal required an agreement between the plaintiffs, the companies, and the insurance carriers. In late 1994, agreement seemed close. Dow Corning provided another pretax charge of $241 million. Combined with additional expected insurance costs, the amounts set aside for injured parties approached $2 billion from Dow Corning and another similar amount from other manufacturers. There were over 19,000 pending lawsuits on this product.

In May of 1995, Dow Corning declared bankruptcy. The company claimed that too many plaintiffs were unwilling to agree to the settlement. Bankruptcy changes the company's whole litigation situation and leaves the final outcome very much in doubt. In 1998, Dow Corning recorded another pretax charge of $1.1 billion as its estimate of total additional costs to be incurred on all claims in bankruptcy, including the breast implant controversy. In 1999, Dow Corning earned $109.7 million and in the first quarter of 2000 earnings were up 24% from the prior year. Perhaps the story is nearly resolved. As this book is printed and used, the final outcome of the case will become clear as the courts rule on pending reorganization plans and discharge of plaintiff claims. However, the facts to date show the difficulty of predicting the cost of litigation. Any time your initial estimate of $25 million is off by a factor of 100, you know your prediction methods have a problem or two.

Source: Corning annual reports for various years.

million and recorded them in the financial statements as an expense, with a related liability. The company later realized that its earlier estimate was low, and the asbestos liability was increased by $544 million.

There are significant philosophical issues about responsibility for the safety of products. There are equally important questions about how to determine scientifically what is safe. Although these are important social questions, our immediate concern is: How should companies measure their obligations, disclose the nature of the obligations, and record these amounts in financial statements? For contingent liabilities, the answer is often that footnote disclosure is the best we can do.

DEBT RATIOS AND INTEREST-COVERAGE RATIOS

We have emphasized the link between the interest rate paid to lenders and the risk associated with the loan. When people take out loans to buy a car or a house, the interest on the loan is often smaller if the down payment is larger. For example, with 5% down the interest rate might be 8%, whereas it would be $7\frac{1}{2}\%$ with a 20% down payment. Lenders feel that the higher a down payment, the less risk they have. Why? Their assumption is that individual buyers who put down more of their own cash (equity) will be more likely to take care of the car and pay off the loan. How does this concept work for corporations? Debt ratios are used to measure the extent to which a company has used borrowing to finance its activity. The more the borrowing, and the less the equity, the riskier it is to lend money to the firm.

Objective 7
Use ratio analysis to assess a company's debt levels.

$$\text{Debt-to-equity ratio} = \frac{\text{Total liabilities}}{\text{Total shareholders' equity}}$$

$$\text{Long-term-debt-to-total-capital ratio} = \frac{\text{Total long-term debt}}{\text{Total shareholders' equity} + \text{Long-term debt}}$$

$$\text{Debt-to-total-assets ratio} = \frac{\text{Total liabilities}}{\text{Total assets}}$$

$$\text{Interest-coverage ratio} = \frac{\text{Pretax income} + \text{Interest expense}}{\text{Interest expense}}$$

debt-to-equity ratio Total liabilities divided by total shareholders' equity.

long-term-debt-to-total-capital ratio Total long-term debt divided by total shareholders' equity plus long-term debt.

debt-to-total-assets ratio Total liabilities divided by total assets.

interest-coverage ratio Pretax income plus interest expense divided by interest expense.

Note that the first three ratios are alternate ways of expressing what part of the firm's resources is obtained by borrowing and what part is invested by the owners. The interest-coverage ratio more directly measures the firm's ability to meet its interest obligation.

In comparing two companies, you observe that one company has little debt with a debt-to-total-assets ratio of 20%. The second company has a much higher ratio of 80%. How would you expect their interest coverage ratios to compare?

ANSWER
A low debt-to-total-assets ratio should be associated with a high interest-coverage ratio. Why? Because low relative debt means low interest costs. Interest costs are low for two reasons: (1) a small amount of debt on which to pay interest and (2) low interest rates because a small amount of borrowing creates less risk than large borrowings. All else equal, when debt levels and interest costs are low, we would expect interest coverage to be high.

Ratios by Industry & Country

Symbol	Company	Industry	Country	Debt-to-Equity Ratio
DELL	Dell	Computers	United States	.10
CPQ	Compaq	Computers	United States	.11
IBM	IBM	Computers	United States	1.40
LLY	Eli Lilly	Drugs	United States	.47
MRK	Merck	Drugs	United States	.47
XOM	ExxonMobil	Oil	United States	.19
RD	Royal Dutch	Oil	Netherlands	.23
REP	Repsol	Oil	Spain	1.52
F	Ford	Autos	United States	8.90

Source: Various Web sites and Calculations from Annual Reports

The table at the top of the page provides values for the debt-to-equity ratio that demonstrate the variation among industries and among countries. The debt burden varies greatly from firm to firm and industry to industry. For example, retailing companies, utilities, and transportation companies tend to have debt of more than 60% of their assets, which gives a debt-to-equity ratio of 1.5. Computer companies and drug companies have much lower debt levels. The very high value of 8.9 for Ford reflects the fact that Ford is not only an automobile manufacturer but also a very large financial institution, Ford Motor Credit Company, and auto leasing company, Hertz.

Debt-to-equity ratios that were thought to be too high a few years ago are becoming commonplace today. The average debt-to-total-assets ratio for major U.S. industrial companies grew from about 35% in 1960 to nearly 60% today.

SUMMARY PROBLEMS FOR YOUR REVIEW

PROBLEM ONE

Suppose that on December 31, 2000, ExxonMobil issued $12 million face value of 10-year, 10% debentures at par.

Required

1. Prepare an analysis of the following items: (a) issuance of the debentures; (b) first two semiannual interest payments; and (c) payment of the maturity value. Use the balance sheet equation (similar to Exhibit 8-3).
2. Prepare journal entries for the items in requirement 1.

SOLUTION TO PROBLEM ONE

1. See Exhibit 8-5.

2.

12/31/00:	Cash	12,000,000	
	Bonds payable		12,000,000
6/30/01:	Interest expense	600,000	
	Cash		600,000

Exhibit 8-5

Analysis of ExxonMobil's Bond Transactions: Problem One

($ in Thousands)

	A	**=**	**L**	**+**	**SE**
	Cash		*Bonds Payable*		*Retained Income*
Exxon Mobil's records					
1. Issuance	12,000		12,000		
2. Semiannual interest					
6 months ended					⎡Increase⎤
6/30/01	−600				−600 ⎢Interest⎢
12/31/01	−600				−600 ⎣Expense⎦
3. Maturity value					
(final payment)	−12,000		−12,000		
Bond-related totals*	−12,000		0		−12,000

* Totals after all 20 interest payments (20 × $600) and payment at maturity.

12/31/01: Interest expense	....	600,000	
Cash	....		600,000
12/31/10: Bonds payable	....	12,000,000	
Cash	....		12,000,000

PROBLEM TWO

Suppose that you are preparing financial statements for Liz Claiborne, Inc., a fashion company that designs and markets many types of clothing and accessories, including the Liz Claiborne and Dana Buchman brands. You notice that there are several lawsuits pending against the company. How would you assess the nature of accounting disclosures required? What choices do you have?

SOLUTION TO PROBLEM TWO

The first step would be to determine the details of the lawsuits and the size of potential losses. The second step would be to get expert legal opinions with respect to the status of the suits. How far along in the process are they? How likely are they to cause changes in the financial statements? The possible actions include (1) recording a liability and recognizing an expense in the income statement, (2) providing a footnote that describes the issue without explicitly recording an amount, or (3) not saying anything because the materiality of the possible loss is small and/or the likelihood of the loss is small.

Not all companies face problems such as those discussed in the text concerning asbestos or medical products liabilities. Liz Claiborne is not the kind of company that typically faces large legal risks. Nevertheless, its January 1, 2000 balance sheet includes a line labeled Commitments and contingencies with no number recorded. The notes describe several risks. For example, the company discloses that 48% of sales are with three customers. This is not a liability, but is disclosed to help alert readers to the fact that Liz Claiborne's sales and collectibility of its receivables are linked to a few large accounts. Another reference is to legal proceedings and says: "The Company is party to several pending legal proceedings and claims. Although the outcome of such actions cannot be determined with certainty, management is of the opinion that the final outcome should not have a material adverse effect on the Company's results of operations or financial position."

PROBLEM THREE

The Solar Kitchen Corporation manufactures and sells energy-efficient additions to provide solar-heated eating areas next to existing kitchens. Because of good styling and marketing to an energy-conscious public, sales have grown briskly. Solar Kitchen has no preexisting deferred tax liability. During 20X0, the following transactions occurred:

1. On January 1, 10,000 new shares of common stock were sold at $100 per share.
2. Half of the proceeds from the stock sale were immediately invested in tax-free bonds yielding 6% per annum. The bonds were held throughout the year, resulting in interest revenue of $500,000 × .06 = $30,000.
3. Sales for the year were $4,500,000, with expenses of $3,800,000 reported under GAAP (exclusive of income tax expense).
4. Tax depreciation exceeded depreciation included in preceding item 3 by $300,000.
5. For financial reporting purposes, warranty costs are calculated at 1% of sales, and the resulting $45,000 is included in the $3,800,000 of expenses. Actual expenditures under warranty were $22,000. The difference is $23,000.

Required

1. Calculate earnings before tax for shareholder reporting.
2. Calculate income tax payable to the tax authorities and income tax expense for shareholder reporting using a 40% tax rate.
3. Make the appropriate journal entry. Assume the 40% tax rate is expected to be maintained.

SOLUTION TO PROBLEM THREE

1. Earnings before taxes for shareholder reporting are:

Sales revenue	$4,500,000
Interest revenue	30,000
Less operating expenses	(3,800,000)
Pretax income	$ 730,000

2. Tax calculations:

	Reporting to Tax Authorities	Reporting to Shareholders
Earnings before tax	$730,000	$730,000
Permanent differences		
Nontaxable interest	(30,000)	(30,000)
Subtotal	700,000	700,000
Timing differences		
Depreciation	(300,000)	—
Warranty expenses	23,000	—
Earnings on which tax is based	423,000	700,000
Tax rate	.40	.40
Income tax payable	$169,200	
Income tax expense reported to shareholders		$280,000

3.

Income tax expense	280,000	
Income tax payable		169,200
Deferred tax liability		110,800

Highlights to Remember

1. **Account for current liabilities.** Liabilities are obligations to pay money or to provide goods or services. An entity's liability level is important to analysts because unpaid liabilities may produce difficulties ranging from an inability to raise additional capital to forced liquidation. To help assess debt levels, financial statements typically separate liabilities requiring payment within 1 year as current liabilities. Accounting for current liabilities is a straightforward extension of procedures covered in earlier chapters. Companies record transactions as they occur, and accruals at the end of a period capture incomplete transactions such as accruing interest, wages, utilities, or taxes.

2. **Design an internal control system for cash disbursements.** Good internal control procedures require that all disbursements be by prenumbered checks. All disbursements should be supported by appropriate documentation that verifies the goods were ordered and received and that billing is consistent with the terms of the order. The goal is to assure all payments are for legitimate authorized transactions.

3. **Explain simple long-term liabilities.** Long-term liabilities involve more complex contracts that convey many rights and responsibilities over long periods of time. Companies initially record bonds, a common long-term liability, at the amount received from investors at issue. During the life of the bond, a company recognizes interest expense each period.

4. **Relate bond covenants to the riskiness of a bond.** Bond covenants restrict the behavior of the borrower or lender under a bond contract. They might require that the bond becomes immediately due and payable under certain conditions. This gives the lender more options if, for example, the debt to total assets ratio becomes very high because the company issues more new debt or suffers profitability problems. When the lender is protected from certain bad outcomes, the risk that the bond will not be repaid is less and the lender may be willing to accept a lower interest rate.

5. **Interpret deferred tax liabilities.** Deferred tax liabilities arise because the timing of tax deductions such as depreciation expense on the company's tax return is often earlier than on the company's books. When this happens, the tax payable immediately is less than it would appear to be if one examined the financial reports. To help investors understand the long-run tax obligations of the company, tax expense is reported as if taxes were paid on the net income reported to shareholders. The company recognizes a deferred tax liability to reflect predictable higher taxes in the future, when these timing differences in the recording of depreciation expense will reverse.

6. **Locate and understand the contingent liabilities information in a company's financial statements.** Contingent liabilities are uncertain in amount and timing of payment. Examples include lawsuits, contract disputes, possible losses on multiyear contracts, and environmental liabilities. Companies use footnote disclosure to alert interested parties to the uncertain, unmeasurable future possibilities.

7. **Use ratio analysis to assess a company's debt levels.** Debt ratios and interest-coverage ratios are two measures used to evaluate the level of a company's indebtedness. The more debt a company has, the more problems it will face if cash flow is inadequate to meet liabilities as they fall due.

Accounting Vocabulary

Assignment Material

Questions

8-1 Distinguish between *current liabilities* and *long-term liabilities*.

8-2 Name and briefly describe five items that are often classified as current liabilities.

8-3 "Withholding taxes really add to employer payroll costs." Do you agree? Explain.

8-4 Distinguish between *employee* payroll taxes and *employer* payroll taxes.

8-5 "Product warranties expense should not be recognized until the actual services are performed. Until then you don't know which products might require warranty repairs." Do you agree? Explain.

8-6 Why do companies require source documents before they will issue a check?

8-7 "If companies pay a bill twice, they are out of luck. No company is going to return the money after receiving it." Do you agree? Explain.

8-8 Distinguish between a *mortgage bond* and a *debenture*. Which is safer?

8-9 Distinguish between *subordinated* and *unsubordinated* debentures.

8-10 "The face amount of a bond is what you can sell it for." Do you agree? Explain.

8-11 "Protective covenants protect the shareholders' interests in cases of liquidation of assets." Do you agree? Explain.

8-12 Bond covenants usually restrict the borrower's rights in various ways. An example might be a restriction that no additional long-term debt could be issued unless the debt-to-total assets ratio was below .5. Who benefits from such a covenant? How?

8-13 Many callable bonds have a call premium for "early" calls. Who does the call premium benefit, the issuer or the purchaser of the bond? How?

8-14 "Restructuring charges recognize in today's income statement expenses that will be incurred in the future." Explain.

8-15 Compare and contrast permanent differences and temporary differences between GAAP and tax reporting.

8-16 "Differences in tax and GAAP rules lead to more depreciation being charged on tax statements than on financial reports to the public." Do you agree? Explain.

8-17 "It is unethical for big companies to recognize a large income tax expense on their income statements reported to the public but to pay a small amount to the government." Do you agree? Explain.

8-18 "A contingent liability is a liability having an estimated amount." Do you agree? Explain.

8-19 "At the balance sheet date, a private high school has lost a court case for an uninsured football injury. The amount of damages has not been set. A reasonable estimate is between $800,000 and $2 million." How should this information be presented in the financial statements?

8-20 Suppose IBM won a lawsuit for $1 million against Innovative Software, a young company with assets of $20 million. Innovative has appealed the suit. How would each company disclose this event in financial statements prepared while the appeal was under way.

8-21 We observe higher debt levels in the automobile industry than in the pharmaceutical industry. Why?

Cognitive Exercises

8-22 Lenders and Covenants

Why would a lender want to add a covenant to a loan contract concerning a maximum debt-to-total assets ratio?

8-23 Vacations and Internal Control

Two of your staff are arguing over the performance of an employee in the accounts receivable area. One is applauding the employee as a hard worker who is dedicated to the company and cites the fact that the employee never takes vacations. The other is saying that the failure to take vacation is not a virtue, but instead it is the source of concern. Which of your subordinates do you side with in this argument?

8-24 Recall of Auto Tires

During 2000, Ford Motor Company and Firestone ended up replacing thousands of Firestone tires on several Ford vehicles. Would you expect this to affect the financial results on the income statements of either company, or would it be covered by the allowance for warranty costs that they had created?

8-25 International Reporting of Liabilities

In financial statements prepared in the United Kingdom, the balance sheets begin with long-lived assets. The current assets and current liabilities are netted together to calculate working capital which is added to long-lived assets to arrive at a total called "total assets minus current liabilities." What are the arguments for structuring the balance sheet one way or the other?

EXERCISES

8-26 German Liabilities

The German company, DaimlerChrysler, one of the world's largest automakers, was formed by the merger of Daimler Benz and Chrysler. It had the following items on its June 30, 1999 balance sheet (German marks in millions):

Cash and cash equivalents	DM 9,099
Trade liabilities	15,786
Inventories	14,985
Additional paid-in capital	17,329
Accrued liabilities	37,695
Financial liabilities	64,488
Other liabilities	10,286
Deferred taxes	5,192
Deferred income	4,510

Required

Prepare the liabilities section of DaimlerChrysler's balance sheet. Include only the items that are properly included in liabilities. Note that the company does not separate current and long-term liabilities.

8-27 Accrued Employee Compensation

Weitz Company had total compensation expense for March of $23,000. The company paid $19,000 to employees during March. The remainder will be paid in April.

Required

1. Prepare the journal entry for recording the compensation expense for March.
2. Suppose salaries and wages payable were $2,000 at the beginning of March. Compute salaries and wages payable at the end of March.

8-28 Sales Taxes

(Alternate is 8-29.) The Long Lake Store is in a midwestern state where the sales tax is 7%. Total sales for the month of September were $400,000, of which $350,000 was subject to sales tax.

Required

1. Prepare a journal entry that summarizes sales (all in cash) for the month.
2. Prepare a journal entry concerning the disbursement for the sales tax.

8-29 Sales Taxes

(Alternate is 8-28.) Most of the food sold in retail stores in California is not subject to sales taxes (for example, candy), but some items are (for example, soft drinks). Apparently, the candy lobbyists were more effective than soft drinks lobbyists when dealing with the state legislature. Most cash registers are designed to record taxable sales and nontaxable sales and automatically add the appropriate sales tax.

The sales for the past week in the local Safeway store were $130,000, of which $30,000 was taxable at a rate of 7%. By using the $A = L + SE$ equation, show the impact on the entity, both now and when the sales taxes are paid at a later date. Also prepare corresponding journal entries.

8-30 Product Warranties

During 20X9, the Perez Appliance Company had sales of $800,000. The company estimates that the cost of servicing products under warranty will average 3% of sales.

Required

1. Prepare journal entries for sales revenue and the related warranty expense for 20X9. Assume all sales are for cash.

2. The liability for warranties was $11,400 at the beginning of 20X9. Expenditures (all in cash) to satisfy warranty claims during 20X9 were $20,400, of which $4,500 was for products sold in 20X9. Prepare the journal entry for the warranty expenditures.

3. Compute the balance in the Liability for Warranties account at the end of 20X9.

8-31 Unearned Revenues

The Reader's Digest Association, Inc., one of the largest publishers of magazines in the world, recently had unearned revenues of $399 million on its March 31 balance sheet. Suppose that during April, Reader's Digest delivered magazines with a sales value of $30 million to prepaid subscribers and sold subscriptions for $37 million.

Required

1. Prepare journal entries for the new subscriptions and the deliveries to prepaid subscribers.

2. Compute the amount in the unearned revenue account at the end of April.

8-32 Priorities of Claims

Ashton Real Estate Corporation is being liquidated. It has one major asset, an office building, which was converted into $19 million cash. The stockholders' equity has been wiped out by past losses. The following claims exist: accounts payable, $3 million; debentures payable, $5 million; first mortgage payable, $13 million.

Required

1. Assume the debentures are not subordinated. How much will each class of claimants receive?

2. If the debentures are subordinated, how much will each class of claimants receive? How much will each class receive if the cash proceeds from the sale of the building amount to only $14.5 million?

8-33 Deferred Taxes

IBM's net sales in 1999 exceeded $37 billion. On its income statement IBM reported the following ($ in millions):

Income before taxes	$11,757
Income tax expense	4,045
Net income	$ 7,712

Taxes due on 1999 taxable income and payments to the government for income taxes related to operations in 1999 were $1,904 million. Assume that the income tax expense and these income tax payments were the only tax-related transactions during 1999.

Required

1. Prepare the journal entry that recognizes the $4,045 million income tax expense and the $1,904 million income tax payment.

2. Compute the change in the deferred income tax liability account for 1999.

8-34 Various Liabilities

(Alternate is 8-35.)

1. Suki Du made a $10,000 savings deposit on August 1. On September 30, the bank recognized 2 months' interest thereon at an annual rate of 6%. On October 1, Du closed her account with the bank. Interest is payable from the date of deposit through the date before withdrawal. Prepare the bank's journal entries.

2. In August the Manchester Opera sold season tickets for £4.8 million cash in advance of the opera season, which begins on September 10. These tickets are for eight performance dates.
    a. What is the effect on the balance sheet of August 31? Prepare the appropriate journal entry for the sale of the tickets.
    b. Assume that six dates remain after September 30. What is the effect on the balance sheet of September 30? Prepare the related summary journal entry for September.
3. AV Corporation sells audio and video equipment. Experience has shown that warranty costs average 4% of sales. Sales for June were $10 million. Cash disbursements for rendering warranty service during June were $360,000. Prepare the journal entries for these transactions.
4. A wholesale distributor gets cash deposits for its returnable bottles. In November, the distributor received $160,000 cash and disbursed $130,000 for bottles returned. Prepare the journal entries for these transactions.
5. The county hospital has lost a lawsuit. Damages were set at $2 million. The hospital plans to appeal the decision to a higher court. The hospital's attorneys are 80% confident of a reversal of the lower court's decision. What liability, if any, should appear on the hospital's balance sheet?

8-35 Various Liabilities
(Alternate is 8-34.)

1. Maytag Corporation sells electric appliances, including automatic washing machines. Experience in recent years has indicated that warranty costs average 3.0% of sales. Sales of washing machines for April were $3.0 million. Cash disbursements and obligations for warranty service on washing machines during April totaled $81,000. Prepare the journal entries prompted by these facts.
2. Pepsi-Cola Company of New York gets cash deposits for its returnable bottles. In November, it received $100,000 cash and disbursed $95,000 for bottles returned. Prepare the journal entries concerning the receipts and returns of deposits.
3. Citibank received a $4,000 savings deposit on April 1. On June 30, it recognized interest thereon at an annual rate of 5%. On July 1, the depositor closed her account with the bank. Prepare the bank's necessary journal entries.
4. The Paramount Theater sold, for $150,000 cash, a "season's series" of tickets in advance of December 31 for five plays, each to be held in successive months, beginning in January.
    a. What is the effect on the balance sheet of December 31? What is the appropriate journal entry for the sale of the tickets?
    b. What is the effect on the balance sheet of January 31? What is the related journal entry for January?
5. Suppose a tabloid newspaper has lost a lawsuit. Damages were set at $500,000. The newspaper plans to appeal the decision to a higher court. The newspaper's attorneys are 90% confident of a reversal of the lower court's decision. What liability, if any, should be shown on the newspaper's balance sheet?

PROBLEMS

8-36 Accounting for Payroll
For the week ended January 27, the Adirondak Manufacturing Company had a total payroll of $200,000. Three items were withheld from employees' paychecks: (1) Social Security (FICA) tax of 7.1% of the payroll; (2) income taxes, which average 21% of the payroll; and (3) employees' savings that are deposited in their Credit Union, which are $10,000. All three items were paid on January 30.

1. Use the balance sheet equation to analyze the transactions on January 27 and January 30.
2. Prepare journal entries for the recording of the items in requirement 1.
3. In addition to the payroll, Adirondak pays (1) payroll taxes of 9% of the payroll, (2) health insurance premiums of $12,000, and (3) contributions to the employees' pension fund of $16,000. Prepare journal entries for the recognition and payment of these additional expenses.

Required

8-37 Analysis of Payroll and Interest
Consider a bank loan of $900,000 to a church on August 31, 20X8. The loan bears interest at 8%. Principal and interest are due in 1 year. The church reports on a calendar-year basis.

1. Prepare an analysis of transactions, using the balance sheet equation. Indicate the entries for the church for August 31, 20X8, December 31, 20X8, and August 31, 20X9. Allocate interest within the year on a straight-line basis. Show all amounts in thousands of dollars.

2. Prepare all the corresponding journal entries keyed previously.

8-38 Bonds Issued at Par

On December 31, 2000, Key Computers issued $10 million of 5-year, 10% debentures at par.

1. Compute the proceeds from issuing the debentures.

2. Using the balance sheet equation format, prepare an analysis of this bond transaction. Show entries for the issuer concerning (a) issuance, (b) first semiannual interest payment, and (c) payment of maturity value.

3. Show all the corresponding journal entries keyed as in requirement 2.

4. Show how the bond-related accounts would appear on the balance sheet as of December 31, 2000, and June 30, 2001. Assume that the semiannual interest payment and amortization due on the balance sheet date have been recorded.

8-39 Bonds Issued at Par

On January 1, 2000, Chen Electronics issued $2 million of 5-year, 11% debentures at par.

1. Compute the proceeds from issuing the debentures.

2. Using the balance sheet equation format, prepare an analysis of this bond transaction. Show entries for the issuer concerning (a) issuance, (b) first semiannual interest payment, and (c) payment of maturity value.

3. Show all the corresponding journal entries keyed as in requirement 2.

4. Show how the bond-related accounts would appear on the balance sheets as of January 1, 2001, and July 1, 2001. Assume that the semiannual interest payment and amortization due on the balance sheet dates have been recorded.

8-40 Convertible Bonds

Sometimes a small company finds it necessary to include a convertibility option to sell bonds at a reasonable interest rate. Commodore Applied Technologies is a young company in the business of separating, destroying, and neutralizing hazardous wastes. In 1993 and 1994, the company issued $4 million of convertible bonds, with each $1 face value of bonds being convertible into one common share of Commodore. The interest rate on the bonds is 8.5%, which is less than the rate the company would have paid to issue bonds without the conversion option.

In 1999, Commodore had revenues of $18.1 million and a net loss of $4.0 million. The company pays no dividends. The market price of Commodore's common shares is about $1.

1. Compute the annual interest received by the holders of the convertible bonds.

2. Suppose the price of one share of Commodore common stock rose to $1.25. If you held some of Commodore's convertible bonds, would you immediately convert your bonds to common stock? Why or why not?

3. Suppose the maturity date of the convertible bonds was rapidly approaching. Would you convert your holdings of the convertible bonds if the price of Commodore stock were $1.25 per share? If the price were $.75 per share? Explain.

8-41 Restructuring

Many well-known companies have incurred restructuring charges in recent years. Consider AT&T. In fiscal 1999, AT&T recorded a $1,506 million pretax restructuring charge. At the end of fiscal 1999, $449 million of these charges remained as liabilities on the balance sheet. After the charge, AT&T's fiscal 1999 income before income taxes was $6,685 million. The company's income before income taxes was $8,307 million in 1998.

1. Prepare the journal entry to record the restructuring charge.

2. Prepare a summary journal entry for the decreases in the accrued restructuring costs account during fiscal 1999. Assume that all the restructuring costs actually incurred in fiscal 1999 were paid in cash.

3. Compute the amount of income before income taxes AT&T would have reported for fiscal 1999 if there had been no restructuring charges. Compare this with the income before income taxes reported in fiscal 1998.

4. Which number, the reported income before income taxes reported in AT&T income statement or the number you computed in requirement 3, would be most useful in predicting AT&T's income before income taxes for fiscal 2000? Explain.

8-42 Deferred Taxes

Cadbury Schweppes is a major global company in beverages and confectionery based in London. Recent sales were more than £5 billion (where £ is the British pound). The company's income statement included the following, using Cadbury Schweppes' terminology (£ in millions):

Profit on ordinary activities before taxation	£592
Tax on profit on ordinary activities	(180)
Profit on ordinary activities after taxation	£412

As a result of operations, the deferred tax liability account increased by £32 million. There was no change in taxes payable.

Required

1. Compute the income taxes paid to the government.
2. Prepare the journal entry to record taxes on ordinary activities.
3. Explain why the amount of income taxes paid to the government was not the same as the amount of income taxes recorded on the income statement.

8-43 The Income Tax Footnote

Corning Incorporated had 1999 operating revenues of approximately $4.8 billion and income before income taxes of $687.2 million. Footnote 6 to the financial statements provided the following:

The provision for income taxes consists of the following:

	1999	1998
	($ in millions)	
Current		
United States	34.0	75.4
State and municipal	2.9	9.2
Foreign	82.8	59.3
Deferred		
United States	51.1	3.8
State and municipal	7.3	(1.0)
Foreign	(1.9)	(0.8)
Net tax expense	$176.2	$145.9

Required

1. Provide the journal entries to record income tax expense for 1999.
2. Compute net income for 1999.

8-44 Debt-to-Equity Ratios

The total debt and stockholders' equity for three companies follows ($ in thousands). The companies are described as follows:

- AT&T provides long-distance phone service and is a large, well-established company.
- Micron Technology is a fast-growing producer of memory products for electronic systems.
- Amgen is a biotechnology company pioneering the development of products based on advances in recombinant DNA.

(in millions)	Total Debt		Stockholders' Equity	
	1999	*1992*	*1999*	*1992*
AT&T	$90,479	$17,122	$78,927	$20,313
Micron Technology	3,001	213	3,964	511
Amgen	1,054	440	3,024	934

1. Compute debt-to-equity ratios for each company for 1992 and 1999.
2. Discuss the differences in the ratios across firms.
3. Discuss the changes in individual company ratios from 1992 to 1999.

8-45 Review of Chapters 7 and 8

Albertson's, Inc., based in Boise, Idaho, operates nearly 2,500 food and drugstores in 37 states. The company's annual report for fiscal 2000 contained the following ($ in millions):

Albertson's, Inc.

	February 3	January 28
	2000	*1999*
Property, plant, and equipment, at cost	$14,000	$13,321
Less accumulated depreciation	5,087	4,776
Net property, plant, and equipment	$ 8,913	$ 8,545
Long-term debt due within 1 year	$ 623	$ 50
Long-term debt	4,805	4,905

Purchases of buildings, machinery, and equipment during fiscal 2000 were 2,098 million and depreciation expense was $854 million.

(The use of T-accounts should help your analysis.)

1. Compute the dollar amounts of:
   a. Accumulated depreciation relating to properties and plants disposed of during fiscal 2000.
   b. Original acquisition cost of properties and plants disposed of during fiscal 2000.
2. Compute the dollar amounts of the net increase or decrease in long-term debt.

8-46 Liabilities for Frequent Flier Miles and Ethics

Most airlines in the United States have frequent flier programs that grant free flights if a customer accumulates enough flight miles on the airline. For example, United Airlines offers a free domestic flight for every 25,000 miles flown on United. Delta Air Lines describes its program as follows in a footnote to the financial statements:

> *The Company sponsors a travel incentive program whereby frequent travelers accumulate mileage credits that entitle them to certain awards including free travel. The company accrues the estimated incremental cost of providing free travel awards under its frequent flyer program when free travel award levels are achieved. The accrued incremental cost is recorded in current liabilities.*

In a recent annual report, American Airlines reported a liability of $270 million for free flights, representing approximately 4 billion flight miles owed to customers. Assuming the average free flight is 2,000 miles, there is a $270 million liability for 2 million flights, an average of $135 per flight. However, some airlines maintain that the true liability is closer to $10 per flight, including the cost of food, insurance, and other miscellaneous expenses. They argue that all other costs would be incurred even in the absence of the person traveling free.

Suppose airlines use one estimate of the cost of these "free" flights for their internal decision making and another for computing the liability for their publicly reported balance sheet. Comment on the ethical issues.

ANNUAL REPORT CASE

8-47 Cisco Annual Report

Refer to Cisco's financial statements in appendix A. Focus on the liabilities section of the balance sheet and footnote 7.

1. Compute the following three ratios at July 29, 2000 and July 31, 1999. Assess the changes in these ratios.

   a. Debt-to-equity ratio.

   b. Debt-to-total-assets ratio.

   c. Interest-coverage ratio.

2. There is a covenant related to Cisco's line of credit. What is the covenant about?

8-48 Financial Statement Research

Identify an industry and select two companies within the industry. Calculate and compare the following ratios between the companies and through time.

1. Debt-to-equity ratio.

2. Debt-to-total-assets ratio.

3. Interest-coverage ratio.

COLLABORATIVE LEARNING EXERCISE

8-49 Characteristics of Bonds

Form groups of three to six persons each. Each person should select a company that has long-term debt in the form of bonds (or debentures). Pick one of the company's bonds, and note the interest rate on the bond. If the company does not list bonds individually, you may need to select one of the groups of bonds that it presents.

Find out as much as you can about the factors that might explain the bond's interest rate. Among the items to look for are characteristics of the bond, such as the size of the issue, the length of the term, and any special features such as subordination, convertibility, and covenants, and characteristics of the company, such as its industry, its debt-equity ratio, and its interest-coverage ratio. Also, try to find out when the bond was issued and the level of prevailing interest rates at the time. (Companies do not usually show the issue date in the footnotes to their financial statements. You might try looking at past annual reports to see when the bonds first appeared on the financial statement.) Prevailing interest rates may be represented by the rates on U.S. Treasury securities. Note the amount by which the interest rate of the bond exceeds the rate of a U.S. Treasury security of the same duration.

After individual students have done their independent research, you should get together and compare results. Do the factors you have identified explain the differences in rates across the companies? How do the factors relate to the riskiness of the bonds? Is the amount by which the bond interest rate exceeds the U.S. Treasury rate related to the bond's riskiness?

INTERNET EXERCISE

8-50 America West Airlines

Go to www.americawestairlines.com to locate America West Airlines' latest annual report. Answer these questions about America West Airlines:

www.prenhall.com/horngren

1. Where does America West Airlines show its liability for frequent flyer miles accrued by passengers? Is this figure an actual or estimated amount?

2. What information does America West Airlines report on deferred taxes? Why do deferred taxes exist?

3. Is America West Airlines subject to regulation under major environmental laws? What effect, if any, will compliance have on the company's financial condition and results of operations?

4. Does America West Airlines have any pending legal proceedings? Which ones are expected to have a material adverse effect on the company's business, financial condition, and results of operations?

5. Are there any lingering effects of America West's 1994 restructuring? What evidence do you see in the financial statements?

VALUING AND ACCOUNTING FOR BONDS AND LEASES

This Lord & Taylor's entrance is one of more than 400 entrances to stores that are part of the May Company. Others include Hecht's and Filene's.

www.prenhall.com/horngren

Learning Objectives

After studying this chapter, you should be able to

1. Compute and interpret present and future values.

2. Value bonds using present value techniques.

3. Account for bond issues over their entire life.

4. Value and account for long-term lease transactions.

5. Evaluate pensions and other postretirement benefits.

Maybe you have never heard of May Department Stores, but you have probably shopped in one of its stores. May Company is a $14 billion retailer operating eight regional department store divisions under 12 trade names including: Foley's, Hecht's, Robinsons-May, Filene's, Lord & Taylor, Kaufmann's, and others. The company owns more than 420 stores across the United States and has plans to open many more over the next 5 years. To accomplish this feat, May will invest $1.4 billion to add 13 million square feet of selling space. That is a lot of money—too much to come from just the results of May's normal operations. How will the company pay for it? May Company will issue long-term debt in the form of bonds and notes to pay for much of this growth.

May's has filed a registration statement with the Securities Exchange Commission (SEC) to permit it to raise $1 billion of new capital in this manner, $200 million of which was raised in February of 2000. Currently May Company has about $4 billion of long-term debt coming due over the next 35 years including annual maturities of $259, $85, $329, $132, and $258 million in the years 2000 to 2004, respectively. You can see that this process is a cyclical one. Each year some existing debt matures and some new debt is issued. When the company is growing, as May Company is, the new debt not only replaces the old, but also increases the total amount borrowed. The proceeds from new borrowings are added to the May Department Stores general funds to cover capital expenditures, acquisitions, working capital needs, and other general corporate purposes.

Why would May want to run up this much debt? From management's perspective, the growth plans and resulting financing needs are a competitive requirement. May has achieved over 20 consecutive years of increasing sales and earnings per share from continuing operations, a fact not lost on investors. Management is taking aggressive measures to maintain this record.

Measuring and reporting long-term liabilities uses fundamental concepts of compound interest, especially present value techniques. In Chapter 8, we focused on the accounting process for simple securities and situations. We did not worry about where the values came from. Now we use present value techniques to value and account for bond issues and for leases, and to interpret disclosures about pensions and other postretirement employee benefits.

You may think that bonds are boring investments that provide semiannual interest payments until they mature and the original principal is repaid. Think again. The resale value of a bond may rise and fall greatly over its life as market conditions change. Large changes in value may accompany general changes in interest rates or changes in the specific circumstances of the issuing firm.

For example, during October 1973, the former American car maker Chrysler issued 8% bonds with principal value of $1,000 maturing in 1998. The bonds were sold at $1,000 because the market rate of interest was also 8% per year.

What was the market price of Chrysler's bonds 9 years after issuance, that is, in October 1982? The listing in the *Wall Street Journal* revealed a price of $491.24. At that time, Chrysler's bond had 16 years (or 32 half yearly interest payments) until maturity. The market value of the bonds was based on the value of the $40 interest payments made every half year ($1,000 × 8% × $\frac{1}{2}$ = $40) and the $1,000 principal payment at maturity. In this chapter we learn why the value of Chrysler's bonds was only $491.24, not $2,280, the total of the 32 payments of $40 and the payment of $1,000 at maturity.

The historical market value of Chrysler's bonds can be found in past issues of *Moody's Bond Record.* Moody's provides bond ratings that measure the likelihood that the issuer will be able to pay back the debt. They range from Aaa (highest) to Baa (middle) to C (lowest). When the Chrysler bonds were issued in 1973, Moody's assigned them an A rating. The following table shows the market value and bond rating in October for 1973 and 1982 to 1993. Why did the price of the bonds fall to $491.24? One reason is that Chrysler bonds became riskier, as indicated by the fall in Moody's rating from A to Caa. During the next year Chrysler's condition improved significantly, its bond rating rose, and owners of these bonds earned a return of 50% including interest and appreciation.

Market Value of Chrysler Bond That Was Issued at Par for $1,000 in October 1973

October	Market Value	Moody's Rating
1973	$ 1,000	A
—	—	—
—	—	—
1982	491.24	Caa
1983	665.00	B 2
1984	621.25	Ba 2
1985	753.75	Baa 3
1986	922.50	Baa 3
1987	840.00	Baa 1
1988	912.50	Baa 1
1989	932.50	Baa 1
1990	750.00	Baa 3
1991	680.00	Ba 3
1992	968.75	B 1
1993	$1,021.25	Baa 3

Chrysler's accounting for these bonds was completely unaffected by these wide swings in value and the associated gains and losses being realized by investors. Chrysler issued the bonds at par and continued to record interest expense and interest payable of $40 per bond every 6 months until the bonds were repaid.

VALUING LONG-TERM LIABILITIES

We have already seen how to value and account for current liabilities. Long-term liabilities are more difficult to value because they involve long time frames. How exactly do lenders and borrowers measure the value of obligations that are not due for at least a year? They use the time value of money, which refers to the fact that a dollar you expect to pay or receive in the future is not worth as much as a dollar you have today. For example, suppose a company owes $105, due in 1 year. It can put $100 in a savings account that pays 5% interest. In 1 year, the original $100 plus the $5 interest earned can be used to pay the $105 obligation. Satisfying the $105 obligation took only 100 of today's dollars. We might express this relationship by saying that $100 is the present value of $105 to be received or paid one year from now when the interest rate is 5%. As you see, accounting has embraced present value approaches in valuing bonds, leases, and pensions.

COMPOUND INTEREST, FUTURE VALUE, AND PRESENT VALUE

Depending on your prior background, these topics may be familiar, in which case skip directly to the heading "Accounting for Bond Transactions," p. 369. This discussion will use amounts from interest tables to solve problems; however, many of you will be using Excel, another spreadsheet, or financial calculators to make these calculations. The mechanism is not important, but the principles are paramount to understanding these liabilities.

When you borrow money, the amount borrowed is known as the loan principal. For the borrower, interest is the cost of using the principal. It is the rental charge for cash, just as rental charges are often made to use an automobile or hotel room. Investing money is basically the same as making a loan. The investor gives money to a company, and that company acts as a borrower. For the investor, interest is the return on investment or the fee for lending money. Contracts that bear interest have many forms, from simple short-term promissory notes to multimillion-dollar issues of bonds.

Calculating the amount of interest depends on the interest rate—a specified percentage of the principal—and the interest period—the time period over which this interest rate is applied.

Simple interest is calculated by multiplying an interest rate by an unchanging principal amount. Because principal amounts increase when you add interest onto them as interest is earned, simple interest is rare in U.S. financial practice. Instead, we see **compound interest,** which is calculated by multiplying an interest rate by a principal amount that increases each time interest is earned. The accumulated interest is added to the principal to become the new principal for the next period.

FUTURE VALUE

Consider an example. Suppose Christina's T-shirt business has $10,000 in cash that is not needed at this moment. Instead of holding the $10,000 in her business checking account, which does not pay interest, she can deposit $10,000 in an account that pays 10% yearly interest, compounded annually. She plans to let the $10,000 remain in the account and earn interest for 3 years. After 3 years, she will withdraw all the money. The amount that will be accumulated in the account, including principal and interest, is called the **future value.**

Objective 1
Compute and interpret present and future values.

simple interest The interest rate multiplied by an unchanging principal amount.

compound interest The interest rate multiplied by a changing principal amount. The unpaid interest is added to the principal to become the principal for the new period.

future value The amount accumulated, including principal and interest.

Compound interest provides interest on interest. That is, interest payments are added to the principal each period, and interest is then earned on the original principal amount and on the amount of added interest. In our Christina example, interest in year one is paid on $10,000: 10% × $10,000 = $1,000. If the interest is not withdrawn, the principal for year two includes the initial $10,000 deposit plus the $1,000 of interest earned in the first year, $11,000. Interest in year two is paid on the $11,000: 10% × $11,000 = $1,100. In the third year interest will thus be earned on $12,100: $12,100 × 10% = 1,210. The future value (FV) of the deposit at the end of 3 years with compound interest would be $13,310:

	Principal	Compound Interest	Balance End of Year
Year 1	$10,000	$10,000 × .10 = $1,000	$11,000
Year 2	11,000	11,000 × .10 = 1,100	12,100
Year 3	12,100	12,100 × .10 = 1,210	13,310

More generally, suppose you invest S dollars for two periods and earn interest at an interest rate i. After one period, the investment would be increased by the interest earned, Si. You would have $S + $Si = $S(1 + i)$. In the second period you would again earn interest ($i[S(1 + i)]$). After two periods you would have:

$$[S(1 + i)] + (i[S(1 + i)]) = S(1 + i)(1 + i) = S(1 + i)^2$$

The general formula for computing the FV of S dollars in n years at interest rate i is

$$FV = S(1 + i)^n$$

In general, n refers to the number of periods the funds are invested. Periods can be years, months, days, or any other time period. However, the interest rate must be consistent with the time period. That is, if n refers to days, i must be expressed as X% per day.

The "force" of compound interest can be staggering. For example:

	Future Values at End of		
Compound Interest	*10 Years*	*20 Years*	*40 Years*
$10,000 × (1.10)^{10} = $10,000 × 2.5937 =	$25,937		
$10,000 × (1.10)^{20} = $10,000 × 6.7275 =		$67,275	
$10,000 × (1.10)^{40} = $10,000 × 45.2593 =			$452,593

Calculating future values and compound interest by hand can be tedious and time consuming. Fortunately, there are tables that do much of the work for you. For example, Table 9-1, shows the future values of $1 for various periods and interest rates. In the table each number is the solution to the expression $(1 + i)^n$. The value of i is given in the column heading. The value of n is given in the row label for number of periods. Notice that the 3-year, 10% future value factor is 1.3310 (the third row, seventh column). This number is calculated as $(1 + .10)^3$. This is consistent with our preceding calculation where we show that $10,000 grows to $13,310 over 3 years ($10,000 × 1.3310 = $13,310).

Suppose you want to know how much $800 will grow to if left in the bank for 9 years at 8% interest. Multiply $800 by $(1 + .08)^9$. The value for $(1 + .08)^9$ is found in the 9-year row and 8% column of Table 9-1.

$$800 × 1.9990 = $1,599.20$$

Table 9-1
Future Value of $1

$$FV = 1(1 + i)^n$$

Periods	3%	4%	5%	6%	7%	8%	10%	12%	14%	16%	18%	20%	22%	24%	25%
1	1.0300	1.0400	1.0500	1.0600	1.0700	1.0800	1.1000	1.1200	1.1400	1.1600	1.1800	1.2000	1.2200	1.2400	1.2500
2	1.0609	1.0816	1.1025	1.1236	1.1449	1.1664	1.2100	1.2544	1.2996	1.3456	1.3924	1.4400	1.4884	1.5376	1.5625
3	1.0927	1.1249	1.1576	1.1910	1.2250	1.2597	1.3310	1.4049	1.4815	1.5609	1.6430	1.7280	1.8158	1.9066	1.9531
4	1.1255	1.1699	1.2155	1.2625	1.3108	1.3605	1.4641	1.5735	1.6890	1.8106	1.9388	2.0736	2.2153	2.3642	2.4414
5	1.1593	1.2167	1.2763	1.3382	1.4026	1.4693	1.6105	1.7623	1.9254	2.1003	2.2878	2.4883	2.7027	2.9316	3.0518
6	1.1941	1.2653	1.3401	1.4185	1.5007	1.5869	1.7716	1.9738	2.1950	2.4364	2.6996	2.9860	3.2973	3.6352	3.8147
7	1.2299	1.3159	1.4071	1.5036	1.6058	1.7138	1.9487	2.2107	2.5023	2.8262	3.1855	3.5832	4.0227	4.5077	4.7684
8	1.2668	1.3686	1.4775	1.5938	1.7182	1.8509	2.1436	2.4760	2.8526	3.2784	3.7589	4.2998	4.9077	5.5895	5.9605
9	1.3048	1.4233	1.5513	1.6895	1.8385	1.9990	2.3579	2.7731	3.2519	3.8030	4.4355	5.1598	5.9874	6.9310	7.4506
10	1.3439	1.4802	1.6289	1.7908	1.9672	2.1589	2.5937	3.1058	3.7072	4.4114	5.2338	6.1917	7.3046	8.5944	9.3132
11	1.3842	1.5395	1.7103	1.8983	2.1049	2.3316	2.8531	3.4785	4.2262	5.1173	6.1759	7.4301	8.9117	10.6571	11.6415
12	1.4258	1.6010	1.7959	2.0122	2.2522	2.5182	3.1384	3.8960	4.8179	5.9360	7.2876	8.9161	10.8722	13.2148	14.5519
13	1.4685	1.6651	1.8856	2.1329	2.4098	2.7196	3.4523	4.3635	5.4924	6.8858	8.5994	10.6993	13.2641	16.3863	18.1899
14	1.5126	1.7317	1.9799	2.2609	2.5785	2.9372	3.7975	4.8871	6.2613	7.9875	10.1472	12.8392	16.1822	20.3191	22.7374
15	1.5580	1.8009	2.0789	2.3966	2.7590	3.1772	4.1772	5.4736	7.1379	9.2655	11.9737	15.4070	19.7423	25.1956	28.4217
16	1.6047	1.8730	2.1829	2.5404	2.9522	3.4259	4.5950	6.1304	8.1372	10.7480	14.1290	18.4884	24.0856	31.2426	35.5271
17	1.6528	1.9479	2.2920	2.6928	3.1588	3.7000	5.0545	6.8660	9.2765	12.4677	16.6722	22.1861	29.3844	38.7408	44.4089
18	1.7024	2.0258	2.4066	2.8543	3.3799	3.9960	5.5599	7.6900	10.5752	14.4625	19.6733	26.6233	35.8490	48.0386	55.5112
19	1.7535	2.1068	2.5270	3.0256	3.6165	4.3157	6.1159	8.6128	12.0557	16.7765	23.2144	31.9480	43.7358	59.5679	69.3889
20	1.8061	2.1911	2.6533	3.2071	3.8697	4.6610	6.7275	9.6463	13.7435	19.4608	27.3930	38.3376	53.3576	73.8641	86.7362
21	1.8603	2.2788	2.7860	3.3996	4.1406	5.0338	7.4002	10.8038	15.6676	22.5745	32.3238	46.0051	65.0963	91.5915	108.4202
22	1.9161	2.3699	2.9253	3.6035	4.4304	5.4365	8.1403	12.1003	17.8610	26.1864	38.1421	55.2061	79.4175	113.5735	135.5253
23	1.9736	2.4647	3.0715	3.8197	4.7405	5.8715	8.9543	13.5523	20.3616	30.3762	45.0076	66.2474	96.8894	140.8312	169.4066
24	2.0328	2.5633	3.2251	4.0489	5.0724	6.3412	9.8497	15.1786	23.2122	35.2364	53.1090	79.4968	118.2050	174.6306	211.7582
25	2.0938	2.6658	3.3864	4.2919	5.4274	6.8485	10.8347	17.0001	26.4619	40.8742	62.6686	95.3962	144.2101	216.5420	264.6978
26	2.1566	2.7725	3.5557	4.5494	5.8074	7.3964	11.9182	19.0401	30.1666	47.4141	73.9490	114.4755	175.9364	268.5121	330.8722
27	2.2213	2.8834	3.7335	4.8223	6.2139	7.9881	13.1100	21.3249	34.3899	55.0004	87.2598	137.3706	214.6424	332.9550	413.5903
28	2.2879	2.9987	3.9201	5.1117	6.6488	8.6271	14.4210	23.8839	39.2045	63.8004	102.9666	164.8447	261.8637	412.8642	516.9879
29	2.3566	3.1187	4.1161	5.4184	7.1143	9.3173	15.8631	26.7499	44.6931	74.0085	121.5005	197.8136	319.4737	511.9516	646.2349
30	2.4273	3.2434	4.3219	5.7435	7.6123	10.0627	17.4494	29.9599	50.9502	85.8499	143.3706	237.3763	389.7579	634.8199	807.7936

The examples in this text use the factors from Table 9-1 and similar tables in this chapter, which are rounded to four decimal places. If you use tables with different rounding, or if you use a hand calculator or personal computer, your answers may differ slightly from those given because of a small rounding error.

PRESENT VALUE

Objective 2
Value bonds using present value techniques.

present value The value today of a future cash inflow or outflow.

Accountants generally use present values instead of future values to record long-term liabilities. The **present value** (PV) is the value today of a future cash inflow or outflow.

Suppose you invest $1.00 today. As shown in the discussion of future values, the $1.00 will grow to $1.06 in 1 year at 6% interest—that is, $1 \times 1.06 = \$1.06$. At the end of the second year its value is $(\$1 \times 1.06) \times 1.06 = \$1 \times (1.06)^2 = \$1.124$.

We know how to calculate the future value of S dollars invested at a known interest rate i for n periods. We can reverse the process to calculate the present value when we know the future value. If

$$FV = S(1 + i)^n$$

then the present value is S, or

$$S = \frac{FV}{(1 + i)^n}$$

If $1.00 is to be received in 1 year, it is worth $1 \div 1.06 = \$.9434$ today. Suppose you invest $.9434 today. In 1 year you will have $.9434 \times 1.06 = \$1.00$. Thus, $0.9434 is the present value of $1.00 a year hence at 6%. If the dollar will be received in 2 years, its present value is $1.00 \div (1.06)^2 = \$.8900$. If $.89 is invested today, it will grow to $1.00 at the end of 2 years. The general formula for the present value (PV) of a future value (FV) to be received or paid in n periods at an interest rate of $i\%$ per period is:

$$PV = \frac{FV}{(1 + i)^n} = FV \times \frac{1}{(1 + i)^n}$$

discount rates The interest rates used in determining present values.

Table 9-2 gives factors for $1/(1 + i)^n$ (which is the present value of $1.00) at various interest rates (often called **discount rates**) over several different periods. Present values are also called discounted values, and the process of finding the present value is discounting. You can think of present values as discounting (decreasing) the value of a future cash inflow or outflow. Why is the value discounted? Because the cash is to be received or paid in the future, not today.

rate of return The amount earned by an investor expressed as a percentage of the amount invested.

Assume that a prominent city is issuing a 3-year non-interest-bearing note payable that promises to pay a lump sum of $1,000 exactly 3 years from now. You desire an interest rate of return of exactly 6%, compounded annually. The interest rate is being earned by the investor and we use the phrase **rate of return** to refer to the amount earned by the investor expressed as a percentage of the amount invested. How much should you be willing to pay now for the 3-year note? The situation is sketched as follows:

End of Year	0	1	2	3
	Present Value			**Future Value**
	? ←			$1,000

The factor in the period 3 row and 6% column of Table 9-2 is .8396. The present value of the $1,000 payment is $1,000 \times .8396 = \$839.60$. You should be willing to pay $839.60 for the $1,000 to be received in 3 years.

Table 9-2
Present Value of $1

$$PV = \frac{1}{(1+i)^n}$$

Periods	3%	4%	5%	6%	7%	8%	10%	12%	14%	16%	18%	20%	22%	24%	25%
1	.9709	.9615	.9524	.9434	.9346	.9259	.9091	.8929	.8772	.8621	.8475	.8333	.8197	.8065	.8000
2	.9426	.9246	.9070	.8900	.8734	.8573	.8264	.7972	.7695	.7432	.7182	.6944	.6719	.6504	.6400
3	.9151	.8890	.8638	.8396	.8163	.7938	.7513	.7118	.6750	.6407	.6086	.5787	.5507	.5245	.5120
4	.8885	.8548	.8227	.7921	.7629	.7350	.6830	.6355	.5921	.5523	.5158	.4823	.4514	.4230	.4096
5	.8626	.8219	.7835	.7473	.7130	.6806	.6209	.5674	.5194	.4761	.4371	.4019	.3700	.3411	.3277
6	.8375	.7903	.7462	.7050	.6663	.6302	.5645	.5066	.4556	.4104	.3704	.3349	.3033	.2751	.2621
7	.8131	.7599	.7107	.6651	.6227	.5835	.5132	.4523	.3996	.3538	.3139	.2791	.2486	.2218	.2097
8	.7894	.7307	.6768	.6274	.5820	.5403	.4665	.4039	.3506	.3050	.2660	.2326	.2038	.1789	.1678
9	.7664	.7026	.6446	.5919	.5439	.5002	.4241	.3606	.3075	.2630	.2255	.1938	.1670	.1443	.1342
10	.7441	.6756	.6139	.5584	.5083	.4632	.3855	.3220	.2697	.2267	.1911	.1615	.1369	.1164	.1074
11	.7224	.6496	.5847	.5268	.4751	.4289	.3505	.2875	.2366	.1954	.1619	.1346	.1122	.0938	.0859
12	.7014	.6246	.5568	.4970	.4440	.3971	.3186	.2567	.2076	.1685	.1372	.1122	.0920	.0757	.0687
13	.6810	.6006	.5303	.4688	.4150	.3677	.2897	.2292	.1821	.1452	.1163	.0935	.0754	.0610	.0550
14	.6611	.5775	.5051	.4423	.3878	.3405	.2633	.2046	.1597	.1252	.0985	.0779	.0618	.0492	.0440
15	.6419	.5553	.4810	.4173	.3624	.3152	.2394	.1827	.1401	.1079	.0835	.0649	.0507	.0397	.0352
16	.6232	.5339	.4581	.3936	.3387	.2919	.2176	.1631	.1229	.0930	.0708	.0541	.0415	.0320	.0281
17	.6050	.5134	.4363	.3714	.3166	.2703	.1978	.1456	.1078	.0802	.0600	.0451	.0340	.0258	.0225
18	.5874	.4936	.4155	.3503	.2959	.2502	.1799	.1300	.0946	.0691	.0508	.0376	.0279	.0208	.0180
19	.5703	.4746	.3957	.3305	.2765	.2317	.1635	.1161	.0829	.0596	.0431	.0313	.0229	.0168	.0144
20	.5537	.4564	.3769	.3118	.2584	.2145	.1486	.1037	.0728	.0514	.0365	.0261	.0187	.0135	.0115
21	.5375	.4388	.3589	.2942	.2415	.1987	.1351	.0926	.0638	.0443	.0309	.0217	.0154	.0109	.0092
22	.5219	.4220	.3418	.2775	.2257	.1839	.1228	.0826	.0560	.0382	.0262	.0181	.0126	.0088	.0074
23	.5067	.4057	.3256	.2618	.2109	.1703	.1117	.0738	.0491	.0329	.0222	.0151	.0103	.0071	.0059
24	.4919	.3901	.3101	.2470	.1971	.1577	.1015	.0659	.0431	.0284	.0188	.0126	.0085	.0057	.0047
25	.4776	.3751	.2953	.2330	.1842	.1460	.0923	.0588	.0378	.0245	.0160	.0105	.0069	.0046	.0038
26	.4637	.3607	.2812	.2198	.1722	.1352	.0839	.0525	.0331	.0211	.0135	.0087	.0057	.0037	.0030
27	.4502	.3468	.2678	.2074	.1609	.1252	.0763	.0469	.0291	.0182	.0115	.0073	.0047	.0030	.0024
28	.4371	.3335	.2551	.1956	.1504	.1159	.0693	.0419	.0255	.0157	.0097	.0061	.0038	.0024	.0019
29	.4243	.3207	.2429	.1846	.1406	.1073	.0630	.0374	.0224	.0135	.0082	.0051	.0031	.0020	.0015
30	.4120	.3083	.2314	.1741	.1314	.0994	.0573	.0334	.0196	.0116	.0070	.0042	.0026	.0016	.0012
40	.3066	.2083	.1420	.0972	.0668	.0460	.0221	.0107	.0053	.0026	.0013	.0007	.0004	.0002	.0001

Suppose interest is compounded semiannually instead of annually. How much should you be willing to pay now? Remember to pay attention to the number of periods involved, not just the number of years. The 3 years become six interest payment periods. The rate per period is half the annual rate, or 6% ÷ 2 = 3%. The factor in the period 6 row and 3% column of Table 9-2 is .8375. You should now be willing to pay $1,000 × 0.8375, or only $837.50 instead of $839.60. Why do you pay less? Because with more frequent compounding the original investment will grow faster.

To see how present values work in conjunction with future values, let us return to our Christina example. Suppose Christina's financial institution promised to pay her a lump sum of $13,310 at the end of 3 years for her investment. How much does Christina need to deposit to earn a 10% rate of return, compounded annually? By using Table 9-2, the period 3 row, and the 10% column, show a factor of .7513. Multiply this factor by the future amount and round to the nearest dollar:

$$PV = .7513 \times \$13,310 = \$10,000$$

 To make sure you have the hang of present values, use Table 9-2 to obtain the present values of:

1. $1,600, @ 20%, to be received at the end of 20 years.
2. $8,300, @ 10%, to be received at the end of 12 years.
3. $8,000, @ 4%, to be received at the end of 4 years.

ANSWERS
1. $1,600 (.0261) = $41.76.
2. $8,300 (.3186) = $2,644.38.
3. $8,000 (.8548) = $6,838.40.

PRESENT VALUE OF AN ORDINARY ANNUITY

annuity Equal cash flows to take place during successive periods of equal length.

An ordinary **annuity** is a series of equal cash flows to take place at the end of successive periods of equal length. In other words, an annuity pays you the same amount at the end of each period for a set period of time. Its present value is denoted PV_A. Assume that you buy a note from a municipality that promises to pay $1,000 at the end of each of 3 years. How much should you be willing to pay for this note if you desire a rate of return of 6%, compounded annually?

You could solve this problem using Table 9-2. First, find the present value of each payment you will receive, and then add the present values as in Exhibit 9-1. You should be willing to pay $943.40 for the first payment, $890.00 for the second, and $839.60 for the third, a total of $2,673.00.

Table 9-3 provides a shortcut method for calculating the present value of an annuity. The present value in Exhibit 9-1 can be expressed as:

$$\begin{aligned} PV_A &= (\$1,000 \times .9434) + (\$1,000 \times .8900) + (\$1,000 \times .8396) \\ &= \$1,000\,(.9434 + .8900 + .8396) \\ &= \$1,000\,(2.6730) \\ &= \$2,673.00 \end{aligned}$$

The three terms in parentheses are the first three numbers from the 6% column of Table 9-2, and their sum is in the third row of the 6% column of Table 9-3: .9434 + .8900 + .8396 = 2.6730. This shortcut is especially valuable if the cash payments or receipts extend over many periods. Consider an annual cash payment of $1,000 for 20 years at 6%. The present value, calculated from Table 9-3, is $1,000 × 11.4699 =

Exhibit 9-1

	End of Year 6% *PV* Factor	Present Value	0	1	2	3
First payment	.9434	$ 943.40 ← $1,000				
Second payment	.8900	890.00 ←————— $1,000				
Third payment	.8396	839.60 ←———————————— $1,000				
		$2,673.00				

$11,469.90. To use Table 9-2 for this calculation, you would have to perform 20 calculations and then add up the 20 products.

The factors in Table 9-3 can be calculated using the following general formula:

$$PV_A = \frac{1}{i}\left[1 - \frac{1}{(1 + i)^n}\right]$$

Applied to our illustration:

$$PV_A = \frac{1}{.06}(1 - .83962) = \frac{.16038}{.06} = 2.6730$$

To make sure you understand present values of annuities, use Table 9-3 to obtain the present values of the following ordinary annuities:

1. $1,600 to be received at the end of each year for 20 years, assuming interest at 20%.
2. $8,300 to be received at the end of each year for 12 years, assuming interest at 10%.
3. $8,000 to be received at the end of each year for 4 years, assuming interest at 4%.

ANSWERS
1. $1,600 (4.8696) = $7,791.36.
2. $8,300 (6.8137) = $56,553.71.
3. $8,000 (3.6299) = $29,039.20.

In particular, note that the higher the interest rate, the lower the present value factor in Table 9-3. Why? Because, at a higher interest rate, you would need to invest less now to obtain the same stream of future annuity payments. For example, for a 10-year annuity the factor declines from 7.7217 for 5% to 6.1446 for 10%.

VALUING BONDS

Bonds create cash flows in many future periods. As a result, bonds are recorded at the present value of all those future payments, discounted at the market interest rate in effect when the liability was incurred. In Chapter 8, we dealt with cases where the coupon rate paid by the bond and the market rate when it was issued were identical and therefore the bond sold at par value. We did not explain the valuation.

A typical bond consists of a promise to pay interest every 6 months until maturity and a promise to pay a lump sum at maturity. Suppose a 2-year $1,000 bond is issued that pays interest of 10%, that is to say the coupon rate is 10%.

Table 9-3
Present Value of Ordinary Annuity of $1

$$PV_A = \frac{1}{i}\left[\frac{1-1}{(1+i)^n}\right]$$

Periods	3%	4%	5%	6%	7%	8%	10%	12%	14%	16%	18%	20%	22%	24%	25%
1	.9709	.9615	.9524	.9434	.9346	.9259	.9091	.8929	.8772	.8621	.8475	.8333	.8197	.8065	.8000
2	1.9135	1.8861	1.8594	1.8334	1.8080	1.7833	1.7355	1.6901	1.6467	1.6052	1.5656	1.5278	1.4915	1.4568	1.4400
3	2.8286	2.7751	2.7232	2.6730	2.6243	2.5771	2.4869	2.4018	2.3216	2.2459	2.1743	2.1065	2.0422	1.9813	1.9520
4	3.7171	3.6299	3.5460	3.4651	3.3872	3.3121	3.1699	3.0373	2.9137	2.7982	2.6901	2.5887	2.4936	2.4043	2.3616
5	4.5797	4.4518	4.3295	4.2124	4.1002	3.9927	3.7908	3.6048	3.4331	3.2743	3.1272	2.9906	2.8636	2.7454	2.6893
6	5.4172	5.2421	5.0757	4.9173	4.7665	4.6229	4.3553	4.1114	3.8887	3.6847	3.4976	3.3255	3.1669	3.0205	2.9514
7	6.2303	6.0021	5.7864	5.5824	5.3893	5.2064	4.8684	4.5638	4.2883	4.0386	3.8115	3.6046	3.4155	3.2423	3.1611
8	7.0197	6.7327	6.4632	6.2098	5.9713	5.7466	5.3349	4.9676	4.6389	4.3436	4.0776	3.8372	3.6193	3.4212	3.3289
9	7.7861	7.4353	7.1078	6.8017	6.5152	6.2469	5.7590	5.3282	4.9464	4.6065	4.3030	4.0310	3.7863	3.5655	3.4631
10	8.5302	8.1109	7.7217	7.3601	7.0236	6.7101	6.1446	5.6502	5.2161	4.8332	4.4941	4.1925	3.9232	3.6819	3.5705
11	9.2526	8.7605	8.3064	7.8869	7.4987	7.1390	6.4951	5.9377	5.4527	5.0286	4.6560	4.3271	4.0354	3.7757	3.6564
12	9.9540	9.3851	8.8633	8.3838	7.9427	7.5361	6.8137	6.1944	5.6603	5.1971	4.7932	4.4392	4.1274	3.8514	3.7251
13	10.6350	9.9856	9.3936	8.8527	8.3577	7.9038	7.1034	6.4235	5.8424	5.3423	4.9095	4.5327	4.2028	3.9124	3.7801
14	11.2961	10.5631	9.8986	9.2950	8.7455	8.2442	7.3677	6.6282	6.0021	5.4675	5.0081	4.6106	4.2646	3.9616	3.8241
15	11.9379	11.1184	10.3797	9.7122	9.1079	8.5595	7.6061	6.8109	6.1422	5.5755	5.0916	4.6755	4.3152	4.0013	3.8593
16	12.5611	11.6523	10.8378	10.1059	9.4466	8.8514	7.8237	6.9740	6.2651	5.6685	5.1624	4.7296	4.3567	4.0333	3.8874
17	13.1661	12.1657	11.2741	10.4773	9.7632	9.1216	8.0216	7.1196	6.3729	5.7487	5.2223	4.7746	4.3908	4.0591	3.9099
18	13.7535	12.6593	11.6896	10.8276	10.0591	9.3719	8.2014	7.2497	6.4674	5.8178	5.2732	4.8122	4.4187	4.0799	3.9279
19	14.3238	13.1339	12.0853	11.1581	10.3356	9.6036	8.3649	7.3658	6.5504	5.8775	5.3162	4.8435	4.4415	4.0967	3.9424
20	14.8775	13.5903	12.4622	11.4699	10.5940	9.8181	8.5136	7.4694	6.6231	5.9288	5.3527	4.8696	4.4603	4.1103	3.9539
21	15.4150	14.0292	12.8212	11.7641	10.8355	10.0168	8.6487	7.5620	6.6870	5.9731	5.3837	4.8913	4.4756	4.1212	3.9631
22	15.9369	14.4511	13.1630	12.0416	11.0612	10.2007	8.7715	7.6446	6.7429	6.0113	5.4099	4.9094	4.4882	4.1300	3.9705
23	16.4436	14.8568	13.4886	12.3034	11.2722	10.3711	8.8832	7.7184	6.7921	6.0442	5.4321	4.9245	4.4985	4.1371	3.9764
24	16.9355	15.2470	13.7986	12.5504	11.4693	10.5288	8.9847	7.7843	6.8351	6.0726	5.4509	4.9371	4.5070	4.1428	3.9811
25	17.4131	15.6221	14.0939	12.7834	11.6526	10.6748	9.0770	7.8431	6.8729	6.0971	5.4669	4.9476	4.5139	4.1474	3.9849
26	17.8768	15.9828	14.3752	13.0032	11.8258	10.8100	9.1609	7.8957	6.9061	6.1182	5.4804	4.9563	4.5196	4.1511	3.9879
27	18.3270	16.3296	14.6430	13.2105	11.9867	10.9352	9.2372	7.9426	6.9352	6.1364	5.4919	4.9636	4.5243	4.1542	3.9903
28	18.7641	16.6631	14.8981	13.4062	12.1371	11.0511	9.3066	7.9844	6.9607	6.1520	5.5016	4.9697	4.5281	4.1566	3.9923
29	19.1885	16.9837	15.1411	13.5907	12.2777	11.1584	9.3696	8.0218	6.9830	6.1656	5.5098	4.9747	4.5312	4.1585	3.9938
30	19.6004	17.2920	15.3725	13.7648	12.4090	11.2578	9.4269	8.0552	7.0027	6.1772	5.5168	4.9789	4.5338	4.1601	3.9950
40	23.1148	19.7928	17.1591	15.0463	13.3317	11.9246	9.7791	8.2438	7.1050	6.2335	5.5482	4.9966	4.5439	4.1659	3.9995

Exhibit 9-2

Computation of Market Value of Bonds
(In Dollars)

	Present Value Factor	Total Present Value	Sketch of Cash Flows by Period				
			0	1	2	3	4
Valuation at 10% per year, or 5% per half-year							
Principal,							
4-period line, Table 9-2							
.8227 × $1,000 = $822.70	.8227	822.70					1,000
Interest,							
4-period line, Table 9-3							
3.5460 × $50 = $177.30	3.5460	177.30		50	50	50	50
Total		1,000.00					
Valuation at 12% per year, or 6% per half-year							
Principal	.7921	792.10					1,000
Interest	3.4651	173.25		50	50	50	50
Total		965.35					
Valuation at 8% per year, or 4% per half-year							
Principal	.8548	854.80					1,000
Interest	3.6299	181.50		50	50	50	50
Total		1,036.30					

Exhibit 9-2 shows how the bond would be valued, using Tables 9-2 and 9-3 and three different effective market interest rates. Exhibit 9-2 calculates the present value of the annuity of interest payments and adds that to the present value of the repayment of face value at maturity. Note that:

1. Although the quoted bond interest rates are expressed as annual rates, interest is actually paid semiannually. Thus, a 10% bond really pays 5% interest each semiannual period. A 2-year bond has 4 periods, a 10-year bond has 20 periods, and so on.

2. The higher the market rate of interest, the lower the present value.

3. When the market interest rate equals the coupon rate of 10%, the bond is worth $1,000. We say such a bond is issued at par. We described the accounting for such a bond in Chapter 8.

4. When the market interest rate of 12% exceeds the 10% coupon rate, the bond sells at a **discount,** $965.35 in this case, that is, for less than the par value of $1,000.

5. When the market interest rate of 8% is less than the 10% coupon rate, the bond sells at a **premium,** $1,036.30 in this case, that is, for more than the par value of $1,000.

discount on bonds The excess of face amount over the proceeds on issuance of a bond.

premium on bonds The excess of the proceeds over the face amount of a bond.

ACCOUNTING FOR BOND TRANSACTIONS

ISSUING AND TRADING BONDS

Bonds are typically sold through a syndicate (special group) of investment bankers called **underwriters.** That is, the syndicate buys the entire issue of bonds from the corporation,

Objective 3
Account for bond
issues over their entire
life.

underwriters A group of
investment bankers that
buys an entire bond or
stock issue from a
corporation and then sells
the securities to the general
investing public.

**coupon rate (nominal
interest rate)** The rate of
interest to be paid on a
bond.

market rate The rate
available on investments in
similar bonds at a moment
in time.

**yield to maturity (effective
interest rate)** The interest
rate that equates market
price at issue to the present
value of principal and
interest.

thus guaranteeing that the company will obtain the funds it needs. The syndicate then sells the bonds to the general investing public.

The company sets the terms of the bond contract with the advice of the investment banker who manages the underwriting syndicate. The terms include the time to maturity, interest payment dates, interest amounts, and size of the bond issue. The rate of interest to be paid by the bond (**coupon rate** or **nominal interest rate**) is usually set as close to the current **market rate** as possible. The market rate is the rate available on investments in similar bonds at a moment in time. Many factors affecting the market rate are discussed here and in Chapter 8, notably general economic conditions, industry conditions, risks of the use of the proceeds, and specific features of the bonds (examples include callability, sinking fund, and convertibility).

On the day of issuance, the proceeds to the issuer may be above par or below par, depending on market conditions. If the proceeds are above par, the bonds have been sold at a premium; if the proceeds are below par, the bonds are sold at a discount. When a bond sells at a discount or premium, the **yield to maturity** (market rate, **effective interest rate**)—the rate of interest demanded by investors in a bond—differs from the nominal interest rate. The interest paid in cash, usually semiannually, is determined by the nominal rate, not the effective rate. The yield to maturity is the interest rate at which all contractual cash flows for interest and principal have a present value equal to the proceeds at issue.

Note that premiums and discounts do not reflect the creditworthiness of the issuer. Instead, they simply reflect differences in the nominal rate and the market rate. These differences often result from the delay between the time a company sets the terms of the bond and when the bond is actually issued.

Bonds typically have a par value of $1,000, but their values are usually expressed in terms of percentages of par. When bonds are traded in markets or on exchanges such as the New York Stock Exchange (NYSE), you can find quotations of their prices in newspaper business sections. A daily quotation for an IBM bond from the August 26, 2000 *New York Times* follows:

12 months			Current					Net
High	*Low*	**Description**	**Yield**	**Volume**	*High*	*Low*	*Last*	**Change**
106	97	IBM $7\frac{1}{2}$S13	7.3	20	$103\frac{1}{4}$	$102\frac{5}{8}$	$102\frac{5}{8}$	—

*The ending price of one $1,000 bond is $102\frac{1}{2}$% of $1,000 = $1,025.00.

current yield Annual
interest payments divided
by the current price of a
bond.

IBM's bonds carrying a $7\frac{1}{2}$% coupon rate and maturing in 2013 closed at a price of $1,025.63 ($102\frac{5}{8}$% of $1,000) at the end of the day. The **current yield** is calculated as the annual interest divided by the current price, or 7.3%. Twenty thousand bonds were traded, each having a face, or par, value of $1,000. The closing price was unchanged from that of the prior day. During the last 52 weeks, the bonds have varied between 97 and 106. Similar reporting occurs in the *Wall Street Journal* and *Barron's*.

The Chrysler example presented earlier showed a sharp drop in value from 1973 to 1982 due to sharply higher interest rates. Extreme increases in general interest rates coincided with increases in Chrysler's firm-specific risk during the period. Interest rates and market values change constantly. Consider the IBM $8\frac{3}{8}$ coupon bond maturing in 2019. In 1990, it was rated an Aaa bond, Moody's highest rating, and sold for $928.75 ($92\frac{7}{8}$) to yield 9.07% if held to maturity. By the end of 1997, it was lower rated on quality. However, its price had risen sharply to $1,168.75 ($116\frac{7}{8}$) and its yield to maturity had fallen to 6.87%. For IBM bonds, the general fall in interest rates during these seven years had a bigger effect than the firm-specific increase in risk.

Today many bonds are trading in a manner similar to the practice in the nineteenth century (i.e., some 150 years ago). When bonds are issued, underwriters play an important role in the design and placement of the issue and earn substantial fees in the process. As existing bonds are traded, getting quotes on a bond may involve calling many brokers. Each broker needs to make a profit so they create a "spread" between the price they pay for a bond and the price at which they will sell it. This is a time honored practice and similar to the one you encounter when traveling internationally. You pay a higher price for the foreign currency when you enter the country than you receive as you leave. In addition, there is probably a "transaction fee" that you pay on each of your currency exchanges.

A number of bond issuers have seen this as an opportunity to inject efficiency and cut out (or reduce) the role of the middleman in bond issuance. Pittsburgh Mayor Tom Murphy used the Internet to auction $55 million of municipal bonds directly to institutional investors in the fall of 1999. Historically, commissions on bond issues were around $5 per bond, but Pittsburgh has been issuing at a cost of half that on the Web. Ford Motor Company and FedEX are selling commercial paper directly to investors on Web sites now. As this is being written, the top 20 issuers of commercial paper are preparing to launch an Internet trading platform for their commercial paper as a joint venture. Some $1.2 trillion of commercial paper is traded.

This is the tip of the iceberg. As the new e-trading opportunities grow, spawned by small, fast-moving innovators, the established firms in the industry will strike back by offering parallel opportunities. The result will surely be reduced trading costs and increased ability to quickly find buyers and sellers.

Even the U.S. government is getting into the game, with U.S. savings bonds. These are basically "zero-coupon" bonds. You invest $25 today and sometime in the future the bond matures and you receive $50. Typically these have been sold at post offices or through payroll deductions. In olden times, children bought savings stamps at a dime apiece and accumulated them until they had enough in their savings book to turn in for one of the bonds. Today, go to the Web site at www.savingsbonds.gov. They accept VISA and Mastercard, though finding out how to do it is a bit clunky. In the first couple of days the site was open in November of 1999, 3,600 bonds were sold.

ASSESSING THE RISKINESS OF BONDS

A key feature in deciding the market rate of interest, and therefore the value of a bond, is a risk assessment of the bond. The higher the risk, the higher the interest rate investors will require before making the investment. An individual investor typically cannot spend the time to do in-depth analysis of each bond offering, so commercial services have developed to offer this service. Moody's and Standard & Poor's Corporation (S&P) are perhaps the best known.

They rate bonds issued by corporations according to their creditworthiness. Higher ratings are safer and therefore companies with better ratings pay lower interest rates. Issuers with high proportions of debt and low interest-coverage ratios usually receive lower bond ratings and therefore pay higher interest rates. Why? Because high debt levels and low interest coverage imply less ability to meet bond obligations and thus place more risk on bondholders. Lower ratings lead to lower prices and therefore higher yields on the bond. As of 1984, 1990, and 1997, the average yields for industrial bonds rated by Moody's were as follows, by rating category.

Rating	Aaa	Aa	A	Baa
Yield 1984	11.76	12.23	12.72	13.34
Yield 1990	9.16	9.58	9.84	11.12
Yield 1997	6.54	6.90	6.95	7.24

Note going across from left to right that in each year the yields rise uniformly as the ratings decrease. Comparing 1990 with 1997 shows that interest rates have fallen significantly during the 1990s. To assign the ratings, S&P often interviews management in addition to analyzing financial data. Aaa bonds have the lowest debt ratios and the highest interest-coverage ratios, as you would expect. Investors will accept a lower yield for debt issued by the least risky companies.

In assessing the riskiness of a company's securities, U.S. analysts rely heavily on the debt level. In the United States, debt obligations are legally enforceable, and many examples exist where creditors have forced a company to liquidate to pay interest or to repay principal. An example from the 1990s is Montgomery Ward.

Financial analysts must adapt to the realities facing the specific companies. In Japan, for example, debt ratios tend to be much higher than they are in the United States. This difference partly reflects banking practices. Japanese banks lend very large sums to the biggest and most creditworthy corporations. Although the transaction has the form of debt, it tends to be part of a very long-term relationship between bank and customer. The banks end up with long-term rights that look somewhat like the rights of a U.S. shareholder.

A mortgage bond, which has a specific lien on particular assets, is an inherently safer investment than the company's debentures, which have no specific lien on any asset. If you consider interest payments to be the return the lender earns for making the loan, it would be reasonable for the interest rate on a mortgage bond to be less than the interest rate on a subordinated debenture bond. It will be useful, as we consider various characteristics of bond contracts and other lending arrangements, to think about whether the feature would make the contract more or less attractive to the lender. The more attractive to the lender, the lower the interest rate. Here we might think of attractiveness in terms of risk. The less risk of default or nonpayment, the more attractive it is to the lender.

Regardless of a particular lien on an asset or other feature, the relative attractiveness of specific bonds depends primarily on the creditworthiness of the issuer. Thus, IBM can issue billions of dollars of unsecured debentures at relatively low interest rates even when compared with the secured mortgage bonds that might be issued by riskier real estate companies.

INTEREST RATES

We have discussed the market interest rate that drives the prices of a bond, but we have not summarized the elements that determine that interest rate. The details of the math are beyond the scope of this text, but the essence deserves mention. The interest rate has three basic components: the real interest rate, the inflation premium, and the firm specific risk component.

1. The *real interest rate* is the return that investors demand because they are delaying their consumption. If you could have an apple now or later, now is better most of the time. Most people would say the real rate of interest historically has been in the 3% range.

2. The *inflation premium* is the extra interest that investors require because they worry that the general price level will change between now and the time they receive their money. This is an expectation, and peoples' expectations vary widely. In some countries inflation rates routinely exceed 100% per year, whereas in the United States recent inflation rates have been closer to 3% per year.

3. Finally, there is the *firm specific risk,* referring to the risk that the firm will not repay the loan or will not pay the interest on time. In either event the investor could lose everything, and at a minimum will have to pursue legal avenues to collect the money

due. This amount ranges widely from 1% or 2% for firms with very good credit ratings to 10% or more for firms facing financial distress.

BONDS ISSUED AT A DISCOUNT

Suppose 10,000 of the two-year 10% coupon bonds described in Exhibit 9-2, p. 369, are issued at a discount on December 31, 2002 when annual market interest rates are 12%. Proceeds of the sale are 10,000 × $965.35 = $9,653,500, which reflects an effective interest rate of 6% per semiannual period, as shown in Exhibit 9-2. Therefore, the company recognizes a discount of $10,000,000 − $9,653,500 = $346,500 at issuance. The discount results from the fact that the company has use of only $9,653,500, not $10,000,000. The journal entry at issue is:

Cash	9,653,500	
Discount on bonds payable	346,500	
Bonds payable		10,000,000

The discount on bonds payable is a contra account. It is deducted from bonds payable. The bonds payable account usually shows the face amount, and the difference between bonds payable and discount on bonds payable is the amount shown on the balance sheet, often referred to as the net carrying amount, the net liability, or simply the book value:

Issuer's Balance Sheet	December 31, 2002
Bonds payable, 10% due December 31, 2004	$10,000,000
Deduct: Discount on bonds payable	346,500
Net liability (book value)	$ 9,653,500

For bonds issued at a discount, interest takes two forms—semiannual cash outlays of 5% × $10 million = $500,000 plus an "extra" lump-sum cash payment of $346,500 at maturity (total payment of $10,000,000 at maturity when only $9,653,500 was actually borrowed). For the issuer, the extra $346,500 is another cost of using the borrowed funds over the four semiannual periods. For the investor, the extra amount represents extra interest in addition to the coupon payments. The issuer should spread the extra $346,500 over all four periods, not simply charge it at maturity. The spreading of the discount over the life of the bonds is called **discount amortization.**

How much of the $346,500 should be amortized each semiannual period? A simple alternative is straight-line amortization:

discount amortization
The spreading of bond discount over the life of the bonds as expense.

Cash interest payment, .05 × $10,000,000	$500,000
Amortization of discount, $346,500 ÷ 4 periods	86,625
Total semiannual interest expense	$586,625

Notice that the amortization of a bond discount increases the interest expense of the issuer. The straight-line amortization is simple to use, but it has the drawback of implying a different effective interest rate each period. During the first 6 months of the life of the bonds, the implied interest rate would be 6.08% ($586,625 interest expense divided by proceeds or carrying value of $9,653,500). The $86,625 of amortized discount would increase the carrying value or book value of the debt to $9,740,125 in the second 6 months, yielding an implied interest rate of 6.02% for the second six months ($586,625 ÷ $9,740,125).

A preferred amortization method that uses a constant interest rate is **effective-interest amortization,** also called the **compound interest method.** The Financial

effective-interest amortization (compound interest method) An amortization method that uses a constant interest rate.

Accounting Standards Board (FASB) requires its use for bond discounts and premiums. The key to effective-interest amortization is that each period bears an interest expense equal to the carrying value of the debt (the net liability or the face amount less unamortized discount) multiplied by the market interest rate in effect when the bond was issued. The product is the effective-interest amount. The difference between the effective-interest amount and the cash interest payment is the amount of discount amortized for the period.

Consider our example with a market rate of 12% (or 6% each semiannual period) when the bond was issued. The effective-interest amortization schedule is shown in Exhibit 9-3. Notice that the discount amortized is not the same amount each period. The balance sheet disclosure of the bond payable is the ending net liability, calculated as the difference between the face or par value and the unamortized discount. Thus at June 30, 2003, the balance sheet would reflect a liability of $9,732,707. The calculation might be shown on the balance sheet or in the footnotes as:

Issuer's Balance Sheets	12/31/02	6/30/03	12/31/03	6/30/04	12/31/04*
Bonds payable, 10% due 12/31/04	$10,000,000	$10,000,000	$10,000,000	$10,000,000	$10,000,000
Deduct: Unamortized discount	346,500	267,293	183,334	94,337	—
Net liability	$ 9,653,500	$ 9,732,707	$ 9,816,666	$ 9,905,663	$10,000,000

*Before payment at maturity.

Exhibit 9-3 shows the worksheet and journal entries for the effective-interest method of amortizing the bond discount. The journal entries are presented in the left column using a discount account and in the right column using only a bonds payable account. Note that the interest expense each period is the market rate of interest at issue times the carrying value or book value of the bond [see column (2) of Exhibit 9-3]. This value increases each semiannual period as the carrying value converges on the maturity value. The cash payment is a constant $500,000, calculated as one-half the coupon rate (10% ÷ 2) times the par value ($10,000,000). Exhibit 9-4 illustrates this information in the context of the accounting equation.

BONDS ISSUED AT A PREMIUM

Accounting for bonds issued at a premium is not difficult after you have mastered bond discounts. The differences are reversed from discount bonds:

1. The cash proceeds *exceed* the face amount.
2. The amount of the contra account Premium on Bonds Payable is *added* to the face amount to determine the net liability reported in the balance sheet.
3. The amortization of bond premium *decreases* the interest expense.

To illustrate, suppose the 10,000 bonds described earlier were issued when annual market interest rates were 8% (and semiannual rates, 4%). Proceeds would be 10,000 × $1,036.30 = $10,363,000 as shown in Exhibit 9-2. Exhibits 9-5 and 9-6 show how the effective-interest method is applied to the bond premium. The key concept remains the same as that for amortization of a bond discount. The interest expense equals the net liability each period multiplied by the market interest rate in effect when the bond was issued. Balance sheets show the net liability calculated as the face amount plus unamortized premium. The premium reduces to zero over the life of the bond as shown at the top of p. 377.

Exhibit 9-3

Effective-Interest Amortization of Bond Discount

For 6 Months Ended	(1) Beginning Net Liability	(2) Effective Interest* @ 6%**	(3) Nominal Interest† @ 5%	(4) Discount Amortized (2)−(3)	Ending Liability Face Amount	Unamortized Discount	Ending Net Liability
12/31/02	—	—	—	—	$10,000,000	$346,500	$9,653,500
6/30/03	$9,653,500	$ 579,207	$ 500,000	$ 79,207	10,000,000	267,293‡	9,732,707
12/31/03	9,732,707	583,959	500,000	83,959	10,000,000	183,334	9,816,666
6/30/04	9,816,666	588,997	500,000	88,997	10,000,000	94,337	9,905,663
12/31/04	9,905,663	594,337	500,000	94,337	10,000,000	0	10,000,000
		$2,346,500	$2,000,000	$346,500			

*Market interest rate when issued times beginning net liability, column (1).

**To avoid rounding errors, an unrounded actual effective rate slightly under 6% was used. The table used to calculate the proceeds of the issue has too few significant digits to calculate the exact present value of a number as large as $10 million. The more exact issue price would be $9,653,489.

†Nominal (coupon interest) rate times par value (face value), for 6 months.

‡$346,500 − $79,207 = $267,293; $267,293 − $83,959 = $183,334; etc.

JOURNAL ENTRIES: USING A DISCOUNT ACCOUNT OR USING BONDS PAYABLE DIRECTLY

12/31/02	1.	Cash	9,653,500		Cash	9,653,500	
		Discount on bonds payable	346,500		Bonds payable		9,653,500
		Bond's payable		10,000,000			
6/30/03	2.	Interest expense	579,207		Interest expense	579,207	
		Discount on bonds payable		79,207	Bonds payable		79,207
		Cash		500,000	Cash		500,000
12/31/03		Interest expense	583,959		Interest expense	583,959	
		Discount on bonds payable		83,959	Bonds payable		83,959
		Cash		500,000	Cash		500,000
6/30/04		Interest expense	588,997		Interest expense	588,997	
		Discount on bonds payable		88,997	Bonds payable		88,997
		Cash		500,000	Cash		500,000
12/31/04		Interest expense	594,337		Interest expense	594,337	
		Discount on bonds payable		94,337	Bonds payable		94,337
		Cash		500,000	Cash		500,000
12/31/04	3.	Bonds payable	10,000,000		Bonds payable	10,000,000	
		Cash		10,000,000	Cash		10,000,000

Exhibit 9-4

Balance Sheet Equation Effects of Effective-Interest Amortization of Bond Discount (Rounded to Thousands of Dollars)

	A	=	L		+	SE
	Cash		Bonds Payable	Discount on Bonds Payable		Retained Income
Issuer's records:						
1. Issuance	+9,654	=	+10,000	−346 [Increase Discount]		
2. Semiannual interest 6 months ended						
6/30/03	−500	=		+79		−579
12/31/03	−500	=		+84 [Decrease		−584 [Increase
6/30/04	−500	=		+89 Discount]		−589 Interest
12/31/04	−500	=		+94		−594 Expense]
3. Maturity value (final payment)	−10,000	=	−10,000	0		
Bond-related totals	−2,346	=	+ 0	+0	+	−2,346

Exhibit 9-5

Effective-Interest Amortization of Bond Premium

For 6 Months Ended	(1) Beginning Net Liability	(2) Effective Interest* @ 4%**	(3) Nominal Interest† @ 5%	(4) Premium Amortized (3)−(2)	Ending Liability Face Amount	Unamortized Premium	Ending Net Liability
12/31/02	—	—	—	—	$10,000,000	$363,000	$10,363,000
6/30/03	$10,363,000	$ 414,517	$ 500,000	$ 85,483	10,000,000	277,517‡	10,277,517
12/31/03	10,277,517	411,098	500,000	88,902	10,000,000	188,615	10,188,615
6/30/04	10,188,615	407,542	500,000	92,458	10,000,000	96,157	10,096,157
12/31/04	10,096,157	403,843	500,000	96,157	10,000,000	0	10,000,000
		$1,637,000	$2,000,000	$363,000			

*Market interest rate when issued times beginning net liability, column (1).
**To avoid rounding errors, an unrounded actual effective rate slightly under 4% was used.
†Nominal (coupon interest) rate times par value (face values), for 6 months.
‡$363,000 − $85,483 = $277,517; $277,517 − $88,902 = $188,615; etc.

JOURNAL ENTRIES: PREMIUM AMORTIZATION (WITHOUT EXPLANATIONS)

```
12/31/02  1.  Cash ...........................  10,363,000
                  Premium on bonds payable .........              363,000
                  Bonds payable ....................          $10,000,000
6/30/03   2.  Interest expense .....................     414,517
              Premium on bonds payable .............      85,483
                  Cash .............................              500,000
12/31/03      Interest expense ....................     411,098
              Premium on bonds payable .............      88,902
                  Cash .............................              500,000
6/30/04       Interest expense ....................     407,542
              Premium on bonds payable .............      92,458
                  Cash .............................              500,000
12/31/04      Interest expense ....................     403,843
              Premium on bonds payable .............      96,157
                  Cash .............................              500,000
12/31/04  3.  Bonds payable .......................  10,000,000
                  Cash ............................           10,000,000
```

Exhibit 9-6

Balance Sheet Equation Effects of Effective-Interest Amortization of Bond Premium
($ Rounded to Thousands)

	A	=	L		+	SE
	Cash		Bonds Payable	Premium on Bonds Payable		Retained Income
Issuer's records						
1. Issuance	+10,363	=	+10,000	+363 [Increase Premium]		
2. Semiannual interest 6 months ended						
6/30/03	−500	=		−85		−415 [Increase Interest Expense]
12/31/03	−500	=		−89 [Decrease Premium]		−411
6/30/04	−500	=		−93		−407
12/31/04	−500	=		−96		−404
3. Maturity value (final payment)	−10,000	=	−10,000			
Bond-related totals	− 1,637	=	+ 0	+ 0	+	−1,637

Issuer's Balance Sheets	12/31/02	6/30/03	12/31/03	6/30/04	12/31/04*
Bonds payable, 10% due 12/31/04	$10,000,000	$10,000,000	$10,000,000	$10,000,000	$ 10,000,000
Add: Premium on bonds payable	363,000	277,517	188,615	96,157	0
Net liability	$10,363,000	$10,277,517	$10,188,615	$ 10,096,157	$10,000,000

*Before payment at maturity.

EARLY EXTINGUISHMENT

Investors do not always hold bonds until maturity. Often they sell the bonds to other investors. Such a sale does not affect the issuer's books unless the issuer is the one doing the buying. Companies do redeem or pay off their own bonds either by purchases on the open market or by exercising their rights to redeem callable bonds. When a company chooses to redeem its own bonds before maturity, the transaction is known as an early extinguishment. Gains or losses on these early extinguishments of debt are computed in the usual manner. That is, the difference between the cash paid and the net carrying amount of the bonds (face less unamortized discount or plus unamortized premium) is the gain or loss.

Consider the bonds issued at a discount and described in Exhibit 9-3. Suppose the issuer purchases all its bonds on the open market for 96 on December 31, 2003 (after all interest payments and amortization were recorded for 2003):

Carrying amount		
Face or par value	$10,000,000	
Deduct: Unamortized discount on bonds*	183,334	$9,816,666
Cash required, 96% of $10,000,000		9,600,000
Difference, gain on early extinguishment of debt		$ 216,666

*See Exhibit 9-3. Of the original $346,500 discount, $79,207 + $83,959 = $163,166 has been amortized, leaving $183,334 of the discount unamortized.

Exhibit 9-7 presents an analysis of the transaction ($ rounded to thousands). The $216,666 gain on extinguishment of debt would be shown on an income statement below operating income as a separate classification called an extraordinary item. The journal entry on December 31, 2003, is:

```
Bond payable .........................    10,000,000
    Discount on bonds payable ............               183,334
    Gain on early extinguishment of debt ....             216,666
    Cash .............................               9,600,000
To record open-market acquisition of
entire issue of 10% bonds at 96
```

Exhibit 9-7

Analysis of Early Extinguishment of Debt on Issuer's Records
($ in Thousands)

	A	=	L		+	SE
	Cash		Bonds Payable	Discount on Bonds Payable		Retained Income
Redemption, December 31, 2003	−9,600	=	−10,000	+183 [Decrease Discount]	+217	[Gain on Early Extinguishment]

BONDS SOLD BETWEEN INTEREST DATES

Bond interest payments are typically made semiannually. Suppose the company in our example had its $10 million worth of 10% bonds printed and ready to be issued on December 31, 2002, but then market conditions delayed the bond issue. On January 31, 2003, a month after the originally planned issue date, the bonds were issued at par. The bond contract still requires the payment of $500,000 interest every 6 months, beginning June 30, 2003.

How does this delay in the issuance date affect the investor? Bonds sold between interest dates command the market price plus accrued interest. If an investor owns a bond for only 5 months but collects interest for a full 6 months, 1 month of interest is unearned. Thus, the market quotations you see for bonds always mean that the investor must pay an extra amount for any unearned interest to be received at the next interest payment date. In our example, the price to be paid is:

Market price of bonds at 100 on 1/31/03	$10,000,000
Accrued interest, $0.10 \times \$10,000,000 \times \frac{1}{12}$	83,333
Market price plus accrued interest	$10,083,333

Note that the $500,000 interest payment due on June 30, 2000, is spread over the first 6 months of 2000 by the straight-line method—that is, with an equal amount to each month even though the bond was in use for only 5 of those 6 months. In this instance, the straight-line method is actually used because the distortion as compared with the effective interest rate is small within a six-month period.

How does the issue date affect the issuer? Exhibit 9-8 presents an analysis of these transactions ($ rounded to thousands). Note that the interest expense for the first half of 2003 is properly measured as $500,000 − $83,333 = $416,667, representing only the 5 months that the money was actually in use. Although the company pays out the full $500,000, this amount is lessened by the extra $83,333 paid by the buyer. The journal entries follow:

1/31/03	Cash	$10,083,333	
	Bonds payable		$10,000,000
	Accrued interest payable		83,333
6/30/03	Accrued interest payable	83,333	
	Interest expense	416,667	
	Cash		500,000

Obviously, the analysis of transactions can be made more complicated by combining the acquisitions of bonds between interest dates with discounts and premiums. However, these are mechanical details that do not involve any new concepts, so we do not need to cover them in detail here.

Exhibit 9-8

Analysis of Bonds Sold between Interest Dates
($ in Thousands)

	A	=	L		+	SE
	Cash		Bonds Payable	Accrued Interest Payable		Retained Income
Issuance, 1/31/03	+10,083	=	+10,000	+83		
Interest payment, 6/30/03	−500	=		−83		−417 [Increase Interest Expense]

NON-INTEREST-BEARING NOTES AND BONDS

Some notes and bonds do not provide semiannual interest payments. Instead, they simply pay a lump sum at a specified date. For example, consider **zero coupon** bonds. These bonds provide no cash interest payments during their life. The name, zero coupon, is completely descriptive. To call such notes non-interest-bearing is a little misleading, though. Investors demand interest revenue. Otherwise, why would they bother investing in the first place? Therefore, zero coupon bonds and notes are sold for less than the face or maturity value. The investor determines their market value at the issuance date by calculating the present value of their maturity value, using the market rate of interest for notes having similar terms and risks. The discount is amortized as interest expense to the borrower (issuer) and as interest revenue to the lender (investor) over the life of the note.

zero coupon A bond or note that pays no cash interest during its life.

Instead of collecting semiannual or other periodic payments, banks often discount both long-term and short-term notes when making loans. Consider a 2-year, "non-interest-bearing," $10,000 face-value note issued on December 31, 2001, when semiannual market interest rates were 5%. In exchange for a promise to pay $10,000 on December 31, 2003, the bank provides the borrower with cash equal to the present value (*PV*) of the $10,000 payment:

$$PV \text{ of } \$1.00 \text{ from Table 9-2, 5\% column, 4-period row} = 0.8227$$
$$PV \text{ of } \$10,000 \text{ note} = \$10,000 \times .8227 = \$8,227$$

The note requires no specific interest payments. However, there is **implicit interest** (or **imputed interest**), which is a form of interest expense that is not explicitly recognized as such in a loan agreement. The imputed interest amount is based on an **imputed interest rate,** which is the market rate that equates the proceeds of the loan with the present value of the loan payments.

implicit interest (imputed interest) An interest expense that is not explicitly recognized in a loan agreement.

In this example, the $10,000 payment on December 31, 2003 will consist of $8,227 repayment of principal and $1,773 ($10,000 − $8,227) of imputed interest. At issue, the note is shown on the borrower's balance sheet as follows:

imputed interest rate The market interest rate that equates the proceeds from a loan with the present value of the loan payments.

Note payable, due December 31, 2003	$10,000
Deduct: Discount on note payable	1,773
Net liability	$ 8,227

Exhibit 9-9

Analysis of Transactions of Borrower, Discounted Notes

	A	=	L		+	SE
	Cash		Notes Payable	Discount on Notes Payable		Retained Income
Proceeds of loan	+ 8,227	=	+10,000	−1,773 [Increase Discount]		
Semiannual amortization						
6 Months ended:						
6/30/02		=		+411		−411
12/31/02		=		+432 [Decrease Discount]		−432 [Increase Interest Expense]
6/30/03		=		+454		−454
12/31/03		=		+476		−476
Payment of note	−10,000	=	−10,000			
Bond-related totals	− 1,773	=	+ 0	+ 0		+ −1,773

Exhibit 9-9 shows how interest expense is recognized for each semiannual period. Each amortization of the discount decreases the discount account and increases the net carrying amount. The appropriate journal entries follow:

12/31/01	Cash	8,227	
	Discount on note payable	1,773	
	Note payable		$10,000
6/30/02	Interest expense	411	
	Discount on note payable		411
12/31/02	Interest expense	432	
	Discount on note payable		432
6/30/03	Interest expense	454	
	Discount on note payable		454
12/31/03	Interest expense	476	
	Discount on note payable		476
	Note payable	10,000	
	Cash		10,000

ACCOUNTING FOR LEASES

Objective 4
Value and account for long-term lease transactions.

lease A contract whereby an owner (lessor) grants the use of property to a second party (lessee) for rental payments.

lessor The owner of property who grants usage rights to the lessee.

lessee The party that has the right to use leased property and makes lease payments to the lessor.

Leasing is a big business. Any asset imaginable, from television sets to cars to buildings, can be acquired via a lease contract. A **lease** is a contract whereby an owner **(lessor)** grants the use of property to a second party **(lessee)** in exchange for rental payments. Our discussion focuses on leasing from the lessee's point of view.

Some lease payments are recorded as expense each time a payment is made. This would surely be true of a month-to-month lease on an apartment for example. However, other leases are actually recorded as liabilities and as assets when the contract is signed. Why? Because, although the ownership of a leased item has not been legally transferred, the lessee has full legal rights to use the item and full legal responsibility for maintaining it and paying for it. To see this most clearly, imagine the lease of a BMW that obligated you to payments of $800 per month for 4 years and gave you the right to buy the BMW at the end of the lease for $1.00. Perhaps you made a $5,000 down payment to enter into the lease. Under the lease contract, you promise to maintain, license, and insure it. These rights and responsibilities are equivalent to ownership, so the leased item is considered an asset even though the lessee does not own it. In fact, you are almost certain to pay the $1.00 and take ownership at the end of the lease.

If this lease were just treated as $800 of expense each month, the reader of your financial statement might think you had more cash available than you really do. You have committed $800 per month to these payments. This obligation is no different than the obligation to make a loan payment, so accountants decided to treat this transaction as if the lessee owns the BMW and as if the money to buy it had been borrowed.

OPERATING AND CAPITAL LEASES

capital lease (financing lease) A lease that transfers substantially all the risks and benefits of ownership to the lessee.

operating lease A lease that should be accounted for by the lessee as ordinary rent expenses.

The names given to the two types of lease accounting are: capital leases and operating leases. **Capital leases** (or **financing leases**) transfer most of the risks and benefits of ownership to the lessee. They are equivalent to installment sales in which the purchase price of an item is paid over time along with interest payments. The leased item must be recorded as if it were sold by the lessor and purchased by the lessee. The BMW lease discussed in the prior section would be a capital lease.

All other leases are **operating leases.** An example is a room or a car rented by the day, week, or month. Operating leases are accounted for as ordinary rent expenses. No balance sheet accounts are affected by operating leases.

Consider a simple example to see how the accounting differs for operating and capital leases. Suppose the Bestick Company can acquire a truck that has a useful life of 4 years and no residual value under either of the following conditions:

Buy Outright	or	Capital Lease

Cash outlays, $50,000
Borrow $50,000 cash to be repaid
  in four equal installments at 12%
  interest compounded annually
		Rental of $16,462 per year, payable
		at the end of each of 4 years

There is no basic difference between an outright purchase or an irrevocable (noncancellable) capital lease for 4 years. The Bestick Company uses the asset for its entire useful life and must pay for repairs, property taxes, and other operating costs under either plan.

Most lease rentals are paid at the start of each payment period, but to ease our computations we assume that each payment of $16,462 will occur at the end of the year. To make the comparison between capital leasing and purchasing, we need to calculate payments on the $50,000 loan in the purchase option:

$$\text{Let } X = \text{loan payment}$$
$$\$50,000 = PV \text{ of annuity of } X \text{ per year for 4 years at 12\%}$$
$$\$50,000 = 3.0373X$$
$$X = \$50,000 \div 3.0373$$
$$X = \$16,462 \text{ per year}$$

Note that this loan payment is exactly equal to the lease payment. Thus, from Bestick's perspective as lessee, both buying outright and capital leasing create an obligation for four $16,462 payments that have a present value of $50,000.

Now suppose this lease contract were treated as an operating lease. Each year the journal entry would be:

```
Rent expense  ...................  16,462
     Cash  ......................           16,462
     To record lease payment
```

No leasehold asset or lease liability would appear on the balance sheet.

Suppose the lease described must be accounted for as a capital lease. Then both a leasehold asset and a lease liability must be placed on the balance sheet at the present value of future lease payments, $50,000 in this illustration. The signing of the capital lease requires the following journal entry:

```
Truck leasehold  .................  50,000
     Capital lease liability  ..........           50,000
     To record lease creation
```

At the end of each of the 4 years, the asset must be amortized. Straight-line amortization, which is used almost without exception, is $50,000 ÷ 4 = $12,500 annually.

The yearly journal entries for the leasehold expense are:

```
Leasehold amortization expense  .....  12,500
     Truck leasehold  .............          12,500
```

In addition, the annual lease payment must be recorded. Each lease payment consists of interest expense plus an amount that reduces the outstanding liability. The effective-interest method is used, as Exhibit 9-10 demonstrates. Study the exhibit before proceeding.

The yearly journal entries for lease payments are:

	YEAR 1		YEAR 2		YEAR 3		YEAR 4	
Interest expense	6,000		4,745		3,339		1,764	
Lease liability	10,462		11,717		13,123		14,698	
Cash		16,462		16,462		16,462		16,462

Exhibit 9-10

Analytical Schedule of Capital Lease Payments

End of Year	(1) Capital Lease Liability at Beginning of Year	(2) Interest Expense at 12% Per Year	(3) Cash for Capital Lease Payment	(4) (3) − (2) Reduction in Lease Liability	(5) (1) − (4) Capital Lease Liability at End of Year
1	50,000	$6,000	$16,462	10,462	$39,538
2	39,538	4,745	16,462	11,717	27,821
3	27,821	3,339	16,462	13,123	14,698
4	14,698	1,764	16,462	14,698	0

Leasehold assets and lease liabilities are illustrated by the following items from the annual report of Kmart for the year ending January 30, 2000:

Kmart Company Footnotes
(Selected Items in Millions)

	End of January	
	2000	*1999*
Assets		
Leased property under capital leases,	$2,038	$2,140
less accumulated amortization	1,167	1,190
	$ 871	$ 950
Liabilities		
Obligations under capital leases	$1,014	$1,091

Kmart's 2000 annual report reveals that "Kmart conducts operations primarily in leased facilities. Kmart store leases are generally for terms of 25 years with multiple five-year renewal options which allow the company the option to extend the life of the lease up to 50 years beyond the initial noncancellable term." Many of these leases also require Kmart to pay taxes, maintenance, and insurance. Generally accepted accounting principles (GAAP) in the United States account for such lease or rental contracts "as if" Kmart borrowed money and purchased the leased stores. Kmart records both an asset (called "leased property under capital leases") and a liability (called a "capital lease obligation") and shows them on the balance sheet. Kmart owned 120 stores in January 2000 and held leases on 2,051 stores.

Explain why the net asset value on capital leases for Kmart of $871 million is not the same as the obligations under capital leases of $1,014 million.

ANSWER

When a company initiates a lease, the capital leased assets and the capital lease obligation are identical. Their values first diverge and then converge over time because of the accounting process. Assets are typically amortized using the straight-line basis. The liability is reduced each period using the effective interest rate method. Under this method, each lease payment includes the payment of interest and the reduction of principal. Because interest is largest in the early period of the loan, reductions in the principal of the loan start off small. Hence, we expect the liability to exceed the asset in most cases.

Exhibit 9-11

Comparison of Annual Expenses: Operating versus Capital Leases

	Operating-Lease Method	Capital-Lease Method			Differences	
Year	*(a)* *Lease* *Payment***	*(b)* *Amortization* *of Asset*†	*(c)* *Interest* *Expense*‡	*(d)* *(b) + (c)* *Total* *Expense*	*(e)* *(a) − (d)* *Difference* *in Pretax* *Income*	*(f)* *Cumulative* *Difference* *in Pretax* *Income*
1	$16,462	$12,500	$ 6,000	$18,500	$(2,038)	$(2,038)
2	16,462	12,500	4,745	17,245	(783)	(2,821)
3	16,462	12,500	3,339	15,839	623	(2,198)
4	16,462	12,500	1,764	14,264	2,198	0
Cumulative expenses	$65,848	$50,000	$15,848	$65,848	$ 0	

*Rent expense for the year under the operating-lease method.

†$50,000 ÷ 4 = $12,500.

‡From Exhibit 9-10.

DIFFERENCES IN INCOME STATEMENTS

Exhibit 9-11 summarizes the major differences between the accounting for operating leases and the accounting for capital leases. The cumulative expenses are the same, $65,848, but the timing differs. In comparison with the operating-lease approach, the capital-lease approach tends to bunch heavier charges in the early years. The longer the lease, the more pronounced the differences will be in the early years. Therefore, immediate reported income is hurt more under the capital-lease approach.

An operating lease affects the income statement as rent expense, which is the amount of the lease payment. A capital lease affects the income statement as amortization (of the asset) plus interest expense (on the liability).

However, treatment varies across the globe. If Kmart were incorporated and issuing financial reports in 17 of the 44 countries whose accounting practices were recently surveyed by the Center for International Financial Analysis & Research, no disclosure of these long-term lease commitments would be required. These countries include Austria, Brazil, Sri Lanka, and Taiwan. Most other countries follow lease disclosure practices similar to those in the United States.

CRITERIA FOR CAPITAL LEASES

Prior to 1976, almost all leases in the United States were reported in financial statements as operating leases. However, analysts criticized many companies for keeping "invisible debt" or using "off-balance sheet financing." These companies treated noncancellable leases, which created a future financial obligation, merely as a monthly rent payment and did not report them on their balance sheets under either assets or liabilities. Authorities created the existing accounting procedures for capital leases as a way of more fairly representing these leases on the balance sheet.

The lease structure determines whether a lease is treated as an operating or capital lease for accounting purposes. Under U.S. GAAP, a capital lease exists if one or more of the following conditions are met:

1. The lessor transfers ownership of the asset to the lessee by the end of the lease term.
2. The lessee can inexpensively purchase the asset from the lessor at the end of the lease.
3. The lease term equals or exceeds 75% of the estimated economic life of the property.
4. At the start of the lease term, the present value of minimum lease payments is at least 90% of the property's fair value.

Managers cannot choose how to treat an existing lease. However, some managers do seek to structure leases so that they do not meet any of the criteria of a capital lease and therefore are not shown on the balance sheet.

PENSIONS AND OTHER POSTRETIREMENT BENEFITS

Objective 5
Evaluate pensions and other postretirement benefits.

pensions Payments to former employees after they retire.

other postretirement benefits Benefits provided to retired workers in addition to a pension, such as life and health insurance.

Most U.S. companies provide retired employees with reduced wages after they stop working. Such payments are commonly called **pensions.** Retirees may also continue to receive health insurance, life insurance, or other employee benefits, which are commonly called **other postretirement benefits.**

Why are pensions and postretirement benefits liabilities? They meet the definition of liabilities as existing obligations to make future payments. We can assess the probable amount of these obligations in present value terms, so they are measurable. In addition, liability recognition is consistent with the accrual accounting system of matching expenses with their associated revenues. Workers "earn" the right to postretirement payments and benefits during their working years. Financial analysts and accountants agree that these benefits should be recognized and recorded as they are earned, years before they are disbursed. As a result, the obligation to provide postretirement benefits is reported as an unpaid liability on the balance sheet. The long time between when the liability is recorded and when it is finally paid causes us to use present value techniques to measure the obligation.

To see how the accounting for pensions and postretirement benefits works, imagine a firm with a 45-year-old employee who has worked for 20 years earning $50,000 per year. She will receive a pension of $25,000 per year after retirement at age 65. To calculate the firm's liability for this pension, assume an interest rate of 10% and a life expectancy of 20 years after retirement. The employee will collect a 20-year annuity, which will have a present value of $212,840 (8.5136 from Exhibit 9-3, p. 375, times $25,000) at retirement. Today, 20 years before retirement, the present value is $31,628 (.1486 from Table 9-2 times $212,840). Firms must disclose this present value calculation of their liability in the notes to their financial statements.

To calculate present values for pensions, firms must estimate employee life expectancy, future work lives, ages at retirement, and levels of future pension payments to retirees. Also, the firm must choose an interest rate. The formal calculations are normally done by actuaries, specialists at making such predictions.

In fact, pension liabilities are effectively provided for each year by setting some money aside as the liability grows. Companies do not just accrue huge pension liabilities during the career of each employee and then pay out the money after retirement. What would happen if the company went out of business before it paid off accrued employee pensions? There would be a lot of angry, and poorer, retirees. Because this problem actually occurred in the 1950s and 1960s, U.S. tax law now provides incentives for companies to make payments into a pension fund that is separate from the company's assets and controlled by a trustee. These payments are made during the employees' working years to assure that assets will be available to meet the pension obligation at retirement. Because significant assets are set aside on behalf of the employees, the major disclosures about pensions occur in footnotes. The footnotes reveal both the present value of the obligation and the current level of assets that are set aside to meet the obligation. IBM's footnotes disclose that as of January 1, 2000, the company set aside $45 billion of assets to cover approximately $34 billion of obligations.

How do companies account for pensions? Suppose a company's current pension expense is $100,000, of which $90,000 is paid in cash to a pension fund. Note the two parts, an expense that represents the increase in the obligation during the current year, and a recording of the cash paid, which is not always equal to the expense. The accounting for pensions has the following basic framework:

	A	=	L	+		SE	
			Accrued				
			Pensions				
	Cash		*Payable*			*Retained Income*	
Current pension expense	−90,000	=	+10,000		−100,000	[Increase] Pension [Expense]	

The journal entry would be:

```
Pension expense ...........................   100,000
    Cash ..................................              90,000
    Accrued pensions payable .............              10,000
To record pension expense for the year
```

   Accounting for the expense of life insurance, health insurance, and similar postretirement benefits is similar to accounting for pensions. The key difference is that the U.S. Congress has not created a special tax incentive to set money aside. Most companies do not set aside specific assets on behalf of employees and therefore the full amount is recorded as a liability. Financial analysts and accountants treat the present value of expected payments as a liability. Increases in the liability are recognized as a current expense.

   Suppose the present value of postretirement benefits is $100,000 at the beginning of 20X1 and $120,000 at the end of the year. The summary journal entry to record the $20,000 increase for 20X1 is:

```
Other postretirement
    benefits expense ....................    $20,000
    Accrued postretirement
        benefits payable .................              $20,000
```

The balance sheets thus include the following:

	December 31	
	20X1	*20X0*
Long-term liabilities:		
Other postretirement benefits	$120,000	$100,000

The following may help put lease and pension liabilities in perspective ($ in millions):

			Footnote Pension Disclosures	
	Total Assets	**Lease Liability**	*Pension Assets*	*Pension Obligation*
AT&T	$169,406	$ —	$21,132	$12,868
Delta Airlines	16,544	196	9,020	8,872
Tricon	3,961	102	290	315
UPS	23,043	516	5,507	4,196

   The first two companies are familiar to most readers. AT&T is a long-distance phone company and Delta is a major U.S. airline. Tricon is the parent of Taco Bell, Pizza Hut, and KFC that was created in a spin-off of these companies from PepsiCo some years go. UPS is the delivery company that competes with FedEX and the U.S. Postal Service. Lease liabilities are relatively small even though these companies were chosen to include fast food and airlines where leasing is a significant activity. Tricon's footnotes reveal that seven times as much in commitments for operating leases of stores exist, but they do not quite meet the requirements to be classified as "capital leases" and recorded as liabilities. UPS leasing is primarily for airplanes.

The pension disclosures reveal several patterns. Generally pension assets exceed pension obligations, which means the companies have set aside more assets than are required to meet existing obligations. These amounts are large relative to the size of the firm. For Delta, the pension assets are over half the size of the operating firm.

Internationally, practice concerning pensions and other postretirement benefits varies widely, mainly because of differences in business practices. For example, many countries provide the majority of retirement income through individual savings or through tax-supported government programs akin to the U.S. Social Security Administration. In these cases, actual company pensions are either extremely small or do not exist, so there is nothing that needs to be reported. In roughly half of the 45 countries examined in a recent survey, it was common practice for pensions to be managed by an independent outside trustee with funding from the sponsoring company through periodic payments to the trustee, in accord with U.S. practice. This separate fund provides substantial security to employees that their future pensions claims will be honored. In the United States, prior to the 1970s, it was very common for companies to go out of business and for their current and future retirees to be left without pensions. Today outside trustees maintain financial assets on behalf of current workers, and the Pension Benefit Guarantee Corporation provides some "pension insurance" for workers.

SUMMARY PROBLEMS FOR YOUR REVIEW

PROBLEM ONE

Suppose that on December 31, 2002, ExxonMobil issued $12 million of 10-year, 10% debentures. Assume that the annual market interest rate at issuance was 14%.

1. Compute the proceeds from issuing the debentures.
2. Prepare an analysis of the following items: (a) issuance of the debentures; (b) first two semiannual interest payments; and (c) payment of the maturity value. Use the balance sheet equation (similar to the presentation in Exhibit 9-4, p. 375). Round to the nearest thousand dollars. Use a bond discount account.
3. Prepare journal entries for the items in requirement 2. Use a bond discount account.

SOLUTION TO PROBLEM ONE

1. Because the market interest rate exceeds the nominal rate, the proceeds will be less than the face amount. This can be computed as the present value (PV) of the 20 interest payments of $600,000 and the $12 million maturity value at 7% per semiannual period:

PV of interest payments: 10.5940 × $600,000	$6,356,400
PV of maturity value: .2584 × $12,000,000	3,100,800
Total proceeds	$9,457,200

2. See Exhibit 9-12.

Exhibit 9-12

Analysis of Exxon's Bond Transactions: Problem Two

($ Rounded to Thousands)

	A	=	L		+	SE
	Cash		Bonds Payable	Discount on Bonds Payable		Retained Income
Exxon's records						
1. Issuance	+9,457		+12,000	−2,543 [Increase Discount]		
2. Semiannual interest						
6 Months ended						
6/30/03	−600			+62 [Decrease	−662* [Increase	
12/31/03	−600			+66 Discount]	−666* Interest Expense]	
3. Maturity value						
(final payment)	−12,000		− 12,000			
Bond-related totals†	−14,543		0	0	−14,543	

*7% × 9,457 = 662; 7% × (9,457 + 62) = 666.

†Totals after payment at maturity and all 20 entries for discount amortization and interest payments are made.

3.

12/31/02:	Cash	9,457,200		
	Discount on bonds payable	2,542,800		
	Bonds payable.		12,000,000	
6/30/03:	Interest expense.	662,004		
	Discount on bonds payable		62,004	
	Cash		600,000	
12/31/03:	Interest expense.	666,344		
	Discount on bonds payable		66,344	
	Cash		600,000	
12/31/12:	Bonds payable.	12,000,000		
	Cash		12,000,000	

PROBLEM TWO

Xerox Corporation plans to enter some new communications business. The company expects to accumulate sufficient cash from its new operations to pay a lump sum of $200 million to Prudential Insurance Company at the end of 5 years. Prudential will lend money on a promissory note now, will take no payments until the end of 5 years, and desires 12% interest compounded annually.

1. How much money will Prudential lend Xerox?

2. Prepare journal entries for Xerox at the inception of the loan and at the end of each of the first 2 years.

SOLUTION TO PROBLEM TWO

The initial step in solving present value problems focuses on a basic question, Which table should I use? No computations should be made until you are convinced that you are using the correct table.

1. Use Table 9-2. The $200 million is a future amount. Its present value is:

$$PV = \$200,000,000 \times \frac{1}{(1 + 0.12)^5}$$

The conversion factor, $1/(1 + 0.12)^5$, is in row 5 and the 12% column. It is .5674.

$$PV = \$200,000,000 \times .5674 = \$113,480,000$$

2.

Cash	113,480,000	
Long-term note payable (or long-term debt)		113,480,000

To record borrowing that is payable in a lump sum at the end of 5 years at 12% interest compounded annually.

Interest expense	13,617,600	
Long-term note payable		13,617,600

To record interest expense and corresponding accumulation of principal at the end of the first year: $0.12 \times \$113,480,000 = \$13,617,600$.

Interest expense	15,251,712	
Long-term note payable		15,251,712

To record interest expense and corresponding accumulation of principal at the end of the second year: $0.12 \times (\$113,480,000 + \$13,617,600)$.

Reflect on the entries for interest. Note how the interest expense becomes larger if no interest payments are made from year to year. This mounting interest expense occurs because the unpaid interest is being added to the principal to form a new higher principal each year.

PROBLEM THREE

Refer to the preceding problem. Suppose Xerox and Prudential agree on a 12% interest rate compounded annually. However, Xerox will pay a total of $200 million in the form of $40 million annual payments at the end of each of the next 5 years. How much money will Prudential lend Xerox?

SOLUTION TO PROBLEM THREE

Use Table 9-3. The $40 million is a uniform periodic payment at the end of a series of years. Therefore, it is an annuity. Its present value is:

$$
\begin{aligned}
PV_A &= \text{Annual payment} \times \text{Present value factor} \\
&= \$40 \text{ million} \times \text{Present value factor for 5 years at 12\%} \\
&= \$40 \text{ million} \times 3.6048 \\
&= \$144,192,000
\end{aligned}
$$

In particular, note that Prudential is willing to lend more than in Problem Two even though the interest rate is the same. Why? Because Prudential will get its money back more quickly.

PROBLEM FOUR

Suppose the Philbrick company enters into a lease to use a machine for 3 years with payments at the end of each year. Lease payments for the 3-year term of the lease are as follows, for a total of $120,000. The lease is treated as a capital lease and an interest rate of 10% is used.

Year 1	$ 40,000
Year 2	40,000
Year 3	40,000
Total minimum rentals	$120,000

1. Calculate the amount to be recorded as the carrying value of the capital leased asset and the capital lease liability as of the beginning of the lease on 12/31/X0.
2. How will the first year's payment be recorded?
3. How will the first year's income statement be affected by the lease?

SOLUTION TO PROBLEM FOUR

1. The present value of a 3-year annuity of $40,000 per year at 10% will be the initial value of the asset and the liability. From Table 9-3, the present value factor is 2.4869.

$$2.4869 \times \$40,000 = \$99,476$$

2. The first year's payment will be for $40,000, part of which is interest and part of which is principal repayment. The interest portion is $.10 \times 99,476 = 9,948$. The journal entry would be:

Interest expense	9,948	
Capital lease obligation	30,052	
Cash		40,000

3. The first year's income statement will show an expense of $9,948 for interest. It will also show depreciation on the capital leased asset of 33,159 calculated on a straight-line basis ($99,476 ÷ 3 years).

Highlights to Remember

1. **Compute and interpret present and future values.** The time value of money is a critical concept for understanding many long-term liabilities. We use present value concepts to value future cash obligation in today's dollars. The basic concept is that a lump sum to be received in the future is worth less today. Thus, present values are always less than future values. The text explains how to apply this concept for lump sums and also for annuities, which are sequences of equal sized payments.
2. **Value bonds using present value techniques.** Bonds are a common long-term liability. We can calculate their current economic value by combining the present value of their future interest payments with the present value of their principal payment. Investors use this procedure to decide on how much to pay for a bond. The calculation uses the market rate of interest appropriate to the company's risk level and the current level of expected inflation. Companies originally record the bond liability at the amount received from investors on issue.
3. **Account for bond issues over their entire life.** During the life of a bond, companies recognize interest expense each period. They use the effective interest rate method to calculate the interest expense each period. They determine the interest paid or payable by multiplying the coupon rate of interest specified in the bond contract by the par value. They determine the interest expense by multiplying the market interest rate when the bond was issued times the book value of the bond. The difference between the two is the amount of the bond discount or premium that is amortized during the period. Amortizing a bond discount increases interest expense and amortizing a bond premium decreases it. The market interest rate depends on the "real rate of interest" that investors require to delay their consumption, the inflation expectation, and the risk associated with the bond. Third parties such as S&P and Moody's evaluate bonds to help investors decide how risky a bond is and, therefore, how much a bond is worth.

4. **Value and account for long-term lease transactions.** Leases are contracts that grant the lessee the right to use property owned by the lessor. Because many leases involve long time periods and place many of the risks of ownership on the lessee, GAAP contains rules to classify some leases as capital leases. Companies account for a capital lease as if the asset were purchased. They create both an asset and a liability when they sign a capital lease. The initial asset and liability values are both equal to the present value of payments required under the lease. The companies amortize the asset over its economic life and they divide the lease payments into interest expense and loan repayment portions using the effective interest amortization of interest. During the life of the lease, the book value of the liability is typically larger than the book value of the asset because of the different amortization methods used.

5. **Evaluate pensions and other postretirement benefits.** The concept of a pension liability requires that measurable obligations for future pension payments and other postretirement benefits be recognized to properly state the balance sheet. Historical precedent leads to footnote disclosure for much of the pension information. On the income statement, the matching principal leads companies to record the change in their liability for future obligations for pensions and other postretirement benefits annually. The details of these calculations are deferred to future accounting courses, but the essence is that companies record the change in the liability as an expense during the current period. Pension disclosures involve footnote presentations of the present value of the obligation as well as the value of pension assets set aside with a trustee on behalf of the employees. For life and health insurance obligations to future retirees, no assets are typically set aside. Thus, financial statements present a significant liability equal to the present value of anticipated future payments for life and health insurance. Both pensions and insurance obligations depend on complex forecasts of future costs, retiree life expectancies, and so forth.

Accounting Vocabulary

annuity, p. 366	effective interest rate, p. 370	operating lease, p. 380
capital lease, p. 380	financing lease, p. 380	other postretirement benefits,
compound interest, p. 361	future value, p. 361	p. 384
compound interest method,	implicit interest, p. 379	pensions, p. 384
p. 373	imputed interest, p. 379	premium on bonds, p. 369
coupon rate, p. 370	imputed interest rate, p. 379	present value, p. 364
current yield, p. 370	lease, p. 380	rate of return, p. 364
discount amortization, p. 373	lessee, p. 380	simple interest, p. 361
discount on bonds, p. 369	lessor, p. 380	underwriters, p. 370
discount rates, p. 364	market rate, p. 370	yield to maturity, p. 370
effective-interest amortization,	nominal interest rate, p. 370	zero coupon, p. 379
p. 373		

Assignment Material

QUESTIONS

9-1 Explain what is meant by the *time value of money.*

9-2 "Future value and present value are two sides of the same coin." Explain.

9-3 "If interest is compounded semiannually instead of annually, you get twice as much interest." Do you agree? Explain.

9-4   How are Table 9-2 (p. 365) and Table 9-3 (p. 368) related to each other?

9-5   Contrast coupon (*nominal*) and *market* interest rates for bonds.

9-6   A company issued bonds with a nominal rate of 10%. At what market rates will the bonds be issued at a discount? At what market rates will they be issued at a premium?

9-7   Why is it important for both companies and investors to assess the riskiness of bonds?

9-8   "The quoted bond interest rates imply a rate per annum, but the bond markets do not mean that rate literally." Explain.

9-9   "When a bond is issued at a discount, there are two components of interest expense." Explain.

9-10   Distinguish between *straight-line* amortization and *effective-interest* amortization.

9-11   What are the three main differences between accounting for a bond discount and accounting for a bond premium?

9-12   "A company that issues zero coupon bonds recognizes no interest expense until the bond matures." Do you agree? Explain.

9-13   Why might a company prefer to lease instead of buy?

9-14   Certain leases are essentially equivalent to purchases. A company must account for such leases as if the asset had been purchased. Explain.

9-15   "A capital lease results in both an asset and a liability on a company's balance sheet." Explain.

9-16   We observe extensive use of capital leases by airlines as a method for financing planes. Why might this be true? Does it make the airline seem to have lower debt ratios?

9-17   "A capital lease and operating lease are recorded differently on the balance sheet, but their effect on the income statement is the same." Do you agree? Explain.

9-18   Discuss which characteristics of a lease are evaluated in deciding whether it is a capital lease.

9-19   "Because a company never knows how much it will have to pay for pensions, no pension liability is recognized. Pension obligations are simply explained in a footnote to the financial statements." Do you agree? Explain.

9-20   Variation in international practice in the accounting for pensions can be explained in part by different financial practices in different countries. Discuss.

COGNITIVE EXERCISES

9-21   Lottery Winnings

The New York Lottery provides prizes that start at $3 million and rise each time someone fails to win the lottery. Participants in the lottery are permitted to chose to receive a lump-sum payment or 26 payments as an annuity. A recent winner of $20 million was surprised on receiving a check for under $10 million? How could you explain this to the winner?

9-22   Pension Payments

Four employees were comparing notes on their pension plans. A man and a woman worked for company A and another man and a woman worked for company B. The pension plans for companies A and B were both "defined contribution" pension plans and all four employees had experienced identical salary progressions during their working years and had made identical contributions to their pension plans. Nonetheless, the two people who worked for company A were able to receive identical annuities during their retirement whereas for company B the man received a higher annuity than the company A employees and the woman who worked for company B received a lower annuity during her retirement than the company A employees did. How do these differences relate to life expectancy differences between men and women?

9-23   Refinancing Bonds

Your treasurer is new to the job and has just noticed that your bonds are trading below par (i.e., at a discount). This officer recommends that you retire the bonds by issuing new bonds because you will have a gain in the process and will reduce your interest payments. Do you believe you should accept the treasurer's recommendation?

9-24   Cash Interest versus Interest Expense

As a lender, you are contemplating a covenant that is based on the interest coverage ratio. A young member of your organization with a fresh MBA degree has suggested that you calculate the ratio using actual cash interest payments each period instead of interest expense each period. You have been asked to discuss this proposal. What do you say?

EXERCISES

9-25   Exercises in Compound Interest

1.   You deposit $6,000. How much will you have in 4 years at 8%, compounded annually? At 12%?

2. A savings and loan association offers depositors a $6,000 lump-sum payment 4 years hence. How much will you be willing to deposit if you desire an interest rate of 8% compounded annually? How much at an interest rate of 12%?

3. Repeat requirement 2, but assume that the interest rates are compounded semiannually.

9-26 Exercises in Compound Interest

A reliable friend has asked you for a loan. You are pondering various proposals for repayment.

1. Repayment of a $20,000 lump sum 4 years hence. How much will you lend if your desired rate of return is (a) 10% compounded annually, (b) 20% compounded annually?

2. Repeat requirement 1, but assume that the interest rates are compounded semiannually.

3. Suppose the loan is to be paid in full by equal payments of $5,000 at the end of each of the next 4 years. How much will you lend if your desired rate of return is (a) 10% compounded annually, (b) 20% compounded annually?

9-27 Compound Interest and Journal Entries

Jenkins Company acquired equipment for a $300,000 promissory note, payable 5 years hence, non-interest-bearing, but having an implicit interest rate of 8% compounded annually. Prepare the journal entry for (1) acquisition of the equipment and (2) interest expense for the first year.

9-28 Compound Interest and Journal Entries

A Munich company has bought some equipment on a contract entailing a DM 100,000 cash down payment and a DM 400,000 lump sum to be paid at the end of 4 years. The same equipment can be bought for DM 394,000 cash. (DM refers to the German mark, a unit of currency).

1. Prepare the journal entry for the acquisition of the equipment.

2. Prepare journal entries at the end of each of the first 2 years. Ignore entries for depreciation.

9-29 Compound Interest and Journal Entries

A newspaper company bought new presses for a $100,000 down payment and $100,000 to be paid at the end of each of 4 years. The applicable imputed interest rate is 10% on the unpaid balance. Prepare journal entries (1) for the acquisition and (2) at the end of the first year.

9-30 Exercises in Compound Interest

1. It is your sixtieth birthday. You plan to work 5 more years before retiring. Then you want to spend $20,000 for a Mediterranean cruise. What lump sum do you have to invest now to accumulate the $20,000? Assume that your minimum desired rate of return is:

a. 5%, compounded annually.

b. 10%, compounded annually.

c. 20%, compounded annually.

2. You want to spend $3,000 on a vacation at the end of each of the next 5 years. What lump sum do you have to invest now to take the five vacations? Assume that your minimum desired rate of return is:

a. 5%, compounded annually.

b. 10%, compounded annually.

c. 20%, compounded annually.

9-31 Exercises in Compound Interest

1. At age 60, you find that your employer is moving to another location. You receive termination pay of $100,000. You have some savings and wonder whether to retire now.

a. If you invest the $100,000 now at 8%, compounded annually, how much money can you withdraw from your account each year so that at the end of 5 years there will be a zero balance?

b. If you invest it at 10%?

2. At 16%, compounded annually, which of the following plans is more desirable in terms of present value? Show computations to support your answer.

	Annual Cash Inflows	
Year	Mining	Farming
1	$100,000	$20,000
2	80,000	40,000
3	60,000	60,000
4	40,000	80,000
5	20,000	100,000
	$300,000	$300,000

9-32 Basic Relationships in Interest Tables

1. Suppose you borrow $20,000 now at 16% interest compounded annually. The borrowed amount plus interest will be repaid in a lump sum at the end of 6 years. How much must be repaid? Use Table 9-1 and basic equation: FV = Present amount X Future value factor.

2. Repeat requirement 1 using Table 9-2 and the basic equation: PV = Future amount $\times$ Present value factor.

3. Assume the same facts as in requirement 1 except that the loan will be repaid in equal installments at the end of each of 5 years. How much must be repaid each year? Use Table 9-3 and the basic equation: PV_A = Future annual amounts $\times$ Conversion factor.

9-33 Deferred Annuity Exercise
It is your twenty-fifth birthday. On your thirtieth birthday, and on three successive birthdays thereafter, you intend to spend exactly $1,000 for a birthday celebration. What lump sum do you have to invest now to have the four celebrations? Assume that the money will earn interest, compounded annually, of 8%.

9-34 Discounted Present Value and Bonds
On December 31, 20X1, a company issued a 3-year $1,000 bond that promises an interest rate of 12%, payable 6% semiannually. Compute the discounted present value of the principal and the interest as of December 31, 20X1, if the market rate of interest for such securities is 12%, 14%, and 10%, respectively. Show your computations, including a sketch of cash flows. Round to the nearest dollar.

9-35 Discounted Present Value and Leases
Suppose Wal-Mart signed a 10-year lease for a new store location. The lease calls for an immediate payment of $20,000 and annual payments of $20,000 at the end of each of the next 9 years. Wal-Mart expects to earn 16% interest, compounded annually, on its investments. What is the present value of the lease payments?

9-36 Bond Quotations
Following is a bond quotation for American Telephone and Telegraph Company (AT&T):

Description	Current Yield	Close	Net Change
AT&T 6S05	6.1	98	$-\frac{3}{8}$

Required

1. How was the current yield of 6.1% calculated?
2. What price (in total dollars) would you have paid for one bond?
3. What was the closing price (in total dollars) for the bond on the preceding day?

9-37 Criteria for Capital Leases

Indicate which of the following leases would be a capital lease and which would be operating leases.

a. Rental of a warehouse for $10,000 per month, renewable annually.

b. Rental of a crane for $8,000 per month on a 6-year lease, with an option to buy for $10,000 at the end of the 6 years.

c. Rental of a computer for $1,000 per month on a 5-year lease. At the end of 5 years the computer is expected to have a fair market value of $2,000.

d. Rental of 10 forklifts for $1,400 per month on an 8-year lease. The value of the forklifts at the end of 12 years is uncertain, but the total economic life is not expected to be more than 10 years.

e. Rental of an automobile on a 3-year lease for $500 per month. The auto will be returned to the dealer after the 3 years.

9-38 Accounting for Pensions

A company's current pension expense is $800,000, of which $200,000 is paid in cash to a trustee. By using the balance sheet equation format, show which accounts are affected by these data. Prepare the corresponding journal entry.

PROBLEMS

9-39 Present Value and Sports Salaries

The *New York Times* reported that Jack Morris, a pitcher, signed a $4 million contract with the Detroit Tigers. His 1988 salary was $1,988,000, and his 1989 salary was $1,989,000. However, $1 million of his 1989 salary was paid in 1988. The *Times* reported that the advance payment increased the contract's value by about $50,000, pushing it over $4 million.

Assume that the contract was signed on December 1, 1987, that the 1988 and 1989 payments were both made on December 1 of the respective years, and that the appropriate discount rate was 10%.

Required

1. What was the present value of the contract on the day it was signed?

2. What would have been the present value of the contract if the $1 million advance payment had been paid in 1989 instead of 1988?

3. How much present value (as of December 1, 1987) did Morris gain by receiving the $1 million payment in 1988 instead of 1989?

4. Do you agree that the contract was worth more than $4 million? Explain.

9-40 Bond Discount Transactions and Straight-Line Amortization

On December 31, 2000, ATP Technology issued $20 million of 10-year, 12% debentures. Proceeds were $18 million.

Show all amounts in thousands of dollars.

Required

1. By using the balance sheet equation format, prepare an analysis of bond transactions. Assume straight-line amortization. Show entries for the issuer concerning (a) issuance, (b) one semiannual interest payment, and (c) payment of maturity value.

2. Show the corresponding journal entries for (a), (b) and (c) in requirement 1.

3. Show how the bond-related accounts would appear on the balance sheets as of December 31, 2000 and 2009.

9-41 Bonds Issued at Par

On December 31, 2000, Alaska Fisheries, Inc. issued $16 million of 10-year, 10% debentures at par.

Required

1. Compute the proceeds from issuing the debentures.

2. By using the balance sheet equation format, prepare an analysis of this bond transaction. Show entries for the issuer concerning (a) issuance, (b) first semiannual interest payment, and (c) payment of maturity value.

3. Show the corresponding journal entries for (a), (b) and (c) in requirement 2.

4. Show how the bond-related accounts would appear on the balance sheet as of December 31, 2000, and June 30, 2001. Assume that the semiannual interest payment and amortization due on the balance sheet date have been recorded.

9-42 Bonds Issued at a Discount

On December 31, 2000, Ruzinski Construction issued $20 million of 10-year, 10% debentures. The market interest rate at issuance was 14%.

Required

1. Compute the proceeds from issuing the debentures.

2. By using the balance sheet equation format, prepare an analysis of this bond transaction. Show entries for the issuer concerning (a) issuance, (b) first semiannual interest payment and discount amortization, and (c) payment of maturity value. Round all amounts to the nearest thousand.

3. Show the corresponding journal entries for (a), (b) and (c) in requirement 2.

4. Show how the bond-related accounts would appear on the balance sheets as of December 31, 2000, and June 30, 2001. Assume that the semiannual interest payment and amortization due on the balance sheet dates have been recorded.

9-43 Bond Discount Transactions

(Alternates are 9-44 and 9-45.) On March 1, 2000, KGI Gas issued $100 million of 20-year, 9% debentures. Proceeds were $91,191 million, implying a market interest rate of 10%.

Show all amounts in thousands of dollars.

Required

1. By using the balance sheet equation format, prepare an analysis of bond transactions. Assume effective-interest amortization. Show entries for the issuer concerning (a) issuance, (b) first semiannual interest payment, and (c) payment of maturity value.

2. Show all the corresponding journal entries for (a), (b), and (c) in requirement 1.

3. Show how the bond-related accounts would appear on the balance sheets as of March 1, 2000 and 2001. Assume the March 1 interest payment and amortization of bond discount have been made.

9-44 Bonds Issued at a Discount

(Alternates are 9-43 and 9-45.) On January 1, 2001, Metro Bus issued $10 million of 5-year, 11% debentures. The market interest rate at issuance was 12%.

Required

1. Compute the proceeds from issuing the debentures.

2. By using the balance sheet equation format, prepare an analysis of this bond transaction. Show entries for the issuer concerning (a) issuance, (b) first semiannual interest payment, and (c) payment of maturity value. Round to the nearest thousand.

3. Show the corresponding journal entries for (a), (b) and (c) in requirement 2.

4. Show how the bond-related accounts would appear on the balance sheets as of January 1, 2001, and July 1, 2001. Assume that the semiannual interest payment and amortization due on the balance sheet dates have been recorded.

9-45 Bond Discount Transactions

(Alternates are 9-43 and 9-44.) Assume that on December 31, 2005, Oslo Tool and Die issued NKR 10 million of 10-year, 10% debentures. Proceeds were NKR 7,881,000; therefore, the market rate of interest was 14%. (NKR is the Norwegian kroner.)

Required

1. By using the balance sheet equation format, prepare an analysis of transactions for Oslo. Key your transactions as follows: (a) issuance, (b) first semiannual interest using effective-interest amortization of bond discount, and (c) payment of maturity value. Round all amounts to the nearest thousand.

2. Prepare corresponding journal entries for (a), (b), and (c) in requirement 1.

3. Show how the bond-related accounts would appear on Oslo's balance sheets as of December 31, 2005, and June 30, 2006. Assume that the semiannual interest payments and amortization have been recorded.

9-46 Bonds Issued at a Premium

(Alternates are 9-47 and 9-48.) On December 31, 2000, Sayers Toyota issued $3 million of 10-year, 12% debentures. The market interest rate at issuance was 10%.

Required

1. Compute the proceeds from issuing the debentures.
2. By using the balance sheet equation format, prepare an analysis of this bond transaction. Show entries for the issuer concerning (a) issuance, (b) first semiannual interest payment and premium amortization, and (c) payment of maturity value. Round all amounts to the nearest thousand.
3. Show the corresponding journal entries for (a), (b) and (c) in requirement 2.
4. Show how the bond-related accounts would appear on the balance sheets as of December 31, 2000, and June 30, 2001. Assume that the semiannual interest payment and amortization due on the balance sheet dates have been recorded.

9-47 Bonds Issued at a Premium

(Alternates are 9-46 and 9-48.) On January 1, 2001, Melbourne Travel issued $4 million of 5-year, 10% debentures. The market interest rate at issuance was 8%.

Required

1. Compute the proceeds from issuing the debentures.
2. By using the balance sheet equation format, prepare an analysis of this bond transaction. Show entries for the issuer concerning (a) issuance, (b) first semiannual interest payment, and (c) payment of maturity value. Round to the nearest thousand.
3. Show the corresponding journal entries for (a), (b) and (c) in requirement 2.
4. Show how the bond-related accounts would appear on the balance sheets as of January 1, 2001, and July 1, 2001. Assume that the semiannual interest payments and amortization due on the balance sheet date have been recorded.

9-48 Bond Premium Transactions

(Alternates are 9-46 and 9-47.) Assume that on December 31, 2001, Zurich Ski Company issued CHF 10 million of 10-year, 10% debentures. Proceeds were CHF 11,359,000; therefore, the market rate of interest was 8%. (CHF is the Swiss franc.)

Required

1. By using the balance sheet equation format, prepare an analysis of transactions for Zurich Ski. Key your transactions as follows: (a) issuance, (b) first semiannual interest using effective-interest amortization of bond discount, and (c) payment of maturity value. Round all amounts to the nearest thousand.
2. Prepare corresponding journal entries for (a), (b), and (c) in requirement 1.
3. Show how the bond-related accounts would appear on Zurich Ski's balance sheets as of December 31, 2001, and June 30, 2002. Assume that the semiannual interest payment and amortization have been recorded.

9-49 Early Extinguishment of Debt

On December 31, 2000, Carribbean Cruises issued $20 million of 10-year, 12% debentures. The market interest rate at issuance was 14%. On December 31, 2001 (after all interest payments and amortization had been recorded for 2001), the company purchased all the debentures for $19 million. Throughout their life, the debentures had been held by a large insurance company.

Required

Show all amounts in thousands of dollars. Round to the nearest thousand.

1. Compute the gain or loss on early extinguishment.
2. By using the balance sheet equation, present an analysis of the transaction on the issuer's books.
3. Show the appropriate journal entry.
4. At what price on December 31, 2001 could Carribbean Cruises redeem the bonds and realize a $500,000 gain?

9-50 Early Extinguishment of Debt

(Alternate is 9-49.) On December 31, 2005, a real estate holding company issued $10 million of 10-year, 12% debentures. The market interest rate at issuance was 12%. Suppose that on December 31, 2006 (after all interest payments and amortization had been recorded for 2006), the company purchased all the debentures for $9 million. The debentures had been held by a large insurance company throughout their life.

Show all amounts in thousands of dollars.

Required

1. Compute the gain or loss on early extinguishment.
2. By using the balance sheet equation, present an analysis of the transaction on the issuer's books.
3. Show the appropriate journal entry.

9-51 Retirement of Bonds
This is a more difficult problem than others in this group. (J. Patel Adapted)

On January 2, 1990, the Newcastle Financial Corporation sold a large issue of Series A £1,000 denomination bonds. The bonds had a stated coupon rate of 6% (annual), had a term to maturity of 20 years, and made semiannual coupon payments. Market conditions at the time were such that the bonds sold at their face value.

During the ensuing 10 years, market interest rates fluctuated widely, and by January 2, 2000, the Newcastle bonds were trading at a price that provided an annual yield of 10%. Newcastle's management was considering purchasing the Series A bonds in the open market and retiring them; the necessary capital was to be raised by a new bond issue—the Series B bonds. Series B bonds were to be £1,000 denomination coupon (semiannual) bonds with a stated annual rate of 8% and a 20-year term. Management felt that these bonds could be sold at a price yielding no more than 10%, especially if the Series A bonds were retired.

Required

1. On January 2, 2000, at what price could Newcastle Financial purchase the Series A bonds? *Hint:* The applicable factors are 5% and 20 periods.
2. Show the journal entries necessary to record the following transactions:
   a. Issue of one Series B bond on January 2, 2000.
   b. Purchase and retirement of one Series A bond on January 2, 2000.
   c. The first coupon payment on a Series B bond on July 2, 2000. Newcastle uses the effective-interest method of accounting for bond premium and discount.
   d. The second coupon payment on a Series B bond on January 2, 2001.
3. By assuming that the Series A issue consisted of 1,000 bonds, how many bonds would be issued in Series B to refinance the series A bonds? How would periodic interest payments change?

9-52 Non-Interest-Bearing Notes
(Alternate is 9-53.) A local bookstore borrowed from a bank on a 1-year note. The face value of the note was $40,000. However, the bank deducted its interest "in advance" at 18% of the face value.

Show the effects on the borrower's records at inception and at the end of the year:

Required

1. By using the balance sheet equation, prepare an analysis of transactions.
2. Prepare journal entries.
3. What was the real rate of interest?

9-53 Non-Interest-Bearing Notes
(Alternate is 9-52.) On July 31, 2001, a veterinarian just beginning a new practice borrowed money from a bank on a 2-year note due on July 31, 2003. The face value of the note was $50,000. However, the bank deducted interest of $10,140 "in advance." Assume annual compounding.

Show the effects on the borrower's records. Show the effects at July 31, 2002 and 2003.

Required

1. By using the balance sheet equation, prepare an analysis of transactions.
2. Prepare journal entries.
3. Calculate the effective annual rate of interest.

9-54 Zero Coupon Bonds
Since 1985, the U.S. Treasury has required issuers of "deep-discount" or "zero coupon" debt securities to use an effective-interest approach to amortization of discount instead of straight-line

amortization. Similarly, buyers of such securities are required to record interest income under the effective-interest rate method. The Treasury claimed that the old tax law, which permitted straight-line amortization of bond discount, resulted in overstatements of deductions in early years for issuers.

Required

1. Assume that General Motors issues a 10-year zero coupon bond having a face amount of $20,000,000 to yield 10%. For simplicity, assume that the 10% yield is compounded annually. Prepare the journal entry for the issuer.

2. Prepare the journal entry for interest expense for the first full year and the second full year using (a) straight-line and (b) effective-interest amortization.

3. Assume an income tax rate of 40%. How much more income tax for the first year would the issuer have to pay because of applying effective-interest instead of straight-line amortization?

4. What kinds of borrowers might prefer these investments over bonds that pay interest immediately?

9-55   Zero Coupon Bonds

Tenet Healthcare Corporation runs more than 110 hospitals and has revenue of more than $10 billion per year. The company included the following information on its balance sheet ($ in millions):

	May 31	
	2000	*1999*
Zero-coupon guaranteed bonds due 2002	$37	$33

Required

Assume that none of the bonds were issued or retired in fiscal 2000.

1. Assume that the bonds were issued on May 31, 1995 at an interest rate of 12%. Prepare the journal entry at issuance. Do not use a discount account.

2. Prepare the journal entry for recording interest expense on the bonds for fiscal 2000. Assume annual compounding of interest.

3. Estimate the face value of the bonds.

9-56   Bonds Sold between Interest Dates

On December 31, 2001, a company had some bonds printed and ready for issuance. But market conditions soured. The bonds were not issued until February 28, 2002, at par. The indenture requires payment of semiannual interest on December 31 and June 30. The face value of the bonds is $10 million. The interest rate is 12%.

Required

1. Compute the total proceeds of the issue on February 28.

2. Prepare an analysis of transactions, using the balance sheet equation. Show amounts in thousands of dollars. Show the effects on the issuer's records on February 28 and June 30, 2002.

3. Prepare corresponding journal entries.

9-57   Capital Lease

The Chicago Packing Company acquired packaging equipment on a capital lease. There were annual lease payments of $40,000 at the end of each of 3 years. The implicit interest rate was 18% compounded annually.

Required

1. Compute the present value of the capital lease.

2. Prepare journal entries at the inception of the lease and for each of the 3 years. Distinguish between the short-term and long-term classifications of the lease.

9-58   Comparison of Operating and Capital Lease

Refer to the preceding problem. Suppose the capital lease were regarded as an operating lease. Ignore income taxes. Fill in the blanks (prepare supporting computations):

	Operating Lease	Capital Lease	Difference
Total expenses			
Year 1	?	?	?
Year 2	?	?	?
Two years together	?	?	?
End of year 1			
Total assets	?	?	?
Total liabilities	?	?	?
Retained income	?	?	?
End of year 2			
Total assets	?	?	?
Total liabilities	?	?	?
Retained income	?	?	?

9-59   Capital or Operating Lease

On December 31, 20X8, Cesar's Wood Products Company has been offered an electronically controlled automatic lathe (a) outright for $100,000 cash or (b) on a noncancellable lease whereby rental payments would be made at the end of each year for 3 years. The lathe will become obsolete and worthless at the end of 3 years. The company can borrow $100,000 cash on a 3-year loan payable at maturity at 16% compounded annually.

Required

1. Compute the annual rental payment, assuming that the lessor desires a 16% rate of return per year.
2. If the lease were accounted for as an operating lease, what annual journal entry would be made?
3. The lease is a capital lease. Prepare an analytical schedule of each lease payment. Show the lease liability at the beginning of the year, interest expense, lease payment, and lease liability at end of year.
4. Prepare an analysis of transactions, using the balance sheet equation format.
5. Prepare yearly journal entries.

9-60   Leases

The following information appeared in a footnote to the 1999 annual report of Delta Air Lines, Incorporated, a June 30 fiscal-year-end company:

The following table summarizes our minimum rental commitments under capital leases and operating leases with initial or remaining terms of more than 1 year as of June 30, 1999:

Years Ending June 30	Capital Leases	Operating Leases
	($ in Millions)	
2000	$ 63	$ 1,020
2001	57	1,030
2002	57	1,040
2003	48	1,020
2004	32	980
After 2004	40	9,440
Total minimum lease payment	$297	$14,530
Less: Amounts representing interest	62	
Present value of future minimum capital lease payments	$235	

1. Suppose the minimum capital lease payments are made in equal amounts on September 30, December 31, March 31, and June 30 of each year. Compute the interest and principal to be paid on capital leases during the first half of fiscal 2000. Do calculations in millions with two decimal places. Assume an interest rate of 8% per annum, compounded quarterly.

2. Prepare the journal entries for the lease payments in requirement 1 on September 30 and December 31, 2000.

3. Suppose the operating leases were capital leases and assume that the payments were $1,000 million per year for 15 years made annually at year-end. If these operating leases were capitalized at 8%, how much would long-term debt increase? Do calculations to closest million.

9-61 Leases

Consider footnote 4 from the 1999 annual report of FedEX:

> Footnote 4:
>
> *The company utilizes certain aircraft, land, facilities, and equipment under capital and operating leases which expire at various dates through 2027. . . . A summary of future minimum lease payments under capital leases and noncancellable operating leases at May 31, 1999 is as follows:*

(Dollars in Millions)	Capital Leases	Operating Leases
2000	$ 15	$ 1,012
2001	15	933
2002	15	876
2003	15	810
2004	15	765
Thereafter	302	8,718
Total	$377	$13,114

1. Footnote 5 contains the minimum future lease payments due under FedEX's capital and operating leases. Compute the net present value of the operating lease payments as of May 31, 1999. Use a 10% implicit interest rate. For ease of computation, assume that each payment is made on May 31 of the designated year (i.e., the first $1,012 million payment is made on May 31, 1998) and that the final payment, labeled "Thereafter," is made on May 31, 2005.

2. Suppose FedEX were to capitalize the operating leases examined in requirement 1. Show the journal entries necessary to:

   a. Capitalize the leases on June 1, 1999. Ignore any prior period adjustments and do not break the lease obligation into current and long-term portions.

   b. Record the first payment on May 31, 2000.

9-62 Effect of Capital Leases

Debbie's Clothing, a chain of specialty women's apparel stores, reported the following information about leases in its annual report ($ in thousands):

	January 31	
	2000	*1996*
Capital lease asset, gross	$1,982	$1,982
Less: Accumulated depreciation	1,387	1,288
Capital lease asset, net	$ 595	$ 694

The only asset under a capital lease is a warehouse and office building. The building has an economic life of 20 years and is being depreciated on a straight-line basis. Debbie's Clothing had income before tax of $39,161,934 in fiscal 2000 (the year ending January 31, 2000).

Required

1. Calculate the depreciation on the warehouse and office building for the fiscal year ending January 31, 2000.
2. On what date was the building placed into service? (*Hint:* How long would it take to build up the accumulated depreciation shown?)
3. The interest on the lease obligation was $257,000 in fiscal 2000. The total lease payment was $550,000. Reconstruct the 2000 journal entry.
4. Suppose this building had met the requirements for an operating lease instead of a capital lease. Calculate the operating income before tax for Debbie's Clothing in fiscal 2000.

9-63 Capital Leases

Home Depot is the leading retailer in the home improvement industry and one of the 10 largest retailers in the United States. The company included the following on its January 28, 2001 balance sheet and footnotes ($ in millions):

Lease assets	213
Capital lease obligations (long term)	227
Capital lease obligations (current)	3

Total capital lease payments scheduled for the fiscal year ended January 30, 2002 are $38,000,000.

Required

1. Prepare the journal entry for the $38,000,000 lease payments. Remember that the lease payment will include the principle payments due for the year plus interest expense accrued for the year.
2. Suppose that lease assets have an average remaining life of 20 years and that no new leases are signed in the fiscal year ending January 30, 2002. Compute the balance in the lease asset account and the total in the capital lease obligations account (long-term and current combined) at January 30, 2002.
3. Explain why the amounts in the lease assets account is not equal to the amount in the lease obligations accounts.

9-64 Pension Liabilities

Bethlehem Steel had a pension liability of $6,115 million and a liability for postretirement benefits other than pensions of $2,750 million at the beginning of 2000. The fair value of plan assets in the pension plan was $6,090 million. Total stockholders' equity was $1,277 million. The total market value of Bethlehem Steel is approximately $524 million, down from $1.2 billion in 1997.

Required

1. Comment on the confidence that employees might have about receiving the benefits due to them.
2. Recognizing pensions and other postretirement benefits as liabilities on the balance sheet has been a controversial topic. Do you think this is important information to disclose to shareholders? Why or why not?

ANNUAL REPORT CASE

9-65 Cisco Annual Report

Examine the annual report for Cisco included in appendix A, especially footnote 8 that describes Leases. Suppose that all operating leases were treated as capital leases. Assume that all the leases were for 10 years and that the lease payments each year are at the same level they were in the year ended July 29, 2000, that is, $302,000,000 per year. Also assume that the implicit interest rate in the leases is 10%.

1. Assume that the operating leases were all capitalized as of July 29, 2000. Compute the amount of the capitalized lease asset and the lease liability that would be added to Cisco's balance sheet.

2. Compute Cisco's debt-to-equity ratio on July 29, 2000, using the balance sheet numbers as reported. Also compute Cisco's debt to equity ratio using numbers that assume the capitalization of operating leases as computed in requirement 1.

3. Comment on the change in debt-to-equity ratio that results from capitalization of the operating leases. What information does this convey to potential investors in Cisco?

9-66 Financial Statement Research

Select any two companies from the airline industry, and find each company's footnote describing its leases. (Possible companies include Alaska Airlines, American Airlines, Continental Airlines, Delta Airlines, Northwest Airlines, United and U.S. Airways, but do not feel restricted to these.) Compute each company's debt-to-equity ratio under each of three assumptions:

1. With leases as reported.
2. With all leases treated as operating leases.
3. With all leases treated as capital leases.

For this calculation assume that all operating lease payments due after the fifth year are spread evenly over years 6 through 15. That is, one-tenth of the remaining lease payments will be made each of the next 10 years. Use a 10% interest rate for computing the present value of the operating leases. Comment on the differences made by the three treatments of leases. Also, comment on the differences in ratios between the two companies.

COLLABORATIVE LEARNING EXERCISE

9-67 Accounting for Pensions

Form groups of two or more students. Divide each group into two debate teams. Each team should be assigned one of the two following positions:

1. Pensions and other postretirement benefits are legitimate liabilities of a company and should be recognized as such on their balance sheets. They are expenses of the periods in which the benefiting employees work, so the obligation to pay them should be accrued at that time.

2. Pensions and other postretirement benefits are not legal liabilities of a company and should not be included among their liabilities on the balance sheet. They are essentially expenses in the period when the benefits are paid.

One team defending each proposition can be given 5 to 10 minutes to present its case, followed by approximately 2 minutes each for rebuttals. Then a general class discussion of the issues can follow. The class might take a vote on which group made the most convincing argument.

INTERNET EXERCISE

9-68 May Department Stores

Go to www.mayco.com to find May Department Stores' financial information. Select *About May,* and click on the annual report.

Answer the following questions about May and its long-term debt:

1. Locate the discussion of *Lease Obligations* in the *Notes to Consolidated Financial Statements.* What percentage of its stores does May own? What type of leases does May report?

www.prenhall.com/horngren

2. How do the operating lease payments affect May's financial statements? Explain how these operating leases are considered "invisible debt."

3. What items comprise May's long-term debt? Is any portion of that debt considered "current"? Where is the current portion reported on the financial statements? Was any long-term debt issued in the most recent year?

4. Describe who is eligible for May's pension and other postretirement benefits. How are these items reported on the financial statements? What discount rate is used for determining the present value of these items?

STATEMENT OF CASH FLOWS

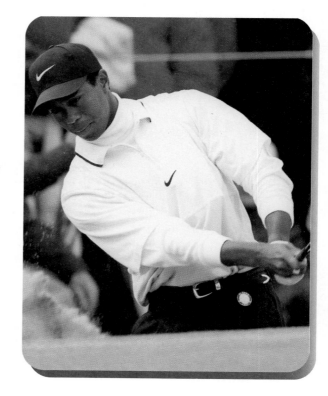

Tiger Woods exits
sandtraps as gracefully
as he collects his
endorsement fees
from Nike.

www.prenhall.com/horngren

Learning Objectives

After studying this chapter, you should be able to

1. Explain the concept of the statement of cash flows.

2. Classify activities affecting cash as operating, investing, or financing activities.

3. Use the direct method to measure cash flows.

4. Determine cash flows from income statement and balance sheet accounts.

5. Use the indirect method to calculate cash flows from operations.

6. Relate depreciation to cash flows provided by operating activities.

7. Reconcile net income to cash provided by operating activities.

8. Adjust for gains and losses from fixed asset sales and debt extinguishments in the statement of cash flows (appendix 10A).

9. Use the T-account approach to prepare the cash flow statement (appendix 10B).

If you watched nothing but commercials on television, you would think the only thing Nike spends its money on is getting athletes to endorse the company's products. We are all familiar with Nike's first endorsement—Michael Jordan of Chicago Bulls basketball fame—but there have been countless others. Runners, hockey and soccer players, and college and professional football teams have all appeared in Nike's commercials or signed other endorsement deals, not to mention swimmers, tennis players, and just about any other sports figure imaginable. Golfer Tiger Woods's deal was for tens of millions over several years. Recently, Nike agreed to pay $120 million over 8 years to sponsor the U.S. Soccer Federation, the governing body for the top men's, women's, and youth teams.

Of course, the company behind the famous Nike "swoosh" needs cash to make the endorsements happen. A quick look at the company's balance sheet tells you that they have plenty—close to $200 million at last count. But if you truly wanted to see where Nike spends its cash, you are better off ignoring the commercials and paying attention to one specific financial report—the statement of cash flows.

Nike reports the cash provided or used by the company for operating, investing, and financing activities giving you a complete picture of how the money was generated and where it has gone. For example, in recent years, operations such as selling merchandise have provided millions in cash for Nike ($760 million in 2000 down from $961 million in 1999). On the other hand, financing activities, primarily $646 million in stock repurchases, have used cash (in contrast to borrowing $314 million as recently as 1997). The constant over time has been aggressive investment, amounting to $440 million in 2000 and $416 million in 1999 for primarily additions to property, plant, and equipment. The net result of all these activities in 2000 was an increase in cash and equivalents of 28% over the previous year.

So far this book has dealt mainly with financial statements based on accrual accounting. Focusing too heavily on accruals and deferrals, though, can make it easy to forget about cash. An understanding of where a company's cash comes from and where it goes is essential to knowing whether the company is in good financial condition.

Given the primary importance of cash, it is not surprising that the statement of cash flows has become one of the central financial statements. It provides a thorough explanation of the changes that occurred in the firm's cash balances during the entire accounting period. The statement of cash flows allows both investors and managers to keep their fingers on the pulse of any company's lifeblood: cash. Companies that lose too much cash become critically ill. The business equivalent of critical illness is bankruptcy. Bankruptcy is loosely used to refer to companies that are unable to meet their obligations. It also refers to firms that seek court protection from their debts under federal law. Court protection allows a firm to delay paying certain obligations while it negotiates an agreement with all its creditors on how to reorganize its business and its debts for the future. Dow Corning and Woolworth's are recent examples of relatively large and seemingly successful companies that have entered bankruptcy and either have been liquidated entirely or have terminated large portions of their business. We observed significant bankruptcies among the dot.coms in 2000–2001.

Every company benefits by tracing its cash flows, and every investor would be wise to check out a company's statement of cash flows before investing. Interestingly, though, not every company prepares a specific statement showing investors its cash flows. The accounting regulations in some countries, such as Austria, India, and Uruguay, do not require any formal statement of cash flows, so investors rarely get such statements. Most countries do require a financial statement like the statement of cash flows, but the contents of these statements can vary widely from country to country. In this chapter, we examine the contents of the statement of cash flows required in the United States and explain what these figures mean to companies and to investors.

OVERVIEW OF STATEMENT OF CASH FLOWS

Companies have not always prepared statements of cash flows. In fact, before 1971, only the balance sheet and income statement were required. That year a statement showing the changes in financial position between balance sheets was added. However, financial problems—mainly inflation—in the 1970s and 1980s caused many economists and accountants to call for a greater emphasis on cash management. In response, in 1987, the FASB required the preparation and presentation of the statement of cash flows in its present form.

Objective 1
Explain the concept of the statement of cash flows.

PURPOSES OF CASH FLOW STATEMENT

The statement of cash flows reports all the cash activities—both receipts and payments—of a company during a given period. It also explains the causes for the changes in cash by providing information about operating, financing, and investing activities. Why does the FASB require a statement of cash flows? Because:

1. It shows the relationship of net income to changes in cash balances. Cash balances can decline despite positive net income and vice versa.
2. It reports past cash flows as an aid to:
   a. Predicting future cash flows
   b. Evaluating the way management generates and uses cash
   c. Determining a company's ability to pay interest and dividends and to pay debts when they are due
3. It identifies changes in the mix of productive assets.

Balance sheets show the status of a company at a single point in time. In contrast, statements of cash flows and income statements show the performance of a company over a period of time. Both explain why the balance sheet items have changed. As the following diagram shows, these statements thus link the balance sheets in consecutive periods:

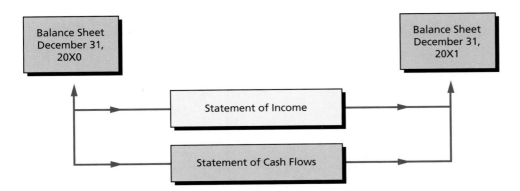

operating management
Concerns the major day-to-day activities that generate revenues and expenses.

financial management
Concerns where to get cash and how to use cash for the benefit of the entity.

The statement of cash flows explains where cash came from during a period and where it went. We should clarify what we mean by *cash* though. Our use of the term refers not only to the bills and coins you normally think of as cash, but to cash equivalents, too. As you should recall, cash equivalents are highly liquid short-term investments that can easily be converted into cash with little delay, such as money market funds and Treasury bills. Hereafter, when we refer to cash, we mean both cash and cash equivalents.

Objective 2
Classify activities affecting cash as operating, investing, or financing activities.

TYPICAL ACTIVITIES AFFECTING CASH

Cash affects and is affected by two primary areas of a firm: its operating management and its financial management. **Operating management** is largely concerned with the major day-to-day activities that generate revenues and expenses. **Financial management** is largely concerned with where to get cash (financing activities) and how to use cash (investing activities). For example, financial managers decide whether to issue or retire long-term debt or additional capital stock and how to invest the capital raised. The statement of cash flows covers the results of both financial management and operating management by reporting on specific operating activities, investing activities, and financing activities.

Operating activities are generally activities or transactions that affect the income statement. For example, sales are linked to collections from customers, and wage expenses are closely tied to cash payments to employees. **Investing activities** involve (1) providing and collecting cash as a lender or as an owner of securities and (2) acquiring and disposing of plant, property, equipment, and other long-term productive assets. **Financing activities** involve obtaining resources as a borrower or issuer of securities and repaying creditors and owners. You should note that financing and investing activities are really

operating activities
Activities that affect the income statement.

investing activities
Activities that involve (1) providing and collecting cash as a lender or as an owner of securities and (2) acquiring and disposing of plant, property, equipment, and other long-term productive assets.

financing activities
Activities that involve obtaining resources as a borrower or an issuer of securities and repaying creditors and owners.

opposite sides of the same coin. For example, when stock is issued for cash to an investor, the issuer treats it as a financing activity and the investor treats it as an investing activity.

The following are typical operating, investing, and financing activities reported in statements of cash flows:

OPERATING ACTIVITIES

Cash Inflows
Collections from customers
Interest and dividends collected
Other operating receipts

Cash Outflows
Cash payments to suppliers
Cash payments to employees
Interest and taxes paid
Other operating cash payments

INVESTING ACTIVITIES

Cash Inflows
Sale of property, plant, and equipment
Sale of securities that are not cash equivalents
Receipt of loan repayments

Cash Outflows
Purchase of property, plant, and equipment
Purchase of securities that are not cash equivalents
Making loans

FINANCING ACTIVITIES

Cash Inflows
Borrowing cash from creditors
Issuing equity securities
Issuing debt securities

Cash Outflows
Repayment of amounts borrowed
Repurchase of equity shares (including the purchase of treasury stock)
Payment of dividends

To see how these activities are treated, consider APT Company, which provides daily cleaning services for homes. Exhibit 10-1 displays APT's financial statements. The company pays all wages in cash daily, and all revenues are collected in cash daily. If these were the only transactions affecting income, APT's net income would equal cash provided by operations. However, APT owns a computer, and depreciation on the computer is allocated to the income statement over the computer's anticipated 3-year life. Because depreciation does not involve a cash flow, it appears on the income statement as an expense but does not affect cash provided by operations.

Cleaning supplies are purchased for cash periodically, but the supplies are not necessarily paid for on delivery. Moreover, supplies are kept in inventory to be used as needed, so all the supplies acquired are not immediately used. The income statement reports the $3,000 of supplies used during the period, and the cash flow statement reports the $3,200 of supplies paid for during the period.

In comparing the income statement and cash flows from operations, you can see that the only differences are for supplies and depreciation. APT Company has only one investing activity, the purchase of a computer, and one financing activity, the payment of cash dividends.

A company raises $1 million by selling common stock and puts $400,000 into marketable securities that are cash equivalents and uses the other $600,000 to buy equipment. What are the effects on the cash flow statement?

ANSWER

The $1 million appears as cash provided by financing activities. The $600,000 appears as a use of cash in the investing section. Because the marketable securities are cash equivalents, the $400,000 does not appear in the investing section; instead it is an increase in cash and cash equivalents.

Exhibit 10-1

APT Company
Financial Statements

Balance Sheets for the Years Ended December 31

	Assets			Liabilities and Stockholders' Equity		
	20X1	20X0			20X1	20X0
Cash	$ 1,200	$ 4,000	Accounts payable		$ 200	$ 200
Supplies	600	400	Stockholders'			
Computer	2,000	0	equity		3,600	4,200
Total assets	$ 3,800	$ 4,400	Total liab. and SE		$3,800	$4,400

Income Statement for the Year Ended December 31, 20X1

Sales		$ 35,000
Wages	$ 20,000	
Depreciation	1,000	
Supplies	3,000	24,000
Net income		$11,000

Statement of Cash Flows for the Year Ended December 31, 20X1

Cash Flows from Operating Activities	
Collections from customers	$ 35,000
Payments to employees	(20,000)
Payments to suppliers	(3,200)
Net cash provided by operating activities	11,800
Cash Flows from Investing Activities	
Cash investment in computer	(3,000)
Net cash used for investing activities	(3,000)
Cash Flows from Financing Activities	
Cash dividend payments	(11,600)
Net cash used for financing activities	(11,600)
Decrease in cash	(2,800)
Cash balance December 31, 20X0	4,000
Cash balance December 31, 20X1	$ 1,200

APPROACHES TO CALCULATING THE CASH FLOW FROM OPERATING ACTIVITIES

Although cash flows from financing and investment activities are fairly easy to summarize at year-end from a review of the checkbook, operating activities are more complex and the calculation of cash flow from operations is similarly complicated. Two approaches can be used to compute **cash flow from operating activities** (or operations). Computing it as collections less operating disbursements is called the **direct method.** Our APT example used this method. Adjusting the previously calculated accrual net income from the income statement to reflect only cash receipts and outlays is called the **indirect method.**

By using the direct method, the cash flow effect of each operating activity is calculated by adjusting the income statement amounts for changes in related asset and liability accounts. Each revenue and expense amount calculated under the accrual method is adjusted to reflect the actual cash paid or received. In contrast, the indirect method considers the same changes in related asset and liability accounts but uses them to adjust the net income number directly to a cash equivalent, instead of adjusting the individual revenue and expense items that comprise net income.

cash flows from operating activities The first major section of the statement of cash flows. It shows the cash effects of transactions that affect the income statement.

direct method In a statement of cash flows, the method that calculates net cash provided by operating activities as collections minus operating disbursements.

indirect method In a statement of cash flows, the method that adjusts the accrual net income to reflect only cash receipts and outlays.

Objective 3
Use the direct method
to measure cash flows.

Under the direct method, we identify the cash part of each item in the income statement. Because depreciation does not use cash, it is not part of the calculation. For APT, which immediately collected the cash it was due and immediately paid out cash it owed, we have only to adjust for supplies. By examining the balance sheet, we see that supplies inventory rose from $400 to $600. This increase suggests APT bought more than it used, so cost of supplies in the income statement was smaller than purchases. However, did APT pay for what it bought? Yes, the company paid for exactly the quantity purchased during the year because the Accounts Payable balance remained unchanged. Therefore, the increases to accounts payable for new purchases had to be identical to the decreases for payments. So if APT paid for all it bought, and it bought $200 more than it sold, the company must have paid for $3,200. Therefore, net cash provided by operating activities must be cash sales of $35,000 less $20,000 in cash wages and $3,200 cash paid for supplies for a net of $11,800, as shown in Exhibit 10-1.

Alternatively, cash flow from operations can be calculated under the indirect method by adjusting the accrual net income figure to reflect only cash transactions. The income statement provides an accrual-based net income of $11,000, which is our starting point. In calculating net income on the income statement, $1,000 of depreciation was deducted, but depreciation involved no cash, so we add it back to get $12,000 ($11,000 plus $1,000). In addition, APT spent $200 more on supplies than it used, so we subtract that $200 as an operating use of cash that does not appear in net income. Thus, by adjusting the accrual net income figure, we again calculate $11,800 ($11,000 + $1,000 − $200).

The FASB prefers the direct method because it shows operating cash receipts and payments in a way that is easier for investors to understand. However, the indirect method is more common. Why? Probably the people who generally prepare the statement are accountants and are use to thinking in terms of net income. The two approaches can be compared as follows:

APT Company Cash Flow from Operating Activities

	Direct Method		Indirect Method	
Collections from customers		$35,000	Net earnings	$11,000
Payments to employees	$20,000		Add depreciation*	1,000
Payments to suppliers	3,200		Deduct supplies†	(200)
Net cash provided by operating activities		$11,800		$11,800

*Depreciation was deducted to compute net earnings but did not involve a cash flow.
†Payments for supplies exceeded the amount charged as expense.

TRANSACTIONS AFFECTING CASH FLOWS FROM ALL SOURCES

APT Company was an intentionally simplified illustration that gave us a first look at the principles behind the statement of cash flows. Now we delve into more detail.

ACTIVITIES AFFECTING CASH

Exhibit 10-2 summarizes the effects of most major transactions on cash. The zeros in the "change in cash" column indicate that the transaction has no effect on cash. For example, sales and purchases on account and even the accrual recording of cost of goods sold have no effect on cash. Most of the items in the list will be familiar to you. We have included several financing transactions that are not covered in detail until chapter 11 on stockholders' equity. However, we wanted the list to be useful as a reference throughout the course.

Exhibit 10-2

Analysis of Effects of Transactions on Cash

Type of Transaction	Change in Cash
Operating Activities	
Sales of goods and services for cash	+
Sales of goods and services on credit	0
Receive dividends or interest	+
Collection of accounts receivable	+
Recognize cost of goods sold	0
Purchase inventory for cash	−
Purchase inventory on credit	0
Pay trade accounts payable	−
Accrue operating expenses	0
Pay operating expenses	−
Accrue taxes	0
Pay taxes	−
Accrue interest	0
Pay interest	−
Prepay expenses for cash	−
Write off prepaid expenses	0
Charge depreciation or amortization	0
Investing Activities	
Purchase fixed assets for cash	−
Purchase fixed assets by issuing debt	0
Sell fixed assets	+
Purchase securities that are not cash equivalents	−
Sell securities that are not cash equivalents	+
Make a loan	−
Financing Activities	
Increase long-term or short-term debt	+
Reduce long-term or short-term debt	−
Sell common or preferred shares	+
Repurchase and retire common or preferred shares	−
Purchase treasury stock	−
Pay dividends	−
Convert debt to common stock	0
Reclassify long-term debt to short-term debt	0

The relationship of these activities to cash should be fairly obvious and straightforward. What is not always obvious is the classification of these activities as operating, investing, or financing. Take interest payments and dividend payments, for example. Both of these represent cash flows to suppliers of capital to the firm. It would seem they might be treated the same, because both are disbursements related to financing activities. However, after much debate, the FASB decided to classify interest payments as cash flows associated with operations and dividend payments as financing cash flows. This classification maintains the long-standing distinction that dividend transactions with the owners (dividends) cannot be treated as expenses, while interest payments to creditors are expenses.

CASH FLOW AND EARNINGS

If both the income statement and the statement of cash flows reconcile the changes the company experiences during the year, you might wonder why both are required. Why should the company not pick the best one? The problem is that each fills a critical information need. The income statement shows how the companies' owners' equity was

On July 29, 2000, Cisco had $5 billion in cash and owned various highly liquid debt securities. Total assets were $33 billion. On December 31, 1999, Ford Motor Company had about $25 billion in cash and near cash, about 10% of total assets. In managing our personal lives we need to do cash planning so that we will have the money we need when we need it, and the corporate world is no different. However, these amounts seem to far exceed normal needs for liquidity. Investors might reasonably ask why such significant asset levels are committed to such low return investments as U.S. Treasury notes and bonds.

There are conventional answers. Cash and cash equivalents provide flexibility. It is often the currency used in merger transactions, something both Cisco and Ford do regularly. In cyclical industries, such as autos, cash helps you through the money-losing years when car and truck sales drop sharply. You might describe the cash levels as precautions against bad economic times, as the minimum level to cover ongoing transactions, or as the speculative amounts needed to fund major unspecified investments.

Cisco is such a rapidly growing company that its problem is a relatively new one. Cash generated from operations was $4.4 billion in 1999, almost triple the level of 2 years earlier. Thus, cash has been accumulating quickly. As fast as Cisco is growing, it does not have enough internal expansion needs to fully utilize the cash. A serious policy decision needs to be made.

Ford has made such a policy decision. Investors and analysts have long criticized Ford's high cash levels and the company has just completed a complex restructuring activity that distributed much of that extra cash to shareholder's. The financial statements for the third quarter of 2000 did not indicate how successful the restructuring was in reducing cash levels, but the prediction is that it will generate about a $10 billion reduction.

Although Cisco and Ford have lived with high cash levels, other companies are devoted to operating with as little cash as possible. A ratio called days operating expenses held in cash (DOEHIC) is often used to asses cash levels. It is calculated by dividing cash levels by daily operating expenses. Before the recapitalization, Ford's DOEHIC was about 80. Many aggressive cash managing firms have 1, 2, or 3 days of cash on hand. The chief financial officer (CFO) of Verizon says, "I hate cash on hand. It is anathema to me." He keeps about 10 days cash on hand. Firms that take such strategies typically use short-term debt to manage through ups and downs in the cash flow cycle. They set up collection and cash management processes so that whenever balances are above the minimum, they pay down any existing debt.

Cash levels seem to depend significantly on management beliefs. They vary widely. In the steel industry Oregon Steel Mills had a DOEHIC of 3 while its competitor WHX has 115 days of cash. Conagra has one day of cash while Tootsie Roll Industries has 6 months.

increased (or decreased) as a result of operations. It matches revenues and expenses using the accrual concepts and provides a valuable measure of economic activity. In contrast, the statement of cash flows explains changes in the cash account rather than owners' equity. The focal point of the statement of cash flows is the net cash flow from operating activities. Frequently, this is called simply cash flow.

THE ECO-BAG COMPANY—A DETAILED EXAMPLE OF THE DIRECT METHOD FOR PREPARING THE STATEMENT OF CASH FLOWS

To see how many of the activities shown in Exhibit 10-2 would affect a real company, consider the Eco-Bag Company, whose financial statements are shown in Exhibit 10-3. Eco-Bag prepares its cash flow statement using the direct method.

Because the statement of cash flows explains the causes for the changes in cash, the first step in developing the statement is always to compute the amount of the change, in this case a decrease of $9,000.

Exhibit 10-3

Eco-Bag Company

Balance Sheet as of December 31 (in Thousands)

Assets	20X2	20X1	Liabilities and Stockholders' Equity	20X2	20X1
Current assets			Current liabilities		
			Accounts payable	$ 74	$ 6
Cash	$ 16	$ 25	Wages and		
Accounts receivable	45	25	salaries payable	25	4
Inventory	100	60			
Total current assets	161	110	Total current liabilities	99	10
Fixed assets, gross	581	330	Long-term debt	125	5
Accum. depreciation	(101)	(110)	Stockholders' equity	417	315
Net	480	220			
			Total liabilities and		
Total assets	$641	$330	stockholders' equity	$641	$330

Eco-Bag Company

Statement of Income for the Year Ended December 31, 20X2 (in Thousands)

Sales		$200
Cost and expenses		
Cost of goods sold	$100	
Wages and salaries	36	
Depreciation	17	
Interest	4	
Total costs and expenses		$157
Income before income taxes		43
Income taxes		20
Net income		$ 23

Eco-Bag Company

Statement of Cash Flows for the Year Ended December 31, 20X2 (in Thousands)

Cash Flows from Operating Activities			
Cash collections from customers		$ 180	
Cash payments			
To suppliers	$ 72		
To employees	15		
For interest	4		
For taxes	20		
Total cash payments		(111)	
Net cash provided by operating activities		$ 69	
Cash Flows from Investing Activities			
Purchases of fixed assets	$ (287)		
Proceeds from sale of fixed assets	10		
Net cash used by investing activities		(277)	
Cash Flows from Financing Activities			
Proceeds from issue of long-term debt	$ 120		
Proceeds from issue of common stock	98		
Dividends paid	(19)		
Net cash provided by financing activities		199	
Net decrease in cash		$ (9)	
Cash, December 31, 20X1		25	
Cash, December 31, 20X2		$ 16	

Cash, December 31, 20X1	$25,000
Cash, December 31, 20X2	16,000
Net decrease in cash	$ 9,000

Our Eco-Bag Company example in Exhibit 10-3 shows how this basic calculation is often shown at the bottom of a statement of cash flows. The net change during the period is added to the beginning cash balance to compute the ending cash balance. However, beginning and ending cash balances are not required in the statement of cash flows. Explaining the net change in cash during the period is all that is necessary.

Eco-Bag Company's statement shows that the excess of cash outflows over cash inflows reduced cash by $9,000. Why does cash decline? Operating activity is contributing additional cash during the year ($69,000), but the cash required for expansion significantly exceeds what operations provides. To support purchases of fixed assets of $287,000, the company raised an additional $199,000 via financing activities, both borrowing and sales of stock. Business expansion usually involves numerous assets, including accounts receivable and inventories. Note that Eco-Bag experienced a significant increase in accounts receivable and inventory during the period, but these increases in current assets were more than offset by rising current liabilities.

Most importantly, this illustration demonstrates how a firm may simultaneously (1) have a significant amount of net income, as computed by accountants on the accrual basis, and yet (2) have a decline in cash that could become severe. Indeed, many growing businesses are desperate for cash even though reported net income zooms upward.

CHANGES IN THE BALANCE SHEET EQUATION

Accountants often prepare the statement of cash flows using the balance sheet approach. The balance sheet equation provides the conceptual basis for all financial statements, including the statement of cash flows. The equation can be rearranged as follows:

$$\text{Assets} = \text{Liabilities} + \text{Stockholders' equity}$$
$$\text{Cash} + \text{Noncash assets} = \text{Liabilities} + \text{Stockholders' equity}$$
$$\text{Cash} = \text{Liabilities} + \text{Stockholders' equity} - \text{Noncash assets (NCA)}$$
$$\text{Cash} = L + SE - NCA$$

Any change (Δ) in cash must be accompanied by a change in one or more items on the right side to keep the equation in balance:

$$\Delta\,\text{Cash} = \Delta\,L + \Delta\,SE - \Delta\,NCA$$

Therefore:

$$\text{Change in cash} = \text{Change in all noncash accounts}$$

or

$$\text{What happened to cash} = \text{Why it happened}$$

The statement of cash flows focuses on the changes in the noncash accounts as a way of explaining how and why the level of cash has gone up or down during a given period. Thus, the major changes in the accounts on the right side of the equation appear in the statement of cash flows as causes of the change in cash. The left side of the equation measures the net effect of the change in cash.

Consider the following summary of 20X2 transactions for Eco-Bag Company. In practice, a company accountant might produce this summary by carefully reviewing the general ledger accounts and combining similar transactions that occurred during the year, that is, combining all the various sales on credit, and so on. Those transactions involving cash have an asterisk (*):

1. Sales on credit, $200,000
*2. Collections of accounts receivable, $180,000
3. Recognition of cost of goods sold, $100,000
4. Purchases of inventory on account, $140,000
*5. Payments of trade accounts payable, $72,000
6. Recognition of wages expense, $36,000
*7. Payments of wages, $15,000
*8. Recognition of interest accrued and paid, $4,000
*9. Recognition and payment of income taxes, $20,000
10. Recognition of depreciation expense, $17,000
*11. Acquisition of fixed assets for cash, $287,000
*12. Sale of fixed assets at book value, $10,000
*13. Issuance of long-term debt, $120,000
*14. Issuance of common stock, $98,000
*15. Declaration and payment of dividends, $19,000

Exhibit 10-4 applies the balance sheet equation to the Eco-Bag Company data. We can see, step by step, how the balance sheet equation produces and explains the statement of cash flows in Exhibit 10-3. The totals in Exhibit 10-4 show that the $9,000 decrease in cash is explained by the changes in the liability, stockholders' equity, and noncash asset accounts, and that all cash transactions have been accounted for. While the information in

Exhibit 10-4

Eco-Bag Company

The Balance Sheet Equation ($ in Thousands)

	Δ Cash	=	ΔL	+ ΔSE	$- \Delta NCA$
Operating activities					
1. Sales on credit		=		+200	$-$ (+200)
*2. Cash collections from customers	+180	=			$-$ ($-$180)
3. Cost of goods sold		=		$-$100	$-$ ($-$100)
4. Inventory purchases on account		=	+140		$-$ (+140)
*5. Payments to suppliers	$-$ 72	=	$-$ 72		
6. Wages and salaries expense		=	+ 36	$-$ 36	
*7. Payments to employees	$-$ 15	=	$-$ 15		
*8. Interest expense paid	$-$ 4	=		$-$ 4	
*9. Income taxes paid	$-$ 20	=		$-$ 20	
Net cash provided by					
operating activities, a subtotal	69				
Expenses not requiring cash					
10. Depreciation		=		$-$ 17	$-$ ($-$ 17)
Net income, a subtotal				+ 23	
Investing activities					
*11. Acquire fixed assets	$-$287	=			$-$ (+287)
*12. Dispose of fixed assets	+ 10	=			$-$ ($-$ 10)
Financing activities					
*13. Issue long-term debt	+120	=	+120		
*14. Issue common stock	+ 98	=		+ 98	
*15. Pay dividends	$-$ 19	=		$-$ 19	
Net changes	$-$ 9	=	+209	+102	$-$ (+320)

Exhibit 10-4 summarizes the elements that caused the changes in cash, they need to be combined and reformatted for final inclusion in a cash flow statement. We turn first to calculating the elements of cash flow from operations.

COMPUTING CASH FLOWS FROM OPERATING ACTIVITIES

The first major section in Eco-Bag Company's statement of cash flows (Exhibit 10-3, p. 413) is cash flows from operating activities. Different companies call this section cash flow from operations, cash provided by operations, or, if operating activities decrease cash, cash used for operations.

Collections from sales to customers are almost always the major operating cash inflows. Correspondingly, disbursements for purchases of goods to be sold and operating expenses are almost always the major operating cash outflows. The amount of inflows (collections) minus the amount of outflows (disbursements) is the net cash provided by—or used up by—operating activities. In Exhibit 10-3, collections of $180,000 minus the $111,000 of operating disbursements equals net cash provided by operating activities, $69,000.

WORKING FROM INCOME STATEMENT AMOUNTS TO CASH AMOUNTS

Objective 4
Determine cash flows from income statement and balance sheet accounts.

Many accountants build the statement of cash flows from the changes in balance sheet items, a few additional facts, and a familiarity with the typical causes of changes in cash. For instance, our Eco-Bag Company example provided the "additional fact" that cash collections from customers for 20X2 was $180,000. Most accounting systems, though, do not provide such additional facts. Therefore, accountants often compute the collections and other cash flow items from figures on the income statement. Let us now examine the detailed calculations for collections and other operating items from Eco-Bag.

a. Eco-Bag Company recognized $200,000 of revenue in 20X2, but the $20,000 increase in accounts receivable suggests that only $180,000 was collected from customers:

	Sales	$200,000
+	Beginning accounts receivable	25,000
	Potential collections	$225,000
−	Ending accounts receivable	45,000
	Cash collections from customers	$180,000

or

Sales	$200,000
Decrease (increase) in accounts receivable	(20,000)
Cash collections from customers	$180,000

Note that an increase in accounts receivable means that sales exceeded collections. Conversely, a decrease in accounts receivable means collections exceeded sales.

b. The difference between the $100,000 cost of goods sold and the $72,000 cash payment to suppliers can be explained by changes in inventory and accounts payable. The $40,000 increase in inventory indicates that purchases exceeded the cost of goods sold by $40,000:

	Ending inventory	$100,000
+	Cost of goods sold	100,000
	Inventory to account for	$200,000
−	Beginning inventory	(60,000)
	Purchase of inventory	$140,000

Although purchases were $140,000, payments to suppliers were only $72,000. Why? Some purchases were made on credit, resulting in a $68,000 increase in trade accounts payable, from $6,000 to $74,000:

Beginning trade accounts payable	$ 6,000
+ Purchases	140,000
Total amount to be paid	$146,000
− Ending trade accounts payable	(74,000)
Accounts paid in cash	$ 72,000

The effects of inventory and trade accounts payable can be combined as follows:

Cost of goods sold	$100,000
Increase (decrease) in inventory	40,000
Decrease (increase) in trade accounts payable	(68,000)
Payments to suppliers	$ 72,000

c. Cash payments to employees were only $15,000 because the wages and salaries expense of $36,000 was offset by a $21,000 increase in wages and salaries payable:

Beginning wages and salaries payable	$ 4,000
+ Wages and salaries expense	36,000
Total to be paid	$40,000
− Ending wages and salaries payable	(25,000)
Cash payments to employees	$15,000

or

Wages and salaries expense	$36,000
Decrease (increase) in wages and salaries payable	(21,000)
Cash payments to employees	$15,000

d. Notice that both interest payable and income taxes payable were zero at the beginning and at the end of 20X2. Therefore, the entire $4,000 interest expense and the $20,000 income tax expense were paid in cash in 20X2.

COMPARISON OF INCOME STATEMENT AND CASH FLOW STATEMENT

Accrual-based measures of revenue and expense are reported in the income statement. Most of these are naturally linked to related asset or liability accounts and the cash effects of the revenue and expense transactions are moderated by changes in their related asset or liability accounts. The balance sheet approach relies on adjusting accrual-based income statement values for changes in asset and liability account balances. The following illustration summarizes the process.

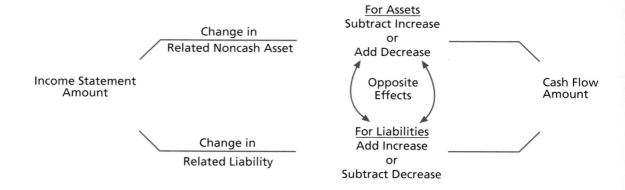

Note that liability changes have opposite effects from asset changes. Each revenue or expense account has a related asset and/or liability account, some examples of which are shown in panel A of Exhibit 10-5.

Panel B of Exhibit 10-5 summarizes the application of this concept to the details of Eco-Bag Company. For example, the $20,000 increase in accounts receivable indicates that not all the sales were collected, so sales revenue is reduced from $200,000 to $180,000, the actual cash collected. Similarly, the $40,000 increase in inventory indicates that we might have paid for more goods than we sold, an additional use of cash. This effect is offset by the increase in accounts payable of $68,000. We delayed the use of cash by increasing our trade credit.

Exhibit 10-5

Comparison of Net Income and Net Cash Provided by Operating Activities

PANEL A: GENERAL CASE—COMMON ADJUSTMENTS TO CONVERT INCOME STATEMENT AMOUNTS TO CASH FLOW AMOUNTS

Income Statement Amount	Related Noncash Asset	Related Liability
Sales revenue	Accounts receivable	Unearned revenue
Cost of goods sold	Merchandise inventory	Accounts payable
Wage expense	Prepaid wages	Wages payable
Rent expense	Prepaid rent	Rent payable
Insurance expense	Prepaid insurance	Insurance payable
Depreciation expense	Plant, property, or equipment	
Amortization expense	Intangible asset	

PANEL B: ECO-BAG COMPANY EXAMPLE

Income Statement		Asset Change −Increases +Decreases	Liability Change +Increases −Decreases		Cash Flow Statement
Sales revenue	$200,000	$(20,000)		=	$180,000
Cost of goods sold	(100,000)	(40,000)	$68,000	=	(72,000)
Wage and salary expense	(36,000)		21,000	=	(15,000)
Interest expense	(4,000)			=	(4,000)
Income taxes	($20,000)			=	(20,000)
Depreciation	(17,000)	17,000			
Net income	$ 23,000	$(43,000)	$89,000		$ 69,000

COMPUTING CASH FLOWS FROM INVESTING AND FINANCING ACTIVITIES

The second and third major sections of the statement of cash flows show **cash flows from investing activities** and **cash flows from financing activities.** The former lists cash flows from the purchase or sale of plant, property, equipment, and other long-lived assets. The latter shows cash flows to and from providers of capital. The idea is that long-lived assets are investments, and sources of capital, such as stocks and bonds, finance the purchase of these investments. If the necessary information concerning these cash flows is not directly available by simply inspecting the cash account, accountants can determine the necessary information by analyzing changes in balance sheet items using the following rules:

- Increases in cash (cash inflows) stem from
    - Increases in liabilities or stockholders' equity
    - Decreases in noncash assets
- Decreases in cash (cash outflows) stem from
    - Decreases in liabilities or stockholders' equity
    - Increases in noncash assets

Consider Eco-Bag Company's balance sheet (Exhibit 10-3, p. 413). All noncash current assets and current liabilities of the company were affected only by operating activities. Three noncurrent accounts—(a) fixed assets, (b) long-term debt, and (c) stockholders' equity—affect the cash flows from investing activities ($277,000 outflow) and financing activities ($199,000 inflow) as follows.

a. Net fixed assets increased by $260,000 in 20X2. Three items usually explain changes in net fixed assets: (1) assets acquired, (2) asset dispositions, and (3) depreciation expense for the period. Therefore:

Increase in net plant assets = Acquisitions − Disposals − Depreciation expense

The elements in this equation explain the company's investing activities. Tracing the cash flow from investing activities requires some knowledge of the year's activity. Sometimes you have only incomplete information and need to solve for the unknown values. For example, you might know the increase in net plant assets, acquisitions of new fixed assets, and depreciation expense without knowing about Eco-Bag Company's asset disposals. The book value of disposals could be computed from the preceding equation:

$$\$260,000 = \$287,000 - \text{Disposals} - \$17,000$$
$$\text{Disposals} = \$287,000 - \$17,000 - \$260,000$$
$$\text{Disposals} = \$10,000$$

Eco-Bag Company received exactly the book value for the assets sold. Appendix 10A discusses disposals for more or less than book value. If the amount of disposals were known, but either acquisitions or depreciation expense were unknown, the missing item could be determined by applying this same equation.

b. Long-term debt increased by $125,000 − $5,000 = $120,000. This increase was due to new long-term debt being issued—a financing activity that increased cash.

c. The $102,000 increase ($417,000 − $315,000) in stockholders' equity can be explained by three factors: (1) issuance of capital stock, (2) net income (or loss), and (3) dividends. Therefore:

Increase in stockholders' equity = New issuance + Net income − Dividends

Suppose you did not know how much new stock had been issued:

$$\$102,000 = \text{New issuance} + \$23,000 - \$19,000$$
$$\text{New issuance} = \$102,000 - \$23,000 + \$19,000$$
$$\text{New issuance} = \$98,000, \text{ an inflow of cash}$$

cash flows from investing activities The second major section of the statement of cash flows describing purchase or sale of plant, property, equipment, and other long-lived assets.

cash flows from financing activities The third major section of the statement of cash flows describing flows to and from providers of capital.

The three sections of the statement of cash flows are related in certain ways, depending on the industry the company is part of and its stage in its growth cycle. The following table suggests eight relationships. The table uses a plus sign (+) to indicate that cash was provided by the activity and a minus (−) to indicate that the activity used cash. The basic activities of operations, investing, and financing are each discussed as follows:

Relationship	1	2	3	4	5	6	7	8
Operating cash flow	+	+	+	+	−	−	−	−
Investing cash flow	+	−	+	−	+	−	+	−
Financing cash flow	+	+	−	−	+	+	−	−

What are the natural/common relationships? In general, companies in dynamic industries with good opportunities are profitable, generate cash from operations (a + in operating cash flow), and make continuous, new investments (a − for investing cash flow). Thus, they are in relationships 2 or 4 (+, −, ?). Which is more common? A profitable, young, growing company would generate cash flow from operations but would be investing in growth prospects rapidly enough as to require additional financing to sustain growth. This is relationship 2 (+, −, +). Relationship 4 describes a firm that is growing more slowly, with operating cash flow sufficient to cover growth while repaying debt.

Some younger, growing firms may still be unprofitable, producing relationship 6 (−, −, +). If profitability is just around the corner, this may be fine. So relationships 2, 4 and 6 are to some extent desirable, or at least normal.

For the most part, investors prefer firms that are growing as represented by the negative investing cash flow in relationships 2, 4, 6, or 8. We have explained why the first three are interesting, but the last one, relationship 8, is a bit strange. Where is the cash coming from for a firm that is using cash in operations while continuing to make new investments and pay off debt? This is unusual and not sustainable and should cause the analyst to examine the firm carefully. It might describe a young start-up that goes to the capital markets every few years for a major infusion of investment capital, and then lives off that capital for several years.

In contrast to the growth perspectives previously discussed, patterns 1, 3, 5 and 7 describe a shrinking firm that is realizing cash from the sale or retirement of assets. This is not generally a healthy situation. Relationships 1 and 3 are generating positive cash flow from operations. 1 is a strange case in that the firm is simultaneously selling assets (disinvesting) and borrowing. All these cash inflows must be aimed at either meeting significant obligations of the firm or financing significant new growth opportunities. This can be ascertained by further analysis. Relationship 3 is a more rational case in that cash generated from operations and sales of assets is being used to retire debt. This is a sustainable situation. Relationships 5 and 7 are both strange in that the firms are not generating cash from operations and are selling assets to provide cash. This may bode ill for the future.

No pattern is fully revealing by itself. Each requires analysis. What has the past pattern been and what is projected for the future? What is the strategic plan behind the pattern? Classifying the pattern is just the first step in understanding the company.

Both the issuance of new shares and the payment of cash dividends are financing activities that affect cash.

NONCASH INVESTING AND FINANCING ACTIVITIES

In our example, Eco-Bag Company did not have any noncash investing or financing activities. Suppose Eco-Bag Company had the following such activities:

1. The firm acquired a $14,000 fixed asset by issuing common stock.
2. The company acquired a small building by signing a mortgage payable for $97,000.
3. The firm converted long-term debt of $35,000 to common stock.

These items affect the balance sheet equation as follows:

Δ Cash	=	Δ L	+ Δ SE		− Δ NCA
1.	0 =		+$14,000 [Increase Common Stock]	−(+$14,000)	[Increase Fixed Asset]
2.	0 = +$97,000	[Increase Mortgage payable]		−(+$97,000)	[Increase Building]
3.	0 = −$35,000	[Decrease Long-term Debt]	+$35,000 [Increase Common Stock]		

None of these transactions affect cash, and therefore they do not belong in a statement of cash flows. However, each transaction could just as easily involve cash. For example, in the first transaction, the company might issue common stock for $14,000 cash and immediately use the cash to purchase the fixed asset. The cash would then need to be traced and appear on the statement of cash flows. Because of the similarities between these noncash transactions and ones involving cash, readers of statements of cash flows should be informed of such noncash activities. Therefore, such items must be included in a separate schedule accompanying the statement of cash flows. Eco-Bag Company's schedule for these additional transactions would be:

Schedule of noncash investing and financing activities
Common stock issued to acquire fixed asset	$14,000
Mortgage payable for acquisition of building	$97,000
Common stock issued on conversion of long-term debt	$35,000

THE CRISIS OF NEGATIVE CASH FLOW

Although investors make important economic decisions on the basis of the so-called bottom line, sometimes earnings numbers do not tell the full story of what is really happening inside a company. Take the case of Prime Motor Inns, at the time, the world's second largest hotel operator, which reported earnings of $77 million on revenues of $410 million for 1989. That is a return on sales (net income ÷ revenues) of nearly 19%. Moreover, in 1989, revenues increased by nearly 11% from the preceding year. Despite its impressive earnings performance, though, Prime lacked the cash to meet its obligations and filed for chapter 11 bankruptcy in September 1990. Under bankruptcy protection, a firm's obligations to its creditors are frozen as management figures out how to pay those creditors. How can a firm with $77 million in earnings file for bankruptcy about a year later?

Although the company's business was owning and operating hotels, much of Prime's reported earnings in 1989 arose from selling hotels. When outside financing for these hotel sales became harder to obtain, Prime financed the sales itself by accepting notes and mortgages receivable from buyers. Of course, Prime soon ran out of hotels to sell, if it wanted to stay in the business. Moreover, the reported gain under accrual accounting often significantly exceeded the cash received. In the year that Prime reported $77 million of net income, an astute analyst would have noted that Prime had a net cash outflow from operations of $15 million. Analyzing the cash flow statement focuses attention on important relationships such as this one.

On July 31, 1992, Prime emerged from bankruptcy with 75 hotels—roughly half of the 141 hotels it had prior to bankruptcy—and a new name, Prime Hospitality Corporation. The new company kept its great stock symbol, "PDQ," and investors who bought the new shares for about $1.50 when the reorganization occurred have done well.

In July of 2000, the price was $9.50, providing those investors a return of 26% per year. Of course, in hindsight that investor might have sold 2 years earlier when the stock peaked at $21.00. The sharp decline followed a year of significant earnings decline, but the cash from operations remains strong. Timing is everything. The shareholders who bought the old company for $35 per share in 1989 watched their investment fall to under $1 in 1 year, while those who bought in 1992 have done quite well.

What pattern in the cash flow statement would have helped to alert the careful analyst to a potential problem at Prime Hospitality Corporation?
ANSWER
Prime was reporting large profits under accrual accounting but operating cash flow was negative. Prime was financing sales by accepting notes and mortgages from buyers. This would have been evident by significant increases in these receivables as compared with prior years.

PREPARING A STATEMENT OF CASH FLOWS — THE INDIRECT METHOD

Objective 5
Use the indirect method to calculate cash flows from operations.

The Eco-Bag Company statement of cash flows in Exhibit 10-3 used the direct method to compute net cash provided by operating activities. The alternative, and often more convenient, indirect method of computing cash flows from operating activities reconciles net income to the net cash provided by operating activities. It also shows the link between the income statement and the statement of cash flows.

RECONCILIATION OF NET INCOME TO NET CASH PROVIDED BY OPERATIONS

In the indirect method, the statement of cash flows begins with net income. Then additions or deductions are made for changes in related asset or liability accounts, that is, for items that affect net income and net cash flow differently. Exhibit 10-6 shows this process for our Eco-Bag example. As we saw in Exhibit 10-5, net cash provided by operating activities exceeds net income by $46,000. If a company uses the direct method, the FASB requires a reconciliation such as Exhibit 10-6 as a supporting schedule to the statement of cash flows.

Consider the following logic applied in the reconciliation in Exhibit 10-6:

1. Depreciation is added back to net income because it was deducted in the computation of net income but it does not represent a use of cash. To calculate cash provided by operations, the depreciation of $17,000 would not have been subtracted. The add-back simply cancels out the earlier deduction.

2. Increases in noncash current assets such as receivables and inventory result in less cash flow from operations. For instance, suppose the $20,000 increase in receivables was a result of credit sales made near the end of the year. The $20,000 sales figure would be included in the computation of net income, but the $20,000 would not have increased cash flow from operations. Therefore, the reconciliation deducts the $20,000 from the net income.

3. Increases in current liabilities such as accounts payable and wages payable result in more cash flow from operations. For instance, suppose the $21,000 increase in wages payable was caused by wages earned near the end of the year, but not yet paid in cash. The $21,000 of noncash wages expense would be deducted in computing net income, but it used no cash. Therefore, the reconciliation adds the $21,000 to net income to offset the noncash expense deduction and thereby show the effect on cash.

Exhibit 10-6

Eco-Bag Company

Reconciliation of Net Income to Net Cash Provided by Operating Activities (in Thousands)

Net income		$23
Adjustments to reconcile net income to net cash provided by operating activities		
Depreciation	$17	
Net increase in accounts receivable	(20)	
Net increase in inventory	(40)	
Net increase in accounts payable	68	
Net increase in wages and salaries payable	21	
Total additions and deductions		46
Net cash provided by operating activities		$69

The general rules for additions and deductions to adjust net income using the indirect method are the same as to those for adjusting the line items of the income statement under the direct method. We focus on current assets and liabilities because they are most often tied to operations.

Depreciation is an allocation of historical cost to expense and does not entail a current outflow of cash. Consider again the calculation of Eco-Bag Company's cash flows in Exhibit 10-6. Why is the $17,000 of depreciation added to net income to compute cash flow? Simply to cancel its deduction in calculating net income. Unfortunately, use of the indirect method may at first glance create an erroneous impression that depreciation is added because it, by itself, is a source of cash. If that were really true, a corporation could merely double or triple its bookkeeping entry for depreciation expense when cash was badly needed. What would happen? Cash provided by operations would be unaffected. Suppose depreciation for Eco-Bag Company is doubled:

Objective 6
Relate depreciation to cash flows provided by operating activities.

	With Depreciation of $17,000	With Depreciation of $34,000
Sales	$200,000	$200,000
All expenses except depreciation (including income taxes)*	(160,000)	(160,000)
Depreciation	(17,000)	(34,000)
Net income	$ 23,000	$ 6,000
Nondepreciation adjustments[†]	29,000	29,000
Add depreciation	17,000	34,000
Net cash provided by operating activities	$ 69,000	$ 69,000

*$100,000 + $36,000 + $4,000 + $20,000 = $160,000

[†]From Exhibit 10-6, $(20,000) + $(40,000) + $68,000 + $21,000 = $29,000

The doubling affects depreciation and net income, but it has no direct influence on cash provided by operations, which, of course, still amounts to $69,000.

RECONCILING ITEMS

We have seen that net income rarely coincides with net cash provided by operating activities. Common additions or deductions to reconcile net income to net cash provided by operating activities are shown in Exhibit 10-7. The majority of listed items have been discussed previously or are logical extensions. For example, depletion expenses arising from natural resources are conceptually the same as those of depreciation.

Objective 7
Reconcile net income
to cash provided by
operating activities.

Exhibit 10-7

Common Reconciling Items

Add charges (expenses) not requiring cash
    Depreciation
    Depletion
    Amortization of assets
    Nonoperating losses
    Amortization of bond discount
Deduct credits to income (revenues) not providing cash
    Nonoperating gains
    Amortization of bond premium
Adjust for changes in current assets and liabilities relating to operating activities

Changes in noncash current assets	**Changes in noncash current liabilities**
deduct increases	add increases
add decreases	deduct decreases
Examples: Accounts receivable inventory	Examples: Accounts payable Wages payable

The new items that deserve discussion are nonoperating gains and losses. Suppose the company sells 10 acres of land it has decided not to use. The land cost $20,000 and is sold for $30,000 in cash. Net income would include a gain of $10,000. The cash flow is $30,000. Note, however, this is not cash from operations, because for most companies ownership of land is an investing activity. To include this properly in the cash flow statement requires that all $30,000 be shown as cash provided by investing activities. The $10,000 gain is subtracted from net income in the reconciliation to avoid including elements of this transaction in both places. It was not a source of operating cash.

THE WINDRIVER CASH FLOW STATEMENT

Exhibit 10-8 contains the 2000 statement of cash flows for WindRiver, a company that "is the leading provider of reliable, innovative software solutions for connected smart devices in the Internet Age." WindRiver is focused on embedded devices, smart devices that are part of other products that enhance the efficiency of a multitude of Web elements. The firm cites a study that predicts growth from 180 million such devices installed worldwide in 1999 to over a billion by 2003. WindRiver's statement contains most of the items described in this chapter, together with many details beyond the scope of this text. Note that WindRiver uses the indirect method in the body of the statement of cash flows to report the cash flows from operating activities. Most companies use this format.

During the 3 years shown, WindRiver had positive cash flow from operations each year. Analysts would be drawn to the large changes in accounts receivable each year that stand out in the cash flow from operations. While revenues were growing at less than 30%, receivables grew at 55%. This is an unsustainable relationship and may indicate collection risk for receivables. The financing section shows that the company had a 3-year pattern of repurchasing common stock, spending more than $25 million in this way. At the same time, the company was issuing new stock in similar amounts in total. In the investing section we observe a pattern of purchases and sales of investment securities. It would come as no surprise that the balance sheet shows about 40% of the assets are investments. The majority of these investments are debt securities. This is common among high-tech companies that are growing rapidly and wish to assure available capital to fund that growth. Much of the capital to support these investments could be traced back to the issuance of convertible subordinated notes in 1998 as seen in financing activities.

Exhibit 10-8

Wind River Systems, Inc.

Consolidated Statements of Cash Flows

	Years Ended January 31,		
In Thousands	*2000*	*1999*	*1998*
Cash flows from operating activities:			
Net income	$ 22,471	$ 25,623	$ 4,326
Adjustments to reconcile net income to net cash provided by operations:			
Depreciation and amortization	10,523	8,531	4,806
Tax benefit from stock plan	5,000	13,400	7,000
Write-off of impaired assets	500	—	—
Deferred income taxes	(92)	(244)	(2,894)
Minority interest in consolidated subsidiary	327	151	88
Acquired in-process research and development	—	—	15,159
Change in assets and liabilities:			
Accounts receivable	(17,695)	(12,552)	(4,449)
Prepaid and other assets	(13,415)	(5,318)	(5,670)
Accounts payable	2,921	(487)	2,015
Accrued liabilities	1,054	(235)	4,387
Accrued compensation	4,305	489	1,050
Income taxes payable	9,417	(729)	2,368
Deferred revenue	7,158	2,164	8,883
Net cash provided by operating activities	32,474	30,793	37,069
Cash flows from investing activities:			
Acquisition of land and equipment	(11,755)	(12,770)	(19,704)
Capitalized software development costs	—	—	(803)
Acquisitions, net of cash acquired	—	—	(20,553)
Purchases of investments	(124,907)	(232,193)	(264,048)
Sales and maturities of investments	118,422	188,231	236,010
Restricted cash	(5,587)	(31,647)	(2,510)
Net cash used in investing activities	(23,827)	(88,379)	(71,608)
Cash flows from financing activities:			
Line of credit	5,094	—	—
Issuance of Common Stock, net	8,861	9,484	4,265
Purchase of treasury stock	(3,997)	(10,006)	(12,364)
Loan to stockholder	(1,900)	—	—
Issuance of convertible subordinated notes, net	—	—	134,925
Net cash provided by (used in) financing activities	8,058	(522)	126,826
Effect of exchange rate changes on cash and cash equivalents	(844)	157	(1,390)
Effect of changing fiscal year of acquired subsidiary	(77)	—	—
Net increase (decrease) in cash and cash equivalents	15,784	(57,951)	90,897
Cash and cash equivalents at beginning of year	42,837	100,788	9,891
Cash and cash equivalents at end of year	$ 58,621	$ 42,837	$100,788
Supplemental disclosures of cash flow information:			
Cash paid for interest	$ 9,414	$ 7,000	—
Cash paid for income taxes	$ 1,995	$ 1,897	$ 3,372

SUMMARY PROBLEMS FOR YOUR REVIEW

PROBLEM ONE

The Buretta Company has prepared the data in Exhibit 10-9.

In December 20X2, Buretta paid $54 million cash for a new building acquired to accommodate an expansion of operations. This purchase was financed partly by a new

Exhibit 10-9

Buretta Company
Income Statement and Statement of Retained Earnings
For the Year Ended December 31, 20X2 (in Millions)

Sales		$100
Less cost of goods sold		
Inventory, December 31, 20X1	$ 15	
Purchases	105	
Cost of goods available for sale	$120	
Inventory, December 31, 20X2	47	73
Gross profit		$ 27
Less other expenses		
General expenses	$ 8	
Depreciation	8	
Property taxes	4	
Interest expense	3	23
Net income		$ 4
Retained earnings, December 31, 20X1		7
Total		$ 11
Dividends		1
Retained earnings, December 31, 20X2		$ 10

Trial Balances

	December 31 (in Millions)		Increase (Decrease)
	20X2	*20X1*	
Debits			
Cash	$ 1	$ 20	$(19)
Accounts receivable	20	5	15
Inventory	47	15	32
Prepaid general expenses	3	2	1
Fixed assets, net	91	50	41
	$162	$92	$ 70
Credits			
Accounts payable for merchandise	$ 39	$ 14	$ 25
Accrued property tax payable	3	1	2
Long-term debt	40	—	40
Capital stock	70	70	—
Retained earnings	10	7	3
	$162	$92	$ 70

issue of long-term debt for $40 million cash. During 20X2, the company also sold fixed assets for their book value of $5 million cash. All sales and purchases of merchandise were on credit.

Because the 20X2 net income of $4 million was the highest in the company's history, Alice Buretta, the chairman of the board, was perplexed by the company's extremely low cash balance.

1. Prepare a statement of cash flows from the Buretta data in Exhibit 10-9 on the next page. Ignore income taxes. You may wish to use Exhibit 10-3 (p. 413) as a guide. Use the direct method for reporting cash flows from operating activities.

2. Prepare a supporting schedule that reconciles net income to net cash provided by operating activities.

3. What does the statement of cash flows tell you about Buretta Company? Does it help you reduce Alice Buretta's puzzlement? Why?

SOLUTION TO PROBLEM ONE

1. See Exhibit 10-10. Cash flows from operating activities were computed as follows ($ in millions):

Sales	$ 100
Less increase in accounts receivable	(15)
Cash collections from customers	$ 85
Cost of goods sold	$ 73
Plus increase in inventory	32
Purchases	$ 105
Less increase in accounts payable	(25)
Cash paid to suppliers	$ 80
General expenses	$ 8
Plus increase in prepaid general expenses	1
Cash payment for general expenses	$ 9
Cash paid for interest	$ 3
Property taxes	$ 4
Less increase in accrued property tax payable	(2)
Cash paid for property taxes	$ 2

2. Exhibit 10-11 reconciles net income to net cash provided by operating activities.

3. The statement of cash flows shows where cash has come from and where it has gone. Operations used $9 million of cash. Why? The statement in Exhibit 10-10,

Exhibit 10-10

Buretta Company
Statement of Cash Flows for the Year Ended December 31, 20X2
(in Millions)

Cash flows from operating activities		
Cash collections from customers		$ 85
Cash payments:		
Cash paid to suppliers	$(80)	
General expenses	(9)	
Interest paid	(3)	
Property taxes	(2)	(94)
Net cash used by operating activities		$ (9)
Cash flows from investing activities		
Purchase of fixed assets (building)	$(54)	
Proceeds from sale of fixed assets	5	
Net cash used by investing activities		(49)
Cash flows from financing activities		
Long-term debt issued	$ 40	
Dividends paid	(1)	
Net cash provided by financing activities		39
Net decrease in cash		$(19)
Cash balance, December 31, 20X1		20
Cash balance, December 31, 20X2		$ 1

Exhibit 10-11

Supporting Schedule to Statement of Cash Flows

Reconciliation of Net Income to Net Cash Provided by Operating
Activities for the Year Ended December 31, 20X2 (in Millions)

Net income (from income statement)	$ 4
Adjustments to reconcile net income to net cash provided by operating activities	
Add: Depreciation, which was deducted in the computation of net income but does not decrease cash	8
Deduct: Increase in accounts receivable	(15)
Deduct: Increase in inventory	(32)
Deduct: Increase in prepaid general expenses	(1)
Add: Increase in accounts payable	25
Add: Increase in accrued property tax payable	2
Net cash used by operating activities	$(9)

which uses the direct method, shows the result clearly: $94 million in cash paid for operating activities exceeded $85 million in cash received from customers. The reconciliation using the indirect method, in Exhibit 10-11, shows why, in a profitable year, operating cash flow could be negative. The three largest items differentiating net income from cash flow are changes in inventory, accounts receivable, and accounts payable. Sales during the period were not collected in full because accounts receivable rose sharply, by $15 million—a 300% increase. Similarly, cash was spent on inventory growth, although much of that growth was financed by increased accounts payable. In summary, large increases in accounts receivable ($15 million) and inventory ($32 million), plus a $1 million increase in prepaid expenses, used $48 million of cash. In contrast, only $39 million, that is, $4 + $8 + $25 + $2 million, was generated. Thus, $9 million was used in operations ($39 − $48).

Investing activities also consumed cash because $54 million was invested in a building, and only $5 million was received from sales of fixed assets, leaving a net use of $49 million. Financing activities did generate $39 million cash, but that was $19 million less than the $58 million used by operating and investing activities ($58 million = $9 million used in operations + $49 million used in investing).

Alice Buretta should no longer be puzzled. The statement of cash flows shows clearly that cash payments exceeded receipts by $19 million. However, she may still be concerned about the depletion of cash. Either operations must be changed so that they do not require so much cash, investment must be curtailed, or more long-term debt or ownership equity must be raised. Otherwise Buretta Company will soon run out of cash.

PROBLEM TWO

To understand how cash flow and net income vary during the life cycle of a business, consider the following example that portrays the 4-year life of a short-lived merchandising company, Trend-2000. The first year the entrepreneurs bought twice as much as they sold because they were building their base inventory levels. Trend-2000 suppliers offered payment terms that resulted in 80% of each year's purchases being paid during that year and 20% in the next year. Sales were for cash with a 100% markup on cost. Selling expenses were constant over the life of the business and were paid in cash. At the end of the fourth year, the suppliers were paid in full and all the inventory was sold. Use the following summary results to prepare four income statements and statements of cash flows from operations for Trend-2000, one for each year of its life.

	Year 1	Year 2	Year 3	Year 4
Purchases	2,000 units	1,500 units	1,500 units	1,000 units
$1 each	$2,000	$1,500	$1,500	$1,000
Sales	1,000 units	1,500 units	2,000 units	1,500 units
$2 each	$2,000	$3,000	$4,000	$3,000
Cost of sales	$1,000	$1,500	$2,000	$1,500
Selling expense	$1,000	$1,000	$1,000	$1,000
Payments to suppliers*	$1,600	$1,600	$1,500	$1,300

*$.8 \times 2,000 = 1,600; (.2 \times 2,000) + (.8 \times 1,500) = 1,600; (.2 \times 1,500) + (.8 \times 1,500) = 1,500; (.2 \times 1,500) + (1.0 \times 1,000) = 1,300.$

SOLUTION TO PROBLEM TWO

	Year 1	Year 2	Year 3	Year 4	Total
Income statement					
Sales	$2,000	$3,000	$4,000	$3,000	$12,000
Cost of sales	1,000	1,500	2,000	1,500	6,000
Selling expenses	1,000	1,000	1,000	1,000	4,000
Net income	$ 0	$ 500	$1,000	$ 500	$ 2,000
Cash flows from Operations: direct method					
Collections	$2,000	$3,000	$4,000	$3,000	$12,000
Payments on account	1,600	1,600	1,500	1,300	6,000
Payments for selling efforts	1,000	1,000	1,000	1,000	4,000
Cash flow from operations	$ (600)	$ 400	$1,500	$ 700	$ 2,000
Cash flows from Operations: indirect method					
Net income	$ 0	$ 500	$1,000	$ 500	$ 2,000
− Increase in inventory	(1,000)				(1,000)
+ Decrease in inventory			500	500	1,000
+ Increase in accounts payable	400				400
− Decrease in accounts payable		(100)		(300)	(400)
Cash flow from operations	$ (600)	$ 400	$1,500	$ 700	$ 2,000

Balance Sheet Accounts at the end of	Year 1	Year 2	Year 3	Year 4
Merchandise inventory	$1,000	$1,000	$ 500	$ 0
Accounts payable	$ 400	$ 300	$ 300	0

This problem illustrates the difference between accrual-based earnings and cash flows. Observe that significant cash outflows occur for operations during the first year as payments to acquire inventory far exceed collections from customers. In fact, it is not until the third year that cash flow from operations exceeds net earnings for the year.

Highlights to Remember

1. **Explain the concept of the statement of cash flows.** The statement of cash flows focuses on the changes in cash and the activities that cause those changes. Accrual-based net income is a useful number, but we also ask: How did our cash position change? How much of the change in cash was caused by operations, how much by investing activities and how much by financing activities.

2. **Classify activities affecting cash as operating, investing, or financing activities.** Operating activities are the typical day-to-day activity of the firm in acquiring or manufacturing products, selling them to customers, and collecting the cash. Investing activities involve buying and selling plant, property, and equipment. It might include buying a whole company as well as specific assets. Financing

activities involve raising or repaying capital such as borrowing from a bank, issuing bonds, or paying dividends to shareholders.

3. **Use the direct method to measure cash flows.** The direct method of calculating net cash provided by operations requires that we restate each income element to reflect the movement of cash. We convert revenue to cash collected from customers, cost of goods sold to cash paid to suppliers, and so on. We then combine these cash items to yield cash from operations.

4. **Determine cash flows from income statement and balance sheet accounts.** The cash flow for an item can be reconstructed by taking the income statement item and adjusting it for changes in the related balance sheet amount. For example, to convert revenue from an accrual measure to a cash measure, we would subtract an increase in accounts receivable during the year from the revenue number or add a decrease in accounts receivable to the revenue number.

5. **Use the indirect method to calculate cash flows from operations.** The more common method for calculating the cash flow from operations is the indirect method, which starts with net income and adjusts it for the differences, typically account by account, between accrual income and operating cash flow. Both the direct and indirect method yield the same result. Depreciation is an example of an amount added back to net income to calculate cash from operations. The logic is that depreciation does not involve the use of cash, although it is deducted in calculating net income. Adding it back eliminates the effect of this noncash item. In addition to depreciation, other items affect the reconciliation of net income to cash from operations. Examples covered in the text through chapter 10 include depletion and amortization of bond premium and discount.

6. **Relate depreciation to cash flows provided by operating activities.** Under the indirect method, depreciation is added to net income because it is an expense not requiring the use of cash. This causes some people to think of depreciation as a source of cash. This is not the case. Increasing depreciation does not affect cash flow unless it affects cash paid for taxes.

7. **Reconcile net income to cash provided by operating activities.** When companies use the direct method to calculate cash flow from operations, they are still required to provide a reconciliation of net income to cash provided from operations. This essentially amounts to preparing a second calculation using the indirect method.

8. **Adjust for gains and losses from fixed asset sales and debt extinguishments in the statement of cash flows (appendix 10A).** Sales of fixed assets are investing activities and debt extinguishments are financing activities. Under the direct method they do not affect cash flows from operations. When using the indirect method, the starting point is net income and net income often includes gains or losses from asset sales or debt repayments. If gains exist, we subtract them from net income to calculate cash provided by operations, and if losses exist, we add them back to net income. The full amount of cash provided or used is then shown in financing or investing as appropriate.

9. **Use the T-account approach to prepare the cash flow statement (appendix 10B).** The T-account approach is a mechanical way to keep track of every change in balance sheet accounts while producing a cash flow statement. It involves a big worksheet that helps calculate the change in every account and position it in the proper section of the cash flow statement.

Objective 8
Adjust for gains and losses from fixed asset sales and debt extinguishments in the statement of cash flows (appendix 10A).

Appendix 10A: More on the Statement of Cash Flows

This appendix describes two common items that affect the statement of cash flows. You do not need to be familiar with these items to have a basic understanding of how the statement of cash flows generally works or is created. However, these two items occur frequently in the statements of cash flows of major corporations, so understanding these items can help you to read real financial statements.

GAIN OR LOSS ON DISPOSAL OF FIXED ASSETS

In the chapter, Eco-Bag Company sold fixed assets for their book value of $10,000. More often a fixed asset is sold for an amount that differs from its book value. Suppose the fixed assets sold by Eco-Bag Company for $10,000 had a book value of $6,000 (original cost = $36,000; accumulated depreciation = $30,000). Therefore, net income would be $27,000, comprising the $23,000 shown in Exhibit 10-3, p. 413 plus a $4,000 gain on disposal of fixed assets. We are assuming no tax effects.

Consider first the disposal's effects on cash and income using the balance sheet equation:

$$\Delta \text{ Cash} = \Delta L + \Delta SE - \Delta NCA$$
$$\text{Proceeds} = \text{Gain} - (-\text{Book value})$$
$$\$10,000 = \$4,000 - (-\$6,000)$$

Although the book value affects the calculation of gain, no cash is involved. The body of the statement of cash flows under the direct method would not include any gains (or losses) from the disposal of fixed assets in the section on operating activities. The disposal of fixed assets is an investing activity, thus the statement of cash flows would show the following item under investing activities:

Proceeds from sale of fixed assets	$10,000

However, consider Exhibit 10-6 on p. 423, which uses the indirect method to reconcile net income to net cash provided by operating activities. If we were to produce a similar reconciliation after our gain on disposal, the new net income of $27,000 would be our starting point. However, this net income figure already includes the $4,000 gain. To avoid double counting, that is, showing inflows of $4,000 in operating activities and $10,000 in investing activities, Eco-Bag Company must deduct from net income the $4,000 gain on disposal:

Net income	$27,000
Plus adjustments in Exhibit 10-6	46,000
Less gain on disposal of fixed assets	(4,000)
Net cash provided by operating activities	$69,000

Losses on the disposal of assets would be treated similarly except that they would be added back to net income. Suppose the book value of the fixed assets sold by Eco-Bag Company was $17,000, creating a $7,000 losts on disposal and net income of $16,000. The reconciliation would show:

Net income	$16,000
Plus adjustments in Exhibit 10-6	46,000
Plus loss on disposal of assets	7,000
Net cash provided by operating activities	$69,000

Losses and gains on disposal are essentially nonoperating items that are included in net income. As such, their effect must be removed from net income when it is reconciled to net cash flow provided by operating activities.

GAIN OR LOSS ON EARLY RETIREMENT OF DEBT

Issuing and retiring debt are financing activities. Any gain or loss on early retirement of debt must be removed from net income in a reconciliation schedule. The process is conceptually the same as gains and losses on sales of fixed assets. The difference is that an outflow of cash to retire the debt is related to the book value of the debt being retired. Suppose Eco-Bag Company paid $37,000 to retire long-term debt with a book value of $34,000, generating a $3,000 loss on retirement of debt. Net income would be $23,000 − $3,000 = $20,000. The balance sheet equation would show:

$$\Delta \text{Cash} = \quad \Delta L \quad + \quad \Delta SE - \Delta NCA$$
$$-\text{Payment} = -\text{Book value} \quad - \text{Loss}$$
$$-\$37,000 = -\$34,000 \quad -\$3,000$$

The $3,000 loss would be added back to net income to determine net cash provided by operating activities:

Net income	$20,000
Plus adjustments in Exhibit 10-6	46,000
Plus loss on retirement of debt	3,000
Net cash provided by operating activities	$69,000

The entire payment for debt retirement would be listed among the financing activities:

Proceeds from issue of long-term debt	$120,000
Payment to retire long-term debt	(37,000)
Proceeds from issue of common stock	98,000
Dividends paid	(19,000)
Net cash provided by financing activities	$162,000

Appendix 10B: T-Account Approach to Statement of Cash Flows

Objective 9
Use the T-account approach to prepare the cash flow statement (appendix 10B).

Many statements of cash flows can be prepared by using the steps described in the body of the chapter. However, analysts confronted with complicated and numerous activities will find the T-account approach easier to use. When constructing any cash flow statement, we know that the increases and decreases of cash due to various activities must add up to the overall change in cash during the year. The T-account approach is simply an easier way of ensuring that all the appropriate activities are identified and treated properly.

To illustrate this approach, we again use the Eco-Bag Company data from Exhibit 10-3, p. 413, and the summary of 20X2 transactions that appears on p. 415. Exhibit 10-12 shows the individual T-accounts for the year, as well as the cash T-account that is divided into sections representing the three categories of cash flows in the statement of cash flows.

This appendix uses T-accounts to produce cash flow information formatted to support preparation of a statement using the direct method. However, the technique helps identify financing and investing cash flows that are the same under both the direct and indirect method. Ultimately, either presentation method requires an understanding of the linkages between cash flow and accrual-based net income.

To employ the T-account approach, reasonably complete re-creations of the summary journal entries for the year are required. The journal entries are shown on page 434, keyed to the entries in Exhibit 10-12. Those involving cash have an asterisk (*).

Exhibit 10-12

Eco-Bag Company

T-Account Approach Using Direct Method Statement of Cash Flows for the Year Ended
December 31, 20X2 (in Thousands)

Cash

Bal. 12/31/X1	25		

Operating Activities

2. Collection of accounts receivable	180	5. Pay accounts payable	72
		7. Pay wages and salaries	15
		8. Pay interest	4
		9. Pay taxes	20

Investing Activities

12. Disposal of fixed assets	10	11. Acquisition of fixed assets	287

Financing Activities

13. Issue long-term debt	120	15. Pay dividends	19
14. Issue common stock	98		
Total debits	408	Total credits	417
		Net decrease	9
Bal. 12/31/X2	16		

Accounts Receivable

Bal. 12/31/X1	25		
1. Sales	200	2. Collections	180
Net Increase	20		
Bal. 12/31/X2	45		

Accounts Payable

		Bal. 12/31/X1	6
5. Payments	72	4. Purchases	140
		Net increase	68
		Bal. 12/31/X2	74

Inventory

Bal. 12/31/X1	60		
4. Purchases	140	2. Cost of goods sold	100
Net increase	40		
Bal. 12/31/X2	100		

Wages and Salaries Payable

		Bal. 12/31/X1	4
7. Payments	15	6. Accruals	36
		Net increase	21
		Bal. 12/31/X2	25

Fixed Assets, Net

Bal. 12/31/X1	220		
11. Acquisition	287	10. Depreciation	17
		12. Disposals	10
Net increase	260		
Bal. 12/31/X2	480		

Long-Term Debt

		Bal. 12/31/X1	5
		13. New issue	120
		Bal. 12/31/X2	125

Stockholder's Equity

		Bal. 12/31/X1	315
3. Cost of goods sold	100	1. Sales	200
		14. New Issue	98
6. Wages	36		
8. Interest	4		
9. Income taxes	20		
10. Depreciation	17		
15. Dividends	19		
Total debits	196	Total credits	298
		Net increase	102
		Bal. 12/31/X2	417

	1.	Sales on credit		
		Accounts receivable	200	
		Sales		200
	*2.	Collection of accounts receivable		
		Cash	180	
		Accounts receivable		180
	3.	Recognition of cost of goods sold		
		Cost of goods sold	100	
		Inventory		100
	4.	Purchases of inventory on credit		
		Inventory	140	
		Trade accounts payable		140
	*5.	Payment of trade accounts payable		
		Trade accounts payable	72	
		Cash		72
	6.	Recognition of wages and salaries expense		
		Wages and salaries expense	36	
		Wages and salaries payable		36
	*7.	Payment of wages and salaries		
		Wages and salaries payable	15	
		Cash		15
	*8.	Recognition of interest accrued and paid		
		Interest expense..................................	4	
		Cash		4
	*9.	Recognition and payment of income taxes		
		Income tax expense	20	
		Cash		20
	10.	Recognition of depreciation expense		
		Depreciation expense	17	
		Fixed assets, net		17
	*11.	Acquisition of fixed assets for cash		
		Fixed assets, net	287	
		Cash		287
	*12.	Sale of fixed assets at book value		
		Cash	10	
		Fixed assets, net		10
	*13.	Issuance of long-term debt		
		Cash	120	
		Long-term debt		120
	*14.	Issuance of common stock		
		Cash	98	
		Stockholders' equity		98
	*15.	Declaration and payment of dividends		
		Dividends declared and paid	19	
		Cash		19

The T-account approach displayed in Exhibit 10-12 is merely another way of applying the balance sheet equation described in the body of the chapter:

Δ Cash	=	Δ Current liabilities	+	Δ Long-term liabilities	+	Δ Stockholders' equity	−	Δ Noncash current assets	−	Δ Fixed assets, net
Δ Cash	=	Δ Accounts and wages payable	+	Δ Long-term debt	+	Δ Stockholders' equity	−	Δ Accounts receivable and inventory	−	Δ Fixed assets, net
9		68		120		102		20		260
		21						40		
		89						60		

Again, we focus on the changes in the noncash accounts to explain why cash changed. The summarized transactions for 20X2 entered in the Cash account are the basis for the preparation of the formal statement of cash flows, as can be seen by comparing the cash account from Exhibit 10-12 with the statement of cash flows in Exhibit 10-3 on p. 413.

Accounting Vocabulary

cash flows from financing
  activities, p. 419
cash flows from investing
  activities, p. 419
cash flows from operating
  activities, p. 409

direct method, p. 409
financing activities, p. 407
financial management, p. 407
indirect method, p. 409

investing activities, p. 407
operating activities, p. 407
operating management, p. 407

Assignment Material

Special note: The following exercises and problems do not involve the indirect method, and therefore can be solved without reading beyond p. 422: 10-30 through 10-33, 10-35 through 10-38, 10-41 through 10-43, 10-47, 10-48, 10-50, 10-52, 10-60, 10-63, and 10-66 through 10-68.

Questions

10-1 "The statement of cash flows is an optional statement included by most companies in their annual reports." Do you agree? Explain.

10-2 What are the purposes of a statement of cash flows?

10-3 Define *cash* equivalents.

10-4 Distinguish between *operating management* and *financial management*.

10-5 What three types of activities are summarized in the statement of cash flows?

10-6 Name four major operating activities included in a statement of cash flows.

10-7 Name three major investing activities included in a statement of cash flows.

10-8 Name three major financing activities included in a statement of cash flows.

10-9 What are the two major ways of computing net cash provided by operating activities?

10-10 Where does interest received or paid appear on the statement of cash flows?

10-11 "Net losses mean drains on cash." Do you agree? Explain.

10-12 Demonstrate how the fundamental balance sheet equation can be recast to focus on cash.

10-13 Why is there usually a difference between the cash collections from customers and sales revenue in a period's financial statements?

10-14 Do all changes in current assets and liabilities affect cash flows from operations? If not, give an example of an account that does not.

10-15 Explain why increases in liabilities increase cash and increases in assets decrease cash.

10-16 Why are noncash investing and financing activities listed on a separate schedule accompanying the statement of cash flows?

10-17 A company acquired a fixed asset in exchange for common stock. Explain how this transaction should be shown, if at all, in the statement of cash flows. Why is your suggested treatment appropriate?

10-18 Suppose a company paid off a $1 million short-term loan to one bank with the proceeds from an identical loan from another bank. The change in the short-term debt account would be zero. Should anything appear in the statement of cash flows? Explain.

10-19 The indirect method for reporting cash flows from operating activities can create an erroneous impression about noncash expenses (such as depreciation). What is the impression, and why is it erroneous?

10-20 An investor's newsletter had the following item: "The company expects increased cash flow in 2002 because depreciation charges will be substantially greater than they were in 2001." Comment.

10-21 "Depreciation is an integral part of a statement of cash flows." Do you agree? Explain.

10-22 XYZ Company's only transaction in 20X1 was the sale of a fixed asset for cash of $20,000. The income statement included only "Gain on sale of fixed asset, $5,000." Correct the following statement of cash flows:

Cash flows from operating activities	
Gain on sale of fixed asset	$ 5,000
Cash flows from investing activities	
Proceeds from sale of fixed asset	20,000
Total increase in cash	$25,000

10-23 The Lawrence Company sold fixed assets with a book value of $5,000 and recorded a $4,000 gain. How should this be reported on a statement of cash flows?

10-24 A company operated at a profit for the year, but cash flow from operations was negative. Why might this occur? What industry or industries might find this a common occurrence?

10-25 A company operated at a loss for the year, but cash flow from operations was positive. Why might this occur? What industry or industries might find this a common occurrence?

Cognitive Exercises

10-26 Cash Flow Patterns and Growth

As an auditor you observed that your client has negative cash flow from operations, negative cash flow from investing, and positive cash flow from financing. All the financing in the current year is from short-term debt with various covenants. The manager on this client has asked you to provide your observations about what the pattern of cash flow tells you about the client's circumstance. How do you respond?

10-27 Cisco and Cash Generation

Cisco is generating increasing amounts of cash from operating activities each year and is unable to fully utilize it in business growth. Hence, the levels of liquid investments are increasing. What would you imagine Cisco management might be considering as a means of using over half of its assets that are currently in cash and liquid investments?

10-28 Amazon and Negative Cash Flow from Operations

In 2000, Amazon.com, the industry leader in online sales of books and other consumer products, used $130 million to support its operating activities and invested another $197 million in purchasing fixed assets and acquiring other businesses. To finance this, it issued over $680 million of new long-term debt. Comment on this strategy.

10-29 Failures to Generate Cash Flow from Operations

You are discussing your investment strategies with a colleague who says, "I would never invest in a company that is not generating both positive earnings and positive cash flow from operations." How do you respond?

Exercises

10-30 Cash Received from Customers

Alpha University Press, Inc., had sales of $750,000 during 20X1, 80% of them on credit and 20% for cash. During the year, accounts receivable increased from $60,000 to $80,000, an increase of $20,000. What amount of cash was received from customers during 20X1?

10-31 Cash Paid to Suppliers

Cost of goods sold for Alpha University Press, Inc., during 20X1 was $500,000. Beginning inventory was $100,000, and ending inventory was $140,000. Beginning trade accounts payable were $24,000, and ending trade accounts payable were $45,000. What amount of cash was paid to suppliers?

10-32 Cash Paid to Employees

Alpha University Press, Inc., reported wage and salary expenses of $250,000 on its 20X1 income statement. It reported cash paid to employees of $210,000 on its statement of cash flows. The beginning balance of accrued wages and salaries payable was $18,000. What was the ending balance in accrued wages and salaries payable? Ignore payroll taxes.

10-33 Simple Cash Flows from Operating Activities

Global Strategy, Inc., provides consulting services. In 20X8, net income was $185,000 on revenues of $470,000 and expenses of $285,000. The only noncash expense was depreciation of $45,000. The company has no inventory. Accounts receivable increased by $5,000 during 20X8, and accounts payable and salaries payable were unchanged.

Required

Prepare a statement of cash flows from operating activities. Use the direct method. Omit supporting schedules.

10-34 Net Income and Cash Flow

Refer to Problem 10-33. Prepare a schedule that reconciles net income to net cash flow from operating activities.

10-35 Investing Activities

Giao Trading Company issued common stock for $300,000 on the first day of 20X8. The company bought fixed assets for $140,000 and inventory for $65,000. Late in the year it sold fixed assets for their book value of $20,000. Half of the inventory was sold for $55,000 during the year. On December 15, excess cash of $60,000 was used to purchase common stock of Franzen Company, which Giao regarded as a long-term investment.

Prepare a statement of cash flows from investing activities for Giao Trading Company.

Required

10-36 Book Value of Asset Disposals

KXYW Broadcasting Company reported net fixed assets of $48 million at December 31, 20X5, and $53 million at December 31, 20X6. During 20X6, the company purchased fixed assets for $10 million and had $4 million of depreciation. Compute the book value of the fixed asset disposals during 20X6.

10-37 Noncash Investing and Financing Activities

Seymour Company had the following items in its statement of cash flows:

Retirement of long-term debt	$560,000
Common stock issued on conversion of preferred shares	340,000
Purchases of marketable securities	225,000
Mortgage assumed on acquisition of warehouse	630,000
Increase in accounts payable	42,000
Note payable issued for acquisition of fixed assets	188,000

Prepare a schedule on noncash investing and financing activities, selecting appropriate items from the preceding list.

Required

10-38 Financing Activities

During 20X8, the Kohl Shipping Company refinanced its long-term debt. It spent DM 160,000 to retire long-term debt due in 2 years and issued DM 200,000 of 15-year bonds at par (DM signifies deutsche mark, the German monetary unit). It then bought and retired common shares for cash of DM 35,000. Interest expense for 20X3 was DM 23,000, of which DM 21,000 was paid in cash; the other DM 2,000 was still payable at the end of the year. Dividends declared and paid during the year were DM 12,000.

Prepare a statement of cash flows from financing activities.

Required

10-39 Depreciation and Cash Flows

(Alternate is 10-49.) Belkview Cafe had sales of $990,000, all received in cash. Total operating expenses were $670,000. All except depreciation were paid in cash. Depreciation of $100,000 was included in the $670,000 of operating expenses. Ignore income taxes.

1. Compute net income and net cash provided by operating activities.
2. Assume that depreciation is tripled. Compute net income and net cash provided by operating activities.

Required

10-40 Gain or Loss on Disposal of Equipment

Icarus Software Company sold five computers. It had purchased the computers 5 years ago for $120,000, and accumulated depreciation at the time of sale was $90,000.

1. Suppose Icarus received $30,000 cash for the computers. How would the sale be shown on the statement of cash flows?
2. Suppose Icarus received $40,000 for the computers. How would the sale be shown on the statement of cash flows (including the schedule reconciling net income and net cash provided by operating activities)?
3. Redo requirement 2 assuming cash received was $20,000.

Required

10-41 Identify Operating, Investing, and Financing Activities

The following listed items were found on a recent statement of cash flows for AT&T. For each item, indicate which section of the statement should contain the item—the operating, investing, or financing section. Also indicate whether AT&T uses the direct or indirect method for reporting cash flows from operating activities.

  a. Net income (loss)
  b. Proceeds from long-term debt issuance
  c. Dividends paid
  d. Capital expenditures net of proceeds from sale or disposal of property, plant, and equipment
  e. Issuance of common shares
  f. Retirements of long-term debt
  g. Increase in inventories
  h. Depreciation and amortization
  i. Increase in short-term borrowing—net

PROBLEMS

10-42 Statement of Cash Flows, Direct Method

Wireless Communications had cash and cash equivalents of $200 million on December 31, 1999. The following items are on the company's statement of cash flows ($ in millions) for the first 6 months of 2000.

Receipts from customers	9,311
Interest paid, net	(140)
Capital expenditures for property and equipment	(1,710)
Purchase of treasury stock	(193)
Sales of marketable securities	191
Retirement of long-term debt	(160)
Payments to suppliers and employees	(7,499)
Issuance of common stock for employee stock plans	251
Dividend payments	(17)
Issuance of long-term debt	135
Other investing activity	(134)
Taxes paid	(167)

Required

Prepare a statement of cash flows for the first 6 months of 2000 using the direct method. Include the balance of cash and cash equivalents at year-end 1999 and calculate the cash balance at June 30, 2000. Omit the schedule reconciling net income to net cash provided by operating activities and the schedule of noncash investing and financing activities.

10-43 Prepare a Statement of Cash Flows, Direct Method

(Alternate is 10-50.) Tubs, Inc. is a wholesale distributor of hot tubs and spas. Its cash balance on December 31, 20X6, was $76 thousand, and net income for 20X7 was $214 thousand. Its 20X7 transactions affecting income or cash follow ($ in thousands):

  a. Sales of $1,400 were all on credit. Cash collections from customers were $1,500.
  b. The cost of items sold was $800. Purchases of inventory totaled $850; inventory and accounts payable were affected accordingly.
  c. Cash payments on trade accounts payable totaled $825.
  d. Accrued salaries and wages: totaled $190 and paid in cash, $200.
  e. Depreciation was $45.
  f. Interest expense, all paid in cash was $11.
  g. Other expenses, all paid in cash totaled $100.

h. Income taxes accrued were $40; income taxes paid in cash were $35.

i. Plant and facilities were bought for $435 cash.

j. Long-term debt was issued for $110 cash.

k. Cash dividends of $39 were paid

Prepare a statement of cash flows using the direct method for reporting cash flows from operating activities. Omit supporting schedules.

Required

10-44 Reconcile Net Income and Net Cash Provided by Operating Activities

(Alternate is 10-51.) Refer to Problem 10-43. Prepare a supporting schedule that reconciles net income to net cash provided by operating activities.

10-45 Cash Provided by Operations

Clorox Company is a leading producer of laundry additives, including Clorox liquid bleach. In 2000, net sales of $4 billion represented almost double the 1997 level and these sales produced earnings of $394 million. To calculate net earnings, Clorox recorded $201 million in depreciation, and other items of revenue and expense not requiring cash increased cash flow from operations by $7 million. Dividends of $189 million were paid during 2000. Among the changes in balance sheet accounts during 2000 were ($ in millions):

Accounts receivable	$ 19	Increase
Inventories	55	Increase
Prepaid expenses	3	Increase
Accounts payable	109	Increase
Accrued liabilities	42	Increase
Income taxes payable	11	Decrease
Other accrued liabilities	7	Decrease

Compute the net cash provided by operating activities using the indirect method.

Required

10-46 Cash Flows from Operating Activities, Indirect Method

Sumimoto Metal Industries, Ltd., is a leading diversified manufacturer of steel products. During 2000, Sumimoto lost ¥145 billion on revenues of approximately ¥1,424 billion (or approximately $13 billion). The following summarized information relates to Sumimoto's statement of cash flows:

	(Billions of Yen)
Depreciation and amortization	¥101.3
Repayments of long-term debt	185.2
Proceeds from long-term debt	110.1
Other noncash operating revenues	16.2
Increase in receivables	21.6
Decrease in inventories	17.9
Gain on sales of marketable securities	40.2
Other decreases in cash from operations due to changes in current assets and liabilities	10.7
Additions to property and equipment	115.8
Increase in payables	36.7

Compute the net cash provided by operating activities. All the information necessary for that task is provided, together with some information related to other elements of the cash flow statement. Note that the format does not include parentheses to differentiate elements that increase cash from those that decrease cash, but the distinction should be clear from the captions.

Required

10-47 Cash Flows from Investing Activities

KLM Royal Dutch Airlines transports approximately 12 million passengers and more than 460 million tons of freight annually. Its revenues in fiscal 2000 topped NLG 10 billion, where NLG is guilders, the monetary unit of the Netherlands. The company's statement of cash flows for fiscal 2000 contained the following items (guilders in millions).

Net capital expenditure on intangible fixed assets	NLG (29)
Net income	743
Repayment of long-term debt	(547)
Net sale of investments in affiliated companies	1,124
Proceeds from issuance of long-term debt	458
Net capital expenditure on tangible fixed assets	(1,292)
Change in operating working capital	(94)

Required Prepare the section "Cash flows from investing activities" for KLM for the 2000 fiscal year. All the items from that section are included in the preceding, along with some items from other sections of the statement of cash flows.

10-48 Cash Flows from Financing Activities

Eli Lilly and Company is a global, research-based corporation that develops, manufactures, and markets pharmaceuticals, medical instruments, diagnostic products, and agricultural products. Its 1999 sales exceeded $10 billion. Lilly's 1999 statement of cash flows included the following items, among others ($ in millions):

Dividends paid	$(1,000.5)
Purchase of common stock and other capital transactions	(1,453.0)
Additions to property and equipment	(528.3)
Depreciation and amortization	439.7
Stock issuances	310.2
Decrease in short-term borrowings	(139.4)
Additions to investments	(162.8)
Additions to long-term debt	843.5
Net income	2,721
Reductions of long-term debt	(13.5)

Required Prepare the section "Cash flows from financing activities" from Eli Lilly's 1999 annual report. All items necessary for that section appear in the preceding. Some items from other sections have been omitted.

10-49 Depreciation and Cash Flows

(Alternate is 10-39.) The following condensed income statement and reconciliation schedule are from the annual report of Cheung Company ($ in millions):

Sales	$376
Expenses	350
Net income	$26

Reconciliation Schedule of Net Income to Net Cash Provided by Operating Activities

Net income	$ 26
Add noncash expenses	
Depreciation	25
Deduct net increase in noncash operating working capital	(17)
Net cash provided by operating activities	$ 34

A shareholder has suggested that the company switch from straight-line to accelerated depreciation on its annual report to shareholders, maintaining that this will increase the cash flow provided by operating activities. According to the stockholder's calculations, using accelerated methods would increase depreciation to $45 million, an increase of $20 million; net cash flow from operating activities would then be $54 million.

Required

1. Suppose Cheung Company adopts the accelerated depreciation method proposed. Compute net income and net cash flow from operating activities. Ignore income taxes.
2. Use your answer to requirement 1 to prepare a response to the shareholder.

10-50 Prepare a Statement of Cash Flows, Direct Method

(Alternate is 10-43.) Osaka Exports, Inc., is a wholesaler of Asian goods. By the end of 20X8, the company's cash balance had dropped to ¥5 million, despite net income of ¥254 million in 20X8. Its transactions affecting income or cash in 20X8 were (¥ in millions):

a. Sales were ¥2,510, all on credit. Cash collections from customers were ¥2,413.
b. The cost of items sold was ¥1,599.
c. Inventory increased by ¥56.
d. Cash payments on trade accounts payable were ¥1,653.
e. Payments to employees were ¥305; accrued wages payable decreased by ¥24.
f. Other operating expenses, all paid in cash, were ¥94.
g. Interest expense, all paid in cash, was ¥26.
h. Income tax expense was ¥105; cash payments for income taxes were ¥108.
i. Depreciation was ¥151.
j. A warehouse was acquired for ¥540 cash.
k. Equipment was sold for ¥47; original cost was ¥206, accumulated depreciation was ¥159.
l. The firm received ¥28 for issue of common stock.
m. Long-term debt was retired for ¥25 cash.
n. The company paid cash dividends of ¥100.

Required

Prepare a statement of cash flows using the direct method for reporting cash flows from operating activities. Calculate the cash balance as of January 1, 20X8. Omit supporting schedules.

10-51 Reconcile Net Income and Net Cash Provided by Operating Activities

(Alternate is 10-44.) Refer to Problem 10-50. Prepare a supporting schedule to the statement of cash flows that reconciles net income to net cash provided by operating activities.

10-52 Prepare Statement of Cash Flows from Income Statement and Balance Sheet

(Alternate is 10-63.) During 20X8, Ralston Tool and Die declared and paid cash dividends of $8,000. Late in the year, the company bought new metal-working machinery for a cash cost of $125,000, financed partly by its first issue of long-term debt. Interest on the debt is payable annually. Several old machines were sold for cash equal to their aggregate book value of $5,000. Taxes were paid in cash as incurred. The following data are in thousands:

Ralston Tool and Die
Income Statement for the Year
Ended December 31, 20X8

Sales		$363
Cost of sales		201
Gross margin		162
Salaries	$82	
Depreciation	40	
Cash operating expenses	15	
Interest	2	139
Income before taxes		23
Income taxes		8
Net income		$ 15

Ralston Tool and Die
Balance Sheets

| | December 31 | | Increase |
	20X8	20X7	(Decrease)
Assets			
Cash and cash equivalents	$ 97	$ 45	$ 52
Accounts receivable	40	55	(15)
Inventories	57	62	(5)
Total current assets	194	162	32
Fixed assets, net	190	110	80
Total assets	$384	$272	$112
Liabilities and Stockholders' Equity			
Accounts payable	$ 21	$ 16	$ 5
Interest payable	2	—	2
Long-term debt	100	—	100
Paid-in capital	220	220	—
Retained income	41	36	5
Total liabilities and stockholders' equity	$384	$272	$112

Required

Prepare a statement of cash flows. Use the direct method for reporting cash flows from operating activities. Omit supporting schedules.

10-53 Indirect Method: Reconciliation Schedule in Body of Statement
Refer to Problem 10-52. Prepare a statement of cash flows that includes a reconciliation of net income to net cash provided by operating activities in the body of the statement.

10-54 Cash Flows, Indirect Method
The Ramez Company has the following balance sheet data ($ in millions):

| | December 31 | | | | December 31 | | |
	20X7	20X6	Change		20X7	20X6	Change
Current assets				Current liabilities			
Cash	$ 15	$ 21	$ (6)	(detailed)	$101	$ 26	$ 75
Receivables, net	50	15	35	Long-term debt	150	—	150
Inventories	94	50	44	Stockholders' equity	208	160	48
Total current assets	$159	$ 86	$ 73				
Plant assets (net of accumulated depreciation)	300	100	200				
Total assets	$459	$186	$273	Total liabilities and stockholders' equity	$459	$186	$273

Net income for 20X7 was $60 million. Net cash inflow from operating activities was $80 million. Cash dividends paid were $12 million. Depreciation was $30 million. Fixed assets were purchased for $230 million, $150 million of which was financed via the issuance of long-term debt outright for cash.

Roberto Ramez, the president and majority stockholder of the Ramez Company, was a superb operating executive. He was imaginative and aggressive in marketing and ingenious and creative in production. But he had little patience with financial matters. After examining the most recent balance sheet and income statement, he muttered, "We've enjoyed 10 years of steady growth; 20X7 was our most profitable ever. Despite such profitability, we're in the worst cash position in our history. Just look at those current liabilities in relation to our available cash! This whole picture of the more you make, the poorer you get, just does not make sense. These statements must be cockeyed."

Required

1. Prepare a statement of cash flows using the indirect method. Include a schedule reconciling net income to net cash provided by operating activities in the body of the statement.

2. By using the statement of cash flows and other information, write a short memorandum to Ramez, explaining why there is such a squeeze on cash.

10-55 Prepare Statement of Cash Flows

The Goldblum Company has assembled the accompanying (a) balance sheets and (b) income statement and statement of retained earnings for 20X9.

Goldblum Company
Balance Sheets as of December 31 (in Millions)

	20X9	20X8	Change
Assets			
Cash	$ 7	$ 20	$(13)
Accounts receivable	45	33	12
Inventory	70	50	20
Prepaid general expenses	4	3	1
Plant assets, net	202	150	52
	$328	$256	$ 72
Liabilities and shareholders' equity			
Accounts payable for merchandise	$ 74	$60	$ 14
Accrued tax payable	3	2	1
Long-term debt	50	—	50
Capital stock	100	100	—
Retained earnings	101	94	7
	$328	$256	$ 72

Goldblum Company
Income Statement and Statement of Retained Earnings for the Year Ended December 31, 20X9 (in Millions)

Sales		$275
Less cost of goods sold		
Inventory, Dec. 31, 19X8	$ 50	
Purchases	185	
Cost of goods available for sale	$235	
Inventory, Dec. 31, 20X9	70	165
Gross profit		$110
Less other expenses		
General expense	$ 51	
Depreciation	40	
Taxes	10	101
Net income		$ 9
Dividends		2
Net income of the period retained		$ 7
Retained earnings, Dec. 31, 20X8		94
Retained earnings, Dec. 31, 20X9		$101

On December 30, 20X9, Goldblum paid $98 million in cash to acquire a new plant to expand operations. This was partly financed by an issue of long-term debt for $50 million in cash. Plant assets were sold for their book value of $6 million during 20X9. Because net income was $9 million, the highest in the company's history, Sidney Goldblum, the chief executive officer, was distressed by the company's extremely low cash balance.

Required

1. Prepare a statement of cash flows using the direct method for reporting cash flows from operating activities. You may wish to use Exhibit 10-3, p. 413, as a guide.

2. Prepare a schedule that reconciles net income to net cash provided by operating activities.

3. What is revealed by the statement of cash flows? Does it help you reduce Mr. Goldblum's distress? Why? Briefly explain to Mr. Goldblum why cash has decreased even though net income was $9 million.

10-56 Balance Sheet Equation

Refer to Problem 10-55, requirement 1. Support your financial statement by using a form of the balance sheet equation. Step by step, show in equation form how each item in the statement of cash flows affects cash.

10-57 Noncash Investing and Financing Activities

The Game Tech Company operates a chain of video game arcades. Among Game Tech's activities in 20X8 were:

1. The firm traded four old video games to another amusement company for one new "Flightime" game. The old games could have been sold for a total of $8,000 cash.

2. The company paid off $50,000 of long-term debt by paying $20,000 cash and signing a $30,000 6-month note payable.

3. The firm issued debt for $60,000 cash, all of which was used to purchase new games for its Northwest Arcade.

4. The company purchased the building in which one of its arcades was located by assuming the $100,000 mortgage on the structure and paying $20,000 cash.

5. Debt holders converted $64,000 of debt to common stock.

6. The firm refinanced debt by paying cash to buy back an old issue at its call price of $21,000 and issued new debt at a lower interest rate for $21,000.

Required

Prepare a schedule of noncash investing and financing activities to accompany a statement of cash flows.

10-58 Comprehensive Statement of Cash Flows

During the past 30 years, Catskill Toys, Inc., has grown from a single-location specialty toy store into a chain of stores selling a wide range of children's products. Its activities in 20X7 included the following:

a. The company purchased 40% of the stock of Seneca Toy Company for $3,848,000 cash.

b. The organization issued $1,906,000 in long-term debt; $850,000 of the proceeds was used to retire debt that became due in 20X7 and was listed on the books at $900,000.

c. The firm purchased property, plant, and equipment for $1,986,000 cash, and sold property with a book value of $576,000 for $500,000 cash.

d. The company signed a note payable for the purchase of new equipment; the obligation was listed at $516,000.

e. Executives exercised stock options for 8,000 shares of common stock, paying cash of $170,000.

f. On December 30, 20X7, the firm bought Sanchez Musical Instruments Company by issuing common stock with a market value of $297,000.

g. The company issued common stock for $3,200,000 cash.

h. The firm withdrew $800,000 cash from a money market fund that was considered a cash equivalent.

i. The company bought $249,000 of treasury stock to hold for future exercise of stock options.

j. Long-term debt of $960,000 was converted to common stock.

k. Selected results for the year follow:

Net income	$ 672,000
Depreciation and amortization	615,000
Increase in inventory	72,000
Decrease in accounts receivable	19,000
Increase in accounts and wages payable	7,000
Increase in taxes payable	25,000
Interest expense	144,000
Increase in accrued interest payable	15,000
Sales	9,739,000
Cash dividends received from investments	152,000
Cash paid to suppliers and employees	8,074,000
Cash dividends paid	240,000
Cash paid for taxes	400,000

Prepare a statement of cash flows for 20X7 using the direct method. Include a schedule that reconciles net income to net cash provided by operating activities. Also include a schedule of noncash investing and financing activities.

Required

10-59 Statement of Cash Flows, Direct and Indirect Methods

Nordstrom, Inc., the Seattle-based fashion retailer, had the following income statement for the year ended January 31, 2000 ($ in millions):

Net sales		$5,124
Costs and expenses		
Cost of sales	$3,360	
Selling, general, and administrative	1,491	
Interest (net)	50	
Less: Other income	(129)	
Total costs and expenses	$ 203	
Earnings before income taxes		$ 332
Income taxes		129
Net earnings		$ 203

The company's net cash provided by operating activities, prepared using the indirect method, was ($ in millions):

Net earnings	$203
Adjustments to reconcile net earnings to net cash provided by operating activities	
Depreciation, amortization, and other	191
Changes in	
Accounts receivable	(30)
Merchandise inventories	(48)
Prepaid expenses	(23)
Accounts payable	51
Accrued salaries and wages	15
Other accrued expenses	7
Income taxes payable	12
Net cash provided by operating activities	$378

Prepare a statement showing the net cash provided by operating activities using the direct method. Assume that all "other income" was received in cash and that prepaid expenses and accrued salaries and wages and other accrued expenses relate to selling, general, and administrative expenses.

10-60 Statement of Cash Flows, Direct Method, for a Utility

The Columbia Energy Group had operating revenues of $1,995 million from providing gas services ranging from exploration and production to pipeline transmission to final distribution to users for the year ending December 31, 1999. The income statement showed operating expenses of $1,346.4 million, other income and (expense) of ($135.2 million), income taxes of $158.2 million, and losses for discontinued operations after tax of $105.8 million. Assume depreciation and depletion affect operating expenses and that other noncash items affect either operating revenue or discontinued operations. The company's statement of cash flows, prepared under the indirect method, also contained the following items (some have been slightly summarized):

	(in Millions)
Issuance of common stock	$ 15.5
Retirement of long-term debt	(52.5)
Dividends paid	(71.8)
Capital expenditures	(462.3)
Issuance of short-term debt	320.7
Other financing activities — net	(173.3)
Acquisitions and other investments	(368.2)
Net Income	249.2
Noncash adjustments	
Depreciation and depletion	229
Other-related to discontinued operations	105.8
Other	121.6
Changes in working capital components	
Accounts receivable	(110.8)
Inventory	41.1
Taxes	72.0
Other	123.5

1. Prepare the statement of cash flows for Columbia Gas using the direct method. Omit the schedule reconciling net income to net cash provided by operating activities.

2. Discuss the relation between operating cash flow and investing and financing needs.

10-61 Interpreting the Statement of Cash Flows

The Kellogg Company statement of cash flows appears in Exhibit 10-13 on facing page. Use that statement to answer two questions.

1. Does Kellogg generate sufficient cash flow from operations to cover ongoing investing activities and pay dividends to its shareholders?

2. How has Kellogg changed its debt-equity ratio during the period 1997 to 1999?

10-62 Cash Flows from Operating Activities

Boise Cascade Corporation, the forest products company with headquarters in Boise, Idaho, reported net income of more than $75 million. The following data are condensed from the company's income statement and balance sheet ($ in thousands):

Revenues	
Sales	$4,184,560
Costs and expenses	
Nondepreciation expenses (summarized)	(3,737,780)
Depreciation	(212,890)
Income from operations	233,890
Interest expense	(116,620)
Interest income	4,130
Income before income taxes	121,400
Income tax provision	46,130
Net income	$ 75,270

Exhibit 10-13

Kellogg Company and Subsidiaries

Consolidated Statement of Cash Flows, Year Ended December 31

(Millions)	1999	1998	1997
Operating activities			
Net earnings	$338.3	$502.6	$546.0
Items in net earnings not requiring (providing) cash			
Depreciation and amortization	288.0	278.1	287.3
Deferred income taxes	(60.5)	46.2	38.5
Restructuring charges, net of cash paid	220.1	62.2	110.8
Disposition-related charges	168.5	—	—
Asset impairment losses	—	—	23.0
Other	65.7	21.7	9.5
Pension and other postretirement benefit contributions	(78.1)	(88.8)	(114.5)
Changes in operating assets and liabilities	(146.8)	(102.3)	(20.8)
Net cash provided by operating activities	**795.2**	**719.7**	**879.8**
Investing activities			
Additions to properties	(266.2)	(373.9)	(312.4)
Acquisitions of businesses	(298.2)	(27.8)	(25.4)
Dispositions of businesses	291.2	—	—
Property disposals	36.6	6.8	5.9
Other	(7.6)	(3.1)	2.6
Net cash used in investing activities	**(244.2)**	**(398.0)**	**(329.3)**
Financing activities			
Net reductions of notes payable			
with maturities less than or equal to 90 days	(410.8)	(152.9)	(374.7)
Issuances of notes payable, with maturities greater than 90 days	292.1	5.5	4.8
Reductions of notes payable, with maturities greater than 90 days	(19.0)	(.8)	(14.1)
Issuances of long-term debt	—	600.0	1,000.0
Reductions of long-term debt	(14.1)	(210.3)	(507.9)
Net issuances of common stock	12.9	15.2	70.7
Common stock repurchases	—	(239.7)	(426.0)
Cash dividends	(388.7)	(375.3)	(360.1)
Net cash used in financing activities	**(527.6)**	**(358.3)**	**(607.3)**
Effect of exchange rate changes on cash	(9.2)	(.2)	(13.8)
Increase (decrease) in cash and cash equivalents	14.2	(36.8)	(70.6)
Cash and cash equivalents at beginning of year	136.4	173.2	243.8
Cash and cash equivalents at end of year	**$150.6**	**$136.4**	**$173.2**

Refer to Notes to Consolidated Financial Statements.

		Increase (Decrease)
Current assets		
Cash	$ 19,781	$ 66
Short-term investments	6,165	639
Receivables	412,558	(9,010)
Inventories	484,972	60,533
Other	74,107	13,038
Total current assets	$997,583	$ 65,266
Current liabilities		
Current portion of long-term debt	$136,731	$106,341
Income taxes payable	140	(4,133)
Notes payable	40,000	40,000
Accounts payable	344,384	(47,158)
Accrued liabilities		
Compensation and benefits	99,530	(14,552)
Interest payable	38,460	(1,611)
Other	99,127	1,261
Total current liabilities	$758,372	$ 80,148

You have determined that other current assets are all operating items, as are other accrued liabilities. Short-term investments are cash equivalents. Depreciation is the only noncash expense. Interest income is all in cash.

Required

1. Prepare a statement of cash flows from operating activities. Use the direct method that begins with cash collections from customers.

2. Reconcile net income to net cash provided by operating activities. (*Hint:* The cash outflow for nondepreciation expense is an aggregation of more specific outflows. There is no way to break the total amount into its component parts.)

10-63 Prepare Statement of Cash Flows from Income Statement and Balance Sheet
(Alternate is 10-52.) Napoli S.A. had the following income statement and balance sheet items (Italian lira in millions):

Income Statement for the Year Ended December 31, 20X8

Sales	L.870
Cost of goods sold	(510)
Gross margin	L.360
Operating expenses	(210)
Depreciation	(60)
Interest	(15)
Income before taxes	L.75
Income taxes	(25)
Net income	L.50
Cash dividends paid	(30)
Total increase in retained earnings	L.20

Balance Sheets

| | December 31 | | Increase |
	20X8	20X7	(Decrease)
Assets			
Cash	L. 20	L. 60	L. (40)
Accounts receivable	240	150	90
Inventories	450	350	100
Total current assets	L. 710	L.560	L.150
Fixed assets, gross	L. 890	L.715	L.175
Accumulated depreciation	(570)	(550)	(20)
Fixed assets, net	L. 320	L.165	L.155
Total assets	L.1,030	L.725	L.305
Liabilities and stockholders' equity			
Trade accounts payable	L. 520	L.300	L.220
Long-term debt	245	180	65
Stockholders' equity	265	245	20
Total liabilities and stockholders' equity	L.1,030	L.725	L.305

During 20X8, Napoli purchased fixed assets for L.315 million cash and sold fixed assets for their book value of L.100 million. Operating expenses, interest, and taxes were paid in cash. No long-term debt was retired.

Prepare a statement of cash flows. Use the direct method for reporting cash flows from operating activities. Omit supporting schedules.

Required

10-64 Miscellaneous Cash Flow Questions

McDonald's Corporation is a well-known provider of food services around the world. McDonald's statement of cash flows for 1999 is reproduced with a few slight modifications as Exhibit 10-14 on page 450. Use that statement and the additional information provided to answer the following questions:

1. In the financing activities section, all parentheses for 1999 have been removed. Which numbers should be put in parentheses?

2. In the investing activities section, all parentheses for 1999 have been removed. Which numbers should be put in parentheses?

3. The 1999 values for the change in cash and cash equivalents and for beginning and end-of-year balances have been omitted and replaced with the letters A, B, and C. Provide the proper values for these three missing numbers.

4. Retained earnings at December 31, 1998 was $13,879.6 million. Estimate the retained earnings balance at December 31, 1999.

5. Comment on the relation between cash flow from operations and cash used for investing activities.

10-65 Statement of Cash Flows, Direct Method, for a Bank

Bank of Granite Corporation is a North Carolina bank with total assets of about $500 million. Its statement of cash flows for 3 months ended March 31, contained the following items ($ in thousands):

Exhibit 10-14

McDonald's Corporation

Consolidated Statement of Cash Flows, Years Ended December 31

(In Millions)	1999	1998
Operating activities		
Net income	$1,947.9	$1,550.1
Adjustments to reconcile to cash provided by operations		
Depreciation and amortization	956.3	881.1
Deferred income taxes	52.9	35.4
Changes in operating working capital items		
Accounts receivable	(81.9)	(29.9)
Inventories, prepaid expenses and other current assets	(47.7)	(18.1)
Accounts payable	(23.9)	(12.7)
Taxes and other liabilities	270.4	337.5
Other	(65.1)	22.9
Cash provided by operations	3,008.9	2,766.3
Investing activities		
Property and equipment expenditures	1,867.8	(1,879.3)
Purchases of restaurant businesses	340.7	(131.0)
Sales of restaurant businesses	241.5	149.0
Property sales	20.9	42.5
Other	315.7	(129.4)
Cash used for investing activities	2,261.8	(1,948.2)
Financing activities		
Net short-term borrowings (repayments)	116.7	(604.2)
Long-term financing issuances	902.5	1,461.5
Long-term financing repayments	682.8	(594.9)
Treasury stock purchases	891.5	(1,089.8)
Common and preferred stock dividends	264.7	(240.5)
Other	193.0	207.6
Cash used for financing activities	626.8	(860.3)
Cash and equivalents increase (decrease)	A	(42.2)
Cash and equivalents beginning of year	B	341.4
Cash and equivalents at end of year	C	$ 299.2

The accompanying financial comments are an integral part of the consolidated financial statements.

Bank of Granite Data

Interest received	$9,521
Net increase in demand deposits	1,174
Net increase in certificates of deposit	4,716
Fees and commissions received	1,365
Proceeds from security sales and maturities	3,900
Purchases of securities	(2,063)
Proceeds from disposals of fixed assets	20
Dividends paid	(811)
Net proceeds from issuance of common stock	268
Net increase in loans	(6,682)
Interest paid	(3,763)
Cash paid to suppliers and employees	(2,967)
Income taxes paid	(518)
Capital expenditures	(518)
Other financing sources of cash	514

Note: Because banks are noticeably different from manufacturing and service companies, their clas-sifications of what constitutes operating, investing, and financing activities also differ. For example, banks treat as financing activities their sales of certificates of deposit. Similarly, the basic deposits that individuals make in the savings bank are treated as financing activities.

Prepare Bank of Granite's statement of cash flows in proper format, using the direct method. Omit the schedule reconciling net income to net cash provided by operating activities.

10-66 Statement of Cash Flows, Direct Method, Interest Expense, Australia

CSR Limited is a leading supplier of building and construction materials headquartered in Sydney, Australia. The company's revenues exceeded A$6 billion, where A$ is the Australian dollar. The following items appeared in CSR's statement of cash flows:

Receipts from customers	A$6,165.7
Purchase of controlled entities	(59.4)
Proceeds from sale of controlled entities	61.4
Payments to suppliers and employees	(5,406.7)
Dividends received	25.0
Net cash from operating activities	670.5
Purchase of property, plant, and equipment	(630.2)
Proceeds from sale of property, plant, and equipment	175.0
Net proceeds from borrowings	138.7
Dividends paid	(296.0)
Other investing activities	43.9
Interest received	12.1
Income taxes paid	(125.6)
Net cash used in investing activities	(409.3)
Proceeds from issue of shares	122.3
Interest paid	(165.3)
Net cash used in financing activities	(200.3)
Net increase in cash	?

Required

1. Prepare a statement of cash flows for CSR Limited using the direct method. Include the proper amount for the net increase in cash. One item, interest paid, is included in a different section of the statement than it would be on a U.S. statement of cash flows. Place it in the section that makes the cash flows in each section total to the amounts given.
2. Where would the interest paid be shown in a statement of cash flows in the United States?
3. Explain why CSR places interest paid where it does.
4. Explain why the FASB in the United States requires the interest paid to be placed in the section you indicated in requirement 2.

10-67 Statement of Cash Flows, Japan

Kansai Electric supplies power to an area of Japan that includes Osaka and Kyoto. Its operating revenues exceed ¥2.5 trillion, and its assets exceed ¥6 trillion. Instead of a statement of cash flows, Kansai Electric provides a statement of receipts and expenditures:

Statement of Receipts and Expenditures, Year Ended March 31
(in Billions of Yen)

Cash balance at beginning of the period	¥	72
Receipts		
Operating revenues		2,545
Nonoperating revenues		109
Bond issue		236
Increase in loans		1,546
Total receipts		4,436
Expenditures		
Operating expenses		1,954
Nonoperating expenses		140
Repayments of bonds		262
Repayments of loans		1,419
Cost of construction		672
Total expenditures		4,447
Cash balance at end of the period	¥	61

From the information in the statement of receipts and expenditures, prepare a statement of cash flows using the direct method.

10-68 British Cash Flow Statement

Lloyds TSB Group is a leading UK-based financial services group. It is the sixth largest UK company, based on market capitalization. Lloyds TSB's consolidated cash flow statement for the year ended December 31 is in Exhibit 10-15.

Discuss the differences between Lloyds TSB's cash flow statement and the statement of cash flows required for U.S. companies.

10-69 T-Account Approach

Study appendix 10B. Refer to the facts concerning the Buretta Company's "Summary Problem for Your Review" in the chapter. Prepare a set of T-accounts that supports the statement of cash flows shown in Exhibit 10-10 (p. 427). Use Exhibit 10-12 (p. 433) as a guide. Key your postings by number.

10-70 T-Account Approach

Study appendix 10B. Refer to the facts concerning the Goldblum Company in problem 10-55. Prepare a set of T-accounts that supports the statement of cash flows. Use Exhibit 10-12 (p. 433) as a guide. Key your postings by number.

Exhibit 10-15

Lloyds TSB Group plc

Consolidated Cash Flow Statement for the Year Ended December 31
(in Millions of Pounds)

Net cash (outflow) inflow from operating activities	£ (771)
Returns on investments and servicing of finance	
Dividends received from associated undertakings	47
Dividends paid	(1,566)
Dividends paid to minority shareholders in group undertakings	(191)
Interest paid on subordinated liabilities (loan capital)	(265)
Interest element of finance lease rental payments	(2)
Net cash outflow from returns on investments and servicing of finance	(1,977)
Tax	
UK corporation tax	(556)
Overseas tax	(59)
Total tax	(615)
Investing activities	
Net disposal of (additions to) fixed asset investments	3,820
Addition to interests in associated undertakings	(4)
Disposal of group undertakings and businesses	3
Additions to tangible fixed assets	(242)
Disposals of tangible fixed assets	329
Purchase of shares from minority shareholders	(683)
Net cash inflow (outflow) from investing activities	3,223
Net cash (outflow) inflow before financing	(140)
Financing	
Issue of subordinated liabilities (loan capital)	557
Issue of ordinary share capital	32
Repayments of subordinated liabilities (loan capital)	(320)
Capital element of finance lease rental payments	(17)
Net cash inflow (outflow) from financing	252
Increase (decrease) in cash and cash equivalents	£ 112

10-71   Interpretation of the Statement of Cash Flows and Ethics

Fleetfoot, Inc., was a successful producer of athletic shoes in the mid-1990s. The company's peak year was 1999. Since then, both sales and profits have fallen. The following information is from the company's 2001 annual report ($ in thousands):

	2001	2000	1999
Net income	$1,500	$4,500	$7,500
Accounts receivable (end of year)	900	1,800	6,000
Inventory (end of year)	1,050	2,100	2,850
Net cash provided by operations	675	1,050	2,250
Capital expenditures	900	1,050	1,350
Proceeds from sales of fixed assets	2,700	1,500	2,250
Net gain on sales of fixed assets			
plus net extraordinary gains	2,250	1,800	2,400

During 2002, short-term loans of $9 million became due. Fleetfoot paid off only $2.25 million and was able to extend the terms on the other $6.75 million. Accounts payable continued at a very low level in 2002, and the company maintained a large investment in corporate equity securities, enough to generate $450,000 of dividends received in 2002. Fleetfoot neither paid dividends nor issued stock or bonds in 2002. Its 2002 statement of cash flows was as follows:

Fleetfoot, Inc.
Statement of Cash Flows for the Year Ended December 31, 2002 (in Thousands)

Cash flows from operating activities		
Net income	$ 1,050	
Adjustments to reconcile net income to net		
cash provided by operating activities		
Depreciation and amortization	600	
Net decrease in accounts receivable	150	
Net decrease in inventory	225	
Investment revenue from equity investments,		
less $900 of dividends received	(600)	
Gains on sales of fixed assets	(2,100)	
Extraordinary loss on building fire	1,200	
Net cash provided by operating activities		$ 525
Cash flows from investing activities		
Purchase of fixed assets	$ (600)	
Insurance proceeds on building fire	3,000	
Sale of plant assets	3,750	
Purchase of corporate equity securities	(2,250)	
Net cash provided by investing activities		3,900
Cash flows from financing activities		
Principal payments on short-term debt to banks	$(2,250)	
Purchase of treasury stock	(900)	
Net cash used for financing activities		(3,150)
Net increase in cash		1,275
Cash, December 31, 1997		1,800
Cash, December 31, 1998		$ 3,075

Required

1. Interpret the statement of cash flows for Fleetfoot.
2. Describe any ethical issues relating to the strategy and financial disclosures of Fleetfoot.

ANNUAL REPORT CASE

10-72 Cisco Annual Report
Examine Cisco's statement of cash flows in appendix A.

Required

1. Explain why Cisco's net cash provided by operating activities was $1,816 million more in the year ended July 29, 2000, than it was in the year ended July 31, 1999. Would you expect a similar increase in the next year? Why or why not?

2. Explain to a nonaccountant what Cisco did with the $6.1 billion of cash generated by operating activities during the year ended July 29, 2000.

3. Suppose a friend of yours commented, "Cisco must have poor financial management. It made more than $2.6 billion in the year ended July 29, 2000, and it generated more than $6.1 billion in cash from operations, yet it paid no dividends and did not repurchase its own stock. It's shareholders got nothing." Answer your friend's question.

10-73 Financial Statement Research
Identify an industry and select two companies within that industry.

Required

1. Determine whether cash flow from operations is stable through time.
2. Relate cash flow from operations to investing and dividend payment needs.
3. Compare cash flow from operations to net income. Explain why they differ.

COLLABORATIVE LEARNING EXERCISE

10-74 Items in the Statement of Cash Flows
Form groups of four to six students each. Each member of the group should select a different company, find its statement of cash flows for a recent year, and make a list of the items included in each section of the statement: operating, investing, and financing activities. Be ready to explain the nature of each item.

Required

1. As a group, make a comprehensive list of all the items the companies listed under cash flows from operating activities. Identify those that are essentially the same but simply differ in terminology, and call them a single item. For each item, explain why and how it affects cash flows from operating activities. Note whether any of the companies selected use the direct method for reporting cash flows from operating activities. (Most companies use the indirect method, despite the fact that the FASB prefers the direct method.) If any use the direct method, separate the items listed under the direct method from those listed under the indirect method.

2. Make another comprehensive list of all the items listed under cash flows from investing activities. Again, combine those that are essentially identical and differ only in terminology. For each item, explain why and how it affects cash flows from investing activities.

3. Make a third comprehensive list, this time including all the items listed under cash flows from financing activities. Again, combine those that are essentially identical and differ only in terminology. For each item, explain why and how it affects cash flows from financing activities.

4. Reconvene as a class. For each of the three sections on the statement of cash flows, have groups sequentially add one item to the list of items included in the statement, simultaneously explaining why it is included in that section. Then identify the items that appear on nearly all cash flow statements and those that are relatively rare.

INTERNET EXERCISE

10-75 Nike
Go to www.nikebiz.com, then select investors to locate Nike's most current financial information.

www.prenhall.com/horngren

1. Take a look at Nike's *Condensed Consolidated Statement of Cash Flows.* Does Nike use the direct or indirect method? How can you tell?

2. Locate *Management's Discussion and Analysis.* Look under the section titled *Liquidity and Capital Resources.* What does management have to say about cash provided by operations?

3. Which is larger: cash provided (or used) by operations or net income for the period? Why is the cash provided by operations different from the amount of net income for the quarter?

4. Why does Nike add depreciation an amortization to net income in the operating activities section?

5. What is the primary reason for cash used (provided) by investing activities in the most recent fiscal period?

6. What is the primary reason for cash used (provided) by financing activities in the most recent fiscal period?

Go to the "Statement of Cash Flows" episode on the *Mastering Accounting* CD-ROM for an interactive, video-enhanced exercise focused on helping CanGo managers understand the difference between direct and indirect methods and the quality of earnings when comparing net income to actual cash flow.

The public has relied on UPS for delivery services for almost a century but has only had access to UPS stock since 1999.

www.prenhall.com/horngren

Learning Objectives

After studying this chapter, you should be able to

1. Describe the rights of shareholders.

2. Differentiate among authorized, issued, and outstanding shares.

3. Contrast bonds, preferred stock, and common stock.

4. Identify the economic characteristics of and accounting for stock splits.

5. Account for both large-percentage and small-percentage stock dividends.

6. Explain and report stock repurchases and other treasury stock transactions.

7. Record conversions of debt for equity or of preferred stock into common stock.

8. Use the rate of return on common equity and book value per share.

United Parcel Service (UPS) has a distinguishing brown fleet of trucks and a distinguished position as the world's largest package delivery company. The company delivers over 12 million packages each business day in over 200 countries from 1.7 million shippers to 6 million recipients. To do this requires about 150,000 delivery vehicles including more than 500 aircraft. UPS is poised to be one of the key beneficiaries of the shift to Web-based businesses. UPS ships over 55% of the goods purchased over the Internet. The firm continues to serve older line, bricks and mortar companies, but the nature of the business is being transformed to a "time-definite" service. It used to be that one shipped items and understood they would get there when they got there, with a sense that knowing the arrival day was rather good service. Today UPS sells not only shipment of the item but also assurance as to its time of arrival, and ability to constantly monitor its progress. Customers need efficient electronic access to the information that allows them to request a pickup, track an order, and serve a customer. They rely on UPS for full logistics support for ordering, scheduling, shipping, and receiving.

In addition to its package delivery service and logistical support, UPS has a company called UPS Capital that lends businesses money, finances inventory, and even buys accounts receivable. It is developing the capability to offer warehousing and order fulfillment services for small-to-medium-sized firms through UPS e-Logistics. It is also launching UPS e-Ventures to help bring to market companies that will serve the needs of Internet-based businesses.

UPS has been a public company only since November 10, 1999. When UPS chose to "go public," it found a receptive audience, raising some $5.5 billion by selling over 109 million shares. The proceeds of the sale were used not only to fund its aggressive growth and development plans but also to purchase shares from employee–shareholders. The company has been employee owned for years and this allowed employees to realize the value of their long investment in the company. Even now, employees and retirees own nearly two-thirds of outstanding shares. Every executive officer has more than 25 years of service with UPS. During its first months of public trading, share prices touched $75 per share before falling as low as $49 and settling in the $53 area by summer's end.

Thus far, we have described transactions affecting assets and liabilities. Now we examine stockholders' equity in more detail. After all, stockholders such as those of UPS want to know details about their interests.

If the accounting equation is to balance, and if we know the amounts of assets and liabilities, the stockholders' equity must be the residual. Economically, this is certainly true. When a company is liquidated, and creditors are paid out of the proceeds, the owners receive whatever is left. It is now time to address issues relating to how we classify and report transactions between a company and its shareholders and how analysts use this information to evaluate the company.

Consider McDonald's, the company that launched chapter 1. The owners' equity section of the McDonald's annual report is reproduced as Exhibit 11-1. Some of what appears there is no surprise because common stock and retained earnings are old friends at this point. However, preferred stock, additional paid-in-capital, unearned employee stock ownership plan (ESOP) compensation, accumulated other comprehensive income, and common stock in treasury are all new. Most of the issues involve explicit transactions between the company and its shareholders. For example, if you had purchased 100 shares of McDonald's in 1984, today you would have many more shares because McDonald's has had six stock splits during that period. During that period some investors received a constant stream of dividends. Others chose to sell their shares back to McDonald's during one of the recurring periods when McDonald's repurchased shares. The last line before the total indicates that at year-end 1999, McDonald's held 309.8 million shares that it had repurchased from former shareholders.

The retained earnings reflects the historic profitability of McDonald's that has enabled it to finance much of its exceptional growth by retaining earnings in the business. Assets of the company reported in the balance sheet total $21 billion and total stock-

Exhibit 11-1

McDonald's Shareholders' Equity

Shareholders' equity		
Preferred stock, no par value; authorized—165.0 million shares;		
issued—none	$ —	$ —
Common stock, $.01 par value;		
authorized, 3.5 billion shares;		
issued—1,660.6 million	16.6	16.6
Additional paid-in capital	1,288.3	989.2
Unearned ESOP compensation	(133.3)	(148.7)
Retained earnings	15,562.8	3,879.6
Accumulated other comprehensive income	(886.8)	(522.5)
Common stock in treasury, at cost; 309.8 and		
304.4 million shares	(6,208.5)	(4,749.5)
Total shareholders' equity	$ 9,639.1	$9,464.7

holder's equity of $9.6 billion represents almost half of that. Note that these accounting values do not correspond to the market value of McDonald's. McDonald's was selling for $30 per share in mid-September 2000, which means its total market value was $40.5 billion ($30 per share times 1,351 million shares—1,661 million issued less 310 million in treasury). This is four times its book value.

A number of the accounting practices for shareholders' equity are based on legal characteristics of corporations, so we make frequent reference to the rights and privileges of shareholders and the consequences of various financing decisions on the firm and its owners.

Internationally there are substantial differences in the structure of corporate/business activity and in accounting procedures used to disclose results. For example, in many countries large corporations are primarily privately owned by a few individuals instead of having broad public ownership and financial reporting as in the United States. In many countries the majority of financing continues to be provided by banks instead of public issuance of bonds. Many formerly planned economies have been transitioning from state-owned-and-operated business entities into private ones; in many countries the government remains the largest employer because it owns many economic entities such as power producers, phone providers, and airlines, not to mention the mail system, which remains a government monopoly even in the United States. From an accounting perspective, the key point is that many diverse legal structures worldwide lead to plentiful international variation in accounting for stockholders' equity.

BACKGROUND ON STOCKHOLDERS' EQUITY

Corporations are entities with perpetual life created in accordance with state laws. The corporate charter specifies the rights of stockholders (or shareholders) that generally include the right to: (1) vote, (2) share in corporate profits, (3) share in any assets left at liquidation, and (4) acquire more shares of subsequent issues of stock. The extent of an individual stockholder's power is determined by the number and type of shares held.

Objective 1
Describe the rights of shareholders.

Corporations hold annual meetings of shareholders, when votes are taken on important matters. For example, the shareholders elect the board of directors. They may also vote on changing employee bonus plans, choosing outside auditors, making decisions to merge, and handling similar matters. Large corporations make heavy use of the proxy system. A **corporate proxy** is a written authority granted by individual shareholders to others (usually members of corporate management) to cast the shareholders' votes. By using a proxy, shareholders may express (vote) their preference without traveling to the site of the annual meeting.

corporate proxy A written authority granted by individual shareholders to others to cast the shareholders' votes.

The ultimate power to manage a corporation almost always resides with the common shareholders, but shareholders of publicly owned corporations usually delegate that power to the company's top managers. The modern large corporation frequently has a team of professional managers, from the chairman of the board downward. Increasingly companies are requiring top managers to own a significant number of shares in the firm. When managers own shares directly or hold stock options to acquire shares, they are more likely to share a common economic interest with shareholders. When the company's stock rises in value, the managers benefit personally.

Stockholders also generally have **preemptive rights,** which are the rights to acquire a proportional amount of any new issues of capital stock. Whenever a company issues new shares of stock, more people can become owners, in which case everyone's percentage of ownership (the percentage of the company held by each owner) decreases. The preemptive privilege allows present shareholders to purchase additional shares directly from the corporation before the shares can be sold to the general public. In this way, the shareholders are able to maintain their percentage of ownership.

preemptive rights The rights to acquire a pro rata amount of any new issues of capital stock.

Perhaps the most important right of common shareholders is limited liability, which means that creditors of the corporation have claims only on the assets owned by the corporation, not on the assets of the owners of the corporation. In contrast, the creditors of a partnership have potential rights against the savings, homes, and automobiles of the individual partners.

We generally think of existing, well-established companies that issued their common stock years ago, but corporations are being formed constantly. Silicon Valley in California, Silicon Alley in New York City, and other high-tech locations have originated thousands of new ventures, some large, some small, some successful, and some not. A complicated marketplace exists in which exciting new ideas are funded. New corporations often start with a few investors and then seek additional funding as their original ideas are shown to be doable, exciting, and profitable. Groups of investors called venture capitalists support exciting ideas early in the process. If these ideas are successfully implemented, the company may issue additional shares that are registered with the SEC. This initial public offering (IPO) is managed by an underwriting firm and the shares are sold to individual investors and to institutional investors such as pension funds, insurance companies, mutual funds, and so on. Regardless of who is involved, and at what stage of the company's growth cycle, the accounting procedures are very similar.

AUTHORIZED, ISSUED, AND OUTSTANDING STOCK

Objective 2
Differentiate among authorized, issued, and outstanding shares.

When a company becomes a corporation, the state in which it operates must approve its articles of incorporation, which detail the number and types of capital stock that can be issued. The total number of shares that may be issued is known as the **authorized shares.** Just because a certain number of shares is authorized does not mean that a company will ever offer that many shares to potential investors. Shares are usually offered in batches over time. When the company receives cash in exchange for stock certificates, the shares become **issued shares.** Shares that are issued and held by the stockholders are called **outstanding shares.**

Sometimes a company buys back shares of stock from its own shareholders. These shares are called **treasury stock.** They are issued, but because the company holds them, they are no longer outstanding. To clarify these issues let us look at an example. As of December 31, 1999, McDonald's had authorized 3.5 billion shares of which 1,660.6 million were issued. Over time, 309.8 million shares had been reacquired and are shown as treasury stock.

authorized shares The total number of shares that may legally be issued under the articles of incorporation.

issued shares The aggregate number of shares sold to the public.

outstanding shares Shares remaining in the hands of shareholders.

treasury stock A corporation's issued stock that has subsequently been repurchased by the company and not retired.

Number of Shares (in Millions)	
Authorized	3,500.0
Deduct: Unissued	1,839.4
Issued	1,660.6
Deduct: Shares held in treasury	309.8
Total shares outstanding	1,350.8

ACCOUNTING FOR STOCK ISSUANCE

To account for a stock issuance, we record the receipt of cash and create a common stock account to represent the ownership interest. In 2000, McDonald's stock was selling for around $30 per share, so a stock issuance of 1 million additional shares could be recorded as:

Cash	30,000,000	
Common Stock		30,000,000

Many companies, however, separate their common stock recognition into two categories, par value and additional paid-in capital. Legally, par value was originally conceived as a measure of protection for creditors because it established the minimum legal liability of a stockholder. In this way, the creditors would be assured that the corporation would have at least a minimum amount of ownership capital, for example, $10 for each share issued. The stockholder had a commitment to invest at least the par value per share in the corporation.

McDonald's shares have a par value of $.01 each. Thus, the actual entry to record issuance of 1 million additional shares would separate out par value as follows:

Cash	30,000,000	
Common stock		10,000
Additional paid-in capital		29,990,000

In practice, the par values are usually set far below the full market price of the shares when issued, as is the case with McDonald's. In some cases, the minimum capital is called stated value instead of par value. Similarly, the language used to describe additional paid-in capital varies widely. For economic purposes, most of these distinctions are of little importance. However, you encounter them in annual reports and must be aware of their meaning. The following illustrates the diversity of practice:

Company	Par Value per Share	Name for Additional Paid-in Capital
AT&T	$1.00	Additional paid-in capital
Coca-Cola	.25	Capital surplus
McDonald's	.01	Additional paid-in capital
Motorola	3.00	Additional paid-in capital
PepsiCo	.0167	Capital in excess of par value
Qualcomm	.0001	Paid-in capital

BUSINESS FIRST
The Legal Perspective

We have defined the accounting rules under GAAP and they are important for investors to understand to assess the risks and returns to ownership of securities. However, many of these terms and practices take on a special legal significance. Every state has its own laws about corporations and the rights and responsibilities of the corporation and its managers and directors. These laws frequently rely on accounting practices.

Consider the par value or stated value of common stock. This arose as a legal requirement to force incorporators to commit a minimum level of cash resources to the firm. The idea was to assure creditors that the owners, who were protected by limited liability for their personal assets, had significant resources at risk in the company. It also served as a limit on the company's ability to distribute resources to its shareholders. The company could not "impair" its legal capital by distributing a dividend that would reduce owner's equity below its legal capital.

Yet today only 13 states still rely heavily on this concept in their rules on corporations. Two of them, Delaware and New York, are very significant states of incorporation for companies, so their rules matter. However, most states have taken different approaches to protecting investors and creditors.

The key issue is the desire of creditors to be sure that the owners of the firm do not misuse resources without paying off their debts first. Lenders have increasingly added covenants to loan documents to limit the ability of the company to pay dividends, to redeem shares, or otherwise to deplete capital prior to repaying borrowed funds. Recently Ben and Jerry's Homemade, the Vermont ice cream maker, disclosed that its loan agreements required specific levels of working capital, current ratio, and tangible net worth. Such contractual requirements provide stronger safety for lenders than the generic state laws about "legal capital" that were embodied in par values and stated values for the common stock.

CASH DIVIDENDS

declaration date The date the board of directors declares a dividend.

date of record The date that determines which shareholders will receive a dividend.

payment date The date dividends are paid.

Dividends are proportional distributions of income to shareholders in a company, usually in the form of cash. In the United States, dividends tend to be paid in equal amounts each quarter, although the board may declare, change, or eliminate a dividend at any time. Some firms tend to pay a special, larger dividend once a year.

No dividend is automatically paid. The company's board of directors votes to approve each dividend. The date on which the board formally announces that it will pay a dividend is called the **declaration date.** The board specifies a **date of record,** a future date that determines which stockholders will receive the dividend. A person who holds the stock on the declaration date, but sells before the date of record, will not receive the dividend. The dividend goes to the person who owns the stock on the date of record. The actual **payment date** is the day the checks are mailed and follows the date of record by a few days or weeks.

No journal entry is required on the date of record, although the company's stock transfer agent must identify all parties to whom dividends will be paid as of that date. If a balance sheet is prepared between declaration and payment, the dividend payable will appear as a liability.

DATE OF DECLARATION

Sept. 26	Retained income	. . . .	20,000	
	Dividends payable	. . . .		20,000
	To record the declaration of dividends to be paid on November 15 to shareholders of record as of October 25			

DATE OF PAYMENT

Nov. 15	Dividends payable	. . . .	20,000	
	Cash	. . . .		20,000
	To pay dividends declared on September 26 to shareholders of record as of October 25			

The amount of cash dividends declared by a board of directors depends on many factors, primarily the market expectations, the current and predicted earnings, and the corporation's current cash position and financial plans concerning spending on plant assets and repayments of debts. Remember that payment of cash dividends requires cash. Thus, the single biggest factor affecting the size of dividends is the availability of cash that is not otherwise committed. It is also true that investors expect companies that have historically paid regular dividends to continue to do so. Ford and General Motors would fall in this category. Investors also expect companies that have not paid dividends because cash was better used to finance expansion will continue to identify growth opportunities requiring additional investment. Microsoft is an example of a company that does not pay cash dividends. The least important factor in the dividend decision is the amount of retained income. Retained income balances matter only when there are legal restrictions on dividend payments in state law or in bond covenants.

Ultimately, changes in dividend patterns are watched very carefully by investors. If a company has maintained a series of uninterrupted dividends over a span of years, it will make an effort to continue such payments even in the face of net losses. In fact, companies occasionally borrow money for the sole purpose of maintaining dividend payments. Elimination and initiation of payments are big events that cause investors to pause and consider carefully what the company's decision means about the future. The careful consideration is necessary because the messages are not completely clear. Consider a company that initiates or increases a dividend. The good news is that it has resources to distribute to shareholders while continuing to grow and do business. The bad news is that it does not have hugely profitable investments to make in its ongoing business that require all the cash it can generate.

The two most common types of stock that companies issue are common stock and preferred stock. Common stock, as the name implies, is the most basic and common type of stock. All corporations have it, and the shareholders who own it have the rights discussed earlier. **Preferred stock** offers owners different rights and preferential treatment. Stock represents a contract between the company and its owners and the terms of preferred stock can involve almost any arrangement the parties select.

For example, preferred stock owners do not usually have voting rights, but they do have a preferred claim on assets. Therefore, at liquidation, preferred stockholders receive any available company assets, up to the amount of their liquidation value, before common stockholders do. The most common preference terms grant preferred stockholders the right to receive dividend payments before common stockholders do.

Preferred stock is like common stock in that dividends are not a legal obligation until the board of directors declares them. With preferred shares, the amount of the dividend is generally specified and does not change over time. While McDonald's has authorized preferred shares, none are currently outstanding. Historically, one McDonald's issue was a 7.72% cumulative preferred stock with a liquidation preference of $50,000 per share. The annual dividend on one share of this preferred was 7.72% times $50,000 or $3,860. The preferred stock usually appears in the top part of the stockholders' equity section of the balance sheet, as illustrated by the preferred stock caption in the McDonald's 1999 annual report in Exhibit 11-1.

CUMULATIVE DIVIDENDS

What happens when the board votes to skip paying a fixed preferred stock dividend? Just because a company can decide not to pay the dividend now does not mean that the company has completely avoided the obligation. Preferred stock dividends are often **cumulative.** Cumulative preferred stock requires that undeclared dividends accumulate and must be paid in the future before any common dividends can be paid. For example, if McDonald's had skipped a $3,860 preferred dividend per share in one year, it would have been required to pay $7,720 for each preferred share the next year before common dividends could be paid. From the standpoint of a common shareholder, accumulated unpaid dividends (called **dividend arrearages**) are somewhat like debt obligations because they must be paid before the common shareholders receive any compensation. Moreover, in the event of liquidation, cumulative unpaid preferred dividends must be paid before common stockholders receive any cash.

To illustrate the operation of cumulative preferred stock, consider Exhibit 11-2. The stockholders' equity of Acumulado Corporation on December 31, 20X0 is shown in panel A, and the consequences of subsequent years of net income and dividends are shown in panel B.

Acumulado's board of directors elects not to declare and pay preferred dividends in 20X1 and 20X2. This decision makes economic sense, given that Acumulado Corporation posted losses both years. You may be thinking that the company had more than enough in retained income to be able to pay the dividends despite the losses, but retained income is not the same as cash. The large retained income balance results from many prior years of profitable operations, but in those prior years the company has reinvested the cash generated by operations into productive business assets. When a firm encounters losses such as Acumulado experienced in 20X1 and 20X2, cash flow may be reduced, and there is often insufficient cash available to pay dividends.

Even though the company skipped making the $5 million annual preferred dividend payments, its obligation to make those payments remained and accumulated, becoming $10 million by the end of 20X2. When operating results improve in 20X3, the board

Objective 3
Contrast bonds, preferred stock, and common stock.

preferred stock Stock that offers owners different rights and preferential treatment.

cumulative A characteristic of preferred stock that requires that undeclared dividends accumulate and must be paid in the future before common dividends.

dividend arrearages Accumulated unpaid dividends on preferred stock.

Exhibit 11-2

Acumulado Corporation Preferred Dividends

PANEL A

Stockholders' Equity, December 31, 20X0		
Preferred stock, no par, cumulative, $5 annual dividend per share		
Issued and outstanding, 1,000,000 shares	$ 50,000,000	
Common stock, no par, 5,000,000 shares	100,000,000	
Retained income	400,000,000	
Total stockholders' equity	$550,000,000	

PANEL B

	Net Income	Preferred Dividends Declared	Preferred Dividends In Arrears	Common Dividends Declared	Ending Balance, Retained Income
20X0					$400,000,000
20X1	$(4,000,000)	—	$ 5,000,000	—	396,000,000
20X2	(4,000,000)	—	10,000,000	—	392,000,000
20X3	21,000,000	$ 3,000,000	12,000,000	—	410,000,000
20X4	49,000,000	17,000,000	—	$ 2,000,000	440,000,000
20X5	32,000,000	5,000,000	—	17,000,000	450,000,000

declares and pays a partial dividend of $3 million leaving $2 million additional arrearages, which raises the total arrearage to $12 million. In 20X4, Acumulado has a banner year and improves profitability and cash flow enough to pay a full dividend and more. Dividends to preferred shareholders of $17 million cover not only the 20X4 dividend but also all accumulated dividends in arrears. With accumulated preferred dividends now completely paid, the firm may pay a dividend to the common shareholders for the first time in 4 years. Note that the ending balance in retained income in each year is equal to the beginning balance, plus net income (or minus a net loss) minus dividends declared.

Would you rather own cumulative or noncumulative preferred stock? In the preceding example, a holder of noncumulative preferred stock would receive nothing in 20X1 or 20X2, $3 million in $20X3 and $5 million in 20X4. The cumulative feature is certainly preferred, but as with most choices, it is not free. Because cumulative preferred shares are more secure, they typically pay a lower dividend than noncumulative shares. The cumulative feature must be explicit in the contract. It is not automatic. Most buyers of preferred shares do insist on cumulative status.

PREFERENCE IN LIQUIDATION

liquidating value A measure of the preference to receive assets in the event of corporate liquidation.

In addition to the cumulative dividend feature, preferred stock usually has a specific liquidating value. The exact **liquidating value** is stated on the stock certificate, and it is often the same as par value. The company would have to pay the full liquidating value (plus dividends in arrears, if any) to all preferred stockholders before it could distribute any assets to common stockholders when the company is liquidated. Of course, before preferred shareholders receive any assets, all debt obligations also have to be paid off.

Consider an illustration of the liquidation of assets when short- and long-term debt, preferred stock, and common stock are all present. Exhibit 11-3 shows how cash is distributed to different claimants. The priority of the claims generally decreases as you move down the chart. The first column presents the book values. The next seven columns show the distributions to each class of claimant under different circumstances.

Exhibit 11-3

Liquidation of Claims under Various Alternatives (in Thousands)

	Account Balances	Assumed Total Cash Proceeds to Be Distributed						
		$1,500	$1,000	$500	$450	$350	$200	$100
Accounts payable	$ 100	$ 100	$ 100	$100	$100	$100	$100	$ 50*
Unsubordinated debentures	100	100	100	100	100	100	100	50*
Subordinated debentures	200	200	200	200	200	150		
Preferred stock ($100 par value and $120 liquidating value per share)	100	120	120	100	50			
Common stock and retained income	500	980	480					
Total liabilities and shareholders' equity	$1,000							
Total cash proceeds distributed		$1,500	$1,000	$500	$450	$350	$200	$100

*Ratio of 50:50 because each has a $100,000 claim.

As you can see, when there is not enough cash to go around, common stockholders are always the last to get paid and often wind up getting nothing. However, in those instances when there is actually excess cash left over, common stockholders get that excess. This illustrates the risks and rewards of stock ownership. When things go well, they go very well indeed. When things go badly, they go very badly. Keep in mind, though, that both common and preferred stockholders are protected by limited liability. They do not have to add additional assets to the company in the event that the company cannot pay off its debts.

OTHER FEATURES OF PREFERRED STOCK

In addition to being cumulative and having liquidation value, preferred stock may have other features. As with our discussion of debt, each feature affects the attractiveness of the stock issue. If you add the cumulative feature to a 5% preferred, investors will pay more for it. Another way to express the same idea would be to say if you add the cumulative feature to a preferred share, you reduce the size of the fixed dividend that investors require to be willing to invest in the preferred stock.

Each of the following features can also affect the attractiveness of the preferred stock. For example, a participating preferred stock ordinarily receives a fixed dividend but can receive higher dividends when the company has a very good year—one in which common stockholders receive especially large dividends. **Participating** means that holders of these shares participate in the growth of the company because they share in the growing amount of dividends. A **callable** preferred stock gives the issuing company the right to purchase the stock back from the owner on payment of the **call price,** or **redemption price.** This call price is typically set 5% to 10% above the par value or issuance price of the stock, to compensate investors for the fact that the stock can be bought back at the issuer's choice.

A **convertible** preferred stock gives the owner the option to exchange the preferred share for shares of common stock. Because the ability to convert the stock can be quite valuable in future years if common stock prices grow significantly, convertible securities typically carry a lower dividend rate. For example, a regular preferred offering of an 8% dividend might sell for the same price as a 7% convertible preferred stock.

It is not possible to describe every imaginable kind of preferred stock because individual investors and issuers have the opportunity to develop a unique security that exactly meets their needs, and they can adapt that security to the particular market conditions they face at the time. In fact, the investment banking community works hard to develop new types of preferred stock that exactly fit the particular needs of certain investors.

participating A characteristic of preferred stock that provides increasing dividends when common dividends increase.

callable A characteristic of bonds or preferred stock that gives the issuer the right to redeem the security at a fixed price.

redemption price (call price) The price at which an issuer can buy back a callable preferred stock or bond, which is typically 5% to 10% above the par value.

convertible A characteristic of bonds or preferred stock that gives the holder the right to exchange the security for common stock.

COMPARING BONDS AND PREFERRED STOCK

Preferred stocks are actually quite similar to bonds. Both are contracts between an investor and an issuer that spell out each party's rights and responsibilities. Preferred stocks and bonds each pay a specific return to the investor. However, they differ greatly as to the size and nature of those returns. The specific return to bondholders is called interest and appears on the earnings statement as an expense. In the United States, interest income is taxable to the recipient and tax deductible to the issuing company. In contrast, the specific return to preferred shareholders is a dividend and represents a distribution of profits. Dividends do not reduce net earnings and are not tax deductible to the issuer. Dividends reduce the retained income account directly. For the recipient, dividends may be fully taxed, partly taxed, or untaxed depending on whether the stockholder is an individual or a corporation and on the quantity of stock that is owned.

Preferred stock and bonds also differ in that bonds have specific maturity dates, at which time they must be repaid, but preferred stock typically has an unlimited life. From the investor's perspective, preferred stock is riskier than bonds because it never matures and the company is not required to declare dividends. It is not always easy to determine whether a security is a debt instrument or an equity interest. Some preferred stock, for example, has a mandatory redemption date. This makes it more similar to a bond.

ADDITIONAL STOCK ISSUANCE

After the company is formed, companies occasionally issue additional shares to investors, to executives, or to current shareholders. There are several motivations and several procedures for additional stock issues. When a firm simply wishes to raise additional equity capital, the process is much like the original stock issue described earlier. Cash is provided by an investor and additional new shares are issued in exchange. Stock options, stock splits, and stock dividends are other procedures for increasing the number of shares held by investors. Each is discussed in the following text.

STOCK OPTIONS

stock options Special rights usually granted to executives to purchase a corporation's capital stock.

Stock options are rights granted to executives or other employees to purchase a specific number of shares of a corporation's capital stock at a specific price for a specific time period. Options are generally given to corporate officers as a form of incentive compensation. The idea is that executives who hold options make money if the value of the stock increases, and the shareholders also make money. The shareholders want executives to make decisions that enhance the stock price. By approving incentive stock option programs, shareholders assure that participating employees have a good reason to work hard and to make the right decisions. For example, suppose UPS granted its top executives options to purchase 30,000 shares of $1 par value common stock at $30 per share, the market price today (date of grant). The options can be exercised over a 5-year span, beginning 3 years from the date of grant. Such options are especially valuable because the executives can gain the benefits of stock price increases without bearing the risks of price declines. However, measurement of the exact value of options at the time of grant is difficult because the future is unknowable. Because these options cannot be sold to others, there are no market prices to be used as guides. Currently accepted accounting attributes zero value to most options as long as the exercise price is the same as or higher than the market price at the date of the grant. Thus, accountants make no entry at the time of grant. However, footnotes in the financial statements must reveal the number and type of options outstanding and an assessment of their value.

Suppose all options are exercised 3 years after the date of grant. The journal entry would be:

Cash	900,000	
Common stock		30,000
Additional paid-in capital		870,000
To record issue of 30,000 shares upon exercise		
of options to acquire them @ $30 per share		

Note that the journal entry is indistinguishable from the issuance of new shares at current market price to new investors. Suppose the market price was $24. An executive would simply buy shares in the open market instead of exercising the option and paying $30. On the other hand, if the market price were $40, the executive would exercise the option to buy at $30 and have the opportunity to either sell immediately and capture the $10 per share gain, or hold the shares in hopes of further appreciation.

How should the granting of an option to an employee affect the income statement? Some stock options are publicly traded. In the hypothetical UPS option just discussed, even when the UPS stock price was exactly $30 investors would pay to buy an option with an exercise price of $30. If the stock price increases, this investor would profit handsomely and if the stock price falls, the investor would lose only the amount initially paid for the option. Think of it as a big "upside gain" and a limited "downside loss." Thus, granting these valuable options is akin to giving employees cash or other items of value and would therefore seem to be properly treated as an expense.

The FASB considered how to report the granting of such options and chose to require extensive disclosures of options, but not to require expense recognition. While the accounting logic for expense recognition is compelling, there are a number of implementation issues, including the issue of how to measure the value of these options. Many entrepreneurs and dynamic companies that use stock options extensively did not want to have to recognize expenses on their income statements. They put significant pressure on Congress and the SEC to resist an earlier FASB proposal for expense recognition. Footnote disclosure of option grants without financial statement recognition was the outcome. Note that the phrase generally accepted accounting principles implies broad agreement regarding accounting practices. The FASB settled for requiring measurement of these options using any one of several techniques and disclosing the calculated values to investors, but this is an area of accounting where you should expect additional developments.

 If you were running an exciting high-tech company, would you include options as a part of the compensation package for people you hired? Why or why not?

ANSWER

Yes, options should be included in the compensation package for many of your employees. Because most companies in high tech do so, it would appear to be a "best practice." Because most companies in high tech do so, it is necessary to attract talent to your firm. The FASB does not require that options be reported as an expense, so it does not lower reported earnings.

STOCK SPLITS AND STOCK DIVIDENDS

The stock issuances discussed so far all involve the exchange of cash from an investor or executive for new shares of the company's stock. Several procedures exist for the company to issue additional shares of stock to its investors without receiving any money. For example, the company could simply issue some additional shares to current investors. In practice, such distributions of new shares take a variety of forms. We examine two of these forms: the stock split and the stock dividend.

ACCOUNTING FOR STOCK SPLITS

Objective 4
Identify the economic characteristics of and accounting for stock splits.

stock split Issuance of additional shares to existing stockholders for no payments by the stockholders.

A **stock split** refers to the issuance of additional shares to existing shareholders without any additional cash payment to the firm. Issuance of one additional share for each share currently owned is called a "two-for-one" split. For example, suppose the Allstar Equipment Company has 100,000 shares outstanding with a market value of $150 per share and par value of $10 per share. The total market value of the stock is thus $15 million. If Allstar Equipment gives each shareholder an additional share for each share owned, the total number of shares would increase to 200,000. If nothing else about the company changes (assets, liabilities, and equity all stay the same), the total value of the outstanding stock should still be $15 million. With 200,000 shares outstanding, though, the market value per share should drop to $75. Shareholders are as well off as they were before because they have paid no additional money and they still have the same proportional ownership interest in the company.

So why bother? Good question, and one for which there is no perfect answer. Many companies do split their stock. A common result is that stock price falls 50%. Thus, one good explanation for issuing a split is that it causes the stock price to fall on a per share basis. If investors like to invest $1,000 to $20,000 at a time, and stocks trade in units of 100 shares, you can see that investors would be attracted to stocks trading in a range between $10 and $200 per share. Most stocks do trade in that range and companies that split are often at the high end of that range. But it is not a requirement. Berkshire Hathaway is an example of a company whose common stock trades at more than $57,000 per share at this writing. Some people argue that the stock split is a way to communicate with shareholders and remind them that their company is growing. It is true that after several stock splits investors realize that they have four times as many shares as they originally bought. However, we would expect a similar pleased reaction from an investor who still had the same original 100 shares but they were valued at four times their purchase price.

Would the accountant need to do anything to acknowledge Allstar's stock issuance? Yes. There are now twice as many shares outstanding. If the company retains a par value of $10 per share, $1 million would need to be added to common stock. Typically this is transferred from additional paid-in capital. This does not change total owner's equity. It merely rearranges it. An alternative is for the $1 million to be transferred from retained income. When this choice is made it is referred to as a stock split "accounted for as a stock dividend."

Sometimes the company decides to adjust par value by exchanging existing shares for twice as many new shares. Assume that Allstar does not just issue an additional share for each current share. Instead, the 100,000 shares of common stock at $10 par value are returned to Allstar in exchange for 200,000 shares of common stock at $5 par value. Nothing changes in the stockholders' equity section except the description of shares authorized, issued, and outstanding. The aggregate par value is unchanged, no cash has changed hands, each owner has the same proportionate interest as before, and each has the same relative voting power.

Panel A of Exhibit 11-4 shows the journal entries for the three approaches to stock splits. Option one is issuing new shares identical to the existing shares with a shift from paid-in-capital to common stock. Option two is identical except it is "accounted for as a dividend" with the transfer from retained earnings to common stock. Option three involves changing the par value, reclaiming all old shares, and issuing new shares with a smaller par value. No journal entry is required because total par value is unchanged. In panel B, each of these outcomes is presented showing the total effect on the shareholder's equity. As noted in panel C, in all three cases, total shareholders' equity is unchanged and the total market value of the firm should be unchanged as well, which implies that the market price of an individual share should be half of its prior value.

Exhibit 11-4

Comparing Three Approaches to Stock Splits

	PANEL A: ALTERNATE JOURNAL ENTRIES		

Option 1. Issue 100,000 new $10.00 par value shares

Additional paid-in capital   1,000,000
      Common stock   1,000,000

Option 2. Issue 100,000 new $10.00 par value shares and "account for it as a stock dividend"

Retained earnings   1,000,000
      Common stock   1,000,000

Option 3. Exchange 200,000 new $5.00 par value shares for the old ones

No entry

PANEL B: ALTERNATE OUTCOMES

	Common Stock	A-P-I-C	Retained Earnings	Owners' Equity
Option 1	$1,000,000	$4,000,000	$6,000,000	$11,000,000
Change	1,000,000	(1,000,000)		
Result	$2,000,000	$3,000,000	$6,000,000	$11,000,000
Option 2	$1,000,000	$4,000,000	$6,000,000	$11,000,000
Change	1,000,000		(1,000,000)	
Result	$2,000,000	$4,000,000	$5,000,000	$11,000,000
Option 3	$1,000,000	$4,000,000	$6,000,000	$11,000,000
No change				

PANEL C: COMMON OUTCOMES

For all three treatments total owners' equity is the same at $11,000,000
For all three treatments the total market value of the firm should remain constant and the two-for-one stock split should cut price per share in half

ACCOUNTING FOR STOCK DIVIDENDS

Stock dividends are also issuances of additional shares to existing shareholders without additional cash payment, but the number of new shares issued is usually smaller than it is in a split, and there is no change in par value. For example, a 10% stock dividend involves issuance of one new share for every 10 currently owned.

LARGE-PERCENTAGE STOCK DIVIDENDS

With stock dividends, new shares are issued and the common stock account is increased to recognize this increase. The amount of the increase depends on the size of the "dividend." U.S. accounting principles require large-percentage stock dividends (typically those 20% or higher) to be accounted for at par or stated value. That means that an accounting entry is made to transfer the par or stated value of the new shares from the retained income account to the common stock account.

As in the case of stock splits, the market value of the outstanding shares tends to adjust completely when a stock dividend is issued. What else happens economically? When firms issue large-percentage stock dividends or splits, they usually lower the per-share dividend proportionately. Consider the Allstar Equipment Company and the effect of possible stock dividends on share price as illustrated in panel C of Exhibit 11-5. Recall that the total market value of the firm will be unchanged by simply changing the number of shares.

If the Allstar Equipment Company chose to double the number of outstanding shares by issuing a stock dividend, the total amount of stockholders' equity would still be unaffected. However, its composition would change as shown in panel A of Exhibit 11-5. Note that this is identical to the result for a two-for-one stock split "accounted for as a

stock dividends
Distribution to stockholders of a small number of additional shares for every share owned without any payment to the company by the stockholders.

Objective 5
Account for stock splits and both large-percentage and small-percentage stock dividends.

Exhibit 11-5

Stock Dividends

Allstar Example: Originally 100,000 Shares, $10 Par Value, $150 Market Value

---

PANEL A: LARGE STOCK DIVIDEND (100%)

Issue 100,000 new $10 par Value Shares Accounted for at Par

Retained earnings	$1,000,000	
Common stock		$1,000,000

	Common Stock	Additional Paid-in-Capital	Retained Earnings	Owners' Equity
Original	$1,000,000	$4,000,000	$6,000,000	$11,000,000
100% Dividend	1,000,000		(1,000,000)	
Result	$2,000,000	$4,000,000	$5,000,000	$11,000,000

PANEL B: SMALL STOCK DIVIDEND (2%)

Issue 2,000 new $10 par Value Shares Accounted for at Market

Retained Earnings	$300,000	
Common Stock		20,000
Additional Paid-in-Capital		280,000

	Common Stock	Additional Paid-in-Capital	Retained Earnings	Owners Equity
Original	$1,000,000	$4,000,000	$6,000,000	$11,000,000
2% Dividend	20,000	280,000	(300,000)	
Result	$1,020,000	$4,280,000	$5,700,000	$11,000,000

PANEL C: MARKET PRICE EFFECTS OF VARIOUS STOCK DIVIDENDS

Stock Dividend	Shares			Post-Dividend Price per Share
	Original	New	Total	
None	100,000		100,000	$150.00 (Original price)
20%	100,000	20,000	120,000	125.00
40%	100,000	40,000	140,000	107.14
60%	100,000	60,000	160,000	93.75
80%	100,000	80,000	180,000	83.33
100%	100,000	100,000	200,000	75.00

---

dividend" that appeared as option 2 in Exhibit 11-4. In substance, there is absolutely no difference between the 100% stock dividend and the two-for-one stock split. Infrequently a company will transfer amounts from additional paid-in capital, as in option 2 for stock splits. Regulations are not ironclad on this issue.

The company does have an economic decision to make. What happens to the cash dividend when a stock dividend or stock split is issued? One possibility is that the dividend is adjusted proportionately. For a 100% stock dividend or a two-for-one stock split, this would mean that the cash dividend per share would be cut in half and total cash dividends would remain unchanged. It is at least as common for the company to increase the total cash dividend being paid. Investors watch this issue carefully to assess the company's belief about future cash flow and future investment opportunity.

SMALL-PERCENTAGE STOCK DIVIDENDS

When a stock dividend of less than 20% is issued, accountants require that the dividend be accounted for at market value, not at par value. This rule is not easy to defend. It is partly the result of tradition and partly because small-percentage stock dividends are most likely to accompany increases in the total dividend payments or other changes in the company's financial policies. It is argued that the decision to increase total dividends communicates management's conviction that future cash flows will rise to support these increased distributions, and this is a positive statement about the firm's prospects.

Panel B of Exhibit 11-5 illustrates the effects of a 2% stock dividend. As before, the individual shareholder receives no assets from the corporation, and the corporation receives no cash from the shareholder. Also, because the overall number of shares and the number of shares held by each investor have both increased, the shareholders' fractional interests are unchanged. If the shareholders sell the dividend shares, their proportionate ownership interest in the company decreases. The major possible economic effect of a stock dividend is to signal increased cash dividend. Suppose the board of the company in our example consistently voted to pay cash dividends of $1 per share. Often this cash dividend level per share is maintained after a small stock dividend. The recipient of the stock dividend can now expect a future annual cash dividend of $1 \times 1,020 = $1,020 instead of $1 \times 1,000 = $1,000. In this case, when the dividend rate per share is maintained, announcing a stock dividend of 2% has the same economic effect as announcing an increase of 2% in the cash dividend.

For small-percentage (under 20%) stock dividends, the company records the transaction by transferring the market value of the additional shares from retained income to common stock and additional paid-in capital. The entry is often referred to as being a "capitalization of retained income." It is basically a signal to the shareholders that $300,000 of retained income is being invested for the long term in productive assets such as plant, property, and equipment. U.S. practice concerning the use of market values in accounting for small-percentage stock dividends is arbitrary and is not consistently adopted worldwide. For example, in Japan these journal entries are recorded at par value. The Japanese practice is one most accountants would support. The U.S. practice compounds the false notion that the recipients are getting a dividend akin to a cash dividend.

WHY USE STOCK SPLITS AND DIVIDENDS?

Experts debate the importance of splits and stock dividends even as companies continue to use them. One observation is that most U.S. common stock sells at under $100 per share. In 2000, Wal-Mart stock sold for approximately $50 per share. During the prior 19 years, the stock split two-for-one on seven occasions. An investor who purchased 1 share in 1981 would have 128 shares in 2000. Without any splits, one original Wal-Mart share would have been worth $6,400 in 2000. After these splits, a "round-lot" of 100 shares costs $100 \times $50 = $5,000, a reasonable investment size. Without the splits, a round-lot would cost $6,400 \times 100 = $640,000. Thus, splits allow the company to maintain the stock price in a trading range accessible to small investors and company employees. If one share cost $6,400, Wal-Mart might not have as many shareholders.

Often a stock split or stock dividend accompanies other announcements, such as new corporate investment strategies or changes in cash dividend levels. Suppose the firm has traditionally paid a special cash dividend at year-end but plans to expand production substantially, which absorbs available cash and makes the payment of this special dividend difficult. The firm might combine the announcement of the planned expansion with an announcement of a small stock dividend. The small-percentage stock dividend does not draw on cash immediately but provides stockholders with an increase in future cash dividends in proportion to the percentage of new shares issued.

RELATION OF DIVIDENDS AND SPLITS

Companies typically use large-percentage stock dividends to accomplish exactly the same purpose as that achieved with a stock split. That is, the companies want to reduce the market price of their shares and simultaneously they want to signal an increase in total dividend payments to shareholders. Stock splits frequently occur in the form of a stock "dividend" to save clerical costs. After all, swapping old $10-par certificates for new $5-par certificates is more expensive than merely printing and mailing additional $10-par certificates.

IBM described its 1999 two-for-one split in the following footnote to the 1999 annual report:

> *On January 26, 1999, the company's Board of Directors approved a two-for-one common stock split effective May 10, 1999. On April 27, 1999, the stockholders of the company approved amendments to the Certificate of Incorporation to increase the number of authorized shares of common stock from 1,875 million to 4,687.5 million, which was required to effect that stock split. In addition, the amendment reduced the par value of the common shares from $.50 to $.20 per share. Common Stockholders of record at the close of business on May 10, 1999, received one additional share for each share held. All share and per share data presented in the Consolidated Financial Statements and notes of this Annual Report reflect the two-for-one stock split.*

IBM had last split its stock in January of 1997. This event was included in the 1996 annual report even though it had not yet occurred. Such items are called "subsequent" events. They are significant items that arise before the financial statements are published but that actually occur after the date on the statements. In the 1997 split, the par value was not changed.

FRACTIONAL SHARES

Corporations ordinarily issue shares in whole units. When shareholders are entitled to stock dividends in amounts equal to fractional units, corporations issue additional shares for whole units plus cash equal to the market value of the fractional amount.

For example, suppose a corporation issues a 3% stock dividend. A shareholder has 160 shares. The market value per share on the date of issuance is $40. Par value is $2. The shareholder would be entitled to .03 × 160 = 4.8 shares. The company would issue four shares plus .8 × ($40) = $32 cash. The journal entry is:

Retained income (4.8 × $40)	192	
Common stock, at par (4 × $2)		8
Additional paid-in capital (4 × $38)		152
Cash (.8 × $40)		32
To issue a stock dividend of 3% to a holder of 160 shares		

THE INVESTOR'S ACCOUNTING FOR DIVIDENDS AND SPLITS

So far, we have focused on how the corporation deals with stock splits and dividends. What about the stockholder? Consider the investor's recording of the transactions described so far. Suppose Investor J bought 1,000 shares of the original issue of Allstar Equipment Company stock for $50 per share:

Investment in Allstar common stock	50,000	
Cash		50,000
To record investment in 1,000 shares of an original issue of Allstar Equipment Company common stock at $50 per share.		

Investor J holds the shares indefinitely. However, if Investor J sold the shares to Investor K at a subsequent price other than $50, a gain or loss would be recorded by J, and K would carry the shares at the amount paid to J. Meanwhile the stockholders' equity of Allstar Equipment Company would be completely unaffected by this sale by one investor to another. The company's underlying shareholder records would simply be changed to delete J and add K as a shareholder.

The following examples show how Investor J would record the stock split, cash dividends, and stock dividends, where each is treated as an independent event, not as sequential events. Note that several events that produced journal entries for Allstar do not cause entries for Investor J:

a. Stock split at 2-for-1:	No journal entry, but a memorandum would be made in the investment account to show that 2,000 shares are now held at a cost of $25 each instead of 1,000 shares at a cost of $50 each		
b. Cash dividends of $2 per share:	Cash .... Dividend income .... To record cash dividends on Allstar Equipment Company stock	2,000	2,000
or:	Alternatively, the following two entries might be used:		
Date of declaration:	Dividends receivable .... Dividend income .... To record dividends declared by Allstar Equipment Company	2,000	2,000
Date of receipt:	Cash .... Dividends receivable .... To record the receipt of cash dividends	2,000	2,000
c. Stock dividends of 2%:	No journal entry, but a memorandum would be made in the investment account to show that [assuming the stock split in (a) had not occurred] 1,020 shares are now owned at an average cost of $50,000 ÷ 1,020, or $49.02 per share		
d. Stock split in form of a 100% dividend:	No journal entry, but a memorandum would be made in the investment account to show that [assuming the stock splits and stock dividends in (a) and (c) had not occurred] 2,000 shares are now owned at an average cost of $25 instead of 1,000 shares @ $50. Note that this memorandum has the same effect as the memorandum in a.		

REPURCHASE OF SHARES

So far we have seen how companies sell shares and how they sometimes issue additional shares to current shareholders. You should not think, though, that stocks always flow out of a company. Sometimes the company brings shares back by repurchasing them. Companies repurchase their own shares for two main purposes: (1) to permanently reduce shareholder claims, called retiring stock, and (2) to temporarily hold shares for later use, most often to be granted as part of employee bonus or stock purchase plans. Temporarily held shares are called *treasury stock* or *treasury shares*.

Objective 6
Explain and report stock repurchases and other treasury stock transactions.

By repurchasing shares, for whatever reason, a company liquidates some shareholders' claims, and total stockholders' equity decreases by the amount of the repurchase. The purpose of the repurchase determines which stockholders' equity accounts are affected. To illustrate the accounting behind repurchasing shares we continue with the now familiar starting point of the Allstar Equipment Company. Recall that Allstar shares have a market value of $150 per share. We can calculate a book value per share as well. It is $110 (total shareholder's equity divided by number of outstanding shares: $11,000,000 ÷ 100,000).

Book value is the term we have frequently used to refer to the value at which an asset or liability is reported in the financial statements. Here book value is expressed in per share terms referring to the historical investment by the shareholders in the company. The total stockholders' equity of $11 million combines the original purchase price of shares in the past (par value plus additional paid-in capital) with the periodic earnings of the firm that have remained in the business (retained income). Dividing it by the number of shares gives the average per share.

Suppose the board of directors has decided that the $150 market value of its shares is "too low." Even though the market value exceeds the book value by $40 per share ($150 − $110), the board may think the market is too pessimistic concerning the company's shares. In time, investors are expected to understand the true value of the company and the market value rises to reflect that value. The board might believe that the best use of corporate cash would be to purchase a portion of the outstanding shares. In this way, the remaining dedicated shareholders would have the sole benefit of the predicted eventual increase in market value per share. Other motives include the desire to change the proportion of debt and equity in use to finance the firm. Buying back shares increases the relative importance of debt.

Buybacks also allow the company to return cash to shareholders without creating expectations of permanent increases in dividends. Buybacks put the cash in the hands of shareholders who want it, because shareholders decide to sell or not sell their shares. Also, selling shareholders have a tax advantage. When they sell, they are taxed only on their gain, the difference between the selling price and the price they paid to acquire the stock. The tax rate on a long-term gain is less than the tax rate on a dividend.

Suppose that you had purchased 100 shares of common stock for $20 per share, and those shares are now selling for $40. Suppose the company wishes to distribute $40 to you either by buying back one share or by issuing a dividend of $.40 per share. Assume a 40% tax rate on ordinary/dividend income and a 20% tax rate on long-term capital gains. In both cases the company distributes $40, but you end up with very different amounts. If it is a dividend, you pay $16 in tax (40% × $40) and end up with $24 in your pocket. If it is a buyback, you pay tax only on the gain. Your tax is only $4 [20% × ($40 − $20) = $4] and wind up with $36 in your pocket. It should come as no surprise that share buybacks have increased significantly in the last decade and dividends play a much smaller role in the economy.

It has become very common for a firm to buy back its own stock. IBM disclosed the following in its 2000 annual report:

> *From time to time, the Board of Directors authorizes the company to repurchase IBM common stock. The company repurchased 61,041,820 common shares at a cost of $6.7 billion and 71,618,800 common shares at a cost of $7.3 billion in 2000 and 1999, respectively.*

Given that IBM had 1.9 billion shares outstanding at year-end 2000, you can see that the firm repurchased about 4% of its shares each year. Note also that the $7 billion per year being used to repurchase shares is far in excess of the approximately $900 million paid out in dividends to shareholders each year. The buyback is similar to a dividend in that both transfer money from the firm to its shareholders and both reduce stockholder's equity. Unlike the dividend, the buyback also reduces the number of shares outstanding and therefore tends to increase the earnings per share being reported. Consider IBM. Reported earnings per share were $4.58 in 2000. If 4% more shares had been outstanding during the year, earnings per share would have been about $4.40.

RETIREMENT OF SHARES

Once shares have been repurchased, they may be retired or held for reissue. Suppose the Board of Allstar Company purchases and retires 5% of its outstanding shares at $150 for a total of 5,000 × $150, or $750,000 cash. These shares were originally issued at $50 per share. The total stockholders' equity is reduced because the $750,000 is charged against the common stock, additional paid-in capital, and retained income accounts. The stock certificates are canceled, and the shares are no longer considered either outstanding or issued as shown in panel A of Exhibit 11-6.

The journal entry reverses the original average paid-in capital per share and charges the additional amount to retained income:

Common stock	50,000	
Additional paid-in capital	200,000	
Retained income	500,000	
Cash		750,000

To record retirement of 5,000 shares of stock for
$150 cash per share. The paid-in capital is
$50 per share ($10 par value + $40 additional
paid-in capital), so the additional $100 per share is
debited to retained income

Exhibit 11-6
Stock Repurchase

PANEL A: REPURCHASED SHARES RETIRED			
	Before Repurchase of 5% of Outstanding Shares	**Changes Because of Retirement**	**After Repurchase of 5% of Outstanding Shares**
Common stock, 100,000 shares @ $10 par	$ 1,000,000	{ −(5,000 shares @ $10 par) = −$50,000	$ 950,000
Additional paid-in capital	4,000,000	{ −(5,000 shares @ $40) = −$200,000	3,800,000
Total paid-in capital	$ 5,000,000	{ −(5,000 @ $100*) = −$500,000	$ 4,750,000
Retained income	6,000,000		5,500,000
Stockholders' equity	$11,000,000		$10,250,000
Book value per common share:			
$11,000,000 ÷ 100,000	$ 110.00		
$10,250,000 ÷ 95,000			$ 107.89

*$150 acquisition price − the $50 (or $10 + $40) originally paid in.

PANEL B: REPURCHASED SHARES HELD AS TREASURY STOCK			
	Before Repurchase of 5% of Outstanding Shares	**Changes Because of Treasury Stock**	**After Repurchase of 5% of Outstanding Shares**
Common stock, 100,000 shares @ $10 par	$ 1,000,000		$ 1,000,000
Additional paid-in capital	4,000,000		4,000,000
Total paid-in capital	$ 5,000,000		$ 5,000,000
Retained income	6,000,000		6,000,000
Total	$11,000,000		$11,000,000
Deduct:			
Cost of treasury stock	—	−$750,000	750,000
Stockholders' equity	$11,000,000		$10,250,000

Book value per common share is calculated on shares outstanding and is identical to the values in panel A.

Note how the book value per share of the outstanding shares has declined from $110.00 to $107.89. The phenomenon is called dilution of the common shareholders' equity. **Dilution** is usually defined as a reduction in shareholders' equity per share or earnings per share that arises from some changes among shareholders' proportionate interests. As a rule, boards of directors avoid dilution. However, boards sometimes favor deliberate dilution if expected future profits will more than compensate for a temporary undesirable reduction in book value per share.

dilution Reduction in stockholders' equity per share or earnings per share that arises from some changes among shareholders' proportional interests.

When IBM repurchased shares in 2000 and 1999 the repurchases were treated differently, than they were in 1998 as the notes disclosed:

> *In 2000 and 1999, the company did not retire the shares it repurchased. . . . The 1998 repurchases resulted in a reduction of $28,498,409 in the stated capital (par value) associated with common stock. In 1998, the company retired the repurchased shares and restored them to the status of authorized but unissued shares.*

TREASURY STOCK

Suppose Allstar's board of directors decides that the 5,000 repurchased shares are classified as treasury stock that will be held only temporarily and then resold. Perhaps the shares are needed for an employee stock purchase plan or for executive stock options. The repurchase decreases stockholders' equity and it is not considered an asset. Why is treasury stock not an asset while it is being held by the company? Because it generates no revenues. Cash dividends are not paid on shares held in the treasury because treasury stock is not considered outstanding:

Shares issued	100,000
Less: Treasury stock	5,000
Total shares outstanding	95,000

If treasury stock is not an asset, then what is it? The Treasury Stock account is a contra account to Owners' Equity just as Accumulated Depreciation is a contra account to related asset accounts. As with the retirement of shares, the purchase of treasury stock decreases stockholders' equity by $750,000 (5,000 shares purchased at $150 per share). Unlike the accounting for retirements, though, common stock at par value, additional paid-in capital, and retained income remain untouched by treasury stock purchases. A separate treasury stock account is a deduction from total stockholders' equity on the balance sheet. Allstar's stockholders' equity section would be affected as shown in panel B of Exhibit 11-6.

Remember that treasury stock is not an asset. A company's holding of shares in another company is an asset; its holding of its own shares is a negative element of stockholders' equity.

Treasury shares are usually resold at a later date, perhaps through an employee stock purchase plan. The sales price usually differs from the acquisition cost. Exhibit 11-7 shows the outcomes when these treasury shares are reissued. Panel A shows the journal entries if reissued at $180 (above the $150 acquisition cost) and panel B shows the result if reissued at $120 (below the $150 acquisition cost). Panel C contains the different shareholder equity sections for each outcome.

The specific accounting practices for transactions in the company's own stock may vary from company to company. Some companies use a last-in, first-out (LIFO) cost flow assumption for treasury shares, some use a first-in, first-out (FIFO) assumption, and some use average cost. Some companies have multiple paid-in-capital accounts and track changes from treasury stock shares in a special account called additional paid-in-capital from treasury stock transactions. However, one rule remains constant. Differences between the acquisition costs and the resale proceeds of treasury stock must never be

Exhibit 11-7

Reissuance of Treasury Shares

Allstar Repurchased 5,000 Shares for $150 per Share Creating a Treasury Stock Balance of $750,000

PANEL A: REISSUE AT $180 PER SHARE		
Cash	900,000	
Treasury stock		750,000
Additional paid-in-capital		150,000

PANEL B: REISSUE AT $120 PER SHARE		
Cash	600,000	
Additional paid-in-capital	150,000	
Treasury stock		750,000

PANEL C: COMPARATIVE BALANCES

	With 5,000 Shares in Treasury @ $150	Reissued @ $180	Reissued @ $120
Common stock	$ 1,000,000	$ 1,000,000	$ 1,000,000
Additional paid-in-capital	4,000,000	4,150,000	3,850,000
	5,000,000	5,150,000	4,850,000
Retained income	6,000,000	6,000,000	6,000,000
Deduct treasury stock	(750,000)		
	$10,250,000	$11,150,000	$10,850,000

reported as expenses, losses, revenues, or gains in the income statement. Why? A corporation's own capital stock is part of its capital structure. It is not an asset of the corporation. A company cannot make profits or losses by buying or selling its own common stock.

There is no important difference between unissued shares and treasury shares. In our example, Allstar could accomplish the same objective by (1) acquiring 5,000 shares, retiring them, and issuing 5,000 "new" shares, or (2) acquiring 5,000 shares and reselling them. While some account balances within stockholders' equity would differ under these alternatives, neither the number of shares outstanding nor the total stockholders' equity would change.

EFFECTS OF REPURCHASES ON EARNINGS PER SHARE

When shares are repurchased and retired or put in treasury, the number of shares outstanding is reduced. This reduction tends to increase earnings per share. For example, suppose that Allstar were generating net income of $950,000 each year. Assume further that the use of $750,000 to repurchase shares would not reduce future net income. Under these circumstances, earnings per share would rise as a result of repurchasing shares:

EPS = net income ÷ average number of shares outstanding				
Before repurchase	$950,000	÷	100,000 shares	= $ 9.50
After purchase	$950,000	÷	95,000 shares	= $10.00

If the same $750,000 were used to pay dividends, the number of shares would remain at 100,000 and the earnings per share (EPS) would remain at $9.50. Note that the only time a repurchase lowers earnings per share is when using cash to repurchase shares leads to lower future earnings.

Cash to Shareholder's: Dividends Vs Buy Backs

During the 2 years 1999 and 1998, total net income for the Coca-Cola Company was $5.9 billion. What did Coca-Cola do with this $5.9 billion in assets generated? It is not surprising that some of it was distributed to shareholders in the form of cash dividends. Total cash dividends were $3.1 billion, resulting in a dividend pay-out ratio (cash dividends to net income) of 53%. What may be a bit surprising is that during this same period, Coca-Cola used $1.6 billion to buy back its own stock.

We often think that cash dividends are the primary method corporations employ to distribute cash to shareholders, but frequently cash used in stock purchases exceeds the amount paid in cash dividends. This was true for Coca-Cola in 1998. One reason firms give is that idle resources within the company could be more efficiently used by individual shareholders. If the excess cash were paid in dividends, all investors would receive cash proportional to their ownership. Some might get more cash than they want or need and would simply turn around and reinvest it. All shareholders would have increased income taxes to pay. In contrast, a share buyback allows shareholders who want cash to sell their shares and raise the cash. These same shareholders are taxed only on their gain, the excess of the price received over the cost incurred historically to acquire the shares.

Another big advantage to the company in returning cash to investors through a buyback is that the size and timing of the buyback are both very flexible. In contrast, if the dividend is increased, it leads to an expectation of maintained high future dividends and it locks the company into the regular quarterly payment pattern.

Firms also use stock purchases to demonstrate confidence in their own prospects. Managers think that investors are more likely to believe company claims of rosy prospects if the investors see the company "putting its money where its mouth is" by buying its own shares. This tactic was employed extensively in the wake of the market crash of October 1987. At the time, in a bid to prop up falling share prices, over 600 firms announced plans to repurchase their own shares. When share prices recovered more quickly than expected, many firms decided not to complete their buyback program. As IBM noted in its 1999 annual report, "From time to time, the Board of Directors authorizes the company to repurchase IBM common stock."

Sources: 1999 Annual Reports of the Coca-Cola Company and IBM.

As an investor would you rather invest in a company that distributes cash via dividends or share repurchases?

ANSWER

The text identifies several issues. A key issue is that investors have more flexibility and better tax treatment with share repurchases than with dividends. With a repurchase, investors sell and convert shares to cash only if they want the cash. If they choose to sell some shares, they may get the low long-term capital gains tax rate on just the gain (if any) on the shares since they purchased them. If the company distributes a dividend, shareholders pay ordinary tax rates on the full amount. Further, if the investors want to maintain their same level of investment in the stock, they must also go to the stock market to buy shares and pay commissions to reinvest the after-tax dollars remaining. Notice that from an accounting standpoint the two alternatives do not have different effects on total stockholders' equity, although they may affect various accounts within stockholders' equity differently. Dividends reduce only retained earnings, whereas the effect of share repurchases depends on the book value of the shares, the market value of the shares, and whether they are retired or held in treasury.

Not all common stock is issued in exchange for cash. In some cases, a company will trade its shares for other assets. In other cases, another corporate security—a bond or preferred stock—is converted to common stock.

Objective 7
Record conversions of debt for equity or of preferred stock into common stock.

NONCASH EXCHANGES

Often a company issues its stock to acquire land, a building, or common stock of another company, or to compensate a person or company for services received. Such exchanges raise the question of the proper dollar value of the transaction to be recorded in both the buyer's and the seller's books. The proper amount is the "fair value" of either the securities or the exchanged assets or services, whichever is easier to determine objectively. This amount should be used by both companies.

CONVERSION OF SECURITIES

When companies issue convertible bonds or convertible preferred stock, the conversion feature makes the securities more attractive to investors and increases the price the issuer receives (or, equivalently, reduces the interest or dividend it must pay). Ultimately, the buyer or some subsequent owner may exercise the conversion privilege. For the issuer the accounts are simply adjusted as if the common stock had been issued initially. This may have significant effects on the companies' proportion of debt and equity and may eliminate some substantial cash commitments previously associated with interest or dividend payments.

For example, suppose Purchaser Company had paid $160,000 for an investment in 5,000 shares of the $1 par value convertible preferred stock of Issuer Company in 20X1. The preferred stock was converted into 10,000 shares of Issuer Company common stock ($1 par value) in 20X8. The accounts of Issuer Company would be affected as shown in Exhibit 11-8.

Purchaser Company has also experienced a change in form of the investment, with no change in historical cost. The carrying value, or book value, of the investment remains $160,000. To show that the form of the investment is now common stock instead of preferred stock, Purchaser Company might use a journal entry to transfer the $160,000 from one investment account to another. Alternatively, it might change subsidiary records that document the composition of a single general ledger account called Investments.

TRACKING STOCK

Sometimes companies issue tracking stock based on one of the parts of the company. Tracking stock is in some ways similar to common stock in that the company can produce separate financial statements for the subunit, it can pay dividends on the tracking stock, and it can issue stock options to employees based on the tracking stock. These tracking shares trade on stock markets just as common shares do. Early examples were created by General Motors (GM) as separate shares for its EDS unit and for Hughes Electronic Corporation. Lately, the concept has become very popular. These shares are viewed as a way to highlight a fast-growing subunit of the business. Thus, Sprint issued Sprint PCS as a tracking stock tied to its wireless business and many companies have created or are contemplating tracking stock tied to their Web ventures, including JCPenney, and Barnes & Noble.

The problem with these shares is that they do not represent voting rights in a separate company and the board of directors of the parent company has great freedom in making

Exhibit 11-8

Analysis of Convertible Preferred Stock

	Assets	=	Liabilities	+	Stockholders' Equity			
	Cash				Preferred Stock	Additional Paid-in Capital, Preferred	Common Stock	Additional Paid-in Capital, Common
Issuance of preferred (20X1)	+ 160,000	=			+5,000	+155,000		
Conversion of preferred (20X8)		=			−5,000	−155,000	+10,000	+150,000

The journal entries would be as follows:

On Issuer's Books

20X1 Cash	160,000	
Preferred stock, convertible		5,000
Additional paid-in capital, preferred		155,000
To record issuance of 5,000 shares of $1 par preferred stock convertible into two common shares for one preferred share		
20X8 Preferred stock, convertible	5,000	
Additional paid-in capital, preferred	155,000	
Common stock		10,000
Additional paid-in capital, common		150,000
To record the conversion of 5,000 preferred shares to 10,000 common shares		

decisions that favor or harm the investors in the subunit. For example, when GM converted the tracking shares on EDS to real shares in a separate company and separated it from GM, it first extracted a $500 million payment from EDS. The total market value of EDS fell by that $500 million and the holders of the tracking stock suffered the loss. Their lawsuit against GM for damages failed. Similarly, when MCI Worldcom and Sprint recently agreed to merge, Sprint shareholders experienced a surge in the value of their investment while shareholders in the tracking stock for Sprint wireless found the value of their shares falling.

RETAINED INCOME RESTRICTIONS

Boards of directors can make decisions that benefit shareholders but hurt creditors. For example, directors might pay such large dividends that payments of creditors' claims would be threatened. To protect creditors, dividend-declaring power is restricted by either state law or contractual obligations, or both. Moreover, boards of directors can voluntarily restrict their declarations of dividends.

States typically do not permit dividends to be declared if those dividends would cause stockholders' equity to be less than total paid-in capital or if stockholders' equity is already less than total paid-in capital. Therefore, retained income must exceed the cost of treasury stock. If there is no treasury stock, retained income must be positive. This restriction limits dividend payments and thus protects the position of the creditors. For example, consider the following ($ in millions):

	Before Dividends	After Dividend Payments of $10	After Dividend Payments of $4
Paid-in capital	$25	$25	$25
Retained income	10	—	6
Total	$35	$25	$31
Deduct:			
Cost of treasury stock	6	6	6
Stockholders' equity	$29	$19	$25

Without restricting dividends to the amount of retained income in excess of cost of the treasury stock, the corporation could pay a dividend of $10 million. This would reduce the stockholders' equity below the paid-in capital of $25 million. With the restriction, unrestricted retained income (and maximum legal payment of dividends) would be $10 million − $6 million, or $4 million. In this case, the existence of treasury stock creates a restriction on the company's ability to declare dividends. The restricted retained income cannot be reduced by dividend declarations.

Most of the time, restrictions of retained income are disclosed by footnotes. Occasionally, restrictions appear as a line item on the balance sheet called **restricted retained income.** Restrictions of retained income are also sometimes called **appropriated retained income** or reserves. The term *reserve* can be misleading. Accountants never use the word reserve to indicate cash set aside for a particular purpose; instead they call such assets a fund. The word **reserve** has one of three broad meanings in accounting: (1) restrictions of dividend declarations, (2) an offset to an asset, or (3) an estimate of a definite liability of indefinite or uncertain amount. An acknowledgment of a restriction on dividend payments is contained in the following reference from a recent Coherent, Inc. annual report:

> *The Company's domestic lines of credit are generally subject to standard covenants related to financial ratios, profitability and dividend payments.*

The United States limits the use of retained earnings reserves. Restrictions tend to arise through state law or contractual agreements. Some other countries, among them France, Germany, the Netherlands, and Japan, allow purely discretionary reserves to be reported. The idea is to disclose specific intentions of management. An international company might use a "reserve for plant expansion" to communicate an intention to reinvest future earnings in new technology instead of increase dividends.

restricted retained income (appropriated retained income) Any part of retained income that may not be reduced by dividend declarations.

reserve Has one of three meanings: (1) a restriction of dividend-declaring power as denoted by a specific subdivision of retained income, (2) an offset to an asset, or (3) an estimate of a definite liability of indefinite or uncertain amount.

OTHER COMPONENTS OF STOCKHOLDERS' EQUITY

Two other elements commonly appear in stockholders' equity and deserve brief mention here. The McDonald's shareholders' equity in Exhibit 11-1 included a deduction of $886.8 million labeled Accumulated Other Comprehensive Income. For McDonald's, a major portion of this item relates to foreign currency translation adjustments. These amounts arise when a company has subsidiary companies in another country. The process of translating Mexican pesos or French francs into U.S. dollars gives rise to some adjustments that affect shareholders' equity. These are discussed in chapter 14. Another potential contributor to other comprehensive income relates to certain unrealized investment gains and losses that are discussed in chapter 12.

The other element of McDonald's shareholders' equity that we have not discussed explicitly is the Unearned Employee Stock Ownership Plan (ESOP) Compensation.

McDonald's is one of many companies that enhances the commitment of its employees to work hard and provide good service by rewarding them with shares of stock. When an ESOP is set up, companies create a separate entity to hold shares on behalf of the employees and create a schedule for future allocations of shares to specific employees. The details of the accounting are beyond our scope, but these programs have become so common that it is important to realize their existence. Some companies, such as United Parcel Service and United Airlines, are primarily owned by the employees, but many companies have significant employee ownership.

FINANCIAL RATIOS RELATED TO STOCKHOLDERS' EQUITY

Objective 8
Use the rate of return on common equity and book value per share.

rate of return on common equity (ROE) Net income less preferred dividends divided by average common equity.

As we have already seen, many ratios aid in evaluating the performance of a company. Not surprisingly, many questions pertaining to stockholders' equity can be answered with ratios. One important question is: How effectively does the company use resources provided by the shareholders? To assess this, analysts relate the net income generated by the firm to the historic investment by its shareholders. The **rate of return on common equity (ROE)** is defined as:

$$\text{Rate of return on common equity} = \frac{\text{Net income} - \text{Preferred dividends}}{\text{Average common equity}}$$

The rate of return on common equity is naturally of great interest to common stockholders. The rate focuses on the company's profitability based on the book value of the common equity. To determine the numerator of the ratio, preferred dividends are subtracted from net income to obtain net income available for common stock. The denominator is the average of the beginning and ending common equity balances. Note that the common equity balance is the total stockholders' equity less the preferred stock at book value. If the liquidating value of a company's preferred stock exceeds the stock's book value, the liquidating value is deducted from the total stockholders' equity to determine the common equity balance. The calculations for Calvin Company are presented in Exhibit 11-9 in which panel A presents comparative stockholders' equity for 2 years together with earnings information and panel B uses that information to calculate ROE.

ROE varies considerably among companies and industries, as follows:

	1999	1996	1993
McDonald's	20.4	19.5	19.0
IBM	38.5	24.8	*
PepsiCo	32.4	16	27
ExxonMobil[†]	12.6	16.0	12.3
DaimlerChrysler[‡]	14.2	31	*

*Denotes a loss year.

[†]ExxonMobil values in 1999, premerger values for Mobil for 1996 and 1993

[‡]DaimlerChrysler values in 1999, premerger values for Chrysler for 1996 and 1993.

ROE patterns can be evaluated in several ways. McDonald's demonstrates a high stable level. In contrast, IBM and Chrysler have highly variable ROE, in part due to losses in 1993. This might arise from difficult business activity, but it is also sometimes related to changes in accounting practice. In chapter 9, we discussed the changes in accounting practice for postretirement benefits. This caused many companies to record very large

Exhibit 11-9

Calvin Company Owners' Equity

PANEL A

	December 31	
	20X2	*20X1*
Stockholders' equity		
10% preferred stock, 100,000 shares, $100 par	$ 10,000,000	$ 10,000,000
Common stock, 5,000,000 shares, $1 par	5,000,000	5,000,000
Additional paid-in capital	35,000,000	35,000,000
Retained income	87,000,000	83,000,000
Total stockholders' equity	$137,400,000	$133,400,000
Net income for the year ended Dec. 31, 20X2	$11,000,000	
Preferred dividends @ $10 per share	1,000,000	
Net income available for common stock	$10,000,000	

PANEL B: ROE

$$\text{Rate of return on common equity} = \frac{\text{Net income} - \text{Preferred dividends}}{\text{Average common equity}}$$

$$= \frac{\$11,000,000 - \$1,000,000}{\frac{1}{2}[(\$133,000,000 - \$10,000,000) + (\$137,400,000 - \$10,000,000)]}$$

$$= \frac{\$10,000,000}{\frac{1}{2}(\$123,000,000 + \$127,400,000)}$$

$$= \frac{\$10,000,000}{\$125,200,000} = 8.0\%$$

one-time expense items. This fact explains Chrysler's 1993 loss. Chrysler recorded a $5 billion charge for the accounting change in 1993 and would have had a ROE of more than 30% that year without the change. On the other hand, further investigation of IBM reveals that its 1993 loss had little to do with the accounting change.

The book value of a company refers to the stockholders' equity, often expressed on a per share basis. When preferred stock is present, the calculation of the **book value per share of common stock** adjusts for the preferred as follows:

book value per share of common stock Stockholders' equity attributable to common stock divided by the number of shares outstanding.

$$\begin{aligned}\text{Book value per share} \\ \text{of common stock}\end{aligned} = \frac{\begin{aligned}\text{Total stockholders' equity} \\ - \text{ Book value of preferred stock}\end{aligned}}{\text{Number of common shares outstanding}}$$

$$= \frac{\$137,400,000 - \$10,000,000}{5,000,000} = \$25.48$$

Suppose the market value for this stock is $35. Note that the book value is much lower than the market value. Shareholders who are paying market value for the stock are paying for what they think future earning power will be instead of the historical cost of assets. Book values are not always useful because they are based on balance sheet values, which show the historical cost of assets. The current value of those assets may differ greatly from their historical cost. As a result, some companies consistently have market prices in excess of book values, or vice versa. Comparing book values with market values is useful because it often reveals the causes behind the difference in values. Many investors express the relation between market and book value as a ratio. For example, in June 2000, Merck had a 1999 book value of about $5.69 and a market value per share over 10 times as large ($74). This produces a **market-to-book ratio** of 13.01 ($74 ÷ $5.69).

market-to-book ratio
Market value per share divided by book value per share.

What do these differences in values mean in the real world? A market value well above the book value may be appropriate if the company has many unrecorded assets or appreciated assets. For example, Merck has valuable patents on various drugs and additional research under way that are not reflected in the book values. Coca-Cola's mid-2000 market value of about $55 substantially exceeded its book value of about $3.85 producing a market-to-book ratio of 14. Why? Presumably, this difference reflects beliefs of investors that Coca-Cola will be able to continue its long-term pattern of rapid sales growth and high return on equity. However, current growth and ROE are well below Coca-Cola's historical levels. In 1997, its market-to-book ratio was 24, consistent with its 10-year average ROE levels of over 40%. ROE in 1999 fell to 25.6%. Variability over time is common. In mid-1992, Ford Motor Company had a $5 market value, a figure below its $5.50 book value. The market-to-book ratio was below one. During a series of bad years for auto sales, Ford suffered losses, had negative ROE, and cut its dividend payment sharply. The market price per share indicated a belief that Ford's production plants and other assets could not be liquidated for their book value. By 1996, Ford had recovered well with a share price ranging from $15 to $20 while book value per share had about doubled to $10. In 1999, Ford was trading around $50 per share with a book value of $22.50. Its ROE had risen to 26.3%.

SUMMARY PROBLEMS FOR YOUR REVIEW

PROBLEM ONE

From the following data, prepare a detailed statement of stockholders' equity for Sample Corporation, December 31, 20X1:

Additional paid-in capital, preferred stock	$ 50,000
Additional paid-in capital, common stock	1,000,000
9% preferred stock, $50 par value, callable at $55, authorized 20,000 shares, issued and outstanding 12,000 shares	
Common stock, no par, stated value $2 per share, authorized 500,000 shares, issued 400,000 shares of which 25,000 shares are held in the treasury	
Dividends payable	90,000
Retained income	2,000,000

The 25,000 shares of treasury stock cost $250,000.

SOLUTION TO PROBLEM ONE

Dividends payable is a liability. It must therefore be excluded from a statement of stockholders' equity:

Sample Corporation Statement of Stockholders' Equity, December 31, 20X1

9% preferred stock, $50 par value, callable at $55, authorized 20,000 shares, issued and outstanding 12,000 shares		$ 600,000
Common stock, no par, stated value $2 per share, authorized 500,000 shares, issued 400,000 shares of which 25,000 shares are held in the treasury		800,000
Additional paid-in capital		
Preferred	$ 50,000	
Common	1,000,000	1,050,000*
Retained income		2,000,000
Subtotal		$4,450,000
Less: Cost of 25,000 shares of common stock reacquired and held in treasury		250,000
Total stockholders' equity		$4,200,000

*Many presentations would not show the detailed breakdown of additional paid-in capital into preferred and common portions.

PROBLEM TWO

B Company splits its $10 par common stock five-for-one. How will its balance sheet and its earnings per share be affected? Assume 2,000 shares are originally outstanding. How would your answer change if the company said that it "accounted for" the split as a stock dividend?

SOLUTION TO PROBLEM TWO

The total amount of stockholders' equity would be unaffected, but there would be 10,000 outstanding shares at $2 par instead of 2,000 shares at $10 par. Earnings per share would be one-fifth of that previously reported, assuming no change in total net income applicable to the common stock.

If the question were framed as "the company recently issued a five-for-one stock split accounted for as a stock dividend," then the par value per share would be retained, and a journal entry would increase the par value account for common stock by $80,000 (8,000 additional shares times $10 par value per share):

Retained earnings	80,000	
Common stock at par		80,000

PROBLEM THREE

C Company distributes a 2% stock dividend on its 1 million outstanding $5 par common shares. The stockholders' equity section before the dividend was:

Common stock, 1,000,000 shares @ $5 par	$ 5,000,000
Additional paid-in capital in excess of par	20,000,000
Retained income	75,000,000
Total stockholders' equity	$100,000,000

The common stock was selling on the open market for $150 per share when the dividend was distributed. How will the stockholders' equity section be affected? If net income were $10.2 million next year, what would be the earnings per share before considering the effects of the stock dividend, and after considering the effects of the stock dividend?

Solution to Problem Three

	Before 2% Stock Dividend	Changes	After 2% Stock Dividend
Common stock, 1,000,000 shares @ $5 par	$ 5,000,000	+(20,000 @ $5)	$ 5,100,000
Additional paid-in capital	20,000,000	+[20,000 @ ($150 − $5)]	22,900,000
Retained income	75,000,000	−(20,000 @ $150)	72,000,000
Total	$100,000,000		$100,000,000

Earnings per share before considering the effects of the stock dividend would be $10,200,000 ÷ 1,000,000, or $10.20. After the dividend: $10,200,000 ÷ 1,020,000, or $10.

Note that the dividend has no effect on net income, the numerator of the earnings-per-share computation. However, it does affect the denominator and causes a mild dilution that, in theory, should be reflected by a slight decline in the market price of the stock.

Problem Four

Metro-Goldwyn-Mayer Film Company declared and distributed a 3% stock dividend. The applicable market value per share was $7.75. The par value of the 966,000 additional shares issued was $1.00 each. The total cash paid to shareholders in lieu of issuing fractional shares was $70,000. Prepare the appropriate journal entry.

Solution to Problem Four

Retained income	7,556,500	
Common stock, $1.00 par value		966,000
Capital in excess of par value		6,520,500
Cash		70,000

To record 3% stock dividend, total shares issued, 966,000 at $7.75, a total market value of $7,486,500. In addition, cash of $70,000 was paid in lieu of issuing fractional shares, total charge to retained earnings was $70,000 + (966,000 × $7.75) = $7,556,500. The account Capital in Excess of Par Value was the description actually used by MGM

Highlights to Remember

1. **Describe the rights of shareholders.** On the balance sheet, stockholders' equity is reported as the book values of the residual interests of a corporation's owners. By incorporating, the company provides limited liability for its owners and provides them with various rights, including the right to vote for the board of directors. Among equity holders, preferred shareholders have more senior claims to dividends and may have other special rights, including cumulative dividends, participating dividends, conversion privileges, and preference in liquidation. Preferred stocks are like bonds.

2. **Differentiate among authorized, issued, and outstanding shares.** Authorized shares are those that the company may issue based on the articles of incorporation of the corporation. Issued shares are those that the company has issued and must be equal to, or less than, the authorized number. Outstanding shares are those that the company has issued and has not repurchased for the treasury and must be equal to, or less than, the issued shares.

3. **Contrast bonds, preferred stock, and common stock.** Bonds, preferred stock and common stock are all claims on the assets of the corporation. Bonds are the senior claim and are specific legal obligations with required dates for payment of interest and repayment of principal. Preferred stock may have many specific rights attached to it, but dividends become obligations only when the board of directors declares them and preferred stock typically has no maturity date. Preferred shareholders typically receive dividends and repayment of principal before common shareholders. Common stock is often called the residual claim because common shareholders typically receive what is left after all other obligations are paid. In liquidation of a failed company, common shareholders may receive little or nothing. On the other hand, when a company grows rapidly and prospers, the value of the common stock may increase much more than the value of either bonds or preferred stock.

4. **Identify the economic characteristics of and account for stock splits.** Stock splits alter the number of shares held by the owners, without altering the economic claims of the shareholders. As a result, typically no change occurs in the total market value of the company, but the value of individual shares changes in proportion to the size of the split or dividend. A two-for-one split would typically cause the market price of the shares to decline by 50%.

5. **Account for both large-percentage and small-percentage stock dividends.** Accounting for stock dividends involves rearranging the owners' equity account balances. Par value accounts, paid-in capital accounts, and retained earnings may be rearranged without changing the total owners' equity. The exact procedure depends on whether the par value of the new shares changes and on the number of additional shares. Similarly, a rearrangement of owners' equity arises when convertible preferred shares are exchanged for common shares.

6. **Explain and report stock repurchases and other treasury stock transactions.** Companies sometimes acquire treasury stock, which are shares of their own stock purchased in the open market. These shares may later be retired, resold, or used to meet obligations under option agreements. Transactions in the company's own stock never give rise to gains and losses and do not affect the income statement. Such transactions with the shareholders give rise only to changes in the equity accounts.

7. **Record conversions of debt for equity or of preferred stock into common stock.** Generally, when debt or preferred stock is converted into common stock, the book values of the debt or preferred are transferred into owners' equity. Part is shown as par or stated value and the remainder, as additional-paid-in capital.

8. **Use the rate of return on common equity and book value per share.** Security analysts use the return on common stockholders' equity as a primary ratio to assess the effectiveness of management and the profitability of the firm. Higher is better. Analysts often compare the market value per share with the book value per share. A high ratio of market value to book value should be associated with growth prospects and possibly unrecorded assets, such as internally developed patents.

Accounting Vocabulary

Assignment Material

QUESTIONS

11-1 What is the purpose of preemptive rights?

11-2 "Common shareholders have limited liability." Explain.

11-3 Can a share of common stock be outstanding but not authorized or issued? Why?

11-4 "Treasury stock is unissued stock." Do you agree? Explain.

11-5 "Cumulative dividends are liabilities that must be paid to preferred shareholders before any dividends are paid to common shareholders." Do you agree? Explain.

11-6 "The liquidating value of preferred stock is the amount of cash for which it can currently be exchanged." Do you agree? Explain.

11-7 What are convertible securities?

11-8 In what way is preferred stock similar to debt, and to common stock?

11-9 Which are riskier, bonds or preferred stock? Why? Whose perspective are you taking, the issuer's or the investor's?

11-10 Why do some accountants want to record an expense when a company grants stock options to its employees?

11-11 Why do you suppose companies offer their employees stock options instead of simply paying higher salaries?

11-12 "The only real dividends are cash dividends." Do you agree? Explain.

11-13 "A 2% stock dividend increases every shareholder's fractional portion of the company by 2%." Do you agree? Explain.

11-14 "A stock split can be achieved by means of a stock dividend." Do you agree? Explain.

11-15 "When companies repurchase their own shares, the accounting depends on the purpose for which the shares are purchased." Explain.

11-16 "When a company retires shares, it must pay the stockholders an amount equal to the original par value and additional capital contributed for those shares plus the stockholders' fractional portion of retained earnings." Do you agree? Explain.

11-17 Why might a company decide to buy back its own shares instead of paying additional cash dividends?

11-18 "Treasury stock is not an asset." Explain.

11-19 "Gains and losses are not possible from a corporation's acquiring or selling its own stock." Do you agree? Explain.

11-20 What is the proper measure for an asset newly acquired through an exchange (e.g., an exchange of land for securities)? Explain.

11-21 Why does a conversion option make bonds or preferred stock more attractive to investors?

11-22 Restrictions on dividend-declaring power may be voluntary or involuntary. Given an example of each.

11-23 Why might a board of directors voluntarily restrict its dividend-declaring power?

11-24 "A company's return on equity (ROE) indicates how much return an investor makes on the investment in the company's shares." Do you agree? Explain.

11-25 "A common stock selling on the market far below its book value is an attractive buy." Do you agree? Explain.

COGNITIVE EXERCISES

11-26   Company Share Prices and Intentions to Repurchase Shares
Your friend has thought about repurchases of common stock by the issuing company and has concluded that this is unethical. Specifically, this friend says that the company knows more than you do and if the company decides to repurchase shares, they are taking advantage of shareholders. How do you respond?

11-27   The Prohibition on Income Recognition from Trading in the Company's Shares
Your friend has considered stock repurchases and thinks that it is proper for the company to buy its own shares and subsequently reissue them, recognizing a profit in doing so that should be reported on the income statement. How do you respond?

11-28   The Meaning of Par Value
Your friend has decided that par value is a meaningless notion and complicates accounting practice without adding value to the financial statements. How do you respond?

11-29 Changes in Stock Prices When the Shares Are Split

Your friend has developed a stock investing strategy that suggests you should always buy the shares of companies when they split their stock or issue large stock dividends. How do you respond?

EXERCISES

11-30 Distinctions between Terms

Disposal Services, Inc., a waste-management company, had 3 million shares of common stock authorized on August 31, 20X2. Shares issued were 2.1 million. There were 200,000 shares held in the treasury. How many shares were issued and outstanding? How many shares were unissued? Label your computations.

11-31 Distinctions between Terms

On January 1, 1999, IBM Corporation had 4,688 million shares of common stock authorized. There were 1,877 million shares issued, and 72 million shares held as treasury stock. How many shares were issued and outstanding? How many shares were unissued? Label your computations.

11-32 Preferences as to Assets

The following are account balances of Reliable Autos, Inc. ($ in thousands): common stock and retained income, $300; accounts payable, $300; preferred stock (5,000 shares; $20 par and $24 liquidating value per share), $100; subordinated debentures, $300; and unsubordinated debentures, $100. Prepare a table showing the distribution of the cash proceeds on liquidation and dissolution of the corporation. Assume cash proceeds of ($ in thousands): $1,500, $1,000, $790, $500, $400, and $200, respectively.

11-33 Issuance of Common Shares

Kawasaki Heavy Industries is a large Japanese company that makes ships, aircraft engines, and many other products in addition to motorcycles. Its 2000 sales of ¥1,150 billion are equivalent to $10,831 million. Kawasaki's balance sheet includes (yen in millions):

Common stock of ¥50 par value, 1,390,595,964 shares issued in 2000	81,427
Capital surplus	24,682

Required

1. Assume that all 1,390,595,964 shares had been issued at the same time. Prepare the journal entry.
2. Is the relationship between the size of the common stock and the size of the capital surplus different from what one might expect to find for a U.S. company? Explain.

11-34 Cumulative Dividends

The Ute Data Services Corporation was founded on January 1, 20X1.

Preferred stock, no par, cumulative $6 annual dividend per share	
Issued and outstanding, 1,000,000 shares	$ 40,000,000
Capital stock, no par, 6,000,000 shares	90,000,000
Total stockholders' equity	$130,000,000

The corporation's subsequent net incomes (losses) were:

20X1	$(5,000,000)
20X2	(4,000,000)
20X3	15,000,000
20X4	30,000,000
20X5	13,000,000

Assume that the board of directors declared dividends to the maximum extent permissible by law. The state prohibits dividend declarations that cause negative retained earnings.

1. Tabulate the annual dividend declarations on preferred and common shares. There is no treasury stock.
2. How would the total distribution to common shareholders change if the preferred were not cumulative?

11-35   Cumulative Dividends

In recent years, the Winslow Company had severe cash flow problems. In 20X4, the company suspended payment of cash dividends on common stock. In 20X5, it ceased payment on its $4 million of outstanding 8% cumulative preferred stock. No common or preferred dividends were paid in 20X5 or 20X6. In 20X7, Winslow's board of directors decided that $1.5 million was available for cash dividends.

Compute the preferred stock dividend and the common stock dividend for 20X7.

11-36   Cash Dividends

If you have a credit card, you have probably dealt with First Data Corporation without knowing it. First Data maintains data for more than 260 million credit and debit cards and processes 1 million credit and debit card transactions every hour. In 1999, First Data declared dividends of $.08 per share paid to an average of 446 million shares. First Data paid dividends every quarter, but for simplicity assume that they declared dividends only once in 1999, on November 15, payable on December 15, to stockholders of record on December 1.

Prepare the journal entries relating to the declaration and payment of dividends by First Data. Include the date on which each journal entry would be made.

11-37   Stock Options

Lyndon Systems granted its top executives options to purchase 5,000 shares of common stock (par $1) at $20 per share, the market price today. The options may be exercised over a 4-year span, starting 3 years hence. Suppose all options are exercised 3 years hence, when the market value of the stock is $30 per share.

Prepare the appropriate journal entry on the books of Lyndon Systems.

11-38   Stock Split

An annual report of Dean Foods Company included the following in the statement of consolidated retained earnings:

Charge for stock split	$4,401,000

The balance sheets before and after the split showed:

	After	Before
Common stock $1 par value	$13,203,000	$8,802,000

Define stock split. What did Dean Foods do to achieve its stock split? Does this conflict with your definition? Explain fully.

11-39   Reverse Stock Split

According to a news story, "The shareholders of QED approved a 1-for-10 reverse split of QED's common stock." Accounting for a reverse stock split applies the same principles as accounting for a regular stock split. QED Exploration, Incorporated was an oil-development company operating in Texas and Louisiana. QED's stockholders' equity section before the reverse split included:

Common stock, authorized 30,000,000 shares, issued 23,530,000 shares	$ 287,637
Additional paid-in capital	3,437,547
Retained income	2,220,895
Less treasury stock, at cost, 1,017,550 shares	(305,250)
Total stockholders' equity	$5,640,829

Required

1. Prepare QED's stockholders' equity section after the reverse stock split.
2. Comment on possible reasons for a reverse split.

11-40 Stock Dividends

Zemex Corporation, a Toronto-based natural resource company, included the following in a footnote to its 1999 financial statements:

Dividends

On October 2, 1998, the Corporation declared a 2% stock dividend to shareholders of record on October 19, 1998, which was paid November 2, 1998. Retained earnings was charged $1,182,000 as a result of the issuance of 165,537 of the Corporation's common shares, and cash payments of $5,000 in lieu of fractional shares.

Required

Prepare the journal entry to record Zemex's stock dividend. Assume a par value of $1 per share.

11-41 Treasury Stock

During 1996, UtiliCorp United, the electric and gas utility company based in Kansas City, repurchased 228,807 of its own shares at an average price of $27.97 per share and held them in the treasury. In 1998, the end of year balance in the treasury stock account was $53.2 and in 1999 it was $5.4.

Required

1. Prepare the journal entry for the 1996 purchase of treasury shares.
2. At the beginning of 1996, UtiliCorp had no treasury stock, and no treasury stock was reissued during 1996. Before accounting for treasury shares, UtiliCorp's total stockholders' equity at the end of 1996 was $1,164.4 million. Compute the total amount of stockholders' equity reported on the company's balance sheet at the end of 1996.
3. The sale of treasury stock in 1999 produced $986 million. Give the journal entry to record the reissuance of these shares.

11-42 Book Value and Return on Equity

Reach Company had net income of $11 million in 20X8. The stockholders' equity section of its 20X8 annual report follows ($ in millions):

	20X8	20X7
Stockholders' equity		
8% Preferred stock, $50 par value, 400,000 shares authorized, 300,000 shares issued	$ 15.0	$ 15.0
Common stock, $1 par, 5 million authorized, 2 million and 1.8 million issued	2.0	1.8
Additional paid-in capital	32.0	30.0
Retained earnings	70.0	65.2
Total stockholders' equity	$119.0	$112.0

Required

1. Compute the book value per share of common stock at the end of 20X8.
2. Compute the rate of return on common equity for 20X8.
3. Compute the amount of cash dividends on common stock declared during 20X8. (*Hint:* Examine the retained earnings T-account.)

11-43 Financial Ratios and Stockholders' Equity

Consider the following data for New York Bankcorp:

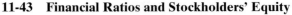

	December 31	
	20X2	*20X1*
Stockholders' equity		
Preferred stock, 200,000 shares,		
$20 par, liquidation value $22	$ 4,000,000	$ 4,000,000
Common stock, 4,000,000 shares,		
$2 par	8,000,000	8,000,000
Additional paid-in capital	5,000,000	5,000,000
Retained income	3,000,000	1,400,000
Total stockholders' equity	$20,000,000	$18,400,000

Net income was $3 million for 20X2. The preferred stock is 10%, cumulative. The regular annual dividend was declared on the preferred stock, and the common shareholders received dividends of $.25 per share. The market price of the common stock on December 31, 20X2 was $10.00 per share.

Required

Compute the following statistics for 20X2: rate of return on common equity, earnings per share of common stock, price–earnings ratio, dividend–payout ratio, dividend–yield ratio, and book value per share of common stock.

11-44 Stockholders' Equity Section

The following are data for the Roselli Corporation.

6% cumulative preferred stock, $40 par value, callable at $42, authorized 100,000 shares, issued and outstanding 80,000 shares	$ 3,200,000
Treasury stock, common (at cost)	4,000,000
Additional paid-in capital, common stock	9,000,000
Dividends payable	100,000
Retained income	15,000,000
Additional paid-in capital, preferred stock	2,000,000
Common stock, $2.50 par value per share, authorized 1.8 million shares, issued 1.2 million shares of which 60,000 are held in the treasury	3,000,000

Required

Prepare a detailed stockholders' equity section as it would appear in the balance sheet at December 31, 20X8.

11-45 Effects on Stockholders' Equity

Indicate the effect (+, −, or 0) on total stockholders' equity of General Services Corporation for each of the following:

1. Operating loss for the period of $900,000.
2. Sale of 100 shares of General Services by Jay Smith to Tom Jones.
3. Declaration of a stock dividend on common stock.
4. Issuance of a stock dividend on common stock.
5. Failing to declare a regular dividend on cumulative preferred stock.
6. Declaration of a cash dividend of $50,000 in total.
7. Payment of item 6.
8. Purchase of 10 shares of treasury stock for $1,000 cash.
9. Sale of treasury stock, purchased in item 8, for $1,200.
10. Sale of treasury stock, purchased in item 8, for $900.

PROBLEMS

11-46 Dividends and Cumulative Preferred Stock

Renton Interiors, Inc., maker of seats and other interior equipment for Boeing aircraft, started 20X8 with the following balance sheet.

6% Cumulative convertible preferred stock, par value $10 a share, authorized 150,000 shares; issued 52,136 shares	$ 521,360
Common stock, par value $.20 a share, authorized 2,000,000 shares, issued 1,322,850 shares	264,570
Additional paid-in capital	2,063,351
Retained income	2,463,951
Less: Treasury stock, at cost	
Preferred stock, 11,528 shares	(80,249)
Common stock, 93,091 shares	(167,549)
Total stockholders' equity	$5,065,434

Required

1. Suppose Renton Interiors had paid no dividends, preferred or common, in the prior year, 20X7. All preferred dividends had been paid through 20X6. Management decided at the end of 20X8 to pay $.05 per share common dividends. Calculate the preferred dividends that would be paid during 20X8. Prepare journal entries for recording both preferred and common dividends. Assume that no preferred or common shares were issued or purchased during 20X8.

2. Suppose 20X8 net income was $450,000. Compute the 20X8 ending balance in the Retained Income account.

11-47 Dividend Reinvestment Plans

Many corporations have automatic dividend reinvestment plans. Individual shareholders may elect not to receive their cash dividends. Instead, an equivalent amount of cash is invested in additional stock (at the current market value) that is issued to the shareholder.

The Coca-Cola Company had the following data at December 31, 1999 ($ in millions):

Coca-Cola Company

Common stock: authorized 5,600,000,000 shares; $.25 par value; issued 3,466,371,904 shares	$ 867
Capital surplus	2,584
Reinvested earnings	20,773
Accumulated other comprehensive income	(1,551)
	22,673
Less treasury stock, at cost (994,796,786 shares)	13,160
	$21,623

Required

1. Coca-Cola declared a quarterly cash dividend of $.16 per share. Suppose that holders of 10% of the company's shares decided to reinvest in the company under an automatic dividend reinvestment plan instead of accepting the cash. The market price of the shares on issuance was $50 per share. Prepare the journal entry (or entries) for these transactions. (*Note:* No dividends are paid on shares held in the treasury.)

2. A letter to the editor of *Business Week* commented:

   > *Stockholders participating in dividend reinvestment programs pay taxes on dividends not really received. If a company would refrain from paying dividends only to take them back as reinvestments, it would save paperwork, and the stockholder would save income tax.*

Do you agree with the writer's remarks? Explain in detail.

11-48 Dividends

(Alternate is 11-49.)

1. The Minneapolis Company issued 400,000 shares of common stock, $5 par, for $30 cash per share on March 31, 20X1. Prepare the journal entry.

2. Minneapolis Company declared and paid a cash dividend of $2 per share on March 31, 20X2. Prepare the journal entry.

3. Minneapolis Company had retained earnings of $9 million by March 31, 20X5. The market value of the common shares was $50 each. A common stock dividend of 5% was declared; the shares were issued on March 31, 20X5. Prepare the journal entry. Also present a tabulation that compares the stockholders' equity section before and after the declaration and issuance of the stock dividend. Also include at the bottom of the tabulation the effects on the overall market value of the stock, the total shares outstanding, and the number of shares and percentage of ownership of an individual owner who originally bought 6,000 shares.

4. What journal entries would be made by the investor who bought 6,000 shares of the Minneapolis common stock and held this investment throughout the time covered in requirements 1, 2, and 3?

5. Refer to requirement 4. Suppose the investor sold 200 shares for $58 each the day after receiving the stock dividend. Prepare the investor's journal entry for the sale of the shares.

11-49 Dividends
(Alternate is 11-48.)

1. Garcia Company issued 600,000 shares of common stock, $1 par, for $10 cash per share on December 31, 20X5. Prepare the journal entry.

2. Garcia Company declared and paid a cash dividend of $.50 per share on December 31, 20X6. Prepare the journal entry. Assume that only the 600,000 shares from part 1 are outstanding.

3. Garcia Company had retained earnings of $7 million by December 31, 20X9. The market value of the common shares was $30 each. A common stock dividend of 3% was declared; the shares were issued on December 31, 20X9. Prepare the journal entry. Also present a tabulation that compares the stockholders' equity section before and after the declaration and issuance of the stock dividend. Also include at the bottom of the tabulation the effects on the overall market value of the stock, the total shares outstanding, and the number of shares and percentage of ownership of an individual owner who originally bought 6,000 shares.

4. What journal entries would be made by the investor who bought 4,000 shares of Garcia Company common stock and held this investment throughout the time covered in requirements 1, 2, and 3?

5. Refer to requirement 4. Suppose the investor sold 100 shares for $33 each the day after receiving the stock dividend. Prepare the investor's journal entry for the sale of the shares.

11-50 Stock Options
AIM Telephones, Inc., was one of the top five independent telecommunications equipment suppliers in the United States. Net income for a recent year was $1,018,000, and AIM paid no cash dividends. During the year, AIM issued 538,522 new shares at an average price of $7.853 per share. In addition, executives exercised stock options for 99,813 shares at an average price of $2.304 per share. The stockholders' equity at the beginning of the year was:

Common stock, par value $.01 per share	$ 39,000
Capital in excess of par value	4,962,000
Retained earnings	1,182,000
Total stockholders' equity	$6,183,000

Required

1. Prepare journal entries for (a) the newly issued shares and (b) the stock options that were exercised. Omit explanations. Round calculations to the nearest thousand dollars.

2. Prepare a statement of stockholders' equity at the end of the year.

3. Suppose all the stock options were exercised when the stock price for AIM was $7.50 per share. How much did the executives gain from exercising the stock options?

4. How much compensation expense did AIM record when the options were granted? When they were exercised?

11-51 Meaning of Stock Splits

A letter of January 31 to shareholders of United Financial, a California savings and loan company, said:

> Once again, I want to take the opportunity of sending you some good news about recent developments at United Financial. Last week the board raised United's quarterly cash dividend $12\frac{1}{2}$ percent and then declared a 5-for-4 stock split in the form of a 25 percent stock dividend. The additional shares will be distributed on March 15 to shareholders of record February 15.

On March 16, the board approved a merger between National Steel Corporation and United Financial. The agreement called for a cash payment of $33.60 on each outstanding United Financial share. The original National Steel offer (in early February) was $42 per share for the 5.8 million shares outstanding.

Required

1. As a recipient of the letter of January 31, you were annoyed by the five-for-four stock split. Prepare a letter to the chairman indicating the reasons for your displeasure.
2. Prepare a response to the unhappy shareholder in requirement 1.
3. A shareholder of United Financial wrote to the chairman in early March: "I'm confused about the change in the agreed upon price per share. I owned 100 shares and thought I'd receive $4,200. Now the price has dropped from $42.00 to $33.60." Prepare a response to the shareholder.

11-52 Stock Dividend and Fractional Shares

The Soderstrom Company declared and distributed a 5% stock dividend. The stockholders' equity before the dividend was:

Common stock, 10,000,000 shares, $1 par	$ 10,000,000
Additional paid-in capital	40,000,000
Retained earnings	50,000,000
Total stockholders' equity	$100,000,000

The market price of Soderstrom's shares was $10 when the stock dividend was distributed. Soderstrom paid cash of $30,000 in lieu of issuing fractional shares.

Required

1. Prepare the journal entry for the declaration and distribution of the stock dividend.
2. Show the stockholders' equity section after the stock dividend.
3. How did the stock dividend affect total stockholders' equity? How did it affect the proportion of the company owned by each shareholder?

11-53 Issuance and Retirement of Shares, Cash Dividends

On January 2, 20X1, Chippewa Investment Company began business by issuing 10,000 shares at $1 par value for $100,000 cash. The cash was invested, and on December 26, 20X1 all investments were sold for $114,000 cash. Operating expenses for 20X1 were $4,000, all paid in cash. Therefore, net income for 20X1 was $10,000. On December 27, the board of directors declared a $.30 per share cash dividend, payable on January 15, 20X2 to owners of record on December 31, 20X1. On January 30, 20X2, the company bought and retired 1,000 of its own shares on the open market for $9.00 each.

Required

1. Prepare journal entries for issuance of shares, declaration and payment of cash dividends, and retirement of shares.
2. Prepare a balance sheet as of December 31, 20X1.

11-54 Issuance, Splits, Dividends

(Alternate is 11-55.)

Required

1. Lopez Company issued 100,000 shares of common stock, $5 par, for $37 cash per share on December 31, 20X1. Prepare the journal entry.
2. Lopez Company had accumulated earnings of $5 million by December 31, 20X5. The board of directors declared a two-for-one stock split and immediately exchanged two $2.50 par shares for each share outstanding. Prepare the journal entry, if any. Present the stockholders' equity section of the balance sheet before and after the split.

3. Repeat requirement 2, but assume that instead of exchanging two $2.50 par shares for each share outstanding, one additional $5 par share was issued for each share outstanding. Lopez said they issued a two-for-one stock split "accounted for as a stock dividend."

4. What journal entries would be made by the investor who bought 2,000 shares of Lopez Company common stock and held this investment throughout the time covered in requirements 1, 2, and 3?

11-55 Issuance, Splits, Dividends

(Alternate is 11-54.) AT&T's December 31, 1999 balance sheet showed total shareowners' equity of $78,927,000,000 and indicated the following detail:

Common stock, par value $1.00 per share	$3,196,000,000

Required

1. Suppose AT&T had originally issued 200 million shares of common stock, $1 par, for $15 cash per share many years ago, for instance, on December 31, 19X1. Prepare the journal entry.

2. AT&T had accumulated earnings of $5 billion by December 31, 19X5. The board of directors declared a two-for-one stock split and immediately exchanged two $.50 par shares for each share outstanding. Prepare the journal entry, if any. Present the stockholders' equity section of the balance sheet before and after the split.

3. Repeat requirement 2, but assume that one additional $1 par share was issued by AT&T for each share outstanding (instead of exchanging shares).

4. What journal entries would be made by the investor who bought 2,000 shares of AT&T common stock and held this investment throughout the time covered in requirements 1, 2, and 3?

11-56 Stock Split and 100% Stock Dividend

The Rubin Company wishes to double its number of shares outstanding. The company president asks the controller how a two-for-one stock split differs from a 100% stock dividend. Rubin has 200,000 shares ($1 par) outstanding at a market price of $30 per share.

The current stockholders' equity section is:

Common shares, 200,000 issued and outstanding	$ 200,000
Additional paid-in capital	2,300,000
Retained income	4,500,000

Required

1. Prepare the journal entry for a two-for-one stock split.
2. Prepare the journal entry for a 100% stock dividend.
3. Explain the difference between a two-for-one stock split and a 100% stock dividend.

11-57 Treasury Stock

(Alternate is 11-64.) Minnesota Mining and Manufacturing Company (3M) presented the following data in its 1999 annual report:

	December 31	
	1999	*1998*
	(in Millions)	
Stockholders' equity		
Common stock		
shares authorized, with 472,016,528 shares issued in 1996 and 1995	$ 296	$ 296
Retained earnings	10,741	9,980
Other	(915)	(858)
Less: Treasury stock	(3,833)	(3,482)
Stockholders' equity, net	$ 6,289	$5,936

1. During 1999, 3M reacquired 9 million treasury shares for $825 million. Give the journal entry to record this transaction.

2. 3M also issued some treasury shares as part of their employee stock option and investment plans. What was the cost of treasury shares issued in 1999?

3. Suppose that on January 7, 2000, 3M used cash to reacquire 175,000 shares for $70 each and held them in the treasury. Prepare the stockholders' equity section after the acquisition of treasury stock. Also prepare the journal entry.

4. Suppose the 175,000 shares of treasury stock are sold for $90 per share. Prepare the journal entry.

5. Suppose the 175,000 shares of treasury stock are sold for $50 per share. Prepare the journal entry.

11-58   Treasury Shares

During 1999 outstanding common shares of General Electric (GE) increased from 3,271,296,000 to 3,284,843,000. GE issued 950,000 new common shares during 1999. Treasury shares were purchased during the year for $7,488 million. A "gain" on the sale of treasury shares of $3,982 million was recorded on those sold that had a cost basis of $3,660 million. GE paid $4,786 million in dividends during the year, and retained income rose from $48,553 million to $54,484 million.

1. Compute the net change in the number of shares of treasury stock during 1999.

2. Compute the cash received from sale of the treasury shares during 1999.

3. The balance in the account "common stock held in the treasury" on January 1, 1999 was $18,739 million. Compute the balance on December 31, 1999.

4. Compute GE's net income for 1999.

5. Comment on the decision to buy treasury stock instead of using the same dollars to pay additional cash dividends.

11-59   Treasury Shares in Switzerland

Nestlé N.A., the Swiss food and beverage company, reported the following in its end-of-year balance sheet [Swiss francs (SF) in millions]:

Shareholders' funds		
Share capital	SF	404
Share premium and reserves		21,802
Less: Own shares		(268)
Total shareholders' funds		SF 21,938

During the year, Nestlé purchased 92,668 of its own shares for SF 111.2 million. Of those shares, 275 were issued on the exercise of stock options. There were no other changes in Nestlé's holdings of its own shares. The balance in the "Own Shares" account at the beginning of year was SF 157.1 million.

1. Restate Nestlé's "Shareholders' Funds" section of its balance sheet using terms more commonly used in the United States.

2. Prepare journal entries for Nestlé's purchase of its own shares during the year.

3. Prepare journal entries for Nestlé's reissue of 275 shares for the exercise of stock options. Assume that the exercise price was SF 500 per share and that the reissued shares were all among those purchased during the year.

4. At the end of the year, Nestlé held a total of 1,021,333 shares of its own stock. Comment on the average price paid for the shares repurchased this year compared with those repurchased previously.

11-60   Repurchase of Shares and Book Value per Share

ExxonMobil repurchased 17 million of its own common shares during 1999. The market price of ExxonMobil shares averaged $57 per share during the year. The condensed 1999 shareholders' equity section of the balance sheet showed (dollars and shares in millions):

Common stock, no par	$ 3,403
Retained earnings and other	75,055
Treasury stock (533 shares)	(12,126)
Other	(2,866)
Total stockholders' equity	$63,466

Required
1. Prepare the journal entry to record the 1999 purchase of treasury shares.
2. Compute the book value per share at December 31, 1999 assuming 3,477 million shares outstanding.
3. Compute the book value per share, assuming that the 1999 treasury stock purchase did not occur.

11-61 Retirement of Shares

Houston Financial Systems, Inc., has the following:

Common stock, 5,000,000 shares @ $2 par	$ 10,000,000
Paid-in capital in excess of par	40,000,000
Total paid-in capital	$ 50,000,000
Retained income	10,000,000
Stockholders' equity	$ 60,000,000
Overall market value of stock @ assumed $40	$200,000,000
Book value per share = $60,000,000 ÷ 5,000,000 = $12	

Required
The company used cash to reacquire and retire 100,000 shares for $40 each. Prepare the stockholders' equity section before and after this retirement of shares. Also prepare the journal entry.

11-62 Disposition of Treasury Stock

Chirac Company bought 10,000 of its own shares for $10 per share. The shares were held as treasury stock. This was the only time Chirac had ever purchased treasury stock.

Required
1. Chirac sold 5,000 of the shares for $12 per share. Prepare the journal entry.
2. Chirac sold the remaining 5,000 shares later for $11 per share. Prepare the journal entry.
3. Repeat requirement 2, assuming the shares were sold for $7 instead of $11 per share.
4. Did you record gains or losses in requirements 1, 2, and 3? Explain.

11-63 Effects of Treasury Stock on Retained Income

Assume that Ming Company has retained income of $10 million, paid-in capital of $25 million, and cost of treasury stock of $6 million.

Required
1. Tabulate the effects of dividend payments of (a) $5 million and (b) $2 million on retained income and total stockholders' equity.
2. Why do states forbid the payment of dividends if retained income does not exceed the cost of any treasury stock on hand? Explain, using the numbers from your answer to requirement 1.

11-64 Treasury Stock

(Alternate is 11-57.) Capetown Company has the following [in rands (R), the South African unit of currency]:

Common stock, 2,000,000 shares @ R3 par	R 6,000,000
Paid-in capital in excess of par	34,000,000
Total paid-in capital	R40,000,000
Retained income	18,000,000
Stockholders' equity	R58,000,000
Overall market value of stock @ assumed R40	R80,000,000
Book value per share = R58,000,000 ÷ 2,000,000 = R29	

1. The company used cash to reacquire 200,000 shares for R40 each and held them in the treasury. Prepare the stockholders' equity section after the acquisition of treasury stock. Also prepare the journal entry.

2. Suppose that all the treasury stock is sold for R50 per share. Prepare the journal entry.

3. Suppose that all the treasury stock is sold for R30 per share. Prepare the journal entry.

4. Recalculate book value after each preceding transaction.

Required

11-65 Treasury Stock

The following information was provided in footnote 7 of the 2000 H. J. Heinz annual report.

Shareholders' Equity

(in Thousands)	Cumulative Preferred Stock $1.70 First Series $10 Par Amount	Common Stock Issued Amount	Issued Shares	In Treasury Amount	In Treasury Shares	Additional Capital Amount
Balance April 28, 1999	$173	$107,774	431,096	$ 2,435,012	(71,969)	$277,652
Reacquired	—	—	—	511,480	12,766	—
Conversion of preferred into common stock	(34)	—	—	(1,170)	(46)	(1,136)
Stock options exercised	—	—	—	(19,681)	(833)	26,830
Other, net	—	—	—	(5,170)	(203)	972
Balance May 3, 2000	$139	$107,774	431,096	$(2,920,471)	(83,653)	$304,318
Authorized Shares— May 3, 2000	14		600,000			

Capital stock: The preferred stock outstanding is convertible at a rate of 1 share of preferred stock into 13.5 shares of common stock. The company can redeem the preferred stock at $28.50 per share.

Provide summary journal entries to account for the treasury stock transactions during the period April 28, 1999 to May 3, 2000. Omit the journal entry for "Other, net."

Required

11-66 Convertible Securities

Suppose Boston Company had paid $200,000 to Hartford Company for an investment in 10,000 shares of the $5 par value preferred stock of Hartford Company. The preferred stock was later converted into 10,000 shares of Hartford Company common stock ($1 par value).

Required

1. Using the balance sheet equation, prepare an analysis of transactions of Boston Company and Hartford Company.

2. Prepare the journal entries to accompany your analysis in requirement 1.

11-67 Issue of Common Shares

Intermec Corporation, a leader in the field of bar code data collection, issued the following common shares during a recent year:

a. Through a public offering 780,000 shares were issued for net cash of $10,765,977, an average price of $13.80 per share.

b. As part of an employee stock purchase plan, 16,900 shares, at $218,093, or $12.90 per share, were received.

c. For the exercise of stock options 88,283 shares, at $355,275, or $4.02 per share, were received.

The stockholders' equity section of Intermec's balance sheet at the beginning of the year was the following:

Common stock: authorized 10,000,000 shares with	
$.60 par value, issued and outstanding 4,510,908 shares	$ 2,706,545
Additional paid-in capital	4,603,092
Retained earnings	8,128,230
Total stockholders' equity	$15,437,867

Net income for the year was $4,008,991. No dividends were paid.

Required

1. Prepare journal entries for the common stock issues in a, b, and c. Omit explanations.
2. Present the stockholders' equity section of the balance sheet at the end of the year.

11-68 Noncash Exchanges

Suppose Cartier Company acquires some equipment from Marseilles Company in exchange for issuance of 10,000 shares of Cartier's common stock. The equipment was carried on Marseilles's books at the FF 520,000 original cost less accumulated depreciation of FF 140,000. Cartier's stock is listed on the Paris Stock Exchange; its current market value is FF 50 per share. Its par value is FF 1 per share.

Required

1. By using the balance sheet equation, show the effects of the transaction on the accounts of Cartier Company and Marseilles Company.
2. Show the journal entries on the books of Cartier Company and Marseilles Company.

11-69 Covenants and Leases

Mitchell Energy and Development Corporation is one of the country's largest oil and gas producers. The notes to its financial statements reveal the existence of certain debt agreement restrictions on the level of consolidated stockholders' equity as well as on various asset-to-debt ratios:

> *The bank credit agreements contain certain restrictions which, among other things, require consolidated stockholders' equity to be equal to at least $300,000,000 and require the maintenance of specified financial and oil and gas reserve and/or asset value to debt ratios.*

Required

1. Given the existence of the asset-to-debt covenants, is Mitchell more likely to be able to enter into operating leases or capital leases without violating the covenants?
2. If Mitchell Energy and Development, Inc., had refused to agree to these conditions at the time of the debt issues, how would it have affected the market price of the debt they issued?

11-70 Financial Ratios

Consider the following data from two companies in very different industries. Adobe Systems is a software company that produces PageMaker, among other products. Xcel Energy (formerly Northern States Power) is an electric utility based in Minneapolis. Both companies have preferred stock. (Amounts except earnings per share and market price are in thousands.)

	Total Assets	Total Liabilities	Net Income	Earnings per Share	Market Price per Share
Adobe Systems	$1,012,285	$ 305,771	$153,277	$2.04	$40
Xcel Energy	6,636,900	2,667,983	231,111	3.82	47

Required

1. Compute the market-to-book ratio and the rate of return on stockholders' equity for both Adobe Systems and Xcel Energy.
2. Explain what might cause the differences in these ratios between the two companies.

11-71 Shareholders' Equity Section

Enron Corporation is a worldwide energy company with annual revenues in excess of $40 billion. Its main activities are in natural gas and electricity. The data at the top of p. 501 are from the company's 1999 annual report ($ in millions).

For the year ended December 31	1999	1998
Other	895	70
Common stock held in treasury, 1,337,714 shares and 9,333,322 shares, respectively	(49)	(195)
Common stock, no par value, 1,200,000,000 shares authorized, 716,865,081 shares and 671,094,552 shares issued, respectively	6,637	5,117
Retained earnings	2,698	2,226
Preferred stock, cumulative, no par value, 1,370,000 shares authorized, 1,296,184 shares and 1,319,848 shares issued, respectively	130	132
Accumulated other comprehensive income	(741)	(162)

Required

1. Prepare Enron's shareholders' equity section of the 1999 balance sheet. Include the amount for total stockholders' equity.

2. Enron paid $355 million of cash dividends on common stock and $66 million of cash dividends on preferred stock in 1999. Compute Enron's net income for 1999.

3. Explain Enron's net acquisition or disposition of treasury shares during 1999. Include the increase or decrease in total number of shares and the average price per share of those acquired or sold. What is the average purchase price of the shares remaining in the treasury at the end of 1999?

11-72 International Perspective

Honda Motor Company provides the following information in its 1997 annual report:

	Yen (Millions)					
	Common Stock	Capital Surplus	Legal Reserve	Retained Earnings	Other	Total Stockholders' Equity
Balance at March 31, 1996	¥86,020	¥171,910	¥25,125	¥1,243,759	(¥382,274)	¥1,144,540
Net income for the year				221,168		221,168
Cash dividends ¥14 per share (note 11)				(13,640)		(13,640)
Transfer to legal reserve (note 11)			543	(543)		—
Conversion of convertible debt (note 10)	8	—				8
Adjustments for the year					36,354	36,354
Balance at March 31, 1997	¥86,028	¥171,910	¥25,668	¥1,450,744	(¥345,920)	¥1,388,430

(10) Common Stock

During the years ended March 31, 1995, 1996, and 1997, the Company issued approximately 462 thousand, 129 thousand, and 19 thousand shares, respectively, of common stock in connection with the conversion of convertible debt. Conversions of convertible debt issued subsequent to October 1, 1982, into common stock and exercise of warrants were accounted for in accordance with the provisions of the Japanese Commercial Code by crediting one-half of the aggregate conversion price equally to the common stock account and the capital surplus account.

(11) Dividends and Legal Reserve

The Japanese Commercial Code provides that earnings in an amount equal to at least 10% of all appropriations of retained earnings that are paid in cash, such as cash dividends and bonuses to directors, shall be appropriated as a legal reserve until such reserve equals 25% of stated capital. This reserve is not available for dividends but may be used to reduce a deficit or may be transferred to stated capital. Certain foreign subsidiaries are also required to appropriate their earnings to legal reserves under laws of the respective countries of domicile.

Cash dividends and appropriations to the legal reserve charged to retained earnings during the years ended March 31, 1995, 1996, and 1997, represent dividends paid out during those years and the related appropriations to the legal reserve. The accompanying consolidated financial statements do not include any provision for the dividend of ¥8 per share aggregating ¥7,794 million to be proposed in June 1997. As at March 31, 1997, the legal reserve of Honda Motor Co., Ltd. equals 25% of stated capital.

Required

1. Give journal entries to record the items shown for fiscal 1997. Omit the item listed under "other."
2. Suppose Honda's legal reserve was still below 25% of stated capital. Give the journal entry that Honda would make for the proposed dividend and transfer to the reserve in June 1997. Assume the transfer is 10% of the dividends.

11-73   Stock Options and Ethics

Bristol-Myers Squibb is one of the largest pharmaceutical companies in the world. In 1999, the company granted executives options to purchase 24,221,950 shares of common stock. Suppose that all shares were granted with an exercise price of $65 per share, which was the market price of the stock on the date the options were granted, and that all options could be exercised anytime between 3 and 5 years from the grant date, provided that the executive still works for Bristol-Myers Squibb.

Assume that at the same time the stock options were issued Bristol-Myers Squibb also issued warrants with the same $65 exercise price that are exercisable any time in the next 5 years. The company received $5 for each such warrant.

Required

1. How much expense was recorded at the issue of each stock option?
2. How much value was there to the executive for each stock option issued?
3. How much did it cost the firm for each stock option that was issued?
4. Might the fact that individual executives hold stock options affect their decisions about declaring dividends? Comment on the ethics of this influence.

ANNUAL REPORT CASE

11-74   Cisco Annual Report

Use Cisco's financial statements and notes contained in appendix A to answer the following questions.

Required

1. Prepare the journal entry to record any dividends declared in the year ended July 29, 2000.
2. Give the journal entry Cisco used to record the issuance stock in the year ended July 29, 2000.
3. What was the average price per share of stock issued in the year ended July 29, 2000?

11-75   Financial Statement Research

Select a company and use its financial statements to answer the following questions.

Required

1. Identify each transaction that affected stockholders' equity during the most recent 2 years.
2. Indicate which accounts were affected and by how much.
3. List any transactions that appear unusual. For example, many companies have a change in shareholders' equity that arises from tax benefits related to stock options. This and a few other common transactions are beyond our scope in this introductory course.

COLLABORATIVE LEARNING EXERCISE

11-76 Price to Book and ROE

Form groups of three to six students each. Each student should pick two companies, preferably from different industries. Find the appropriate data and compute the market-to-book ratio and the rate of return on stockholders' equity (ROE) for each company.

Assemble the group and list the companies selected, together with their market-to-book ratio and ROE. Rank the companies from highest to lowest on price to book ratio. Then rank them on ROE.

Explain why companies rank as they do in each list. Are the rankings similar; that is, is the ranking based on market-to-book similar to the rankings on ROE? Explain why you would or would not expect similarity in the rankings.

INTERNET EXERCISE

11-77 United Parcel Service

Go to www.ups.com to find the home page of United Parcel Service (UPS). Select *UPS Investor Relations*. Click on "*Financials*" to locate UPS's latest annual report.

Answer the following questions about UPS:

www.prenhall.com/horngren

1. Identify the classes of stock that UPS has authorized as of the end of its most recent fiscal period, with their par values. Have all the shares in each category been issued? Can you tell if the shares were issued above par? How?

2. How many additional shares of common stock is UPS able to issue as of its most recent balance sheet date? If these shares were all issued and outstanding, how would the values reported on the balance sheet change? Does UPS have any treasury stock?

3. What is the cause of any changes in the Common Stock accounts during the period?

4. Did UPS declare any stock splits or stock dividends during its most recent 2-year comparative reporting period? If so, what effect did these have on the number of shares of stock outstanding? Why do you think UPS would want to declare a stock split or stock dividend?

5. Does UPS have a stock option plan? Prior to December 31, 1998, how did UPS account for its common stock held for awards and distributions? What effect did Financial Accounting Standards No. 123 and Accounting Principles Board Opinion No. 25 have on how UPS accounts for its stock options?

Go to the "Dividends and Treasury Stock" episode on the *Mastering Accounting* CD-ROM for an interactive, video-enhanced exercise on how CanGo can boost investor confidence after poor quarterly performance reports. The difference between cash and stock dividends is explained.

INTERCORPORATE INVESTMENTS AND CONSOLIDATIONS

This GM vehicle, the Denali, is photographed in front of Mt. McKinley in Alaska, which is called Denali by Alaskans. The Denali, like any GM nameplate, can be financed with a loan from General Motors Acceptance Corporation (GMAC).

www.prenhall.com/horngren

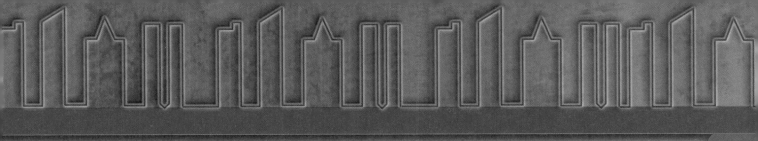

Learning Objectives

After studying this chapter, you should be able to

1. Explain why corporations invest in one another.
2. Account for short-term investments in debt securities and equity securities.
3. Report long-term investments in bonds.
4. Contrast the equity and market methods of accounting for investments.
5. Prepare consolidated financial statements.
6. Incorporate minority interests into consolidated financial statements.
7. Explain the economic and reporting role of goodwill.

Deciding to buy and finance a new car is one of the most important decisions you can make as a consumer. If you have gone through this process, you realize that automakers sell financing (auto loans) as well as automobiles. Wherever you buy a GM car you can also "buy" your financing through a fully owned subsidiary, General Motors Acceptance Corporation (GMAC). Just what is the relationship between General Motors (GM) and GMAC? They are separate entities, each with its own financial records. However, they are so closely related that authorities require them to combine financial records when preparing financial statements for the public.

Pick up the annual report of almost any major company (and even most middle-size companies) and you find *consolidated financial statements*. This term means that the books of two or more separate legal entities have been combined into the statements presented. General Motors describes its statements as follows: "The consolidated financial statements include the accounts of General Motors Corporation and domestic and foreign subsidiaries that are more than 50% owned, principally General Motors Acceptance Corporation (GMAC) and Hughes."

The process of consolidating financial statements used to be an accountant's nightmare. It took days and sometimes nights for many accountants. The consolidated statements filled pages and pages of 13-column paper spreadsheets. Today, thanks to computers and sophisticated software packages, some companies consolidate statements in hours. General Motors takes 3 days, but the combining of statements is really completed after the first day. The next 2 days are spent analyzing worldwide results for possible errors and ensuring an explanation for any deviations from the expected.

You probably know that the Ford Motor Company makes many models of cars and trucks under various Ford nameplates around the world. You may not know that Ford owns Jaguar, the prestigious British luxury car manufacturer. You also may not know that Ford owns 33% of Mazda, the popular Japanese auto manufacturer. Why did Ford buy

Jaguar and part of Mazda? Why not all of Mazda? Is the accounting different for 100% ownership than for 33%? We are not able to answer all the strategic questions, but we address some of the explanations and we explain how the accounting differs between these two cases, and why.

The acquisition game continues. Ford purchased Volvo on March 31, 1999 and purchased Land Rover in early 2000. The open question is how can Ford streamline the production process or the selling process of these acquired companies. For example, can they make Land Rover more cost effective by designing future models to share parts with current Ford products? Can they learn things about technology from either company that enhances the quality of other Ford products? Both of these outcomes have already occurred for the Jaguar acquisition.

However, Ford is not just an acquirer. In June 2000, it distributed shares in a separate company, Visteon, to its shareholders. Visteon is the second largest supplier of automotive parts in the world. Ford believes that creating it as a separate company, without any ownership interest by Ford, will allow Visteon to increase its share of non-Ford business from 12% to 20% of its total business in a few years.

Examples throughout the chapter stress the fact that investments in securities (and disinvestments) arise from many different motives. The accounting for such investments differs depending on the purpose of the investment, on whether the investment is an equity or debt security, and on the degree of control the investor has over the issuer of the security.

AN OVERVIEW OF CORPORATE INVESTMENTS

Objective 1
Explain why
Corporations invest in
one another.

As noted previously, when a firm has an excess of cash, smart managers should invest the cash instead of letting it remain idle in the company's checking account. Just as it makes sense for individuals to invest their extra money, it makes sense for a corporation to earn interest income by investing temporarily idle cash. These investments can take on many different forms.

In many instances, companies invest in both short-term and long-term debt securities issued by governments, banks, or other corporations. For example, Ford classified $13.1 billion of marketable securities as current assets on its balance sheet and also owned $817 million in debt securities classified as noncurrent investments by its Financial Services subsidiary as of December 31, 2000.

In addition to debt securities, companies also invest in other corporations' equity securities. These investments are typically long-term investments; when they are large enough, they allow the investing company varying degrees of control over the company issuing the securities. Such investments are common and arise from various motivations. Ford bought Jaguar in 1989 for approximately $2.5 billion after a fierce competition with General Motors (GM). GM already owned Lotus, and Chrysler acquired Lamborghini, so Ford was determined to acquire its own European luxury car maker. These major U.S. auto companies were all committed to a strategy that required a full range of automobile offerings, including a luxury nameplate. Ford has significantly changed the way Jaguar does business by implementing many Ford manufacturing practices, design practices, and quality initiatives. The response in the marketplace has been positive although it has taken almost a decade to realize the improvements. Ford's motives in acquiring 33% of

Mazda were different. Ford does not control Mazda the way it does Jaguar. Instead, the two companies function as partners who share various production efficiencies and technical know-how.

CORPORATE MARRIAGE AND DIVORCE

Corporate mergers can be a little like marriages. The challenge is to combine and retain the right combination of people and products to succeed over the long haul. Many companies acquire other companies on a regular basis. For example, Cisco, Microsoft, Intel, Oracle, and other technology companies often buy smaller, innovative young companies to capture their new ideas and, often, their talented employees. In other cases, firms buy large similar companies hoping to integrate the two firms and create cost savings from eliminating duplications. The Exxon/Mobil merger and the British Petroleum/Amoco/ARCO merger are recent examples in the oil industry. Both included significant reductions in total employment of the combined firms.

Just as not all marriages work, not all business combinations work. This outcome is disturbingly common. *Forbes* (October 30, 2000) cited a study by Big Five accounting firm KPMG that concluded that over half of all deals destroy shareholder value and an additional third offer no benefit. By this reckoning only one-sixth of business combinations are desirable. KPMG found that smaller companies were more likely to be successful with mergers. *Forbes* speculated that it may be because smaller companies are more careful and less likely to do deals to impress the public or create growth for the sake of growth. What if the combination does not work? At the worst, the combined company's assets are sold off, the proceeds are distributed to creditors, and the company disappears.

Less extreme possibilities exist, however. Often the parent company simply sells off a distinct business unit or subsidiary company. An interesting alternative is called a spin-off, which occurs when shares in a subsidiary are distributed to the shareholders of the parent. For example, PepsiCo recently spun off its food operations, which included Pizza Hut, Taco Bell, and KFC, to create a new company called Tricon. Tricon became a completely separate entity with its own board of directors, management, assets, liabilities, and owners. The spin-off energized Tricon, whose stock rose from $30 at the spin-off in mid-1997 to over $70 by early 1999. Unfortunately, the path reversed in the subsequent year. In mid-2000, the company's shares were trading around $34. The former parent, PepsiCo also had ups and downs though not as extreme. At the spin-off PepsiCo was about $35, fell as low as $28, and rose as high as $45 during the ensuing years to close at around $40 in mid-2000.

Spin-offs often separate dissimilar business segments to create opportunities for more creative and innovative growth. They allow managers of the spun-off company to be compensated more directly based on the performance of the new, often smaller, company. Historically, companies that were spun off have performed well and investors who held the shares they received in the spin-off or who acquired the companies when they were initially available as separate firms have earned substantial profits. A recent study of 146 spin-offs over 30 years concluded that investments in shares of spun-off firms outperform the stock market by an average of 35% in their first 3 years as separate companies.

Sometimes a company does not believe the market is fully valuing all of what it does. By spinning off or selling some shares in a subsidiary, the value of the subsidiary becomes more obvious. The subsidiary then prepares and distributes its own financial statements, and its separately traded shares have an observable share price. In late 1999, IPC Communications, which makes high-tech telephone sets for Wall Street trading desks, spun off a piece of its IXNet subsidiary that makes telecommunications networks for those same customers. Similarly IDT, which sells prepaid phone cards, sold some shares in its Net2Phone subsidiary, which makes software for phone calls over the Internet. In the

How does a company increase the odds that its business combination will be one of the successful ones? The KPMG study referred to in the text cites shoddy due diligence, a lack of synergy between the two companies, too little planning, and lousy execution as common reasons for failure. The recipe for a successful acquisition is to avoid these pitfalls. More specifically, the *Forbes* article recommends:

1. Do not wait for a deal to come to you. Investment bankers and company brokers represent companies that wish to be acquired. They create a packet of information and make presentations to possible acquirers. *Forbes* advises a more active approach, looking for the right partner and being willing to convince them to be acquired instead of choosing among companies who are formally for sale.

2. Stick to your knitting. Expansion should be aimed at doing what you already do more effectively or at modest expansions of the scope of the business. There have been periodic episodes in which conglomerate mergers were popular. These involve buying very diverse businesses on the grounds that management is management and larger is better. These mergers have failed at an even higher rate than usual.

3. Know what you are buying. "Due diligence" is the phrase for carefully investigating the target company. It refers to the corporate equivalent of kicking the tires or having a mechanic examine a potential car purchase. Common important questions include: What is the order backlog? Will critical employees stay? Is the debt subject to a change of ownership clause? Is the company subject to unrecorded liabilities such as environmental pollution or extensive periods of deferred maintenance that leave plant, property, and equipment in need of repair? What are customers and competitors doing? The list is long.

4. Learn their tribal customs. Perhaps the biggest problem that mergers face is that the two companies have very different work cultures. This is easily illustrated with international examples. Consider a U.S. company headed by a rapid decision maker. Although the U.S. buyer might be willing to sign an agreement immediately, a Swiss seller might want to think about it awhile. Although the U.S. buyer might be able to act alone, a Chinese seller might expect to bring many managers into the negotiation to be sure that a consensus was reached. The process for sealing the deal is suggestive about ongoing managerial expectations that differ around the world and even coast to coast in the United States.

5. Start integration well before the deal is closed. If the most difficult task is the merger of workforces and overcoming cultural differences, the preparation for these tasks must start early and receive total attention.

Notice that the accounting issues do not make the list of do's and don'ts. There are important steps in bringing the financial accounting for the combining companies together, but they are rarely critical to the success.

Forbes, "The Race to Embrace," October 30, 2000, pp. 184–191.

fast-paced technology markets, these corporate names and identities may be reshuffled many times during the life of this textbook.

After companies create intercorporate linkages, their accountants must develop ways to report on the financial results of these complicated entities. In 1994, Ford increased its ownership in Hertz from 49% to 100%. That change in ownership significantly altered the way Ford accounts for the relationship. In 1996, Ford increased its ownership of Mazda from 25% to 33%, but this change did not alter the fundamental accounting for the relationship. As we will see, current accounting procedures for intercorporate linkages are tied directly to the percentage of ownership, with 20% and 50% being the critical percentages at which accounting treatment changes.

Once the company chooses an accounting procedure that determines how a relationship is to be measured, there is also a question about *where* it is to be reported on the balance sheet, among current or long-term assets. Investments are classified on a balance sheet according to purpose or intention. An investment should be carried as a current asset if it is a short-term investment, one the owner expects to convert to cash. Other investments are classified as noncurrent assets and usually appear as either (1) a separate investments category between current assets and property, plant, and equipment, or (2) a part of other assets below the plant assets category.

SHORT-TERM INVESTMENTS

Objective 2
Account for short-term investments in debt securities and equity securities.

As its name implies, a **short-term investment** is a temporary investment of otherwise idle cash in marketable securities. **Marketable securities** are notes, bonds, or stocks that can be easily sold. A company's short-term investment portfolio (total of securities owned) usually consists of short-term debt securities and short-term equity securities. The investments are highly liquid (easily convertible into cash) and have stable prices.

Ordinarily, companies expect to convert items classified as short-term investments into cash within a year after the date on the balance sheet on which they appear. In actuality some of these securities are not converted into cash and are held beyond a 12-month period. Nevertheless, these investments are still classified as current assets if management intends to convert them into cash when needed. The key point is that conversion to cash is immediately available at the option of management.

Short-term debt securities consist largely of government- and business-issued notes and bonds with maturities of 1 year or less. They pay a fixed amount of interest, which is usually why investors purchase them. Typically, debt security investments include short-term obligations of banks, called **certificates of deposit,** and **commercial paper,** consisting of short-term notes payable issued by large corporations with top credit ratings. They also include **U.S. Treasury obligations,** which refer to interest-bearing notes, bonds, and bills issued by the federal government. All these debt securities may be held until maturity or may be resold in securities markets.

Short-term equity securities consist of capital stock (shares of ownership) in other corporations. Companies, as well as individuals, regularly buy and sell equity securities on the New York Stock Exchange (NYSE) or other stock exchanges. If the investing firm intends to sell the equity securities it holds within 1 year or within its normal operating cycle, then the securities are considered a short-term investment.

At acquisition, companies record these securities at cost. How they are reported after acquisition depends on whether they are classified as trading securities, available-for-sale securities, or held-to-maturity securities. You can see these three categories in the footnote to Ford's 1999 financial statements shown in Exhibit 12-1.

Trading securities are short-term investments, including both debt and equity securities, that the company buys with the intent to resell them shortly. Companies list such securities among current assets on their balance sheets and measure them at market value (or fair value). As shown in Exhibit 12-1, $190 million of Ford's short-term investments in its Financial Services operations are trading securities.

Held-to-maturity securities are debt securities that the company purchases with the intent to hold them until they mature. They are shown on the balance sheet at amortized cost, not market value. In chapter 10, we examined the amortization of premiums and discounts on bonds payable by the issuer of the debt. Corporations that invest in bonds use the same approach, as illustrated later in this chapter. Unlike trading securities, which are always classified as short-term because of the owner's intention, held-to-maturity securities are classified according to the time remaining until they mature. If the time to maturity is less than 1 year, they are short-term investments, and thus current

short-term investment A temporary investment in marketable securities of otherwise idle cash.

marketable securities Any notes, bonds, or stocks that can readily be sold.

short-term debt securities Largely notes and bonds with maturities of 1 year or less.

certificates of deposit Short-term obligations of banks.

commercial paper Short-term notes payable issued by large corporations with top credit ratings.

U.S. Treasury obligations Interest-bearing notes, bonds, and bills issued by the U.S. government.

short-term equity securities Capital stock in other corporations held with the intention to liquidate within 1 year as needed.

trading securities Current investments in equity or debt securities held for short-term profit.

Exhibit 12-1

Ford Motor Company, Financial Services Sector
1999 Marketable and Other Securities Footnote

Investments in Securities at December 31, 1999 ($ in Millions)

	Amortized Cost	Unrealized Gains	Unrealized Losses	Book/ Fair Value
Trading securities	$190	$—	$—	$190
Available-for-sale securities				
Debt securities issued by the U.S. government and agencies	89	—	3	86
Municipal securities	18	—	1	17
Debt securities issued by non-U.S. governments	19	—	—	19
Corporate securities	156	—	6	150
Mortgage-backed securities	202	—	7	195
Equity securities	28	43	2	69
Total available-for-sale securities	512	43	19	536
Held-to-maturity securities				
Debt securities issued by the U.S. government and agencies	6	—	—	6
Corporate securities	1			1
Total held-to-maturity securities	7			7
Total investments in securities	$709	$43	$19	$733

held-to-maturity securities Debt securities that the investor expects to hold until maturity.

available-for-sale securities Investments in equity or debt securities that are not held for active trading but may be sold before maturity.

assets. Otherwise, they are long-term investments, and thus noncurrent assets. Only $7 million of Ford's Financial Services investments are held-to-maturity securities.

Available-for-sale securities include all debt and equity securities that are neither trading securities nor held-to-maturity securities. They include equity securities that the company does not intend to sell in the near future and debt securities that the company neither plans to sell shortly nor to hold to maturity. Ford provides separate lines under this category for many different types of securities held by its Financial Services operations. Note that most are debt securities of one type or another issued by the U.S. treasury, municipalities, foreign governments, or corporations. The amount reported on the balance sheet is the market value of $536 million, which is $24 million greater than the original cost of these securities.

The total investments by the Financial Services operations of Ford, the amount shown on Ford's balance sheet, is the $733 million shown at the bottom of the far right-hand column of Exhibit 12-1. It is the market value of trading securities and available-for-sale securities and the amortized cost of the held-to-maturity securities.

CHANGES IN MARKET PRICES OF SECURITIES

You now know how short-term investments are shown on the balance sheet. How do we account for the returns on these investments?

Held-to-maturity investments are easiest to account for because interest revenue is the only return received on such securities. Changes in market value are ignored. Interest revenue appears directly on the income statement, increasing income and therefore increasing stockholders' equity.

Returns on trading securities and available-for-sale securities come in two forms: (1) dividend or interest revenue, and (2) changes in market value. The former are recorded on the income statement when earned for all securities. However, we account for changes in market value differently for trading securities than for available-for-sale securities.

As the market value of trading securities changes, companies report the gains from increases in price and the losses from decreases in price in the income statement. In contrast, the gains and losses that arise as market values of available-for-sale securities rise and fall are not shown on the income statement. Instead, we add such unrealized gains and losses to a separate valuation allowance account in the stockholders' equity section of the balance sheet. This account increases stockholders' equity for securities whose price has increased since purchase. It decreases stockholders' equity for securities that have experienced a drop in prices. Ford shows $19 million of unrealized losses and $43 million of unrealized gains on available-for-sale securities, for a net increase in stockholders' equity of $24 million.

Notice that increases in prices of both trading securities and available-for-sale securities increase stockholders' equity, and decreases in prices decrease stockholders' equity. For trading securities, the increase or decrease is part of retained earnings because the gains and losses are included in net income. For available-for-sale securities, the increase or decrease is in a separate valuation account included in owners' equity.

We call this method of accounting for trading securities and available-for-sale securities the market method. Under the **market method,** the reported asset values in the balance sheet are the market values of the publicly traded securities. Suppose two companies acquire identical assets at the same price on the same day, but one company reported them as trading securities and the other reported them as available-for-sale securities. The two companies would report identical asset values on their balance sheets, but they would differ in how they report changes in those market values. Assume that the portfolio of assets purchased by the two companies cost $50 million and had the market values at the end of four subsequent periods shown in Exhibit 12-2 ($ in millions).

market method Method of accounting for trading securities changes affect the income statement; for available-for-sale securities a valuation allowance appears in owners' equity.

Exhibit 12-2 shows the results for four periods. Most companies present the market value directly as a single line on the balance sheet. The valuation adjustment provides a linkage to cost and shows that the valuation allowance in stockholders' equity for available-for-sale securities has a balance equal to the difference between historical cost and market.

The unrealized gain (loss) for trading securities affects net income and therefore also increases (decreases) retained income. Over the four periods, the loss of $5 million and gains of $2 million and $7 million provide a net increase in retained income of $4 million ($9 million of gains less $5 million of losses).

Exhibit 12-2
Financial Statement Presentation
Trading Securities and Available-for-Sale Securities

	End of Period			
	1	*2*	*3*	*4*
Assumed market value	50	45	47	54
Balance sheet presentation—both methods				
Short-term investment at cost	50	50	50	50
Valuation adjustment to market	0	(5)	(3)	4
Carrying value	50	45	47	54
For trading securities				
Income statement presentation				
Unrealized gain (loss) on changes in market	0	(5)	2	7
For available-for-sale-securities				
Additional balance sheet presentation				
Balance in valuation allowance in stockholders' equity	0	(5)	(3)	4

The journal entries for the two classes of securities for periods 2, 3, and 4 would appear as follows, without explanations:

PERIOD	TRADING SECURITIES			AVAILABLE-FOR-SALE SECURITIES		
2	Unrealized loss	5		Valuation Allowance	5	
	Marketable Securities		5	Marketable Securities		5
3	Marketable Securities	2		Marketable Securities	2	
	Unrealized gain		2	Valuation Allowance		2
4	Marketable Securities	7		Marketable Securities	7	
	Unrealized gain		7	Valuation Allowance		7

In Exhibit 12-2, the carrying value on the balance sheet is identical for both trading and available-for-sale securities. However, the numbers shown for trading and available-for-sale securities in the bottom half of the table are the same in period two but not in periods three and four. Explain.

ANSWER

The carrying values on the balance sheet are the same, but for trading securities gains and losses appear in the income statement. The income statement amounts show the change in market value each period. In contrast, available-for-sale securities do not affect the income statement. Instead, a valuation allowance is shown in owners' equity that reflects the difference between market value and cost at the end of each period. In the second period, the change in market value is also the end-of-period difference between cost and market, so both securities show ($5). However, in period three, the change shown in the income statement for trading securities is $2 based on the increase in value during the period. For available-for-sale securities, the difference between market and cost is ($3), which is the net cumulative result of the ($5) loss in period two and the $2 gain in period three.

COMPREHENSIVE INCOME

For many companies, especially some in high-tech industries, it is common to invest in other companies and to treat the investment as an available-for-sale security. The change in the economic value of the firm is not fully revealed in the income statement because the increase or decrease in value of these securities is shown only on the balance sheet: among assets because the market value of the asset is reported, and in owners' equity because the difference between cost and market is included in owners' equity. To understand the changes during the year, comprehensive income is reported as well as net income. Comprehensive income includes both net income and changes in the value of available-for-sale securities. Cisco provides a good example.

In the balance sheet, included in owners' equity, Cisco reports "Accumulated other comprehensive income of $3,530 million in 2000 and $298 million in 1999." The year-to-year change is explained in the consolidated statements of shareholders' equity by calculating a comprehensive income number that combines various elements as follows ($ in millions):

Net income	$ 2,668
Change in net unrealized gains on investments	3,240
Translation adjustments	(8)
	$ 5,900

Two issues are noteworthy. For Cisco, the change in value of investments exceeded net income. The other element of comprehensive income arises from changes in foreign currencies and tends to be small compared with variations in the value of investments from year to year.

LONG-TERM INVESTMENTS IN BONDS

Objective 3
Report long-term investments in bonds.

Chapter 10 explained the basic approach issuing firms use to account for bonds payable. Recall that the issuer amortizes bond discounts and premiums as periodic adjustments of interest expense. Investing firms use a similar method to account for bonds held to maturity. However, although the issuer typically keeps a separate account for unamortized discounts and premiums, investors do not (although they could if desired).

BONDS-HELD-TO-MATURITY

Exhibit 12-3 should look familiar to you. It is the same as Exhibit 9-3 except that our perspective has changed from issuer to that of investor. Therefore, we use the phrase book value to refer to the first column instead of the label net liability used in Exhibit 9-3. Recall that book value is a general term referring to the amount reported in financial statements under generally accepted accounting principles.

Exhibit 12-3 shows the values for 10,000 two-year bonds paying interest semiannually with a face value of $1,000 each and a 10% coupon rate (5% interest every 6 months). The bonds were issued to yield 12%. Because they pay only a 10% coupon interest rate, they are sold at a discount. Therefore, despite the face value of $10,000,000, an investor acquiring the whole issue would initially pay only $9,653,500. Interest (rental payment for the $9,653,500) takes two forms—four semiannual cash receipts of $500,000 (5% × $10 million), plus an extra lump-sum receipt of $346,500 ($10 million face value less amount paid at issue) at maturity.

The extra $346,500 to be paid at maturity (the amount of the discount) relates to the use of the proceeds over the 2 years. Therefore, like the issuer, the investor amortizes the discount:

	6/30/03	12/31/03	6/30/04	12/31/04
Semiannual interest revenue:				
Cash interest payments, .05 × $10 million	$500,000	$500,000	$500,000	$500,000
Amortization of $346,500 discount*	79,207	83,959	88,997	94,337
Semiannual revenue	$579,207	$583,959	$588,997	$594,337

*For the amortization schedule, see column 4 of exhibit 12-3. Note that $79,207 + $83,959 + $88,997 + $94,337 = $346,500.

Exhibit 12-3

Effective-Interest Amortization of Bond Discount

For 6 Months Ended	(1) Beginning Book Value	(2) Effective Interest @ 6%*	(3) Nominal Interest @ 5%	(4) Discount Amortized (2) − (3)	Ending Book Value		
					Face Amount	*Unamortized Discount*	*Ending Book Value*
12/31/02	—	—	—	—	$10,000,000	$346,500	$ 9,653,500
6/30/03	$9,653,500	$579,207	$500,000	$79,207	10,000,000	267,293†	9,732,707
12/31/03	9,732,707	583,959	500,000	83,959	10,000,000	183,334†	9,816,666
6/30/04	9,816,666	588,997	500,000	88,997	10,000,000	94,337	9,905,663
12/31/04	9,905,663	594,337	500,000	94,337	10,000,000	0	10,000,000

*To avoid rounding errors, an unrounded actual effective rate slightly under 6% was used.
†$346,500 − $79,207 = $267,293; $267,293 − $83,959 = $183,334; etc.

Exhibit 12-4

Accounting for Bonds

		Investor's Records					Issuer's Records		
12/31/02	1.	Investment in bonds	9,653,500		1.	Cash	9,653,500	
		Cash		9,653,500		Discount on bonds payable	346,500	
						Bonds payable		10,000,000
6/30/03	2.	Cash	500,000		2.	Interest expense	579,207	
		Investment in bonds	79,207			Discount on bonds payable		79,207
		Interest revenue		579,207		Cash		500,000
12/31/03		Cash	500,000			Interest expense	583,959	
		Investment in bonds	83,959			Discount on bonds payable		83,959
		Interest revenue		583,959		Cash		500,000
6/30/04		Cash	500,000			Interest expense	588,997	
		Investment in bonds	88,997			Discount on bonds payable		88,997
		Interest revenue		588,997		Cash		500,000
12/31/04		Cash	500,000			Interest expense	594,337	
		Investment in bonds	94,337			Discount on bonds payable		94,337
		Interest revenue		594,337		Cash		500,000
12/31/04	3.	Cash	10,000,000		3.	Bonds payable	10,000,000	
		Investment in bonds		10,000,000		Cash		10,000,000

As Exhibit 12-3 shows, the discount is used to make up the difference between the coupon interest rate of 10% and the market interest rate of 12%. Amortization of a discount increases the interest revenue of investors. (Investor accounting for bonds issued at a premium is similar except that amortization of premium decreases the interest revenue of investors.)

Exhibit 12-4 shows how the investor and the issuer account for the bonds throughout the bonds' lives. Note that interest revenue and interest expense are identical in each period.

EARLY EXTINGUISHMENT OF INVESTMENT

Suppose in our example that the issuer buys back all its bonds on the open market for $9.6 million on December 31, 2003 (after all interest payments and amortization were recorded for 2003). The investor's loss is calculated in panel A of Exhibit 12-5. The journal entries for the investor and the issuer are shown in panel B.

Recall that this same extinguishment of debt was initially analyzed from the issuer's viewpoint in chapter 9. Note that for the issuer to extinguish the bonds early, either the bond must grant the issuer the right to repay the debt early or the investor must choose to sell the bonds back to the issuer.

THE MARKET AND EQUITY METHODS FOR INTERCORPORATE INVESTMENTS

Objective 4
Contrast the equity and market methods of accounting for investments.

Many companies invest in the equity securities of another company. The accounting for equity securities from the issuer's point of view was discussed in chapter 11. The investor's accounting depends on the relationship between the "investor" and the "investee." The question is: How much can the investor influence the operations of the investee? For example, the holder of a small number of shares in a company's stock cannot affect how the company invests its money, conducts its business, or declares and pays its dividends. We call this type of investor a passive investor. Such investors use the market method, under which the investment is carried at market value and dividends are recorded as income when received.

Exhibit 12-5

Early Extinguishment

PANEL A: INVESTOR'S LOSS

Carrying amount		
Face or par value	$10,000,000	
Deduct: Unamortized discount on bonds*	183,334	$9,816,666
Cash received		9,600,000
Difference, loss on sale		$ 216,666

*The remaining discount is $88,997 + $94,337 = $183,334, or $346,500 − $79,207 − $83,959 = $183,334.

PANEL B: JOURNAL ENTRIES AT DECEMBER 31, 2003

Investor's Records		Issuer's Records	
Cash 9,600,000		Bonds payable 10,000,000	
Loss on disposal of bonds 216,666		Discount on bonds payable	183,334
Investment in bonds	9,816,666	Gain on early	
To record the sale of bonds		extinguishment	216,666
on the open market		Cash	9,600,000

As an investor acquires more substantial holdings of a company's stock, that investor's ability to influence the company changes. A stockholder with 2% or 3% ownership of a company has little difficulty making appointments to speak with company management. At 5% ownership, U.S. law requires the investor to report the ownership publicly in a filing with the SEC. As ownership interest rises to 20% and beyond, the investor begins to affect decisions, to appoint directors, and so on.

Once the investor has "significant influence," a term that GAAP defines as about 20% to 25% ownership, the market method no longer reflects the economic relationship between the potentially active investor and the investee (or **affiliated company**). In the United States, such an investor must use the **equity method,** which records the investment at acquisition cost and makes adjustments for the investor's share of dividends and earnings or losses experienced by the investee after the date of investment. As a result, the investor's share of the investee's earnings increases the book value at which the investment is carried and reported. Likewise, dividends received from the investee and the investor's share of the investee's losses reduce this carrying amount.

Many companies have "significant influence" stock ownership in other, usually smaller, companies. For example, Corning Inc., a technology company that is the world's leader in fiber-optic cable, holds such ownership in several companies. One such company is the Indian glass company, Samcor Glass Limited, in which Corning recently held a 45% interest.

Let us take a look at an example of how the market and equity methods might be applied. Suppose Buyit Corporation invests $80 million in each of two companies, Passiveco and Influential. Influential has a total market value of $200 million, generates earnings of $30 million, and pays dividends of $10 million. Because of its $80 million investment, Buyit owns 40% ($80 million ÷ $200 million) of Influential and must account for that investment using the equity method. Passiveco, however, has a total market value of $800 million, generates earnings of $120 million, and pays dividends of $40 million. Buyit thus owns only 10% ($80 million ÷ $800 million) of Passiveco and must use the market method to account for this investment.

To compare the methods, consider how Buyit is affected differently by investee earnings and dividends, as shown in Exhibit 12-6. Panel A shows the effects on the balance sheet equation and panel B shows the different journal entries for the two cases. The

affiliated company A company that has 20% to 50% of its voting shares owned by another company.

equity method Accounting for an investment at acquisition cost, adjusted for the investor's share of dividends and earnings or losses of the investee subsequent to the date of investment.

Exhibit 12-6

Comparing Market and Equity Methods

PANEL A: EFFECTS ON THE BALANCE SHEET EQUATION

	Market Method—Passiveco*				Equity Method—Influential**			
	A		**=**	**L + SE**	**A**		**=**	**L + SE**
	Cash	*Investments*		*Liab.*	*SE*	*Cash*	*Investments*	*Liab.*	*SE*
1. Acquisition	−80	+80	=			−80	+80	=	
2. a. Net income of Passiveco	No entry and no effect								
b. Net income of Influential							+12	=	+12
3. a. Dividends from Passiveco	+ 4		=		+4				
b. Dividends from Influential						+ 4	− 4	=	
Effects for year	−76	+80	=		+4	−76	+88	=	+12

*Passiveco: Under the market method, the investment account is unaffected. The dividend increases the cash amount by $4 million. Dividend revenue increases stockholders' equity by $4 million.

**Influential: Under the equity method, the investment account has a net increase of $8 million for the year. The dividend increases the cash account by $4 million and reduces investments. Investment revenue increases stockholders' equity by $12 million.

PANEL B: JOURNAL ENTRIES

Cost Method—Passiveco			Equity Method—Influential		
1. Investment in Passiveco	80		1. Investment in Influential	80	
Cash		80	Cash		80
2. No entry			2. Investment in Influential	12	
			Investment revenue†		12
3. Cash	4		3. Cash	4	
Dividend revenue‡		4	Investment in Influential		4

†Frequently called "equity in earnings of affiliated companies."

‡Frequently called "dividend income."

example assumes that the market values of Passiveco and Influential do not change during the period.

Under the market method, Buyit recognizes income when dividends are received. While the income statement and retained earnings are affected, Buyit's investment account is unaffected by the event. Under the equity method, Buyit recognizes income as it is earned by Influential instead of when dividends are received. Cash dividends from Influential do not affect net income; they increase cash and decrease the investment balance. In a sense, Buyit's claim on Influential grows by its share of Influential's net income. The dividend is a partial liquidation of Buyit's "claim." The receipt of a dividend is similar to the collection of an account receivable. The revenue from a sale of merchandise on account is recognized when the receivable is created; to include the collection also as revenue would be double-counting. Similarly, it would be double-counting to include the $4 million of dividends as income after the $12 million of income is already recognized in Buyit's income statement as it is earned.

The major reason for using the equity method instead of the market method is that the equity method does a better job of recognizing increases or decreases in the economic resources that the investor can influence. The reported net income of an "equity" investor (an investor who owns more than 20% of a company and thus uses the equity method) is increased by its share of net income or decreased by its share of net loss recognized by the investee.

Why does GAAP not permit shares accounted for under the equity method to be carried as an asset valued at market price? One explanation is that market prices are only good estimates of sales prices when small transactions occur. For example, 1.8 million of the 153 million outstanding shares of Tricon changed hands on February 3, 2000, a typical day. An investor who wanted to sell 100, 1,000 or even 10,000 shares could do so at about the $29 per share market price observed that day. However, if an investor owned 30% of Tricon and wanted to sell those 46 million shares, it could have a huge effect on the market price, potentially driving it down sharply. Thus, quoted market prices are not good measures of the value of large ownership interests. In addition, observed market prices may not be good estimates of the value of larger equity interests because the investor and investee have significant business relationships. For example, they may be customer and supplier or have joint R&D enterprises, or they may have overlapping boards of directors. In such cases, sale of a large investment interest might also mean significant changes to future business relationships and therefore changes in the value of the investee.

CONSOLIDATED FINANCIAL STATEMENTS

So far we have dealt with partial ownership of one company by another. Sometimes, though, as in the case of Ford and Jaguar, one company buys 100% of another company. In other cases, one company buys a majority (over 50%) share of a second company and effectively takes control of that second company. In these cases, a parent–subsidiary relationship exists. The **parent company** is the owner, and the **subsidiary** is the "owned" company that is fully owned or controlled by the parent. Keep in mind that subsidiaries are not folded into the parent company but instead remain separate legal entities from their parents. One parent can have numerous subsidiaries. Ford Motor Company actually has 60 different subsidiaries just in the United States, as well as several others, including Jaguar, outside the United States.

Sometimes acquisitions are part of an integrated strategy to grow the business. Consider Corning, Inc. the previously mentioned world leader in fiber-optic cable. Corning and Siemens, a German company, had two joint ventures in which they cooperated and some major markets in which they competed. In February of 2000, Corning announced the acquisition of the fiber-optic businesses of Siemens, including acquiring Siemens's share of their two joint ventures. This was the most recent in a series of steps by Corning to grow its fiber-optic business and solidify its worldwide leadership. It had expanded its internal production capability by 50% recently and had announced another 50% expansion planned for the near future. It had acquired a number of smaller companies and had committed to technological leadership, not only in the fiber-optic cable, but also in various supporting materials and technology to effectively use fiber-optic networks worldwide. Corning was well rewarded for this focused growth and new initiatives. Its stock price was at $30 per share in August of 1998 and reached $300 in August of 2000, for a compound annual growth rate of 216% per year.

Why have subsidiaries? Why not integrate the smaller companies into the larger parent to create a single legal entity? The reasons include limiting the liabilities in a risky venture, saving income taxes, conforming with government regulations with respect to a part of the business, doing business in a foreign country, and expanding in an orderly way while retaining the ability to subsequently contract by selling or spinning off the separate corporate subsidiary. For example, there are often tax advantages for the sellers when an acquisition involves the capital stock of a going concern instead of its individual assets.

Objective 5
Prepare consolidated financial statements.

parent company A company owning more than 50% of the voting shares of another company, called the subsidiary company.

subsidiary A corporation owned or controlled by a parent company through the ownership of more than 50% of the voting stock.

Sometimes foreign subsidiaries face more favorable treatment from their country of residence than a foreign parent corporation would experience. When Pepsi spun off Tricon, the transaction was easier and less costly because KFC, Pizza Hut, and Taco Bell were all existing separate subsidiary corporations.

So how do we account for subsidiaries if they are their own legal entities? We must start by accounting for them separately. Each subsidiary has its own set of financial statements that are independent of the parent's statements. Of course, the financial performance of a subsidiary affects the financial performance of the parent. Therefore, anyone who owns stock in a parent company needs to know how the subsidiaries are doing. If you own stock in Ford, you probably do not want to read over 60 sets of financial statements just to find out the overall value of your stock. **Consolidated statements** solve this problem by combining the financial positions and earnings reports of the parent company with those of its subsidiaries into an overall report as if they were a single entity.

Consolidated statements have been common in the United States since the turn of the century, when interconnected corporate entities first began to appear in the form of "holding companies," a parent with many subsidiaries. J. P. Morgan's U.S. Steel, formed in 1901, is a classic example. As recently as 1977, consolidated accounts were rare in Japan. In 1977, the law was changed, and both "parent-only" and supplemental consolidated statements became publicly available, although the consolidated statements were generally released later. Accounting reform continues in Japan. In March of 2000 consolidated statements and cash-flow statements became compulsory. In 2001 and 2002 market value accounting becomes required for various investments. *The Wall Street Journal* suggested these most recent changes will spur major restructuring as Japanese companies are forced to acknowledge bad investments in affiliates. In 1992, the Seventh Company Law Directive required full implementation of consolidation by members of the European Union. Similarly, the International Accounting Standards Board (IASB) encourages this trend.

consolidated statements Combinations of the financial positions and earnings reports of the parent company with those of various subsidiaries into an overall report as if they were a single entity.

THE ACQUISITION

To illustrate the concept of consolidated financial statements, consider two companies: the parent (P) and a subsidiary (S). Initially, they are separate companies with assets of $650 million and $400 million, respectively. P acquires all the stock of S by purchasing the shares from their current owners for $213 million paid in cash. The transaction is illustrated in panel A of Exhibit 12-7. Exhibit 12-7 shows the balance sheets of the two companies before and after this transaction in panel B. Panel C shows the journal entries for the acquisition. Figures in this and subsequent tables are in millions.

This purchase transaction is a simple exchange of one asset for another, from P's perspective. In terms of the balance sheet equation, cash declines by $213 million, and the asset account, Investment in S, increases by the same amount. The subsidiary S is entirely unaffected from an accounting standpoint, although it now has one centralized owner with unquestionable control over all economic decisions S may make in the future. In this example, the purchase price and the "investment in S" equal the stockholders' equity of the acquired company. Note that the $213 million purchase price is paid to the former owners of S as private investors. The $213 million is not an addition to the existing assets and stockholders' equity of S. That is, the books of S are unaffected by P's investment and P's subsequent accounting thereof. S still exists as a separate legal entity but with a new owner, P.

Each legal entity keeps its own set of books. Interestingly, no books are kept for the consolidated entity. Instead, working papers are used to prepare the consolidated statements as shown schematically in Exhibit 12-8.

Exhibit 12-7

Before and After the Acquisition, Parent (P) Buys Subsidiary (S) for $213

PANEL A: THE EVENTS

100% Purchase of S by P

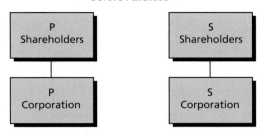

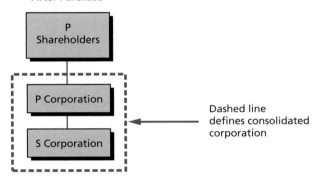

PANEL B: THE BALANCE SHEETS

	Before Purchase		After Purchase	
	S	*P*	*S*	*P*
Cash	$100	$300	$100	$ 87
Net plant	300	350	300	350
Investment in S				213
Total assets	$400	$650	$400	$650
Accounts payable	$187	$100	$187	$100
Bonds payable	—	100	—	100
Stockholders' equity	213	450	213	450
Total liabilities and SE	$400	$650	$400	$650

The following journal entries occur:

PANEL C: THE JOURNAL ENTRIES

P Books

Investment in S	213	
Cash		213

S Books

No entry

Exhibit 12-8

Preparing Consolidated Statements

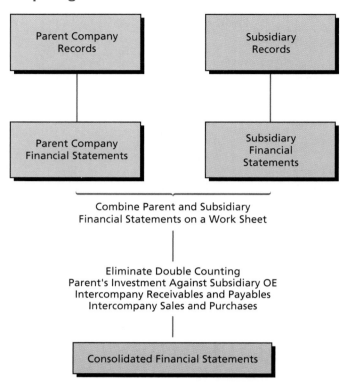

How do we consolidate the financial statements? Basically, we add up the individual financial statement values of the parent and all the subsidiaries. Consider a consolidated balance sheet prepared immediately after P's acquisition of S. The consolidated statement shows the details of all assets and liabilities of both the parent and the subsidiary. The Investment in S account on P's books represents P's investment in S, which is, in essence, really composed of all the assets and liabilities of S. This same amount is represented in S's books by stockholders' equity. If the consolidated statements simply add the individual balance sheet values of S and P, the $213 amount is represented twice, once as P's investment in S account, and again in S's stockholders' equity. The consolidated statements cannot count this amount twice because true assets and liabilities will be misstated. We can avoid this double-counting by eliminating the investment in S on P's books, and the stockholders' equity on S's books.

On the work sheet for consolidating the balance sheet, the entry to eliminate the double-counting of ownership interest in journal format is:

Stockholders' equity (on S books)	213	
Investment in S (on P books)		213

Separately, after the purchase, P has assets of $650 and S has assets of $400, so you might think the consolidated company would have assets totaling $1,050. However, when we consolidate and eliminate the double-counting of the investment amount in S, the consolidated assets are $1,050 − $213, or $837. The consolidated result, expressed in terms of the accounting equation, is:

100% Ownership

	Assets			=	Liabilities	+	Stockholders' Equity
	Investment in S	+	*Cash and Other Assets*	=	*Accounts Payable, etc.*	+	*Stockholders' Equity*
P's accounts, Jan. 1							
Before acquisition			650	=	200	+	450
Acquisition of S	+213		−213	=			
S's accounts, Jan. 1			400	=	187	+	213
Intercompany eliminations	−213			=			−213
Consolidated, Jan. 1	0	+	837	=	387	+	450

AFTER ACQUISITION

After the initial acquisition, P accounts for its long-term investment in S by the same equity method used to account for an unconsolidated ownership interest of 20% through 50%. Suppose S has a net income of $50 million for the subsequent year (year one). If the parent company P were reporting alone using the equity method, it would account for the net income of its subsidiary by increasing its Investment in S account and its Stockholders' Equity account (in the form of retained income) by 100% of $50 million.

The income statements for the year are (numbers in millions assumed):

	P	S	Consolidated
Sales	$900	$300	$1,200
Expenses	800	250	1,050
Operating income	$100	$ 50	$ 150
Investment revenue*	50	—	
Net income	$150	$ 50	

*Pro rata share (100%) of subsidiary net income, often called equity in earnings of affiliate or subsidiary.

P's parent-company-only income statement would show its own sales and expenses plus its proportional share of S's net income (as the equity method requires). This is shown in the leftmost column of the preceding table. The journal entry on P's books is:

```
Investment in S  ..............................   50
    Investment revenue* ......................        50
```
*Or "equity in net income of subsidiary."

To avoid counting the $50 million net income twice—once as S's net income and again as P's investment revenue—P must eliminate it in consolidation. Thus, after P records this year's result, the amount that will eliminate the investment in S on the work sheet used for consolidating the balance sheets is $213 + $50 = $263, which is P's new Investment in S balance and S's Stockholders' Equity.

Exhibit 12-9 reflects the changes in P's accounts, S's accounts, and the consolidated accounts ($ in millions). Review at this point to see that consolidated statements are the summation of the individual accounts of two or more separate legal entities. They are prepared periodically via work sheets. The consolidated entity does not have a separate continuous set of books like the legal entities. Moreover, a consolidated income statement is

Exhibit 12-9
Consolidation Work Sheet

	Assets			= Liabilities	+	Stockholders' Equity
	Investment in S	+	*Cash and Other Assets*	= *Accounts Payable, etc.*	+	*Stockholders' Equity*
P's accounts						
Beginning of year	+213	+	437	= 200	+	450
Operating income			+100	=		+100*
Share of S income	+50			=		+50*
End of year	263	+	537	= 200	+	600
S's accounts						
Beginning of year			400	= 187	+	+213
Net income			+50	=		+50*
End of year			450	= 187	+	263
Intercompany eliminations	−263			=		−263
Consolidated, end of year	0	+	987	= 387	+	600

*Changes in the retained income portion of stockholders' equity.

merely the summation of the revenue and expenses of the separate legal entities being consolidated after eliminating double-counting. The income statement for P shows the same $150 million net income as the consolidated income statement. The difference is that P's "parent-only" income statement shows its 100% share of S as a single $50 million item, whereas the consolidated income statement combines the detailed revenue and expense items for P and S.

INTERCOMPANY ELIMINATIONS

When accountants consolidate the financial records of two companies, they must be careful to avoid double-counting any items. Exhibit 12-9 emphasizes elimination of the parent's investment account and the subsidiary's owners' equity. In many cases, the parent and subsidiary do business together, which can lead to another type of double-counting. For example, suppose S charges P $12 for products that cost S $10, and the sale is made on credit. The following journal entries are made by each firm on its separate books:

P's RECORDS		
Merchandise inventory	12	
Accounts payable		12

S's RECORDS		
Accounts receivable	12	
Sales revenue		12
Cost of goods sold	10	
Merchandise inventory		10

However, has anything happened economically? No—as far as the consolidated entity is concerned, the product is just moved from one location to another. If P paid cash to S, the cash just shifts from "one pocket to another." So this transaction is not an important one from the perspective of the consolidated company, and it should be eliminated. It is important that each separate legal entity keeps track of its own transactions for its own records. The accountant can always later undo these intercompany transactions when the consolidation is done. The accountant needs to eliminate the intercompany receivable and payable, eliminate the costs and revenues, and be sure the inventory is carried at its cost to the consolidated company, $10. All these eliminations can be made using the following consolidation journal entries on the consolidation work sheet.

Accounts payable (P)	12	
Accounts receivable (S)		12
Sales revenue (S)	12	
Cost of goods sold (S)		10
Merchandise inventory (P)		2

The parenthetical letters show whose records contain the account balances. Remember, these entries are not recorded on the individual records of either company, only in the consolidation work sheet.

MINORITY INTERESTS

Objective 6
Incorporate minority interests into consolidated financial statements.

minority interests   The outside shareholders' interests, as opposed to the parent's interests, in a subsidiary corporation.

Our example of the consolidation of P and S assumes that P purchased 100% of S. However, in reality, companies often purchase less than 100% of a subsidiary. One company can control another with just 51% of the shares. For example, Corning owns 51% of Corning Asahi Video Products Company, and the remainder is owned by Asahi Glass America, Inc. Corning consolidates Asahi Video into its consolidated financial statements. But Asahi Glass has a claim on some of the consolidated assets and has a claim on some of Asahi Video's earnings. These claims are called **minority interests.** Minority interests represent the rights of nonmajority shareholders in the assets and earnings of a company that is consolidated into the accounts of its major shareholder. On the consolidated 1998 earnings statement, Corning shows a reduction of net income of $60.9 million due to "Minority interest in earnings of subsidiaries." On the consolidated balance sheet, Corning shows a $346.1 million "Minority interest in subsidiary companies." Some of these amounts relate to Asahi and some are related to other companies and other subsidiaries.

To apply this concept to our example, assume that our parent company (P) bought only 90% of S. Exhibit 12-10, using the basic figures of the previous example, shows the overall approach to a consolidated balance sheet immediately after the acquisition. In panel A, the graphic shows that some shareholders of S continue to have a minority interest in the consolidated entity. P's 90% of S's cost 0.90 × $213, or $192 million. The minority interest is 10%, or $21 million. (All dollar amounts are rounded to the nearest million.) Panel B illustrates that the investment is shown at cost on P's records and in consolidation that the minority interest appears at $21 million. You can think of the minority interest as representing the interests of those shareholders who own the 10% of the subsidiary stockholders' equity that is not owned by the parent company.

The 90% acquisition is assumed to occur on January 1. Suppose S has net income of $50 million for the year. The same basic procedures are followed by P and by S in their individual income statements regardless of whether S is 100% owned or 90% owned. P reports either 100% or 90% of S's earnings as a line item on P's income statement labeled something like equity in earnings of subsidiary. However, the presence of a minority interest changes the consolidated income statement. In consolidation, all the income is combined and then the 10% share due to minority shareholders is subtracted. We illustrate this in panel A of Exhibit 12-11. Note that the parent only income statement shows net income of $145 as does the consolidated income statement in the far right column.

Panel B shows how the minority interest from the income statement during the year serves to increase the level of the minority interest on the balance sheet at year-end. Note that the minority interest of $21 that existed on January 1 has been increased by $5 during the year to reflect the minority shareholders' 10% interest in the year's net income of $50. As indicated in the intercompany elimination near the bottom of panel B, the eliminating entry on the work sheet used for consolidating the balance sheet is:

Stockholders' equity (on S books)	263	
Investment in S (on P books)		237
Minority interest (on consolidated statements)		26

Exhibit 12-10

90% Purchase of S: P Pays Cash to Some S Shareholders; Some S Shareholders Retain Minority Interest

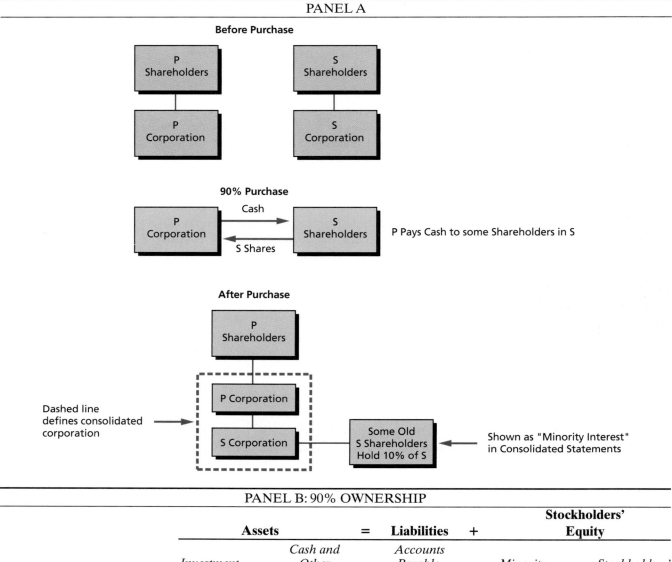

PANEL A

Before Purchase

90% Purchase

After Purchase

Dashed line defines consolidated corporation

Shown as "Minority Interest" in Consolidated Statements

PANEL B: 90% OWNERSHIP

	Assets		=	Liabilities	+	Stockholders' Equity		
	Investment in S	+ Cash and Other Assets =		Accounts Payable, etc.	+	Minority Interest	+	Stockholders' Equity
P's accounts, Jan. 1								
Before acquisition		650	=	200			+	450
Acquisition of 90% of S	+192	−192	=					
S's accounts, Jan. 1		400	=	187			+	213
Intercompany eliminations	−192		=			+21		−213
Consolidated, Jan. 1	0	858	=	387		21	+	450

DEFINING CONTROL

Intercorporate investments occur worldwide, and different countries have made different choices about how to define control and about when to consolidate the financial results of two related companies. Consolidation is appropriate when one entity can

Exhibit 12-11

Effect of 90% Ownership During the Year

PANEL A: THE INCOME STATEMENT			
	P	**S**	**Consolidated**
Sales	$900	$300	$1,200
Expenses	800	250	1,050
Operating income	$100	$ 50	$ 150
Investment Revenue*	45	—	
Net income	$145	$ 50	
Minority interest (10%) in subsidiary's net income			5
Net income to consolidated entity			$ 145

*Pro rata share (90%) of subsidiary net income, often called equity in earnings of affiliate or subsidiary.

PANEL B: THE BALANCE SHEET								
	Assets			**=**	**Liabilities**	**+**	**Stockholders' Equity**	
	Investment in S	+	*Cash and Other Assets*	=	*Accounts Payable, etc.*	+	*Minority Interest*	+	*Stockholders' Equity*
P's accounts								
Beginning of year, before acquisition			650	=	200		+	450
Acquisition	192		−192	=				
Operating income			+100	=				+100
Share of S income	+45			=				+45
End of year	237	+	558	=	200		+	595
S's accounts								
Beginning of year			400	=	187		+	213
Net income			+50	=				+50
End of year		+	450	=	187		+	263
Intercompany eliminations	−237			=			+26**	−263
Consolidated, end of year	0	+	1,008	=	387	+	26**	+	595

**Beginning minority interest plus minority interest in net income: $21 + .10(50) = 21 + 5 = 26$.

direct the use of the assets of another company. In Australia, the definition of control and the decision to consolidate two firms is complex and relies on a combination of factors, including not only whether one firm owns 50% of another but also whether it can control the membership of the board of directors and whether other investors own significant concentrated blocks of stock. Thus, an Australian parent company might own only 40% of a subsidiary company but might control it because the parent has an influence over the board of directors or because not enough other shareholders care enough to outvote the parent.

In the United States, GAAP specifies three methods for accounting for intercorporate investments, and currently "bright line" tests are used to choose among them. For ownership of less than 20%, the market method is used, above 50%, consolidation generally is required, and between the two, the equity method is used. As this is being written, the FASB is debating whether to modify U.S. GAAP. If it does, it will no doubt move toward the more common and flexible definitions of control currently in use internationally.

Changing the rules of control can have some interesting consequences. Consider the case of USAir, a major airline in the United States that has one of the highest cost structures in the business. While United converted to employee ownership and American reached agreement on employee participation in profits during the early 1990s, USAir struggled to engage its employees in similar agreements. The various unions have demanded representation on the board of directors as part of an arrangement to reduce wages and increase scheduling flexibility. USAir Chairman, Seth Schofield, may have favored such a plan, but could not accept it because British Airways PLC, then owner of 24% of USAir, adamantly opposed any voting role for the unions. Of the shares, 24% provided British Airways with significant authority. Times change and at this writing United Airlines has offered to acquire USAir and the regulatory agencies in Washington are trying to decide whether such a merger can significantly reduce competition. At the same time, United's employees, who are the primary owners of the company, are trying to decide whether to approve the merger.

Another interesting case of control concerns Joseph Antonini, former chairman of Kmart, a direct competitor of Wal-Mart. Kmart was the bigger company 15 years ago, and many predicted that Wal-Mart would never exceed Kmart on any financial measure. But Sam Walton, Wal-Mart's founder, generated spectacular growth while Kmart languished. Years after Wal-Mart passed Kmart, the board still supported Antonini. What finally led to his dismissal? CALPERS, the California pension system, and other institutional

BUSINESS FIRST
Merger Lessons

When one company buys another, the expectation is that it will be a good deal. Why else should it be done? However, many acquisitions do not work. The reasons are many and investors have developed a healthy skepticism. Typically, when mergers are announced, the stock price of the acquiring company falls, while the stock price of the target company rises sharply. At this writing an announcement by JDS Uniphase is much in the news. JDS has announced an agreement to purchase SDL. Both are fiber-optic component companies. The transaction is a share-for-share exchange, 3.8 shares of JDS for each share of SDL. JDS stock fell 13% on July 10, the day of the announcement, while SDL stock rose almost 9%.

This merger may be great. The two companies are very similar and JDS is an experienced company in the acquisition game, although usually with smaller, more easily integrated targets. Historically, however, the list of failed mergers is long. For example, AT&T bought NCR after a long pursuit for $7.4 billion in 1991. NCR was spun off to shareholders in 1995 in a deal valued at $3.4 billion, a $4 billion loss. When the merger occurred the CEO's message was about attaining a level of growth and success that the companies could not have attained separately. The explanation for the spin-off was that the "complexity of trying to manage these different busi-

nesses began to overwhelm the advantages of integration." Similarly, Novell bought WordPerfect for $1.4 billion in 1994 and sold it for $124 million in 1996, a $1.3 billion loss. Novell aspired to become a "software powerhouse" and settled for what it does best, "networking software."

Sometimes a wave of mergers passes through an industry. In the pharmaceutical industry the wave involved purchase of pharmacy-benefit managers. The wave was initiated by Merck's purchase of a benefits manager for $6.6 billion in 1993, followed by similar purchases by Smithkline Beecham and Eli Lilly in 1994. Merck's acquisition has been retained and Merck-Medco revenues now account for about 50% of Merck's total revenues (although only 5% of earnings). Smithkline sold its 1994, $2.3 billion investment in 1999 for $700 million at a loss of $1.6 billion (70%) and Lilly sold its $4 billion investment for $1.5 billion in 1998 at a loss of $2.5 billion (63%).

Perhaps the most common problems are cultural and related to the integration of two different cultures. Sometimes the strategic plan is simply a bad plan. Of course, many mergers work well. At this writing recent mergers of Travelers with Citicorp, Daimler Benz with Chrysler, Exxon with Mobil, and BP with Amoco and with Arco seem to be moving forward reasonably well. Time will tell.

holders of Kmart stock decided enough was enough. While none of them owned enough shares to have significant influence over the Kmart board, their collective voice was loud and clear. The Kmart board finally agreed and replaced Antonini and changed direction.

PURCHASED GOODWILL

The example in the previous section on consolidated financial statements assumed that the acquisition cost of Company S by Company P was equal to the book value of Company S. However, the total purchase price paid by P often exceeds the book values of the assets acquired. In fact, the purchase price also often exceeds the sum of the fair market values (current values) of the identifiable individual assets less the liabilities. Such excess of purchase price over fair market value is called **goodwill** or purchased goodwill or, more accurately, excess of cost over fair value of net identifiable assets of businesses acquired. For example, Philip Morris paid $13 billion for Kraft, but only $2 billion was assigned to identifiable individual assets. The remaining $11 billion was goodwill.

goodwill The excess of the cost of an acquired company over the sum of the fair market value of its identifiable individual assets less the liabilities.

Why would Philip Morris rather buy Kraft as a going concern than pay less to buy trucks, buildings, copying machines, accounting systems, and so on that would produce the products that Kraft produces? When customers consider a purchase, they know that Kraft offers reliable quality. Customers pay more for Kraft products than they would for an unbranded cheese. When grocery stores lay out their shelf space, they offer Kraft more space in better locations than they allow for unbranded, unknown products. Customers are more prone to buy well-displayed products in prime locations. These established patterns and reputations are why Kraft's goodwill is valuable.

ACCOUNTING FOR GOODWILL

To see the impact of goodwill on the consolidated statements, refer to our initial example on consolidations, where there was an acquisition of a 100% interest in S by P for $213 million. Suppose the price were $40 million higher, or a total of $253 million cash. For simplicity, assume that the fair values of the individual assets of S are equal to their book values. This means that the entire excess of purchase price over existing book value is goodwill. The balance sheets immediately after the acquisition are developed in Exhibit 12-12. As suggested in the table, the eliminating entry on the work sheet for consolidating the balance sheet is:

Objective 7
Explain the economic and reporting role of goodwill.

Stockholders' equity (on S books)	213	
Goodwill (on consolidated balance sheet)	40	
Investment in S (on P books)		253

GOODWILL AND ABNORMAL EARNINGS

As you might suspect, the final price paid by the purchaser of an ongoing business is the culmination of a bargaining process. Therefore, the exact amount paid for goodwill is subject to the negotiations concerning the total purchase price. A popular logic for determining the maximum price follows.

Goodwill is fundamentally the price paid for "excess" or "abnormal" earning power. The steps to value the abnormal earning power are summarized in panel A of Exhibit 12-13. Essentially we determine the market value of the identifiable assets of an ordinary company (M in this case) and treat that as the reasonable cost of acquiring the ordinary earnings the company generates ($80,000 in this case). The market value is 10 times earnings. Company N has identical assets worth $800,000 but also has location, human resource, or reputation advantages that allow it to earn an extra $20,000 more than

Exhibit 12-12
Creating Goodwill

	Assets			=	Liabilities	+	Stockholders' Equity
	Investment in S	+	*Cash and Other Assets*	=	*Accounts Payable, etc.*	+	*Stockholders' Equity*
P's accounts							
Before acquisition			650	=	200	+	450
Acquisition	+253		−253	=			
S's accounts			400	=	187	+	213
Intercompany							
eliminations	−213			=			−213
Consolidated	40*	+	797	=	387	+	450

*The $40 million "goodwill" would appear in the consolidated balance sheet as a separate intangible asset account. It is often shown as the final item in a listing of assets.

Company M. We calculate a price for these abnormal earnings using a multiple of six. The multiples of 10 times earnings and 6 times earnings are arbitrary. Actual values differ from year to year and from company to company. These earnings are not worth as much per dollar as ordinary earnings because they are likely to be harder to maintain. The total value of Company N is $920,000, as shown in panel B of Exhibit 12-13.

This discussion may help explain why Ford would rather buy Jaguar than start its own luxury car line. It may help explain why Ford paid $2 billion more for Jaguar than its physical assets were worth. Several Japanese manufacturers have proved it is possible to create new prestige labels: the Lexus and the Infiniti. However, these may be a notch below Jaguar in price and status. Also, new labels lack the generations of image building that lead people to conceive of success as being able to own a Jaguar. Ford made a strategic choice about the future extra income that the Jaguar name will provide. Only time will tell if the $2 billion investment in goodwill was worth it, not to mention the additional investment to transform Jaguar production processes made by Ford in the 1990s. Some analysts are saying great things about the quality and performance of the Jaguars hitting the streets in 2001 and those on the drawing boards.

AMORTIZATION OF GOODWILL

Does goodwill last forever? Some might argue that it can. After all, McDonald's and CocaCola have enjoyed good reputations for decades. However, take a look at a company like Atari, the old computer maker. In the early 1980s, Atari was huge, as one of the first makers of home video games. Now, however, you probably do not even recognize the name. Also realize that for reputations to persist, the company must continue to advertise, to produce a quality product, and to satisfy its customers. Coke and Pepsi are internationally known, distributed, and consumed, and they command a premium price over their generic competitors. Yet if one gave up the cola wars, the other would quickly gain market share. So goodwill can be maintained by continuous effort, but it does not have perpetual life. Goodwill is not impervious to events. In Europe in the late 1990s, concern over impurity in some bottles of Coca Cola created quite a ruckus and led to a drop in market share. Coke had to take immediate action to limit the effects of these events.

How do accountants reflect this limited life in financial statements? International practice ranges from immediate write-off of goodwill against stockholders' equity to treating goodwill as infinitely lived. Notice that in both cases net income was unaffected

Exhibit 12-13

Valuation of Goodwill

PANEL A: COMPUTATION OF VALUES		
	Ordinary Company M	**Extraordinary Company N**
1. Fair market value of identifiable assets, less liabilities	$800,000	$800,000
2. Normal annual earnings on net assets at 10%	80,000	80,000
3. Actual average annual earnings for past 5 years (including for Company N an excess or abnormal return of $20,000)	80,000	100,000
4. Maximum price paid for normal annual earnings is 10 times line 2	800,000	800,000
5. Maximum price paid for abnormal annual earnings (which are riskier and thus less valuable per dollar of expected earnings) is six times $20,000	—	120,000*
6. Maximum price a purchaser is willing to pay for the company (line 1 plus line 5)	800,000	920,000

*This is the most the purchaser is willing to pay for goodwill.

PANEL B: VALUE OF COMPANY N

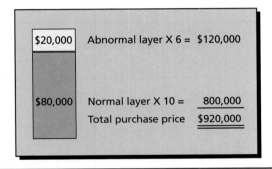

by the presence of goodwill. Prior to 2001, U.S. GAAP required that goodwill purchased after 1970 be amortized as an expense against net income over the period benefited, not to exceed 40 years. The 40-year maximum was arbitrary and reflected the negotiated nature of many accounting principles. People could live with that flexibility. Footnote disclosures of amortization practices for Ford and British Petroleum (BPAmoco) are reproduced as follows:

Ford:

Goodwill represents the excess of the purchase price over the fair value of the net assets of acquired companies and is being amortized using the straight-line method principally over 40 years.

BPAmoco:

Goodwill is the excess of purchase consideration over the fair value of net assets acquired. It is capitalized and amortized over its estimated useful economic life, limited to a maximum period of 20 years.

Exhibit 12-14

Ford Motor Company and Subsidiaries

① Consolidated Statement of Income for the Year Ended December 31, 1999 (in Millions)

Automotive		
Sales	$136,973	
Total costs and expenses	128,594	
Operating income	8,379	
Net interest income	31	
③ Equity in net (income) of affiliated companies	(82)	
Net (expense)/revenue from transactions with financial services	45	
Income before income taxes—automotive		$ 8,447
Financial services		
Revenues	$ 25,585	
Total costs and expenses	23,051	
Net revenue from transactions with automotive	45	
Income before income taxes—Financial Services		$ 2,579
Total company		
Income before income taxes		$11,026
Provision for income taxes		3,670
Income before minority interests		7,356
② Minority interests in net income of subsidiaries		119
Net income		$ 7,237

Ford Motor Company and Subsidiaries

① Consolidated Balance Sheet December 31, 1999 (in Millions)

Assets		
Automotive		
Total current assets	$ 44,091	
③ Equity in net assets of affiliated companies	2,744	
Property, net	42,317	
Other assets	16,029	
Total automotive assets	105,181	
Financial Services		
Total Financial Services assets	171,048	
Total assets	$276,229	
Liabilities and stockholders' equity		
Automotive		
Total current liabilities	$41,391	
Long-term debt	10,542	
② Minority interests in net assets of subsidiaries	177	
Other liabilities	35,580	
Deferred income taxes	1,376	
Total automotive liabilities	89,066	
Financial Services		
Total Financial Services liabilities	159,626	
Total stockholders' equity	27,537	
Total liabilities and stockholders' equity	$276,229	

Cisco acquires companies frequently and had $4 billion of goodwill on its July 28, 2000 balance sheet. Due to the dynamic industry in which it operates, it amortized goodwill more rapidly than either Ford or BPAmoco. "Amortization is computed using the straight-line method over the economic lives of the respective assets, generally 3 to 5 years."

During the year 2000, the FASB debated how goodwill should be treated. Initially the board proposed that the amortization period be shortened to a maximum of 20 years. This would have further reduced the reported earnings of companies that purchased significant amounts of goodwill. In a series of public meetings and discussions many groups encouraged the board to rethink its decision. Among their arguments was that amortization lead to a misstatement of both the balance sheet and the income statement. When companies purchase other companies the market value of the transaction leads to a reliable arms-length valuation of the goodwill. Unless something happens to that goodwill, it should continue to be reported as an asset. Moreover, when companies successfully maintain the value of their brands they do so by significant outlays on such items as advertising, brand management, and often research and development. These costs appear in the income statement and reflect the cost of maintaining the brand. To amortize the original investment in the brand in addition to these maintenance costs overstates the total costs for the year and therefore understates net income. Responding to this logic, the board reversed course and issued a rule that requires periodic reassessment of the goodwill and a write-down of the goodwill only when its asset value becomes impaired.

PERSPECTIVE ON CONSOLIDATED STATEMENTS

Exhibit 12-14 provides summarized financial statements for Ford Motor Company for 1999. The circled items 1, 2, and 3 in the exhibit deserve special mention:

1.   The headings indicate that these are consolidated financial statements.

2.   Minority interests typically appear on the balance sheet, just above stockholders' equity. For Ford, the minority interest is rather small, shown as "Minority interest in net assets of subsidiaries" of $177 million. In the income statement, the "Minority interests in net income of subsidiaries" appears as $119 million and is deducted to arrive at final net income of $7,237 million.

3.   "Affiliated companies" are discussed in Ford's footnotes as follows: "Affiliates that are 20%–50% owned, principally Mazda Motor Corporation and Auto Alliance International, Inc., and subsidiaries where control is expected to be temporary, principally investments in certain dealerships, are generally accounted for on an equity basis." In the balance sheet, the "Equity in net assets of affiliated companies" appears with automotive assets in the amount of $2,744 million. On the income statement, the caption "Equity in net income of affiliated companies" describes the income associated with these affiliates in the amount of $82 million.

      In 1990, these affiliates contributed a net loss of $96.6 million to Ford's consolidated income statement and in 1994, income of $271 million. These observations from prior years do not necessarily provide useful information about the performance of Mazda and Auto Alliance, however, because ownership interests change over time. For example, in May of 1996, Ford increased its investment in Mazda from 24.5% to 33.4%. To help you understand the relationship between the consolidated financial statements and Ford's actual corporate structure, consider the simplified version of Ford Motor Company shown at the top of the next page

The FASB requires that all subsidiaries be consolidated. That is, all subsidiaries, regardless of their line of business or the parent company's line of business, are an

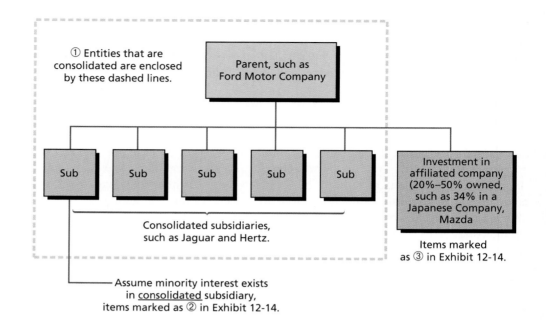

① Entities that are consolidated are enclosed by these dashed lines.

Parent, such as Ford Motor Company

Sub Sub Sub Sub Sub

Investment in affiliated company (20%–50% owned, such as 34% in a Japanese Company, Mazda

Consolidated subsidiaries, such as Jaguar and Hertz.

Items marked as ③ in Exhibit 12-14.

Assume minority interest exists in <u>consolidated</u> subsidiary, items marked as ② in Exhibit 12-14.

integral part of the complete consolidated entity. As a result, the FASB believes that not consolidating some subsidiaries would result in significant amounts of the overall company's assets, liabilities, revenues, and expenses being left out, which would make the consolidated statements less useful.

There are exceptions to the general rule, but they are rare. One exception is that a subsidiary shall not be consolidated if control is likely to be temporary or if that control does not rest with the majority owner. This exception actually applies to Ford. As you might have noted from our discussion of item 3 for Ford's consolidated statements, the company sometimes owns dealerships that it plans to quickly resell to a new dealer. Because the ownership of these dealerships is temporary, Ford does not consolidate them. Ford's statements reflect the consolidation of a manufacturing company with a financing company. Ford has chosen to structure the statements to clearly separate these two parts of its economic activity. The assets and liabilities of the Financial Services activity are listed separately as are the revenue and expense components. The footnotes provide additional detail on both segments of the business. Financial analysts pay particular attention to understanding the distinct parts of a business as they make predictions about the future.

EQUITY AFFILIATES, MINORITY INTEREST, AND THE STATEMENT OF CASH FLOWS

A company with equity affiliates (firms for which the investor uses the equity method) may use the direct method or the indirect method to prepare its cash flow statement. If it uses the direct method, no special problem arises because only the cash received from the affiliate as a dividend appears. However, if the indirect method is used, net earnings are increased by the investor's share of its affiliates' earnings or are decreased by its share of the affiliates' loss. To calculate cash flow from operations, we must adjust reported income. Suppose the investor had net income of $7.6 million, including equity in earnings of an affiliate of $2.5 million, and received $1.3 million in dividends from the affiliate. Cash flow is $1.3 million. Because net earnings includes $2.5 million, the indirect method must adjust net earnings by $2.5 million − $1.3 million = $1.2 million, the amount of the equity in earnings that was not received in cash.

Elements of the Operating Activities section of Cornings' Consolidated Statement of Cash Flows for 1999 are reproduced as follows. The key numbers are in bold type.

Corning's share of the earnings of affiliated companies exceeded the dividends received by $61.4 million in 1999. This excess is often called "undistributed earnings." The income statement shows that Corning reported equity in earnings of $112.3 million in 1999, which is included in the $515.8 million of net income.

Corning Incorporated
Operating Activities Section Consolidated Statements of Cash Flows

	Year Ended December 31		
(In millions)	1999	1998	1997
Cash Flows from Operating Activities:			
Net income	$515.8	$421.3	$461.5
Adjustments to reconcile net income to net cash provided by operating activities of continuing operations:			
Income from discontinued operations	(4.8)	(66.5)	(30.9)
Depreciation and amortization	408.3	320.1	305.0
Non-operating gains	(30.0)	(40.4)	
Provision for impairment and restructuring, net of cash spent	1.4	61.3	
Employee benefit expense in excess of (less than) cash funding	(17.1)	39.4	36.2
Equity in earnings of associated companies in excess of dividends received	**(61.4)**	**(33.9)**	**(13.8)**
Minority interest in earnings of subsidiaries in excess of dividends paid	**50.5**	**8.3**	**39.7**
(Gains) losses on disposition of properties and investments	8.8	8.9	(6.4)
Deferred tax provision	36.3	2.0	0.3
Other	25.3	31.0	3.8
Changes in operating assets and liabilities:			
Accounts receivable	(152.1)	(61.9)	(74.0)
Inventories	(81.3)	(19.6)	(62.7)
Other current assets	(6.8)	(13.6)	(10.3)
Accounts payable and other current liabilities	156.0	16.0	51.1
Net Cash Provided by Operating Activities of Continuing Operations	848.9	672.4	699.5

 From the information about Corning, calculate the dividends paid by the unconsolidated equity affiliates to Corning during 1999.

ANSWERS

We can compute that dividends of $50.9 million were received in 1999 from equity affiliates ($112.3 million of equity in earnings reported on the income statement less the $61.4 million "undistributed" portion shown as "Equity in earnings of associated companies in excess of dividends received" in the statement of cash flow).

The Operating Section of the Cash Flow statement also refers to minority interests in earnings of subsidiaries in excess of dividends paid amounting to $50.5, which is added back to net income to calculate cash flow from operations. The logic is similar to equity earnings. Here the full income statement reduces consolidated net income by 66.8 representing claims of minority shareholders. However, only $16.3 million was distributed to the minority shareholders through cash dividends. The $50.5 million represents the portion that was not paid in cash.

PURCHASED RESEARCH AND DEVELOPMENT

The basic rule in an acquisition is that the assets of the acquired company are included on the books of the acquiring company at their fair market value on the date of acquisition. Research and development that a company acquires creates a special problem. Recall that purchased patents that represent the legal right to exclusive use of a process that has been fully developed are recorded at cost by the purchaser and amortized. In contrast, R&D conducted by a company must be expensed immediately even though it may give rise to a patent in the future and may have long-term value for the firm. When a company buys another company, one of the assets it acquires (and pays for) is R&D that is in process. The buyer pays a price for this asset, but the buyer is not allowed to record it on the books as an asset. The buyer must expense it immediately.

Cisco often buys other companies and its income statement shows this practice. In the income statement for the year ended July 29, 2000 Cisco deducted "in-process research and development" of $1,373 million. This was in addition to R&D conducted by Cisco directly that lead to $2,704 million of expense. Thus, of total expenses of $8,947 million, $4,077 was for R&D ($1,373 plus $2,704).

Standard setters and analysts are concerned about this practice and the FASB is currently evaluating alternative rules. The issue is that in a purchase transaction the buyer has fully evaluated the value of in-process R&D and has decided to pay for it as part of the purchase price. Many would argue that this valuation is at arm's length and as reliable as the valuation attached to plant, property, and equipment or other assets being acquired. However, the balance sheet does not show this as an asset. Moreover, immediate expensing of this cost means that future income statements do not appropriately bear an expense for the expiration of this acquired asset. Recall that Cisco amortizes its intangible assets rapidly, perhaps over 3 years. By immediately deducting the $1,373 million, its income statements over the next 3 years show $454 million per year more in income before tax. This is approximately 10% of its income before tax of $4,343 million in 2000.

SUMMARY OF ACCOUNTING FOR EQUITY SECURITIES

Exhibit 12-15 summarizes all the relationships in intercorporate investments. Take a few moments to reconcile the Ford financial statements in Exhibit 12-14 with Exhibit 12-15. In particular, note that minority interests arise only in conjunction with consolidated subsidiaries. Why? Because consolidated balance sheets and income statements assume that the parent company owns and controls 100% of the detailed assets, liabilities, sales, and expenses of the subsidiary companies. Thus, if a minority interest were not recognized, the stockholders' equity and net income of the consolidated enterprise would overstate the claims of the parent company shareholders.

In contrast, minority interests do not arise in connection with the accounting for investments in affiliated companies. Why? Because no detailed assets, liabilities, revenues, and expenses of the affiliated companies are included in the consolidated statements. The investor's interests in these companies have been recognized on a proportional basis only.

As we have seen, the accounting for investments in common stock depends on the nature of the investment:

1. Investments that represent more than a 50% ownership interest are usually consolidated. A subsidiary is a corporation controlled by another corporation. The usual condition for control is ownership of a majority (more than 50%) of the outstanding voting stock.

Exhibit 12-15

Summary of Accounting for Equity Securities

Item in Exhibit 12-14	Percentage of Ownership	Type of Accounting	Balance Sheet Effects	Income Statement Effects	Major Journal Entries
①	100%	Consolidation	Individual assets, individual liabilities added together. For subsidiaries purchased for more than the fair value of identifiable assets, goodwill is shown	Individual revenues, individual expenses added together. If goodwill exists, it must be amortized against net income	None, except in work sheets for preparing consolidated statements; to eliminate reciprocal accounts, to avoid double-counting, and to recognize any goodwill
②	Greater than 50% and less than 100%	Consolidation	Same as 1, but recognition given to minority interest in liability section	Same as 1, but recognition given to minority interest near bottom of statement when consolidated net income is computed	Same as 1, but recognition of minority interests is included in work sheet entries

③	20% to and including 50%	Equity method	Investment carried at cost plus pro rata share of subsidiary earnings less dividends received	Equity in earnings (losses) of *affiliated* or *associated* companies shown on one line as addition to (deduction from) income	Investment xx
					  Equity in earnings xx
					  To record earnings
					Cash xx
					  Investment xx
					  To record dividends received

	Below 20%	Market method	Investment carried at market	For trading securities changes affect the income statement. For available-for-sale securities a valuation allowance appears in owners' equity	Marketable securities xx
					  Unrealized gains xx
					  To record appreciation
					Marketable securities xx
					  Valuation allowance xx
					  To record appreciation

2. The equity method is generally used for a 20% through 50% interest because such a level of ownership creates a presumption that the owner has the ability to exert significant influence. Under the equity method, the cost at date of acquisition is adjusted for the investor's share of the earnings or losses of the investee subsequent to the date of investment. Dividends received from the investee reduce the carrying amount of the investment.

3. Marketable equity securities are generally carried at market value. These investments are typically passive in the sense that the investor exerts no significant influence on the investee.

SUMMARY PROBLEMS FOR YOUR REVIEW

PROBLEM ONE

The following is a summary of material from Dow Chemical's annual report as of December 31, 1999 ($ in millions):

	$
Marketable securities and interest-bearing deposits	706
Total current assets	8,847
Investments:	
Investment in nonconsolidated affiliates	1,359
Other investments	2,872
Noncurrent receivables	390
Total investments	4,621
Properties	24,276
Less: Accumulated depreciation	15,786
Net property	8,490
Goodwill	1,834
Deferred charges and other assets	1,707
Total	$25,499

Note that the statements are somewhat compressed and no detail for current assets is shown. Current assets may include some smaller holdings of equity securities that are valued at market.

Dow also shows "Minority interests in subsidiary companies" of $408 million among its liabilities.

Required

1. Suppose "Marketable securities" included a $24 million portfolio of equity securities. Their market values on the following March 31, June 30, and September 30 were $20, $23, and $28 million, respectively. Compute the following:
   a. Carrying amount of the portfolio on each of the three dates.
   b. Gain (loss) on the portfolio for each of the three quarters.

2. Suppose the $2,872 million of "Other investments" included a $9 million investment in the debentures of an affiliate that was being held to maturity. The debentures had a par value of $10 million and a 10% nominal rate of interest, payable June 30 and December 31. Their market rate of interest when the investment was made was 12%. Prepare the Dow journal entry for the semiannual receipt of interest.

3. Suppose Dow's 20% to 50% owned companies had net income of $200 million. Dow received cash dividends of $70 million from these companies. No other transactions occurred. Prepare the pertinent journal entries. Assume that on average Dow owns 40% of the companies.

SOLUTION TO PROBLEM ONE

1. Amounts are in millions.

   a. Market: $20, $23, and $28.

   b. $20 − $24 = $4 loss; $23 − $20 = $3 gain; $28 − $23 = $5 gain. Gain or loss would be reported in the income statement for trading securities or in the stockholders' equity section for securities available-for-sale.

2.
Cash	500,000	
Other investments (in bonds)	40,000	
Interest revenue		540,000

   Six months' interest earned is
   .5 × .12 × $9,000,000 = $540,000
   Amortization is $540,000 − cash received of
   .5 × .10 × $10,000,000 = $540,000 − $500,000

3.
Investments in 20% to 50% owned companies	80,000,000	
Investment revenue		80,000,000
To record 40% share of $200 million income		
Cash.......................................	70,000,000	
Investments in 20% to 50% owned companies ...		70,000,000
To record dividends received from 20% to 50% owned companies		

PROBLEM TWO

1. Review the section on minority interests, pp. 523–524. Suppose P buys 60% of the stock of S for a cost of .60 × $213, or $128 million. The total assets of P consist of this $128 million plus $522 million of other assets, a total of $650 million. The S assets and equities are unchanged from the amount given in the example on p. 524. Prepare an analysis showing what amounts would appear in a consolidated balance sheet immediately after the acquisition.

2. Suppose S has a net income of $50 million for the year, and P has an operating income of $100 million. Other details of their income statements are as described in the example on p. 525. Prepare an analysis showing what amounts would appear in a consolidated income statement and year-end balance sheet.

SOLUTION TO PROBLEM TWO

1.

	Assets			=	Liabilities	+		Stockholders' Equity	
	Investment in S	+	Cash and Other Assets	=	Accounts Payable, etc.	+	Minority Interest	+	Stockholders' Equity
P's accounts, Jan. 1:									
Before acquisition			650	=	200			+	450
Acquisition of 60% of S	+128		−128	=					
S's accounts, Jan. 1			400	=	187			+	213
Intercompany eliminations	−128			=			+85		−213
Consolidated, Jan. 1	0	+	922	=	387	+	85	+	450

2.

	P	S	Consolidated
Sales	$900	$300	$1,200
Expenses	800	250	1,050
Operating income	$100	$ 50	$ 150
Pro rata share (60%) of unconsolidated subsidiary net income	30	—	
Net income	$130	$ 50	
Outside interest (40%) in consolidated subsidiary net income (minority interest in income)			20
Net income to consolidated entity			$ 130

	Assets			=	Liabilities	+	Stockholders' Equity		
	Investment in S	+	Cash and Other Assets	=	Accounts Payable, etc.	+	Minority Interest	+	Stockholders' Equity
P's accounts									
Beginning of year	128	+	522*	=	200			+	450
Operating income			+100	=				+	+100
Share of S income	+30			=					+ 30
End of year	158	+	622	=	200			+	580
S's accounts									
Beginning of year			400	=	187			+	213
Net income			+50	=					+50
End of year			450	=	187			+	263
Intercompany eliminations	−158			=			+105†		−263
Consolidated, end of year	0	+	1,072	=	387	+	105	+	580

*650 beginning of year − 128 for acquisition = 522.
†85 beginning of year + .40 × (50) = 85 + 20 = 105.

Highlights to Remember

1. **Explain why corporations invest in one another.** Corporate investments arise for many reasons. Smaller investments are intended to create a relationship that leads to communication and sharing of information. As investments rise in size, the investor obtains more influence over the investee leading to changes in the behavior of both parties. When investments exceed 50% ownership of the investee, the investor obtains control sufficient to dictate behavior. The owner totally controls decision making and dictates what is made, to whom it is sold, from whom parts are purchased, how activity is financed, whether dividends are paid, what new assets are purchased, and so on.

2. **Account for short-term investments in debt securities and equity securities.** The accounting for intercorporate investments depends on the purpose of the investment, on whether it is an equity or debt security, and on the level of control the investor has over the issuer of the security. For short-term debt securities and short-term equity securities, accounting is at market. Trading securities are held to be resold, and the gains and losses from changes in market value go directly to the income statement. Marketable securities that are available-for-sale are reported at

market in the balance sheet, but gains and losses are carried in a separate account in stockholders' equity until the securities are sold.

3. **Report long-term investments in bonds.** When the investor's intention is to hold debt securities to maturity, the investor's accounting uses the effective interest rate method in the same manner that the issuer does. That is, discount and premium are amortized to affect interest revenue. For equity securities held for the long term, the accounting is linked to the investor's level of control of the issuer of the equity security. For ownership interests of less than 20%, accounting for equity securities requires classification as either available-for-sale or trading. The accounting is based on fair value.

4. **Contrast the equity and market methods of accounting for investments.** As the ownership interest ranges from 20% to 50%, the increasing control the investor can exert over the issuer leads to earnings recognition in the income statement, proportional to the percentage of ownership. The investment account is increased by this share of the issuer's earnings (or decreased by a proportionate share of losses). When dividends are received, the investment account is decreased with no effect on earnings. This is called the equity method.

5. **Prepare consolidated financial statements.** As the ownership interest exceeds 50%, the investor controls the subsidiary. Consolidation is appropriate, which involves combining all the assets and liabilities of the related corporate entities. For 100%-owned subsidiaries, the main concern is the elimination of intercompany transactions: sales, receivables, and payables.

6. **Incorporate minority interests into consolidated financial statements.** Minority interests are the rights of other shareholders in consolidated subsidiaries that are more than 50% owned and therefore consolidated, but are not 100% owned. They are treated much like the equity interests of an investor. On the income statement, the minority interests are deducted in arriving at net income available to common shareholders of the consolidated entity. On the balance sheet, the minority interests are an historical measure of the claims of minority shareholders on the assets of consolidated subsidiaries.

7. **Explain the economic and reporting role of goodwill.** Goodwill refers to the excess of the purchase price of an acquired company over the market value of its identifiable assets. Economically, it arises because the acquired firm has created the ability to earn extraordinary returns by creating market power. The market power might take the form of an exceptional brand name, such as Coca-Cola has developed. Because of the brand recognition, Coca-Cola can sell soft drinks at higher prices and earn higher returns than unbranded colas. U.S. policy makers have changed the requirement to amortize goodwill over a period not to exceed 40 years. In the future, goodwill will be written off only when it is impaired. Going forward, goodwill will remain an asset unless management concludes that the value of the goodwill has declined.

Accounting Vocabulary

affiliated company, p. 515
available-for-sale securities, p. 510
certificates of deposit, p. 509
commercial paper, p. 509
consolidated statements, p. 518
equity method, p. 515
goodwill, p. 527

held-to-maturity securities, p. 510
market method, p. 511
marketable securities, p. 509
minority interests, p. 523
parent company, p. 517
short-term debt securities, p. 509

short-term equity securities, p. 509
short-term investment, p. 509
subsidiary, p. 517
trading securities, p. 509
U.S. Treasury obligations, p. 509

Assignment Material

QUESTIONS

12-1 Why is *marketable securities* an ill-chosen term to describe short-term investments?

12-2 Distinguish among trading securities, available-for-sale securities and held-to-maturity securities.

12-3 "The cost method is applied to investments in short-term securities." Do you agree? Explain.

12-4 "Increases in the market price of short-term investments become gains on the income statement; decreases become losses." Do you agree? Explain.

12-5 Suppose an investor buys a $1,000 face value bond for $950, a discount of $50. Will amortization of the discount increase or decrease the investor's interest income? Explain.

12-6 What is the equity method?

12-7 "The equity method is usually used for long-term investments." Do you think this is appropriate? Explain.

12-8 Contrast the *market* method with the *equity* method.

12-9 What criterion is used to determine whether a parent–subsidiary relationship exists?

12-10 Why have subsidiaries? Why not have the corporation take the form of a single legal entity?

12-11 Suppose Company A buys 100% of the common shares of Company B for cash. How does Company B record the receipt of this cash on its books?

12-12 Why does a consolidated balance sheet require "eliminating entries"?

12-13 "A consolidated income statement will show more income than a parent-company-only statement when both the parent and subsidiary have positive net income." Do you agree? Explain.

12-14 What is a minority interest?

12-15 Distinguish between *control of* a company and *significant influence over* a company.

12-16 "Goodwill is the excess of purchase price over the book values of the individual asset acquired." Do you agree? Explain.

12-17 Does GAAP require amortization of goodwill against net income? If not, when does goodwill decrease?

12-18 Why might a company prefer to own 19.9% interest in an affiliate instead of a 20.1% interest?

12-19 When is there justification for not consolidating majority-owned subsidiaries?

12-20 Suppose P company received $20,000 in cash dividends from Y company, a 40%-owned affiliated company. Y company's net income was $80,000. How will P's statement of cash flows show these items using the direct method?

12-21 Why do minority interests arise in connection with consolidated statements, but not with investments in affiliated companies?

12-22 Would you expect the consolidated income statement to report higher net income than shown in the parent's separate financial statements?

COGNITIVE EXERCISES

12-23   Consequences of Marking to Market

As president of a young technology company, you and your chief financial officer are discussing your great success in investing in other high-growth companies in your industry. When you raised $20 million in capital, you actually needed $10 million immediately so you invested the other $10 million in a portfolio of dynamic companies. Over the last year the value of these companies doubled. You are trying to figure out how next year's reported income will compare with this year's if you liquidate that portfolio and invest it in the core business.

12-24   Scoping Out an Acquisition Strategy

You recently hired a young MBA who is advising you that you should grow more aggressively and suggesting that you should do so by acquiring other small companies. Your cookware and tableware importing business has been quite successful, but you are not sure that this new employee's plan to acquire a series of retail cooking/kitchenware stores makes sense. What issues would you raise in discussing this proposal?

12-25   Accounting Consequences of Changing Ownership Interest

You own 19% of a company that you do business with and are considering buying another 5% of the company. They provide a great product and great service. Their share price has been rising because of their potential. However, they are currently not profitable from an accounting perspective because they are doing a great deal of research and development. You have asked your CFO to advise you about the consequences of this increase in your ownership position. What would you expect the CFO to say?

12-26   Transactions between Companies

Your company has sales of $100 million and profits of $10 million. A similar, smaller company with sales of $25 million and profits of $5 million appears to be an attractive merger candidate. You currently buy 50% of the smaller company's production. The CEO has indicated that this would be a great acquisition because it would increase sales by 25% and profits by 50%. As CFO what issues do you raise concerning this proposed purchase and the CEO's analysis.

EXERCISES

12-27 Trading Securities
The McMillan Company has a portfolio of trading securities consisting of common and preferred stocks. The portfolio cost $160 million on January 1. The market values of the portfolio were ($ in millions): March 31, $150; June 30, $138; September 30, $152; and December 31, $170.

Required

1. Prepare a tabulation showing the balance sheet presentations and income statement presentations for interim reporting purposes.
2. Show the journal entries for quarters 1, 2, 3, and 4.

12-28 Available-for-Sale Securities
The MacGregor Company has a portfolio of securities identical to that of the McMillan Company (see Exercise 12-27). However, MacGregor classified the portfolio as available-for-sale securities. The portfolio cost $160 million on January 1. The market values of the portfolio were ($ in millions): March 31, $150; June 30, $138; September 30, $152; and December 31, $170.

Required

1. Prepare a tabulation showing the balance sheet presentations and income statement presentations for interim reporting purposes.
2. Show the journal entries for quarters 1, 2, 3, and 4.

12-29 Bond Discount Transactions
On December 31, 2001, a company purchased $1 million of 10-year, 10% debentures for $885,295. The market interest rate was 12%.

Required

1. Using the balance sheet equation format, prepare an analysis of bond transactions. Assume effective-interest amortization. Show entries for the investor concerning (a) purchase, (b) first semiannual interest payment, and (c) payment of maturity value.
2. Show the corresponding journal entries for preceding (a), (b), and (c).
3. Show how the bond investment would appear on the balance sheets as of December 31, 2001, and June 30, 2002.

12-30 Bond Premium Transactions
On December 31, 2001, the Guzman Company purchased $1 million of 10-year, 10% debentures for $1,135,915. The market interest rate was 8%.

Required

1. Using the balance sheet equation format, prepare an analysis of transactions for the investor's records. Key your transactions as follows: (a) purchase, (b) first semiannual interest payment using effective-interest amortization of bond premium, and (c) payment of maturity value.
2. Prepare sample journal entries for (a), (b), and (c) in requirement 1.
3. Show how the bond-related accounts would appear on the balance sheets as of December 31, 2001, and June 30, 2002.

12-31 Market Method or Equity Method
Yukon Outdoor Equipment acquired 25% of the voting stock of Bearpaw Snowshoes for $40 million cash. In year one, Bearpaw had a net income of $28 million and paid a cash dividend of $16 million.

Required

1. Using the equity and the market methods, show the effects of the three transactions on the accounts of Yukon Outdoor Equipment. Use the balance sheet equation format. Also show the accompanying journal entries. Assume constant market value for Bearpaw.
2. Which method, equity or market, would Yukon use to account for its investment in Bearpaw? Explain.

12-32 Equity Method
Company X acquired 30% of the voting stock of Company Y for $90 million cash. In Year one, Y had a net income of $50 million and paid cash dividends of $20 million.

Required

Prepare a tabulation that uses the equity method of accounting for X's investment in Y. Show the effects on the balance sheet equation. What is the year-end balance in the Investment in Y account under the equity method?

12-33 Consolidated Statements
Able and Baker companies had the following balance sheets at December 31, 20X8 ($ in thousands):

	Able	Baker
Assets		
Cash	$ 400	$100
Net plant	1,800	400
Total assets	$2,200	$500
Liabilities and stockholders' equity		
Accounts payable	175	$ 80
Long-term debt	425	220
Stockholders' equity	1,600	200
Total liabilities and stockholders' equity	$2,200	$500

On January 1, 20X9, Able purchased 100% of the common stock of Baker for $200,000.

Required

1. Prepare a balance sheet for Able Company immediately after its purchase of Baker Company.

2. Prepare a balance sheet for the consolidated entity immediately after the purchase of Baker Company.

3. Suppose Able Company had net income of $250,000 in 20X9 (before recognizing its share of Baker's income) and Baker Company had net income of $60,000 in 20X9. Neither company sold items to the other. What was the 20X9 consolidated net income?

12-34 Minority Interest

Suppose P company owns 95% of S company and S company earns $100,000. What is the amount of the minority interest shown in P company's consolidated income statement? What is the amount of the minority interest shown in S company's individual income statement?

12-35 Goodwill

Megasoft, Inc. purchased 100% of the common shares of Zenatel for $570,000 on January 1, 20X7. Zenatel's balance sheet just before the acquisition was ($ in thousands):

Cash	$ 90
Net fixed assets	220
Total assets	$310
Liabilities	$240
Stockholders' equity	70
Total liabilities and stockholders' equity	$310

The fair market value of Zenatel's assets and liabilities was equal to their book values.

Required

1. Compute the amount of goodwill Megasoft would recognize on this purchase. Where would this goodwill appear on Megasoft's financial statements?

2. Suppose Megasoft elected to amortize this goodwill over 20 years. Megasoft's 20X7 net income from all operations excluding those of Zenatel were $150,000. Zenatel had a net loss of $10,000. Compute consolidated net income for 20X7.

12-36 Affiliated Companies

Suppose P company owns 40% of S company. S company earns $200,000 and pays total dividends of $50,000 to its shareholders. What appears in the consolidated income statement of P company as a result of S company's activity? What would be the change in the account titled Investment in equity affiliates on P company's balance sheet?

12-37 Consolidations in Japan

A few years ago, Japan's finance ministry issued a directive requiring the 600 largest Japanese companies to produce consolidated financial statements. The previous practice had been to use parent-company-only statements. A story in *Business Week* said,

> *Financial observers hope that the move will help end the tradition-honored Japanese practice of "window dressing" the parent company financial*

results by shoving losses onto hapless subsidiaries, whose red ink was seldom revealed. . . . When companies needed to show a bigger profit, they would sell their product to subsidiaries at an inflated price. . . . Or the parent company charged a higher rent to a subsidiary company using its building.

Required

Could a parent company follow the quoted practices and achieve window dressing in its parent-only financial statements if it used the equity method of accounting for its intercorporate investments? Explain.

PROBLEMS

12-38 Trading Securities
On a recent December 31, Pennzoil Company held a portfolio of trading equity securities that cost $660,100,000 and had a market value of $955,182,000. Assume that the same portfolio was held until the end of the first quarter of the subsequent year. The market value of the portfolio was $980,160,000 at January 31, $941,187,000 at February 29, and $959,550,000 at March 31.

Required

1. Prepare a tabulation showing the balance sheet presentation and income statement presentation for monthly reporting purposes.
2. Show the journal entries for January, February, and March.
3. How would your answer to requirement 1 change if the securities were classified as available-for-sale?

12-39 Short-Term Investments
The VanDankan Company has the following footnote to its financial statements:

> Note 4: Short-Term Investments
>
> *The company holds the following short-term investments at December 31 (in thousands):*

	Cost	Market Value
Trading securities		
U.S. Government Bonds	680,000	670,000
Held-to-maturity securities		
Bonds issued by Beta Corporation	540,000	560,000
Available-for-sale securities		
Common shares of Gamma Corp.	300,000	770,000

Required

1. Compute the amount that VanDankan would show on its balance sheet for short-term investments.
2. Suppose the market values of the three securities at the beginning of the year had been:

U.S. Government bonds	685,000
Bonds issued by Beta Corp.	550,000
Common shares of Gamma Corp.	710,000

Prepare journal entries to recognize the changes in market values that would be recorded in VanDankan's books during the year.

12-40 Early Extinguishment of an Investment
On December 31, 2002, an insurance company purchased $10 million of 10-year, 10% debentures for $8,852,950. On December 31, 2003 (after all interest payments and amortization had been recorded for 2003), the insurance company sold all the debentures for $9.2 million. The market interest rate at issuance was 12%.

1. Compute the gain or loss on the sale for the insurance company (i.e., the investor).
2. Prepare the appropriate journal entries for the insurance company (i.e., the investor).

12-41   Consolidated Statements

Consider the following for Chow Company (the parent) as of December 31, 20X8:

	Chow	Subsidiary*
Assets	$800,000	$200,000
Liabilities to creditors	$300,000	$ 80,000
Stockholder's equity	500,000	120,000
Total equities	$800,000	$200,000

*60% owned by Chow.

The $800,000 of assets of Chow include a $72,000 investment in the subsidiary. The $72,000 includes Chow's pro rata share of the subsidiary's net income for 20X8. Chow's sales were $870,000 and operating expenses were $802,000. These figures exclude any pro rata share of the subsidiary's net income. The subsidiary's sales were $550,000 and operating expenses were $510,000. Prepare a consolidated income statement and a consolidated balance sheet.

12-42   Consolidated Financial Statements and Minority Interest

The parent company owns 90% of the common stock of Company S-1 and 60% of the common stock of Company S-2. The balances as of December 31, 20X4, in the condensed accounts follow:

	($ in thousands)		
	Parent	*S-1*	*S-2*
Sales	300,000	80,000	100,000
Investment in subsidiaries*	72,000	—	—
Other assets	128,000	90,000	20,000
Liabilities to creditors	100,000	20,000	5,000
Expenses	280,000	90,000	95,000
Stockholders' equity, including current net income	100,000	70,000	15,000

*Carried at equity in subsidiaries.

Prepare a consolidated balance sheet as of December 31, 20X4, and a consolidated income statement for 20X4 ($ in millions of dollars).

12-43   Consolidated Financial Statements

Company P acquired a 100% voting interest in Company S for $110 million cash at the start of the year. Immediately before the business combination, each company had the following condensed balance sheet accounts ($ in millions):

	P	S
Cash and other assets	$500	$150
Accounts payable, etc.	$200	$ 40
Stockholders' equity	300	110
Total liab. & stk. eq.	$500	$150

1. Prepare a tabulation of the consolidated balance sheet accounts immediately after acquisition. Use the balance sheet equation format.
2. Suppose P and S have the following results for the year:

	P	S
Sales	$600	$180
Expenses	450	160

Prepare income statements for the year for P, S, and the consolidated entity. Assume that neither P nor S sold items to the other.

3. Present the effects of the operations for the year on P's accounts and on S's accounts, using the balance sheet equation. Also tabulate the consolidated balance sheet accounts at the end of the year. Assume that liabilities are unchanged.

4. Suppose S paid a cash dividend of $10 million. What accounts in requirement 3 would be affected and by how much?

12-44 Minority Interests

This alters the preceding problem. However, this problem is self-contained because all the facts are reproduced as follows. Company P acquired an 80% voting interest in Company S for $88 million cash at the start of the year. Immediately before the business combination, each company had the following condensed balance sheet accounts ($ in millions):

	P	S
Cash and other assets	$500	$150
Accounts payable, etc.	$200	$ 40
Stockholders' equity	300	110
Total liab. & stk. eq.	$500	$150

Required

1. Prepare a tabulation of the consolidated balance sheet accounts immediately after acquisition. Use the balance sheet equation format.

2. Suppose P and S have the following results for the year:

	P	S
Sales	$600	$180
Expenses	450	160

Prepare income statements for the year for P, S, and the consolidated entity. Assume that neither P nor S sold items to the other.

3. Using the balance sheet equation format, present the effects of the operations for the year on P's accounts and on S's accounts. Also tabulate consolidated balance sheet accounts at the end of the year. Assume that liabilities are unchanged.

4. Suppose S paid a cash dividend of $10 million. What accounts in requirement 3 would be affected and by how much?

12-45 Goodwill and Consolidations

This alters problem 12-44. However, this problem is self-contained because all the facts are reproduced later. Company P acquired a 100% voting interest in Company S for $150 million cash at the start of the year. Immediately before the business combination, each company had the following condensed balance sheet accounts ($ in millions):

	P	S
Cash and other assets	$500	150
Accounts payable, etc.	$200	$ 40
Stockholders' equity	300	110
Total liab. & stk. equity	$500	$150

Assume that the fair values of the individual assets of S were equal to their book values.

Required

1. Prepare a tabulation of the consolidated balance sheet accounts immediately after the acquisition. Use the balance sheet equation format.

2. Suppose the book values of the S individual assets are equal to their fair market values except for equipment. The net book value of equipment is $30 million and its fair market value is $50 million. The equipment has a remaining useful life of 4 years. Straight-line depreciation is used.

   a. Describe how the consolidated balance sheet accounts immediately after the acquisition would differ from those in requirement 1. Be specific as to accounts and amounts.

   b. By how much will consolidated income differ in comparison with the consolidated income that would be reported if all equipment had fair value equal to its book value on S's books as in requirement 1?

12-46 Purchased Goodwill

Consider the following balance sheets ($ in millions):

	Company A	Company B
Cash	150	15
Inventories	60	25
Plant assets, net	60	30
Total assets	270	70
Common stock and paid-in surplus	70	30
Retained income	200	40
Total liab. & stk. equity	270	70

Company A paid $100 million to Company B stockholders for all their stock. The "fair value" of the plant assets of Company B is $50 million. The fair value of cash and inventories is equal to their carrying amounts. Companies A and B continued to keep separate books.

Required

1. Prepare a tabulation showing the balance sheets of companies A and B, intercompany eliminations, and the consolidated balance sheet immediately after the acquisition.

2. Suppose that $60 million instead of $50 million of the total purchase price of $100 million could logically be assigned to the plant assets. How would the consolidated accounts be affected?

3. Refer to the facts in requirement 2. Suppose Company A had paid $110 million instead of $100 million. State how your tabulation in requirement 2 would change.

12-47 Effects of Goodwill on the Income Statement

Consider the following:

1. Philip Morris purchased General Foods for $5.6 billion. Philip Morris could assign only $1.7 billion to identifiable individual assets. What is the amount of goodwill created by the acquisition?

2. The Gannett Company, Inc., publisher of many newspapers, including *USA Today,* purchased radio stations KKBQ-AM and FM in Houston and WDAE-AM in Tampa for a total of $41 million. A footnote in the annual report stated that goodwill is "amortized over a period of 40 years." Assume that both purchases were made on January 2 and that Gannett could assign only $33 million to identifiable individual assets. What is the minimum amount of amortization of goodwill for the first year under pre-2000 GAAP? Could the entire amount be written off immediately? Explain.

12-48 Allocating Total Purchase Price to Assets

Two Hollywood companies had the following balance sheet accounts as of December 31, 20X7 ($ in millions):

	Cinemon	Bradley Productions		Cinemon	Bradley Productions
Cash and receivables	$ 30	$ 22	Current liabilities	$ 50	$ 20
Inventories	120	3	Common stock	100	10
Plant assets, net	150	95	Retained income	150	90
Total assets	$300	$120	Total liab. and stk. eq.	$300	$120
Net income for 20X7	$ 19	$ 4			

On January 4, 20X8, these entities combined. Cinemon issued $180 million of its shares (at market value) in exchange for all the shares of Bradley, a motion picture division of a large company. The inventory of films acquired through the combination had been fully amortized on Bradley's books.

During 20X8, Bradley received revenue of $21 million from the rental of films from its inventory. Cinemon earned $20 million on its other operations (i.e., excluding Bradley) during 20X8. Bradley broke even on its other operations (i.e., excluding the film rental contracts) during 20X8.

Required

1. Prepare a consolidated balance sheet for the combined company immediately after the combination. Assume that $80 million of the purchase price was assigned to the inventory of films.

2. Prepare a comparison of Cinemon's net income between 20X7 and 20X8 where the cost of the film inventories would be amortized on a straight-line basis over 4 years. What would be the net income for 20X8 if the $80 million were assigned to goodwill instead of the inventory of films and goodwill was not amortized?

12-49 Prepare Consolidated Financial Statements

From the following data, prepare a consolidated balance sheet and an income statement for Midlands Data Corporation. All data are in millions and pertain to operations for 20X2 or to December 31, 20X2:

Short-term investments at cost, which approximates current market	$ 35
Income tax expense	90
Accounts receivable, net	110
Minority interest in subsidiaries	90
Inventories at average cost	390
Dividends declared and paid on preferred stock	10
Equity in earnings of affiliated companies	20
Paid-in capital in excess of par	82
Interest expense	25
Retained income	218
Investments in affiliated companies	100
Common stock, 10 million shares, $1 par	10
Depreciation and amortization	20
Accounts payable	200
Cash	55
First-mortgage bonds, 10% interest, due December 31, 20X8	80
Property, plant, and equipment, net	120
Preferred stock, 2 million shares, $50 par, dividend rate is $5 per share, each share is convertible into one share of common stock	100
Accrued income taxes payable	30
Cost of goods sold and operating expenses, exclusive of depreciation and amortization	710
Subordinated debentures, 11% interest, due December 31, 20X9	100
Minority interest in subsidiaries' net income	20
Goodwill	100
Net sales and other operating revenue	960

12-50 Minority Interest

The consolidated financial statements of Anchor Gaming, Inc., include the accounts of Colorado Grande Enterprises, Inc., an 80%-owned subsidiary. Anchor Gaming makes gambling machines and runs casinos. Colorado Grande Enterprises operates the Colorado Grande Casino in Cripple Creek, 45 miles from Colorado Springs. Colorado Grande Enterprises is Anchor Gaming's only consolidated subsidiary with minority interests. A recent Anchor Gaming income statement contained the following:

Income before minority interest and taxes	$56,987,737
Taxes	21,000,702
Minority interest in earnings of consolidated subsidiary	310,607
Net income	$35,676,428

Anchor Gaming's Minority interest in consolidated subsidiary account listed $672,955 at the beginning of the year. Colorado Grande Enterprises paid no dividends during the year. Anchor Gaming did not buy or sell any of its interest in Colorado Grande Enterprises during the year.

Required

1. Compute the net income of Colorado Grande Enterprises for the year.
2. What proportion of Anchor Gaming's $35,676,428 net income was contributed by Colorado Grande Enterprises?
3. Compute Anchor Gaming's balance in "Minority interest in consolidated subsidiary" at the end of the year.
4. Comment on the reason for including a line for minority interest in the income statement and balance sheet of Anchor Gaming.

12-51 Acquisition of RCA

The stockholders of RCA approved the sale of 100% of RCA's common stock to General Electric for $66.50 per share. Of the votes cast, over 90% were in favor of the $6.28 billion cash sale, the largest nonoil acquisition at the time. Assume that the $6.28 billion price was twice RCA's book value.

Required

1. Suppose the fair market values of RCA's net assets totaled $6.28 billion. Prepare the journal entry or entries to record the acquisition on General Electric's books.
2. Suppose the fair market values of RCA's tangible assets were equal to their book values. Fair market value of identifiable intangible assets was $800 million; their useful life was 8 years. None of the intangible assets appeared on RCA's balance sheet. Prepare the journal entry or entries to record the acquisition on General Electric's books.
3. Refer to requirement 2. Assume that the acquisition took place on January 2. Prepare the December 31 journal entry or entries to recognize the first year's amortization of the intangible assets. Assume that goodwill is not amortized.
4. Assume that the acquisition occurred on July 1 and that RCA's net income for the year was $500 million. RCA's net income was earned at a constant rate per unit of time during the year. How much of that net income would appear in General Electric's consolidated net income for the year ended December 31?

12-52 Equity Method and Cash Flows

Moscow Resources Company owns a 40% interest in Siberia Mining Company. Moscow uses the equity method to account for the investment. During 20X6, Siberia had net income of 100 million rubles and paid cash dividends of 70 million rubles. Moscow's net income, including the effect of its investment in Siberia, was 486 million rubles.

Required

1. In reconciling Moscow's net income with its net cash provided by operating activities, the net income must be adjusted for Moscow's pro rata share of the net income of Siberia. Compute the amount of the adjustment. Will it be added to or deducted from net income?
2. Under the direct method, the dividends paid by Siberia will affect the amounts Moscow lists under operating, investing, or financing activities. Which type(s) of activity will be affected? By how much? Will the amount(s) be cash inflows or cash outflows?

12-53 Effect of Transactions under the Equity Method

Coca-Cola's footnotes to its 1999 financial statements revealed ($ in millions):

	December 31	
	1999	*1998*
Equity method investments	$6,442	$6,291

Coca-Cola's share of the net loss of these equity method investments was $184 million in 1999, and it received dividends from those companies of $108 million. During 1999, Coca-Cola actually had some complicated transactions involving some of these equity investments. For purposes of this problem assume that no equity investments were sold during 1999.

Required

1. Compute the additional investment that Coca-Cola made in its equity affiliates during 1999. *Hint:* Use a T-account to aid your analysis.
2. Describe how the income and dividends from equity investments would affect the cash flow statement. Coca-Cola uses the indirect method for cash flows from operations.

12-54 Equity Method, Consolidation, and Minority Interest

On January 2, 20X6, Jordan Shoe Company purchased 40% of Sports Clothing Company (SCC) for $2.0 million cash. Before the acquisition, Jordan had assets of $10 million and stockholders' equity of $8 million. SCC had stockholders' equity of $5 million and liabilities of $1 million, and the fair values of its assets were equal to their book values.

SCC reported 20X6 net income of $400,000 and declared and paid dividends of $200,000. Assume that Jordan and SCC had no sales to one another. Separate income statements for Jordan and SCC were as follows:

	Jordan Shoe Company	Sports Clothing Company
Sales	$12,500,000	$4,400,000
Expenses	11,100,000	4,000,000
Operating income	$ 1,400,000	$ 400,000

Required

1. Prepare the journal entries for Jordan Shoe (a) to record the acquisition of SCC and (b) to record its share of SCC net income and dividends for 20X6.
2. Prepare Jordan Shoe's income statement for 20X6 and calculate the balance in its investments in SCC as of December 31, 20X6.
3. Suppose Jordan had purchased 80% of SCC for $4 million. Using the balance sheet equation format, prepare a tabulation of the consolidated balance sheet immediately after acquisition. Prepare the journal entries for both Jordan and SCC to record the acquisition. Omit explanations.
4. Prepare a consolidated income statement for 20X6, using the facts of requirement 3.

12-55 Equity Investments

Corning Inc.'s 1999 Consolidated Statements of Income reported equity in earnings of associated companies of $112.3 million. Its consolidated balance sheets included investments in associated companies of $421.9 million in 1999 and $323.9 million in 1998. The consolidated statements of cash flow indicated that the equity in earnings of associated companies were more than the dividends received from these companies in 1999 by $61.4 million.

Required

1. Compute the amount of net investment or disinvestment in associated companies, if any, during 1999.
2. Suppose these associated companies were 40% owned and that Corning had acquired another 40% of these companies on the last day of 1999. Describe how the financial statements for 1999 would change as a result. Your answer should identify the accounts that would probably change and the direction of the probable change.

12-56 Intercorporate Investments and Statements of Cash Flow

The 20X6 balance sheet of Global Resources Corp. contained the following three assets:

ASSIGNMENT MATERIAL **549**

	20X6	20X5
Long-term debt investments held-to-maturity	$ 166,000	$ 166,000
Investment in Alberta Mining Company, 43% owned	$ 981,000	$ 861,000
Investment in Sutter Gold Company, 25% owned	$1,145,000	$1,054,000

The long-term-debt investments were shown at cost, which equaled maturity value. Interest income was $14,000 for these debt investments, which had been owned for several years. The equity method was used to account for both Alberta Mining and Sutter Gold. Results for 20X6 included:

	Alberta Mining Company	Sutter Gold Company
Global Resources Corp. pro rata share of net income	$120,000	$100,000
Cash dividends received by Global Resources Corp.	$ 40,000	$ 0

Global Resources reported net income of $696,000 and depreciation of $129,000 in 20X6.

A schedule that reconciles net income to net cash provided by operating activities contained the following:

Net income	$696,000
Depreciation	129,000
Increase in noncash working capital	(16,000)

Note: The increase in noncash working capital is the net change in current assets and liabilities other than cash.

Required   Given the available data, complete the reconciliation.

12-57 Intercorporate Investments and Ethics

Hans Rasmussen and Alex Renalda were best friends at a small undergraduate college and they fought side-by-side in the jungles of Vietnam. On returning to the United States, they went their separate ways to pursue MBA degrees, Hans to a prestigious East Coast business school and Alex to an equally prestigious West Coast school. However, 30 years later, their paths crossed again.

By 1999, Alex had become president and CEO of Medusa Electronics after 21 years with the firm. Hans had started working for American Airlines, but had left after 9 years to start his own firm, Rasmussen Transport. In April of 1999, Rasmussen Transport was near bankruptcy when Hans approached his old friend for help. Alex Renalda answered his friend's call, and Medusa Electronics bought 19% of Rasmussen Transport.

In 2002, Rasmussen was financially stable and Medusa was struggling. In fact, Alex Renalda thought his job as CEO might be in jeopardy if Medusa did not report income up to expectations. Late in 2002, Alex approached Hans with a request—quadruple Rasmussen's dividends so that Medusa could recognize $760,000 of investment income. Medusa had listed its investment in Rasmussen as an available-for-sale security, so changes in the market value of Rasmussen were recorded directly in stockholders' equity. However, dividends paid were recognized in Medusa's income statement. Although Rasmussen had never paid dividends of more than 25% of net income, and it had plenty of use for excess cash, Hans felt a deep obligation to Alex. Thus, he agreed to a $4 million dividend on net income of $4.17 million.

Required
1. Why does the dividend policy of Rasmussen Transport affect the income of Medusa Electronics? Is this consistent with the intent of the accounting principles relating to the market and equity methods for intercorporate investments? Explain.
2. Comment on the ethical issues in the arrangements between Hans Rasmussen and Alex Renalda.

ANNUAL REPORT CASE

12-58 Cisco Annual Report

Cisco includes the following two items on its balance sheet for the year ended July 29, 2000 ($ in millions):

Short-term investments	$ 1,291
Long-term investments	13,688

1. How does Cisco determine whether an investment is short term or long term?
2. How does Cisco measure the balance sheet value of these investments?
3. Suppose that the book value on July 29, 2000 was the same as the cost of the short-term investments. Suppose further that the maturity value of Cisco's short-term investments on July 29, 2000 was 1.2 million. During the next year, all the investments matured, and Cisco received the face value of 1.2 million for the securities. Prepare the journal entry or entries required by the securities transactions during the year. Include any gains or losses that would be recognized.

12-59 Financial Statement Research

Select five companies in any industry. Review each company's financial statements to determine whether an acquisition occurred during the most recent year. For each acquisition, identify as much as possible concerning each of the following:

1. Did the company use cash or stock?
2. What percentage of the target was purchased?
3. Can you determine whether the acquired company was previously either a customer or a supplier of the acquiring company? If so, which one?

COLLABORATIVE LEARNING EXERCISE

12-60 International Perspective on Consolidation

Form groups of four to six students. Each student should pick a country from the following list:

Australia	Japan
France	Sweden
Germany	United Kingdom
Italy	

Find out the policy on consolidating financial statements in the country you select. If possible, find out when consolidated statements were first required and what criteria are used to determine what subsidiaries should be consolidated.

Meet as a group and share your information. What generalizations can you draw from the policies you found? Propose explanations for the differences you find among countries. Discuss the effect of consolidation policies on comparisons of financial statements across countries.

INTERNET EXERCISE

12-61 General Motors

Go to www.gm.com to locate the General Motors (GM) home page. Select *The Company* and click on *Investor Information*. Then, select the most recent annual report.

Answer these questions about GM:

www.prenhall.com/horngren

1. What business segments do the consolidated financial statements of GM include? How are the operations of these segments interrelated?
2. What clues do you find that intercompany eliminations have been performed? What effect did this activity have on net income?
3. What information does GM provide about its marketable securities shown on the consolidated balance sheets? Can you tell which ones are classified as trading securities? Where do the net unrealized gains on available-for-sale securities appear in the financial statements?
4. Did GM report any goodwill? Why would GM want to pay more than the value of the net assets of a company it acquired?

Competition for the fast-food dollar on this Chicago street is just one example of a battle fought city-by-city and country-by-country, around the world.

www.prenhall.com/horngren

Learning Objectives

After studying this chapter, you should be able to

1. Locate and use the many sources of information about company performance.

2. Analyze the components of a company using trend analysis and other techniques.

3. Use the basic financial ratios to guide your thinking.

4. Evaluate corporate performance using ROA, ROE, and EVA.

5. Calculate EPS under complex circumstances.

6. Adjust for nonrecurring items.

Chapter 1 opened with a discussion of McDonald's, and we should now consider some additional questions an investor might ask in evaluating this company. During the 12 months from May 1999 to May 2000, McDonald's shares traded as low as $29 and as high as $49. The *Wall Street Journal* reported a closing price of $37.88 on May 1, 2000, up some 31% from its low point. McDonald's was selling at a price-earnings ratio of about 27. This price earnings ratio was up sharply from the level of 20 that McDonald's experienced in 1997.

What happened to cause investor sentiment to change during the year and to cause price earnings ratios to rise so significantly from 1997? Some events were economy-wide. The stock market did fabulously from 1997 to 2000 with strong earnings growth and low inflation. Price-earnings ratios rose across the board during this period. McDonald's benefited as did most companies. The federal budget was moving toward balance, the world was generally at peace, and life was good.

In February 1997, McDonald's experienced a 3-day, $5.00, decline of 9% in value that *Business Week* called "the discount dip." McDonald's dropped the price of Big Macs and McMuffins to 55 cents. Consumers probably thought "great," more value, but investors figured it was bad news if McDonald's nearly gave away burgers to increase sales. Investors want rising sales, yes; however, more than that, they want rising profits. Analysts estimated that sales would have to rise 2% just to cover the effect of lower prices and noted that Burger King would not sit still while this happened.

This sales campaign also raised questions as to whether it made sense for McDonald's to continue its U.S. expansion in the face of tightening markets. After opening 1,130 units in 1995 and 726 stores in 1996, plans to open 720 more in 1997 worried investors. Adding almost 10% more stores each year in a crowded market worried investors who still remembered the failed 1996 launch of "Deluxe" sandwiches. These were the high-priced adult sandwiches that did not attract a lot of business and seriously injured the McDonald's image of a pro-kid, happy-meal haven.

Many of these worries proved false 3 years later. Prices had stabilized and growth had continued. The company added 3,500 restaurants during the period and added some 15 more countries to its international presence. During 2000, McDonald's intended to open new restaurants at the rate of five per day. McDonald's has been expanding from its simple roots by adding new brands including Donatos Pizza, Chipotle Mexican Grill, Boston Market, and Aroma Café (United Kingdom).

Adding stores should increase sales in total, but may decrease average sales per restaurant. The 1999 annual report indicated "The number of new restaurants affects average sales as new restaurants historically have taken a few years to reach long-term volumes." But a good question would be: How are sales in existing McDonald's going? The answer in 1997 was that "same store" sales had fallen in 9 of the last 10 quarters. By 1999, this trend had reversed with McDonald's reporting that "in 1999 and 1998, comparable [same store] sales drove the increases in U.S. average annual sales per restaurant. Another important statistic is that some 64% of McDonald's operating income in 1999 came from overseas business, up from 60% in 1997. Separate forecasts of domestic and international growth and profitability can improve the accuracy of forecasts for the whole company and improve investment decisions.

Of course, good financial analysis requires that we understand how the business works. Much of McDonald's business is done through franchises. If the people owning and running the franchises are not happy, they do not deliver the focused, quality service and product that makes people associate McDonald's with the break they deserve today. Interviews with franchise owners in 1997 revealed that only 26% supported some policies, down from 86% in 1995. One owner of four franchises pointed out that her third franchise lost money and the fourth was 42% below sales projections. One response by McDonald's was the "Made for You" program. This involved installing "new food preparation systems in virtually all restaurants in the United States and Canada to produce fresher, better tasting food at the speed of McDonalds's. The system also supports future growth through product development because it can more easily accommodate an expanded menu." Owner's were provided financial incentives up to $12,500 per restaurant to support the conversions.

McDonald's is a great company with one of the world's most recognized brands. But investors want to know where the company is on its growth curve. Potential franchise investors want to decide whether 2000 or 2003 is the right year to buy. The analysis methods in this chapter summarize many of the techniques such investors use to answer these questions.

financial statement analysis
Using financial statements to assess a company's performance.

In prior chapters, we concentrated on how to collect financial data, and how to prepare and evaluate financial statements. You know that the accountant's goal in preparing financial statements is to provide usable information to anyone who wants it. **Financial statement analysis** involves using the information so that we fully understand the story it tells about the company.

Different people read financial statements for different reasons. Suppliers might want to see if a customer can afford a price hike. Customers might want to know if a company will still be around in a year to honor a warranty. Managers, creditors, investors, and the CEO's mother all have their purposes for reading the statements. Our focus is on the investor. Investors read financial statements either to check on their current investments or to plan their future ones. Investors analyze financial statements to determine whether their beliefs about the company have been borne out and to develop expectations about the future.

How do we get the future out of financial statements? Throughout the book we have shown you various ratios and other tools of analysis, so you should have at least a clue as to how it is done. Ratios focus your attention and direct your questions. This chapter integrates the tools you have already seen and teaches you several new ones as we focus on financial statement analysis. Most of the chapter deals with ratios and how to understand the financial statements as prepared under GAAP.

SOURCES OF INFORMATION ABOUT COMPANIES

Objective 1
Locate and use the many sources of information about company performance.

Publicly available information takes on many forms. The now familiar annual report is important because of its completeness and its reliability, given the attestation of an independent third-party auditor. In addition to the financial statements (income statement, balance sheet, statement of cash flows, and statement of stockholders' equity) we have already seen, annual reports usually contain:

1. Footnotes to the financial statements
2. A summary of the accounting principles used
3. Management's discussion and analysis of the financial results
4. The auditor's report
5. Comparative financial data for a series of years
6. Narrative information about the company

The Cisco annual report included in appendix A of this book provides examples of each of the items listed. In addition to the annual reports distributed to shareholders, companies also prepare reports for the Securities and Exchange Commission (SEC). Form 10-K presents financial statement data in greater detail than do the financial statements in annual reports. Form 10-Q includes quarterly financial statements, so it provides more timely, although less complete, information than do the annual reports. Other SEC reports are required for specific events, such as the issuance of common shares or debt. All SEC filings are available to any investor and most are available on the World Wide Web. See the Prentice-Hall Web site for easy access to Edgar, the SEC electronic information source.

Both annual reports and SEC reports are issued well after the events being reported have occurred. More timely information can be found in periodic company press releases, which provide the public with news about company developments, including the following:

1. Changes in personnel
2. Changes in dividends
3. Issuance or retirement of debt
4. Acquisition or sale of assets or business units
5. New products
6. New orders
7. Changes in production plans
8. Financial results

Press releases provide the basis for articles appearing in the financial press, such as local newspapers, the *Wall Street Journal, Business Week, Forbes, Fortune,* and *Barron's. Industry Standard* and *Red Herring* are examples of new publications that concentrate on news about young dynamic companies and high-tech industries. Members of the financial press decide which information in press releases will be interesting and important. For example, the *Tulsa World* newspaper in Oklahoma may report in great detail about local oil exploration and production. The *Washington Post* in Washington, DC, probably would not cover these issues but would instead provide up-to-date news on local companies and government business. National publications, such as the *Wall Street Journal,* would not provide as much detail in these specific areas as either the *Tulsa World* or the *Washington Post.*

Investors also rely on the other articles, reports, and analyses that appear in the financial press. Services such as Value Line, Moody's Investors Services, and Standard and Poor's (S&P's) Industrial Surveys also provide investors with useful information, as do credit agencies such as Dun & Bradstreet. In addition, stockbrokers prepare company analyses for their clients, and private investment services and newsletters supply information to their subscribers.

The Internet is changing the way that investing is done. Many investors now purchase and sell securities electronically without ever talking to a broker. Commissions for such transactions are down by more than 90% from the rates that existed 3 years ago. Also, much information is available electronically. Many Internet browsers provide continuous information on security prices and access to analysts' reports on various industries and securities. Much of this information is free but some requires purchase of certain items, for the investor to have a brokerage account with the firm or for the user to subscribe to a service.

BUSINESS FIRST
Who Do You Believe?

Web sites and focused business newscasts have increased the speed with which information reaches the markets. This change allows investors to understand more and to act more quickly, generally making stock prices more reliable. This question remains: Is every news item "news"? Companies provide press releases to news wires such as PR Newswire or Internet Wire who distribute the releases to subscribing news agencies such as CNBC or the *New York Times* who distribute the news via TV or newspaper. When individual investors or institutional investors see surprising news, they act quickly; buying or selling as the information dictates.

On August 25, 2000, some investors were hurt badly by a fraudulent news release. It was front-page news the next day for the *New York Times.* Emulex was the company. It closed on Thursday at $113. On Friday a press release at about 9:30 A.M. eastern time, just before the markets opened, indicated that the company was restating its earnings for the quarter from a profit of 25 cents to a loss of 15 cents, that earnings for the last 2 years would also be revised, and that its CEO had resigned. The stock dropped rapidly at an accelerating pace, in response to this news. By the time the company on the West Coast could respond to the news (about 7:00 A.M. Pacific time, 10:00 A.M. eastern Time), the stock had fallen to $28.50, down 75%. The NASDAQ halted trading in response to the company's request. Trading resumed after 1 P.M. eastern time at near the prior close.

The company had assured the markets that the "news" was false. People reassessed their beliefs about the company and the stock closed for the day at $106. Billions of paper dollars were made and lost during the day and the people who sold at $28.50 suffered real losses. The people who bought at $28.50 made triple their money for the day. Unfortunately, some of them were probably the perpetrators of the scam. These culprits have not yet been found, though many regulators are looking and there will be huge fines and jail time awaiting them.

Our markets work only because such events are rare. In this case Internet Wire seems to have forwarded a "press release" and others picked it up and responded to falling share prices by emphasizing the "news" surrounding the price fall. A lot of damage was done before the company had a chance to correct the record. No doubt there will be litigation over which news agencies acted inappropriately, but the lesson for all is clear. It is not enough to simply repeat what others have said. The premier news agencies should confirm such explosive news with the company or with the other sources responsible.

Source: *New York Times,* August 26, 2000, p. A1.

Investors should always get information before they invest, and the sources we have described tend to provide plenty. Of course, some large investors can demand even more information. For example, banks or other creditors making multimillion-dollar loans can ask for a set of projected financial statements or other estimates of predicted results, known as **pro forma statements.** Not every investor can demand pro forma statements, but not every investor needs to. There is so much information available to the public that wading through it all can take a good deal of time. Although there is much to be gained from other sources, our discussion focuses on analyzing the information contained in the financial statements themselves. However, sometimes examining that information necessarily directs the analyst to other information that is required to resolve an issue.

pro forma statement A carefully formulated expression of predicted results.

OBJECTIVES OF FINANCIAL STATEMENT ANALYSIS

Different types of investors expect different types of returns. Equity investors expect both dividends and an increase in the value of the stock they hold. Creditors, however, expect to receive interest and the return of their loan principal. Although the types of returns they expect are different, equity investors and creditors both risk not receiving those returns. Therefore, both types of investors use financial statement analysis to (1) predict their expected returns and (2) assess the risks associated with those returns.

Creditors mainly want to know about short-term liquidity and long-term solvency. **Short-term liquidity** refers to how much cash a company has on hand to meet current payments, such as interest, wages, taxes, and so on, as they become due. Conversely, **long-term solvency** refers to a company's ability to generate cash to repay long-term debts to creditors as they mature.

short-term liquidity An organization's ability to meet current payments as they become due.

long-term solvency An organization's ability to generate enough cash to repay long-term debts as they mature.

In contrast, equity investors are more concerned with profitability and future security prices. Why? Because dividend payments depend on how profitable operations are, and stock prices depend on the market's assessment of the company's future prospects. Investors gain when they receive dividends and when the values of their securities rise. Rising profits spur both events. Actually, creditors also want to know about profitability because the profitable operations that drive stock prices to higher levels also provide the cash to repay loans and finance growth.

Both creditors and equity investors are interested in what will happen in a company's future. What good to them is financial statement analysis, which deals solely with past events? Financial statement analysis helps creditors and equity investors because past performance is often a good indicator of future performance. Trends in past sales, operating expenses, and net income often continue, so financial statement analysis of past performance gives clues to future returns.

EVALUATING TRENDS AND COMPONENTS OF THE BUSINESS

There are several ways of looking at financial statement information. One of the most popular methods involves comparing financial trends from one year to the next. A second method focuses on examining the components of the business. At one level, the composition of the business involves the relationship among elements reported in the financial statements. We have already examined many ratios that do this: the current ratio, the inventory turnover ratio, the rate of return on common equity (ROE) and so on. Components can also be thought of as business units or geographic segments. For example, Philip Morris has a food business and a tobacco business, and operates in the United States and many other regions of the world. Investors and analysts could focus on any one, or better yet, all these dimensions in trying to predict the future of Philip Morris.

Objective 2
Analyze the components of a company using trend analysis and other techniques.

TREND ANALYSIS

Annual reports contain financial statements for the current and previous year, and the amounts of key financial items for at least the last 5 years and often for 10 or 11. Not surprisingly, the longer histories of information tend to be published by the companies whose 10-year histories are impressive. In evaluating trends, these numbers may or may not be adequate. Many supplemental sources provide much longer and richer access to information by archiving and adjusting older information. Many colleges and universities now have Compustat PC, a CD-ROM data collection that provides 20 years of financial information extracted from the financial statements. Multiple services are arising to provide rich information for financial analysis. Trends are nothing more than predictable patterns that have been observed in the past and are expected to continue into the future. The aging composition of the U.S. population is a classic example of a trend.

The essence of trend analysis in accounting is to identify a pattern in the past, a trend. Then you ask yourself why that trend exists and whether you expect it to continue. Often this pattern of questions forces you to ask more questions. If sales have been growing steadily, but inventories have not, can this continue or will future inventory growth require substantial additional investment? If inventories have been growing steadily but sales have not, why is someone buying so much inventory?

Trend analysis also prompts investors to ask themselves what could cause the trends to end. In spring of 2000, for example, investors worried that after an extraordinary period of economic growth with stable prices, tight labor markets, and growing affluence of consumers might cause prices to rise (inflation). To control inflation the Federal Reserve Bank might decide to raise interest rates. Rising interest rates hurt many industries. Banks are hurt because they must pay more for the money that they lend. Automobile

Exhibit 13-1

Oxley Company
Statement of Income (in Thousands Except Earnings per Share)

	For the Year Ended December 31, 20X2	For the Year Ended December 31, 20X1	Increase (Decrease) Amount	Percentage
Sales	$999	$800	$199	24.9%
Cost of goods sold	399	336	63	18.8
Gross profit (or gross margin)	$600	$464	$136	29.3
Operating expenses				
Wages	$214	$150	$ 64	42.7
Rent	120	120	0	0.0
Miscellaneous	100	50	50	100.0
Depreciation	40	40	0	0.0
Total operating expenses	$474	$360	$114	31.7
Operating income (or operating profit)	$126	$104	$ 22	21.2
Other revenue and expense				
Interest revenue	36	36	0	0.0
Deduct: Interest expense	(12)	(12)	0	0.0
Income before income taxes	$150	$128	$ 22	17.2
Income tax expense	60	48	12	25.0
Net income	$ 90	$ 80	$ 10	12.5
Earnings per common share*	$ .45	$ .40	$ .05	12.5%

*Dividends per share, $.40 and $.20, respectively. For publicly held companies, there is a requirement to show earnings per share on the face of the income statement, but it is not necessary to show dividends per share. Calculation of earnings per share: $90,000 ÷ 200,000 = $.45, and $80,000 ÷ 200,000 = $.40.

manufacturers are hurt because car buyers face higher car payments when interest rates rise and therefore buy fewer cars. The same analysis follows for builders of new houses. In contrast, rising interest rates often help companies such as Home Depot, which serves the home owners' needs for home improvement materials. Why? Because people who would like to move up to a nicer home and conclude interest rates are too high, often decide to remodel their existing home instead. These examples illustrate how you might think about trends in sales and profits in particular industries.

To see how trend analysis works, let us examine the income statements and balance sheets from Oxley Company, a retailer of nursery products for lawns and gardens, shown in Exhibits 13-1 and 13-2. The first two columns show Oxley's information for the last 2 years. The third column shows the amount of the change in each item from 20X1 to 20X2. Finally, the fourth column shows the percentage change, computed as follows:

$$\text{Percentage change 20X1 to 20X2} = \frac{\text{Amount of change}}{\text{20X1 amount}} \times 100$$

Exhibit 13-2
Oxley Company Balance Sheet
(in Thousands)

	December 31		Increase (Decrease)	
	20X2	*20X1*	*Amount*	*Percentage*
Assets				
Current assets				
Cash	$150	$ 57	$ 93	163.2%
Accounts receivable	95	70	25	35.7
Accrued interest receivable	15	15	0	0.0
Inventory of merchandise	20	60	(40)	(66.7)
Prepaid rent	10	—	10	*
Total current assets	$290	$202	$ 88	43.6
Long-term assets				
Long-term note receivable	288	288	0	0.0
Equipment, less accumulated depreciation				
of $120 and $80	80	120	(40)	(33.3)
Total assets	$658	$610	$ 48	7.9%
Liabilities and stockholders' equity				
Current liabilities				
Accounts payable	$ 90	$ 65	$ 25	38.5%
Accrued wages payable	24	10	14	140.0
Accrued income taxes payable	16	12	4	33.3
Accrued interest payable	9	9	0	0.0
Unearned sales revenue	—	5	(5)	(100.0)
Note payable—current portion	80	—	80	*
Total current liabilities	$219	$101	$118	116.8
Long-term note payable	40	120	(80)	(66.7)
Total liabilities	$259	$221	$ 38	17.2
Stockholders' equity				
Paid-in capital†	$102	$102	$ 0	0.0
Retained income	297	287	10	3.5
Total stockholders' equity	$399	$389	$ 10	2.6
Total liabilities and stockholders' equity	$658	$610	$ 48	7.9%

*When the base-year amount is zero, no percentage of change can be computed.

†Details are often shown in a supplementary statement or in footnotes. In this case, there are 200,000 common shares outstanding, $.25 par per share, or 200,000 × $.25 = $50,000. Additional paid-in capital is $52,000.

For example, Oxley's accounts receivables increased 35.7%:

$$\text{Percentage change} = \frac{\$95{,}000 - \$70{,}000}{\$70{,}000} \times 100 = 35.7\%$$

Both the amount and the percentage changes are needed to recognize trends and understand their true meaning. For example, although the sales increase of $199,000 is larger than the $22,000 increase in operating income, the percentage increase is only slightly larger—24.9% to 21.2%. Similarly, the 140% increase in accrued wages payable seems large, but the increase is only $14,000, a relatively small amount in the overall picture. Remember that unlike the amounts of change, the percentage changes cannot be added or subtracted to obtain subtotals.

Changes in dollar amount and percentage terms help analysts to see patterns, such as a rise in sales or a decrease in inventories. Although recognizing patterns is key, understanding what caused those patterns is even more important. In our example, why did current assets increase by 43.6% while equipment decreased by 33.3%? This question is generated by an apparent inconsistency. If current assets are increasing, it suggests the company is growing, but a growing company might be expected to be acquiring new equipment as well. Answering such a question often reveals a specific company strategy or some characteristic of the market. For example, it might be that the original equipment was not being fully utilized in 20X1 and that as the company grew, the equipment was fully utilized and more sales occurred without requiring more investment. Alternatively, the company may have been able to rent additional equipment to support sales growth because the growth was concentrated during short periods of the year. Similar questions motivated by inconsistencies might include: Why did cash and accounts receivable increase, while inventories plummeted? Why did current liabilities increase 116.8% while long-term liabilities decreased 66.7%? Answers to such questions say a lot about how a company is run, how it will perform in the future, and whether it would be a good investment.

An analyst would note that Oxley Company's sales increase of 24.9% exceeds the 18.8% increase in cost of goods sold, causing a 29.3% increase in gross profit. That is good news. However, operating expenses increased by 31.7% with only two items, wages and miscellaneous expenses, causing the increase. In total, the nearly 25% increase in sales led to only a 12.5% increase in net income. Investors know that the most powerful growth occurs because people are dying to acquire your product. Top-line, revenue growth that leads to increasing net income is highly desirable. However, when sales grow 25% and net income grows less, something is wrong. Has the company gotten top-heavy, hiring too many managers and not enough production and sales people?

Good analysts develop pictures in their heads about how changes in one financial statement item should affect another. When relationships do not look as good as expected, the issue is whether a crisis exists. When relationships look better than expected, the question is whether this excellent situation can be sustained. To see how trends develop over time, analysts often look at several years' worth of a company's financial information. Exhibit 13-3 shows a 5-year summary of key items for Oxley Company with selected percentage of growth rates. For example, percentage changes in sales are:

20X2

$$\left(\frac{\$999 - \$800}{\$800}\right) \times 100 = 24.9\%$$

20X1

$$\left(\frac{\$800 - \$765}{\$765}\right) \times 100 = 4.6\%$$

20X0

$$\left(\frac{\$765 - \$790}{\$790}\right) \times 100 = (3.2\%)$$

20Y9

$$\left(\frac{\$790 - \$694}{\$694}\right) \times 100 = 13.8\%$$

Exhibit 13-3

Oxley Company

Five-Year Financial Summary (in Thousands, Except per
Share Amounts)

	For the Year Ended December 31				
	20X2	*20X1*	*20X0*	*20Y9*	*20Y8*
Income statement data					
Sales	$999	$800	$765	$790	$694
Gross profit	600	464	448	460	410
Operating income	126	104	85	91	78
Net income	90	80	62	66	56
Earnings per share	.45	.40	.31	.33	.28
Dividends per share	.40	.20	.20	.20	.15
Balance sheet data (as of December 31)					
Total assets	$658	$610	$590	$585	$566
Total liabilities	259	221	241	258	265
Stockholders' equity	399	389	349	327	301

By applying the present value techniques of chapter 9, we can see that the 4-year average compound growth rate of sales has been 9.53%. This precise value was obtained with a calculator. Using the tables in chapter 9, we can approximate the value. The future value multiple is 1.44 ($999 ÷ $694 = 1.44). In Table 9-1 in chapter 9, p. 383, the future value factor for 4 years for 8% is 1.3605 and for 10% is 1.4641. The observed value of 1.44 falls near the upper end of this range, so it must be closer to 10% than to 8%. Our 9.53% value qualifies.

What caused these highly variable sales growth rates? Thoughtful analysts might conclude that weather and rates of new home construction play a role. Perhaps the sales decline in 20X0 was caused by a recession, and the sales increase in 20X2 involved a new product. Understanding these causes can help in assessing how Oxley has performed and how it might perform in the future.

COMMON-SIZE STATEMENTS

To aid comparisons with a company's prior years or comparisons of companies that differ in size, income statements and balance sheets are often analyzed using **common-size statements** in which the components are assigned a relative percentage. Oxley's common-size statements appear in Exhibit 13-4, side by side with the income statements from Exhibit 13-1 and the condensed balance sheets from Exhibit 13-2.

The income statement percentages are based on sales = 100%. Then each element of the income statement is expressed as a percentage of sales. In 20X1, gross margin was 58%, rising to 60% in 20X2. To understand the importance of this improvement in Oxley's gross margin, we might compare it to a specific competitor's values, or to industry averages. It is good to realize that gross margins improved, but did they improve as much as a competitor's did? Did they improve as much as most industry members did? The common-size statements translate raw dollar values for gross margins into percentage values that can be easily compared with the performance of others.

The behavior of each expense in relation to changes in total revenue is often revealing. That is, which expenses go up or down as sales fluctuate? For example, during these 2 years, rent, depreciation, and interest have been fixed in total but have decreased in relation to sales. In contrast, the wages have increased in total and as a percentage of sales. The latter is not a welcome sign. Exhibit 13-4 indicates that wages in 20X1 were

common-size statements
Financial statements in which components are expressed in relative percentages.

Exhibit 13-4

Oxley Company

Common-Size Statements (in Thousands Except Percentages)

	For the Year Ended December 31			
	20X2		*20X1*	
Statement of income				
Sales	$999*	100%	$800	100%
Cost of goods sold	399	40	336	42
Gross profit (or gross margin)	$600*	60%	$464	58%
Wages	$214	21%	$150	19%
Rent	120	12	120	15
Miscellaneous	100	10	50	6
Depreciation	40	4	40	5
Operating expenses	$474	47%	$360	45%
Operating income	$126	13%	$104	13%
Other revenue and expense	24	2	24	3
Pretax income	$150	15%	$128	16%
Income tax expense	60	6	48	6
Net income	$ 90	9%	$ 80	10%

	December 31			
	20X2		*20X1*	
Balance sheet				
Current assets	$290	44%	$202	33%
Long-term note receivable	288	44	288	47
Equipment, net	80	12	120	20
Total assets	$658	100%	$610	100%
Current liabilities	$219	33%	$101	16%
Long-term note	40	6	120	20
Total liabilities	$259	39%	$221	36%
Stockholders' equity	399	61	389	64
Total liab. and stk. eq.	$658	100%	$610	100%

*Note the use of dollar signs in columns of numbers. Frequently, they are used at the top and bottom only and not for every subtotal. Their use by companies depends on the preference of management.

$150 ÷ $800 = 19% of sales, whereas wages in 20X2 were $214 ÷ $999 = 21% of sales. A manager confronted with this information might ask who was hired and what they were doing. An investor would ask similar questions but would have a slightly harder time finding the answers. If we learned that wages rose because we hired some people to open a new location where no revenues were yet being generated, we might view this pattern as very reasonable. Alternatively, if we had more people working in the same locations with no greater business, we might conclude that management had gotten lazy.

component percentages
Elements of financial statements that express each component as a percentage of the total.

The balance sheet percentages in Exhibit 13-4 are based on total assets = 100%. They are often referred to as **component percentages** because they measure each component of the financial statements as a percentage of the total. Current liabilities are more prominent as a percentage of the total assets at the end of 20X2. What is the cause of the change? The explanation is that $80,000 of the long-term note came due in 20X2 and became a current liability.

MANAGEMENT'S DISCUSSION AND ANALYSIS

A required section of annual reports, called **management's discussion and analysis** (often called **MD&A**), generally discusses both trends and component percentages. The MD&A section explains the major changes in the income statement, liquidity, and capital resources. Space devoted to MD&A has increased dramatically in recent years.

Exhibit 13-5 contains excerpts from the chairman's letter in the 1998 annual report of PepsiCo. These 2 pages present an overview/summary of the material that is covered in the 12 pages of Management Discussion and Analysis. The total annual report is 44 pages long. The first 10 pages are colorful, graphic introductory information about the company in the form of a letter from Roger Enrico, the Chairman of the Board and CEO. Another 14 pages are the President's Letter and the MD&A. The rest is financial statements and accompanying notes. PepsiCo's report follows a U.S. trend toward shorter, less expensive annual reports. Since 1996, the report has been reduced from 52 pages, primarily by reducing the number of glossy, expensive photos and charts and by using lesser quality paper for the financial data.

The message is very upbeat about sales and income performance but, as Enrico points out, investors did not fare well. In fact, in May of 2000, the stock price stood at $38.50, basically the same as its price in December of 1997. In contrast, from 1986 to 1996 PepsiCo provided returns to shareholders well above market averages. One of the biggest changes for PepsiCo was the 1997 disposition of the restaurant business. The company transferred Taco Bell, Pizza Hut, and Kentucky Fried Chicken to a new company called Tricon and distributed Tricon shares to PepsiCo shareholders. This is called a spin-off. Tricon shares did no better than PepsiCo's. Tricon's share price of $31.50 in May of 2000 was about the same as its initial price when it was created in 1997.

management's discussion and analysis (MD&A) A required section of annual reports that concentrates on explaining the major changes in the income statement, liquidity, and capital resources.

BUSINESS FIRST

Roger Enrico and the "Power of One"

The April 10, 2000 edition of *Business Week* had a feature story, titled "PepsiCo's New Formula," by John Byrne, a senior editor. Roger Enrico is the Chairman and CEO of PepsiCo and rose to that position in 1996 from a career with PepsiCo that included heading each of the major business units. Byrne cites one wag who noted that in 1996 "Coke was kicking Pepsi's can." Enrico wasted no time in responding to the problems at Pepsi when he took over. He immediately shed the restaurant businesses and proceeded to change the ownership structure of the PepsiCo bottlers and to buy Tropicana. He also revised the international strategy. Historically, PepsiCo had challenged Coca-Cola at every turn in every international market, with little success. Coke had gotten to most of these markets early and was firmly entrenched. Enrico reoriented the strategy to focus on large international markets where soft drinks were not yet well established, including China and India. However, none of these strategic decisions is the "new formula" referred to in the title of the article. The new formula is the "Power of One," which refers to the powerful interplay between the snack and beverage businesses of PepsiCo. When Pepsi-Cola merged with Frito-Lay 35 years ago, the head of Pepsi said to his counterpart, "You make them thirsty and I'll give them something to drink." Enrico realized the power of this link and has made it the basis of a new pitch to grocery stores, where the battle for the location and amount of display space is key to consumer products. He pitches side-by-side placement of Frito snack products with Pepsi beverages. They have found that getting stores to display the products together adds significantly to sales growth rates of both products. Placement of such displays at the end of an aisle adds more. During 1999, Enrico visited a small Mexican shop owner to congratulate him on becoming the 8,000th retailer in Mexico to adopt the "Power of One." In Mexico, these joint displays have fueled a 36% increase in sales for PepsiCo products.

Roger A. Enrico
Chairman and Chief
Executive Officer

Dear Friends:

The PepsiCo associates on our cover have a lot to smile about these days. Thanks to them and our colleagues around the world, we had a terrific 1999.
Every one of our five operating divisions posted growth in revenue, volume and operating profit. Every one generated excess cash. And nearly every one gained market share. On a pro forma basis, we posted revenue growth of 6% in snacks, 4% in beverages and 10% in juices. Operating profits grew 11% in snacks, 2% in beverages and a whopping 55% in juices. Our cash provided by operations totaled $3 billion and our return on invested capital was a very healthy 20%.

As the numbers show, PepsiCo today is lean and strong. Even better, we're focused squarely on three great businesses full of opportunity: Frito-Lay snacks, Pepsi-Cola beverages and Tropicana juices.

It's no accident. We've transformed PepsiCo with the goal of being one of the world's very best and fastest growing consumer products companies—a premier performer delivering healthy, consistent financial results quarter after quarter, year after year.

And we've come a long way. Just look at how our numbers today compare with four years ago:

- Sales are more than one-third lower, yet earnings are higher;
- Operating free cash flow of $2 billion is also higher;
- Return on invested capital has risen from about 15% to 20%;
- Operating profit margin has risen from 10% to 15%;
- Shifting to less capital-intensive businesses has reduced our capital spending from 6.9% of sales to 5.5%;

- Net debt has been reduced from $8 billion to $2 billion.

During those four years we returned $10.6 billion to shareholders—$7.6 billion in share repurchases plus $3 billion in dividends.

And I'd add that in that time we've become arguably the single most important supplier to U.S. retailers in terms of their sales growth, profit and cash flow.

So why didn't our stock reflect our progress? It's a point of great frustration for me, and I'm sure for you as well. I believe we're doing the right things both strategically and financially. Our earnings met or beat Wall Street expectations in every quarter of 1999. Virtually every securities analyst who covers us rates PepsiCo a "buy." And we outpaced our food and beverage peers.

For all that, though, consumer products companies have been out of favor with investors. To me that's not an excuse, it's a challenge. It means we must work even harder to tell our story. And with our transformation complete, I plan to devote a lot more time to showing investors exactly why PepsiCo is a financial gem well capable of double-digit profit growth, strong cash flow and a return on invested capital above 20%.

It's a challenge I welcome. In fact, I've never been more optimistic about PepsiCo—not just because our financial picture is so much brighter, but also because today this company and the consumer are absolutely in sync. We're sharply focused on meeting the demand for convenient foods and drinks. It's a global opportunity measured in the hundreds of billions of dollars. And it's growing.

From Mexico to Miami to Malaysia, people are pressed for time, so they're eating fewer traditional meals and snacking more. They want convenient food that tastes great.

That puts PepsiCo right in the "sweet spot" of the food and beverage arena—the center of growth today and in the future. That's crucial if you want to stand out among premier companies.

Which gets me to an important question: What exactly is it that enables the best consumer product companies to grow year in and year out?

It seems to me the great companies share five basic qualities:

1. Leadership market positions
2. Strong, well-recognized brands
3. Good growth prospects
4. Globally diverse portfolios
5. Advantaged business systems.

Today PepsiCo measures up well on all of these. Let me show you.

Exhibit 13-5 *(continued)*

1 Leadership Market Positions

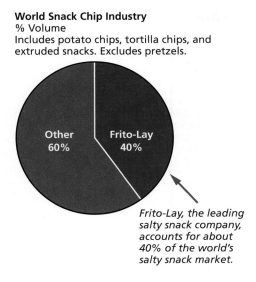

World Snack Chip Industry
% Volume
Includes potato chips, tortilla chips, and
extruded snacks. Excludes pretzels.

*Frito-Lay, the leading
salty snack company,
accounts for about
40% of the world's
salty snack market.*

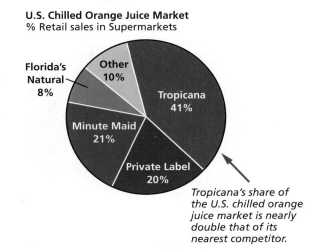

U.S. Chilled Orange Juice Market
% Retail sales in Supermarkets

*Tropicana's share of
the U.S. chilled orange
juice market is nearly
double that of its
nearest competitor.*

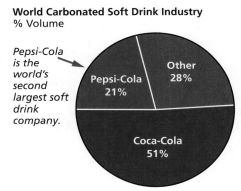

World Carbonated Soft Drink Industry
% Volume

*Pepsi-Cola
is the
world's
second
largest soft
drink
company.*

2 Strong, Well-Recognized Brands

Our brand strength is especially striking in the huge U.S. supermarket channel. We have nine of the top-10 salty snacks, three of the top-10 soft drink brands and four of the top-10 refrigerated juice brands.

3 Good Growth Prospects

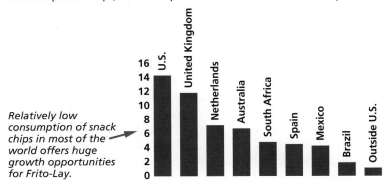

Annual Per Capita Consumption of Snack Chips
In Pounds
Includes potato chips, tortilla chips and extruded snacks. Excludes pretzels.

*Relatively low
consumption of snack
chips in most of the
world offers huge
growth opportunities
for Frito-Lay.*

Exhibit 13-5 *(continued)*

4   Globally Diverse Portfolios

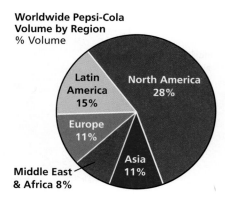

**Worldwide Pepsi-Cola
Volume by Region**
% Volume

Pepsi-Cola brands are available in some 160 countries and command the number one or two position in some 50 of these markets. Outside North America two of our largest and fastest growing businesses are in India and China, which include more than a third of the world's population.

5 Advantaged Business Systems

The way we take our products to market gives us compelling advantages—from our product innovation capabilities to our patented manufacturing processes, to the vast scale of our manufacturing and distribution systems.

While most companies rely on third-party distributors, the bulk of our products go to market through our own (or our bottlers') "direct store distribution" systems. These systems give us great control of our business and provide clear benefits to retailers.

We take our products to customers in our own trucks and even put them on the shelves. So our snacks and beverages are fresh, well displayed and handled carefully—all crucial in selling impulse foods.

We've got so much going for us—so much promise and 116,000 terrific employees to make it happen. You can understand why I'm confident PepsiCo will earn a place among the very best of the world's premier consumer product companies.

Roger A. Enrico
Chairman of the Board and Chief Executive Officer

SEGMENT REPORTING

Exhibit 13-6 provides useful information concerning PepsiCo's business segments by type of business—snack foods and beverages—and breaks the information down by geographic region. The notes to the financial statements indicate, "In 1998, we adopted Statement of Financial Accounting Standards No. 131, Disclosures about Segments of a Business Enterprise and Related Information, which is based on management reporting." This means that PepsiCo reports its segment data consistent with the way it manages the business. In 1999, the company changed the way it owned and managed its bottling businesses, and this annual report presents the historical results for 1997 and 1998 restated to be consistent and comparable with

Exhibit 13-6

Segment Disclosures for PepsiCo, December 31, 1999

BUSINESS SEGMENTS			
	1999	**1998**	**1997**
Net sales			
Frito-Lay			
North America	$ 7,865	$ 7,474	$ 6,967
International	3,750	3,501	3,409
Pepsi-Cola			
North America	2,605	1,389	1,344
International	1,771	1,600	1,935
Tropicana	2,253	722	—
New PepsiCo	18,244	14,686	13,655
Bottling operations/investments	2,123	7,662	7,262
	$20,367	$22,348	$20,917
Operating Profit			
Frito-Lay			
North America	$ 1,580	$ 1,424	$ 1,388
International	406	367	318
Pepsi-Cola			
North America	751	732	755
International	108	99	(67)
Tropicana	170	40	—
Combined segments	3,015	2,662	2,394
Corporate	(250)	(202)	(142)
New PepsiCo	2,765	2,460	2,252
Bottling operations/investments	53	124	410
	$ 2,818	$ 2,584	$ 2,662
Total assets			
Frito-Lay			
North America	$ 4,013	$ 3,915	$ 3,650
International	4,170	4,039	3,583
Pepsi-Cola			
North America	729	547	600
International	1,454	1,177	1,814
Tropicana	3,708	3,661	—
Combined segments	14,074	13,339	9,647
Corporate	1,008	215	2,160
Bottling operations/investments	2,469	9,106	8,294
	$17,551	$22,660	$20,101
GEOGRAPHIC AREAS			
Net sales			
United States	$11,772	$ 8,782	$ 7,630
International	6,472	5,904	6,025
Combined segments	18,244	14,686	13,655
Bottling operations/investments	2,123	7,662	7,262
	$20,367	$22,348	$20,917
Long-lived assets			
United States	$ 7,980	$ 6,732	$ 3,700
International	4,867	4,276	3,306
Combined segments	12,847	11,008	7,006
Bottling operations/investments	—	6,702	6,311
	$12,847	$17,710	$13,317

the reorganized management structure in use in 1999. Such restatements are crucial to allow investors to make useful comparisons through time and to use trends in making projections about the future. This exhibit includes results for sales and profit, and geographical information on assets, but the annual report also includes information by segment on assets, amortization and depreciation, noncash items, capital spending, and investments.

Notice that the exhibit presents information in a manner that allows the analyst to concentrate on the Frito-Lay and Pepsi-Cola business segments in North America or internationally, while it consolidates the Tropicana business worldwide. This reporting structure mirrors how PepsiCo manages the activities. Notes to these disclosures emphasize the international diversity of a branded company such as PepsiCo. For example, snack products include primarily salty snacks in North America including Lay's and Ruffles potato chips and Doritos and Tostitos tortilla chips as well as Fritos. In Mexico, PepsiCo has Sabrita brand snack foods and Alegro and Gamesa brand sweet snacks.

How can we use segment data to make projections about PepsiCo's future? Total sales for PepsiCo fell from $20,917 million in 1997 to $20,367 million in 1999. You could conclude that consumption of these products was falling because of health concerns. Parents around the country had decided to say no to soft drinks and salty snacks. This would lead you to project a further decline moving into 2000.

Segment analysis quickly reveals the errors of such conclusions. Observe that, in North America, Frito-Lay sales have risen an average of 6.25% per year since 1997. You might forecast continued growth at that rate for next year. You could proceed in a similar way for other elements but you would quickly encounter questions. Why did international Pepsi sales fall and then rise again? What might we predict going forward? We would discover some strategic choices to reduce activity in some parts of the world combined with the economic crisis in Russia that led to reduced demand for beverages and changes in the value of the ruble (the Russian currency) that further depressed beverage sales when reported in U.S. dollars.

Tropicana sales are also a little difficult to predict based on this disclosure, so we would consult other information in the report to learn that PepsiCo acquired Tropicana in 1998 and the sales reported in 1998 are those occurring after acquisition. Notes to the report provide information that Tropicana sales would have been $2,048 million for all of 1998. From this we can see that sales grew about 10% in 1999. Similar searching is required to interpret the sharp drop in Bottling Operations sales from $7,662 million in 1998 to $2,132 million in 1999. Again the explanation is in the notes and relates to accounting norms surrounding a business transaction. PepsiCo restructured its bottling operations. It used to own the bottlers and it transferred many of its owned operations to a new company. It owns less than 50% of the new company, therefore, PepsiCo's sales do not include the new company's sales after the April 6, 1999 transfer. Because PepsiCo accounts for its interest in the new entity using the equity method as described in detail in chapter 12, PepsiCo does not include any of the new company's sales with its own in 2000, the year we are forecasting. Instead we need to consider the profitability of the bottling operations and the effect in producing equity earnings for PepsiCo.

The separation of the bottling operation adds yet another complexity to the story. Notice that Pepsi-Cola North America reported sales of $1,389 million in 1998 and $2,605 million in 1999 for a resounding growth rate in sales of 88%. Should we expect that growth rate to repeat? What caused it? A phone call to Investor Relations at PepsiCo revealed that this was another accounting-based result that could easily be misleading. When the bottlers were spun off, some sales that used to be included with the bottlers results in prior years were reclassified to the Pepsi-Cola activity for 1999. Thus, the real growth in sales to third parties by PepsiCo North America was nothing like 88%. The reclassification of some of the sales has inflated the growth rate because 1998 was not restated under the new definition. This is an example of things that appear too good to be true, often are. The financial statements provide a basis for analysis and the analysis generates additional questions. Investors and analysts sometimes have to go to the company for resolution of their questions. The good news is that the investor relations units in companies are willing and able to help clarify issues such as this one.

The PepsiCo example is more complicated than most. The company is restructuring itself by reducing the level of involvement in the bottling business and adopting the equity method of accounting for the reduced ownership interest. It is adding Tropicana to the business. This complexity has made communicating useful information to analysts and investors more difficult. PepsiCo's accountants are looking forward to a year from now when year-to-year comparisons will again be more straightforward. For those who are currently studying accounting, the message has two parts. Evaluating segment data forces us to ask important questions that help us truly understand the business. Moreover, truly understanding the business requires not only understanding what is sold and how much is made but also interpreting how financial reports summarize dynamic changes in the business.

In 1999, 64% of PepsiCo's $18,244 million in sales were snacks and 36% were beverages. Suppose you predicted snack sales to grow 8% and beverage sales to grow 5%. What would be your prediction of sales for the year 2000?

ANSWER
1. Snack sales equal .64 × $18,244 × 1.08 = $12,610.
2. Beverage sales equal .36 × $18,244 × 1.05 = $6,896.
3. Projected sales would be the total of $19,506 for a weighted-average growth of about 7%.

FINANCIAL RATIOS

Objective 3
Use the basic financial ratios to guide your thinking.

Although many analysis methods exist, the cornerstone of financial statement analysis is the use of ratios. Exhibit 13-7 groups some of the most popular ratios into four categories. Most of these ratios have been introduced in earlier chapters, as indicated in the second column (a dash in the column means that the ratio is being introduced in this chapter for the first time). We provide this summary to avoid the need to search for definitions in prior material.

EVALUATING FINANCIAL RATIOS

There are three main types of comparisons used to evaluate financial ratios: (1) with a company's own historical ratios (called **time-series comparisons**), (2) with general rules of thumb or **benchmarks,** and (3) with ratios of other companies or with industry averages (called **cross-sectional comparisons**).

Some annual reports support time-series trend analysis by providing comparative ratios for 5 or 10 years. For example, the 2000 annual report of Taiwan Semiconductor provides a 5-year history on some 30 relationships including familiar ratios such as the debt ratio, times interest earned, and return on assets (ROA). Such a display allows you to quickly assess managerial effectiveness in several areas. The Taiwan Semiconductor material permits an analyst to conclude that the company has significantly improved its profitability since 1997 while maintaining essentially the same capital structure but using its assets much more effectively.

time-series comparisons Comparisons of a company's financial ratios with its own historical ratios.

benchmarks General rules of thumb specifying appropriate levels for financial ratios.

cross-sectional comparisons Comparisons of a company's financial ratios with the ratios of other companies or with industry averages.

RATIOS

Ratios are useful for financial analysis by investors because ratios capture critical dimensions of the economic performance of the entity. How might ratios pay off for managers? Increasingly, ratios are a tool that managers use to guide, measure, and reward workers. If

Exhibit 13-7
Some Typical Financial Ratios

Typical Name of Ratio	Introduced in Chapter	Numerator	Denominator	Using Appropriate Oxley Numbers Applied to December 31 of Year	
				20X2	20X1
Short-term liquidity ratios					
Current ratio	4	Current assets	Current liabilities	290 ÷ 219 = 1.3	202 ÷ 101 = 2.0
Quick ratio	4	Cash + marketable securities + receivables	Current liabilities	(150 + 0 + 95) ÷ 219 = 1.1	(57 + 0 + 70) ÷ 101 = 1.3
Average collection period in days	5	Average accounts receivable × 365	Sales	[1/2(95 + 70) × 365] ÷ 999 = 30†	Unknown*
Inventory turnover	6	Cost of goods sold	Average inventory at cost	399 ÷ 1/2(20 + 60) = 10	Unknown*
Long-term solvency ratios					
Total debt to total assets	8	Total liabilities	Total assets	259 ÷ 658 = 39.4%	221 ÷ 610 = 36.2%
Total debt to equity	8	Total liabilities	Stockholders' equity	259 ÷ 399 = 64.9%	221 ÷ 389 = 56.8%
Interest coverage	8	Income before interest and taxes	Interest expense	(150 + 12) ÷ 12 = 13.5	(128 + 12) ÷ 12 = 11.7
Profitability ratios					
Return on stockholders' equity (ROE)	4, 11	Net income	Average stockholders' equity	90 ÷ 1/2(399 + 389) = 22.8%	Unknown*
Gross profit rate or percentage	4	Gross profit or gross margin	Sales	600 ÷ 999 = 60%	464 ÷ 800 = 58%
Return on sales	4	Net income	Sales	90 ÷ 999 = 9%	80 ÷ 800 = 10%
Asset turnover	—	Sales	Average total assets available	999 ÷ 1/2(658 + 610) = 1.6	Unknown*
Pretax return on operating assets	—	Operating income	Average total assets available	126 ÷ 1/2(658 + 610) = 19.9%	Unknown*
Earnings per share	2	Net income less dividends on preferred stock, if any	Average common shares outstanding	90 ÷ 200 = $.45	80 ÷ 200 = $.40
Market price and dividend ratios					
Price-earnings	2	Market price of common share (assume $4 and $3)	Earnings per share	4 ÷ 45 = 8.9	3 ÷ 40 = 7.5%
Dividend-yield	2	Dividends per common share	Market price of common share (assume $4 and $3)	.40 ÷ 4 = 10.0%	.20 ÷ 3 = 6.7%
Dividend-payout	2	Dividends per common share	Earnings per share	.40 ÷ .45 = 89%	.20 ÷ .40 = 50%

*Insufficient data available because the *beginning* balance sheet balances for 20X1 are not provided. Without them, the *average* investment in receivables, inventory, total assets, or stockholders' equity during 20X1 cannot be computed.

†This may be easier to see as follows: Average receivables = 1/2(95 + 70) = 82.5. Average receivables as a percentage of annual sales = 82.5 ÷ 999 = 8.25%. Average collection period = 8.25% × 365 days = 30 days.

managers compensate workers for actions that make the company more profitable, workers are likely to do the right thing. Thus, some companies give workers a bonus if the company generates a ROE of more than 20% or if earnings per share (EPS) exceeds a specific number. Hewitt Associates, a compensation consulting firm, reports that 60% of the 1,941 large companies the firm surveyed had profit-sharing programs. Such programs are based on the solid view that when profits rise, workers are doing the right thing and should share in the benefits.

Duke Power Company decided that profit may not be the right measure for rewarding employees. Suppose profit increases because you raise more capital and expand the company. Should the workers necessarily earn more? Duke Power decided to reward workers based on two factors: success in meeting goals and ROE. For one worker, the goal might be defined as reduced injuries and for another, as improved customer service. However, everyone earns more for meeting ROE targets. ROE is a good measure of efficiency because it can be improved by increasing profitability (the return on sales) and also by increasing the efficiency with which assets are employed (asset turnover).

Programs such as the one at Duke Power are increasing. Managers often use the phrase "open-book management" to describe this process in which the goal is to assure that workers understand the finances of the company and believe it is their responsibility to help improve financial performance. Southwest Airlines sponsored a quiz for its employees concerning various levels of costs the company faced. People who tracked down the data in the company newsletter and submitted their quiz were eligible to win free travel. *Open-Book Management* by John Case provides many examples of companies that have applied these principles. Now many certified public accountants (CPA's) and other business consultants include training for open-book management principles as one of their specialties.

Let us examine some specific ratios by comparing those for Oxley Company in Exhibit 13-7 with some of the Dun & Bradstreet ratios for 1,712 retail nurseries and garden stores:

Dun and Bradstreet Ratios

	Current Ratio	Quick Ratio	Average Collection Period (Days)	Total Debt to Stockholders' Equity (Percent)	Return on Sales (Percent)	Return on Stockholders' Equity (Percent)
1,712 Companies						
Upper quartile	4.2	1.5	5.5	32.3	6.1	30.2
Median	2.0	0.5	11.3	92.8	2.5	12.6
Lower quartile	1.3	0.2	23.0	230.7	0.5	2.6
Oxley*	1.3	1.1	30.0	64.9	9.0	22.8

*Ratios are from exhibit 13-7. Please consult that exhibit for an explanation of the components of each ratio.

Dun and Bradstreet ranks the individual ratios from best to worst. The ratio ranked in the middle is the median. The upper quartile is the ratio ranked halfway between the median and the best value. The lower quartile is the ratio ranked halfway between the median and the worst value. The concept of best and worst must be taken with a grain of salt. Different analysts may have different ideas about what is good and what is bad. For example, a short-term creditor would think that a very high current ratio was good, because it means the assets are there to repay the debt. From management's perspective, however, a very high current ratio may be bad and show that the company is maintaining higher levels of inventory and receivables than it should. Let us take a look at how analysts would interpret some of the main types of ratios.

Oxley is above the median level of net-income-based ratios and has a reasonable debt level. The long collection period means Oxley has a lot of receivables. It is unclear whether the long collection period is a problem or just an odd practice of Oxley's. The analyst must ask management about it. What are the possibilities? Oxley could have a lot of deadbeat customers, which is bad news. Alternatively, most companies similar to Oxley may require bank cards and not have any "real" receivables whereas Oxley actually lets local buyers have credit terms on their large purchases. You must understand the business and be aware of what the norms are before you evaluate the specifics of one company. Although the current ratio is low, the quick ratio is high, which means Oxley should have enough liquid funds to manage current obligations.

How might analysts think about specific liquidity ratios? Changes in average collection period and inventory turnover can alert investors and creditors to problems. For example, a decrease in inventory turnover may suggest that a company's sales staff is no longer doing a very good job or that the company's products have fallen out of favor with the buying public. An alternative to the "sales are falling" explanation is the "inventory is rising" explanation. Suppose manufacturing is producing product at a rapid pace beyond what current buyers want. Inventory builds faster than sales, and the turnover falls.

Similarly, an increase in the average collection period of receivables may indicate that the company has started selling to buyers who are credit risks or that the company has gotten lazy in its collection efforts. Whether the inventory turnover of 10 and the average collection period of 30 days are "fast" or "slow" depends on past performance and the performance of similar companies. Inventory turnover is not available from Dun & Bradstreet on an industry-comparable basis. The average collection period for Oxley is nearly three times as long as the industry median of 11.3 days. Perhaps most firms give large discounts for prompt payment and Oxley does not.

A company with many cash sales may have a short average collection period for total sales, even though there may be long delays in receiving payments for items sold on credit. Suppose half of Oxley's sales were for cash and half were on open credit. The average collection period for credit sales would be:

$$\frac{(1/2)(95 + 70) \times 365}{(1/2)(999)} = 60 \text{ days}$$

To compare this average for credit sales with the given industry average collection period, we must adjust the industry average for credit sales. Suppose only one-fourth of the sales in retail nurseries are on credit. The industry median collection period for credit accounts would be $11.3 \div (1/4) = 45.2$ days. Many analysts use sales on account in the denominator of the average collection period to remove this interpretation problem.

Oxley's debt-to-equity ratio of 64.9% is below the industry median of 92.8%, which suggests that the company has a better than average ability to pay its debts on time. Typically, companies with heavy debt in relation to ownership capital are in greater danger of suffering net losses or even insolvency when business conditions sour. Why? Because revenues and many expenses decline, but interest expenses and maturity dates do not change.

Oxley's ROE of 22.8% is above the industry median of 12.6%. What explains Oxley's superior performance? Two additional profitability ratios help explain it. The return on sales has fallen from 10% to 9% but still places Oxley well above the upper quartile for nurseries and garden stores according to Dun & Bradstreet. Also, Oxley is very efficient when using its assets to generate sales. Various additional ratios can be used to assess the role of operating performance and financial performance in the overall success of the company.

OPERATING PERFORMANCE AND FINANCIAL PERFORMANCE

Measures of overall profitability, such as ROE (see p. 160), are affected by both operating and financing choices. Financial management is concerned with where the company gets cash and how it uses that cash to its benefit. Operating management is concerned with the day-to-day activities that generate revenues and expenses. Ratios to assess operating efficiency should not be affected by financial management performance.

Objective 4
Evaluate corporate
performance using
ROA, ROE, and EVA.

OPERATING PERFORMANCE

In general, we evaluate the overall success of an investment by comparing our investment returns with the amount of investment we initially made:

$$\text{Rate of return on investment} = \frac{\text{Income}}{\text{Invested capital}} \tag{1}$$

In various settings, we find it useful to define income differently, sometimes as net earnings and sometimes as either pretax income from operations or earnings before interest and taxes **(EBIT).** We also define invested capital differently, sometimes as the stockholders' equity and other times as the total capital provided by both debt and equity sources. These choices are determined by the purpose of the analysis. For example, an investor in common stock would be more concerned about the ROE, whereas a lender is more concerned with how effectively borrowed capital is being used to generate cash in support of interest payments.

EBIT Earnings before interest and taxes.

Because the measurement of operating performance should not be influenced by how assets are financed, it is best measured by **pretax operating rate of return on total assets** also called simply **return on total assets (ROA):**

pretax operating rate of return on total assets (return on total assets— ROA) Operating income divided by average total assets available.

$$\begin{array}{c}\text{Pretax operating rate}\\\text{of return on total assets}\end{array} = \frac{\text{Operating income}}{\text{Average total assets available}} \tag{2}$$

The right side of equation 2 consists of two important ratios:

$$\frac{\text{Operating income}}{\text{Average total assets available}} = \frac{\text{Operating income}}{\text{Sales}} \times \frac{\text{Sales}}{\begin{array}{c}\text{Average total}\\\text{assets available}\end{array}} \tag{3}$$

These relationships are displayed for Oxley Company in Exhibit 13-8.

The right-side terms in equation 3 are often called the **operating income percentage on sales** and the **total asset turnover (asset turnover),** respectively. Equation 3 may be reexpressed:

operating income percentage on sales Operating income divided by sales.

$$\begin{array}{ccc}\begin{array}{c}\text{Pretax operating rate}\\\text{of return on total assets}\end{array} = & \begin{array}{c}\text{Operating income}\\\text{percentage on sales}\end{array} \times \text{Total asset turnover} \\ 19.9\% & = & 12.6\% & \times & 1.576 \text{ times}\end{array} \tag{4}$$

total asset turnover (asset turnover) Sales divided by average total assets available.

Equation 4 highlights that operating income percentage and turnover, by themselves, each increases the rate of return on total assets. Unfortunately, these ratios are sometimes calculated on after-tax amounts, so peculiarities of the income tax laws may sometimes distort results. You know how you calculate a number but may not always be sure how published numbers are calculated.

This decomposition of the pretax return on total assets can also be applied to the return on equity. In this case, the numerator is after-tax earnings and the invested capital is owner's equity. A third component called leverage is added that emphasizes the effects

Exhibit 13-8

Major Ingredients of Return on Total Assets

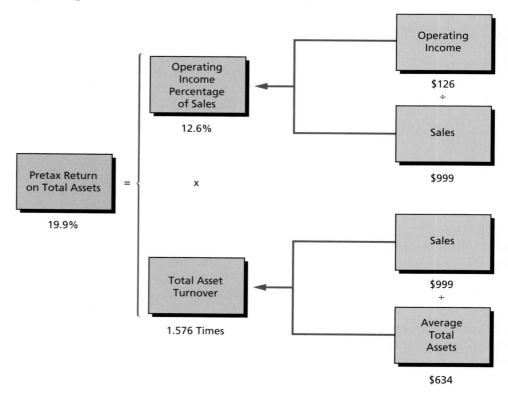

on ROE associated with the use of debt. This decomposition is often referred to as DuPont analysis because it was developed some years ago by a very talented group of financial analysts working at DuPont. The decomposition would be:

$$ROE = \text{Return on sales} \times \text{Asset turnover} \times \text{Leverage}$$

$$= \frac{\text{Net income}}{\text{Sales}} \times \frac{\text{Sales}}{\text{Average total assets}} \times \frac{\text{Average total assets}}{\text{Average stockholders' equity}}$$

FINANCIAL PERFORMANCE

Good financial performance requires an appropriate balance of debt and equity financing. In addition to deciding how much debt is appropriate, a firm must choose how much to borrow short-term, for example, accounts payable and some bank debt, and how much to borrow by issuing bonds or other longer term debt. Short-term debt must be quickly repaid or refinanced. When the borrower encounters trouble and cannot repay, it is also difficult to refinance. Lenders prefer healthy, profitable borrowers, not troubled ones. Such problems are especially severe during periods when interest rates are rising, because each new refinancing occurs at a higher interest rate, and the cash flow needed to cover interest payments rises.

Long-term investments are usually financed by long-term capital: debt or stock. Debt is often a more attractive vehicle to companies than is common stock because (1) interest payments are deductible for income tax purposes, but dividends are not, and (2) ownership rights to voting and profits are kept by the present shareholders.

Trading on the Equity

Most companies have two basic types of long-term financing: long-term debt and stockholders' equity. The total of long-term financing is often called the **capitalization,** or simply **capital structure** of a corporation. Suppose a company has long-term debt (bonds payable) and common stock as its capital structure. The common shareholders enjoy the benefits of all income in excess of interest on the bonds.

Trading on the equity (also referred to as using **financial leverage, leveraging**, or in the United Kingdom, **gearing**) means using money borrowed at fixed interest rates to try to enhance the rate of return on common shareholders' equity. There are costs and benefits to shareholders from trading on the equity. The costs are interest payments and increased risk, and the benefits are the larger returns to the common shareholders—as long as overall income is large enough.

To illustrate, imagine companies A, B, and C shown in Exhibit 13-9. Each is in the same industry, with $80,000 of assets and with the same rate of ROA each year. However, the annual ROA varies from 20% in year one, to 10% in year two, and 5% in year three. The three companies have chosen very different capital structures. Company A has no debt, Company B has $30,000 in debt, and Company C has $60,000 in debt. Company B pays 10% interest, while the more heavily indebted Company C must pay 12%. How do the shareholders fare in these three companies in different years? Exhibit 13-9 summarizes the results.

The first column of Exhibit 13-9 gives the income before interest expense. To focus clearly on leverage, this example ignores taxes. Recall that we calculate the return on assets as

$$\text{Pretax operating rate of return on total assets} = \frac{\text{Operating income (income before interest and taxes)}}{\text{Average total assets}}$$

capitalization (capital structure) Owners' equity plus long-term debt.

trading on the equity (financial leverage, leveraging, gearing) Using borrowed money at fixed interest rates with the objective of enhancing the rate of return on common equity.

Exhibit 13-9
Trading on the Equity-Effects of Debt on Rates of Return

	(1) Income before Interest	(2) Interest Expense	(3) Net Income	(4) Stockholders' Equity	(5) Return on Equity
	(ROA × Assets)*	(Debt × Interest Rate)+	(1) − (2)		(3) ÷ (4)
Year one: 20% ROA					
Company A	$16,000	$ 0	$16,000	$80,000	20%
Company B	16,000	3,000	13,000	50,000	26%
Company C	16,000	7,200	8,800	20,000	44%
Year two: 10% ROA					
Company A	$ 8,000	$ 0	$ 8,000	$80,000	10%
Company B	8,000	3,000	5,000	50,000	10%
Company C	8,000	7,200	800	20,000	4%
Year three: 5% ROA					
Company A	$ 4,000	$ 0	$ 4,000	$80,000	5%
Company B	4,000	3,000	1,000	50,000	2%
Company C	4,000	7,200	(3,200)	20,000	(16%)

*All three companies have $80,000 in assets.

+Company A, no debt; Company B, $30,000 in debt at 10%; Company C, $60,000 in debt at 12%.

Therefore, income before interest and taxes equals ROA times average total assets. In this instance, we assume a constant ROA for each firm, but we vary the ROA from one year to the next. We can calculate operating income each year by multiplying ROA for the year times the constant asset level of $80,000. The interest expense differs by company because each has a different level of debt, but for any company it does not change from year to year. Our primary interest is the effect of leverage on the level of the rate of ROE.

What do we learn from Exhibit 13-9? First, a debt-free, or unlevered, company has identical ROA and ROE. Note that equity-financed, unlevered Company A's ROE and ROA are identical in each year: 20%, 10%, and 5%. Second, when a company has an ROA greater than its interest rate, ROE exceeds ROA. This situation is called favorable financial leverage and describes both companies B and C in year one. They earn 20% on their assets and pay either 10% or 12% on their debt. The earnings in excess of the interest cost increase earnings available to shareholders.

Year two is interesting because Company B has an ROA of 10%, which equals its interest rate. Thus, like Company A, Company B has a ROE of 10%. In contrast, Company C experiences unfavorable financial leverage. Because its 10% ROA is less than its 12% interest cost, its ROE falls sharply to 4%. Year three further stresses the effects of leverage in poor years. When ROA falls noticeably below the firm's interest cost, ROE falls sharply as well. Company B falls to an ROE of 2%, while the more highly leveraged Company C faces a loss year and negative ROE.

When a company is unable to earn at least the interest rate on the money borrowed, the return on equity is lower than it would be for the debt-free company. If earnings are low enough that the interest and principal payments on debt cannot be made, a company may be forced into bankruptcy. The possibility of bankruptcy increases the risk to the common stockholders even more than it does to debt holders. Remember, debt holders collect their claims before stockholders do.

Obviously, the more stable the income, the less dangerous it is to trade on the equity. Therefore, regulated utilities such as electric, gas, and telephone companies tend to have a much heavier proportion of debt than do manufacturers of computers or steel. Historically, these regulated companies have had a stable customer base and were somewhat protected from competition. Government regulations helped assure that prices would be sufficiently high to ensure a profit. The breakup of AT&T as the dominant national phone company and current efforts to introduce more competition among electric utility companies may produce changes in these historical patterns of leverage. The prudent use of debt is part of intelligent financial management.

ECONOMIC VALUE ADDED

We calculate ROA and ROE directly from the financial statements. They measure performance by relating an income statement number to investment levels reported in the balance sheet. Economic value added (EVA) is a related performance measure developed and trademarked by Stern Stewart and Company. The idea is that a firm must earn more than it must pay for its capital if it is to increase in value. This is like saying that a firm must earn more than the interest rate on borrowing for borrowing to be favorable. When we refer to capital in EVA, we are referring to all capital, both debt and equity. The cost of that capital is a weighted average of interest cost and the returns required by equity investors. Let us assume that this weighted average cost of capital is 10%. Furthermore, assume that a company has $1 million in invested capital. Then the company is adding value if its net operating profit after tax exceeds 10% of $1 million, or $100,000.

If the net operating profit after tax were $120,000, for example, we would calculate the EVA as $120,000 − $100,000 = $20,000. If this firm were generating only $70,000 of net operating profit after tax, we would say that EVA was a negative $30,000 ($70,000 − $100,000). Here value is being lost, and it would be preferable to dissolve the company and return the capital to the creditors and owners. In applying EVA, managers often make adjustments to the accounting results. Without exploring all such adjustments, we consider one, research and development expenditures. Although accountants require companies to expense R&D immediately, all agree that it has some economic value and that the expensing procedure is a conservative approach. EVA proponents argue that it is better to arbitrarily assume a 5-year life than no life and they restate the financial statement accordingly.

Suppose a company spent $50,000 per year on R&D, every year. If the company capitalized this with a 5-year life, annual amortization of R&D in the income statement would still be $50,000, but there would be higher assets and higher owner's equity.

Many companies have adopted EVA as an internal management tool, including AT&T, Coca-Cola, CSX, Eli Lilly, and Monsanto. They believe that this procedure helps them allocate, manage, and redeploy scarce capital resources such as heavy equipment, working capital, and real estate. Eli Lilly includes a calculation of EVA as 1 of 13 elements in its 1999 financial highlights. Its EVA analysis indicates that Lilly reports adding $1.5 billion dollars of value.

INCOME TAX EFFECTS

Because interest payments are deductible as an expense for income tax purposes but dividends are not, if all other things are equal, the use of debt is less costly to the corporation than is equity. Consider raising additional capital of $10 million either through long-term debt or through preferred stock. The typical preferred stock is a part of shareholders' equity, and the dividend thereon is not deductible for income tax purposes. Moreover, the rate of preferred dividends is usually higher than is the rate of interest because the preferred stockholders have a greater risk due to their lower priority claim on the total assets of a company. Assume an interest rate of 10% for debt and a preferred dividend rate of 11%. The income tax rate is 40%. Compare the effects on net income less preferred dividends of these two methods as shown in the accompanying table.

	$10 Million Long-Term Debt	$10 Million Preferred Stock
Income before interest expense (assumed)	$5,000,000	$5,000,000
Interest expense at 10% of long-term debt	1,000,000	—
Income before income taxes	$4,000,000	$5,000,000
Income tax expense at 40%	1,600,000	2,000,000
Net income	$2,400,000	$3,000,000
Dividends to preferred shareholders at 11%	—	1,100,000
Net income less dividends	$2,400,000	$1,900,000
Pretax cost of capital raised	10%	11%
After-tax cost of capital raised		
$600,000* ÷ $10,000,000	6%	
$1,100,000 ÷ $10,000,000		11%
*Interest expense	$1,000,000	
Income tax savings because of interest deduction:		
.40 × $1,000,000	400,000	
Interest expense after tax savings	$ 600,000	

You should note three points:

1. Interest is tax deductible, so its after-tax cost can be considerably less than that of dividends on preferred stock (6% versus 11%). In other words, net income attributable to common shareholders can be substantially higher if debt is used.

2. Interest is an expense, whereas preferred dividends are not. Therefore, net income is higher if preferred shares are used ($3 million versus $2.4 million). Note that trading on the equity can benefit the common stockholders by the issuance of either long-term debt securities or preferred stock, provided that there are sufficient earnings on the additional assets acquired.

3. Failure to pay interest is an act of bankruptcy, which gives creditors rights to control or liquidate the company. Failure to pay dividends has less severe consequences.

MEASURING SAFETY

Investors in debt securities want assurance that future operations will easily provide enough cash for the company to make the scheduled payments of interest and principal. Debt securities often have provisions aimed at reducing investor risk, such as the right to repossess assets or the right to receive payment before common stockholders do. However, because they kick in only when the company is in danger of defaulting on the loans, these provisions are nowhere near as valuable as a pattern of growing earnings. Bondholders prefer to avoid the trouble and costs of foreclosure or bankruptcy litigation. They would much rather have a steady stream of interest and repayments of principal provided by a company with good, steady earnings.

times interest earned
Income before interest expense and income taxes divided by interest expense. Synonym for interest coverage.

Debt-to-equity ratios are popular measures of risk. But they do not focus directly on the major concern of the holders of long-term debt: the ability to make debt payments on schedule. A ratio that focuses on interest-paying ability is interest coverage (see, p. 363, also called **times interest earned**), calculated as income before interest expense and income taxes divided by interest expense. For example, in Exhibit 13-7, interest coverage is 5.0 times.

A rule of thumb or benchmark for debt investors is that the interest coverage should be at least five times, even in the poorest year in a span of 7 to 10 years. The numerator in this equation does not deduct income taxes because interest expense is deductible for income tax purposes. In effect, income taxes, as a periodic "claim" on earnings, are calculated after interest is deducted. For instance, if the numerator were only $1 million, interest would be paid, leaving a net taxable income of zero. This tax-deductibility feature is a major reason why bonds are used much more widely than preferred stock.

PROMINENCE OF EARNINGS PER SHARE

Throughout this text, we have viewed earnings as a basic reporting element in the financial statements. We have noted that earnings are often expressed on a per share basis (EPS) and that EPS is itself a component in the price–earnings ratio. Up to this point, though, we have kept EPS simple by considering only common stock. In reality, EPS can be a bit more complicated. We now turn to issues that complicate EPS.

Objective 5
Calculate EPS under complex circumstances.

WEIGHTED-AVERAGE SHARES AND PREFERRED STOCK

When the outstanding shares are all common stock, the primary complication is the calculation of weighted-average shares in the following equation (numbers assumed):

$$\text{Earnings per share} \atop \text{of common stock} = \frac{\text{Net income}}{\text{Weighted-average number of shares}\atop\text{outstanding during the period}}$$

$$= \frac{\$1,000,000}{800,000} = \$1.25$$

How would the 800,000 weighted-average shares be calculated? Suppose 750,000 shares were outstanding at the beginning of a calendar year, and 200,000 additional shares were issued on October 1 (3 months before the end of the year). The weighted average is based on the number of months that the shares were outstanding during the year. The basic computation can be accomplished in two different ways:

750,000 × Weighting of 12/12 = $750,000		750,000 × 9/12 = $562,500
200,000 × Weighting of 3/12 = 50,000	*or*	950,000 × 3/12 = 237,500
Weighted-average shares $800,000		$800,000

In this example, the number of shares outstanding rose because additional shares were issued. This might have occurred because some executives exercised some stock options and acquired more shares. The company might have simply issued a block of additional shares to outside investors at the current market price. The number of shares could also decline during the year due to purchase of shares for the treasury.

A second complication arises if shares of nonconvertible preferred stock are outstanding. The dividends on preferred stock for the current period, whether or not paid, should be deducted in calculating earnings applicable to common stock (figures assumed):

$$\text{Earnings per share}\atop\text{of common stock} = \frac{\text{Net income} - \text{Preferred dividends}}{\text{Weighted-average number of shares}\atop\text{outstanding during the period}}$$

$$= \frac{\$1,000,000 - \$200,000}{800,000} = \$1.00$$

Further, to assure comparability of historical summaries of EPS, we must adjust for changes in capitalization structure, for example, stock splits and stock dividends. As an example, Cisco had a two-for-one stock split in June 1999. In the 1999 historical summary, 1998 earnings per share are reported to be $.65. If you actually looked at the 1998 annual report, the EPS reported there would be $1.30. Why? Because the investor wants to be able to compare the year-to-year performance in terms of today's shares. Because each 1998 share outstanding counts as two 1999 shares, Cisco must adjust 1998 EPS to allow meaningful comparisons.

BASIC AND DILUTED EPS

EPS calculations become a bit more complex when companies have convertible securities, stock options, or other financial instruments that can be exchanged for, or converted to, common shares. For example, suppose a firm has some convertible preferred stock outstanding:

Convertible preferred stock at 5%, $100 par, each share convertible into two common shares	100,000 shares
Common stock	1,000,000 shares

The basic EPS computation follows (numbers assumed):

Computation of earnings per share	
Net income	$10,500,000
less preferred dividends	500,000
Net income to common stock	$10,000,000
Earnings per share of common stock	
$10,000,000 ÷ 1,000,000 shares	$ 10.00

However, note how EPS would be affected if the preferred stock were converted, that is, exchanged for common stock. EPS will be "diluted," or reduced. We can calculate EPS as if conversion had occurred at the beginning of the period. No preferred dividends would be paid but there would be more shares outstanding:

Net income	$10,500,000
less preferred dividends	0
Net income to common stock	$10,500,000
Earnings per share of common stock—assuming conversion	
$10,500,000 ÷ 1,200,000 shares	$ 8.75

The dilution of common stock caused by the conversion is $10.00 − $8.75 = $1.25 per share. Diluted EPS assumes the conversion of all potentially dilutive securities. In 1999, Cisco reported basic EPS of $.65 and diluted EPS of $.62. If all options were exercised, Cisco would experience an increase of 185 million shares.

DISCLOSURE OF NONRECURRING ITEMS

Objective 6
Adjust for nonrecurring items.

One of the main ideas behind financial statement analysis is evaluating or estimating a firm's future prospects. When estimating the future, though, we need to distinguish the elements of the current financial statements that reflect recurring aspects of the firm from those that represent one-time events or items that will not continue. These nonrecurring items fall into four major categories: special items, extraordinary items, discontinued operations, and accounting changes. Three of the four are illustrated, with related numbers in bold type in the income statement of E.I. du Pont in Exhibit 13-10.

SPECIAL ITEMS

special items Expenses that are large enough and unusual enough to warrant separate disclosure.

Special items are large and unusual items. They appear in the income statement as a separately identified amount. Companies have substantial flexibility in deciding when to treat something as a special item. Recently, the most common special item has been restructuring charges. A restructuring occurs when a firm decides to substantially change the size, scope, or location of a part of the business. It often involves relocation, plant closings, and reductions in personnel. The costs typically are incurred over an extended period of time, often several years, but GAAP requires that the total costs be estimated and recorded when the plan is made. In 1994, the FASB and the SEC acted to assure that restructuring charges did not include costs that will benefit future periods. Specifically, restructuring cannot include relocation and training costs for people who will continue to work for the firm. These costs must still be properly matched to future revenues. A special item would appear as a separate line item among operating expenses, with any necessary discussion or explanation in the footnotes. The $524 million restructuring charge in E.I. du Pont's 1999 income statement in Exhibit 13-10 illustrates this point.

How would an analyst use this information to project future operating income? Because a restructuring of such magnitude is rare, the analyst might argue that the expense of $524 million is nonrecurring. Continuing operating profit projections would be based on 1999 operating income before deducting restructuring charges: $1,690 million + $524 million or $2,214 million.

Notice that because special items are reported with other expenses, they are reported before tax. Taxable income is thus reduced as is income tax expense. If we assume a 40% tax rate, the special item reduced taxable income by $524 million and therefore reduced the tax provision by 40% of $524 million, or $210 million. The special item's after-tax effect would be $524 − (.40 × $524) = $314 million. In estimating future net income, the analyst would add back $314 million to reported net income.

Exhibit 13-10

E.I. du Pont de Nemours and Company and Consolidated Subsidiaries

Consolidated Income Statement, Dollars in Millions, Except per Share

	1999	1998
Sales	$26,918	$24,767
Other income	974	981
Total	27,892	25,748
Cost of goods sold and other operating charges	16,991	15,556
Selling, general, and administrative expenses	2,595	2,115
Depreciation	1,444	1,452
Amortization of goodwill and other intangible assets	246	108
Research and development expense	1,617	1,308
Interest expense	535	520
Purchased in-process research and development	2,250	1,443
Restructuring charges	**524**	**633**
Total	26,202	23,135
Income from continuing operations before income taxes		
and minority interests	1,690	2,613
Provision for income taxes (note 6)	1,410	941
Minority interests in earnings of consolidated subsidiaries	61	24
Income from continuing operations	219	1,648
Discontinued operations (note 7)		
Income from operations of discontinued business,		
net of income taxes	—	594
Gain on disposal of discontinued business, net of income taxes	**7,471**	**2,439**
Income before extraordinary item	7,690	4,681
Extraordinary charge from early extinguishment of debt,		
net of income taxes (note 8)	—	**(201)**
Net Income	$ 7,690	$ 4,480
Basic earnings (loss) per share of common stock (note 9)		
Continuing operations before extraordinary item	$ .19	$ 1.45
Discontinued operations	**6.89**	**2.69**
Before extraordinary item	7.08	4.14
Extraordinary charge	—	(.18)
Net income	$ 7.08	$ 3.96
Diluted earnings (loss) per share of common stock (note 9)		
Continuing operations before extraordinary item	$ .19	$ 1.43
Discontinued operations	**6.80**	**2.65**
Before extraordinary item	6.99	4.08
Extraordinary charge	—	**(.18)**
Net income	$ 6.99	$ 3.90

In 1999, however, life would not be quite that easy for the equity analyst trying to assess the future earnings of DuPont. For one thing, DuPont has reported such restructuring costs in each of the last 3 years in amounts ranging from $340 million to $633 million. Although the items are large and it is important to highlight them, it is not obvious that they are unusual and nonrecurring. The evidence is exactly the opposite. The notes that describe these as "Employee separations costs and write-down of assets" occupy two full pages in the report. For example, the company attributes elements of the 1999 charge to three business areas: agriculture and nutrition, nylon, and polyester.

One piece was the write-off of $45 million of intangible assets.

> *The company had previously established an intangible asset related to the acquisition of exclusive rights to market a product under a long-term contract that included the purchase of stipulated minimum quantities. Due to significantly lower than expected sales, the company notified the supplier that it will not purchase the minimum quantity and therefore will forego the right to exclusively market the product.*

In each area there were multiple items, including write-offs such as this one and severance of employees.

It is likely that an analyst would conclude that costs of this type will continue to be incurred in different parts of the business in different years and therefore future predictions would be based on the $1,690 million of income from continuing operations without adjusting for these special items. Adjustment would be more appropriate for a company that had not experienced such costs in prior years but was making what appears to be a one-time adjustment in employment levels and asset values in one primary business area.

EXTRAORDINARY ITEMS

extraordinary items Items that are unusual in nature and infrequent in occurrence that are shown separately, net of tax, in the income statement.

Extraordinary items result from events that must have both an unusual nature and an infrequency of occurrence. Therefore, write-downs of receivables and inventories are ordinary items, as are gains or losses on the sale of fixed assets. The effects of a strike and many foreign currency revaluations are also ordinary items. However, the financial effects of an earthquake or government expropriation are likely to qualify as extraordinary items. Interestingly enough, the effects of most floods are not considered extraordinary. Why not? Because most floods occur in areas that are prone to certain amounts of flooding, thus a flood there is not an unusual occurrence. Basically, an event or transaction should be presumed to be ordinary unless the evidence clearly supports its classification as extraordinary.

The few events and items that are considered extraordinary must be excluded from regular operating income calculations. Extraordinary items are presented separately on the income statement. They are reported net of tax, which means that the figure presented includes any tax effect an item might have (remember, most items that increase/decrease income also increase/decrease taxes).

In an average year, fewer than 10% of major U.S. companies report an extraordinary item. Fewer than 5% have an extraordinary item greater than 10% of their net income. Most of the extraordinary items arise from extinguishment of debt. The FASB requires debt extinguishments to be treated in this manner, although they do not truly meet the definition of extraordinary. Perhaps the goal is to prevent companies from using conscious decisions to redeem debt early to affect the amounts being reported as ordinary operating income. For example, in the absence of this rule, companies could redeem debt at a gain when operating results were poor. In 1998, DuPont extinguished some debt (see Exhibit 13-10). Note 8 to the financial statements reveals ($ in millions):

> *In September 1998 the company redeemed various outstanding notes and debentures with an aggregate principal value of $1,633. The extraordinary charge of $201, net of a tax benefit of $74, principally represents call premium and unamortized discount. The effective income tax rate of 26.9 percent reflects the mix of U.S. and international operations.*

A tragic illustration of an extraordinary charge was caused by criminal tampering with Tylenol capsules. People died as a result of cyanide being put into the product. The manufacturer, Johnson & Johnson (J&J), took immediate action to pull all products from store shelves while tracing the source of the problem. J&J reported the following on its income statement ($ in millions):

Earnings before extraordinary charge	$146.5
Extraordinary charge—costs associated with the withdrawal of Tylenol capsules (less applicable tax relief of $50.0)	50.0
Net earnings	$ 96.5

DISCONTINUED OPERATIONS

Discontinued operations involve the termination (closing or sale) of a segment of the business, not just of a single plant or location. Many large companies have several discrete business segments. For example, PepsiCo has a beverage business and a snack food business. If a company discontinues any segment, it should report the results of continuing operations separately from those of discontinued operations, although both must be reported on the income statement. Any gain or loss from the disposal of a segment of a business must be reported with the related results of discontinued operations and not as an extraordinary item. As with extraordinary items, discontinued operations are shown on the income statement net of tax.

In a comparative income statement, the income or loss of the discontinued segment's operations needs to be shown separately for all past years that segment operated. Otherwise, the company's current financial status, which no longer includes the discontinued segment, would not be comparable to its past financial status. In Exhibit 13-10, DuPont separately discloses the income from its Conoco subsidiary in 1998, $594 million net of tax. The gain on disposition of Conoco is spread across 2 years because of the timing of the transactions involved and totals approximately $10 billion.

The structure of the income statement makes it easy to understand the huge effect of this transaction on DuPont's performance in 1998 and 1999. Note that income from continuing operations dropped significantly in 1999 from $1,648 million to $219 million although net income nearly doubled. EPS is a very important summary measure and DuPont has appropriately decomposed the EPS number by separately disclosing the effect of the discontinued operations and the extraordinary charge in the calculation of EPS.

ACCOUNTING CHANGES

The presentation of the effects of an accounting change is net of tax and is separated from ongoing operations in the same section of the income statement that contains discontinued

discontinued operations
The termination of a business segment. The results are reported separately, net of tax, in the income statement.

operations. Changes of accounting method that are treated this way arise from changes in FASB requirements. When the FASB changes its rules, it often requires a major one-time recognition. Such a change in reporting for postretirement insurance and health costs affected many U.S. companies in 1992 and 1993. This led to large charges against income. At the same time, many companies adopted the new FASB rule on taxes that caused some companies to realize one-time additional expense and caused other companies to show increased income. Few companies have reported significant accounting changes since 1994, but the following examples illustrate the importance of some of the 1992/1993 accounting changes ($ in millions):

	Bethlehem Steel	IBM	PepsiCo
Income before accounting change	$(260.2)	$(6,865)	$1,302
After-tax effect of change	(290.1)	1,900	(928)
Net income	$(550.3)	$(4,965)	$ 374

Bethlehem Steel's loss on the accounting change almost doubled its loss, IBM's gain on the accounting change reduced its loss, while PepsiCo's loss on the accounting change dropped its income by some 75%.

INTERNATIONAL ISSUES

Internationally, financial statement analysis is significantly complicated by a variety of factors. Throughout the text, we have considered differences in accounting methods used. In addition, we should stress the obvious but easily forgotten differences in the language of reporting and the currency of measurement. For example, most U.S. analysts cannot read financial statements in Japanese and do not readily "have a feel for" the value of yen versus dollars. Last, but not least, is the fact that different structures for security markets, different tax laws, and different preferences among citizens of different countries all affect the relative value of financial assets.

VALUATION ISSUES

Accounting data are critically important to deciding on the value of a company. We have already examined a number of ratios that help in this effort. Exhibit 13-11 presents some of the fundamental price and valuation information that the Excite Web portal provides to investors at **http://quicken.excite.com.** This material is a joint venture among Excite, Charles Schwab (an online broker), and Quicken (a financial analysis software provider). It is illustrative of information provided by many financial services.

The information is for four companies identified by ticker symbol. YUM is Tricon, the restaurant activity spun off by PepsiCo, MCD is McDonald's, WEN is Wendy's International, and OSI is Outback Steakhouses. All four companies are in the fast- or convenience-food industry and compete with each other. Reviewing this information gives us an opportunity to emphasize the importance of financial information to valuation and to explain a few common ratios and values that we have not given significant attention. The four stocks trade at similar prices per share and have all shown significant share price variation during the period from November 1999 to November 2000. YUM and MCD are trading at the lower end of their 52-week range and WEN and OSI at the higher end. The 60-month beta is a measure of how closely the stock of the company follows general market conditions. A value of one indicates the stock moves proportionally to the market. Only OSI moves more than the market. On a typical day, if the market moved up

Exhibit 13-11

Fundamentals of Fast- or Convenience-Food Industry

Tricon (YUM), McDonald's (MCD), Wendy's (WEN), and Outback (OSI)

Source: Excite Money & Investing by Quicken.com

PRICE AND VALUATION

Ticker Symbol	Current Price	52-Week Range	60-Month Beta	EPS	Price-Earnings
YUM	30	23.56–46.25	.66	$3.92	10.6
MCD	32.38	26.37–49.56	.84	$1.39	21.6
WEN	22.44	14.00–24.56	.62	$1.32	16.2
OSI	28.19	20.75–34.43	1.18	$1.57	15.6

	PEG Ratio	Price/Sales	Price/Book	12-Month Return	5-yr Return
YUM	.6	.75	N/S*	−25.2%	N/C*
MCD	1.7	4.11	4.69	−30.1%	46.2%
WEN	.9	1.19	2.48	−36.0%	16.8%
OSI	.8	1.22	2.77	6.5%	14.5%

GROWTH TRENDS

	Latest Annual Income (mil)	1-yr Income Growth	5-yr Income Growth	Latest Annual Revenue (mil)	1-yr Revenue Growth	5-yr Revenue Growth
YUM	$627.0	−32.1%	N/C*	$7,822.0	−10.1%	N/C*
MCD	$1,947.9	11.2%	6.6%	$13,259.3	7.0%	7.4%
WEN	$166.6	26.8%	7.1%	$2,072.2	9.6%	6.2%
OSI	$124.3	24.5%	21.5%	$1,646.0	24.8%	22.9%

	Latest Annual EPS	1-yr EPS Growth	5-yr EPS Growth	Annual Dividend/Share	Dividend Yield	5-yr Dividend Growth Rate
YUM	$3.92	−27.9%	N/C*	$0.00	0.0%	N/C*
MCD	$1.39	13.8%	8.0%	$0.86	2.7%	−6.6%
WEN	$1.32	31.8%	6.0%	$0.24	1.0%	−1.2%
OSI	$1.57	18.5%	18.1%	$0.00	0.0%	N/C*

FINANCIAL STRENGTH

	Total Debt/Equity	Current Total Debt (mil)	Current Ratio	Quick Ratio	Current Inventory Turnover	Current Receivable Turnover
YUM	N/S*	$2,502.0	.5	.4	35.7	25.8
MCD	.75	$7,967.8	.5	.3	69.8	20.2
WEN	.24	$ 252.8	1.2	1.0	43.8	25.6
OSI	.00	$ 1.7	1.4	1.2	132.5	154.1

MANAGEMENT EFFECTIVENESS

	Return on Assets	5-yr Avg. Return on Assets	Return on Equity	5-yr Avg. Return on Equity	Revenue/ Employee (000's)	Income/ Employee (000's)
YUM	15.8%	7.8%	N/S*	.0%	$ 34	$ 2
MCD	9.3%	8.9%	20.2%	18.6%	$ 45	$ 6
WEN	8.8%	7.7%	15.6%	13.3%	$313	$25
OSI	14.6%	13.9%	17.9%	18.4%	$ 47	$ 4

(*continued*)

Exhibit 13-11 (continued)

Fundamentals of Fast- or Convenience-Food Industry

Tricon (YUM), McDonald's (MCD), Wendy's (WEN), and Outback (OSI)
(Source: Excite Money & Investing by Quicken.com)

		SHARE INFORMATION			
Ticker Symbol	Market Cap (mil)	Shares Outstanding (000's)	Number of Institutional Shareholders	Shares Held by Institutions (000's)	% Held by Institutions
YUM	$ 4,388.04	146,268	680	101,831	69.8
MCD	$42,757.76	1,320,703	1,739	791,265	59.9
WEN	$ 2,546.41	113,489	534	65,822	57.9
OSI	$ 2,195.64	77,894	415	54,924	70.5

Data as of 11/02/2000.

*N/C - Not calculable; *N/S - Negative stockholders' equity.

10%, OSI would be expected to move up slightly more (11.8%). Although their prices are reasonably similar, their EPS numbers range from $1.32 to $3.92 and therefore their P-E ratios vary significantly, with YUM at the low end and McDonald's over twice as high. The next three items relate price to the growth rate (PEG), to sales, and to book value. Note that McDonald's price is the highest relative to all three of these measures. YUM shows N/S for price/book, which indicates that YUM has negative shareholders' equity. This affects many of the ratios calculated for YUM.

This industry has not been in favor with investors during 2000, with only OSI generating positive returns for investors, 6.5% versus losses exceeding 25% for all three of the others. The next four sets of data provide growth rates for 1 and 5 years for income, revenue, EPS, and dividends. Outback is growing the most quickly on the first three measures but not for dividends. Outback pays no dividends.

Outback is also at or near the top on most of the ratios and turnover measures. This suggests high liquidity (current and quick ratios) and efficient resource utilization (turnovers and returns on assets and equity). The data include revenue generated per employee, and here Wendy's stands out, generating levels some 10 times higher than its competitors.

In the final several categories it becomes clear that McDonald's is much larger than the other three companies. McDonald's market capitalization, the total market price of its outstanding shares, is 10 times larger than the other companies. It has three times as many institutional shareholders. These institutional shareholders are sophisticated investors such as pension funds and insurance companies. However, although OSI has the fewest institutional shareholders, it actually has the largest percentage of its shares owned by this group.

So what might an analyst conclude? There are always more questions. What is the company planning? How many new stores are under construction? Is growth in sales occurring in existing stores or only in new ones? How are competitors changing the industry dynamics? Have burgers become old hat? Analysts would pursue some of these issues before reaching a conclusion, but at first blush, Outback Steakhouse looks very promising. It has outperformed the others recently and therefore has momentum in its favor. Moreover, its pricing is well below that of McDonald's measured on P-E, price-sales, and price-book. Because its growth rates are so high, we would expect it to also be high priced (in relative terms) and it is not. If the investigation of its plans for expansion was encouraging and sales in existing stores were doing well, it appears to be the pick from these four firms for investment today.

The P-E ratio is a useful tool for relating the price of a company's stock to the earnings it is generating. Some would argue that low P-E stocks might be undervalued and high P-E stocks might be overvalued. This is the view of people who are called "value investors." These investors seek securities that the market is currently undervaluing. They would not blindly buy low P-E stocks but would use low P-E as a screen to identify securities that are likely candidates for purchase. They would then consider many other factors in determining the best investments.

The opposite view is that the best investments are growth stocks. "Growth investors" believe that high P-E stocks are likely to be high growth stocks. The price is "high" because investors see strong growth prospects ahead. Again the growth investor would use high P-Es to identify a group of stocks to evaluate more carefully.

Who is right? How do we relate P-E ratios to growth? When are we paying too much for future growth? As of June, 2000 the average P-E on stocks in the S&P was about 24. While this was high relative to long-term norms of around 14 or 15, it was down from recent levels. Share prices fell slightly in early 2000 while earnings continued to increase so both the numerator and denominator of this ratio changed in directions that lower the ratio.

One way to relate P-E ratios directly to earnings growth rates is called the price-earnings growth (PEG) ratio. It is calculated as the P-E ratio divided by the earnings growth rate. The P-E ratio could be calculated on historical earnings, current earnings, or forecasted earnings. Similarly, the earnings growth rate could be historical, current, or forecasted. Many analysts would prefer a current P-E ratio and a forecasted 5-year earnings growth rate.

Consider Corning, Inc., the manufacturer of fiber-optic cable and photonic materials to serve the Internet and other communications channels. In July of 2000, Corning was trading at about $90 per share on a split-adjusted basis up from a 52-week low of $20. The P-E ratio for Corning was a hefty 147. This looks very high relative to an S&P norm of 24. However, Corning's earnings grew about 50% in the last year. Thus, the PEG ratio was 3. Similarly, Cisco has a robust P-E ratio at 183 but its growth rate is also about 50% for a PEG ratio of 3.7. During the last part of 2000 these companies fell sharply in price as the tech industry fell generally. By February 2001 Corning was at $33, with a PEG of .9 and Cisco's P-E was 62 with a PEG of 1.4.

What are norms for the PEG ratio? *Business Week* (June 26, 2000) cited the average S&P PEG ratio as 1.5 at that time and indicated it had peaked in January of 1999 at 2.0. In June, 2000, *Business Week* cited a couple of attractive investments based on PEG ratios including Citigroup (1.31), FedEx (1.21), Target Group (1.21), and Texaco (1.37). Of course, different investment advisers set different ranges. The Motley Fool Website **(www.fool.com)** provides a definition of the PEG ratio and its own investment advice on using the ratio:

.50 or less	Buy
.50 to .65	Look to buy
.65 to 1.00	Hold
1.00 to 1.30	Look to sell
1.30 to 1.70	Consider shorting
Over 1.70	Short

Notice that two of the securities that *Business Week* recommends buying, based on their PEG ratios, fall in the "consider shorting" category for the Motley Fools. Thus, the PEG ratio helps inform our analysis, and it moderates knee jerk reactions to P-E ratios, but it is just a tool to help focus our attention.

RELATING CASH FLOW AND NET INCOME

For the healthiest of firms both net income and cash flow from operations are positive, but there are four logical possible combinations of positive and negative net income and cash flow from operations and it is useful to think about what they might mean.

Relationship	1	2	3	4
Cash flow from operations	+	+	−	−
Net income	+	−	+	−

In relationship one, the two positive values confirm the profitability of the company. In the fourth case, the uniform negative values are again in agreement. When either of these patterns appear, and continue, for multiple periods, the implications are straightforward.

What about case two? This is common in some industries. Consider high capital investment industries with large depreciation charges or rapidly growing companies in capital-intensive industries. If a declining-balance depreciation method is used, large depreciation charges may create losses even though operating cash flow is positive. One might examine several years to assess the pattern. Another example is real estate, where the economic returns to the company include both current operating performance and appreciation of the underlying property. The accounting model does not record appreciation in real estate, so it does not appear in the income statement. Thus, you could have negative net income even though cash flow was sufficient to cover all expenses and the investment was appreciating consistently.

Case three is often a red flag for trouble, but may also represent the case of a rapidly growing firm. The difference between cash flow and net income is depreciation and accruals of current assets and liabilities. A very rapidly growing firm may be investing heavily in inventory for new stores and granting credit to new customers with the result that current assets are growing very quickly. Thus, all the sales are not collected now and additional cash is being invested in inventory. This may be a very good situation. However, this pattern is also observed in cases where the top-line sales figure is not growing quickly, but inventory and accounts receivable are. This is very bad. It tends to indicate bad management, slow-moving merchandise, and failure to manage credit. This pattern often precedes bankruptcy. The FASB requires a statement of cash flows for a reason. Net income does not tell the whole story.

SUMMARY PROBLEM FOR YOUR REVIEW

PROBLEM

Exhibit 13-12 contains a condensed income statement and balance sheet for Nautica Enterprises, Inc. The company that began 15 years ago with a six-item outerwear collection of clothing, has expanded to include a wide assortment of fashion-oriented men's apparel, and now has three distinct brands and a significant international presence.

1. Compute the following ratios: (a) current ratio, (b) quick ratio, (c) average collection period, (d) inventory turnover, (e) total debt to total assets, (f) return on sales, and (g) return on stockholders' equity.

2. Compare your computed values to the values that follow for Nike.

Exhibit 13-12

Nautica Enterprises, Inc. and Subsidiaries
Consolidated Statement of Earnings

(amounts in thousands, except share data)	Year Ended March 4, 2000	Year Ended February 27, 1999	Year Ended February 28, 1998
Net sales	$ 621,286	$ 552,650	$ 484,832
Cost of goods sold	323,195	287,021	252,698
Gross profit	298,091	265,629	232,134
Selling, general and administrative expenses	229,975	178,293	149,044
Net royalty income	(5,748)	(5,281)	(5,738)
Operating profit	73,864	92,617	88,828
Other income			
Investment income, net	2,067	4,016	3,781
Minority interest in loss of consolidated subsidiary	—	405	785
Earnings before provision for income taxes	75,931	97,038	93,394
Provision for income taxes	29,768	38,330	36,976
Net earnings	$ 46,163	$ 58,708	$ 56,418
Net earnings per share of common stock			
Basic	$ 1.33	$ 1.53	$ 1.44
Diluted	$ 1.26	$ 1.45	$ 1.35
Weighted-average number of common shares outstanding			
Basic	34,805,000	38,430,000	39,081,000
Diluted	36,597,000	40,529,000	41,729,000

(continued)

Nike 2000	
Current ratio	1.9
Quick ratio	1.0
Average collection period	60.0
Inventory turnover	4.0
Total debt to total assets	.32
Return on sales	.06
ROE	.19

SOLUTION

1. a.   Current ratio

= Current assets ÷ Current liabilities

= 256,456 ÷ 88,225 = 2.91

b.   Quick ratio

= (Cash + Short-term Investments
  + Receivables) ÷ Current liabilities

= 168,743 ÷ 88,225 = 1.91

c.   Average collection period = (Average accounts receivable × 365) ÷ Sales

= [((107,609 + 102,471) ÷ 2) × 365] ÷ 621,286

= 61.7

d.   Inventory turnover

= Cost of goods sold ÷ Average inventory

= 323,195 ÷ [(73,879 + 70,212) ÷ 2]

= 4.49

Exhibit 13-12 (continued)

Nautica Enterprises, Inc. and Subsidiaries
Consolidated Balance Sheets

(amounts in thousands, except share data)	March 4, 2000	February 27, 1999
Assets		
Current Assets		
Cash and cash equivalents	$ 27,143	$ 15,498
Short-term investments	33,991	55,049
Accounts receivable—net of allowances of $9,046 in 2000 and $5,640 in 1999	107,609	102,471
Inventories	73,879	70,212
Prepaid expenses and other current assets	5,453	5,434
Deferred tax benefit	8,381	7,369
Total current assets	256,456	256,033
Property, plant and equipment—at cost,		
less accumulated depreciation and amortization	81,674	64,524
Other Assets	13,808	11,777
	$351,938	$332,334
Liabilities and stockholder's equity		
Current liabilities		
Current maturities of long-term debt	$ —	$ 50
Accounts payable—trade	29,048	29,596
Accrued expenses and other current liabilities	49,384	40,298
Income taxes payable	9,793	6,523
Total current liabilities	88,225	76,467
Long-term debt—net	—	50
Commitments and contingencies		
Stockholders' Equity		
Preferred stock—par value $.01; authorized, 2,000,000 shares; no shares issued	—	—
Common stock—par value $.10; authorized, 100,000,000 shares; issued, 42,696,000 shares in 2000 and 42,604,000 shares in 1999	4,270	4,260
Additional paid-in capital	67,559	66,813
Retained earnings	322,045	275,882
Accumulated other comprehensive income (loss)	—	(35)
Common stock in treasury at cost; 8,964,000 shares in 2000 and 5,596,000 shares in 1999	(130,161)	(91,103)
	263,713	255,817
	$351,938	$332,334

e. Total debt to total assets = Total liabilities ÷ Total assets

= (Total assets − Stockholders' equity) ÷ Total assets

= (351,938 − 263,713) ÷ 351,938

= .25

f. Return on sales = Net income ÷ Sales

= 46,163 ÷ 621,286

= .07 or 7%

g. ROE $\quad\quad\quad = $ Net income ÷ Average stockholder's equity

$\quad\quad\quad\quad\quad\quad\quad\quad = 46{,}163 \div [(263{,}713 + 255{,}817) \div 2]$

$\quad\quad\quad\quad\quad\quad\quad\quad = .18 \text{ or } 18\%$

2. Nautica has higher current and quick ratios for higher short-term liquidity. This could also suggest that current assets are excessive. Accounts receivable levels are less favorable for Nautica compared with Nike, given the slightly longer collection period. On the other hand, Nautica has better inventory turnover than that of Nike. Nautica has more debt than Nike and a lower return on sales. The differences are generally small and their overall performance measured by ROE is similar.

Highlights to Remember

1. **Locate and use the many sources of information about company performance.** Financial and operating information is available from many sources, including daily newspapers. Various regulations in the United States require the issuance of annual reports and govern their content. In addition, publicly traded companies must disclose particular information by filing 10-K, 8-K, and other forms with the SEC on a periodic basis. Financial information is provided to aid investors in assessing the risk and return of a potential investment. Creditors are particularly concerned about the solvency and liquidity of the issuer, while equity investors are more interested in profitability.

2. **Analyze the components of a company using trend analysis and other techniques.** Trend analysis is a form of financial statement analysis that concentrates on changes in the financial statements through time. It involves comparing relationships for a period of years or quarters. We can construct common-size financial statements by expressing the elements of the balance sheet as a percentage of total assets and the elements of the income statement as a percentage of total revenue. They enchance the ability to compare one company with another or to conduct a trend analysis over time.

3. **Use the basic financial ratios to guide your thinking.** The basic financial ratios allow us to put numbers in perspective. By relating one part of the financial statements to another, they facilitate questions such as "Given the change in revenues, was the change in accounts receivable reasonable?" and "Is the company's inventory level, given its size, comparable to industry norms?" The chapter reviews the ratios presented throughout the text. Liquidity ratios deal with the immediate ability to make payments. Solvency ratios deal with the longer term ability to meet obligations. Creditors often incorporate such ratios into debt covenants to protect lenders' rights. Investors use profitability ratios to assess operating efficiency and performance. At the end of the chapter, we revisit these questions using actual performance information reported on the Excite Web portal and introduce additional performance measures including price-sales, price-book and multiple growth measures. When one company stands out on measures including ROA and ROE and is growing quite rapidly, but is not the highest priced based on P-E, price-sales, and price-book, this suggests a possible investment opportunity.

4. **Evaluate corporate performance using ROA, ROE, and EVA.** Return on equity (ROE) is the most fundamental profitability ratio for equity investors because it relates income to the shareholder's investment. ROE is one of several related elements that focuses on the profitable use of all assets. It can be further divided into the return on sales and the total asset turnover. EVA refers to economic value added. It compares an adjusted earnings number with the minimum amount that should have been earned given the total capital in use. If the adjusted earnings exceeds the required return, calculated as the weighted-average cost of capital times the capital in use, then the company has added economic value during the period.

5. **Calculate EPS under complex circumstances.** Earnings per share (EPS) is a fundamental measure of performance. This chapter introduces some complexities in calculating EPS. Because preferred shares receive preference as to dividends, their dividends are deducted from earnings in the numerator. Because shares outstanding may change during the year, the denominator is calculated as a weighted average over the year. The presence of options and convertible securities creates a potential to issue new shares that dilute current shareholders' interests. Therefore, companies report both basic and diluted EPS when significant options and conversion features exist.

6. **Adjust for nonrecurring items.** Special items, extraordinary items, discontinued operations, and accounting changes are categories of unusual and possibly nonrecurring items. Separately disclosing these allows analysts to refine forecasts of future performance based on current operations. Income statements include special items with other expenses on a before-tax basis, but identify them separately. In contrast, income statements show extraordinary items, discontinued items, and accounting changes separately, below earnings from operations and net of their individual tax effects.

Accounting Vocabulary

asset turnover, p. 573
benchmarks, p. 569
capital structure, p. 575
capitalization, p. 575
common-size statement, p. 561
component percentages, p. 562
cross-sectional comparisons, p. 569
discontinued operations, p. 583
EBIT, p. 573

extraordinary items, p. 582
financial leverage, p. 575
financial statement analysis, p. 554
gearing, p. 575
leveraging, p. 575
long-term solvency, p. 557
management's discussion and analysis (MD&A), p. 563
operating income percentage on sales, p. 573

pretax operating rate of return on total assets, p. 573
pro forma statement, p. 557
return on total assets (ROA), p. 573
short-term liquidity, p. 557
special items, p. 580
time-series comparisons, p. 569
times interest earned, p. 578
total asset turnover, p. 573
trading on the equity, p. 575

Assignment Material

QUESTIONS

13-1 Why do decision makers use financial statement analysis?

13-2 In addition to the basic financial statements, what information is usually presented in a company's annual report?

13-3 Give three sources of information for investors besides accounting information.

13-4 "Financial statements report on *history*. Therefore they are not useful to creditors and investors who want to predict *future* returns and risk." Do you agree? Explain?

13-5 How do information demands of creditors differ from those of equity investors?

13-6 "It's always a bad sign when revenues increase at a faster percentage rate than does net income." Do you agree? Explain.

13-7 Suppose you wanted to evaluate the financial performance of IBM over the last 10 years. What factors might affect the comparability of a firm's financial ratios over such a long period of time?

13-8 How do common-size statements aid comparisons with other companies?

13-9 What information is presented in the "management's discussion and analysis" (MD&A) section of annual reports?

13-10 Ratios are often grouped into four categories. What are the categories?

13-11 Suppose you compared the financial statements of an airline and a grocery store. Which would you expect to have the higher values for the following ratios: debt-to-equity ratio, current ratio, inventory turnover ratio, average collection period, and return on equity? Explain.

13-12 Name three types of comparisons that are useful in evaluating financial ratios.

13-13 Suppose you worked for a small manufacturing company and the president said that you must improve your current ratio. Would you interpret this to mean that you should increase it or decrease it? How might you do so?

13-14 Suppose the current ratio for your company changed from 2-to-1 to become 1.8-to-1. Would you expect the level of working capital to increase or to decrease? Why?

13-15 Suppose you work for a small local department store that manages its own accounts receivable with a private charge card. Your boss has told you to improve the average collection period from 30 to 20 days. How would you go about this? What are the risks in your proposal that might affect the company negatively?

13-16 Distinguish between operating management and financial management.

13-17 What two measures of operating performance are combined to give the pretax operating return on total assets?

13-18 "Trading on the equity means exchanging bonds for stock." Do you agree? Explain.

13-19 "Borrowing is a two-edged sword." Do you agree? Explain.

13-20 Why are companies with heavy debt in relation to ownership capital in greater danger when business conditions sour?

13-21 "The tax law discriminates against preferred stock and in favor of debt." Explain.

13-22 "Any company that has income before interest and taxes greater than its interest expense is a relatively safe investment for creditors." Do you agree? Explain.

13-23 What causes the "dilution" in diluted EPS?

13-24 How does the accounting for special items differ from the accounting for extraordinary items?

13-25 "Separate reporting of the results of discontinued operations aids predicting future net income." Do you agree? Explain.

13-26 Suppose you wanted to compare the financial statements of Colgate-Palmolive and Procter & Gamble. What concerns might you have in comparing their various ratios?

COGNITIVE EXERCISES

13-27 EVA
Your CEO has heard a lot about EVA as a management tool. This officer understands that the basic concept is to calculate an estimate of true economic profit by subtracting an appropriate charge for the firms cost of capital from its operating profit. However, the CEO wonders why focusing on EVA is any better than focusing on ROE. Can you help explain the concept?

13-28 Assessing Value
Your accounting teacher has been talking about how important accounting numbers are in valuing a firm, and yet many of the people you know who invest are always talking about growth as the important measure. Who is right?

13-29 Investment Advice on the Internet
Your friend Barry just called to say that you should consider investing in ABC Company because the high-flying chat room on the Internet had 20 buy recommendations posted and not a single sell recommendation. Barry says that the chat room has examples of investments recommended there that have doubled in value in just a few months. What do you think?

13-30 Which P-E
Your investment advisor called to suggest buying ABC Company and noted that its P-E was only 20 and the rest of the companies in its industry had P-Es of around 28. You looked in the *Wall Street Journal* and found they reported a P-E of 32 for ABC Company and an average P-E of around 30. How can you make sense of this?

EXERCISES

13-31 Common-Size Statements
Following is a condensed income statement for Microsoft for the year ended June 30, 2000.

	Microsoft (in Millions)
Total revenues	$22,956
Total cost of revenues	3,002
Gross profit	19,954
Total operating expenses	9,017
Operating income	10,937
Other income, net	3,338
Income before income taxes	14,275
Provision for income taxes	4,854
Net income	$ 9,421

Required

1. Prepare common-size income statements for Microsoft.
2. Using data in the appendix and using the same summarized income statement items as for Microsoft, prepare a common-size income statement for Cisco for 2000.
3. Compare the two companies by using the common-size statements.

13-32 Computation of Ratios

MCI Worldcom, the long-distance telephone company, included the income statement and balance sheets in Exhibit 13-13 in its 1999 annual report. Additional information includes average common shares outstanding of 2,815 million in 1999 and market price per share of $50 at December 31, 1999 and $20 in October 2000. Calculate ratios that include price on both dates. No dividends were paid on common stock.

Required

Compute the following ratios:

1.	Current ratio		7.	Return on stockholders' equity
2.	Quick ratio		8.	Gross profit rate
3.	Average collection period		9.	Return on sales
4.	Total debt to total assets		10.	Asset turnover
5.	Total debt to equity		11.	Pretax return on operating assets
6.	Interest coverage		12.	Earnings per share

Exhibit 13-13
MCI Worldcom, Inc. and Subsidiaries

CONSOLIDATED STATEMENTS OF OPERATIONS

	For the Years Ended December 31,	
(In Millions, Except per Share Data)	*1999*	*1998*
Revenues	$37,120	$18,169
Operating expenses		
Line costs	15,951	8,534
Selling, general and administrative	8,935	4,563
Depreciation and amortization	4,354	2,289
In-process research and development and other charges	(8)	3,725
Total	29,232	19,111
Operating income (loss)	7,888	(942)
Other income (expense)		
Interest expense	(966)	(692)
Miscellaneous	242	44
Income (loss) before income taxes, minority interests, cumulative effect of accounting change and extraordinary items	7,164	(1,590)
Provision for income taxes	2,965	877
Income (loss) before minority interests, cumulative effect of accounting change and extraordinary items	4,199	(2,467)
Minority interests	(186)	(93)
Income (loss) before cumulative effect of accounting change and extraordinary items	4,013	(2,560)
Cumulative effect of accounting change (net of income taxes of $22 in 1998)	—	(36)
Extraordinary items (net of income taxes of $78 in 1998)	—	(129)
Net income (loss)	4,013	(2,725)
Distributions on subsidiary trust mandatorily redeemable preferred securities	63	18
Preferred dividend requirement	9	24
Net income (loss) applicable to common shareholders	$ 3,941	$(2,767)

(continued)

Exhibit 13-13 (Continued)

MCI Worldcom, Inc. and Subsidiaries

CONSOLIDATED BALANCE SHEETS

	December 31	
(In Millions, Except Share Data)	*1999*	*1998*
Assets		
Current assets		
Cash and cash equivalents	$ 876	$ 1,727
Marketable securities	6	—
Accounts receivable, net of allowance for bad debts		
of $1,122 in 1999 and $920 in 1998	5,746	5,309
Deferred tax asset	2,565	2,546
Other current assets	1,131	1,187
Total current assets	10,324	10,769
Property and equipment		
Transmission equipment	14,689	12,271
Communications equipment	6,218	5,400
Furniture, fixtures and other	7,424	6,092
Construction in progress	5,397	3,080
	33,728	26,843
Accumulated depreciation	(5,110)	(2,275)
	28,618	24,568
Goodwill and other intangible assets	47,308	47,285
Other assets	4,822	4,470
	$91,072	$87,092
Liabilities and shareholders investment		
Current liabilities		
Short-term debt and current maturities of long-term debt	$ 5,015	$ 4,757
Accounts payable	2,557	1,771
Accrued line costs	3,721	3,903
Other current liabilities	5,916	5,749
Total current liabilities	17,209	16,180
Long-term liabilities, less current portion		
Long-term debt	13,128	16,448
Deferred tax liability	4,877	2,870
Other liabilities	1,223	1,855
Total long-term liabilities	19,228	21,173
Commitments and contingencies	—	—
Minority interests	2,599	3,700
Company obligated mandatorily redeemable		
preferred securities of subsidiary trust holding		
solely junior subordinated deferrable interest		
debentures of the company and other redeemable		
preferred securities	798	798
Shareholders' investment		
Common stock, par value $.01 per share; authorized:		
5,000,000,000 shares; issued and outstanding:		
2,849,743,843 shares in 1999 and 2,776,758,726		
shares in 1998	28	28
Additional paid-in capital	52,108	50,173
Retained earnings (deficit)	(928)	(4,869)
Unrealized holding gain on marketable equity securities	575	122
Cumulative foreign currency translation adjustment	(360)	(28)
Treasury stock, at cost, 6,765,316 shares in 1999 and 1998	(185)	(185)
Total shareholders' investment	51,238	45,241
	$91,072	$87,092

13-33 Common Stock Ratios and Book Value

The Somar Corporation has outstanding 400,000 shares of 8% preferred stock with a $100 par value and 10 million shares of common stock of $1 par value. The current market price of the common is $24, and the latest annual dividend rate is $2 per share. Common treasury stock consists of 500,000 shares costing $7 million. The company has $150 million of additional paid-in capital, $15 million of retained income, and $12 million of investments in affiliated companies. Net income for the current year is $20 million.

Required

Compute the following:

1. Total stockholders' equity
2. Common price-earnings ratio
3. Common dividend-yield percentage
4. Common dividend-payout percentage
5. Book value per share of common

13-34 Rate-of-Return Computations

1. Sapporo Company reported a 4% operating margin on sales, an 8% pretax operating return on total assets, and 2 billion yen of total assets. Compute (a) operating income, (b) total sales, and (c) total asset turnover.

2. Glasgow Corporation reported £900 million of sales, £48 million of operating income, and a total asset turnover of four times. Compute (a) total assets, (b) operating margin percentage on sales, and (c) pretax operating return on total assets.

3. Compare the two companies.

13-35 Return on Assets

The Home Depot, Inc. is the leading retailer in the home improvement industry and ranks among the largest retailers in the United States. Some data from the company's financial statements for the years ended January 30, 2000 and January 31, 1999 follow ($ in millions):

	2000	1999
Sales	$38,434	$30,219
Operating income	3,795	2,661
Net income	2,320	1,614
Property, plant, and equipment, net	10,227	8,160
Total assets	17,081	13,465
Stockholders' equity	12,341	8,740

Required

1. Compute Home Depot's pretax operating return on total assets for the year ended January 30, 2000.

2. Compute the operating income percentage on sales and total asset turnover. Show how these two ratios determine the pretax operating return on total assets.

13-36 Trading on the Equity

Bayol Company has assets of $600 million, bonds payable of $300 million, and stockholders' equity of $300 million. The bonds bear interest at 10% per annum. Carmody Company, which is in the same industry, also has assets of $600 million and stockholders' equity of $600 million. Prepare a comparative tabulation of Carmody Company and Bayol Company for each of 3 years. Show income before interest, interest, net income, return on assets, and return on stockholders' equity.

The income before interest for both companies was: year one, $60 million; year two, $30 million; and year three, $90 million. Ignore income taxes. Show all monetary amounts in millions of dollars. Comment on the results.

13-37 Using Debt or Equity

The O'Hare Corporation is trying to decide whether to raise additional capital of $40 million through a new issue of 12% long-term debt or of 10% preferred stock. The income tax rate is 40%. Compute net income less preferred dividends for these alternatives. Assume that income before interest expense and taxes is $10 million. Show all dollar amounts in thousands. What is the after-tax cost of capital for debt and for preferred stock expressed in percentages? Comment on the comparison. Compute times interest earned for the first year.

13-38 Debt versus Preferred Stock

In 1996, Bell Atlantic Corporation provided telephone services to several middle-Atlantic states. Subsequently, it merged with NYNEX, a local New York phone company, and during 2000 it finalized additional mergers with Vidafone and GTE. It has done well for shareholders. A $100 investment in 1984 would be valued at $1,588 in December of 1999. In 1999, the company had operating income before taxes and interest of $8,495 million. Long-term debt was $18,463 million. The company has no preferred stock outstanding, although 10 million shares are authorized.

Suppose $8,000 million of preferred stock with a dividend rate of 11% had been issued instead of $8,000 million of the long-term debt. The debt had an effective interest rate of 7%. Assume that the income tax rate is 40%.

Required

Compute net income and net income attributable to common shareholders under (a) the current situation with $18,463 million of long-term debt and no preferred stock, and (b) the assumed situation with $8,000 million of preferred stock and $10,463 million of long-term debt.

13-39 Earnings per Share

Ford Motor Company had net income of $7,237 million and paid preferred dividends of $15 million in 1999. An average of 1,210 million common shares were outstanding during the year.

Required

1. Compute Ford's earnings per share of common stock in 1999.
2. Suppose all preferred stock was convertible into 35 million shares of common stock. Compute diluted earnings per share.

13-40 EPS and Times Interest Earned Computations

Baltimore Shipping Company has outstanding 500,000 shares of common stock, $4 million of 8% preferred stock, and $8 million of 10% bonds payable. Its income tax rate is 40%.

1. Assume the company has $6 million of income before interest and taxes. Compute (a) EPS and (b) number of times bond interest has been earned.
2. Assume $3 million of income before interest and taxes, and make the same computations.

13-41 Discontinued Operations

Nokia, a Finnish company based in Helsinki, is a leading international telecommunications company that employs 31,700 people in 45 countries. The company's income statement ended with the following three lines [Finnish marks (FIM) in millions]:

Profit from continuing operations	FIM 3,044
Discontinued operations	219
Net profit	FIM 3,263

Required

Suppose the operations in place at the end of the year continued into the next year with exactly the same results as before. What net profit would you expect Nokia to report in the next year? Explain.

13-42 Interpretation of Changes in Ratios

Consider each of the following as an independent case:

a. Increase in cash dividends.

b. Decrease in interest-coverage.

c. Increase in return on sales.

d. Increase in the price-earnings ratio.

e. Reduction in accounts receivable turnover.

f. Increase in current ratio.

Required

1. From the point of view of a manager of the company, indicate which of these items indicate good news and which indicate bad news. Explain your reasoning for each.

2. Would any of these items be viewed differently by an investor than by a manager? If so, which ones? Why?

13-43 Common-Size Statements
(Alternate is 13-50.) Price-Break and Low-Cost are both discount store chains. Condensed income statements and balance sheets for the two companies are shown in Exhibit 13-14. Amounts are in thousands.

Exhibit 13-14

Financial Statements for Price-Break and Low-Cost

INCOME STATEMENTS

($ in thousands)	Price-Break	Low-Cost
	Year Ended December 31, 20X9	
Sales	$905,600	$491,750
Cost of sales	602,360	301,910
Gross profit	303,240	189,840
Operating expenses	184,130	147,160
Operating income	119,110	42,680
Other revenue (expense)	(21,930)	6,270
Pretax income	97,180	48,950
Income tax expense	38,870	19,580
Net income	$ 58,310	$ 29,370

BALANCE SHEETS

($ in thousands)	Price-Break December 31 20X9	Price-Break December 31 20X8	Low-Cost December 31 20X9	Low-Cost December 31 20X8
Assets				
Current assets				
Cash	$ 9,100	$ 10,700	$ 8,200	$ 6,900
Marketable securities	8,300	8,300	4,100	3,800
Accounts receivable	36,700	37,100	21,300	20,500
Inventories	155,600	149,400	105,100	106,600
Prepaid expenses	17,100	16,900	8,800	8,400
Total current assets	226,800	222,400	147,500	146,200
Property and equipment, net	461,800	452,300	287,600	273,500
Other assets	14,700	13,900	28,600	27,100
Total assets	$703,300	$688,600	$463,700	$446,800
Liabilities and stockholders' equity				
Liabilities				
Current liabilities (summarized)	$ 91,600	$ 93,700	$ 61,300	$ 58,800
Long-term debt	156,700	156,700	21,000	21,000
Total liabilities	248,300	250,400	82,300	79,800
Stockholders' equity	455,000	438,200	381,400	367,000
Total liabilities and stockholders' equity	$703,300	$688,600	$463,700	$446,800

1. Prepare common-sized statements for Price-Break and Low-Cost for 20X9.
2. Compare the financial performance for 20X9 and financial position at the end of 20X9 for Price-Break with the performance and position of Low-Cost. Use only the statements prepared in requirement 1.
3. Calculate and compare ROE for the two firms.

13-44 Financial Ratios

(Alternate is 13-46.) This problem uses the same data as 13-43, but it can be solved independently. Price-Break and Low-Cost are both discount store chains. Condensed income statements and balance sheets for the two companies are shown in Exhibit 13-14. Amounts are in thousands.

Additional information:

- Cash dividends per share: Price-Break, $2.00; Low-Cost, $1.50.
- Market price per share: Price-Break, $30; Low-Cost, $40.
- Average shares outstanding for 20X9: Price-Break, 15 million; Low-Cost, 7 million.

1. Compute the following ratios for both companies for 20X9: (a) current, (b) quick, (c) average collection period, (d) inventory turnover, (e) total debt to total assets, (f) total debt to total equity, (g) return on stockholders' equity, (h) gross profit rate, (i) return on sales, (j) asset turnover, (k) pretax return on assets, (l) earnings per share, (m) price-earnings, (n) dividend yield, and (o) dividend payout.
2. Compare the liquidity, solvency, profitability, and market price and dividend ratios of Price-Break with those of Low-Cost.

13-45 Trend Analysis

Merck & Company, the pharmaceutical company, has frequently been ranked among America's most admired companies by *Fortune* magazine. The 1998 and 1999 income statements and balance sheets are in Exhibit 13-15 on page 600. A few categories are slightly condensed.

1. Prepare an income statement and balance sheet for Merck & Company that has two columns, one showing the amount of change between 1998 and 1999 and the other showing the percentage of change.
2. Identify and discuss the most significant changes between 1998 and 1999.

13-46 Financial Ratios

(Alternate is 13-44.) Merck & Company is the largest company in the health-care industry in the United States. Two recent income statements and balance sheets are in Exhibit 13-15. Additional 1999 data are:

- Cash dividends, $1.10 per share
- Market price per share, $90
- Average common shares outstanding, $2,347,800,000

Compute the following ratios for Merck & Company for 1999: (a) current, (b) quick, (c) average collection period, (d) total debt to total assets, (e) total debt to total equity, (f) return on stockholders' equity, (g) return on sales, (h) asset turnover, (i) pretax return on assets, (j) earnings per share, (k) price-earnings, (l) dividend yield, and (m) dividend payout. Total debt includes current liabilities, long-term debt, and deferred income taxes and noncurrent liabilities.

13-47 Trend Analysis and Common-Size Statements

Ryan Company furnished the condensed data shown in Exhibit 13-16 on page 602.

1. Prepare a trend analysis for Ryan's income statement and balance sheet that compares 20X3 with 20X2.
2. Prepare common-size income statements for 20X3 and 20X2 and balance sheets for December 31, 20X3 and December 31, 20X2 for Ryan Company.
3. Comment on Ryan Company's performance and position for 20X3 compared with 20X2.

Exhibit 13-15

Merck & Company Inc. and Subsidiaries
(Years Ended December 31, $ in Millions Except per Share Amounts)

CONSOLIDATED STATEMENT OF INCOME		
	1999	**1998**
Sales	$32,714.0	$26,898.2
Costs, expenses and other		
Materials and production	17,534.2	13,925.4
Marketing and administrative	5,199.9	4,511.4
Research and development	2,068.3	1,821.1
Acquired research	51.1	1,039.5
Equity income from affiliates	(762.0)	(884.3)
Gains on sales of businesses	—	(2,147.7)
Other (income) expense, net	3.0	499.7
	24,094.5	18,765.1
Income before taxes	8,619.5	8,133.1
Taxes on income	2,729.0	2,884.9
Net income	$ 5,890.5	$ 5,248.2
Basic earnings per common share	$ 2.51	$ 2.21
Earnings per common share assuming dilution	$ 2.45	$ 2.15

CONSOLIDATED STATEMENT OF RETAINED EARNINGS		
Balance, January 1	$20,186.7	$17,291.5
Net income	5,890.5	5,248.2
Common stock dividends declared	(2,629.3)	(2,353.0)
Balance, December 31	$23,447.9	$20,186.7

CONSOLIDATED STATEMENT OF COMPREHENSIVE INCOME		
Net income	$ 5,890.5	$ 5,248.2
Other comprehensive income (loss)		
Net unrealized gain (loss) on investments, net of tax and net income realization	25.6	(5.6)
Minimum pension liability, net of tax	3.8	(24.7)
	29.4	(30.3)
Comprehensive income	$ 5,919.9	$ 5,217.9

(continued)

13-48 Financial Ratios
Consider the data for Ryan Company in Exhibit 13-16.

Required

1. Compute the following ratios for each of the last 2 years, 20X2 and 20X3:
   a. Percentage of net income to stockholders' equity.
   b. Gross profit rate.
   c. Percent of net income to sales.
   d. Ratio of total debt to stockholders' equity.
   e. Inventory turnover.
   f. Current ratio.
   g. Average collection period for accounts receivable.

2. For each of the following items, indicate whether the change from 20X2 to 20X3 for Ryan Company seems to be favorable or unfavorable, and identify the ratios you computed previously that most directly support your answer. The first two items that follow are given as an example.
   a. Return to owners, favorable, a.
   b. Gross profit rate, unchanged, b.

Exhibit 13-15 (continued)

Merck & Company Inc. and Subsidiaries
(Years Ended December 31, $ in Millions Except per Share Amounts)

CONSOLIDATED BALANCE SHEET

	1999	1998
Assets		
Current assets		
Cash and cash equivalents	$ 2,021.9	$ 2,606.2
Short-term investments	1,180.5	749.5
Accounts receivable	4,089.0	3,374.1
Inventories	2,846.9	2,623.9
Prepaid expenses and taxes	1,120.9	874.8
Total current assets	11,259.2	10,228.5
Investments	4,761.5	3,607.7
Property, plant, and equipment (at cost)		
Land	259.2	228.8
Buildings	4,465.8	3,664.0
Machinery, equipment, and office furnishings	7,385.7	6,211.7
Construction in progress	2,236.3	1,782.1
	14,347.0	11,886.6
Less allowance for depreciation	4,670.3	4,042.8
	9,676.7	7,843.8
Goodwill and other intangibles (net of accumulated amortization of $1,488.7 million in 1999 and $1,123.9 million in 1998)	7,584.2	8,287.2
Other assets	2,353.3	1,886.2
	$35,634.9	$31,853.4
Liabilities and Stockholders' Equity		
Current liabilities		
Accounts payable and accrued liabilities	$ 4,158.7	$ 3,682.1
Loans payable and current portion of long-term debt	2,859.0	624.2
Income taxes payable	1,064.1	1,125.1
Dividends payable	677.0	637.4
Total current liabilities	8,758.8	6,068.8
Long-term debt	3,143.9	3,220.8
Deferred income taxes and noncurrent liabilities	7,030.1	6,057.0
Minority interests	3,460.5	3,705.0
Stockholders' equity		
Common stock, one cent par value		
Authorized—5,400,000,000 shares		
Issued—2,968,030,509 shares	29.7	29.7
Other paid-in capital	5,920.5	5,614.5
Retained earnings	23,447.9	20,186.7
Accumulated other comprehensive income (loss)	8.1	(21.3)
	29,406.2	25,809.6
Less treasury stock, at cost		
638,953,059 shares—1999		
607,399,428 shares—1998	16,164.6	13,007.8
Total stockholders' equity	13,241.6	12,801.8
	$35,634.9	$31,853.4

Exhibit 13-16

Ryan Company

Balance Sheets and Income Statements (in Thousands)

	December 31		
	20X3	*20X2*	*20X1*
Cash	$ 30	$ 25	$ 20
Accounts receivable	90	70	50
Merchandise inventory	80	70	60
Prepaid expenses	10	10	10
Land	30	30	30
Building	70	75	80
Equipment	60	50	40
Total assets	$370	$330	$290
Accounts payable	$ 50	$ 40	$ 30
Taxes payable	20	15	10
Accrued expenses payable	15	10	5
Long-term debt	45	45	45
Paid-in capital	150	150	150
Retained income	90	70	50
Total liab. and stk. eq.	$370	$330	$290

	Year Ended December 31	
	20X3	*20X2*
Sales (all on credit)	$800	$750
Cost of goods sold	(440)	(410)
Operating expenses	(300)	(295)
Pretax income	60	45
Income taxes	(20)	(15)
Net income	$ 40	$ 30

c. Ability to pay current debts on time.
d. Collectibility of receivables.
e. Risks of insolvency.
f. Salability of merchandise.
g. Return on sales.
h. Overall accomplishment.
i. Future stability of profits.
j. Coordination of buying and selling functions.
k. Screening of risks in granting credit to customers.

13-49 Computation of Financial Ratios

The financial statements of the Ito Company are shown in Exhibit 13-17.

Required

Compute the following for the 20X8 financial statements.

1. Pretax return on total assets.
2. Divide your answer to requirement 1 into two components: operating income percentage of sales and total asset turnover.
3. After-tax rate of return on total assets. Be sure to add the after-tax interest expense to net income.

Exhibit 13-17
The Ito Company

BALANCE SHEETS

	December 31	
(Yen in Millions)	*20X8*	*20X7*
Assets		
Current assets		
Cash	¥ 2,000	¥ 2,000
Short-term investments		1,000
Receivables, net	5,000	4,000
Inventories at cost	11,000	8,000
Prepayments	1,000	1,000
Total current assets	¥19,000	¥16,000
Plant and equipment, net	22,000	23,000
Total assets	¥41,000	¥39,000
Liabilities and Stockholders' Equity		
Current liabilities		
Accounts payable	¥10,000	¥ 6,000
Accrued expenses payable	500	500
Income taxes payable	1,500	1,500
Total current liabilities	¥12,000	¥ 8,000
8% bonds payable	¥10,000	¥10,000
Stockholders' equity		
Preferred stock, 12%, par value		
$100 per share	¥ 5,000	¥ 5,000
Common stock, $5 par value	4,000	4,000
Premium on common stock	8,000	8,000
Unappropriated retained earnings	1,000	3,000
Reserve for plant expansion	1,000	1,000
Total stockholders' equity	¥19,000	¥21,000
Total liab. and stk. eq.	¥41,000	¥39,000

STATEMENT OF INCOME AND RECONCILIATION OF RETAINED EARNINGS

(Yen in Thousands)	Year Ended December 31, 20X8	
Sales (all on credit)		¥44,000
Cost of goods sold		32,000
Gross profit on Sales		¥12,000
Other operating expenses		
Selling expenses	¥5,000	
Administrative expenses	2,000	
Depreciation	1,000	8,000
Operating income		¥ 4,000
Interest expense		800
Income before income taxes		¥ 3,200
Income taxes at 40%		¥ 1,280
Net income		¥ 1,920
Dividends on preferred stock		600
Net income for common stockholders		¥ 1,320
Dividends on common stock		3,320
Net income retained		¥(2,000)
Unappropriated retained earnings, December 31, 20X7		3,000
Unappropriated retained earnings, December 31, 20X8		¥ 1,000

4. Rate of return on total stockholders' equity. Did the preferred and common stockholders benefit from the existence of debt? Explain fully.

5. Rate of return on common stockholders' equity. This ratio is the amount of net income available for the common stockholders, divided by total stockholders' equity less the par value of preferred stock. Did the common stockholders benefit from the existence of preferred stock? Explain fully.

6. Calculate inventory turnover. How would Ito have been helped if they had been able to maintain the level of inventory from 20X7?

13-50 Common-Size Statements

(Alternate is 13-43.) Exhibit 13-18 contains the slightly condensed income statement and balance sheets of Minnesota Mining and Manufacturing Company (3M), a multinational company with sales over $15.6 billion.

Exhibit 13-18

Minnesota Mining and Manufacturing Company (3M) and Subsidiaries

CONSOLIDATED STATEMENT OF INCOME		
Years Ended December 31		
(Amounts in Millions, Except per Share Amounts)	*1999*	*1998*
Net sales	$15,659	$15,021
Operating expenses		
Cost of goods sold	8,852	8,705
Restructuring charge—inventory	—	39
Total cost of goods sold	8,852	8,744
Selling, general and administrative expenses	3,879	3,784
Restructuring charge (credit)—other	(28)	454
Total	12,703	12,982
Operating income	2,956	2,039
Other income and expense		
Interest expense	109	139
Investment and other income—net	(33)	(52)
Total	76	87
Income before income taxes,		
minority interest and extraordinary loss	2,880	1,952
Provision for income taxes	1,032	685
Minority interest	85	54
Income before extraordinary loss	1,763	1,213
Extraordinary loss from early extinguishment		
of debt—net of income taxes	—	(38)
Net income	$ 1,763	$ 1,175
Weighted average common shares outstanding—basic	402.0	403.3
Earnings per share—basic		
Income before extraordinary loss	$ 4.39	$ 3.01
Extraordinary loss	—	(.10)
Net income	$ 4.39	$ 2.91
Weighted average common shares outstanding—diluted	406.5	408.0
Earnings per share—diluted		
Income before extraordinary loss	$ 4.34	$ 2.97
Extraordinary loss	—	(.09)
Net income	$ 4.34	$ 2.88

(continued)

Exhibit 13-18 (continued)

Minnesota Mining and Manufacturing Company (3M) and Subsidiaries

CONSOLIDATED BALANCE SHEET

At December 31 ($ in Millions)	1999	1998
Assets		
Current assets		
Cash and cash equivalents	$ 387	$ 211
Other securities	54	237
Accounts receivable—net	2,778	2,666
Inventories	2,030	2,219
Other current assets	817	886
Total current assets	6,066	6,219
Investments	487	623
Property, plant and equipment—net	5,656	5,566
Other assets	1,687	1,745
Total	$13,896	$14,153
Liabilities and Stockholders' Equity		
Current liabilities		
Short-term debt	$ 1,130	$1,492
Accounts payable	1,008	868
Payroll	361	487
Income taxes	464	261
Other current liabilities	856	1,114
Total current liabilities	3,819	4,222
Long-term debt	1,480	1,614
Other liabilities	2,308	2,381
Stockholders' equity—net	6,289	5,936
Shares outstanding—1999: 398,710,817		
1998: 401,924,248		
Total	$13,896	$14,153

Required

1. Prepare common-size statements for 3M for 1998 and 1999.
2. Comment on the changes in component percentages from 1998 to 1999.

13-51 Liquidity Ratios

Exhibit 13-18 contains the slightly condensed income statement and balance sheets of Minnesota Mining and Manufacturing Company (3M), maker of Scotch brand tapes.

Required

1. Compute the following ratios for 1999: (a) current, (b) quick, (c) average collection period, and (d) inventory turnover.
2. Assess 3M's liquidity compared with the following industry averages:

Current ratio	1.8 times
Quick ratio	1.0 times
Average collection period	41.6 days
Inventory turnover	4.5 times

13-52 Solvency Ratios

Exhibit 13-18 contains the income statement and balance sheets of Minnesota Mining and Manufacturing Company (3M), a diversified manufacturing company with operations in the United States and 51 other countries.

1. Compare the following ratios for 1999: (a) total debt to total assets and (b) total debt to total equity.

2. Assess 3M's solvency compared with the following industry averages:

Total debt to total assets	57.4%
Total debt to total shareholders' equity	115.3%

13-53 Profitability Ratios

Exhibit 13-18 contains the income statement and balance sheets of Minnesota Mining and Manufacturing Company (3M), a technology company with over 100 technologies. A corporate objective is for significant sales to be generated by new products introduced in the last 5 years.

1. Compute the following ratios for 1999: (a) return on stockholders' equity, (b) gross profit rate, (c) return on sales, (d) asset turnover, (e) pretax return on assets, and (f) earnings per share.

2. Assess 3M's profitability in 1999 compared with the following industry averages:

Return on stockholders' equity	12%
Gross profit rate	32%
Return on sales	3.2%
Asset turnover	2.66 times
Pretax return on assets	7.7%
Earnings per share	$1.94

13-54 Market Price and Dividend Ratios

Exhibit 13-18 contains the income statement and balance sheets of Minnesota Mining and Manufacturing Company (3M), a leader in bringing new technology-based products to the market. In 1999, 3M paid cash dividends of $2.32 per share, the market price was $95 per share and EPS was $4.34.

1. Compute the following ratios for 1999: (a) price–earnings, (b) dividend–yield, (c) dividend–payout and market to book value.

2. Assess 3M's market price and dividend ratios compared with the following industry averages:

Price–earnings	30
Dividend–yield	2.8%
Dividend–payout	46%
Market to book value	Not available

13-55 Income Ratios and Asset Turnover

The following data are from the 1999, 1998, and 1995 annual reports of McDonald's Corporation. There are more than 27,000 McDonald's restaurants in 120 countries:

	1999	1998	1995
Rate of return on stockholders' equity	20.4%	18.97%	19.36%
Operating income percentage on sales	25%	24.63%	26.56%
Total asset turnover (sales ÷ average assets)	.65	.65	.68
Average total assets	$20,384	$16,400 million	$14,504 million
Interest and other nonoperating expenses	$ 436	$ 382 million	$ 432 million
Income tax expense	$ 936	$ 678 million	$ 742 million

1. Complete the following condensed income statement for 1999. Round to the nearest million.

Required

	1999
Sales	$?
Operating expenses	?
Operating income	$?
Interest and other nonoperating expenses	?
Pretax income	$?
Income tax expense	?
Net income	$?

2. Compute the following for 1999 and 1995:
   a. Pretax operating rate of return on total assets.
   b. Rate of return on sales.
   c. Average stockholders' equity.
3. Compare the values for 1999 to 1995.

13-56 Income Ratios and Asset Turnover

Tribune Company, publisher of the *Chicago Tribune* and owner of the Chicago Cubs baseball team, included the following data in its 1999 annual report to stockholders (amounts in millions except for percentages):

Net income	$1,480
Total assets	
Beginning of year	5,936
End of year	8,798
Net income as a percentage of	
Total revenue	46%
Average stockholders' equity	51%

Surprised by the very high net income as percentage of total revenue and average stockholders' equity, you found that $1,700 million of the income before taxes arose from nonoperating gains. You also calculated a tax rate of 39% for the Tribune. Using this data, compute the following values for 1999:

Required

1. Net income as a percentage of average assets.
2. Total revenues.
3. Average stockholders' equity.
4. Asset turnover, using two different approaches.
5. Compare the computed 1999 values to the 1994 net income as a percentage of total revenue and average stockholders' equity of 11.2% and 19.9% and the 1996 values of 15.5% and 25.5%.
6. Comment on the growth in revenue from 1996 level of $2.4 billion.

13-57 Industry Identification

Exhibit 13-19 presents common-size financial statements and selected ratio values for nine companies from the following industries:

1. Department store
2. Telecommunications
3. Pharmaceutical
4. Petroleum
5. Newspaper
6. Grocery
7. Consumer products

Exhibit 13-19

(For Problem 13-57)

(Columns May Not Add Due to Rounding)

	A	B	C	D	E	F	G	H	I
	%	%	%	%	%	%	%	%	%
Balance sheet									
Cash & marketable securities	13.86	3.71	1.28	1.67	1.32	0.00	1.21	1.57	3.54
Current receivables	13.85	14.52	15.73	18.30	7.90	3.87	2.94	0.00	17.09
Inventories	0.00	10.78	7.95	19.23	0.97	2.48	22.62	34.90	11.62
Other current assets	2.16	11.20	1.96	2.73	2.93	0.69	1.85	0.67	3.20
Total current assets	29.87	40.20	26.91	41.93	13.12	7.04	28.63	37.15	35.46
Net property, plant, & equip.	55.35	48.14	61.39	43.22	36.93	84.64	49.91	1.41	32.37
Other noncurrent assets	14.78	11.66	11.69	14.86	49.95	8.31	21.47	61.45	32.18
Total assets	100.00	100.00	100.00	100.00	100.00	100.00	100.00	100.00	100.00
Current liabilities	19.17	46.90	32.30	21.91	14.38	9.35	36.31	29.84	24.90
Long-term liabilities	25.82	16.70	26.43	48.69	36.37	50.64	50.87	51.85	45.43
Owners' equity	55.02	36.40	41.27	29.40	49.25	40.02	12.82	18.31	29.68
Total liabilities & owners' eq.	100.00	100.00	100.00	100.00	100.00	100.00	100.00	100.00	100.00
Income statement									
Revenue	100.00	100.00	100.00	100.00	100.00	100.00	100.00	100.00	100.00
Cost of sales	51.85	20.58	54.41	61.71	53.56	32.11	72.80	76.81	51.57
Gross profit	48.15	79.42	45.59	38.29	46.44	67.89	27.20	23.19	46.43
Interest expense	1.15	1.21	0.68	3.15	1.19	5.28	1.42	6.39	1.14
Research & development	0.00	13.21	0.77	0.00	0.00	0.00	0.00	0.00	0.00
Selling, general, & admin.	28.42	35.89	8.09	27.25	37.48	23.03	21.19	11.79	31.50
Other expenses (income)	0.17	−0.43	27.00	0.50	−8.66	9.57	−0.15	1.05	1.09
Depreciation & amortization	8.82	3.38	4.60	3.40	0.00	13.35	2.09	1.56	3.10
Income taxes	3.64	6.25	2.85	1.73	7.37	6.04	1.11	0.91	3.95
Net Income	5.96	19.80	1.60	2.26	9.05	10.63	1.53	1.49	7.65
Ratios									
Current ratio	1.56	0.86	0.83	1.91	0.91	0.75	0.79	1.24	1.42
Long-term debt as % of equity	33.29	11.80	27.49	124.44	30.64	75.70	314.43	274.09	96.08
Return on sales	5.96	19.80	1.62	2.26	9.05	10.63	1.53	1.49	7.65
Return on assets	5.75	21.34	2.62	1.90	6.72	4.79	4.75	1.22	9.75
Return on equity	11.59	58.42	6.28	6.34	13.56	12.27	46.69	8.08	31.37
Inventory turnover	INF	2.20	9.83	2.88	32.45	5.66	10.05	2.33	5.62
Times interest earned	9.37	22.59	8.98	2.26	14.63	4.16	2.91	1.36	11.15

8. Utility
9. Home building

Required   Use your knowledge of general business practices to match the industries to the company data.

13-58 Choosing Potential Investments among Delivery Companies

Exhibit 13-20 presents some financial information for United Parcel Service (UPS) and FedEx. Which do you believe is the preferred investment based on this information gathered in the Fall of 2000? Be prepared to defend your answer.

13-59 Choosing Potential Investments among Retailers

Exhibit 13-21 presents some financial information for Wal-Mart, Kmart, JCPenney, and Home Depot. Which do you believe is the preferred investment based on this information gathered in the fall of 2000? Be prepared to defend your answer.

13-60 EVA at Briggs & Station

Briggs & Stratton Corporation is the world's largest maker of air-cooled gasoline engines for outdoor power equipment. The company's engines are used by the lawn and garden equipment

Exhibit 13-20

Investments in Delivery Companies

FedEx Corporation (FDX) and United Parcel Service Incorporated CL B (UPS)

PRICE AND VALUATION

Ticker Symbol	Current Price	52-Week Range	60-Month Beta	EPS	Price-Earnings
FDX	46 3/4	30.56–47.93	1.06	$2.32	19.7
UPS	60.56	49.50–76.93	N/C*	$ .77	25.0

	PEG Ratio	Price/Sales	Price/Book	12-Month Return	5-yr Return
FDX	1.2	.58	2.81	−4.9%	151.0%
UPS	1.7	3.09	7.53	N/C*	N/C*

GROWTH TRENDS

	Latest Annual Income (mil)	1-yr Income Growth	5-yr Income Growth	Latest Annual Revenue (mil)	1-yr Revenue Growth	5-yr Revenue Growth
FDX	$688.3	8.9%	19.7%	$18,256.9	10.0%	14.7%
UPS	$883.0	307.8%	N/C*	$27,052.0	11.6%	N/C*

	Latest Annual EPS	1-yr EPS Growth	5-yr EPS Growth	Annual Dividend/Share	Dividend Yield	5-yr Dividend Growth Rate
FDX	$2.32	11.3%	12.0%	$0.00	0.0%	N/C*
UPS	$0.77	275.4%	N/C*	$0.68	1.1%	N/C*

FINANCIAL STRENGTH

Ticker Symbol	Total Debt/Equity	Current Total Debt (mil)	Current Ratio	Quick Ratio	Current Inventory Turnover	Current Receivable Turnover
FDX	.37	$1,918.0	1.2	1.0	32.7	7.9
UPS	.19	$3,197.0	1.7	1.4	N/A*	N/A*

MANAGEMENT EFFECTIVENESS

Ticker Symbol	Return on Assets	5-yr Avg. Return on Assets	Return on Equity	5-yr Avg. Return on Equity	Revenue Employee (000's)	Income/ Employee (000's)
FDX	6.0%	5.1%	14.4%	12.6%	$195	$7
UPS	3.8%	7.0%	7.1%	15.7%	$ 85	$8

SHARE INFORMATION

Ticker Symbol	Market Cap (mil)	Shares Outstanding (000's)	Number of Institutional Shareholders	Shares Held by Institutions (000's)	% Held by Institutions
FDX	$13,325.53	285,038	797	165,286	58.0%
UPS	$69,163.77	1,142,023	477	67,032	46.1%

Data as of 11/04/2000.

*N/A - Not available; *N/C - Not calculable.

Exhibit 13-21

Retailers

Home Depot (HD), Kmart (KM), JCPenney (JCP), and Wal-mart (WMT)

PRICE AND VALUATION

Ticker Symbol	Current Price	52-Week Range	60-Month Beta	EPS	Price-Earnings
HD	41 1/4	34.68–70.00	.96	$1.00	36.7
KM	6.25	5.06–12.25	1.00	$0.81	N/C*
JCP	11.19	8.68–27.50	.46	$1.16	N/M*
WMT	47.38	41.43–70.25	1.06	$1.25	34.3

Ticker Symbol	PEG Ratio	Price/Sales	Price/Book	12-Month Return	5-yr Return
HD	1.1	3.41	6.92	21.9%	324.9%
KM	.7	.11	.51	−52.2%	−19.3%
CP	1.2	.16	.45	−59.3%	−56.1%
WMT	1.8	1.48	7.53	30.9%	301.3%

GROWTH TRENDS

Ticker Symbol	Latest Annual Income (mil)	1-yr Income Growth	5-yr Income Growth	Latest Annual Revenue (mil)	1-yr Revenue Growth	5-yr Revenue Growth
HD	$2,320.0	32.4%	29.6%	$ 38,434.0	24.6%	23.0%
KM	$ 403.0	−98.3%	N/C*	$ 35,925.0	3.6%	1.0%
JCP	$ 336.0	−94.2%	−30.0%	$ 32,510.0	3.3%	9.7%
WMT	$5,575.0	24.6%	16.9%	$165,013.0	22.7%	14.0%

Ticker Symbol	Latest Annual EPS	1-yr EPS Growth	5-yr EPS Growth	Annual Dividend/Share	Dividend Yield	5-yr Dividend Growth Rate
HD	$1.00	32.9%	27.1%	$0.16	0.4%	23.6%
KM	$0.81	−100.0%	N/C*	$0.00	0.0%	N/C*
JCP	$1.16	−99.5%	−44.1%	$0.50	4.5%	1.7%
WMT	$1.25	24.3%	17.5%	$0.24	0.5%	14.4%

FINANCIAL STRENGTH

Ticker Symbol	Total Debt/Equity	Current Total Debt (mil)	Current Ratio	Quick Ratio	Current Inventory Turnover	Current Receivable Turnover
HD	.06	$ 797.0	1.6	.3	5.2	64.7
KM	.45	$ 2,755.0	1.9	.1	4.1	N/C*
JCP	1.00	$ 6,064.0	1.9	.4	3.9	12.3
WMT	.85	$22,624.0	.9	.1	7.0	143.3

MANAGEMENT EFFECTIVENESS

Ticker Symbol	Return on Assets	5-yr Avg. Return on Assets	Return on Equity	5-yr Avg. Return on Equity	Revenue Employee (000's)	Income/ Employee (000's)
HD	13.6%	11.2%	18.8%	16.8%	$213	$13
KM	2.7%	.7%	6.4%	1.1%	$134	$ 0
JCP	1.6%	2.8%	5.0%	9.5%	$113	$ 0
WMT	7.9%	7.9%	21.6%	19.6%	$159	$ 5

(continued)

Exhibit 13-21 (continued)

Retailers

Home Depot (HD), Kmart (KM), JCPenney (JCP), and Wal-Mart (WMT)

		SHARE INFORMATION			
Ticker Symbol	**Market Cap (mil)**	**Shares Outstanding (000's)**	**Number of Institutional Shareholders**	**Shares Held by Institutions (000's)**	**% Held by Institutions**
HD	$ 95,531.13	2,315,906	2,316	1,386,788	59.8%
KM	$ 3,000.62	480,099	643	291,564	60.6%
JCP	$ 2,931.87	262,067	699	181,693	69.4%
WMT	$211,592.68	4,466,336	2,412	1,555,526	34.8%

Data as of 11/04/2000.

*N/C - Not calculable; *N/M - Not meaningful.

industry. According to the company's 1999 Annual Report, "management subscribes to the premise that the value of Briggs & Stratton is enhanced if the capital invested in the company's operations yields a cash return that is greater than that expected by the provider of capital."

The following data are from Briggs & Stratton's 1999 Annual Report (thousands of dollars):

	1999	**1998**
Adjusted operating profit	$187,994	$131,546
Cash taxes	65,255	41,102
Invested capital	697,887	716,112
Cost of capital	10.3%	10.0%

1. Compute the economic value added for Briggs & Stratton for 1998 and 1999.
2. Did Briggs & Stratton's overall performance improve from 1998 to 1999? Explain.

13-61 EVA and MVA

EVA is discussed in the text as an annual measure that considers whether the current year's operating performance produced results that exceeded the firm's cost of capital. Another way to say it is: Did we earn enough to justify the significant investment that investors have made in the company? In addition to this annual measure, there is a related concept called market value added (MVA). This is defined as market value of equity minus invested equity capital (book value). In years when EVA is positive, MVA should increase and in years when EVA is negative, MVA should fall. In fact, this does not happen exactly because some portion of a company's stock valuation is about its own performance and some portion is about the overall performance of the economy.

We have worked with many prominent companies in this book. Try to match the following four companies to their 1999 MVA ranking among the top 1000, as reported by *Fortune* magazine. Explain your reasoning.

The four companies, listed alphabetically, are Cisco, Ford, GM, and Kmart. The four 1999 rankings on MVA are 8, 43, 978, and 1,000, respectively.

Required

13-62 Comparing Merck and Eli Lilly

In November of 2000, the following relationships held for Merck and Eli Lilly. Which would you expect to have the larger EVA in 1999? Why?

	Merck	**Eli Lilly**
Share price	$87.75	$88.00
EPS	$ 2.45	$ 2.46
P-E	31.3	31.5
PEG ratio	2.5	2.4
Book value per share	$ 5.69	$ 4.60
Shares outstanding (billions)	2.3	1.1

13-63   MD&A and Ethics

If certain conditions are met, the SEC requires companies to disclose information about future events that are reasonably likely to materially affect the firms' operations. Many companies are understandably reluctant to disclose such information. After all, positive predictions may not materialize and negative predictions may unduly alarm the investors. What ethical considerations should a company's managers consider when deciding what prospective information to disclose in the MD&A section of the annual report?

ANNUAL REPORT CASE

13-64   Cisco Annual Report

Use the financial statements and notes of Cisco in appendix A to respond to the questions that follow.

Required

1. Calculate return on common stockholders' equity for the year ended July 29, 2000. Compare it with the value for the year ended July 31, 1999.
2. Calculate the current ratio for the year ended July 29, 2000 and compare it with the value for the year ended July 31, 1999.
3. Calculate debt-to-total-assets for the year ended July 29, 2000. Compare it with the value for the year ended July 31, 1999.

13-65   Financial Statement Research

Choose two companies in each of two industries.

Required

Calculate the return on assets, return on equity, and return on sales for each of the companies. Compare and contrast the two companies in each industry and the averages for each industry.

COLLABORATIVE LEARNING EXERCISE

13-66   Operating Return on Total Assets

Form groups of four to six students. Each student should choose an industry (a different industry for each student in the group) and pick two companies in that industry. Compute the following for each of the companies:

1. Operating income percentage on sales.
2. Total asset turnover.
3. Pretax operating rate of return on total assets.

Get together as a group and list the industries and the three ratios for each company in the industry. Examine how the ratios differ between the two companies within each industry compared with the differences between industries. As a group, prepare two lists of possible explanations for the differences in ratios. The first list should explain why ratios of two companies within the same industry might differ. The second list should explain why ratios differ by industry.

INTERNET EXERCISE

www.prenhall.com/horngren

13-67   Dell

Go to www.dell.com to locate Dell's home page. Select *About Dell*, then *Investor Relations*. Click on *Annual Reports* to find the most recent version.

Answer the following questions about Dell:

1. Where in Dell's annual report do you find a trend and a component percentage analysis? Which key ratios does Dell provide for investors? Examine the trend in the liquidity ratios presented. Is the trend positive or negative? What factors influenced the trend?
2. What is Dell's dividend policy? Have there been any stock splits? If you were an equity investor, how would you interpret this information?

3. Where does Dell report geographic segment information? What segments exist? Which is the largest? Which is experiencing the greatest percentage of growth?

4. Calculate Dell's debt-to-equity ratio for the last two fiscal years. What is the trend? What effect does additional financing have on net income, and on EPS?

5. What is the amount of Dell's EPS for the most recent fiscal year? What factors influenced the change from the last period to the current period?

chapter 14

CONCEPTUAL FRAMEWORK AND MEASUREMENT TECHNIQUES

At Dell Computer Corporation financial analysts are using various techniques to evaluate the financial condition of customers and suppliers.

www.prenhall.com/horngren

Learning Objectives

After studying this chapter, you should be able to

1. Describe the FASB's conceptual framework.

2. Identify the qualities that make information valuable.

3. Explain how accounting differences could produce differing income for similar companies.

4. Differentiate between financial capital and physical capital.

5. Incorporate changing prices into income measurement using four different methods.

6. Compare U.S. GAAP with other countries' standards.

7. Discuss the role of the International Accounting Standards Board (IASB) in setting standards.

There is an old saying that "beauty is in the eye of the beholder." Depending on who you are, you may find beauty and meaning in places others do not. When looking at accounting information, its usefulness is like beauty—meaning is found in the eye of the beholder. The information serves a purpose in decision making, but the types of decisions made differ with the individual user.

When an organization prepares financial statements, it recognizes that the reported results will be used by different people in different ways. For example, investment analysts, brokers, and investors look at reported performance to determine whether a particular company is worthy of investment. At Piper Jaffray, corporate financial data are analyzed regularly so that recommendations can be made to clients to buy, sell, or hold stocks. Banks such as Bank of America use financial reports to determine creditworthiness. When an organization seeks a line of credit or loans, the financial statements are used to get a picture of the applicant's economic health. Even businesses use financial reports to examine the status of current and potential business partners. Dell Computer Corporation employs analysts who keep an eye on how their suppliers are doing. If a problem arises with a supplier, it could seriously affect whether Dell meets its own commitments and financial targets.

The analyses may differ among decision makers, but they all rely on the same conceptual framework that guides the creation of the financial reports. When prepared according to generally accepted accounting principles, investors, bankers, analysts, and others can count on finding meaning, value, and reliability in the accounting information. However, it is important to conduct your analysis with a careful eye toward choices that a company makes among permitted principles. When the companies under analysis include non–U.S. companies, the possible variability in principles grows substantially.

The essence of the related topics in this chapter involves the questions: What are we trying to measure and what principles should we bring to the task? Throughout the book, we have included some international examples and some discussion of basic principles. In this chapter, we integrate these discussions. You have now considered enough details of the accounting process to address some underlying issues in a more integrated manner. Many countries have confronted the problem of selecting accounting principles, and they have reached different conclusions. In the United States, we allow a wide range of choices in method. In this chapter, we examine some of the reasons for this practice.

CONCEPTUAL FRAMEWORK OF ACCOUNTING

For years, accountants have sought a consistent set of concepts underlying accounting practice. But GAAP remains a patchwork that has evolved slowly over many years. The key element of this patchwork is that people accept it. Some accounting rules seem inconsistent with others and changes occur one at a time. For example, the lower-of-cost-or-market (LCM) basis was applied differently to inventories, to short-term investments, and to long-term investments in prior years. The recent acceptance of the market method of accounting for most short-term investments has made the conservatism of LCM relevant only in the inventory arena.

FASB's Conceptual Framework

Objective 1
Describe the FASB's conceptual framework.

Between 1978 and 1984, the Financial Accounting Standards Board (FASB) issued four Statements of Financial Accounting Concepts (SFACs) relating to business enterprises. The statements provide the conceptual framework used by the FASB. The FASB makes accounting policy by choosing the accounting measurements and disclosure methods for financial reporting. The board's function might be called rule making, standard setting, or regulation, but the essence is that the FASB exercises judgment in choosing among alternatives. Because there are no objective criteria to guide the FASB in making its decisions, the conceptual framework summarized in Exhibit 14-1 was created to guide the exercise of judgment and increase the consistency between standards.

Are the statements in Exhibit 14-1 the final word in U.S. accounting practice? No. Accounting policy is too complex to remain fixed over time. The FASB has to adjust it to changes in the world of business, such as changes in technology, business practice, economics, and so on. Progress comes in fits and starts and is considered too fast by some and too slow by others. One person's improvement is often another person's impairment. A key for the FASB is getting everyone to accept its decisions and statements.

The FASB has a good batting record. Of the 140 some statements it has issued, only a few have been opposed. How does the FASB get such compliance? For one reason, the board involves various constituencies at every stage of the debate, including the public accounting firms, corporate preparers, and analysts who use the information. So it solicits opinions and works to create a consensus around good accounting. It also compromises when necessary to get acceptance. Of course, a conceptual framework, plausible logic, and compelling facts all increase the odds of winning support from diverse interests.

Exhibit 14-1

Statements of Financial Accounting Concepts for Business Enterprises

Statement	Highlights
SFAC No. 1, Objectives of Financial Reporting by Business Enterprises	• Accounting should provide information useful for making economic decisions • Statements should focus on external users, such as creditors and investors • Information should aid the prediction of cash flows • Earnings based on accrual accounting provide a better measure of performance than do cash receipts and disbursements
SFAC No. 2, Qualitative Characteristics of Accounting Information	• Usefulness is evaluated in relation to the purposes to be served • Different information is useful for different decisions • Decision usefulness is the primary characteristic in the hierarchy of desirable characteristics • Both relevance and reliability are necessary for information to be useful • Relevance requires timeliness and either predictive or feedback value • Reliable information must faithfully represent the item being measured and be verifiable and neutral • Comparability and consistency aid usefulness • To be useful, information must be material, that is, reported amounts must be large enough to make a difference in decisions • Benefits from using information should exceed its cost
SFAC No. 3, Elements of Financial Statements of Business Enterprises	• This statement defines the ten building blocks that comprise financial statements: (1) assets, (2) liabilities, (3) equity, (4) investments by owners, (5) distributions to owners, (6) comprehensive income, (7) revenues, (8) expenses, (9) gains, and (10) losses
SFAC No. 5, Recognition and Measurement in Financial Statements of Business Enterprises	• This specifies what information should be included in financial statements and when • All components of financial statements are important, not just a single "bottom-line" number • A statement of financial position provides information about assets, liabilities, and equity; it does not show the market value of the entity • Earnings measure periodic performance; comprehensive income recognizes all effects on equity except investments by or distributions to owners • Financial statements are based on the concept of financial capital maintenance • Measurement is and will continue to be based on nominal units of money • Revenue is recognized when it is earned and realized (or realizable) • Information based on current prices, if reliable and more relevant than alternative information, should be reported if costs involved are not too high

*SFAC nos. 4 and 6 relate to nonbusiness entities and are not summarized here.

Until the early 1930s, when the Securities and Exchange Commission (SEC) was created by Congress, accounting practices in the United States evolved in accordance with the best professional judgment of certified public accountants (CPAs) and managers. Then private and public regulators entered the picture. Today, the SEC is legally charged with setting accounting standards but has delegated that responsibility to the FASB.

The term *generally accepted* is a key part of the familiar term *generally accepted accounting principles*. When the FASB considers a financial accounting standard, assorted interested parties present arguments to support their favored choices. The standards issued are often compromises among the contending interests. Therefore, the standards are not necessarily products of airtight logic.

The FASB's task is not only technical but also political in the sense that the FASB must convince interested persons about the wisdom of the board's decisions. The FASB has encountered only an occasional failure to obtain acceptance. One early example was Statement No. 19 in which the FASB mandated specific accounting standards for oil and gas exploration, only to be overturned by SEC action requiring that firms be granted continued opportunity to choose between two methods.

More recently, the board issued an exposure draft that would have required firms to record an expense in their income statements when they issued stock options to executives. In the face of strong opposition from managers around the country and spirited discussion in Congress, the FASB ultimately decided to accept disclosure of such costs in footnotes instead of the income statement itself.

Of course, in retrospect, the FASB probably won more than it lost. True, they did not require expense recognition in the income statement, but on the other hand, they did require substantially increased disclosure in the footnotes. When the information is in the footnotes to be read and interpreted, the security analysts and interested investors quickly understand what is going on.

CHOOSING AMONG REPORTING ALTERNATIVES

Objective 2
Identify the qualities that make information valuable.

The FASB must make difficult decisions about reporting requirements. For example, should stock options for executives be treated as an expense? How should the expense for nonpension retirement benefits be measured and disclosed? Should assets and liabilities be shown at historical cost or current market value? The list could go on and on.

How does the FASB decide that one level of disclosure or one measurement method is acceptable and another is not? The main decision criterion is always cost versus benefit. Accounting should improve decision making. This is a benefit. However, accounting information is an economic good that is costly to produce. The FASB must choose rules whose decision-making benefits exceed their costs. Unfortunately, these costs and benefits are hard to measure and sometimes even hard to identify.

Many would say that the United States has the best accounting standards in the world. Because our standards are good, they would argue that U.S. corporations have very easy and cheap access to both debt and equity financing. Investors have confidence in the disclosures. Others would point out that because the United States requires more disclosure than any other country, many international companies list their shares in exchanges in London, Tokyo, and other capital cities where the accounting regulations are less difficult to meet. This costs the New York Stock Exchange (NYSE) and other U.S. exchanges a lot of business and it makes it harder for U.S. investors to buy shares in some premier international companies.

Exhibit 14-2

Qualities that Increase the Value of Information

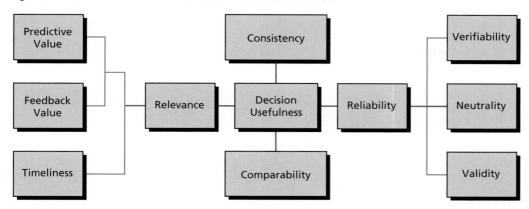

Source: Adapted from *Qualitative Characteristics of Accounting Information* (Stamford, CT: FASB, 1980), p. 15.

The costs of providing information include costs to both providers and users. Providers incur costs for data collecting and processing, auditing, and educating preparers. In addition, disclosure of sensitive information can lead to lost competitive advantages or increased labor union pressures. These provider costs are often passed along to the user via higher prices. They then become user costs. User costs also include the costs of education, analysis, and interpretation.

The benefits of accounting information are sometimes harder to pinpoint than are the costs. A major effort by countries in the former Soviet Union and in other emerging market economies has been to create an infrastructure of financial markets and relevant information to guide the economy. However, the specific benefits of a particular proposal are harder to articulate than the general benefits of an intelligent system of accounting rules and procedures.

Because these broad benefits can be hard to measure or even see, the FASB has come up with a set of easily identified characteristics of information that lead to increased benefits, as shown in Exhibit 14-2. The main characteristic is decision usefulness. If accounting information is not useful in making decisions, it provides no benefit. The rest of the characteristics are aspects of decision usefulness.

ASPECTS OF DECISION USEFULNESS

You might notice that accuracy is not a quality that is mentioned explicitly. This is intentional. Note that materiality is a fundamental concept of accounting. We want to know the important issues. Tell us what might change our mind. Do so in a consistent, comparable way so we can compare one company with another and trace a company through time. We do not expect IBM to report its earnings to the penny. We settle for hundreds of millions as being precise enough and accurate enough. So the qualities emphasized in Exhibit 14-2 have to do with meaningful, valuable, reliable information on which people can agree.

Relevance and reliability are the two main qualities that make accounting information useful for decision making. **Relevance** refers to whether the information makes a difference to the decision maker. **Reliability** means that the information can be counted on to represent faithfully the condition of the company, given the rules in use. Accounting is filled with trade-offs between relevance and reliability. Consider the $1.7 billion balance sheet value of Weyerhaeuser Company's timberlands, which are recorded at original cost.

relevance The capability of information to make a difference to the decision maker.

reliability A quality of information meaning that it can be counted on to represent faithfully the condition of the company.

Exhibit 14-3

Frequently Encountered Terminology in Conceptual Frameworks of Accounting

Term	Short Description	Example and Chapter coverage in this Text*
Cost and benefits	Accounting information that is an economic good, that should be gathered as long as its benefits exceed its costs	Decisions that must be improved sufficiently to justify recording current values in addition to historical costs; mainly in ch. 4, 7
Relevance	Capability of information to make a difference to the decision maker	Report of cash in bank that is essential to determine how much money to borrow, ch. 3, 14
Reliability	Dependability of information as representing what it purports to represent	The cost of the land that was $1 million 2002 dollars; ch. 4, 14
Verifiability (objectivity)	Characteristic of information that allows it to be checked to be sure it is correct	Cash that has high verifiability, accounts receivable less, inventories less yet, depreciable assets even less, and so on; ch. 1, 3, 14
Validity (representational faithfulness)	Correspondence between numbers and objects or events portrayed	The historical cost/constant dollar cost of the land described may be $1 million 2002 dollars, but that represents neither the current cost or market value; ch. 14
Consistency	Applying the same accounting methods over a series of reporting periods	Use of FIFO inventory over a series of years, not FIFO for 2 years, LIFO for 3 years, and so on; ch. 6
Neutrality (evenhandedness)	A quality of information implying that it is objective and without bias	An example of lack of neutrality that may clarify: The MACRS depreciation system for tax purposes is constructed from arbitrary economic lives and an accelerated schedule to encourage investment; ch. 14
Materiality	An item is material if the judgment of a reasonable person would change by its omission or misstatement	An error of $100 of revenue that would be immaterial for a firm with $100,000 of revenue but material for a firm with $1,000 of revenue; ch. 4
Conservatism	Response to uncertainties; avoids recognition of income based on inadequate evidence but requires recognition of losses when assets are impaired or liabilities incurred; when in doubt, write it off	Charging all research and development (R&D) costs to expenses as incurred; applying lower-of-cost-or-market methods (LCM) to asset valuation; ch. 5, 7, 12
Continuity (going concern)	Assumption that an entity will continue indefinitely or at least will not be liquidated in the near future	Letterhead stationery on hand is classified as supplies or rubbish, depending on the continuity assumption; ch. 4
Entity	The unit of accountability	A parent corporation, a subsidiary, a retail store; ch. 1, 12
Accrual accounting	Record financial effects in the periods affected regardless of when cash is received or paid	Recognizing receivables and payables when promise to pay is made and matching expenses with revenues; ch. 2, 3, 4
Recognition	Formally incorporating an item in accounts and financial statements; an element may be recognized (recorded) or unrecognized (unrecorded)	Revenue recognition requires revenues to be earned and realized; increases or decreases in the value of land may be earned but unrealized; advance payments on subscriptions may be realized but not earned; ch. 1, 2, 4, 5
Matching and cost recovery	Matching, that is relating, revenues and expenses to each other in a particular period	Sales commission expenses are "matched" directly against related sales; sales salaries, costs of heating, and depreciation are "matched" against current revenues because their benefits are exhausted in the current period; ch. 2, 4, 5, 14

*Many of these criteria or basic ideas underlie this entire textbook.

Much of the land was purchased more than 50 years ago. The historical cost is reliable, but not very relevant. In contrast, the current value of the land is more relevant, but estimates of this current value are subjective and thus might not be reliable. Which quality is more important? That answer depends on the specific decision being made. However, the most desirable information is both reliable and relevant. The prevailing view in the United States is that many current market value estimates are not sufficiently reliable to be included in the accounting records, even though they are more relevant. However, in some countries, current market values are routinely used. For example, BPAmoco used market values when it subtracted the "replacement cost of sales" in obtaining "replacement cost operating profit" of £17,350 million in 2000.

As you can see in Exhibit 14-2, both relevance and reliability have their own characteristics. For information to be relevant, it must help decision makers either predict the outcomes of future events (predictive value) or confirm or update past predictions (feedback value). Relevant information must also be available on a timely basis, that is, before a decision maker has to act.

Reliability is characterized by verifiability (or objectivity), neutrality, and validity. **Verifiability** means that information can be checked to make sure it is correct. It also means that measured amounts have the same value each time the measurement is made. The historical cost of an item is verifiable because we can easily check records to verify that the amounts are correct. In contrast, estimates or appraisals are not verifiable. **Validity** (also called **representational faithfulness**) means the information provided represents the events or objects it is supposed to represent. **Neutrality,** or freedom from bias, means that information is objective and is not weighted unfairly. For example, information that focuses heavily on the benefits of one option while ignoring the benefits of another option is not neutral and does not help lead to a fair decision. Neutrality suggests that allowable depreciation methods should effectively match depreciation expense with revenue but should not be chosen to encourage or discourage investment.

The final items affecting decision usefulness are comparability and consistency. Information is more useful if it can be compared with similar information about other companies or with similar information for other reporting periods. For example, financial results for two companies are hard to compare if one company uses first-in, first-out (FIFO) and the other uses last-in, first-out (LIFO). Comparisons cannot be made over time if a company keeps changing its accounting methods.

verifiability A quality of information meaning that it can be checked to make sure that it is correct.

validity (representational faithfulness) A correspondence between the accounting numbers and the objects or events those numbers purport to represent.

neutrality A quality of information meaning that it is objective and free from bias.

OVERVIEW OF KEY CONCEPTS

Exhibit 14-3 presents an overview of key accounting concepts covered in this text, where in the text they appear, and a concrete example of each. This table should be a handy guide for recalling and comparing major ingredients of accounting's conceptual framework.

MEASURING INCOME

Measuring income is easily the most controversial subject in accounting. The most popular approach to income measurement, the historical-cost method, is based on actual costs of acquiring assets. This is the primary method underlying U.S. GAAP. However, the label *historical cost* does not completely define the way income is measured. Disputes often occur in applying the historical-cost method. The majority of these disputes center on timing. For example, when are revenues recognized? When do the costs of assets become expenses? In addition, in recent years, a few exceptions to historical cost have worked their way into GAAP, most notably in the valuation of marketable securities. Let us take a look at some of the issues concerning the historical-cost method.

REVENUE RECOGNITION

Objective 3
Explain how accounting differences could produce differing income for similar companies.

Under accrual accounting, revenue is usually recorded when goods or services are delivered to customers. However, there are some exceptions to this rule. For example, companies taking on long-run construction projects often recognize revenue using a percentage-of-completion method. Consider the builder of an ocean liner. Such a company might take well over a year to finish and deliver a given product. Spreading expected costs and revenues over the life of the contract, based on the work accomplished, allows income recognition in each year and realistically portrays the economic process. Otherwise, all the net income would appear in one chunk on completion of the project, as if it had been earned on a single day.

Also, in very rare cases, revenue can be recorded in proportion to cash collections under long-run installment contracts. An illustration is the retail sales of undeveloped lots. The receivables may be collectible over decades instead of months, and there is no reliable basis for estimating how likely it is that the full amount will ever be collected.

Not knowing whether a receivable will be collected does not always delay the recording of revenue. Many accountants regard the revenue as realized but provide an ample allowance for uncollectible accounts. For example, hospitals can recognize revenue on the accrual basis as their services are delivered. However, because many hospital debts go unpaid, hospitals must offset some of this revenue with an account for bad debts expense.

EXPENSE RECOGNITION

GAAP also allow accountants to choose when to recognize certain expenses. Comparing two companies can be difficult if each chooses a different method for recognizing major expenses. To achieve comparability, analysts often reconstruct a company's financial statements to place them on a basis consistent with other companies in the same industry.

Suppose two companies, Miami Marine (MM) and Sarasota Sailboats (SS), began business in the same industry in 20X1. Each company would have reported amounts from panel A of Exhibit 14-4, depending on the accounting method chosen.

For stockholder reporting purposes, the choice of accounting policies can have a dramatic effect on operating income before taxes. Assume that MM takes one extreme stance; SS takes the other extreme. As panel B of Exhibit 14-4 shows, the choices of LIFO, accelerated depreciation, and immediate write-off of product introduction costs cause MM's operating income to be $50,000. In contrast, SS's operating income is $120,000.

Many managers seek to maximize reported earnings by choosing the accounting policies favored by SS. Others tend to be more conservative and choose the MM policies. The point here is that similar operations may be portrayed differently in income statements. Note that all the data are the same as far as the underlying cash flows are concerned. Also recall that over the life of the business either set of methods would produce identical results.

Someday accounting procedures may become more standardized and financial statements will be easier to compare. Until then, companies will have to disclose all the practices used in creating their financial statements. Why? Because once analysts know what methods are in use by different companies, the analysts can revise the financial statements to put them on a comparable basis so comparisons are meaningful.

STATEMENT OF ACCOUNTING POLICIES

How and where do companies disclose the accounting methods they used to create their financial statements? The disclosure usually appears as a separate summary of significant accounting policies preceding the footnotes of financial statements. Exhibit 14-5 displays some of the items in a typical summary, that of Corning Incorporated from its 1999 annual report. We have discussed many of the items identified, although a few, including details of foreign currency translation and income tax accounting, are topics for more advanced accounting texts.

Exhibit 14-4

Income Effects of Accounting Differences

PANEL A: LIST OF ITEMS

	Amount	Difference
Beginning inventory	$ 0	
Purchases	270,000	
Ending inventory, if FIFO is used	110,000 ⎫	
Ending inventory, if LIFO is used	70,000 ⎭	$40,000
Depreciation, if accelerated is used	20,000 ⎫	
Depreciation, if straight-line is used	10,000 ⎭	10,000
Product introduction costs, original total amount	30,000 ⎫	
Product introduction costs, amortized amount	10,000 ⎭	20,000
Revenue	400,000	
Other expenses	100,000	

PANEL B: INCOME STATEMENTS FOR THE YEAR ENDED DECEMBER 31, 20X1 ($ IN THOUSANDS)

	Individual Effects				
	(1) Miami Marine *(LIFO, Accelerated, Immediate Write-off)*	*(2)* *Change from LIFO to FIFO*	*(3)* *Change from Accelerated to Straight-line*	*(4)* *Change from Immediate Write-off to Amortization*	*(5)* Sarasota Sailboat *(FIFO, Straight-line, Amortization)*
Revenue	$400				$400
Expenses					
Cost of goods sold	200	$40			160
Depreciation	20		$10		10
Product introduction costs	30			$20	10
Other expenses	100				100
Total expenses	350	—	—	—	280
Operating income before income taxes	$ 50	$40	$10	$20	$120

INCOME MEASUREMENT WHEN PRICES CHANGE

Sometimes historical costs do not measure income properly. Accountants tend to agree that income is best described as the return on capital invested by shareholders. By examining the relationship of income to capital in greater detail, we can discover circumstances when historical cost leads to incorrect and misleading measures of income.

Objective 4
Differentiate between financial capital and physical capital.

INCOME OR CAPITAL

At first glance, the concept of income seems straightforward. Income is a company's increase in wealth during a period. It is the amount that could be paid out to shareholders at the end of the period, while still leaving the company as well off as it was at the beginning of the period. In essence, shareholders invest capital and expect a return *on* the capital and an eventual return *of* the capital. To measure the shareholders' return on capital, the company first measures the resources required to maintain invested capital at its

Exhibit 14-5

Corning Incorporated and Subsidiary Companies

Notes to Supplemental Consolidated Financial Statements, (in Millions, Except Share and per Share Amounts)
Selected items

---

1. Summary of Significant Accounting Policies

Principles of Consolidation: The consolidated financial statements include the accounts of all entities controlled by Corning. All significant intercompany accounts and transactions are eliminated.

The equity method of accounting is used for investments in associated companies which are not controlled by Corning and in which Corning's interest is generally between 20% and 50%.

The preparation of financial statements in conformity with generally accepted accounting principles requires management to make estimates and assumptions that affect the reported amounts of assets and liabilities and to disclose contingent assets and liabilities at the date of the financial statements and the reported amounts of revenues and expenses during the reporting period. Actual results could differ from those estimates.

Cash and Cash Equivalents: Short-term investments, comprised of repurchase agreements and debt instruments with original maturities of three months or less, are considered cash equivalents.

Marketable Securities: Corning's marketable securities consist of equity securities classified as available-for-sale which are stated at estimated fair value based primarily upon market quotes. Unrealized gains and losses, net of tax, are computed on the basis of specific identification and are reported as a separate component of accumulated other comprehensive income in shareholders' equity until realized. A decline in the value of any marketable security

below cost that is deemed other than temporary is charged to earnings, resulting in a new cost basis for the security.

Inventories: Corning historically used the last-in, first-out (LIFO) method for approximately 40% of its inventories, with the remaining inventories valued on a first-in, first-out (FIFO) basis. In the second quarter of 1999, Corning changed its method of determining the cost of its LIFO inventories to the FIFO method. As a result of declining costs and prices for such inventories, Corning believes that the use of the FIFO method results in a more current inventory valuation at period end dates and minimizes the likelihood of lower-of-cost-or-market valuation issues.

Property and Depreciation: Land, buildings and equipment are recorded at cost. Depreciation is based on estimated useful lives of properties using straight-line and accelerated methods. The estimated useful lives range from 20–40 years for buildings and 3–20 years for the majority of Corning's equipment.

Taxes on Income: Corning uses the asset and liability approach to account for income taxes. Under this method, deferred tax assets and liabilities are recognized for the expected future tax consequences of differences between the carrying amounts of assets and liabilities and their respective tax bases using enacted tax rates in effect for the year in which the differences are expected to reverse. The effect on deferred tax assets and liabilities of a change in tax rates is recognized in income in the period when the change is enacted.

---

original level. Any profit above and beyond this level of maintained capital is income. Traditional historical-cost accounting would state that maintaining capital requires keeping resources equal to the dollar value of the original investment. Under this financial concept of income, any excess dollar amount is income, the return on capital.

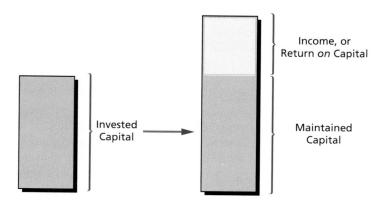

In contrast to the financial concept, some accountants and managers define capital as a physical concept, based on the company's real productive capacity. They identify the physical resources that make up capital at the beginning of the period, such as plant, property, equipment, and inventory. To maintain that capital, the company must set aside enough end-of-period resources (dollars) to replace the beginning-of-period physical capacity. Only resources in excess of those required to replicate the initial productive capacity are considered income.

Consider an example in which a company begins with owners' investment (capital) of $1,000. That $1,000 is used immediately to purchase 500 units of inventory. The inventory is sold a year later for $1,500. The cost of replacing the 500 units of inventory has risen to $1,200. The year began with financial capital of $1,000 that is immediately transformed into 500 units of physical capital (inventory). At the end of the year, there is $1,500 and no inventory. Suppose management wanted to keep the initial level of capital to begin a new year but also to pay investors a return on their investment. How much can the company pay out?

The simple answer is that the company can pay out its cash to the extent it is not needed to maintain the initial level of capital. However, what capital are we maintaining? If we are maintaining financial capital, income is based on the $1,500 sales less the $1,000 level of financial investment, which equals $500. Calculating income based on maintaining financial capital is known as **financial capital maintenance.** Conversely, if we are maintaining physical capital, income is based on the $1,500 less the cost of maintaining a 500-unit inventory. That cost is now $1,200, so income would be only $300 ($1,500 − $1,200). Calculating income based on maintaining physical capital is known as **physical capital maintenance.** Do you see how using historical costs to determine income might be a problem in this example? Historical cost is a financially driven concept. In a world of changing prices in which physical capital maintenance is important, historical cost overstates income. If dividend distributions are based on historical cost, $500 will be distributed, inventories will not be fully replaced, and prior levels of activity will not be maintainable.

financial capital maintenance A concept of income measurement whereby income emerges only after financial resources are recovered.

physical capital maintenance A concept of income measurement whereby income emerges only after recovering an amount that allows physical operating capability to be maintained.

	Financial Capital Maintenance	**Physical Capital Maintenance**
Sales	$1,500	$1,500
Cost of goods sold	1,000	1,200
Income	$ 500	$ 300

COMPLAINTS ABOUT HISTORICAL COST

A pet theme of politicians and other critics of business is the "unconscionable" or "obscene" profits reported by American companies. In response, many business executives insist that our traditional historical-cost basis for measuring income overstates profits during a time of rising prices. These overstated profits also cause their companies to pay more income taxes than they should.

The importance of this issue varies to some extent by industry. Industries with huge investments in plant and equipment tend to be most affected. For instance, consider NYNEX, a telephone company that emerged from the breakup of the Bell system, and subsequently merged into Bell Atlantic. In a period of high inflation, NYNEX reported net income of $1,095 million. This would have been a net loss of $82 million if depreciation had been adjusted for inflation. In 2001, inflation was fairly low, around 3% per year, so annual effects are small. Even so, if an asset was purchased in 1980, its historical cost would probably be about half of its replacement cost. This would mean its depreciation would be half of what depreciation should be under a physical capital maintenance concept.

The soaring inflation of the late 1970s in the United States raised many questions about the usefulness of traditional historical-cost financial statements. The FASB responded by issuing Statement No. 33. "Financial Reporting and Changing Prices." The statement required no changes in the primary financial statements. However, it required large companies to include supplementary inflation-adjusted schedules in their annual reports.

Statement No. 33 was experimental, and its requirements were in place for 8 years. By 1987, inflation had subsided, and the FASB decided that inflation-adjusted disclosures would no longer be required. Although U.S. companies do not need to report inflation-adjusted numbers, a basic knowledge about reporting the effects of changing prices is useful for at least four reasons: (1) high inflation is still present in many countries, and most accounting reports in those countries report the effects of inflation; (2) if history is any indication, higher inflation rates will return to the United States sooner or later, and when they do, readers of financial statements will again become concerned with inflation-adjusted statements; (3) cumulative effect of even a 2% or 3% rate is substantial; and (4) understanding the limitations of traditional financial statements is enhanced by knowing how inflation affects (or does not affect) such financial statements.

ALTERNATIVES TO HISTORICAL-COST INCOME MEASUREMENT

inflation A general decline in the purchasing power of the monetary unit.

nominal dollars Those dollars that are not restated for fluctuations in the general purchasing power of the monetary unit.

constant dollars Dollar measurements that are restated in terms of current purchasing power.

historical cost The amount of originally paid to acquire an asset.

current cost Generally, the cost to replace an asset.

When prices of resources do not change, financial and physical capital maintenance give identical measures of income. However, price changes are a fact of life. Some price changes are a result of **inflation,** a general decline in the purchasing power of the dollar (or other monetary unit) or a general increase in the average cost of goods and services. Other price changes are specific to a product. For example, the price of computing power has been declining steadily for decades as a result of improved technology, although most products had stable or rising prices.

Changing prices, and particularly inflation, have caused accountants to consider two types of changes in financial reporting: (1) Switch from measuring transactions in **nominal dollars** which are dollar measurements that are not restated for fluctuations in the general purchasing power of the monetary unit, to **constant dollars,** which are dollar values restated in terms of current purchasing power, (2) instead of reporting the **historical cost** of an asset, which is the amount originally paid to acquire it, use the **current cost,** which is generally the cost to replace it. As our previous example indicates, using historical costs implies financial capital maintenance, and using current costs implies physical capital maintenance. Traditional accounting uses nominal (instead of constant) dollars and historical (instead of current) costs. Such accounting has almost exclusively dominated financial reporting in the United States for at least 100 years.

The two proposed changes, which can be applied separately or jointly, address separate but related problems caused by changing prices: (1) Constant-dollar disclosures account for general changes in the purchasing power of the dollar, and (2) current-cost disclosures account for changes in specific prices. The two approaches create the following four alternatives for measuring income:

Objective 5
Incorporate changing prices into income measurement using four different methods.

	Historical Cost	Current Cost
Nominal Dollars	1 Historical cost/ nominal dollars	2 Current cost/ nominal dollars
Constant Dollars	3 Historical cost/ constant dollars	4 Current cost/ constant dollars

We use the Greystone Company situation to compare these four basic methods of income measurement. Greystone has the following comparative balance sheets at December 31 (based on historical costs in nominal dollars):

	20X1	20X2
Cash	$ 0	$10,500
Inventory, 400 and 100		
units, respectively	8,000	2,000
Total assets	$8,000	$12,500
Original paid-in capital	$8,000	$ 8,000
Retained income	—	4,500
Stockholders' equity	$8,000	$12,500

The company acquired all 400 units of inventory at $20 per unit (total of $8,000) on December 31, 20X1, and held the units until December 31, 20X2. On December 31, 20X2, 300 units were sold for $35 per unit (total of $10,500 cash). The replacement cost of the inventory at that date was $30 per unit. The government monitors price levels by calculating how much a particular collection of items, called a market basket, would cost at various points in time. Suppose the market basket cost $300 on December 31, 20X1 and $330 on December 31, 20X2. You can see that the cost rose 10%. The $30 change is 10% of the original value of $300 (($330 − $300) ÷ $300 = 10%).

For ease of reference, an index is often created, so future price levels can be expressed in terms of a base year. If we set December 31, 20X1 as the base year and set the index to 100 on that date, we can express the index value on December 31, 20X2 as 110. This is calculated by dividing the 20X2 value by the 20X1 dollar value ($330 ÷ $300 = 110). This means that a bundle of goods that cost $100 on December 31, 20X1 will cost $110 on December 31, 20X2. You could also predict that because of inflation, a bundle of goods that cost $200 in 20X1 would cost $220 in 20X2 ($200 × 110 = $220). We assume that these are the company's only transactions, and for simplicity, we ignore income taxes. Exhibit 14-6 shows Greystone's balance sheets and income statements prepared according to each of the four methods for measuring income.

HISTORICAL COST/NOMINAL DOLLARS

The first two columns of Exhibit 14-6 show financial statements prepared using the time-honored historical-cost/nominal-dollar approach (method 1). Basically, this method measures invested capital in nominal dollars. It is the most popular approach to income measurement and is the primary method in U.S. GAAP, which we have referred to as historical cost. Operating income (which equals net income in this case) is $4,500, the excess of realized revenue ($10,500 in 20X2) over the "not restated" $6,000 historical costs of assets used in obtaining that revenue. As we know, when this conventional accrual basis of accounting is used, an exchange transaction is ordinarily necessary before revenues (and resulting incomes) are recognized. Thus, no income generally appears until the asset is sold, and intervening price fluctuations are ignored.

CURRENT COST/NOMINAL DOLLARS

The second set of financial statements in Exhibit 14-6 illustrates a current-cost method that has especially strong advocates in the United Kingdom and Australia (method 2). This method uses current cost/nominal dollars. The focus is on income from continuing

Exhibit 14-6

Greystone Company

Four Major Methods to Measure Income and Capital (in Dollars)*

	Nominal Dollars**				Constant Dollars**			
	(Method 1) Historical Cost		(Method 2) Current Cost		(Method 3) Historical Cost		(Method 4) Current Cost	
Balance sheets as of								
December 31	20X1	20X2	20X1	20X2	20X1	20X2	20X1	20X2
Cash	—	10,500	—	10,500	—	10,500	—	10,500
Inventory, 400 and 100 units, respectively	8,000	2,000***	8,000	3,000†	8,800††	2,200††	8,800††	3,000†
Total assets	8,000	12,500	8,000	13,500	8,800	12,700	8,800	13,500
Original paid-in capital	8,000	8,000	8,000	8,000	8,800†††	8,800†††	8,800†††	8,800†††
Retained income (confined to income from continuing operations)		4,500		1,500		3,900		1,500
Revaluation equity (accumulated holding gains)				4,000				3,200
Total liab. & stk. eq.	8,000	12,500	8000	13,500	8,800	12,700	8,800	13,500
Income statements for 20X2								
Sales, 300 units @ $35		10,500		10,500		10,500		10,500
Cost of goods sold, 300 units		6,000***		9,000†		6,600††		9,000†
Income from continuing operations (to retained income)		4,500		1,500		3,900		1,500
Holding gains (losses)§								
On 300 units sold				3,000§§				2,400§§§
On 100 unsold units				1,000§§				800§§§
Total holding gains§ (to revaluation equity)				4,000				3,200

*Assumptions: Inventory, historical cost—$20/unit; inventory, current cost—$30/unit; beginning index—100; ending index—110.

**Nominal dollars are not restated for a general price index, whereas constant dollars are restated.

***100 × $20,
  300 × $20.

†100 × $30,   ††110/100 × $8,000,   †††110/100 × $8,000.
  300 × $30.   110/100 × $2,000,
                 110/100 × $6,000.

§Many advocates of the current-cost method favor showing these gains in a completely separate statement of holding gains instead of a part of the income statement. Others favor including some or all of these gains as a part of income for the year.

§§300 × ($30 − $20),   §§§$9,000 − [(110/100) × $6,000] = $2,400   or   300 × [30 − (110/100) × $20] = $2,400.
  100 × ($30 − $20). $3,000 − [(110/100) × $2,000] = $800   or   100 × [$30 − (110/100) × $20] = $800.

operations. This model emphasizes that operating income should be income that is "distributable" to shareholders while maintaining physical capital. That is, Greystone could pay dividends in an amount of only $1,500, leaving enough assets to allow for replacement of the inventory that has just been sold.

Critics of traditional accounting claim that the $4,500 historical-cost measure of income from continuing operations is misleading because it overstates the net amount of distributable assets. If a $4,500 dividend were paid, the company would not be able to continue operations at the same level as before. The current cost statement reports only the $1,500 profit available after replacing the inventory. The $3,000 difference between the two operating incomes ($4,500 − $1,500 = $3,000) is frequently referred to as an *inventory profit* or an *inflated profit.* Why? Because under the traditional method 1, this amount counts as profit, although it actually needs to be spent on inventory. The $3,000 can be considered an overstatement of profit because the extra inventory replacement cost is being ignored.

HOLDING GAINS AND PHYSICAL CAPITAL

The current-cost method stresses a separation between income from continuing operations, which is defined as the excess of revenue over the current costs of the assets consumed in obtaining that revenue, and holding gains (or losses), which are increases (or decreases) in the replacement costs of the assets held during the current period. The current-cost method recognizes the impact of intervening price fluctuations on a company when the values of its assets change.

Accountants differ sharply on how to account for holding gains. The "correct" accounting depends on distinctions between capital and income. That is, income cannot occur until invested capital is "recovered" or "maintained." The issue of capital versus income is concretely illustrated in Exhibit 14-6. The advocates of a physical concept of capital maintenance claim that all holding gains (both those gains related to the units sold and the gains related to the units unsold) should be excluded from income and become a part of stockholders' equity called **revaluation equity.** Why? Because holding gains represent the amount that must be reinvested to maintain physical capital at its beginning-of-the-year level. Holding gains become part of capital, not a return on capital.

revaluation equity A part of stockholders' equity that includes all holding gains that are excluded from income.

The $4,000 revaluation equity has two parts. The inventory holding gains on the 300 units that were sold contributes $3,000. This is the $10 per unit increase in value during the period times the number of units. In addition, the 100 units that have remained in inventory are now being shown at their $30 current replacement cost instead of the $20 historical cost. This $10 per unit difference represents another $1,000 of revaluation equity.

HISTORICAL COST/CONSTANT DOLLARS

Method 3 of Exhibit 14-6 shows the results of applying general index numbers to historical costs. Essentially, the income measurements in each year are restated in terms of constant dollars (which possess the same general purchasing power of the current year) instead of the nominal dollars (which possess different general purchasing powers of various years).

Because of inflation, dollars spent or received in 20X2 have a different value than do dollars spent or received in 20X1. Adding 20X1 dollars to 20X2 dollars is like adding apples and oranges. Constant-dollar accounting measures all items on the 20X2 financial statements, including the items from previous years, in 20X2 dollars to aid comparability.

Consider the objections to method 1. Deducting 6,000 in 20X1 dollars from 10,500 in 20X2 dollars to obtain $4,500 is akin to deducting 60 centimeters from 105 inches and calling the result 45 centimeters. That sort of nonsensical arithmetic can get you in trouble, but accountants have been paid well for years for performing similar arithmetic. It has worked because inflation rates have been relatively low.

Method 3, historical cost/constant dollars, shows how to remedy the foregoing objections. General indexes may be used to restate the amounts of historical-cost/nominal-dollar method 1. Examples of such indexes are the gross national product (GNP) implicit price deflator and the consumer price index (CPI) for all urban consumers. You may have noticed in the popular press continuing discussion about whether the CPI is being measured properly. This obscure issue is very important because the increases that many retirees get in their Social Security payments are tied directly to such indices. Index numbers are used to gauge the relationship between current conditions and some norm or base condition (which is assigned the index number of 100). For our purpose, a **general price** index compares the average price of a group of goods and services at one date with the average price of a similar group at another date.

general price index An index that compares the average price of a group of goods and services at one date with the average price of a similar group at another date.

A price index is an average. It does not measure the behavior of the individual component prices. Some individual prices may move in one direction, and some may move in another. For example, the general consumer price level may soar while the prices of eggs and chickens decline. During 1997, the CPI rose slightly whereas crude oil prices fell sharply. During 2000 the CPI continued to rise slowly while crude oil and natural gas prices rose very significantly.

specific price index An index used to approximate the current costs of particular assets or types of assets.

Do not confuse general indexes, which are used in constant-dollar accounting, with specific indexes. The two have entirely different purposes. Sometimes **specific price indexes** are used as a means of approximating the current costs of particular assets or types of assets. That is, companies use specialized indexes to inexpensively approximate current costs without hiring professional appraisers. For example, Inland Steel has used the engineering news record construction cost index to value most of its property, plant, and equipment for purposes of using the current-cost method.

Maintaining Invested Capital

The historical-cost/constant-dollar approach (method 3) is not a fundamental departure from historical costs. Instead it maintains that all historical costs to be matched against revenue should be restated on some constant-dollar basis so that all revenues and all expenses are expressed in dollars of the same (usually current) purchasing power. The restated figures are actually historical costs expressed in constant dollars via the use of a general price index.

The current dollar is typically employed because readers of financial statements tend to think in such terms instead of terms of old dollars with significantly different purchasing power. The original units in inventory would be updated on each year's balance sheet along with their effect on stockholders' equity. For example, the December 31, 20X1 balance sheet would be restated for comparative purposes on December 31, 20X2:

	Not Restated Cost	**Multiplier**	**Restated Cost**
Inventory	$8,000	110/100	$8,800
Original paid-in capital	8,000	110/100	8,800

To extend the illustration, suppose all the inventory was held for two full years. The general price index rose from 110 to 132 during 20X3. The December 31, 20X2 balance sheet items would be restated for comparative purposes on December 31, 20X3, using 20X3 dollars:

	Not Restated Cost **12/31/X2**	**Multiplier**	**Restated Cost** **12/31/X3**
Inventory	$8,800	132/110	$10,560*
Original paid-in capital	8,800	132/110	10,560*

*The same restated 20X3 result could be tied to 20X1, the year of acquisition:
Inventory $8,000 × 132/100 = $10,560
Original paid-in capital $8,000 × 132/100 = $10,560.

BUSINESS FIRST
Price Indices

Price indices are used to measure the changing value of a currency over time. The basic notion is to track the changing price paid for a constant item. For example, you could ask about the changing cost of a McDonald's hamburger over time and use the change as a measure of the change in the purchasing power of the dollar. These hamburgers cost $.15 40 years ago and they cost something like $1.05 in 2000. To create a price index we would set 1960 equal to 100 and calculate the value of the McDonald's price index in 2000 as $1.05 ÷ $.15 = 700. The price of a McDonald's hamburger is 7 times its price 40 years ago.

This does not measure the overall price level effectively and general price indices are aimed at overall cost. Thus, we construct a market basket of items that people buy. For example, a representative market basket for people living in the United States in 2000 would include food, clothing, lodging, medical care, transportation, taxes, and entertainment. To construct an index we would determine the proportion of an average person's costs of living represented by these items and then weight the items. If people spend half their income on food and half on lodging, and the index on food rose 20% from 100 to 120 and the index on lodging rose 12% from 100 to 112, we could calculate these persons' cost of living index as 116 (($\frac{1}{2} \times 120$) + ($\frac{1}{2} \times 112$)).

The most familiar index of this sort in the United States is probably the consumer price index (CPI). The CPI is calculated by the Bureau of Labor Statistics and is published by the federal government. Investors watch for the release of monthly updates on the CPI to assess the extent to which inflation is changing and whether inflation levels will begin to cause troubles for consumers and business people. The fact that inflation has been moderate in the United States for many years provides constancy and enables us to rely on historical cost financial statements. In countries where high levels of inflation are common, financial statements are often adjusted using techniques described in the text and contracts are often adjusted as well. You may be willing to agree to perform a task over 3 years for a specific amount of money, if you can predict what that money will buy during that time. However, in periods of high inflation or rapidly changing inflation the buyer and seller may write a contract that "indexes" the price of the contract to the changing value of the currency. Such contracts are the norm in countries with patterns of significant annual inflation.

There is one overall CPI but many subcomponents for people interested in particular issues. For example, the CPI can be calculated for urban consumers or for specific components of the shopping basket such as food. The McDonald's hamburger rose slightly more rapidly in price than the general price level. The CPI went from 29 in 1960 to 168 in 2000. The general price level in 2000 is 5.8 times its level in 1960 (168 ÷ 29 = 5.8), a slower rate of increase than the seven-fold increase we calculated for McDonald's hamburgers. The CPI is set as 1982–1984 = 100.

The restated amount is just that—a restatement of original cost in terms of current (20X3) dollars. It is not a gain in any sense. Therefore, this approach should not be confused with "current-cost" accounting. Using this approach, if the specific current cost of the inventory goes up or down but the average price level remains unchanged, the restated cost also remains unchanged. Just as a ruler can be 12 inches or 30.5 centimeters, the inventory can be $8,000 in 20X1 dollars or $10,560 in 20X3 dollars.

The restated historical-cost approach fits with the concept of maintaining the general purchasing power of the invested capital in total instead of maintaining "specific invested capital" item by item. You could think of it as a financial concept of capital maintenance expressed in constant dollars.

CURRENT COST/CONSTANT DOLLARS

Method 4 of Exhibit 14-6 shows the results of applying general index numbers together with current costs. As the footnotes of the exhibit explain in more detail, the nominal gains reported under method 2 are adjusted so that only gains in constant dollars are reported. For example, suppose you buy 100 units on December 31, 20X1 for $2,000 cash. If the current replacement cost of your inventory at December 31, 20X2 is $3,000 but the general price index has risen from 100 to 110, your nominal gain is $1,000, but your "real" gain in constant dollars in 20X2 is only $800: the $3,000 current cost minus the restated historical cost of $2,000 × 1.10 = $2,200.

Suppose the 100 units are held throughout 20X3 while the general price index rises from 110 to 132. The replacement cost rises from $30 to $34, a nominal holding gain for 20X3 of $4 × 100 = $400. However, the current-cost/constant-dollar approach (method 4) would report a real holding loss in 20X3:

	December 31		
	20X1	*20X2*	*20X3*
Original cost restated for changes in the price level	$2,000	$2,200	$2,640
Current cost	2,000	3,000	3,400
Increase in current cost		1,000*	400*
Increase due to price level		200†	440†
Holding gain (loss)		$ 800	$ (40)

*3,000 − 2,000 = 1,000, and 3,400 − 3,000 = 400.
†2,200 − 2,000 = 200 and 2,640 − 2,200 = 440.

Many accountants disagree on the relative merits of using historical-cost approaches versus using current-cost approaches to income measurement. However, most accountants agree that using constant dollars would be an improvement if for no other reason than improved comparability.

BUSINESS FIRST
The Case of Daimler Benz

Daimler Benz, the prominent German conglomerate, manufactures the Mercedes automobile and does significant business in many other industries. It recently acquired Chrysler, formerly the third largest of the U.S. automobile manufacturers. However, early in the 1990s Daimler had already made an entry into the United States capital markets by being the first German company to seek to list its securities on U.S. exchanges. Daimler had a long record of consistent earnings under German accounting. Many analysts felt that German accounting was fairly conservative. German accounting called for reserves and expense recognition in such a way as to reduce earnings below what they might have been for the same company in the United States.

In filing with the U.S. SEC, Daimler had to reconcile its German GAAP financial statements to what would have been reported using U.S. GAAP. Under German

GAAP, Daimler reported earnings of DM 168 million, but under U.S. GAAP, those earnings fell to a loss of DM 949 million. The four biggest differences were as follows:

German GAAP earnings	DM 168
Differences	
Provisions, reserves and valuations	(1,615)
Pensions and other postretirement benefits	(135)
Financial instruments	(293)
Deferred taxes	920
Other (net)	6
U.S. GAAP earnings	DM(949)

Apparently, German GAAP was not so conservative, after all.

This text has focused on U.S. GAAP while mentioning practices of other countries throughout. The most basic aspects of accounting are consistent throughout the world. For example, double-entry systems, accrual accounting, and the income statement and balance sheet are used worldwide. However, as you have already seen in some cases, there are many differences in accounting around the world. Accounting practices differ among countries for a variety of reasons, such as differences in government, economic systems, culture, and traditions. We briefly discuss how accounting in the United Kingdom, France, Germany, and Japan differs from that in the United States.

Objective 6
Compare U.S. GAAP with other countries' standards.

DIFFERENCES IN TAX AND INFLATION ACCOUNTING

One major area of differences in financial reporting is the influence of the income tax law on reporting to shareholders. Methods in the United States for reporting to tax authorities differ from those used for reporting to shareholders. In contrast, tax reporting and shareholder reporting are identical in many countries. For example, France has a "plan compatible" that specifies a national uniform chart of accounts used for both tax returns and reporting to shareholders. German financial reporting is also determined primarily by tax laws. If accounting records are not kept according to strict tax laws, the German tax authorities can reject the records as a basis for taxation. Similarly, in Japan, certain principles are allowed for tax purposes only if they are also used for shareholder reporting. When such principles provide tax advantages, there is a tendency for companies to use them for reporting to shareholders. This "tax conformity" concept appears occasionally in the United States as in the LIFO/FIFO conformity rule, but it is uncommon.

In addition to the influence of the tax law, financial reporting of income taxes differs among countries. For example, in Argentina, income tax expenses are recognized in financial statements only when payments are made to the government; in contrast, most countries, including the United States, Great Britain, the Netherlands, and Canada, accrue taxes when the related income is recognized. This process of deferred tax accounting was discussed in chapter 8. Sweden and Switzerland are two other countries that do not recognize deferred taxes.

Another significant difference among countries is the extent to which financial statements account for inflation. In the 1980s, the FASB experimented with requiring supplementary disclosure of inflation-adjusted numbers, but subsequently concluded that the costs exceeded the benefits. Now no requirements for such supplementary disclosure exist in the United States. In contrast, many countries require full or partial adjustments for inflation for reporting to both shareholders and tax authorities. For example, until recently, Brazil experienced persistent double- and triple-digit inflation rates and required all statements to be adjusted for changes in the general price level in the manner described earlier in this chapter. Such inflation-adjusted statements are used for both tax and shareholder reporting. In many countries, the requirement is linked to the level of inflation being experienced.

The Netherlands has been a leader in the application of current replacement-cost measurements to financial accounts, although it has no formal requirement mandating either historical cost or replacement cost. French financial statements include a partial inflation adjustment, using replacement cost for fixed assets. Similarly, Sweden allows (but does not require) the revaluation of certain property, plant, and equipment. Mexico requires inflation adjustments, but allows either price-level adjustments or current-cost statements.

Not surprisingly, countries that have experienced the lowest inflation rates have been the slowest to recognize inflation in their accounting statements. Japan has no recognition of inflation, and Germany has recommended supplementary disclosures, but few companies have responded.

ACCOUNTING PRINCIPLES IN SELECTED COUNTRIES

The Companies' Laws in the United Kingdom provide general guidance for accounting standards, and details are specified by the Accounting Standards Board, a private-sector body sponsored by the accountancy profession. U.K. companies can use either historical-cost or current-cost accounting, or a mixture of the two. For example, BPAmoco reports both "historical cost operating profit" and "replacement cost operating profit" on its income statement. LIFO is not allowed for either tax or shareholder reporting. Research expenditures are charged to expense, but development expenses can be capitalized. Purchased goodwill is usually written off immediately.

France leads the way in standardizing accounting. Companies must use a National Uniform Chart of Accounts and abide by extensive financial reporting requirements. Accounting records are considered legal control devices more than they are considered sources of information for decision makers. Accounting methods such as LIFO and capitalization of leases are not allowed. Research and development (R&D) costs can be capitalized but must be amortized over no more than 5 years, and goodwill is amortized over 5 to 25 years. Future pension obligations are not recognized as liabilities. Two unusual reporting requirements exist in France: (1) companies must publish an annual social balance sheet relating to environmental matters and employee conditions and benefits, and (2) companies must publish comprehensive financial forecasts.

Tax law dominates financial reporting in Germany. Whatever is reported to shareholders must also be reported to tax authorities. Therefore, accounting standards are based on statutes and court decisions, and they are not necessarily directed at producing statements useful for decision making. Both FIFO and LIFO are allowed, but they must correspond to the physical flow of inventory. Goodwill must be written off over 15 years. Depreciation is based on specific tax-depreciation schedules. Cash flow statements are not required, but many companies provide them anyway. Consolidated statements are required, but exceptions are granted for many companies. Although German accounting standards have grown closer to U.S. standards since World War II, they remain significantly different.

Accounting and finance play a smaller role in Japanese companies and in the Japanese economy than they do in other industrialized countries. Accounting is dominated by the central government, especially the Ministry of Finance. There is extensive cross-ownership among Japanese firms, and banks are often heavily involved with companies to whom they lend money. Debt capital is used much more than is equity capital. Because large creditors can obtain extensive information easily, there is less need for public financial disclosure to capital market participants such as individual investors. Japan almost reveres historical-cost accounting. Current-cost data cannot be given even as supplementary information. Consolidated statements are required of more companies, as the primary disclosure. Goodwill is based on the difference between purchase price and book value (not fair market value) of net assets acquired. Goodwill, R&D expenditures, and many other intangible assets must be written off over 5 years or less. Few leases are capitalized, and pension obligations are not recognized as liabilities.

In general, Japanese accounting standards are very conservative. One study showed that the average net income for a Japanese firm is 58% below the amount that would be reported using U.S. accounting standards. This is one of the reasons that price–earnings (P-E) ratios of Japanese firms have historically far exceeded those of U.S. firms.

This section has presented only a sample of the differences in international accounting standards. Until recently, few people were very concerned about these differences. However, the growing globalization of business is creating much current interest in common, worldwide standards. There are too many cultural, social, and political differences among countries to expect complete worldwide standardization of financial reporting in the near future. In fact, complete standardization could be harmful, because it could mask true cultural and economic differences among countries. However, the trend is clear. The International Federation of Accountants (IFAC) is leading the way toward more standardization of accounting measurement and reporting practices throughout the world.

THE INTERNATIONAL ACCOUNTING STANDARDS BOARD

The International Accounting Standards Board (IASB) is an independent, private sector body of 14 members, formed in 2001 to harmonize the accounting principles that companies throughout the world use for financial reporting. The IASB follows a predecessor organization formed in 1973 through an agreement made by professional accountancy bodies from Australia, Canada, France, Germany, Japan, Mexico, the Netherlands, the United Kingdom and Ireland, and the United States of America.

Objective 7
Discuss the role of the International Accounting Standards Board (IASB) in setting standards.

For international accounting standards (IAS) to be widely used, they must be accepted by securities regulators in many countries. A breakthrough in gaining such acceptance came in 2000 when the International Organization of Securities Commissions (IOSCO) and the Council of European Economic and Finance Ministers (ECOFIN) endorsed the standards. IOSCO represents 158 organizations that represent securities regulators in most countries of the world, including the SEC in the United States, while ECOFIN represents the countries of the European Union. Acceptance of a core set of international accounting standards to be used globally by all companies seems to be just around the corner.

International accounting standards (IAS) should help to increase the international flow of capital. People and organizations in every country seek opportunities to invest in companies worldwide. Companies also seek capital in global markets to fuel their expansion and growth. Information prepared in an understandable way makes such investments easier for everyone to evaluate and enhances comparisons of one investment to another.

International acceptance has been good. Many countries accept financial statements prepared under IAS, including Australia, Belgium, France, Germany, Japan, United Kingdom, and the United States. Nevertheless, this "acceptance" is often conditional. For example, Australia allows IAS reporting only for non-Australian companies. This type of restriction is common. The United States takes this a step further. It also requires non-U.S. companies to reconcile their IAS results to totals that would have been reported under U.S. GAAP.

Some countries do not allow IAS reporting for their publicly traded companies, including Brazil and Mexico, both of which require reporting under their national GAAP. More common is a requirement that local companies report under local GAAP and non-national companies report using the GAAP of their home country.

How different are IASC standards from those of the U.S. GAAP emphasized in this book? Not very. The standards are easily recognized by those familiar with U.S. practice, although the standards do differ in some important details. However, most of the differences can be relatively easily understood. For example, inventory accounting must use lower-of-cost-or-market method (LCM) under both sets of standards. However, while IASC standards permit use of LIFO, it must be accompanied by disclosure of LCM FIFO, weighted-average, or current-cost results. IASC standards also give companies permission to provide supplemental disclosures about changing prices.

FOREIGN-CURRENCY ISSUES

Today, companies conduct business in various countries and so must learn to do business using different currencies. Two problems arise. One problem is accounting for day-to-day transactions that occur in foreign currencies. Another problem is consolidating a subsidiary that exists in another country and does its own accounting in the currency of that country.

foreign-currency exchange rates The number of units of one currency that can be exchanged for one unit of another currency.

These issues are important because of fluctuating **foreign-currency exchange rates.** The foreign-currency exchange rate specifies how many units of one currency are required to obtain one unit of another currency. Recently, the conversion rate of Japanese yen into U.S. dollars has been approximately .0094. This means that 1 yen buys .94 cents. The relation could instead be expressed as the conversion rate of U.S. dollars into Japanese yen, which would be ¥106. One U.S. dollar buys 106 Japanese yen. If conversion rates were constant, no accounting problems would arise, but the rates often change significantly. Forty years ago, the conversion rate of dollars into yen was ¥360. In the spring of 1991, it was around ¥138, and in the spring of 1995, around ¥90. From 1995 to 2000, the yen fluctuated in value falling as low as ¥145.

ACCOUNTING FOR TRANSACTIONS IN FOREIGN CURRENCIES

If a U.S. firm exports an automobile to Japan for $10,000, the sale is often on credit and denominated in yen. The customer owes ¥1,060,000 (because the conversion rate at the time of the sale was ¥106). The U.S. firm records the sale in dollars, and the receivable would be $10,000 on its books. After 1 month, the Japanese buyer remits ¥1,060,000 to the U.S. seller. Suppose the yen has fallen (or weakened) against the dollar, and the new exchange rate is ¥110. When the yen is converted to dollars, the seller ends up with only $9,636 (¥1,060,000 ÷ ¥110). The transaction has given rise to a loss for the U.S. seller of $364.00, which would be recorded as follows:

Cash	. . . .	$9,636
Loss on currency fluctuation	. . . .	364
Accounts receivable	. . . .	$10,000.00

If the currency exchange rate moved in the other direction it would give rise to a gain. Many companies use sophisticated financial transactions to eliminate the effect of currency fluctuations, but these hedging transactions and their accounting are covered in more advanced courses.

CONSOLIDATING INTERNATIONAL STATEMENTS

The previous section dealt with a company in one country doing business with a company in another country. A more complex problem arises in an international parent–subsidiary relationship. Suppose a U.S. company (parent) owns a Japanese company (subsidiary, or sub) doing business in Japan in yen. At the end of the year the parent must consolidate the sub's financial data with its own and create a single set of statements. What exchange rate should be used?

GAAP requires that different exchange rates be used for different elements of the financial statements. Assets and liabilities of the sub are translated at the year-end exchange rate. The common stock account is translated at the historical rate existing when the sub was created. The average exchange rate during the year is used to account for the transactions in the income statement. These translated net income figures annually increase the retained earnings of the parent. Over time, the parent's retained earnings reflect yen translations of annual incomes at different exchange rates. The problem is apparent. If the assets of the sub equal its liabilities plus its owners' equity denominated in yen, and different rates are used to translate assets, liabilities, and equity, then the consolidated balance sheet expressed in U.S. dollars is forced out of balance. To bring it back in balance a translation adjustment is created, which is reported as part of stockholders' equity. Details of computing this **translation adjustment** are beyond the scope of this text.

translation adjustment An account in stockholders' equity that arises when a foreign subsidiary is consolidated.

The stockholders' equity sections of most multinational firms include foreign currency translation adjustments that are included in the retained earnings element— comprehensive income. The composition of comprehensive income is often disclosed in the footnotes. The title and amount of the translation adjustment and total stockholders' equity for some international companies follow (in millions):

Company	Account Name	Amount	Total SE
ExxonMobil	Cumulative foreign exchange translation adjustment	($2,300)	$63,466
Eli Lilly	Foreign currency translation	(376)	5,013
McDonald's	Foreign currency translation adjustment	(887)	9,639

SUMMARY PROBLEMS FOR YOUR REVIEW

PROBLEM ONE

In 1970, a parcel of land (parcel 1) was purchased for $1,200. An identical parcel (parcel 2) was purchased today for $3,600. The general-price-level index has risen from 100 in 1970 to 300 now. Fill in the blanks in the following table:

Parcel	(1) Historical Cost Measured in 1970 Purchasing Power	(2) Historical Cost Measured in Current Purchasing Power	(3) Historical Cost as Originally Measured
1	_____	_____	_____
2	_____	_____	_____
Total	======	======	======

1. Compare the figures in the three columns. Which total presents a nonsense result. Why?
2. Does the write-up of parcel 1 in column 2 result in a gain? Why?
3. Assume that these parcels are the only assets of the business. There are no liabilities. Prepare a balance sheet for each of the three columns.

SOLUTION TO PROBLEM ONE

Parcel	(1) Historical Cost Measured in 1970 Purchasing Power	(2) Historical Cost Measured in Current Purchasing Power	(3) Historical Cost as Originally Measured
1	$1,200	$3,600	$1,200
2	1,200	3,600	3,600
Total	$2,400	$7,200	$4,800

1. The addition in column 3 produces a nonsense result. In contrast, the other sums are the results of applying a standard unit of measure. The computations in columns 1 and 2 are illustrations of a restatement of historical cost in terms of a common dollar, a standard unit of measure. Such computations have frequently been called adjustments for changes in the general price level. Whether the restatement is made using the 1970 dollar or the current dollar is a matter of

personal preference. After all, columns 1 and 2 yield equivalent results. Restatement in terms of the current dollar (column 2) is most popular because the current dollar has more meaning than does the old dollar to the reader of the financial statements.

2. The mere restatement of identical assets in terms of different but equivalent measuring units cannot be regarded as a gain. Expressing parcel 1 as $1,200 in column 1 and $3,600 in column 2 is like expressing parcel 1 in terms of, for example, either 1,200 square yards or $9 \times 1,200 = 10,800$ square feet. Surely, the "write-up" from 1,200 square yards to 10,800 square feet is not a gain. It is merely another way of measuring the same asset. That is basically what general-price-level accounting is all about. It says you cannot measure one plot of land in square yards and another in square feet and add them together before converting to some common measure. Unfortunately, column 3 fails to perform such a conversion before adding the two parcels together; hence the total is meaningless.

3. The only items on the balance sheets would be:

	(1)	(2)	(3)
Land	$2,400	$7,200	$4,800
Paid-in capital	$2,400	$7,200	$4,800

Note that (1) is expressed in 1970 dollars, (2) is in current dollars, and (3) is a mixture of 1970 and current dollars.

Note that the construction of this problem forces current cost and constant dollar equivalence. The general price index rose by a factor of 3 from an index value of 100 to 300 whereas the specific price of the land rose by exactly the same amount from $1,200 to $3,600.

PROBLEM TWO

Reexamine Exhibit 14-6, p. 628. Suppose the replacement cost at December 31, 20X2 had been $25 instead of $30. Suppose also that the general price index had been 120 instead of 110. All other facts are unchanged. Use four columns to prepare balance sheets as of December 31, 20X2 (only) and income statements for 20X2 under the four concepts shown in Exhibit 14-6.

SOLUTION TO PROBLEM TWO

The solution is in Exhibit 14-7. In particular, compare methods 2 and 4. The current cost of inventory items has risen 25% during a period when the general level has risen 20%.

Note too that the historical-cost/constant-dollar concept restates the old historical-cost amounts in 20X2 dollars instead of 20X1 dollars by multiplying the old dollars by 120/100.

Highlights to Remember

1. **Describe the FASB's conceptual framework.** Accountants have sought a conceptual framework for years, but financial accounting standards are still largely set on a piecemeal basis. The FASB is in charge of setting standards and determining accounting practice. This is no easy task because the FASB must not only

Exhibit 14-7

Solution Exhibit for Summary Problem Two

	Nominal Dollars		Constant Dollars	
	(Method 1) Historical Cost*	*(Method 2)* Current Cost	*(Method 3)* Historical Cost	*(Method 4)* Current Cost
Balance Sheets, December 31, 20X2				
Cash	10,500	10,500	10,500	10,500
Inventory, 100 units	2,000	2,500**	2,400†	2,500**
Total assets	12,500	13,000	12,900	13,000
Original paid-in capital	8,000	8,000	9,600††	9,600††
Retained income (confined to income from continuing operations)	4,500	3,000	3,300	3,000
Revaluation equity (accumulated holding gains)	—	2,000	—	400
Total stockholders' equity	12,500	13,000	12,900	13,000
Income statements for 20X2				
Sales, 300 units @ $35	10,500	10,500	10,500	10,500
Cost of goods sold, 300 units	6,000	7,500**	7,200†	7,500**
Income from continuing operations	4,500	3,000	3,300	3,000
Holding gains (losses)				
On 300 units sold		1,500†††		300§
On 100 unsold units		500†††		100§
Total holding gains		2,000		400

*Numbers are the same as in exhibit 14-6 except replacement cost and the price index and related calculations.

**100 × $25	†120/100 × $2,000	††120/100 × $8,000.	†††300 × ($25 − $20)
300 × $25.	120/100 × $6,000.		100 × ($25 − 20).

§$7,500 − [(120/100) × 6,000] = $300
$2,500 − [(120/100) × 2,000] = $100.

choose the best possible practices but also get companies to comply with the standards. The FASB is responsible only for U.S. accounting standards.

2. **Identify the qualities that make information valuable.** A number of characteristics increase the value of information, including relevance, consistency, reliability, and comparability. The most important of these are (1) relevance, which means the information has the ability to alter a decision, and (2) reliability, which means the information is a faithful representation of reality. Reliability includes the concepts of verifiability, neutrality, and validity.

3. **Explain how accounting differences could produce differing income for similar companies.** GAAP in the United States allows managers and accountants to choose a company's exact accounting policies. The choice made influences the pattern of earnings the company reports. In periods of rising prices, for example, LIFO yields lower net income than FIFO. For a growing firm, accelerated depreciation yields lower net income than that of straight-line depreciation. Publicly held companies must publish a statement of their accounting policies as a part of their annual financial reports. This allows analysts and others to interpret the effects of accounting choices on the income levels reported.

4. **Differentiate between financial capital and physical capital.** The concept of financial capital leads us to compare one period with the next based on the dollar value of assets in place without regard to changes in the purchasing power of the

dollar from period to period. Maintaining financial capital from year to year means continuing a stable level of financial investment. Physical capital refers to the productive assets in place including inventory, plant, and equipment. If prices are rising, it takes more financial capital over time to maintain a given level of physical capital.

5. **Incorporate changing prices into income measurement using four different methods.** The matching of historical costs with revenue is the generally accepted means of measuring net income. However, in times of changing prices, this may overstate the economic income of the firm because net income includes an element of "inventory gain." Two approaches are common in attempts to moderate this problem. Some critics suggest using general price indices to adjust all historical costs so that all expenses are measured in current dollars of the same purchasing power. Such adjustments do not represent a departure from historical cost. A more fundamental change is to base net income computations on some version of current or replacement costs. Proponents of current-cost accounting claim that such a measure is a better gauge of the distinctions between income (the return on capital) and capital maintenance (the return of capital). Current-cost accounting is an explicit adaptation of a concept of physical capital maintenance. The fourth approach to this problem combines the constant-dollar and current-cost approaches.

6. **Compare U.S. GAAP with other countries' standards.** Accounting standards vary from country to country and probably will for years to come. Common differences include several issues discussed in this chapter, including accounting for price level changes and for foreign currency fluctuations. Some differences originate in the economic and social histories of various countries. Countries in the Anglo tradition often have different practices than countries from the Spanish tradition. Similarly, the practices in Japan are a melding of traditional practices moderated by the infusion of some Anglo practices following the Second World War. Some of the differences are passionately defended on both sides based on what is "right." Other differences stem from different emphases, for example, a focus on investors in a market economy or on the needs of lenders and government officials in a more controlled economy.

7. **Discuss the role of the International Accounting Standards Board (IASB) in setting standards.** The IASB is an independent body established in 2001 to create harmony in accounting practices and a single GAAP that can be used worldwide. The IASB continues the substantial progress of its predecessor and many countries now allow companies trading publicly on their exchanges to report financial results using international accounting standards (IAS). Others require modifications to IAS. For example, the United States requires that IAS results be reconciled to the results that would have been reported under U.S. GAAP. Progress toward harmony of accounting standards will certainly continue.

Accounting Vocabulary

constant dollars, p. 626
current cost, p. 626
financial capital maintenance, p. 625
foreign currency exchange rate, p. 636
general price index, p. 630
historical cost, p. 626

inflation, p. 626
neutrality, p. 621
nominal dollars, p. 626
physical capital maintenance, p. 625
relevance, p. 619
reliability, p. 619

representational faithfulness, p. 621
revaluation equity, p. 629
specific price index, p. 630
translation adjustment, p. 636
validity, p. 621
verifiability, p. 621

Assignment Material

QUESTIONS

14-1 "A conceptual framework is too theoretical to be of practical value." Do you agree? Explain.

14-2 What are the major objectives of financial reporting as chosen by the FASB?

14-3 "Now that the FASB has a conceptual framework, accounting policy making is simply a matter of mechanically applying the framework to issues that arise." Do you agree? Explain.

14-4 "Accounting policy making is a political endeavor." Do you agree? Explain.

14-5 What is the fundamental cost-benefit test in accounting policy making?

14-6 Name three types of costs of producing accounting information.

14-7 "It is better to be roughly right than precisely wrong." Interpret this statement in light of the qualitative characteristics of accounting.

14-8 "The ability of a dozen independent accountants to apply the same measurement methods and obtain the same result is an example of validity." Do you agree? Explain.

14-9 "Neutrality underscores a fundamental approach that should be taken by the FASB." Describe the approach.

14-10 "Timing of expense recognition is not important. The important thing is that all expenses eventually be recognized on the income statement." Do you agree? Explain.

14-11 What is a statement of accounting policies?

14-12 Distinguish between the physical and the financial concepts of maintenance of invested capital.

14-13 "The FASB no longer requires reporting of inflation-adjusted data in annual reports. Therefore, there is no reason to study inflation-adjusted financial statements." Do you agree? Explain.

14-14 "The choice among accounting measures income is often expressed as either historical-cost accounting or general-price-level accounting or current-cost accounting." Do you agree? Explain.

14-15 What is the common meaning of current cost?

14-16 Explain how net income is measured under the current-cost approach.

14-17 "All holding gains should be excluded from income." What is the major logic behind this statement?

14-18 Explain what a general price index represents.

14-19 Distinguish between general indexes and specific indexes.

14-20 "Specific indexes are used in nominal-dollar accounting but not in constant-dollar accounting." Do you agree? Explain.

14-21 "Accounting policies differ so much from country to country that accountants trained in one country have difficulty practicing in another, even if there is no language barrier." Do you agree? Explain.

14-22 How have high inflation rates influenced accounting policies in many countries?

14-23 Do you expect common, worldwide accounting standards within the next decade? Explain.

COGNITIVE EXERCISES

14-24 Taxes and Inventory Profits
The United States uses cost-based accounting for tax purposes. Corporate leaders are complaining that this causes firms to pay taxes on phantom profits (or inventory profits) and they believe that inventories should be indexed or that current replacement cost should be used for calculating cost of goods sold for tax purposes. Would you support this argument?

14-25 Inventory Economics
Which is the more supportable inventory method from an economic perspective, FIFO or LIFO?

14-26 Depreciation Economics
Which is more supportable from an economic perspective, SL or DDB?

14-27 Managing Money in Inflationary Times
Most people in the United States seem to think that inflation is under control at the turn of the millennium, on the order of 3% or so. Suppose you had a very different belief and expected inflation to resurface in 2003 and 2004. In 2002, you face a decision about whether to call (repay) some 9% callable bonds that are due in 2010 and possibly need to borrow again in 3 years. The alternative is to accumulate excess cash over the next several years and invest it until it is needed in 2005. What would you recommend? Why?

EXERCISES

14-28 Statements of Financial Accounting Concepts

By using your own words, describe the basic contents of Statements of Financial Accounting Concepts Numbers 1, 2, 3, and 5. Use only one sentence for each statement. Make each sentence as informative as possible.

14-29 Costs and Benefits of Information

The FASB requires companies to include a liability for postretirement benefits on their balance sheets. Postretirement benefits are items such as health insurance that are provided to retired employees. Many companies argued against such a requirement. They maintained that the costs would exceed the benefits.

Required

1. Discuss the potential costs and benefits of mandatory reporting of a liability for postretirement benefits on companies' balance sheets.
2. Assess the relevance and reliability of measuring and reporting such a liability.

14-30 Characteristics of Information

International Paper Company shows the following under long-term assets in its balance sheet for 2000 ($ in millions):

Forestlands	$5,966

A footnote described the forestlands as 12 million acres in the United States, 1.5 million acres in Brazil, and 820,000 acres in New Zealand that are "stated at cost, less cost of timber harvested." The average cost of the timberlands is $417 per acre. Suppose the current market price is estimated to be between $600 and $1,000 per acre, providing a best estimate of total market value of $800 × 14.32 million = $11,456 million.

Required

1. Which measure, the $5,966 million or $11,456 million, is more relevant? What characteristics make it relevant?
2. Which measure is more reliable? What characteristics make it reliable?
3. If you were an investor considering the purchase of common stock in International Paper, which measure would be most valuable to you? Explain.

14-31 Effect of Inventory and Depreciation Methods on Income

Langdon Building Supply began business on January 2, 20X1, with a cash investment by shareholders of $100,000. Management immediately purchased inventory for $60,000 and a machine for $40,000. The machine has a useful life of 4 years and no salvage value.

The inventory was sold during 20X1 for $110,000, and it was replaced at a cost of $70,000. Ignore taxes.

Required

1. Compute operating income assuming Langdon uses FIFO and straight-line depreciation.
2. Compute operating income assuming Langdon uses LIFO and double-declining-balance (DDB) depreciation.
3. Compare the answers in requirements 1 and 2. Does the choice of accounting method make a difference? Explain.

14-32 Effects of Transactions on Financial Statements

For each of the following numbered items, select the lettered transaction that indicates its effect on the corporation's financial statements. If a transaction has more than one effect, list all applicable letters. Assume that the total current assets exceed the total current liabilities both before and after every transaction described.

NUMBERED TRANSACTIONS

1. Purchase of inventory on open account.
2. Payment of trade account payable.

3. Sale on account at a gross profit.
4. Collection of account receivable.
5. Issue of new shares in a three-for-one split of common stock.
6. Sale for cash of a factory building at a selling price that substantially exceeds the book value.
7. The destruction of a building by fire. Insurance proceeds, collected immediately, slightly exceed book value.
8. The appropriation of retained earnings as a reserve for contingencies.
9. Issuance of additional common shares as a stock dividend.

LETTERED EFFECTS

a. Increases working capital.
b. Decreases working capital.
c. Increases current ratio.
d. Decreases current ratio.
e. Increases the book value per share of common stock.
f. Decreases the book value per share of common stock.
g. Increases total retained earnings.
h. Decreases total retained earnings.
i. Increases total stockholders' equity.
j. Decreases total stockholders' equity.
k. None of the above.

14-33 Financial and Physical Capital Maintenance

Natalie's Neighborhood Grocery began business on January 2, 20X8, with a cash investment of $140,000, which was used to immediately purchase inventory. One-half of the inventory was sold for $120,000 during January and was not replaced before the end of the month. The cost to replace the inventory would have been $90,000 on January 31.

1. Using the financial capital maintenance concept, compute operating income for January. **Required**
2. Using the physical capital maintenance concept, compute income for January.

14-34 Holding Gains

Suquamish Cedar Mill had cedar logs that were purchased for $40,000 on March 1, 20X8. During March, Congress passed a law severely restricting the cutting of cedar trees, so the replacement cost of the logs jumped to $60,000. On March 31, half of the logs were sold for $34,000.

Compute the holding gain on the logs for the month of March under (a) the historical-cost/nominal-dollar method and (b) the current-cost/nominal-dollar method. **Required**

14-35 Inventory in Constant Dollars

On December 31, 20X1, Hannon Company bought inventory for $18,000. During 20X2, half of the inventory was sold, and on December 31, 20X2, the inventory that was sold was replaced at a cost of $11,000. The price index was 110 on 12/31/X1 and 121 on 12/31/X2.

Compute the inventory reported on the balance sheets of 12/31/X1 and 12/31/X2 assuming that **Required** Hannon uses (a) the historical-cost/nominal-dollar method of accounting and FIFO and (b) the historical-cost/constant-dollar method of accounting.

14-36 Meaning of General Index Applications and Choice of Base Year

Alamo County Hospital acquired land in mid-1980 for $5 million. In mid-2000, it acquired a substantially identical parcel of land for $8 million. The general-price-level index annual averages were 2000, 210.0; 1990, 100.0; and 1980, 60.0.

1. In four columns, show the computations of the total cost of the two parcels of land **Required** expressed in (a) costs as traditionally recorded, (b) dollars of 2000 purchasing power, (c) 1990 purchasing power, and (d) 1980 purchasing power.
2. Explain the meaning of the figures that you computed in requirement 1.

PROBLEMS

14-37 Revenue Recognition and Percentage-of-Completion

Van Danken Company contracted to build a large river bridge for the city of Amsterdam. The board of directors is about to meet to decide whether to adopt the completed-contract or the percentage-of-completion method of accounting. The percentage-of-completion method recognizes income based on incurred costs to date, divided by these known costs plus the estimated future costs to complete the contract. It computes an applicable percentage as follows:

$$\text{Percentage of completion} = \frac{\text{Costs incurred to date}}{\left(\begin{array}{c}\text{Cost incurred} \\ \text{to date}\end{array}\right) + \left(\begin{array}{c}\text{Estimated additional} \\ \text{costs to compute}\end{array}\right)}$$

The percentage is applied to the total contract price to determine the recognized revenue for the period.

Van Danken began business on January 1, 20X8. Construction activity for the year ended December 31, 20X8, revealed [Netherlands guilders (NG) in millions]:

Total contract price	NG 88
Billings through December 31, 20X8	35
Cash collections	28
Contract costs incurred	45
Estimated additional costs to complete the contract	15

Any work remaining to be done is expected to be completed in 20X9. Ignore selling and other expenses as well as income taxes.

Required

Prepare a schedule computing the amount of revenue and income that would be reported for 20X8 under:

a. The completed-contract method.

b. The percentage-of-completion method (based on estimated costs).

14-38 Recognition Criteria

Fortune reported on a Supreme Court decision related to accrual accounting. The Internal Revenue Service (IRS) and several casinos disagreed on when to recognize revenue and expenses for progressive slot machines. These slot machines have no limit to the payoff. They pay a lucky winner the money others have put into the machine since the last payoff (less the house takeout, of course). The longer since the last win, the larger the jackpot. Progressive slots pay off on an average every four and one-half months.

Suppose that on December 31, 20X5, Harrah's Casino had a progressive slot machine that had not paid off recently. In fact, $900,000 had been placed in the machine since its last payoff on February 13, 20X5. Assume that the house's takeout is 5%.

The IRS regarded the $900,000 as revenue but allowed no expense until a payoff occurred. The casinos argued that an expense equal to 95% of the revenue will eventually be incurred, and accrual accounting would require recognition of the expense at the same time as the revenue is recorded.

Required

1. How much revenue should Harrah's recognize in 20X5 from the machine? Explain fully.
2. How much expense should Harrah's recognize in 20X5 from the machine? Explain fully.
3. The IRS argued that no expense should be recognized until a payoff to the winner had been made. What do you suppose was the basis for their argument?
4. If the IRS won, how would the tax return report these events in 20X6 if the machine paid off after an additional $200,000 was wagered?
5. Suppose you are a gambler who uses accrual accounting. How would you account for $1,000 placed into the progressive slot machine described earlier? Is this consistent with your answers to requirements 1 and 2? Why or why not?

14-39 Nature of Capital, Income, Revenue

(M. Wolfson, adapted) Here is a letter written by the financial vice president of Acurex Corporation, a manufacturer of energy, environmental, and agricultural equipment:

Dear Professor:

We are engaged in a somewhat unusual government contract with the Department of Energy as a demonstration, or "showcase," program. We are designing and constructing a fuel delivery system for industrial boilers in which we will cost-share 35% of the total cost with the government. In return, we are awarded immediate title to all the equipment involved, including the government's 65% portion.

It seems to me that there is some real logic in reflecting the government's gift of 65% of total cost in current earnings, subject only to a test of net realizable value. I'd appreciate your thoughts.

Sincerely,

The company's net income the previous year was $1,007,000.

Required

Suppose the cost of the fuel delivery system is $1.2 million. This consists of about $600,000 in "hard assets" (equipment, etc.) and about $600,000 in designing costs. Via journal entries, show at least two ways in which the government contract could be reflected in Acurex's books, assuming the costs are all incurred prior to the end of the year. What is the effect of your two ways on the year's pretax income?

14-40 Japanese Annual Reports

Ishikawajima-Harima Heavy Industries Company, Limited is a large Japanese manufacturing firm with sales of nearly ¥1 trillion (equivalent to more than $10 billion at current exchange rates). Ishikawajima-Harima Heavy Industries maintains its records and prepares its financial statements in accordance with generally accepted accounting principles and practices in Japan. Selected parts of the company's 2000 footnotes on "Significant Accounting Policies" follow:

Basis of Financial Statements

The accompanying consolidated financial statements of Ishikawajima-Harima Heavy Industries Co., Ltd. and consolidated subsidiaries have been prepared from the financial statements filed with the Minister of Finance as required by the Japanese Securities and Exchange Law in accordance with accounting principles and practices generally accepted in Japan.

Sales Recognition

Net sales from contracts are recognized at the time the contracts are completed.

Allowance for Doubtful Receivables

The allowance for doubtful receivables is provided by adding amounts estimated individually for uncollectible receivables to the maximum amount permitted by the Corporate Income Tax Law of Japan.

Inventories

Finished goods, work in process and contracts in process are stated principally at identified cost, and raw materials and supplies are stated principally at the lower of cost or market, cost being determined by the moving-average method.

Marketable Securities and Investment Securities

Marketable securities and investment securities, other than common stocks listed on stock exchanges, are stated principally at cost as determined by the moving-average method. Common stocks listed on stock exchanges are stated principally at the lower of cost or market, cost being determined by the moving-average method.

Property, Plant and Equipment and Intangible Assets

Depreciation of plant and equipment is computed principally by the declining-balance method based on the estimated useful lives of the assets as stipulated by the Corporate Income Tax Law and regulations of Japan.

Income Taxes

The Companies record income taxes currently payable based upon taxable income determined in accordance with the applicable tax laws, and do not recognize deferred income taxes arising from timing differences in the recognition of income and expenses for financial statement and income tax purposes.

Leases

Noncancellable lease transactions of the Companies are accounted for as operating leases regardless of whether such leases are classified as operating leases or finance leases, except that lease agreements which stipulate the transfer of ownership of the leased property to the lessee are accounted for as finance leases.

Required Identify the accounting policies used by Ishikawajima-Harima Heavy Industries that would not generally be used in the United States.

14-41 Effects of Various Accounting Methods on Net Income

You are the manager of Tsumagari Company, a profitable new company that has high potential growth. It is nearing the end of your first year in business and you must make some decisions concerning accounting policies for financial reporting to stockholders. Your controller and your CPA have gathered the following information (all figures in millions except tax rate):

Revenue	¥40,000
Beginning inventory	0
Purchases	24,000
Ending inventory—if LIFO is used	6,000
Ending inventory—if FIFO is used	8,000
Depreciation—if straight-line is used	1,500
Depreciation—if double-declining-balance is used	3,000
Store-opening costs	4,000
Store-opening costs (amortized amount)	800
Other expenses	2,000
Income tax rate	40%
Common shares outstanding	2,000

DDB depreciation is to be used for tax purposes regardless of the method chosen for reporting to stockholders. For all other items, assume that the same method is used for tax purposes and for financial reporting purposes.

Required
1. Prepare a columnar income statement such as in panel B of Exhibit 14-4 on p. 623. In column 1, show the results using LIFO, DDB depreciation, and direct write-off of store-opening costs. Show earnings per share as well as net income. In successive columns, show the separate effects on net income and earnings per share of substituting the alternative methods: column 2, FIFO inventory; column 3, straight-line depreciation; and column 4, amortization of store-opening costs. In column 5, show the total results of choosing all the alternative methods (columns 2 through 4). Note that in columns 2 through 4 only single changes from column 1 should be shown; that is, column 3 does not show the effects of columns 2 and 3 together, and column 4 does not show the effects of columns 2, 3, and 4 together.
2. As the manager, which accounting policies would you adopt? Why?

14-42 Effects of Various Accounting Methods on Income

General Electric had the following data in its 1999 annual report (in millions of dollars except for EPS):

Total revenues	$111,630
Cost of goods and services sold	45,958
Depreciation	4,908
Other expenses (summarized here)	45,187
Total expenses	96,053
Earnings before income taxes	15,577
Provision for income taxes	4,860
Net earnings	$ 10,717
Net earnings per share (in dollars)	$ 3.22

Inventories on December 31, 1999, were $7,007 million and on December 31, 1998, were $6,049 million. If FIFO had been used instead of LIFO, the FIFO inventories would have been higher by $1,209 million at December 31, 1999, and $744 million at December 31, 1998.

The company stated that most depreciation is computed by accelerated methods, primarily sum-of-the-years'-digits. General Electric's marginal 1999 income tax rate was 35%.

Required

Suppose General Electric had used straight-line depreciation for reporting to shareholders, resulting in depreciation and amortization expense of $3,908 million instead of $4,908 million in 1999. Also, suppose the company had used FIFO instead of LIFO. Recast all the preceding data for 1999, including the amount earned per common share. Show supporting computations.

14-43 Four Versions of Income and Capital

Asia Pacific Trading Company has the following comparative balance sheets as of December 31 (based on historical costs in nominal dollars):

	20X4	20X5
Cash	$ —	$4,500
Inventory, 100 and 40 units, respectively	5,000	2,000
Total assets	$5,000	$6,500
Paid-in capital	$5,000	$5,000
Retained income	—	1,500
Stockholders' equity	$5,000	$6,500

The general-price-level index was 140 on December 31, 20X4, and 161 on December 31, 20X5. The company had acquired 100 units of inventory on December 31, 20X4, for $50 each and held them throughout 20X5. On December 31, 20X5, 60 units were sold, each for $75 cash. The replacement cost of the inventory at that date was $60 per unit. Assume that these are the only transactions. Ignore income taxes.

Required

Use four sets of columns to prepare comparative balance sheets as of December 31, 20X4 and 20X5, and income statements for 20X5 using (1) historical cost/nominal dollars, (2) current cost/nominal dollars, (3) historical cost/constant dollars, and (4) current cost/constant dollars.

14-44 Concepts of Income

Suppose you are in the business of investing in land and holding it for resale. On December 31, 20X7, a parcel of land had a historical cost of $200,000 and a current value (measured via use of a specific price index) of $600,000; the general price level had doubled since the land was acquired. Suppose also that the land was sold a year later on December 31, 20X8 for $720,000. The general price level rose by 5% during 20X8.

Required

1. Prepare a tabulation of income from continuing operations and holding gains for 20X8, using the four methods illustrated in Exhibit 14-6.
2. In your own words, explain the meaning of the results, giving special attention to what income represents.

14-45 LIFO and Current Costs

Inman Company began business on December 31, 20X1, when it acquired 100 units of inventory for $40 per unit. It held the inventory until December 31, 20X2, when it acquired 100 more units for $60 per unit and sold 150 units for $80 each. Assume that these are the company's only transactions, and ignore income taxes.

Required

1. Compute operating income using the historical-cost/nominal-dollars method and the FIFO inventory method.
2. Compute operating income using the historical-cost/nominal-dollars method and the LIFO inventory method.

3. Compute operating income using the current-cost/nominal-dollars method.
4. Explain the differences in operating income in requirements 1, 2, and 3.
5. Does historical-cost/nominal-dollars operating income using LIFO give results that approximate current-cost operating income? Why or why not?

14-46 Reporting on Changing Prices

Transamerica Corporation, a large diversified company, reported operating income of $151 million on sales of $5,399 million. After adjusting for changes in specific prices (current costs), operating income was $107 million. Three other amounts reported were related to holding gains ($ in millions):

Effect of increase in general price level	$64
Excess of increase in specific prices over increase in general price level	23
Increase in specific prices of inventories and property and equipment held during the year	$87

Required

1. Identify the holding gain under the current-cost/nominal-dollars method.
2. Identify the holding gain under the current-cost/constant-dollars method.
3. Explain why the holding gain in requirement 1 differs from that in requirement 2.

14-47 Depreciation and Price-Level Adjustments

Shreck Legal Services purchased a computer with networking services for $400,000. This computer has an expected life of 4 years and an expected residual value of zero. Straight-line depreciation is used. The general price index is 100 at the date of acquisition; it increases 20 points annually the next 3 years. The results follow:

Year	Price-Level Index	Historical-Cost/ Nominal-Dollars Depreciation	Multiplier	Historical-Cost/ Constant-Dollars Depreciation as Recorded
1	100	$100,000	$\frac{100}{100}$	$100,000
2	120	100,000	$\frac{120}{100}$	120,000
3	140	100,000	$\frac{140}{100}$	140,000
4	160	100,000	$\frac{160}{100}$	160,000
		$400,000		

Required

1. Convert the figures in the last column so that they are expressed in terms of fourth-year dollars. For example, the $120,000 second-year dollars would have to be restated by multiplying by 160/120.
2. Suppose in requirement 1 that revenue easily exceeds expenses for each year and that cash equal to the annual depreciation charge was invested in a non-interest-bearing cash account. If amounts equal to the unadjusted depreciation charge were invested each year, would sufficient cash have accumulated to equal the general purchasing power of $400,000 invested in the asset 4 years ago? If not, what is the extent of the total financial deficiency measured in terms of fourth-year dollars?
3. Suppose in requirement 2 that amounts equal to the constant-dollar depreciation for each year were used. What is the extent of the total financial deficiency?

4. Suppose in requirement 3 that the amounts were invested each year in assets that increased in value at the same rate as the increase in the general price level. What is the extent of the total financial deficiency?

14-48 Revenues in Constant Dollars

Alcoa, the aluminum company, reported the following total revenues ($ in millions):

	1999	1996	1994	1992
Historical basis	$16,323	$13,061	$ 9,904	$9,492
In average 1999 dollars	?	13,868	11,133	?

The average consumer price index was 166.6 in 1999, 156.9 in 1996, and 140.3 in 1992.

Compute the following:

Required

1. Total revenues for 1992 in average 1999 dollars. Round to the nearest million.
2. Total revenues for 1999 in average 1999 dollars. Round to the nearest million.
3. Percentage increase in revenues between 1992 and 1999 on a historical-cost basis.
4. Percentage increase in revenues between 1992 and 1999 in average 1999 dollars.
5. Average consumer price index for 1994.

14-49 Effects of General versus Specific Price Changes

The following data are from the annual reports of Gannett Company, owner of 120 newspapers; and Goodyear Tire and Rubber Company:

(In Millions)	Gannett	Goodyear
Increase in specific prices of assets held during the year*	$45.8	$ (4.7)
Less effect of increase in general price level	37.5	252.0
Excess of increase in specific prices over increase in the general price level†	$ 8.3	$(256.7)

*Holding gain using current-cost/nominal-dollars method.
†Holding gain using current-cost/constant-dollars method.

Required

Compare and contrast the relationship between changes in the general price level and changes in the prices of the specific assets of each of the companies.

14-50 Ethics and Business Practices

Ethical considerations affect business decisions of many companies. Consider the brief descriptions of how ethics affects each of the following three companies:

> A. Baxter International, Inc.— This health-care company adopted an aggressive environmental and ethical policy in 1990. The company met its goal of having all its facilities in the United States achieve "state of the art" environmental status by 1993. Between 1990 and 1993 it reduced emissions of 17 toxic substances by 94%. In three years it reduced hazardous waste by 49%. In 1993 the company increased the percentage of women in its workforce from 46% to 52% and the percentage of minorities from 28% to 29%. This was just the beginning. In 1999 Baxter was one of the first companies to publish a Sustainability Report. Baxter characterizes sustainable development as "development that meets the needs of the present without compromising the ability of future generations to meet their own needs." The executive summary of their report continues "Sustainability challenges Baxter and other organizations to satisfy a 'triple bottom line' of environmental quality, social responsibility and economic prosperity." (See the Baxter International Web site.)

B.   SC Johnson Wax—Since its founding in 1896, Johnson Wax has been committed to putting something back into the community. As described in Management Accounting, the company contributes a minimum of 5% of pretax profits to charities. It also promotes employee involvement in community service activities. Two areas where Johnson Wax has been especially supportive are education and the environment. From elementary schools through colleges and universities, a variety of programs improve the quality of education and thereby the quality of Johnson Wax's workforce. Consistent with this commitment, in 2000, Johnson Wax endowed a chair at the Johnson School at Cornell University in support of sustainable enterprise. For the environment, Johnson Wax first makes its operations as environmentally friendly as possible. In addition, the company supports numerous outside environmental activities that improve the communities in which it operates. Underlying the philanthropic vision is the belief that Johnson Wax will eventually benefit from contributing to worthy social causes. Because Johnson Wax is a private company, they are not as accountable to security markets as are public firms and they do not suffer from the wide swings in share price associated with short-term fluctuations in profitability.

C.   Calvert Social Investment Fund—Calvert is one of the largest of U.S. mutual funds devoted to "ethical investing." In 2000, Calvert directed more than $6 billion into companies who "make a significant contribution to society through their products and services and through the way they do business." Calvert focuses on environmental issues, labor relations, product safety, and human rights as issues that distinguish ethical companies. Thus, Calvert might avoid companies that damage the environment, make weapons, sell tobacco or alcohol, discriminate in employment, or use animals in testing products. Each fund has its own standards.

Required

Describe how ethical issues might affect the decisions of each company. Do you believe these firms view ethical behavior as primarily a cost or a benefit? List some specific costs for each company and some potential benefits.

14-51   Comprehensive Review: Reconstruct Transactions

Childrobics, Inc. was incorporated in New York State. The company owned and operated indoor recreation facilities for children and their families in the New York metropolitan area. The company prepared financial statements on February 28, for the period since incorporation. Slightly revised versions of the company's balance sheet and statement of cash flows are in Exhibit 14-8. Footnotes pointed out that, in exchange for a note payable of $250,000, the creditors supplied $146,000 in cash and $104,000 in property and equipment.

Required

Compute amounts to replace each of the question marks in Childrobic's balance sheet.

ANNUAL REPORT CASE

14-52   Cisco Annual Report

Examine the income statement of Cisco and footnotes 2 and 4 with regard to depreciation and amortization.

Required

1. Suppose that Cisco had extended the period over which depreciation and amortization are calculated to be twice the time period they actually used in 2000. Compute the revised income before income taxes for the year ended July 29, 2000.

2. How could you estimate the amount of depreciation and amortization that Cisco would report in 2001 assuming that existing lives used in 2000 were retained and sales and other activity in 2001 was at the same level as 2000.

3. How could you estimate the amount of depreciation and amortization that Cisco would report in 2001 assuming that existing lives used in 2000 were doubled as suggested in requirement 1.

14-53   Financial Statement Research

Select any company. Be sure that amounts are available for both beginning and ending inventory and depreciation and amortization for the most recent fiscal year.

Exhibit 14-8

Childrobics, Inc.

BALANCE SHEET FEBRUARY 28

Assets

Current assets

Cash		$?

Property and equipment

At cost	$?	
Accumulated depreciation	?	
Net		?
Other assets		25,300
Total assets		$?

Liabilities and stockholders' equity

Current liabilities

Accounts payable and accrued expenses	$?	
Deferred revenue	?	
Note payable	?	
Total current liabilities		$?

Stockholders' equity

Common stock—$.01 par value, 25,000,000 shares authorized, 975,000 shares issued and outstanding	?	
Additional paid-in capital	?	
Retained earnings	?	
Total stockholders' equity		?
Total liabilities and stockholders' equity		$?

STATEMENT OF CASH FLOWS FOR THE PERIOD ENDED FEBRUARY 28

Operating activities

Net income	$ 2,516	
Adjustment to reconcile net income to net cash provided by operating activities		
Depreciation	10,947	
Change in assets and liabilities		
Accounts payable and accrued expenses	59,871	
Deferred revenue—customer deposits	13,450	
Net cash—operating activities		$ 86,784

Investing activities

Purchases of property and equipment	$(192,583)	
Expenditures for other assets	(25,300)	
Net cash—investing activities		(217,883)

Financing activities

Loans	$ 146,000	
Common stock	25,000	
Net cash—financing activities		171,000
Net increase in cash		39,901
Cash—beginning of period		0
Cash—end of period		$ 39,901

Suppose your company changed its inventory and depreciation methods beginning with the start of the most recent fiscal year. Prior-year results were not restated. Therefore, balance sheet amounts at the beginning of the year were unaffected by the changes.

The changes caused the ending inventory value to be 10% lower than the amount shown in the statements and the annual depreciation and amortization to be 20% greater. (Such changes might result from a switch from FIFO to LIFO and from straight-line to accelerated depreciation. However, assume the given changes regardless of the inventory and depreciation methods currently being used.)

Required

1. Compute the revised income before taxes for the most recent fiscal year.
2. Determine the company's effective tax rate. Then compute the revised provision for income taxes, net income, and net income per share for your company in the most recent fiscal year.
3. Assume that your company reports the same cost of sales on its tax and shareholder income statements. However, the tax statement includes the new depreciation and amortization, that is, it is 20% higher on the tax statement than on shareholder reports. Now assume that the inventory method is changed as specified in the problem for both tax and shareholder reports, while the depreciation and amortization is changed in the shareholder report only. This makes tax and shareholder reports identical. What would be the effect of the change in tax reporting on the income taxes shown on the income statement for shareholder reporting? What would be the effect on the taxes currently payable and the deferred taxes on the reports to shareholders?
4. Assume that the changes in requirement 3 are allowed for both tax and shareholder reporting. What factors would affect your company's decision about whether to make the changes?

COLLABORATIVE LEARNING EXERCISE

14-54 Understanding Financial Statements

Form groups of four to six students each. Each group should pick a company that has a corporate or division headquarters in the local or regional area. Contact a top financial person at the company to arrange an interview. The person should have some responsibility for the company's financial statements. The person might be the chief financial officer (CFO), controller, accounting manager, or even treasurer at some companies.

Before the interview, the group should meet and study the company's annual report, focusing on the financial statements. Prepare at least six questions about the financial statements.

The questions can form the basis of the interview. The goal, besides answering the questions, is to determine how the company decides on the accounting policies and practices to be used in the financial statements. For example, how does the company decide on an inventory policy (FIFO, LIFO, or weighted average), depreciation method (especially if it uses something other than straight line), amount of allowance for uncollectible accounts, and classification of short-term investments (trading securities, available-for-sale securities, and held-to-maturity securities)?

Each group should be prepared to share with the entire class what it learns about accounting policy choices at the company it selected.

INTERNET EXERCISE

www.prenhall.com/horngren

14-55 McDonald's

Go to www.mcdonalds.com to locate McDonald's home page. Select *Investor* and then *Annual Reports*. Answer the following questions about McDonald's:

1. Read McDonald's *Summary of Significant Accounting Policies* following the financial statements. What is McDonald's policy for advertising costs? Why do you think the company handles costs this way? The policy is an example of which accounting principle?
2. Locate McDonald's discussion of *Nonoperating (Income) Expense*. Would these miscellaneous expenses be considered "material"? How can you tell? Is the impact of fluctuating foreign currencies on cash considered material? How do you know? (*Hint:* Look in the *Summary of Significant Accounting Policies.*)

3. McDonald's uses accrual-basis accounting to prepare its financial statements. What evidence do you see of this?

4. McDonald's operates restaurants in over 118 countries. In addition to translating foreign currencies to the U.S. dollar for reporting, what else does the company do to its reported figures that helps readers better interpret the financial information? (*Hint:* Take a look at the data reported for *Systemwide Sales.*)

5. What is McDonald's accounting policy for foreign currency? How does this affect McDonald's financial reports?

APPENDIX A*

2000 ANNUAL REPORT

DISCOVER ALL THAT'S
POSSIBLE ON THE **INTERNET**

CISCO SYSTEMS, INC.

These are the financial review portions of the 2000 annual report of Cisco Systems, reprinted by Prentice Hall for educational purposes.

SELECTED FINANCIAL DATA[1]

Five Years Ended July 29, 2000 (In millions, except per-share amounts)

	July 29, 2000	July 31, 1999	July 25, 1998	July 26, 1997	July 28, 1996
Net sales	**$18,928**	$12,173	$8,489	$6,452	$4,101
Net income	**$ 2,668**[2]	$ 2,023[3]	$1,331[4]	$1,047[5]	$ 915[6]
Net income per common share—basic	**$ 0.39**	$ 0.30	$ 0.21	$ 0.17	$ 0.16
Net income per common share—diluted	**$ 0.36**[2]	$ 0.29[3]	$ 0.20[4]	$ 0.17[5]	$ 0.15[6]
Shares used in per-common share calculation—basic*	**6,917**	6,646	6,312	6,007	5,758
Shares used in per-common share calculation—diluted*	**7,438**	7,062	6,658	6,287	6,008
Total assets	**$32,870**	$14,893	$9,043	$5,504	$3,647

* Reflects the two-for-one stock split effective March 2000.

[1] All historical financial information has been restated to reflect the acquisitions that were accounted for as poolings of interests (see Note 3 to the Consolidated Financial Statements).

[2] Net income and net income per common share include in-process research and development expenses of $1.37 billion, amortization of goodwill and purchased intangible assets of $291 million, acquisition-related costs of $62 million, payroll tax on stock option exercises of $51 million, and net gains realized on minority investments of $531 million. Pro forma net income and diluted net income per common share, excluding these items net of tax of $0, were $3.91 billion and $0.53, respectively.

[3] Net income and net income per common share include in-process research and development expenses of $471 million, amortization of goodwill and purchased intangible assets of $61 million, and acquisition-related costs of $16 million. Pro forma net income and diluted net income per common share, excluding these items net of tax benefits of $54 million, were $2.52 billion and $0.36, respectively.

[4] Net income and net income per common share include in-process research and development expenses of $594 million, amortization of goodwill and purchased intangible assets of $23 million, and net gains realized on minority investments of $5 million. Pro forma net income and diluted net income per common share, excluding these items net of tax benefits of $67 million, were $1.88 billion and $0.28, respectively.

[5] Net income and net income per common share include in-process research and development expenses of $508 million, amortization of goodwill and purchased intangible assets of $11 million, and net gains realized on minority investments of $152 million. Pro forma net income and diluted net income per common share, excluding these items net of tax benefits of $7 million, were $1.42 billion and $0.23, respectively.

[6] Net income and net income per common share include amortization of goodwill and purchased intangible assets of $14 million. Pro forma net income and diluted net income per common share, excluding this item net of a tax benefit of $2 million, were $927 million and $0.15, respectively.

MANAGEMENT'S DISCUSSION AND ANALYSIS OF FINANCIAL CONDITION AND RESULTS OF OPERATIONS

All historical financial information has been restated to reflect the acquisitions that were accounted for as poolings of interests (see Note 3 to the Consolidated Financial Statements).

FORWARD-LOOKING STATEMENTS

Certain statements contained in this Annual Report, including, without limitation, statements containing the words "believes," "anticipates," "estimates," "expects," "projections," and words of similar import, constitute "forward-looking statements." You should not place undue reliance on these forward-looking statements. Our actual results could differ materially from those anticipated in these forward-looking statements for many reasons, including risks faced by us described in the Risk Factors sections, among others, included in the documents we file with the Securities and Exchange Commission ("SEC"), including our most recent reports on Form 10-K, Form 8-K, and Form 10-Q, and amendments thereto.

COMPARISON OF FISCAL 2000 AND FISCAL 1999

Net sales in fiscal 2000 were $18.93 billion, compared with $12.17 billion in fiscal 1999, an increase of 55.5%. The increase in net sales was primarily a result of increased unit sales of switch, router, and access products; growth in the sales of add-on boards that provide increased functionality; optical transport products; and maintenance, service, and support sales (see Note 12 to the Consolidated Financial Statements).

We manage our business on four geographic theaters: the Americas; Europe, the Middle East, and Africa ("EMEA"); Asia Pacific; and Japan. Summarized financial information by theater for fiscal 2000 and 1999 is presented in the following table (in millions):

	Amount		Percentage of Net Sales	
Years Ended	July 29, 2000	July 31, 1999	July 29, 2000	July 31, 1999
Net sales:				
Americas	$12,924	$ 8,088	68.3%	66.4%
EMEA	4,770	3,216	25.2	26.4
Asia Pacific	1,705	825	9.0	6.8
Japan	935	566	4.9	4.7
Sales adjustments	(1,406)	(522)	(7.4)	(4.3)
Total	$18,928	$12,173	100.0%	100.0%

The revenue growth for each theater was primarily driven by market demand and the deployment of Internet technologies and business solutions.

Gross margin in fiscal 2000 was 64.4%, compared with 65.0% in fiscal 1999. The following table shows the standard margins for each theater:

Years Ended	July 29, 2000	July 31, 1999
Standard margins:		
Americas	72.8%	72.2%
EMEA	75.1%	74.0%
Asia Pacific	71.3%	71.0%
Japan	78.8%	77.0%

The net sales and standard margins by geographic theater differ from the amounts recognized under generally accepted accounting principles because we do not allocate certain sales adjustments, production overhead, and manufacturing variances and other related costs to the theaters. Sales adjustments relate to revenue deferrals and reserves, credit memos, returns, and other timing differences.

Standard margins increased for all geographic theaters as compared with fiscal 1999. The decrease in the overall gross margin was primarily due to shifts in product mix, introduction of new products, which generally have lower margins when first released, higher production-related costs, the continued pricing pressure seen from competitors in certain product areas, and the above-mentioned sales adjustments, which were not included in the standard margins.

We expect gross margin may be adversely affected by increases in material or labor costs, heightened price competition, increasing levels of services, higher inventory balances, introduction of new products for new high-growth markets, and changes in channels of distribution or in the mix of products sold. We believe gross margin may additionally be impacted due to constraints relating to certain component shortages that currently exist in the supply chain. We may also experience a lower gross margin as the product mix for access and optical product volume grows.

We have recently introduced several new products, with additional new products scheduled to be released in the future. Increase in demand would result in increased manufacturing capacity, which in turn would result in higher inventory balances. In addition, our vendor base is capacity-constrained, and this could result in increased cost pressure on certain components. If product or related warranty costs associated with these new products are greater than we have experienced, gross margin may be adversely affected. Our gross margin may also be impacted by geographic mix, as well as the mix of configurations within each product group. We continue to expand into third-party or indirect-distribution channels, which generally results in a lower gross margin. In addition, increasing third-party and indirect-distribution channels generally results in greater difficulty in forecasting the mix of our product, and to a certain degree, the timing of orders from our customers. Downward pressures on our gross margin may be further impacted by other factors, such as increased percentage of revenue from service provider markets, which may have lower margins or an increase in product costs, which could adversely affect our future operating results.

Research and development ("R&D") expenses in fiscal 2000 were $2.70 billion, compared with $1.66 billion in fiscal 1999, an increase of 62.6%. R&D expenses, as a percentage of net sales, increased to 14.3% in fiscal 2000, compared with 13.7% in fiscal 1999. The increase reflected our ongoing R&D efforts in a wide variety of areas such as data, voice, and video integration, digital subscriber line ("DSL") technologies, cable modem technology, wireless access, dial access, enterprise switching, optical transport, security, network management, and high-end routing technologies, among others. A significant portion of the increase was due to the addition of new personnel, partly through acquisitions, as well as higher expenditures on prototypes and depreciation on additional lab equipment. We also continued to purchase technology in order to bring a broad range of products to the market in a timely fashion. If we believe that we are unable to enter a particular market in a timely manner with internally developed products, we may license technology from other businesses or acquire businesses as an alternative to internal R&D. All of our R&D costs are expensed as incurred. We currently expect that R&D expenses will continue to increase in absolute dollars as we continue to invest in technology to address potential market opportunities.

Sales and marketing expenses in fiscal 2000 were $3.95 billion, compared with $2.46 billion in fiscal 1999, an increase of 60.1%. Sales and marketing expenses, as a percentage of net sales, increased to 20.8% in fiscal 2000, compared with 20.2% in fiscal 1999. The increase was principally due to an increase in the size of our direct sales force and related commissions, additional marketing and advertising investments associated with the introduction of new products, the expansion of distribution channels, and general corporate branding. The increase also reflected our efforts to invest in certain key areas, such as expansion of our end-to-end networking strategy and service provider coverage, in order to be positioned to take advantage of future market opportunities. We currently expect that sales and marketing expenses will continue to increase in absolute dollars.

General and administrative ("G&A") expenses in fiscal 2000 were $633 million, compared with $381 million in fiscal 1999, an increase of 66.1%. G&A expenses, as a percentage of net sales, increased to 3.3% in fiscal 2000, compared with 3.1% in fiscal 1999. G&A expenses for fiscal 2000 and 1999 included acquisition-related costs of approximately $62 million and $16 million, respectively. Excluding the acquisition-related costs, the increase in G&A expenses was primarily related to the addition of new personnel and investments in infrastructure. We intend to keep G&A expenses relatively constant as a percentage of net sales; however, this depends on the level of acquisition activity and our growth, among other factors.

Amortization of goodwill and purchased intangible assets included in operating expenses was $291 million in fiscal 2000, compared with $61 million in fiscal 1999. Amortization of goodwill and purchased intangible assets primarily relates to various purchase acquisitions (see Note 3 and Note 4 to the Consolidated Financial Statements). Amortization of goodwill and purchased intangible assets will continue to increase as we acquire companies and technologies.

MANAGEMENT'S DISCUSSION AND ANALYSIS OF FINANCIAL CONDITION AND RESULTS OF OPERATIONS

The amount expensed to in-process research and development ("in-process R&D") arose from the purchase acquisitions completed in fiscal 2000 (see Note 3 to the Consolidated Financial Statements).

The fair values of the existing products and patents, as well as the technology currently under development, were determined using the income approach, which discounts expected future cash flows to present value. The discount rates used in the present value calculations were typically derived from a weighted-average cost of capital analysis and venture capital surveys, adjusted upward to reflect additional risks inherent in the development life cycle. These risk factors have increased the overall discount rate for acquisitions in the current year. We consider the pricing model for products related to these acquisitions to be standard within the high-technology communications equipment industry. However, we do not expect to achieve a material amount of expense reductions or synergies as a result of integrating the acquired in-process technology. Therefore, the valuation assumptions do not include significant anticipated cost savings.

The development of these technologies remains a significant risk due to the remaining effort to achieve technical viability, rapidly changing customer markets, uncertain standards for new products, and significant competitive threats from numerous companies. The nature of the efforts to develop the acquired technologies into commercially viable products consists principally of planning, designing, and testing activities necessary to determine that the products can meet market expectations, including functionality and technical requirements. Failure to bring these products to market in a timely manner could result in a loss of market share or a lost opportunity to capitalize on emerging markets and could have a material adverse impact on our business and operating results.

The following table summarizes the significant assumptions underlying the valuations for our significant purchase acquisitions completed in fiscal 2000 and 1999 (in millions, except percentages):

Acquired Company	Acquisition Assumptions	
	Estimated Cost to Complete Technology at Time of Acquisition	Risk-Adjusted Discount Rate for In-Process R&D
FISCAL 2000		
Monterey Networks, Inc.	$ 4	30.0%
The optical systems business of Pirelli S.p.A.	$ 5	20.0%
Aironet Wireless Communications, Inc.	$ 3	23.5%
Atlantech Technologies	$ 6	37.5%
JetCell, Inc.	$ 7	30.5%
PentaCom, Ltd.	$13	30.0%
Qeyton Systems	$ 6	35.0%
FISCAL 1999		
Summa Four, Inc.	$ 5	25.0%
Clarity Wireless, Inc.	$42	32.0%
Selsius Systems, Inc.	$15	31.0%
PipeLinks, Inc.	$ 5	31.0%
Amteva Technologies	$ 4	35.0%

Regarding our purchase acquisitions completed in fiscal 2000 and 1999, actual results to date have been consistent, in all material respects, with our assumptions at the time of the acquisitions. The assumptions primarily consist of an expected completion date for the in-process projects, estimated costs to complete the projects, and revenue and expense projections once the products have entered the market. Shipment volumes of products from the above-acquired technologies are not material to our overall financial results at the present time. Therefore, it is difficult to determine the accuracy of overall revenue projections early in the technology or product life cycle. Failure to achieve the expected levels of revenue and net income from these products will negatively impact the return on investment expected at the time that the acquisitions were completed and potentially result in impairment of any other assets related to the development activities.

Interest and other income, net, was $577 million in fiscal 2000, compared with $330 million in fiscal 1999. The increase was primarily due to interest income related to the general increase in cash and investments, which was generated from our operations. Net gains realized on minority investments were $531 million in fiscal 2000. The net gains realized on minority investments were not material in fiscal 1999.

Our pro forma effective tax rate for fiscal 2000 was 30.0%. The actual effective tax rate was 38.6%, which included the impact of nondeductible in-process R&D and acquisition-related costs. Our future effective tax rates could be adversely affected if earnings are lower than anticipated in countries where we have lower effective rates or by unfavorable changes in tax laws and regulations. Additionally, we have provided a valuation allowance on certain of our deferred tax assets because of uncertainty regarding their realizability due to expectation of future employee stock option exercises (see Note 11 to the Consolidated Financial Statements).

COMPARISON OF FISCAL 1999 AND FISCAL 1998

Net sales in fiscal 1999 were $12.17 billion, compared with $8.49 billion in fiscal 1998, an increase of 43.4%. The increase in net sales was primarily a result of increased unit sales of LAN switching products, access servers, high-performance WAN switching and routing products, and maintenance service contracts.

Gross margin in fiscal 1999 was 65.0%, compared with 65.6% in fiscal 1998. The decrease in the overall gross margin was primarily due to our continued shift in revenue mix toward our lower-margin products and the continued pricing pressure seen from competitors in certain product areas.

R&D expenses in fiscal 1999 were $1.66 billion, compared with $1.05 billion in fiscal 1998, an increase of 58.1%. R&D expenses, as a percentage of net sales, increased to 13.7% in fiscal 1999, compared with 12.4% in fiscal 1998. The increase reflected our ongoing R&D efforts in a wide variety of areas such as data, voice, and video integration, DSL technologies, cable modem technology, wireless access, dial access, enterprise switching, security, network management, and high-end routing technologies, among others. A significant portion of the increase was due to the addition of new personnel, partly through acquisitions, as well as higher expenditures on prototypes and depreciation on additional lab equipment.

Sales and marketing expenses in fiscal 1999 were $2.46 billion, compared with $1.58 billion in fiscal 1998, an increase of 56.1%. Sales and marketing expenses, as a percentage of net sales, increased to 20.2% in fiscal 1999, compared with 18.6% in fiscal 1998. The increase was principally due to an increase in the size of our direct sales force and related commissions, television advertising campaigns to build brand awareness, additional marketing and advertising costs associated with the introduction of new products, and the expansion of distribution channels. The increase also reflected our efforts to invest in certain key areas, such as expansion of our end-to-end networking strategy and service provider coverage, in order to be positioned to take advantage of future market opportunities.

G&A expenses in fiscal 1999 were $381 million, compared with $247 million in fiscal 1998, an increase of 54.3%. G&A expenses, as a percentage of net sales, increased to 3.1% in fiscal 1999, compared with 2.9% in fiscal 1998. The increase was primarily related to additional personnel and acquisition-related costs of $16 million.

Amortization of goodwill and purchased intangible assets included in operating expenses was $61 million in fiscal 1999, compared with $23 million in fiscal 1998. Amortization of goodwill and purchased intangible assets increased as we acquired companies and technologies.

Interest and other income, net, in fiscal 1999 was $330 million, compared with $196 million in fiscal 1998. Interest income rose primarily as a result of additional investment income on our increased investment balances.

MANAGEMENT'S DISCUSSION AND ANALYSIS OF FINANCIAL CONDITION AND RESULTS OF OPERATIONS

RECENT ACCOUNTING PRONOUNCEMENTS

In June 1998, the Financial Accounting Standards Board ("FASB") issued Statement of Financial Accounting Standards No. 133, "Accounting for Derivative Instruments and Hedging Activities" ("SFAS 133"). SFAS 133, as amended, establishes accounting and reporting standards for derivative instruments and hedging activities. It requires an entity to recognize all derivatives as either assets or liabilities on the balance sheet and measure those instruments at fair value. We do not expect the initial adoption of SFAS 133 to have a material effect on our operations or financial position. We are required to adopt SFAS 133 in the first quarter of fiscal 2001.

In September 1999, the FASB issued Emerging Issues Task Force Topic No. D-83, "Accounting for Payroll Taxes Associated with Stock Option Exercises" ("EITF D-83"). EITF D-83 requires that payroll tax paid on the difference between the exercise price and the fair value of acquired stock in association with an employee's exercise of stock options be recorded as operating expenses. Payroll tax on stock option exercises of $51 million was expensed in fiscal 2000.

In December 1999, the SEC issued Staff Accounting Bulletin No. 101, "Revenue Recognition in Financial Statements" ("SAB 101"). SAB 101, as amended, summarizes certain of the SEC's views in applying generally accepted accounting principles to revenue recognition in financial statements. At this time, we do not expect the adoption of SAB 101 to have a material effect on our operations or financial position; however, the SEC's final guidance for implementation has not been released to date. We are required to adopt SAB 101 in the fourth quarter of fiscal 2001.

LIQUIDITY AND CAPITAL RESOURCES

Cash and cash equivalents, short-term investments, and investments were $20.50 billion at July 29, 2000, an increase of $10.28 billion from July 31, 1999. The increase was primarily a result of $5.00 billion of net unrealized gains on publicly held investments and $7.70 billion of cash generated by operating and financing activities partially offset by investing activities, including net capital expenditures of $1.09 billion, purchases of technology licenses of $444 million, and investments in lease receivables of $535 million.

Accounts receivable increased 83.9% during fiscal 2000. Days sales outstanding in receivables increased to 37 days for fiscal 2000, from 32 days for fiscal 1999. The increase in accounts receivable and days sales outstanding was due, in part, to growth in total net sales combined with conditions in a number of markets, resulting in longer payment terms.

Inventories increased 87.2% during fiscal 2000; however, inventory turns remained constant at 7.8 times. The increase in inventory levels reflected new product introductions, continued growth in our two-tier distribution system, and increased purchases to secure the supply of certain components. Inventory management remains an area of focus as we balance the need to maintain strategic inventory levels to ensure competitive lead times with the risk of inventory obsolescence due to rapidly changing technology and customer requirements.

At July 29, 2000, we had a line of credit totaling $500 million, which expires in July 2002. There have been no borrowings under this agreement (see Note 7 to the Consolidated Financial Statements).

We have entered into several agreements to lease 448 acres of land located in San Jose, California, where our headquarters operations are established, and 759 acres of land located in Boxborough, Massachusetts; Salem, New Hampshire; Richardson, Texas; and Research Triangle Park, North Carolina, where we have expanded certain R&D and customer-support activities. In connection with these transactions, we have pledged $1.29 billion of our investments as collateral for certain obligations of the leases. We anticipate that we will occupy more leased property in the future that will require similar pledged securities; however, we do not expect the impact of this activity to be material to our liquidity position (see Note 8 to the Consolidated Financial Statements).

We believe that our current cash and cash equivalents, short-term investments, line of credit, and cash generated from operations will satisfy our expected working capital, capital expenditure, and investment requirements through at least the next 12 months.

QUANTITATIVE AND QUALITATIVE DISCLOSURES ABOUT MARKET RISK

We maintain an investment portfolio of various holdings, types, and maturities. These securities are generally classified as available for sale and, consequently, are recorded on the balance sheet at fair value with unrealized gains or losses reported as a separate component of accumulated other comprehensive income, net of tax. Part of this portfolio includes minority equity investments in several publicly traded companies, the values of which are subject to market price volatility. For example, as a result of recent market price volatility of our publicly traded equity investments, we experienced a $111 million after-tax unrealized loss during the third quarter of fiscal 2000 and a $1.83 billion after-tax unrealized gain during the fourth quarter of fiscal 2000 on these investments. We have also invested in numerous privately held companies, many of which can still be considered in the start-up or development stages. These investments are inherently risky as the market for the technologies or products they have under development are typically in the early stages and may never materialize. We could lose our entire initial investment in these companies. We also have certain real estate lease commitments with payments tied to short-term interest rates. At any time, a sharp rise in interest rates could have a material adverse impact on the fair value of our investment portfolio while increasing the costs associated with our lease commitments. Conversely, declines in interest rates could have a material impact on interest earnings for our investment portfolio. We do not currently hedge these interest rate exposures.

INVESTMENTS

The following table presents the hypothetical changes in fair values in the financial instruments held at July 29, 2000 that are sensitive to changes in interest rates. These instruments are not leveraged and are held for purposes other than trading. The modeling technique used measures the change in fair values arising from selected potential changes in interest rates. Market changes reflect immediate hypothetical parallel shifts in the yield curve of plus or minus 50 basis points ("BPS"), 100 BPS, and 150 BPS over a 12-month horizon. Beginning fair values represent the principal plus accrued interest and dividends of the interest rate-sensitive financial instruments at July 29, 2000. Ending fair values are the market principal plus accrued interest, dividends, and reinvestment income at a 12-month horizon. The following table estimates the fair value of the portfolio at a 12-month horizon (in millions):

Issuer	Valuation of Securities Given an Interest Rate Decrease of X Basis Points			Fair Value as of	Valuation of Securities Given an Interest Rate Increase of X Basis Points		
	(150 BPS)	(100 BPS)	(50 BPS)	July 29, 2000	50 BPS	100 BPS	150 BPS
U.S. government notes and bonds	$2,350	$2,329	$2,307	$2,285	$2,262	$2,240	$2,218
State, municipal, and county government notes and bonds	3,666	3,632	3,598	3,564	3,529	3,494	3,459
Corporate notes and bonds	3,296	3,266	3,235	3,204	3,173	3,141	3,110
Total	$9,312	$9,227	$9,140	$9,053	$8,964	$8,875	$8,787

A 50 BPS move in the Federal Funds Rate has occurred in nine of the last 10 years; a 100 BPS move in the Federal Funds Rate has occurred in six of the last 10 years; and a 150 BPS move in the Federal Funds Rate has occurred in four of the last 10 years.

QUANTITATIVE AND QUALITATIVE DISCLOSURES ABOUT MARKET RISK

The following analysis presents the hypothetical changes in fair values of public equity investments that are sensitive to changes in the stock market. These equity securities are held for purposes other than trading. The modeling technique used measures the hypothetical change in fair values arising from selected hypothetical changes in each stock's price. Stock price fluctuations of plus or minus 15%, plus or minus 35%, and plus or minus 50% were selected based on the probability of their occurrence. The following table estimates the fair value of the publicly traded corporate equities at a 12-month horizon (in millions):

	Valuation of Securities Given X% Decrease in Each Stock's Price			Fair Value as of	Valuation of Securities Given X% Increase in Each Stock's Price		
	(50%)	(35%)	(15%)	July 29, 2000	15%	35%	50%
Corporate equities	$3,112	$4,046	$5,291	$6,225	$7,159	$8,404	$9,337

Our equity portfolio consists of securities with characteristics that most closely match the S&P Index or companies traded on the NASDAQ National Market. The NASDAQ Composite Index has shown a 15% movement in each of the last three years and a 35% and 50% movement in at least one of the last three years.

We also have an investment in KPMG Consulting, Inc. in the principal amount of $1.05 billion of Series A Mandatorily Redeemable Convertible Preferred Stock, which carries a 6% dividend rate on the original issue price until converted to common stock. Conversion is at our option upon or after the completion of an initial public offering of KPMG Consulting, Inc. We have not included the investment in the above sensitivity analyses due to the nature of this investment.

LEASES

We are exposed to interest rate risk associated with leases on our facilities where payments are tied to the London Interbank Offered Rate ("LIBOR"). We have evaluated the hypothetical change in lease obligations held at July 29, 2000 due to changes in the LIBOR. The modeling technique used measures hypothetical changes in lease obligations arising from selected hypothetical changes in the LIBOR. The hypothetical market changes reflected immediate parallel shifts in the LIBOR curve of plus or minus 50 BPS, 100 BPS, and 150 BPS over a 12-month period. The results of this analysis were not material in comparison to our financial results.

FOREIGN EXCHANGE FORWARD AND OPTION CONTRACTS

We enter into foreign exchange forward contracts to offset the impact of currency fluctuations on certain nonfunctional currency assets and liabilities, primarily denominated in Australian, Canadian, Japanese, Korean, and several European currencies, primarily the euro and British pound. We also periodically hedge anticipated transactions with purchased currency options.

The foreign exchange forward and option contracts we enter into generally have original maturities ranging from one to three months. We do not enter into foreign exchange forward and option contracts for trading purposes. We do not expect gains or losses on these contracts to have a material impact on our financial results (see Note 8 to the Consolidated Financial Statements).

CONSOLIDATED STATEMENTS OF OPERATIONS
(In millions, except per-share amounts)

Years Ended	July 29, 2000	July 31, 1999	July 25, 1998
NET SALES	$18,928	$12,173	$8,489
Cost of sales	6,746	4,259	2,924
GROSS MARGIN	12,182	7,914	5,565
Operating expenses:			
Research and development	2,704	1,663	1,052
Sales and marketing	3,946	2,465	1,579
General and administrative	633	381	247
Amortization of goodwill and purchased intangible assets	291	61	23
In-process research and development	1,373	471	594
Total operating expenses	8,947	5,041	3,495
OPERATING INCOME	3,235	2,873	2,070
Net gains realized on minority investments	531	–	5
Interest and other income, net	577	330	196
INCOME BEFORE PROVISION FOR INCOME TAXES	4,343	3,203	2,271
Provision for income taxes	1,675	1,180	940
NET INCOME	$ 2,668	$ 2,023	$1,331
Net income per common share—basic	$ 0.39	$ 0.30	$ 0.21
Net income per common share—diluted	$ 0.36	$ 0.29	$ 0.20
Shares used in per-common share calculation—basic	6,917	6,646	6,312
Shares used in per-common share calculation—diluted	7,438	7,062	6,658

See Notes to Consolidated Financial Statements.

CONSOLIDATED BALANCE SHEETS

(In millions, except par value)

	July 29, 2000	July 31, 1999
ASSETS		
Current assets:		
Cash and cash equivalents	$ 4,234	$ 913
Short-term investments	1,291	1,189
Accounts receivable, net of allowances for doubtful accounts of $43 at 2000 and $27 at 1999	2,299	1,250
Inventories, net	1,232	658
Deferred tax assets	1,091	580
Prepaid expenses and other current assets	963	171
Total current assets	11,110	4,761
Investments	13,688	7,032
Restricted investments	1,286	1,080
Property and equipment, net	1,426	825
Goodwill and purchased intangible assets, net	4,087	460
Lease receivables	527	500
Other assets	746	235
TOTAL ASSETS	$32,870	$14,893
LIABILITIES AND SHAREHOLDERS' EQUITY		
Current liabilities:		
Accounts payable	$ 739	$ 374
Income taxes payable	233	630
Accrued compensation	1,317	679
Deferred revenue	1,386	724
Other accrued liabilities	1,521	631
Total current liabilities	5,196	3,038
Commitments and contingencies (Note 8)		
Deferred tax liabilities	1,132	–
Minority interest	45	44
Shareholders' equity:		
Preferred stock, no par value: 5 shares authorized; none issued and outstanding	–	–
Common stock and additional paid-in capital, $0.001 par value: 20,000 shares authorized; 7,138 and 6,821 shares issued and outstanding at 2000 and 1999, respectively	14,609	5,731
Retained earnings	8,358	5,782
Accumulated other comprehensive income	3,530	298
Total shareholders' equity	26,497	11,811
TOTAL LIABILITIES AND SHAREHOLDERS' EQUITY	$32,870	$14,893

See Notes to Consolidated Financial Statements.

CONSOLIDATED STATEMENTS OF CASH FLOWS

(In millions)

Years Ended	July 29, 2000	July 31, 1999	July 25, 1998
Cash flows from operating activities:			
Net income	$ 2,668	$ 2,023	$ 1,331
Adjustments to reconcile net income to net cash provided by operating activities:			
Depreciation and amortization	863	489	329
Provision for doubtful accounts	40	19	43
Provision for inventory allowances	339	151	161
Deferred income taxes	(782)	(247)	(76)
Tax benefits from employee stock option plans	2,495	837	422
Adjustment to conform fiscal year ends of pooled acquisitions	(18)	1	–
In-process research and development	1,279	379	436
Gains on minority investments	(92)	–	–
Change in operating assets and liabilities:			
Accounts receivable	(1,043)	45	(166)
Inventories	(887)	(443)	(267)
Prepaid expenses and other current assets	(249)	(101)	21
Accounts payable	286	111	32
Income taxes payable	(365)	217	155
Accrued compensation	576	285	123
Deferred revenue	662	385	156
Other accrued liabilities	369	174	165
Net cash provided by operating activities	6,141	4,325	2,865
Cash flows from investing activities:			
Purchases of short-term investments	(2,473)	(1,250)	(1,611)
Proceeds from sales and maturities of short-term investments	2,481	1,660	1,751
Purchases of investments	(14,778)	(5,632)	(3,561)
Proceeds from sales and maturities of investments	13,240	1,994	1,107
Purchases of restricted investments	(458)	(1,101)	(527)
Proceeds from sales and maturities of restricted investments	206	560	337
Acquisition of property and equipment	(1,086)	(602)	(429)
Purchases of technology licenses	(444)	(95)	–
Acquisition of businesses, net of cash and cash equivalents	24	(19)	–
Net investment in lease receivables	(535)	(310)	(171)
Other	(554)	(190)	1
Net cash used in investing activities	(4,377)	(4,985)	(3,103)
Cash flows from financing activities:			
Issuance of common stock	1,564	947	555
Other	(7)	7	(7)
Net cash provided by financing activities	1,557	954	548
Net increase in cash and cash equivalents	3,321	294	310
Cash and cash equivalents, beginning of fiscal year	913	619	309
Cash and cash equivalents, end of fiscal year	$ 4,234	$ 913	$ 619

See Notes to Consolidated Financial Statements.

CONSOLIDATED STATEMENTS OF SHAREHOLDERS' EQUITY

(In millions)

	Common Stock Number of Shares	Common Stock and Additional Paid-In Capital	Retained Earnings	Accumulated Other Comprehensive Income	Total Shareholders' Equity
BALANCE AT JULY 26, 1997	6,163	$ 1,814	$2,478	$ 40	$ 4,332
Net income	–	–	1,331	–	1,331
Change in net unrealized gains on investments	–	–	–	28	28
Translation adjustments	–	–	–	(10)	(10)
Comprehensive income	–	–	–	–	1,349
Issuance of common stock	280	555	–	–	555
Tax benefits from employee stock option plans	–	422	–	–	422
Pooling of interests acquisitions	6	12	(9)	–	3
Purchase acquisitions	42	536	–	–	536
BALANCE AT JULY 25, 1998	6,491	3,339	3,800	58	7,197
Net income	–	–	2,023	–	2,023
Change in net unrealized gains on investments	–	–	–	234	234
Translation adjustments	–	–	–	6	6
Comprehensive income	–	–	–	–	2,263
Issuance of common stock	300	947	–	–	947
Tax benefits from employee stock option plans	–	837	–	–	837
Pooling of interests acquisitions	4	38	(42)	–	(4)
Purchase acquisitions	26	570	–	–	570
Adjustment to conform fiscal year ends of pooled acquisitions	–	–	1	–	1
BALANCE AT JULY 31, 1999	6,821	5,731	5,782	298	11,811
Net income	–	–	2,668	–	2,668
Change in net unrealized gains on investments	–	–	–	3,240	3,240
Translation adjustments	–	–	–	(8)	(8)
Comprehensive income	–	–	–	–	5,900
Issuance of common stock	219	1,564	–	–	1,564
Tax benefits from employee stock option plans	–	3,077	–	–	3,077
Pooling of interests acquisitions	20	75	(74)	–	1
Purchase acquisitions	78	4,162	–	–	4,162
Adjustment to conform fiscal year ends of pooled acquisitions	–	–	(18)	–	(18)
BALANCE AT JULY 29, 2000	7,138	$14,609	$8,358	$3,530	$26,497

See Notes to Consolidated Financial Statements.

NOTES TO CONSOLIDATED FINANCIAL STATEMENTS

1. DESCRIPTION OF BUSINESS

Cisco Systems, Inc. and its subsidiaries ("Cisco" or the "Company") is the worldwide leader in networking for the Internet. Cisco hardware, software, and service offerings are used to create Internet solutions so that individuals, companies, and countries have seamless access to information—regardless of differences in time and place. Cisco solutions provide competitive advantage to our customers through more efficient and timely exchange of information, which in turn leads to cost savings, process efficiencies, and closer relationships with their customers, prospects, business partners, suppliers, and employees. These solutions form the networking foundation for companies, universities, utilities, and government agencies worldwide.

2. SUMMARY OF SIGNIFICANT ACCOUNTING POLICIES

Fiscal Year The Company's fiscal year is the 52 or 53 weeks ending on the last Saturday in July. Fiscal 2000, 1999, and 1998 were 52-week, 53-week, and 52-week fiscal years, respectively.

Principles of Consolidation The Consolidated Financial Statements include the accounts of Cisco Systems, Inc. and its subsidiaries. All significant intercompany accounts and transactions have been eliminated.

Cash and Cash Equivalents The Company considers all highly liquid investments purchased with an original or remaining maturity of less than three months at the date of purchase to be cash equivalents. Substantially all cash and cash equivalents are custodied with three major financial institutions.

Investments The Company's investments comprise U.S., state, and municipal government obligations; corporate debt securities; and public corporate equity securities. Investments with maturities of less than one year are considered short-term and are carried at fair value. All investments are primarily held in the Company's name and custodied with two major financial institutions. The specific identification method is used to determine the cost of securities disposed. At July 29, 2000 and July 31, 1999, substantially all of the Company's investments were classified as available for sale. Unrealized gains and losses on these investments are included as a separate component of shareholders' equity, net of any related tax effect.

The Company also has certain other minority investments in nonpublicly traded companies. These investments are included in other assets on the Company's balance sheet and are generally carried at cost. The Company monitors these investments for impairment and makes appropriate reductions in carrying values when necessary.

Inventories Inventories are stated at the lower of cost or market. Cost is computed using standard cost, which approximates actual cost on a first-in, first-out basis.

Restricted Investments Restricted investments consist of U.S. government obligations with maturities of more than one year. These investments are carried at fair value and are restricted as to withdrawal. Restricted investments are held in the Company's name and custodied with two major financial institutions.

Fair Value of Financial Instruments Carrying amounts of certain of the Company's financial instruments, including cash and cash equivalents, accrued compensation, and other accrued liabilities, approximate fair value because of their short maturities. The fair values of investments are determined using quoted market prices for those securities or similar financial instruments.

Concentrations Cash and cash equivalents are primarily maintained with three major financial institutions in the United States. Deposits held with banks may exceed the amount of insurance provided on such deposits. Generally, these deposits may be redeemed upon demand and, therefore, bear minimal risk.

The Company performs ongoing credit evaluations of its customers and, with the exception of certain financing transactions, does not require collateral from its customers.

The Company receives certain of its components from sole suppliers. Additionally, the Company relies on a limited number of hardware manufacturers. The inability of any supplier or manufacturer to fulfill supply requirements of the Company could materially impact future operating results.

NOTES TO CONSOLIDATED FINANCIAL STATEMENTS

Revenue Recognition The Company generally recognizes product revenue when persuasive evidence of an arrangement exists, delivery has occurred, fee is fixed or determinable, and collectibility is probable. Revenue from service obligations is deferred and generally recognized ratably over the period of the obligation. The Company makes certain sales to partners in two-tier distribution channels. These partners are generally given privileges to return a portion of inventory and participate in various cooperative marketing programs. The Company recognizes revenue to two-tier distributors based on estimates which approximate the point products have been sold by the distributors and also maintains accruals and allowances for all cooperative marketing and other programs. The Company accrues for warranty costs, sales returns, and other allowances based on its experience.

Lease Receivables Cisco provides a variety of lease financing services to its customers to build, maintain, and upgrade their networks. Lease receivables represent the principal balance remaining in sales-type and direct-financing leases under these programs. These leases typically have two to three year terms and are collateralized by a security interest in the underlying assets.

Advertising Costs The Company expenses all advertising costs as incurred.

Software Development Costs Software development costs, which are required to be capitalized pursuant to Statement of Financial Accounting Standards No. 86, "Accounting for the Costs of Computer Software to Be Sold, Leased, or Otherwise Marketed," have not been material to date.

Depreciation and Amortization Property and equipment are stated at cost less accumulated depreciation and amortization. Depreciation and amortization is computed using the straight-line method over the estimated useful lives of the assets. Estimated useful lives of 24 to 30 months are used on computer equipment and related software and production and engineering equipment and five years for office equipment, furniture, and fixtures. Depreciation and amortization of leasehold improvements is computed using the shorter of the remaining lease term or five years.

Goodwill and Purchased Intangible Assets Goodwill and purchased intangible assets are carried at cost less accumulated amortization. Amortization is computed using the straight-line method over the economic lives of the respective assets, generally three to five years.

Income Taxes Income tax expense is based on pre-tax financial accounting income. Deferred tax assets and liabilities are recognized for the expected tax consequences of temporary differences between the tax bases of assets and liabilities and their reported amounts.

Computation of Net Income per Common Share Basic net income per common share is computed using the weighted-average number of common shares outstanding during the period. Diluted net income per common share is computed using the weighted-average number of common and dilutive common equivalent shares outstanding during the period. Dilutive common equivalent shares consist of stock options. Share and per-common share data for all periods presented reflect the two-for-one stock split effective March 2000.

Foreign Currency Translation Assets and liabilities of non-U.S. subsidiaries that operate in a local currency environment are translated to U.S. dollars at exchange rates in effect at the balance sheet date with the resulting translation adjustments recorded directly to a separate component of shareholders' equity. Income and expense accounts are translated at average exchange rates during the year. Where the U.S. dollar is the functional currency, translation adjustments are recorded in income.

Derivatives The Company enters into foreign exchange forward contracts to minimize the short-term impact of foreign currency fluctuations on assets and liabilities denominated in currencies other than the functional currency of the reporting entity. All foreign exchange forward contracts are highly inversely correlated to the hedged items and are designated as, and considered effective as, hedges of the underlying assets or liabilities. Gains and losses on the contracts are included in interest and other income, net, and offset foreign exchange gains or losses from the revaluation of intercompany balances or other current assets and liabilities denominated in currencies other than the functional currency of the reporting entity. Fair values of foreign exchange forward contracts are determined using published rates. If a derivative contract terminates prior to maturity, the investment is shown at its fair value with the resulting gain or loss reflected in interest and other income, net. The Company periodically hedges anticipated transactions with purchased currency options. The premium paid is amortized over the life of the option while any intrinsic value is recognized in income during the same period as the hedged transaction.

Minority Interest Minority interest represents the preferred stockholders' proportionate share of the equity of Cisco Systems, K.K. (Japan). At July 29, 2000, the Company owned all issued and outstanding common stock amounting to 73.2% of the voting rights. Each share of preferred stock is convertible into one share of common stock at any time at the option of the holder.

Use of Estimates The preparation of financial statements and related disclosures in conformity with accounting principles generally accepted in the United States requires management to make estimates and assumptions that affect the amounts reported in the Consolidated Financial Statements and accompanying notes. Estimates are used for, but not limited to, the accounting for the allowance for doubtful accounts, inventory allowances, depreciation and amortization, sales returns, warranty costs, taxes, and contingencies. Actual results could differ from these estimates.

Impairment of Long-Lived Assets Long-lived assets and certain identifiable intangible assets to be held and used are reviewed for impairment whenever events or changes in circumstances indicate that the carrying amount of such assets may not be recoverable. Determination of recoverability is based on an estimate of undiscounted future cash flows resulting from the use of the asset and its eventual disposition. Measurement of an impairment loss for long-lived assets and certain identifiable intangible assets that management expects to hold and use are based on the fair value of the asset. Long-lived assets and certain identifiable intangible assets to be disposed of are reported at the lower of carrying amount or fair value less costs to sell.

Recent Accounting Pronouncements In June 1998, the Financial Accounting Standards Board ("FASB") issued Statement of Financial Accounting Standards No. 133, "Accounting for Derivative Instruments and Hedging Activities" ("SFAS 133"). SFAS 133, as amended, establishes accounting and reporting standards for derivative instruments and hedging activities. It requires an entity to recognize all derivatives as either assets or liabilities on the balance sheet and measure those instruments at fair value. Management does not expect the initial adoption of SFAS 133 to have a material effect on the Company's operations or financial position. The Company is required to adopt SFAS 133 in the first quarter of fiscal 2001.

In September 1999, the FASB issued Emerging Issues Task Force Topic No. D-83, "Accounting for Payroll Taxes Associated with Stock Option Exercises" ("EITF D-83"). EITF D-83 requires that payroll tax paid on the difference between the exercise price and the fair value of acquired stock in association with an employee's exercise of stock options be recorded as operating expenses. Payroll tax on stock option exercises of $51 million was expensed in fiscal 2000.

In December 1999, the Securities and Exchange Commission ("SEC") issued Staff Accounting Bulletin No. 101, "Revenue Recognition in Financial Statements" ("SAB 101"). SAB 101, as amended, summarizes certain of the SEC's views in applying generally accepted accounting principles to revenue recognition in financial statements. At this time, management does not expect the adoption of SAB 101 to have a material effect on the Company's operations or financial position; however, the SEC's final guidance for implementation has not been released to date. The Company is required to adopt SAB 101 in the fourth quarter of fiscal 2001.

Reclassifications Certain reclassifications have been made to prior year balances in order to conform to the current year presentation.

3. BUSINESS COMBINATIONS

Pooling of Interests Combinations

In fiscal 2000, the Company acquired StratumOne Communications, Inc. ("StratumOne"); TransMedia Communications, Inc. ("TransMedia"); Cerent Corporation ("Cerent"); WebLine Communications Corporation ("WebLine"); SightPath, Inc. ("SightPath"); InfoGear Technology Corporation ("InfoGear"); and ArrowPoint Communications, Inc. ("ArrowPoint"), which were accounted for as poolings of interests. All historical financial information has been restated to reflect these acquisitions. In addition, the historical financial information has been restated to reflect the acquisition of Fibex Systems ("Fibex"), which was completed in the fourth quarter of fiscal 1999 and accounted for as a pooling of interests. These transactions are summarized as follows (in millions):

Acquisition Date	Acquired Company	Shares of Cisco Stock Issued, Including Options Assumed	Fair Value of Acquisition
May 1999	Fibex	11.5	$ 314
September 1999	StratumOne	13.3	$ 435
September 1999	TransMedia	13.9	$ 407
November 1999	Cerent	200.0	$6,900
November 1999	WebLine	8.6	$ 325
May 2000	SightPath	11.4	$ 800
June 2000	InfoGear	4.7	$ 301
June 2000	ArrowPoint	90.2	$5,700

NOTES TO CONSOLIDATED FINANCIAL STATEMENTS

All of these acquired companies used a calendar year end. In order for all companies to operate on the same fiscal year, operations for the one-month period ending July 31, 1999, which were not significant to the Company, have been reflected as an adjustment to retained earnings in fiscal 2000. No significant adjustments were necessary to conform accounting policies. However, the companies' historical results have been adjusted to reflect the elimination of previously provided valuation allowances on deferred tax assets. There were no intercompany transactions requiring elimination in any period presented. The following table shows the historical results for the periods prior to the mergers of these entities (in millions):

	Nine Months Ended April 29, 2000	Years Ended July 31, 1999	Years Ended July 25, 1998
Net sales:			
Cisco	$13,147	$12,154	$8,488
Fibex	–	3	–
StratumOne	–	–	–
TransMedia	–	–	–
Cerent	35	10	–
WebLine	1	3	1
SightPath	–	–	–
InfoGear	–	–	–
ArrowPoint	25	3	–
Total	$13,208	$12,173	$8,489
Net income (loss):			
Cisco	$ 1,932	$ 2,096	$1,355
Fibex	–	(13)	(3)
StratumOne	(3)	(6)	(1)
TransMedia	(4)	(7)	–
Cerent	(15)	(31)	(9)
WebLine	(3)	(4)	(2)
SightPath	(8)	(2)	–
InfoGear	(15)	(5)	(5)
ArrowPoint	(12)	(5)	(4)
Total	$ 1,872	$ 2,023	$1,331

In fiscal 1999, the Company acquired GeoTel Communications Corporation and approximately 68 million shares of common stock were exchanged and options were assumed for a fair value of $2 billion. The transaction was accounted for as a pooling of interests and all periods presented prior to fiscal 1999 were restated.

Other Pooling of Interests Combinations Completed as of July 29, 2000

The Company has also completed a number of other pooling transactions during the three years ended July 29, 2000. The historical operations of these entities were not material to the Company's consolidated operations on either an individual or aggregate basis; therefore, prior period financial statements have not been restated for these acquisitions. These transactions are summarized as follows (in millions):

Fiscal Year	Acquired Company	Shares of Cisco Stock Issued, Including Options Assumed	Fair Value of Acquisition
1998	Precept Software, Inc.	6.0	$ 84
1999	Sentient Networks, Inc.	4.0	$131
2000	Cocom A/S	1.9	$ 66
2000	V-Bits, Inc.	2.8	$128
2000	Growth Networks, Inc.	5.6	$355
2000	Altiga Networks, Inc.	6.3	$335
2000	Compatible Systems Corporation	3.8	$232

Purchase Combinations

During the three years ended July 29, 2000, the Company completed a number of purchase acquisitions. The Consolidated Financial Statements include the operating results of each business from the date of acquisition. Pro forma results of operations have not been presented because the effects of these acquisitions were not material on either an individual or an aggregate basis.

The amounts allocated to in-process research and development ("in-process R&D") were determined through established valuation techniques in the high-technology communications equipment industry and were expensed upon acquisition because technological feasibility had not been established and no future alternative uses existed. Amounts allocated to goodwill and purchased intangible assets are amortized on a straight-line basis over periods not exceeding five years. A summary of purchase transactions is outlined as follows (in millions):

Acquired Company	Consideration	In-Process R&D Expense	Form of Consideration and Other Notes to Acquisition
FISCAL 2000			
Monterey Networks, Inc.	$ 517	$354	Common stock and options assumed; $14 in liabilities assumed; goodwill and other intangibles recorded of $154
The optical systems business of Pirelli S.p.A.	$2,018	$245	Common stock; $362 in liabilities assumed; goodwill and other intangibles recorded of $1,717
Aironet Wireless Communications, Inc.	$ 835	$243	Common stock and options assumed; $34 in liabilities assumed; goodwill and other intangibles recorded of $589
Atlantech Technologies	$ 179	$ 63	Cash of $92; common stock and options assumed; $1 in liabilities assumed; goodwill and other intangibles recorded of $140
JetCell, Inc.	$ 203	$ 88	Cash of $5; common stock and options assumed; $2 in liabilities assumed; goodwill and other intangibles recorded of $137
PentaCom, Ltd.	$ 102	$ 49	Cash of $26; common stock and options assumed; goodwill and other intangibles recorded of $40
Qeyton Systems	$ 887	$260	Common stock; goodwill and other intangibles recorded of $567
Other	$ 228	$ 71	Cash of $31; common stock and options assumed; $5 in liabilities assumed; goodwill and other intangibles recorded of $155
FISCAL 1999			
Summa Four, Inc.	$ 129	$ 64	Common stock and options assumed; $16 in liabilities assumed; goodwill and other intangibles recorded of $29
Clarity Wireless, Inc.	$ 153	$ 94	Common stock and options assumed; goodwill and other intangibles recorded of $73
Selsius Systems, Inc.	$ 134	$ 92	Cash of $111; options assumed; goodwill and other intangibles recorded of $41
PipeLinks, Inc.	$ 118	$ 99	Common stock and options assumed; goodwill and other intangibles recorded of $11
Amteva Technologies, Inc.	$ 159	$ 81	Common stock and options assumed; $9 in liabilities assumed; goodwill and other intangibles recorded of $85
Other	$ 58	$ 41	Common stock and options assumed; goodwill and other intangibles recorded of $18
FISCAL 1998			
Dagaz Technologies, Inc.	$ 130	$127	Cash of $108; $18 in common stock; liabilities assumed of $4
LightSpeed International, Inc.	$ 161	$143	Common stock and options assumed; other intangibles recorded of $15
WheelGroup Corporation	$ 124	$ 97	Common stock and options assumed; goodwill and other intangibles recorded of $38
NetSpeed International, Inc.	$ 252	$179	Cash of $12; common stock and options assumed; liabilities assumed of $18; goodwill and other intangibles recorded of $76
Other	$ 51	$ 48	Cash of $38 and options assumed

NOTES TO CONSOLIDATED FINANCIAL STATEMENTS

Other Purchase Combinations Completed as of July 29, 2000

In fiscal 2000, the Company acquired Maxcomm Technologies, Inc.; Calista, Inc.; Tasmania Network Systems, Inc.; Internet Engineering Group, LLC; Worldwide Data Systems, Inc.; and Seagull Networks, Ltd. for a total purchase price of $228 million, paid in common stock and cash. Total in-process R&D related to these acquisitions amounted to $71 million.

Total in-process R&D expense in fiscal 2000, 1999, and 1998 was $1.37 billion, $471 million, and $594 million, respectively. The in-process R&D expense that was attributable to stock consideration for the same periods was $1.28 billion, $379 million, and $436 million, respectively.

4. BALANCE SHEET DETAIL

The following tables provide details of selected balance sheet items (in millions):

	July 29, 2000	July 31, 1999
INVENTORIES, NET:		
Raw materials	$ 145	$ 143
Work in process	472	198
Finished goods	496	282
Demonstration systems	119	35
Total	$1,232	$ 658
PROPERTY AND EQUIPMENT, NET:		
Leasehold improvements	$ 607	$ 289
Computer equipment and related software	908	639
Production and engineering equipment	407	238
Office equipment, furniture, and fixtures	1,083	685
	3,005	1,851
Less, accumulated depreciation and amortization	(1,579)	(1,026)
Total	$1,426	$ 825
GOODWILL AND PURCHASED INTANGIBLE ASSETS, NET:		
Goodwill	$2,937	$ 157
Purchased intangible assets	1,558	395
	4,495	552
Less, accumulated amortization	(408)	(92)
Total	$4,087	$ 460

The following table presents the details of the amortization of goodwill and purchased intangible assets as reported in the Consolidated Statements of Operations:

Years Ended	July 29, 2000	July 31, 1999	July 25, 1998
Reported as:			
Cost of sales	$ 25	$ 1	$ –
Operating expenses	291	61	23
Total	$316	$62	$23

5. LEASE RECEIVABLES

Lease receivables represent sales-type and direct-financing leases resulting from the sale of the Company's and complementary third-party products and services. These lease arrangements typically have terms from two to three years and are usually collateralized by a security interest in the underlying assets. The net lease receivables are summarized as follows (in millions):

	July 29, 2000	July 31, 1999
Gross lease receivables	$1,310	$663
Unearned income and other reserves	(195)	(83)
Total	1,115	580
Less, current portion	(588)	(80)
Long-term lease receivables, net	$ 527	$500

Contractual maturities of the gross lease receivables at July 29, 2000 were $588 million in fiscal 2001, $354 million in fiscal 2002, $337 million in fiscal 2003, $29 million in fiscal 2004, and $2 million in fiscal 2005. Actual cash collections may differ from the contractual maturities due to early customer buyouts or refinancings. The current portion of lease receivables is included in prepaid expenses and other current assets.

6. INVESTMENTS

The following tables summarize the Company's investments in securities (in millions):

JULY 29, 2000	Amortized Cost	Gross Unrealized Gains	Gross Unrealized Losses	Fair Value
U.S. government notes and bonds	$ 2,317	$ –	$ (32)	$ 2,285
State, municipal, and county government notes and bonds	3,592	13	(41)	3,564
Corporate notes and bonds	3,222	1	(19)	3,204
Corporate equity securities	641	5,621	(37)	6,225
Mandatorily redeemable convertible preferred stock	987	–	–	987
Total	$10,759	$5,635	$(129)	$16,265
Reported as:				
Short-term investments				$ 1,291
Investments				13,688
Restricted investments				1,286
Total				$16,265

JULY 31, 1999	Amortized Cost	Gross Unrealized Gains	Gross Unrealized Losses	Fair Value
U.S. government notes and bonds	$ 2,187	$ –	$ (29)	$ 2,158
State, municipal, and county government notes and bonds	5,177	5	(44)	5,138
Corporate notes and bonds	1,145	–	(17)	1,128
Corporate equity securities	288	615	(26)	877
Total	$ 8,797	$ 620	$(116)	$ 9,301
Reported as:				
Short-term investments				$ 1,189
Investments				7,032
Restricted investments				1,080
Total				$ 9,301

NOTES TO CONSOLIDATED FINANCIAL STATEMENTS

Net gains realized on minority investments were $531 million in fiscal 2000. The net gains realized on minority investments that were attributable to noncash activity were $92 million in fiscal 2000. The net gains realized on minority investments were not material in fiscal 1999 and were $5 million in fiscal 1998.

The following table summarizes debt investment and mandatorily redeemable convertible preferred stock maturities (including restricted investments) at July 29, 2000 (in millions):

	Amortized Cost	Fair Value
Less than one year	$ 1,753	$ 1,744
Due in 1–2 years	1,930	1,922
Due in 2–5 years	4,218	4,161
Due after 5 years	2,217	2,213
Total	$10,118	$10,040

7. LINE OF CREDIT

At July 29, 2000, the Company had a syndicated credit agreement under the terms of which a group of banks committed a maximum of $500 million on an unsecured, revolving basis for borrowings of various maturities. The commitments made under this agreement expire on July 1, 2002. Under the terms of the agreement, borrowings bear interest at a spread over the London Interbank Offered Rate based on certain financial criteria and third-party rating assessments. As of July 29, 2000, this spread was 17.5 basis points. From this spread, a commitment fee of 5.5 basis points is assessed against any undrawn amounts. The agreement includes a single financial covenant that places a variable floor on tangible net worth, as defined, if certain leverage ratios are exceeded. There have been no borrowings under this agreement to date.

8. COMMITMENTS AND CONTINGENCIES

Leases

The Company has entered into several agreements to lease 448 acres of land located in San Jose, California, where it has established its headquarters operations, and 759 acres of land located in Boxborough, Massachusetts; Salem, New Hampshire; Richardson, Texas; and Research Triangle Park, North Carolina, where it has expanded certain research and development and customer-support activities.

All of the leases have initial terms of five to seven years and options to renew for an additional three to five years, subject to certain conditions. At any time during the terms of these leases, the Company may purchase the land. If the Company elects not to purchase the land at the end of each of the leases, the Company has guaranteed a residual value of $624 million.

The Company has also entered into agreements to lease certain buildings standing or to be constructed on the land described above. The lessors of the buildings have committed to fund up to a maximum of $1.40 billion (subject to reductions based on certain conditions in the respective leases) for the construction of the buildings, with the portion of the committed amount actually used to be determined by the Company. Rent obligations for the buildings commenced on various dates and will expire at the same time as the land leases.

The Company has options to renew the building leases for an additional three to five years, subject to certain conditions. The Company may, at its option, purchase the buildings during or at the end of the terms of the leases at approximately the amount expended by the lessors to construct the buildings. If the Company does not exercise the purchase options by the end of the leases, the Company will guarantee a residual value of the buildings as determined at the lease inception date of each agreement (approximately $748 million at July 29, 2000).

As part of the above lease transactions, the Company restricted $1.29 billion of its investment securities as collateral for specified obligations of the lessors under the leases. These investment securities are restricted as to withdrawal and are managed by a third party subject to certain limitations under the Company's investment policy. In addition, the Company must maintain a minimum consolidated tangible net worth, as defined.

The Company also leases office space in Santa Clara, California; Chelmsford, Massachusetts; and for its various U.S. and international sales offices.

Future annual minimum lease payments under all noncancelable operating leases as of July 29, 2000 are as follows (in millions):

Fiscal Year

2001	$ 302
2002	299
2003	310
2004	251
2005	237
Thereafter	1,506
Total	$2,905

Rent expense totaled $229 million, $123 million, and $90 million for fiscal 2000, 1999, and 1998, respectively.

Foreign Exchange Forward and Option Contracts

The Company conducts business on a global basis in several major currencies. As such, it is exposed to adverse movements in foreign currency exchange rates. The Company enters into foreign exchange forward contracts to reduce the impact of certain currency exposures. These contracts hedge exposures associated with nonfunctional currency assets and liabilities denominated in Australian, Canadian, Japanese, Korean, and several European currencies, primarily the euro and British pound.

The Company does not enter into foreign exchange forward contracts for trading purposes. Gains and losses on the contracts are included in interest and other income, net, and offset foreign exchange gains or losses from the revaluation of intercompany balances or other current assets and liabilities denominated in currencies other than the functional currency of the reporting entity. The Company's foreign exchange forward contracts generally range from one to three months in original maturity.

The Company periodically hedges anticipated transactions with purchased currency options. A purchased currency option's premium is amortized over the life of the option while any intrinsic value is recognized in income during the same period as the hedged transaction. The deferred premium and intrinsic value from hedging anticipated transactions were not material at July 29, 2000. In the unlikely event that the underlying transaction terminates or becomes improbable, the remaining premium or deferred intrinsic value will be recorded in the Consolidated Statements of Operations. The Company does not purchase currency options for trading purposes. Foreign exchange forward and option contracts as of July 29, 2000 are summarized as follows (in millions):

	Notional Amount	Carrying Value	Fair Value
Forward contracts:			
Assets	$1,377	$ (5)	$(15)
Liabilities	$1,500	$12	$ 37
Option contracts:			
Assets	$ 561	$12	$ 14

The Company's foreign exchange forward and option contracts contain credit risk to the extent that its bank counterparties may be unable to meet the terms of the agreements. The Company minimizes such risk by limiting its counterparties to major financial institutions. In addition, the potential risk of loss with any one party resulting from this type of credit risk is monitored. Management does not expect any material losses as a result of default by other parties.

Legal Proceedings

The Company is subject to legal proceedings, claims, and litigation arising in the ordinary course of business. While the outcome of these matters is currently not determinable, management does not expect that the ultimate costs to resolve these matters will have a material adverse effect on the Company's consolidated financial position, results of operations, or cash flows.

NOTES TO CONSOLIDATED FINANCIAL STATEMENTS

9. SHAREHOLDERS' EQUITY

Authorized Shares

On November 10, 1999, the shareholders of the Company approved an increase to the authorized number of shares of common stock from 5.40 billion to 10 billion shares. On March 20, 2000, the Board of Directors of the Company approved an increase to the authorized number of shares of common stock from 10 billion to 20 billion shares relating to the two-for-one stock split distributed on March 22, 2000.

Stock Split

The Board of Directors authorized the splitting of the Company's common stock on a two-for-one basis for shareholders of record on February 22, 2000 and the resulting shares from the split were distributed on March 22, 2000. All references to share and per-share data for all periods presented have been adjusted to give effect to this two-for-one stock split.

Shareholders' Rights Plan

In June 1998, the Board of Directors approved a Shareholders' Rights Plan ("Rights Plan"). The Rights Plan is intended to protect shareholders' rights in the event of an unsolicited takeover attempt. It is not intended to prevent a takeover of the Company on terms that are favorable and fair to all shareholders and will not interfere with a merger approved by the Board of Directors. Each right entitles shareholders to buy a unit equal to a portion of a new share of Series A Preferred Stock of the Company. The rights will be exercisable only if a person or a group acquires or announces a tender or exchange offer to acquire 15% or more of the Company's common stock.

In the event the rights become exercisable, the Rights Plan allows for Cisco shareholders to acquire, at an exercise price of $108 per right owned, stock of the surviving corporation having a market value of $217, whether or not Cisco is the surviving corporation. The rights, which expire in June 2008, are redeemable for $0.00017 per right at the approval of the Board of Directors.

Preferred Stock

Under the terms of the Company's Articles of Incorporation, the Board of Directors may determine the rights, preferences, and terms of the Company's authorized but unissued shares of preferred stock.

Comprehensive Income

The components of comprehensive income, net of tax, are as follows (in millions):

Years Ended	July 29, 2000	July 31, 1999	July 25, 1998
Net income	$2,668	$2,023	$1,331
Other comprehensive income (loss):			
Change in net unrealized gains on investments, net of tax of $1,762, $144, and $17 in fiscal 2000, 1999, and 1998, respectively	3,240	234	25
Reclassification for net unrealized gains previously included in net income, net of tax of $2 in fiscal 1998	–	–	3
Net unrealized gains	3,240	234	28
Change in accumulated translation adjustments	(8)	6	(10)
Total	$5,900	$2,263	$1,349

10. EMPLOYEE BENEFIT PLANS

Employee Stock Purchase Plan

The Company has an Employee Stock Purchase Plan (the "Purchase Plan") under which 222 million shares of common stock have been reserved for issuance. Eligible employees may purchase a limited number of shares of the Company's common stock at 85% of the market value at certain plan-defined dates. The Purchase Plan terminates on January 3, 2005. In fiscal 2000, 1999, and 1998, seven million, 10 million, and 14 million shares, respectively, were issued under the Purchase Plan. At July 29, 2000, 123 million shares were available for issuance under the Purchase Plan.

Employee Stock Option Plans

The Company has two main stock option plans: the 1987 Stock Option Plan (the "Predecessor Plan") and the 1996 Stock Incentive Plan (the "1996 Plan"). The Predecessor Plan was terminated in 1996. All outstanding options under the Predecessor Plan were transferred to the 1996 Plan. However, all outstanding options under the Predecessor Plan continue to be governed by the terms and conditions of the existing option agreements for those grants.

The maximum number of shares under the 1996 Plan was initially limited to the 620 million shares transferred from the Predecessor Plan. However, under the terms of the 1996 Plan, the share reserve increased each December for the three fiscal years beginning with fiscal 1997, by an amount equal to 4.75% of the outstanding shares on the last trading day of the immediately preceding November. In fiscal 1999, the Company's shareholders approved the extension of the automatic share increase provision of the 1996 Plan for an additional three-year period.

Although the Board of Directors has the authority to set other terms, the options are generally 20% or 25% exercisable one year from the date of grant and then ratably over the following 48 or 36 months, respectively. Options issued under the Predecessor Plan generally had terms of four years. New options granted under the 1996 Plan expire no later than nine years from the grant date. A summary of option activity follows (in millions, except per-share amounts):

		Options Outstanding	
	Options Available for Grant	Options	Weighted-Average Exercise Price per Share
BALANCE AT JULY 26, 1997	96	810	$ 4.05
Granted and assumed	(282)	282	10.00
Exercised	–	(168)	2.40
Canceled	48	(48)	4.59
Additional shares reserved	314	–	–
BALANCE AT JULY 25, 1998	176	876	6.25
Granted and assumed	(245)	245	22.22
Exercised	–	(210)	3.09
Canceled	22	(22)	10.85
Additional shares reserved	359	–	–
BALANCE AT JULY 31, 1999	312	889	11.22
Granted and assumed	(295)	295	52.10
Exercised	–	(176)	5.75
Canceled	37	(37)	22.70
Additional shares reserved	339	–	–
BALANCE AT JULY 29, 2000	**393**	**971**	**$24.19**

The Company has, in connection with the acquisitions of various companies, assumed the stock option plans of each acquired company. During fiscal 2000, a total of approximately 31 million shares of the Company's common stock have been reserved for issuance under the assumed plans and the related options are included in the preceding table.

In 1997, the Company adopted a Supplemental Stock Incentive Plan (the "Supplemental Plan") under which options can be granted or shares can be directly issued to eligible employees. Officers and members of the Company's Board of Directors are not eligible to participate in the Supplemental Plan. Nine million shares have been reserved for issuance under the Supplemental Plan, of which 9,000 shares are subject to outstanding options and 66,600 shares have been issued in fiscal 2000.

NOTES TO CONSOLIDATED FINANCIAL STATEMENTS

The following table summarizes information concerning outstanding and exercisable options at July 29, 2000 (in millions, except number of years and per-share amounts):

Range of Exercise Prices	Options Outstanding			Options Exercisable	
	Number Outstanding	Weighted-Average Remaining Contractual Life (in Years)	Weighted-Average Exercise Price per Share	Number Exercisable	Weighted-Average Exercise Price per Share
$ 0.01– 5.56	229	5.20	$ 5.23	188	$ 4.44
5.57–12.27	258	6.16	9.56	162	8.95
12.28–28.61	194	7.49	23.59	63	22.47
28.62–54.53	241	8.34	49.91	5	31.02
54.54–72.56	49	8.64	65.65	–	–
Total	971	6.87	$24.19	418	$ 9.22

At July 31, 1999 and July 25, 1998, approximately 370 million and 312 million outstanding options, respectively, were exercisable. The weighted-average exercise prices for outstanding options were $5.75 and $3.64 at July 31, 1999 and July 25, 1998, respectively.

The Company is required under Statement of Financial Accounting Standards No. 123, "Accounting for Stock-Based Compensation" ("SFAS 123"), to disclose pro forma information regarding option grants made to its employees based on specified valuation techniques that produce estimated compensation charges. These amounts have not been reflected in the Company's Consolidated Statements of Operations because no compensation charge arises when the price of the employees' stock options equals the market value of the underlying stock at the grant date, as in the case of options granted to the Company's employees. Pro forma information under SFAS 123 is as follows (in millions, except per-share amounts):

Years Ended	July 29, 2000	July 31, 1999	July 25, 1998
Net income—as reported	$2,668	$2,023	$1,331
Net income—pro forma	$1,549	$1,487	$1,074
Basic net income per common share—as reported	$ 0.39	$ 0.30	$ 0.21
Diluted net income per common share—as reported	$ 0.36	$ 0.29	$ 0.20
Basic net income per common share—pro forma	$ 0.22	$ 0.22	$ 0.17
Diluted net income per common share—pro forma	$ 0.21	$ 0.21	$ 0.16

The fair value of each option grant is estimated on the date of grant using the Black-Scholes option pricing model with the following weighted-average assumptions:

	Employee Stock Option Plans			Employee Stock Purchase Plan		
	July 29, 2000	July 31, 1999	July 25,1998	July 29, 2000	July 31, 1999	July 25,1998
Expected dividend yield	0.0%	0.0%	0.0%	0.0%	0.0%	0.0%
Risk-free interest rate	6.4%	5.1%	5.7%	5.3%	4.9%	5.4%
Expected volatility	33.9%	40.2%	35.6%	43.3%	47.2%	44.8%
Expected life (in years)	3.1	3.1	3.1	0.5	0.5	0.5

The Black-Scholes option pricing model was developed for use in estimating the fair value of traded options that have no vesting restrictions and are fully transferable. In addition, option pricing models require the input of highly subjective assumptions including the expected stock price volatility. The Company uses projected volatility rates which are based upon historical volatility rates trended into future years. Because the Company's employee stock options have characteristics significantly different from those of traded options, and because changes in the subjective input assumptions can materially affect the fair value estimate, in management's opinion, the existing models do not necessarily provide a reliable single measure of the fair value of the Company's options. The weighted-average estimated fair values of employee stock options granted during fiscal 2000, 1999, and 1998 were $19.44, $8.40, and $3.57 per share, respectively.

The above pro forma disclosures under SFAS 123 are also not likely to be representative of the effects on net income and net income per common share in future years, because they do not take into consideration pro forma compensation expense related to grants made prior to fiscal 1996.

Employee 401(k) Plans

The Company sponsors the Cisco Systems, Inc. 401(k) Plan (the "Plan") to provide retirement benefits for its employees. As allowed under Section 401(k) of the Internal Revenue Code, the Plan provides tax-deferred salary deductions for eligible employees. The Company also has other 401(k) plans that it sponsors. These plans arose from acquisitions of other companies and are not material to the Company on either an individual or aggregate basis.

Employees may contribute from 1% to 15% of their annual compensation to the Plan, limited to a maximum annual amount as set periodically by the Internal Revenue Service. The Company matches employee contributions dollar for dollar up to a maximum of $1,500 per year per person. All matching contributions vest immediately. In addition, the Plan provides for discretionary contributions as determined by the Board of Directors. Such contributions to the Plan are allocated among eligible participants in the proportion of their salaries to the total salaries of all participants. The Company's matching contributions to the Plan totaled $34 million, $20 million, and $15 million in fiscal 2000, 1999, and 1998, respectively. No discretionary contributions were made in fiscal 2000, 1999, or 1998.

11. INCOME TAXES

The provision for (benefit from) income taxes consisted of (in millions):

Years Ended	July 29, 2000	July 31, 1999	July 25, 1998
Federal:			
Current	$1,843	$1,164	$855
Deferred	(652)	(221)	(54)
	1,191	943	801
State:			
Current	282	112	87
Deferred	(118)	(24)	(8)
	164	88	79
Foreign:			
Current	332	151	74
Deferred	(12)	(2)	(14)
	320	149	60
Total provision for income taxes	$1,675	$1,180	$940

NOTES TO CONSOLIDATED FINANCIAL STATEMENTS

The Company paid income taxes of $327 million, $301 million, and $440 million in fiscal 2000, 1999, and 1998, respectively. Income before provision for income taxes consisted of (in millions):

Years Ended	July 29, 2000	July 31, 1999	July 25, 1998
United States	$2,544	$2,092	$1,950
International	1,799	1,111	321
	$4,343	$3,203	$2,271

The items accounting for the difference between income taxes computed at the federal statutory rate and the provision for income taxes consisted of:

Years Ended	July 29, 2000	July 31, 1999	July 25, 1998
Federal statutory rate	35.0%	35.0%	35.0%
Effect of:			
State taxes, net of federal tax benefit	1.9	2.2	2.2
Foreign sales corporation	(1.9)	(1.6)	(2.4)
Foreign income at other than U.S. rates	(1.6)	(1.0)	–
Nondeductible in-process R&D	8.1	3.9	6.4
Tax-exempt interest	(1.8)	(1.9)	(1.6)
Tax credits	(1.6)	(1.2)	(1.4)
Other, net	0.5	1.5	3.2
Total	38.6%	36.9%	41.4%

U.S. income taxes and foreign withholding taxes were not provided for on a cumulative total of approximately $411 million of undistributed earnings for certain non-U.S. subsidiaries. The Company intends to reinvest these earnings indefinitely in operations outside the United States. The components of the deferred tax assets (liabilities) follow (in millions):

	July 29, 2000	July 31, 1999
ASSETS		
Allowance for doubtful accounts and returns	$ 418	$ 185
In-process R&D	265	163
Inventory allowances and capitalization	94	57
Accrued state franchise tax	–	32
Depreciation	41	28
Deferred revenue	177	65
Credits and net operating loss carryforwards	1,023	–
Other	451	256
Gross deferred tax assets	2,469	786
Valuation allowance	(299)	–
Total deferred tax assets	2,170	786
LIABILITIES		
Purchased intangible assets	(257)	(88)
Unrealized gain on investments	(1,954)	(192)
Total deferred tax liabilities	(2,211)	(280)
Total	$ (41)	$ 506

The noncurrent portion of the deferred tax liabilities, which totaled $74 million at July 31, 1999, is included in other assets.

The Company has provided a valuation allowance on certain of its deferred tax assets because of uncertainty regarding their realizability due to expectation of future employee stock option exercises. Deferred tax assets of approximately $963 million at July 29, 2000 pertain to certain tax credits and net operating loss carryforwards resulting from the exercise of employee stock options. When recognized, the tax benefit of these credits and losses will be accounted for as a credit to shareholders' equity rather than as a reduction of the income tax provision.

As of July 29, 2000, the Company's federal and state net operating loss carryforwards for income tax purposes were approximately $496 million and $865 million, respectively. If not utilized, the federal net operating loss carryforwards will begin to expire in fiscal 2020, and the state net operating loss carryforwards will begin to expire in fiscal 2005. As of July 29, 2000, the Company's federal and state tax credit carryforwards for income tax purposes were approximately $678 million and $197 million, respectively. If not utilized, the federal and state tax credit carryforwards will begin to expire in fiscal 2005.

The Company's income taxes payable for federal, state, and foreign purposes have been reduced, and the deferred tax assets increased, by the tax benefits associated with dispositions of employee stock options. The Company receives an income tax benefit calculated as the difference between the fair market value of the stock issued at the time of exercise and the option price, tax effected. These benefits were credited directly to shareholders' equity and amounted to $3.08 billion, $837 million, and $422 million for fiscal 2000, 1999, and 1998, respectively. Benefits reducing taxes payable amounted to $2.49 billion, $837 million, and $422 million for fiscal 2000, 1999, and 1998, respectively. Benefits increasing gross deferred tax assets amounted to $582 million in fiscal 2000.

12. SEGMENT INFORMATION AND MAJOR CUSTOMERS

The Company's operations involve the design, development, manufacture, marketing, and technical support of networking products and services. The Company offers end-to-end networking solutions for its customers. Cisco products include routers, LAN and ATM switches, dial-up access servers, and network-management software. These products, integrated by the Cisco IOS® software, link geographically dispersed LANs, WANs, and IBM networks.

The Company conducts business globally and is managed geographically. The Company's management relies on an internal management system that provides sales and standard cost information by geographic theater. Sales are attributed to a theater based on the ordering location of the customer. The Company's management makes financial decisions and allocates resources based on the information it receives from this internal management system. The Company does not allocate research and development, sales and marketing, or general and administrative expenses to its geographic theaters as management does not use this information to measure the performance of the operating segments. Management does not believe that allocating these expenses is material in evaluating a geographic theater's performance. Information from this internal management system differs from the amounts reported under generally accepted accounting principles due to certain corporate level adjustments not included in the internal management system. These corporate level adjustments are primarily sales adjustments relating to revenue deferrals and reserves, credit memos, returns, and other timing differences. Based on established criteria, the Company has four reportable segments: the Americas; Europe, the Middle East, and Africa ("EMEA"); Asia Pacific; and Japan.

NOTES TO CONSOLIDATED FINANCIAL STATEMENTS

Summarized financial information by theater for fiscal 2000, 1999, and 1998, as taken from the internal management system discussed previously, is as follows (in millions):

Years Ended	July 29, 2000	July 31, 1999	July 25, 1998
Net sales:			
Americas	$12,924	$ 8,088	$5,732
EMEA	4,770	3,216	2,114
Asia Pacific	1,705	825	535
Japan	935	566	459
Sales adjustments	(1,406)	(522)	(351)
Total	$18,928	$12,173	$8,489
Gross margin:			
Americas	$ 9,412	$ 5,836	$4,261
EMEA	3,581	2,380	1,565
Asia Pacific	1,215	586	395
Japan	737	436	340
Standard margins	14,945	9,238	6,561
Sales adjustments	(1,406)	(522)	(351)
Production overhead	(455)	(255)	(207)
Manufacturing variances and other related costs	(902)	(547)	(438)
Total	$12,182	$ 7,914	$5,565

The standard margins by geographic theater differ from the amounts recognized under generally accepted accounting principles because the Company does not allocate certain sales adjustments, production overhead, and manufacturing variances and other related costs to the theaters. The above table reconciles the net sales and standard margins by geographic theater to net sales and gross margin as reported in the Consolidated Statements of Operations by including such adjustments.

Enterprise-wide information provided on geographic sales is based on the ordering location of the customer. Property and equipment information is based on the physical location of the assets. The following table presents net sales and property and equipment information for geographic areas (in millions):

	July 29, 2000	July 31, 1999	July 25,1998
Net sales:			
United States	$ 12,013	$ 7,454	$5,232
International	8,321	5,241	3,608
Sales adjustments	(1,406)	(522)	(351)
Total	$ 18,928	$12,173	$8,489
Property and equipment, net:			
United States	$ 1,242	$ 711	$ 537
International	184	114	72
Total	$ 1,426	$ 825	$ 609

The following table presents net sales for groups of similar products and services (in millions):

Years Ended	July 29, 2000	July 31, 1999	July 25, 1998
Net sales:			
Routers	$ 7,611	$ 5,196	$3,856
Switches	7,509	5,167	3,613
Access	2,396	1,127	630
Other	2,818	1,205	741
Sales adjustments	(1,406)	(522)	(351)
Total	$18,928	$12,173	$8,489

Substantially all of the Company's assets at July 29, 2000 and July 31, 1999 were attributable to U.S. operations. In fiscal 2000, 1999, and 1998, no single customer accounted for 10% or more of the Company's net sales.

13. NET INCOME PER COMMON SHARE

The following table presents the calculation of basic and diluted net income per common share (in millions, except per-share amounts):

Years Ended	July 29, 2000	July 31, 1999	July 25, 1998
Net income	$2,668	$2,023	$1,331
Weighted-average shares—basic	6,917	6,646	6,312
Effect of dilutive securities:			
Employee stock options	521	416	346
Weighted-average shares—diluted	7,438	7,062	6,658
Net income per common share—basic	$ 0.39	$ 0.30	$ 0.21
Net income per common share—diluted	$ 0.36	$ 0.29	$ 0.20

14. SUBSEQUENT EVENTS (UNAUDITED)

Pending Business Combinations

The Company announced definitive agreements to acquire HyNEX, Ltd.; Netiverse, Inc.; Komodo Technology, Inc.; NuSpeed Internet Systems, Inc.; IPmobile, Inc.; and PixStream Incorporated for a total purchase price of approximately $1.76 billion, payable in common stock and cash. These acquisitions will be accounted for as purchases and are expected to close in the first quarter of fiscal 2001.

REPORT OF INDEPENDENT ACCOUNTANTS

To the Board of Directors and Shareholders of Cisco Systems, Inc.

In our opinion, the accompanying consolidated balance sheets and the related consolidated statements of operations and of shareholders' equity and of cash flows present fairly, in all material respects, the financial position of Cisco Systems, Inc. and its subsidiaries at July 29, 2000 and July 31, 1999, and the results of their operations and their cash flows for each of the three years in the period ended July 29, 2000, in conformity with accounting principles generally accepted in the United States. These financial statements are the responsibility of the Company's management; our responsibility is to express an opinion on these financial statements based on our audits. We conducted our audits of these statements in accordance with auditing standards generally accepted in the United States, which require that we plan and perform the audit to obtain reasonable assurance about whether the financial statements are free of material misstatement. An audit includes examining, on a test basis, evidence supporting the amounts and disclosures in the financial statements, assessing the accounting principles used and significant estimates made by management, and evaluating the overall financial statement presentation. We believe that our audits provide a reasonable basis for the opinion expressed above.

PricewaterhouseCoopers LLP

San Jose, California
August 8, 2000

SUPPLEMENTARY FINANCIAL DATA[1] (Unaudited)

(In millions, except per-share amounts)

	July 29, 2000	April 29, 2000	Jan. 29, 2000	Oct. 30, 1999	July 31, 1999	May 1, 1999	Jan. 23, 1999	Oct. 24, 1998
Net sales	$5,720	$4,933	$4,357	$3,918	$3,558	$3,172	$2,845	$2,598
Gross margin	$3,662	$3,172	$2,818	$2,530	$2,297	$2,059	$1,857	$1,701
Net income	$ 796[2]	$ 641[3]	$ 816[4]	$ 415[5]	$ 605[6]	$ 632[7]	$ 279[8]	$ 507[9]
Net income per common share—basic*	$ 0.11	$ 0.09	$ 0.12	$ 0.06	$ 0.09	$ 0.09	$ 0.04	$ 0.08
Net income per common share—diluted*	$ 0.11[2]	$ 0.08[3]	$ 0.11[4]	$ 0.06[5]	$ 0.08[6]	$ 0.09[7]	$ 0.04[8]	$ 0.07[9]

* Reflects the two-for-one stock split effective March 2000.

(1) All historical financial information has been restated to reflect the acquisitions that were accounted for as poolings of interests (see Note 3 to the Consolidated Financial Statements).

(2) Net income and net income per common share include in-process research and development expenses of $461 million, payroll tax on stock option exercises of $26 million, amortization of goodwill and purchased intangible assets of $169 million, acquisition-related costs of $37 million, and net gains realized on minority investments of $344 million. Pro forma net income and diluted net income per common share, excluding these items net of tax of $53 million, were $1.20 billion and $0.16, respectively.

(3) Net income and net income per common share include in-process research and development expenses of $488 million, payroll tax on stock option exercises of $25 million, amortization of goodwill and purchased intangible assets of $51 million, and net gains realized on minority investments of $156 million. Pro forma net income and diluted net income per common share, excluding these items net of tax benefits of $44 million, were $1.01 billion and $0.13, respectively.

(4) Net income and net income per common share include in-process research and development expenses of $43 million, amortization of goodwill and purchased intangible assets of $47 million, acquisition-related costs of $25 million, and net gains realized on minority investments of $31 million. Pro forma net income and diluted net income per common share, excluding these items net of tax benefits of $3 million, were $897 million and $0.12, respectively.

(5) Net income and net income per common share include in-process research and development expenses of $381 million and amortization of goodwill and purchased intangible assets of $24 million. Pro forma net income and diluted net income per common share, excluding these items net of tax benefits of $6 million, were $814 million and $0.11, respectively.

(6) Net income and net income per common share include in-process research and development expenses of $81 million, amortization of goodwill and purchased intangible assets of $19 million, and acquisition-related costs of $16 million. Pro forma net income and diluted net income per common share, excluding these items net of tax benefits of $11 million, were $710 million and $0.10, respectively.

(7) Net income and net income per common share include amortization of goodwill and purchased intangible assets of $19 million. Pro forma net income and diluted net income per common share, excluding this item net of a tax benefit of $6 million, were $645 million and $0.09, respectively.

(8) Net income and net income per common share include in-process research and development expenses of $349 million and amortization of goodwill and purchased intangible assets of $12 million. Pro forma net income and diluted net income per common share, excluding these items net of tax benefits of $34 million, were $606 million and $0.09, respectively.

(9) Net income and net income per common share include in-process research and development expenses of $41 million and amortization of goodwill and purchased intangible assets of $11 million. Pro forma net income and diluted net income per common share, excluding these items net of tax benefits of $3 million, were $556 million and $0.08, respectively.

STOCK MARKET INFORMATION

Cisco common stock (NASDAQ symbol CSCO) is traded on the NASDAQ National Market. The following table sets forth the range of high and low closing prices for each period indicated, adjusted to reflect the two-for-one split effective March 2000:

	2000		1999		1998	
	High	Low	High	Low	High	Low
First quarter	$37.00	$29.38	$17.32	$10.97	$ 9.37	$ 7.75
Second quarter	$57.63	$35.00	$26.67	$15.19	$10.05	$ 8.10
Third quarter	$80.06	$54.75	$29.69	$23.78	$12.31	$ 9.44
Fourth quarter	$71.44	$50.55	$33.53	$26.09	$17.20	$11.74

The Company has never paid cash dividends on its common stock and has no present plans to do so. There were approximately 60,150 shareholders of record at July 29, 2000.

DIRECTORS AND OFFICERS

Directors

Carol A. Bartz [2] [4] [5] [6] [8]
Chairman and Chief Executive Officer
Autodesk, Inc.

Larry R. Carter
Senior Vice President, Finance and Administration
Chief Financial Officer and Secretary
Cisco Systems, Inc.

John T. Chambers [1] [4] [5] [6] [8]
President and Chief Executive Officer
Cisco Systems, Inc.

Mary Cirillo [3] [7]
Chairman and Chief Executive Officer
OPCENTER, LLC

James F. Gibbons, Ph.D. [2] [4]
Reid Weaver Dennis Professor of Electrical Engineering and
Special Consul to the President for Industrial Relations Stanford
University

Edward R. Kozel [7] [8]
Managing Member
Open Range Ventures

James C. Morgan [2]
Chairman and Chief Executive Officer
Applied Materials, Inc.

John P. Morgridge [1] [5] [6] [7]
Chairman of the Board
Cisco Systems, Inc.

Arun Sarin [3] [5]
Chief Executive Officer
InfoSpace, Inc.

Donald T. Valentine [1] [5] [7]
General Partner
Sequoia Capital

Steven M. West [3]
President and Chief Executive Officer
Entera, Inc.

Jerry Yang
Cofounder and Chief Yahoo!
Yahoo!

(1) Member of the Executive Committee
(2) Member of the Compensation/Stock Option Committee
(3) Member of the Audit Committee
(4) Member of the Nomination Committee
(5) Member of the Acquisition Committee
(6) Member of the Special Stock Option Committee
(7) Member of the Investment/Finance Committee
(8) Member of the Special Acquisition Committee

Officers

Larry R. Carter
Senior Vice President, Finance and Administration
Chief Financial Officer and Secretary

John T. Chambers
President and Chief Executive Officer

Gary J. Daichendt
Executive Vice President
Worldwide Operations

Charles H. Giancarlo
Senior Vice President
Small/Medium Business Line of Business
Consumer Line of Business

Richard J. Justice
Senior Vice President
Worldwide Field Operations

Carl Redfield
Senior Vice President, Manufacturing and
Worldwide Logistics

James Richardson
Senior Vice President, Enterprise Line of Business and
Internet Communications Software Group

Michelangelo Volpi
Senior Vice President, Chief Strategy Officer

OTHER SENIOR VICE PRESIDENTS

Douglas C. Allred
Senior Vice President, Customer Advocacy

Vernon E. Altman
Senior Vice President, Strategic Business Partnerships

Barbara Beck
Senior Vice President, Human Resources

Susan L. Bostrom
Senior Vice President, Internet Business Solutions Group

Howard S. Charney
Senior Vice President, Office of the President

William G. Conlon
Senior Vice President
Customer Advocacy Global Support Operations

Doug Dennerline
Senior Vice President
U.S. Enterprise and Federal Sales

Kevin A. DeNuccio
Senior Vice President
Worldwide Service Provider Field Operations

Richard Freemantle
Senior Vice President, Asia Pacific

Kevin J. Kennedy
Senior Vice President
Service Provider Line of Business and
Cisco IOS® Technologies Division

David Kirk
Senior Vice President
Internet Communications Software Group

Mario Mazzola
Senior Vice President, New Business Ventures

William R. Nuti
Senior Vice President, EMEA Operations

Randy Pond
Senior Vice President, Operations

Daniel Scheinman
Senior Vice President, Corporate Affairs

Cas Skrzypczak
Senior Vice President
Customer Advocacy for Service Provider and
Consumer Lines of Business

Peter Solvik
Senior Vice President, Chief Information Officer

SHAREHOLDER INFORMATION

Online Annual Report

We invite you to visit our online interactive report at
www.cisco.com/annualreport/2000. In this version
you will find our shareholders' letter in multiple
languages, a financial section, and additional
company and product information. This Web-based
report complements our printed report, giving you
a comprehensive understanding of Cisco Systems.

Cisco recently introduced the iQ Web site and
iQ magazine with additional information to help
business executives implement effective Internet
business solutions. *iQ* magazine is the senior
executive's atlas to the Internet economy. Using
the successful models of Cisco and its customers,
the site and magazine detail how businesses
can harness the power of the Internet to gain a
competitive advantage and increase profitability.
Visit the site at **www.cisco.com/go/iqmagazine.**

Investor Relations

For further information on the Company, additional
copies of this report, Form 10-K, or other financial
information, contact:

Investor Relations
Cisco Systems, Inc.
170 West Tasman Drive
San Jose, CA 95134-1706
(408) 227-CSCO (2726)

You may also contact us by sending an e-mail to
investor-relations@cisco.com or by visiting the
Investor Relations section on the Company's Web
site at www.cisco.com.

Transfer Agent and Registrar

Fleet National Bank
(f/k/a BankBoston, N.A.)
c/o EquiServe Limited Partnership
P.O. Box 8040
Boston, MA 02266-8040
www.equiserve.com
(800) 730-6001

Independent Accountants

PricewaterhouseCoopers LLP
San Jose, CA

Legal Counsel

Brobeck, Phleger & Harrison LLP
Palo Alto, CA

Notice of Annual Meeting

Paramount's Great America
Paramount Theater
1 Great America Parkway
Santa Clara, CA
November 14, 2000
10 a.m. Pacific Standard Time

GLOSSARY

accelerated depreciation Any depreciation method that writes off depreciable costs more quickly than the ordinary straight-line method based on expected useful life.

account A summary record of the changes in a particular asset, liability, or owners' equity.

account format A classified balance sheet with the assets at the left.

account payable A liability that results from a purchase of goods or services on open account.

accounting The process of identifying, recording, summarizing, and reporting economic information to decision makers.

accounting controls The methods and procedures for authorizing transactions, safeguarding assets, and ensuring the accuracy of the financial records.

Accounting Principles Board (APB) The predecessor to the Financial Accounting Standards Board.

accounting system A set of records, procedures, and equipment that routinely deals with the events affecting the financial performance and position of the entity.

accounts receivable (trade receivables, receivables) Amounts owed to a company by customers as a result of delivering goods or services and extending credit in the ordinary course of business.

accounts receivable turnover Credit sales divided by average accounts receivable.

accrual basis Accounting method that recognizes the impact of transactions on the financial statements in the time periods when revenues and expenses occur.

accrue To accumulate a receivable or payable during a given period even though no explicit transaction occurs.

accumulated depreciation (allowance for depreciation) The cumulative sum of all depreciation recognized since the date of acquisition of the particular assets described.

adjustments (adjusting entries) End-of-period entries that assign the financial effects of implicit transactions to the appropriate time periods.

administrative controls All methods and procedures that facilitate management planning and control of operations.

affiliated company A company that has 20% to 50% of its voting shares owned by another company.

aging of accounts receivable An analysis that considers the composition of year-end accounts receivable based on the age of the debt.

AICPA American Institute of Certified Public Accountants, the leading organization of the auditors of corporate financial reports.

allowance for uncollectible accounts (allowance for doubtful accounts, allowance for bad debts, reserve for doubtful accounts) A contra asset account that measures the amount of receivables estimated to be uncollected.

allowance method Method of accounting for bad debt losses using estimates of the amount of sales that will ultimately be uncollectible and a contra asset account, allowance for doubtful accounts.

amortization When referring to long-lived assets, it usually means the allocation of the costs of intangible assets to the periods that benefit from these assets.

annual report A combination of financial statements, management discussion and analysis, and graphs and charts that is provided annually to investors.

annuity Equal cash flows to take place during successive periods of equal length.

APB Opinions A series of thirty-one opinions of the Accounting Principles Board, many of which are still the "accounting law of the land."

assets Economic resources that are expected to help generate future cash inflows or help reduce future cash outflows.

audit An examination of transactions and financial statements made in accordance with generally accepted auditing standards.

audit committee A committee of the board of directors that oversees the internal accounting controls, financial statements, and financial affairs of the corporation.

auditor A person who examines the information used by managers to prepare the financial statements and attests to the credibility of those statements.

auditor's opinion (independent opinion) A report describing the auditor's examination of transactions and financial statements. It is included with the financial statements in an annual report issued by the corporation.

authorized shares The total number of shares that may legally be issued under the articles of incorporation.

available-for-sale securities Investments in equity or debt securities that are not held for active trading but may be sold before maturity.

bad debt recoveries Accounts receivable that were written off as uncollectible but then collected at a later date.

bad debts expense The cost of granting credit that arises from uncollectible accounts.

balance The difference between the total left-side and right-side amounts in an account at any particular time.

balance sheet (statement of financial position, statement of financial condition) A financial statement that shows the financial status of a business entity at a particular instant in time.

balance sheet equation Assets = Liabilities + Owners' equity

basket purchase The acquisition of two or more types of assets for a lump-sum cost.

bench marks General rules of thumb specifying appropriate levels for financial ratios.

bonds Formal certificates of debt that include (1) a promise to pay interest in cash at a specified annual rate plus (2) a promise to pay the principal at a specific maturity date.

book of original entry A formal chronological record of how the entity's transactions affect the balances in pertinent accounts.

book value (net book value, carrying amount, carrying value) The balance of an account shown on the books, net of any contra accounts. For example, the book value of equipment is its acquisition cost minus accumulated depreciation.

book value per share of common stock Stockholders' equity attributable to common stock divided by the number of shares outstanding.

call premium The amount by which the redemption price of a callable bond exceeds par.

callable A characteristic of bonds or preferred stock that gives the issuer the right to redeem the security at a fixed price.

callable bonds Bonds subject to redemption before maturity at the option of the issuer.

capital A term used to identify owners' equities for proprietorships and partnerships.

capital lease (financing lease) A lease that transfers substantially all the risks and benefits of ownership to the lessee.

capitalization (capital structure) Owners' equity plus long-term debt.

capitalized A cost that is added to an asset account, as distinguished from being expensed immediately.

capital stock certificate (stock certificate) Formal evidence of ownership shares in a corporation.

cash basis Accounting method that recognizes the impact of transactions on the financial statements only when cash is received or disbursed.

cash discounts Reductions of invoice prices awarded for prompt payment.

cash dividends Distributions of cash to stockholders that reduce retained income.

cash equivalents Highly liquid short-term investments that can easily be converted into cash.

cash flows from financing activities The third major section of the statement of cash flows describing flows to and from providers of capital.

cash flows from investing activities The second major section of the statement of cash flows describing purchase or sale of plant, property, equipment, and other long-lived assets.

cash flows from operating activities The first major section of the statement of cash flows. It shows the cash effects of transactions that affect the income statement.

certificates of deposit Short-term obligations of banks.

certified public accountant (CPA) In the United States, a person earns this designation by a combination of education, qualifying experience, and the passing of a two-day written national examination.

charge A word often used instead of debit.

chart of accounts A numbered or coded list of all account titles.

classified balance sheet A balance sheet that groups the accounts into subcategories to help readers quickly gain a perspective on the company's financial position.

common-size statements Financial statements expressed in component percentages.

commercial paper A short-term debt contract issued by prominent companies that borrow directly from investors.

Commercial paper Short-term notes payable issued by large corporations with top credit ratings.

common stock (capital stock) Stock representing the class of owners having a "residual" ownership of a corporation.

compensating balances Required minimum cash balances on deposit when money is borrowed from banks.

component percentages Elements of financial statements that express each component as a percentage of the total.

compound entry An entry for a transaction that affects more than two accounts.

compound interest The interest rate multiplied by a changing principal amount. The unpaid interest is added to the principal to become the principal for the new period.

conservatism Selecting the methods of measurement that yield lower net income, lower assets, and lower stockholders' equity.

consistency Conformity from period to period with unchanging policies and procedures.

consolidated statements Combinations of the financial positions and earnings reports of the parent company with those of various subsidiaries into an overall report as if they were a single entity.

constant dollars Dollar measurements that are restated in terms of current purchasing power.

contingent liability A potential liability that depends on a future event arising out of a past transaction.

contra account A separate but related account that offsets or is a deduction from a companion account. An example is accumulated depreciation.

contra asset A contra account that offsets an asset.

convertible A characteristic of bonds or preferred stock that gives the holder the right to exchange the security for common stock.

convertible bonds Bonds that may, at the holder's option, be exchanged for other securities.

copyrights Exclusive rights to reproduce and sell a book, musical composition, film, and similar items.

corporate proxy A written authority granted by individual shareholders to others to cast the shareholders' votes.

corporation A business organization that is created by individual state laws.

cost-benefit criterion As a system is changed, its expected additional benefits should exceed its expected additional costs.

cost of goods available for sale Sum of beginning inventory plus current year purchases.

cost of goods sold (cost of sales) The original acquisition cost of the inventory that was sold to customers during the reporting period.

cost recovery The concept by which some purchases of goods or services are recorded as assets because their costs are expected to be recovered in the form of cash inflows (or reduced cash outflows) in future periods.

cost valuation Process of assigning specific historical costs to items counted in the physical inventory.

coupon rate (nominal interest rate) The rate of interest to be paid on a bond.

credit An entry or balance on the right side of an account.

creditor A person or entity to whom money is owed.

cross referencing The process of numbering or otherwise specifically identifying each journal entry and each posting.

cross-sectional comparisons Comparisons of a company's financial ratios with the ratios of other companies or with industry averages.

cumulative A characteristic of preferred stock that requires that undeclared dividends accumulate and must be paid in the future before common dividends.

current assets Cash plus assets that are expected to be converted to cash or sold or consumed during the next twelve months or within the normal operating cycle if longer than a year.

current cost Generally, the cost to replace an asset.

current liabilities Liabilities that fall due within the coming year or within the normal operating cycle if longer than a year.

current ratio (working capital ratio) Current assets divided by current liabilities.

current yield Annual interest payments divided by the current price of a bond.

cutoff error Failure to record transactions in the correct time period.

data processing The totality of the procedures used to record, analyze, store, and report on chosen activities.

date of record The date when ownership is fixed for determining the right to receive a dividend.

days to collect accounts receivable (average collection period) 365 divided by accounts receivable turnover.

debenture A debt security with a general claim against all assets instead of a specific claim against particular assets.

debit An entry or balance on the left side of an account.

debt-to-equity ratio Total liabilities divided by total shareholders' equity.

debt-to-total-assets ratio Total liabilities divided by total assets.

debtor A person or entity that owes money to another.

declaration date The date the board of directors declares a dividend.

deferred charges Similar to prepaid expenses, but they have longer term benefits.

deferred tax liability An obligation arising because of predictable future taxes, to be paid when a future tax return is filed.

depletion The process of allocating the cost of natural resources to the periods in which the resources are used.

depreciable value The amount of the acquisition cost to be allocated as depreciation over the total useful life of an asset. It is the difference between the total acquisition cost and the predicted residual value.

depreciation The systematic allocation of the acquisition cost of long-lived or fixed assets to the expense accounts of particular periods that benefit from the use of the assets.

depreciation schedule The listing of depreciation amounts for each year of an asset's useful life.

dilution Reduction in stockholders' equity per share or earnings per share that arises from some changes among shareholders' proportional interests.

direct method In a statement of cash flows, the method that calculates net cash provided by operating activities as collections minus operating disbursements.

discontinued operations The termination of a business segment. The results are reported separately, net of tax, in the income statement.

discount amortization The spreading of bond discount over the life of the bonds as expense.

discount on bonds The excess of face amount over the proceeds upon issuance of a bond.

discount rates The interest rates used in determining present values.

dividend arrearages Accumulated unpaid dividends on preferred stock.

dividend-payout ratio Common dividends per share divided by earnings per share.

dividend-yield ratio Common dividends per share divided by market price per share.

double-declining-balance depreciation (DDB) The most popular form of accelerated depreciation. It is computed by doubling the straight-line rate and multiplying the resulting DDB rate by the beginning book value.

double-entry system The method usually followed for recording transactions, whereby at least two accounts are always affected by each transaction.

earnings per share (EPS) Net income divided by average number of common shares outstanding.

EBIT Earnings before interest and taxes.

effective-interest amortization (compound interest method) An amortization method that uses a constant interest rate.

entity An organization or a section of an organization that stands apart from other organizations and individuals as a separate economic unit.

equity method Accounting for an investment at acquisition cost, adjusted for the investor's share of dividends and earnings or losses of the investee subsequent to the date of investment.

expenditures The purchases of goods or services, whether for cash or on credit.

expenses Decreases in owners' equity that arise because goods or services are delivered to customers.

explicit transactions Events such as cash receipts and disbursements, credit purchases, and credit sales that trigger nearly all day-to-day routine entries.

extraordinary items Items that are unusual in nature and infrequent in occurrence that are shown separately, net of tax, in the income statement.

F.O.B. destination Seller pays freight costs from the shipping point of the seller to the receiving point of the buyer.

F.O.B. shipping point Buyer pays freight costs from the shipping point of the seller to the receiving point of the buyer.

FASB Statements The FASB's rulings on generally accepted accounting principles (GAAP).

financial accounting The field of accounting that serves external decision makers, such as stockholders, suppliers, banks, and government agencies.

Financial Accounting Standards Board (FASB) A private-sector body that determines generally accepted accounting standards in the United States.

financial capital maintenance A concept of income measurement whereby income emerges only after financial resources are recovered.

financial management Concerns where to get cash and how to use cash for the benefit of the entity.

financial statement analysis Using financial statements to assess a company's performance.

financing activities Activities that involve obtaining resources as a borrower or issuer of securities and repaying creditors and owners.

finished goods inventory The accumulated costs of manufacture for goods that are complete and ready for sale.

first-in, first-out (FIFO) This method of accounting for inventory assigns the cost of the earliest acquired units to cost of goods sold.

fiscal year The year established for accounting purposes.

franchises (licenses) Privileges granted by a government, manufacturer, or distributor to sell a product or service in accordance with specified conditions.

freight in (inward transportation) An additional cost of the goods acquired during the period, which is often shown in the purchases section of an income statement.

freight out The transportation costs borne by the seller of merchandise and often shown as a "shipping expense."

future value The amount accumulated, including principal and interest.

general journal The most common example of a book of original entry; a complete chronological record of transactions.

general ledger The collection of accounts that accumulates the amounts reported in the major financial statements.

general price index An index that compares the average price of a group of goods and services at one date with the average price of a similar group at another date.

generally accepted accounting principles (GAAP) A term that applies to the broad concepts or guidelines and detailed practices in accounting, including all the conventions, rules, and procedures that make up accepted accounting practice at a given time.

going concern convention (continuity convention) The assumption that in all ordinary situations an entity persists indefinitely.

goodwill The excess of the cost of an acquired company over the sum of the fair market value of its identifiable individual assets less the liabilities.

gross profit (gross margin) The excess of sales revenue over the cost of the inventory that was sold.

gross profit percentage (gross margin percentage) Gross profit divided by sales.

gross profit percentage Gross profit as a percentage of sales.

gross sales Total sales revenue before deducting sales returns and allowances.

held-to-maturity securities Debt securities that the investor expects to hold until maturity.

historical cost The amount originally paid to acquire an asset.

holding gain (inventory profit) Increase in the replacement cost or other measure of current value of the inventory held during the current period.

implicit interest (imputed interest) An interest expense that is not explicitly recognized in a loan agreement.

implicit transactions Events (such as the passage of time) that do not generate source documents or visible evidence of the event and are not recognized in the accounting records until the end of an accounting period.

improvement (betterment, capital improvement) An expenditure that is intended to add to the future benefits from an existing fixed asset.

imputed interest rate The market interest rate that equates the proceeds from a loan with the present value of the loan payments.

income (profit, earnings) The excess of revenues over expenses.

income statement (statement of earnings, operating statement) A report of all revenues and expenses pertaining to a specific time period.

indirect method In a statement of cash flows, the method that adjusts the accrual net income to reflect only cash receipts and outlays.

inflation A general decline in the purchasing power of the monetary unit.

intangible assets Rights or economic benefits, such as franchises, patents, trademarks, copyrights, and goodwill, that are not physical in nature.

interest-coverage ratio Pretax income plus interest expense divided by interest expense.

interest rate The percentage applied to a principal amount to calculate the interest charged.

interim periods The time spans established for accounting purposes that are less than a year.

internal control System of checks and balances that assures all actions ocurring within the company are in accordance with organizational objectives.

International Accounting Standards Board (IASB) An organization charged with responsibility for developing a common set of accounting standards to be used throughout the world.

inventory Goods held by a company for the purpose of sale to customers.

inventory shrinkage Inventory reductions from theft, breakage, or losses of inventory.

inventory turnover The cost of goods sold divided by the average inventory held during the period.

investing activities Activities that involve (1) providing and collecting cash as a lender or as an owner of securities and (2) acquiring and disposing of plant, property, equipment, and other long-term productive assets.

invoice A bill from the seller to a buyer indicating the number of items shipped, their price, and any additional costs (such as shipping) along with payment terms, if any.

issued shares The aggregate number of shares sold to the public.

journal entry An analysis of the effects of a transaction on the accounts, usually accompanied by an explanation.

journalizing The process of entering transactions into the journal.

keying of entries (cross-referencing) The process of numbering or otherwise specifically identifying each journal entry and each posting.

last-in, first-out (LIFO) This inventory method assigns the most recent costs to cost of goods sold.

lease A contract whereby an owner (lessor) grants the use of property to a second party (lessee) for rental payments.

leasehold The right to use a fixed asset for a specified period of time, typically beyond one year.

leasehold improvement Investments by a lessee in items that are not permitted to be removed from the premises when a lease expires, such as installation of new fixtures, panels, walls, and air-conditioning equipment.

ledger The records for a group of related accounts kept current in a systematic manner.

lessee The party that has the right to use leased property and makes lease payments to the lessor.

lessor The owner of property who grants usage rights to the lessee.

liabilities Economic obligations of the organization to outsiders or claims against its assets by outsiders.

LIFO layer (LIFO increment) A separately identifiable additional segment of LIFO inventory.

LIFO reserve The difference between a company's inventory valued at LIFO and what it would be under FIFO.

limited liability A feature of the corporate form of organization whereby corporate creditors ordinarily have claims against the corporate assets only. The owners' personal assets are not subject to the creditors' grasp.

line of credit An agreement with a bank to provide automatically short-term loans up to some preestablished maximum.

liquidating value A measure of the preference to receive assets in the event of corporate liquidation.

liquidation Converting assets to cash and paying off outside claims.

long-lived assets Resources that are held for an extended time, such as land, buildings, equipment, natural resources, and patents.

long-term-debt-to-total-capital ratio Total long-term debt divided by total shareholders' equity plus long-term debt.

long-term liabilities Obligations that fall due beyond one year from the balance sheet date.

long-term solvency An organization's ability to generate enough cash to repay long-term debts as they mature.

lower-of-cost-or-market method (LCM) The superimposition of a market-price test on an inventory cost method.

management accounting The field of accounting that serves internal decision makers, such as top executives, department heads, college deans, hospital administrators, and people at other management levels within an organization.

management reports Explicit statements in annual reports of publicly held companies that management is responsible for all audited and unaudited information in the annual report.

management's discussion and analysis (MD&A) A required section of annual reports that concentrates on explaining the major changes in the income statement, liquidity, and capital resources.

marketable securities Any notes, bonds, or stocks that can readily be sold. The term is often used as a synonym for short-term investments.

market rate The rate available on investments in similar bonds at a moment in time.

market to book ratio Market value per share divided by book value per share.

matching The recording of expenses in the same time period as the related revenues are recognized.

materiality convention The concept that an item should be included in a financial statement if its omission or misstatement would tend to mislead the reader of the financial statements under consideration.

minority interests The outside shareholders' interests, as opposed to the parent's interests, in a subsidiary corporation.

mortgage bond A form of long-term debt that is secured by the pledge of specific property.

multiple-step income statement An income statement that contains one or more subtotals that highlight significant relationships.

negotiable Legal financial contracts that can be transferred from one lender to another.

net income The remainder after all expenses have been deducted from revenues.

net loss The difference between revenues and expenses when expenses exceed revenues.

net sales Total sales revenue reduced by sales returns and allowances.

neutrality A quality of information meaning that it is free from bias.

nominal dollars Those dollars that are not restated for fluctuations in the general purchasing power of the monetary unit.

nominal interest rate (contractual rate, coupon rate, stated rate) A contractual rate of interest paid on bonds.

nominal interest rate Synonym for coupon rate.

notes payable Promissory notes that are evidence of a debt and state the terms of payment.

open account Buying or selling on credit, usually by just an "authorized signature" of the buyer.

operating activities Activities that affect the income statement.

operating cycle The time span during which cash is used to acquire goods and services, which in turn are sold to customers, who in turn pay for their purchases with cash.

operating income (operating profit) Gross profit less all operating expenses.

operating income percentage on sales Operating income divided by sales.

operating lease A lease that should be accounted for by the lessee as ordinary rent expenses.

operating management Is mainly concerned with the major day-to-day activities that generate revenues and expenses.

other postretirement benefits Benefits provided to retired workers in addition to a pension, such as life and health insurance.

outstanding shares Shares remaining in the hands of shareholders.

owner' equity The residual interest in the organization's assets after deducting liabilities.

paid-in capital The total capital investment in a corporation by its owners both at and subsequent to the inception of business.

paid-in capital in excess of par value When issuing stock, the difference between the total amount received and the par value.

parent company   A company owning more than 50% of the voting shares of another company, called the subsidiary company.

participating   A characteristic of preferred stock that provides increasing dividends when common dividends increase.

partnership   A form of organization that joins two or more individuals together as co-owners.

par value (stated value)   The nominal dollar amount printed on stock certificates.

patents   Grants by the federal government to an inventor, bestowing (in the United States) the exclusive right for 17 years to produce and sell the invention.

payment date   The date dividends are paid.

pensions   Payments to former employees after they retire.

percentage of accounts receivable method   An approach to estimating bad debts expense and uncollectible accounts at year-end using the historical relations of uncollectibles to accounts receivable.

percentage-of-completion method   Method of recognizing revenue on long-term contracts as production occurs.

percentage of sales method   An approach to estimating bad debts expense and uncollectible accounts based on the historical relations between credit sales and uncollectibles.

period costs   Items identified directly as expenses of the time period in which they are incurred.

periodic inventory system   The system in which the cost of goods sold is computed periodically by relying solely on physical counts without keeping day-to-day records of units sold or on hand.

permanent differences   Revenue or expense items that are recognized for tax purposes but not recognized under GAAP, or vice versa.

perpetual inventory system   A system that keeps a running, continuous record that tracks inventories and the cost of goods sold on a day-to-day basis.

physical capital maintenance   A concept of income measurement whereby income emerges only after recovering an amount that allows physical operating capability to be maintained.

physical count   The process of counting all the items in inventory at a moment in time.

pooling-of-interests method   A way of accounting for the combination of two corporations based on the book values of the acquired company's net assets, as distinguished from the purchase method.

posting   The transferring of amounts from the journal to the appropriate accounts in the ledger.

preemptive rights   The rights to acquire a pro-rata amount of any new issues of capital stock.

preferred stock   Stock that offers owners different rights and preferential treatments.

premium on bonds   The excess of the proceeds over the face amount of a bond.

present value   The value today of a future cash inflow or outflow.

pretax income   Income before income taxes.

pretax operating rate of return on total assets (return on total assets (ROA))   Operating income divided by sales.

price-earnings ratio (P-E)   Market price per share of common stock divided by earnings per share of common stock.

principal (face amount)   The loan amount that a borrower promises to repay at a specific maturity date.

private accountants   Accountants who work for businesses, as well as government agencies, and other nonprofit organizations.

privately owned   A corporation owned by a family, a small group of shareholders, or a single individual, in which shares of ownership are not publicly sold.

private placement   A process whereby notes are issued by corporations when money is borrowed from a few sources, not from the general public.

product costs   Costs that are linked with revenues and are charged as expenses when the related revenue is recognized.

profitability   The ability of a company to provide investors with a particular rate of return on their investment.

pro forma statement   A carefully formulated expression of predicted results.

promissory note   A written promise to repay principal plus interest at specific future dates.

protective covenant (covenant)   A provision stated in a bond, usually to protect the bondholders' interests.

public accountants   Accountants who offer services to the general public on a fee basis including auditing, tax work, and management consulting.

public accounting   The field of accounting where services are offered to the general public on a fee basis.

publicly owned   A corporation in which shares in the ownership are sold to the public.

purchase method   A way of accounting for the acquisition of one company by another, based on the market prices paid for the acquired company's assets.

purchase order   A document that specifies the items ordered and the price to be paid by the ordering company.

rate of return   The amount earned by an investor expressed as a percentage of the amount invested.

rate of return on common equity (ROE)   Net income less preferred dividends divided by average common equity.

raw material inventory   Includes the cost of materials held for use in the manufacturing of a product.

receiving report   A document that specifies the items received by the company and the condition of the items.

recognition　A test for determining whether revenues should be recorded in the financial statements of a given period. To be recognized, revenues must be earned and realized.

reconcile a bank statement　To verify that the bank balance for cash is consistent with the accounting records.

redemption price (call price)　The price at which an issuer can buy back a callable preferred stock or bond, which is typically 5% to 10% above the par value.

relevance　The capability of information to make a difference to the decision maker.

reliability　The quality of information that assures decision makers that the information captures the conditions or events it purports to represent.

replacement cost　The cost at which an inventory item could be acquired today.

report format　A classified balance sheet with the assets at the top.

reserve　Has one of three meanings: (1) a restriction of dividend-declaring power as denoted by a specific subdivision of retained income, (2) an offset to an asset, or (3) an estimate of a definite liability of indefinite or uncertain amount.

residual value (terminal value, disposal value, salvage value, scrap value)　The amount received from disposal of a long-lived asset at the end of its useful life.

restricted retained income (appropriated retained income)　Any part of retained income that may not be reduced by dividend declarations.

restructuring　A significant makeover of part of the company typically involving the closing of plants, firing of employees, and relocation of activities.

retailer　A company that sells items directly to the final users, individuals.

retained income (retained earnings, reinvested earnings)　Additional owners' equity generated by income or profits.

return on sales ratio　Net income divided by sales.

return on stockholders' equity ratio　Net income divided by invested capital (measured by average stockholders' equity).

revaluation equity　A part of stockholders' equity that includes all holding gains that are excluded from income.

revenues (sales)　Increases in owners' equity arising from increases in assets received in exchange for the delivery of goods or services to customers.

sales allowance (purchase allowance)　Reduction of the original selling price.

sales returns (purchase returns)　Products returned by the customer.

Securities and Exchange Commission (SEC)　The agency designated by the U.S. Congress to hold the ultimate responsibility for authorizing the generally accepted accounting principles for companies whose stock is held by the general investing public.

series　Different groups of preferred shares issued at different times with different features.

short-term debt securities　Largely notes and bonds with maturities of one year or less.

short-term equity securities　Capital stock in other corporations held with the intention to liquidate within one year as needed.

short-term investment　A temporary investment in marketable securities of otherwise idle cash.

short-term liquidity　An organization's ability to meet current payments as they become due.

simple entry　An entry for a transaction that affects only two accounts.

simple interest　The interest rate multiplied by an unchanging principal amount.

single-step income statement　An income statement that groups all revenues together and then lists and deducts all expenses together without drawing any intermediate subtotals.

sinking fund　A pool of cash or securities set aside for meeting certain obligations.

sinking fund bonds　Bonds with indentures that require the issuer to make annual payments to a sinking fund.

sole proprietorship　A separate organization with a single owner.

solvency　An entity's ability to meet its immediate financial obligations as they become due.

source documents　The supporting original records of any transaction.

special items　Expenses that are large enough and unusual enough to warrant separate disclosure.

specific identification method　This inventory method concentrates on the physical linking of the particular items sold.

specific price index　An index used to approximate the current costs of particular assets or types of assets.

specific write-off method　This method of accounting for bad debt losses assumes all sales are fully collectible until proved otherwise.

statement of cash flows (cash flow statement)　A required statement that reports the cash receipts and cash payments of an entity during a particular period.

statement of income and retained income　A statement that includes a statement of retained income at the bottom of an income statement.

statement of retained income　A statement that lists the beginning balance in retained income, followed by a description of any changes that occurred during the period, and the ending balance.

stock dividends Distribution to stockholders of additional shares of any class of the distributing company's stock, without any payment to the company by the stockholders.

stock options Special rights usually granted to executives to purchase a corporation's capital stock.

stock split Issuance of additional shares to existing stockholders for no payments by the stockholders.

stockholders' equity (shareholders' equity) Owners' equity of a corporation. The excess of assets over liabilities of a corporation.

straight-line depreciation A method that spreads the depreciable value evenly over the useful life of an asset.

subordinated debentures Debt securities whose holders have claims against only the assets that remain after the claims of general creditors are satisfied.

subsidiary A corporation owned or controlled by a parent company through the ownership of more than 50% of the voting stock.

T-account Simplified version of ledger accounts that takes the form of the capital letter T.

tangible assets (fixed assets, plant assets) Physical items that can be seen and touched, such as land, natural resources, buildings, and equipment.

tax rate The percentage of taxable income paid to the government.

times interest earned Income before interest expense and income taxes divided by interest expense. Synonym for interest coverage.

time-series comparisons Comparisons of a company's financial ratios with its own historical ratios.

timing differences (temporary differences) Differences between net income and taxable income that arise because some revenue and expense items are recognized at different times for tax purposes than for reporting purposes.

total asset turnover (asset turnover) Sales divided by average total assets available.

trade discounts Reductions to the gross selling price for a particular class of customers.

trademarks Distinctive identifications of a manufactured product or of a service taking the form of a name, a sign, a slogan, a logo, or an emblem.

trading on the equity (financial leverage, leveraging, gearing) Using borrowed money at fixed interest rates with the objective of enhancing the rate of return on common equity.

trading securities Current investments in equity or debt securities held for short-term profit.

transaction Any event that both affects the financial position of an entity and can be reliably recorded in money terms.

treasury stock A corporation's issued stock that has subsequently been repurchased by the company and not retired.

trial balance A list of all accounts in the general ledger with their balances.

trust indenture A contract whereby the issuing corporation of a bond promises a trustee that it will abide by stated provisions.

turnover A synonym for sales or revenues in many countries outside the United States.

U.S. Treasury obligations Interest-bearing notes, bonds, and bills issued by the U.S. government.

uncollectible accounts (bad debts) Receivables determined to be uncollectible because debtors are unable or unwilling to pay their debts.

underwriters A group of investment bankers that buys an entire bond or stock issue from a corporation and then sells the securities to the general investing public.

unearned revenue (revenue received in advance, deferred revenue, deferred credit) Revenue received and recorded before it is earned.

unit depreciation A depreciation method based on units of service when physical wear and tear is the dominating influence on the useful life of the asset.

unsubordinated debenture A bond that is unsecured by specific pledged assets, giving its owner a general claim with a priority like an account payable.

useful life (economic life) The number of years before an asset wears out or becomes obsolete, whichever comes first.

validity (representational faithfulness) A correspondence between the accounting numbers and the events or objects those numbers purport to represent.

verifiability A quality of information meaning that it can be checked to make sure that it is correct.

weighted-average method This inventory method computes a unit cost by dividing the total acquisition cost of all items available for sale by the number of units available for sale.

wholesaler An intermediary that sells inventory items to retailers.

work in process inventory Includes the cost incurred for partially completed items, including raw materials, labor, and other costs.

working capital The excess of current assets over current liabilities.

write-down A reduction in the assumed cost of an item in response to a decline in value.

yield to maturity (effective interest rate) The interest rate that equates market price at issue to the present value of principal and interest.

zero coupon A bond or note that pays no cash interest during its life.

INDEX

PHOTO CREDITS